RUTH AND BOAZ.

The Works of
of
John Bunyan.

VOL. III.

The Ascent of Christiana

THE

COMPLETE WORKS

OF

JOHN BUNYAN,

AUTHOR OF "THE PILGRIM'S PROGRESS."

EDITED,

WITH ORIGINAL INTRODUCTIONS, NOTES, AND MEMOIR OF THE AUTHOR,

BY HENRY STEBBING, D.D., F.R.S.,

RECTOR OF ST. MARY SOMERSET WITH ST. MARY MOUNTHAW, UPPER THAMES STREET, LONDON.

Illustrated with Engravings on Steel and Wood.

IN FOUR VOLUMES.

VOL. III.

1970

Georg Olms
Verlag
Hildesheim · New York

Johnson
Reprint Corporation
New York

First reprinting 1970, Johnson Reprint Corporation

Printed in the United States of America

CONTENTS OF VOLUME III.

CONTENTS.

PREFATORY REMARKS

THE HOLY WAR.

THE first edition of Milton's *Paradise Lost* appeared in 1667: that of *Paradise Regained* in 1671. Bunyan's *Holy War* was first published in 1682. No comparison can be instituted between these works; but it is almost impossible to read the beginning of *The Holy War* without feeling assured that Bunyan was well acquainted with Milton, and derived the general idea of this work from the poems of his great contemporary. Utterly unlike both in plan and execution, they both speak

> " Of man's first disobedience, and the fruit
> Of that forbidden tree, whose mortal taste
> Brought death into the world, and all our woe."

Having started with the same object in view, they immediately separate : Milton to pursue it along a path opened for him by the sublimest energy of sanctified imagination ; Bunyan to seek it along the by-paths and curious turnings of a track discovered to him by the habits of a simple but active and well exercised invention. As we accompany the former, our minds become impressed with the grandeur of a mighty woe : we are humbled, terrified ; but still sensible of a presence which dignifies our grief. Our converse with the latter produces a very different feeling. Anger, disappointment, contempt, become the prevailing emotions of our hearts. The extreme folly of betrayed man is so conspicuously exhibited, that we are often tempted to smile at him as a miserable dupe, rather than pity him as the victim of a fallen archangel. There is this contrast between the sentiments produced by Milton and Bunyan ; and in all the considerations of literature, and even in some religious points, the former is immeasurably the superior.

The effort which has been made to prove that certain resemblances exist between Bunyan's *Pilgrim's Progress* and Caxton's *Pylgrimage of the Sowle*, and other early works, deserves all the praise due to ingenious research, but it serves little purpose unless in respect to Bunyan's mental cultivation. Caxton and Wynkin de Worde had not laboured in vain for the men of a following generation. Their curious little volumes were dispersed throughout the land ; and had not become worm-eaten when Bunyan began to love books. They were not curiosities as they now are. Though confined in the nineteenth century to the cabinets of the rich collector, they were then in the hands of every man who had learnt to read. And so it was in regard to the entire series of printed books from the beginning of the sixteenth century.

But had Bunyan the disposition to make use of these various sources of instruction ? Was he really that " man of one book," so proverbially spoken of as invincible in controversy ? Is there any indication in his mental character which would lead to such a belief ? His numerous works furnish a satisfactory answer to all these questions. They prove a general cultivation of mind, and such as could only have been attained to by much careful and general reading. There is no poverty of language, no obscurity or affectation, even in those of his theological writings where the subject was most likely to trammel him with difficulties. Mere good sense, or natural ability, will not give men such a command of artificial language. The most fluent thinker will be the least contented with the expression of his thoughts till he has learnt through what forms they may be sent with the least waste. Bunyan was a wise man in all these respects. He loved to speak with a quiet, concealed irony of his ignorance of Latin, and other scholastic acquirements; but from the age of twenty he had studied English as only such men can study that or any other language.

Theological reading was his chief and proper employment ; and had his mind been differently constructed, we might have believed that he became an author solely from his acquaintance with the divines of his own age, and that immediately preceding it. But he had this remarkable characteristic of a poetic temperament : he was a dreamer from his youth. Wild, fanciful, and ardent, his thoughts were always wandering in search of something remote from the world and his own narrow experience. The gloom which so frequently enveloped all his visions was no less the result of an extreme sensibility. That it warned him of awful and real dangers, and drove him to the brink of despair, did not diminish its importance as an element of his genius. It furnished him with the most powerful motives to seek for light and sympathy in the productions of other minds, similarly constituted, but better disciplined and informed.

Whatever might be his feelings at a later period, he could have no disposition, at first, to confine his reading to the severe lessons of theology. Both the character of his mind and the circumstances through which it had to trace its way into the open world of light and beauty, necessarily sent him to the poets, and other imaginative writers. In them he would find thoughts analogous to his own. It required less time and patience to read a poem than to study any of the works which he subsequently mastered. Poetical fiction was as various as it was enticing. If he could read Spenser, he could also read Homer in Chapman's bold, deep-rolling verses. Fairfax enabled him to become acquainted with all the sweet romance and noble chivalry of Tasso's *Jerusalem Delivered ;* and Harrington with the marvels of Ariosto. These authors were made English for popular use. They floated on the very surface of the common, general literature. The taste for reading was not universal as in our time ; but for all who did read, such were the books and authors which met them at every step of their progress. Should it even then seem improbable that Bunyan took the pains, or found opportunity, to pore into Caxton, Wynkin de Worde, or works in Norman French, it is very far from unlikely that he gradually became well acquainted with the authors whose writings were then universally known and admired.

But allowing this, Bunyan's *Holy War* is still to be regarded as one of the most extraordinary productions of original talent. *The Pilgrim's Progress* represents in lively colours the journey of an individual believer, free to pursue his course, and generally walking in such an open daylight of reality, that there is little difficulty in reducing the allegory to the common experience of life. We ever see the man before us. Whether climbing a hill, or tracing his way through a valley, he is surrounded with mystical forms and shadows, but he himself is substance : an actual man, never lost to us in the crowd of personified virtues and vices,—a friend, whose name is no sooner mentioned than memory gives us his form and history.

This is not the case with the class of impressions left on the mind by *The Holy War.* It requires a much greater effort of thought to imagine the human soul under the form of a populous city, and to trace its history as such, than to create some one character, and invest him with the power of making virtues or vices visible by their effects. Neither author nor reader is far out of the track of common invention in this experiment. But the old metaphysical idea that the soul is a world in itself, is a very unsubstantial basis for a long narrative. For a man to believe this of his own soul, he must subject himself to a long training in the school of mysticism. To extend the notion, and believe that the wonder is repeated in every soul which exists, and that there are as many universes, or, at least, capital cities, as there are souls, requires a further culture of this kind. Bunyan adopted the abstract idea of the human soul. It is necessary that his readers should understand this ; and that they should look with their teacher's eyes upon the wonderful city, of the fall and recovery of which he proposes to write the history.

The introductory description is well conceived. We see the magnificent and beautiful city reposing in joyous tranquillity. Its inhabitants are true-hearted, wise, and loving ; and its founder and sovereign, Shaddai, great above the greatest of monarchs. A hostile prince, as bold and subtle as he is evil, resolves to gain possession of this city. He discusses his project with the most devoted of his adherents. They agree to prepare an expedition. The plan is speedily laid and executed. By a mixture of fraud and violence Mansoul falls under the power of Diabolus. Its worthiest inhabitants are put to death, or thrown into prison ; and the condition of the city is wholly changed. After a certain period, during which every passion that can disturb or debase human nature is at work, the great Sovereign, Shaddai, determines to send an army, and expel the invader of this part of his dominions. The conduct of the force is entrusted to captains of approved skill and valour ; but they fail to recover the city. An appeal is made for additional help. The request is granted ; and Emmanuel himself, the Son of Shaddai, hastens to the siege. His attack is irresistible. Diabolus in vain proposes to yield on terms. One messenger after another is sent to the triumphant Prince. He scorns the artifices of the discomfited enemy ; and both the chief and his adherents are driven out with horrible confusion.

A full account is given of the proceedings which followed this victory. The citizens, and the great dignitaries among them, who had one and all proved unfaithful to their proper Monarch, expected nothing less than immediate death. But the Conqueror was full of clemency and mercy. After proofs had been given of genuine humility and penitence, pardon was proclaimed ; a new charter was granted the city ; and, to its infinite benefit and satisfaction, a Lord Chief Secretary, equal in nature to Shaddai and Emmanuel, was thenceforward to be its guide and teacher.

After these important events, there are still dangers to be encountered, and Mansoul is wholly indebted for its preservation to the wisdom of the Lord Chief Secretary, and the tender care exercised by Emmanuel. But Diabolus is ever on the watch, and he has an ally in the very heart of the city. This is Mr. Carnal-security, the son of Mr. Self-conceit, and his wife, Lady Fear-nothing. By degrees, other enemies of Shaddai appeared among the inhabitants. They had hidden themselves in holes and corners till the danger which threatened them was past. The people being now lapped in ease and comfort, they came forth from their concealment. Sin speedily followed in the train of these foes of the good Emmanuel. The city of Mansoul was again upon the point of being lost; when means were found, in the deep and wonderful counsels of Shaddai, to place it finally in a state of peace and glory.

This outline of the narrative will enable the reader to understand how large a circle Bunyan had to fill up with various characters, and how active that invention must have been which enabled him not only to show these characters as living and active, but to find for them all proper situations and employments. Every faculty of the mind is personified, and has its office and post of honour. The passions are leaders in one or the other of the hostile armies. These higher officers being fitted with appointments, the most minute scrutiny is instituted to discover what modes of thought even; what lurking feelings and dispositions may exist. As soon as detected they are brought out, named, dressed in proper habiliments, and made soldiers, statesmen, friends or traitors, as the plot may require. The skill with which the armies are kept in movement, marched and countermarched; the political ingenuity exhibited in the debates of the opposite parties; the ready foresight with which the attack on this or that side is anticipated, reminds us of what is related, whether fabulously or truly, of certain remarkable chess-players, who can wondrously survey the mimic field of battle extending over four boards at the same time. Bunyan never loses sight of a single man. He makes every character perform its part to the uttermost. There is a marvellous sustained energy in the conduct of the war through all its stages. Even the interval of peace is filled up with action. Never did a party bent upon some evil design exercise a more laborious subtlety than that attributed to the faction in Mansoul. That must indeed have been a pains-taking, penetrating observation of human nature which enabled the author to describe so well what the most cunning counsellor could only have attempted by becoming skilful in such a study. The ruling passion is, in each case, kept distinct from all others; and, however base, is true to itself from beginning to end. In the ranks of the army, and in the council chamber of the friends of Shaddai, grace and virtue execute their offices with equal particularity and force. They speak the language of wisdom and holiness. We recognise manly firmness, sedate prudence, and heroic self-devotion in these loyal servants of their Lord, in the same way in which they might be looked for among men most familiarly known to us for their eminent and extensive usefulness.

But it is obvious that while the attention is thus powerfully directed to so many objects which have in effect an outward existence, the mind has little disposition to look inward upon its own movements; or to believe that all this vast concourse of personages, generals, and statesmen, with mighty armies at their back, or crowds of political partizans, are, in reality, existing in its own little self—are, in fact, only a part of itself, or its own creation. The language of simple thought or reflection disposes to reflection; but when fancy is employed to present a multifarious crowd of busy actors, and events succeed events in ceaseless succession upon an ever-varying scene, the contrary effect is produced, and an inter—, often a long one, must be allowed before the mind can transfer its faith in the outward images to the reality of its own affections.

It is generally known that *The Holy War* has never enjoyed so great a popularity as *The Pilgrim's Progress*. This may be easily accounted for. The latter not only creates a readier sympathy, as a picture of individual life, but there is a charm in its style, and in a large proportion of its incidents, of which *The Holy War* is almost wholly destitute. It has none of that sweet, earnest tenderness which breathes such beauty over the scenes of the earlier narrative. The difference of purpose in the two works had some share in giving them this opposite character. But there are points in the progress of *The Holy War* at which, had he been so inclined, the author might have both softened the sternness and greatly increased the interest of his story, by some intermixture of pathos with the severer elements of his style. The want of this blending of colours—the absence of all appeals to the mild affections and sympathies of life, must always tend to limit the popularity of *The Holy War*. Bunyan's mind was full of vigour, and abounded in bold and healthy thought when he wrote this remarkable book. But he could hardly have been in the same temper in which he conceived the design of *The Pilgrim's Progress*. Then he felt and wrote as one under the influence of the gentlest spirit, affectionate, sympathizing, and looking out for all the sweet and lovely objects that can be met with on the path of Christian holiness. The sternest chronicler of actual war, when speaking of battles and defeated enemies, could not breathe a rougher or haughtier spirit than this historian of Mansoul.

H. S.

THE HOLY WAR,

MADE BY SHADDAI UPON DIABOLUS,

FOR THE REGAINING OF THE METROPOLIS OF THE WORLD;

OR,

THE LOSING AND TAKING AGAIN OF THE TOWN OF MANSOUL.

" I have used similitudes."—Hos. xii. 10.

TO THE READER.

'Tis strange to me, that they that love to tell
Things done of old, yea, and that do excel
Their equals in Historiology,
Speak not of Mansoul's wars, but let them lie
Dead, like old fables, or such worthless things,
That to the reader no advantage brings;
When men, let them make wha' they will their
    own,
Till they know this, are to themselves unknown.

Of stories I well know there's divers sorts,
Some foreign, some domestic; and reports
Are thereof made, as fancy leads the writers;
(By books a man may guess at the inditers.)

Some will again of that which never was,
Nor will be, feign (and that without a cause)
Such matter, raise such mountains, tell such things
Of men, of laws, of countries, and of kings;
And in their story seem to be so sage,
And with such gravity clothe every page,
That though their frontispiece say all is vain,
Yet to their way disciples they obt   .

But, readers, I have somewhat else to do,
Than with vain stories thus to trouble you:
What here I say some men do know so well,
They can with tears of joy the story tell.

The town of Mansoul is well known to many,
Nor are her troubles doubted of by any
That are acquainted with those histories
That Mansoul and her wars anatomize.

Then lend thine ear to what I do relate
Touching the town of Mansoul, and her state;
How she was lost, took captive, made a slave;
And how against him set, that should her save;
Yea, how by hostile ways she did oppose
Her Lord, and with his enemy did close.
For they are true; he that will them deny,
Must needs the best of records vilify.

For my part, I myself was in the town,
Both when 'twas set up, and when pulling down,
I saw Diabolus in his possession,
And Mansoul also under his oppression.
Yea, I was there when she own'd him for lord,
And to him did submit with one accord.

When Mansoul trampled upon things divine,
And wallowed in filth as doth a swine;
When she betook herself unto her arms,
Fought her Emmanuel, despised his charms;
Then I was there, and did rejoice to see
Diabolus and Mansoul so agree.

Let no man, then, count me a fable-maker,
Nor make my name or credit a partaker
Of their derision; what is here in view,
Of mine own knowledge I dare say is true.

I saw the Prince's armed men come down
By troops, by thousands, to besiege the town;
I saw the captains, heard the trumpets sound,
And how his forces cover'd all the ground;
Yea, how they set themselves in battle 'ray,
I shall remember to my dying day.

I saw the colours waving in the wind,
And they within to mischief how combined,
To ruin Mansoul, and to make away
Her *primum mobile* without delay.

I saw the mounts cast up against the town,
And how the slings were placed to beat it down.
I heard the stones fly whizzing by mine ears;
(What longer kept in mind, than got in fears?)
I heard them fall, and saw what work they made,
And how old Mors did cover with his shade
The face of Mansoul, and I heard her cry,
Woe worth the day, " In dying I shall die!"

I saw the battering-rams, and how they play'd
To beat ope Ear-gate; and I was afraid

Not only Ear-gate, but the very town
Would by those battering-rams be beaten down.

I saw the fights, and heard the captains shout,
And in each battle saw who faced about;
I saw who wounded were, and who were slain,
And who, when dead, would come to life again.

I heard the cries of those that wounded were,
(While others fought like men bereft of fear;)
And while the cry, Kill! kill! was in mine ears,
The gutters ran, not so with blood as tears.

Indeed the captains did not always fight,
But then they would molest us day and night:
Their cry, Up, fall on, let us take the town!
Kept us from sleeping, or from lying down.
I was there when the gates were broken ope,
And saw how Mansoul then was stript of hope.
I saw the captains march into the town,
How there they fought, and did their foes cut down.

I heard the Prince bid Boanerges go
Up to the castle, and there seize his foe;
And saw him and his fellows bring him down
In chains of great contempt quite through the town.

I saw Emmanuel when he possest
His town of Mansoul; and how greatly blest
The town, his gallant town of Mansoul was,
When she received his pardon, loved his laws.

When the Diabolonians were caught,
When tried, and when to execution brought,
Then I was there; yea, I was standing by
When Mansoul did the rebels crucify.

I also saw Mansoul clad all in white,
And heard her Prince call her his heart's delight;
I saw him put upon her chains of gold,
And rings and bracelets, goodly to behold.

What shall I say? I heard the people's cries,
And saw the Prince wipe tears from Mansoul's eyes.
I heard the groans, and saw the joy of many;
Tell you of all, I neither will, nor can I;
But by what here I say, you well may see
That Mansoul's matchless wars no fables be.

Mansoul, the desire of both Princes was,
One keep his gain would, t'other gain his loss;
Diabolus would cry, The town is mine!
Emmanuel would plead a right divine
Unto his Mansoul; then to blows they go,
And Mansoul cries, "These wars will me undo!"
Mansoul, her wars seemed endless in her eyes,
She's lost by one, becomes another's prize;

And he again that lost her last would swear,
Have her I will, or her in pieces tear.

Mansoul, it was the very seat of war;
Wherefore her troubles greater were by far
Than only where the noise of war is heard,
Or where the shaking of a sword is fear'd!
Or only where small skirmishes are fought,
Or where the fancy fighteth with a thought.

She saw the swords of fighting men made red,
And heard the cries of those with them wounded.
Must not her frights, then, be much more by far
Than theirs that to such doings strangers are?
Or theirs that hear the beating of a drum,
But not made fly for fear from house and home?

Mansoul not only heard the trumpet sound,
But saw her gallants gasping on the ground;
Wherefore we must not think that she could rest
With them whose greatest earnest is but jest;
Or where the blust'ring threatenings of great wars
Do end in parleys, or in wording jars.

Mansoul, her mighty wars, they did portend
Her weal, or woe, and that world without end;
Wherefore she must be more concern'd than they
Whose fears begin and end the self-same day;
Or where none other harm doth come to him
That is engaged, but loss of life or limb;
As all must needs confess that now do dwell
In Universe, and can this story tell.

Count me not, then, with them who to amaze
The people, set them on the stars to gaze;
Insinuating with much confidence
That each of them is now the residence
Of some brave creatures; yea, a world they will
Have in each star, though it be past their skill
To make it manifest to any man
That reason hath, or tell his fingers can.

But I have too long held thee in the porch,
And kept thee from the sunshine with a torch.
Well, now go forward, step within the door,
And there behold five hundred times much more
Of all sorts of such inward rarities
As please the mind will, and will feed the eyes
With those which if a Christian thou wilt see
Not small, but things of greatest moment be.

Nor do thou go to work without my key,
(In mysteries men soon do lose their way,)
And also turn it right if thou wouldst know
My riddle, and wouldst with my heifer plough.
It lies there in the window. Fare thee well,
My next may be to ring thy passing bell.

JOHN BUNYAN.

THE HOLY WAR.

In my travels, as I walked through many regions and countries, it was my chance to happen into that famous continent of Universe. A very large and spacious country it is: it lieth between the two poles, and just amidst the four points of the heavens. It is a place well watered, and richly adorned with hills and valleys, bravely situate; and for the most part, at least where I was, very fruitful; also well peopled, and a very sweet air.

The people are not all of one complexion, nor yet of one language, mode, or way of religion; but differ as much as, it is said, do the planets themselves: some are right and some are wrong, even as it happeneth to be in lesser regions.

In this country, as I said, it was my lot to travel; and there travel I did, and that so long, even till I learned much of their mother-tongue, together with the customs and manners of them among whom I was. And, to speak truth, I *A natural state pleasing to the flesh.* was much delighted to see and hear many things which I saw and heard among them: yea, I had, to be sure, even lived and died a native among them, so was I *Christ.* taken with them and their doings, had not my Master sent for me home to his house, there to do business for him, and to oversee business done.

Now there is, in this gallant country of Universe, a fair and delicate town, *Man.* a corporation called Mansoul; a town, for its building so curious, for its situation so commodious, for its privileges so advantageous, (I mean, with reference to its original,) that I may say of it, as was said before of the continent in which it is placed, "There is not its equal under the whole heaven."

As to the situation of this town, it lieth just between the two worlds: and the first founder and builder of it, so far as by the *Scriptures.* best and most authentic records I can gather, was one Shad- *The Almighty. Gen. i. 26.* dai; and he built it for his own delight. He made it the mirror and glory of all that he made, even the top-piece, beyond anything else that he did in that country. Yea, so goodly a town was Mansoul when *Created. angels.* first built, that, it is said by some, the gods, at the setting up thereof, came down to see it, and sang for joy; and as he made it goodly to behold, so also mighty to have dominion over all the country round about. Yea, all were commanded to acknowledge Mansoul for their metropolitan, all were enjoined to do homage to it. Ay, the town itself had positive commission, and power from her King, to demand service of all, and also to subdue any that anywise denied to do it.

There was reared up in the midst of this town a most famous and stately palace; *The heart.* for strength, it might be called a castle; for pleasantness, a paradise; for largeness, a place so copious as to contain all *Eccles. iii. 11.* the world. This palace the King Shaddai intended but for himself alone, and not another with him: partly because of his own delights, and partly because he would not that the terror of strangers should be upon the town. This place Shaddai made also a garrison of; but committed the keeping of it only to the men of the town.

The walls of the town were well built; yea, so

fast and firm were they knit and *The powers of the soul.* compact together, that had it not been for the townsmen themselves, they could not have been shaken or broken for ever.

For here lay the excellent wisdom of him that built Mansoul, that the walls could *The body.* never be broken down nor hurt by the most mighty adverse potentates, unless the townsmen gave consent thereto.

This famous town of Mansoul had five gates, in at which to come, out at which to go; and these were made likewise answerable to the walls, to wit, impregnable, and such as could never be opened nor forced but by the will and leave of those within. The names of the gates were these: Ear-gate, Eye-gate, Mouth-gate, Nose-gate, and Feel-gate.

The five senses.

Other things there were that belonged to the town of Mansoul, which if you adjoin to these, will yet give further demonstration to all of the glory and strength of the place. It had always a sufficiency of provision within its walls : it had the best, most wholesome, and excellent law that then was extant in the world. There was not a rascal, rogue, or traitorous person then within its walls : they were all true men, and fast joined together: and this, you know, is a great matter. And to all these it had always, so long as it had the goodness to keep true to Shaddai, the king, his countenance, his protection, and it was his delight, &c.

The state of Mansoul at first.

Well, upon a time there was one Diabolus, a mighty giant, made an assault upon this famous town of Mansoul, to take it, and make it his own habitation. This giant was king of the blacks or negroes, and a most raving prince he was. We will, if you please, first discourse of the original of this Diabolus, and then of his taking of this famous town of Mansoul.

The devil.

Sinners, the fallen angels.

This Diabolus is indeed a great and mighty prince, and yet both poor and beggarly. As to his original, he was at first one of the servants of King Shaddai, made, and taken, and put by him into most high and mighty place, yea, and was put into such principalities as belonged to the best of his territories and dominions.

The origin of Diabolus.

This Diabolus was made son of the morning, and a brave place he had of it: it brought him much glory, and gave him much brightness; an income that might have contented his Luciferian heart, had it not been insatiable, and enlarged as hell itself.

Isa. xiv. 12.

Well; he seeing himself thus exalted to greatness and honour, and raging in his mind for higher state and degree, what doth he but begins to think with himself, how he might be set up as lord over all, and have the sole power under Shaddai. Now that did the king reserve for his Son, yea, and had already bestowed it upon him; wherefore he first consults with himself what had best to be done; and then breaks his mind to some other of his companions, to the which they also agreed. So, in fine, they came to this issue, that they should make an attempt upon the King's Son to destroy him, that the inheritance might be theirs. Well, to be short, the treason, as I said, was concluded, the time appointed, the word given, the rebels rendezvoused, and the assault attempted. Now the King and his Son being all, and always eye, could not but discern all passages in his dominions; and he having always love for his Son, as for

2 Pet. ii. 4.
Jude 6.

himself, could not, at what he saw, but be greatly provoked and offended : wherefore what does he but takes them in the very nick, and first trip that they made towards their design, convicts them of their treason, horrid rebellion, and conspiracy that they had devised, and now attempted to put into practice, and casts them altogether out of all place of trust, benefit, honour, and preferment : this done, he banishes them the court, turns them down into the horrible pits, as fast bound in chains, never more to expect the least favour from his hands, but to abide the judgment that he had appointed, and that for ever.

And yet, now, they being thus cast out of all place of trust, profit, and honour, and also knowing that they had lost their prince's favour for ever, being banished his courts, and cast down to the horrible pits, you may be sure they would now add to their former pride what malice and rage against Shaddai, and against his Son, they could. Wherefore, roving and ranging in much fury from place to place, if perhaps they might find something that was the King's to revenge by spoiling of that themselves on him ; at last they happened into this spacious country of Universe, and steer their course towards the town of Mansoul : and considering that that town was one of the chief works and delights of King Shaddai, what do they, but after counsel taken, make an assault upon that. I say, they knew that Mansoul belonged unto Shaddai ; for they were there when he built it, and beautified it for himself. So when they had found the place, they shouted horribly for joy, and roared on it as a lion upon the prey ; saying, " Now we have found the prize, and how to be revenged on King Shaddai for what he hath done to us." So they sat down and called a council of war; and considered with themselves what ways and methods they had best to engage in, for the winning to themselves this famous town of Mansoul ; and these four things were then propounded to be considered of :

1 Pet. v. 8.

A council of war.

First. Whether they had best all of them to show themselves in this design to the town of Mansoul ?

Proposals.

Secondly. Whether they had best to go and sit down against Mansoul, in their now ragged and beggarly guise?

Thirdly. Whether they had best show to Mansoul their intentions, and what design they came about ; or whether to assault it with words and ways of deceit ?

Fourthly. Whether they had not best to some of their companions to give out private orders to take the advantage, if they see one or more of the principal townsmen, to shoot them ; if thereby they should judge their cause and design will the better be promoted ?

First. It was answered to the first of these proposals in the negative ; to wit, that it would not be best that all should show themselves before the town, because the appearance of many of them might alarm and fright the town; whereas a few, or but one of them, was not so likely to do it. And to enforce this advice to take place, it was added further. that if Mansoul was frighted, or did take the alarm, "it is impossible," said Diabolus (for he spake now), "that we should take the town: for that none can enter into it without its own consent. Let, therefore, but few, or but one, assault Mansoul, and, in mine opinion," said Diabolus, "let me be he." Wherefore to this they all agreed; and then to the second proposal they came, namely,

Secondly. Whether they had best to go and sit down before Mansoul in their now ragged and beggarly guise?

To which it was answered also in the negative, By no means; and that because, though the town of Mansoul had been made to know, and to have to do, before now, with things that are invisible; they did never as yet see any of their fellow-creatures in so sad and rascally condition as they: and this was the advice of that fierce Alecto. Then said Apollyon, "The advice is pertinent; for even one of us appearing to them as we are now, must needs both beget and multiply such thoughts in them as will both put them into a consternation of spirit, and necessitate them to put themselves upon their guard; and if so," said he, "then, as my Lord Alecto said but now, it is in vain for us to think of taking the town." Then said that mighty giant, Beelzebub, "The advice that already is given is safe; for, though the men of Mansoul have seen such things as we were once, yet hitherto they did never behold such things as we now are. And it is best, in mine opinion, to come upon them in such a guise as is common to and most familiar among them." To this when they had consented, the next thing to be considered was, In what shape, hue, or guise, Diabolus had best to show himself, when he went about to make Mansoul his own. Then one said one thing, and another the contrary. At last Lucifer answered, That, in his opinion, it was best that his lordship should assume the body of some of those creatures that they of the town had dominion over: "for," quoth he, "these are not only familiar to them, but, being under them, they will never imagine that an attempt should by them be made upon the town; and, to blind all, let him assume the body of one of these Gen. iii. 1. beasts that Mansoul deems to be Rev. xx. 1, 2. wiser than any of the rest." This advice was applauded of all; so it was determined that the giant Diabolus should assume the dragon; for that he was, in those days, as familiar with the town of Mansoul, as now is the bird with the boy; for nothing that was in its primitive state was at all amazing to them. Then they proceeded to the third thing, which was,

Thirdly. Whether they had best show their intentions, or the design of his coming to Mansoul, or no?

This also was answered in the negative, because of the weight that was in the former reasons, to wit, for that Mansoul were a strong people, a strong people in a strong town, whose wall and gates were impregnable (to say nothing of their castle), nor can they by any means be won but by their own consent. "Besides," said Legion (for he gave answer to this), "a discovery of our intentions may make them send to their king for aid; and if that be done, I know quickly what time of day it will be with us; therefore let us assault them in all pretended fairness, covering of our intentions with all manner of lies, flatteries, delusive words; feigning of things that never will be, and promising of that to them which they shall never find: this is the way to win Mansoul, and to make them of themselves to open their gates to us; yea, and to desire us too to come in to them.

"And the reason why I think that this project will do, is, because the people of Mansoul now are every one simple and innocent; all honest and true: nor do they as yet know what it is to be assaulted with fraud, guile, and hypocrisy. They are strangers to lying and dissembling lips; wherefore we cannot, if thus we be disguised, by them at all be discerned; our lies shall go for true sayings, and our dissimulations for upright dealings. What we promise them, they will in that believe us; especially if in all our lies and feigned words we pretend great love to them, and that our design is only their advantage and honour." Now there was not one bit of a reply against this; this went as current down as doth the water down a steep descent; wherefore they go to consider of the last proposal, which was,

Fourthly. Whether they had not best to give out orders to some of their company, to shoot some one or more of the principal of the townsmen; if they judge that their cause may be promoted thereby?

This was carried in the affirmative; and the man that was designed by this stratagem to be destroyed, was one Mr. Resistance, otherwise called Captain Resistance; and a great man in Mansoul this Captain Resistance was; and a man that the giant Diabolus, and his band, more feared than they feared the whole town of Mansoul besides. Now who should be the actor to do the murder? that was the next: and they appointed one Tisiphane, a fury of the lake, to do it.

They thus having ended their council of war, rose up, and assayed to do as they had determined: they marched towards Mansoul, but all in a manner invisible, save one, only one; nor did he approach the town in his own likeness, but under the shape and in the body of the dragon. *The result of their council.*

So they drew up, and sat down before Ear-gate; for that was the place of hearing for all without the town, as Eye-gate was the place of perspection. So, as I said, he came up with his train to the gate, and laid his ambuscado for Captain Resistance, within bowshot of the town. This done, the giant ascended up close to the gate, and called to the town of Mansoul for audence. Nor took he any with him but one Ill-pause, who was his orator in all difficult matters. Now, as I said, he being come up to the gate (as the manner of those times was), sounded his trumpet for audience; at which the chief of the town of Mansoul, such as my Lord Innocent, my Lord Will-be-will, my Lord Mayor, Mr. Recorder, and Captain Resistance, came down to the wall to see who was there, and what was the matter. And my Lord Will-be-will, when he had looked over, and saw who stood at the gate, demanded what he was, wherefore he was come, and why he roused the town of Mansoul with so unusual a sound?

Diabolus then, as if he had been a lamb, began his oration, and said, "Gentlemen of the famous town of Mansoul, I am, as you may perceive, no far dweller from you, but

Diabolus, his oration.

near, and one that is bound by the King to do you my homage, and what service I can: wherefore, that I may be faithful to myself and to you, I have somewhat of concern to impart unto you: wherefore grant me your audience, and hear me patiently. And, first, I will assure you, it is not myself but you, not mine but your advantage, that I seek by what I now do, as will full well be made manifest, by that I have opened my mind unto you. For, gentlemen, I am, to tell you the truth, come to show how you may obtain great and ample deliverance from a bondage that, unawares to yourselves, you are captivated and enslaved under." At this the town of Mansoul began to prick up its ears. "And what is it, pray? what is it?" thought they. And he said, "I have somewhat to say to you concerning your King, concerning his law, and also touching yourselves. Touching your King, I know he is great and potent; but yet all that he hath said to you is neither true, nor yet for your advantage. 1. It is not true; for that wherewith he hath hitherto awed you shall not come to pass, nor be fulfilled, though you do the thing that he hath forbidden. But if there was danger, what a slavery is it to live always in fear of the greatest Diabolus' subtlety made up of lies. of punishments, for doing so small and trivial a thing as eating of a little fruit is! 2. Touching his laws, this I say, further, they are both unreasonable, intricate, and intolerable. Unreasonable, as was hinted before, for that the punishment is not proportioned to the offence: there is great difference and disproportion betwixt the life and an apple; yet the one must go for the other, by the law of your Shaddai. But it is also intricate, in that he saith, first, you may eat of *all*; and yet, after, forbids the eating of *one*. And then, in the last place, it must needs be intolerable; forasmuch as that fruit, which you are forbidden to eat of, (if you are forbidden any,) is that, and that alone, which is able, by your eating, to minister to you a good as yet unknown by you. This is manifest by the very name of the tree; it is called The Tree of Knowledge of Good and Evil: and have you that knowledge as yet? No, no; nor can you conceive how good, how pleasant, and how much to be desired to make one wise, it is, so long as you stand by your King's commandment. Why should you be holden in ignorance and blindness? Why should you not be enlarged in knowledge and understanding? And now, ah, ye inhabitants of the famous town of Mansoul! to speak more particularly to yourselves, you are not a free people, you are kept both in bondage and slavery, and that, by a grievous threat, no reason being annexed, but, So I will have it; so it shall be. And is it not grievous to think on, that that very thing that you are forbidden to do, might you but do it, would yield you both wisdom and honour? for then your eyes will be opened, and you shall be as gods. Now since this is thus," quoth he, "can you be kept by any prince in more slavery, and in greater bondage, than you are under this day? You are made underlings, and are wrapt up in inconveniences, as I have well made appear: for what bondage greater than to be kept in blindness? Will not reason tell you, that it is better to have eyes than to be without them? and so to be at liberty to be better than to be shut up in a dark and stinking cave?"

Captain Resistance slain. And, just now, while Diabolus was speaking these words to Mansoul, Tisiphane shot at Captain Resistance, where he stood on the gate, and mortally wounded him in the head; so that he, to the amazement of the townsmen, and the encouragement of Diabolus, fell down dead quite over the wall. Now when Captain Resistance was dead, (and he was the only man of war in the town,) poor Mansoul was wholly left naked of courage, nor had she now any heart to resist; but this was as the devil would have it. Then stood forth that he, Mr. Ill-pause, that Diabolus brought with him, who was his orator; and he addressed himself to speak to the town of Mansoul; the tenor of whose speech here follows:—

Ill-pause. "Gentlemen," quoth he, "it is my master's happiness, that he has this day a quiet and teachable auditory; Mr. Ill-pause, his speech to the town of Mansoul. and it is hoped by us that we shall prevail with you not to cast off good advice: my master has a very great love for you: and although, as he very well knows that he runs the hazard of the anger of King Shaddai, yet love to you will make him do more than that. Nor doth there need that a word more should be spoken to confirm for truth what he hath said; there is not a word but carries in it self-evidence in its bowels; the very name of the tree may put an end to all controversy in this matter. I therefore, at this time, shall only add this advice to you, under and by the leave of my lord," (and with that he made Diabolus a very low congee:) "Consider his words, look on the tree, and the promising fruit thereof; remember, also, that yet you know but little, and that this is the way to know more: and if your reasons be not conquered to accept of such good counsel, you are not the men that I took you to be." But when the townsfolk saw that the tree was good for food, and that it was pleasant to the eye, and a tree to be desired to make one wise, they did as old Ill-pause advised; they took and did eat thereof.

Now this I should have told you before, that even then, when this Ill-pause was making of his speech to the townsmen, my Lord Innocency (whether My Lord Innocency's death. by a shot from the camp of the giant, or from a sinking qualm that suddenly took him, or rather by the stinking breath of that treacherous villain, old Ill-pause, for so I am most apt to think) sunk down in the place where he stood, nor could he be brought to life again. Thus these two brave men died: brave men I call them, for they were the beauty and glory of Mansoul so long as they lived therein: nor did there now remain any more a noble spirit in Mansoul; they all fell down and yielded obedience to Diabolus, and became his slaves and vassals, as you shall hear.

Now these being dead, what do the rest of the townsfolk, but, as men that had found a fool's paradise, they presently, as afore was hinted, fall The town taken, and how. to prove the truth of the giant's words: and, first, they did as Ill-pause had taught them; they looked, they considered, they were taken with the forbidden fruit : " they took thereof, and did eat ;" and having eaten, they became immediately drunken therewith ; so they opened the gates, both Ear-gate and Eye-gate, and let in Diabolus, with all his bands, quite forgetting their good Shaddai, his law, and the judgment that he had annexed, with solemn threatening, to the breach thereof.

Diabolus, having now obtained entrance in at the gates of the town, marches up to the middle thereof, to make his conquest as sure as he could ; and finding, by this time, the affections of the people warmly inclining to him, he, as thinking it was best striking while the iron is hot, made this further deceivable speech unto them, saying, " Alas, my poor Mansoul ! I have done thee indeed this service, as to promote thee to honour, and to greaten thy liberty ; but, alas, alas ! poor Mansoul, thou wantest now one to defend thee ; for, assure thyself, that when Shaddai shall hear what is done, he will come ; for sorry will he be that thou hast broken his bonds, and cast his cords away from thee. What wilt thou do ? Wilt thou, after enlargement, suffer thy privileges to be invaded and taken away ? or what wilt thou resolve with thyself ?" Then they all, with one consent, said to this bramble, " Do thou reign over us."

He is entertained for their king. So he accepted the motion, and became the king of the town of Mansoul. This being done, the next thing was to give him possession of the castle, and so of the whole strength of the town. Wherefore into the castle he goes—it was that which Shaddai built in Mansoul, for his own delight and pleasure : this now was become a den and hold for the giant, Diabolus. Now having got possession of this stately palace, or castle, what doth he, but make it a garrison for himself, and strengthens and fortifies it with all sorts of provision against the King Shaddai, or those that should endeavour the regaining of it to him and his obedience again.

This done, but not thinking himself yet secure enough, in the next place he bethinks himself of new modelling the town : and so he does, setting up one and putting down another at pleasure. Wherefore, my Lord Mayor, whose name was my Lord Understanding, and Mr. Recorder, whose name was Mr. Conscience, those he puts out of place and power.

My Lord Mayor is turned out of place. 2 Cor. x. 4, 5. As for my Lord Mayor, though he was an understanding man, and one, too, that had complied with the rest of the town of Mansoul in admitting the giant into the town, yet Diabolus thought not fit to let him abide in his former lustre and glory, because he was a seeing man, wherefore he darkened it, not only by taking from him his office and power, but by building a high and strong tower, just between the sun's reflections and the windows of my lord's palace ; by which means his house and all, and the whole of his habitation, was made as dark as darkness itself, and thus, being alienated from the light, he became as one that was born blind. To this his house my lord was confined, Eph. iv. 18, 19. as to a prison ; nor might he upon his parole go further than within his own bounds. And now, had he had a heart to do for Mansoul, what could he do for it, or wherein could he be profitable to her ? So then, so long as Mansoul was under the power and government of Diabolus, and so long it was under him as it was obedient to him, which was even until by a war it was rescued out of his hand ; so long my Lord Mayor was rather an impediment in, than an advantage to, the famous town of Mansoul.

The Recorder put out of place. As for Mr. Recorder, before the town was taken, he was a man well read in the laws of his king, and also a man of courage and faithfulness to speak truth at every occasion ; and he had a tongue as bravely hung, as he had a head filled with judgment. Now, this man Diabolus could by no means abide, because, though he gave his consent to his coming into the town, yet he could not by all wiles, trials, stratagems, and devices, that he could use, make him wholly his own. True, he was much degenerated from his former king, and also much pleased with many of the giant's laws and service. But all this would not do, forasmuch as he was not wholly his : he would now and then think upon Shaddai, and have dread of his law upon him, and then he would speak with a voice as great against Diabolus as when a lion roareth : yea, and would also, at certain times, when his fits were upon him, (for, you must know, that sometimes he had terrible fits,) make the whole town of Mansoul shake with his voice ; and therefore the new king of Mansoul could not abide him.

Diabolus, therefore, feared the Recorder more than any that was left alive in the town of Mansoul, because, as I said, his words did shake the whole town ; they were like the rattling thunder, and also like thunder-claps. Since, therefore, the giant could not make him wholly his own, what doth he do, but studies all that he could to debauch the old gentleman, and, by debauchery, to stupify his mind, and more harden his heart in ways of vanity. And as he attempted so he accomplished his design ; he debauched the man, and, by little and little, so drew him into sin and wickedness that at last he was not only debauched as at first, and so by consequence defiled, but was almost (at last, I say) past all conscience of sin. And this was the farthest Diabolus could go. Wherefore, he bethinks him of another project, and that was, to per-The town taken off from heeding of him. suade the men of the town that Mr. Recorder was mad, and so not to be regarded. And for this he urged his fits, and said, " If he be himself, why doth he not do thus always? But," quoth he, " as all mad folks have their fits, and in them their raving language, so hath this old and doating gentleman." Thus, by one means or another, he quickly got Mansoul to slight, neglect, and despise whatever Mr. Recorder could say. For, besides what already you have heard, Diabolus had a way to make the old gentleman, when he was merry, unsay and deny what he in his fits had affirmed. And, indeed, this was the next way to make himself ridiculous, and to cause that no man should regard him. Also, now he never *How conscience becomes so ridiculous, as with carnal men it is.* spake freely for King Shaddai, but always by force and constraint. Besides, he would at one time be hot against that at which at another he would hold his peace, so uneven was he now in his doings. Sometimes he would be as if fast asleep, and again sometimes as dead, even then when the whole town of Mansoul was in her career after vanity, and in her dance after the giant's pipe.

Wherefore, sometimes, when Mansoul did use to be frighted with the thundering voice of the Recorder that was, and when they did tell Diabolus of it, he would answer, that what the old gentleman said, was neither of love to him, nor pity to them, but of a foolish fondness that he had to be prating; and so would hush, still, and put all to quiet again. And that he might leave no argument unurged that might tend to make them secure, he said, and said it often, "O Mansoul! consider that, notwithstanding the old gentleman's rage, and the rattle of his high and thundering words, you hear nothing of Shaddai himself;" (when, liar and deceiver that he was, every outcry of Mr. Recorder against the sin of Mansoul was the voice of God in him to them!) But he goes on, and says, "You see that he values not the loss nor rebellion of the town of Mansoul; nor will he trouble himself with calling of his town to a reckoning, for their giving up themselves to me. He knows, that though ye were his, now you are lawfully mine; so, leaving us one to another, he now hath shaken his hands of us.

"Moreover, O Mansoul!" quoth he, "consider how I have served you, even to the utmost of my power; and that with the best that I have, could get, or procure for you in all the world: besides, I dare say that the laws and customs that you now are under, and by which you do homage to me, do yield you more solace and content than did the paradise that at first you possessed. Your liberty, also, as yourselves do very well know, has been greatly widened and enlarged by me: whereas I found you a pent-up people, I have not laid any restraint upon you; you have no law, statute, or judgment of mine to fright you: I call none of you to account for your doings except the *Conscience.* madman, you know who I mean: I have granted you to live, each man like a prince in his own, even with as little control from me as I myself have from you."

And thus would Diabolus hush up and quiet the town of Mansoul, when the Recorder that was did at times molest them; yea, and with such cursed orations as these would set the whole *Men sometimes angry with their consciences.* town in a rage and fury against the old gentleman; yea, the rascal crew at sometimes would be for destroying of him. They have often wished, in my hearing, that he had lived a thousand miles off from them: his company, his words, yea, the sight of him, and especially when they remembered how in old times he did use to threaten and condemn them, (for all he was now so debauched,) did terrify and afflict them sore.

But all wishes were vain; for, I do not know how, unless by the power of Shaddai, and his wisdom, he was preserved in being amongst them. Besides, his house was as strong as a castle, and stood hard to a stronghold of the town; moreover, if at any time *Ill thoughts.* any of the crew or rabble attempted to make him away, he could pull up the sluices, and let in such floods as *Of fears.* would drown all round about him.

But to leave Mr. Recorder, and to come to my Lord Will-be-will, another of the gentry of the famous town of Mansoul. This *The will.* Will-be-will was as high-born as any man in Mansoul, and was as much, if not more, a freeholder, than many of them were: besides, if I remember my tale aright, he had some privilege peculiar to himself in the famous town of Mansoul. Now, together with these, he was a man of great strength, resolution, and courage, nor in his occasion could any turn him away. But, I say, whether he was proud of his estate, privileges, strength, or what, (but sure it was through pride or something,) he scorns now to be a slave in Mansoul; and therefore resolves to bear office under Diabolus, that he might, such a one as he was, be a petty ruler and governor in Mansoul: and headstrong man that he was! thus he began betimes; for this man, when Diabolus did make his oration at Ear-gate, was one of the first that was for consenting to his words, and for accepting of his counsel as wholesome, and that was for the opening of the gate, and for letting him into the town: wherefore Diabolus had a kindness for him, and therefore he designed for him a place; and perceiving the valour and stoutness of the man, he coveted to have him for one of his great ones, to act and do in matters of the highest concern.

So he sent for him, and talked with him of that secret matter which lay in his breast; but there needed not much persuasion in the *The will takes place under Diabolus.* case; for as at first he was willing that Diabolus should be let into the town, so now he was as willing to serve him there. When the tyrant, therefore, perceived the willingness of my lord to serve him, and that his mind stood bending that way, he forthwith made him the captain of the castle, governor of *Heart. Flesh. Senses.* the wall, and keeper of the gates of

Mansoul: yea, there was a clause in his commission, that nothing without him should be done in all the town of Mansoul; so that now, next to Diabolus himself, who but my Lord Will-be-will in all the town of Mansoul; nor could anything now be done but at his will and pleasure throughout the town of Mansoul. He had also one Mr. Mind for his clerk; a man to speak on, every way like his master; for he and his lord were in principle one, and in practice not far asunder. And now was Mansoul brought under to purpose, and made to fulfil the lusts of the will and of the mind.

Rom. viii. 7.

Eph. ii. 2, 3.

But it will not out of my thoughts, what a desperate one this Will-be-will was, when power was put into his hand. First, he flatly denied that he owed any suit or service to his former prince and liege lord. This done, in the next place he took an oath, and swore fidelity to his great master, Diabolus, and then, being stated and settled in his places, offices, advancements, and preferments, oh, you cannot think, unless you had seen it, the strange work that this workman made in the town of Mansoul!

First, he maligned Mr. Recorder to death; he would neither endure to see him, nor to hear the words of his mouth: he would shut his eyes when he saw him, and stop his ears when he heard him speak. Also he could not endure that so much as a fragment of the law of Shaddai should be anywhere seen in the town. For example, his clerk, Mr. Mind, had some old, rent, and torn parchments of the law of good Shaddai in his house: but when Will-be-will saw them he cast them behind his back. True, Mr. Recorder had some of the laws in his study; but my lord could by no means come at them: he also thought, and said, that the windows of my old Lord Mayor's house were always too light for the profit of the town of Mansoul. The light of a candle he could not endure. Now nothing at all pleased Will-be-will, but what pleased Diabolus his lord.

The carnal will opposeth conscience.

Neh. ix. 26.

Corrupt will loves a dark understanding.

There was none like him to trumpet about the streets the brave nature, the wise conduct, and great glory of the king, Diabolus. He would range and rove throughout all the streets of Mansoul, to cry up his illustrious lord; and would make himself even as an abject, among the base and rascal crew, to cry up his valiant prince. And, I say, when and wheresoever he found these vassals, he would even make himself as one of them. In all ill courses, he would act without bidding, and do mischief without commandment.

Vain thoughts.

The Lord Will-be-will also had a deputy under him, and his name was Mr. Affection, one that was also greatly debauched in his principles, and answerable thereto in his life: he was wholly given to the flesh, and therefore

Rom. i. 25.

they called him Vile-Affection. Now there was he and one Carnal Lust, the daughter of Mr. Mind, ("like to like," quoth the devil to the collier,) that fell in love and made a match, and were married: and, as I take it, they had several children, as Impudent, Blackmouth, and Hate-Reproof. These three were black boys; and besides these they had three daughters, as Scorn-Truth and Slight-God, and the name of the youngest was Revenge; these were all married in the town, and also begot and yielded many bad brats, too many to be inserted. But to pass by this:

A match betwixt Vile-Affection and Carnal Lust.

When the giant had thus engarrisoned himself in the town of Mansoul, and had put down and set up whom he thought good, he betakes himself to defacing. Now there was in the market-place of Mansoul, and also upon the gates of the castle, an image of the blessed King Shaddai: this image was so exactly engraven, (and it was engraven in gold,) that it did the most resemble Shaddai himself of anything that then was extant in the world. This he basely commanded to be defaced, and it was as basely done by the hand of Mr. No-Truth. Now, you must know, that as Diabolus had commanded, and that by the hand of Mr. No-Truth the image of Shaddai was defaced, he likewise gave order that the same Mr. No-Truth should set up in its stead the horrid and formidable image of Diabolus, to the great contempt of the former King, and debasing of his town of Mansoul.

Moreover, Diabolus made havoc of all remains of the laws and statutes of Shaddai that could be found in the town of Mansoul; to wit, such as contained either the doctrines of morals, with all civil and natural documents: also relative severities he sought to extinguish. To be short, there was nothing of the remains of good in Mansoul, which he and Will-be-will sought not to destroy; for their design was to turn Mansoul into a brute, and to make it like to the sensual sow, by the hand of Mr. No-Truth.

All law-books destroyed that could be so.

When he had destroyed what law and good orders he could, then, further to effect his design, namely, to alienate Mansoul from Shaddai her King, he commands, and they set up his own vain edicts, statutes, and commandments, in all places of resort or concourse in Mansoul, to wit, such as gave liberty to the lusts of the flesh, the lusts of the eyes, and the pride of life, which are not of Shaddai, but of the world. He encouraged, countenanced, and promoted lasciviousness and all ungodliness there. Yea, much more did Diabolus to encourage wickedness in the town of Mansoul; he promised them peace, content, joy, and bliss, in doing his commands, and that they should never be called to an account for their not doing the contrary. And let this serve to give a taste to them that love to hear tell of what is done beyond their knowledge, afar off in other countries.

1 John ii. 16.

Now Mansoul being wholly at his beck, and brought wholly to his bow, nothing was heard or seen therein, but that which tended to set up him.

But now he, having disabled the Lord Mayor and Mr. Recorder from bearing of office in Mansoul, and seeing that the town, before he came to it, was the most ancient of corporations in the world, and fearing, if he did not maintain greatness, they at any time should object that he had done them an injury; therefore, I say, that they might see that he did not intend to lessen their grandeur, or to take from them any of their advantageous things, he did choose for them a Lord Mayor and a Recorder himself; and such as contented them at the heart, and such also as pleased him wondrous well.

The name of the Mayor that was of Diabolus' making, was the Lord Lustings, a man that had neither eyes nor ears; *The new Lord Mayor.* all that he did, whether as a man or as an officer, he did it naturally as doth the beast; and that which made him yet the more ignoble, though not to Mansoul, yet to them that beheld, and were grieved for its ruins, was that he never could savour good, but evil.

The Recorder was one whose name was Forget-Good, and a very sorry fellow he was; he could remember nothing *The new Recorder.* but mischief, and to do it with delight. He was naturally prone to do things that were hurtful, even hurtful to the town of Mansoul, and to all the dwellers there. These two, therefore, by their power and practice, examples, and smiles upon evil, did much more grammar, and settled the common people in hurtful ways; for who doth not perceive, but when those that sit aloft are vile and corrupt themselves, they corrupt the whole region and country where they are?

Besides these, Diabolus made several burgesses and aldermen in Mansoul; such as *He doth make them new Aldermen, and who.* out of whom the town, when it needed, might choose them officers, governors, and magistrates; and these are the names of the chief of them: Mr. Incredulity, Mr. Haughty, Mr. Swearing, Mr. Whoring, Mr. Hard-Heart, Mr. Pitiless, Mr. Fury, Mr. No-Truth, Mr. Stand-to-Lies, Mr. False-Peace, Mr. Drunkenness, Mr. Cheating, Mr. Atheism; thirteen in all. Mr. Incredulity is the eldest, and Mr. Atheism the youngest of the company.

There was also an election of common-councilmen, and others: as bailiff, serjeants, constables, and others, but all of them, like to those aforenamed, being either fathers, brothers, cousins, or nephew to them; whose names, for brevity sake, I omit to mention.

When the giant had thus far proceeded in his *He buildeth three strong-holds.* work, in the next place he betook him to build some strongholds in the town; and he built three that seemed to be impregnable. The first he called the hold of Defiance, because it was made to command the whole town, and to keep it from the knowledge of its ancient King. The second he called Midnight-Hold, because it was built on purpose to keep Mansoul from the true knowledge of itself. The third was called Sweet-Sin-Hold, because by that he fortified Mansoul against all desires of good. The first of these holds stood close by Eye-gate, that as much as might be, light might be darkened there. The second was built hard by the old castle, to the end that that might be made more blind, if possible. And the third stood in the market-place.

He that Diabolus made governor over the first of these, was one Spite-God, a most blasphemous wretch. He came with the whole rabble of them that came against Mansoul at first, and was himself one of themselves. He that was made the governer of Midnight-Hold was one Love-no-Light; he was also one of them that came first against the town. And he that was made the governor of the hold called Sweet-Sin-Hold, was one whose name was Love-Flesh; he was also a very lewd fellow, but not of that country where the others are bound. This fellow could find more sweetness, when he stood sucking of a lust, than he did in all the Paradise of God.

And now Diabolus thought himself safe: he had taken Mansoul; he had engarrisoned himself therein; he had put down the old officers, and had set up new ones; he had defaced the image of Shaddai, and had set up his own; he had spoiled the old law-books, and had promoted his own vain lies; he had made him new magistrates, and set up new aldermen; he had built him new holds, and had manned them for himself. And all this he did to make himself secure, in case the good Shaddai or his Son should come to make an incursion upon them.

Now you may well think, that, long before this time, word by some or other could *Tidings carried to the court of what had happened to Mansoul.* not but be carried to the good King Shaddai, how his Mansoul, in the continent of Universe, was lost: and that the runagate giant Diabolus, once one of his Majesty's servants, had, in rebellion against the King, made sure thereof for himself. Yea, tidings were carried and brought to the King thereof, and that to a very circumstance.

As first how Diabolus came upon Mansoul (they being a simple people, and innocent) with craft, subtlety, lies, and guile: Item, That he had treacherously slain the right noble and valiant captain, their Captain Resistance, as he stood upon the gate with the rest of the townsmen: Item, How my brave Lord Innocent fell down dead (with grief, some say, or with being poisoned with the stinking breath of one Ill-pause, as say others) at the hearing of his just Lord and rightful Prince, Shaddai, so abused by the mouth of so filthy a Diabolonian as that varlet Ill-pause was. The messenger further told, that after this Ill-pause had made a short oration to the townsmen in behalf of Diabolus, his master, the simple town, believing that what was said was true, with one consent did open Ear-gate, the chief gate of the corporation, and did let him with his crew into a possession of the famous town of Mansoul. He further showed how Diabolus had served the Lord Mayor, and Mr. Recorder; to wit, that he had put them from all place of power and trust. Item, He showed also, that my Lord Will-be-will was turned a very rebel and runagate, and that so was one Mr. Mind, his clerk; and that they two did range and revel it all the town over, and teach the wicked ones their way. He said, moreover, that this Will-be-will was put into great trust, and particularly that Diabolus had put into Will-be-will's hand all the strong places in Mansoul; and that Mr. Affection was made my Lord Will-be-will's deputy, in his most rebellious affairs. Yea, said the messenger, this monster, Lord Will-be-will, has openly disavowed his King Shaddai, and hath horribly given his faith and plighted his troth to Diabolus.

Also, said the messenger, besides all this, the new king, or rather rebellious tyrant, over the once famous, but now perishing, town of Mansoul, has set up a Lord Mayor and a Recorder of his own. For Mayor, he has set up one Mr. Lustings; and for Recorder, Mr. Forget-Good; two of the vilest of all the town of Mansoul. This faithful messenger also proceeded, and told what a sort of new burgesses Diabolus had made; also that he had built several strong forts, towers, and strongholds in Mansoul. He told, too, the which I had almost forgot, how Diabolus had put the town of Mansoul into arms, the better to capacitate them on his behalf to make resistance against Shaddai, their king, should he come to reduce them to their former obedience.

Now the tidings-teller did not deliver his relation of things in private, but in open court, the King and his Son, high lords, chief captains, and nobles, being all there present to hear. But by that they had heard the whole of the story, it would have amazed one to have seen, had he been there to behold it, what sorrow and grief, and compunction of spirit there was among all sorts, to think that famous Mansoul was now taken: only the King and his Son foresaw all this long before, yea, and sufficiently provided for the relief of Mansoul, though they told not everybody thereof. Yet, because they also would have a share in condoling of the misery of Mansoul, therefore they also did, and that at the rate of the highest degree, bewail the losing of Mansoul. The King said plainly, that "it grieved him at the heart," and you may be sure that his Son was not a whit behind him. Thus they gave conviction to all about them, that they had love and compassion for the famous town of Mansoul. Well, when the King and his Son were

Grief at court to hear the tidings.

Gen. vi. 5, 6.

retired into the privy-chamber, there they again consulted about what they had designed before, to wit, that as Mansoul should in time be suffered to be lost, so as certainly it should be recovered again. Recovered, I say, in such a way, as that both the King and his Son would get themselves eternal fame and glory thereby. Wherefore, after this consult, the Son of Shaddai, (a sweet and comely person, and one that had always great affection for those that were in affliction, but one that had mortal enmity in his heart against Diabolus because he was designed for it, and because he sought his crown and dignity,) this Son of Shaddai, I say, having stricken hands with his Father, and promised that he would be his servant to recover his Mansoul again, stood by his resolution, nor would he repent of the same. The purport of which agreement was this, to wit, That at a certain time, prefixed by both, the King's Son should take a journey into the country of Universe, and there, in a way of justice and equity, by making amends for the follies of Mansoul, he should lay the foundation of her perfect deliverance from Diabolus, and from his tyranny.

The secret of his purpose.

The Son of God.

Isa. xlix. 5.
1 Tim. i. 15.
Heb. xiii. 14.

A brave design on foot for the town of Mansoul.

Moreover, Emmanuel resolved to make, at a time convenient, a war upon the giant Diabolus, even while he was possessed of the town of Mansoul; and that he would fairly, by strength of hand, drive him out of his hold, his nest, and take it to himself, to be his habitation.

By the Holy Ghost.

This now being resolved upon, order was given to the Lord Chief Secretary, to draw up a fair record of what was determined, and to cause that it should be published in all the corners of the kingdom of Universe. A short breviate of the contents thereof you may, if you please, take here as follows:

The Holy Scriptures.

"Let all men know, who are concerned, that the Son of Shaddai, the great King, is engaged, by covenant to his Father, to bring his Mansoul to him again: yea, and to put Mansoul, too, through the power of his matchless love, into a far better and more happy condition than it was in before it was taken by Diabolus."

These papers, therefore, were published in several places, to the no little molestation of the tyrant, Diabolus: "for now," thought he, "I shall be molested, and my habitation will be taken from me."

But when this matter, I mean this purpose of the King and his Son, did at first take air at court, who can tell how the high lords, chief captains, and noble princes that were there, were taken with the business! First, they whispered it one to another, and after that it began to ring out throughout the King's palace, all wondering at the glorious design that, between the King and his Son, was on foot

Among the angels.

for the miserable town of Mansoul; yea, the courtiers could scarce do anything, either for the King or kingdom, but they would mix, with the doing thereof, a noise of the love of the King and his Son that they had for the town of Mansoul.

Nor could these lords, high captains, and princes be content to keep this news at *Diabolus perplexed at the news.* court; yea, before the records thereof were perfected, themselves came down and told it in Universe. At last it came to the ears, as I said, of Diabolus, to his no little discontent; for you must think it would perplex him to hear of such a design against him. Well, but after a few casts in his mind, he concluded on these four things:

First. That this news, this good tidings, if possible, should be kept from the ears of the town of Mansoul: "for," said he, "if they shall once come to the knowledge that Shaddai, their former King, and Emmanuel, his Son, are contriving of good for the town of Mansoul, what can be expected by me, but that Mansoul will make a revolt from under my hand and government, and return again to him?"

Now, to accomplish this his design, he renews his flattery with the Lord Will-be-Will, and also gives him strict charge and command that he should keep watch by day and by night at all the gates of the town, especially Ear-gate and Eye-gate; "for I hear of a design," quoth he, "a design to make us all traitors, and that Mansoul will be reduced to its first bondage again. I hope they are but flying stories," quoth he; "however, let no such news by any means be let into Mansoul, lest the people be dejected thereat: I think, my lord, *The will engaged against the gospel.* it can be no welcome news to you— I am sure it is none to me: and I think, that at this time it should be all our wisdoms and care to nip the head of all such rumours as shall tend to trouble our people; wherefore I desire, my lord, that you will in this matter do as I say. Let there be strong guards daily kept at every gate of the town. Stop also and examine from whence such come that you perceive do from far come hither to trade: nor let them by any means be admitted into Mansoul, unless you shall plainly perceive that they are *All good thoughts and words in the town are to be suppressed.* favourers of our excellent government. I command, moreover," said Diabolus, "that there be spies continually walking up and down the town of Mansoul; and let them have power to suppress and destroy any that they shall perceive to be plotting against us, or that shall prate of what by Shaddai and Emmanuel is intended."

This, therefore, was accordingly done: my Lord Will-be-Will hearkened to his lord and master, went willingly after the commandment, and, with all the diligence he could, kept any that would from going out abroad, or that sought to bring these tidings to Mansoul, from coming into the town.

Secondly. This done, in the next place Diabolus, that he might make Mansoul as sure as he could, frames and *A new oath imposed upon Mansoul.* imposes a new oath and horrible covenant upon the townsfolk:

To wit, "That they should never desert him, nor his government, nor yet betray him, nor seek to alter his laws; but that they should own, confess, stand by, and acknowledge him for their rightful king, in defiance to any that do, or hereafter shall, by any pretence, law, or title whatever, lay claim to the town of Mansoul;" thinking belike that Shaddai had no power to absolve them from this covenant with death, and agreement with hell. Nor did the silly Mansoul stick or boggle at all at this most monstrous engagement, but, as if it had been a sprat in the mouth of a whale, they swallowed it without any chewing. Were they troubled at it? Nay, they rather bragged and boasted of their so brave fidelity to the tyrant, their pretended king; swearing, that they would never be changelings, nor forsake their old lord for a new.

Thus did Diabolus tie poor Mansoul fast; but jealousy, that never thinks itself strong enough, put him in the next place upon another exploit, which was, yet more, if possible, to debauch this town of Mansoul: wherefore he caused, by the hand of one Mr. Filth, an odious, *Odious atheistical pamphlets, and filthy ballads and romances.* nasty, lascivious piece of beastliness, to be drawn up in writing, and to be set upon the castle gates: whereby he granted and gave licence to all his true and trusty sons in Mansoul to do whatever their lustful appetites prompted them to do, and that no man was to let, hinder, or control them, upon pain of incurring the displeasure of their prince.

Now this he did for these reasons:

1. That the town of Mansoul might be yet made weaker and weaker, and so more unable, should tidings come that their redemption was designed, to believe, hope, or consent to the truth thereof; for Reason says, "The bigger the sinner, the less grounds of hopes of mercy."

2. The second reason was, If perhaps Emmanuel, the Son of Shaddai their King, by seeing the horrible and profane doings of the town of Mansoul, might repent, though entered into a covenant of redeeming them, of pursuing that covenant of their redemption; for he knew that Shaddai was holy, and that his Son, Emmanuel, was holy; yea, he knew it by woeful experience: for, for the iniquity and sin of Diabolus was he cast from the highest orbs. Wherefore, what more rational than for him to conclude, that thus for sin it might fare with Mansoul! But, fearing also lest this knot should break, he bethinks himself of another, to wit:

3. To endeavour to possess all hearts in the town of Mansoul, that Shaddai was raising of an army to come to overthrow and utterly to destroy this town of Mansoul; and this he did to forestal any tidings that might come to their ears

of their deliverance; "for," thought he, "if I first bruit this, the tidings that shall come after will all be swallowed up of this: for what else will Mansoul say when they shall hear that they must be delivered, but that the true meaning is, Shaddai intends to destroy them?"

The place of hearing and of considering. Wherefore he summons the whole town into the market-place, and there, with deceitful tongue, thus he addresses himself unto them:

"Gentlemen, and my very good friends, you are all, as you know, my legal subjects, and men of the famous town of Mansoul; you know how, from the first day I have been with you until now, I have behaved myself among you, and what liberty and great privileges you enjoyed under my government; I hope to your honour and mine, and also to your content and delight. Now, my famous Mansoul, a noise of trouble there is abroad, of trouble to the town of Mansoul; sorry am I thereof, for your sakes. For I have received but now, by the post, from my Lord Lucifer, (and he useth to have good intelligence,) that your old King Shaddai is raising of an army to come against you, to destroy you root and branch: and this, O Mansoul! is now the cause that at this time I have called you together, namely, to advise what in this juncture is best to be done. For my part, I am but one, and can with ease shift for myself, did I list to seek my own ease, and to leave my Mansoul in all the danger: but my heart is so firmly united to you, and so unwilling am I to leave you, that I am willing to stand and fall with you, to the utmost hazard that shall befall me. What say you, O my Mansoul! will you now desert your old friend; or do you think of standing by me?"

Then, as one man, with one mouth, they cried out together, "Let him die the death that will not!"

Then said Diabolus again, "It is in vain for us to hope for quarter, for this King knows not how to show it. True, perhaps, he, at his first sitting down before us, will talk of, and pretend to, mercy, that thereby, with the more ease, and less trouble, he may again make himself the master of Mansoul; whatever, therefore, he shall say, believe not one syllable or tittle of it, for all such language is but to overcome us; and to make us, while we wallow in our blood, the trophies of his merciless victory. My mind is, therefore, that we resolve to the last man to resist him, and not to believe him upon any terms; *for in at that door will come our danger.* But shall we be flattered out of our lives? I hope you know more of the rudiments of politics, than to suffer yourselves so pitifully to be served.

Very deceivable language.

"But suppose he should, if he gets us to yield, save some of our lives, or the lives of some of them that are underlings in Mansoul, what help will that be to you that are the chief of the town, especially of you whom I have set up, and whose greatness has been procured by you through your

faithful sticking to me? And suppose, again, that he should give quarter to every one of you, be sure he will bring you into that bondage under which you were captivated before, or a worse, and then what good will your lives do you? Shall you, with him, live in pleasure, as you do now? No, no. You must be bound by laws that will pinch you, and be made to do that which at present is hateful to you. I am for you, if you are for me; and it is better to die valiantly, than to live like pitiful slaves. But, I say, the life of a slave will be counted a life too good for Mansoul now: blood, blood, nothing but blood, is in every blast of Shaddai's trumpet against poor Mansoul now. Pray be concerned; I hear he is coming up; and stand to your arms, that now, while you have any leisure, I may learn you some feats of war. Armour for you I have, and by me it is; yea, and it is sufficient for Mansoul, from top to toe; nor can you be hurt by what his force can do, if you shall keep it well girt and fastened about you. Come, therefore, to my castle, and welcome, and harness yourselves for the war. There is helmet, breast-plate, sword, and shield, and what not, that will make you fight like men.

Lying language.

He is afraid of losing of Mansoul.

"1. My helmet, otherwise called a head-piece, is hope of doing well at last, what lives soever you live. This is that which they had, who said, that they should have peace, though they walked in the wickedness of their heart, to add drunkenness to thirst: a piece of approved armour this is; and whoever has it, and can hold it, so long no arrow, dart, sword, or shield, can hurt him; this, therefore, keep on, and thou wilt keep off many a blow, my Mansoul.

"2. My breast-plate is a breast-plate of iron. I had it forged in mine own country, and all my soldiers are armed therewith. In plain language, it is a hard heart; a heart as hard as iron, and as much past feeling as a stone; the which if you get and keep, neither Mercy shall win you, nor Judgment fright you. This, therefore, is a piece of armour most necessary for all to put on that hate Shaddai, and that would fight against him under my banner.

"3. My sword is a tongue that is set on fire of hell, and that can bend itself to speak evil of Shaddai, his Son, his ways, and people; use this, it has been tried a thousand times twice told; whoever hath it, keeps it, and makes that use of it as I would have him, can never be conquered by mine enemy.

"4. My shield is unbelief, or calling into question the truth of the word, or all the sayings that speak of the judgment that Shaddai has appointed for wicked men: use this shield; many attempts he has made upon it, and sometimes, it is true, it has been bruised; but they that have writ of the wars of Emmanuel against my servants have testified that 'he could do no mighty work there, because of their unbelief.' Now to handle this weapon of mine aright, it is not to believe things because they are true, of what sort, or by whomsoever asserted. If he speaks of judgment, care not for it; if he speaks of mercy, care not for it; if he promises, if he swear that he would do to Mansoul, if it turns, no hurt, but good. Regard

not what is said; question the truth of all; for this is to wield the shield of unbelief aright, and as my servants ought and do; and he that doth otherwise, loves me not, nor do I count him but an enemy to me.

"5. Another part or piece," said Diabolus, "of mine excellent armour is, a dumb and prayerless spirit, a spirit that scorns to cry for mercy, let the danger be ever so great: wherefore be you, my Mansoul, sure that you make use of this. What! cry for quarter? Never do that, if you would be mine. I know you are stout men, and am sure that I have clad you with that which is armour of proof: wherefore to cry to Shaddai for mercy, let that be far from you. Besides all this, I have a maul, firebrands, arrows, and death, all good hand-weapons, and such as will do execution."

After he had thus furnished his men with armour and arms, he addressed himself to them in such like words as these: " Remember." quoth

he, "that I am your rightful king; and that you have taken an oath, and entered into covenant, to be true to me and my cause : I say, remember this, and show yourselves stout and valiant men of Mansoul. Remember, also, the kindness that I have always showed to you ; and that, without your petition, I have granted to you external things : wherefore the privileges, grants, immunities, profits, and honours, wherewith I endowed you, do call for, at your hands, returns of loyalty, my lion-like men of Mansoul ; and when so fit a time to show it, as when another shall seek to take my dominion over you into their own hands? One word more, and I have done: Can we but stand, and overcome this one shock or brunt, I doubt not but in little time all the world will be ours ; and when that day comes, my true hearts, I will make you kings, princes, and captains, and what brave days shall we have then!"

Diabolus, having thus armed and fore-armed his servants and vassals, in Mansoul, against their good and lawful King Shaddai, in the next place he doubleth his guards at the gates of the town, and he takes himself to the castle, which was his stronghold. His vassals, also, to show their wills, and supposed, but ignoble gallantry, exercise themselves in their arms every day, and teach one another feats of war; they also defied their enemies, and sang up the praises of their tyrant; they threatened also what men they would be, if ever things should rise so high as a war between Shaddai and their king.

They of Mansoul show their loyalty to the giant.

Now all this time the good King, the King Shaddai, was preparing to send an army to recover the town of Mansoul again from under the tyranny of their pretended king, Diabolus : but he thought good, at the first, not to send them by the hand and conduct of brave Emmanuel his Son, but under the hand of some of his servants, to see first by them the temper of Mansoul, and whether by them they would be won to the obedience of their King. The army consisted of above forty thousand, all true men ; for they came from the King's own court, and were those of his own choosing.

Shaddai prepareth an army for the recovery of Mansoul.

The word of God.

They came up to Mansoul under the conduct of four stout generals, each man being a captain of ten thousand men ; and these are their names and their signs :—The name of the first was Boanerges ; the name of the second was Captain Conviction ; the name of the third was Captain Judgment ; and the name of the fourth was Captain Execution. These were the captains that Shaddai sent to regain Mansoul.

The captains' names.

These four captains, as was said, the King thought fit, in the first place, to send to Mansoul to make an attempt upon it ; for indeed, generally, in all his wars he did use to send these four captains in the van ; for they were very stout and rough-hewn men,

Psalm lx. 4.

men that were fit to break the ice, and to make their way by dint of sword, and their men were like themselves.

To each of these captains the King gave a banner, that it might be displayed, because of the goodness of his cause, and because of the right that he had to Mansoul.

First, to Captain Boanerges, for he was the chief; to him, I say, was given ten thousand men: his ensign was Mr. Thunder: he bare the black colours, and his escutcheon was three burning thunderbolts.

The second captain was Captain Conviction; to him was also given ten thousand men: his ensign's name was Mr. Sorrow: he did bare the pale colours, and his escutcheon was the book of the law wide open, from whence issued a flame of fire.

The third captain was Captain Judgment; to him was given ten thousand men: his ensign's name was Mr. Terror: he bare the red colours, and his escutcheon was a burning fiery furnace.

The fourth captain was Captain Execution; to him was given ten thousand men: his ensign was one Mr. Justice: he also bare the red colours, and his escutcheon was a fruitless tree, with an axe lying at the root thereof.

These four captains, as I said, had every one of them under his command ten thousand men, all of good fidelity to the King, and stout at their military actions.

Well, the captains and their forces, their men and under-officers, being had upon a day by Shaddai into the field, and there called all over by their names, were then and there put into such harness as became their degree, and that service that now they were going about for their king.

Now, when the King had mustered his forces, (for it is he that mustereth the host to the battle,) he gave unto the captains their several commissions, with charge and commandment, in the audience of all the soldiers, that they should take heed faithfully and courageously to do and execute the same. Their commissions were, for the substance of them, the same in form, though, as to name, title, place and degree of the captains, there might be some, but very small, variation: and here let me give you an account of the matter and sum contained in their commission.

A Commission from the great Shaddai, King of Their Commission. *Mansoul, to his trusty and noble captain, the Captain Boanerges, for his making war upon the town of Mansoul.*

"Oh, thou Boanerges, one of my stout and thundering captains, over one ten thousand of my valiant and faithful servants, go thou in my name, with this thy force, to the miserable town of Mansoul; and when thou comest thither, offer them first conditions of peace; and command them, that, casting off the yoke and tyranny of the wicked Diabolus, they return to me, their rightful Prince and Lord: command them, also, that they cleanse themselves from all that is his in the town of Mansoul, and look to thyself, that thou hast good satisfaction touching the truth of their obedience. Thus, when thou hast commanded them, if they in truth submit thereto, then do thou, to the uttermost of thy power, what in thee lies, to set for me a garrison in the famous town of Mansoul; nor do thou hurt the least native that moveth or breatheth therein, if they will submit themselves to me; but treat thou such as if they were thy friend or brother; for all such I love, and they shall be dear unto me; and tell them that I will take a time to come unto them, and to let them know that I am merciful.

"But if they shall, notwithstanding thy summons, and the producing of thy authority, resist, stand out against thee, and rebel; then do I command thee to make use of all thy cunning, power, might, and force, to bring them under by strength of hand. Farewell."

Thus you see the sum of their commissions; for, as I said before, for the substance of them, they were the same that the rest of the noble captains had.

Wherefore, they having received, each commander, his authority at the hand of their King, the day being appointed, and the place of their rendezvous prefixed, each commander appearing in such gallantry as became his cause and calling · so, after a new entertainment from Shaddai, with flying colours they set forward to march towards the famous town of Mansoul. Captain Boanerges led the van, Captain Conviction and Captain Judgment made up the main body, and Captain Execution brought up the rear. They then, having a great way to go, for the town of Mansoul was far off from the court of Shaddai, they marched through the regions and countries of many people, not hurting or abusing any, but blessing wherever they came. They also lived upon the King's cost in all the way they went.

Having travelled thus for many days, at last they came within sight of Mansoul; the which when they saw, the captains could for their hearts do no less than for a while bewail the condition of the town; for they quickly saw how that it was prostrate to the will of Diabolus, and to his ways and designs.

Well, to be short, the captains came up before the town, march up to Ear-gate, sit down there, for that was the place of hearing. So, when they had pitched their tents, and entrenched themselves, they addressed themselves to make their assault.

Now the townsfolk, at first beholding so gallant a company, so bravely accoutred, and so excellently disciplined, having on their glittering armour, and displaying of their flying colours, could not but come out of their houses and gaze. But the cunning fox, Diabolus, fearing that the people, after this sight, should, on a sudden summons, open

The world are convinced by the well-ordered life of the godly.

the gates to the captains, came down with all haste from the castle, and made them retire into the body of the town; who, when he had them there, made this lying and deceivable speech unto them:

Diabolus alienates their minds from them. "Gentlemen," quoth he, "although you are my trusty and well-beloved friends, yet I cannot but a little chide you for your late uncircumspect action, in going out to gaze on that great and mighty force that but yesterday sat down before, and have now entrenched themselves, in order to the maintaining of a siege against the famous town of Mansoul. Do you know who they are? whence they come? and what is their purpose in sitting down before the town of Mansoul? They are they of *That's false, Satan!* whom I have told you long ago, that they would come to destroy this town, and against whom I have been at the cost to arm you with cap-a-pie for your body, besides great fortifications for your mind. Wherefore, then, did you not rather, even at the first appearance of them, cry out, fire the beacons, and give the whole town an alarm concerning them, that we might all have been in a posture of defence, *Satan greatly afraid of God's ministers, that they will set Mansoul against him.* and been ready to have received them with the highest acts of defiance? then had you showed yourselves men to my liking; whereas, by what you have done, you have made me half afraid; I say, half afraid, that when they and we shall come to push a pike, I shall find you want courage to stand it out any longer. Wherefore have I commanded a watch, and that you should double your guards at the gates? Wherefore have I endeavoured to make you as hard as iron, and your hearts as a piece of the nether millstone? Was it, think you, that you might show yourselves women; and that you might go out like a company of innocents to gaze on your mortal foes? *He stirs them up to bid defiance to the ministers of the Word.* Fie, fie! put yourselves into a posture of defence; beat up the drum, gather together in warlike manner, that our foes may know, that before they shall conquer this corporation, there are valiant men in the town of Mansoul.

"I will leave off now to chide, and will not further rebuke you; but I charge you, that, henceforwards, you let me see no more such actions. Let not, henceforward, a man of you, without order first obtained from me, so much as show his head over the wall of the town of Mansoul. You have now heard me; do as I have commanded, and you shall cause me that I dwell securely with you, and that I take care as for myself, so for your safety and honour also. Farewell."

When sinners hearken to Satan, they are set in a rage against godliness. Now were the townsmen strangely altered; they were as men stricken with a panic fear: they ran to and fro through the streets of the town of Mansoul, crying out, "Help! help! the men that turn the world upside down are come hither also." Nor could any of them be quiet after; but still, as men bereft of wit, they cried out, "The destroyers of our peace and people are come." This went down with Diabolus. "Ah!" quoth he to himself, "this I like well; now it is as I would have it; now you show your obedience to your prince. Hold you but here, and then let them take the town, if they can."

Well, before the King's forces had sat before Mansoul three days, Captain Boa- *The King's trumpet sounded at Ear-gate.* nerges commanded his trumpeter to go down to Ear-gate: and there, in the name of the great Shaddai, to summon Mansoul to give audience to the message that he in his Master's name was to them commanded to deliver. So the trumpeter, whose name was Take-heed-what-you-hear, went up, as he was commanded, to Ear-gate, and there sounded his trumpet for a hearing; but there *They will not hear.* was none that appeared, that gave answer or regard, for so had Diabolus commanded. So the trumpeter returned to his captain, and told him what he had done, and also how he had sped; whereat the captain was grieved, but bid the trumpeter go to his tent. Again *A second summons.* Captain Boanerges sendeth his trumpeter to Ear-gate, to sound as before for a hearing; but they again kept close, came not out, nor would they give him an answer, so observant were they of the command of Diabolus, their king. Then the captains and other field-officers called a council of war, to consider what further was to be done for the gaining of the town of Mansoul: and, after some close and thorough debate upon the contents of their commissions, they concluded yet to give to the town, by the hand of the fore-named trumpeter, another summons to hear; but if that should be refused, said they, and that the town shall stand it out still, then they determined, and bid the trumpeter tell them so, that they would endeavour by what means they could to compel them by force to the obedience of their King.

So Captain Boanerges commanded his trumpeter to go up to Ear-gate again, *A third summons.* and, in the name of the great King Shaddai, to give it a very loud summons to come down without delay to Ear-gate, there to give audience to the King's most noble captains. So the trumpeter went, and did as he was commanded; he went up to Ear-gate, and sounded his trumpet, and gave a third summons to Mansoul. He said, moreover, that if this they should still refuse to do, the captains of his Prince would with might come down upon them, and endeavour to reduce them to their obedience by force.

Then stood up my Lord Will-be-will, who was the governor of the town—this Will-be-will was that apostate of whom mention was made before—and the keeper of the gates of Mansoul. He, therefore, with big and ruffling words, demanded of the trumpeter who he was, whence he came, and what was the cause of his making so hideous a noise at the gate, and speaking such insufferable words against the town of Mansoul?

The trumpeter answered, "I am servant to the most noble captain, Captain Boanerges, general of the forces of the great King Shaddai, against whom both thyself, with the whole town of Mansoul, have rebelled, and lift up the heel; and my master, the captain, hath a special message to his town, and to thee as a member thereof: the which if you of Mansoul shall peaceably hear, so; and if not, you must take what follows."

Then said the Lord Will-be-will, "I will carry thy words to my lord, and will know what he will say."

But the trumpeter soon replied, saying, "Our message is not to the giant, Diabolus, but to the miserable town of Mansoul: nor shall we at all regard what answer by him is made, nor yet by any for him; we are sent to this town to recover it from under his cruel tyranny, and to persuade it to submit, as in former times it did, to the most excellent King Shaddai."

Then said the Lord Will-be-will, "I will do your errand to the town."

The trumpeter then replied, "Sir, do not deceive us, lest in so doing you do deceive yourselves much more." He added, moreover, "For we are resolved, if in peaceable manner you do not submit yourselves, then to make a war upon you, and to bring you under by force. And of the truth of what I now say, this shall be a sign unto you: you shall see the black flag, with its hot, burning thunderbolts, set upon the mount to-morrow, as a token of defiance against your prince, and of our resolutions to reduce you to your Lord and rightful King."

The trumpeter returns to the camp. So the said Lord Will-be-will returned from off the wall, and the trumpeter came into the camp.

When the trumpeter was come into the camp, the captains and officers of the mighty King Shaddai came together to know if he had obtained a hearing, and what was the effect of his errand. So the trumpeter told, saying, "When I had sounded my trumpet, and had called aloud to the town for a hearing, my Lord Will-be-will, the governor of the town, and he that hath charge of the gates, came up, when he heard me sound, and, looking over the wall, he asked me what I was, whence I came, and what was the cause of my making this noise? So I told him my errand, and by whose authority I brought it. 'Then,' said he, 'I will tell it to the governor, and to Mansoul:' and then I returned to my lords."

Carnal souls make a wrong interpretation of the design of a gospel ministry. Then said the brave Boanerges, "Let us yet for a while lie still in our trenches, and see what these rebels will do." Now when the time drew nigh that audience by Mansoul was to be given to the brave Boanerges and his companions, it was commanded that all the men of war throughout the whole camp of

Shaddai should, as one man, stand to their arms, and make themselves ready, if the town of Mansoul shall hear, to receive it forthwith to mercy: but if not, to force a subjection. So, the day being come, the trumpeters sounded, and that throughout the whole camp, that the men of war might be in a readiness for that which then should be the work of the day. But when they that were in the town of Mansoul heard the sound of the trumpets throughout the camp of Shaddai, and thinking no other but that it must be in order to storm the corporation, they at first were put to great consternation of spirit: but, after they were a little settled again, they also made what preparation they could for a war, if they did storm, else to secure themselves.

Well, when the utmost time was come, Boanerges was resolved to hear their answer; wherefore he sent out his trumpeter again, to summons Mansoul to a hearing of the message that they had brought from Shaddai; so he went and sounded, and the townsmen came up, but made Ear-gate as sure as they could. Now when they were come up to the top of the wall, Captain Boanerges desired to see the Lord Mayor; but my Lord Incredulity was then Lord Mayor, for he came in the room of my Lord Lustings. So Incredulity he came up and showed himself over the wall. But when the Captain Boanerges had set his eyes upon him, he cried out aloud, "This is not he; where is my Lord Understanding, the ancient Lord Mayor of the town of Mansoul? for to him I would deliver my message."

Then said the giant (for Diabolus was also come down) to the captain, "Mr. Captain, you have, by your boldness, given to Mansoul at least four summons, to subject herself to your King, by whose authority I know not; nor will I dispute that now. I ask, therefore, what is the reason of all this ado? or what would you be at, if you know yourselves?"

Then Captain Boanerges, whose were the black colours, and whose escutcheon was the three burning thunderbolts, *Boanerges obtains a hearing.* (taking no notice of the giant, or of his speech,) thus addressed himself to the town of Mansoul: "Be it known unto you, O unhappy and rebellious Mansoul! that the most gracious King, the great King Shaddai, my master, hath sent me unto you, with commission" (and so he showed to the town his broad seal,) "to reduce you to his obedience. And he hath commanded me, in case you yield upon my summons, to carry it to you as if you were my friend or brother; but he also hath bid, that if, after summons to submit, you still stand out and rebel, we should endeavour to take you by force."

Then stood forth Captain Conviction, and said, (his were the pale colours, and for *The speech of Captain Conviction.* an escutcheon he had the book of the law wide open, &c.) "Hear, O Mansoul! Thou, O Mansoul, wast once famous for innocency, but now thou art degenerated into lies and deceit. Thou hast heard what my brother, the Captain Boanerges, hath said, and it is your wisdom, and will be your happiness to stoop to, and accept of conditions of peace and mercy when offered; especially when offered by one against whom thou hast rebelled, and one who is of power to tear thee in pieces, for so is Shaddai our King; nor when he is angry can any thing stand before him? If you say you have not sinned, nor acted rebellion against our King, the whole of your doings, since the day that you cast off his service, (and there was the beginning of your sin,) will sufficiently testify against you: what else means your hearkening to the tyrant, and your receiving him for your king? What means else your rejecting of the laws of Shaddai, and your obeying of Diabolus? Yea, what means this your taking up of arms against, and the shutting of your gates upon us, the faithful servants of your King? Be ruled, then, and accept of my brother's invitation, and overstand not the time of mercy, but agree with thine adversary quickly. Ah, Mansoul! suffer not thyself to be kept from mercy, and to be run into a thousand miseries, by the flattering wiles of Diabolus: perhaps that piece of deceit may attempt to make you believe that we seek our own profit in this our service: but know, it is obedience to our King, and love to your happiness, that is the cause of this undertaking of ours.

"Again, I say to thee, O Mansoul, consider if it be not amazing grace, that Shaddai should so humble himself as he doth. Now he, by us, reasons with you, in a way of entreaty and sweet persuasions, that you would subject yourselves to him. Has he that need of you, that we are sure you have of him? No, no; but he is merciful, and will not that Mansoul should die, but turn to him and live." (2 Cor. v. 18.)

Then stood forth Captain Judgment, whose Captain Judgment, his speech. were the red colours, and for an escutcheon he had the burning fiery furnace; and he said, "O ye, the inhabitants of the town of Mansoul, that have lived so long in rebellion and acts of treason against the King Shaddai; know, that we come not to-day to this place, in this manner, with our message, of our own minds, or to revenge our own quarrel; it is the King my Master that hath sent us to reduce you to your obedience to him; the which if you refuse in a peaceable way to yield, we have commission to compel you thereto. And never think of yourselves, nor yet suffer the tyrant Diabolus to persuade you to think, that our King, by his power, is not able to bring you down, and to lay you under his feet; for he is the former of all things; and if he touches the mountains, they smoke. Nor will the gate of the King's clemency stand always open: for the day that shall burn like an oven is before him: yea, it hasteth greatly, it slumbereth not. O Mansoul, is it little in thine eyes, that our King doth offer thee mercy, and that after so many provocations? Yea, he still holdeth out his golden sceptre to thee, and will not yet suffer his gate to be shut against thee; wilt thou provoke him to do it? If so, consider of what I say; to thee it is opened no more for ever. If thou sayest thou shalt not see him, yet judgment is before him; therefore trust thou in him. Yea, because there is wrath, beware lest he take thee away with his stroke; then a great ransom cannot deliver thee. Will he esteem thy riches? No, not gold nor all the forces of strength. He hath prepared his throne for judgment: for he will come with fire, and with his chariots, like a whirlwind, to render his anger with fury, and his rebukes with flames of fire. Therefore, O Mansoul, take heed, lest after thou hast fulfilled the judgment of the wicked, justice and judgment should take hold of thee." (Job xxxvi. 14, 18. Ps. ix. 7. Is. lxvi. 15.)

Now while Captain Judgment was making of this oration to the town of Mansoul, it was observed by some that Diabolus trembled. But he proceeded in his parable, and said, "Oh, thou woeful town of Mansoul! wilt thou not yet set open thy gate to receive us, the deputies of thy King, and those that would rejoice to see thee live? Can thine heart endure, or can thine hands be strong, in the day that he shall deal in judgment with thee? (Ezek. xxii. 14.) I say, canst thou endure to be forced to drink, as one would drink sweet wine, the sea of wrath that our King has prepared for Diabolus and his angels? Consider betimes, consider."

Then stood forth the fourth captain, the noble Captain Execution, and said: "O The speech of town of Mansoul, once famous, but Captain Execution. now like the fruitless bough, once the delight of the high ones, but now a den for Diabolus; hearken also to me, and to the words that I shall speak to thee in the name of the great Shaddai. Behold, 'the axe is laid to the root of the tree; every tree, therefore, that bringeth not forth good fruit, is hewn down and cast into the fire.' (Matt. iii. 7—10.)

"Thou, O town of Mansoul, hast hitherto been this fruitless tree; thou bearest nought but thorns and briers. Thy evil fruit bespeaks thee not to be a good tree; thy grapes are grapes of gall, thy clusters are bitter. Thou hast rebelled against thy King; and lo, we, the power and force of Shaddai, are the axe that is laid to thy roots. What sayest thou? Wilt thou turn? I say, again, tell me, before the first blow is given, wilt thou turn? Oh, turn, turn! Our axe must first be laid to thy root, before it be laid at thy root; it must first be laid to thy root in a way of threatening, before it is laid at thy root by way of execution: and between these two is required thy repentance, and this is all the time that thou hast. What wilt thou do? wilt thou turn, or shall I smite? If I fetch my blow, Mansoul, down you go: for I have commission to lay my axe at, as well as to, thy roots; nor will anything, but yielding to our King, prevent doing of execution. What art thou fit for, O Mansoul, if mercy prevent not, but to be hewn down and cast into the fire and burnt ?

" O Mansoul! patience and forbearance do not act for ever; a year, or two, or three, they may, but, if thou provoke by a three years' rebellion, (and thou hast already done more than this,) then what follows, but ' cut it down ?' nay, ' after that thou shalt cut it down ?' (Luke xiii. 9.) And dost thou think that these are but threatenings, or that our King has not power to execute his words ? O Mansoul, thou wilt find that in the words of our King, when they are by sinners made little or light of, there is not only threatenings, but burning coals of fire.

" Thou hast been a cumber-ground long already, and wilt thou continue so still ? Thy sin has brought this army to thy walls, and shall it bring it in judgment to do execution into thy town ? Thou hast heard what the captains have said, but as yet thou shuttest thy gates; speak out, Mansoul, wilt thou do so still, or wilt thou accept of conditions of peace ?"

These brave speeches of these four noble captains, the town of Mansoul refused to hear; yet a sound thereof did beat against Ear-gate, though *Mansoul desires time to make answer.* the force thereof could not break it open. In fine, the town desired a time to prepare their answer to these demands. The captains then told them, " that if they would throw out to them one Ill-pause, that was in the town, that they might reward him according to his works, then they would give them time to consider; but if they would not cast him to them over the wall of Mansoul, then they would give them none: " for," said they, " we know, that so long as Ill-pause draws breath in Mansoul, all good consideration will be confounded, and nothing but mischief will come thereon."

Then Diabolus who was there present, being loth *Diabolus interrupts them, and sends Incredulity to answer them.* to lose his Ill-pause, because he was his orator, (and yet be sure he had, could the captains have laid their fingers on him,) was resolved at this instant to give them answer by himself; but then, changing his mind, he commanded the then Lord Mayor, the Lord Incredulity, to do it, saying, " My Lord, do you give these runagates an answer, and speak out, that Mansoul may hear and understand you."

So Incredulity, at Diabolus's command, began, *His speech.* and said, " Gentlemen, you have here, as we do behold, to the disturbance of our prince, and the molestation of the town of Mansoul, camped against it; but from whence you come we will not know; and what you are we will not believe. Indeed, you tell us in your terrible speech that you have this authority from Shaddai; but by what right he commands you to do it, of that we shall yet be ignorant.

" You have, also, by the authority aforesaid, summoned this town to desert her lord, and, for protection, to yield up herself to the great Shaddai, your King; flatteringly telling her, that if she will do it, he will pass by, and not charge her with her past offences.

" Further, you have also, to the terror of the town of Mansoul, threatened with great and sore destructions to punish this corporation, if she consents not to do as your wills would have her.

" Now, captains, from whencesoever you come, and though your designs be never so *The true picture of unbelief.* right, yet know ye, that neither my Lord Diabolus, nor I, his servant, Incredulity, nor yet our brave Mansoul, doth regard either your persons, message, or the King that you say hath sent you : his power, his greatness, his vengeance, we fear not; nor will we yield to all your summonses.

As for the war that you threaten to make upon us, we must therein defend ourselves as well as we can; and, know ye, that we are not without wherewithal to bid defiance to you. And, in short, (for I will not be tedious,) I tell you that we take you to be some vagabond runagate crew, that, having shaken off all obedience to your king, have gotten together in tumultuous manner, and are ranging from place to place, to see if, through the flatteries you are skilled to make on the one side, and threats wherewith you think to fright on the other, to make some silly town, city, or country, to desert their place, and leave it to you: but Mansoul is none of them.

" To conclude : We dread you not, we fear you not, nor will we obey your summons; our gates we keep shut upon you, our place we will keep you out of; nor will we long thus suffer you to sit down before us. Our people must live in quiet : your appearance doth disturb them; wherefore, arise, with bag and baggage, and begone, or we will let fly from the walls against you."

This oration, made by old Incredulity, was seconded by desperate Will-be-will, in words to this effect.

" Gentlemen, we have heard your demands, and the noise of your threats, and have *The speech of the Lord Will-be-will.* heard the sound of your summons; but we fear not your force, we regard not your threats, but will still abide as you found us. And we command you, that in three days' time you cease to appear in these parts, or you shall know what it is once to dare offer to rouse the lion, Diabolus, when asleep in the town of Mansoul."

The Recorder, whose name was Forget-Good, he also added as followeth :

" Gentlemen, my lords, as you see, have with mild and gentle words answered *The speech of Forget-good, the Recorder.* your rough and angry speeches; they have, moreover, in my hearing, given you leave quietly to depart as you came, wherefore take their kindness and begone. We might have come out with force upon you, and have caused you to feel the dint of our swords; but as we love ease and quiet ourselves, so we love not to hurt or molest others."

Then did the town of Mansoul shout for joy; as if by Diabolus and his crew some great advantage had been gotten of the captains. They also rang the bells, and made merry, and danced upon the walls.

The town resolved to withstand the captains.

Diabolus also returned to the castle, and the Lord Mayor and Recorder to their place; but the Lord Will-be-will took special care that the gates should be secured with double guards, double bolts, and double locks and bars. And that Ear-gate especially might the better be looked to, (for that was the gate in at which the King's forces sought most to enter,) the Lord Will-be-will made one old Mr. Prejudice, an angry and ill-conditioned fellow, captain of the ward at that gate; and put under his power sixty men, called Deaf-men; men advantageous for that service, forasmuch as they mattered no words of the captains nor of their soldiers.

Now when the captains saw the answer of the great ones, and that they could not get a hearing from the old natives of the town, and that Mansoul was resolved to give the King's army battle; they prepared themselves to receive them, and to try it out by the power of the arm. And, first, they made their force more formidable against Ear-gate; for they knew that unless they could penetrate that, no good could be done upon the town. This done they put the rest of their men in their places. After which they gave out the word, which was, *Ye must be born again.* Then they sounded the trumpet; then they in the town made them answer, with shout against shout, charge against charge, and so the battle began. Now they in the town had planted upon the tower over Ear-gate two great guns, the one called High-mind, and the other Heady. Unto these two guns they trusted much; they were cast in the castle by Diabolus's founder, whose name was Mr. Puff-up: and mischievous pieces they were. But so vigilant and watchful when the captains saw them were they, that though sometimes their shot would go by their ears with a whizz, yet they did them no harm. By these two guns the townsfolk made no question but greatly to annoy the camp of Shaddai, and well enough to secure the gate; but they had not much cause to boast of what execution they did, as by what follows will be gathered.

The captains resolved to give them battle.

The guns planted upon Ear-gate.

The famous Mansoul had also some other small pieces in it, of the which they made use against the camp of Shaddai.

They from the camp also did as stoutly, and with as much of that as may, in truth, be called valour, let fly as fast at the town, and at Ear-gate: for they saw, unless they could break open Ear-

gate, it would be but in vain to batter the wall. Now the King's captains had brought with them several slings, and two or three battering-rams: with their slings, therefore, they battered the houses and people of the town, and with their rams they sought to brake Ear-gate open.

The sentence and power of the word.

The camp and the town had several skirmishes and brisk encounters; while the captains, with their engines, made many brave attempts to break open or beat down the tower that was over Ear-gate, and at the said gate to make their entrance: but Mansoul stood it out so lustily, through the rage of Diabolus, the valour of the Lord Will-be-will, and the conduct of old Incredulity, the Mayor, and Mr. Forget-good, the Recorder, that the charge and expense of that summer's wars, on the King's side, seemed to be almost quite lost, and the advantage to return to Mansoul; but when the captains saw how it was, they made a fair retreat, and entrenched themselves in their winter quarters. Now in this war you must needs think there was much loss on both sides, of which be pleased to accept of this brief account following:

The King's captains, when they marched from the court to come up against Mansoul to war, as they came crossing over the country, they happened to light upon three young fellows that had a mind to go for soldiers; proper men they were, and men of courage and skill, to appearance. Their names were Mr. Tradition, Mr. Human-wisdom, and Mr. Man's-invention. So they came up to the captains, and proffered their services to Shaddai. The captains then told them of their design, and bid them not to be rash in their offers; but the young men told them they had considered the thing before, and that hearing they were upon their march for such a design, came hither on purpose to meet them, that they might be listed under their excellencies. Then Captain Boanerges, for that they were men of courage, listed them into his company, and so away they went to the war.

An account of this war, with reference to the loss on both sides.

Now, when the war was begun, in one of the briskest skirmishes, so it was that a company of the Lord Will-be-will's men sallied out of the sallyport, or postern of the town, and fell in upon the rear of Captain Boanerges' men where these three fellows happened to be; so they took them prisoners, and away they carried them into the town, where they had not laid long in durance, but it began to be noised about the streets of the town, what three notable prisoners the Lord Will-be-will's men had taken, and brought in prisoners out of the camp of Shaddai. At length, tidings thereof were carried to Diabolus to the castle, to wit, what my Lord Will-be-will's men had done, and whom they had taken prisoners.

Then Diabolus called for Will-be-will, to know the certainty of this matter. So he asked him, and he told him. Then did the giant send for the prisoners, who when they were come, demanded of them who they were, whence they came, and what they did in the camp of Shaddai? and they told him. Then he sent them to ward again. Not many days after, he sent for them to him again, and then asked them if they would be willing to serve him against their former captains. They then told him that they did not so much live by religion, as by the fates of fortune; and that, since his lordship was willing to entertain them, they should be willing to serve him. Now, while things were thus in hand, there was one Captain Anything, a great doer in the town of Mansoul, and to this Captain Anything did Diabolus send these men, with a note under his hand, to receive them into his company; the contents of which letter were thus:—

"Anything, my darling,—The three men that are the bearers of this letter have a desire to serve me in the war; nor know I better to whose conduct to commit them than to thine; receive them, therefore, in my name, and as need shall require make use of them against Shaddai and his men. Farewell."

So they came, and he received them, and he made two of them serjeants; but he made Mr. Man's-invention his ancient-bearer. But thus much for this, and now to return to the camp.

They of the camp did also some execution upon the town; for they did beat down the roof of the old Lord Mayor's house, and so laid him more open than he was before. They had almost, with a sling, slain my Lord Will-be-will outright, but he made a shift to recover again. But they made a notable slaughter among the aldermen, for with one only shot they cut off six of them; to wit, Mr. Swearing, Mr. Whoring, Mr. Fury, Mr. Stand-to-lies, Mr. Drunkenness, and Mr. Cheating.

The roof of old Incredulity's house beat down.

Six aldermen slain.

They also dismounted the two guns that stood upon the tower over Eargate, and laid them flat in the dirt. I told you before, that the King's noble captains had drawn off to their winter quarters, and had there entrenched themselves and their carriages, so as, with the best advantage to their King, and the greatest annoyance to the enemy, they might give seasonable and warm alarms to the town of Mansoul. And this design of them did so hit, that I may say they did almost what they would to the molestation of the corporation.

The two great guns dismounted.

For now could not Mansoul sleep securely as before, nor could they now go to their debaucheries with that quietness as in times past; for they had from the camp of Shaddai such frequent warm and terrifying alarms, first at one gate and then at another, and again at all the gates at once, that they were broken as to former peace: yea, they had their alarms so frequently, and that when the nights were at longest, the weather

The effects of convictions, though common, if abiding.

coldest, and so, consequently, the season most unseasonable, that that winter was to the town of Mansoul a winter by itself; sometimes the trumpets would sound, and sometimes the slings would whirl the stones into the town. Sometimes ten thousand of the King's soldiers would be running round the walls of Mansoul at midnight, shouting, and lifting up the voice for the battle. Sometimes, again, some of them in the town would be wounded, and their cry and lamentable voice would be heard, to the great molestation of the now languishing town of Mansoul. Yea, so distressed with those that laid siege against them were they, that I dare say Diabolus, their king, had in these days his rest much broken.

In these days, as I was informed, new thoughts, and thoughts that began to run counter one to another, began to possess the minds of the men of the town of Mansoul. Some would say, "There is no living thus." Others would then reply, "This will be over shortly." Then would a third stand up and answer, "Let us turn to the King Shaddai, and so put an end to these troubles." And a fourth would come in with a fear, saying, "I doubt he will not receive us."

The old gentleman, too, the Recorder, that was so before Diabolus took Mansoul, he also began to talk aloud, and his words were now to the town of Mansoul as if they were great claps of thunder. No noise now so terrible to Mansoul as was his, with the noise of the soldiers, and the shoutings of the captains.

Conscience speaks.

Also things began to grow scarce in Mansoul; now the things that her soul lusted after were departing from her. Upon all her pleasant things there was a blast, and burning instead of beauty. Wrinkles now, and some shows of the shadow of death, were upon the inhabitants of Mansoul. And now, oh how glad would Mansoul have been to have enjoyed quietness and satisfaction of mind, though joined with the meanest condition in the world!

A famine in Mansoul.

The captains, also, in the deep of the winter, did send, by the mouth of Boanerges' trumpeter, a summons to Mansoul, to yield up herself to the King, the great King Shaddai. They sent it once, and twice, and thrice; not knowing but that at some time there might be in Mansoul some willingness to surrender up themselves unto him, might they but have the colour of an invitation to do it under. Yea, so far as I could gather, the town had been surrendered up to them before now, had it not been for the opposition of old Incredulity, and the fickleness of the thoughts of my Lord Will-be-will. Diabolus also began to rave; wherefore Mansoul, as to yielding, was not yet all of one mind; therefore they still lay distressed under these perplexing fears.

They are summoned again to yield.

I told you but now, that they of the King's army had this winter sent three times to Mansoul, to submit herself.

The first time the trumpeter went, he went with words of peace, telling of them, that the captains, the noble captains of Shaddai, did pity and bewail the misery of the now perishing town of Mansoul, and were troubled to see them so much at a stand in the way of their own deliverance. He said, moreover, that the captains bid him tell them, that if now poor Mansoul would humble herself, and turn, her former rebellious and most notorious treasons should, by their merciful King, be forgiven them, yea, and forgotten too. And having bid them beware that they stood not in their own way, that they opposed not themselves, nor made themselves their own losers, he returned again into the camp.

The second time the trumpeter went, he did treat them a little more roughly; for, after sound of trumpet, he told them, that their continuing in their rebellion did but chafe and heat the spirit of the captains, and that they were resolved to make a conquest of Mansoul, or to lay their bones before the town walls.

He went again the third time, and dealt with them yet more roughly; telling of them, that now, since they had been so horribly profane, he did not know, not certainly know, whether the captains were inclined to mercy or judgment. "Only," said he, "they commanded me to give you a summons to open the gates unto them." So he returned and went into the camp.

These three summonses, and especially the two last, did so distress the town, that they presently call a consultation, the result of which was this, that my Lord Will-be-will should go up to Ear-gate, and there, with sound of trumpet, call to the captains of the camp for a parley. Well, the Lord Will-be-will sounded upon the wall; so the captains came up in their harness, with their ten thousands at their feet. The townsmen then told the captains that they had heard and considered their summons, and would come to an agreement with them, and with their King Shaddai, upon such certain terms, articles, and propositions, as, with and by the order of their prince, they to them were appointed to propound; to wit, they would agree upon these grounds to be one people with them:

The town sounds for a parley.

" 1. If that those of their own company, as the new Lord Mayor, and their Mr. Forget-Good, with their brave Lord Will-be-will, might, under Shaddai, be still the governors of the town, castle, and gates of Mansoul.

" 2. Provided that no man that now serveth under their great giant, Diabolus, be by Shaddai cast out of house, harbour, or the freedom that he hath hitherto enjoyed in the famous town of Mansoul.

" 3. That it shall be granted them, that they of the town of Mansoul shall enjoy certain of their rights and privileges; to wit, such as have formerly been granted them, and that they have long lived in the enjoyment of, under the reign of their king,

Diabolus, that now is, and long has been, their only lord and great defender.

" 4. That no new law, officer, or executioner of law or office, shall have any power over them, without their own choice and consent.

" These be our propositions, or conditions of peace : and upon these terms," said they, " we will submit to your king."

But when the captains had heard this weak and feeble offer of the town of Mansoul, and their high and bold demands, they made to them again, by their noble captain, the Captain Boanerges, this speech following :

" Oh, ye inhabitants of the town of Mansoul, when I heard your trumpet sounded for a parley with us, I can truly say I was glad; but when you said you were willing to submit yourselves to our King and Lord, then I was yet more glad; but when, by your silly provisos and foolish cavils, you lay the stumbling-block of your iniquity before your own faces, then was my gladness turned into sorrow, and my hopeful beginnings of your return into languishing fainting fears.

" I count that old Ill-pause, the ancient enemy of Mansoul, did draw up those proposals that now you present us with, as terms of an agreement; but they deserve not to be admitted to sound in the ear of any man that pretends to have service for Shaddai. We do, therefore, jointly, and that with the highest disdain, refuse and reject such things, as the greatest of iniquities.

" But, O Mansoul, if you will give yourselves into our hands, or rather into the hands of our King, and will trust him to make such terms with you and for you as shall seem good in his eyes, (and I dare say they shall be such as you shall find to be most profitable to you,) then we will receive you, and be at peace with you ; but if you like not to trust yourselves in the arms of Shaddai, our King, then things are but where they were before, and we know also what we have to do."

Then cried out old Incredulity, the Lord Mayor, and said, " And who, being out of the hands of their enemies, as you see we are now, will be so foolish as to put the staff out of their own hands into the hands of they know not who? I, for my part, will never yield to so unlimited a proposition. Do we know the manner and temper of their King? It is said by some, that he will be angry with his subjects, if but the breadth of a hair they chance to step out of the way ; and of others, that he requireth of them much more than they can perform. Wherefore, it seems, O Mansoul, to be thy wisdom to take good heed what thou doest in this matter ; for if you once yield, you give up yourselves to another, and so you are no more your own. Wherefore, to give up yourselves to an unlimited power, is the greatest folly in the world ; for now you indeed may repent, but can never justly complain. But do you indeed know, when you are his, which of you he will kill,

Unbelief never is profitable in talk, but always speaks mischievously.

and which of you he will save alive ; or whether he will not cut off every one of us, and send out of his own country another new people, and cause them to inhabit this town ?"

This speech of the Lord Mayor undid all, and threw flat to the ground their hopes of an accord ; wherefore, the captains returned to their trenches, to their tents, and to their men, as they were ; and the mayor to the castle, and to his king.

Now Diabolus had waited for his return, for he had heard that they had been at their points. So, when he was come into the chamber of state, Diabolus saluted him with,—" Welcome, my lord ; how went matters betwixt you to-day ?" So the Lord Incredulity, (with a low congee,) told him the whole of the matter, saying : Thus and thus said the captains of Shaddai, and thus and thus said I. The which, when it was told to Diabolus, he was very glad to hear it, and said, " My Lord Mayor, my faithful Incredulity, I have proved thy fidelity above ten times already, but never yet found thee false. I do promise thee, if we rub over this brunt, to prefer thee to a place of honour, a place far better than to be Lord Mayor of Mansoul ; I will make thee my universal deputy, and thou shalt, next to me, have all nations under thy hand ; yea, and thou shalt lay hands upon them, that they may not resist thee ; nor shall any of our vassals walk more at liberty, but those that shall be content to walk in thy fetters."

Now came the Lord Mayor out from Diabolus, as if he had obtained a favour indeed ; wherefore, to his habitation he goes in great state, and thinks to feed himself well enough with hopes, until the time came that his greatness should be enlarged.

But now, though the Lord Mayor and Diabolus did thus well agree, yet this repulse to the brave captains put Mansoul into a mutiny ; for while old Incredulity went into the castle to congratulate his lord with what had passed, the old Lord Mayor, that was so before Diabolus came to the

The understanding and conscience begin to receive conviction, and they set the soul in a hubbub.

town, to wit, my Lord Understanding, and the old Recorder, Mr. Conscience, getting intelligence of what had passed at Ear-gate, (for you must know that they might not be suffered to be at that debate lest they should then have mutinied for the captains ;) but, I say, they got intelligence of what had passed there, and were much concerned therewith ; wherefore, they, getting some of the town together, began to possess them with the reasonableness of the noble captains' demands, and with the bad consequences that would follow upon the speech of old Incredulity, the Lord Mayor ; to wit, how little reverence he showed therein, either to the captains, or to their King ; also how he implicitly charged them with unfaithfulness and treachery ; " for what less," quoth he, " could be made of his words, when he said he would not yield to their proposition ? and added moreover a supposition, that he would destroy us, when before he had sent us word that

he would show us mercy ?" The multitude, being now possessed with the conviction of the evil that old Incredulity had done, began to run *A mutiny in* together by companies in all places, *Mansoul.* and in every corner of the streets of Mansoul ; and first they began to mutter, then to talk openly ; and after that they ran to and fro, and cried as they ran, " Oh the brave captains of Shaddai! would we were under the government of the captains, and of Shaddai their King !" When the Lord Mayor had intelligence that Mansoul was in an uproar, down he comes to appease the people, and thought to have quashed their heat with the bigness and the show of his countenance. But when they saw him, they came running upon him, and had doubtless done him a mischief had he not betaken himself to home. However, they strongly assaulted the house where he was, to have pulled it down about his ears ; but the place was too strong, so they failed of that. So he, taking some courage, addressed himself out at a window to the people in this manner :

" Gentlemen, what is the reason that there is here such an uproar to-day ?"

Then answered my Lord Understanding, " It is even because thou and thy master have carried it not rightly, and as you should, to the captains of Shaddai ; for in three things you are faulty. First, in that you would not let Mr. Conscience and myself be at the hearing of your discourse. Secondly, in that you propounded such terms of peace to the captains, by no means could be granted, unless they had intended that their Shaddai should have been only a titular prince ; and that Mansoul should still have had power, by law, to have lived in all lewdness and vanity before him, and so, by consequence, Diabolus should still here be king in power, and the other only king in name. Thirdly, for that thou didst thyself, after the captains had showed us upon what conditions they would have received us to mercy, even undo all again with thy unsavoury, and unseasonable, and ungodly speech."

When old Incredulity had heard this speech, he cried out, " Treason ! treason ! To *Sin and the* your arms, to your arms, O ye, the *soul at odds.* trusty friends of Diabolus in Mansoul !"

Under. " Sir, you may put upon my words what meaning you please ; but I am sure that the captains of such a high lord as theirs is deserved a better treatment at your hands."

Then said old Incredulity, " This is but little better. But, Sir," quoth he, " what I spake I spake for my prince, for his government, and the quieting of the people, whom, by your unlawful actions, you have this day set to mutiny against us."

Then replied the old Recorder, whose name was Mr. Conscience, and said, " Sir, you ought not thus to retort upon what my Lord Understanding hath said. It is evident enough that he hath spoken the truth, and that you are an enemy to Mansoul; be convinced, then, of the evil of your saucy and malapert language, and of the grief that you have put the captains to; yea, and of the damages that you have done to Mansoul thereby. Had you accepted of the conditions, the sound of the trumpet and the alarm of war had now ceased about the town of Mansoul; but that dreadful sound abides, and your want of wisdom in your speech has been the cause of it."

Incred. Then said old Incredulity: "Sir, if I live, I will do your errand to Diabolus, and there you shall have an answer to your words. Meanwhile we will seek the good of the town, and not ask counsel of you."

Und. "Sir, your prince and you are both foreigners to Mansoul, and not the natives thereof. And who can tell but that when you have brought us into greater straits, when you also shall see that yourselves can be safe by no other means than by flight, you may leave us and shift for yourselves, or set us on fire, and go away in the smoke, or by the light of our burning, and so leave us in our ruins."

Incred. "Sir, you forget that you are under a governor, and that you ought to demean yourself like a subject; and know ye, when my Lord the King shall hear of this day's work, he will give you but little thanks for your labour."

Now while these gentlemen were thus in their chiding words, down come, from the walls and the gates of the town, the Lord Will-be-will, Mr. Prejudice, Old Ill-pause, and several of the new-made aldermen and burgesses, and they asked the reason of the hubbub and tumult. And with that every man began to tell his own tale, so that nothing could be heard distinctly. Then was a silence commanded, and the old fox Incredulity began to speak. "My Lord," quoth he, "here are a couple of peevish gentlemen that have, as a fruit of their bad dispositions, and, as I fear, through the advice of one Mr. Discontent, tumultuously gathered this company against me this day, and also attempted to run the town into acts of rebellion against our prince."

Then stood up all the Diabolonians that were present, and affirmed these things to be true.

Now when they that took part with my Lord Understanding and with Mr. Conscience, perceived that they were like to come to the worst, for that force and power was on the other side, they came in for their help and relief. So a great company was on both sides. Then they on Incredulity's side would have had the two old gentlemen presently away to prison; but they on the other side said they should not. Then they began to cry up parties again; the Diabolonians cried up old Incredulity, Forget-good, the new aldermen, and their great one, Diabolus; and the other party, they as fast cried up Shaddai, the captains, his laws, their mercifulness, and applauded their conditions and ways. Thus the bickerment went a

Men of arms come down.

A great confusion.

while; at last they passed from words to blows, and now there were knocks on both sides. The good old gentleman, Mr. Conscience, was knocked down twice by one of the Diabolonians, whose name was Mr. Benumbing. And my Lord Understanding had like to have been slain with a harquebus, but that he that shot wanted to take his aim aright. Nor did the other side wholly escape, for there was one Mr. Rash-head, a Diabolonian, that had his brains beaten out by Mr. Mind, the Lord Will-be-will's servant; and it made me laugh to see how old Mr. Prejudice was kicked and tumbled about in the dirt. For, though a while since he was made captain of a company of the Diabolonians, to the hurt and damage of the town, yet now they had got him under their feet; and I will assure you he had, by some of the Lord Understanding's party, his crown soundly cracked to boot. Mr. Anything, also, he became a brisk man in the broil, but both sides were against him, because he was true to none. Yet he had for his malapertness one of his legs broken, and he that did it wished it had been his neck. Much harm more was done on both sides, but this must not be forgotten; it was now a wonder to see my Lord Will-be-will so indifferent as he was; he did not seem to take one side more than another, only it was perceived that he smiled to see how old Prejudice was tumbled up and down in the dirt. Also when Captain Anything came halting up before him, he seemed to take but little notice of him.

They fall from words to blows.

A hot skirmish.

Harm done on both sides.

Now when the uproar was over, Diabolus sends for my Lord Understanding, and Mr. Conscience, and claps them both up in prison, as the ringleaders and managers of this most heavy riotous rout in Mansoul. So now the town began to be quiet again, and the prisoners were used hardly; yea, he thought to have made them away, but that the present juncture did not serve for that purpose, for that war was in all their gates. But let us return again to our story. The captains, when they were gone back from the gate, and were come into the camp again, called a council of war, to consult what was further for them to do. Now some said, Let us go up presently and fall upon the town, but the greatest part thought rather better it would be to give them another summons to yield; and the reason why they thought this to be best was, because that, so far as could be perceived, the town of Mansoul now was more inclinable than heretofore. And if, said they, while some of them are in a way of inclination, we should by ruggedness give them distaste, we may set them further from closing with our summons than we would be willing they should.

Wherefore to this advice they agreed, and called a trumpeter, put words into his mouth, set him

The two old gentlemen put in prison, as the authors of this revel rout.

The captains call a council, and consult what to do.

his time, and bid him God speed. Well, many

The result is, they send another trumpeter to summon the town to yield.

hours were not expired before the trumpeter addressed himself to his journey. Wherefore, coming up to the wall of the town, he steereth his course to Ear-gate, and there sounded, as he was commanded. They, then, that were within came out to see what was the matter, and the trumpeter made them this speech following :—

"O hard-hearted and deplorable town of Man-

The summons itself.

soul, how long wilt thou love thy sinful, sinful simplicity, and ye fools delight in your scorning? As yet despise you the offers of peace and deliverance? As yet will ye refuse the golden offers of Shaddai, and trust to the lies and falsehoods of Diabolus? Think you, when Shaddai should have conquered you, that the remembrance of these your carriages towards him will yield you peace and comfort? or that, by ruffling language, you can make him afraid as a grasshopper? Doth he entreat you for fear of you? Do you think that you are stronger than he? Look to the heavens, and behold, and consider the stars, how high are they? Can you stop the sun from running his course, and hinder the moon from giving her light? Can you count the number of the stars, or stay the bottles of heaven? Can you call for the waters of the sea, and cause them to cover the face of the ground? Can you behold every one that is proud, and abase him, and bind their faces in secret? Yet these are some of the works of our King, in whose name, this day, we come up unto you, that you may be brought under his authority. In his name, therefore, I summon you again to yield up yourselves to his captains."

At this summons the Mansoulians seemed to be

The town at a stand.

at a stand, and knew not what answer to make; wherefore Diabolus forthwith appeared, and took upon him to do it himself, and thus he begins, but turns his speech to them of Mansoul :—

"Gentlemen," quoth he, "and my faithful sub-

Diabolus makes a speech to the town; and endeavours to terrify it with the greatness of God.

jects, if it is true that this summoner hath said concerning the greatness of their King, by his terror you will always be kept in bondage, and so be made to sneak. Yea, how can you now, though he is at a distance, endure to think of such a mighty one? And if not to think of him while at a distance, how can you endure to be in his presence? I, your prince, am familiar with you, and you may play with me as you would with a grasshopper. Consider, therefore, what is for your profit, and remember the immunities that I have granted you. Farther, if all be true that this man hath said, how comes it to pass that the subjects of Shaddai are so enslaved ·in all places where they come? None in the universe so unhappy as they; none so trampled upon as they. Consider, my Mansoul. Would thou wert as loth to leave me

as I am loth to leave thee! But consider, I say, the ball is yet at thy foot; liberty you have, if you know how to use it; yea, a king you have too, if you can tell how to love and obey him."

Upon this speech, the town of Mansoul did again harden their hearts yet more

He drives Mansoul into despair.

against the captains of Shaddai. The thoughts of his greatness did quite quash them, and the thoughts of his holiness sunk them in despair. Wherefore, after a short consultation, they, of the Diabolonian party they were, sent back this word by the trumpeter, "That, for their parts, they were resolved to

Mansoul grows worse and worse.

stick to their king, but never to yield to Shaddai. So it was but in vain to give them any further summons, for they had rather die upon the place than yield." And now things seemed to be gone quite back, and Mansoul to be out of reach or call; yet the captains, who knew what their Lord could do, would not yet be beat out of heart. They therefore send them another summons, more sharp and severe than the last; but the oftener they were sent to, to be reconciled to Shaddai, the further off they were. "As they called them, so they went from them;" yea, "though they called them to the Most High." (Hos. xi. 2, 7.)

So they ceased that way to deal with them any more, and inclined to think of another way. The captains, there-

The captains leave off to summons, and betake themselves to prayer.

fore, did gather themselves together, to have free conference among themselves, to know what was yet to be done to gain the town, and to deliver it from the tyranny of Diabolus. And one said after this manner, and another after that. Then stood up the right noble, the Captain Conviction, and said, "My brethren, mine opinion is this :—

"First. That we continually play our slings into the town, and keep it in a continual alarm, molesting of them day and night; by thus doing, we shall stop the growth of their rampant spirit. For a lion may be tamed by continual molestations.

"Second. This done, I advise that, in the next place, we, with one consent, draw up a petition to our Lord Shaddai; by which, after we have showed our King the condition of Mansoul, and of affairs here, and have begged his pardon for our no better success, we will earnestly implore his Majesty's help, and that he will please to send us more force and power; and some gallant and well-spoken commander to head them; that so his Majesty may not lose the benefit of these his good beginnings, but may complete his conquest upon the town of Mansoul."

To this speech of the noble Captain Conviction, they, as one man, consented: and agreed that a petition should forthwith be drawn up, and sent by a fit man away to Shaddai with speed. The contents of the petition were thus :—

"Most gracious and glorious King, the Lord of the best world, and the builder of the town of

Mansoul: we have, dread Sovereign, at thy commandment, put our lives in jeopardy, and at thy bidding made a war upon the famous town of Mansoul. When we went up against it, we did, according to our commission, first offer conditions of peace unto it. But they, great King, set light by our counsel, and would none of our reproof. (Matt. xxii. 5. Prov. i. 25—30. Zech. x. 11, 12.) They were for shutting of the gates, and for keeping us out of the town. They also mounted their guns, they sallied out upon us, and have done us what damage they could; but we pursued them, with alarm upon alarm, requiting of them with such retribution as was meet, and have done some execution upon the town. Diabolus, Incredulity, and Will-be-will are the great doers against us; now we are in our winter quarters, but so as that we do yet with a high hand molest and distress the town. Once, as we think, had we had but one substantial friend in the town, such as would but have seconded the sound of our summons as they ought, the people might have yielded themselves. But there were none but enemies there, nor any to speak in behalf of our Lord to the town; wherefore, though we have done as we could, yet Mansoul abides in a state of rebellion against thee. Now, King of kings, let it please thee to pardon the unsuccessfulness of thy servants, who have been no more advantageous in so desirable a work as the conquering of Mansoul is; and send, Lord, as we now desire, more forces to Mansoul, that it may be subdued; and a man to head them, that the town may both love and fear. We do not thus speak because we are willing to relinquish the wars, for we are for laying of our bones against the place; but that the town of Mansoul may be won for thy Majesty. We also pray thy Majesty for expedition in this matter, that, after their conquest, we may be at liberty to be sent about other thy gracious designs. Amen."

The petition thus drawn up was sent away with haste to the King, by the hand of *Who carried* that good man, Mr. Love-to-Man- *this petition.* soul.

When this petition was come to the palace of the *To whom it was* King, who should it be delivered to, *delivered.* but to the King's Son. So he took it and read it, and because the contents of it pleased him well, he mended, and also in some things added to the petition himself. So, after he had made such amendments and additions as he thought convenient, with his own hand, he carried it in to *The King re-* the King; to whom when he had *ceives it with* with obeisance delivered it, he put *gladness.* on authority, and spake to it himself.

Now the King, at the sight of the petition, was glad; but how much more, think you, when it was seconded by his Son? It pleased him also to hear that his servants that camped against Mansoul were so hearty in the work, and so steadfast in their resolves, and that they had already got some ground upon the famous town of Mansoul.

Wherefore the King called to him Emmanuel, his Son, who said, "Here am I, *The King calls* my Father." Then said the King, *his Son, and* "Thou knowest, as I do myself, *tells him that* the condition of the town of Man- *he shall go to* soul, and what we have purposed, *conquer the* and what thou hast done to redeem *town of Man-* it. Come now, therefore, my Son, *soul, and he is* and prepare thyself for the war, for thou shalt go to my camp at Mansoul. Thou shalt also there prosper, and prevail, and conquer the town of Mansoul.

Then said the King's Son, "Thy law is within my heart. I delight to do thy will." (Heb. x.) This

is the day that I have longed for, and the work
that I have waited for all this while.

He solaceth himself with the thoughts of this work.
Grant me, therefore, what force thou shalt in thy wisdom think meet, and I will go, and will deliver from Diabolus, and from his power, thy perishing town of Mansoul. My heart has been often pained within me for the miserable town of Mansoul; but now it is rejoiced, but now it is glad." And with that he leaped over the mountains for joy; saying, " I have not in my heart thought anything too dear for Mansoul; the day of vengeance is in mine heart for thee, my Mansoul; and glad am I that thou, my Father, hast made me the Captain of their salvation. (Heb. ii. 10.) And I will now begin to plague all those that have been a plague to my town of Mansoul, and will deliver it from their hand."

When the King's Son had said thus to his Father, it presently flew like lightning round about at court; yea, it there became the only talk what Emmanuel was to go to do for the famous town of

The highest peer in the kingdom covets to go on this design.
Mansoul. But you cannot think how the courtiers too were taken with this design of the Prince. Yea, so affected were they with this work, and with the justness of the war, that the highest lord and greatest peer of the kingdom did covet to have commissions under Emmanuel, to go to help to recover again to Shaddai the miserable town of Mansoul.

Then was it concluded that some should go and carry tidings to the camp, that Emmanuel was to come to recover Mansoul, and that he would bring along with him so mighty, so impregnable a force, that he could not be resisted. But oh, how ready were the high ones at court to run like lackeys to carry these tidings to the camp that was at Mansoul! Now when the captains perceived that the King would send Emmanuel his Son, and that it also delighted the Son to be sent on this errand by the great Shaddai, his Father, they also, to

The camp shout for joy when they hear the tidings.
show how they were pleased at the thoughts of his coming, gave a shout that made the earth rend at the sound thereof. Yea, the mountains did answer again by echo, and Diabolus himself did totter and shake.

For you must know, that though the town of Mansoul itself was not much, if at all, concerned with the project—for, alas for them, they were wofully besotted, for they chiefly regarded their

Diabolus afraid at the news of his coming.
pleasure and their lusts—yet Diabolus their governor was; for he had his spies continually abroad, who brought him intelligence of all things, and they told him what was doing at court against him, and that Emmanuel would shortly certainly come with a power to invade him. Nor was there any man at court, nor peer of the kingdom, that Diabolus so feared as he feared this Prince. For if you remember, I showed you before that Diabolus had

felt the weight of his hand already. So that, since it was he that was to come, this made him the more afraid. Well, you see how I have told you that the King's Son was engaged to come from the court to save Mansoul, and that his Father had made him the Captain of the forces. The time, therefore, of his setting forth being now expired, he addressed himself for his march, and taketh with him, for his power, five noble captains and their forces.

The Prince addresses himself for his journey.

The first was that famous captain, the noble Captain Credence. His were the red colours, and Mr. Promise bore them; and for an escutcheon he had the holy lamb and golden shield. And he had ten thousand men at his feet. (John i. 29. Eph. vi. 16.)

The second was that famous captain, the Captain Goodhope. His were the blue colours; his standard-bearer was Mr. Expectation, and for an escutcheon he had the three golden anchors. And he had ten thousand men at his feet. (Heb. vi. 19.)

The third captain was that valiant captain, the Captain Charity. His standard-bearer was Mr. Pitiful. His were the green colours; and for his escutcheon he had three naked orphans embraced in the bosom. And he had ten thousand men at his feet. (1 Cor. xiii.)

The fourth was that gallant commander, the Captain Innocent. His standard-bearer was Mr. Harmless; his were the white colours, and for his escutcheon he had the three golden doves. (Heb. x. 16.)

The fifth was the truly loyal and well-beloved captain, the Captain Patience. His standard-bearer was Mr. Suffer-long; his were the black colours, and for an escutcheon he had three arrows through the golden heart. (Heb. vi. 12.)

These were Emmanuel's captains, these their standard-bearers, their colours, and their escutcheons, and these the men under their command. So, as was said, the brave Prince took his march to go to the town of Mansoul. Cap-

Faith and Patience do the work.
tain Credence led the van, and Captain Patience brought up the rear. So the other three, with their men, made up the main body; the Prince himself riding in his chariot at the head of them.

But when they set out for their march, oh how the trumpets sounded, their armour glittered, and how the colours waved in the wind! The Prince's armour was all of gold, and it shone

Their march.
like the sun in the firmament. The captains' armour was of proof, and was in appearance like the glittering stars. There were also some from the court that rode reformades, for the love that they had to the King Shaddai, and for the happy deliverance of the town of Mansoul.

Emmanuel also, when he had thus set forward to go to recover the town of Mansoul, took with him, at the commandment of his Father, fifty-four battering rams, and twelve slings, to whirl

stones withal. Every one of these was made of pure gold; and these they carried with them in the heart and body of their army, all along as they went to Mansoul.

The Holy Bible, containing 66 books.

So they marched till they came within less than a league of the town. And there they lay till the first four captains came thither, to acquaint him with matters. Then they took their journey to go to the town of Mansoul, and unto Mansoul they came. But when the old soldiers that were in the camp saw that they had new forces to join with, they again gave such a shout before the walls of the town of Mansoul that it put Diabolus into another fright. So they sat down before the town, not now as the other four captains did, to wit, against the gates of Mansoul only; but they environed it round on every side, and beset it behind and before; so that now, let Mansoul look which way it will, it saw force and power lie in siege against it. Besides, there were mounts cast up against it.

The forces joined with rejoicing.

Mansoul beleaguered round.

The Mount Gracious was on the one side, and Mount Justice was on the other; further, there were several small banks and advance-grounds, as Plain-truth Hill, and No-sin Banks, where many of the slings were placed against the town. Upon Mount Gracious were planted four, and upon Mount Justice were planted as many; and the rest were conveniently placed in several parts round about the town. Five of the best battering rams, that is, of the biggest of them, were placed upon Mount Hearken; a mount cast up hard by Ear-gate, with intent to break that open.

Mounts cast up against it.

Now, when the men of the town saw the multitude of the soldiers that were come up against the place, and the rams and slings, and the mounts on which they were planted, together with the glittering of the armour and the waving of their colours, they were forced to shift and shift, and again to shift their thoughts, but they hardly changed for thoughts more stout, but rather for thoughts more faint. For though before they thought themselves sufficiently guarded, yet now they began to think that no man knew what would be their hap or lot.

The heart of Mansoul begins to fail.

When the good Prince Emmanuel had thus beleaguered Mansoul, in the first place he hangs out the white flag, which he caused to be set among the golden slings that were planted upon Mount Gracious. And this he did for two reasons: 1. To give notice to Mansoul that he could and would yet be gracious, if they turned to him. 2. And that he might leave them the more without excuse, should he destroy them, they continuing in their rebellion.

The white flag hung out.

So the white flag, with the three golden doves on it, was hanged out for two days together, to give them time and space to consider. But they, as was hinted before, as if they were unconcerned, made no reply to the favourable signal of the Prince. Then he commanded, and they set the red flag upon that mount called Mount Justice. It was the red flag of

The red flag hung out.

Captain Judgment, whose escutcheon was the burning fiery furnace, and this also stood waving before them in the wind for several days together. But look how they carried it under the white flag when that was hanged out, so did they also when the red one was, and yet he took no advantage of them.

Then he commanded again that his servants would hang out the black flag of defiance against them, whose escutcheon was the three burning

The black flag hung out. thunderbolts. But as unconcerned was Mansoul at this as at those that went before. But when the Prince saw that neither mercy, nor judgment, nor execution of judgment, would or could come near the heart of Mansoul, he was touched with much compunction, and said, " Surely this strange carriage of the town of Mansoul does rather arise from ignorance

Christ makes not war as the world does. of the manner and feats of war, than from a secret defiance of us, and abhorrence of their own lives; or, if they know the manner of the war of their own, yet not the rites and ceremonies of the wars in which we are concerned, when I make wars upon mine enemy Diabolus."

Therefore, he sent to the town of Mansoul, to let them know what he meant by those signs and

He sends to know if they would have mercy or justice. ceremonies of the flag, and also to know of them which of the things they would choose, whether grace and mercy, or judgment and the execution of judgment. All this while they kept their gates shut with locks, bolts, and bars, as fast as they could; their guards also were doubled, and their watch made as strong as they could. Diabolus also did pluck up what heart he could to encourage the town to make resistance.

The townsmen also made answer to the Prince's messenger, in substance, according to that which follows :—

" Great Sir, as to what by your messenger you

The townsfolk's answer. have signified to us, whether we will accept of your mercy or fall by your justice, we are bound by the law and custom of this place, and can give you no positive answer. For it is against the law, government, and the prerogative royal of our king, to make either peace or war without him. But this we will do ; we will petition that our prince will come down to the wall, and there give you such treatment as he shall think fit, and profitable for us."

When the good Prince Emmanuel heard this answer, and saw the slavery and bondage of the people, and how much content they were to abide

Emmanuel grieved at the folly of Mansoul. in the chains of the tyrant Diabolus, it grieved him at the heart. And, indeed, when at any time he perceived that any were contented under the slavery of the giant, he would be affected with it.

But to return again to our purpose. After the town had carried this news to Diabolus, and had told him, moreover, that the Prince that lay in the leaguer without the wall, waited upon them for

Diabolus afraid. an answer, he refused, and huffed as well as he could, but in heart he was afraid. Then, said he, I will go down to the gates myself, and give him such an answer as I think fit. So he went down to Mouth-gate, and there addressed himself to speak to Emmanuel, but in such language as the town understood not; the contents whereof were as follows :—

" O thou great Emmanuel, Lord of all the world, I know thee that thou art the Son of

His speech to the Prince. the great Shaddai ! Wherefore art thou come to torment me, and to cast me out of my possession ? This town of Mansoul, as thou very well knowest, is mine, and that by twofold right. 1. It is mine by right of conquest : I won it in the open field. And shall the prey be taken from the mighty, or the lawful captive be delivered ? 2. This town of Mansoul is mine also by their subjection. They have opened the gates of their town unto me, they have sworn fidelity to me, and have openly chosen me to be their king. They have also given their castle

Heart. into my hands ; yea, they have put the whole strength of Mansoul under me. Moreover, this town of Mansoul hath disavowed thee ; yea, they have cast thy law, thy name, thy image, and all that is thine, behind their back, and have accepted, and set up in their room, my law, my name, mine image, and all that ever is mine. Ask else thy captains, and they will tell thee that Mansoul hath, in answer to all their summons, shown love and loyalty to me ; but always disdain, despite, contempt, and scorn to thee and thine. Now, thou art the Just One, and the Holy, and shouldst do no iniquity ; depart then, I pray thee, therefore, from me, and leave me to my just inheritance, peaceably."

This oration was made in the language of Diabolus himself. For, although he can, to every man, speak in their own language, else he could not tempt them all as he does, yet he has a language proper to himself, and it is the language of the infernal cave, or black pit.

Wherefore the town of Mansoul, poor hearts, understood him not, nor did they see how he crouched and cringed, while he stood before Emmanuel their prince. Yea, they all this while took him to be one of that power and force that by no means could be resisted. Wherefore, while he was thus entreating that he might yet have his residence there, and that Emmanuel would not take it from him by force, the inhabitants boasted even of his valour, saying, " Who is able to make war with him ?"

Well, when this pretended king had made an end of what he would say, Emmanuel, the golden Prince, stood up and spake, the contents of whose words follow :—

" Thou deceiving one," said he, " I have in my Father's name, in mine own name, and on the behalf and for the good of this wretched town of Mansoul, somewhat to say unto thee. Thou pretendest a right, a lawful right, to the deplorable town of Mansoul, when it is most apparent to all my Father's court, that the entrance which thou hast obtained in at the gates of Mansoul was through thy lies and falsehood. Thou beliedst my Father, thou beliedst his law, and so deceivedst the people of Mansoul. Thou pretendest that the people have accepted thee for their king, their captain, and right liege lord, but that also was by the exercise of deceit and guile. Now, if lying wiliness, sinful craft, and all manner of horrible hypocrisy, will go in my Father's court for equity and right, in which court thou must be tried, then will I confess unto thee that thou hast made a lawful conquest. But, alas! what thief, what tyrant, what devil is there that may not conquer after this sort? But I can make it appear, O Diabolus, that thou, in all thy pretences to a conquest of Mansoul, hast nothing of truth to say. Thinkest thou this to be right, that thou didst put the lie upon my Father, and madest him, to Mansoul, the greatest deluder in the world? And what sayest thou to thy perverting, knowingly, the right purport and intent of the law? Was it good also that thou madest a prey of the innocency and simplicity of the now miserable town of Mansoul? Yea, thou didst overcome Mansoul by promising to them happiness in their transgressions against my Father's law, when thou knewest, and couldst not but know, hadst thou consulted nothing but thine own experience, that that was the way to undo them. Thou hast also thyself, O thou master of enmity, of despite, defaced my Father's image in Mansoul, and set up thine own in its place, to the great contempt of my Father, the heightening of thy sin, and to the intolerable damage of the perishing town of Mansoul. Thou hast, moreover, as if all these were but little things with thee, not only deluded and undone this place, but, by thy lies and fraudulent carriage, hast set them against their own deliverance. How hast thou stirred them up against my Father's captains, and made them to fight against those that were sent of him to deliver them from their bondage? All these things and very many more thou hast done against thy light, and in contempt of my Father and of his law; yea, and with design to bring under his displeasure for ever the miserable town of Mansoul. I am therefore come to avenge the wrong that thou hast done to my Father, and to deal with thee for the blasphemies wherewith thou hast made poor Mansoul blaspheme his name. Yea, upon thy head, thou prince of the infernal cave, will I require it.

"As for myself, O Diabolus, I am come against thee by lawful power, and to take, by strength of hand, this town of Mansoul out of thy burning fingers. For this town of Mansoul is mine, O Diabolus, and that by undoubted right, as all shall see that will diligently search the most ancient and most authentic records, and I will plead my title to it, to the confusion of thy face.

"First. For the town of Mansoul, my Father built and did fashion it with his hand. The palace also that is in the midst of that town, he built it for his own delight. This town of Mansoul, therefore, is my Father's, and that by the best of titles; and he that gainsays the truth of this must lie against his soul.

"Second. O thou master of the lie, this town of Mansoul is mine.

"1. For that I am my Father's heir, his first-born, and the only delight of his heart. I am therefore come up against thee in mine own right, even to recover mine own inheritance out of thine hand. (Heb. i. 2. John xvi. 15.)

"2. But further, as I have a right and title to Mansoul, by being my Father's heir, so I have also by my Father's donation. His it was, and he gave it me (John xvii.); nor have I at any time offended my Father, that he should take it from me and give it to thee. Nor have I been forced by playing the bankrupt to sell, or set to sale to thee, my beloved town of Mansoul. (Isa. l. 1.) Mansoul is my desire, my delight, and the joy of my heart. But,

"3. Mansoul is mine by right of purchase. I have bought it, O Diabolus, I have bought it to myself. Now, since it was my Father's and mine, as I was his heir, and since also I have made it mine by virtue of a great purchase, it followeth, that by all lawful right the town of Mansoul is mine, and that thou art an usurper, a tyrant, and traitor, in thy holding possession thereof. Now, the cause of my purchasing of it was this: Mansoul had trespassed against my Father; now, my Father had said, that in the day that they broke his law they should die. Now, it is more possible for heaven and earth to pass away, than for my Father to break his word. (Matt. v. 18.) Wherefore, when Mansoul had sinned indeed by hearkening to thy lie, I put in and became a surety to my Father, body for body, and soul for soul, that I would make amends for Mansoul's transgressions; and my Father did ac- O sweet Prince, cept thereof. So when the time Emmanuel. appointed was come, I gave body for body, soul for soul, life for life, blood for blood, and so redeemed my beloved Mansoul.

"4. Nor did I do this to the halves; my Father's law and justice, that were both concerned in the threatening upon transgression, are both now satisfied, and very well content that Mansoul should be delivered.

"5. Nor am I come out this day against thee but by commandment of my Father; it was he that said unto me, Go down and deliver Mansoul. Wherefore, be it known unto thee, O thou fountain of deceit, and be it also known to the foolish town of Mansoul, that I am not come against thee this day without my Father.

"And now," said the golden-headed Prince, "I have a word to the town of Mansoul;" but as soon as mention was made that he had a word to speak to the besotted town of Mansoul, the gates were double guarded, and all men commanded not to give him audience; so he proceeded, and said, "O unhappy town of Mansoul, I cannot but be touched with pity and compassion for thee. Thou hast accepted of Diabolus for thy king, and art become a nurse and minister of Diabolonians against thy Sovereign Lord. Thy gates thou hast opened to him, but hast shut them fast against me; thou hast given him a hearing, but hast stopped thine ears at my cry; he brought to thee thy destruction, and thou didst receive both him and it. I am come to thee bringing salvation, but thou regardest me not. Besides, thou hast, as with sacrilegious hands, taken thyself, with all that was mine in thee, and hast given all to my foe, and to the greatest enemy my Father has. You have bowed and subjected yourselves to him; you have vowed and sworn yourselves to be his. Poor Mansoul! what shall I do unto thee? Shall I save thee? shall I destroy thee? What shall I do unto thee? shall I fall upon thee and grind thee to powder, or make thee a monument of the richest grace? What shall I do unto thee? Hearken, therefore, thou town of Mansoul, hearken to my word, and thou shalt live. I am merciful, Mansoul, and thou shalt find me so; shut me not out of thy gates. (Sol. Song v. 2.)

" O Mansoul, neither is my commission nor inclination at all to do thee any hurt; why fliest thou so fast from thy friend, and stickest so close to thine enemy? Indeed, I would have thee, because it becomes thee, to be sorry for thy sin; but do not despair of life, this great force is not to hurt thee, but to deliver thee from thy bondage, and to reduce thee to thy obedience. (Luke ix. 56. John xii. 47.)

" My commission, indeed, is to make a war upon Diabolus thy king, and upon all Diabolonians with him; for he is the strong man armed, that keeps the house, and I will have him out; his spoils I must divide, his armour I must take from him, his hold I must cast him out of, and must make it an habitation for myself. And this, O Mansoul, shall Diabolus know, when he shall be made to follow me in chains, and when Mansoul shall rejoice to see it so.

" I could, would I now put forth my might, cause that forthwith he should leave you and depart; but I have it in my heart so to deal with him, as that the justice of the war that I shall make upon him may be seen and acknowledged by all. He hath taken Mansoul by fraud, and keeps it by violence and deceit; and I will make him bare and naked in the eyes of all observers. All my words are true; I am mighty to save, and will deliver my Mansoul out of his hand."

This speech was intended chiefly for Mansoul, but Mansoul would not have the hearing of it. They shut up Ear-gate, they barricaded it up, they kept it locked and bolted; they set a guard thereat, and commanded that no Mansoulonian should go out to him, nor that any from the camp should be admitted into the town; all this they did, so horribly had Diabolus enchanted them to do, and seek to do for him, against their rightful Lord and Prince; wherefore no man, nor voice, nor sound of man that belonged to the glorious host, was to come into the town.

So when Emmanuel saw that Mansoul was thus involved in sin, he calls his army together, since now also his words were despised, and gave out a commandment throughout all his host to be ready against the time appointed. Now, forasmuch as there was no way lawfully to take the town *Emmanuel prepares to make war upon Mansoul.* of Mansoul, but to get in by the gates, and at Eargate as the chief, therefore he commanded his captains and commanders to bring their rams, their slings, and their men, and place them at Eye-gate and Ear-gate, in order to his taking the town.

When Emmanuel had put all things in readiness to give Diabolus battle, he sent again to know of the town of Mansoul, if in peaceable manner they would yield themselves, or whether they were yet resolved to put him to try the utmost extremity. Then they, together with Diabolus their king, called a council of war, and resolved upon certain propositions that should be offered to Emmanuel, if he will accept thereof, so they agreed; and then the next was, who should be sent on this errand. Now there was in the town of Mansoul an old man, a Diabolonian, and his name was Mr. Loth-to-stoop, a stiff man in his way, and a great doer for Diabolus; him therefore they sent, and put into his mouth what he should say. So he went, and *Diabolus sends by the hand of his servant, Mr. Loth-to-stoop, and by him he propounds conditions of peace.* came to the camp to Emmanuel; and when he was come, a time was appointed to give him audience. So at the time he came, and after a Diabolonian ceremony or two, he thus began, and said, " Great Sir, that it may be known unto all men how good-natured a prince my master is, he hath sent me to tell your Lordship that he is very willing, rather than to go to war, to deliver up into your hands one-half of the town of *Mark this.* Mansoul. (Titus i. 16.) I am therefore to know if your Mightiness will accept of this proposition."

Then said Emmanuel, " The whole is mine by gift and purchase, wherefore I will never lose one-half."

Then said Mr. Loth-to-stoop, " Sir, my master hath said, that he will be content *Mark this.* that you shall be the nominal and titular Lord of all, if he may possess but a part." (Luke xiii. 25.)

Then Emmanuel answered, " The whole is mine really; not in name and word only: wherefore I will be the sole Lord and possessor of all, or of none at all of Mansoul."

Then Mr. Loth-to-stoop said again, " Sir, behold the condescension of my master! He says that he will be content, *Mark this.* if he may but have assigned to him some place in Mansoul as a place to live privately in, and you shall be Lord of all the rest." (Acts v. 1—5.)

Then said the golden Prince, " All that the Father giveth me, shall come to me; and of all that he hath given me I will lose nothing, no, not a hoof, nor a hair. I will not therefore grant him, no, not the least corner in Mansoul to dwell in; I will have all to myself."

Then Loth-to-stoop said again, " But, Sir, suppose that my lord should resign the whole town to you, only with this **Mark this.** proviso, that he sometimes, when he comes into this country, may, for old acquaintance sake, be entertained as a wayfaring man for two days, or ten days, or a month, or so; may not this small matter be granted?"

Then said Emmanuel, " No; he came as a wayfaring man to David, nor did he stay long with him, and yet it had like to have cost David his soul. (2 Sam. xii. 1—5.) I will not consent that he ever should have any harbour more there."

Then said Mr. Loth-to-stoop, " Sir, you seem to be very hard. Suppose my master should yield to all that your Lordship hath said, provided that **Sins and** his friends and kindred in Mansoul **carnal lusts.** may have liberty to trade in the town, and to enjoy their present dwellings; may not that be granted, Sir?"

Then said Emmanuel, " No: that is contrary to my Father's will; for all, and all manner of Diabolonians that now are, or that at any time shall be found in Mansoul, shall not only lose their lands and liberties, but also their lives." (Rom. vi. 13. Gal. v. 24. Col. iii. 5.)

Then said Mr. Loth-to-stoop again, " But, Sir, may not my master and great lord, by letters, by passengers, by acci- **Mark this.** dental opportunities, and the like, maintain, if he shall deliver up all unto thee, some kind of old friendship with Mansoul?" (John x. 8.)

Emmanuel answered, " No, by no means; forasmuch as any such fellowship, friendship, intimacy, or acquaintance, in what way, sort, or mode soever maintained, will tend to the corrupting of Mansoul, the alienating of their affections from me, and the endangering of their peace with my Father."

Mr. Loth-to-stoop yet added further, saying, " But, great Sir, since my master **Mark this.** hath many friends, and those that are dear to him in Mansoul, may he not, if he shall depart from them, even of his bounty and good nature, bestow upon them, as he sees fit, some tokens of his love and kindness that he had for them, to the end that Mansoul, when he is gone, may look upon such tokens of kindness once received from their old friend, and remember him who was once their king, and the merry times that they sometimes enjoyed one with another, while he and they lived in peace together."

Then said Emmanuel, " No; for if Mansoul come to be mine, I shall not admit of, nor consent that there should be the least scrap, shred, or dust of Diabolus left behind, as tokens or gifts bestowed upon any in Mansoul, thereby to call to remembrance the horrible communion that was betwixt them and him." (Rom. vi. 12, 13.)

" Well, Sir," said Mr. Loth-to-stoop, " I have one thing more to propound, and **Mark this.** then I am got to the end of my commission. Suppose that when my master is gone from Mansoul, any that yet shall live in the town should have such business of high concerns to do, that if they be neglected the party shall be undone; and suppose, Sir, that nobody can help in that case so well as my master and lord; may not now my master be sent for upon so urgent an occasion as this? Or if he may not be admitted into the town, may not he and the person concerned meet in some of the villages near Mansoul, and there lay their heads together, and there consult of matters?" (2 Kings i. 3, 6, 7.)

This was the last of those ensnaring propositions that Mr. Loth-to-stoop had to propound to Emmanuel on behalf of his master Diabolus; but Emmanuel would not grant it, for he said, " There can be no case, or thing, or matter, fall out in Mansoul, when thy master shall be gone, that may not be salved by my Father; besides, it will be a great disparagement to my Father's wisdom and skill to admit any from Mansoul to go out to Diabolus for advice, when they are bid before, in everything, by prayer and supplication, to let their request be made known to my Father. (1 Sam. xxviii. 15. 2 Kings i. 2, 3.) Further, this, should it be granted, would be to grant that a door should be set open for Diabolus and the Diabolonians in Mansoul, to hatch, and plot, and bring to pass treasonable designs, to the grief of my Father and me, and to the utter destruction of Mansoul."

When Mr. Loth-to-stoop had heard this answer, he took his leave of Emmanuel and **Loth-to-stoop** departed, saying, that he would do **departs.** word to his master concerning this whole affair. So he departed and came to Diabolus to Mansoul, and told him the whole of the matter, and how Emmanuel would not admit, no, not by any means, that he, when he was once gone out, should for ever have anything more to do, either in, or with any that are of, the town of Mansoul. When Mansoul and Diabolus had heard this relation of things, they with one consent concluded to use their best endeavour to keep Emmanuel out of Mansoul, and sent old Ill-pause, of whom you have heard before, to tell the Prince and his captains so. So the old gentleman came up to the top of Ear-gate, and called to the camp for a hearing; who, when they gave audience, he said, " I have in **A speech of Old** commandment from my high Lord **Ill-pause to** to bid you to tell it to your Prince **the camp.** Emmanuel, that Mansoul and their king are resolved to stand and fall together, and that it is in vain for your Prince to think of ever having of Mansoul in his hand, unless he can take it by force." So some went and told to Emmanuel what old Ill-pause, a Diabolonian in Mansoul, had said. Then said the Prince, " I must try the power of my sword, for I will not, for all the rebellions and repulses that Mansoul has made against me, raise my siege and depart, but will assuredly take my Mansoul, and deliver it from the hand of her enemy." (Eph. vi. 17.) And with that he gave out a commandment that Captain Boanerges, Captain Conviction, Captain Judgment, and Captain Execution, should *They must fight.* forthwith march up to Ear-gate with trumpets sounding, colours flying, and with shouting for the battle. Also he would *Preparations to the battle.* that Captain Credence should join himself with them. Emmanuel, moreover, gave order that Captain Good-hope and Captain Charity should draw themselves up before Eye-gate. He bid also that the rest of his Captains, and their men, should place themselves for the best of their advantage against the enemy, round about the town; and all was done as he had commanded. Then he bid that the word should be given forth, and the word was at that time "Emmanuel." Then was an alarm sounded, and the battering-rams were played, and the slings did whirl stones into the town amain, and thus the battle began. Now Diabolus himself did manage the townsmen in the war, and that at every gate; wherefore their resistance was the more forcible, hellish, and offensive to Emmanuel. Thus was the good Prince engaged and entertained by Diabolus and Mansoul for several days together. And a sight worth seeing it was, to behold how the captains of Shaddai behaved themselves in this war.

And first for Captain Boanerges, not to under-*Boanerges plays the man.* value the rest, he made three most fierce assaults, one after another, upon Ear-gate, to the shaking of the posts thereof. Captain Conviction, he also made up as fast with Boanerges as possibly he could, and both discerning that the gate began to yield, they commanded that the rams should still be played against it. Now Captain Conviction going up very near to *Conviction wounded.* the gate, was with great force driven back, and received three wounds in the mouth. And those that rode *Angels.* Reformades, they went about to encourage the captains.

For the valour of the two captains made mention of before, the Prince sent for them to his pavilion, and commanded that awhile they should rest themselves, and that with somewhat they should be refreshed. Care also was taken for Captain Conviction, that he should be healed of his wounds. The Prince also gave to each of them a chain of gold, and bid them yet be of good courage. Nor *Good-hope and Charity play the men at Eye-gate.* did Captain Good-hope nor Captain Charity come behind in this most desperate fight, for they so well did behave themselves at Eye-gate, that they had almost broken it quite open. These also had a reward from their Prince, as also had the rest of the captains, because they did valiantly round about the town.

In this engagement several of the officers of Diabolus were slain, and some of the townsmen wounded. For the officers, there was one Captain *Captain Boasting slain.* Boasting slain. This Boasting thought that nobody could have shaken the posts of Ear-gate, nor have shaken the heart of Diabolus. Next to him there was one

Captain Secure slain; this Secure used to say that the blind and lame in Mansoul were *Captain Secure slain.* able to keep the gates of the town against Emmanuel's army. (2 Sam. v. 6.) This Captain Secure did Captain Conviction cleave down

the head with a two-handed sword, when he received himself three wounds in his mouth. Besides these, there was one Captain Brag-*Captain Brag-man slain.* man, a very desperate fellow, and he was captain over a band of those that threw firebrands, arrows, and death; he also received, by the hand of Captain Good-hope at Eye-gate, a mortal wound in the breast.

There was, moreover, one Mr. Feeling, but he was no captain, but a great stickler to encourage Mansoul to rebellion, he received a *Mr. Feeling hurt.* wound in the eye by the hand of one of Boanerges' soldiers, and had by the captain himself been slain, but that he made a sudden retreat.

But I never saw Will-be-will so daunted in all my life: he was not able to do as he was wont; and some say that he also received *Will-be-will hurt.* a wound in the leg, and that some of the men in the Prince's army have certainly seen him limp, as he afterwards walked on the wall.

I shall not give you a particular account of the names of the soldiers that were slain in the town, for many were maimed and wounded, and slain; for when they saw that *Many of the soldiers in Mansoul slain.* the posts of Ear-gate did shake, and Eye-gate was well-nigh broken quite open; and also that their captains were slain, this took away the hearts of many of the Diabolonians; they fell also by the force of the shot that were sent by the golden slings into the midst of the town of Mansoul.

Of the townsmen there was one *Love-no-good wounded.* Love-no-good, he was a townsman, but a Diabolonian, he also received his mortal wound in Mansoul, but he died not very soon. Mr. Ill-pause also who was the man that came along with Diabolus when at first he attempted the taking

Ill-pause wounded. of Mansoul, he also received a grievous wound in the head, some say that his brain-pan was cracked; this I have taken notice of, that he was never after this able to do that mischief to Mansoul as he had done in times past. Also old Prejudice and Mr. Anything fled.

Now when the battle was over, the Prince com-

The white flag hung out again. manded that yet once more the white flag should be set upon Mount Gracious, in sight of the town of Mansoul; to show that yet Emmanuel had grace for the wretched town of Mansoul.

When Diabolus saw the white flag hanging out

Diabolus's new prank. again, and knowing that it was not for him, but Mansoul, he cast in his mind to play another prank, to wit, to see if Emmanuel would raise his siege and be gone, upon promise of a reformation. So he comes down to the gate one evening, a good while after the sun was gone down, and calls to speak with Emmanuel, who presently came down to the gate, and Diabolus saith unto him:

"Forasmuch as thou makest it appear by thy

His speech to Emmanuel. white flag, that thou art wholly given to peace and quiet, I thought meet to acquaint thee that we are ready to accept thereof upon terms which thou mayest admit.

"I know that thou art given to devotion, and that holiness pleases thee; yea, that thy great end in making a war upon Mansoul is that it may be an holy habitation. Well, draw off thy forces from the town, and I will bend Mansoul to thy bow.

"I will lay down all acts of hostility against

Diabolus would be Emmanuel's deputy, and he would turn reformer. thee, and will be willing to become thy deputy, and will, as I have formerly been against thee, now serve thee in the town of Mansoul. And more particularly: 1. I will persuade Mansoul to receive thee for their Lord, and I know that they will do it the sooner when they shall understand that I am thy deputy. 2. I will show them wherein they have erred, and that transgression stands in the way to life. 3. I will show them the holy law unto which they must conform, even that which they have broken. 4. I will press upon them the necessity of a reformation according to thy law. 5. And, moreover, that none of these things may fail, I myself, at my own proper cost and charge, will set up and maintain a sufficient ministry, besides lecturers, in Mansoul. 6. Thou shalt receive, as a token of our subjection to thee continually, year by year, what thou shalt think fit to lay and levy upon us, in token of our subjection to thee."

Then said Emmanuel to him, "O full of deceit,

The answer. how movable are thy ways! How often hast thou changed and rechanged, if so be thou mightest still keep posses-

sion of my Mansoul, though, as has been plainly declared before, I am the right heir thereof? Often hast thou made thy proposals already, nor is this last a whit better than they. And failing to deceive when thou showedst thyself in thy black, thou hast now transformed thyself into an angel of light, and wouldest, to deceive, be now as a minister of righteousness. (2 Cor. xi. 14.)

"But know thou, O Diabolus, that nothing must be regarded that thou canst propound, for nothing is done by thee but to deceive; thou

Diabolus has no conscience to God, nor love to Mansoul. neither hast conscience to God, nor love to the town of Mansoul; whence then should these thy sayings arise, but from sinful craft and deceit? He that can of list and will propound what he pleases, and that wherewith he may destroy them that believe him, is to be abandoned with all that he shall say. But if righteousness be such a beauty-spot in thine eyes now, how is it that wickedness was so closely stuck to by thee before? But this is by the by. Thou talkest now of a reformation in Mansoul, and that thou thyself, if I will please, will be at the head of that reformation, all the while knowing that the greatest proficiency that man can make in the law, and the righteousness thereof, will amount to no more for the taking away of the curse from Mansoul than just nothing at all; for a law being broken by Mansoul, that had before, upon a supposition of the breach thereof, a curse pronounced against him for it of God, can never, by his obeying of the law, deliver himself therefrom. To say nothing of what a reformation is like to be, set up in Mansoul, when the devil is become the corrector of vice. Thou knowest that all that

He knows that that will do no good, which yet he propounds for the health of Mansoul. thou hast now said in this matter is nothing but guile and deceit; and is, as it was the first, so is it the last card that thou hast to play. Many there be that do soon discern thee when thou showest them thy cloven foot; but in thy white, thy light, and in thy transformation thou art seen but of a few. But thou shalt not do thus with my Mansoul, O Diabolus, for I do still love my Mansoul.

"Besides, I am not come to put Mansoul upon works to live thereby, should I do so, I should be like unto thee; but I am come that by me, and by what I have and shall do for Mansoul, they may to my Father be reconciled, though by their sin they have provoked him to anger, and though by the law they cannot obtain mercy.

"Thou talkest of subjecting of this town to good, when none desireth it at thy hands.

All things must be new in Mansoul. I am sent by my Father to possess it myself, and to guide it by the skilfulness of my hands into such a conformity to him as shall be pleasing in his sight. I will therefore possess it myself, I will dispossess and cast thee out; I will set up mine own standard in the midst of them; I will also govern them by new laws, new officers, new motives, and new ways.

Yea, I will pull down this town and build it again, and it shall be as though it had not been, and it shall then be the glory of the whole universe."

When Diabolus heard this, and perceived that *Diabolus confounded.* he was discovered in all his deceits, he was confounded and utterly put to a non-plus; but having in himself the fountain of iniquity, rage, and malice against both Shaddai and his Son, and the beloved town of Mansoul, what doth he but strengthen himself what he could, to give fresh battle to the noble Prince Emmanuel? So then, now we must have another fight before the town of Mansoul is taken. Come up then to the mountains you that love to see military actions, and behold by both sides how the fatal blow is given : while one seeks to hold, and the other seeks to make himself master of the famous town of Mansoul.

Diabolus, therefore, having withdrawn himself *New preparations for to fight.* from the wall to his force that was in the heart of the town of Mansoul, Emmanuel also returned to the camp; and both of them, after their divers ways, put themselves into a posture fit to bid battle one to another.

Diabolus, as filled with despair of retaining in *Diabolus despairs of holding of Mansoul, and therefore contrives to do it what mischief he can.* his hands the famous town of Mansoul, resolved to do what mischief he could, if indeed he could do any, to the army of the Prince, and to the famous town of Mansoul; for, alas! it was not the happiness of the silly town of Mansoul that was designed by Diabolus, but the utter ruin and overthrow thereof; as now is enough in view. Wherefore he commands his officers that they should then, when they see that they could hold the town no longer, do it what harm and mischief they could; rending and tearing of men, women, and children. (Mark ix. 26, 27). For, said he, we had better quite demolish the place, and leave it like a ruinous heap, than so leave it that it may be an habitation for Emmanuel.

Emmanuel again, knowing that the next battle would issue in his being made master of the place, gave out a royal commandment to all his officers, high captains, and men of war, to be sure to show themselves men of war against Diabolus, and all Diabolonians; but favourable, merciful, and meek to all the old inhabitants of Mansoul. Bend, therefore, said the noble Prince, the hottest front of the battle against Diabolus and his men.

So the day being come, the command was given, and the Prince's men did bravely stand to their arms; and did, as before, bend their main force against Ear-gate, and Eye-gate. The word was *The battle joined, and they fight on both sides fiercely.* then, "Mansoul is won," so they made their assault upon the town. Diabolus also, as fast as he could with the main of his power, made resistance from within, and his high lords and chief captains for a time fought very cruelly against the Prince's army.

But after three or four notable charges by the Prince and his noble captains, Ear- *Ear-gate broken open.* gate was broken open, and the bars and bolts wherewith it was used to be fast shut up against the Prince, were broken into a thousand pieces. Then did the Prince's trumpets sound, the captains shout, the town shake, and Diabolus retreat to his hold. Well, when the Prince's forces had broken open the gate, himself came up and did set his throne in it; also he set his standard thereby upon a mount, that before *The Prince's standard set up, and the slings are played still at the castle.* by his men was cast up to place the mighty slings thereon. The mount was called Mount Hear-well; there, therefore, the Prince abode, to wit, hard by the going in at the gate. He commanded also that the golden slings should yet be played upon the town, especially against the castle, because for shelter thither was Diabolus retreated. Now from Ear-gate the street was straight, even to the house of Mr. Recorder that so was before Diabolus took the town, and hard by his house stood the castle, which Diabolus for a long time had made his irksome den. The captains, therefore, did quickly clear that street by the use of their slings, so that way was made up to the heart of the town. Then did the Prince command that Captain Boanerges, Captain Conviction, and Captain Judgment should forthwith march up the town to the old gentle- *Conscience. They go up to the Recorder's house.* man's gate. Then did the captains in most warlike manner enter into the town of Mansoul, and marching in with flying colours, they came up to the Recorder's house, and that was almost as strong as was the castle. Battering rams they took also with them to plant against the castle-gates. When they were come to the house of Mr. Conscience, they knocked and demanded entrance. Now the old gentleman, not knowing as yet fully their design, kept his gates shut all the time of this fight. Wherefore Boanerges demanded entrance at his *They demand entrance.* gates, and no man making answer, he gave it one stroke with the head of a ram, and this made the old gentleman to shake, and his house to tremble and totter. Then came Mr. Recorder down to the gate, and, as he could, with quivering lip, he asked who was there. Boanerges answered, We are the captains and commanders of the great Shaddai, and of the blessed Emmanuel his Son, and we demand possession of your house for the use of our noble Prince. And with that the battering-ram gave the gate another shake; this made the old gentleman tremble the more, yet durst he not but open the gate. *They go in.* Then the king's forces marched in, namely, the three brave captains mentioned before. Now the Recorder's house was a place of much convenience for Emmanuel, not only because it was near to the castle, and strong, but also because it was large, and fronted the castle, the den where now Diabolus was; for he was now afraid to come out of his hold. As for Mr. Recorder, the captains carried it very reservedly to

They do keep themselves reserved from the Recorder.

him; as yet he knew nothing of the great designs of Emmanuel; so that he did not know what judgment to make, nor what would be the end of such thundering beginnings. It was also presently noised in the town, how the Recorder's house was possessed, his rooms taken up, and his palace

His house the seat of war.

made the seat of the war; and no sooner was it noised abroad, but they took the alarm as warmly, and gave it out to others of his friends, and you know as a snow-ball loses nothing by rolling, so in little time the whole town was possessed that they must expect nothing from the Prince but destruction; and the ground of the business was this. The Recorder was afraid, the Recorder trembled, and the captains

carried it strangely to the Recorder, so many came to see: but when they with their own eyes did behold the captains in the palace, and their battering rams ever playing at the castle-gates to beat

The office of Conscience when he is awakened.

them down, they were riveted in their fears, and it made them as in amaze. And, as I said, the man of the house would increase all this, for whoever came to him, or discoursed with him, nothing would he talk of, tell them, or hear, but that death and destruction now attended Mansoul.

"For," quoth the old gentleman, "you are all of you sensible that we all have been traitors to that once despised, but now famously victorious and glorious Prince Emmanuel. For he now, as you see, doth not only lie in close siege about us, but hath forced his entrance in at our gates; moreover, Diabolus flees before him, and he hath, as you behold, made of my house a garrison against the castle, where he is. I, for my part, have transgressed greatly, and he that is clean it is well for him. But, I say, I have transgressed greatly in keeping of silence when I should have spoken, and

in perverting of justice when I should have executed the same. True, I have suffered something at the hand of Diabolus, for taking part with the laws of King Shaddai; but that, alas! what will that do? Will that make compensation for the rebellions and treasons that I have done, and have suffered without gainsaying, to be committed in the town of Mansoul? Oh, I tremble to think what will be the end of this so dreadful and so ireful a beginning!"

Now, while these brave captains were thus busy in the house of the old Recorder, Captain Execution was as busy in other parts

The brave exploits of Captain Execution.

of the town, in securing the back streets, and the walls. He also hunted the Lord Will-be-will sorely; he suffered him not to rest in any corner. He pursued him so hard, that he drove his men from him, and made him glad to thrust his head into a hole. Also, this mighty warrior did cut three of the Lord Will-be-will's officers down to the ground; one was old Mr. Prejudice, he

Old Prejudice slain.

that had his crown cracked in the mutiny; this man was made by Lord Will-be-will keeper of Ear-gate, and fell by the hand of Captain Execution. There was also one Mr. Backward-to-all-but-naught, and he also was one of Lord Will-be-will's officers, and was the captain of the two guns that once were mounted on the top of Ear-gate; he also was cut down to the ground by the hands of Captain Execution. Besides these two, there was another, a third, and his name was Captain Treacherous, a vile man this was, but one that Will-be-will did put a great deal of confidence in; but him also did this Captain Execution cut down to the ground with the rest.

He also made a very great slaughter among my Lord Will-be-will's soldiers, killing many that were stout and sturdy, and wounding of many that for Diabolus were nimble and active. But all these were Diabolonians; there was not a man, a native of Mansoul, hurt.

Other feats of war were also likewise performed by other of the captains, as at Eye-gate, where Captain Good-hope and Captain Charity had a charge, was great execution done; for the Captain Good-hope, with his own hands, slew

Captain Good-hope doth slay Captain Blindfold.

one Captain Blindfold, the keeper of that gate; this Blindfold was captain of a thousand men, and they were they that fought with mauls; he also pursued his men, slew many, and wounded more, and made the rest hide their heads in corners.

There was also at that gate Mr. Ill-pause, of whom you have heard before; he

And old Ill-pause.

was an old man, and had a beard that reached down to his girdle: the same was he that was orator to Diabolus; he did much mischief in the town of Mansoul, and fell by the hand of Captain Good-hope.

What shall I say? the Diabolonians in these days lay dead in every corner, though too many yet were alive in Mansoul.

Now, the old Recorder, and my Lord Understanding, with some others of the chief of the

The old townsmen meet and consult.

town, to wit, such as knew they must stand and fall with the famous town of Mansoul, came together upon a day, and after consultation had, did jointly agree to draw up a petition, and to send it to Emmanuel, now while he sat in the gate of Man-

The town does petition, and are answered with silence.

soul. So they drew up their petition to Emmanuel, the contents whereof were this, That they, the old inhabitants of the now deplorable town of Mansoul, confessed their sin, and were sorry that they had offended his princely Majesty, and prayed that he would spare their lives.

Upon this petition he gave no answer at all, and that did trouble them yet so much the more. Now, all this while the captains that were in the Recorder's house were playing with the battering-rams at the gates of the castle, to beat them down. So, after some time, labour, and travail, the gate

The castle gates broke open.

of the castle that was called Impregnable was beaten open, and broken into several splinters; and so a way made to go up to the hold in which Diabolus had hid himself. Then was tidings sent down to Ear-gate, for Emmanuel still abode there, to let him know that a way was made in at the gates of the castle of Mansoul. But oh, how the trumpets at the tidings sounded throughout the Prince's camp, for that now the war was so near an end, and Mansoul itself of being set free!

Then the Prince arose from the place where he

Emmanuel marches into Mansoul.

was, and took with him such of his men of war as were fittest for that expedition, and marched up the street of Mansoul to the old Recorder's house.

Now, the Prince himself was clad all in armour of gold, and so he marched up the town with his standard borne before him; but he kept his countenance much reserved all the way as he went, so that the people could not tell how to gather to themselves love or hatred by his looks. Now, as he marched up the street, the townsfolk came out at every door to see, and could not but be taken with his person, and the glory thereof, but wondered at the reservedness of his countenance; for as yet he spake more to them by his actions and works than he did by words or smiles. But also poor Mansoul, as in such cases all are apt to do, they interpreted the carriages of

How they interpret Emmanuel's carriages.

Emmanuel to them, as did Joseph's brethren his to them, even all the quite contrary way. For, thought they, if Emmanuel loved us, he would show it to us by word or carriage; but none of these he doth, therefore Emmanuel hates us. Now, if Emmanuel

hates us, then Mansoul shall be slain, then Mansoul shall become a dunghill. They knew that they had transgressed his Father's law, and that against him they had been in with Diabolus his enemy. They also knew that the Prince Emmanuel knew all this; for they were convinced that he was as an Angel of God, to know all things that are done in the earth. And this made them think that their condition was miserable, and that the good Prince would make them desolate.

And, thought they, what time so fit to do this in as now, when he has the bridle of Mansoul in his hand. And this I took special notice of, that the inhabitants, notwithstanding all this, could not, no, they could not, when they see him march through the town, but cringe, bow, bend, and were ready to lick the dust of his feet. They also wished a thousand times over, that he would become their Prince and Captain, and would become their protection. They would also one to another talk of the comeliness of his person, and how much for glory and valour he outstripped the great ones of the world. But, poor hearts, as to themselves, their thoughts would change, and go upon all manner of extremes; yea, through the working of them backward and forward, Mansoul became as a ball tossed, and as a rolling thing before the whirlwind. (Isa. xvii. 13 : xxii. 18)

Now, when he was come to the castle gates, he commanded Diabolus to appear, and

He comes up to the castle, and commands Diabolus to surrender himself.

to surrender himself into his hands. But oh, how loth was the beast to appear! How he stuck at it! how he shrunk! ay, how he cringed! Yet out he came to the Prince. Then Emmanuel commanded, and they took Diabolus and bound him fast in chains, the better to reserve him to the judgment that he had appointed for him. But Diabolus stood up to entreat for himself, that Emmanuel would not send him into the deep, but suffer him to depart out of Mansoul in peace.

When Emmanuel had taken him and bound him in chains, he led him into the

He is taken and bound in chains.

market-place, and there, before Mansoul, stripped him of his armour in which he boasted so much before. This now was one of the acts of triumph of Emmanuel over his enemy; and all the while that the giant was stripping, the trumpets of the golden Prince did sound amain; the captains also shouted, and the soldiers did sing for joy. Then was Mansoul called upon to behold the beginning of Em-

Mansoul must behold it.

manuel's triumph over him in whom they so much had trusted, and of whom they so much had boasted in the days when he flattered them.

Thus having made Diabolus naked in the eyes of Mansoul, and before the commanders of the Prince, in the next place he com-

He is bound to his chariot wheels.

mands that Diabolus should be bound with chains to his chariot-wheels. Then leaving of some of his forces, to wit, Captain Boanerges, and Captain Conviction, as a guard for the castle gates, that resistance might be made on his behalf, if any that heretofore followed Dia-

The Prince rides in triumph over him in the sight of Mansoul.

bolus should make an attempt to possess it, he did ride in triumph over him quite through the town of Mansoul, and so out at, and before the gate called Eye-gate, to the plain where his camp did lie. (Eph. iv.)

But you cannot think unless you had been there, as I was, what a shout there was in Emmanuel's camp when they saw the tyrant bound by the hand of their noble Prince, and tied to his chariot-

They sing.

wheels! And they said, He hath led captivity captive; he hath spoiled principalities and powers; Diabolus is subjected to the power of his sword, and made the object of all derision!

Those also that rode Reformades, and that came

The Reformades' joy.

down to see the battle, they shouted with that greatness of voice, and sung with such melodious notes, that they caused them that dwell in the highest orbs to open their windows, put out their heads, and look down to see the cause of that glory. (Luke xv. 7, 10.)

The townsmen also, so many of them as saw this sight, were as it were, while they looked, betwixt the earth and the heavens. True, they

The men of Mansoul taken with Emmanuel.

could not tell what would be the issue of things as to them, but all things were done in such excellent methods; and I cannot tell how, but things in the management of them seemed to cast a smile towards the town, so that their eyes, their heads, their hearts, and their minds, and all that they had, were taken and held, while they observed Emmanuel's order.

So when the brave Prince had finished this part of his triumph over Diabolus his foe, he turned him up in the midst of his contempt and shame, having given him a charge no more to be a possessor of Mansoul. Then went he from Emmanuel, and out of the midst of his camp to inherit the parched places in a salt land, seeking rest but finding none. (Matt. xii. 43.)

Now Captain Boanerges and Captain Conviction were both of them men of very great majesty, their faces were like the faces of lions, their words like the roaring of the sea; and they still quartered in Mr. Conscience's house, of whom mention was made before. When therefore the high and mighty Prince had thus far finished his triumph over Diabolus, the townsmen had more leisure to view and to behold the actions of these noble captains. But the

The carriages of Boanerges, and of Captain Conviction, do crush the spirit of Mansoul.

captains carried it with terror and dread in all that they did, and you may be sure that they had private instructions so to do, that they kept the town under continual heartaching, and caused, in their apprehension, the well-being of Mansoul for the future, to hang in doubt before them, so that, for some considerable

time, they neither knew what rest, or ease, or peace, or hope meant.

Nor did the Prince himself, as yet, abide in the town of Mansoul, but in his royal pavilion in the camp, and in the midst of his Father's forces. So at a time convenient, he sent special orders to Captain Boanerges to summons Mansoul, the whole of the townsmen, into the castle-yard, and then and there, before their faces, to take my Lord Understanding, Mr. Conscience, and

The Prince commands, and the captains put the three chiefs of Mansoul in ward.

that notable one the Lord Will-be-will, and put them all three in ward, and that they should set a strong guard upon them there, until his pleasure concerning them were further known. The which orders, when the captains had put them in execution, made no small addition to the fears of the town of Mansoul; for now, to their thinking, were their former fears of the ruin of Mansoul confirmed. Now, what death they should die, and how long they should be in dying, was that which most perplexed their heads and hearts. Yea, they were afraid that Emmanuel would command them all into the deep, the place that the prince Diabolus was afraid of; for they knew that they had deserved it. Also to die by the sword in the face of the town, and in the open way of disgrace, from the hand of so good and so holy a Prince, that, too, troubled them sore.

Mansoul greatly distressed

The town was also greatly troubled for the men that were committed to ward, for that they were their stay and their guide, and for that they believed that if those men were cut off, their execution would be but the beginning of the ruin of the town of Mansoul. Wherefore what do they, but together with the men in prison,

They send a petition to Emmanuel, by the hand of Mr. Would-live.

draw up a petition to the Prince, and sent it to Emmanuel by the hand of Mr. Would-live. So he went and came to the Prince's quarters, and presented the petition; the sum of which was this:—

"Great and wonderful potentate, victor over Diabolus, and conqueror of the town of Mansoul, We, the miserable inhabitants of that most woful corporation, do humbly beg that we may find favour in thy sight, and remember not against us former transgressions, nor yet the sins of the chief of our town, but spare us according to the greatness of thy mercy, and let us not die, but live in thy sight; so shall we be willing to be thy servants, and if thou shalt think fit, to gather our meat under thy table. Amen."

So the petitioner went as was said with his petition to the Prince, and the Prince took it at his hand, but sent him away with silence. This still afflicted the town of Mansoul, but yet considering that

They are answered with silence.

now they must either petition or die—for now they could not do anything else—therefore they consulted again, and sent another petition, and this petition was much after the form and method of the former.

But when the petition was drawn up, by whom should they send it was the next question; for they would not send this by him by whom they sent the first, for they thought that the Prince had taken some offence at the manner of his deport- ment before him; so they attempted *They petition again.* to make Captain Conviction their messenger with it, but he said that he neither durst, nor would petition Emmanuel for traitors; nor be to the Prince an advocate for rebels. Yet withal, said he, our Prince is good, *They cannot tell by whom to send it.* and you may adventure to send it by the hand of one of your town, provided he went with a rope about his head, and pleaded nothing but mercy.

Well, they made, through fear, their delays as long as they could, and longer than delays were good; but fearing at last the dangerousness of them, they thought, but with many a fainting in their minds, to send their petition by Mr. Desires- awake; so they sent for Mr. Desires-awake. Now he dwelt in a very mean cottage in Mansoul, and he came at his neighbours' request So they told him what they had done, and what they would do concerning petitioning, and that they did desire of him that he would go therewith to the Prince.

Then said Mr. Desires-awake, why should not I *Mr. Desires- awake goes with the pe- tition to the Prince.* do the best I can to save so famous a town as Mansoul from deserved destruction? They therefore deli- vered the petition to him, and told him how he must address himself to the Prince, and wished him ten thousand good speeds. So he comes to the Prince's pavilion as the first, and asked to speak with his Majesty; so word was carried to Emmanuel, and the Prince came out to the man. When Mr. Desires-awake saw the Prince, he fell flat, with his face to the ground, and cried out, Oh that Mansoul might live before thee! and with that he presented the petition. The which when the Prince had read, he turned away *His entertain- ment.* for a while and wept, but, refrain- ing himself, he turned again to the man, who all this while lay crying at his feet as at the first, and said to him, Go thy way to thy place, and I will consider of thy requests.

Now you may think that they of Mansoul that had sent him, what with guilt, and what with fear, lest their petition should be rejected, could not but look with many a long look, and that too with strange workings of heart to see what would be- come of their petition. At last, they *His return and answer to them that sent him.* saw their messenger coming back; so, when he was come, they asked him how he fared, what Emmanuel said, and what was become of the petition? But he told them that he would be silent till he came to the prison to my Lord Mayor, my Lord Will-be-will, and Mr. Recorder. So he went forwards towards the prison-house where the men of Mansoul lay bound. But oh, what a multitude flocked after to hear what the messenger said. So when he was come

and had shown himself at the grate of the prison, my Lord Mayor himself looked as white as a clout, the Recorder also did quake; but they asked and said, Come, good Sir, what did the great Prince say to you? Then said Mr. Desires-awake, when I came to my Lord's pavilion, I called, and he

came forth; so I fell postrate at his feet, and de- livered to him my petition, for the greatness of his person and the glory of his countenance would not suffer me to stand upon my legs. Now, as he re- ceived the petition, I cried, Oh that Mansoul might live before thee! So when for a while he had looked thereon, he turned him about and said to his servant, Go thy way to thy place again, and I will consider of thy request. The messenger added moreover, and said, The Prince to whom you sent me is such a one for beauty and glory, that whoso sees him must both love and fear him; I, for my part, can do no less; but I know not what will be the end of these things. At this answer they were all at a stand; both they *Mansoul con- founded at the answer.* in prison, and they that followed the messenger thither to hear the news; nor knew they what or what manner of in- terpretation to put upon what the Prince had said. Now, when the prison was cleared of the throng, the prisoners among themselves began to comment upon Emmanuel's words. My Lord Mayor said that the answer did not look with a *The prisoners' judgment upon the Prince's answer.* rugged face; but Will-be-will said it betokened evil; and the Recorder, that it was a messenger of death.

Now, they that were left, and that stood behind, and so could not so well hear what the prisoners said, some of them catched hold of one piece of a sen- tence, and some on a bit of another; some took hold of what the messenger said, and some of the prisoners' judgment thereon; so *Misgiving thoughts breed confusion in Mansoul.* none had the right understanding of things; but you cannot imagine what work these people made, and what a confusion there was in Mansoul now.

For presently they that had heard what was

said, flew about the town; one crying one thing, and another the quite contrary, and both were sure enough they told true, for they did hear, they said, with their ears what was said, and therefore could not be deceived. One would say, We must all be killed; another would say, We must all be saved; and a third would say that the Prince would not be concerned with Mansoul; and a fourth, that the prisoners must be suddenly put to death. And, as I said, every one stood to it that he told his tale the rightest, and that all others but he were out. Wherefore Mansoul had now molestation upon molestation, nor could any man know on what to rest the sole of his foot; for one would go by now, and as he went, if he heard his neighbour tell his tale, to be sure he would tell the quite contrary, and both would stand in it that he told the truth. Nay, some of them had got this story by the end, that the Prince did intend to put Mansoul to the sword. And now it began to

Mansoul in perplexity. be dark; wherefore poor Mansoul was in sad perplexity all that night until the morning.

But, so far as I could gather, by the best information that I could get, all this hubbub came through the words that the Recorder said, when he told them that in his judgment the Prince's answer was a messenger of death. It was this

What will guilt do? that fired the town, and that began the fright in Mansoul; for Mansoul, in former times, did use to count that Mr. Recorder was a seer, and that his sentence was equal to the best of oracles, and thus was Mansoul a terror to itself.

And now did they begin to feel what was the effects of stubborn rebellion, and unlawful resistance against their Prince. I say, they now began to feel the effects thereof by guilt and fear, that now had swallowed them up, and who more involved in the one, but they who were most in the other; to wit, the chief of the town of Mansoul. To be brief, when the fame of the fright was out of the town, and the prisoners had a little recovered themselves, they take to themselves some

They resolve to petition again. heart, and think to petition the Prince for life again. So they did draw up a third petition, the contents whereof were this :—

" Prince Emmanuel the Great, Lord of all

Their petition. worlds, and master of mercy, We, thy poor, wretched, miserable, dying town of Mansoul, do confess unto thy great and glorious majesty that we have sinned against thy Father and thee, and are no more worthy to be called thy Mansoul, but rather to be cast into the pit. If thou wilt slay us, we have deserved it. If thou wilt condemn us to the deep, we cannot but say thou art righteous. We cannot complain, whatever thou dost, or however thou carriest it towards us. But oh, let mercy reign; and let it be extended to us! Oh let mercy take hold upon us, and free us from our transgressions, and we

will sing of thy mercy and of thy judgment. Amen."

This petition, when drawn up, was designed to be sent to the Prince as the first, but who should carry it, that was Prayer attended with difficulty. the question. Some said, Let him do it that went with the first; but others thought not good to do that, and that because he sped no better. Now, there was an old man in the town and his name was Mr. Good-deed; a man that bare only the name, but had nothing of the nature of the thing. Now, some were for sending of him, but the Recorder Old Good-deed propounded as a fit person to carry the petition; the old Recorder opposes it, and he is rejected. was by no means for that, for, said he, we now stand in need of, and are pleading for mercy, wherefore to send our petition by a man of his name will seem to cross the petition itself. Should we make Mr. Good-deed our messenger when our petition cries for mercy?

" Besides," quoth the old gentleman, " should the Prince now, as he receives the petition, ask him and say, What is thy name? as nobody knows but he will, and he should say, Old Good-deed; what, think you, would Emmanuel say but this, Ay! is old Good-deed yet alive in Mansoul? then let old Good-deed save you from your distresses. And if he says so, I am sure we are lost; nor can a thousand of old Good-deeds save Mansoul."

After the Recorder had given in his reasons why old Good-deed should not go with this petition to Emmanuel, the rest of the prisoners and chief of Mansoul opposed it also, and so old Good-deed was laid aside, and they agreed to send Mr. Desires-awake again; so they sent for him, and desired him that he would a second time go with their petition to the Prince, and he readily told them he would. But they bid him that in any wise he would take heed that in no word or carriage he gave offence to the Prince, for by doing so, for ought we can tell, you may bring Mansoul into utter destruction, said they.

Now, Mr. Desires-awake, when he saw that he must go of this errand, besought that they would grant that Mr. Wet-eyes might go Mr. Desires-awake goes again, and takes one Wet-eyes with him. with him. Now, this Wet-eyes was a near neighbour of Mr. Desires, a poor man, a man of a broken spirit, yet one that could speak well to a petition. So they granted that he should go with him. Wherefore they addressed themselves to their business. Mr. Desires put a rope upon his head, and Mr. Wet-eyes went with hands wringing together. Thus they went to the Prince's pavilion.

Now, when they went to petition this third time, they were not without thoughts that by often coming they might be a burden to the Prince. Wherefore, when they were come to the Their apology for their coming again. door of his pavilion, they first made their apology for themselves, and for their coming to trouble Emmanuel so often; and they said that they came not hither to-day for that they delighted in being troublesome, or for that they delighted to hear themselves talk, but for that necessity caused them to come to his Majesty. They could, they said, have no rest day nor night, because of their transgressions against Shaddai, and against Emmanuel his Son. They also thought that some misbehaviour of Mr. Desires-awake the last time might give distaste to his Highness, and so caused that he returned from so merciful a Prince empty, and without countenance. So, when they had made this apology, Mr. Desires-awake cast himself prostrate upon the ground as at the first, at the feet of the mighty Prince, saying, Oh that Mansoul might live before thee! And so he delivered his petition. The Prince then having read the petition, turned aside awhile, as before, and, coming again to the place where The Prince talketh with them. the petitioner lay on the ground, he demanded what his name was, and of what esteem in the account of Mansoul; for that he, above all the multitude in Mansoul, should be sent to him upon such an errand. Then said the man to the Prince, "Oh Mr. Desires' free speech to the Prince. let not my Lord be angry; and why inquirest thou after the name of such a dead dog as I am? Pass by, I pray thee, and take no notice of who I am, because there is, as thou very well knowest, so great a disproportion between me and thee. Why the townsmen chose to send me on this errand to my Lord is best known to themselves, but it could not be for that they thought that I had favour with my Lord. For my part, I am out of charity with myself; who then should be in love with me? Yet live I would, and so would I that my towns-men should, and because both they and myself are guilty of great transgressions, therefore they have sent me, and I am come in their names to beg of my Lord for mercy. Let it please thee, there-fore, to incline to mercy, but ask not what thy servants are."

Then said the Prince, " And what is he that is become thy companion in this so weighty a matter?" So Mr. Desires told Emmanuel that he was a poor neighbour of his, and one of his most intimate associates, and his name, said he, may it please your most excellent Majesty, is Wet-eyes, of the town of Mansoul. I know that there are many of that name that are nought, but I hope it will be no offence to my Lord that I have brought my poor neighbour with me.

Then Mr. Wet-eyes fell on his face to the ground, and made this apology for his coming with his neighbour to his Lord :—

" Oh my Lord," quoth he, " what I am I know Mr. Wet-eyes' apology for his coming with his neighbour. not myself, nor whether my name be feigned or true, especially when I begin to think what some have said, namely, that this name was given me because Mr. Repentance was my father. Good men have bad children, and the sincere do oftentimes beget hypocrites. My mother also

called me by this name from my cradle, but whe-ther because of the moistness of my brain, or because of the softness of my heart, I cannot tell. I see dirt in mine own tears, and filthiness in the bottom of my prayers. But I pray thee," (and all this while the gentleman wept,) " that thou wouldst not remember against us our transgressions, nor take offence at the unqualifiedness of thy servants, but mercifully pass by the sin of Mansoul, and refrain from the glorifying of thy grace no longer."

So at his bidding they arose, and both stood trembling before him, and he spake to them to this purpose :—

" The town of Mansoul hath grievously rebelled against my Father, in that they The Prince's answer. have rejected him from being their king, and did choose to themselves for their cap-tain, a liar, a murderer, and a runagate slave. For this Diabolus, and your pretended prince, though once so highly accounted of by you, made rebel-lion against my Father and me, even in our palace and highest court there, thinking to become a prince and king. But being there The original of Diabolus. timely discovered and apprehended, and for his wickedness bound in chains, and sepa-rated to the pit with those who were his compa-nions, he offered himself to you, and you have received him.

" Now this is, and for a long time hath been an high affront to my Father, wherefore my Father sent to you a powerful army to reduce you to your obedience. But you know how those men, their captains, and their counsels, were esteemed of you, and what they received at your hand. You re-belled against them, you shut your gates upon them, you bid them battle, you fought them, and fought for Diabolus against them. So they sent to my Father for more power, and I with my men are come to subdue you. But as you treated the servants, so you treated their Lord. You stood up in hostile manner against me, you shut up your gates against me, you turned the deaf ear to me, and resisted as long as you could ; but now I have made a conquest of you. Did you cry me mercy so long as you had hopes that you might prevail against me? But now I have taken the town, you cry. But why did you not cry before, when the white flag of my mercy, the red flag of justice, and the black flag that threatened execution were set up to cite you to it? Now I have conquered your Diabolus, you come to me for favour, but why did you not help me against the mighty? Yet I will consider your petition, and will answer it so as will be for my glory.

" Go, bid Captain Boanerges and Captain Con-viction bring the prisoners out to me into the camp to-morrow, and say you to Captain Judg-ment and Captain Execution, Stay you in the castle, and take good heed to yourselves that you keep all quiet in Mansoul until you hear further from me." And with that he turned himself from them, and went into his royal pavilion again.

So the petitioners having received this answer from the Prince, returned as at the first to go to their companions again. But they had not gone far, but thoughts began to work in their minds that no mercy as yet was intended by the Prince to Mansoul; so they went to the place where the prisoners lay bound; but these workings of mind about what would become of Mansoul had such strong power over them, that by that they were come unto them that sent them, they were scarce able to deliver their message.

But they came at length to the gates of the town (now the townsmen with earnestness were waiting for their return) where many met them, to know what answer was made to the petition. Then they cried out to those that were sent, What news from the Prince, and what hath Emmanuel said? But they said that they must, as before, go up to the prison, and there deliver their mes- *Of Inquisitive thoughts.* sage. So away they went to the prison, with a multitude at their heels. Now, when they were come to the grates of the prison, they told the first part of Emmanuel's speech to the prisoners; to wit, how he reflected *The messengers, in telling their tale, fright the prisoners.* upon their disloyalty to his Father and himself, and how they had chose and closed with Diabolus, had fought for him, hearkened to him, and been ruled by him, but had despised him and his men. This made the prisoners look pale; but the messengers proceeded, and said, He, the Prince, said, moreover, that yet he would consider your petition, and give such answer thereto as would stand with his glory. And as these words were spoken, Mr. Wet-eyes gave a great sigh. At this they were all of them struck into their dumps, and could not tell what to say. Fear also possessed them in a marvellous manner; and death seemed to sit upon some of their eyebrows. Now, there was in the company a notable sharp-witted fellow, *Old Inquisitive.* a mean man of estate, and his name was old Inquisitive. This man asked the petitioners if they had told out every whit of what Emmanuel said. And they answered, Verily, no. Then said Inquisitive, I thought so, indeed. Pray, what was it more that he said unto you? Then they paused awhile; but at last they brought out all, saying, "The Prince did bid us bid Captain Boanerges and Captain Conviction bring the prisoners down to him to-morrow; and that Captain Judgment and Captain Execution should take charge of the castle and town till they should hear further from him." They said also that when the Prince had commanded them thus to do, he immediately turned his back upon them, and went into his royal pavilion.

But oh, how this return, and especially this last clause of it, that the prisoners must go out to the Prince into the camp, brake all their loins in pieces! Wherefore, with one voice, they set up a cry that reached up to the heavens. This done, each of the three prepared himself to die; and the Re- corder said unto them, This was the thing that I feared; for they concluded that *Conscience.* to-morrow, by that the sun went down, they should be tumbled out of the world. The whole town also counted of no other but that, in their time and order, they must all drink of the same cup. Wherefore the town of Mansoul spent that night in mourning, and sackcloth and ashes. The prisoners also, when the time was come for them to go down before the Prince, dressed themselves in mourning attire, with ropes upon their heads. The whole town of Mansoul also showed themselves upon the wall, all clad in mourning weeds, if, perhaps, the Prince, with the sight thereof might be moved with compassion. But oh, how the busybodies that were *Vain thoughts.* in the town of Mansoul did now concern themselves! They did run here and there through the streets of the town by companies, crying out as they ran in tumultuous wise, one after one manner, and another the quite contrary, to the almost utter distraction of Mansoul.

Well, the time is come that the prisoners must go down to the camp, and appear before the Prince. And thus was the manner of their *The prisoners had to trial.* going down. Captain Boanerges went with a guard before them, and Captain Conviction came behind, and the prisoners went down bound in chains in the midst; so, I say, the prisoners went in the midst, and the guard went with flying colours behind and before, but the prisoners went with drooping spirits.

Or, more particularly thus :—

The prisoners went down all in mourning; they put ropes upon themselves; they *How they went.* went on smiting of themselves on the breasts, but durst not lift up their eyes to heaven. Thus they went out at the gate of Mansoul, till they came into the midst of the Prince's army, the sight and glory of which did greatly heighten their affliction. Nor could they now longer forbear, but cry out aloud, Oh unhappy men! Oh wretched men of Mansoul! Their chains still mixing their dolorous notes with the cries of the prisoners, made noise more lamentable.

So, when they were come to the door of the Prince's pavilion, they cast themselves prostrate upon the place. Then one went in and told his Lord that the prisoners were come down. The Prince then ascended a throne of state, and sent for the prisoners in; who, when they came, did tremble before him; also they covered their faces with shame. Now, as they drew *They fall down prostrate before him.* near to the place where he sat, they threw themselves down before him. Then said the Prince to the Captain Boanerges, Bid the prisoners stand upon their feet. Then they stood trembling before him, and he said, "Are you the men that here- *They are upon their trial.* tofore were the servants of Shaddai?" And they said, "Yes, Lord, yes." Then said the Prince again, "Are you the men that did suffer yourselves to be corrupted and defiled by that abominable one, Diabolus?" And they said "We did more than suffer it, Lord; for we chose it of our own mind." The Prince asked further, saying, "Could you have been content that your slavery should have continued under his tyranny as long as you had lived?" Then said the prisoners, "Yes, Lord, yes; for his ways were pleasing to our flesh, and we were grown aliens to a better state." "And did you," said he, "when I came up against this town of Mansoul, heartily wish that I might not have the victory over you?" "Yes, Lord, yes," said they. Then said the Prince, "And what punishment is it, think you, that you deserve at my hand for these and other your high and mighty sins?" And they said, "Both death and the deep, Lord; for we have deserved no less." He asked again if they had aught to say for themselves, why the sentence that they confessed that they had deserved should not be passed upon them? And they said, "We *They condemn themselves.* can say nothing, Lord; thou art just, for we have sinned." Then said the Prince, "And for what are those ropes on your heads?" *Sins.* The prisoners answered, "These ropes are to bind us withal to the place of execution, if mercy be not pleasing in thy sight." So he further asked, if all the men in the town of Mansoul were in this confession as they? *Powers of the soul.* And they answered, "All the natives, Lord; but for the Diabolonians that came into our town when *Corruptions and lusts.* the tyrant got possession of us, we can say nothing for them."

Then the Prince commanded that a herald should *A victory proclaimed.* be called, and that he should, in the midst and throughout the camp of Emmanuel proclaim, and that with sound of trumpet, that the Prince, the Son of Shaddai, had, in his Father's name and for his Father's glory, gotten a perfect conquest and victory over Mansoul, and that the prisoners should follow him, and say, Amen. So this was done as he had *Joy for the victory.* commanded. And presently the music that was in the upper region sounded melodiously. The captains that were in the camp shouted, and the soldiers did sing songs of triumph to the Prince, the colours waved in the wind, and great joy was everywhere: only it was wanting as yet in the hearts of the men of Mansoul.

Then the Prince called for the prisoners to come *They are pardoned, and are commanded to proclaim it to-morrow in Mansoul.* and to stand again before him, and they came and stood trembling. And he said unto them, "The sins, trespasses, iniquities, that you, with the whole town of Mansoul, have from time to time committed against my Father and me, I have power and commandment from my Father to forgive to the town of Mansoul; and do forgive you accordingly." And having so said, he gave them written in parchment, and sealed with seven seals, a large and general pardon, commanding both my Lord Mayor, my Lord Will-be-will, and Mr. Recorder, to proclaim, and cause it to be proclaimed to-morrow by that the sun is up, throughout the whole town of Mansoul.

Moreover, the Prince stripped the prisoners of their mourning weeds, and gave *Their rags are taken from them.* them "beauty for ashes, the oil of joy for mourning, and the garment of praise for the spirit of heaviness." (Is. lxi. 3.)

Then he gave, to each of the three, jewels of gold, and precious stones, and took *A strange alteration.* away their ropes, and put chains of gold about their necks, and ear-rings in their ears. Now the prisoners, when they did hear the gracious words of Prince Emmanuel, and had beheld all that was done unto them, fainted almost quite away; for the grace, the benefit, the pardon, was sudden, glorious, and so big, that they were not able, without staggering, to stand up under it. Yea, my Lord Will-be-will swooned outright; but the Prince stepped to him, put his everlasting arms under him, embraced him, kissed him, and bid him be of good cheer, for all should be performed according to his word. He also did kiss, and embrace, and smile upon the other two, that were Will-be-will's companions, saying, "Take these as further tokens of my love, favour, and compassion to you; and I charge you, that you, Mr. Recorder, tell in the town of Mansoul what you have heard and seen."

Then were their fetters broken to pieces before their faces, and cast into the air, and *Their guilt.* their *steps* were enlarged under them. Then they fell down at the feet of the Prince, and kissed his feet, and wetted them with tears; also they cried out with a mighty strong voice, saying, "Blessed be the glory of the Lord from this place." (Eze. iii. 12.) So they were bid rise up, and go to the town, and tell to Mansoul what the Prince had done. He commanded also that one with a pipe and tabor should *They are sent home with pipe and tabor.* go and play before them all the way into the town of Mansoul. Then was fulfilled what they never looked for, and they were made to possess that which they never dreamed of. The Prince also called *Captain Credence guards them home.* for the noble Captain Credence, and commanded that he and some of his officers should march before the noblemen of Mansoul, with flying colours, into the town. He gave also unto Captain Credence a charge, that about that time that *When faith and pardon meet together, judgment and execution depart from the heart.* the Recorder did read the general pardon in the town of Mansoul, that at that very time he should with flying colours march in at Eye-gate, with his ten thousands at his feet, and that he should go until he came by the high street of the town, up to the castle gates, and that himself should take possession thereof against his Lord came thither. He commanded, moreover, that he should bid Captain Judgment and Captain Execution to leave the stronghold to him, and to withdraw from Mansoul, and to return into the camp with speed unto the Prince.

And now was the town of Mansoul also delivered from the terror of the first four captains and their men.

Well, I told you before how the prisoners were entertained by the noble Prince Emmanuel, and how they behaved themselves before him, and how he sent them away to their home with pipe and tabor going before them. And now you must think that those of the town that had all this while waited to hear of their death, could not but be exercised with sadness of mind, and with thoughts that pricked like thorns. Nor could their thoughts be kept to any one point; the wind blew with them all this while at great uncertainties; yea, their hearts were like a balance that had been disquieted with a shaking hand. But, at last, as they with many a long look looked over the wall of Mansoul, they thought that they saw some returning to the town; and thought again, Who should they be too, who should they be! At last they discerned that they were the prisoners; but can you imagine how their hearts were surprised with wonder, especially when they perceived also in what equipage and with what honour they were sent home? They

went down to the camp in black, but they came back to the town in white; they went down to the camp in ropes, they came back in chains of gold; they went down to the camp with their feet in fetters, but came back with their steps enlarged under them; they went also to the camp looking for death, but they came back from thence with assurance of life; they went down to the camp with heavy hearts, but came back again with pipe and tabor playing before them. So, so soon as they were come to Eye-gate, the poor and tottering town of Mansoul adventured to give a shout, and they gave such a shout as made the captains in the prince's army leap at the sound thereof.

A strange alteration.

Alas for them, poor hearts! who could blame them, since their dead friends were come to life again? for it was to them as life from the dead, to see the ancients of the town of Mansoul to shine in such splendour. They looked for nothing but the axe and the block; but behold! joy and gladness, comfort and consolation, and such melodious notes attending of them that was sufficient to make a sick man well. So, when they came up, they saluted each other with Welcome! welcome! and blessed be he that has spared you. (Isa. xxxiii. 24.) They added also, "We see it is well with you, but how must it go with the town of Mansoul?" and "Will it go well with the town of Mansoul?" said they. Then answered them the Recorder and my Lord Mayor, "Oh tidings! glad tidings! good tidings of good and of great joy to poor Mansoul!" Then they gave another shout that made the earth to ring again. After this, they inquired yet more particularly how things went in the camp, and what message they had from Emmanuel to the town. So they told them all passages that had happened to them at the camp, and every thing that the Prince did to them. This made Mansoul wonder at the wisdom and grace of the Prince Emmanuel. Then they told them what they had received at his hands for the whole town of Mansoul; and the Recorder delivered it in these words, "*Pardon, pardon,* Oh, the joy of *pardon for Mansoul;* and this shall pardon of sin! Mansoul know to-morrow." Then he commanded, and they went and summoned Mansoul to meet together in the market-place to-morrow, there to hear their general pardon read.

But who can think what a turn, what a change, what an alteration this hint of things did make in the countenance of the town of Mansoul! No man of Mansoul could sleep that night for joy; in every house there was joy and music, singing and making *Town-talk* merry, telling and hearing of Man- *of the* soul's happiness, was then all that *King's mercy.* Mansoul had to do; and this was the burden of all their song, " Oh, more of this at the rising of the sun! more of this to-morrow!" Who thought yesterday, would one say, that this day would have been such a day to us! And who thought, that saw our prisoners go down in irons, that they would have returned in chains of gold! yea, they that judged themselves as they went to be judged of their judge, were by his mouth acquitted, not for that they were innocent, but of the Prince's mercy, and sent home with pipe and tabor. But is this the common custom of Princes? do they use to show such kind of favours to traitors? No! this is only peculiar to Shaddai, and unto Emmanuel his Son.

Now morning drew on apace, wherefore the Lord Mayor, the Lord Will-be-will, and Mr. Recorder came down to the market-place at the time that the Prince had appointed, where the townsfolk were waiting for them; and when they came, they came in that attire and in that glory that the Prince had put them into the day before, and the street was lightened with their glory. So the Mayor, Recorder, and my Lord Will-be-will drew down to Mouth-gate, which was at the lower end of the market-place, because that of old time was the place where they used to read public matters. Thither, therefore, they came in their robes, and their tabret went before them. Now the eagerness of the people to know the full of the matter was great.

Then the Recorder stood up upon his feet, and *The manner* first beckoning with his hand for *of reading the* silence, he read out with loud voice *pardon.* the pardon. But when he came to these words, " The Lord, the Lord God, merciful and gracious, pardoning iniquity, transgression, and sin " (Ex. xxxiv. 6); and to these, " All manner of sin and blasphemy shall be forgiven," &c. (Mark iii. 28); they could not forbear but leap for joy. For this you must know, that there was conjoined herewith every man's name in Mansoul; also the seals of the pardon made a brave show.

When the Recorder had made an end of reading *Now they tread* the pardon, the townsmen ran up upon *upon the flesh.* the walls of the town, and leaped and skipped thereon for joy; and bowed themselves seven times with their faces towards Emmanuel's *Lively and warm* pavilion, and shouted out aloud for *thoughts.* joy, and said, " Let Emmanuel live for ever!" Then order was given to the young

men in Mansoul, that they should ring the bells for joy. So the bells did ring, and the people sing, and the music go in every house in Mansoul.

When the Prince had sent home the three prisoners of Mansoul with joy, and pipe, and tabor, he commanded his captains with *The carriage of* all the field officers and soldiers *the camp.* throughout his army, to be ready in that morning, that the Recorder should read the pardon in Mansoul to do his further pleasure. So the morning, as I have showed, being come, just as the Recorder had made an end of reading the pardon, Emmanuel commanded that all the trumpets in the camp should sound, that the colours should be displayed, half of them upon Mount Gracious, and half of them upon Mount Justice. He commanded also that all the captains should show themselves in all their harness, and that the soldiers should shout for joy. Nor was Captain *Faith will not* Credence, though in the castle, *be silent when* silent in such a day, but he, from *Mansoul is* the top of the hold showed himself *saved.* with sound of trumpet to Mansoul, and to the Prince's camp.

Thus have I showed you the manner and way that Emmanuel took to recover the town of Mansoul from under the hand and power of the tyrant Diabolus.

Now, when the Prince had completed these, the outward ceremonies of his joy, he again commanded that his captains and sol- *The Prince dis-* diers should show unto Mansoul *plays his graces* some feats of war. So they pre- *before Mansoul.* sently addressed themselves to this work. But oh, with what agility, nimbleness, dexterity, and bravery did these military men discover their skill in feats of war to the now gazing town of Mansoul!

They marched, they counter-marched, they opened to the right and left, they divided and subdivided, they closed, they wheeled, made good their front and rear with their right and left wings, and twenty things more, with that aptness, and then were all as they were again, *They are ra-* that they took, yea, ravished the *vished at the* hearts that were in Mansoul, to be- *sight of them.* hold it. But add to this, the handling of their arms, the managing of their weapons of war, were marvellous taking to Mansoul and me.

When this action was over, the whole town of Mansoul came out as one man to the Prince in the camp to thank him, and praise him for his abundant favour, and to beg that it would please his grace to come unto Mansoul with *They beg that* his men, and there to take up their *the Prince and* quarters for ever. And this they *his men will* did in most humble manner, bowing *dwell with them* themselves seven times to the ground before him. Then said he, " All peace be to you." So the town came nigh, and touched with the hand the top of his golden sceptre, and they said, Oh that the Prince Emmanuel, with his captains and men of war, would dwell in Mansoul for ever; and that his battering rams and slings might be lodged in her for the use and service of the Prince, and for the help and strength of Mansoul. "For," said they, "we have room for thee, we have room for thy men, we have also room for thy weapons of war, and a place to make a magazine for thy Say, and hold to carriages. Do it, Emmanuel, and it, Mansoul. thou shalt be King and Captain in Mansoul for ever. Yea, govern thou also according to all the desire of thy soul, and make thou governors and princes under thee of thy captains and men of war, and we will become thy servants, and thy laws shall be our direction."

They added, moreover, and prayed his Majesty to consider thereof; "for," said they, "if now, after all this grace bestowed upon us thy miserable town of Mansoul, thou shouldest withdraw, thou and thy captains from us, the town of Mansoul will die. Yea," said they, "our blessed Emmanuel, if thou shouldest depart from us now thou hast done so much good for us, and showed so much mercy unto us, what will follow but that our joy will be as if it had not been, and our enemies will a second time come upon us with more rage than at the first. Wherefore, we beseech thee, oh thou the desire of our eyes, and the strength and life of our poor town, accept of this motion that now we have made unto our Lord, and come and dwell in the midst of us, and let us be thy people. Besides, Their fears. Lord, we do not know but that to this day many Diabolonians may be yet lurking in the town of Mansoul, and they will betray us when thou shalt leave us, into the hand of Diabolus again; and who knows what designs, plots, or contrivances have passed betwixt them about these things already; loth are we to fall again into his horrible hands. Wherefore, let it please thee to accept of our palace for thy place of residence, and of the houses of the best men in our town for the reception of thy soldiers, and their furniture."

Then said the Prince, "If I come to your town, The Prince's will you suffer me further to prose- question to Man- cute that which is in mine heart soul. against mine enemies and yours; yea, will you help me in such undertakings?"

They answered, "We know not what we shall Their answer. do; we did not think once that we should have been such traitors to Shaddai as we have proved to be; what then shall we say to our Lord? Let him put no trust in his saints, let the Prince dwell in our castle, and make of our town a garrison, let him set his noble captains, and his warlike soldiers over us. Yea, let him conquer us with his love, and overcome us with his grace, and then surely shall he be but with us, and help us, as he was, and did that morning that our pardon was read unto us, we shall comply with this, our Lord, and with his ways, and fall in with his word against the mighty.

"One word more, and thy servants have done, and in this will trouble our Lord no more. We know not the depth of the wisdom of thee our Prince. Who could have thought that had been ruled by his reason, that so much sweet as we do now enjoy should have come out of those bitter trials wherewith we were tried at the first? but Lord, let light go before, and let love come after; yea, take us by the hand, and lead us by thy counsels, and let this always abide upon us, that all things shall be for the best for thy servants, and come to our Mansoul, and do as it pleaseth thee. Or, Lord, come to our Mansoul, do what thou wilt, so thou keepest us from sinning, and makest us serviceable to thy majesty."

Then said the Prince to the town of Mansoul again, "Go, return to your houses in peace; I will willingly in this He consenteth to dwell in Man- comply with your desires. I will soul, and pro- remove my royal pavilion, I will miseth to come in to-morrow. draw up my forces before Eye-gate to-morrow, and so will march forwards into the town of Mansoul. I will possess myself of your castle of Mansoul, and will set my soldiers over you; yea, I will yet do things in Mansoul that cannot be paralleled in any nation, country, or kingdom under heaven."

Then did the men of Mansoul give a shout, and returned unto their houses in peace; they also told to their kindred and friends the good that Emmanuel had promised to Mansoul. And to-morrow, said they, he will march into our town, and take up his dwelling, he and his men, in Mansoul.

Then went out the inhabitants of the town of Mansoul with haste to the green Mansoul's pre- trees, and to the meadows, to gather paration for his boughs and flowers, therewith to reception. strew the streets against their Prince, the Son of Shaddai, should come; they also made garlands, and other fine works, to betoken how joyful they were, and should be to receive their Emmanuel into Mansoul; yea, they strewed the street quite from Eye-gate to the Castle-gate, the place where the Prince should be. They also prepared for his coming what music the town of Mansoul would afford, that they might play before him to the palace, his habitation.

So, at the time appointed, he makes his approach to Mansoul, and the gates were set open for him, there also the ancients and elders of Mansoul met him, to salute him with a thousand welcomes. Then he arose and entered Mansoul, he and all his servants. The elders of Mansoul did also go dancing before him till he came to the castle gates. And this was the manner of his He enters the going up thither. He was clad in town of Mansoul, his golden armour, he rode in his and how. royal chariot, the trumpets sounded about him, the colours were displayed, his ten thousands went up at his feet, and the elders of Mansoul danced before him. And now were the walls of the famous town of Mansoul filled with the tramplings of the inhabitants thereof, who went up thither to view the approach of the blessed Prince, and his royal army. Also the casements, windows, balconies, and tops of the houses were all now filled with persons of all sorts to behold how their town was to be filled with good.

Now, when he was come so far into the town as to the Recorder's house, he commanded that one should go to Captain Credence, to know whether the castle of Mansoul was prepared to entertain his Royal Presence, for the preparation of that was left to that Captain, and word was brought that it was. (Acts xv. 9.) Then was Captain Credence commanded also to come forth with his power to meet the Prince, the which was, as he had commanded, done, and he conducted him into the castle. (Eph. iii. 17.) This done, the Prince that night did lodge in the castle with his mighty captains and men of war, to the joy of the town of Mansoul.

Now, the next care of the townsfolk was, how the captains and soldiers of the Prince's army should be quartered among them, and the care was *The townsmen covet who shall have most of the soldiers that belong to the Prince.* not how they should shut their hands of them, but how they should fill their houses with them; for every man in Mansoul now had that esteem of Emmanuel and his men, that nothing grieved them more than because they were not enlarged enough, every one of them to receive the whole army of the Prince; yea, they counted it their glory to be waiting upon them, and would in those days run at their bidding like lacqueys. At last they came to this result:—

1. That Captain Innocency should quarter at *How they were quartered in the town of Mansoul.* Mr. Reason's. 2. That Captain Patience should quarter at Mr. Mind's. This Mr. Mind was formerly the Lord Will-be-will's clerk, in time of the late rebellion. 3. It was ordered that Captain Charity should quarter at Mr. Affection's house. 4. That Captain Good-hope should quarter at my Lord Mayor's. Now, for the house of the Recorder, himself desired, because his house was next to the castle, and because from him it was ordered by the Prince, that, if need be, the alarm should be given to Mansoul; it was, I say, desired by him that Captain Boanerges and Captain Conviction should take up their quarters with him, even they and all their men. 5. As for Captain Judgment and Captain Execution, my Lord Will-be-will took them, and their men to him, because he was to rule under the Prince for the good of the town of Mansoul now, as he had before, under the tyrant Diabolus, for the hurt and damage thereof. (Rom. vi. 19; Eph. iii. 17.) 6. And throughout the rest of the town were quartered Emmanuel's forces, but Captain Credence with his men abode still in the castle. So the Prince, his captains, and his soldiers were lodged in the town of Mansoul.

Now the ancients and elders of the town of Mansoul thought that they never *Mansoul inflamed with their Prince Emmanuel.* should have enough of the Prince Emmanuel; his person, his actions, his words, and behaviour, were so pleasing, so taking, so desirable to them. Wherefore, they prayed him, that though the castle of Mansoul was his place of residence, and they desired that he might dwell there for ever, yet that he would often visit the streets, houses, and people of Mansoul. For, said they, dread Sovereign, thy presence, thy looks, thy smiles, thy words, are the life, and strength, and sinews of the town of Mansoul.

Besides this, they craved that they might have, without difficulty or interruption, *They have access unto him.* continual access unto him; so for that very purpose he commanded that the gates should stand open, that they might there see the manner of his doings, the fortifications of the place, and the royal mansion-house of the Prince. When he spake, they all stopped their *They learn of him.* mouths and gave audience; and when he walked, it was their delight to imitate him in his goings.

Now, upon a time, Emmanuel made a feast for the town of Mansoul, and upon the feasting-day the townsfolk were come to the castle to partake of his banquet. And he feasted them with all manner of outlandish food—food that grew not in the fields of Mansoul, nor in all the whole kingdom of Universe. It was food that came from his Father's court, and so there was dish *Promise after promise.* after dish set before them, and they were commanded freely to eat. But still, when a fresh dish was set before them, they would whisperingly say to each other, "What is it?" (Exod. xvi. 15.) For they wist not what to call it. They drank also of the water that was made wine; and were very merry with him. There *Brave entertainment.* was music also all the while at the table, and man did eat angels' food, and had honey given him out of the rock. So Mansoul did eat the food that was peculiar to the court, yea, they had now thereof to the full. (Ps. lxxviii. 24, 25.)

I must not forget to tell you that as at this table there were musicians, so they were not those of the country, nor yet of the town of Mansoul, but they were the masters of the songs that were sung at the court of Shaddai.

Now, after the feast was over, Emmanuel was for entertaining the town of Mansoul *Riddles.* with some curious riddles of secrets drawn up by his Father's secretary, by the skill and wisdom of Shaddai; the like to these there is not in any kingdom. These riddles *The Holy Scriptures.* were made upon the King Shaddai himself, and upon Emmanuel his Son, and upon his wars and doings with Mansoul.

Emmanuel also expounded unto them some of those riddles himself, but oh, how they were lightened! They saw what they never saw, they could not have thought that such rarities could have been couched in so few and such ordinary words. I told you before whom these riddles did concern; and as they were opened, the people did evidently see it was so. Yea, they did gather that the things themselves were a kind of portraiture, and that of Emmanuel himself; for when they read in the scheme where the riddles were writ, and looked in the face of the Prince, things looked so like the one to the other that Mansoul could not forbear but say, This is the Lamb, this is the Sacrifice, this is the Rock, this is the Red Cow, this is the Door, and this is the Way; with a great many other things more.

And thus he dismissed the town of Mansoul. But can you imagine how the people of the corporation were taken with this entertainment? Oh, *The end of that banquet.* they were transported with joy, they were drowned with wonderment, while they saw and understood, and considered what their Emmanuel entertained them withal, and what mysteries he opened to them; and when they were at home in their houses, and in their most retired places, they could not but sing of him, and of his actions. Yea, so taken were the townsmen now with their Prince, that they would sing of him in their sleep.

Now it was in the heart of the Prince Emmanuel *Mansoul must be new modeled.* to new model the town of Mansoul, and to put it into such a condition as might be more pleasing to him, and that might best stand with the profit and security of the now flourishing town of Mansoul. He provided also against insurrections at home, and invasions from abroad; such love had he for the famous town of Mansoul. Wherefore he first of all commanded *The instruments of war mounted.* that the great slings that were brought from his Father's court when he came to the war of Mansoul, should be mounted, some upon the battlements of the castle some upon the towers, for there were towers in the town of Mansoul, towers new built by Emmanuel since he came thither. There was also an *A nameless terrible instrument in Mansoul.* instrument invented by Emmanuel, that was to throw stones from the castle of Mansoul, out at Mouthgate; an instrument that could not be resisted, nor that would miss of execution; wherefore for the wonderful exploits that it did when used, it went without a name, and it was committed to the care of, and to be managed by the brave captain, the Captain Credence, in case of war.

This done, Emmanuel called the Lord Will-be-*Lord Will-be-will promoted.* will to him, and gave him in commandment to take care of the gates, the wall, and towers in Mansoul. Also the Prince gave him the militia into his hand; and a special charge to withstand all insurrections and tumults that might be made in Mansoul, against the peace of our Lord the King, and the peace and tranquillity of the town of Mansoul. He also gave him in commission, that if he found any of the Diabolonians lurking in any corner in the famous town of Mansoul, he should forthwith apprehend them, and stay them, or commit them to safe custody, that they may be proceeded against according to law.

Then he called unto him the Lord Understanding, who was the old Lord Mayor, *My Lord Mayor put into place.* he that was put out of place when Diabolus took the town, and put him into his former office again, and it became his place for his life-time. He bid him also that he should build him a palace near Eye-gate, and that he should build it in fashion like a tower for defence. He bid him also that he should read in the revelation of mysteries all the days of his life, that he might know how to perform his office aright. He also made Mr. Knowledge, the Recorder; *Mr. Knowledge made Recorder.* not of contempt to old Mr. Conscience, who had been Recorder before; but for that it was in his princely mind to confer upon Mr. Conscience another employ; of which he told the old gentleman he should know more hereafter.

Then he commanded that the image of Diabolus should be taken down from the place where it was set up, and that they should destroy *The image of the Prince and his Father set up again in Mansoul.* it utterly, beating of it into powder, and casting it unto the wind, without the town wall; and that the image of Shaddai his Father should be set up again, with his own, upon the castle gates, and that it should be more fairly drawn than ever; forasmuch as both his father and himself were come to Mansoul in more grace and mercy than heretofore. (Rev. xxii. 4.) He would also that his name should be fairly engraven upon the front of the town, and that it should be done in the best of gold, for the honour of the town of Mansoul.

After this was done, Emmanuel gave out a commandment that those three great Diabolonians should be apprehended; namely, the two late Lord Mayors; to wit, Mr. Incredulity, Mr. Lustings, and Mr. Forget-good, the Recorder. Besides these, there were some of them that Diabolus made burgesses and aldermen in Mansoul, that were committed to ward by the hand of the now valiant, and now right noble, the brave Lord Will-be-will. And these were their names, Alder- *Some Diabolonians committed to prison under the hand of Mr. Trueman the keeper.* man Atheism, Alderman Hardheart, and Alderman False-peace. The burgesses were Mr. No-truth, Mr. Pitiless, Mr. Haughty, with the like. These were committed to close custody; and the jailer's name was Mr. Trueman; this Trueman was one of those that Emmanuel brought with him from his Father's court, when at the first he made a war upon Diabolus in the town of Mansoul.

After this, the Prince gave a charge that the three strongholds, that at the command of Diabolus the Diabolonians built in Mansoul, should be demolished and utterly pulled down; of which holds *Diabolus's strongholds pulled down.*

and their names, with their captains and governors, you read a little before. But this was long in doing, because of the largeness of the places, and because the stones, the timber, the iron, and all rubbish, was to be carried without the town.

When this was done, the Prince gave order that the Lord Mayor and Aldermen of Mansoul should call a court of judicature for the trial and execution of the Diabolonians in the corporation, now under the charge of Mr. Trueman the jailer.

A court to be called to try the Diabolonians.

Now when the time was come, and the court set, commandment was sent to Mr. Trueman the jailer, to bring the prisoners down to the bar. Then were the prisoners brought down, pinioned, and chained together, as the custom of the town of Mansoul was. So when they were presented before the Lord Mayor, the Recorder, and the rest

The prisoners brought to the bar.

of the honourable bench, first, the jury was empanelled, and then the witnesses sworn. The names of the jury were these: Mr. Belief, Mr. True-heart, Mr. Upright, Mr. Hate-bad, Mr. Love-God, Mr. See-truth, Mr. Heavenly-mind, Mr. Moderate, Mr. Thankful, Mr. Good-work, Mr. Zeal-for-God, and Mr. Humble. The names of the witnesses were Mr. Know-all, Mr. Tell-true, Mr. Hate-lies, with my Lord Will-be-will and his man, if need were.

The jury impanelled, and the witnesses sworn.

So the prisoners were set to the bar; then said Mr. Do-right, for he was the town-clerk, Set Atheism to the bar, jailer. So he was set to the bar. Then said the Clerk, "Atheism, hold up thy hand. Thou art here indicted by the name of Atheism, an intruder upon the town of Mansoul, for that thou hast perniciously and

Do-right the Clerk.

Atheism set to the bar; his indictment.

doultishly taught and maintained that there is no God; and so no heed to be taken to religion. This thou hast done against the being, honour, and glory of the King, and against the peace and safety of the town of Mansoul. What sayest thou, art thou guilty of this indictment, or not?"

His plea. *Atheism.* Not guilty.

Crier. Call Mr. Know-all, Mr. Tell-true, and Mr. Hate-lies, into the court. So they were called, and they appeared.

Clerk. Then said the Clerk, "You, the witnesses for the King, look upon the prisoner at the bar; do you know him?"

Know. Then said Mr. Know-all, "Yes, my Lord, we know him, his name is Atheism; he has been a very pestilent fellow for many years in the miserable town of Mansoul."

Clerk. You are sure you know him.

Know. Know him! Yes, my Lord; I have here-

tofore too often been in his company, to be at this time ignorant of him. He is a Diabolonian, the son of a Diabolonian, I knew his grandfather, and his father.

Clerk. Well said. He standeth here indicted by the name of Atheism, &c., and is charged that he hath maintained and taught that there is no God, and so no heed need be taken to any religion. What say you, the King's witnesses, to this? Is he guilty, or not?

Know. My Lord, I and he were once in Villains' Lane together, and he at that time did briskly talk of diverse opinions, and then and there I heard him say that for his part he did believe that there was no God. But, said he, I can profess one, and be as religious too, if the company I am in, and the circumstances of other things, said he, shall put me upon it.

Clerk. You are sure you heard him say thus.

Know. Upon mine oath I heard him say thus.

Then said the Clerk, Mr. Tell-true, "What say you to the King's judges, touching the prisoner at the bar?"

Tell. My Lord, I formerly was a great companion of his, for the which I now repent me, and I have often heard him say, and that with very great stomachfulness, that he believed there was neither God, angel, nor spirit.

Clerk. Where did you hear him say so?

Tell. In Blackmouth Lane, and in Blasphemers' Row, and in many other places besides.

Clerk. Have you much knowledge of him?

Tell. I know him to be a Diabolonian, the son of a Diabolonian, and a horrible man to deny a Deity; his Father's name was Never-be-good, and he had more children than this Atheism. I have no more to say.

Clerk. Mr. Hate-lies, look upon the prisoner at the bar; do you know him?

Hate. My Lord, this Atheism is one of the vilest wretches that ever I came near, or had to do with in my life. I have heard him say that there is no God; I have heard him say that there is no world to come, no sin, nor punishment hereafter; and moreover, I have heard him say that it was as good to go to a whore-house, as to go to hear a sermon.

Clerk. Where did you hear him say these things?

Hate. In Drunkards' Row, just at Rascal Lane's end, at a house in which Mr. Impiety lived.

Clerk. Set him by, jailer, and set Mr. Lustings to the bar.

Lustings set to the bar.

Mr. Lustings, thou art here indicted by the name of Lustings, an intruder upon the town of Mansoul, for that thou hast devilishly and traitorously taught, by practice and filthy words, that it is lawful and profitable to man to give way to his carnal desires; and that thou, for thy part, hast not, nor never wilt deny thyself of any sinful delight, as long as thy name is Lustings. How sayest thou, art thou guilty of this indictment or not?

His indictment.

Lust. Then said Mr. Lustings, "My Lord, I am a man of high birth, and have been used to pleasures and pastimes of greatness. I have not been wont to be snubbed for my doings, but have been left to follow my will as if it were law. And it seems strange to me that I should this day be called into question for that, that not only I, but also all men do either secretly or openly countenance, love, and approve of."

His plea.

Clerk. Sir, we concern not ourselves with your greatness, though the higher the better you should have been; but we are concerned, and so are you now, about an indictment preferred against you. How say you, are you guilty of it, or not?

Lust. Not guilty.

Clerk. Crier, call upon the witnesses to stand forth and give their evidence.

Crier. Gentlemen, you the witnesses for the King, come in, and give in your evidence for our Lord the King against the prisoner at the bar.

Clerk. Come, Mr. Know-all, look upon the prisoner at the bar; do you know him?

Know. Yes, my Lord, I know him.

Clerk. What is his name?

Know. His name is Lustings; he was the son of one Beastly, and his mother bare him in Flesh Street; she was one Evil-concupiscence's daughter. I knew all the generation of them.

Clerk. Well said. You have here heard his indictment, what say you to it, is he guilty of the things charged against him or not?

Know. My Lord, he has, as he saith, been a great man indeed; and greater in wickedness than by pedigree, more than a thousand fold.

Clerk. But what do you know of his particular actions, and especially with reference to his indictment?

Know. I know him to be a swearer, a liar, a sabbath-breaker; I know him to be a fornicator, and an unclean person; I know him to be guilty of abundance of evils. He has been to my knowledge a very filthy man.

Clerk. But where did he use to commit his wickednesses, in some private corners, or more open and shamelessly?

Know. All the town over, my Lord.

Clerk. Come, Mr. Tell-true, what have you to say for our Lord the King against the prisoner at the bar?

Tell. My Lord, all that the first witness has said, I know to be true, and a great deal more besides.

Clerk. Mr. Lustings, do you hear what these gentlemen say?

Lust. I was ever of opinion that the happiest life that a man could live on earth, was to keep himself back from nothing that he desired in the world; nor have I been false at any time to this opinion of mine, but have lived in the love of my notions all my days. Nor was I ever so churlish, having found such sweetness in them myself, as to keep the commendations of them from others.

His second plea.

Court. Then said the court, "There hath proceeded enough from his own mouth to lay him open to condemnation, wherefore set him by, jailer, and set Mr. Incredulity to the bar."

Incredulity set to the bar.

Clerk. Mr. Incredulity, thou art here indicted by the name of Incredulity, an intruder upon the town of Mansoul, for that thou hast feloniously and wickedly, and that when thou wert an officer in the town of Mansoul, made head against the captains of the great King Shaddai, when they came and demanded possession of Mansoul; yea, thou didst bid defiance to the name, forces, and cause of the King, and didst also, as did Diabolus thy captain, stir up and encourage

Incredulity set to the bar.

His indictment.

the town of Mansoul to make head against, and resist the said force of the King. What sayest thou to this indictment? Art thou guilty of it, or not?

Then said Incredulity, "I know not Shaddai;

His plea. I love my old prince, I thought it my duty to be true to my trust, and to do what I could to possess the minds of the men of Mansoul, to do their utmost to resist strangers and foreigners, and with might to fight against them. Nor have I, nor shall I change my opinion, for fear of trouble, though you at present are possessed of place and power.

Court. Then said the court, "The man, as you see, is incorrigible; he is for maintaining his villainies by stoutness of words, and his rebellion with impudent confidence; and, therefore, set him by, jailer, and set Mr. Forget-good to the bar."

Forget-good set to the bar.

Clerk. Mr. Forget-good, thou art here indicted

Forget-good set to the bar. by the name of Forget-good, an intruder upon the town of Mansoul,

His indictment. for that thou, when the whole affairs of the town of Mansoul were in thy hand, didst utterly forget to serve them in what was good, and didst fall in with the tyrant Diabolus against Shaddai the King, against his captains, and all his host, to the dishonour of Shaddai, the breach of his law, and the endangering of the destruction of the famous town of Mansoul. What sayest thou to this indictment? Art thou guilty, or not guilty?

Then said Forget-good, "Gentlemen, and at

His plea. this time my judges, as to the indictment by which I stand of several crimes accused before you, pray attribute my forgetfulness to mine age, and not to my wilfulness; to the craziness of my brain, and not to the carelessness of my mind, and then I hope I may by your charity be excused from great punishment, though I be guilty."

Then said the court, "Forget-good, Forget-good, thy forgetfulness of good was not simply of frailty, but of purpose, and for that thou didst loathe to keep virtuous things in thy mind. What was bad thou couldst retain, but what was good thou couldst not abide to think of; thy age, therefore, and thy pretended craziness, thou makest use of to blind the court withal, and as a cloak to cover thy knavery. But let us hear what the witnesses have to say for the King against the prisoner at the bar—is he guilty of this indictment, or not?"

Hate. My Lord, I have heard this Forget-good say that he could never abide to think of goodness, no, not for a quarter of an hour.

Clerk. Where did you hear him say so?

Hate. In All-base Lane, at a house next door to the sign of the Conscience-seared-with-an-hot-iron.

Clerk. Mr. Know-all, what can you say for our Lord the King against the prisoner at the bar?

Know. My Lord, I know this man well, he is a Diabolonian, the son of a Diabolonian, his father's name was Love-naught, and for him, I have often heard him say that he counted the very thoughts of goodness the most burthensome thing in the world.

Clerk. Where have you heard him say these words?

Know. In Flesh Lane, right opposite to the church.

Then said the clerk, "Come, Mr. Tell-true, give in your evidence concerning the prisoner at the bar about that for which he stands here, as you see, indicted before this honourable court."

Tell. My Lord, I have heard him often say he had rather think of the vilest thing than of what is contained in the holy Scriptures.

Clerk. Where did you hear him say such grievous words?

Tell. Where? in a great many places; particularly in Nauseous Street, in the house of one Shameless; and in Filth Lane, at the sign of the Reprobate, next door to the Descent-into-the-pit.

Court. Gentlemen, you have heard the indictment, his plea, and the testimony of the witnesses. Jailer, set Mr. Hard-heart to the bar.

He is set to the bar.

Clerk. Mr. Hard-heart, thou art here indicted by the name of Hard-heart, an intruder upon the town of Mansoul, *Hard-heart set to the bar.* for that thou didst most desperately and wickedly possess the town of Mansoul with impenitency and obdurateness, and didst keep them from remorse and sorrow for their evils, all the time of their apostasy from, and rebellion against, the blessed King Shaddai. What sayest thou to this indictment? Art thou guilty, or not guilty?

Hard. My Lord, I never knew what remorse or sorrow meant in all my life; I am impenetrable, I care for no man; nor can I be pierced with men's griefs, their groans will not enter into my heart; whomever I mischief, whomever I wrong, to me it is music, when to others mourning.

Court. You see the man is a right Diabolonian, and has convicted himself. Set him by, jailer, and set Mr. False-peace to the bar.

Falsepeace set to the bar.

"Mr. False-peace, thou art here indicted by the name of False-peace, an intruder *False-peace set* upon the town of Mansoul, for that *to the bar.* thou didst most wickedly and satanically bring, hold, and keep the town of Mansoul, both in her apostasy, and in her hellish rebellion, in a false, groundless, and dangerous peace, and damnable security, to the dishonour of the King, the transgression of his law, and the great damage of the town of Mansoul. What sayest thou? Art thou guilty of this indictment, or not?"

Then said Mr. False-peace, "Gentlemen, and you now appointed to be my judges, *His plea.* I acknowledge that my name is Mr. Peace, but that my name is False-peace I utterly deny. If your honours will please to send for any that do intimately know me, or for the midwife that laid my mother of me, or for the gossips that were at my christening, they will any, or all of them prove that my name is not False-peace, but

He denies his name.

Peace. Wherefore, I cannot plead to this indictment, forasmuch as my name is not inserted therein. And as is my true name, so also are my conditions. I was always a man that loved to live at quiet, and what I loved myself, that I thought others might love also. Wherefore, when I saw any of my neighbours to labour under a disquieted mind, I endeavoured to help them what I could, and instances of this good temper of mine many I could give; as,

"1. When at the beginning our town of Mansoul did decline the ways of Shaddai, they some of them afterwards began to have disquieting reflections upon themselves for what they had done; but I, as one troubled to see them disquieted, presently sought out means so get them quiet again. 2. When the ways of the old world and of Sodom were in fashion, if anything happened to molest those that were for the customs of the present times, I laboured to make them quiet again, and to cause them to act without molestation. 3. To come nearer home, when the wars fell out between Shaddai and Diabolus, if at any time I saw any of the town of Mansoul afraid of destruction, I often used by some way, device, invention, or other to labour to bring them to peace again. Wherefore, since I have always been a man of so virtuous a temper, as some say a peace-maker is, and if a peace-maker be so deserving a man as some have been bold to attest he is, then let me, gentlemen, be accounted by you, who have a great name for justice and equity in Mansoul, for a man that deserveth not this inhuman way of treatment, but liberty, and also a license to seek damage of those that have been my accusers."

Then said the Clerk, " Crier, make a proclamation."

Crier. " O yes, forasmuch as the prisoner at the bar hath denied his name to be that which is mentioned in the indictment, the court requireth that if there be any in this place that can give information to the court of the original and right name of the prisoner, they would come forth and give in their evidence, for the prisoner stands upon his own innocency."

Then came two into the court and desired that they might have leave to speak what they knew concerning the prisoner at the bar; the name of the one was Search-truth, and the name of the other Vouch-truth. So the court demanded of these men if they knew the prisoner, and what they could say concerning him, for he stands, said they, upon his own vindication.

Then said Mr. Search-truth, "My Lord, I—"

Court. Hold, give him his oath; then they sware him. So he proceeded.

Search. My Lord, I know, and have known this man from a child, and can attest that his name is False-peace. I knew his father, his name was

Mr. Flatter, and his mother, before she was married, was called by the name of Mrs. Sooth-up; and these two, when they came together, lived not long without this son, and when he was born they called his name False-peace. I was his playfellow, only I was somewhat older than he; and when his mother did use to call him home from his play, she used to say, " False-peace, False-peace, come home quick, or I'll fetch you." Yea, I knew him when he sucked; and though I was then but little, yet I can remember that when his mother did use to sit at the door with him, or did play with him in her arms, she would call him twenty times together, " My little False-peace, my pretty False-peace," and " Oh my sweet rogue, False-peace;" and again, " Oh my little bird, False-peace; and how do I love my child!" The gossips also know it is thus, though he has had the face to deny it in open court.

Then Mr. Vouch-truth was called upon to speak what he knew of him. So they sware him. Then said Mr. Vouch-truth, " My Lord, all that the former witness hath said is true; his name is his False-peace, the son of Mr. Flatter and of Mrs. Sooth-up his mother. And I have in former times seen him angry with those who have called him anything else but False-peace, for he would say that all such did mock and nickname him, but this was in the time when Mr. False-peace was a great man, and when the Diabolonians were the brave men in Mansoul."

Court. Gentlemen, you have heard what these two men have sworn against the prisoner at the bar. And now Mr. False-peace, to you, you have denied your name to be False-peace, yet you see that these honest men have sworn that this is your name. As to your plea, in that you are quite besides the matter of your indictment, you are not by it charged for evil doing, because you are a man of peace, or a peace-maker among your neighbours; but for that you did wickedly, and satanically, bring, keep, and hold the town of Mansoul both under its apostasy from, and in its rebellion against its King, in a false, lying, and damnable peace, contrary to the law of Shaddai, and to the hazard of the destruction of the then miserable town of Mansoul. All that you have pleaded for yourself is, that you have denied your name, &c., but here you see we have witnesses to prove that you are the man.

For the peace that you so much boast of making among your neighbours, know that peace that is not a companion of truth and holiness, but that which is without this foundation, is grounded upon a lie, and is both deceitful and damnable; as also the great Shaddai hath said; thy plea therefore has not delivered thee from what by the indictment thou art charged with, but rather it doth fasten all upon thee.

But thou shalt have very fair play, let us call the witnesses that are to testify as to matter of fact, and see what they have to say for our Lord the King against the prisoner at the bar.

Clerk. Mr. Know-all, what say you for our Lord the King against the prisoner at the bar?

Know. My Lord, this man hath of a long time made it, to my knowledge, his business to keep the town of Mansoul in a sinful quietness in the midst of all her lewdness, filthiness, and turmoils, and hath said, and that in my hearing, "Come, come, let us fly from all trouble, on what ground soever it comes, and let us be for a quiet and peaceable life, though it wanteth a good foundation."

Clerk. Come, Mr. Hate-lies, what have you to say?

Hate. My Lord, I have heard him say that peace, though in a way of unrighteousness, is better than trouble with truth.

Clerk. Where did you hear him say this?

Hate. I heard him say it in Folly-yard, at the house of one Mr. Simple, next door to the sign of the Self-deceiver. Yea, he hath said this to my knowledge twenty times in that place.

Clerk. We may spare further witness, this evidence is plain and full. Set him by, jailer, and set Mr. No-truth to the bar.
No-truth set to the bar.
Mr. No-truth, thou art here indicted by the name of No-truth, an intruder upon the town of Mansoul, for that thou hast
His indictment.
always, to the dishonour of Shaddai, and the endangering of the utter ruin of the famous town of Mansoul, set thyself to deface and utterly to spoil all the remainders of the law and image of Shaddai that have been found in Mansoul, after her deep apostasy from her king to Diabolus, the envious tyrant. What sayest thou? Art thou guilty of this indictment, or not?

No-truth. Not guilty, my Lord.

Then the witnesses were called, and Mr. Know-all did first give in his evidence against him.

Know. My Lord, this man was at the pulling down of the image of Shaddai; yea, this is he that did it with his own hands. I myself stood by and saw him do it, and he did it at the commandment of Diabolus. Yea, this Mr. No-truth did more than this, he did also set up the horned image of the beast Diabolus in the same place. This also is he that, at the bidding of Diabolus, did rend and tear and cause to be consumed all that he could of the remainders of the law of the King, even whatever he could lay his hands on, in Mansoul.

Clerk. Who saw him do this besides yourself?

Hate. I did, my Lord, and so did many more besides; for this was not done by stealth, or in a corner, but in the open view of all, yea, he chose himself to do it publicly, for he delighted in the doing of it.

Clerk. Mr. No-truth, how could you have the face to plead not guilty, when you were so manifestly the doer of all this wickedness?

No-truth. Sir, I thought I must say something, and as my name is, so I speak. I have been advantaged thereby before now, and did not know but by speaking no truth I might have reaped the same benefit now.

Clerk. Set him by, jailer, and set Mr. Pitiless to the bar. Mr. Pitiless, thou art
here indicted by the name of Piti-
Pitiless set to the bar. His indictment.
less, an intruder upon the town of Mansoul, for that thou didst most traitorously and wickedly shut up all bowels of compassion, and wouldst not suffer Mansoul to condole her own misery when she had apostatized from her rightful King, but didst evade, and at all times turn her mind awry from those thoughts that had in them a tendency to lead her to repentance. What sayest thou to this indictment? Guilty, or not guilty?

"Not guilty of pitilessness; all I did was to cheer up, according to my name, for my name is not Pitiless, but Cheer-up: and I could not abide to see Mansoul incline to melancholy."

Clerk. How! do you deny your name, and say it is not Pitiless, but Cheer-up? Call for the witnesses. What say you, the witnesses, to this plea?

Know. My Lord, his name is Pitiless; so he hath writ himself in all papers of concern wherein he has had to do. But these Diabolonians love to counterfeit their names: Mr. Covetuousness covers himself with the name of Good-husbandry, or the like; Mr. Pride can, when need is, call himself Mr. Neat, Mr. Handsome, or the like, and so of all the rest of them.

Clerk. Mr. Tell-true, what say you?

Tell. His name is Pitiless, my Lord; I have known him from a child, and he hath done all that wickedness whereof he stands charged in the indictment; but there is a company of them that are not acquainted with the danger of damning, therefore they call all those melancholy that have serious thoughts how that state should be shunned by them.

Clerk. Set Mr. Haughty to the bar, jailer. Mr. Haughty, thou art here indicted
by the name of Haughty, an in-
Haughty set to the bar. His indictment.
truder upon the town of Mansoul, for that thou didst most traitorously and devilishly teach the town of Mansoul to carry it loftily and stoutly against the summons that was given them by the captains of the King Shaddai. Thou didst also teach the town of Mansoul to speak contemptuously and vilifyingly of their great King Shaddai; and didst moreover encourage, both by words and example, Mansoul to take up arms, both against the King and his son Emmanuel. How sayest thou? Art thou guilty of this indictment, or not?

Haughty. Gentlemen, I have always been a man of courage and valour, and have not used, when under the greatest clouds, to sneak or hang down the head like a bulrush; nor did it at all at any time please me to see men vail their bonnets to those that have opposed them; yea, though their adversaries seemed to have ten times the advantage of them. I did not use to consider who was my foe, nor what the cause was in which I was engaged. It was enough to me if

I carried it bravely, fought like a man, and came off a victor.

Court. Mr. Haughty, you are not here indicted for that you have been a valiant man, nor for your courage and stoutness in times of distress, but for that you have made use of this your pretended valour to draw the town of Mansoul into acts of rebellion, both against the great King and Emmanuel his Son. This is the crime and the thing wherewith thou art charged in and by the indictment. But he made no answer to that.

Now when the court had thus far proceeded against the prisoners at the bar, then they put them over to the verdict of their jury, to whom they did apply themselves after this manner :—

" Gentlemen of the jury, you have been here, and have seen these men, you have heard their indictments, their pleas, and what the witnesses have testified against them ; now what remains, is, that you do forthwith withdraw yourselves to some place, where without confusion you may consider of what verdict, in a way of truth and righteousness, you ought to bring in for the King against them, and so bring it in accordingly."

Then the jury, to wit, Mr. Belief, Mr. True-heart, Mr. Upright, Mr. Hate-bad, *The jury withdraw.* Mr. Love-God, Mr. See-truth, Mr. Heavenly-mind, Mr. Moderate, Mr. Thankful, Mr. Humble, Mr. Good-work, and Mr. Zeal-for-God, withdrew themselves in order to their work. Now when they were shut up by themselves they fell to discourse among themselves, in order to the drawing up of their verdict.

And thus Mr. Belief, for he was the foreman, began ; " Gentlemen," quoth he, " for the men, the prisoners at the bar, for my part I believe that they all deserve death." " Very right," said Mr. True-heart, " I am wholly of your opinion." " Oh, what a mercy is it," said Mr. Hate-bad, " that such villains as these are apprehended !" " Ay, ay," said Mr. Love-God, " this is one of the joyfullest days that ever I saw in my life." Then said Mr. See-truth, " I know that if we judge them to death, our verdict shall stand before Shaddai himself." " Nor do I at all question it," said Mr. Heavenly-mind ; he said, moreover, " When all such beasts as these are cast out of Mansoul, what a goodly town will it be then !" Then said Mr. Moderate, " It is not my manner to pass my judgment with rashness ; but for these, their crimes are so notorious, and the witness so palpable, that that man must be wilfully blind who saith the prisoners ought not to die." " Blessed be God," said Mr. Thankful, " that the traitors are in safe custody. " And I join with you in this upon my bare knees," said Mr. Humble. " I am glad also," said Mr. Good-work. Then said the warm man, and true-hearted Mr. Zeal-for-God, " Cut them off, they have been the plague, and have sought the destruction of Mansoul."

Thus, therefore, being all agreed in their verdict, they come instantly into the court.

Clerk. Gentlemen of the jury answer all to your names ; Mr. Belief, one ; Mr. *They are agreed* True-heart, two ; Mr. Upright, *of their verdict,* three ; Mr. Hate-bad, four ; Mr. *and bring them* Love-God, five ; Mr. See-truth, *in guilty.* six ; Mr. Heavenly-mind, seven ; Mr. Moderate, eight ; Mr. Thankful, nine ; Mr. Humble, ten ; Mr. Good-work, eleven ; and Mr. Zeal-for-God, twelve ; good men and true, stand together in your verdict ; are you all agreed ?

Jury. Yes, my Lord.

Clerk. Who shall speak for you ?

Jury. Our Foreman.

Clerk. You, the gentlemen of the jury, being impannelled for our Lord the King to serve here in a matter of life and death, have heard the trials of each of these men, the prisoners at the bar. What say you, are they guilty of that, and those crimes for which they stand here indicted, or are they not guilty ? *The verdict.*

Foreman. Guilty, my Lord !

Clerk. Look to your prisoners, jailer.

This was done in the morning, and in the afternoon they received the sentence of death according to the law.

The jailer, therefore, having received such a charge, put them all in the inward prison, to preserve them there till the day of execution, which was to be the next day in the morning.

But now to see how it happened, one of the prisoners, Incredulity by name, in *Incredulity* the interim betwixt the sentence *breaks prison.* and time of execution, brake prison, and made his escape, and gets him away quite out of the town of Mansoul, and lay lurking in such places and holds as he might, until he should again have opportunity to do the town of Mansoul a mischief for their thus handling of him as they did.

Now when Mr. Trueman the jailer perceived that he had lost his prisoner, he was in a heavy taking, because he, that prisoner we speak of, was the very worst of all the gang ; wherefore first, he goes and acquaints my Lord Mayor, Mr. Recorder, and my Lord Will-be-will with the matter, and to get of them an order to make a search for him throughout the town of Mansoul. So an order he got, and search was made, but no such man could now be found in all the town of Mansoul.

All that could be gathered was that he had lurked a while about the outside of the town, and that here and there one or other had a glimpse of him as he did make his escape out of Mansoul ; one or two also did affirm that they saw him without the town, going a-pace quite over the plain. Now when he was quite gone, it was affirmed by one Mr. Did-see, that he ranged all *He is gone to* over dry places, till he met with *Diabolus.* Diabolus, his friend ; and where should they meet one another but just upon Hell-gate-hill.

But oh, what a lamentable story did the old gentleman tell to Diabolus, concerning what sad alteration Emmanuel had made in Mansoul !

As first, how Mansoul had, after some delays,

He tells Diabolus what Emmanuel now is doing in Mansoul. received a general pardon at the hands of Emmanuel, and that they had invited him into the town, and that they had given him the castle for his possession. He said, moreover, that they had called his soldiers into the town, coveted who should quarter the most of them; they also entertained him with the timbrel, song, and dance. " But that," said Incredulity, " that is the sorest vexation to me is, that he hath pulled down, O father, thy image, and set up his own; pulled down thy officers, and set up his own. Yea, and Will-be-will, that rebel, who, one would have thought should never have turned from us, he is now in as great favour with Emmanuel as ever he was with thee. But besides all this, this Will-be-will has received a special commission from his master to search for, to apprehend, and to put to death all, and all manner of Diabolonians that he shall find in Mansoul; yea, and this Will-be-will has taken and committed to prison already, eight of my lord's most trusted friends in Mansoul. Nay, further, my lord, with grief I speak it, they have been all arraigned, condemned, and, I doubt, before this, executed in Mansoul. I told my lord of eight, and

myself was the ninth, who should assuredly have drunk of the same cup, but that through craft, I, as thou seest, have made my escape from them."

When Diabolus had heard this lamentable story *Diabolus yells at the news.* he yelled, and snuffed up the wind like a dragon, and made the sky to look dark with his roaring; he also sware that he would try to be revenged on Mansoul for this. So they, both he and his old friend, Incredulity, concluded to enter into great consultation how they might get the town of Mansoul again.

Now before this time, the day was come in which the prisoners in Mansoul were to be executed. (Rom. viii. 13.) So they were brought to the cross, and that by Mansoul, in most solemn manner. (Rom. vi. 12—14.) For the Prince said that this should be done by the hand of the town of Mansoul, " that I may see," said he, " the forwardness of my now redeemed Mansoul to keep my word, and to do my commandments; and that I may bless Mansoul in doing this deed. Proof of sincerity pleases me well; let Mansoul, therefore, first lay their hands upon these Diabolonians to destroy them." (Gal. v. 24.)

So the town of Mansoul slew them according to the word of their Prince; but when the prisoners were brought to the cross to die, you can hardly believe what troublesome work Mansoul had of it to put the Diabolonians to death; for the men, knowing that they must die, and all of them having implacable enmity in their heart to Mansoul, what did they but took courage at the cross, and there resisted the men of the town of Mansoul. Wherefore the men of Mansoul were *The assistance of more grace.* forced to cry out for help to the captains and men of war. Now the great Shaddai had a secretary in the town, and he was a great lover of the men of Mansoul, and he was at the place of execution also; so he hearing the men of Mansoul cry out against the strugglings and unruliness of the prisoners, rose up from his place, and came and put his hands upon the hands of the men of Mansoul. So they *Execution done.* crucified the Diabolonians that had been a plague, a grief, and an offence to the town of Mansoul. (Rom. viii. 13.)

Now when this good work was done, the Prince came down to see, to visit, and to *The Prince comes down to congratulate them.* speak comfortably to the men of Mansoul, and to strengthen their hands in such work. And he said that by this act of theirs he had proved them, and found them to be lovers of his person, observers of his laws, and such as had also respect to his honour. He said, moreover, to show them that they by this should not be losers, nor their town weakened by the loss of them, that he would make them another captain, and that of one of themselves. And that this captain should be the ruler of a thousand, for the good and benefit of the now flourishing town of Mansoul.

He promises to make them a new captain.

So he called one to him whose name was Waiting, and bid him go quickly up to the Castle-gate, and inquire there for one Mr. Experience, that waiteth upon that noble captain, the Captain Credence, and bid him come hither to me. So the messenger that waited upon the good Prince Emmanuel went and said as he was commanded. Now the young gentleman was waiting to see the captain train and muster his men in the castle-yard. Then said Mr. Waiting to him, "Sir, the Prince would that you should come down to his Highness forthwith." So he brought him down to Emmanuel, and he came and made obeisance before him. Now the men of the town knew Mr. Experience well, for he was born and bred in the town of Mansoul; they also knew him to be a man of conduct, of valour, and a person prudent in matters; he was also a comely person, well spoken, and very successful in his undertakings. Wherefore the hearts of the townsmen were transported with joy, when they saw that the Prince himself was so taken with Mr. Experience, that he would needs make him a captain over a band of men.

Experience must be the new captain.

Mansoul takes it well.

So with one consent they bowed the knee before Emmanuel, and with a shout said, "Let Emmanuel live for ever!" Then said the Prince to the young gentleman whose name was Mr. Experience, "I have thought good to confer upon thee a place of trust and honour in this my town of Mansoul;" then the young man bowed his head and worshipped. "It is," said Emmanuel, "that thou shouldst be a captain, a captain over a thousand men in my beloved town of Mansoul." Then said the captain, "Let the King live." So the Prince gave out orders forthwith to the King's Secretary, that he should draw up for Mr. Experience a commission, to make him a captain over a thousand men; "and let it be brought to me," said he, "that I may set to my seal." So it was done as it was commanded. The commission was drawn up, brought to Emmanuel, and he set his seal thereto. Then, by the hand of Mr. Waiting, he sent it away to the Captain.

His commission sent him.

Now, so soon as the captain had received his commission, he soundeth his trumpet for volunteers, and young men come to him apace, yea, the greatest and chiefest men in the town sent their sons to be listed under his command. Thus Captain Experience came under command to Emmanuel, for the good of the town of Mansoul. He had for his lieutenant one Mr. Skilful, and for his cornet one Mr.

His under officers.

Memory. His under-officers I need not name. His colours were the white colours for the town of Mansoul, and his escutcheon was the dead lion and dead bear. (1 Sam. xvii. 36, 37.) So the Prince returned to his royal palace again.

Now, when he was returned thither, the elders of the town of Mansoul, to wit, the Lord Mayor, the Recorder, and the Lord Will-be-will, went to congratulate him, and in special way to thank him for his love, care, and the tender compassion which he showed to his ever-obliged town of Mansoul. So, after a while, and some sweet communion between them, the townsmen having solemnly ended their ceremony, returned to their place again.

Emmanuel also at this time appointed them a day wherein he would renew their charter, yea, wherein he would renew and enlarge it, mending several faults therein that Mansoul's yoke might be yet more easy. (Matt. xi. 28—30.) And this he did without any desire of theirs, even of his own frankness and noble mind. So, when he had sent for and seen their old one, he laid it by and said, "Now that which decayeth and waxeth old, is ready to vanish away." (Heb. viii. 13.) He said, moreover, the town of Mansoul shall have another, a better, a new one, more steady and firm by far. An epitome hereof take as follows:—

He renews their charter.

"Emmanuel, Prince of peace, and a great lover of the town of Mansoul, I do, in the name of my Father, and of mine own clemency, give, grant, and bequeath to my beloved town of Mansoul: First, Free, full, and everlasting forgiveness of all wrongs, injuries, and offences done by them against my Father, me, their neighbour, or themselves. (Heb. viii. 12). Secondly, I do give them the holy law, and my testament, with all that therein is contained, for their everlasting comfort and consolation. (John xv. 8—14.) Thirdly, I do also give them a portion of the self-same grace and goodness that dwells in my Father's heart and mine. (2 Pet. i. 4; 2 Cor. vii. 1; 1 John iv. 16.) Fourthly, I do give, grant, and bestow upon them freely, the world, and what is therein, for their good; and they shall have that power over them as shall stand with the honour of my father, my glory, and their comfort; yea, I grant them the benefits of life and death, and of things present, and things to come. (1 Cor. iii. 21, 22.) This privilege, no other city, town, or corporation, shall have but my Mansoul only. Fifthly, I do give and grant them leave, and free access to me in my palace, at all seasons, to my palace above or below, there to make known their wants to me. (Heb. x. 19, 20.) And I give them, moreover, a promise that I will hear and redress all their grievances. (Matt. vii. 7.) Sixthly, I do give, grant to, and invest the town of Mansoul with full power and authority to seek out, take, enslave, and destroy all, and all manner of Diabolonians, that at any time from whencesoever, shall be found straggling in, or about the town of Mansoul. Seventhly, I do further grant to my beloved town of Mansoul that they shall have authority not to suffer any foreigner, or stranger, or their seed, to be free in and of the blessed town of Mansoul, nor to share in the excellent privileges thereof. (Eph. iv. 22.) But that all the grants, privileges, and immunities, that I bestow upon the famous town of Mansoul, shall be for those the old natives and true inhabitants thereof, to them I say, and to their right seed after them. (Col. iii. 5—9.) But all Diabolonians of what sort, birth, country, or kingdom soever, shall be debarred a share therein."

So, when the town of Mansoul had received at the hand of Emmanuel, their gracious charter, which in itself is infinitely more large than by this lean epitome is set before you, they carried it to audience, that is, to the market-place, and there Mr. Recorder read it in the presence of all the people. (2 Cor. iii. 3; Jer. xxxi. 33.) This being *Their charter set upon their castle gates.* done, it was had back to the castle-gates, and there fairly engraven upon the doors thereof, and laid in letters of gold, to the end that the town of Mansoul, with all the people thereof, might have it always in their view, or might go where they might see what a blessed freedom their Prince had bestowed upon them, that their joy might be increased in themselves, and their love renewed to their great and good Emmanuel. (Heb. viii. 10).

But what joy, what comfort, what consolation, *Joy renewed in Mansoul.* think you, did now possess the hearts of the men of Mansoul! The bells ringed, the minstrels played, the people danced, the captains shouted, the colours waved in the wind, and the silver trumpets sounded, and the Diabolonians now were glad to hide their heads, for they looked like them that had been long dead.

When this was over, the Prince sent again for the elders of the town of Mansoul, and communed with them about a ministry that he intended to establish among them, such a ministry that might open unto them, and that might instruct them in the things that did concern their present and future state.

"For," said he, "you of yourselves, without you have teachers and guides, will not be able to know, and if not to know, to be sure, not to do the will of my Father." (Jer. x. 23; 1 Cor. ii. 14.)

At this news, when the elders of Mansoul brought it to the people, the whole town came *The common good thoughts.* running together, for it pleased them well, as whatever the Prince now did, pleased the people, and all with one consent implored his Majesty, that he would forthwith establish such a ministry among them as might teach them both law and judgment, statute and commandment, that they might be documented in all good and wholesome things. So he told them that he would grant them their requests, and would establish two among them, one that was of his Father's court, and one that was a native of Mansoul.

"He that is from the court," said he, "is a person of no less quality and dignity than is my Father and I, and he is the Lord Chief Secretary of my Father's house; for he is, and always has been, the chief dictator of all my Father's laws; a person altogether well skilled in all mysteries, and knowledge of mysteries, as is my Father, or as myself is. Indeed, he is one with us in nature, and also as to loving of, and being faithful to, and in, the eternal concerns of the town of Mansoul.

"And this is he," said the Prince, "that must be your chief teacher, for it is he, and he only, that can teach you clearly in all high and supernatural things. (1 Thess. i. 5, 6.) He and he only it is that knows the ways and methods of my Father at court, nor can any like him show how the heart of my Father is at all times, in all things, upon all occasions, towards Mansoul; for as no man knows the things of a man, but that spirit of a man which is in him, so the things of my Father knows no man but this his high and mighty Secretary. Nor can any, as he, tell Mansoul how and what they shall do to keep themselves in the love of my Father. He also it is that can bring lost things to your remembrance, and that can tell you things to come. This teacher therefore must of necessity have the pre-eminence, both in your affections and judgment, before your other teacher. (Rom. viii. 26.) His personal dignity, the excellency of his teaching, also the great dexterity that he hath to help you to make and draw up petitions to my Father for your help, and to his pleasing (Jude 20; Eph. vi. 18), must lay obligations upon you to love him, fear him, and to take heed that you grieve him not. (Rev. ii. 7, 11, 17, 29; Eph. iv. 30.)

"This person can put life and vigour into all he says, yea, and can also put it into your hearts. This person can make seers of you, and can make you tell what shall be hereafter. (Acts xxi. 10, 11.) By this person you must frame all your petitions to my Father and me, and without his advice and counsel first obtained, let nothing enter into the town or castle of Mansoul, for that may disgust and grieve this noble person. (Isa. lxiii. 10.)

"Take heed, I say, that you do not grieve this minister; for if you do, he may fight against you; and should he once be moved by you, to set himself against you, against you in battle array, that will distress you more than if twelve legions should from my Father's court be sent to make war upon you.

"But, as I said, if you shall hearken unto him, and shall love him; if you shall devote yourselves to his teaching, and shall seek to have converse, and to maintain communion with him; you shall find him ten times better than is the whole world to any. Yea, he will shed abroad the love of my Father in your hearts, and Mansoul will be the wisest and most blessed of all people." (1 Cor. xiii. xiv.; Rom. v. 5.)

Then did the Prince call unto him the old gentleman, who afore had been the Recorder of Mansoul, Mr. Conscience, by name, and told him that forasmuch as he was well skilled in the law and government of the town of Mansoul, and was also well spoken, and could pertinently deliver to them his Master's will in all terrene and domestic matters, therefore he would also make him a minister for, in, and to the goodly town of Mansoul, in all the laws, statutes, and judgments of the famous town of Mansoul. "And thou must," said the Prince, "confine thyself to the teaching of moral virtues, to civil and natural

Conscience made a minister.

duties; but thou must not attempt to presume to be a revealer of those high and supernatural mysteries that are kept close in the bosom of Shaddai my Father, for those things know no man, nor can any reveal them, but my Father's Secretary only.

"Thou art a native of the town of Mansoul, but the Lord Secretary is a native with my Father; wherefore, as thou hast knowledge of the laws and customs of the corporation, so he of the things and will of my Father. Wherefore, O Mr. Conscience, although I have made thee a minister and a preacher in the town of Mansoul, yet as to the

things which the Lord Secretary knoweth, and shall teach to this people, there thou must be his scholar, and a learner, even as the rest of Mansoul are.

"Thou must, therefore, in all high and supernatural things go to him for information and knowledge; for though there be a spirit in man, this person's inspiration must give him understanding. (Job. xxxiii. 8.) Wherefore, O thou Mr. Recorder, keep low and be humble, and remember that the Diabolonians that kept not their first charge, but left their own standing, are now made

prisoners in the pit; be therefore content with thy station. I have made thee my Father's vicegerent on earth, in such things of which I have made mention before. And thou, take thou power to teach them to Mansoul; yea, and to impose them with whips and chastisements, if they shall not willingly hearken to do thy commandments.

His power in Mansoul.

"And, Mr. Recorder, because thou art old, and through many abuses made feeble, therefore I give thee leave and licence to go when thou wilt to my fountain, my

His liberty.

conduit, and there to drink freely of the blood of my grape, for my conduit does always run wine. Thus doing, thou shalt drive from thy heart and stomach all foul, gross, and hurtful humours. It will also lighten thine eyes, and will strengthen thy memory for the reception and keeping of all that the King's most noble Secretary teacheth." (Heb. v. 14.)

When the Prince had thus put Mr. Recorder, that once so was, into the place and office of a minister to Mansoul, and the man had thankfully accepted thereof, then did Emmanuel address himself in a particular speech to the townsmen themselves :—

"Behold," said the Prince to Mansoul, " my love and care towards you. I have added, to all that is past, this mercy, to appoint you preachers ; the most noble Secretary to teach you in all high and sublime mysteries ; and this gentleman," pointing to Mr. Conscience, " is to teach you in all things human and domestic ; for therein lieth his work. He is not, by what I have said, debarred of telling to Mansoul anything that he hath heard and received at the mouth of the Lord High Secretary ; only he shall not attempt to presume to pretend to be, a revealer of those high mysteries himself ; for the breaking of them up, and the discovery of them to Mansoul, layeth only in the power, authority, and skill of the Lord High Secretary himself. Talk of them he may, and so may the rest of the town of Mansoul ; yea, and may, as occasion gives them opportunity, press them upon each other, for the benefit of the whole. These things, therefore, I would have you observe and do, for it is for your life, and the lengthening of your days.

The Prince's speech to Mansoul.

A licence to Mansoul.

" And one thing more to my beloved Mr. Recorder, and to all the town of Mansoul. You must not dwell in, nor stay upon anything of that which he hath in commission to teach you, as to your trust and expectation of the next world ; of the next world, I say, for I purpose to give another to Mansoul, when this with them is worn out, but for that you must wholly and solely have recourse to, and make stay upon his doctrine, that is your teacher after the first order. Yea, Mr. Recorder himself must not look for life from that which he himself revealeth ; his dependence for that must be founded in the doctrine of the other preacher. Let Mr. Recorder also take heed that he receive not any doctrine or point of doctrine, that are not communicated to him by his superior teacher ; nor yet within the precincts of his own formal knowledge."

Now, after the Prince had thus settled things in the famous town of Mansoul, he proceeded to give to the elders of the corporation a necessary caution, to wit, how they should carry it to the high and noble captains that he had, from his Father's court, sent or brought with him to the famous town of Mansoul.

He gives them caution about the captains.

" These captains," said he, " do love the town of Mansoul, and they are picked men, picked out of abundance, as men that best suit, and that will most faithfully serve in the wars of Shaddai against the Diabolonians, for the preservation of the town of Mansoul. I charge you, therefore," said he, " O ye inhabitants of the now flourishing town of Mansoul, that you carry it not ruggedly or untowardly to my captains or their men ; since, as I said, they are picked and choice men, men chosen out of many for the good of the town of Mansoul. I say, I charge you, that you carry it not untowardly to them ; for though they have the hearts and faces of lions, when at any time they shall be called forth to engage and fight with the King's foes, and the enemies of the town of Mansoul, yet a little discountenance cast upon them from the town of Mansoul will deject and cast down their faces, will weaken and take away their courage. Do not, therefore, O my beloved, carry it unkindly to my valiant captains and courageous men of war, but love them, nourish them, succour them, and lay them in your bosoms, and they will not only fight for you, but cause to fly from you all those Diabolonians that seek, and will, if possible, be your utter destruction.

" If, therefore, any of them should, at any time, be sick or weak, and so not able to perform that office of love which with all their hearts they are willing to do, and will do also when well and in health, slight them not, nor despise them, but rather strengthen them, and encourage them, though weak and ready to die, (Heb. xii. 12 ;) for they are your fence, and your guard, your wall, your gates, your locks, and your bars. And although, when they are weak, they can do but little, but rather need to be helped by you, than that you should then expect great things from them, yet when well, you know what exploits, what feats and warlike achievements they are able to do, and will perform for you.

" Besides, if they be weak, the town of Mansoul cannot be strong ; if they be strong, then Mansoul cannot be weak ; your safety, therefore, doth lie in their health, and in your countenancing of them. (Isa. xxxv. 3.) Remember also that if they be sick, they catch that disease of the town of Mansoul itself. (Rev. iii. 2 ; 1 Thess. v. 14.)

" These things have I said unto you, because I love your welfare, and your honour. Observe, therefore, O my Mansoul, to be punctual in all things that I have given in charge unto you, and that not only as a town corporate, and so to your officers and guard, and guides in chief, but to you as you are a people whose well-being, as single persons, depends on the observation of the orders and commandments of their Lord.

" Next, O my Mansoul, I do warn you of that of which notwithstanding that reformation that at present is wrought among you, you have need to be warned about. Wherefore hearken diligently unto me. I am now sure, and you will know hereafter, that there are yet of the Diabolonians remaining in the town of Mansoul; Diabolonians that are sturdy and implacable, and that do already while I am with you, and that will yet more when I am from you, study, plot, contrive, invent, and jointly attempt to bring you to desolation, and so to a state far worse than that of the Egyptian bondage; they are the avowed friends of Diabolus, therefore look about you; they used heretofore to lodge with their prince in the castle, when Incredulity was the Lord Mayor of this town. (Mark vii. 21, 22.) But since my coming hither, they lie more in the outsides, and walls, and have made themselves dens, and caves, and holes, and strongholds therein. Wherefore, O Mansoul, thy work, as to this, will be so much the more difficult and hard. (Rom. vii. 18.) That is, to take, mortify, and put them to death according to the will of my Father. Nor can you utterly rid yourselves of them, unless you should pull down the walls of your town, the which I am by no means willing you should. Do you ask me, What shall we do then? Why, be you diligent, and quit you like men, observe their holds, find out their haunts, assault them, and make no peace with them. Wherever they haunt, lurk, or abide, and what terms of peace soever they offer you, abhor, and all shall be well betwixt you and me. And that you may the better know them from those that are the natives of Mansoul, I will give you this brief schedule of the names of the chief of them, and they are these that follow: The Lord Fornication, the Lord Adultery, the Lord Murder, the Lord Anger, the Lord Lasciviousness, the Lord Deceit, the Lord Evil-eye, Mr. Drunkenness, Mr. Revelling, Mr. Idolatry, Mr. Witchcraft, Mr. Variance, Mr. Emulation, Mr. Wrath, Mr. Strife, Mr. Sedition, and Mr. Heresy. These are some of the chief, O Mansoul, of those that will seek to overthrow thee for ever. These, I say, are the skulkers in Mansoul; but look thou well into the law of thy King, and there thou shalt find their physiognomy, and such other characteristical notes of them, by which they certainly may be known.

A caution about the Diabolonians that yet remain in Mansoul.

The names of some of the Diabolonians in Mansoul.

"These, O my Mansoul, and I would gladly that you should certainly know it, if they be suffered to run and range about the town as they would, will quickly, like vipers, eat out your bowels, yea, poison your captains, cut the sinews of your soldiers, break the bar and bolts of your gates, and turn your now most flourishing Mansoul into a barren and desolate wilderness, and ruinous heap. Wherefore, that you may take courage to yourselves to apprehend these villains wherever you find them, I give to you, my Lord Mayor, my Lord Will-be-will, and Mr. Recorder, with all the inhabitants of the town of Mansoul, full power and commission to seek out, to take, and to cause to be put to death by the cross, all, and all manner of Diabolonians, when and wherever you shall find

A commission to destroy the Diabolonians in Mansoul.

them to lurk within, or to range without the walls of the town of Mansoul.

"I told you before, that I had placed a standing ministry among you, not that you have but these with you, for my four first captains who came against the master and lord of the Diabolonians that was in Mansoul, they can, and if need be, and if they be required, will not only privately inform, but publicly preach to the corporation both good and wholesome doctrine, and such as shall lead you in the way; yea, they will set up a weekly, yea, if need be, a daily lecture in thee, O Mansoul; and will instruct thee in such profitable lessons, that if heeded, will do thee good at the end. And take good heed that you spare not the men that you have a commission to take and crucify.

"Now, as I have set out before your eyes the vagrants and runagates by name, so I will tell you that among yourselves some of them shall creep in to beguile you, even such as would seem, and that in appearance are, very rife and hot for religion. And they, if you watch not, will do you a mischief, such an one as at present you cannot think of. These, as I said, will show themselves to you in another hue than those under description before. Wherefore, Mansoul, watch and be sober, and suffer not thyself to be betrayed."

A caution.

When the Prince had thus far new modelled the town of Mansoul, and had instructed them in such matters as were profitable for them to know, then he appointed another day, in which he intended, when the townsfolk came together, to bestow a further badge of honour upon the town of Mansoul; a badge that should distinguish them from all the people, kindreds, and tongues that dwell in the kingdom of Universe. Now, it was not long before the day appointed was come, and the Prince and his people met in the King's palace, where first Emmanuel made a short speech unto them, and then did for them as he had said, and unto them as he had promised.

Another privilege for Mansoul.

"My Mansoul," said he, "that which I now am about to do, is to make you known to the world to be mine, and to distinguish you also in your own eyes, from all false traitors that may creep in among you."

His speech to Mansoul.

Then he commanded that those that waited upon him should go and bring forth out of his treasury those white and glistering robes, "that I," said he, "have provided and laid up in store for my Mansoul." So the white garments were fetched out of his treasury, and laid forth to the eyes of the people. Moreover, it was granted to them that they should take them and put them on, according, said he, to your size and stature. So the people were put into white, into fine linen, white and clean. (Rev. xix. 8.)

White robes.

Then said the Prince unto them, "This, O Mansoul, is my livery, and the badge by which mine are known from the servants of others. Yea, it is that which I grant to all that are mine, and without which no man is permitted to see my face. Wear them therefore for my sake who gave them unto you; and also if you would be known by the world to be mine."

But now, can you think how Mansoul shone? It was fair as the sun, clear as the moon, and terrible as an army with banners. (Sol. Song vi.)

The Prince added further, and said, "No prince, potentate, or mighty one of Universe, giveth this livery but myself; behold therefore, as I said before, you shall be known by it to be mine.

"And now," said he, "I have given you my livery, let me give you also in commandment concerning them; and be sure that you take good heed to my words. First, Wear them daily, day by day, lest you should at sometimes appear to others as if you were none of mine. Secondly, Keep them always white, for, if they be soiled, it is dishonour to me. (Eccle. ix. 8.) Thirdly, Wherefore gird them up from the ground, and let them not lag with dust and dirt. Fourthly, Take heed that you lose them not, lest you walk naked, and they see your shame. (Rev. iii. 2.) Fifthly, But if you should sully them, if you should defile them, —the which I am greatly unwilling you should, and the prince Diabolus would be glad if you would—then speed you to do that which is written in my law, that yet you may stand, and not fall before me, and before my throne. (Luke xxi. 36.) Also this is the way to cause that I may not leave you nor forsake you while here, but may dwell in this town of Mansoul for ever." (Rev. vii. 15—17.)

And now was Mansoul, and the inhabitants of it, as the signet upon Emmanuel's right hand; where was there now a town, a city, a corporation that could compare with Mansoul? a town redeemed from the hand and from the power of

The glorious state of Mansoul.

Diabolous; a town that the King Shaddai loved, and that he sent Emmanuel to regain from the prince of the infernal cave, yea, a town that Emmanuel loved to dwell in, and that he chose for his royal habitation; a town that he fortified for himself, and made strong by the force of his army. What shall I say? Mansoul has now a most excellent Prince, golden captains and men of war, weapons proved, and garments as white as snow. Nor are these benefits to be counted little, but great. Can the town of Mansoul esteem them so, and improve them to that end and purpose for which they are bestowed upon them.

When the Prince had thus completed the modelling of the town, to show that he had great delight in the work of his hands, and took pleasure in the good that he had wrought for the famous and flourishing Mansoul, he commanded, and they set his standard upon the battlements of the castle. And then,

First, He gave them frequent visits, not a day

now but the elders of Mansoul must come to him, or he to them, into his palace. Now they must walk and talk together of all the great things that he had done, and yet further promised to do for the town of Mansoul. (2 Cor. vi. 16.) Thus would he often do with the Lord Mayor, my Lord Will-be-will, and the honest subordinate preacher Mr. Conscience, and Mr. Recorder. But oh, how graciously, how lovingly, how courteously, and tenderly did this blessed prince now carry it towards the town of Mansoul! In all the streets, gardens, orchards, and other places where he came, to be sure the poor should have his blessing and benediction; yea, he would kiss them, and if they were ill, he would lay hands on them, and make them well. The captains also he would daily, yea, sometimes hourly encourage with his presence and goodly words. For you must know that a smile from him upon them would put more vigour, more life and stoutness into them, than would anything else under heaven.

The Prince would now also feast them, and be with them continually. Hardly a week would pass but a banquet must be had betwixt him and them. (1 Cor. v. 8.) You may remember that some pages before we made mention of one feast that they had together, but now to feast them was a thing more common; every day with Mansoul was a feast day now. Nor did he, when they returned to their places, send them empty away, either they must have a ring, a gold chain, a bracelet, a white stone, or something; so dear was Mansoul to him now; so lovely was Mansoul in his eyes.

A token of marriage.
A token of honour.
A token of beauty.
A token of pardon.

Secondly, When the elders and townsmen did not come to him, he would send in much plenty of provision unto them, meat that came from court, wine and bread that were prepared for his Father's table. Yea, such delicates would he send unto them, and therewith would so cover their table, that whoever saw it confessed that the like could not be seen in any kingdom.

Thirdly, If Mansoul did not frequently visit him as he desired they should, he would walk out to them, knock at their doors, and desire entrance, that amity might be maintained betwixt them and him. If they did hear and open to him, as commonly they would, if they were at home, then would he renew his former love, and confirm it too with some new tokens and signs of continued favour. (Rev. iii. 20; Sol. Song v. 2.)

And was it not now amazing to behold, that in that very place where sometimes Diabolus had his abode, and entertained his Diabolonians to the almost utter destruction of Mansoul, the Prince of princes should sit eating and drinking with them, while all his mighty captains, men of war, trumpeters, with the singing men and singing women of his Father, stood round about to wait upon them! Now did Mansoul's cup run over, now did her conduits run sweet

Mansoul's glory.

F

wine, now did she eat the finest of the wheat, and drink milk and honey out of the rock! Now she said, How great is his goodness! for since I found favour in his eyes, how honourable have I been!

The blessed prince did also order a new officer in the town, and a goodly person he was; his name was Mr. God's-peace. (Col. ii. 15.) This man

was set over my Lord Will-be-will, my Lord Mayor, Mr. Recorder, the subordinate Preacher, Mr. Mind, and over all the natives of the town of Mansoul. Himself was not a native of it, but came with the Prince Emmanuel from the court. He was a great acquaintance of Captain Credence and Captain Good-hope; some say they were kin, and I am of that opinion too. (Rom. xv. 13.) This man, as I said, was made governor of the town in general, especially over the castle, and Captain Credence was to help him there. And I made great observation of it, that so long as all things went in Mansoul as this sweet-natured gentleman would, the town was in most happy condition. Now there were no jars, no chiding, no interferings, no unfaithful doings in all the town of Mansoul, every man in Mansoul kept close to his own employment. The gentry, the officers, the

Holy conceptions. soldiers, and all in place observed
Good thoughts. their order. And as for the women and children of the town, they followed their business joyfully, they would work and sing, work and sing from morning till night; so that quite through the town of Mansoul now, nothing was to be found but harmony, quietness, joy, and health. And this lasted all that summer.

But there was a man in the town of Mansoul, and his name was Mr. Carnal-security. This man did, after all this mercy bestowed on this corporation, bring the town of Mansoul into great and grievous slavery and bondage. A brief account of him and of his doings take as followeth :—

The story of Mr. Carnal-security.

When Diabolus at first took possession of the town of Mansoul, he brought thither with himself a great number of Diabolonians, men of his own condition. Now among these there was one whose name was Mr. Self-conceit, and a *Mr. Self-con-* notable brisk man he was, as any *ceit.* that in those days did possess the town of Mansoul. Diabolus then perceiving this man to be active and bold, sent him upon many desperate designs, the which he managed better, and more to the pleasing of his Lord, than most that came with him from the dens could do. Wherefore finding of him so fit for his purpose, he preferred him, and made him next to the great Lord Will-be-will, of whom we have written so much before. Now the Lord Will-be-will being in those days very well pleased with him, and with his achievements, gave him his daughter, the Lady Fear-nothing, to wife. Now of my Lady Fear-nothing did this *Carnal-security's* Mr. Self-conceit beget this gentle- *original.* man Mr. Carnal-security. Wherefore there being then in Mansoul those strange kinds of mixtures, it was hard for them in some cases to find out who were natives, who not; for Mr. Carnal-security sprang from my Lord Will-be-will by mother's side, though he had for his father a Diabolonian by nature.

Well, this Carnal-security took much after his father and mother; he was self-con- ceited, he feared nothing, he was *His qualities.* also a very busy man; nothing of news, nothing of doctrine, nothing of alteration, or talk of altera- tion, could at any time be on foot in Mansoul, but be sure Mr. Carnal-security would be at the head or tail of it; but to be sure he would decline those that he deemed the weakest, and stood always with them, in his way of standing, that he supposed was the strongest side.

Now when Shaddai the mighty, and Emmanuel his Son made war upon Mansoul to take it, this Mr. Carnal-security was then in town, and was a great doer among the people, encouraging them in their rebellion, putting of them upon hardening of themselves in their resisting of the King's forces; but when he saw that the town of Mansoul was taken and converted to the use of the glorious Prince Emmanuel, and when he also saw what was become of Diabolus, and how he was unroosted, and made to quit the castle in the greatest con- tempt and scorn, and that the town of Mansoul was well lined with captains, engines of war, and men, and also provision, what doth he but slily wheel about also; and as he had served Diabolus against the good Prince, so he feigned that he would serve the prince against his foes.

And having got some little smattering of

Emmanuel's things by the end, being bold, he ventures himself into the company of the townsmen, and attempts also to chat among them. Now *How Mr. Carnal-security begins the misery of Mansoul.* he knew that the power and strength of the town of Mansoul was great, and that it could not but be pleasing to the people if he cried up their might and their glory. Wherefore he beginneth his tale with the power and strength of Mansoul, and affirmed that it was impregnable. Now magnifying their captains, and their slings, and their rams; then crying up their fortifications and strongholds; and lastly, the assurances that they had from their Prince that Mansoul should be happy for ever. But when he saw that some of the men of the town were tickled and taken with his discourse, he makes it his business, and walking from street to street, house to house, and man to man, he at last brought Mansoul to dance after his pipe, and to grow almost as carnally secure as himself; so from talking they went to feasting, and from feasting to sporting; and so to some other matters. Now Emmanuel was yet in the town of Mansoul, and he wisely observed their doings. My Lord Mayor, my Lord Will-be-will, and Mr. Recorder, were also all taken with the words of this tattling Diabolonian gentleman, forgetting that their Prince had given them warning before to take heed that they were not beguiled with any Diabolonian sleight. He had *It is not grace received, but grace improved, that preserves the soul from temporal dangers.* further told them that the security of the now flourishing town of Mansoul, did not so much lie in her present fortifications and force, as in her so using of what she had as might oblige her Emmanuel to abide within her castle. For the right doctrine of Emmanuel was, that the town of Mansoul should take heed that they forget not his Father's love and his; also that they should so demean themselves as to continue to keep themselves therein. Now this was not the way to do it, namely, to fall in love with one of the Diabolonians, and with such an one too as Mr. Carnal-security was, and to be led up and down by the nose by him. They should have heard their Prince, feared their Prince, loved their Prince, and have stoned this naughty pack to death, and took care to have walked in the ways of their Prince's prescribing, for then should their peace have been as a river, when their righteousness had been like the waves of the sea.

Now when Emmanuel perceived that, through the policy of Mr. Carnal-security, the hearts of the men of Mansoul were chilled, and abated in their practical love to him; first, he bemoans them, and condoles their state with the Secretary, saying, O *Emmanuel bemoans Mansoul.* that my people had hearkened unto me, and that Mansoul had walked in my ways! I would have fed them with the finest of the wheat, and with honey out of the rock would I have sustained them. (Ps. lxxxi. 16.) This done, he said in his heart, I will return to the court, and go to my place, till Mansoul shall consider and acknowledge their offence. And he did so, and the cause and manner of his going away from them was thus:—

The cause was, for that Mansoul declined him, as is manifest in these particulars. 1. They left off their former way of visiting of him, they came not to his royal palace as afore. 2. They did not regard, nor yet take notice that he came, or came not to visit them. 3. The love-feasts that had wont to be between their Prince and them, though he made them still, and called them to them, yet they neglected to come at them, or to be delighted with them. 4. They waited not for his counsels, but began to be headstrong and confident in themselves, concluding that now they were strong and invincible, and that Mansoul was secure and beyond all reach of the foe, and that her state must needs be unalterable for ever.

Now, as was said, Emmanuel perceiving that by the craft of Mr. Carnal-security, the town of Mansoul was taken off from their dependance upon him, and upon his Father by him, and set upon what by them was bestowed upon it; he first, as I said, bemoaned their state, then he used means to make them understand that the way that they went on in was dangerous. For he sent my Lord High Secretary to them, to forbid them such ways; but twice when he came to them he found them at dinner in Mr. Carnal-security's parlour, and perceiving also that they were not willing to reason about matters concerning their good, *They grieve the Holy Ghost and Christ.* he took grief and went his way. The which when he had told to the Prince Emmanuel, he took offence, and was grieved also, and so made provision to return to his Father's court.

Now the methods of his withdrawing, as I was saying before, were thus, 1. Even while he was yet with them in Mansoul, he kept himself close and more retired than formerly. 2. His speech was not now, if he came in their company, so pleasant and familiar as formerly. 3. Nor did he, as in times past, send to Mansoul from his table those dainty bits which he was wont to do. 4. Nor when they came to visit him, as now and then they would, would he be so easily spoken with as they found him to be in times past. They might now knock once, yea twice, but he would *The working of their affections.* seem not at all to regard them; whereas formerly, at the sound of their feet, he would up and run, and meet them half-way, and take them too, and lay them in his bosom.

But thus Emmanuel carried it now, and by this his carriage he sought to make them bethink themselves and return to him. But, alas! they did not consider, they did not know his ways, they regarded not, they were not touched with these, nor with the true remembrance of former favours. Wherefore what does he but in private manner withdraw himself, first from his palace, then to the gate of the town, and so away from Mansoul he goes, till they should acknowledge their offence, and more earnestly seek his face. (Hosea v. 15.) Mr. God's-peace also laid down his commission, and would for the present act no longer in the town of Mansoul. (Ezek. xi. 21.)

Thus they walked contrary to him, and he again by way of retaliation, walked contrary to them. (Lev. xxvi. 21—24.) But, alas! by this time they were so hardened in their way, and had so drunk in the doctrine of Mr. Carnal-security, that the departing of their Prince touched them not, nor was he remembered by them when gone; and so of consequence, his absence not condoled by them. (Jer. ii. 32.)

Now there was a day wherein this old gentleman A trick put upon Mr. Godly-fear. Mr. Carnal-security did again make a feast for the town of Mansoul, and there was at that time in the town one Mr. Godly-fear, one now but little set by, though formerly one of great request. This man old Carnal-security had a mind, if possible, to gull and debauch, He goes to the feast and sits there like a stranger. and abuse as he did the rest, and therefore he now bids him to the feast with his neighbours; so the day being come they prepare, and he goes and appears with the rest of the guests; and being all set at the table, they did eat and drink, and were merry even all but this one man. For Mr. Godly-fear sat like a stranger, and did neither eat, nor was merry. The which when Mr. Carnal-security perceived, he presently addressed himself in a speech thus to him:—

Carn. Mr. Godly-fear, are you not well? you Talk betwixt Mr. Carnal-security and Mr. Godly-fear. seem to be ill of body or mind, or both. I have a cordial of Mr. For-get-good's making, the which, sir, if you will take a dram of, I hope it may make you bonny and blithe, and so make you more fit for we feasting companions.

Godly. Unto whom the good old gentleman discreetly replied, "Sir, I thank you for all things courteous and civil, but for your cordial I have no list thereto. But a word to the natives of Mansoul—you the elders and chief of Mansoul, to me it is strange to see you so jocund and merry, when the town of Mansoul is in such woful case."

Carn. Then said Mr. Carnal-security, "You want sleep, good sir, I doubt. If you please lie down and take a nap, and we, meanwhile, will be merry."

Godly. Then said the good man as follows, "Sir, if you were not destitute of an honest heart, you could not do as you have done, and do."

Carn. Then said Mr. Carnal-security, "Why?"

Godly. "Nay, pray interrupt me not. It is true the town of Mansoul was strong, and, with a proviso, impregnable; but you, the townsmen, have weakened it, and it now lies obnoxious to its foes; nor is it a time to flatter, or be silent. It is you, Mr. Carnal-security, that have wilily stripped Mansoul, and driven her glory from her; you

have pulled down her towers, you have broken down her gates, you have spoiled her locks and bars.

"And now to explain myself. From that time that my lords of Mansoul and you, sir,· grew so great, from that time the strength of Mansoul has been offended, and now he is arisen and is gone. If any shall question the truth of my words, I will answer him by this, and such like questions: Where is the Prince Emmanuel? When did a man or woman in Mansoul see him? When did you hear from him, or taste any of his dainty bits? You are now a feasting with this Diabolonian monster, but he is not your prince. I say, therefore, though enemies from without, had you taken heed, could not have made a prey of you, yet since you have sinned against your Prince, your enemies within have been too hard for you."

Carn. Then said Mr. Carnal-security, "Fie, fie, Mr. Godly-fear, fie; will you never shake off your timorousness? Are you afraid of being sparrow-blasted? Who hath hurt you? Behold I am on your side, only you are for doubting, and I am for being confident. Besides, is this a time to be sad in? A feast is made for mirth; why then do ye now, to your shame and our trouble, break out into such passionate melancholy language, when you should eat, and drink, and be merry?"

Godly. Then said Mr. Godly-fear again, "I may well be sad, for Emmanuel is gone from Mansoul. I say again, he is gone, and you, sir, are the man that has driven him away; yea, he is gone without so much as acquainting the nobles of Mansoul with his going, and if that is not a sign of his anger, I am not acquainted with the methods of godliness.

"And now, my lords and gentle- His speech to the elders of Mansoul. men, for my speech is still to you, your gradual declining from him did provoke him gradually to depart from you, the which he did for some time, if perhaps you would have been made sensible thereby, and have been renewed by humbling of yourselves; but when he saw that none would regard, nor lay these fearful beginnings of his anger and judgment to heart, he went away from his place, and this I saw with mine eye. Wherefore now, while you boast, your strength is gone, you are like the man that had lost his locks that before did wave about his shoulders. You may with this lord of your feast shake yourselves, and conclude to do as at other times; but since without him you can do nothing, and he is departed from you, turn your feast into a sigh, and your mirth into lamentation."

Then the subordinate preacher, old Mr. Conscience by name, he that of old was Conscience startled. Recorder of Mansoul, being startled at what was said, began to second it thus.

Con. "Indeed, my brethren," quoth he, "I fear that Mr. Godly-fear tells us true: I, for my part, have not seen my prince a long season. I cannot remember the day for my part. Nor can I answer Mr. Godly-fear's question. I doubt, I am afraid that all is naught with Mansoul."

Godly. "Nay, I know that you shall not find him in Mansoul, for he is departed and gone; yea, and gone for the faults of the elders, and for that they rewarded his grace with unsufferable unkindnesses."

Then did the subordinate Preacher look as if he They are all would fall down dead at the table, aghast. also all there present, except the man of the house, began to look pale and wan. But having a little recovered themselves, and jointly agreeing to believe Mr. Godly-fear and his sayings, they began to consult what was best to be done (now Mr. Carnal-security was gone into his withdrawing room, for he liked not such dumpish doings), both to the man of the house for drawing them into evil, and also to recover Emmanuel's love.

And with that, that saying of their Prince came very hot into their minds, which he had bidden them do to such as were false prophets that should They consult arise to delude the town of Mansoul. and burn their So they took Mr. Carnal-security, feast-master's house. concluding that he must be he, and burned his house upon him with fire, for he also was a Diabolonian by nature.

So when this was past and over, they bespeed themselves to look for Emmanuel their prince, and they sought him, but they found him not. (Sol. Song v. 6.) Then were they more confirmed in the truth of Mr. Godly-fear's sayings, and began also severely to reflect upon themselves for their so vile and ungodly doings, for they concluded now that it was through them that their prince had left them.

Then they agreed and went to my Lord Secre- They apply tary, him whom before they refused themselves to to hear, him whom they had grieved the Holy Ghost: but he is with their doings, to know of him, grieved, &c. for he was a seer and could tell where Emmanuel was, and how they might direct a petition to him. But the Lord Secretary would not admit them to a conference about this matter, nor would admit them to his royal place of abode, nor come out to them to show them his face, or intelligence. (Isa. lxiii. 10. Eph. iv. 30. 1 Thess. v. 19.)

And now was it a day, gloomy and dark, a day of clouds and of thick darkness with Mansoul. Now they saw that they had been foolish, and began to perceive what the company and prattle of Mr. Carnal-security had done, and what desperate damage his swaggering words had brought poor Mansoul into. But what further it was like to cost them, that they were ignorant of. Now Mr. Godly-fear began again to be in repute with the men of the town: yea, they were ready to look upon him as a prophet.

Well, when the Sabbath-day was come, they went to hear the subordinate Preacher; but oh how he did thunder and lighten this day! His text was that in the prophet Jonah, "They that observe lying vanities forsake their own mercies." (Jon. ii. 8.) But there was then A thundering such power and authority in that sermon. sermon, and such a dejection seen in the countenances of the people that day, that the like hath seldom been heard or seen. The people, when sermon was done, were scarce able to go to their homes, or to betake themselves to their employs the week after, they were so sermon-smitten, and also so sermon-sick by being smitten, that they knew not what to do. (Hos. v. 13.)

He did not only show to Mansoul their sin, but did tremble before them, under the sense of his own, still crying out of himself, as he preached to them, "Unhappy The subordinate man that I am! that I should do so Preacher doth wicked a thing! That I! a preacher! fault, and be- whom the prince did set up to teach pliance with to Mansoul his law, should myself Mr. Carnal- live senseless, and sottishly here, and security. be one of the first found in transgression. This transgression also fell within my precincts, I should have cried out against the wickedness, but I let Mansoul lie wallowing in it, until it had driven Emmanuel from its borders." With these things he also charged all the lords and gentry of Mansoul, to the almost distracting of them. (Psalms lxxxviii.)

About this time also there was a great sickness in the town of Mansoul, and most A great sickness of the inhabitants were greatly in Mansoul. afflicted; yea, the captains also, and men of war, were brought thereby to a languishing condition, and that for a long time together; so that in case of an invasion, nothing could to purpose now have been done, either by the townsmen or field officers. Oh how many pale faces, weak hands, feeble knees, and staggering men were now seen to walk the streets of Mansoul. Here were groans, there pants, and yonder lay those that were ready to faint. (Heb. xii. 12, 13. Rev. iii. 2.)

The garments too which Emmanuel had given them were but in a sorry case; some were rent, some were torn, and all in a nasty condition; some also did hang so loosely upon them, that the next bush they came at was ready to pluck them off. (Isa. iii. 24.)

After some time spent in this sad and desolate condition, the subordinate Preacher called for a day of fasting, and to humble themselves for being so wicked against the great Shaddai, and his Son; and he desired that captain Boanerges would preach. So he consented to do it, and the day was come, and his text was this, "Cut it down, why cumbereth it the ground?" Boanerges doth and a very smart sermon he made preach to Man- upon the place. First, he showed soul. what was the occasion of the words, to wit, because the fig-tree was barren; then he showed what was contained in the sentence, to wit, repentance, or utter desolation. He then showed also by whose authority this sentence was pronounced, and that was by Shaddai himself. And lastly, he showed the reasons of the point, and then concluded his sermon. But he was very pertinent in the application, insomuch that he made poor Mansoul tremble. For this sermon, as well as the former, wrought much upon the hearts of the men of Mansoul; yea, it greatly helped to keep awake those that were roused by the preaching that went before. So that now throughout the whole town there was little or nothing to be heard or seen but sorrow and mourning, and woe.

Now, after sermon they got together and consulted what was best to be done. *They consult what to do.* "But," said the subordinate Preacher, "I will do nothing of mine own head, without advising with my neighbour, Mr. Godly-fear. For if he had afore, and understood more of the mind of our Prince than we, I do not know but he also may have it now, even now we are turning again to virtue."

So they called and sent for Mr. Godly-fear, and he forthwith appeared; then they desired that he would further show his opinion about what they had best to do. Then said the old *Mr. Godly-fear's advice.* gentleman as followeth: "It is my opinion that this town of Mansoul should, in this day of her distress, draw up and send an humble petition to their offended Prince Emmanuel, that he in his favour and grace will turn again unto you, and not keep anger for ever."

When the townsmen had heard this speech, they

did with one consent agree to his advice; so they did presently draw up their request, and the next was, But who shall carry it? at last *They send the Lord Mayor to court.* they did all agree to send it by my Lord Mayor. So he accepted of the service, and addressed himself to his journey; and went and came to the court of Shaddai, whither Emmanuel the Prince of Mansoul was gone. But the gate was shut, and a strict watch kept thereat, so that the petitioner was forced to stand without for a great while together. (Lam. iii. 8.) Then he desired that some would go in to the Prince and tell him who stood at the gate, and what his business was. So one went and told to Shaddai, and to Emmanuel his Son, that the Lord Mayor of the town of Mansoul stood without at the gate of the King's court, desiring to be admitted into the presence of the Prince, the King's Son. He also told what was the Lord Mayor's errand, both to the King and his Son Emmanuel. But the Prince would not come down, nor admit that the gate should be opened to him, but sent him an answer to this effect: They have turned the back unto me, and not their face; but now, in the time of their trouble, they say to me, Arise and save us. (Lam. iii. 44.) But can they not now go to Mr. Carnal-security, to whom they went when they turned from me, and make him their leader, and their lord, and their protection, now *A dreadful answer.* in their trouble? Why now in their trouble do they visit me, since in their prosperity they went astray? (Jer. ii. 27, 28.)

This answer made my Lord Mayor look black in the face; it troubled, it perplexed, it rent him sore. (Lam. iv. 7, 8.) And now he began again to see what it was to be familiar with Diabolonians, such as Mr. Carnal-security was. When he saw that at court, as yet, there was little help to be expected, either for himself, or *The Lord Mayor returns, and how.* friends in Mansoul, he smote upon his breast and returned weeping, and all the way bewailing the lamentable state of

Mansoul. Well, when he was come within sight of the town, the elders and chief of the people of Mansoul went out at the gate to meet him, and to salute him, and to know how he sped at court. But

The state of Mansoul now. he told them his tale in so doleful a manner, that they all cried out, and mourned and wept. Wherefore they threw ashes and dust upon their heads, and put sackcloth upon their loins, and went crying out through the town of Mansoul; the which when the rest of the townsfolk saw, they all mourned and wept. This, therefore, was a day of rebuke, and trouble, and of anguish to the town of Mansoul, and also of great distress.

After some time, when they had somewhat *They consult again.* refrained themselves, they came together to consult again what by them was yet to be done; and they asked advice, as they did before, of that Rev. Mr. Godly-fear,

Mr. Godly-fear's advice. who told them, that there was no way better than to do as they had done, nor would he that they should be discouraged at all with what they had met with at court; yea, though several of their petitions should be answered with nought but silence or rebuke; "for," said he, "it is the way of the wise Shaddai to make men wait and to exercise patience, and it should be the way of them in want to be willing to stay his leisure."

Then they took courage, and sent again, and *See now what is the work of a backsliding saint awakened.* again, and again, and again; for there was not now one day, nor an hour that went over Mansoul's head, wherein a man might not have met upon the road one or other riding post, sounding the horn from Mansoul to the court of the King Shaddai; and all with letters petitionary in behalf *Groaning desires.* of, and for the Prince's return to Mansoul. The road, I say, was now full of messengers, going and returning, and meeting one another; some from the court, and some from Mansoul, and this was the work of the miserable town of Mansoul all that long, that sharp, that cold, and tedious winter.

Now, if you have not forgot, you may yet remember that I told you before, that *A memento.* after Emmanuel had taken Mansoul, yea, and after that he had new modelled the town, there remained in several lurking places of the corporation many of the old Diabolonians, that either came with the tyrant when he invaded and took the town, or that had there, by reason of unlawful mixtures, their birth, and breeding, and bringing up. And their holes, dens, and lurking places were in, under, or about the wall of the town. Some of their names are the Lord Fornication, the Lord Adultery, the Lord Murder, the Lord Anger, the Lord Lasciviousness, the Lord Deceit, the Lord Evil-eye, the Lord Blasphemy, and that horrible villain, the old and dangerous Lord Covetousness. These, as I told you, with many more, had yet their abode in the town

of Mansoul, and that after that Emmanuel had driven their prince Diabolus out of the castle.

Against these the good Prince did grant a commission to the Lord Will-be-will and *Mansoul heeded not her Prince's caution, nor put his commission into execution.* others; yea, to the whole town of Mansoul, to seek, take, secure, and destroy any or all that they could lay hands of; for that they were Diabolonians by nature, enemies to the Prince, and those that sought to ruin the blessed town of Mansoul. But the town of Mansoul did not pursue this warrant, but neglected to look after, to apprehend, to secure, and to destroy these Diabolonians. Wherefore, what do these villains, but by degrees take courage to put forth their heads, and to show themselves to the inhabitants of the town; yea, and as I was told, some of the men of Mansoul grew too familiar with some of them, to the sorrow of the corporation, as you yet will hear more of in time and place.

Well, when the Diabolonian lords that were left perceived that Mansoul had, through sinning, offended Emmanuel their Prince, *The Diabolonians plot.* and that he had withdrawn himself and was gone, what do they but plot the ruin of the town of Mansoul. So upon a time they met together at the hold of one Mr. Mischief, who also was a Diabolonian, and there consulted how they might deliver up Mansoul into the hand of Diabolus again. Now some advised one way, and some another, every man according to his own liking. At last, my Lord Lasciviousness propounded whether it might not be best, in the first place, for some of those that were Diabolonians in Mansoul, to adventure to offer themselves for servants to some of the natives of the town. For, said he, if they so do, and Mansoul shall accept of them, they may for us, and for Diabolus our lord, make the taking of the town of Mansoul more easy than otherwise it will be. But then stood up the Lord Murder, and said, "This may not be done at this time, for Mansoul is now in a kind of rage; because by our friend, Mr. Carnal-security, she hath been once ensnared already, and made to offend against her Prince; and how shall she reconcile herself unto her Lord again, but by the heads of these men? Besides, we know that they have in commission to take and slay us wherever they shall find us; let us therefore be wise as foxes; when we are dead we can do them no hurt, but while we live we may." Thus when they had tossed the matter to and fro, they jointly agreed that a letter should forthwith be *They send to hell for advice.* sent away to Diabolus in their name; by which the state of the town of Mansoul should be showed him, and how much it is under the frowns of their Prince; we may also, said some, let him know our intentions, and ask of him his advice in the case.

So a letter was presently framed, the contents of which was this—

" *To our great Lord, the Prince Diabolus, dwelling below in the Infernal Cave.*

"O great Father, and mighty Prince Diabolus, We, the true Diabolonians, yet remaining in the rebellious town of Mansoul, having received our beings from thee, and our nourishment at thy hands, cannot with content and quiet endure to behold, as we do this day, how thou art dispraised, disgraced, and reproached among the inhabitants of this town ; nor is thy long absence at all delightful to us, because greatly to our detriment.

The copy of their letter.

"The reason of this our writing unto our Lord is, for that we are not altogether without hope that this town may become thy habitation again ; for it is greatly declined from its Prince Emmanuel, and he is up-risen, and is departed from them ; yea, and though they send, and send, and send, and send after him to return to them, yet can they not prevail, nor get good words from him.

"There has been also of late, and is yet remaining, a very great sickness and faintings among them, and that not only upon the poorer sort of the town, but upon the lords, captains, and chief gentry of the place ; we only, who are of the Diabolonians by nature, remain well, lively, and strong, so that through their gre t transgression on the one hand, and their dangercus sickness on the other, we judge they lay open to thy hand and power. If therefore it shall stand with thy horrible cunning, and with the cunning of the rest of the princes with thee, to come and make an attempt to take Mansoul again, send us word, and we shall to our utmost power be ready to deliver it into thy hand. Or, if what we have said, shall not by thy fatherhood be thought best, and most meet to be done, send us thy mind in a few words, and we are all ready to follow thy counsel, to the hazarding of our lives, and what else we have.

"Given under our hands the day and date above written, after a close consultation at the house of Mr. Mischief, who yet is alive, and hath his place in our desirable town of Mansoul."

Mr. Profane is carrier, and he brings the letter to Hell-gate-hill, and there presents it to Cerberus, the porter.

When Mr. Profane, for he was the carrier, was come with his letter to Hell-gate-hill, he knocked at the brazen gates for entrance. Then did Cerberus, the porter, for he is the keeper of that gate, open to Mr. Profane, to whom he delivered his letter which he had brought from the Diabolonians in Mansoul. So he carried it in and presented it to Diabolus his lord, and said, "Tidings, my lord, from Mansoul, from our trusty friends in Mansoul."

Then came together from all places of the den Beelzebub, Lucifer, Apollyon, with the rest of the rabblement there, to hear what news from Mansoul. So the letter was broken up and read, and Cerberus he stood by. When the letter was openly read,

Deadman's bell, and how it went.

and the contents thereof spread into all corners of the den, command was given that, without let or stop, Deadman's bell should be rung for joy. So the bell was rung, and the princes rejoiced that Mansoul was like to come to ruin. Now the clapper of the bell went, "The town of Mansoul is coming to dwell with us, make room for the town of Mansoul." This bell, therefore, they did ring, because they did hope that they should have Mansoul again.

Now, when they had performed this their horrible ceremony, they got together again to consult what answer to send to their friends in Mansoul, and some advised one thing, and some another ; but, at length, because the business required haste, they left the whole business to the Prince Diabolus, judging him the most proper lord of the place. So he drew up a letter as he thought fit, in answer to what Mr. Profane had brought, and sent it to the Diabolonians that did dwell in Mansoul, by the same hand that had brought theirs to him, and this was the contents thereof :

" *To our offspring, the high and mighty Diabolonians, that yet dwell in the town of Mansoul, Diabolus, the great Prince of Mansoul, wisheth a prosperous issue and conclusion of those many brave enterprises, conspiracies, and designs, that you of your love and respect to our honour, have in your hearts to attempt to do against Mansoul.*

"Beloved children and disciples, my Lord Fornication, Adultery, and the rest, we have here, in our desolate den, received, to our highest joy and content, your welcome letter, by the hand of our trusty Mr. Profane ; and to show how acceptable your tidings were, we rung out our bell for gladness, for we rejoiced as much as we could, when we perceived that yet we had friends in Mansoul, and such as sought our honour and revenge in the ruin of the town of Mansoul. We also rejoice to hear that they are in a degenerated condition, and that they have offended their Prince, and that he is gone. Their sickness also pleaseth us, as doth also your health, might, and strength. Glad also would we be, right horribly beloved, could we get this town into our clutches again. Nor will we be sparing of spending our wit, our cunning, our craft, and hellish inventions, to bring to a wished conclusion this your brave beginning, in order thereto.

"And take this for your comfort, our birth and our offspring, that shall we again surprise it and take it, we will attempt to put all your foes to the sword, and will make you the great lords and captains of the place. Nor need you fear, if ever we get it again, that we after that shall be cast out any more, for we will come with more strength, and so lay far more fast hold than at the first we did. Besides, it is the law of that Prince that now they own, that if we get them a second time they shall be ours for ever. (Matt. xii. 43—45.)

" Do you, therefore, our trusty Diabolonians, yet more pry into, and endeavour to spy out, the weakness of the town of Mansoul. We also would that you yourselves do attempt to weaken them more and more. Send us word also by what means you think we had best to attempt the regaining thereof; to wit, whether by persuasion to a vain and loose life, or whether by tempting them to doubt and despair, or whether by blowing up of the town by the gunpowder of pride and self-conceit. Do ye also, oh ye brave Diabolonians and true sons of the pit, be ye always in a readiness to make a most hideous assault within, when we shall be ready to storm it without. Now speed you in your project, and we in our desires, the utmost power of our gates, which is the wish of your great Diabolus, Mansoul's enemy, and him that trembles when he thinks of judgment to come! All the blessings of the pit be upon you, and so we close up our letter.

" Given at the pit's mouth, by the joint consent of all the princes of darkness, to be sent to the force and power that we have yet remaining in Mansoul, by the hand of Mr. Profane. —By me, DIABOLUS."

This letter, as was said, was sent to Mansoul, to the Diabolonians that yet remained there, and that yet inhabited the wall, from the dark dungeon of Diabolus, by the hand of Mr. Profane, by whom *Profane comes home again.* they also in Mansoul sent theirs to the pit. Now when this Mr. Profane had made his return, and was come to Mansoul again, he went and came as he was wont to the house of Mr. Mischief, for there was the conclave, and the place where the contrivers were met. Now when they saw that their messenger was returned safe and sound, they were greatly gladed thereat. Then he presented them with his letter which he had brought from Diabolus for them, the which, when they had read and considered, did much augment their gladness. They asked him after the welfare of their friends, as how their Lord Diabolus, Lucifer, and Beelzebub did, with the rest of those of the den. To which this Profane made answer, " Well, well, my lords, they are well, even as well as can be in their place." They also, said he, did ring for joy at the reading of your letter, as you will perceive by this when you read it.

Now, as was said, when they had read their letter, and perceived that it encouraged them in their work, they fell to their way of contriving again, to wit, how they might complete their Diabolonian design upon Mansoul. And the first thing that they agreed upon was, to keep all things from Mansoul as close as they could. Let it not be known, let not Mansoul be acquainted with what we design against it. The next thing

was, how, or by what means, they should try to bring to pass the ruin and overthrow of Mansoul, and one said after this manner, and another said after that. Then stood up Mr. Deceit, and said, " My right Diabolonian friends, our lords, and the high ones of the deep dungeon, do propound unto us these three ways :

" 1. Whether we had best to seek its ruin by making of Mansoul loose and vain ? 2. Or whether by driving them to doubt and despair ? 3. Or whether by endeavouring to blow them up by the gunpowder of self-conceit ?

" Now, I think, if we shall tempt them to pride, that may do something ; and if we tempt them to wantonness, that may help. But, in my mind, if we could drive them into desperation, that would knock the nail on the head, for then we should have them, in the first place, question the truth of the love of the heart of their Prince towards them, and that will disgust him much. This, if it works well, will make them leave off quickly their way of sending petitions to him ; then farewell earnest solicitations for help and supply, for then this conclusion lies naturally before them, As good do nothing as do to no purpose." So to Mr. Deceit they unanimously did consent.

Then the next question was, " But how shall we do to bring this our project to pass ?" And it was answered by the same gentleman *Take heed, Mansoul!* that this might be the best way to do it : " Even let," quoth he, " so many of our friends as are willing to venture themselves for the promoting of their prince's cause, disguise themselves with apparel, change their names, and go into the market like far-countrymen, and proffer to let themselves for servants to the famous town of Mansoul, and let them pretend to do for their masters as beneficially as may be, for by so doing they may, if Mansoul shall hire them, in little time so corrupt and defile the corporation, that her now Prince shall be not only further offended with them, but in conclusion shall spew them out of his mouth. And when this is done, our prince Diabolus shall prey upon them *Take heed, Mansoul!* with ease ; yea, of themselves they shall fall into the mouth of the eater." (Nah. iii. 12.)

This project was no sooner propounded but was as highly accepted, and forward were all Diabolonians now to engage in so delicate an enterprise ; but it was not thought fit that all should do thus, wherefore they pitched upon two or three, namely, the Lord Covetousness, the Lord Lasciviousness, and the Lord Anger. The Lord Covetousness called himself by the name of Prudent-thrifty, the Lord Lasciviousness called himself *Take heed, Mansoul!* by the name of Harmless-mirth, and the Lord Anger called himself by the name of Good-zeal.

So upon a market-day they came into the market-place—three lusty fellows they were to look on —and they were clothed in sheeps'-russet, which was also now in a manner as white as were the white robes of the men of Mansoul.

Take heed, Mansoul! Now the men could speak the language of Mansoul well. So, when they were come into the market-place, and had offered to let themselves to the townsmen, they were presently taken up, for they asked but little wages, and promised to do their masters great service.

Mr. Mind hired Prudent-thrifty, and Mr. Godly-fear hired Good-zeal. True, this fellow Harmless-mirth did hang a little in hand, and could not so soon get him a master as the others did, because the town of Mansoul was now in Lent; but after awhile, because Lent was almost out, the Lord Will-be-will hired Harmless-mirth to be both his waiting-man and his lacquey, and thus they got them masters.

These villains now being got thus far into the houses of the men of Mansoul, quickly began to do great mischief therein; for being filthy, arch, and sly, they quickly corrupted the families where they were; yea, they tainted their masters much, especially this Prudent-thrifty, and him they call Harmless-mirth. True, he that went under the vizor of Good-zeal, was not so well liked of his master, for he quickly found that he was but a counterfeit rascal; the which when the fellow perceived, with speed he made his escape from the

house, or I doubt not but his master had hanged him.

Well, when these vagabonds had thus far carried on their design, and had corrupted the town as much they could, in the next place they considered with themselves at what time their prince Diabolus without, and themselves within the town, should make an attempt to seize upon Mansoul; and they all agreed upon this, that a market-day

A day of worldly cumber. would be the best for that work. For why? Then will the townsfolk be busy in their ways. And always take this for a rule, When people are most busy in the world, they least fear a surprise. We also then, said they, shall be able with less suspicion to gather ourselves together for the work of our friends and lords; yea, and in such a day, if we shall attempt our work, and miss it, we may, when they shall give us the rout, the better hide ourselves in the crowd, and escape.

These things being thus far agreed upon by them, they wrote another letter to Diabolus, and sent it by the hand of Mr. Profane, the contents of which were this—

Look to it, Mansoul! " The Lords of Looseness send to the great and high Diabolus, from our dens, caves, holes, and strongholds in and about the wall of the town of Mansoul, greeting:

" Our great lord, and the nourisher of our lives, Diabolus; how glad we were when we heard of your fatherhood's readiness to comply with us, and help forward our design in our attempts to ruin Mansoul! None can tell but those who, as we do, set themselves against all appearance of good, when and wheresoever we find it. (Rom. vii. 21, Gal. v. 17.)

" Touching the encouragement that your greatness is pleased to give us to continue to devise, contrive, and study the utter desolation of Mansoul, that we are not solicitous about, for we know right well that it cannot but be pleasing and profitable to us to see our enemies, and them that seek our lives, to die at our feet or fly before us. We therefore are still contriving, and that to the best of our cunning, to make this work most facile and easy to your lordships, and to us.

" First, we considered of that most hellishly-cunning, compacted, threefold project, that by you was propounded to us in your last; and have concluded, that though to blow them up with the gunpowder of pride would do well, and to do it by tempting them to be loose and vain will help on; yet to contrive to bring them into the gulf of desperation, we think, will be best of all. Now we, who are at your beck, have thought of two ways to do this:—First, we, for our parts, will make them as vile as we can; and then you with us, at a time appointed, shall be ready to fall upon them with the utmost force, And, of all the nations that are at your whistle, we think that an army of Doubters may be the most likely to attack and overcome the town of Mansoul. Thus shall we overcome these enemies; else the pit shall open her mouth upon them, and desperation shall thrust them down into it. We have also, to effect this so much by us desired design, sent already three of our trusty Diabolonians among them; they are disguised in garb, they have changed their names, and are now accepted of them; to wit, Covetousness, Lasciviousness, and Anger. The name of Covetousness is changed to Prudent-thrifty; and him Mr. Mind has hired, and is almost become as bad as our friend. Lasciviousness has changed his name to Harmless-mirth, and he is got to be the Lord Will-be-will's lacquey, but he has made his master very wanton. Anger changed his name into Good-zeal, and was entertained by Mr. Godly-fear, but the peevish old gentleman took pepper in the nose, and turned our companion out of his house. Nay, he has informed us since that he ran away from him, or else his old master had hanged him up for his labour.

"Now these have much helped forward our work and design upon Mansoul; for notwithstanding the spite and quarrelsome temper of the old gentleman last mentioned, the other two ply their business well, and are like to ripen the work apace.

"Our next project is, that it be concluded that you come upon the town upon a market-day, and that when they are upon the heat of their business; for then to be sure they will be most secure, and least think that an assault will be made upon them. They will also at such a time be less able to defend themselves, and to offend you in the prosecution of our design. And we, your trusty, and we are sure your beloved ones, shall, when you shall make your furious assault without, be ready to second the business within. So shall we, in all likelihood, be able to put Mansoul to utter confusion, and to swallow them up before they can come to themselves. If your serpentine heads, most subtle dragons, and our highly esteemed lords can find out a better way than this, let us quickly know your minds.

"To the Monsters of the Infernal Cave, from the house of Mr. Mischief in Mansoul, by the hand of Mr. Profane."

Now all the while that the raging runagates, and hellish Diabolonians, were thus contriving the ruin of the town of Mansoul, they, to wit, the poor town itself, was in a sad and woeful case; partly because they had so grievously offended Shaddai and his Son, and partly because that the enemies thereby got strength within them afresh, and also because though they had by many petitions made suit to the Prince Emmanuel, and to his Father Shaddai, by him, for their pardon and favour, yet, hitherto, obtained they not one smile; but contrariwise, through the craft and subtlety of the domestic Diabolonians, their cloud was made to grow blacker and blacker, and their Emmanuel to stand at further distance.

The sad state of Mansoul!

The sickness also did still greatly rage in Mansoul, both among the captains and the inhabitants of the town; their enemies and their enemies only were now lively and strong, and like to become the head, whilst Mansoul was made the tail.

By this time, the letter last mentioned, that was written by the Diabolonians that yet lurked in the town of Mansoul, was conveyed to Diabolus in the black den, by the hand of Mr. Profane. He carried the letter by Hell-gate-hill as before, and conveyed it by Cerberus to his lord.

But when Cerberus and Mr. Profane did meet, they were presently as great as beggars, and thus they fell into discourse about Mansoul, and about the project against her.

Cerb. Ah! old friend, quoth Cerberus, art thou come to Hell-gate-hill again! By St. Mary, I am glad to see thee.

Prof. Yes, my lord, I am come again about the concerns of the town of Mansoul.

Cerb. Prithee, tell me what condition is that town of Mansoul in at present?

Talk between him and Cerberus.

Prof. In a brave condition, my lord, for us, and for my lords, the lords of this place I trow, for they are greatly decayed as to godliness, and that is as well as our heart can wish; their Lord is greatly out with them, and that doth also please us well. We have already also a foot in their dish, for our Diabolonian friends are laid in their bosoms, and what do we lack but to be masters of the place. Besides, our trusty friends in Mansoul are daily plotting to betray it to the lords of this town; also the sickness rages bitterly among them, and that which makes up all, we hope at last to prevail.

Cerb. Then said the Dog of Hell-gate, "No time like this to assault them; I wish that the enterprise be followed close, and that the success desired may be soon effected. Yea, I wish it for the poor Diabolonians' sakes, that live in the continual fear of their lives in that traitorous town of Mansoul."

Prof. The contrivance is almost finished, the lords in Mansoul that are Diabolonians are at it day and night, and the others are like silly doves, they want heart to be concerned with their state, and to consider that ruin is at hand. Besides, you may, yea, must think, when you put all things together, that there are many reasons that prevail with Diabolus to make what haste he can.

Cerb. Thou hast said as it is, I am glad things are at this pass. Go in, my brave Profane, to my lords, they will give thee for thy welcome as good a *corunto* as the whole of this kingdom will afford. I have sent thy letter in already.

Then Mr. Profane went into the den, and his Lord Diabolus met him, and saluted him with, "Welcome, my trusty servant, I have been made glad with thy letter." The rest of the lords of the pit gave him also their salutations. Then Profane, after obeisance made to them all, said, "Let Mansoul be given to my Lord Diabolus, and let him be her king for ever." And with that the hollow belly and yawning gorge of hell gave so loud and hideous a groan—for that is the music of that place—that it made the mountains about it totter, as if they would fall in pieces.

Profane's entertainment.

Now after they had read and considered the letter, they consulted what answer to return, and the first that did speak to it was Lucifer.

Lucif. Then said he, "The first project of the Diabolonians in Mansoul is like to be lucky, and to take; to wit, that they will by all the ways and means they can, make Mansoul yet more vile and filthy; no way to destroy a soul like this; this is *probatum est.* Our old friend Balaam went this way and prospered many years ago; let this therefore stand with us for a maxim, and be to Diabolonians for a general rule in all ages, for nothing can make this to fail but grace, in which I would hope that this town has no share. (Num. xxxi. 16. Rev. ii. 14.) But whether to fall upon them on a market-day, because of their cumber in business, that I would should be under debate. And there is more reason why this head should be debated, than why some other should; because upon this will turn the whole of what we shall attempt. If we time not our business well, our whole project may fail. Our friends the Diabolonians say that a market-day is best, for then will Mansoul be most busy, and have fewest thoughts of a surprise. But what if also they should double their guards on those days—and methinks nature and reason should teach them to do it—and what if they should keep such a watch on those days as the necessity of their present case doth require? Yea, what if their men should be always in arms on those days? Then you may, my lords, be disappointed in your attempts, and may bring our friends in the town to utter danger of unavoidable ruin."

They consult what answer to give to the letter.

Cumberments are dangerous.

They had need do it.

Beel. Then said the great Beelzebub, "There is something in what my lord hath said, but his conjecture may or may not fall out. Nor hath my lord laid it down as that which must not be receded from, for I know that he said it only to provoke to a warm debate thereabout. Therefore we must understand, if we can, whether the town of Mansoul have such sense and knowledge of her decayed state, and of the design that we have on foot against her, as doth provoke her to set watch and ward at her gates,

A lesson for Christians.

and to double them on market days. But if, after inquiry made, it shall be found that they are asleep, then any day will do, but a market-day is best; and this is my judgment in this case."

Diab. Then quoth Diabolus, "How should we know this?" And it was answered, "Inquire about it at the mouth of Mr. Profane." So Profane was called in and asked the question, and he made his answer as follows—

Prof. My lords, so far as I can gather, this is at present the condition of the town of Mansoul. They are decayed in their faith and love; Emmanuel their Prince has given them the back; they send often by petition to fetch him again, but he maketh not haste to answer their request, nor is there much reformation among them.

Profane's description of the present state of Mansoul.

Diab. I am glad that they are backward to a reformation, but yet I am afraid of their petitioning. However, their looseness of life is a sign that there is not much heart in what they do, and without the heart things are little worth. But go on, my masters, I will divert you, my lords, no longer.

Beel. If the case be so with Mansoul, as Mr. Profane has described it to be, it will be no great matter what day we assault it; not their prayers nor their power will do them much service.

Apoll. When Beelzebub had ended his oration, then Apollyon did begin. "My opinion," said he, "concerning this matter is, that we go on fair and softly, not doing things in a hurry. Let our friends in Mansoul go on still to pollute and defile it, by seeking to draw it yet more into sin, for there is nothing like sin to devour Mansoul. If this be done, and it takes effect, Mansoul of itself will leave off to watch, to petition, or anything else that should tend to her security and safety; for she will forget her Emmanuel, she will not desire his company, and can she be gotten thus to live, her Prince will not come to her in haste. Our trusty friend, Mr. Carnal-security, with one of his tricks, did drive him out of the town, and why may not my Lord Covetousness, and my Lord Lasciviousness, by what they may do, keep him out of the town? And this I will tell you, not because you know it not, that two or three Diabolonians, if entertained and countenanced by the town of Mansoul, will do more to the keeping of Emmanuel from them, and towards making of the town of Mansoul your own, than can an army of a legion that should be sent out from us to withstand him.

Dreadful advice against Mansoul.

"Let, therefore, this first project that our friends in Mansoul have set on foot be strongly and diligently carried on with all cunning and craft imaginable; and let them send continually, under one guise or another, more and other of their men to play with the people of Mansoul; and then, perhaps, we shall not need to be at the charge of making a war upon them; or if that must of necessity

Dreadful advice against Mansoul.

be done, yet the more sinful they are, the more unable, to be sure, they will be to resist us, and then the more easily we shall overcome them. And besides, suppose—and that is the worst that can be supposed—that Emmanuel should come to them again, why may not the same means, or the like, drive him from them once more? Yea, why may he not by their lapse into that sin again, be driven from them for ever, for the sake of which he was at the first driven from them for a season? And if this should happen, then away go with him his rams, his slings, his captains, his soldiers, and he leaveth Mansoul naked and bare. Yea, will not this town, when she sees herself utterly forsaken of her Prince, of her own accord open her gates again unto you, and make of you as in the days of old? But this must be done by time; a few days will not effect so great a work as this."

So soon as Apollyon had made an end of speaking, Diabolus began to blow out his own malice, and to plead his own cause; and he said, "My lords and powers of the cave, my true and trusty friends, I have with much impatience, as becomes me, given ear to your long and tedious orations. But my furious gorge and empty paunch so lusteth after a repossession of my famous town of Mansoul, that, whatever comes out, I can wait no longer to see the events of lingering projects. I must, and that without further delay, seek by all means I can to fill my insatiable gulf with the soul and body Look to it Mansoul. of the town of Mansoul. Therefore, lend me your heads, your hearts, and your help, now I am going to recover my town of Mansoul."

When the lords and princes of the pit saw the flaming desire that was in Diabolus to devour the miserable town of Mansoul, they left off to raise any more objections, but consented to lend him what strength they could; though, had Apollyon's advice been taken, they had far more fearfully distressed the town of Mansoul. But, I say, they were willing to lend him what strength they could, not knowing what need they might have of him, when they should engage for themselves, as he. Wherefore, they fell to advising about the next thing propounded, to wit, what soldiers they were, and also how many, with whom Diabolus should go against the town of Mansoul to take it; and after some debate, it was concluded, according as in the letter the Diabolonians had suggested, that none was more fit for that expedition than an army of terrible Doubters. They, therefore, concluded to send against Mansoul an army of sturdy Doubters. The number thought fit to be employed in that service was between twenty and thirty thousand. So then, the result An army of Doubters raised to go against the town of Mansoul. of that great council of those high and mighty lords was, that Diabolus should even now, out of hand, beat up his drum for men in the land of Doubting, which land lieth upon the confines

of the place called Hell-gate-hill, for men that might be employed by him against the miserable town, Mansoul. It was also concluded that these lords themselves should help him in the war, and that they would, to that end, head The princes of the pit go with them. and manage his men. So they drew up a letter and sent back to the Diabolonians that lurked in Mansoul, and that waited for the back-coming of Mr. Profane, to signify to them into what method and forwardness they at present had put their design. The contents whereof now followeth.

"*From the dark and horrible Dungeon of Hell, Diabolus, with all the Society of the Princes of Darkness, sends to our trusty ones, in and about the walls of the town of Mansoul, now impatiently waiting for our most devilish answer to their venomous and most poisonous design against the town of Mansoul.*

"Our native ones, in whom from day to day we boast, and in whose actions all the year long we do greatly delight ourselves, we received your welcome, because highly-esteemed, letter, at the hand of our trusty and greatly beloved, the old gentleman, Mr. Profane; and do give you to understand that when we had broken it up, and had read the contents thereof, to·your amazing memory be it spoken, our yawning hollow-bellied place, where we are, made so hideous and yelling a noise for joy, that the mountains that stood round about Hell-gate-hill had like to have been shaken to pieces at the sound thereof.

"We could also do no less than admire your faithfulness to us, with the greatness of that subtlety that now hath showed itself to be in your heads to serve us against the town of Mansoul. For you have invented for us so excellent a method for our proceeding against that rebellious people, a more effectual cannot be thought of by all the wits of hell. The proposals, therefore, which now at last you have sent us, since we saw them, we have done little else but highly approved and admired them.

"Nay, we shall, to encourage you in the profundity of your craft, let you know, that, at a full assembly and conclave of our princes and principalities of this place, your project was discoursed, and tossed from one side of our cave to the other, by their mightinesses; but a better, and as was by themselves judged, a more fit and proper way by all their wits could not be invented, to surprise, take, and make our own, the rebellious town of Mansoul.

"Wherefore, in fine, all that was said that varied from what you had in your letter propounded, fell of itself to the ground, and yours only was stuck to by Diabolus the prince; yea, his gaping gorge and vaunting paunch was on fire to put your invention into execution.

"We, therefore, give you to understand that our stout, furious, and unmerciful Diabolus, is raising for your relief, and the ruin of the rebellious town of Mansoul, more than twenty thousand Doubters to come against that people. They are all stout and sturdy men, and men that of old have been accustomed to war, and that can therefore well endure the drum. I say, he is doing of this work of his with all the possible speed he can; for his heart and spirit is engaged in it. We desire, therefore, that as you have hitherto stuck to us, and given us both advice and encouragement thus far; that you still will prosecute our design, nor shall you lose, but be gainers thereby; yea, we intend to make you the lords of Mansoul.

"One thing may not by any means be omitted, that is, those with us do desire that every one of you that are in Mansoul would still use all your power, cunning, and skill, with delusive persuasions, yet to draw the town of Mansoul into more sin and wickedness, even that sin may be finished and bring forth death.

"For thus it is concluded with us, that the more vile, sinful, and debauched the town of Mansoul is, the more backward will be their Emmanuel to come to their help, either by presence, or other relief; yea, the more sinful, the more weak, and so the more unable will they be to make resistance when we shall make our assault upon them to swallow them up. Yea, that may cause that their mighty Shaddai himself may cast them out of his protection; yea, and send for his captains and soldiers home, with his slings and rams, and leave them naked and bare, and then the town of Mansoul will of itself open to us, and fall as the fig into the mouth of the eater. Yea, to be sure that we then with a great deal of ease shall come upon her and overcome her.

"As to the time of our coming upon Mansoul, we as yet have not fully resolved upon that, though at present some of us think as you, that a market-day, or a market-day at night, will certainly be the best. However, do you be ready, and when you shall hear our roaring drum without, do you be as busy to make the most horrible confusion within. (1 Pet. v. 8.) So shall Mansoul certainly be distressed before and behind, and shall not know which way to betake herself for help. My Lord Lucifer, my Lord Beelzebub, my Lord Apollyon, my Lord Legion, with the rest salute you, as does also my Lord Diabolus, and we wish both you, with all that you do or shall possess, the very self-same fruit and success for their doing, as we ourselves at present enjoy for ours.

"From our dreadful confines in the most fearful Pit, we salute you, and so do those many legions here with us, wishing you may be as hellishly prosperous as we desire to be ourselves. By the Letter-carrier, Mr. Profane."

Then Mr. Profane addressed himself for his return to Mansoul, with his errand from the horrible pit to the Diabolonians that dwelt in that town. So he came up the stairs from the deep to the mouth of the cave where Cerberus was. Now when Cerberus saw him, he asked how matters did go below, about, and against the town of Mansoul.

Prof. Things go as well as we can expect. The letter that I carried thither was highly approved, and well liked by all my lords, and I am returning to tell our Diabolonians so. I have an answer to it here in my bosom, that I am sure will make our masters that sent me glad; for the contents thereof is to encourage them to pursue their design to the utmost, and to be ready also to fall on within, when they shall see my Lord Diabolus beleaguering of the town of Mansoul.

Cerb. But does he intend to go against them himself?

Prof. Does he! Ay, and he will take along with him more than twenty thousand, all sturdy Doubters, and men of war, picked men, from the land of Doubting, to serve him in the expedition. *The land from the which the Doubters do come.*

Cerb. Then was Cerberus glad, and said, "And is there such brave preparations a-making to go against the miserable town of Mansoul? And would I might be put at the head of a thousand of them, that I might also show my valour against the famous town of Mansoul."

Prof. Your wish may come to pass; you look like one that has mettle enough, and my lord will have with him those that are valiant and stout. But my business requires haste.

Cerb. Ay, so it does. Speed thee to the town of Mansoul with all the deepest mischiefs that this place can afford thee. And when thou shalt come to the house of Mr. Mischief, the place where the Diabolonians meet to plot, tell them that Cerberus doth wish them his service, and that if he may, he will with the army come up against the famous town of Mansoul.

Prof. That I will. And I know that my lords that are there will be glad to hear it, and to see you also.

So after a few more such kind of compliments, Mr. Profane took his leave of his friend Cerberus, and Cerberus again, with a thousand of their pit-wishes, bid him haste with all speed to his masters. The which when he had heard, he made obeisance, and began to gather up his heels to run.

Thus therefore he returned, and went and came to Mansoul, and going as afore to the house of Mr. Mischief, there he found the Diabolonians assembled, and waiting for his return. Now when he was come, and had presented himself, he also delivered to them his letter, and adjoined this compliment to them therewith: "My Lords from the confines of the pit, the high and mighty principalities and powers of the den salute you here, the true Diabolonians of the town of Mansoul. Wishing you always the most proper of their benedictions, for the great service, high attempts, and brave achievements that you have put yourselves upon, for the restoring, to our prince Diabolus, the famous town of Mansoul." *Profane returned again to Mansoul.*

This was therefore the present state of the miserable town of Mansoul: she had offended her Prince, and he was gone; she had encouraged the powers of hell, by her foolishness, to come against her, to seek her utter destruction.

True, the town of Mansoul was somewhat made sensible of her sin, but the Diabolonians were gotten into her bowels; she cried, but Emmanuel was gone, and her cries did not fetch him as yet again. Besides, she knew not now whether ever or never he would return and come to his Mansoul again, nor did they know the power and industry of the enemy, nor how forward they were to put in execution that plot of hell that they had devised against her.

They did indeed still send petition after petition to the Prince, but he answered all with silence. They did neglect reformation, and that was as Diabolus would have it, for he knew, if they regarded iniquity in their heart, their King would not hear their prayer; they therefore did still grow weaker and weaker, and were as a rolling thing before the whirlwind. They cried to their King for help, and laid Diabolonians in their bosoms; what, therefore, should a king do to them? Yea, there seemed now to be a mixture in Mansoul, the Diabolonians and the Mansoulians would walk the streets together. Yea, they began to seek their peace, for they thought that since the sickness had been so mortal in Mansoul, it was in vain to go to handy-gripes with them. Besides, the weakness of Mansoul was the strength of their enemies; and the sins of Mansoul the advantage of the Diabolonians. The foes of Mansoul did also now begin to promise themselves the town for a possession; there was no great difference now betwixt Mansoulians and Diabolonians, both seemed to be *Good thoughts,* masters of Mansoul. Yea, the Dia- *good concep-* bolonians increased and grew, but *tions, and good* the town of Mansoul diminished *desires.* greatly. There was more than eleven thousand of men, women, and children that died by the sickness in Mansoul.

But now, as Shaddai would have it, there was *The story of* one whose name was Mr. Pry-well, *Mr. Pry-well.* a great lover of the people of Mansoul. And he, as his manner was, did go listening up and down in Mansoul to see and to hear, if at any time he might, whether there was any design against it or no. For he was always a jealous man, and feared some mischief sometime would befall it, either from the Diabolonians within, or from some power without. Now, upon a time it so happened, as Mr. Pry-well went listening here and there, that he lighted upon a place called Vile-hill, in Mansoul, where Diabolonians used to meet; so hearing a muttering—you must know that it was in the night—he softly drew near to *The Diabolonian* hear; nor had he stood long under *plot discovered,* the house-end, for there stood a *and by whom.* house there, but he heard one confidently affirm that it was not or would not

be long before Diabolus should possess himself again of Mansoul, and that then the Diabolonians did intend to put all Mansoulians to the sword, and would kill and destroy the King's captains, and drive all his soldiers out of the town.

He said, moreover, that he knew there were about twenty thousand fighting men prepared by Diabolus for the accomplishing of this design, and that it would not be months before they all should see it. When Mr. Pry-well had heard this story, he did quickly believe it was true, wherefore he went forthwith to my Lord Mayor's house, and acquainted him therewith; who, sending for the subordinate Preacher, brake the business to him, and he as soon gave the alarm to *Understanding.* the town—for he was now the chief *Conscience.* preacher in Mansoul—because as yet my Lord Secretary was ill at ease. And this was the way that the subordinate Preacher did take to alarm the town therewith: the same hour he caused the Lecture-bell to be rung, so the people came together; he gave them then a short exhortation to watchfulness, and made Mr. Pry-well's news the argument thereof. "For," said he, "a horrible plot is contrived against Mansoul, even to massacre us all in a day; nor is this story to be slighted, for Mr. Pry-well is the author thereof. Mr. Pry-well was always a lover of Mansoul, a sober and judicious man, a man that is no tattler, nor raiser of false reports, but one that loves to look into the very bottom of matters, and talks nothing of news but by very solid arguments. I will call him, and you shall hear him your own selves."

So he called him, and he came and told his tale so punctually, and affirmed its truth *Pry-well tells* with such ample grounds, that Man- *his news to* soul fell presently under a convic- *Mansoul.* tion of the truth of what he said. The Preacher did also back him, saying, "Sirs, it is not irrational for us to believe it, for we have provoked Shaddai to anger, and have sinned Emmanuel out of the town; we have had too much correspondence with Diabolonians, and have forsaken our former mercies; no marvel then if the enemy, both within and without, should plot our ruin; and what time like this to do it? The sickness is now in the town, and we have been made weak thereby. Many a good meaning man is dead, and the Diabolonians of late grow stronger and stronger.

"Besides," quoth the subordinate Preacher, "I have received from this good truth-teller this one inkling further, that he understood by those that he overheard, that several letters have lately passed between the Furies and the Diabolonians, in order to our destruction." When Mansoul heard all this, and not being able to gainsay it, *They take* they lift up their voice and wept. *alarm.*

Mr. Pry-well did also, in the presence of the townsmen, confirm all that their subordinate Preacher had said. Wherefore they now set afresh to be-

wail their folly, and to a doubling of petitions to
Shaddai and his Son. They also
brake the business to the captains,
high commanders, and men of war
in the town of Mansoul, entreating of them to use
the means to be strong, and to take good courage,
and that they would look after their harness, and
make themselves ready to give Diabolus battle, by
night and by day, shall he come, as they are informed he will, to beleaguer the town of Mansoul.

They tell the thing to the captains.

When the captains heard this, they being always
true lovers of the town of Mansoul, what do they,
but like so many Samsons, they
shake themselves, and come together
to consult and contrive how to de-
feat those bold and hellish contrivances that were
upon the wheel, by the means of Diabolus and
his friends, against the now sickly, weakly, and
much impoverished town of Mansoul; and they
agreed upon the following particulars :—

They come together to consult.

1. That the gates of Mansoul should be kept
shut, and made fast with bars and
locks ; and that all persons that went
out, or came in, should be very strictly examined
by the captains of the guards (1 Cor. xvi. 13) ; to
the end, said they, that those that are managers of
the plot amongst us may either, coming or going,
be taken ; and that we may also find out who are
the great contrivers amongst us of our ruin. (Lam.
iii. 40.)

Their agree-ment.

2. The next thing was, that a strict search should
be made for all kind of Diabolonians throughout
the whole town of Mansoul; and every man's
house, from top to bottom, should be looked into,
and that too, house by house, that if possible a
further discovery might be made of all such among
them as had a hand in these designs. (Heb. xii.
15, 16.)

3. It was further concluded upon, that wheresoever or with whomsoever any of the Diabolonians
were found, that even those of the town of Mansoul that had given them house and harbour,
should to their shame, and the warning of others,
do penance in the open place. (Jer. ii. 34 ; v. 26.
Ezek. xvi. 52.)

4. It was moreover resolved by the famous town
of Mansoul, that a public fast, and a day of humiliation should be kept throughout the whole corporation, to the justifying of their Prince, the
abasing of themselves before him for their transgressions against him, and against Shaddai his
Father. (Joel. i. 14 ; ii. 15, 16.) It was further
resolved, that all such in Mansoul as did not on
that day endeavour to keep that fast, and to
humble themselves for their faults, but that should
mind their worldly employs, or be found wandering up and down the streets, should be taken for
Diabolonians, and should suffer as Diabolonians,
for such their wicked doings.

5. It was farther concluded then, that with
what speed and with what warmth of mind they
could, they would renew their humiliation for sin,

and their petitions to Shaddai for help ; they also
resolved to send tidings to the court of all that
Mr. Pry-well had told them. (Jer. xxxvii. 4, 5.)

6. It was also determined that thanks should be
given by the town of Mansoul to Mr. Pry-well for
his diligent seeking of the welfare
of their town ; and further, that forasmuch as he was so naturally in-
clined to seek their good, and also to undermine
their foes, they gave him a commission of Scout-
master-general, for the good of the town of Mansoul.

Mr. Pry-well is made Scout-master-general.

When the corporation, with their captains, had
thus concluded, they did as they had said ; they
shut up their gates, they made for Diabolonians
strict search, they made those with whom any
were found to do penance in the open place.
They kept their fast, and renewed their petitions
to their Prince, and Mr. Pry-well managed his
charge, and the trust that Mansoul had put in his
hands with great conscience, and
good fidelity ; for he gave himself
wholly up to his employ, and that not only within
the town, but he went out to pry, to see, and to
hear.

Mr. Pry-well goes a scouting.

And not many days after, he provided for his
journey, and went towards Hell-gate-hill, into the
country where the Doubters were, where he heard
of all that had been talked of in Mansoul, and he
perceived also that Diabolus was almost ready for
his march. So he came back with speed, and
calling the captains and elders of Mansoul together,
he told them where he had been,
what he had heard, and what he
had seen. Particularly, he told them that Diabolus was almost ready for his march, and that he
had made old Mr. Incredulity, that once brake
prison in Mansoul, the general of his army ; that
his army consisted all of Doubters, and that their
number was above twenty thousand. He told,
moreover, that Diabolus did intend to bring with
him the chief princes of the infernal pit, and that he
would make them chief captains over his Doubters.
He told them, moreover, that it was certainly true
that several of the black-den would, with Diabolus,
ride Reformades to reduce the town of Mansoul to
the obedience of Diabolus their prince.

He returns with great news.

He said, moreover, that he understood by the
Doubters, among whom he had been, that the
reason why old Incredulity was made general of
the whole army, was because none truer than he
to the tyrant ; and because he had an implacable
spite against the welfare of the town of Mansoul.
Besides, said he, he remembers the affronts that
Mansoul has given, and he is resolved to be revenged of them. But the black princes shall be
made high commanders, only Incredulity shall be
over them all, because, which I had almost forgot,
he can more easily, and more dexterously beleaguer
the town of Mansoul than can any of the princes
besides. (Heb. xii. 1.)

Now when the captains of Mansoul, with the

elders of the town, had heard the tidings that Mr. Prywell did bring, they thought it expedient without further delay, to put into execution the laws that, against the Diabolonians, their Prince had made for them, and given them in commandment to manage against them. Wherefore, forthwith a diligent and impartial search was made in all houses in Mansoul for all and all manner of Diabolonians. Now in the house of Mr. Mind, and in the house of the great Lord Will-be-will were two Diabolonians found. In Mr. Mind's house was one Lord Covetousness found, but he had changed his name to Prudent-thrifty. In my Lord Will-be-will's house, one Lasciviousness was found; but he had changed his name to Harmless-mirth. These two the captains and elders of the town of Mansoul took, and committed them to custody under the hand of Mr. Trueman the

Some Diabolonians taken in Mansoul, and committed to prison.

jailer; and this man handled them so severely, and loaded them so well with irons, that in time they both fell into a very deep consumption, and died in the prison-house; their masters also, according to the agreement of the captains and elders, were brought to take penance in the open place to their shame, and for a warning to the rest of the town of Mansoul.

Now this was the manner of penance in those days. The persons offending, being made sensible of the evil of their doings, were enjoined open confession of their faults, and a strict amendment of their lives.

Penance, what.

After this, the captains and elders of Mansoul sought yet to find out more Diabolonians, wherever they lurked, whether in dens, caves, holes, vaults, or where else they could, in or about the wall or town of Mansoul. But though they could plainly see their footing, and so follow them, by their tract

and smell, to their holds, even to the mouths of their caves and dens, yet take them, hold them, and do justice upon them, they could not, their ways were so crooked, their holds so strong, and they so quick to take sanctuary there.

But Mansoul did now with so stiff a hand rule over the Diabolonians that were left, that they were glad to shrink into corners. Time was when they durst walk openly, and in the day, but now they were forced to embrace privacy, and the night—time was when a Mansoulian was their companion, but now they counted them deadly enemies. This good change did Mr. Prywell's intelligence make in the famous town of Mansoul.

By this time Diabolus had finished his army, which he intended to bring with him for the ruin of Mansoul; and had set over them captains, and other field-officers, such as liked his furious stomach best. Himself was lord paramount, Incredulity was general of his army. Their highest captains shall be named afterwards, but now for their officers, colours, and escutcheons.

1. Their first captain was Captain Rage, he was captain over the Election-doubters; his were the red colours, his standard-bearer was Mr. Destructive, and the great red dragon he had for his escutcheon. (Rev. xii. 3, 4, 13—17.)

Diabolus's army.

2. The second captain was Captain Fury, he was captain over the Vocation-doubters; his standard-bearer was Mr. Darkness, his colours were those that were pale, and he had for his escutcheon the fiery flying serpent. (Num. xxi.)

3. The third captain was Captain Damnation, he was captain over the Grace-doubters; his were the red colours, Mr. No-life bare them, and he had for his escutcheon the black den. (Matt. xxii. 13; Rev. ix. 1.)

4. The fourth captain was the Captain Insatiable, he was captain over the Faith-doubters; his were the red colours, Mr. Devourer bare them, and he had for an escutcheon the yawning jaws. (Prov. xxvii. 20; Ps. xi. 6.)

5. The fifth captain was Captain Brimstone, he

was captain over the Perseverance-doubters; his also were the red colours, Mr. Burning bare them, and his escutcheon was the blue and stinking flame. (Ps. xi. 6; Rev. xiv. 11.)

6. The sixth captain was Captain Torment, he was captain over the Resurrection-doubters; his colours were those that were pale, Mr. Gnaw was his ancient-bearer, and he had the black worm for his escutcheon. (Mark ix. 44—48.)

7. The seventh captain was Captain No-ease, he was captain over the Salvation-doubters; his were the red colours, Mr. Restless bare them, and his escutcheon was the ghastly picture of death. (Rev. vi. 8; xiv. 11.)

8. The eighth captain was the Captain Sepulchre, he was captain over the Glory-doubters; his also were the pale colours, Mr. Corruption was his ancient-bearer, and he had for his escutcheon a skull, and dead men's bones. (Jer. v. 16; ii. 25.)

9. The ninth captain was Captain Past-hope, he was captain of those that are called the Felicity-doubters; his ancient-bearer was Mr. Despair; his also were the red colours, and his escutcheon was the hot iron and the hard heart. (1 Tim. iv. 2. Rom. ii. 5.

These were his captains, and these were their forces, these were their ancients, these were their colours, and these were their escutcheons. Now, over these did the great Diabolus make superior captains, and they were in number seven, as, namely, the Lord Beelzebub, the Lord Lucifer, the Lord Legion, the Lord Apollyon, the Lord Python, the Lord Cerberus, and the Lord Belial; these seven he set over the captains, and Incredulity was lord-general, and Diabolus was king.

The Reformades also, such as were like themselves, were made some of them captains of hundreds, and some of them captains of more, and thus was the army of Incredulity completed.

So they set out at Hell-gate-hill, for there they had their rendezvous, from whence they came with a straight course upon their march toward the town of Mansoul. Now, as was hinted before, the town had, as Shaddai would have it, received from the mouth of Mr. Prywell the alarm of their coming before. Wherefore they set a strong watch at the gates, and had also doubled their guards, they also mounted their slings in good places, where they might conveniently cast out their great stones, to the annoyance of the furious enemy.

Nor could those Diabolonians that were in the town do that hurt as was designed they should, for Mansoul was now awake. But, alas! poor people, they were sorely affrighted at the first appearance of their foes, and at their sitting down before the town, especially when they heard the roaring of their DRUM. (1 Pet. v. 8.) This, to speak truth was amazingly hideous to hear; it frighted all men seven miles round, if they were but awake and heard it. The streaming of their colours were also terrible and dejecting to behold.

When Diabolus was come up against the town, first he made his approach to Ear-gate and gave it a furious assault, supposing, as it seems, that his friends in Mansoul had been ready to do the work within; but care was taken of that before, by the vigilance of the captains. Wherefore, missing of the help that he expected from them, and finding of his army warmly attended with the stones that the slingers did sling—for that I will say for the captains, that considering the weakness that yet was upon them, by reason of the long sickness that had annoyed the town of Mansoul, they did gallantly behave themselves—he was forced to make some retreat from Mansoul, and to intrench himself and his men in the field, without the reach of the slings of the town. (James iv. 7.)

He makes an assault upon Ear-gate, and is repelled.

He retreats and intrenches himself.

Now, having intrenched himself, he did cast up four mounts against the town, the first he called Mount Diabolus, putting his own name thereon, the more to affright the town of Mansoul; the other three he called thus, Mount Alecto, Mount Megæra, and Mount Tisiphone; for these are the names of the dreadful furies of hell. Thus he began to play his game with Mansoul, and to serve it as doth the lion his prey, even to make it fall before his terror. But, as I said, the captains and soldiers resisted so stoutly, and did so much execution with their stones, that they made him, though against stomach, to retreat, wherefore Mansoul began to take courage.

He casts up mounts against the town.

Now, upon Mount Diabolus, which was raised on the north side of the town, there did the tyrant set up his standard, and a fearful thing it was to behold, for he had wrought in it by devilish art, after the manner of an escutcheon, a flaming flame, fearful to behold, and the picture of Mansoul burning in it.

Diabolus, his standard set up.

When Diabolus had thus done, he commanded that his drummer should every night approach the walls of the town of Mansoul, and so to beat a parley, the command was to do it at a-nights, for in the day-time they annoyed him with their slings, for the tyrant said that he had a mind to parley with the now trembling town of Mansoul, and he commanded that the drum should beat every night, that through weariness they might at last—if possibly at the first they were unwilling, yet—be forced to do it.

So his drummer did as commanded; he arose and did beat his drum. But when his drum did go, if one looked towards the town of Mansoul, behold darkness and sorrow, and the light was darkened in the heaven thereof. No noise was ever heard upon earth more terrible, except the voice of Shaddai when he speaketh. But how did Mansoul tremble! It now looked for nothing but forthwith to be swallowed up. (Isa. v. 30.)

Mansoul trembles at the noise of his drum.

When this drummer had beaten for a parley, he

made this speech to Mansoul : " My master has bid me tell you, that if you willingly submit, you shall have the good of the earth, but if you shall be stubborn, he is resolved to take you by force." But by that the fugitive had done beating of his drum, the people of Mansoul had betaken themselves to the captains that were in the castle, so that there was none to regard, nor to give this drummer an answer, so he proceeded no further that night, but returned again to his master to the camp.

When Diabolus saw that by drumming he could not work out Mansoul to his will, the next night he sendeth his drummer without his drum, still to let the townsmen know, that he had a mind to parley with them. But when all came to all, his parley was turned into a summons to the town to deliver up themselves, but they gave him neither heed nor hearing, for they remembered what at first it cost them to hear him a few words.

The next night he sends again, and then who should be his messenger to Mansoul but the terrible Captain Sepulchre ; so Captain Sepulchre came up to the walls of Mansoul, and made this oration to the town—

" O ye inhabitants of the rebellious town of Mansoul ! I summon you, in the name of the Prince Diabolus, that without any more ado you set open the gates of your town, and admit the great Lord to come in. But if you shall still rebel, when we have taken to us the town by force, we will swallow you up as the grave ; wherefore if you will hearken to my summons, say so, and if not, then let me know.

Mansoul summoned by Captain Sepulchre.

" The reason of this my summons," quoth he, " is, for that my Lord is your undoubted prince and lord, as you yourselves have formerly owned. Nor shall that assault that was given to my Lord, when Emmanuel dealt so dishonourably by him, prevail with him to lose his right, and to forbear to attempt to recover his own. Consider then, O Mansoul, with thyself, wilt thou show thyself peaceable or no ? If thou shalt quietly yield up thyself, then our old friendship shall be renewed, but if thou shalt yet refuse and rebel, then expect nothing but fire and sword."

When the languishing town of Mansoul had heard this summoner and his summons, they were yet more put to their dumps, but made to the captain no answer at all, so away he went as he came.

But after some consultation among themselves, as also with some of their captains, they applied themselves afresh to the Lord Secretary for counsel and advice from him, for this Lord Secretary was their chief preacher, as also is mentioned some pages before, only now he was ill at ease, and of him they begged favour in these two or three things—

They address themselves to their good Lord Secretary.

1. That he would look comfortably upon them, and not to keep himself so much retired from them as formerly. Also that he would be prevailed with to give them a hearing, while they should make known their miserable condition to him. But to this he told them as before, that as yet he was but ill at ease, and therefore could not do as he had formerly done.

2. The second thing that they desired was, that he would be pleased to give them his advice about their now so important affairs, for that Diabolus was come and set down before the town with no less than twenty thousand Doubters. They said, moreover, that both he and his captains were cruel men, and that they were afraid of them. But to this he said, " You must look to the law of the Prince, and there see what is laid upon you to do."

3. Then they desired that his Highness would help them to frame a petition to Shaddai, and unto Emmanuel his Son, and that he would set his own hand thereto, as a token that he was one with them in it ; " for," said they, " my lord, many a one have we sent, but can get no answer of peace, but now, surely one with thy hand unto it may obtain good for Mansoul."

But all the answer that he gave to this was that they had offended their Emmanuel, and had also grieved himself, and that therefore they must as yet partake of their own devices.

The cause of his being ill at ease.

This answer of the Lord Secretary fell like a millstone upon them, yea, it crushed them so that they could not tell what to do, yet they durst not comply with the demands of Diabolus, nor with the demands of his captain. So then, here were the straits that the town of Mansoul was betwixt when the enemy came upon her, her foes were ready to swallow her up, and her friends did forbear to help her. (Lam. i. 3.)

The sad straits of Mansoul.

Then stood up my Lord Mayor, whose name was my Lord Understanding, and he began to pick and pick, until he had picked comfort out of that seemingly bitter saying of the Lord Secretary, for thus he descanted upon it : First, said he, this unavoidably follows upon the saying of our Lord that we must yet suffer for our sins. Second. But, quoth he, the words yet sound as if at last we should be saved from our enemies, and that after a few more sorrows Emmanuel will come and be our help. Now the Lord Mayor was the more critical in his dealing with the Secretary's words, because my Lord was more than a prophet, and because none of his words were such but that at all times they were most exactly significant, and the townsmen were allowed to pry into them, and to expound them to their best advantage.

A comment upon the Lord Secretary's speech.

So they took their leaves of my Lord, and returned, and went, and came to the captains, to whom they did tell what my Lord High Secretary had said, who, when they had heard it, were all of the same opinion as was my Lord Mayor himself; the captains therefore began to take some courage unto them, and to prepare to make some brave attempt upon the camp of the enemy, and to destroy all that were Diabolonians, with the roving Doubters that the tyrant had brought with him to destroy the poor town of Mansoul.

So all betook themselves forthwith to their places, the captains to theirs, the *The town of Mansoul in order.* Lord Mayor to his, the subordinate Preacher to his, and my Lord Will-be-will to his. The captains longed to be at some work for their Prince, for they delighted in warlike achievements. The next day, therefore, they came together and consulted, and, after consultation had, they resolved to give an answer to the captain of Diabolus with slings, and so they did at the rising of the sun on the morrow; for Diabolus had adventured to come nearer again, but the sling-stones were, to him and his, like hornets. (Zech. ix. 15.) For as there is nothing to the town of Mansoul so terrible as the roaring of Diabolus's drum, so there is nothing to Diabolus so terrible *Words applied against him by faith.* as the well playing of Emmanuel's slings. Wherefore Diabolus was forced to make another retreat, yet further off from the famous town of Mansoul. Then did the Lord Mayor of Mansoul cause the bells to be rung, and that thanks should be sent to the Lord High Secretary by the mouth of the subordinate Preacher; for that by his words the captains and elders of Mansoul had been strengthened against Diabolus.

When Diabolus saw that his captains and soldiers, high lords, and renowned, were frightened, and beaten down by the stones that came from the golden slings of the Prince of the town of Mansoul, he bethought himself, and said, I will try to catch them by fawning, I will try to flatter them into my net. (Rev. xii. 10.)

Wherefore after a while he came down again to *Diabolus changes his way.* the wall, not now with his drum, nor with Captain Sepulchre, but having so all-besugared his lips, he seemed to be a very sweet-mouthed, peaceable prince, designing nothing for humour sake, nor to be revenged on Mansoul for injuries by them done to him, but the welfare, and good, and advantage of the town and people therein, was now, as he said, his only design. Wherefore, after he had called for audience, and desired that the townsfolk would give it to him, he proceeded in his oration, and said :—

"Oh! the desire of my heart, the famous town of Mansoul! How many nights have I watched, and how many weary steps have I taken, if, perhaps, I might do thee good. (1 Pet. v. 8.) Far be it, far be it from me, to desire to make a war upon you, if ye will but willingly and quietly deliver up yourselves unto me. You know that you were mine of old (Matt. iv. 8, 9 ; Luke iv. 6, 7.) Remember, also, that so long as you enjoyed me for your lord, and that I enjoyed you for my subjects, you wanted for nothing of all the delights of the earth, that I, your lord and prince, could get for you ; or that I could invent to make you bonny and blithe withal. Consider, you never had so many hard, dark, troublesome, and heart-afflicting hours, while you were mine, as you have had since you revolted from me ; nor shall you ever have peace again until you and I become one as before. Be but prevailed with to embrace me again, and I will grant, yea, enlarge your old charter with abundance of privileges ; so that your licence and liberty shall be to take, hold, enjoy, and make your own, all that is pleasant from the east to the west. Nor shall any of those incivilities wherewith you have offended me, be ever charged upon you by me, so long as the sun and moon endureth. Nor shall any of those dear friends of mine, that now, for the fear of you, lie lurking in dens, and holes, and caves in Mansoul, be hurtful to you any more ; yea, they shall be your servants, and shall minister unto you of their substance, and of whatever shall come to hand. I need speak no more, you know them, and have some time since been much delighted in their company, why then should we abide at such odds ? Let us renew our old acquaintance and friendship again.

"Bear with your friend ; I take the liberty at this time to speak thus freely unto you. The love that I have to you presses me to do it, as also does the zeal of my heart for my friends with you ; put me not therefore to further trouble, nor yourselves to further fears and frights. Have you I will, in a way of peace or war ; nor do you flatter yourselves with the power and force of your captains, or that your Emmanuel will shortly come in to your help, for such strength will do you no pleasure.

"I am come against you with a stout and valiant army, and all the chief princes of the den are even at the head of it. Besides, my captains are swifter than eagles, stronger than lions, and more greedy of prey than are the evening-wolves. What is Og of Bashan ! What is Goliah of Gath ! And what is a hundred more of them to one of the least of my captains ! How then shall Mansoul think to escape my hand and force ?"

Diabolus having thus ended his flattering, fawning, deceitful, and lying speech to the famous town of Mansoul, the Lord Mayor replied upon him as follows :—

"O Diabolus, prince of darkness, and master of all deceit ; thy lying flatteries we *The Lord Mayor's answer.* have had and made sufficient probation of, and have tasted too deeply of that destructive cup already ; should we therefore again hearken unto thee, and so break the commandments of our great Shaddai, to join in affinity with thee ; would not our Prince reject us, and cast us off for ever ; and being cast off by him, can the place that he has prepared for thee, be a place of rest for us ; Beside, O thou that art empty and void of all truth, we are rather ready to die by the hand, than to fall in with thy flattering and lying deceits."

When the tyrant saw that there was little to be got by parleying with my Lord Mayor, he fell into a hellish rage, and resolved that again, with his army of Doubters, he would another time assault the town of Mansoul.

So he called for his drummer, who beat up for his men (and while he did beat, Mansoul did shake), to be in a readiness to give battle to the corporation; then Diabolus drew near with his army, and thus disposed of his men. Captain Cruel, and Captain Torment, these he drew up and placed against Feel-gate, and commanded them to sit down there for the war. And he also appointed that if need were, Captain No-ease should come in to their relief.

At Nose-gate he placed the Captain Brimstone and Captain Sepulchre, and bid them look well to their ward, on that side of the town of Mansoul. But at Eye-gate he placed that grim-faced one, the Captain Past-hope, and there also now he did set up his terrible standard.

Now Captain Insatiable was to look to the carriage of Diabolus, and was also appointed to take into custody, that, or those persons, and things, that should at any time as prey be taken from the enemy.

Now Mouth-gate the inhabitants of Mansoul kept for a sally-port, wherefore that they kept strong, for that was it, by, and out of which the towns-folk did send their petitions to Emmanuel their Prince; that also was the gate from the top of which the captains did play their slings at the enemies, for that gate stood somewhat ascending, so that the placing of them there, and the letting of them fly from that place, did much execution The use of against the tyrant's army; wherefore Mouth-gate. for these causes, with others, Diabolus sought, if possible, to stop up Mouth-gate with dirt.

Now as Diabolus was busy and industrious in preparing to make his assault upon the town of Mansoul without, so the captains and soldiers in the corporation were as busy in preparing within; they mounted their slings, they set up their banners, they sounded their trumpets, and put themselves in such order as was judged most for the annoyance of the enemy and for the advantage of Mansoul, and gave to their soldiers orders to be ready at the sound of the trumpet for war. The The Lord Will- Lord Will-be-will also, he took the be-will plays charge of watching against the the man. rebels within, and to do what he could to take them while without, or to stifle them within their caves, dens, and holes, in the townwall of Mansoul. And to speak the truth of him, ever since he did penance for his fault, he has showed as much honesty and bravery of spirit as Jolly and any in Mansoul; for he took one Griggish taken Jolly, and his brother Griggish, the and executed. two sons of his servant Harmlessmirth, for to that day, though the father was

committed to ward, the sons had a dwelling in the house of my lord. I say he took them, and with his own hands put them to the cross. And this was the reason why he hanged them up, after their father was put into the hands of Mr. Trueman, the jailer; they, his sons, began to play his pranks, and to be ticking and toying with the daughters of their lord; nay, it was jealoused that they were too familiar with them, the which was brought to his lordship's ear. Now, his lordship, being unwilling unadvisedly to put any man to death, did not suddenly fall upon them, but set watch and spies to see if the thing was true; of the which he was soon informed, for his two servants, whose names were Find-out and Tell-all, catched them together in uncivil manner more than once or twice, and went and told their lord. So when my Lord Will-be-will had sufficient ground to believe the thing was true, he takes the two young Diabolonians, for such they were, for their father was a Diabolonian born, and has them to Eye-gate, where he raised a very high cross just in the face of Diabolus, The place of and of his army, and there he their execution. hanged the young villains in defiance to Captain Past-hope, and of the horrible standard of the tyrant.

Now this Christian act of the brave Lord Will-be-will did greatly abash Captain Past-hope, discourage the army of Diabolus, put fear into the Diabolonian runagates in Mansoul, and put strength and courage into the captains that belonged to Emmanuel the prince; Mortification of for they without did gather, and sin is a sign of that, by this very act of my lord, hope of life. that Mansoul was resolved to fight, and that the Diabolonians within the town could not do such things as Diabolus had hopes they would. Nor was this the only proof of the brave Lord Will-be-will's honesty to the town, nor of his loyalty to his Prince, as will afterwards appear.

Now when the children of Prudent-thrifty, who dwelt with Mr. Mind—for Thrift left children with Mr. Mind, when he was also com- Mr. Mind plays mitted to prison, and their names the man. were Gripe and Rake-all; these he begat of Mr. Mind's bastard-daughter, whose name was Mrs. Hold-fast-bad—I say, when his children perceived how the Lord Will-be-will had served them that dwelt with him, what do they but, lest they should drink of the same cup, endeavour to make their escape? But Mr. Mind being wary of it, took them and put them in hold in his house till morning, for this was done over night, and remembering that by the law of Mansoul, all Diabolonians were to die, (and to be sure they were at least by father's side such, and some say by mother's side too,) what does he but takes them and puts them in chains, and carries them to the self-same place where my lord hanged his two before, and there he hanged them.

The townsmen also took great encouragement

at this act of Mr. Mind, and did what they could to have taken some more of these Diabolonian troublers of Mansoul; but at that time the rest lay so close that they could not be apprehended; so they set against them a diligent watch, and went every man to his place.

Mansoul set against the Diabolonians.

I told you a little before that Diabolus and his army were somewhat abashed and discouraged at the sight of what my Lord Will-be-will did, when he hanged up those two young Diabolonians; but his discouragement quickly turned itself into furious madness and rage against the town of Mansoul, and fight it he would. Also the townsmen, and captains within, they had their hopes and their expectations heightened, believing at last the day would be theirs, so they feared them the less. Their subordinate Preacher too made a sermon about it, and he took that theme for his text, "Gad, a troop shall overcome him; but he shall overcome at the last." (Gen. xlix. 19.) Whence he showed that though Mansoul should be sorely put to it at the first, yet the victory should most certainly be Mansoul's at the last.

So Diabolus commanded that his drummer should beat a charge against the town, and the captains also that were in the town sounded a charge against them; but they had no drum, they were trumpets of silver with which they sounded against them. Then they which were of the camp of Diabolus came down to the town to take it, and the captains in the castle, with the slingers at Mouth-gate, played upon them amain. And now there was nothing heard in the camp of Diabolus but horrible rage and blasphemy; but in the town good words, prayer, and singing of psalms. The enemy replied with horrible objections, and the terribleness of their drum; but the town made answer with the slapping of their slings, and the melodious noise of their trumpets. And thus the fight lasted for several days together, only now and then they had some small intermission, in the which the townsmen refreshed themselves, and the captains made ready for another assault.

With heart and mouth.

The captains of Emmanuel were clad in silver armour, and the soldiers in that which was of proof; the soldiers of Diabolus were clad in iron, which was made to give place to Emmanuel's engine-shot. In the town some were hurt, and some were greatly wounded. Now the worst on it was, a surgeon was scarce in Mansoul, for that Emmanuel at present was absent. Howbeit, with the leaves of a tree the wounded were kept from dying; yet their wounds did greatly putrify, and some did grievously stink. (Rev. xxii. 2; Psalm xxxviii. 5.) Of these were wounded, to wit,

My Lord Reason, he was wounded in the head. Another that was wounded was the brave Lord Mayor, he was wounded in the eye.

Who of Mansoul were wounded.

Another that was wounded was Mr. Mind, he received his wound about the stomach.

The honest subordinate Preacher also, he received a shot not far off the heart, but none of these were mortal.

Many also of the inferior sort were not only wounded, but slain outright.

Now in the camp of Diabolus were wounded and slain a considerable number. For instance:

Hopeful thoughts.

Captain Rage, he was wounded, and so was Captain Cruel.

Captain Damnation was made to retreat and to intrench himself further off of Mansoul; the standard also of Diabolus was beaten down, and his standard-bearer, Captain Much-hurt, had his brains beat out with a sling-stone, to the no little grief and shame of his prince Diabolus.

Who in the camp of Diabolus were wounded and slain.

Many also of the Doubters were slain outright, though enough of them are left alive to make Mansoul shake and totter. Now the victory that day being turned to Mansoul, did put great valour into townsmen and captains, and did cover Diabolus's camp with a cloud, but withal it made them far more furious. So the next day Mansoul rested, and commanded that the bells should be rung; the trumpets also joyfully sounded, and the captains shouted round the town

The victory did turn that day to Mansoul.

My Lord Will-be-will also was not idle, but did notable service within against the domestics of the Diabolonians that were in the town, not only by keeping of them in awe, for he lighted on one at last whose name was Mr. Anything, a fellow of whom mention was made before; for it was he, if you remember, that

My Lord Will-be-will taketh one Anything, and one Loosefoot, and committeth them to ward.

brought the three fellows to Diabolus whom the Diabolonians took out of Captain Boanerges' company ; and that persuaded them to list themselves under the tyrant, to fight against the army of Shaddai ; my Lord Will-be-will did also take a notable Diabolonian, whose name was Loose-foot ; this Loose-foot was a scout to the vagabonds in Mansoul, and that did use to carry tidings out of Mansoul to the camp, and out of the camp to those of the enemies in Mansoul ; both these my lord sent away safe to Mr. Trueman the jailer, with a commandment to keep them in irons ; for he intended then to have them out to be crucified, when it would be for the best to the corporation, and most for the discouragement of the camp of the enemies.

My Lord Mayor also, though he could not stir The captains consult to fall upon the enemy. about so much as formerly, because of the wound that he lately received, yet gave he out orders to all that were the natives of Mansoul to look to their watch, and stand upon their guard, and, as occasion should offer, to prove themselves men.

Mr. Conscience, the preacher, he also did his utmost to keep all his good documents alive upon the hearts of the people of Mansoul.

Well, awhile after, the captains and stout ones of the town of Mansoul agreed and resolved upon a time to make a sally out upon the camp of Diabolus, and this must be done in the night, and there was the folly of Mansoul, for the night is always the best for the enemy, but the worst for Mansoul to fight in ; but yet they would do it, their courage was so high ; their last victory also still stuck in their memories.

So the night appointed being come, the Prince's They fight in the night, who do lead the van. brave captains cast lots who should lead the van in this new and desperate expedition against Diabolus, and against his Diabolonian army, and the lot fell to Captain Credence, to Captain Experience, and to Captain Good-hope to lead the forlorn hope. This Captain Experience the Prince created such when himself did reside in the town of Mansoul ; How they fall on. so, as I said, they made their sally out upon the army that lay in the siege against them ; and their hap was to fall in with the main body of their enemies. Now Diabolus and his men being expertly accustomed to night work, took the alarm presently, and were as ready to give them battle, as if they had sent them word of their coming. Wherefore to it they went amain, and blows were hard on every side ; the hell-drum also was beat most furiously, while the trumpets of the Prince most sweetly sounded. And thus the battle was joined, and Captain Insatiable looked to the enemies' carriages, and waited when he should receive some prey.

The Prince's captains fought it stoutly, beyond They fight bravely. what indeed could be expected they should ; they wounded many ; they made the whole army of Diabolus to make a retreat. But I cannot tell how, but the brave Captain Credence, Captain Good-hope, and Captain Experience, as they were upon the pursuit, cutting down, and following hard after the enemy in the rear, Captain Credence stumbled Captain Credence hurt. and fell, by which fall he caught so great a hurt that he could not rise till Captain Experience did help him up, at which their men were put in disorder ; the captain also was so full of pain that he could not forbear The rest of the captains faint. FAITH ESSENTIAL. but aloud to cry out ; at this the other two captains fainted, supposing that Captain Credence had received his mortal wound : their men also were more disordered, and had no list to fight. Now Diabolus being very observing though at this time as yet he was put to the worst, perceiving that a halt was made among the men that were the pursuers, what does he but taking it for granted that the cap- Diabolus takes courage. tains were either wounded or dead ; he therefore makes at first a stand, then faces about, and so comes up upon the Prince's army with as much of his fury as hell could help him to, and his hap was to fall in just among the three captains, Captain Credence, Captain Good-hope, and Captain Experience, and did cut, wound, and pierce them so dreadfully, that The Prince's forces beaten. what through discouragement, what through disorder, and what through the wounds that now they had received, and also the loss of much blood, they scarce were able, though they had for their power the three best bands in Mansoul, to get safe into the hold again.

Now, when the body of the Prince's army saw how these three captains were put Satan sometimes makes saints eat their own words. to the worst, they thought it their wisdom to make as safe and good a retreat as they could, and so returned by the sally-port again, and so there was an end of this present action. Diabolus flushed. But Diabolus was so flushed with this night's work that he promised himself, in few days, an easy and complete conquest over the town of Mansoul ; wherefore, on the day He demands the town. following, he comes up to the sides thereof with great boldness, and demands entrance, and that forthwith they deliver themselves up to his government. The Diabolonians, too, that were within, they began to be somewhat brisk, as we shall show afterward.

But the valiant Lord Mayor replied, that what he got he must get by force, for as The Lord Mayor's answer. long as Emmanuel their Prince was alive, though he at present was not so with them as they wished, they should never consent to yield Mansoul up to another.

And with that the Lord Will-be-will stood up and said, " Diabolus, thou master of Brave Will-be-will's speech. the den, and enemy to all that is good, we, poor inhabitants of the town of Mansoul, are too well acquainted with thy rule and government, and with the end of those things that for certain will follow submitting to thee, to do it.

Wherefore, though while we were without know-ledge we suffered thee to take us, as the bird that saw not the snare fell into the hands of the fowler, yet, since we have been turned from darkness to light, we have also been turned from the power of Satan to God. And though, through thy subtilty, and also the subtilty of the Diabolonians within, we have sustained much loss, and also plunged ourselves into much perplexity, yet give up our-selves, lay down our arms, and yield to so horrid a tyrant as thou, we shall not: die upon the place we choose rather to do. Besides, we have hopes that in time deliverance will come from court unto us, and therefore we yet will maintain a war against thee."

This brave speech of the Lord Will-be-will, *The captains encouraged.* with that also of the Lord Mayor, did somewhat abate the boldness of Diabolus, though it kindled the fury of his rage. It also succoured the townsmen and captains, yea, it was as a plaster to the brave Captain Credence's wound; for you must know that a brave speech now, when the captains of the town came home routed, and when the enemy took courage and boldness at the success that he had obtained, to draw up to the walls and demand entrance as he did, was in season, and also advantageous.

The Lord Will-be-will also did play the man within, for while the captains and soldiers were in the field, he was in arms in the town, and wherever by him there was a Diabolonian found, they were forced to feel the weight of his heavy hand, and also the edge of his penetrating sword; many therefore of the Diabolonians he wounded, as the Lord Cavil, the Lord Brisk, the Lord Pragmatic, and the Lord Murmur; several also of the meaner sort he did sorely maim, though there cannot at this time an account be given you of any that he slew outright. The cause, or rather the advantage, that my Lord Will-be-will had at this time to do thus, was, for that the captains were gone out to fight the enemy in the field. For now, thought the Diabolonians within, is our time to stir and make an uproar in the town; what do they there-fore but quickly get themselves into a body, and fall forthwith to hurricaning in Mansoul, as if now nothing but whirlwind and tempest should be there; wherefore, as I said, he takes this opportunity *Will-be-will's gallantry.* to fall in among them with his men, cutting and slashing with courage that was undaunted, at which the Diabolonians, with all haste, dispersed themselves to their holds, and my lord to his place as before.

This brave act of my lord did somewhat revenge the wrong done by Diabolus to the captains, and *Nothing like faith to crush Diabolus.* also did let them know that Mansoul was not to be parted with for the loss of a victory or two; wherefore the wing of the tyrant was clipped again—as to boast-ing, I mean—in comparison of what he would have done, if the Diabolonians had put the town to the same plight to which he had put the captains.

Well, Diabolus yet resolves to have the other bout with Mansoul; for, thought he, since I beat them once, I may beat them twice; wherefore he commanded his men to be ready at *He tries what he can do upon the sense and feeling of the Christian.* such an hour of the night, to make a fresh assault upon the town, and he it gave out in special that they should bend all their force against Feel-gate, and attempt to break into the town through that; the word that then he did give to his officers and soldiers was "*Hell-fire.*" "And," said he, "if we break in upon them, as I wish we do, either with some or with all our force, let them that break in look to it, that they forget not the word. And let nothing be heard in the town of Mansoul but Hell-fire, Hell-fire, Hell-fire!" The drummer was also to beat without ceasing, and the standard-bearers were to display their colours, the soldiers too were to put on what courage they could, and to see that they played manfully their parts against the town.

So the night was come, and all things by the tyrant made ready for the work; he suddenly makes his assault upon Feel-gate, and after he had a while struggled there, he throws the gates wide open. For the truth is, those gates were but weak, and so most easily made to yield. When Diabolus had thus far made his attempt, he placed his captains, to wit, Torment and No-ease there, so he attempted to press forward, but the Prince's captains came down upon him, and made his entrance more difficult than he desired. And, to speak the truth, they made what resistance they could, but the three of their best and most valiant captains being wounded, and by their wounds made much incapable of doing the town that service they would, and all the rest having more than their hands full of the Doubters, and their captains that did follow Diabolus, they were overpowered with force, nor could they keep him out of the town. Wherefore the Prince's men and their captains betook themselves to the castle, as to the strong-hold of the town, and this they did partly for their own security, partly for the security of the town, and partly, or rather chiefly, to preserve to Em-manuel the prerogative-royal of Mansoul, for so was the castle of Mansoul.

The captains, therefore, being fled into the castle, the enemy, without much resistance, possess them-selves of the rest of the town, and spreading themselves as they went into every corner, they cried out as they marched, according to the com-mand of the tyrant, "Hell-fire, Hell-fire, Hell-fire!" so that nothing for a while throughout the town of Mansoul could be heard but the direful noise of "Hell-fire," together with the roaring of Diabolus's drum. And now did the clouds hang *The sad fruits of apostacy.* black over Mansoul, nor to reason did anything but ruin seem to attend it. Diabolus also quartered his soldiers in the houses of the inhabitants of the town of Mansoul. Yea, the subordinate Preacher's house was as full of these outlandish Doubters as ever it could hold; and so was my Lord Mayor's, and my Lord Will-be-will's also. Yea, where was there a corner, a cottage, a barn, or a hog-stye, that now were not full of these vermin? yea, they turned the men of the town out of their houses, and would lie in their beds, and sit at their tables themselves. Ah, poor Mansoul! Now thou feelest the fruits of sin, and what venom was in the flattering words of Mr. Carnal-security! They made great havoc of whatever they laid their hands on; yea, they fired the town in several places, many young children also were by them dashed in pieces, yea, those that were yet unborn they destroyed in their mothers' wombs; for you must needs think that it could not now be otherwise; for what conscience, what pity, what bowels of compassion can any expect at the hands of outlandish Doubters? many in Mansoul that were women, both young and old, they forced, ravished, and beast-like abused, so that they swooned, miscarried, and many of them died, and so lay at the top of every street, and in all by-places of the town.

And now did Mansoul seem to be nothing but a den of dragons, an emblem of hell, and a place of total darkness. Now did Mansoul lie almost like the barren wilderness, nothing but nettles, briers, thorns, weeds, and stinking things, seemed now to cover the face of Mansoul. I told you before how that these Diabolonian Doubters turned the men of Mansoul out of their beds; and now I will add, they wounded them, they mauled them, yea, and almost brained many of them. Many, did I say, yea, most, if not all of them; Mr. Conscience they so wounded, yea, and his wounds so festered, that Sad work among he could have no ease day nor night, the townsmen. but lay as if continually upon a rack: but that Shaddai rules all, certainly they had slain him outright. My Lord Mayor they so abused that they almost put out his eyes, and had not my Lord Will-be-will got into the castle, they intended to have chopped him all to pieces, for they did look upon him, as his heart now stood, to be one of Satan has a par- the very worst that was in Mansoul ticular spite against a sancti- against Diabolus and his crew. And, fied will. indeed, he hath showed himself a man, and more of his exploits you will hear of afterwards.

Now a man might have walked for days together in Mansoul, and scarce have seen one in the town that looked like a religious man. Oh the fearful state of Mansoul now! Now every corner swarmed with outlandish Doubters; red-coats and The soul full of black-coats walked the town by idle thoughts clusters, and filled up all the houses and blasphemies. with hideous noises, vain songs, lying stories, and blasphemous language against Shaddai and his Son. Now, also, those Diabolonians that lurked in the walls, and dens, and holes that were in the town of Mansoul, came forth and showed themselves, yea, walked with open face in company with the Doubters that were in Mansoul. Yea, they had more boldness now to walk the streets, to haunt the houses, and to show themselves abroad, than had any of the honest inhabitants of the now woful town of Mansoul.

But Diabolus and his outlandish men were not at peace in Mansoul, for they were not there entertained as were the captains and forces of Emmanuel; the townsmen did browbeat them what they could; nor did they partake or make destruction of any of the necessaries of Mansoul, but that which they seized on against the townsmen's will; what they could they hid from them, and what they could not they had with an ill-will. They, poor hearts, had rather have had their room than their company, but they were at present their captives, and their captives for the present they were forced to be. (Rom. vii.) But, I say, they discountenanced them as much as they were able, and showed them all the dislike that they could.

The captains also from the castle did hold them in continual play with their slings, to the chasing and fretting of the minds of the enemies. True, Diabolus made a great many at- Mr. Godly-fear tempts to have broken open the is made gates of the castle, but Mr. Godly- keeper of the castle gates. fear was made the keeper of that; and he was a man of that courage, conduct, and valour, that it was in vain, as long as life lasted within him, to think to do that work, though mostly desired, wherefore all the attempts that Diabolus made against him were fruitless. I have wished sometimes that that man had had the whole rule of the town of Mansoul.

Well, this was the condition of the town of Mansoul for about two years and a half; the body of the town was the seat of war; The town of the people of the town were driven Mansoul the into holes. and the glory of Man- seat of war. soul was laid in the dust; what rest then could be to the inhabitants, what peace could Mansoul have, and what sun could shine upon it? Had the enemy lain so long without in the plain against the town, it had been enough to have famished them; but now when they shall be within, when the town shall be their tent, their trench, and fort against the castle that was in the town, when the town shall be against the town, and shall serve to be a defence to the enemies of her strength and life; I say, when they shall make use of the forts and town-holds to secure themselves in, even till they shall take, spoil, and demolish Heart. the castle, this was terrible; and yet this was now the state of the town of Mansoul.

After the town of Mansoul had been in this sad and lamentable condition for so long a time as I have told you, and no petitions that they presented their Prince with all this while could prevail, the inhabitants of the town, to wit, the elders and chief of Mansoul gathered together, and after some time spent in condoling their miserable state, and this miserable judgment coming upon them, they agreed together to draw up yet another petition, and to send it away to Emmanuel for relief. But Mr. Godly-fear stood up and answered, that he knew that his Lord the Prince never did, nor ever would receive a petition for these matters from the hand of any whoever, unless the Lord Secretary's hand was to it; and this, quoth he, is the reason that you prevailed not all this while. Then they said, they would draw up one, and get the Lord Secretary's hand to it. But Mr. Godly-fear answered again, that he knew also that the Lord Secretary would not set his hand to any petition that himself had not a hand in composing and drawing up; and besides, said he, the Prince doth know my Lord Secretary's hand from all the hands in the world, wherefore he cannot be deceived by any pretence whatever; wherefore my advice is, that you go to my Lord, and implore him to lend you his aid. Now he did yet abide in the castle where all the captains and men-at-arms were.

Mr. Godly-fear's advice about drawing up of a petition to the Prince.

So they heartily thanked Mr. Godly-fear, took his counsel, and did as he had bidden them; so they went and came to my Lord, and made known the cause of their coming to him, to wit, that since Mansoul was in so deplorable a condition, his highness would be pleased to undertake to draw up a petition for them to Emmanuel, the Son of the mighty Shaddai, and to their King and his Father by him.

Then said the Secretary to them, " What petition is it that you would have me draw up for you ?" But they said, " Our Lord knows best the state and condition of the town of Mansoul, and how we are backslidden and degenerated from the Prince; thou also knowest who is come up to war against us, and how Mansoul is now the seat of war. My Lord knows, moreover, what barbarous usages our men, women, and children have suffered at their hands, and how our home-bred Diabolonians do walk now with more boldness than dare the townsmen in the streets of Mansoul. Let our Lord, therefore, according to the wisdom of God that is in him, draw up a petition for his poor servants to our Prince Emmanuel." " Well," said the Lord Secretary, " I will draw up a petition for you, and will also set my hand thereto." Then said they, " But when shall we call for it at the hands of our Lord ?" But he answered, " Yourselves must be present at the doing of it. Yea, you must put your desires to it. True, the hand and pen shall be mine, but the ink and paper must be yours, else how can you say it is your petition ? nor have I need to petition for myself, because I have not offended."

The Secretary employed to draw up a petition for Mansoul.

He also added as followeth : " No petition goes from me in my name to the Prince, and so to his Father by him, but when the people that are chiefly concerned therein do join in heart and soul in the matter, for that must be inserted therein."

So they did heartily agree with the sentence of the Lord, and a petition was forthwith drawn up for them. But now who should carry it ? that was the next. But the Secretary advised that Captain Credence should carry it, for he was a well-spoken man. They therefore called for him, and propounded to him the business. " Well," said the captain, " I gladly accept of the motion; and though I am lame, I will do this business for you with as much speed, and as well as I can."

The contents of the petition were to this purpose :—

" O our Lord and Sovereign Prince Emmanuel, the potent, the long-suffering Prince; grace is poured into thy lips, and to thee belongs mercy and forgiveness, though we have rebelled against thee. We who are no more worthy to be called thy Mansoul, nor yet fit to partake of common benefits, do beseech thee, and thy Father by thee, to do away our transgressions. We confess that thou mightest cast us away for them, but do it not for thy name's sake ; let the Lord rather take an opportunity, at our miserable condition, to let out his bowels and compassions to us; we are compassed on every side, Lord, our own backslidings reprove us; our Diabolonians within our town fright us, and the army of the angel of the bottomless pit distresses us. Thy grace can be our salvation, and whither to go but to thee we know not.

The petition.

" Furthermore, O gracious Prince, we have weakened our captains, and they are discouraged, sick, and, of late, some of them grievously worsted and beaten out of the field by the power and force of the tyrant. Yea, even those of our captains in whose valour we did formerly use to put most of our confidence, they are as wounded men. Besides, Lord, our enemies are lively, and they are strong, they vaunt and boast themselves, and do threaten to part us among themselves for a booty. They are fallen also upon us, Lord, with many thousand Doubters, such as with whom we cannot tell what to do ; they are all grim-looked, and unmerciful ones, and they bid defiance to us and thee.

" Our wisdom is gone, our power is gone, because thou art departed from us, nor have we what we may call ours but sin, shame, and confusion of face for sin. Take pity upon us, O Lord, take pity upon us, thy miserable town of Mansoul, and save us out of the hands of our enemies. Amen."

This petition, as was touched afore, was handed by the Lord Secretary, and carried to the court by the brave and most stout Captain Credence. Now he carried it out at Mouth-gate, for that, as I said, was the sally-port of the town ; and he went and came to Emmanuel with it. Now how it came out, I do not know, but for certain it did, and that so far as to reach the ears of Diabolus. Thus I conclude, because that the tyrant had it presently by the end, and charged the town of Mansoul with it, saying, "Thou rebellious and stubborn-hearted *Satan cannot abide prayer.* Mansoul, I will make thee to leave off petitioning; art thou yet for petitioning? I will make thee to leave off." Yea, he also knew who the messenger was that carried the petition to the Prince, and it made him both to fear and rage.

Wherefore he commanded that his drum should be beat again, a thing that Mansoul could not abide to hear; but when Diabolus will have his drum beat, Mansoul must abide the noise. Well, the drum was beat, and the Diabolonians were gathered together.

Then said Diabolus, "O ye stout Diabolonians, be it known unto you that there is treachery hatched against us in the rebellious town of Mansoul; for albeit the town is in our possession, as you see, yet these miserable Mansoulians have attempted to dare, and have been so hardy as yet to send to the court of Emmanuel for help. This I give you to understand, that ye may yet know how to carry it to the wretched town of Mansoul. Wherefore, O my trusty Diabolonians, I command that yet more and more ye distress this town of Mansoul, and vex it with your wiles, ravish their women, deflower their virgins, slay their children, brain their ancients, fire their town, and what other mischief you can; and let this be the reward of the Mansoulians from me, for their desperate rebellions against me."

This you see was the charge, but something stepped in betwixt that and execution, for as yet there was but little more done than to rage.

Moreover, when Diabolus had done thus, he went the next way up to the castle-gates, and demanded that, upon pain of death, the gates should be opened to him, and that entrance should be given him and his men that followed after. To whom Mr. Godly-fear replied—for he it was that had the charge of that gate—that the gate should not be opened unto him, nor to the men that followed after him. He said, moreover, that Mansoul, when she had suffered awhile, should be made perfect, strengthened, settled. (1 Pet. v. 10.)

Then said Diabolus, "Deliver me then the men *Satan cannot abide faith.* that have petitioned against me, especially Captain Credence that carried it to your Prince; deliver that varlet into my hands, and I will depart from the town."

Then up starts a Diabolonian, whose name was *Mr. Fooling.* Mr. Fooling, and said, "My lord offereth you fair; it is better for you that one man perish, than that your whole Mansoul should be undone."

But Mr. Godly-fear made him this replication, "How long will Mansoul be kept out of the dungeon when she hath given up her faith to Diabolus? As good lose the town as lose Captain Credence; for if one be gone, the other must follow." But to that Mr. Fooling said nothing.

Then did my Lord Mayor reply, and said, "O thou devouring tyrant, be it known unto thee, we shall hearken to none of thy words; we are resolved to resist thee as long as a captain, a man, a sling, and a stone to throw at thee, shall be found in the town of Mansoul." But Diabolus answered, "Do you hope, do you wait, do you *Diabolus rages.* look for help and deliverance? You have sent to Emmanuel, but your wickedness sticks too close in your skirts to let innocent prayers come out of your lips. Think you that you shall be prevailers and prosper in this design? You will fail in your wish. You will fail in your attempts; for is it not only I, but your Emmanuel is against you. (Ps. xlii. 10.) Yea, it is he that hath sent me against you to subdue you; for what then do you hope, or by what means will you escape?"

Then said the Lord Mayor, "We have sinned indeed, but that shall be no help to *The Lord Mayor's speech just at the time of the return of Captain Credence.* thee, for our Emmanuel has said it, and that in great faithfulness: 'And him that cometh to me I will in no wise cast out.' He hath also told us, O our enemy, that all manner of sin and blasphemy shall be forgiven to the sons of men. Therefore we dare not despair, but will look for, wait for, and hope for deliverance still."

Now by this time Captain Credence was returned and come from the court from Emmanuel to the castle of Mansoul, and he returned to them with a packet. So my Lord Mayor hearing that Captain Credence was come, withdrew himself from the noise of the roaring of the tyrant, and left him to yell at the wall of the town, or against the gates of the castle. So he came up to the captain's lodgings, and saluting him, he asked him

of his welfare, and what was the best news at court? But when he asked Captain Credence that, the water stood in his eyes. Then said the captain, "Cheer up, my lord, for all will be well in time:" and with that he first produced his packet, and laid it by, but that the Lord Mayor and the rest of the captains took for a sign of good tidings. Now a season of grace being come, he sent for all the captains and elders of the town that were here and there in their lodgings in the castle, and upon their guard, to let them know that Captain Credence was returned from the court, and that he had something in general, and something in special, to communicate to them. So they all came up to him, and saluted him, and asked him concerning his journey, and what was the best news at the court? And he answered them as he had done the Lord Mayor before, that all would be well at last. Now when the captain had thus saluted them, he opened his packet, and thence did draw out his several notes for those that he had sent for. And the first note was for my Lord Mayor, wherein was signified:

The packet opened.

That the Prince Emmanuel had taken it well that my Lord Mayor had been so true and trusty in his office, and the great concerns that lay upon him for the town and people of Mansoul; also he bid him to know that he took it well that he had been so bold for his Prince Emmanuel, and had engaged so faithfully in his cause against Diabolus. He also signified at the close of his letter, that he should shortly receive his reward.

A note for my Lord Mayor.

The second note that came out was for the noble Lord Will-be-will, wherein there was signified, that his Prince Emmanuel did well understand how valiant and courageous he had been for the honour of his Lord, now in his absence, and when his name was under contempt by Diabolus. There was signified also that his Prince had taken it well that he had been so faithful to the town of Mansoul in his keeping of so strict a hand and eye over, and so strict a rein upon the necks of the Diabolonians that did still lie lurking in their several holes in the famous town of Mansoul.

A note for the Lord Will-be-will.

He signified, moreover, how that he understood that my lord had with his own hand done great execution upon some of the chief of the rebels there, to the great discouragement of the adverse party, and to the good example of the whole town of Mansoul, and that shortly his lordship should have his reward.

The third note came out for the subordinate Preacher, wherein was signified, that his Prince took it well from him that he had so honestly and so faithfully performed his office, and executed the trust committed to him by his Lord while he exhorted, rebuked, and forewarned Mansoul according to the laws of the town. He signified, moreover, that he took well at his hand that he called to fasting, to sackcloth and ashes, when Mansoul was under her revolt. Also that he called for the aid of the Captain Boanerges to help in so weighty a work, and that shortly he also should receive his reward.

A note for the subordinate Preacher.

The fourth note came out for Mr. Godly-fear, wherein his Lord thus signified, that his lord-ship observed that he was the first of all the men in Mansoul that detected Mr. Carnal-security, as the only one that through his subtilty and cunning had obtained for Diabolus, a defection and decay of goodness in the blessed town of Mansoul. Moreover, his Lord gave him to understand that he still remembered his tears and mourning for the state of Mansoul. It was also observed by the same note, that his Lord took notice of his detecting of this Mr. Carnal-security at his own table among his guests, in his own house, and that in the midst of his jolliness, even while he was seeking to perfect his villanies against the town of Mansoul. Emmanuel also took notice that this reverend person, Mr. Godly-fear, stood stoutly to it at the gates of the castle against all the threats and attempts of the tyrant, and that he had put the townsmen in a way to make their petition to their Prince, so as that he might accept thereof, and as they might obtain an answer of peace; and that therefore shortly he should receive his reward.

A note for Mr. Godly-fear.

After all this, there was yet produced a note which was written to the whole town of Mansoul, whereby they perceived that their Lord took notice of their so often repeating of petitions to him, and that they should see more of the fruits of such their doings in time to come. Their Prince did also therein tell them, that he took it well that their heart and mind now at last abode fixed upon him and his ways, though Diabolus had made such inroads upon them, and that neither flatteries on the one hand, nor hardships on the other, could make them yield to serve his cruel designs. There was also inserted at the bottom of this note, that his Lordship had left the town of Mansoul in the hands of the Lord Secretary, and under the conduct of Captain Credence, saying, Beware that you yet yield yourselves unto their governance, and in due time you shall receive your reward.

A note for the town of Mansoul.

So, after the brave Captain Credence had delivered his notes to those to whom they belonged, he retired himself to my Lord Secretary's lodgings, and there spends time in conversing with him; for they two were very great, one with another, and did indeed know more how things would go with Mansoul than did all the townsmen besides. The Lord Secretary also loved the Captain Credence dearly; yea, many a good bit was sent him from my Lord's table; also he might have a show of countenance when the rest of Mansoul lay under the clouds; so after some time for converse was spent, the captain betook himself to his chambers to rest. But it was not long after, but my lord did send for the captain again. So the captain came to him, and they greeted one another with usual salutations. Then said the captain to the Lord Secretary, "What hath my lord to say to his servant?" So the Lord Secretary took him, and had him aside, and after a sign or two of more favour, he said, "I have made thee the Lord's lieutenant over all the forces in Mansoul, so that from this day forward all men in Mansoul shall be at thy word, and thou shalt be he that shall lead in, and that shalt lead out Mansoul. Thou shalt therefore manage, according to thy place, the war for thy Prince, and for the town of Mansoul, against the force and power of Diabolus, and at thy command shall the rest of the captains be.

Now the townsmen began to perceive what interest the captain had, both with the court, and also with the Lord Secretary in Mansoul; for no man before could speed when sent, nor bring such good news from Emmanuel as he. Wherefore what do they, after some lamentation that they made no more use of him in their distresses, but send by their subordinate Preacher to the Lord Secretary, to desire him that all that ever they were and had, might be put under the government, care, custody, and conduct of Captain Credence.

So their preacher went and did his errand, and received this answer from the mouth of his Lord, that Captain Credence should be the great doer in all the King's army against the King's enemies, and also for the welfare of Mansoul. So he bowed to the ground, and thanked his Lordship, and returned and told his news to the townsfolk. But all this was done with all imaginable secrecy, because the foes had yet great strength in the town. But to return to our story.

When Diabolus saw himself thus boldly confronted by the Lord Mayor, and perceived the stoutness of Mr. Godly-fear, he fell *Diabolus rages.* into a rage, and forthwith called a council of war, that he might be revenged on Mansoul. So all the princes of the pit came together, and old Incredulity in the head of them, with all the captains of his army. So they consult what to do. Now, the effect and conclusion of the council that day was, how they might take the castle; because they could not conclude themselves masters of the town so long as that was in the possession of their enemies. So one advised this way, and another advised that; but when they could not agree in their verdict, Apollyon, the president of the council, stood up, and thus he began : " My brotherhood," quoth he, " I have two things to propound unto you, and my first is this; let us withdraw ourselves from the town into the plain again, for our presence here will do us no good, because the castle is yet in our enemy's hands; nor is it possible that we should take that, so long as so many brave captains are in it, and that this bold fellow Godly-fear is made the keeper of the gates of it.

" Now, when we have withdrawn ourselves into the plain, they, of their own accord, will be glad of some little ease; and it may be, of their own accord, they again may begin to be remiss; and even their so being will give them a bigger blow than we can possibly give them ourselves. But if that should fail, our going forth of the town

may draw the captains out after us, and you know what it cost them when we fought them in the field before. Besides, can we but draw them out into the field, we may lay an ambush behind the town, which shall, when they are come forth abroad, rush in, and take possession of the castle." But Beelzebub stood up, and replied, saying, " It is impossible to draw them all off from the castle ; some you may be sure will lie there to keep that ; wherefore it will be but in vain thus to attempt, unless we were sure that they will all come out." He therefore concluded that what was done must be done by some other means ; and the most likely means that the greatest of their heads could invent, was that which Apollyon had advised to before, to wit, to get the townsmen again to sin. " For," said he, " it is not our being in the town, nor in the field, nor our fighting, nor our killing of their men, that can make us the masters of Mansoul ; for so long as one in the town is able to lift up his finger against us, Emmanuel will take their parts ; and if he shall take their parts, we know what time a-day it will be with us. Wherefore, for my part," quoth he, " there is, in my judgment, no way to bring them into bondage to us, like inventing a way to make them sin." (2 Pet. ii. 18—21.) " Had we," said he, " left all our Doubters at home, we had done as well as we have done now, unless we could have made them the masters and governors of the castle ; for Doubters at a distance, are but like objections repelled with arguments. Indeed, can we but get them into the hold, and make them possessors of that, the day will be our own. Let us therefore withdraw ourselves into the plain, not expecting that the captains in Mansoul should follow us, but yet, I say, let us do this, and before we so do, let us advise again with our trusty Diabolonians that are yet in their holds of Mansoul, and set them to work to betray the town to us ; for they indeed must do it, or it will be left undone for ever." By these sayings of Beelzebub—for I think it was he that gave this counsel—the whole conclave was forced to be of his opinion : to wit, that the way to get the castle was to get the town to sin. Then they fell to inventing by what means to do this thing.

Then Lucifer stood up and said, " The counsel of Beelzebub is pertinent : now the way to bring this to pass, in mine opinion, is this : let us withdraw our force from the town of Mansoul, let us do this, and let us terrify them no more, either with summons or threats, or with the noise of our drum, or any other awakening means. Only let us lie in the field at a distance, and be as if we regarded them not ; for frights I see do but awaken them, and make them stand more to their arms. I have also another stratagem in my head : you know Mansoul is a market-town ; and a town that delights in commerce ; what therefore if some of our Diabolonians shall feign themselves far countrymen, and shall go out and bring to the market of Mansoul some of our wares to sell; and what matter at what rates they sell their wares, though it be but for half the worth. Now, let those that thus shall trade in their market, be those that are witty and true to us, and I will lay my crown to pawn it will do. There are two that are come to my thoughts already, that I think will be arch at this work, and they are Mr. Penny-wise-pound-foolish, and Mr. Get-i'th'-hundred-and-lose-i'th'-shire; nor is this man with the long name at all inferior to the other. What also if you join with them Mr. Sweet-world, and Mr. Present-good; they are men that are civil and cunning, but our true friends and helpers. Let these with as many more engage in this business for us, and let Mansoul be taken up in much business, and let them grow full and rich, and this is the way to get ground of them; remember ye not that thus we prevailed upon Laodicea, and how many at present do we hold in this snare? (Rev. iii. 17.) Now when they begin to grow full, they will forget their misery, and if we shall not affright them they may happen to fall asleep, and so be got to neglect their town-watch, their castle-watch, as well as their watch at the gates.

"Yea, may we not by this means so cumber Mansoul with abundance, that they shall be forced to make of their castle a warehouse instead of a garrison fortified against us, and a receptacle for men of war? Thus if we go tour goods and commodities thither, I reckon that the castle is more than half ours. Besides, could we so order it that it should be filled with such kind of wares, then if we made a sudden assault upon them, it would be hard for the captains to take shelter there. Do you know that of the parable, The deceitfulness of riches choke the word. (Luke viii. 14.) And again, When the heart is overcharged with surfeiting and drunkenness, and the cares of this life, all mischief comes upon them unawares. (Luke xxi. 34—36.)

"Furthermore, my lords," quoth he, "you very well know that it is not easy for a people to be filled with our things, and not to have some of our Diabolonians as retainers to their houses and services. Where is a Mansoulian that is full of this world, that has not for his servants and waiting-men, Mr. Profuse, or Mr. Prodigality, or some other of our Diabolonian gang, as Mr. Voluptuous, Mr. Pragmatical, Mr. Ostentation, or the like? Now these can take the castle of Mansoul, or blow it up, or make it unfit for a garrison for Emmanuel; and any of these will do. Yea, these, for aught I know, may do it for us sooner than an army of twenty thousand men. Wherefore, to end as I began, my advice is, that we quietly withdraw ourselves, not offering any further force, or forcible attempts upon the castle, at least at this time, and let us set on foot our new project, and let us see if that will not make them destroy themselves."

This advice was highly applauded by them all, and was accounted the very master-piece of hell·

to wit, to choke Mansoul with a fulness of this world, and to surfeit her heart with the good things thereof. But see how things meet together; just as this Diabolonian council was bro- *Captain Credence receives that from his Prince which he understandeth not.* ken up, Captain Credence received a letter from Emmanuel, the contents of which was this, That upon the third day he would meet him in the field in the plains about Mansoul. "Meet me in the field!" quoth the captain, "what meaneth my Lord by this? I know not what he meaneth by meeting of me in the field." So he took the note in his hand, and did carry it to my Lord Secretary, to ask his thoughts thereupon; for my Lord was a seer in all matters concerning the King, and also for the good and comfort of the town of Mansoul. So he showed my Lord the note, and desired his opinion thereof: "for my part," quoth Captain Credence, "I know not the meaning thereof." So my Lord did take and read it, and after a little pause he said, "The Diabolonians have had against Mansoul a great consultation to-day; they have, I say, this day been contriving the utter ruin of the town; and the result of their council is, to set Mansoul into such a way, which, if taken, will surely make her destroy herself. And to this end they are making ready for their own departure out of the town, intending to betake themselves to the field again, and there to lie till they shall see whether this their project will take or no. But be thou ready, with the men of thy Lord, for on the third day they will be in the plain; there to fall upon the Diabolonians; for the Prince will by that time be in the field; yea, by that it is break of day, sun rising, or before, and that with a mighty force against *The riddle expounded to Captain Credence.* them. So he shall be before them, and thou shalt be behind them, and betwixt you both their army shall be destroyed."

When Captain Credence heard this, away goes he to the rest of the captains, and tells them what a note he had a while since received from the hand of Emmanuel. "And," said he, "that which was dark therein, has my Lord, the Lord Secretary, expounded unto me." He told them moreover, what by himself, and by them, must be done to answer the mind of their Lord. Then were the captains glad, and Captain Credence commanded that all the King's trumpeters should ascend to the battlements of the castle, and there in the audience of Diabolus, and of the whole town of Mansoul, make the best music that heart could invent. The trumpeters then did as they were commanded. They got themselves up to the top of the castle, and thus they began to sound; then did Diabolus start, and said, What can be the meaning of this, they neither sound boot and saddle, nor horse and away, nor a charge? What do these madmen mean, that yet they should be so merry and glad? Then answered him one of themselves and said, "This is for joy that their Prince Emmanuel is coming to relieve the town of Mansoul; that to this end he is at the head of an army, and that this relief is near."

The men of Mansoul also were greatly concerned at this melodious charm of the trumpets. They said, yea, they answered one another, saying, "This can be no harm to us; surely this can be no harm to us." Then said the Diabolonians, "What had we best to do?" And it was answered, it was best to quit the town; and that, said one, " Ye may do in pursuance of your last council, and by so doing, also be better able to give the enemy battle, should an army from without come upon us." So on the second day they withdrew themselves from Mansoul, and abode in the plains without; but they encamped themselves before Eye-gate, in what terrene and terrible manner they could. The reason why they would not abide in the town, besides the reasons that were debated in their late conclave, was, for that they were not possessed of the stronghold, and because, said they, we shall have more convenience to fight, and also to fly, if need be, when we are encamped in the open plains. Besides, the town would have been a pit for them rather than a place of defence, had the Prince come up, and enclosed them fast therein. Therefore they betook themselves to the field, that they might also be out of the reach of the slings, by which they were much annoyed all the while that they were in the town.

Diabolus withdraws from the town, and why.

Well, the time that the captains were to fall upon the Diabolonians being come, they eagerly prepared themselves for action; for Captain Credence had told the captains over night that they should meet their Prince in the field to-morrow. This therefore made them yet far more desirous to be engaging the enemy, for, " You shall see the Prince in the field to-morrow," was like oil to a flaming fire; for of a long time they had been at a distance, they therefore were for this the more earnest and desirous of the work. So, as I said, the hour being come, Captain Credence, with the rest of the men of war, drew out their forces before it were day by the sally-port of the town. And being all ready, Captain Credence went up to the head of the army, and gave to the rest of the captains the word, and so they to their under-officers and soldiers. The word was, " The sword of the Prince Emmanuel, and the shield of Captain Credence," which is, in

The time come for the captains to fight them.

They draw out into the field.

the Mansoulian tongue, " The word of God and faith." Then the captains fell on, and began roundly to front, and flank, and rear Diabolus's camp.

Now they left Captain Experience in the town, because he was yet ill of his wounds which the Diabolonians had given him in the last fight. But when he perceived that the captains were at it, what does he, but, calling for his crutches with haste, gets up, and away he goes to the battle, saying, "Shall I lie here when my brethren are in the fight? and when Emmanuel the Prince will

show himself in the field to his servants?" But when the enemy saw the man come with his crutches, they were daunted yet the more; for, thought they, what spirit has possessed these Mansoulians that they fight us upon their crutches! Well the captains, as I said, fell on, and did bravely handle their weapons, still crying out and shouting, as they laid on blows, " The sword of the Prince Emmanuel, and the shield of Captain Credence."

Now when Diabolus saw that the captains were come out, and that so valiantly they surrounded his men, he concluded, that for the present, nothing from them was to be looked for but blows, with the dints of their two-edged swords.

Wherefore he also falls on upon the Prince's army with all his deadly force. So the battle was

The battle joined. joined. Now who was it that at first Diabolus met with in the fight, but Captain Credence on the one hand, and the Lord Will-be-will on the other; now Will-be-will's blows were like the blows of a giant, for that man had a strong arm, and he fell in upon the Election-doubters—for they were the life-guard of Diabolus—and he kept them in play a good while, cutting and battering shrewdly. Now when Captain Credence saw my Lord engaged, he did stoutly fall on, on the other hand, upon the same company, also; so they put them to great disorder. Now Captain Goodhope had engaged the Vocation-doubters, and they were sturdy men, but the captain was a valiant man. Captain Experience did also send him some aid, so he made the Vocation-doubters to retreat. The rest of the armies were hotly engaged, and that on every side, and the Diabolonians did fight stoutly. Then did my Lord Secretary command that the slings from the castle should be played, and his men could throw stones at an hair's breadth. But after a while, those that were made to fly before the captains of the Prince did begin to rally again, and they came up stoutly upon the rear of the Prince's army, wherefore the Prince's army began to faint, but remembering that they should see the face of their Prince by and by, they took courage, and a very fierce battle was fought. Then shouted the captains, saying, "The sword of the Prince Emmanuel and the shield of Captain Credence," and with that Diabolus gave back, thinking that more aid had been come. But no Emmanuel as yet appeared;

They both retreat, and, in the time of respite, Captain Credence makes a speech to his soldiers. moreover, the battle did hang in doubt, and they made a little retreat on both sides. Now, in the time of respite, Captain Credence bravely encouraged his men to stand to it, and Diabolus did the like as well as he could. But Captain Credence made a brave speech to his soldiers, the contents whereof here follow— "Gentlemen soldiers, and my brethren in this design, it rejoiceth me much to see in the field for our Prince this day, so stout and so valiant an army, and such faithful lovers of Mansoul. You have hitherto, as hath become you, shown yourselves men of truth and courage against the Diabolonian forces, so that, for all their boast, they have not yet much cause to boast of their gettings. Now take to yourselves your wonted courage, and show yourselves men even this once only, for in a few minutes after the next engagement this time, you shall see your Prince show himself in the field, for we must make this second assault upon this tyrant Diabolus, and then Emmanuel comes."

No sooner had the captain made this speech to his soldiers, but one Mr. Speedy came post to the captain from the Prince, to tell him that Emmanuel was at hand. This news, when the captain had received, he communicated to the other field-officers, and they again to their soldiers and men of war. Wherefore, like men raised from the dead, so the captains and their men arose, made up to the enemy, and cried as before, "The sword of the Prince Emmanuel, and the shield of Captain Credence."

The Diabolonians also bestirred themselves and made resistance as well as they could, but in this last engagement the Diabolonians lost their courage, and many of the Doubters fell down dead to the ground. Now when they had been in heat of battle about an hour or more, Captain Credence lift up his eyes and saw, and behold Emmanuel came, and he came with colours flying, trumpets sounding, and the feet of his men scarce touched the ground, they hasted with that celerity towards the captains that were engaged. Then did Credence wind with his men to the townward, and gave to Diabolus the field. So Emmanuel came upon him on the one side, and the enemy's place was betwixt them both; then again they fell to it afresh, and now it was but a little while more but Emmanuel and Captain Credence met, still trampling down the slain as they came.

But when the captains saw that the Prince was come, and that he fell upon the Diabolonians on the other side, and that Captain Credence and his Highness had got them up betwixt them, they shouted, they so shouted that the ground rent again, saying, "The sword of Emmanuel and the shield of Captain Credence." Now when Diabolus saw that he and his forces were so hard beset by the Prince and his princely army, what does he, and the lords of the pit that were with him, but make their escape and forsake their army, and leave them to fall by the hand of Emmanuel, and of his noble Captain Credence; so they fell all down slain before them, before the Prince, and before his royal army; there was not left so much as one Doubter alive; they lay spread upon the ground dead men, as one would spread dung upon the land.

The victory falls to Emmanuel, and to his men, who slay all.

When the battle was over, all things came into order in the camp; then the captains and elders of Mansoul came together to salute Emmanuel, while without the corporation; so they saluted him and welcomed him, and that with a thousand welcomes, (Sol. Song, viii. 1), for that he was come to the borders of Mansoul again; so he smiled upon them and said, "Peace be to you." Then they addressed themselves to go to the town; they went then to go up to Mansoul, they, the Prince, with all the new forces that now he had brought with him to the war. Also all the gates of the town were set open for his reception, so glad were they of his blessed return. And this was the

Mansoul salutes the Prince without; he addresses himself to go into the town.

manner and order of this going of his into Mansoul.

First, as I said, all the gates of the town were set open, yea the gates of the castle also; the elders too of the town of Mansoul placed themselves at *The manner of* the gates of the town to salute him *his going in.* at his entrance thither; and so they did, for as he drew near and approached towards the gates, they said, "Lift up your heads, O ye gates; and be ye lift up, ye everlasting doors; and the King of glory shall come in." And they answered again, "Who is the King of glory?" and they made return to themselves, "The Lord strong and mighty, the Lord mighty in battle. Lift up your heads, O ye gates; even lift *them* up ye everlasting doors." (Ps. xxiv. 7—9.)

Secondly, It was ordered also by those of Mansoul, that all the way from the town-gates to those of the castle, his blessed Majesty should be entertained with the song, by them that had could best skill in music in all the town of Mansoul; then did the elders and the rest of the men of Mansoul answer one another as Emmanuel entered the town, till he came at the castle-gates, with songs and sound of trumpets, saying, "They have seen thy goings, O God, *even* the goings of my God, my King in the sanctuary." So "the singers went before, the players on instruments *followed* after; among *them were* the damsels playing with timbrels." (Ps. lxviii. 25.)

Thirdly, Then the captains—for I would speak a word of them—they in their order waited on the Prince as he entered into the gates of Mansoul. Captain Credence went before, and Captain Good-hope with him; Captain Charity came behind with other of his companions, and Captain Patience followed, after all, and the rest of the captains—some on the right hand, some on the left—accompanied Emmanuel into Mansoul. And all the while the colours were displayed, the trumpets sounded, and continual shoutings were among the soldiers. The Prince himself rode into the town in his armour, which was all of beaten gold, and in his chariot—the pillars of it were of silver, the bottom thereof of gold, the covering of it was of purple, the midst thereof being paved with love for the daughters of the town of Mansoul.

Fourthly, When the Prince was come to the entrance of Mansoul, he found all the streets strewed with lilies, and flowers curiously decked *Good and joyful* with boughs and branches from the *thoughts.* green trees that stood round about the town. Every door also was filled with persons who had adorned every one their fore-part against their house, with something of variety and singular excellency to entertain him withal as he passed in the streets; they also themselves, as Emmanuel passed by, did welcome him with shouts and acclamations of joy, saying, "Blessed be the Prince that cometh in the name of his Father Shaddai."

Fifthly, At the castle-gates the elders of Mansoul, to wit, the Lord Mayor, the Lord Will-be-

will, the subordinate Preacher, Mr. Knowledge, Mr. Mind, with other of the gentry of the place, saluted Emmanuel again. They bowed before him, they kissed the dust of his feet, they thanked, they blessed, and praised his Highness for not taking advantage against them for their sins, but rather had pity upon them in their misery, and returned to them with mercies, and to build up their Mansoul for ever. Thus was he had up straightway to the castle; for that was the royal palace, and the place where his honour was to dwell; the which was ready prepared for his Highness by the presence of the Lord Secretary and the work of Captain Credence. So he entered in.

Sixthly, Then the people and commonalty of the town of Mansoul came to him into the castle to mourn and to weep, and to lament for their wickedness, by which they had forced him out of the town. So they, when they were come, bowed themselves to the ground seven times, they also wept, they wept aloud, and asked forgiveness of the Prince, and prayed that he would again, as of old, confirm his love to Mansoul.

To the which the great Prince replied, "Weep not, but 'Go your way, eat the fat and drink the sweet, and send portions unto them for whom nought is prepared; for the joy of the Lord is your strength.' (Neh. viii. 10.) I am returned to Mansoul with mercies, and my name shall be set up, exalted, and magnified by it." He also took these inhabitants and kissed them, and laid them in his bosom.

Moreover, he gave to the elders of Mansoul, and to each town-officer, a chain of gold *The holy con-* and a signet. He also sent to their *ceptions of* wives, ear-rings, and jewels, and *Mansoul.* bracelets, and other things. He also bestowed upon the true-born children of Mansoul many precious things.

When Emmanuel the Prince had done all these things for the famous town of Mansoul, then he said unto them, first, "Wash your garments, then put on your ornaments, and then come to me into the castle of Mansoul." (Exod. ix. 8.) So they went to the fountain that was set open for Judah and Jerusalem to wash in (Zec. xiii. 1), and there they washed, and there they made their garments white, and came again to the Prince into the castle, and thus they stood before him. (Rev. vii. 14, 15.)

And now there was music and dancing throughout the whole town of Mansoul, and that because their Prince had again granted to them his presence and the light of his countenance, the bells also did ring, and the sun shone comfortably upon them for a great while together.

The town of Mansoul did also now more throughly seek the destruction and ruin of all remaining Diabolonians that abode in the walls and the dens that they had in the town of Mansoul, for there was of them that had to this day escaped with life and limb from the hand of their suppressors in the famous town of Mansoul.

But my Lord Will-be-will was a greater terror to them now than ever he had been before ; forasmuch as his heart was yet more fully bent to seek, contrive, and pursue them to the death ; he pursued them night and day, and did put them now to sore distress, as will afterwards appear.

After things were thus far put into order in the famous town of Mansoul, care was taken and order given by the blessed Prince Emmanuel, that the townsmen should, without further delay, appoint

Orders given out to bury the dead. some to go forth into the plain to bury the dead that were there—the dead that fell by the sword of Emmanuel and by the shield of the Captain Credence—lest the fumes and ill savours that would arise from them might infect the air, and so annoy the famous town of Mansoul. This also was a reason of this order, to wit, that as much as in Mansoul lay, they might cut off the name, and being, and remembrance of those enemies from the thought of the famous town of Mansoul and its inhabitants.

So order was given out by the Lord Mayor—that wise and trusty friend of the town of Mansoul—that persons should be employed about this necessary business ; and Mr. Godly-fear and one Mr. Upright were to be overseers about this matter ; so persons were put under them to work in the fields and to bury the slain that lay dead in the plains. And these were their places of employment—some were to make the graves, some to bury the dead, and some were to go to and fro in the plains, and also round about the borders of Mansoul, to see if a skull, or a bone, or a piece of a bone of a Doubter was yet to be seen above ground anywhere near the corporation ; and if any were found, it was ordered that the searchers that searched should set up a mark thereby, and a sign, that those that were appointed to bury them might find it, and bury it out of sight, that the name and remembrance of a Diabolonian Doubter might be blotted out from under heaven. And that the children, and they that were to be born in Mansoul, might not know, if possible, what a skull, what a bone, or a piece of a bone of a Doubter was.

So the buriers, and those that were appointed for that purpose, did as they were commanded, they buried the Doubters, and all the skulls and bones, and pieces of bones of Doubters wherever they found them, and so they cleansed the plains. Now also Mr. God's-peace took up his commission and acted again as in former days.

Thus they buried in the plains about Mansoul, the Election-doubters, the Vocation-doubters, the Grace-doubters, the Perseverance-doubters, the Resurrection-doubters, the Salvation-doubters, and the Glory-doubters, whose captains were Captain Rage, Captain Cruel, Captain Damnation, Captain Insatiable, Captain Brimstone, Captain Torment, Captain No-ease, Captain Sepulchre, and Captain Past-hope, and old Incredulity was under Diabolus their general ; there were also the seven heads of their army, and they were the Lord Beelzebub, the Lord Lucifer, the Lord Legion, the Lord Apollyon, the Lord Python, the Lord Cerberus, and the Lord Belial. But the princes and the captains, with old Incredulity their general, did all of them make their escape, so their men fell down slain by the power of the Prince's forces, and by the hands of the men of the town of Mansoul. They also were buried, as before related, to the exceeding great joy of the now famous town of Mansoul. They that buried them, buried also with them their arms, which were cruel instruments of death ; their weapons were arrows, darts, mauls, firebrands, and the like ; they buried also their armour, their colours, banners, with the standard of Diabolus, and what else soever they could find that did but smell of a Diabolonian Doubter.

Now when the tyrant was arrived at Hell-gate-hill, with his old friend Incredulity, they immediately descended the den, and having there, with their fellows, for a while condoled their misfortune and great loss that they sustained against the town of Mansoul, they fell at length into a passion, and revenged they would be for the loss that they sustained before the town of Mansoul, wherefore they presently call a council to contrive *The tyrant resolves to have yet a bout with Mansoul.* yet further what was to be done against the famous town of Mansoul ; for their yawning paunches could not wait to see the result of their Lord Lucifer's and their Lord Apollyon's counsel that they had given before, for their raging gorge thought every day even as long as a short-for-ever, until they were filled with the body and soul, with the flesh and bones, and with all the delicates of Mansoul. They therefore resolve to make another attempt upon the town of Mansoul, and that by an army mixed, and made up, partly of Doubters and partly of Bloodmen. A more particular account now take of both.

The Doubters are such as have their name from their nature, as well as from the lord *An army of Doubters and Bloodmen.* and kingdom where they are born ; their nature is to put a question upon every one of the truths of Emmanuel, and their country is called the Land of Doubting, and that land lieth off, and furthest remote to the north, between the Land of Darkness and that called the Valley of the Shadow of Death. For though the Land of Darkness, and that called the Land of the Shadow of Death, be sometimes *Of the country of the Doubters and of the Bloodmen, where they lie.* called as if they were one and the self-same place, yet indeed they are two, lying but a little way asunder, and the Land of Doubting points in, and lieth between them. This is the Land of Doubting, and these that came with Diabolus to ruin the town of Mansoul are the natives of that country.

The Bloodmen are a people that have their name derived from the malignity of their nature, and from the fury that is in them to execute it upon the town of Mansoul ; their land lieth under the Dog-star, and by that they are governed as to their intellectuals.

The name of their country is the Province of Loath-good, the remote parts of it are far distant from the Land of Doubting, yet they do both butt and bound upon the hill called Hell-gate-hill. These people are always in league with the Doubters, for they jointly do make question of the faith and fidelity of the men of the town of Mansoul, and so are both alike qualified for the service of their prince.

Now of these two countries did Diabolus, by the beating of his drum, raise *The number of his new army.* another army against the town of Mansoul, of five and twenty thousand strong. There were ten thousand Doubters and fifteen thousand Bloodmen, and they were put under several captains for the war, and old Incredulity was again made general of the army.

As for the Doubters, their captains were five of the seven that were heads of the last Diabolonian army, and these are their names, Captain Beelzebub, Captain Lucifer, Captain Apollyon, Captain Legion, and Captain Cerberus, and the captains that they had before were some of them made lieutenants, and some ensigns in the army.

But Diabolus did not count that in this expedition of his, these Doubters would prove his principal men, for their manhood had been tried before, also the Mansoulians had put them to the worst, only he did bring them to multiply a number, and to help, if need was, at a pinch; but his trust he put in his Bloodmen, for that they were all rugged villains, and he knew that they had done feats heretofore.

As for the Bloodmen, they also were under command, and the names of their captains were, *The captains of the Bloodmen.* Captain Cain, Captain Nimrod, Captain Ishmael, Captain Esau, Captain Saul, Captain Absalom, Captain Judas, and Captain Pope.

1. Captain Cain was over two bands, to wit, the zealous and the angry Bloodmen; his standard-bearer bare the red colours, and his escutcheon was the murdering club. (Gen. iv. 8.)

2. Captain Nimrod was captain over two bands, to wit, the tyrannical and encroaching Bloodmen; his standard-bearer bare the red colours, and his escutcheon was the great blood-hound. (Gen. x. 8.)

3. Captain Ishmael was captain over two bands, to wit, over the mocking and scornful Bloodmen; his standard-bearer bare the red colours, and his escutcheon was one mocking at Abraham's Isaac. (Gen. xxi. 9, 10.)

4. Captain Esau was captain over two bands, to wit, the Bloodmen that grudged that another should have the blessing, also over the Bloodmen that are for executing their private revenge upon others; his standard-bearer bare the red colours, and his escutcheon was one privately lurking to murder Jacob. (Gen. xxvii. 42—45.)

5. Captain Saul was captain over two bands, to wit, the groundlessly jealous, and the devilishly furious Bloodmen; his standard-bearer bare the red colours, and his escutcheon was three bloody darts cast at harmless David. (1 Sam. xviii. 10; xix. 10; xx. 33.)

6. Captain Absalom was captain over two bands, to wit, over the Bloodmen that will kill a father or a friend for the glory of this world, also over those Bloodmen that will hold one fair in hand with words, till they shall have pierced him with their swords; his standard-bearer did bare the red colours, and his escutcheon was the son a-pursuing his father's blood. (2 Sam. xv. xvi. xvii.)

7. Captain Judas was over two bands, to wit, the Bloodmen that will sell a man's life for money, and those also that will betray their friend with a kiss; his standard-bearer bare the red colours, and his escutcheon was thirty pieces of silver and the halter. (Mat. xxvi. 14—16.)

8. Captain Pope was captain over one band, for all these spirits are joined in one under him; his standard-bearer bare the red colours, and his escutcheon was the stake, the flame, and the good man in it. (Rev. xiii. 7, 8. Dan. xi. 33.)

Now the reason why Diabolus did so soon rally another force after he had been beaten out of the field was, for that he put mighty confidence in his army of Bloodmen, for he put a great deal of more trust in them than he did before in *The conditions of the Blood-men, their stoutness and valour.* his army of Doubters, though they had also often done great service for him in the strengthening of him in his kingdom. But these Bloodmen he had proved them often, and their sword did seldom return empty. Besides, he knew that these, like mastiffs, would fasten upon any, upon father, mother, brother, sister, prince, or governor, yea, upon the Prince of princes. And that which encouraged him the more, was for that they once did force Emmanuel out of the kingdom of Universe, and why, thought he, may they not also drive him from the town of Mansoul?

So this army of five and twenty thousand strong, was, by their general, the Lord In- *They sit down before Man-soul.* credulity, led up against the town of Mansoul. Now Mr. Pry-well, the scoutmaster-general, did himself go out to spy, and he did bring Mansoul tidings of their coming; wherefore they shut up their gates and put themselves in a posture of defence against these new Diabolonians that came up against the town.

So Diabolus brought up his army and beleaguered the town of Mansoul; the Doubters were placed about Feel-gate, and the Bloodmen set down before Eye-gate and Ear-gate.

Now when this army had thus encamped themselves, Incredulity did, in the name of Diabolus, his own name, and in the name of the Bloodmen and the rest that were with him, send a summons as hot as a red hot iron to Mansoul to yield to their demands, threatening that if they still stood it out against them, they would presently burn down Mansoul with fire. For you must know, that as for the Bloodmen, they were not so much that Mansoul should be surrendered, as that Mansoul should be destroyed and cut off out of the land of the living. True, they send to them to surrender, but should they so do, that would not stanch or quench the thirsts of these men. (Is. lix. 7.) They must have blood, the blood of Mansoul, else they die; and it is from hence that they have their name. (Ps. xxvi. 9, 10. Is. lix. 7. Jer. xxii. 17.) Wherefore these Bloodmen he reserved while now that they might, when all his engines proved ineffectual, as his last and sure card, be played against the town of Mansoul.

Now when the townsmen had received this red hot summons, it begat in them at present some changing and interchanging thoughts, but they jointly agreed, in less than half an hour, to carry the summons to the Prince, the which they did when they had writ at the bottom of it, " Lord, save Mansoul from bloody men." (Ps. lix. 2.)

So he took it and looked upon it, and considered it, and took also notice of that short petition that the men of Mansoul had written at the bottom of it, and called to him the noble Captain Credence, and bid him go, and take Captain Patience with him, and go and take care of that side of Mansoul that was beleaguered by the Bloodmen. (Heb. vi. 12, 15.) So they went and did as they were commanded, the Captain Credence went and took Captain Patience, and they both secured that side of Mansoul that was besieged by the Bloodmen.

Then he commanded that Captain Good-hope and Captain Charity, and my Lord Will-be-will, should take charge of the other side of the town, " And I," said the Prince, " will set my standard upon the battlements of your castle, and do you three watch against the Doubters." This done, he again commanded that the brave captain, the Captain Experience, should draw up his men in the market-place, and that there he should exercise them day by day before the people of the town of Mansoul. Now this siege was long, and many a fierce attempt did the enemy, especially those called the Blood-men, make upon the town of Mansoul, and many a shrewd brush did some of the townsmen meet with from them, especially Captain Self-denial, who, I should have told you before, was commanded to take care of Ear-gate and Eye-gate now against the Bloodmen. This Captain Self-denial was a young man, but stout, and a townsman of Mansoul, as Captain Experience also was. And Emmanuel, at his second return to Mansoul, made him a captain over a thousand of the Mansoulians, for the good of the corporation. This captain, therefore, being a hardy man, and a man of great courage, and willing to venture himself for the good of the town of Mansoul, would now and then sally out upon the Bloodmen and give them many notable alarms, and entered several brisk skirmishes

with them, and also did some execution upon them; but you must think that this could not easily be done, but he must meet with brushes himself, for he carried several of their marks in his face; yea, and some in some other parts of his body.

So, after some time spent for the trial of the faith, and hope, and love of the town of Mansoul, the Prince Emmanuel upon a day *Emmanuel pre-* calls his captains and men of war *pares to give* together, and divides them into two *the enemy bat-* companies; this done, he commands *tle. How he or-* *dereth his* them at a time appointed, and that in the morning *men.* very early, to sally out upon the enemy, saying, " Let half of you fall upon the Doubters, and half of you fall upon the Bloodmen. Those of you that go out against the Doubters, kill and slay, and cause to perish so many of them as by any means you can lay hands on, but for you that go out against the Bloodmen, slay them not, but take them alive."

So, at the time appointed, betimes in the morning the captains went out, as they were commanded, against the enemies; Captain Good-hope, Captain Charity, and those that were joined with them, as Captain Innocent and Captain Experience, went out against the Doubters; and Captain Credence and Captain Patience, with Captain Self-denial, and the rest that were to join with them, went out against the Bloodmen.

Now those that went out against the Doubters drew up into a body before the plain, *The Doubters* and marched on to bid them battle; *put to flight.* but the Doubters, remembering their last success, made a retreat, not daring to stand the shock, but fled from the Prince's men, wherefore they pursued them, and in their pursuit slew many, but they could not catch them all. Now those that escaped went some of them home, and the rest, by fives, nines, and seventeens, like wanderers, went straggling up and down the country, where they, upon the barbarous people, showed and exercised many of their Diabolonian actions; nor did these people rise up in arms against them, but suffered themselves to be enslaved by them. They would also after this show themselves in companies before the town of Mansoul, but never to abide it, for if Captain Credence, Captain Good-hope, or Captain Experience did but show themselves, they fled.

Those that went out against the Bloodmen did as they were commanded, they forbore *The Bloodmen* to slay any, but sought to compass *are taken, and* them about. But the Bloodmen, *how.* when they saw that no Emmanuel was in the field, concluded also that no Emmanuel was in Mansoul, wherefore they, looking upon what the captains did, to be, as they called it, a fruit of the extravagancy of their wild and foolish fancies, rather despised them than feared them; but the captains, minding their business, at last did compass them round, they also that had routed the Doubters came in amain to their aid; so in fine, after some little struggling—for the Bloodmen also would have run for it, only now it was too late—for though they are mischievous and cruel where they can overcome, yet all Bloodmen are chicken-hearted men when they once come to see themselves matched and equalled—so the captains took them, and brought them to the Prince.

Now when they were taken, had before the Prince, and examined, he found them to be of three several counties, though they all came out of one land.

They are brought to the Prince, and found to be of three sorts.

1. One sort of them came out of Blindmanshire, and they were such as did ignorantly what they did. (1 Tim. i. 13—15. Matt. v. 44.)

2. Another sort of them came out of Blindzealshire, and they did superstitiously what they did. (Luke vi. 22.)

3. The third sort of them came out of the town of Malice, in the county of Envy, and they did what they did out of spite and implacableness. (Jn. xvi. 2.)

For the first of these, to wit, they that came out of Blindmanshire, when they saw where they were, and against whom they had fought, they trembled, and cried as they stood before him ; and as many of these as asked him mercy, he touched their lips with his golden sceptre. (Acts. ix. 5—6.)

They that came out of Blindzealshire, they did not as their fellows did, for they pleaded that they had a right to do what they did, because Mansoul was a town whose laws and customs were diverse from all that dwelt thereabouts. Very few of these could be brought to see their evil; but those that did, and asked mercy, they also obtained favour. (John viii. 40.)

They that came out of the town of Malice, that is in the county of Envy, they neither wept nor disputed, nor repented, but stood gnawing of their tongues before him for anguish and madness, because they could not have their will upon Mansoul. (Rev. ix. 20, 21.) Now these last, with all those of the other two sorts that did not unfeignedly ask pardon for their faults, those he made to enter into sufficient bond to answer for what they had done against Mansoul and against her King, at the great and general assizes to be holden for our Lord the King, where he himself should appoint for the country and kingdom of Universe.

The Bloodmen are bound over to the day of judgment.

So they became bound, each man for himself, to come in when called upon, to answer before our Lord the King for what they had done as before.

And thus much concerning this second army that were sent by Diabolus to overthrow Mansoul.

But there were three of those that came from the land of Doubting, who, after they had wandered and ranged the country awhile, and perceived that they had escaped, were so hardy as to thrust themselves, knowing that yet there were in the town Diabolonians—I say they were so hardy as to thrust themselves into Mansoul among them. Three, did I say? I think

Three or four of the Doubters go into Mansoul, are entertained, and by whom.

there were four. Now, to whose house should these Diabolonian Doubters go, but to the house of an old Diabolonian in Mansoul, whose name was Evil-questioning : a very great enemy he was to Mansoul, and a great doer among the Diabolonians there. Well, to this Evil-questioning's house, as was said, did these Diabolonians come—you may be sure that they had directions how to find the way thither; so he made them welcome, pitied their misfortune, and succoured them with the best that he had in his house. Now, after a little acquaintance, and it was not long before they had that, this old Evil-questioning asked the Doubters if they were all of a town—he knew that they were all of one kingdom. And they answered, no, nor not of one shire neither; for I, said one, am an Election-doubter; I, said another, am a Vocation-doubter; then, said the third, I am a Salvation-doubter; and the fourth said he was a Grace-doubter. "Well," quoth the old gentleman, "be of what shire you will, I am persuaded that you are down boys; you have the very length of my foot, are one with my heart, and shall be welcome to me." So they thanked him, and were glad that they had found themselves a harbour in Mansoul. Then said Evil-questioning to them, "How many of your company might there be that came with you to the siege of Mansoul?" And they answered, "There were but ten thousand Doubters in all, for the rest of the army consisted of fifteen thousand Bloodmen." "These Bloodmen," quoth they, "border upon our country; but, poor men, as we hear, they were every one taken by Emmanuel's forces." "Ten thousand !" quoth the old gentleman, "I'll promise you that is a round company. But how came it to pass, since you were so mighty a number, that you fainted, and durst not fight your foes ?" "Our general," said they, "was the first man that did run for it." "Pray," quoth their landlord, "who was that your cowardly general ?" "He was once the Lord Mayor of Mansoul," said they. "But pray call him not a cowardly general ; for whether any, from the east to the west, has done more service for our prince, Diabolus, than has my Lord Incredulity, will be a hard question for you to answer. But had they catched him, they would for certain have hanged him ; and we promise you hanging is but a bad business." "Then," said the old gentleman, "I would that all the ten thousand Doubters were now well armed in Mansoul, and myself in the head of them, I would see what I could do." "Ay," said they, "that would be well if we could see that; but wishes, alas! what are they?" And these words were spoken aloud. "Well," said old Evil-questioning, "take heed that you talk not too loud ; you must be quat and close, and must take care of yourselves while you are here, or, I'll assure you, you will be snapt."

"Why?" quoth the Doubters.

"Why?" quoth the old gentleman; "why, because both the Prince and Lord Secretary, and

Talk betwixt the Doubters and old Evil-questioning.

their captains and soldiers, are all at present in town; yea, the town is as full of them as ever it can hold. And, besides, there is one whose name is Will-be-will, a most cruel enemy of ours, and him the Prince has made keeper of the gates, and has commanded him that, with all the diligence he can, he should look for, search out, and destroy all and all manner of Diabolonians. And if he lighteth upon you, down you go, though your heads were made of gold."

And now to see how it happened. One of the *They are over-* Lord Will-be-will's faithful soldiers, *heard.* whose name was Mr. Diligence, stood all this while listening under old Evil-questioning's eaves, and heard all the talk that had been betwixt him and the Doubters that he entertained under his roof.

The soldier was a man that my lord had much confidence in, and that he loved dearly; and that both because he was a man of courage, and also a man that was unwearied in seeking after Diabolonians to apprehend them.

Now this man, as I told you, heard all the talk *They are dis-* that was between old Evil-question- *covered.* ing and these Diabolonians; wherefore, what does he but go to his lord, and tells him what he had heard. "And sayest thou so, my trusty?" quoth my lord. "Ay," quoth Diligence, "that I do; and if your lordship will be pleased to go with me, you shall find it as I have said." "And are they there?" quoth my lord; "I know Evil-questioning well, for he and I were great in the time of apostacy. But I know not now where he dwells." "But I do," said his man; "and, if your lordship will go, I will lead you the way to his den." "Go!" quoth my lord, "that I will. Come, my Diligence, let us go find them out." So my lord and his man went together the direct way to his house. Now, his man went before, to show him his way, and they went till they came even under old Mr. Evil-questioning's wall. Then said Diligence,' 'Hark! my lord; do you know the old gentleman's tongue when you hear it?" "Yes," said my lord, "I know it well; but I have not seen him many a day. This I know; he is cunning. I wish he doth not give us the slip." "Let me alone for that," said his servant, Diligence. "But how shall we find the door?" quoth my lord. "Let me alone for that, too," said his man. So he had my Lord Will-be-will about, and showed him the way to the door. Then my lord, without more ado, broke open the door, rushed into the house, and caught them all five together, even as *They are ap-* Diligence, his man, had told him. *prehended,* So my lord apprehended them, and *and committed* led them away, and committed them *to prison.* to the hand of Mr. Trueman, the jailer, and commanded, and he did put them in ward. This done, my Lord Mayor was acquainted in the morning with what my Lord Will-be-will had done overnight, and his lordship rejoiced much at the news, not only because there were Doubters apprehended,

but because that old Evil-questioning was taken, for he had been a very great trouble to Mansoul, and much affliction to my Lord Mayor himself. He had also been sought for often, but no hand could ever be laid upon him till now.

Well, the next thing was to make preparation to try these five that by my lord had been apprehended, and that were in the hands of Mr. Trueman, the jailer. So the day was set, and the court called and come together, and *They are* the prisoners brought to the bar. *brought to trial.* My Lord Will-be-will had power to have slain them when at first he took them, and that without any more ado; but he thought it at this time more for the honour of the Prince, the comfort of Mansoul, and the discouragement of the enemy, to bring them forth to public judgment.

But, I say, Mr. Trueman brought them in chains to the bar, to the town-hall, for that was the place of judgment. So, to be short, the jury was pannelled, the witnesses sworn, and the prisoners tried for their lives. The jury was the same that tried Mr. No-truth, Pityless, Haughty, and the rest of their companions.

And first old Questioning himself was set to the bar; for he was the receiver, the entertainer, and comforter of these Doubters, that by nation were outlandish men; then he was bid to hearken to his charge, and was told that he had liberty to object, if he had aught to say for himself. So his indictment was read; the manner and form here follows—

"Mr. Questioning, thou art here indicted by the name of Evil-questioning, an in- *His indict-* truder upon the town of Mansoul, *ment.* for that thou art a Diabolonian by nature, and also a hater of the Prince Emmanuel, and one that hast studied the ruin of the town of Mansoul. Thou art also here indicted for countenancing the King's enemies, after wholesome laws made to the contrary: For, 1. Thou hast questioned the truth of her doctrine and state. 2. In wishing that ten thousand Doubters were in her. 3. In receiving, in entertaining, and encouraging of her enemies that came from their army unto thee. What sayest thou to this indictment, Art thou guilty, or not guilty?"

"My lord," quoth he, "I know not the meaning of this indictment, forasmuch as I *His plea.* am not the man concerned in it; the man that standeth by this charge, accused before this bench, is called by the name of Evil-questioning, which name I deny to be mine, mine being Honest-inquiring. The one indeed sounds like the other; but I trow, your lordships know, that between these two there is a wide difference; for I hope that a man, even in the worst of times, and that too amongst the worst of men, may make an honest inquiry after things, without running the danger of death."

Will. Then spake my Lord Will-be-will, for he was one of the witnesses: "My lord, and you the honourable bench, and magistrates of the town of Mansoul, you all have heard with your ears that the prisoner at the bar has denied his name, and so thinks to shift from the charge of the indictment. But I know him to be the man concerned, and that his proper name is Evil-questioning. I have known him, my lord, above this thirty years; for he and I—a shame it is for me to speak it—were great acquaintance, when Diabolus, that tyrant, had the government of Mansoul; and I testify that he is a Diabolonian by nature, and enemy to our Prince, and a hater of the blessed town of Mansoul. He has, in times of rebellion, been at, and lain in my house, my lord, not so little as twenty nights together; and we did use to talk then, for the substance of talk, as he, and his Doubters have talked of late; true I have not seen him many a day. I suppose that the coming of Emmanuel to Mansoul has made him to change his lodgings, as this indictment has driven him to change his name; but this is the man my lord."

The Lord Will-be-will's testimony.

Then said the court unto him, "Hast thou any more to say?"

Evil. "Yes," quoth the old gentleman, "that I have; for all that as yet has been said against me, is but by the mouth of one witness, and it is not lawful for the famous town of Mansoul, at the mouth of one witness, to put any man to death.

Dilig. Then stood forth Mr. Diligence, and said, "My Lord, as I was upon my watch such a night, at the head of Bad Street, in this town, I chanced to hear a muttering within this gentleman's house; then thought I, what is to do here? So I went up close, but very softly, to the side of the house, to listen, thinking, as indeed it fell out, that there I might light upon some Diabolonian conventicle. So, as I said, I drew nearer and nearer, and when I was got up close to the wall, it was but a while before I perceived that there were outlandish men in the house; but I did well understand their speech, for I have been a traveller myself. Now hearing such language in such a tottering cottage as this old gentleman dwelt in, I clapt mine ear to a hole in the window, and there heard them talk as followeth. This old Mr. Questioning asked these Doubters what they were, whence they came, and what was their business in these parts? And they told him to all these questions, yet he did entertain them. He also asked what numbers there were of them, and they told him ten thousand men. He then asked why they made no more manly assault upon Mansoul? And they told him; so he called their general coward for marching off when he should have fought for his Prince. Further, this old Evil-questioning wished, and I heard him wish, would all the ten thousand Doubters were now in Mansoul, and himself in the head of them. He bid them also to take heed and lie quat, for if they were taken they must die, although they had heads of gold."

Mr. Diligence's testimony.

Then said the court, "Mr. Evil-questioning, here is now another witness against you, and his testimony is full: 1. He swears that you did receive these men into your house, and that you did nourish them there, though you knew that they were Diabolonians, and the King's enemies. 2. He swears that you did wish ten thousand of them in Mansoul. 3. He swears that you did give them advice to be quat and close lest they were taken by the King's servants. All which manifesteth that thou art a Diabolonian; for hadst thou been a friend to the King, thou wouldest have apprehended them."

Evil. Then said Evil-questioning, "To the first of these I answer, the men that came into mine house were strangers, and I took them in, and is it now become a crime in Mansoul for a man to entertain strangers? That I did also nourish them is true, and why should my charity be blamed? As for the reason why I wished ten thousand of them in Mansoul, I never told it to the witnesses, nor to themselves. I might wish them to be taken, and so my wish might mean well to Mansoul, for aught that any yet knows. I did also bid them take heed that they fell not into the captain's hands; but that might be because I am unwilling that any man should be slain; and not because I would have the King's enemies, as such, escape."

My Lord Mayor then replied, "That though it was a virtue to entertain strangers, yet it was treason to entertain the King's enemies. And for what else thou hast said, thou dost by words but labour to evade, and defer the execution of judgment. But could there be no more proved against thee but that thou art a Diabolonian, thou must for that die the death by the law; but to be a receiver, a nourisher, a countenancer, and a harbourer of others of them, yea, of outlandish Diabolonians; yea, of them that came from far, on purpose to cut off and destroy our Mansoul—this must not be borne."

Then said Evil-questioning, "I see how the game will go; I must die for my name, and for my charity." And so he held his peace.

Then they called the outlandish Doubters to the bar; and the first of them that was arraigned was the Election-doubter; so his indictment was read, The Election-doubter tried. and because he was an outlandish man, the substance of it was told him by an interpreter; to wit, that he was there charged with being an enemy of Emmanuel the Prince, a hater of the town of Mansoul, and an opposer of her most wholesome doctrine.

Then the judge asked him if he would plead?
His plea. But he said only this, that he confessed that he was an Election-doubter, and that that was the religion that he had ever been brought up in: and said, moreover, "If I must die for my religion, I trow, I shall die a martyr, and so I care the less."

Judge. Then it was replied, "To question election, is to overthrow a great doctrine of the gospel; to wit, the omniscience, and power, and will of God; to take away the liberty of God with his creature; to stumble the faith of the town of Mansoul; and to make salvation to depend upon works, and not upon grace. It also belied the word, and disquieted the minds of the men of Mansoul; therefore, by the best of laws he must die."

Then was the Vocation-doubter called, and set The Vocation-doubter tried. to the bar; and his indictment for substance was the same with the other, only he was particularly charged with denying the calling of Mansoul.

The judge asked him also what he had to say for himself?

So he replied that he never believed that there was any such thing as a distinct and powerful call of God to Mansoul; otherwise than by the general voice of the Word; nor by that neither, otherwise than as it exhorted them to forbear evil, and to do that which is good, and in so doing, a promise of happiness is annexed.

Then said the Judge, "Thou art a Diabolonian: and hast denied a great part of one of the most experimental truths of the Prince of the town of Mansoul; for he has called, and she has heard a most distinct and powerful call of her Emmanuel, by which she has been quickened, awakened, and possessed with heavenly grace to desire to have communion with her Prince, to serve him, and do his will, and to look for her happiness merely of his good pleasure. And for thine ab-

horrence of this good doctrine thou must die the death."

Then the Grace-doubter was called, and his indictment was read; and he replied The Grace-doubter tried. thereto, that though he was of the land of Doubting, his father was the offspring of a Pharisee, and lived in good fashion among his neighbours, and that he taught him to believe, and believe it I do, and will, that Mansoul shall never be saved freely by grace.

Then said the Judge, "Why, the law of the Prince is plain: 1. Negatively, 'Not of works.' 2. Positively, 'By grace you are saved.' (Rom. iii. Eph. ii.) And thy religion settleth in and upon the works of the flesh; for the works of the law are the works of the flesh. Besides, in saying as thou hast done, thou hast robbed God of his glory, and given it to a sinful man; thou hast robbed Christ of the necessity of his undertaking, and the sufficiency thereof, and hast given both these to the works of the flesh. Thou hast despised the work of the Holy Ghost, and hast magnified the will of the flesh, and of the legal mind. Thou art a Diabolonian, the son of a Diabolonian; and for thy Diabolonian principles thou must die."

The court then having proceeded thus far with them, sent out the jury, who forthwith brought them in guilty of death. Then stood up the Recorder, and addressed himself to the prisoners: "You, the prisoners at the bar, you Their sentence to die. have been here indicted, and proved guilty of high crimes against Emmanuel our Prince, and against the welfare of the famous town of Mansoul; crimes for which you must be put to death; and die ye accordingly."

So they were sentenced to the death of the cross. The place assigned them for execu- The places of tion was that where Diabolus drew their death assigned. up his last army against Mansoul; save only that old Evil-questioning was hanged at the top of Bad Street, just over against his own door.

When the town of Mansoul had thus far rid themselves of their enemies, and of the troublers of their peace, in the next place, a strict commandment was given out, that yet my Lord Willbe-will should, with Diligence his man, search for, and do his best to apprehend, what town-Diabolonians were yet left alive in Mansoul. The names of several of them were: Mr. Fooling, Mr. Letgood-slip, Mr. Slavish-fear, Mr. No-love, Mr. Mistrust, Mr. Flesh, and Mr. Sloth. It was also commanded that he should apprehend Mr. Evil-questioning's children that he left behind him, and that they should demolish his house. The children that he left behind were these: Mr. Doubt, and he was his eldest son; the next to him was Legal-life, Unbelief, Wrong-thoughts-of-Christ, Clip-promise, Carnal-sense, Live-by-feeling, Self-love. All these he had by one wife, and her name was No-hope. She was the kinswoman of old Incredulity; for he was her uncle, and, when her father, old Dark, was dead, he took her, and brought her up; and, when she was marriageable, he gave her to this old Evil-questioning to wife.

Now, the Lord Will-be-will did put into execution his commission, with great Diligence, his man. He took Fooling in the streets, and hanged him up in Want-wit-alley, over against his own Fooling taken. house. This Fooling was he that would have had the town of Mansoul deliver up Captain Credence into the hands of Diabolus, provided that then he would have withdrawn his force out of the town. He also took Mr. Let-good-slip one day as he was busy in the market, and executed him according to law. Now, there was an honest poor man in Mansoul, and his name was Mr. Meditation, one of no great account in the days of apostacy, but now of repute with the best of the town. This man, therefore, they were willing to prefer; now Mr. Let-good-slip had a great deal of wealth heretofore in Mansoul, and at Emmanuel's coming it was sequestered to the use of the Prince; this, therefore, was now given to Mr. Meditation, to improve for the common good, and after him to his son, Mr. Think-well; this Think-well he had by Mrs. Piety, his wife, and she was the daughter of Mr. Recorder.

After this my Lord apprehended Clip-promise, now because he was a notorious villain, for by his doings much of the King's coin was abused, therefore he was made a public example. He was arraigned and judged to be first set in the pillory, then to be whipt by all the children and servants in Mansoul, and then to be hanged till he was dead. Some may wonder at the severity of this man's punishment, but those that are honest traders in Mansoul, are sensible of the great abuse that one clipper of promises in little time may do to the town of Mansoul. And, truly, my judgment is, that all those of his name and life should be served even as he.

He also apprehended Carnal-sense, and put him in hold; but how it came about I cannot tell, but he brake prison and made his escape. Yea, and the bold villain will not yet quit the town, but lurks in the Diabolonian dens a days, and haunts like a ghost honest men's houses a nights. Wherefore there was a proclamation set up in the market-place in Mansoul, signifying that whosoever should discover Carnal-sense, and apprehend him and slay him, should be admitted daily to the Prince's table, and should be made keeper of the treasure of Mansoul. Many, therefore, did bend themselves to do this thing, but take him and slay him they could not, though often he was discovered.

But my Lord took Mr. Wrong-thoughts-of-Christ, and put him in prison, and he died there, though it was long first, for he died of a lingering consumption.

Self-love was also taken and committed to custody; Self-love taken. but there were many that were allied to him in Mansoul, so his judgment was deferred, but at last Mr. Self-

denial stood up and said, if such villains as these may be winked at in Mansoul, I will lay down my commission. He also took him from the crowd, and had him among his soldiers, and there he was brained. But some in Mansoul muttered at it, though none durst speak plainly, because Emmanuel was in town. But this brave act of Captain Self-denial came to the Prince's ears, so he sent for him, and made him a lord Captain Self-denial made a Lord. in Mansoul. My Lord Will-be-will also obtained great commendations of Emmanuel for what he had done for the town of Mansoul.

Then my Lord Self-denial took courage, and set to pursuing of the Diabolonians with my Lord Will-be-will; and they took Live-by-feeling, and they took Legal-life, and put them in hold till they died. But Mr. Unbelief was a nimble jack, him they could never lay hold of, though they attempted to do it often. He, therefore, and some few more of the subtilest of the Diabolonian tribe, did yet remain in Mansoul, to the time that Mansoul left off to dwell any longer in the kingdom of Universe. But they kept them to their dens and holes; if one of them did appear or happen to be seen in any of the streets of the town of Mansoul, the whole town would be up in arms after them, yea the very children in Mansoul would cry out after them as after a thief, and would wish that they might stone them to death with stones. And now did Mansoul arrive to some good degree of peace and quiet, her Prince also The peace of Mansoul, she minds her trade. did abide within her borders, her Captains also, and her soldiers did their duties, and Mansoul minded her trade that she had with the country that was afar off; also she was busy in her manufacture. (Isa. xxxiii. 17. Phil. iii. 20. Prov. xxxi.)

When the town of Mansoul had thus far rid themselves of so many of their enemies, and the troublers of their peace, the Prince sent to them, and appointed a day wherein he would at the market-place meet the whole people, and there give them in charge concerning some further matters, that if observed, would tend to their further safety and comfort, and to the condemnation and destruction of their home-bred Diabolonians. So the day appointed was come, and the townsmen met together; Emmanuel also came down in his chariot, and all his captains in their state attending of him, on the right hand and on the left. Then was an O yes made for silence, and after some mutual carriages of love, the Prince began, and thus proceeded:

"You, my Mansoul, and the beloved of mine heart, many and great are the pri- Emmanuel's speech to Mansoul. vileges that I have bestowed upon you; I have singled you out from others, and have chosen you to myself, not for your worthiness, but for mine own sake. I have also redeemed you, not only from the dread of my Father's law, but from the hand of Diabolus. This

I have done because I loved you, and because I have set my heart upon you to do you good. I have also, that all things that might hinder thy way to the pleasures of paradise might be taken out of the way, laid down for thee, for thy soul, a plenary satisfaction, and have bought thee to myself; a price, not of corruptible things, as of silver and gold, but a price of blood, mine own blood, which I have freely spilt upon the ground to make thee mine. So I have reconciled thee, O my Mansoul, to my Father, and intrusted thee in the mansion-houses that are with my Father in the royal city where things are, O my Mansoul, that eye hath not seen, nor hath entered into the heart of man to conceive.

"Besides, O my Mansoul, thou seest what I have done, and how I have taken thee out of the hands of thine enemies; unto whom thou hast deeply revolted from my Father, and by whom thou wast content to be possessed, and also to be destroyed. I came to thee first by my law, then by my gospel, to awaken thee, and show thee my glory. And thou knowest what thou wast, what thou saidst, what thou didst, and how many times thou rebelledst against my Father and me; yet I left thee not; as thou seest this day, but came to thee, have borne thy manners, have waited upon thee, and after all accepted of thee, even of my mere grace and favour; and would not suffer thee to be lost, as thou most willingly wouldst have been. I also compassed thee about, and afflicted thee on every side, that I might make thee weary of thy ways, and bring down thy heart with molestation to a willingness to close with thy good and happiness. And when I had gotten a complete conquest over thee, I turned it to thy advantage.

"Thou seest also what a company of my Father's host I have lodged within thy borders—captains and rulers, soldiers and men of war, engines and excellent devices to subdue and bring down thy foes; thou knowest my meaning, O Mansoul. And they are my servants, and thine too, Mansoul. Yea, my design of possessing of thee with them, and the natural tendency of each of them is to defend, purge, strengthen, and sweeten thee for myself, O Mansoul, and to make thee meet for my Father's presence, blessing, and glory; for thou, my Mansoul, art created to be prepared unto these.

"Thou seest, moreover, my Mansoul, how I have passed by thy backslidings, and have healed thee. Indeed I was angry with thee, but I have turned mine anger away from thee, because I loved thee still, and mine anger and mine indignation is ceased in the destruction of thine enemies, O Mansoul. Nor did thy goodness fetch me again unto thee, after that I for thy transgressions have hid my face, and withdrawn my presence from thee. The way of backsliding was thine, but the way and means of thy recovery was mine. I invented the means of thy return; it was I that made an hedge and a wall, when thou wast beginning to turn to things in which I delighted not. It was I that made thy sweet, bitter; thy day, night; thy smooth ways thorny; and that also confounded all that sought thy destruction. It was I that set Mr. Godly-fear to work in Mansoul. It was I that stirred up thy conscience and understanding, thy will and thy affections, after thy great and woful decay. It was I that put life into thee, O Mansoul, to seek me, that thou mightest find me, and in thy finding, find thine own health, happiness, and salvation. It was I that fetched the second time the Diabolonians out of Mansoul; and it was I that overcame them, and that destroyed them before thy face.

"And now, my Mansoul, I am returned to thee in peace, and thy transgressions against me are as if they had not been. Nor shall it be with thee as in former days, but I will do better for thee than at thy beginning. For yet a little while, O my Mansoul, even after a few more times are gone over thy head, I will—but be not thou troubled at what I say—I will take down this famous town of Mansoul, stick and stone to the ground. (1 Chron. xxix. 30.) And will carry the stones thereof, and the timber thereof, and the walls thereof, and the dust thereof, and the inhabitants thereof, into mine own country, even into the kingdom of my Father; and will there set it up in such strength and glory, as it never did see in the kingdom where now it is placed. I will even there set it up for my Father's habitation, for, for that purpose it was at first erected in the kingdom of Universe; and there will I make it a spectacle of wonder, a monument of mercy, and the admirer of its own mercy. There shall the natives of Mansoul see all that of which they have seen nothing here; there shall they be equal to those unto whom they have been inferior here. And there shalt thou, O my Mansoul, have such communion with me, with my Father, and with your Lord Secretary, as is not possible here to be enjoyed, nor ever could be, shouldest thou live in Universe the space of a thousand years.

"And there, O my Mansoul, thou shalt be afraid of murderers no more; of Diabolonians and their threats no more. There, there shall be no more plots, nor contrivances, nor designs against thee, O my Mansoul. There thou shalt no more hear the evil tidings, or the noise of the Diabolonian drum. There thou shalt not see the Diabolonian standard-bearers, nor yet behold Diabolus his standard. No Diabolonian mount shall be cast up against thee there, nor shall there the Diabolonian standard be set up to make thee afraid. There thou shalt not need captains, engines, soldiers, and men of war. There thou shalt meet with no sorrow, nor grief, nor shall it be possible that any Diabolonian should again, for ever, be able to creep into thy skirts, burrow in thy walls, or be seen again within thy borders all the days of eternity. Life shall there last longer than here you are able to desire it should, and yet it shall always be sweet and new, nor shall any impediment attend it for ever.

"There, O Mansoul, thou shalt meet with many of those that have been like thee, and that have been partakers of thy sorrows; even such as I have chosen, and redeemed and set apart as thou for my Father's court and city royal. All they will be glad in thee, and thou, when thou seest them, shall be glad in thine heart.

"There are things, O Mansoul, even things of thy Father's providing and mine, that never were seen since the beginning of the world, and they are laid up with my Father, and sealed up among his treasures for thee, till thou shalt come thither to enjoy them. I told you before that I would remove my Mansoul, and set it up elsewhere; and where I will set it, there are those that love thee, and those that rejoice in thee now, but how much more when they shall see thee exalted to honour. My Father will then send them for you to fetch you; and their bosoms are chariots to put you in. And you, O my Mansoul, shall ride upon the wings of the wind. They will come to convey, conduct, and bring you to that; when your eyes see more, that will be your desired haven. (Ps. lxviii. 17.)

"And thus, O my Mansoul, I have showed unto thee what shall be done to thee hereafter, if thou canst hear, if thou canst understand; and now I will tell thee what at present must be thy duty and practice, until I shall come and fetch thee to myself, according as is related in the Scriptures of truth.

"First, I charge thee that thou dost hereafter keep more white and clean the liveries which I gave thee before my last withdrawing from thee. Do it, I say, for this will be thy wisdom. They are in themselves fine linen, but thou must keep them white and clean. This will be your wisdom, your honour, and will be greatly for my glory. When your garments are white, the world will count you mine. Also when your garments are white, then I am delighted in your ways; for then your goings to and fro will be like a flash of lightning, that those that are present must take notice of, also their eyes will be made to dazzle thereat. Deck thyself therefore according to my bidding, and make to thyself by my law straight steps for thy feet, so shall thy King greatly desire thy beauty, for he is thy Lord, and worship thou him.

"Now that thou mayest keep them as I bid thee, I have, as I before did tell thee, provided for thee an open fountain to wash thy garments in. Look therefore that thou wash often in my fountain, and go not in defiled garments; for as it is to my dishonour and my disgrace, so it will be to thy discomfort, when you shall walk in filthy garments. (Zec. iii. 3, 4.) Let not therefore my garments, your garments, the garments that I gave thee, be defiled or spotted by the flesh. (Jude 23.) Keep thy garments always white, and let thy head lack no ointment.

"My Mansoul, I have ofttimes delivered thee from the designs, plots, attempts, and conspiracies of Diabolus, and for all this I ask thee nothing, but that thou render not to me evil for my good, but that thou bear in mind my love, and the continuation of my kindness to my beloved Mansoul, so as to provoke thee to walk, in thy measure, according to the benefit bestowed on thee. Of old the sacrifices were bound with cords to the horns of the golden altar. Consider what is said to thee, O my blessed Mansoul.

"O my Mansoul, I have lived, I have died; I live, and will die no more for thee. I live that thou mayest not die. Because I live thou shalt live also. I reconciled thee to my Father by the blood of my cross, and being reconciled thou shalt live through me. I will pray for thee, I will fight for thee, I will yet do thee good.

"Nothing can hurt thee but sin; nothing can grieve me but sin; nothing can make thee base before thy foes but sin. Take heed of sin, my Mansoul.

"And dost thou know why I at first, and do still suffer Diabolonians to dwell in thy walls, O Mansoul? It is to keep thee wakening, to try thy love, to make thee watchful, and to cause thee yet to prize my noble captains, their soldiers, and my mercy.

"It is also that yet thou mayest be made to remember what a deplorable condition thou once wast in. I mean when, not some, but all did dwell, not in thy walls, but in thy castle, and in thy stronghold, O Mansoul!

"O my Mansoul, should I slay all them within, many there be without that would bring thee into bondage; for were all those within cut off, those without would find thee sleeping, and then as in a moment they would swallow up my Mansoul. I therefore, left them in thee, not to do thee hurt, the which they yet will, if thou hearken to them, and serve them; but to do thee good, the which they must, if thou watch and fight against them. Know, therefore, that whatever they shall tempt thee to, my design is that they should drive thee, not further off, but nearer to my Father, to learn thee war, to make petitioning desirable to thee, and to make thee little in thine own eyes. Hearken diligently to this, my Mansoul.

"Show me then thy love, my Mansoul, and let not those that are within thy walls take thy affections off from him that hath redeemed thy soul. Yea, let the sight of a Diabolonian heighten thy love to me. I came once, and twice, and thrice to save thee from the poison of those arrows that would have wrought thy death; stand for me, thy friend, my Mansoul, against the Diabolonians, and I will stand for thee before my Father, and all his court. Love me against temptation, and I will love thee notwithstanding thine infirmities.

"O my Mansoul, remember what my captains, my soldiers, and mine engines have done for thee. They have fought for thee, they have suffered by thee, they have borne much at thy hands to do thee good, O Mansoul. Hadst thou not had them to help thee, Diabolus had certainly made a hand of thee. Nourish them, therefore, my Mansoul. When thou dost well, they will be well ; when thou dost ill, they will be ill, and sick, and weak. Make not my captains sick, O Mansoul, for if they be sick, thou canst not be well; if they be weak thou canst not be strong ; if they be faint, thou canst not be stout and valiant for thy King, O Mansoul. Nor must thou think always to live by sense, thou must live upon my Word. Thou must believe, O my Mansoul, when I am from thee, that yet I love thee, and bear thee upon mine heart for ever.

"Remember, therefore, O my Mansoul, that thou art beloved of me; as I have therefore taught thee to watch, to fight, to pray, and to make war against my foes, so now I command thee to believe that my love is constant to thee. O my Mansoul, how have I set my heart, my love upon thee, watch. Behold, I lay none other burden upon thee than what thou hast already; hold fast till I come."

AN ADVERTISEMENT TO THE READER.

Some say the Pilgrim's Progress is not mine,
Insinuating as if I would shine
In name and fame by the worth of another,
Like some made rich by robbing of their brother.
Or that so fond I am of being sire,
I'll father bastards ; or, if need require,
I'll tell a lie in print to get applause.
I scorn it : John such dirt-heap never was,
Since God converted him. Let this suffice
To show why I my Pilgrim patronize.

It came from mine own heart, so to my head,
And thence into my fingers trickled ;
Then to my pen, from whence immediately
On paper I did dribble it daintily.

Manner and matter too was all mine own,
Nor was it unto any mortal known,
'Till I had done it. Nor did any then
By books, by wit, by tongues, or hand, or pen,
Add five words to it, or write half a line
Thereof : the whole, and every whit, is mine.

Also, for this thine eye is now upon,
The matter in this manner came from none
But the same heart, and head, fingers, and pen,
As did the other. Witness all good men ;
For none in all the world, without a lie,
Can say that this is mine, excepting I.

I write not this of any ostentation,
Nor 'cause I seek of men their commendation ;
I do it to keep them from such surmise,
As tempt them will my name to scandalize.
Witness my name, if anagram'd to thee,
The letters make, *Nu hony in a B.*

                                        JOHN BUNYAN.

NOTES.

NOTE 1, p. 7.—" *A Council of War.*"]—The resemblance between the leading idea of this assembly and of that described in the *Paradise Lost*, is far too close to be ascribed to accident. Bunyan had seized upon Milton's wonderful recital with the natural vigour and delight of his ardent fancy ; but he wished to make it profitable to his own purposes as a popular teacher. This could only be accomplished by reducing the characters and scenes in Milton from their gigantic proportions to a somewhat less than natural size; or by converting the sublime and awful into a rough and homely familiarity. With these changes, he could make the groundwork of Milton's narrative, and even his personages, available to his own humble design. This he has done; and an intelligent reader may find much to interest him in comparing the two descriptions of the council of war, with the several circumstances and dialogues, as given by one of the greatest of poets, and by one of the most useful of teachers. The question might be put by a curious inquirer, whether, had Bunyan been the first to handle such a theme, Milton would have conceived the idea of exalting it from the humble level of Bunyan's conception, and by a process the reverse of Bunyan's, converting the most homely images into forms of terrible and surpassing grandeur. It is not at all improbable that Milton would have done this had the *Holy War* fallen into his hands under favourable circumstances. Some of the most grotesque tales and traditions have been invested by the genius of poets with a pathos and beauty very foreign to their original shape.

NOTE 2, p. 10.—" *King Shaddai.*"]—Shaddai is an authorized and well-chosen name for the Almighty Ruler of the universe. A reader unaccustomed to the style of such writers as Bunyan, feels some difficulty in reconciling to his taste the mixture of proper names and titles with such appellations as "My Lord Understanding," "Mr. Conscience," "Mr. Swearing," "Mr. Stand-to-lies," "Mr. Drunkenness," and so on. The main objection to such names is the excess of their simplicity—their too plain and open meaning. In ordinary writing, it is the author's aim to bring out and show the principal characters with which he has to do by a gradual display of their temper and principles. The reader's chief interest consists in watching their words; tracing their course of action, till, one after another, their peculiarities come to light, and the ruling passion is discovered amid all the deceits and intricacies of the heart. There is a most agreeable excitement in this process of detecting the carefully-concealed characteristics of a selfish nature. But this pleasure is lost when the personages with whom we are concerned come before us broadly designated, the very fringes of their garments covered with the names of their virtues or vices. Knowing at once what they are, we foretell their history; and the moral is so much the less impressive or forcible as it is learnt with the less effort of thought or attention. Bunyan has contrived to introduce so much action into his story, that his use of trivial names is readily excused. They would have rendered an ordinary recital flat and wearisome, but they are lost sight of and forgotten in the rush of unexpected incidents.

NOTE 3, p. 16.—" *To be drawn up in writing,*" *&c.*]— This proclamation, making licentiousness a law, is evidently based upon the unhappy accounts given of the Anabaptists of Munster, and other parts of the continent, and, in Bunyan's time, remembered as the chronicles of yesterday. Terrible as is the representation of the fiction, it only simply describes what were the actual facts during the reign of Antinomian fanaticism. The subtlety of Satan was proved in this case by the most skilful use of all the means in his power to subvert common sense, as well as morals. His success was so pre-eminent, that every succeeding generation

has learned to look with dread at any repetition of the experiment. Just as the odious wretch, described by Bunyan, set up his proclamation, so did the Anabaptists of Munster suffer John of Leyden openly to trample under foot the laws of God. This miserable fanatic having fortified himself in Munster, was crowned by his wretched followers in the month of June, 1534, and proclaimed king of the whole earth. One of the first acts of his sovereignty was to emancipate "the saints" from the restraint of a single marriage. This was described as a legal bondage, unfitting the state of liberty to which they were exalted. He soon numbered in his own household fifteen wives. His followers had a number proportioned to their dignity in his spiritual kingdom. Every other principle established as a rule of conduct corresponded with this: and had the terrible movement thus begun been permitted to succeed, the real world would, in a very few years, have been precisely in the condition of the fictitious city of Mansoul, when in its lowest state of depravity and bondage. The old leaven of Anabaptism had not quite worn itself out when the *Holy War* was written. More than occasional allusions are made to this fact in the course of the narrative.

NOTE 4, pp. 21—23.—The whole of this conference is admirably described. Whether tried by Scripture, or by the experience of men's hearts, it is equally and wonderfully truthful. The approaches, the merciful forbearance of God, would, after a certain amount of suffering for sin, be readily acknowledged and welcomed, could some indulgence be still rendered to favourite vices and follies. There is something which each and every man would surrender for the sake of safety ; but the question ought never to be, how much am I willing to yield ? for, as long as there is any limiting or measuring, there can be no treaty with God. "Am I ready to submit, to give up myself, and all which concerns me, to his will ?" This is the only question which goes to the point, or to which it can be of any avail to return an answer. The conditions of "My Lord Will-be-will," and of "Mansoul," are precisely those insisted upon by men who have begun to tremble for their souls, and would just put themselves in a state of safety. They must have a reserve in the world, and a retreat somewhere about its borders; both are required. The reserve, in the way of pleasures or possessions, is needed in case the peace and blessings of holiness should prove unsatisfying ; and the retreat, to provide against misgivings, or a final breaking of the covenant with heaven. But no such considerations can be allowed where God is concerned. The rebel owes an infinite debt of gratitude for the offer of pardon, and it is equally his duty and interest to accept it, though only to be had by an unconditional and unquestioning surrender both for time and eternity.

NOTE 5, p. 33.—" *Great Sir,*" *&c. &c.*]—It must be remembered that the people who thus spoke were under the government of a tyrant and usurper. Had they not been subject to an unlawful rule, their words would only have expressed a loyal and proper sentiment. Much of the moral of the lesson depends upon this point.

NOTE 6, p. 39.—The readers of Froissart, Holinshed, and other old chroniclers, will be reminded of these authors by many passages in the *Holy War*. Bunyan evidently knew and relished them. However he became acquainted with such sources of information, he had made good use of his opportunities. His descriptions, are doubtless, enlivened by his own vivid recollections of actual scenes and events ; but they perpetually exhibit signs of a knowledge to be gained from books only. To suppose him wanting in these resources is to throw a doubt upon his authorship.

NOTE 7, p. 65.—" *Hardly a week would pass,*" *&c.*]— This account of the frequent banquetings enjoyed by the people, now rich in their Prince's favour, answers to the pictures drawn of the primitive church. In those times, when faith and love were in their freshest state of vigour, every act of public worship was accompanied, or followed, by the feast of communion. This, till formalism and hypocrisy invaded the sanctuary, diffused an air of joy and festivity through the assembly; and Bunyan's description, with its sweet and sober gaiety, only answered to a daily reality.

NOTE 8, p. 79.—" *Mr. Prywell, a great lover of,*" &c.]— A better name than Prywell might have been found for this " great lover of the people of Mansoul;" but the narrative of his proceedings is striking and ingenious. It is pleasant to watch him on his stealthy path, taking advantage of the night to go and listen at the very door of the enemy's house. The diligence of my Lord Mayor, the speed with which the preacher roused the town, and the measures taken for its safety, are described with such quiet simplicity, that the whole account wins an assent to its truthfulness, and we hardly care to inquire whether it be the literal or the spiritual truth to which we thus assent. It need scarcely be observed, that the preacher is called " subordinate," because, as a type of preachers generally, he is under the Holy Spirit, described, and, as we have already remarked, not well described, by the harsh-sounding title of " Lord Secretary."

NOTE 9, p. 86.—" *There was nothing heard in,*" &c.]— Bunyan, during his brief military career, had had sufficient opportunities of observing how differently two hostile armies may regard the claims of religious duty. History tells us that on the eve of the great battle of Hastings, the English passed the night in revelry, while the Normans employed themselves in acts of devotion. A similar contrast was shown on the eve of the battle of Cressy, though in this case it was the English who prayed, and the French who feasted. But with Cromwell's army it was not an occasional event which led to acts of religion. The sternest discipline of a church could not have produced more remarkable manifestations of earnest, wakeful, severe zeal, than such as were common among the soldiers of the Commonwealth. We have seen that it is very questionable to which of the armies Bunyan himself belonged. The determination of this matter is of no great consequence; on whichever side he stood, the contrast between his own and the opposite party would be equally obvious. However reckless in his conduct, or daring under strange temptations to blasphemy, he never lost his sense of the worth of holiness. Among the fiercest and most licentious of the cavalier troops, he would not forget that they were defying heaven; and that while they had taken upon them to defend their church and their king, they were, in reality, warring against the only power by which kings reign, and princes decree judgment. Short as was the time during which Bunyan continued in the field, it served him as a means of education, of which he made no small use in authorship.

NOTE 10, p. 94.—" *May we not so cumber,*" &c.]—The insecurity in which an over-anxious attention to the interests of commerce may thus place a nation, has been lately alluded to by a celebrated and noble orator. He has probably read Bunyan, and some recollection, more or less perfect, may have put him in mind of the startling picture here drawn of Satan plotting with traders to prevent a trading community from thinking of its dangers or enemies. Bunyan's homely style is to many persons of refined taste like a veil made of sackcloth, and they are unwilling to believe that it can conceal any but the most ordinary features. Where this taste is accompanied with a more robust character of intellect, the veil is accounted nothing, and a steady gaze at the features which it concealed is sufficient to inspire trust and admiration.

NOTE 11.—It is not unworthy of remark, that, from the beginning to the end of this remarkable book, Bunyan almost equally divides the exercise of his invention between the stratagems of war, and the niceties of law and justice. This may be accounted for partly by the nature of the story; but it is still more attributable to the influence which the events of his life exercised on his intellectual habits. He had been a soldier, and had never forgotten what he had seen in the camp, and on the battle-field. Law had been made familiar to him by a more painful experience; but he loved it notwithstanding. His acute mind delighted in its perilous distinctions, and adventurous issues.

PREFATORY REMARKS

LIGHT FOR THEM THAT SIT IN DARKNESS.

LIGHT may be wanting to the human understanding from a variety of circumstances. A different measure of light may be referred to at different times; and, by comparison, that may be darkness to one man, or even at various periods of the same man's life, which, in other cases, will be regarded as light. This enters into the consideration of every careful teacher. The multitudes that sit in darkness are not all wrapped in the folds of the same cloud. Shadows fall upon a man according to the objects among which he moves. Even in broad daylight, he may, if he please, walk in gloom, and the darkness of night itself becomes more or less deep according as we walk in open or secret paths.

In the concerns of the mind, or soul, it is very evident, that a distinction should be made between the darkness which arises from an original want of light, and that which follows upon the loss, or occasional failure of light. If the difference in state and temper in these cases be forgotten, the lessons given with the hope of dispelling the darkness will commonly fail of their due effect. Nothing is sooner or more instinctively felt than the injury inflicted by a wrongly directed lesson on religion. The man who has long been familiar with the literal truth, but has never experienced the power of faith, is not in darkness in the same way as the man who meekly yearns for a Saviour, but knows not where to find him. Were a religious teacher to give the former the catechetical instruction, most needful for the latter, not only would his pains be lost, but harm would be done. The man who is again and again told that which does not meet his case, feels tempted either to turn from it with disregard, or to reject it as utterly wanting in the life and reality to which he is left insensible. If it fail to affect him now, when it is repeated with marked distinctness and earnestness, this failure seems to justify his persevering infidelity, or indifference. The formal teacher may be supposed to have done his best; to have exercised sound judgment; to have placed the facts and lessons with which he is concerned in the most profitable points of view. When this process is exhausted, he may, if competent to the task, begin another with stricter attention to the mental or spiritual state of the learner. But the error of pressing instruction not needed, or not adapted to the state of the soul, often proves an invincible bar to any after success, however benevolently sought.

The same, or no less, danger is to be apprehended from the notion, that a person who has none of that elementary knowledge which catechetical instruction might afford, can be safely addressed as only wilfully ignorant; or as immersed in the darkness of his selfishness and earthly affections. If ignorance be the consequence of adverse circumstances rather than of pride or indifference, it can hardly be connected with the notion of moral guilt. The reproofs, the arguments, and exhortations which would be eminently proper in the latter case, would be highly inapplicable in that of a man who had never been admitted to the study of Christian evidence or doctrine. He could hardly fail to hear, with a painful and perplexed feeling, persuasions to cultivate a state of mind for which he had no preparation; or rebukes for want of faith, or delight in doctrines to which he was a stranger.

In either case, the evil is of great practical importance. The man who is not well grounded in the principles of religion must be taught them before he is appealed to on points of spiritual experience; and the man who has long been familiar with the fundamental truths of the gospel, but has not profited by his knowledge, must be shown not how to repeat his creed more fluently, but how to detect those secret corruptions and perverted feelings of the heart, which render his knowledge of no avail. There is darkness in both cases; darkness which, if unremoved, cannot but peril the salvation of the soul. Charity prompts the believer in the gospel to do his best towards delivering his neighbour from so dangerous a state; but he must know with whom he is dealing, and not treat the case of simple want, as if it were one where medicine is needed, or the distempered soul, as if it only required knowledge.

While this broad distinction exists between the two classes of those who sit in darkness, and who require so different a mode of address, there is still another to be observed of almost equal importance.

In both classes there will be some who are anxiously looking for the appearance of the day-star—who feel the darkness about them cold and horrible, and cry for light as for the saving power of a failing nature. There will be also those to whom the darkness is no felt or acknowledged distress—who regard it with indifference, or indulge it as a convenient cloak for their follies and deformities. A great difference of treatment is necessary with minds so differently disposed. Reproof, in the one case, may sound like a fatal discouragement : in the other, it will be almost an essential element of instruction.

The cautions necessary for a teacher may often be made applicable to the learner. We greatly retard our own advancement in religious knowledge by neglecting to consider the particular character of our defects. It is as bad for us to suppose that we need more intellectual instruction when the darkness is in our will rather than in our minds, as it is for a teacher to catechise us, when our hearts may be saying, " Teach us to pray." Take the other side, and the self-inquiry is equally necessary. A man may easily deceive himself into the notion that he is sufficiently well acquainted with Christian doctrine. But, not supposing any defect of understanding, the distractions of common life may have prevented his giving due attention to the subject, and his views may consist of the notions which he has gleaned only from his intercourse with the world. If such a man flatter himself that he need merely some better training in sentiment, and that it would be an unnecessary act of humiliation, should he submit to be taught as a little child, he is never likely to attain to a saving knowledge of the truth.

Bunyan's *Light for them that sit in Darkness*, may be profitably read with a view to the principles here suggested. He had too practical a mind, and possessed too much experience, not to have respect to the variety of characters which he wished to influence.

                                                                                    H. S.

LIGHT FOR THEM THAT SIT IN DARKNESS;

OR,

A DISCOURSE OF JESUS CHRIST:

AND THAT HE UNDERTOOK TO ACCOMPLISH, BY HIMSELF, THE ETERNAL REDEMPTION OF SINNERS

ALSO,

HOW THE LORD JESUS ADDRESSED HIMSELF TO THIS WORK—WITH UNDENIABLE DEMONSTRATIONS
THAT HE PERFORMED THE SAME.

OBJECTIONS TO THE CONTRARY ANSWERED.

" Christ hath redeemed us from the Curse of the Law, being made a curse for us."—GAL. iii. **13.**

THE AUTHOR TO THE READER.

GENTLE READER,—It was the great care of the Apostle Paul to deliver his gospel to the churches in its own simplicity, because, *so* it is the power of God unto salvation to every one that believeth; and if it was his care so to deliver it to us, it should be ours to seek so to continue it; and the rather, because of the unaptness of the minds, even of the saints themselves, to retain it without commixture. For, to say nothing of the projects of hell, and of the cunning craftiness of some that lie in wait to deceive even the godly themselves, as they are dull of hearing, so much more dull in receiving and holding fast the simplicity of the gospel of Jesus Christ. From their sense, and reason, and unbelief, and darkness, arise many imaginations and high thoughts, which exalt themselves against the knowledge of God, and the obedience of Jesus Christ, wherefore they themselves have much ado to stand complete in all the will of God. And were they not concerned in electing love, by which they are bound up in the bundle of life, and blessed with the enjoyment of saving grace, which enlighteneth their souls and maintaineth their faith and hope, they would not only be assaulted, and afflicted with their own corruptions, but, as others, overcome thereby.

· Alas! how ordinary a thing is it for professors to fall from the knowledge they have had of the glorious gospel of the blessed God, and to be turned unto fables, seducing spirits, and doctrines of devils, through the intoxications of delusions, and the witchcraft of false preachers.

Now this, their swerving from the gospel, ariseth—1st, either from their not having, or,

having, not retaining the true knowledge of the person of the Lord Jesus Christ: or, 2nd, from their not believing the true causes of his coming into the world, with his doing and suffering there. Upon one or both these accounts, I say it is that they everlastingly perish; for, if they have not, and do not also retain the knowledge of his person, they want the *He*, on whom, if they believe not, they must die in their sins; and if they know not the reason of his coming, doing, and suffering, they are in the same condition also.

Now, those professors that have had some knowledge of these things, and yet have lost them, it hath come thus to pass with them, because they first lost the knowledge of themselves, and of their sins. They know not themselves to be such nothing-ones as the Scripture reporteth them to be, nor their sins to be so heinous as the law hath concluded; therefore, they either turn again with the dog to his vomit, or adhere to a few of the rags of their own fleshly righteousness, and so become pure in their own eyes, yet are not purged by blood from their filthiness.

For the person and doings of Jesus Christ are only precious to them that get and retain the true knowledge of themselves, and the due reward of their sins by the law. These are desolate, being driven out of all; these embrace the rock instead of a shelter. The sensible sinner receiveth him joyfully.

And because a miscarriage in this great truth is the most dangerous and damning miscarriage, therefore should professors be the more fearful of swerving aside therefrom. The man that rejecteth the true knowledge of the person of the Lord Jesus, and the causes of his doing and suffering in the world, takes the next way to be guilty of that transgression that is not to be purged with sacrifice for ever; that *fearful* transgression, for which is left *no* offering *at all,* nor anything to be expected by the person transgressing, but fearful judgment, and fiery indignation, which shall devour the adversary.

Now, for their sakes that have not sinned this sin, for their sakes that are in danger thereof, but yet not overcome, for their sakes have I written this little book; wherein is largely, and yet with few words, discovered the doctrine of the person, and doings, and sufferings of Christ, with the true cause thereof; also a removal of those objections that the crafty children of darkness have framed against the same.

And I have been the more plain and simple in my writing, because the sin against the Holy Ghost is in these days more common than formerly, and the way unto it more beautified with colour and pretence of truth. I may say of the way to this sin, it is, as was once the way to Jerusalem, strewed with boughs and branches, and by some there is cried a kind of Hosanna to them that are treading these steps to hell. Oh, the plausible pretences, the golden names, the feigned holiness, the demure behaviours mixed with damnable hypocrisy, that attends the persons that have forsaken the Lord Jesus, that have despised his person, trampled upon him, and counted the blood of the covenant wherewith he was sanctified, an unholy thing! They have crucified him to themselves, and think that they can go to heaven without him; yea, pretend they love him, when they hate him; pretend they have him, when they have cast him off; pretend they trust in him, when they bid defiance to his undertakings for the world.

Reader, let me beseech thee to hear me patiently; read, and consider, and judge. I have presented thee with that which I have received from God; and the holy men of God, who spake as they were moved by the Holy Ghost, do bear me witness. Thou wilt say, All pretend to this. Well, but give me the hearing, take me to the Bible, and let me find in thy heart no favour if thou find me to swerve from the standard.

I say again, receive my doctrine; I beseech thee, in Christ's stead, receive it. I know it to be the way of salvation. I have ventured my own soul thereon with gladness; and if all the souls in the world were mine, as mine own soul is, I would, through God's grace, venture every one of them there. I have not writ at a venture, nor borrowed my doctrine from libraries. I depend upon the sayings of no man: I found it in the Scriptures of truth, among the true sayings of God.

I have done when I have exhorted thee to pray, and give heed to the words of God as revealed in the holy writ. The Lord Jesus Christ himself give thee light and life by faith in him; to whom, with the Father, and the good Spirit of grace, be glory and dominion, now and for ever. Amen.

           JOHN BUNYAN.

LIGHT FOR THEM THAT SIT IN DARKNESS.

" Of this man's seed hath God, according to his Promise, raised unto Israel a Saviour, Jesus."—ACTS xiii. 23.

THESE words are part of a sermon which Paul preached to the people that lived at Antioch in Pisidia, where also inhabited many of the Jews. The preparation to his discourse he thus begins, ver. 16: "Men of Israel, and ye that fear God, give audience;" by which, having prepared their minds to attend, he proceeds, and gives a particular relation of God's peculiar dealings with his people Israel, from Egypt to the time of David their king, of whom he treateth particularly—

That he was the son of Jesse, that he was a king, that God raised him up in mercy, that God gave testimony of him, that he was a man after God's own heart, that he should fulfil all his will. (ver. 22.)

And this he did of purpose, both to engage them the more to attend, and because they well knew that of the fruit of his loins God had promised the Messiah should come.

Having thus, therefore, gathered up their minds to hearken, he presented them with his errand; to wit, that the Messiah was come, and that the promise was indeed fulfilled, that a Saviour should be born to Israel. "Of this man's seed," saith he, "hath God, according to the promise, raised unto Israel a Saviour, Jesus."

In this assertion he concludeth, 1. That the promise had kept its due course in presenting a Saviour to Israel; to wit, in David's loins—"Of this man's seed." 2. That the time of the promise was come, and the Saviour was revealed—"God hath raised unto Israel a Saviour." 3. That Jesus of Nazareth, the son of Joseph, was he—"He hath raised unto Israel a Saviour, Jesus."

From these things we may inquire for the explication of the words :—First, What this Jesus is. Second, What it was for this Jesus to be of the seed of David. Third, What it was for Jesus to be of this man's seed according to the promise. Fourth, And what it was for him to be raised unto Israel. These things may give us light into what shall be spoken after.

Quest. 1.—First. What this Jesus is.

He is God, and had personal being from before all worlds; therefore, not such an one as took being when he was formed in the world; he is God's natural son, the eternal son of his begetting and love. " God sent forth his Son ;" he was, and was his Son before he was revealed. " What is his name, and what is his Son's name, if thou canst tell ? " (Prov. xxx. 4. Ezek. xxi. 10.) He hath an eternal generation, such as none can declare ; nor man, nor angel. (Isa. liii. 8.) He was the delight of his Father before he had made either mountain or hill. While as yet he had not made the earth or the fields, or the highest part of the dust of the world, all things were made by him, and without him was not any thing made that was made, and he is before all things, and by him all things consist. It is he with whom the Father consulted when he was about to make man ; when he intended to overthrow Babel, and when he sent Isaiah to harden the hearts of Israel. (Prov. viii. 26. John i. 3. Heb. i. 2, 3. Col. i. 17. Gen. i. 26 ; xi. 7. Isa. vi. 8.) This is the person intended in the text. Hence also he testifies of himself, that he came down from the Father ; that he had glory with him before the world was. And " what and if you shall see the Son of man ascend up where he was before ? " (John vi. 62 ; xvii. 5 ; xvi. 28.)

Quest. 2.—Second. What was it for Jesus to be of David's seed ?

To be of David's seed is to spring from his loins, to come of his race according to the flesh : and therefore as he is David's God, so likewise is he David's Son ; the root and also the offspring of David ; and this the Lord himself acknowledgeth, saying, " I am the root," or God, " and the offspring," and Son " of David, and the bright and morning star." (Rev. xxii. 16.) This is indeed the great mystery, the mystery of godliness. " If David called him Lord, how is he then his Son ? " (Luke ii. 4. Rom. i. 3. 2 Tim. ii. 8. Matt. xxii. 45.) And hence it is that he is said to be " wonderful," because he is both God and man in one person. " To us a child is born, to us a Son is given ; and the government shall be upon his shoulder, and his name shall be called Wonderful." (Isa. ix. 6.) Wonderful indeed ! Wonderful God, Wonderful man, Wonderful God-man, and so a Wonderful Jesus and Saviour. He also hath wonderful love, bore wonderful sorrows for our wonderful sins, and obtained for his a wonderful salvation.

Quest. 3.—Third. What was it for Jesus to be of this man's seed according to the promise ?

1. This word " promise " doth sometimes comprehend all the promises which God made to our fathers, from the first promise to the last ; and so the Holy Ghost doth call them. " The promise made unto the fathers, God hath fulfilled the same to us their children." (Acts xiii. 32, 33.) 2. But the word " promise " here doth in special intend that which God made to David himself. " Men and brethren," said Peter, " let me freely speak unto you of the patriarch David, that he is both dead and buried, and his sepulchre is with us unto this day. Therefore, being a prophet, and knowing that God had sworn with an oath to him, that of the fruit of his loins according to the flesh, he would raise up Christ to sit on his throne, he, seeing this before, spake of the resurrection of Christ," &c. (Acts ii. 29, 30.)

Quest. 4.—Fourth. What was it for Jesus to be raised thus up of God to Israel ?

Here we have two things to consider of : 1. Who Israel is. 2. What it was for Jesus to be raised up unto them.

1. Who Israel is. By " Israel " sometimes we should understand the whole stock of Jacob, the natural children of his flesh ; for that name they have of him ; for he obtained it when he wrestled with the angel, and prevailed, and it remained with his seed in their generations. (Gen. xxxii.) By " Israel " we are to understand all those that God hath promised to Christ. The children of the promise are counted for the seed—the elect Jews and Gentiles. These are called the Israel of God, and the seed of Abraham, whom Jesus in special regarded in his undertaking the work of man's redemption. (Rom. ix. 6. Gal. vi. 16. Heb. ii. 14—16.)

2. What it was for Jesus to be raised up unto them.

These words, " raised up," is diversely taken in the Scripture. (1.) It is taken for " sending ; " as when he saith, he raised them up judges, saviours, and prophets, he means, he sent them such ; and thus he raised up Jesus ; that is, " he sent him." (Judges ii. 16, 18 ; iii. 9, 15. Amos ii. 11.) " I came not," saith he, " of myself, but he sent me. But the Father which sent me gave me a commandment." (John xii. 49.) (2.) To be raised up intimateth one vested with power and authority. Thus he raised up David to be the king of Israel ; he anointed him, and invested him with kingly power. (1 Sam. xvi. 13. Acts xiii. 22.) And thus was Jesus Christ raised up. Hence he is called, " the horn of salvation : " " He hath raised up for us an horn of salvation in the house of his servant David." (Luke i. 69.) (3.) To be raised up intimateth quickening and strengthening, to oppose and overcome all opposition. Thus was Jesus raised up from under sin, death, the rage of the world, and hell, that day that God raised him out of the grave.

Thus, therefore, was Jesus raised up to Israel ; that is, he was sent, authorized, and strengthened

I 2

to, and in the work of their salvation, to the completing of it.

The words thus opened do lay before us these two observations: *First*. That in all ages God gave his people a promise, and so ground for a believing remembrance that he would one day send them a Saviour. *Second*. That when Jesus was come into the world, then was that promise of God fulfilled.

To begin with the first: That in all ages God gave his people a promise, and so ground for a believing remembrance that he would one day send them a Saviour.

This Zacharias testifies when he was filled with the Holy Ghost; for speaking of the Messiah, or the Saviour, he saith that God spake of him by the mouth of all the prophets which have been since the world began; to which I will add that of Peter; "Yea, and all the prophets from Samuel, and those that follow after, as many as have spoken, have likewise foretold of these days." (Luke i. 69, 70. Acts iii. 24.)

From these texts it is evident that in every generation or age of the world God did give his people a promise, and so ground for a believing remembrance, that he would one day send them a Saviour; for indeed the promise is not only a ground for remembrance, but for a believing remembrance. What God saith is sufficient ground for faith, because he is truth, and cannot lie or repent. But that is not all; his heart was engaged, yea, all his heart, in the promise which he spoke, of sending us a Saviour.

From this observation I shall make inquiry into these three things: *First*. What it is to be a Saviour. *Second*. How it appears that God in all ages gave his people a promise that he would one day send them a Saviour. *Third*. That this was ground for a believing remembrance that a Saviour should one day come.

First. What it is to be a Saviour.

1. This word "Saviour" is easy to be understood, it being all one with Deliverer, Redeemer, &c. "A Saviour, Jesus;" both words are of the same signification, and are doubled, perhaps to teach us, that the person mentioned in the text is not called "Jesus" only to distinguish him from other men (for names are given to distinguish); but also, and especially, to specify his office: his name is "Saviour," because it was to be his work, his office, his business in the world. "His name shall be called Jesus, for he shall save his people from their sins." (Matt. i. 21.)

2. This word "Saviour" is a word so large, that it hath place in all the undertakings of Christ; for whatever he doth in his mediation he doth as a Saviour. He interposed between God and man as a Saviour. He engaged against sin, the devil, death, and hell, as a Saviour, and triumphed over them by himself as a Saviour.

3. The word "Saviour," as I said, is all one with Redeemer, Deliverer, Reconciler, Peace-maker, or the like; for though there be variation in the terms, yet Saviour is the intendment of them all. By redeeming he becomes a Saviour, by delivering he becomes a Saviour, by reconciling he becomes a Saviour, and by making peace he becometh a Saviour. But I pass this now, intending to speak more to the same question afterwards.

Second. How it appears that God in all ages gave his people a promise that he would one day send them a Saviour.

It appears evidently, for so soon as man had sinned, God came to him with an heart full of promise, and continued to renew, and renew, till the time of the promised Messiah to be revealed, was come.

1. He promised him under the name of "the seed of the woman," after our first fathers had sinned: "I will put enmity between thee and the woman, and between thy seed and her seed: it shall break thy head, and thou shalt bruise his heel." (Gen. iii. 15.) This the Apostle hath his eye upon when he saith, "when the fulness of the time was come, God sent forth his Son made of a woman, made under the law, to redeem them that were under the law." (Gal. iv. 4, 5.)

2. God renewed this promise to Abraham, and there tells him Christ should be his seed; saying, "In thy seed shall all families of the earth be blessed." (Gen. xii. 3.) "Now," saith St. Paul, "to Abraham and his seed was the promise made." He saith not, And to seeds, as of many; but as of one, "And to thy seed, which is Christ." (Gal. iii. 16.)

3. He was promised in the time of Moses under the name of a "prophet:" "I will raise them up," saith God to him, "a prophet of their brethren, like unto thee." (Deut. xviii. 18.) This Peter expounds of Christ, "For Moses truly said unto the fathers, A prophet shall the Lord your God raise up unto you of your brethren, like unto me; him shall you hear in all things whatsoever he shall say unto you." (Acts iii. 22.)

4. He promised him to David under the title of a "Son;" saying, "I will be to him a Father, and he shall be to me a Son." (2 Sam. vii. 14.) For this the Apostle expounded of the Saviour; saying, "Thou art my Son, this day have I begotten thee;" and again, "I will be to him a Father, and he shall be to me a Son." (Heb. i. 5.)

5. He was promised in the days of Uzziah, Jotham, Ahaz, and Hezekiah, kings of Judah.

(1.) By the name of a branch: "In that day shall the branch of the Lord be beautiful and glorious."

(2.) Under the name of the "Son of a virgin:" "Therefore the Lord himself shall give you a sign: Behold, a virgin shall conceive, and bear a Son, and thou shalt call his name Immanuel." This Matthew expounds of Christ. (Isa. vii. 14. Matt. i. 22.)

(3.) He was promised under the name of a "rod:" "There shall come forth a rod out of the stem of Jesse, and a branch shall grow cut of his roots, and the Spirit of the Lord shall rest upon him." This answereth the text, David was the son of Jesse, and Christ the son of David. (Isa. ii. 1, 2.)

(4.) He is promised under the title of a "king:" "Behold, a king shall rule in righteousness; and a man shall be for a hiding-place for the wind, and a covert from the tempest; as rivers of waters in a dry place, as the shadow of a great rock in a weary land." (Isa. xxxii. 1, 2.)

(5.) He was promised under the name of an "elect servant:" "Behold my servant, whom I uphold; mine elect, in whom my soul delighteth. I have put my Spirit upon him; he shall bring forth judgment to the Gentiles. He shall not cry, nor lift up, nor cause his voice to be heard in the streets. A bruised reed shall he not break, and smoking flax shall he not quench." (Matt. xii. 17—20.)

(6.) He was promised to Jeremiah under the name of "the Lord our Righteousness:" "Behold, the days come, saith the Lord, that I will raise unto David a righteous Branch, and a king shall reign and prosper: he shall execute judgment in the earth. In his days Judah shall be saved, and Israel shall dwell safely; and this is the name wherewith he shall be called, THE LORD OUR RIGHTEOUSNESS." (Jer. xxiii. 5, 6.)

(7.) He was promised by the prophet Ezekiel under the name of "David a shepherd:" "And I will set one shepherd over them, and he shall feed them, even my servant David, he shall feed them; and he shall be their shepherd, and I the Lord will be their God, and my servant David a prince among them; I the Lord have spoken it." (Ezek. xxxiv. 23.)

(8.) He was promised by the prophet Daniel under the name of "Messiah, or Christ, the most holy:" "And after threescore and two weeks shall tne Messiah be cut off, but not for himself." (Dan. ix. 26.)

(9.) He was promised by the prophet Micah under the name of the "ruler in Israel:" "But thou, Bethlehem Ephratah, though thou be little among the thousands of Judah, yet out of thee shall he come, that is to be ruler in Israel." (Mic. v. 2.)

(10.) He was promised by Haggai as "the desire of all nations:" "I will shake all nations, and the desire of all nations shall come, and I will fill this house with glory, saith the Lord of hosts." (Hag. ii. 7.)

(11.) He was promised by Zechariah under the name of "servant and branch:" "For, behold, I will bring forth my servant the branch:" and again, "Behold the man whose name is the Branch; he shall grow up out of his place, and he shall build the temple of the Lord, and he shall bear the glory." (Zech. iii. 8; vi. 12, 13.)

(12.) He was promised by Malachi under the name of "the Lord," and "the messenger of the covenant:" "Behold, I send my messenger, and he shall prepare the way before me: and the Lord whom ye seek shall suddenly come to his temple; even the messenger of the covenant whom ye delight in; behold, he shall come, saith the Lord of hosts." (Mal. iii. 1.)

Indeed, the Scriptures of the Old Testament are filled with promises of the Messias to come, prophetical promises, typical promises; for all the types and shadows of the Saviour are virtually so many promises.

6. Having, therefore, touched upon the prophetical, I will briefly touch the typical promises also; for as God spake at sundry times to the fathers, so also in divers manners, prophetically, providentially, typically, and all of the Messias. (Heb. i. 1.)

The types of the Saviour were various. First. Sometimes he was typed out *by men*. Second. Sometimes *by beasts*. Third. Sometimes *by insensible creatures*.

First. He was typed forth sometimes *by men*. Adam was his type in many things, especially as he was the head and father of the first world. He was "the figure of him that was to come." (Rom. v. 14.) Moses was his type as mediator, and as builder of the tabernacle. (Heb. iii. 2, 3.) Aaron was his type as he was high priest, and so was Melchisedec before him. (Heb. v. 4, 5; vii. 1, 21.) Samson was his type in the effects of his death; for as Samson gave his life for the deliverance of Israel from the Philistines, Christ gave his life to deliver us from sin and devils. Joshua was his type in giving the land of Canaan to Israel, as Jesus will give the kingdom of heaven to the elect. (Heb. iv. 8.) David was his type in many things, especially in his subduing of Israel's enemies, and feeding them; hence he is sometimes called David their king, and David their shepherd. (Ezek. xxxiv. 23, 24.) Solomon was his type in his building the temple, and in his peaceable kingdom. Hence it is said, "He shall build the temple of the Lord;" and again, "Of his government and peace there shall be no end."

Second. *Beasts were his types*. To instance some:

1. The paschal lamb was his type. (Exod. xii.) In its spotlessness. Christ was a "a lamb without blemish and without spot." (1 Pet. i. 18, 19.) In its being roasted, it was a figure of the cursed death of Christ, for to be roasted bespake one accursed. (Jer. xxix. 22. Gal. iii. 13.) In that it was to be eaten: "He that eateth my flesh, and drinketh my blood," saith Christ, "hath eternal life." (John vi. 54.) In that its blood was to be sprinkled upon the doors of their houses, for the destroying angel to look on. The blood of Christ is sprinkled upon the elect, for the justice of God to look on. (Heb. ix. 1 Pet. i. 2.) By eating the paschal lamb the people went out of Egypt; by feeding upon Christ by faith, we come from under the Egyptian darkness, tyranny of Satan, &c.

2. The red cow was his type. (Num. xix. 2, &c.) In that she was to be without blemish. In that she was to be slain without the camp. "Jesus also, that he might sanctify the people with his own blood, suffered without the gate." (Heb. xiii. 12.) In that her flesh was to be burnt; a type of the grievous death of Christ. Her ashes was to be carried into a clean place without the camp; a type of the clean sepulchre, where the body of Jesus was laid. (John xix. 38—41.)

There were also divers other sacrifices, as bulls, goats, and birds; which were types of him, which I here omit.

Third. *Insensible creatures were his types.*

1. As, The manna in the wilderness. (Ex. xvi.) And that, as it came down from heaven; for so did Christ: "I came down from heaven," saith he; and again, "I am the living bread which came down from heaven." (John vi. 51.) The manna was to be eaten; so is Christ by faith: "If any man eat of this bread, he shall live for ever; and the bread that I will give is my flesh, which I will give for the life of the world." (John vi. 51.) The manna was to be gathered daily; so is Christ to be daily eaten. The manna was all the bread that Israel had in the wilderness; Christ is all the bread that believers have in this life for their souls. The manna came not by Moses' law, neither comes Christ by our merits: "Moses gave you not that bread from heaven, but my Father giveth you the true bread from heaven." (John vi. 32.)

2. Again; the rock that gave them out water for their thirst was a type of him. (Num. xx.) They "did all drink of the same spiritual drink, for they drank of that spiritual Rock that followed them, and that Rock was Christ." (1 Cor. x. 4.) This rock was his type in four things:—(1.) It gave drink to the people in the wilderness when they were come out of Egypt; Christ gives drink to them that forsake the world for him. (2.) The rock yielded water by being smitten by Moses' rod; Christ giveth drink, even his blood, by being stricken by Moses' law. (Num. xx. 11. Isa. liii.) (3.) The water out of this rock was given to the thirsty: "I will give to them that is a-thirst," saith Christ, "of the fountain of the water of life freely." (Rev. xxi. 6.) (4.) The water of the rock in the wilderness ran after the people; they drank of that rock that followed them: "He opened the rock, and the waters gushed out; they ran in dry places like a river." (Ps. cx. 41.) Christ also is said by that type to follow us: "They drank of that rock that followed them, and that rock was Christ." (1 Cor. x. 4.)

3. Again; the Mount Moriah was his type. That mount stood in Jerusalem; Christ also stands in his church. Upon that rock was built the temple (2 Chron. iii. 1); and "upon this rock," saith Christ, "will I build my church, and the gates of hell shall not prevail against it." (Matt. xvi. 18.)

Other things might be urged, but these being virtually of the force of the promise, and also as a key to open them, therefore I thought good to place them here with the promises; because, as they are standing with them, so they are written to beget faith in the same Lord Jesus Christ.

Third. I come now to the third thing, to wit, That these promises were ground for a believing remembrance that a Saviour should one day come.

There is a remembering, and a believing remembering, or such a remembering that begetteth and maintaineth faith in the heart. Jacob had a believing remembrance, when he said, "I have waited for thy salvation, O Lord." (Gen. xlix. 18.) And so had David when he cried, "O that the salvation of Israel was come out of Zion." (Ps. liii. 6.) These, with Simeon and Anna, had not remembrance only, but a believing remembrance, that God would send them a Saviour. They had the promise not in the book only, but in their hearts. This gospel was mixed in them with faith; therefore they, with their fellows, remembered and believed, or made the promise the ground of their believing, that God would one day send them a Saviour.

Let me make some *Use of this Doctrine.*

Here we may see how much the heart of God was set upon the salvation of sinners: he studied it, contrived it, set his heart on it, and promised, and promised, and promised to complete it, by sending one day his Son for a Saviour. (Eph. i. 2. 2 Sam. xiv. 14. Tit. i. 2.) No marvel, therefore, if when he treateth of the new covenant, in which the Lord Jesus is wrapped, and presented in a word of promise to the world, that he saith, I will do it assuredly "with my whole heart, and with my whole soul." (Jer. xxxii. 41.)

Now this is of singular comfort to sensible sinners; yea, what greater ground of consolation to such, than to hear that the God against whom they have sinned, should himself take care to provide us a Saviour. There are some poor sinners in the world that have given such way to discouragement, from the sense of the greatness of their sins, that they dare not think upon God, nor the sins which they have committed; but the reason is, because they are ignorant that God's heart was wrapt up in this good work of providing and sending a Saviour. Let such hearken now to the call of God: "Return unto me, for I have redeemed thee." (Isa. xliv. 22.) Oh! turn again, hearken; the heart of God is much [set upon mercy, from the beginning of the world he resolved and promised, ay, and sware we should have a Saviour.

Second. I now proceed to the *second observation.* That when Jesus was come into the world, then was the promise of God fulfilled, namely, that he would one day send us a Saviour.

Take three texts for the confirmation of this point: 1. "This is of a truth that prophet that should come into the world." (John vi. 14.)

Nazareth, looking towards the Plain of Esdraelon

These words were spoken of them that were present at that miracle of Jesus, when he fed five thousand with five barley loaves, which a lad had about him in the company; for these men, when they had seen the miracle, being amazed at it, made confession of him to be the Saviour. 2. "Lord, I believe thou art the Christ, the Son of God, which should come into the world." (John ix. 27.) 3. "This is a faithful saying, and worthy of all acceptation, that Christ Jesus came into the world to save sinners." (1 Tim. i. 15.)

For the explaining of this observation, I will briefly handle three questions: First. How this Jesus is to be distinguished from others of that name. Second. What it was for this Jesus to come into the world. Third. What it was for him to come to be a Saviour.

Quest. First. For the first, The Jesus in the text is distinguished from all others of that name.

1. By the manner of his birth. He was born of a virgin, a virgin espoused to a man whose name was Joseph; but he "knew her not till she had brought forth her first-born son, and he called his name Jesus." (Matt. i. 25.)

2. He is distinguished from others of that name by the place of his birth; to wit, Bethlehem, the city of David; there he must be born, there he was born. (John vii. 42. Matt. ii. 4—6.)

3. He is distinguished by his lineage: He came "of the house and lineage of David." (Luke ii. 4—6.)

4. He is distinguished by the time of his birth; to wit, the time of the prophets prefixed. (Gal. iv. 4.)

5. But his common distinction is, "Jesus of Nazareth;" by his name he is distinguished one and twenty times in the New Testament. (1.) His enemies called him, "Jesus of Nazareth." (Matt. xxvi. 71. Mark xiv. 67. John xviii. 5.) (2.) His disciples called him "Jesus of Nazareth." (Matt. xxi. 11. Luke xxiv. 19. John i. 45. Acts ii. 22.) (3.) The angels called him "Jesus of Nazareth." (Mark xvi. 6.) (4.) And he calleth himself "Jesus of Nazareth." (Acts xxii. 8.) (5.) Yea, and he goeth also by the name of "Jesus of Nazareth" among the devils. (Mark i. 24. Luke iv. 34.)

He was called "Jesus of Nazareth" because he dwelt there with his mother Mary and her husband. Nazareth was his city where he had been brought up, whither for shelter Joseph carried him when he came up out of Egypt with him; in Nazareth was his common abode, until the time that John was cast into prison. (Luke iv. 16. Matt. ii. 23; iv. 12, 13.) Wherefore he might well say, "I am Jesus of Nazareth." Yea, though he was now in heaven; for heaven shall not make us forget what countrymen we were when we lived in the world. Jesus, you see here, though glorified in heaven, yet forgets not what countryman he was when he dwelt in the world. "I am Jesus of Nazareth," saith he, I am the Jesus that thou persecutest; and that thou mayest know I am he, I tell thee I dwelt once in the city of Nazareth in Galilee; Joseph and my mother Mary brought me up there, and there I dwelt with them many years. "I am Jesus of Nazareth, whom thou persecutest." (Acts xxii. 8.)

Quest. Second. What was it for Jesus to come into the world?

Answ. Not his coming in, or by his Spirit in his people; for so he was never out of the world. Neither is it his appearance in his ordinances. Nor that coming of his by which he destroyed antichrist. Nor his appearing in his dreadful providences or judgments. But by the coming of Jesus, according to the text, we are to understand that, or such a coming, whereby he was manifest to the God-man in one person—God in our flesh without us, or distinct in his own person by himself; such a coming by which he was manifested to be in all points like as men are, sin only excepted; such a coming, wherein, or by which, the Son of God became also the Son of man.

First, For the further clearing of this, you find it expressly said, he was "born into the world;" Mary, "of whom was born Jesus." Now, when Jesus was born, it is said, "Where is he that is born king of the Jews?" Herod "demanded of them where Christ should be born." (Matt. i. 16; ii. 1—4. Luke i. 35; ii. 11.)

Now, that this was fulfilled according to the very word of the text, without any juggle, evasion, or cunningly devised fable, consider—

1. He is called the first-born of this woman; the male child that opened her womb. (Luke ii. 7, 23.)

2. He was not born till nourished in her womb the full time, according to the time of life. And so it was that while they were at Bethlehem, the days were accomplished that she should be delivered, and she brought forth her first-born Son, and wrapt him in swaddling clothes, and laid him in a manger. (Luke ii. 6, 7.)

3. She also continued in her separation at the birth of Jesus, as other women at the birth of their children, until "the days of her purification, according to the law of Moses, were accomplished." (Luke ii. 22.)

4. Himself, also, as other Hebrew children, was brought to Jerusalem to present him unto the Lord: "As it is written in the law of Moses, Every male that openeth the womb shall be called holy unto the Lord." (Luke ii. 23, 24.)

5. Thus Jesus also, as other Hebrew children, when the set day was come, was circumcised. "And when eight days were accomplished for the circumcising of the child, his name was called Jesus, which was so named of the angel before he was conceived in the womb." (Luke ii. 21.)

6. After this he is often called the young child, the child Jesus; and further it is said of him, that he grew, that he increased in wisdom and stature. (Matt. ii. 20, 21. Luke ii. 40, 52.)

Behold, with what diligence, even to a circumstance, the Holy Ghost sets forth the birth of the Lord Jesus, and all to convince the incredulous world of the true manner of the coming of the Saviour into the world.

Second. The reality of the manhood of this Lord Jesus is yet further manifest, and that— 1. By those natural infirmities that attend human flesh. 2. By the names the prophets gave him in the days of the Old Testament and the New.

1. By those natural infirmities that attend human flesh. As, at his birth he could not go, but as carried by his parents. He was sensible of hunger, (Luke iv. 2). He was sensible of thirst, (John xix. 28). He was sensible of weariness, (John iv. 6). He was nourished by sleep, (Mark iv. 34). He was subject to grief, (Mark iii. 5). He was subject to anger, (Mark iii. 5). He was subject to weep, (John xi. 35. Luke xix. 41). He had joy as a man, and rejoiced, (Matt. xi. 27. Luke x. 21). These things, I say, Jesus was subject to as a man, as the Son of the Virgin.

2. The reality of his manhood is yet made manifest by the names the prophets gave him, both in the Old Testament and in the New. As,

(1.) He is called the "seed." The seed of the woman, the seed of Abraham, the seed of David, by which is meant, he was to come of their children. (Gen. iii. 15; xii. 22. Gal. iii. 16, 17. Rom. i. 4.)

(2.) Therefore it is added (where mention is made of the fathers), "of whom, as concerning the flesh, Christ came." He was made of the seed of David according to the flesh; and hence, again, he calleth himself the offspring of David; therefore, I say, he is said to be of their flesh, their loins, and is called their Son. (Rom. i. 4; ix. 5. Acts ii. 30. Rev. xxii. 16.)

(3.) He therefore is frequently called " a man, and the Son of man :" "Then shall you see the Son of man coming in the clouds of heaven." "When the Son of man shall come in his glory, and all the holy angels with him." " This man, because he continueth ever, hath an unchangeable priesthood." " It is therefore necessary that this man have somewhat also to offer." (Matt. xxvi. 63; xxv. 30, 31. Heb. vii. 24; viii. 3; x. 12.)

(4.) What shall I say? Himself gave undeniable demonstration of all this, when he said, he was dead; when he called to Thomas to put his finger to, and behold his hands, to reach to him his hand and thrust it into his side, and bid him he should not be faithless, but believing. At another time, when he stood in the midst of the eleven, as they were troubled with the thoughts of unbelief, he said, " Behold my hands and my feet, that it is I myself; handle me, and see; for a spirit hath not flesh and bones, as ye see me have." (John xx. 27. Luke xxiv. 39.)

Thus have I showed you what it was for Jesus to come into the world; namely, to be born of a woman, to take flesh, and to become God-man in one person. I come now to the *third question;* but before I speak particularly to that, I will produce further testimony that we find upon record concerning the truth of all this.

Particular Testimonies that this coming of Jesus is his coming to save us.

1. *Simeon the Just* gives testimony of him. " And the Holy Ghost was upon him, and it was revealed unto him by the Holy Ghost that he should not see death before he had seen the Lord's Christ. And he came by the Spirit into the temple; and when the parents brought in the child Jesus, to do for him after the custom of the law, then took he him up in his arms, and blessed God, and said, Lord, now lettest thou thy servant depart in peace, for mine eyes have seen thy salvation." (Luke ii. 25—32.)

2. *The Testimony of Anna.*—Anna, a prophetess, one " of a great age, which departed not from the temple, but served God with fasting and prayer night and day. And she coming in at the same instant, gave thanks likewise unto the Lord, and spake of him to all that looked for redemption in Jerusalem." (Luke ii. 26—28.)

3. *The Testimony of John Baptist.* — John Baptist, as he fulfilled his ministry, he cried concerning this Jesus, " Behold the Lamb of God, that taketh away the sins of the world. And he," saith John, " that sent me to baptize with water, the same said unto me, Upon whom thou shalt see the Spirit descending and abiding," or remaining, " the same is he which shall baptize with the Holy Ghost. And I saw, and bare record that this is the Son of God." (John i. 29—34.)

4. *The Testimony of the Star and Wise Men.*— The star that appeared at his birth in the east, and that coasted through the heavens till it came over the place where the young child Jesus was, that star gave testimony that he was the Saviour. This star alarmed many, especially the wise men of the east, who were brought by it from afar to worship him. " And lo, the star which they saw in the east, went before them till it came and stood over where the young child was. And when they saw the star, they rejoiced with exceeding great joy. And when they were come into the house, they saw the young child with Mary his mother, and fell down and worshipped him; and when they had opened their treasures, they presented unto him gifts, gold, and frankincense, and myrrh." (Matt. ii. 9—11.)

5. *The Testimony of the Angels.*—(1.) To Mary herself: " And in the sixth month the angel Gabriel was sent from God unto a city of Galilee named Nazareth, to a virgin espoused to a man whose name was Joseph, and the virgin's name was Mary. And the angel came in unto her, and said, Hail, thou that art highly favoured. And the angel said unto her, Fear not, Mary, for thou

hast found favour with God. And, behold, thou shalt conceive in thy womb, and bring forth a son, and shalt call his name Jesus. He shall be great, and shall be called the Son of the Highest. And the Lord God shall give unto him the throne of his father David, and he shall reign over the house of Jacob for ever, and of his kingdom there shall be no end." (Luke i. 26—33.) (2.) The angels' testimony to the shepherds, as they were feeding their flocks in the fields by night : " And lo, the angel of the Lord came upon them, and the glory of the Lord shined round about them, and they were sore afraid ; and the angel said unto them, Fear not, for behold, I bring you good tidings of great joy, which shall be to all people ; for unto you is born this day in the city of David, a Saviour, which is Christ the Lord." (Luke ii. 9—11.) (3.) How the angels solemnized his birth among themselves : " And suddenly there was with the angel a multitude of heavenly host, praising God, and saying, Glory to God in the highest ; and on earth peace, good-will towards men." (ver. 13, 14.)

6. *The Testimony of God the Father.*—(1.) When he was baptized : " And Jesus, when he was baptized, went up straightway out of the water ; and, lo, the heavens were open unto him, and he saw the Spirit of God descending like a dove, and lighting upon him ; and, lo, a voice from heaven, saying, This is my beloved Son, in whom I am well pleased." (Matt. iii. 16, 17.) (2.) The Father's testimony concerning the trans-figuration : " And he took Peter, and James, and John, and went up into a mountain to pray. And as he prayed, the fashion of his countenance was altered, and his raiment was white and glittering," &c. And there appeared Moses and Elias talking with him, and a cloud from heaven overshadowed them ; at which the three disciples began to be afraid. Then " there came a voice out of the cloud saying, This is my beloved Son, hear him." (Luke ix. 28—35.) This is that testimony of God which Peter speaks of, saying, " We have not followed cunningly devised fables, when we made known unto you the power and coming of our Lord Jesus Christ, but were eye-witnesses of his majesty ; for he received from God the Father honour and glory, when there came such a voice to him from the excellent glory, This is my beloved Son, in whom I am well pleased. And this voice which came from heaven we heard, when we were with him in the holy mount." (2 Pet. i. 16—18.) (3.) God gave testimony of him by signs and wonders : " Believest thou not that I am in the Father, and the Father in me ? The words that I speak unto you, I speak not of myself, but the Father that dwelleth in me, he doth the works." " God also bearing them witness," that preached salvation by Jesus, " both with signs and wonders, and with divers miracles and gifts of the Holy Ghost, according to his own will." (John xiv. 10. Heb. ii. 4.)

Concerning Jesus, how he put himself upon the test among his adversaries.

The Lord Jesus also putteth himself upon the test among his adversaries divers ways.

First. He urgeth the time of the appearing of the Messias to be come : " The time is fulfilled, and the kingdom of God is at hand ; repent ye, and believe the gospel." (Mark i. 15.)

For this he had a three-fold proof : 1. The heathens had invaded and taken the land, according to that of Daniel. (ix. 25, 26.) 2. The sceptre was departed from Judah, according to that of Jacob. (Gen. xlix. 10.) To which also suited that prophecy : " Before the child shall know to refuse the evil, and choose the good, the land which thou abhorrest shall be forsaken of both her kings." (Isa. vii. 16.) 3. The Roman emperor had not only subdued the nation, and put down the kingly race of the Jews, but had set up and established his own power over them. In the fifteenth year of the reign of Tiberius Cæsar, Pontius Pilate was Governor of Judea ; Herod was Tetrarch of Galilee ; Philip, Tetrarch of Iturea ; and Lysanius, Tetrarch of Abilene ; all heathens, and of Tiberius his making.

Besides, the kingly race of Judah was at this time become so low by reason of the Roman oppression, that the chief of them were put to get their living by their own hands. Even Joseph, the supposed father of Jesus, was then become a carpenter. Poor man ! when Jesus was born, he was fain to thrust into a stable—for there was in the inn no room for such guests as they. The offering also which was brought unto God at the time when Jesus was presented unto the Lord was two turtle-doves, or two young pigeons ; a sacrifice allowed only for them that were poor, and could provide no bigger : " And if she be not able to bring a lamb, then she shall bring two turtle-doves, or two young pigeons, the one for a burnt-offering, the other for a sin-offering." (Lev. xii. 8.) Besides, Jesus himself saith, " Foxes have holes, and the birds of the air have nests, but the Son of man hath not whereon to lay his head."

Now, I say, all these things were so apparent to the Jews, that they could not object ; they felt the Romans were come, they knew the sceptre was gone, they smarted under the Roman tyranny, and knew the kingly race of Judea was overthrown. How, then, could they object, that the time was not come for Christ to be born ?

Further. The people was generally convinced that the time was come, and therefore, saith the text, " they were in expectation." And as all the people were in expectation, and all men mused in their hearts of John, whether he was the Christ or not (Luke iii. 15), the unbiassed people, observing the face of things, could do no other but look for the Messias. And hence it is, that the Lord Jesus gives the Pharisees—those mortal enemies of his—such sore rebukes, saying, " O ye hypocrites, ye can discern the face of the sky, but can ye not discern the signs of the times?" The kingdom is lost, the heathens are come, and the sceptre is departed from Judah. "Ye hypocrites, ye can discern the face of the sky, and of the earth; but how is it that ye do not discern this time?" (Matt. xvi. 3. Luke xii. 56.)

Second. He yet again puts himself upon the test, by the miracles which he wrought before them: "Believe me, that I am in the Father, and the Father in me, or else believe me for the very works' sake." (John xiv. 11.) "For the works which the Father hath given me to finish, the same works that I do, bear witness of me, that the Father hath sent me." (John v. 36.)

This proof they could not withstand, but granted that he did many miracles, while they did nothing. "Then gathered the chief priests and Pharisees a council, and said, What do we? for this man doeth many miracles. If we let him alone, all men will believe on him, and the Romans shall come and take away both our place and nation." (John xi. 47, 48.)

Yea, so did Jesus confound them, that by their own records and laws, by which they were to prove persons clean or unclean, they, in reading their lectures, did justify him, and overthrow themselves.

For instance, it was written in their law: "If he that hath an issue spit upon him that is clean," that spittle should make him unclean. (Lev. xv. 8.) Now Jesus, whom they counted most unclean, because he said he was the Son of God, as they thought speaking blasphemy, he spits upon people and makes them whole. He spat, and made clay with the spittle, and with that clay made a blind man see. (John ix. 6.) Also he spat on the eyes of another, and made him see. (Mark viii. 23—25.) Again, he spat, and with his spittle touched the tongue of one that was dumb, and made him speak immediately. (Mark vii. 33—35.) Thus he proved himself clear of their accusations, and maintained before them that by their law he was guiltless, and the Son of God; for the miracles which he wrought were to prove him so to be.

Again; in their law it was written, that whoso touched the altar of incense should be holy. (Exod. xxix. 37.) A woman with a bloody issue touched him, and is whole of her plague. (Mark v. 28.) Yea, they brought to him many diseased persons; "and besought him that they might only touch the hem of his garment; and as many as touched were made perfectly whole." (Matt. xiv. 36.)

Thus was he justified before them out of their own law, and had his glory manifest before their faces, to their everlasting confusion and contempt.

Indeed, the Jews did make one objection against Jesus Christ, that seemed to them to have weight in it; and that was because he first began to appear, and manifested his glory, in Cana of Galilee. At this, I say, they stumbled; it was

their sore temptation; for still, as some affirmed him to be the Christ, others as fast objected, "Shall Christ come out of Galilee?" "Art thou also of Galilee? Search and look, for out of Galilee ariseth no prophet." (John ii. 1, 11; vii. 40—42, 52.)

But this their stumble might arise either (1), From the cruelty of Herod; or (2), From their own not observing, and keeping in mind the alarm that God gave them at his birth.

1. It might arise or be occasioned through the cruelty of Herod; for Jesus was born in Bethlehem, the city where David dwelt. But when Herod sent out to kill him, and for his sake killed all the young children in Bethlehem, then was Joseph warned by an angel of God to take the young child and his mother, and fly into Egypt; and so he did, and was there till the death of Herod. (Matt. ii. 1, 13, 16.) After this, the angel comes to them in Egypt, and bids them take the young child, and return into the land of Israel; wherefore they arose and went: but hearing that Herod's son, that tyrant, ruled in the room of his father, they were afraid to go to Bethlehem, but turned aside into the parts of Galilee, where they remained till the time of his showing to Israel.

2. This stumble of theirs might arise from their not observing and keeping in mind the alarm that God gave them of his birth. (1.) God began to give them the alarm at the birth of John the Baptist, where was asserted that he was to go before the face of the Lord Jesus, and to prepare his ways. "And fear came upon all that dwelt round about them; and all these sayings were noised abroad throughout all the hill country of Judea." (Luke i. 65.) (2.) Again; what a continuation of this alarm was there also at the birth of Jesus, which was about three months after John Baptist was born! Now comes a strange star over the country, to lead men of the East to the stable where Jesus was born; and now was Herod, the priests, the scribes, and also the city of Jerusalem, awakened and sore troubled: for it was noised by the wise men, that Christ, the King and Saviour, was born. Besides the shepherds, Simeon and Anna gave notice of him to the people; they should therefore have retained the memory of these things, and have followed God in all his dark providences, until his Sun of Righteousness should arise among them, with healing under his wings.

3. I may add another cause of their stumble: They did not understand the prophecies that went before of him. (1.) He was come to them out of Egypt: "Out of Egypt have I called my Son." (Matt. ii. 15.) (2.) He turned aside into Cana of Galilee, and dwelt in the city of Nazareth, "that it might be fulfilled which was spoken by the prophets, He shall be called a Nazarene." (Matt. ii. 23.) (3.) That saying also was to be fulfilled, "The land of Zabulon, and the land of Naphthalim, by the way of the sea beyond Jordan, Galilee of the

Gentiles; the people that sat in darkness saw a great light, and to them that sat in the region and shadow of death, light is sprung up." (Matt. iv. 15, 16.)

At these things, then, they stumbled, and it was a great judgment of God upon them. Besides, there seemed to be a contradiction in the prophecies of the Scriptures concerning his coming. He was to be born in Bethlehem, and yet to come out of Egypt. How should he be the Christ, and yet come out of Galilee, out of which ariseth no prophet? Thus they stumbled.

Hence note, that though the prophecies and promises be full and plain, as these were, that he should be born in Bethlehem, yet men's sins may cause them to be fulfilled in such obscurity, that instead of having benefit thereby, they may stumble and split their souls thereat. Take heed, then; hunt not Christ from plain promises with Herod, hunt him not from Bethlehem, lest he appear to your amazement and destruction from Egypt, or in the land of Zabulon. But thus much to the second question, to wit, What it was for Jesus to come into the world?

I come now to the third question.

Quest. Third. What it was for him to come to be a Saviour?

For the further handling of this question I must show: First. What it is to be a Saviour. Second. What it is to come to be a Saviour. Third. What it is for Jesus to come to be a Saviour. To these three briefly:

First. What it is *to be* a Saviour.

1. A Saviour supposeth some in misery, and himself one that is to deliver them.

2. A Saviour is either such an one ministerially or meritoriously.

Ministerially, is when one person engageth, or is engaged by virtue of respect or command from superiors, to go and obtain by conquest or the king's redemption, the captives or persons grieved by the tyranny of an enemy. And thus were Moses and Joshua, and the judges and kings of Israel, Saviours: "Thou deliverest them into the hand of their enemies, who vexed them; and in the time of their trouble, when they cried unto thee, thou heardest them from heaven; and according to thy manifold mercies thou gavest them saviours, who saved them out of the hand of their enemies." (Neh. ix. 27.) Thus was Jesus Christ a Saviour; he was engaged by virtue of respect and command from God to obtain, by conquest and redemption, the captives or persons grieved; God sent his Son to be the Saviour of the world. (John iv. 42.)

Meritoriously, is when the person engaging shall, at his own proper cost and charge, give a sufficient value and price for those he redeemeth. Thus those under the law were redeemed by the money called redemption money: "And Moses gave the money of those that were redeemed unto Aaron and to his sons." (Num. iii. 46—51.)

And thus was Jesus Christ a Saviour. He paid full price to Divine justice for sinners, even his own precious blood: "Forasmuch as ye know that ye were not redeemed from your vain conversation, received by tradition from your fathers with corruptible things, as silver and gold, but with the precious blood of Christ." (1 Pet. i. 18, 19.)

And forasmuch as, in man's redemption, the undertaker must have respect, not only to the paying of a price, but also to the getting of a victory; for there is not only justice to satisfy, but death, devil, hell, and the grave to conquer: therefore hath he also by himself gotten victory over these. He hath abolished death. (2 Tim. i. 10.) He hath destroyed the devil. (Heb. ii. 14, 15.) He hath been the destruction of the grave. (Hos. xiii. 14.) He hath gotten the keys of hell. (Rev. i. 17—19.) And this, I say, he did by himself at his own proper cost and charge, when he triumphed over them upon his cross. (Col. ii. 14, 15.)

Second. What it is *to come to be* a Saviour?

1. To come to be one, supposeth one ordained, and fore-prepared for that work. "Then said he, Lo, I come, a body hast thou prepared me." (Heb. x. 5, 7.)

2. To come to be a Saviour supposeth one commissionated or authorized to that work. "The Spirit of the Lord is upon me, because he hath anointed me," authorized me, "to preach the gospel to the poor: he has sent me to bind up the broken-hearted, to preach deliverance to the captives, and recovering of sight to the blind, and to set at liberty them that are bruised." (Luke iv. 18.) And upon this account it is, that he is so often called "Christ," or the "Anointed one;" the anointed Jesus, or Jesus, the anointed Saviour. "Thou art the Christ the Son of God, that should come into the world." "This Jesus whom I preach unto you is Christ." He "testified to the Jews that Jesus was Christ," and he "confounded the Jews which dwelt at Damascus, proving" by the Scriptures "that this is the very Christ," (John xi. 27;) the very anointed of God, or he whom God authorized and qualified to be the Saviour of the world.

3. To come to be a Saviour, supposeth a resolution to do that work before he goeth back: "I will ransom them from the power of the grave; I will redeem them from death: O death, I will be thy plague; O grave, I will be thy destruction; repentance shall be hid from mine eyes." (Hos. xiii. 14.)

And as he resolved, so hath he done:

(1.) He hath purged our sins. (Heb. i. 2, 3.) (2.) He hath perfected for ever, by one offering, them that are sanctified. (Heb. x. 14.) (3.) He hath obtained eternal redemption for them. (Heb. ix. 12. See further, 2 Tim. i. 10; Heb. ix. 26; Col. ii. 15; Heb. vi. 18.)

Third. I come now to the third question, What is it for *Jesus to come to be* a Saviour?

1. It is the greatest discovery of man's misery and inability to save himself therefrom, that ever was made in the world. Must the Son of God himself come down from heaven, or can there be no salvation? Cannot one sinner save another? Cannot man by any means redeem his brother, nor give to God a ransom for him? Cannot an angel do it? Cannot all the angels do it? No; Christ must come and die to do it.

2. It is the greatest discovery of the love of God that ever the world had, for God so to love the world as to send his Son! For God so to commend his love to the world, as to send it to them in the blood of his Son! Amazing love! (John iii. 16. Rom. v. 8.)

3. It is the greatest discovery of the condescension of Christ that ever the world had. (1.) That he should not come to be ministered unto, but to minister; and to give his life a ransom for many. (Matt. xx. 28.) (2.) That he should be manifest for this purpose, that he might destroy the works of the devil. (1 John iii. 8.) (3.) That he should come that we "might have life, and that we might have it more abundantly." (John x. 10.) (4.) That the Son of God should " come to seek and to save that which was lost." (Luke xix. 10.) (5.) That he should not come to judge the world, but to save the world." (John xi. 47.) (6.) That "Christ Jesus should come into the world to save sinners, of whom I am chief." (1 Tim. i. 15.) (7.) That he should "love us, and wash us from our sins in his own blood." (Rev. i. 5.) What amazing condescension and humility is this! (Phil. ii. 6, 9.)

How Jesus Christ addressed himself to the work of our Redemption.

I come, then, in the next place, to show you how Jesus Christ addressed himself to the work of man's redemption.

The Scripture saith, "he became poor;" that he made himself of no reputation, and took upon him the form of a servant; that he humbled himself unto death, even the death of the cross. But particularly—*First*. He took upon him our flesh. *Second*. He was made under the law. *Third*. He took upon him our sins. *Fourth*. He bore the curse due to our sins.

First. He took upon him our flesh. I showed you before that he came in our flesh, and now I must show you the reason of it: namely, because that was the way to address himself to the work of our redemption. Wherefore, when the Apostle treated of the incarnation of Christ, he addeth withal the reason, to wit, that he might be capable to work out the redemption of men.

There are three things to be considered in this first head:

First. That he took our flesh for this reason, that he might be a Saviour. *Second*. How he took flesh, that he might be our Saviour. *Third*. That it was necessary that he should take our flesh, if indeed he will be our Saviour.

For the first, That he took our flesh for this reason, that he might be a Saviour: "For what the law could not do, in that it was weak through the flesh, God, sending his own Son in the likeness of sinful flesh, and for sin, condemned sin in the flesh." (Rom. viii. 3.)

The sum of the words is, Forasmuch as the law could do us no good, by reason of the inability that is in our flesh to do it (for the law can do us no good until it be fulfilled), and because God had a desire that good should come to us, therefore did he send his Son in our likeness, clothed with flesh, to destroy by his doing the law, the tendency of the sin that dwells in our flesh. He therefore took our flesh, that our sin, with its effects, might by him be condemned and overcome.

The reason, therefore, why he took flesh, is, because he would be our Saviour: "Forasmuch, then, as the children are partakers of flesh and blood, he also likewise took part of the same, that through death he might destroy him that had the power of death, that is the devil; and deliver them who through the fear of death were all their lifetime subject to bondage." (Heb. ii. 14, 15.)

In these words it is asserted, that he took our flesh for certain reasons:

1. Because the children, the heirs of heaven, are partakers of flesh and blood. "Forasmuch, then, as the children are partakers of flesh and blood, he also himself took part of the same." Had the children, the heirs, been without flesh, he himself had not taken it upon him; had the children been angels, he had taken upon him the nature of angels; but because the children were partakers of flesh, therefore leaving angels, or refusing to take hold of angels, he took flesh and blood, the nature of the children, that he might put himself into a capacity to save and deliver the children. Therefore it follows, that "through death he might destroy him that had the power of death, that is the devil."

2. This, therefore, was another reason, that he might destroy the devil.

The devil had bent himself against the children; he is their adversary, and goeth forth to make war with them. "The devil, your adversary:" "And he went to make war with the remnant of her seed." (1 Pet. v. 8. Rev. 12, 17.) Now the children could not destroy him, because he had already cast them into sin, defiled their nature, and laid them under the wrath of God. Therefore Christ puts himself among the children, and into the nature of the children, that he might, by means of his dying in their flesh, destroy the devil; that is, take away sin, his work, that he might destroy the works of the devil; for sin is the great engine of hell, by which he overthroweth all that perish. Now this did Christ destroy, by taking on him the similitude of sinful flesh; of which more anon.

3. "That he might destroy him that had the power of death, that is the devil, and deliver them." This was the thing in chief intended, that he might deliver the children, that he might deliver them

from death, the fruit of their sin, and from sin, the sting of that death. " That he might deliver them, who through the fear of death, were all their lifetime subject to bondage." He took flesh, therefore, because the children had it; and that he might die for the children, and deliver them from the works of the devil; that he might deliver them. No deliverance had come to the children if the Son of God had not taken their flesh and blood. Therefore he took our flesh that he might be our Saviour.

Again, in a Saviour there must be not only merit, but compassion and sympathy; because the children who are to live by faith, are not yet come to the inheritance. " It behoveth him, therefore, in all things to be made like unto his brethren, that he might be a merciful and faithful High-priest in things pertaining to God, to make reconciliation for the sins of the people." (Heb. ii. 17, 18.)

Two reasons are rendered in this text, why he must take flesh; namely, that he might be their Priest, to offer sacrifice, to wit, his body and blood for them; and that he might be merciful and faithful, to pity and preserve them unto the kingdom appointed for them.

Mark you, therefore, how the Apostle, when he asserteth that the Lord Jesus took our flesh, urgeth the reason why he took our flesh: that he might destroy the devil and death, that he might deliver them. It behoved him, therefore, to be made like unto his brethren, that he might be merciful and faithful, that he might make reconciliation for the sins of the people. The reason, therefore, why he took our flesh is declared, to wit, that he might be our Saviour. And hence you find it so often recorded, He hath " slain the enmity by his flesh;" " And you, who were sometimes aliens and enemies in your minds by wicked works, yet now hath he reconciled, in the body of his flesh, through death, to present you holy and unblameable in his sight." (Eph. ii. 15, 16. Col. i. 21, 22.)

How he took flesh.

Second. I come now to the second question, to wit—how he took our flesh. This must be inquired into, for his taking flesh was not after the common way; never any took man's flesh upon him as he, since the foundation of the world.

1. He took not our flesh like Adam, who was formed out of the ground : " who was made of the dust of the ground." (Gen. ii. 7; iii. 19). 2. He took not our flesh as we do by carnal generation. Joseph knew not his wife, neither did Mary know any man, till she had brought forth her first-born Son. (Matt. i. 25; Luke i. 34). 3. He took flesh, then, by the immediate working and overshadowing of the Holy Ghost. And hence it is said expressly, " She was found with child of the Holy Ghost." (Matt. i. 18.) " Now the birth of Jesus Christ was on this wise : when as his mother Mary was espoused to Joseph," before they came together, " she was found with child of the Holy Ghost." And hence, again, when Joseph doubted

of her honesty, (for he perceived she was with child, and knew he had not touched her,) the angel of God himself comes down to resolve his doubt, and said, "Joseph, thou son of David, fear not to take unto thee Mary thy wife, for that which is conceived in her is of the Holy Ghost." (Matt. i. 20.)

But, again, though the Holy Ghost was that by which the child Jesus was formed in the womb, so as to be without carnal generation—yet was he not formed in her without, but by, her conception. " Behold, thou shalt conceive in thy womb, and bring forth a Son, and shall call his name Jesus." (Luke i. 31.) Wherefore he took flesh not only in, but of the Virgin. Hence he is called her Son, the seed of the woman. And hence it is also that he is called the seed of Abraham, the seed of David; their seed according to the flesh. (Gen. xii.)

And this the work he undertook, required: 1. It required that he should take our flesh. 2. It required that he should take our flesh without sin, which could not be had he taken it by reason of a carnal generation; for so all children are conceived in, and polluted with sin. (Ps. li.) And the least pollution, either of flesh or spirit, had utterly disabled him for the work, which to do he came down from heaven. Therefore, " such an High-priest became us, who is holy, harmless, undefiled, separate from sinners, and made higher than the heavens." (Heb. vii. 26.)

This mystery of the incarnation of the Son of God was thus completed, I say, that he might be in all points like as we are, yet without sin; for sin in the flesh disableth, and maketh incapable to do the commandment. Therefore was he thus made, thus made of a woman; and this the angel assigneth as the reason of this his marvellous incarnation: " The holy Ghost," saith he, " shall come upon thee, and the power of the Highest shall overshadow thee; therefore also that holy thing that shall be born of thee shall be called the Son of God." (Luke i. 35.)

The overshadowing of the Holy Ghost, and the power of the Highest, the Father and the Holy Ghost, brought this wonderful thing to pass, for Jesus is a wonderful one in his conception and birth. This mystery is that next to the mystery of three persons in one God. It is a great mystery : " Great is the mystery of godliness; God was manifested in the flesh."

The conclusion is, that Jesus Christ took our flesh that he might be a Saviour; and that he might be our Saviour indeed, he thus took our flesh.

That it was necessary that he should take our flesh, if he will be our Saviour.

Third. I come now to the third thing, namely, that it was necessary that he should take our flesh if he will be our Saviour.

1. And that, first, from the nature of the work: His work was to save man, sinking man; man that was " going down to the pit." (Job xxxiv. 24.) Now, he that will save him that is sinking must

take hold on him ; and since he was not to save a man, but men, therefore it was necessary that he should take hold, not of one person, but of the common nature, clothing himself with part of the same. He took not hold of angels, but took on him the seed of Abraham : for that flesh was the same with the whole lump of the children, to whom the promise was made, and comprehended in it the body of them that shall be saved, even as in Adam was comprehended the whole world at first. (Rom. v.) Hence we are said to be chosen in him, to be gathered, being in him, to be dead by him, to be risen with him, and to be set with him, or in him, in heavenly places already.

This then was the wisdom of the great God, that the eternal Son of his love should take hold of, and so secure the sinking souls of perishing sinners by assuming their flesh.

2. The manner of his doing the work of a Saviour did call for his taking of our flesh. He must do the work by dying : " Ought not Christ to have suffered ? Christ must needs have suffered," or else no glory follows. (Luke xxiv. 26 : Acts xvii. 3). The prophets " testified beforehand the sufferings of Christ, and the glory that should follow." (1 Pet. i. 11.) Yea, they did it by the Spirit, even by the Spirit of Christ himself. This Spirit, then, did bid them tell the world, yea, testify, that Christ must suffer, or no man be blest with glory ; for the threatening of death and the curse of the law lay in the way between heaven gates and the souls of the children, for their sins ; wherefore he that will save them must answer Divine justice, or God must lie in saving them without inflicting the punishment threatened. Christ then must needs have suffered ; the manner of the work laid a necessity upon him to take our flesh upon him ; he must die, he must die for us, he must die for our sins. And this was effectually foretold by all the bloody sacrifices offered under the law ; the blood of bulls, and the blood of lambs, the blood of rams, and the blood of calves, and the blood of goats and birds. These bloody sacrifices, what did they signify, what were they figures of, but of the bloody sacrifice of the body of Jesus Christ ? their blood being a shadow of his blood, and their flesh being a shadow of his flesh.

Therefore, when God declared that he took no pleasure in them, because they could not make the worshippers perfect as pertaining to the conscience, then comes Jesus Christ to offer his sinless body and soul for the sin of the people : " For it is not possible that the blood of bulls and goats should take away sin. Wherefore, when he cometh into the world, he saith, Sacrifices and offerings thou wouldst not, but a body hast thou prepared me ; in burnt-offerings and sacrifices for sin thou hast had no pleasure. Then said I, Lo, I come ; in the volume of the book it is written of me, to do thy will, O God." Since burnt-offerings cannot do thy will, my body shall ; since the blood of bulls and goats cannot do thy will, my blood shall. Then follows, By the will of God " we are sanctified

through the offering up of the body of Jesus Christ once for all." (Heb. x. 4—10.)

3. The end of the work required that Christ, if he will be our Saviour, should take upon him our flesh. The end of our salvation is, that we might enjoy God, and that he by us might be glorified for ever and ever.

(1.) That we might enjoy God, " I will dwell in them, and they shall be my people, and I will be their God." This indwelling of God, and consequently our enjoyment of him, begins first in its eminency, by his possessing our flesh in the person of Jesus Christ. Hence his name is called " Emmanuel, God with us ;" and " the word was made flesh, and dwelt among us." The flesh of Christ is the tabernacle which the Lord pitched, according to that saying : " The tabernacle of God is with men, and he will dwell with them, and they shall be his people, and God himself shall be with them, and be their God." (Rev. xxi. 3.) Here God beginneth to discover his glory, and to be desirable to the sons of men.

God could not communicate himself to us, nor take us into the enjoyment of himself, but with respect to that flesh which his Son took of the Virgin, because sin stood betwixt. Now this flesh only was the holy lump, in this flesh God could dwell ; and forasmuch as this flesh is the same with ours, and was taken up with intent that what was done in and by that should be communicated to all the children, therefore through that doth God communicate of himself unto his people. " God was in Christ, reconciling the world unto himself." (2 Cor. v. 19.) And " I am the way," saith Christ, " no man cometh to the Father but by me." (John xiv. 6.)

That passage to the Hebrews is greatly to our purpose ; We have boldness, brethren, " to enter into the holiest," the place where God is, " by the blood of Jesus, by a new and living way, which he hath consecrated for us through the veil, that is to say, his flesh." (Heb. x. 19, 20.)

Wherefore by the flesh and blood of Christ we enter into the holiest ; through the veil, saith he, that is to say, his flesh.

(2.) As the end of our salvation is that we might enjoy God, so also it is that he by us might be glorified for ever : " That God in all things might be glorified through Jesus Christ our Lord."

Here, indeed, will the mystery of his grace, wisdom, justice, power, holiness, and glory, inhabit eternal praise, while we that are counted worthy of the kingdom of God shall admire at the mystery, and see ourselves, without ourselves, even by the flesh and blood of Christ, through faith therein, effectually and eternally saved. Oh, this will be the burden of our eternal joy : God loved us, and gave his Son for us ; Christ loved us, and gave his flesh for our life, and his blood for our eternal redemption and salvation !

That Christ was made under the Law.

Second. But, secondly, Christ was made under

the law: "When the fulness of the time was come, God sent forth his Son, made of a woman, made under the law." (Gal. iv. 4.)

Of right, being found in flesh, he must needs be under the law, for that there is not any creature above or without law to God; but this is not the point in hand. Christ was not therefore under the law, because he was found in flesh, but he took flesh, and designedly put himself, or was made, under the law; wherefore it is added, he was made under the law, "to redeem," to redeem them that were under the law. Wherefore here is a design, a heavenly contrivance and device on foot. Christ is made, that is, by design subjected under the law, for the sake and upon the account of others, "to redeem them that were under the law."

Made under the law; that is, put himself into the room of sinners, into the condition of sinners; made himself subject to the same pains and penalties we are obnoxious to. We were under the law, and it had dominion over us, bound us upon pain of eternal damnation to do completely all things written in the law. This condition Christ put himself into, that he might redeem; for assuredly we had else perished.

The law had dominion over us, and since we had sinned, of right it pronounced the curse, and made all men subject to the wrath of God. Christ, therefore, did not only come into our flesh, but also into our condition, into the valley and shadow of death where we were, and where we are, as we are sinners. He that is under the law, is under the edge of the axe. When David was to go to visit his brethren, and to save them from the hand of Goliath, he was to look how his brethren feared, and to "take their pledge." (1 Sam. xvii. 18.) This is true of Jesus Christ; when he came to save us from the hand of death and the law, he looked how his brethren fared, took to heart their deplorable condition, and put himself into the same plight, to wit, under the law, that he might redeem them that were under the law.

I told you before, that he came sinless into the world, that he had a miraculous conception, and wonderful birth: and here you see a reason for it, he was to be put, or made under the law, "to redeem." He that will be made under the law to redeem, had need be sinless and spotless himself; for the law findeth fault with the least, and condemneth man for the first beginning of sin.

Without this, then, there could not have been redemption, nor any the sons of God by adoption: no redemption, because the sentence of death had already passed upon all; no sons by adoption, because that is the effect of redemption. "God sent forth his Son, made of a woman, made under the law, that we might receive the adoption of sons." Christ, then, by being made under the law, hath recovered his from under the law, and obtained for them the privilege of the adoption of sons. For as I told you before, Christ stood a

common person, presenting in himself the whole lump of the promised seed, or the children of the promise; wherefore he comes under the law for them, takes upon him to do what the law required of them, takes upon him to do it for them.

He began, therefore, at the first tittle of the law, and going in man's flesh, for man, through the law, he becomes "the end of the law for righteousness, for every one that believeth." The *end* of the law; what is the end of the law but perfect and sinless obedience? that is the end of the law, both with respect to its nature, and the cause of its being imposed. God gave the law, that complete righteousness should by that be found upon men; but because sin was got into man's flesh, therefore this righteousness, by us, could not be completed. Now comes Christ the Lord into the world, clothes himself with the children's flesh, addresseth himself to the work of their redemption, is made under the law; and going through every part of the law without sin, he becometh "the end of the law for" justifying "righteousness to every one that believeth." (Rom. x. 4.) For he obeyed not the law for himself, he needed no obedience thereto: it was we that needed obedience, it was we that wanted to answer the law; we wanted it, but could not obtain it, because then the law was weak through the flesh; therefore God sent his own Son, and he did our duty for us, even to become the end of the law to every one that believeth. In this, therefore, Christ laboured for us, he was made under the law to redeem. Therefore, as I said before, it behoved him to be sinless, because the law binds over to answer for sin at the bar of the judgment of God. Therefore did his Godhead assume our human flesh, in a clean and spotless way, that he might come under "the law, to redeem them that were under the law." For, consisting of two natures, and the personality lying in the Godhead, which gave value and worth to all things done for us by the manhood, the obedience takes denomination from thence, to be the obedience of God. The Son's righteousness, the Son's blood; the righteousness of God, the blood of God. (Heb. v. 8, 9. Phil. iii. 9. Acts xx. 28. 1 John iii. 16.)

Thus Jesus Christ came into the world under the law to redeem; not simply as God, but God-man, both natures making one Christ. The Godhead, therefore, did influence and give value to the human flesh of Christ in all its obedience to the law; else there would have been wanting that perfection of righteousness which only could answer the demands and expectation of the justice of God, to wit, perfect righteousness by flesh.

But the second person in the Godhead, the Son, the Word, coming under the law for men in their flesh, and subjecting himself by that flesh to every tittle and demand of the law, all and every whit of what was acted and done by Jesus Christ, God-man, for us, it was and is the righteousness of God: and since it was not done for himself, but for us, as he saith in the text, "to redeem," the righteousness by which we are set free from the law is none other but the righteousness that alone resideth in the person of the Son of God.

And that it is absolutely necessary thus it should be is evident, both with respect to God, and also with respect to man.

1. With respect to God. The righteousness is demanded by God; therefore he that comes to redeem must present before God a righteousness absolutely perfect; this can be done by none but God. 2. With respect to man. Man was to present this righteousness to God, therefore must the undertaker be man. Man for man, and God for God, God-man between God and men. This Daysman can lay his hand upon us both, and bring God and man together in peace. (John ix. 33.)

Quest. But some may say, What need of the righteousness of one that is naturally God? had Adam, who was but a mere man, stood in his innocency and done his duty, he had saved himself and all his posterity.

Ans. Had Adam stood, he had so long secured himself from the wages of sin, and posterity so long as they were in him. But had Adam sinned, yea, although he had not defiled his nature with filth, he could never after that have redeemed himself from the curse of the law, because he was not equal with God; for the curse of the law is the curse of God; but no man can deliver himself from the curse of God, having first transgressed. This is evident, because angels, for sin, lie bound in chains, and can never deliver themselves. He, therefore, that redeemeth man from under the law, must not only do all the good that the law requireth, but bear all the penalty that is due by the law for sin.

Should an angel assume human flesh, and in that flesh do the law, this righteousness would not redeem a sinner; it would be but the righteousness of an angel, and so, far short of such a righteousness as can secure a sinner from the wrath of God. But "thou shalt love the Lord thy God with all thy soul, with all thy heart, with all thy mind, with all thy strength." If there were no more required of us now to redeem ourselves, it would be utterly impossible for us to do it, because in the best there is sin, which will intermix itself with every duty of man. This being so, all the heart, all the soul, all the strength, and all the mind, to the exact requirement of the justice of the law, can never be found in a natural man.

Besides; for this work there is required a perfect memory, always to keep in mind the whole duty of man, the whole of every tittle of all the law, lest sin come in by forgetfulness: a perfect knowledge and judgment, lest sin come in by ignorance: an everlasting unweariedness in all, lest sin and continual temptations tire the soul, and cause it to fail before the whole be done.

For the accomplishing this last, he must have:

1. A perfect willingness, without the least thought to the contrary. 2. Such an hatred of sin as is not to be found but in the heart of God. 3. A full delight in every duty, and that in the midst of all temptations. 4. A continuing in all things to the well-pleasing of the justice of God.

I say, should the penalty of the law be taken off, should God forgive the penalty and punishment due to sins that are past, and only demand good works now, according to the tenor of the law, no man could be saved; there would not be found that heart, that soul, that mind, and that strength anywhere in the world.

This, therefore, must cease for ever, unless the Son of God will put his shoulder to the work; but, blessed be God, he hath done it: "When the fulness of the time was come, God sent forth his Son, made of a woman, made under the law, to redeem them that are under the law."

Christ took upon him our Sins.

Third. But, thirdly, Christ our Saviour takes upon him our sins. This is another step to the work of our redemption. He hath made him to be sin for us. Strange doctrine! a fool would think it blasphemy, but Truth hath said it. Truth, I say, hath said, not that he was made to be sin; but that God made him to be sin, "He hath made him to be sin for us." (2 Cor. v. 21.)

This, therefore, showeth us how effectually Christ Jesus undertook the work of our redemption: He was made to be sin for us. Sin is the great block and bar to our happiness; sin is the procurer of all miseries to men, both here and for ever. Take away sin, and nothing can hurt us; for death temporal, death spiritual, and death eternal is the wages of sin. (Rom. vi. 23.)

Sin, then, and man for sin, is the object of the wrath of God. If the object of the wrath of God, then is his case most dreadful; for who can bear, who can grapple with the wrath of God? Men cannot, angels cannot, the whole world cannot. All, therefore, must sink under sin, but he who is made to be sin for us; he only can bear sins, he only can bear them away, and therefore were they laid upon him. "The Lord laid upon him the iniquities of us all." (Isa. liii. 6.)

Mark, therefore, and you shall find that the reason why God made him to be sin for us was, "that we might be made the righteousness of God in him." He took our flesh, he was made under the law, and was made to be sin for us, that the devil might be destroyed, that the captives might be redeemed, and made the righteousness of God in him.

And forasmuch as he saith that God "hath made him to be sin," it declareth that the design of God, and the mystery of his will and grace, was in it. "He hath made him to be sin." God hath done it, that we might be made the righteousness of God in him. There was no other way; the wisdom of heaven could find no other way; we could not by other means stand just before the justice of God.

Now, what remains, but that we who are reconciled to God by faith in his blood are quit, discharged, and set free from the law of sin and death? Yea, what encouragement to trust in him, when we read, that God "made him to be sin for us."

Quest. But how was Jesus Christ made of God to be sin for us?

Ans. Even so as if himself had committed all our sins; that is, they were as really charged upon him as if himself had been the actor and committer of them all. "He hath made him to be sin;" not only as a sinner, but as sin itself. He was as the sin of the world, that day he stood before God in our stead. Some, indeed, will not have Jesus Christ our Lord to be made sin for us; their wicked reasons think this to be wrong judgment in the Lord: it seems, supposing that because they cannot imagine how it should be, therefore God, if he does it, must do it at his peril, and must be charged with doing wrong judgment, and so things that become not his heavenly Majesty. But against this duncish sophistry we set Paul and Isaiah, the one telling us still, "The Lord laid on him the iniquities of us all;" and the other, that "God made him to be sin for us."

But these men, as I suppose, think it enough for Christ to die under that notion only, not knowing nor feeling the burden of sin, and the wrath of God due thereto. These make him as senseless in his dying, and as much without reason, as a silly sheep or goat, who also died for sin, but so as in name, in show, and shadow only. They felt not the proper weight, guilt, and judgment of God for sin. But thou, sinner, who art so in thine own eyes, and who feelest guilt in thine own conscience, know thou that Jesus Christ, the Son of the living God in flesh, was made to be sin for thee, or stood sensibly guilty of all thy sins before God, and bare them in his own body upon the cross.

God charged our sins upon Christ, and that in their guilt and burden; what remaineth, but that the charge was real or feigned? If real, then he hath either perished under them, or carried them away from before God; if they were charged but feignedly, then did he but feignedly die for them, then shall we have but feigned benefit by his death, and but a feigned salvation at last; not to say how this cursed doctrine chargeth God and Christ with hypocrisy—the one in saying, he made Christ to be sin; the other, that he bare our sin; when, indeed, our guilt and burden never was really upon him.

Quest. But might not Christ die for our sins, but he needs must bear their guilt or burden?

Ans. He that can sever sin and guilt, sin and the burden, each from other, laying sin and no guilt, sin and no burden on the person that dieth for sin, must do it only in his own imaginary head. No scripture, nor reason, nor sense, under-

standeth, or feeleth sin when charged without its guilt or burden.

And here we must distinguish between sin charged and sin forgiven. Sin forgiven may be seen without guilt or burden, though I think not without shame in this world; but sin charged, and that by the justice of God—for so it was upon Christ—this cannot be but guilt and the burden, as inseparable companions, must unavoidably lie on that person. Poor sinner, be advised to take heed of such deluded preachers, who, with their tongues smoother than oil, would rob thee of that excellent doctrine, "God hath made him to be sin for us;" for such, as I said, do not only present thee with a feigned deliverance and forgiveness, with a feigned heaven and happiness, but charge God and the Lord Jesus as mere impostors, who, while they tell us that Christ was made of God to be sin for us, affirm that it was not so really, suggesting this sophistical reason, No wrong judgment comes from the Lord. I say again, this wicked doctrine is the next way to turn the gospel, in thy thoughts, to no more than a cunningly-devised fable, (2 Pet. i. 16;) and to make Jesus Christ in his dying for our sins, as brutish as the paschal lamb in Moses' law.

Wherefore, distressed sinner, when thou findest it recorded in the word of truth that Christ died for our sins, and that God hath made him to be sin for us, then do thou consider of sin as it is—a transgression against the law of God; and that as such, it procureth the judgment of God, torments and afflicts the mind with guilt, and bindeth over the soul to answer it. Sever not sin and guilt asunder, lest thou be a hypocrite like these wicked men, and rob Christ of his true sufferings. Besides, to see sin upon Christ, but not its guilt, to see sin upon Christ, but not the legal punishment, what is this but to conclude, that either there is no guilt and punishment in sin, or that Christ bare our sin, but we the punishment? for the punishment must be borne, because the sentence is gone out from the mouth of God against sin.

Do thou, therefore, as I have said, consider of sin as a transgression of the law (1 John iii. 4), and a provoker of the justice of God; which done, turn thine eye to the cross, and behold those sins in the guilt and punishment of them sticking in the flesh of Christ. "God condemned sin in the flesh" of Christ. (Rom. viii. 3.) "He bare our sins *in* his own body on the tree." (1 Pet. ii. 24.)

I would only give thee this caution; not sin, in the nature of sin; sin was not so in the flesh of Christ; but sin in the natural punishment of it, to wit, guilt, and the chastising hand of justice. "He was wounded for our transgressions, he was bruised for our iniquities; the chastisements of our peace were upon him, and by his stripes we are healed." (Isa. liii. 5.)

Look, then, upon Christ crucified to be as the sin of the world, as if he only had broken the law; which done, behold him perfectly innocent in himself, and so conclude, that for the transgression of God's people he was stricken; that when the Lord made him to be sin, he made him to be sin *for us.*

He was made a Curse for us.

Fourth.—As he was made flesh under the law, and also sin, so he was made a curse for us. " Christ hath redeemed us from the curse of the law, being made a curse for us; as it is written, Cursed is every one that hangeth on a tree." This sentence is taken out of Moses, being passed there upon them that for sin are worthy of death: " And if a man have committed a sin worthy of death, and thou hang him on a tree, his body shall not remain all night upon the tree, but thou shalt in any wise bury him that day, for he that is hanged is accursed of God." (Deut. xxi. 22, 23.) By this sentence Paul concludeth that Jesus Christ was justly hanged, because sin worthy of death was upon him; sin, not of his own, but ours. Since, then, he took our sins, he must be cursed of God; for sin is sin, wherever it lies; and justice is justice, wherever it finds it: wherefore, since Jesus Christ will bear our sin, he must be " numbered with the transgressors," and counted worthy to die the death.

He that committeth sin is worthy of death. This, though Christ did not personally do, his members, his body, which is his church, did; and since he would undertake for them with God, and stand in their sins before the eyes of his justice, he must die the death by the law.

Sin and the curse cannot be severed. Sin must be followed with the curse of God: sin, therefore, being removed from us to the back of Christ, thither goes also the curse; for if sin be found upon him, he is the person worthy to die, worthy by our sins. Wherefore Paul here setteth forth Christ clothed with our sins, and so taking from us the guilt and punishment. What punishment but the wrath and displeasure of God? Christ " hath redeemed us from the curse of the law, being made a curse for us."

In this word " curse " are two things comprised:—

1. The reality of sin; for there can be no curse where there is no sin, either of the person's own, or made to be his by his own consent or the imputation of Divine justice. And since sins are made to be Christ's by imputation, they are his, though not naturally, yet really, and consequently the wages due. He hath made him to be sin; he was made a curse for us.

2. This word "curse" compriseth, therefore, the punishment of sin, that punishment properly due to sin from the hand of God's justice; which punishment standeth in three things: (1.) In charging sin upon the body and soul of the person concerned; and hence we read that both the body and soul of Christ " were made an offering for sin." (Isa. liii. 10. Heb. x. 10.) (2.) The punishment standeth in God's inflicting of the just merits of

sin upon him that standeth charged therewith, and that is death in its own nature and strength; to wit, death with the sting thereof: " The sting of death is sin." This death did Christ die, because he died for our sins. (3.) The sorrows and pains of this death, therefore, must be undergone by Jesus Christ.

Now there are divers sorrows in death: 1. Such sorrows as brutes are subject to. 2. Such sorrows as persons are subject to, that stand in sin before God. 3. Such sorrows as those undergo who are swallowed up of the curse and wrath of God for ever. Now so much of all kinds of sorrows as the imputation of our sin could justly bring from the hand of Divine justice, so much of it he had. 1. He had death. 2. He had the sting of death, which is sin. 3. He was forsaken of God, but could not by any means have those sorrows which they have that are everlastingly swallowed up of them. It was not possible that he should be holden of it. For where sin is charged and borne, there must of necessity follow the wrath and curse of God. Now where the wrath and curse of God is, there must of necessity follow the effects, the natural effects. I say, the natural effects; to wit, the sense, the sorrowful sense of the displeasure of an infinite Majesty, and his chastisements for the sin that hath provoked him. There are effects natural, and effects accidental; those accidental, are such as show from our weakness, whilst we wrestle with the judgment of God, to wit, hellish fear, despair, rage, blasphemy, and the like; these were not incident to Jesus Christ, he being in his own person every way perfect. Neither did he always endure the natural effects; his merits relieved and delivered him. God loosed the pains of death, " because it was not possible he should be holden of it." Christ, then, was made a curse for us, for he did bear our sin; the punishment, therefore, from the revenging hand of God, must needs fall upon him.

Wherefore, by these four things, we see how Christ became our Saviour; he took hold of our nature, was born under the law, was made to be sin, and the accursed of God for us. And observe it; all this, as I said before, was the handiwork of God. God made him flesh, made him under the law; God made him to be sin, and also a curse for us. The Lord bruised him, the Lord put him to grief, the Lord made his soul an offering for sin: not for that he hated him, considering him in his own harmless, innocent, and blessed person; for he was daily his delight; but by an act of grace to usward were our iniquities laid upon him, and he in our stead bruised and chastised for them. God loved us, and made him a curse for us. He was made a curse for us, " that the blessing of Abraham might come on the Gentiles, through faith in Jesus Christ." (Gal. iii. 14.)

Further Demonstration of this Truth.

Before I pass this truth, I will present thee,

courteous reader, with two or three demonstrations for its further confirmation.

First. That Christ did bear our sin and curse is clear, because he died, and that without a mediator.

1. He died: death is the wages of sin. Now if death be the wages of sin, and that be true that Christ did die and not sin, either the course of justice is perverted, or else he died for our sins; there was " no cause of death in him," yet he died. (Acts xiii. 28.) He did no evil, guile was not found in his mouth, yet he received the wages of sin. (1 Pet. ii. 22.) Sin, therefore, though not of his own, was found upon him, and laid to his charge, because he died. "Christ died for our sins," Christ "gave himself for our sins." (1 Cor. xv. 1—3. Gal. i. 4.)

He, then, that will conclude that Christ did not bear our sin, chargeth God foolishly, for delivering him up to death; for laying on him the wages, when in no sense he deserved the same. Yea, he overthroweth the whole gospel, for that hangeth on this hinge: " Christ died for our sins."

Obj. But all that die do not bear the curse of God for sin.

Ans. But all that die without a mediator do. Angels died the cursed death, because Christ took not hold of them; and they for whom Christ never prayeth, they die the cursed death, for they perish everlastingly in the unutterable torments of hell. Christ, too, died that death which is the proper wages of sin, for he had none to stand for him. " I looked," saith he, " and there was none to help; I wondered that there was none to uphold: therefore mine own arm brought salvation unto me." " And he saw that there was no man, and he wondered that there was no intercessor; therefore his arm brought salvation unto him, and his righteousness sustained him." (Isa. lxiii. 5; lix. 16.)

Christ then died, or endured the wages of sin, and that without an intercessor, without one between God and him: he grappled immediately with the eternal justice of God, who inflicted on him death, the wages of sin: there was no man to hold off the hand of God; justice had his full blow at him, and made him a curse for sin. He died for sin without a mediator. He died the cursed death.

Second. A second thing that demonstrateth that Christ died the cursed death for sin: it is, the frame of spirit that he was in at the time that he was to be taken.

Never was poor mortal so beset with the apprehensions of approaching death as was this Lord Jesus Christ; amazement beyond measure, sorrow that exceeded seized upon his soul. " My soul," saith he, " is exceeding sorrowful, even unto death." (Matt. xxvi. 38.) " And he began," saith Mark, " to be sore amazed, and to be very heavy," (xiv. 33.)

Add to this, that Jesus Christ was better able to grapple with death, even better able to do it alone, than the whole world joined all together. 1. He was anointed with the Spirit without measure. (John iii. 34.) 2. He had all grace perfect in him. (John i. 16.) 3. Never any had so much of his Father's love as himself. (Prov. viii. 23—30.) 4. Never none so harmless, and without sin as he, and consequently never man had so good a conscience as he. (Heb. vii. 26.) 5. Never none prepared such a stock of good works to bear him company at the hour of death as he. 6. Never none had greater assurance of being with the Father eternally in the heavens than he. And yet, behold, when he comes to die, how weak is he, how amazed at death, how heavy, how exceeding sorrowful! and, I say, no cause assigned but the approach of death.

Alas! how often is it seen that we poor sinners can laugh at destruction when it cometh; yea, and " rejoice exceedingly when we find the grave," (Job iii. 22,) looking upon death as a part of our portion; yea, as that which will be a means of our present relief and help. (1 Cor. iii. 22.) This, Jesus Christ could not do, considering as dying for our sin, but the nearer death the more heavy and oppressed with the thoughts of the revenging hand of God. Wherefore he falls into an agony, and sweats; not after the common rate, as we do when death is severing body and soul: " His sweat was as it were great drops (clodders) of blood falling down to the ground." (Luke xxii. 44.)

What, I say, should be the reason, but that death assaulted him with his sting? If Jesus Christ had been to die for his virtues only, doubtless he would have borne it lightly, and so he did as he died, bearing witness to the truth, " He endured the cross, and despised the shame." (Heb. xii. 2.) How have the martyrs despised death, and, as it were, not been careful of that, having peace with God by Jesus Christ, scorning the most cruel torments that hell and men could devise and invent! but Jesus Christ could not do so, as he was a sacrifice for sin; he died for sin, he was made a curse for us. Oh, my brethren, Christ died many deaths at once; he made his grave with the wicked, and with the rich in his death. Look how many thousands shall be saved, so many deaths did Jesus die; yet it was but once he died. He died thy death, and my death, and so many deaths as all our sins deserved, who shall be saved from the wrath to come.

Now, to feign that these sorrows, and this bloody agony was not real, but in show only, what greater condemnation can be passed upon Jesus Christ, who loved to do all things in the most unfeigned simplicity! It was therefore because of sin, the sin that was put into the death he died, and the curse of God that was due to sin, that made death so bitter to Jesus Christ, " It is Christ that died." The Apostle speaks as if never any died but Christ, nor indeed did there, so wonderful a death as he. (Rom. viii. 34.) Death, considered simply as it is, a deprivation of natural life, could not have these effects in a person personally more righteous than an angel. Yea, even carnal wicked men, not awakened in their conscience, how securely can they die! It must therefore also be concluded, that the sorrows and agony of Jesus Christ came from a higher cause, even from the guilt of sin, and from the curse of God that was now approaching for that sin.

It cannot be attributed to the fear of men; their terror could not make him afraid; that was contrary to his doctrine, and did not become the dignity of his person; it was sin, sin, sin, and the curse due to sin.

Third. It is evident that Christ did bear and die the cursed death for sin, from the carriage and dispensations of God towards him.

1. From the carriage of God. God now becomes as an enemy to him. (1.) He forsakes him. "My God, my God, why hast thou forsaken me?" Yea, the sense of the loss of God's comfortable presence abode with him even till he gave up the ghost. (2.) He dealeth with him as with one that hath sinned; he chastiseth him, he bruiseth him, he striketh and smiteth him (Isa. liii.); and was pleased, that is, his justice was satisfied, in so doing. "It pleased the Lord to bruise him; he hath put him to grief."

These things could not be, had he only considered him in his own personal standing. Where was the righteous forsaken? Without the consideration of sin, he doth not willingly afflict nor grieve the children of men; that is, not out of pleasure, or without sufficient cause.

Jesus Christ, then, since he is under this withdrawing, chastising, bruising, and afflicting displeasure of God, he is all that time under sin, under our sins, and therefore thus accursed of God, his God.

1. Not only the carriage of God, but his dispensations, his visible dispensations, plainly declare that he stood before God in our sins. Vengeance suffered him not to live; wherefore God delivered him up: "He spared not his own Son, but delivered him up for us all." (Rom. viii. 32.) (1.) He delivered him into the hands of men. (Mark ix. 31.) (2.) He was delivered into the hands of sinners. (Luke xxiv. 7.) (3.) He was delivered unto death. (Rom. iv. 25.) (4.) Yea, so delivered up, as that they both had him to put him to death, and God left him for that purpose in their hands; yea, was so far off from delivering him, that he gave way to all things that had a tendency to take his life from the earth.

Now may men do what they will with him; he was delivered to their will.

Judas may sell him; Peter may deny him; all his disciples forsake him; the enemy apprehends him, binds him: they have him away like a thief to Caiaphas, the high priest, in whose house he is mocked, spit upon: his beard is twitched from his cheeks; now they buffet him, and scornfully bow the knee before him; yea, "his visage is so marred more than any man's, and his form more than the sons of men." (Isa. lii. 14.)

Now he is sent to the governor, defaced with blows and blood, who delivereth him into the hands of his soldiers: they whip him, crown him with thorns, and stick the points of the thorns fast in his temples, by a blow with a staff in their hand; now is he made a spectacle to the people, and then sent away to Herod, who, with his men of war, set him at nought, no God appearing for his help.

In fine, they at last condemn him to death, even to the death of the cross, where they hang him up by wounds made through his hands and his feet, between the earth and the heavens, where he hanged for the space of six hours, to wit, from nine in the morning till three in the afternoon: no God yet appears for his help. While he hangs there, some rail at him, others wag their head, others tauntingly say, "He saved others, himself he cannot save;" some divide his raiment, casting lots for his garments before his face; others mockingly bid him come down from the cross; and when he desireth succour, they give him vinegar to drink: no God yet appears for his help.

Now the earth quakes, the rocks are rent, the sun becomes black, and Jesus still cries out that he was forsaken of God; and presently boweth his head and dies. (Read Matt. xxvi.; xxvii. Mark xiv.; xv. Luke xxii.; xxiii. John xviii.; xix.)

And for all this there is no cause assigned from God but sin. "He was wounded for our transgressions, he was bruised for our iniquities: the chastisement of our peace was upon him; and by his stripes we are healed." (Isa. liii. 5.)

The sum, then, is, that Jesus Christ, the Lord, by taking part of our flesh, became a public person, not doing nor dying in a private capacity, but in the room and stead of sinners, whose sin deserved death, and the curse of God; all which Jesus Christ bare in his own body upon the tree. I conclude, then, that my sin is already crucified, and accursed in the death and curse Christ underwent.

I come, now, to some objections:—

Obj. 1. Christ never was a sinner: God never supposed him to be a sinner: neither did our sins become really his. God never reputed him so to have been; therefore, hate or punish him as a sinner he could not; for no false judgment can belong to the Lord.

Ans. 1. That Christ was not a sinner personally, by acts or doings of his own, is granted; and in this sense it is true that God did never suppose him to be a sinner, nor punished him as such a sinner; nor did he really, if by really you understand naturally, become our sin, nor did God ever repute him so. 2. But that Christ stood before God in our sins, and that God did not only suppose him so to stand, but set him in them, put them upon him, and counted them as his own, is so true, that he cannot at present be a Christian that denies it. "The Lord hath laid upon him the iniquities of us all." (Isa. liii. 6.) 3. So, then, though God did not punish him for sin of his own committing, yet he punished him for sin of our committing. "The just suffered for the unjust." (1 Pet. iii. 18.) 4. Therefore, it is true, that though Christ did never really become sin of his own, he did really become our sin, did really become our curse for sin. If this be denied, it follows that he became our sin but feignedly, that he was made our curse, or a curse for us, but in appearance, show, or in dissimulation; but no such action or work can proceed of the Lord. He did, then, really lay our sin and his curse upon him for our sin.

Obj. 2. But if Christ indeed hath suffered for our sins, and endured for them that curse that of justice is due thereto, then hath he also endured for us the proper torments of hell, for they are the wages of our sins.

Ans. Many things might be said in answer to this objection. But, briefly: First. What God chargeth upon the soul for sin is one thing, and what followeth upon that charge is another. Second. A difference in the person suffering may make a difference in the consequences that follow upon the charge. Let us then consider of both these things.

First. The charge is sin, God charged him with our sins. The person then stands guilty before the judgment of God. The consequences are: 1. The person charged sustains or suffereth the wrath of God. 2. This wrath of God is expressed, and inflicted on body and soul.

The consequences are: God forsaketh the person charged, and being left, if he cannot stand, he falleth under the power of guilt and horror of the same.

If the person utterly fall under this charge, as not being able to wrestle with and overcome this wrath of God, then despair, horror of hell, rage, blasphemy, darkness, and damnable anguish immediately swallow him up, and he lieth for ever and ever in the pains of hell, a monument of eternal vengeance.

Now, that Christ underwent the wrath of God it is evident, because he bare our curse; that God forsook him, he did with strong crying and tears acknowledge; and, therefore, that he was under the soul-afflicting sense of the loss of God's favour, and under the sense of his displeasure, must needs flow from the premises.

Second. But now, because Christ Jesus the Lord was a person infinitely differing from all others that fall under the wrath of God, therefore those things that flow from damned sinners could not flow from him.

1. Despair would not rise in his heart, for his flesh did rest in hope; and said, even when he suffered, "Thou wilt not leave my soul in hell." (Acts ii. 27.)

2. The everlastingness of the punishment, therefore, not the terrors that accompany such, could not fasten upon him; for he knew at last that God would justify him, or approve of his works, that they were meritorious. And mark, everlasting punishment is not the proper wages of sin, but under a supposition that the person suffering be not able to pay the debt. "Thou shalt not depart thence, till thou hast paid the very last mite." (Luke xii. 59.) The difference, then, of the persons suffering may make a difference, though not in the nature of the punishment, yet in the duration and consequences of it.

(1.) Christ under the sentence was, as to his own personal acts only, altogether innocent; the damned only altogether sinners. (2.) Christ had in him, even then, the utmost perfection of all graces and virtues; but the damned, the perfection of sin and vileness. (3.) Christ's humanity had still union with his Godhead; the damned, union only with sin. (4.) Now an innocent person, perfect in all graces, as really God as man, can better wrestle with the curse for sin, than either sinful men or angels.

While they despair, Christ hopes. While they blaspheme, Christ submits. While they rage, Christ justifies God. While they sink under the burthen of sin and wrath, Christ recovereth by virtue of his worthiness: "Thou wilt not leave my soul in hell, neither wilt thou suffer thy Holy One to see corruption." He was God's Holy One, and his holiness prevailed.

So that it follows not, that because Christ did undergo the curse due to our sins, he therefore must have those accidental consequences which are found to accompany damned souls.

Obj. 3. But the Scripture saith that the wages of sin is everlasting punishment: "Depart from me, ye cursed, into everlasting fire, prepared for the devil and his angels." (Matt. xxv. 41.)

Ans. This objection is partly answered already, in the answer to that foregoing. But further,

1. Consider, the wages of sin is death, and punishment under the wrath of God: till those that die the death for sin have paid the utmost farthing. (Matt. v. 26.)

2. So, then, the everlastingness of the punishment lieth here; if the person suffering be not able to make amends to justice for the sins for which he suffereth; else justice neither would, nor could, because it is just, keep such still under punishment.

3. The reason, then, why fallen angels and damned souls have an everlastingness of punishment allotted them, is because, by what they suffer, they cannot satisfy the justice of God.

4. The conclusion then is, though the rebukes of God for sin by death and punishment after be the rebukes of eternal vengeance, yet the eternity of that punishment is for want of merit; could the

damned merit their own deliverance, justice would let them go.

5. It is one thing, therefore, to suffer for sin by the stroke of eternal justice, and another thing to abide for ever a sufferer there : Christ did the first, the damned do the second.

6. His rising, therefore, from the dead the third day doth nothing invalidate his sufferings, but rather showeth the power of his merit. And here I would ask a question, Had Christ Jesus been more the object of faith, if weakness and endless infirmity had kept him under the curse, than by rising again from the dead, want of merit causing the one, sufficiency thereof causing the other ?

7. If men will not believe that Christ hath removed the curse, because he is risen again, they would much more strongly have doubted it, had he been still in the grave. But oh, amazing darkness ! to make that an argument, that his sufferings wanted merit, which to God himself is sufficient proof that he hath purged our sins for ever : " For this man, after he had offered up one sacrifice for sins for ever, sat down on the right hand of God." (Heb. x. 12.)

Obj. 4. But the Scripture saith, Christ is our example, and that is in his very death.

Ans. Christ in his sufferings and death is both sacrifice and example.

First. A sacrifice : " Christ our passover is sacrificed for us." And again, " He gave himself for us, an offering and a sacrifice to God for a sweet-smelling savour." And thus he made reconciliation for iniquity, and brought in everlasting righteousness. (1 Cor. v. 7. Eph. v. 1, 2. Dan. ix. 24.)

Second. He was also in his sufferings exemplary, and that in several particulars. 1. In his meek deportment, while he was apprehended. (Isa. liii. 7.) 2. In doing them good that sought his life. (Luke xxii. 50, 51.) 3. In his praying for his enemies when they were in their outrage. (Luke xxiii. 34.) 4. " When he was reviled, he reviled not again ; when he suffered, he threatened not ; but committed himself to him that judgeth righteously." (1 Pet. ii. 23.)

In these respects, I say, he was exemplary, and brought honour to his profession by his good behaviour ; and oh, how beautiful would Christianity be in the eyes of men, if the disciples of our Lord would more imitate him therein !

But what ? because Christ is our pattern, is he not our passover ? or, because we should in these things follow his steps, died he not for our sins ? Thus to conclude, would not only argue thee very erroneous, but such a conclusion would overthrow the gospel ; it being none other but a great slight of Satan to shut out the whole by a part, and to make us blasphemers while we plead for holiness.

Look then for the death of Christ under a double consideration : 1. As he suffered from the hand of God. 2. As he suffered from the hand of men.

Now as he suffered by God's hand, so he suffered for sin ; but as he suffered from men, so he suffered for righteousness' sake.

Observe then, that as he suffered for sin, so no *man* took away his life ; but as he suffered for righteousness' sake, so *they* slew him by wicked hands. What is it then ? Christ must needs have suffered, and the wisdom of God had so ordained, that " those things which God before had showed by the mouth of all his prophets, that Christ should suffer, he hath so fulfilled." (Acts iii. 18.) Thus, therefore, we ought to distinguish of the causes and ends of the death of Christ.

Again ; as Christ suffered for sin, so he would neither be taken at man's pleasure, nor die at man's time : 1. Not at man's pleasure ; and hence it was that they so often sought his life in vain, for his hour was not yet come, to wit, the hour in which he was to be made a sacrifice for our sin. (John xiii. ; xvii. 1, 2 ; xviii. 1, 2.) 2. Not at their time ; but, contrary to all expectation, when the due time was come, " he bowed his head, and gave up the ghost." (John xix. 30.)

And for this last work he had power given him of God, that is, power to die when he would. " I have power," said he, " to lay down my life, and I have power to take it again." This power never man had before. This made the centurion wonder, and made Pontius Pilate marvel : and, indeed, well they might, for it was as great a miracle as any he wrought in his life. It demonstrated him to be the Son of God. (Mark xv. 38, 39.) The centurion, knowing that according to nature he might have lived longer, concluded, therefore, that his dying at that instant was not but miraculously. And when he " saw that he so cried out, and gave up the ghost, he said, Truly this man was the Son of God ! "

And the reason why he had power to die was, that he might offer his offering willingly and at the season.

1. Willingly. " If his offering be a burnt sacrifice of the herd, let him offer a male without blemish ; he shall offer it of his own voluntary will, at the door of the tabernacle of the congregation before the Lord." (Lev. i. 3.) 2. He must offer it at the season, " Thou shalt keep this ordinance," the passover, " in his season." (Exod. xiii. 10.)

Now both these offerings having immediate respect to the offering of the body of Christ for sin (for he came in the room of all burnt sacrifices), the passover was also a type of him. (Heb. x. 3— 6. 1 Cor. v. 7, 8.) Therefore, he being now the priest as well as sacrifice, must have power and will to offer his sacrifice with acceptation ; and this the Scripture testifies he did, where it saith, " In due time Christ died for the ungodly." (Rom. v. 6.) In due time, that is, at the time appointed, at the acceptable time.

Thou must, therefore, unless thou art willing to be deceived, look upon the sufferings of Christ under a double consideration, and distinguish between his suffering as our example, and his suffering for our sins. And know, that as he suffered as our example, so he suffereth only for righteousness' sake from the hands of wicked men; but as he suffered for our sins, so he suffered, as being by God reputed wicked, the punishment that was due to sin, even the dreadful curse of God. Not that Christ died two deaths, one after another; but he died at the same time upon a double account, for his righteousness' sake from men—for our sins from the hand of God. And, as I said before, had he only suffered for righteousness' sake, death had not so amazed him, nor had he been so exceeding heavy in the thoughts of it; that had never put him into an agony, nor made him sweat as it were great drops of blood. Besides, when men suffer only for righteousness' sake, God does not use to hide his face from them, to forsake them, and make them accursed; but "Christ hath delivered us from the curse of the law, being made a curse for us."

Obj. 5. But if indeed Christ hath paid the full price for us by his death, in suffering the punishment that we should have done, wherefore is the Scripture so silent as not to declare that by his death he hath made satisfaction?

Ans. No man may teach God knowledge; he knoweth best how to deliver his mind in such words and terms as best agree with his eternal wisdom, and the consciences of those that are truly desirous of salvation, being over-burdened with the guilt of sin. Perhaps the word "satisfaction" will hardly be found in the Bible; and where is it said in so many words, God is dissatisfied with our sins? yet it is sufficiently manifest, that there is nothing that God hateth but sin, and sinners for the sake of sin. What meant he by turning Adam out of Paradise, by drowning the old world, by burning up Sodom with fire and brimstone from heaven? What meant he by drowning of Pharaoh, by causing the ground to swallow up Corah and his company, and by his destroying Israel in the wilderness, if not to show that he was dissatisfied with sin? That God is also satisfied, yea, more than satisfied by Christ's sufferings, for our sins, is apparent; for, granting that he died for them, as these Scriptures declare: Isa. liii. 1 Cor. xv. 1—4. Gal. i. 4. 1 Cor. v. 8. 2 Cor. v. 21. Gal. iii. 13. 1 Pet. ii. 24; iii. 18. 1 John ii. 2; iii. 16; iv. 14. Rev. i. 5; v. 9. Isa. xlix. 4—6.

1. It is apparent, because it is said that God smelled in that offering of the body of Christ for our sins a sweet-smelling savour. "He gave himself for us an offering and a sacrifice to God, for a sweet-smelling savour." (Eph. v. 2.)

2. It is apparent, because it is said expressly that God for Christ's sake doth now forgive. "Be ye kind one to another, tender-hearted, forgiving one another, even as God for Christ's sake hath forgiven you." (Eph. iv. 32.)

3. It is apparent that God is satisfied with Christ's blood for our sins, because he hath declared that he can justify those that believe in, or rely upon that blood for life, in a way of justice and righteousness: "Being justified freely by his grace, through the redemption that is in Jesus Christ; whom God hath set forth to be a propitiation through faith in his blood, to declare his righteousness for the remission of sins that are past, through the forbearance of God. To declare, I say, at this time his righteousness; that he might be just, and the justifier of him that believeth in Jesus." (Rom. iii. 24—26.)

Now, I say, to object against such plain testimonies, what is it but, 1. To deny that Christ died for sin; or to conclude, 2. That having so done, he is still in the grave: or, 3. That there is no such thing as sin: or, 4. No such thing as revenging justice in God against it: or, 5. That we must die ourselves for our sins: or, 6. That sin may be pardoned without a satisfaction: or, 7. That every man may merit his own salvation. But "without shedding of blood there is no remission." (Heb. ix. 22.)

To avoid, therefore, these cursed absurdities, it must be granted that Jesus Christ by his death did make satisfaction for sin.

But the word "satisfaction" may not be used by the Holy Ghost, perhaps for that it is too short and scanty a word to express the blessedness that comes to sinners by the blood of Christ.

1. To make satisfaction, amounts to no more than completely to answer a legal demand for harms and injuries done. Now this, when done to the full, leaveth the offender there where he was before he committed the injury. Now if Christ had done no more than this, he had only paid our debt, but had not obtained eternal redemption for us.

2. For a full satisfaction given by this man for harms done by another, may neither obtain the love of the person offended, nor the smallest gift which the person offending hath not deserved. Suppose I owe to this man ten thousand talents, and another should pay him every farthing, there remaineth over and above, by that complete satisfaction, not one single halfpenny for me. Christ hath therefore done more than to make satisfaction for sin by his blood. He hath also "made us kings and priests to God and his Father," and we "shall reign with him for ever and ever." (Rev. i. 6; xxii. 5.)

But take a few more scriptures for the proof of the doctrine afore asserted.

First. We have redemption through his blood.

1. Redemption from sin. (Eph. i. 7.) 2. Redemption from death. (Heb. ii. 14, 15. Hos. xiii. 14.) 3. Redemption from Satan. (Heb. ii. 14.) 4. Redemption from the world. (Gal. i. 4.) 5. Redemption to God. (Rev. v. 9.) 6. Eternal redemp-

tion : " Neither by the blood of goats and calves, but by his own blood, he entered in once into the holy place, having obtained eternal redemption for us." (Heb. ix. 12.)

Second. We are said also to be washed in his blood. 1. Our persons are washed : He " loved us, and washed us from our sins in his own blood." (Rev. i. 5.) 2. His blood washeth also our performances : " Our robes are washed, and made white in the blood of the Lamb." (Rev. vii. 14.)

Third. We are said to be purged by his blood. 1. Purged from sin before God : " When he had by himself purged our sins, he sat down on the right hand of God." (Heb i. 3.) 2. Purged from evil consciences : " How much more shall the blood of Christ, who through the eternal Spirit offered himself without spot to God, purge your conscience from dead works to serve the living God ?" (Heb. ix. 14.)

Fourth. We are said to be made nigh to God by his blood: " But now in Christ Jesus, ye who sometimes were afar off are made nigh by the blood of Christ." (Eph. ii. 13.)

Fifth. Peace is said to be made by his blood. 1. Peace with God. (Col. i. 20.) 2. Peace of conscience. (Heb. x. 19—23.) 3. Peace one with another. (Eph. ii. 14.)

Sixth. We are said to be justified by his blood : " Much more then, being now justified by his blood, we shall be saved from wrath through him." (Rom. v. 9.) Justified, that is acquitted : 1. Acquitted before God. (Eph. v. 26.) 2. Acquitted before angels. (Matt. xxviii. 5.) 3. Acquitted by the law. (Rom. iii. 21—23.) 4. Acquitted in the court of conscience. (Heb. ix. 14.)

Seventh. We are said to be saved by his blood. (Rom. v. 8, 9.)

Eighth. We are said to be reconciled by his blood. (Col. i. 20—22.)

Ninth. We are said to be sanctified by his blood. (Heb. xiii. 12.)

Tenth. We are said to be admitted into the holiest by his blood. (Heb. x. 19.)

Eleventh. We are said to have eternal redemption by his blood. (Heb. ix. 12.)

Yea, lastly, This blood which was once spilt upon the cross, will be the burden of our song in heaven itself for ever and ever. (Rev. v. 9.)

Now if we be redeemed, washed, purged, made nigh to God, have peace with God; if we stand just before God, are saved, reconciled, sanctified, admitted into the holiest; if we have eternal redemption by his blood, and if his blood will be the burden of our song for ever; then hath Christ paid the full price for us by his death, then hath he done more than made satisfaction for our sins.

SEVERAL DEMONSTRATIONS MORE, PROVING THE FORMER DOCTRINE.

But before I conclude this answer, I will give you nine or ten more undeniable demonstrations to satisfy you, if God will bless them to you, in the truth of this great doctrine, to wit, that Jesus Christ by what he hath done hath paid the full price to God for the souls of sinners, and obtained eternal redemption for them.

The First Demonstration.

And, first, I begin with his resurrection : That God who delivered him up unto death, and that made him a curse for sin, that God raised him up from the dead. " But God raised him from the dead." (Acts iii. 15.) Now, considering that at his death he was charged with our sins, and accursed to death for our sins, that justice that delivered him up for them must have amends made to him before he acquit him from them ; for there can be no change in justice. Had he found him in our sins in the grave, as he found him in them upon the tree, (for he had them in his body on the tree, 1 Pet. ii. 24,) he had left him there as he left him upon the tree ; yea, he had as surely rotted in the grave as ever he died on the tree. But when he visited Christ in the grave, he found him a holy, harmless, undefiled, and spotless Christ, and therefore he raised him up from the dead : " He raised him up from the dead, having loosed the pains of death ; because it was not possible that he should be holden of it." (Acts ii. 24.)

Quest. But why not possible now to be holden of death ?

Ans. Because the cause was removed. Sin was the cause : " He died for our sins ;" " He gave himself for our sins." (1 Cor. xv. 1—3. Gal. i. 4.) These sins brought him to death ; but when God, that had made him a curse for us, looked upon him into the grave, he found him there without sin, and therefore loosed the pains of death ; for justice saith, This is not possible, because not lawful, that he who lieth sinless before God should be swallowed up of death ; therefore he raised him up.

Quest. But what did he do with our sins ? for he had them upon his back.

Ans. It is said he took them away : " Behold the Lamb of God, that taketh away the sins of the world." It is said he put them away : " Now once in the end of the world hath he appeared to put away sin by the sacrifice of himself." (1 John i. 29. Heb. ix. 26.) That is, by the merit of his undertaking he brought into the world, and set before the face of God, such a righteousness that outweigheth, and goeth far beyond that sin, and so did hide sin from the sight of God ; hence he that is justified is said to have his sins hid and covered : " Blessed is the man whose transgressions are forgiven, and whose sin is covered," (Ps. xxxii. 1 ;) covered with the righteousness of Christ. " I spread my skirt over thee, and covered thy nakedness," thy sins. (Ezek. xvi. 8.) Christ Jesus, therefore, having by the infiniteness of his merit taken away, put away, or hidden our sins from the face of God, therefore he raised him up from the dead.

You find in that 16th of Leviticus mention made of two goats; one was to be slain for a sin-offering, the other to be left alive. The goat that was slain was a type of Christ's death, the other of his merit. Now this living goat, he carried away the sins of the people into the land of forgetfulness: "And Aaron shall lay both his hands upon the head of the live goat, and confess over him all the iniquities of the children of Israel, and all their transgressions in all their sins, putting them upon the head of the goat, and shall send him away by the hands of a fit man into the wilderness; and the goat shall bear upon him all their iniquities unto a land not inhabited." (Lev. xvi. 21, 22.) Thus did Jesus Christ bear away, by the merit of his death, the sins and iniquities of them that believe; wherefore, when God came to him in the grave, he found him holy and undefiled, and raised him up from the dead.

And observe it, as his death was for our sin, so his rising again was for our discharge; for both in his death and resurrection he immediately respected our benefits; he died for us, he rose from the dead for us. "He was delivered for our offences, and was raised again for our justification." (Rom. iv. 25.) By his death he carried away our sins, by his rising he brought to us justifying righteousness.

There are five circumstances also attending his resurrection, that show us how well pleased God was with his death.

1. It must be solemnized with the company, attendance and testimony of angels. (Matt. xxviii. 1—8. Luke xxiv. 3—7. John xx. 11, 12.)

2. At, or just upon his resurrection, the graves, where many of the saints for whom he died lay asleep, did open, and they followed the Lord in full triumph over death: "The graves were opened, and many bodies of saints which slept arose, and came out of their graves after his resurrection, and went into the holy city, and appeared unto many." (Matt. xxvii. 52, 53.) These saints coming out of their graves after him, what a testimony is it that he for them had taken away sin, and destroyed him that had the power of death; yea, what a testimony was it that he had made amends to God the Father, who granted him at his resurrection to have presently out of the grave, of the price of his blood, even the bodies of many of the saints which slept! He was declared to be the Son of God with power by the Spirit of holiness, and the resurrection from the dead. It saith not, by his resurrection, though that be true; but by the resurrection, meaning the resurrection of the bodies of the saints which slept, because they rose by virtue of his blood, and by that he was with power declared to be the Son of God. They, I say, were part of his purchase, some of them for whom Christ died. Now for God to raise them, and that upon, and by virtue of his resurrection, what is it but an open

declaration from heaven that Christ by his death hath made amends for us, and obtained eternal redemption for us?

_c._ When he was risen from the dead, God, to confirm his disciples in the faith of the redemption that Christ had obtained by his blood, brings him to the church, presents him to them alive, shows him openly, sometimes to two or three, sometimes to eleven or twelve, and once to above five hundred brethren at once. (Acts i. 3; x. 40. Luke xxiv. 13—16. John xx. 19; xxi. 1—23. 1 Cor. xv. 3—8.)

4. At his resurrection, God gives him the keys of hell and of death. (Rev. i. 18.) Hell and death are the effects and fruits of sin. "The wicked shall be turned into hell," and "the wages of sin is death." But what then are sinners the better for the death and blood of Christ? Oh, they that dare venture upon him are much the better, for they shall not perish unless the Saviour will damn them, for he hath the keys of hell and of death. "Fear not," saith he, "I am not the first and the last; I am he that liveth and was dead, and behold, I am alive for evermore, and have the keys of hell and death." These were given him at his resurrection, as if God had said, My Son, thou hast spilt thy blood for sinners; I am pleased with it, I am delighted in thy merits, and in the redemption which thou hast wrought; in token hereof, I give thee the keys of hell and of death; I give thee all power in heaven and earth; save who thou wilt, deliver who thou wilt, bring to heaven who thou wilt.

5. At Christ's resurrection, God bids him ask the heathen of him, with a promise to give him the uttermost parts of the earth for his possession. This sentence is in the second Psalm, and is expounded by Paul's interpretation of the words before, to be spoken to Christ at his resurrection: "Thou art my Son, this day have I begotten thee." I have begotten thee, that is saith Paul, from the dead. (Acts xiii. 33, 34.)

He hath raised up Jesus again, as it is also written in the second Psalm, "Thou art my Son, this day have I begotten thee." Now mark, at his raising him from the dead, he bids him ask, "Ask of me," and that "the heathen;" as if God had said, My Son, thy blood hath pacified and appeased my justice; I can now, in justice for thy sake, forgive poor mortals their sin; ask them of me, ask them, though they be heathens, and I will give them to thee, to the utmost ends of the earth. This is then the first demonstration to prove that Jesus Christ, by what he hath done, hath paid full price to God for the souls of sinners, and obtained eternal redemption for them; namely, his being raised again from the dead.

The Second Demonstration.

Second. A second thing that demonstrateth this truth is, that he ascended, and was received up into heaven. "So after the Lord had spoken to them, he was received up into heaven." (Matt. xvi. 9.) This demonstration consisteth of two parts: First. Of his ascending. Second. Of his being received.

First. For his ascending: "He is ascended on high." (Eph. iv. 8.) This act of ascending answereth to the high-priest under the law, who, after they had killed the sacrifice, he was to bring the blood into the most holy place, to wit, the inner temple, the way to which was ascending or going up.

Now, consider the circumstances that attended his ascending, when he went to carry his blood to present it before the mercy-seat; and you will find they all say amends is made to God for us.

1. At this he is again attended, and accompanied with angels. (Acts i. 10, 11.)

2. He ascended with a shout, and with the sound of a trumpet, with "Sing praises, sing praises, sing praises." (Ps. xlvii. 6.)

3. The enemies of man's salvation are now tied to his chariot-wheels. When he ascended on high, he led captivity captive; that is, he led death, devils, and hell, and the grave, and the curse captive, for these things were our captivity. And thus did Deborah prophecy of him, when she cried, "Arise, Barak, and lead thy captivity captive, thou son of Abinoam." This David also foresaw when he said, "Thou hast ascended on high, thou hast led captivity captive." (Ps. lxviii. 18.)

4. The apostles must be the beholders of his going up, and must see the cloud receive him out of their sight. (Acts i. 9—12.)

The consideration of these things strongly enforceth this conclusion, that he hath spoiled what would have spoiled us, had he not by his blood-shed taken them away. And I say, for God to adorn him with all this glory in his ascension; THUS to make him ride conqueror up into the clouds; THUS to go up with the sound of trumpet, with shout of angels, and with songs of praises; and, let me add, to be accompanied also with those that rose from the dead after his resurrection, who were the very price of his blood: this does greatly demonstrate, that Jesus Christ, by what he hath done, hath paid a full price to God for the souls of sinners, and obtained eternal redemption for them; he had not else rid thus in triumph to heaven.

Second. I come now to his being received: "He was received up into heaven." The high-priest under the law, when he ascended into the holiest, he was there to offer the blood; which holiest was the type of heaven. (Exod. xix. 10, 11. Heb. ix. 24.) But because the sacrifice under the law could not make them that did the service perfect, as pertaining to the conscience; therefore they were to stand, not to sit; to come out again, not tarry there. "For it is not possible that the blood of bulls and goats should take away sin; wherefore, when he cometh into the world he saith, Sacrifices and offerings thou wouldst not,

but a body hast thou prepared me. In burnt-offerings and sacrifices for sin thou hast had no pleasure. Then said he, Lo, I come (in the volume of thy book it is written of me) to do thy will, O God." (Heb. x. 4—6.)

Christ, therefore, in his entering into heaven, did it as high-priest of the church of God; therefore neither did he go in without blood. Wherefore, when he came to be "an high-priest of good things to come, by a greater and more perfect tabernacle, not made with hands; that is to say, not of this building; neither by the blood of bulls and goats, but by his own blood; he entered in once into the holy place, having obtained eternal redemption for us." (Heb. ix. 12—14.) He entered in, having obtained, or because he obtained, eternal redemption for us. But to pass that:

Consider ye now also those glorious circumstances that accompany his approach to the gates of the everlasting habitation.

First. The everlasting gates are set, yea, bid stand open: Be ye open, "ye everlasting doors, and the King of glory shall come in." This King of glory is Jesus Christ, and the words are a prophecy of his glorious ascending into the heavens, when he went up as the high-priest of the church, to carry the price of his blood into the holiest of all. "Lift up your heads, O ye gates; even lift them up, ye everlasting doors; and the King of glory shall come in." (Ps. xxiv. 7—9.)

Second. At his entrance he was received, and the price accepted which he paid for our souls. Hence it is said, he entered in by his blood; that is, by the merit of it. To receive, is an act of complacency and delight, and includeth well-pleasedness in the person receiving, who is God the Father: and considering that this Jesus, now received, is to be received upon our account, or as undertaking the salvation of sinners—for he entered into the heavens for us—it is apparent that he entered thither by virtue of his infinite righteousness which he accomplished for us upon the earth.

Third. At his reception he received glory, and that also for our encouragement: "God raised him up, and gave him glory, that our faith and hope might be in him." (1 Pet. i. 19—21.) He gave him glory, as a testimony that his undertaking the work of our redemption was accepted of him.

1. He gave glory, first, to his person, in granting him to sit at his own right hand; and this he had, I say, for, or upon the account of the work he accomplished for us in the world, when he had offered up one sacrifice for sins, for ever, he sat down on the right hand of God, and this by God's appointment: "Sit thou at my right hand." (Heb. x. 12.) This glory is the highest; it is above all kings, princes, and potentates in this world; it is above all angels, principalities, and powers in heaven. "He is gone into heaven, and is on the right hand of God; angels, and

authorities, and powers being made subject unto him." (1 Pet. iii. 32.)

2. He gave glory to his name,—to his name, *Jesus,* that name being exalted above every name : " He hath given him a name above every name, that at the name of Jesus every knee should bow, of things in heaven, and things on earth, and things under the earth ; and that every tongue should confess that Jesus Christ is Lord, to the glory of God the Father." (Phil. ii. 9—11.)

This name is said, in another place, to be a name above every name that is named, "not only in this world but also in that which is to come." (Eph. i. 21.)

But should *Jesus* have been such a name, since he undertook for sinners, had this undertaker failed in his work, if his work had not been accepted with God, even the work of our redemption by his blood ? No, verily ; it would have stunk in the nostrils both of God and man, it would have been the most abhorred name. But *Jesus* is the name ; *Jesus,* he was called in order to his work : " His name shall be called *Jesus,* for he shall save ; " he was so named of the angel before he was conceived in the womb ; and he goeth by that name now he is in heaven ; by the name Jesus, " Jesus of Nazareth," because he once dwelt there. This name, I say, is the highest name, the everlasting name : the name that he is to go by, to be known by, to be worshipped by, to be glorified by ; yea, the name by which also most glory shall redound to God the Father. Now what is the signification of this name, but *Saviour ?* This name he hath, therefore, for his work's sake ; and because God delighted in his undertaking, and was pleased with the price he had paid for us, therefore the Divine Majesty hath given him it, hath made it high, and hath commanded all angels to bow unto it. Yea, it is the name in which he resteth, and by which he hath magnified all his attributes.

(1.) This is the name by which sinners should go to God the Father. (2.) This is the name through which they obtain forgiveness of sins and *any* thing, " If you ask any thing in my name, I will do it." (John xiv. 14.) (3.) This is the name through which our spiritual services and sacrifices are accepted, and by which an answer of peace is returned unto our bosoms. (1 Pet. ii.) But more of this anon. (4.) At *this* name, devils tremble ; at *this* name, angels bow the head ; at *this* name, God's heart openeth ; at *this* name, the godly man's heart is comforted ; *this* name, none but devils hate it, and none but those that must be damned despise it. " No man speaking by the Holy Ghost calls Jesus accursed," or accounteth him still dead, and his blood ineffectual to save the world.

3. He hath also given him the glory of office.

(1.) He is there a Priest for ever, intercepting betwixt the Divine presence, and all that hate us, by his blood ; sin, Satan, death, hell, the law, the grave, or the like, cannot be heard, if his blood be presented to God, as the atonement for us. This is called the blood of sprinkling, which speaks better things than the blood of Abel. By this blood he entered into heaven, by this blood he secureth from wrath, "all that come unto God by him." But should his blood have had a voice in heaven to save withal, had it not merited first, even in the shedding of it, the ransom and redemption of souls ? It is true, a man whose blood cannot save, may, with Abel's, cry out for vengeance and wrath on the head of him that sheds it ; but *this* blood speaks for better things, this blood speaks for souls, for sinners, for pardon, " having obtained eternal redemption for us."

(2.) He is there a forerunner for us : " Whither the forerunner is for us entered, even Jesus." (Heb. vi. 20.) This office of harbinger is distinct from, though it comes by virtue of his priestly office ; therefore they are both mentioned in the text : " Whither the forerunner is for us entered, even Jesus, made an High-priest for ever, after the order of Melchisedec." He is therefore our forerunner, by virtue of his priesthood, his blood giving worth to all he does.

In this office of harbinger, or forerunner, he prepareth for believers their dwelling-places in the heavens, their dwelling-places, according to their place, state, calling, service, or work, in his body the church : " In my Father's house," saith he, " are many mansions ; if it were not so, I would have told you. I go to prepare a place for you." (John xiv. 2.)

This is that is mentioned in the 47th Psalm : " He shall choose our inheritance for us, the excellency of Jacob whom he loved." But should he have had power to choose our inheritance for us, to prepare our dwelling-places ; should he have power to give, even heaven itself, to a company of poor men, had he not in the first place obtained by his blood the deliverance of our souls from death ?

(3.) He is there a prophet for us, by which office of his he hath received to communicate the whole will of the eternal God, so far as is fit for us to know in this world, or in that which is to come. Hence he is called the prophet of the church : " The Lord shall raise you up a prophet," " and this is of a truth that prophet that should come into the world." But this office he hath also now in heaven, by virtue of the blood he shed for us upon earth. Hence the new testament is called " the new testament in his blood ;" and his blood is said to be " the blood of the everlasting covenant," or testament ; yea, such virtue doth his blood give to the new testament, or covenant of grace, as that severed from that it is nothing worth ; " for a testament is of force after men are dead ; otherwise it is of no strength at all while the testator liveth." (Heb. ix. 17.) So that every word of God, which he hath by Christ given to us for our everlasting consolation, is dipt in blood, is founded in blood, and stands good to sinners purely (I mean with respect to merit), upon the account of blood, or because his blood that was shed for us on the cross prevailed for us for the remission of our sins. Let no man think to receive any benefit by Christ's prophetical office, by any of the good words of grace, and forgiveness of sins, that are sprinkled up and down in the New Testament; that looketh not for that good to come to him for the sake of that blood by which this testament is established; for "neither was the first testament dedicated without blood; for when Moses had spoken every precept to all the people according to the law, he took the blood of calves, and of goats with water, and scarlet wool, and hyssop, and sprinkled both the book and all the people, saying, This is the blood of the testament which God hath enjoined unto you." (Heb. ix. 18—20.)

The prophetical office of Christ standeth of two parts: first, in promises of grace; secondly, in directions of worship; but neither is this last, to wit, the doctrine of worship, or our subjection to that worship, of any value, any further than as sprinkled also with his blood: for as in the first testament, the tabernacle and all the vessels of the ministry were sprinkled with blood, and it was necessary that so it should be; so the heavenly things themselves must be also purified with sacrifices, but yet with better sacrifice than these; for now, not Moses, but Christ, doth sprinkle, not with blood of calves, but with his own blood, neither as entered into places made with hands, but from heaven doth Jesus sprinkle all that doctrine of worship, and subjection of his saints thereto, which is of his own instituting and commanding. (Heb. ix. 23—26.)

(4.) He hath received there the office of a king, by which he ruleth in the church, and over all things for her sake. The government is laid upon his shoulders; the Lord God hath given him the throne of his father David. Hence it is that he saith, "All power is given me in heaven and in earth;" but now this kingly office, he hath it by his blood, because he humbled himself to death, therefore God hath highly exalted him, and given him the highest name. And hence, again, he is called a *Lamb* upon the throne: "In the midst of the throne, and of the four beasts, and in the midst of the elders, stood a Lamb as it had been slain, having seven horns;" a demonstration of kingly power. But mark, he was a Lamb upon the throne, he had his horns as a lamb. Now by *Lamb*, we are to understand, not only his meek and sweet disposition, but his sacrifice; for he was as a lamb to be slain and sacrificed; and so his having a throne and seven horns, as a lamb, giveth us to understand, that he obtained this dignity of king by his blood. "When he had by himself purged our sins, he sat down on the right hand of the majesty in the heavens." (Heb. i. 8.) When "he had offered up one sacrifice for sins for ever, he sat down on the right hand of God." (Heb. x. 12.)

Now, put all these together, to wit, his resurrection from the dead, his ascension, and his exalta-tion to office; and remember also that the person thus exalted is the same Jesus of Nazareth that sometime was made accursed of God for sin, and also that he obtained this glory by virtue of the blood that was shed for us; and it must unavoid-ably follow, that Jesus Christ, by what he hath done, hath paid full price to God for sinners, and obtained eternal redemption for them.

The Third Demonstration.

But to proceed: A third demonstration that Jesus Christ, by what he hath done, hath paid full price to God for sinners, and obtained eternal redemption for them, is, because he hath received for them the holy Spirit of God.

"This Jesus hath God raised up, whereof," said Peter, "we are all witnesses. Therefore, being by the right hand of God exalted, and having received of the Father the promise of the Holy Ghost, he hath shed forth that which ye now see and hear." (Acts. ii. 32, 33.)

The receiving of the Holy Ghost at the hand of the Father, who had bruised him before for the transgressions of his people; the receiving of it, I say, upon his resurrection, and that to give them for whom, just before, he had spilt his blood to make an atonement for their souls, argueth, that the Divine Majesty found rest and content in that precious blood, and found it full price for the sinners for whom he shed it.

And if you consider the necessity of the giving of this good Spirit to men, and the benefit that they receive by his coming upon them, you will see yet more into the truth now contended for. First. Then of the necessity of giving this good Spirit. Second. And then of the benefit which we receive at his coming.

First. Of the necessity of its being given.

1. Otherwise Jesus could never have been proved to be the Saviour; for the promise was, that Messias should have the Spirit given him; given him to communicate: "As for me, this is my covenant with them, saith the Lord, My Spirit which is upon thee, and my words which I have put in thy mouth," meaning the Redeemer, (ver. 20,) "shall not depart out of thy mouth, nor out of the mouth of thy seed, nor out of the mouth of thy seed's seed, saith the Lord, from henceforth and for ever." (Isa. lix. 20, 21.)

Here is the promise of the Spirit to be given to Christ, and by him to his seed for ever. And this was signified long before, in the anointing of Aaron and his sons: "And thou shalt anoint Aaron and his sons, and consecrate them." (Exod. xxx. 30.)

This Spirit Jesus promised to send unto his, at his exaltation on the right hand of God. The Spirit, I say, in the plentiful pourings of it out. True, the church in all ages had something of it by virtue of the suretyship of the Lord Jesus; but this, in comparison of what was to come into the church after his resurrection, is not reckoned a pouring forth; therefore pourings forth thereof are reserved to the time of the ascension and exaltation of this Jesus: " I will pour out of my Spirit in *those* days."

Hence Jesus reserves it till his going away, and it is expressly said, " The Holy Ghost was not yet given, because Jesus was not yet glorified." Accordingly did the apostles wait after his resurrection for the pouring forth of the Holy Ghost, and at the set time did receive it, by the giving of which he declared himself to be the Son of God and Saviour of the world. (John xiv. 26; xv. 26; xvi. 7. Acts i. 4, 5. Joel ii. 28. Acts ii. 16, 17. John vii. 39. Rom. i. 4.)

2. Without the giving of the Holy Ghost there had wanted a testimony that his gospel was the gospel of Messias. Moses his ministration was confirmed by signs and wonders and mighty deeds, both in Egypt, in the wilderness, and at the Red Sea; wherefore it was necessary that the doctrine of redemption by blood, which is the doctrine of the gospel of this Jesus, should be also confirmed with signs following. Hence both himself and apostles did as frequently work miracles and do mighty deeds, as his ministers now do preach; which signs, and miracles, and wonders, confirmed their doctrine, though themselves, both master and scholar, were in appearance the most considerable mean; yea, they by the means of the Holy Ghost, have so ratified, confirmed, and settled the gospel in the world, that no philosopher, tyrant, or devil hath been able hitherto to move it out of its place. He confirmed the "word with signs following." (Mark xvi. 20.)

3. As the giving of the Holy Ghost was necessary thus, so was it necessary also to strengthen them that were intrusted with his gospel: (1.) To preach it effectually. (2.) To stand to it boldly. (3.) And to justify it to be the doctrine of Messias incontrollably.

(1.) To preach it effectually: in demonstration of the Spirit. (2.) To stand to it boldly : " Then Peter, filled with the Holy Ghost," said, " And they saw the boldness of Peter and John." (2 Cor. vi. 4, 6. Acts viii. 13.) (3.) To justify the doctrine incontrollably : " I will give you a mouth and wisdom, which all your adversaries shall not be able to resist or gainsay." (Luke xxi. 15.) " And they were not able to resist the wisdom and Spirit by which he spake." (Acts. vi. 10.)

Now I say, that God should give the Holy Ghost to Jesus to confirm this gospel, redemption from sin by his blood; what is it but that by his blood he hath paid full price to God for sinners, and obtained eternal redemption for them?

But, again; the benefit which we receive at the coming of the Holy Ghost doth more demonstrate this truth. Hath Christ purchased sinners, and are they the price of his blood? Yes. But how doth that appear? Why, because by the Holy Ghost which he hath received to give us, we are fitted for the inheritance which by his blood is prepared for us.

1. By the Spirit of God we are quickened and raised from a state of sin; but that we could not be, were it not that an atonement is made for us first, by the blood of Christ our Saviour. This is true; for they that are quickened by the Holy Ghost are quickened by it through the word of the gospel, which offereth justification to sinners through faith in his blood; yea, we are said to be quickened together with him, dead and risen with him; yet so as by the Spirit of God.

2. We are not only quickened by the Holy Ghost, but possessed therewith; it is given to dwell in our hearts. "Because ye are sons, God hath sent forth the Spirit of his Son into your hearts" (Gal. iv. 6); which Spirit is also our earnest for heaven, until the redemption of the purchased possession; that is, until our body, which is the purchased possession, be redeemed also out of the grave by the power of the same mighty Spirit of God. (Eph. i. 13, 14.)

3. By this Holy Spirit we are made to believe. (Rom. xv. 13.)

4. By this Holy Spirit we are helped to pray, and call God Father.

5. By this Holy Spirit we are helped to understand and apply the promises.

6. By this Holy Spirit the joy of heaven, and the love of God, is shed abroad in the hearts of the saved.

7. By this Holy Spirit we are made to wait for the hope of righteousness by faith; that is, to stand fast through our Lord Jesus in the day when he shall judge the world.

And all this is the fruit of redemption by blood; of redemption by the blood of Christ.

This is yet further evident—(1.) Because the work of the Spirit is to lead us into the sayings of Christ; which, as to our redemption from death, are such as these : " I lay down my life, that you may have life;" " I give my life a ransom for many;" and, " The bread which I will give is my flesh, which I will give for the life of the world." (2.) Because the Spirit, in the wisdom of heaven, is not counted a sufficient testimony on earth, but as joined with the blood of Christ: " There are three that bear witness on earth, the Spirit, the water, and the blood;" these are the witnesses of God. The Spirit, because it quickeneth; the blood, because it hath merited; and the water, to wit, the word, because by that we are clean as to life and conversation. (1 John v. 8. Eph. v. 26. Rom. viii. 16. Ps. cxix. 9.) (3.) Because, as by the Spirit, so we are sanctified by faith in the blood of Jesus. (Heb. xiii. 12.) (4.) Because, when most full of the Spirit, and when that doth work most mightily in us, we are then most in the belief and admiring apprehensions of our deliverance from death by the blood of Jesus. (Rev. v. 9; xv.) (5.) The Holy Ghost breatheth nowhere so as in the ministry of this doctrine; this doctrine is sent with the Holy Ghost from heaven; yea, as I have hinted, one of the great works of the Holy Ghost, under the Old Testament, was to testify of the sufferings of Christ, and the glory that should follow. (1 Pet. i. 11, 12.)

Put all these things together, and see if Jesus Christ, by what he hath done, hath not paid full price to God for sinners; if he "hath not obtained eternal redemption for them."

The Fourth Demonstration.

That Jesus Christ, by what he hath done, hath paid full price to God for sinners, and obtained eternal redemption for them, is evident, if you consider how the preaching thereof hath been from that time to this a mighty conqueror over all kind of sinners. What nation, what people, what kind of sinners have not been subdued by the preaching of a crucified Christ? He upon the white horse with his bow and his crown hath conquered, doth conquer, and goeth forth yet "conquering, and to conquer." (Rev. vi. 2.) "And I," saith he, "if I be lifted up from the earth, will draw all men unto me." (John xii. 32.) But what was it to be lifted up from the earth? Why, it may be expounded by that saying: "As Moses lifted up the serpent in the wilderness, so must the Son of man be lifted up, that whosoever believeth in him might not perish, but have everlasting life." (John iii. 14, 15.)

He was then lifted up, when he was hanged upon a tree between the heavens and the earth as the accursed of God for us. The revelation of this, it conquers all nations, tongues, and people. "And they sang a new song, saying, Thou art worthy to take the book, and to open the seals thereof, for thou wast slain, and hast redeemed us to God by thy blood, out of every kindred and tongue, and people, and nation." (Rev. v. 9.) Hence the Apostle Paul chose, above all doctrines, to preach up a crucified Christ, and resolved so to do: "For I determined," saith he, "not to know anything among you, save Jesus Christ, and him crucified." (1 Cor. ii. 2.)

First. The doctrine of forgiveness of sin conquered his very murderers. They could not withstand the grace; those bloody ones, that would kill him whatever it cost them, could stand no longer, but received his doctrine, fell into his bosom, and obtained the salvation which is in Christ Jesus. "They shall look upon him whom they have pierced, and mourn for him, as one mourneth for his only son; and they shall be in bitterness for him, as one is in bitterness for his first-born." (Zech. xii. 10.) Now was the Scripture eminently fulfilled, when the kindness of a crucified Christ broke to pieces the hearts of them that had before been his betrayers and murderers. Now was there a great mourning in Jerusalem; now was there wailing and lamentation mixed with joy and rejoicing.

Second. Though Paul was mad, exceeding mad against Jesus Christ of Nazareth, yea, though he was his avowed enemy, seeking to put out his name from under heaven, yet the voice from heaven, "I am Jesus," &c., "I am the Saviour," how did it conquer him, make him throw down his arms, fall down at his feet, and accept of the forgiveness of sins freely by grace, through redemption by faith in his blood.

Third. They at Samaria, though before Philip preached to them, worshipped and admired the devil in Magus, yet when they believed Philip's preaching of Christ unto them, and forgiveness of sins through faith in his name, great joy was amongst them, and they were baptized both men and women. (Acts viii.) "He preached," saith the text, "the things concerning the kingdom of God, and the name of Jesus Christ;" that is, all the blessings of life, through the name of Jesus Christ; for he is the Mediator, and without his blood come no spiritual blessings to men.

Fourth. How was the sturdy jailer overcome by a promise of forgiveness of sins by faith in Jesus Christ. It stopped his hand of self-murder; it eased him of the gnawings of a guilty conscience and fears of hell-fire, and filled his soul with rejoicing in God. (Acts xvi. 30—34.)

Fifth. How were those that used curious arts, that were next to, if not, witches indeed; I say, how were they prevailed upon, and overcome by the word of God, which is the gospel of good tidings, through faith in the blood of Christ. (Acts xix. 17, 18.)

Sixth. How were the Ephesians, who were sometimes far from God; how, I say, were they made nigh by the blood of Christ. (Eph. ii. 13.)

Seventh. The Colossians, though sometimes dead in their sins, yet how were they quickened by God, through the forgiveness of all their trespasses; and they had that through his blood. (Col. i. 14; ii. 13.)

What shall I say? No man could as yet stand before, and not fall under the revelation of the forgiveness of sins through a crucified Christ; as hanged, as dying, as accursed for sinners; he draws all men unto him, men of all sorts, of all degrees.

Shall I add, how have men broken through all difficulties to Jesus, when he hath been discovered to them? Neither lions, nor fires, nor sword, nor famine, nor nakedness, nor peril; neither death, nor life, nor angels, nor principalities, nor powers, nor things present, nor things to come, nor height, nor depth, nor any other creature, shall be able to separate us from the love of God, which is in Christ Jesus our Lord. (Rom. viii. 35—39.)

The Fifth Demonstration.

That Jesus Christ, by what he hath done, hath paid full price to God for sinners, and obtained eternal redemption for them, is evident, by the peace and holiness that, by that doctrine, possesseth men's souls: the souls of men awakened, and that continue so. By awakened men, I mean such as through the revelation of their sin and misery, groan under the want of Jesus to save them, and that continue sensible that they needs must perish if his benefits be not bestowed upon them; for otherwise the gospel ministereth neither peace nor holiness to any of the souls of the sons of. men; that is to say, not saving peace and holiness. The gospel of grace and salvation is above all doctrines the most dangerous, if in word only it be received by graceless men; if it be not attended with a revelation of men's need of a Saviour; if it be not accompanied in the soul by the power of the Holy Ghost. For such men as have only the notions of it, are of all men liable to the greatest sins, because there wanteth in their notions the power of love, which alone can constrain them to love Jesus Christ. And this is the reason of these scriptures: "They turn the grace of God into wantonness;" "They turn the grace of our God into lasciviousness." (Jude iv.)

For some, when they hear of the riches of grace through Christ, that hearing not being attended with the faith and love which is in Christ Jesus, those men receive the notions of this good doctrine only to cloak their wickedness, and to harden themselves in their villanies.

Others, when they hear, being leavened before with the leaven of some other doctrine,—some doctrine of the righteousness of the world, or doctrine of devils,—forthwith make head against, and speak evil of the blessed doctrine; and because some that profess it are not cleansed from their filthiness of flesh and spirit, and do not perfect holiness in the fear of God, therefore others conclude that all that profess it are such, and that the doctrine itself tendeth to encourage, or at least, to tolerate licentiousness, as they imagined and affirmed of Paul, that he should say, "Let us do evil, that good may come." (Rom. iii. 8.)

The ground of that wicked conclusion of theirs was, because he by the allowance of God affirmed that, as sin had reigned unto death, so grace reigned unto life in a way of righteousness by Jesus Christ our Lord. Nay, then, says the adversary, we may be as unholy as we will, and that by the doctrine you preach; for if where sin abounds, grace abounds more, the consequence of a wicked life is but the heightening, advancing, and magnifying of grace. But what saith the Apostle? My conclusions are true, that grace doth reign above sin, but to say, "Let us therefore sin," that man's damnation is just; because such an one abuseth, and maketh the most devilish use of the blessedest doctrine that ever was heard of in the world among men. Besides, it is evident that such know not the power thereof; nor have felt or savoured its blessedness; for where this gospel cometh in truth, it naturally produceth *peace* and *holiness*.

First. Peace. He is our peace; he is the Prince of peace; he giveth peace in his high places. This word "peace" hath in it a double respect.

1. It respecteth God. He hath "made peace by the blood of his cross;" that is, he hath made peace for us with God, having appeased the rigour of his law, and satisfied justice for us. Hence it is said: "The peace of God, which passeth all understanding, shall keep your hearts and minds through Christ Jesus." (Col. i. 20. Phil. iv. 7.) "The peace of God," that is, the doctrine of reconciliation by Christ's being made to be sin for us, *that* shall keep the heart, that is, from despair or fainting, under apprehensions of weakness and justice. But yet, this peace of God cannot be apprehended, nor be of any comfort to the heart, but as the man looks for it through Christ Jesus. Therefore that clause is added, "through Christ Jesus;" for he is peace-maker, it is he that reconcileth us to God "in the body of his flesh through death;" for by his doing and suffering he presented God with everlasting righteousness for sinners. Upon this we have peace with God. Hence Christ is called King of righteousness first, "first being by interpretation King of righteousness, and after that also King of Salem, which is King of peace." (Heb. vii. 1, 2.) For he could not make peace with God, betwixt us and him, but by being first the Lord of righteousness, the Lord our righteousness; but having first completed righteousness, he then came and preached peace, and commanded his ambassadors to make proclamation of it to the world, (2 Cor. v. 19, 21;) for it was want of righteousness that caused want of peace. Now, then, righteousness being brought in, it followeth that he hath made peace. "For he is our peace, who hath made both one, and hath broken down the middle wall of partition between us. Having abolished in his flesh the enmity, even the law of commandments, contained in ordinances, for to make in himself of twain one new man, so making peace; and that he might reconcile both unto God in one body by the cross, having slain the enmity thereby; and came and preached peace to you that were afar off, and to them that were nigh. For through him we both have access, by one Spirit unto the Father." (Eph. ii. 14—18.)

2. This word "peace" respecteth our inward quietness of heart, which we obtain by beholding this reconciliation made by Christ, with God, for us. "Being justified by faith, we have peace with God through our Lord Jesus Christ." (Rom. v. 1.) "The God of peace fill you with all joy and peace in believing." (Rom. xv. 13.)

This "peace" is expressed diversely. (1.) Sometimes it is called quietness; for it calms the soul from those troublous fears of damning, because of sin: "And the work of righteousness shall be peace, and the effect of righteousness, quietness and assurance for ever." (Isa. xxxii. 17.) (2.) Sometimes it is called "boldness;" for by the blood of Christ a man hath encouragement to approach unto God: "Having, brethren, boldness to enter into the holiest by the blood of Jesus by a new and living way which he hath consecrated for us through the vail, that is to say, his flesh." (Heb. x. 19, 20.)   (3.) It is sometimes called " confidence;" because by Jesus Christ we have not only encouragement to come to God, but confidence, that if we ask anything according to his will, he not only heareth, but granteth the request which we put up to him. (1 John v. 14.)   " In whom we have boldness and access with confidence, by the faith of Jesus." (Eph. iii. 12.) (4.) Sometimes this peace is expressed by " REST," because a man having found a sufficient fulness to answer all his wants, he sitteth down, and looks no further for satisfaction : " Come unto me, all ye that labour and are heavy laden, and I will give you rest." (Matt. xi. 28.)   (5.) It is expressed by " singing," because the peace of God, when it is received into the soul by faith, putteth the conscience into a heavenly and melodious frame : " And the ransomed of the Lord shall return, and come to Zion with songs, and everlasting joy upon their heads ; they shall obtain joy and gladness, and sorrow and sighing shall fly away." (Isa. xxxv. 10.)   (6.) Sometimes it is expressed or discovered by a heavenly glorying and boasting in Jesus Christ, because this peace causeth the soul to set its face upon its enemies with faith of a victory over them for ever by its Lord Jesus : " Let him that glorieth, glory in the Lord," (Jer. ix. 23, 24 ;) and, " My soul shall make her boast in the Lord ; the humble shall hear thereof, and be glad." (Ps. xxxiv. 2.)   (7.) Sometimes it is expressed or discovered by joy, " joy unspeakable ;" because the soul, having seen itself reconciled to God, hath not only quietness, but such apprehensions do now possess it of the unspeakable benefits it receiveth by Christ with respect to the world to come, that it is swallowed up with them : " Whom having not seen, ye love ; in whom, though now ye see him not, yet believing, ye rejoice with joy unspeakable, and full of glory." (1 Pet. i. 8.)   (8.) Lastly, It is expressed or discovered by the triumph that ariseth sometimes in the hearts of the believers; for they at times are able to see death, sin, the devil, and hell, and all adversity conquered by and tied as captives at the chariot-wheels of Jesus Christ ; taken captive, I say, and overthrown for ever !   " Thanks be to God, who causeth us always to triumph in Christ." (2 Cor. ii. 14.)   " O clap your hands, O ye people ; sing unto God with the voice of triumph." (Ps. xlvii. 1.)

Now that all this should be a cheat, is impossible, that is, it is impossible that believers should thus have peace with God through the blood of his cross, he having not paid full price to God for them ; especially if you consider, that the authors of this peace are all the three in the Godhead, and that upon a double account.

1. In that they have given us a gospel of peace, (Rom. x. 15,) or a New Testament, which propoundeth peace with God through the redemption that is in Christ. (1 Thess. ii. 9.)   Now as this is called the gospel of peace, so it is called, the gospel of God. (2 Thess. i. 8.)   The gospel of Christ. (Rom. xv. 19.)   A gospel indited by the Holy Ghost. (1 Thess. iv. 8.)   I say, therefore, that redemption and salvation, being that through Christ, and the truth thereof proclaimed by the Father, the Word, and the Holy Ghost, in the word of the truth of the gospel, it must needs be that we who believe shall be saved, " if we hold the confidence and the rejoicing of the hope firm unto the end."

2. As the three in the Godhead are the authors of this peace, by inditing for us the gospel of peace, or the good tidings of salvation by Jesus Christ, so they are the authors of our peace, by working with that word of the gospel in our hearts.   And hence—(1.) The Father is called the God of peace : " Now the God of peace be with you all." (Rom. xv. 33.)   " And the very God of peace sanctify you." (1 Thess. v. 23.)   And because he is the God of peace, therefore he filleth those that believe in his Christ with joy and peace through believing.   (2.) Again, Christ is called the Prince of peace ; therefore the prayer is, " Grace be with you, and peace, from God the Father, and the Lord Jesus Christ." (2 Thess. i. 2.) (3.) The Holy Ghost also is the author of this peace, this inward peace ; even " righteousness and peace, and joy in the Holy Ghost." (Rom. xiv. 17.)

And I say, as I also have already said, the procuring or meritorious cause of this peace, is the doings and sufferings of Christ.   Therefore by his doings and sufferings he paid full price to God for sinners, and obtained eternal redemption for them ; else God would never have indited a proclamation of peace for them, and the tenor of that proclamation to be the worthiness of the Lord Jesus : yea, he would never have wrought with that word in the heart of them that believe, to create in them peace, peace.

Second. As peace with God is an evidence (the blood of Christ being the cause thereof), that Christ hath by it paid full price to God for sinners, so holiness in their hearts, taking its beginning from this doctrine, makes this fifth demonstration of double strength.

1. That holiness, true gospel holiness, possesseth our hearts by this doctrine, it is evident ; because the ground of holiness, which is the Spirit of God in us, is ministered to us by this doctrine.   When the Apostle had insinuated that the Galatians were bewitched, because they had turned from the doctrine of Christ crucified, he demands of them, whether " they received the Spirit by the works of the law, or by the hearing of faith ?" (Gal. iii. 1—4.) That is, whether the Spirit took possession of their souls by their obedience to the Ten Commandments, or by their giving credit to the doctrine of the forgiveness of their sins by faith in this crucified Christ ; strongly concluding not by the

law, but by the hearing, or preaching of faith ; that is, of the Lord Jesus as crucified, who is the object of faith.

2. As this doctrine conveyeth the ground or groundwork, which is the Spirit, so also it worketh in the heart those three graces, faith, hope, love, all which as naturally purify the heart from wickedness, as soap, or nitre, cleanseth the cloth. He purified "their hearts by faith," by faith in Christ's blood. "And every one that hath this hope in him, purifieth himself, even as he is pure." And also love, you shall see what that doth, if you look into the text: Acts. xv. 9. 1 John iii. 3, 4. 1 Cor. xiii. Now I say, this faith groundeth itself in the blood of Christ; hope waiteth for the full enjoyments of the purchase of it, in another world; and love is begot, and worketh by the love that Christ hath expressed by his death, and by the kindness he presented us with in his heart's blood, (Rom. iii. 24. 1 Cor. xv. 19. 2 Cor. v. 14.)

Besides, What arguments so prevailing, as such as are purely gospel? To instance a few. (1.) What stronger than a free forgiveness of sins ? " A certain man had two debtors, the one owed him five hundred pence, and the other fifty; and when they had nothing to pay, he frankly forgave them both ; tell me therefore which of them will love him most ?" (Luke vii. 41, 42, 47.) (2.) What stronger argument to holiness, than to see, that though forgiveness comes free to us, yet it cost Christ Jesus heart-blood to obtain it for us? "Herein is love, not that we loved God, but that he loved us, and sent his Son to be the propitation for our sins." And this love of God in giving his Christ, and of Christ, in dying for us, there is no argument stronger to prevail with a sensible and awakened sinner to judge "he should live to him that died for him, and rose again." (2 Cor. v. 15.) (3.) What stronger argument to holiness than this : " If any man sin, we have an advocate with the Father, Jesus Christ the righteous ?" (1 John ii. 1.) Unsanctified and graceless wretches know not how to use these words of God ; the hypocrites also fly in our faces, because we thus urge them; but a heart that is possessed with gospel ingenuity, or, to speak more properly, that is possessed with gospel grace, and with divine considerations, cries, If it be thus, oh, let me never sin against God ! "for the love of Christ constrains me." (2 Cor. v. 14.) (4.) What greater argument to holiness, than to see the Holy Scriptures so furnished with promises of grace and salvation by Christ, that a man can hardly cast his eye into the Bible, but he espieth one or another of them ? Who would not live in such a house, or be a servant to such a prince, who, besides his exceeding in good conditions, hath gold and silver as common in his palace as stones are by the highway side ? " Having therefore, these promises, dearly beloved, let us cleanse ourselves from all filthiness of flesh and spirit, perfecting holiness in the fear of God." (2 Cor. vii. 1.)

(5.) What greater argument to holiness, than to have our performances, though weak and infirm from us, yet accepted of God in Jesus Christ ? (1 Pet. ii. 4—6.) (6.) What greater argument to holiness, than to have our soul, our body, our life hid, and secured with Christ in God ? " Mortify, therefore, your members that are upon the earth, fornication, uncleanness, inordinate affection, evil concupiscence, and covetousness, which is idolatry." (Col. iii. 1, 5.) (7.) What greater argument to holiness, than to be made the members of the body, of the flesh, and of the bones of Jesus Christ ? " Shall I, then, take the members of Christ, and make them the members of a harlot? God forbid." (Eph. v. 30. 1 Cor. vi. 15.)

Now all these, and five times as many more, having their foundation in the love, blood, and righteousness of Christ, and operating in the soul by faith, are the great arguments unto that holiness to which is annexed eternal life. It is worth our observing, that in Acts xxvi. at the 18th, the inheritance belongs " to them that are sanctified by faith in Jesus Christ ;" for all other pretences to holiness, they are but a stolen semblance of that which is true and acceptable; though it is common for even that which is counterfeit to be called by the deluded the true ; and to be reckoned to be in them that are utter strangers to faith, and the holiness that comes by faith. " But whosoever compoundeth any like it, or whosoever putteth any of it upon a stranger, shall even be cut off from his people." (Exod. xxx. 23.) God knoweth which is holiness that comes by faith and in forgiveness of sins, and acceptance with God, through Christ ; and God knows which is only such feignedly ; and accordingly will he deal with sinners in that great day of God Almighty.

The Sixth Demonstration.

That Jesus Christ, by what he hath done, hath paid full price to God for sinners, and obtained eternal redemption for them, is evident, because prayers are accepted of God only upon the account and for the sake of the name of Jesus Christ: " Verily, verily, I say unto you, whatsoever ye shall ask the Father in my name, he will give it you." (John xvi. 23.) In my name, in the name of Jesus Christ of Nazareth, in the name of him that came into the world to save sinners, by dying for them a grievous, bloody death ; in his name that hath by himself put away sin, and brought unto God acceptable righteousness for sinners ; in his name. Why in his name, if he be not accepted of God ? why in his name, if his undertakings for us are not well-pleasing to God ? But by these words, " In my name," are insinuated, that his person and performances, as our undertaker, are accepted by the Father of spirits. We may not go in our own names, because we are sinners; not in the name of one another, because all are sinners. But why not in the name of an angel ? Because they are not those that did undertake for us ; or had they, they could not have done our work for us. "He putteth no trust in his saints; yea, the heavens are not clean in his sight." (Job iv. 18; xv. 15.) It may further be objected:

Since Jesus Christ is God equal with the Father, and so hath naturally the same power to give as the Father, why should the Father rather than the Son be the great giver to the sinners of the world? and why may we not go to Christ in the name of the Father, as well as to the Father in the name of Christ? I say, how can these things be solved, but by considering that sin and justice put a *necessity* upon it, that thus must our salvation be obtained. Sin and justice could not reconcile, nor could a means be found out to bring the sinner and a holy God together, but by the intercepting of the Son, who must take upon him to answer justice, and that by taking our sins from before the face of God by bloody sacrifice, not by blood of others, as the high-priests under the law: "For, as every high-priest is ordained to offer gifts and sacrifices, it is of necessity that this man have somewhat also to offer;" (Heb. viii. 3;) which offering and sacrifice of his being able to perfect for ever them that are sanctified and set apart for eternal life, therefore the name of the person that offered (even Jesus, made of God a high-priest) is acceptable with God; yea, therefore is he made for ever, by his doing for us, the appeaser of the justice of God, and the reconciler of sinners to him. Hence it is, that *his* name is that which it behoveth us to mention when we come before God, for what God hath determined in his counsels of grace to bestow upon sinners; because for his name's sake he forgiveth them. "I write to you, little children, because your sins are forgiven you for his name's sake." (1 John ii. 12.) "To him give all the prophets witness, that through his name, whosoever believeth in him shall receive remission of sins." (Acts x. 43.)

They therefore that would obtain the forgiveness of sins, must ask it of God, through the name of Jesus; and he that shall sensibly and unfeignedly do it, he shall receive the forgiveness of them. "Whatsoever ye shall ask the Father in my name, he will give it you." Hence it is evident that he hath not only paid full price to God for them, but also obtained eternal redemption for them.

And it is observable, the Lord Jesus would have his disciples make a proof of this, and promiseth, that if they do, they shall experimentally find it so: "Hitherto," saith he, "ye have asked nothing in my name: ask, and ye shall receive, that your joy may be full." (John xvi. 24.) As who should say, O my disciples, you have heard what I have promised to you, even that my Father shall do for you whatsoever ye shall ask him in my name. Ask now, therefore, and prove me, if I shall not make my words good: ask, I say, what you need, and see if you do not receive it to the joying of your hearts. "At that day ye shall ask·in my name, and I say not unto you, that I will pray the Father for you." I do not bid you ask in my name, as if the Father was yet hard to be reconciled, or unwilling to accept you to mercy; my coming into the world was the design of my Father, and the effect of his love to sinners; but there is sin in you, and justice in God; therefore that you to him might be reconciled, I am made of my Father mediator: wherefore ask in my name; for, "there is none other name given under the heavens among men whereby they must be saved." (Acts iv. 12.) Ask in my name; love is let out to you through me; it is let out to you by me in a way of justice, which is the only secure way for you. Ask in my name, and my Father will love you. "The Father himself loveth you, because you have loved me, and have believed that I came out from God." (John xvi. 27.) My Father's love is set first upon me, for my name is chief in his heart, and all that love me are beloved of my Father, and shall have what they need, if they ask in my name.

But, I say, what cause would there be to ask in his name more than in the name of some other, since justice was provoked by our sin, if he had not undertook to make up the difference that by sin was made betwixt justice and us? For though there be in this Jesus infinite worth, infinite righteousness, infinite merit; yet if he make not with these interest for us, we get no more benefit thereby than if there were no mediator. But this worth and merit is in him for us, for he undertook to reconcile us to God; it is therefore that his name is with God so prevailing for us poor sinners, and therefore that we ought to go to God in his name. Hence, therefore, it is evident that Jesus Christ hath paid full price to God for sinners, and obtained eternal redemption for them.

The Seventh Demonstration.

That Jesus Christ, by what he hath done, hath paid full price to God for sinners, &c., is evident because we are commanded also to give God thanks in his name: "By him, therefore, let us offer the sacrifice of praise continually, that is, the fruit of our lips, giving thanks in his name." (Heb. iii. 15.)

"By him, therefore?" Wherefore? Because he also, that he might "sanctify us with his own blood, suffered without the gate." (ver. 12.)

He sanctified us with his blood; but why should the Father have thanks for this? Even because the Father gave him for us, that he might die to sanctify us with his blood: "Giving thanks to the Father, which hath made us meet to be partakers of the inheritance of the saints in light; who hath delivered us from the power of darkness, and hath translated us into the kingdom of his dear Son; in whom we have redemption through his blood, even the forgiveness of sins." (Col. i. 12—14.) The Father is to be thanked, for the contrivance was also his; but the blood, the righteousness, or that worthiness, for the sake of which we are accepted of God, is the worthiness of his own dear Son. As it is meet, therefore, that God should have thanks, so it is necessary that he have it in his name for whose sake we are indeed accepted of him.

Let us therefore by him offer praise, first, for the gift of his Son, and for that we stand quit through him in his sight; and that in despite of all inward weakness, and that in despite of all outward enemies.

When the Apostle had taken such a view of himself as to put himself into a maze, with an outcry also, "Who shall deliver me?" he quiets himself with this sweet conclusion, "I thank God through Jesus Christ." (Rom. vii. 24, 25.) He found more in the blood of Christ to save him, than he found in his own corruptions to damn him; but that could not be, had he not paid full price for him, had he not obtained eternal redemption for him. And can a holy and just God require that we give thanks to him in his name, if it was not effectually done for us by him?

Further; when the Apostle looks upon death and the grave, and strengtheneth them by adding to them sin and the law, saying, "The sting of death is sin, and the strength of sin is the law," he presently added, "But thanks be to God, which giveth us the victory, through Jesus Christ." (1 Cor. xv.) The victory over sin, death, and the law, the victory over these through our Lord Jesus Christ; but God hath given us the victory; but it is through our Lord Jesus Christ, through his fulfilling the law, through his destroying death, and through his bringing in everlasting righteousness. Elisha said to the king of Israel, that had it not been that he regarded the person of Jehoshaphat, he would not look to him, nor regard him, (2 Kings iii. 14;) nor would God at all have looked to, or regarded thee, but that he respected the person of Jesus Christ.

"Let the peace of God, therefore, rule in your hearts, to the which also you are called in one body, and be you thankful." (Col. iii. xv.) The peace of God, of that we have spoken before. But how should this rule in our hearts? He by the next words directs you: "Let the word of Christ dwell in you richly;" that is, the word that makes revelation of the death and blood of Christ, and of the peace that is made with God for you thereby.

"Giving thanks always for all things unto God and the Father, in the name of our Lord Jesus Christ." (Eph. v. 20.) For all things; for all things come to us through this name Jesus—redemption, translation, the kingdom, salvation, with all the good things wherewith we are blessed.

These are the works of God; he gave his Son, and he brings us to him, and puts us into his kingdom; that is, his true body, which Jeremiah calleth a putting among the children, and a "giving us a goodly heritage of the hosts of nations." (Jer. iii. 19. John vi.)

"Now thanks be to God, which causeth us always to triumph in Christ." (2 Cor. ii. 11.) See here, our cause of triumph is through Christ Jesus; and God causeth us through him to triumph, first and chiefly, because Christ Jesus hath done our work for us, hath pleased God for our sins, hath spoiled the powers of darkness. God gave Jesus Christ to undertake our redemption; Christ did undertake it, did engage our enemies, and spoiled them. He "spoiled principalities and powers, and made a show of them openly, triumphing over them" upon the cross. (Col. ii. 14, 15.) Therefore it is evident that he paid full price to God for sinners with his blood, because God commands us to give thanks to him in his name, through his name: "And whatsoever ye do in word or deed, do all in the name of the Lord Jesus, giving thanks unto God and the Father by him." (Col. iii. 17.)

Take this conclusion from the whole: no thanks are accepted of God that come not to him in the name of his Son; his Son must have the glory of conveying our thanks to God, because he was he that by his blood conveyeth his grace to us.

The Eighth Demonstration.

In the next place; that Jesus Christ, by what he hath done, hath paid full price to God for sinners, and obtained eternal redemption for them is evident, because he was exhorted to wait for, and to expect the full and glorious enjoyment of the eternal redemption, at the second coming of the Lord from heaven: "Let your loins be girded about, and your lights burning, and you yourselves like unto men that wait for their Lord, that when he cometh and knocketh ye may open unto him immediately." (Luke xii. 35, 36.)

Jesus Christ hath obtained by his blood eternal redemption for us, and hath taken it up now in the heavens, is, as I have showed, preparing for us there everlasting mansions of rest; and then he will come again for us. This coming is intended in this text, and this coming we are exhorted to wait for; and that I may more fully show the truth of this demonstration, observe these following texts:

1. It is said, he shall choose our inheritance for us: "He shall choose our inheritance for us; the excellency of Jacob whom he loved. Selah. God is gone up with a shout," &c. (Ps. xlvii. 4, 5.) These latter words intend the ascension of Jesus Christ; his ascension, when he had upon the cross made reconciliation for iniquity; his ascension into the heavens to prepare our mansions of glory for us. For our inheritance is in the heavens; our house, our hope, our mansion-house, and our incorruptible and undefiled inheritance is in heaven. (2 Cor. v. 1, 2. Col. i. 5, 6. John xiv. 1, 2. 1 Pet. i. 3—5.)

This is called the eternal inheritance, of which

we that are called have received the promise already. This inheritance, I say, he is gone to choose for us in the heavens, because by his blood he obtained it for us. (Heb. ix. 12.) And this we are commanded to wait for ; but how ridiculous, yea, how great a cheat would this be, had he not by his blood obtained it for us !

2. We wait for his Son from heaven, whom he raised from the dead, even Jesus Christ, which delivered us from the wrath to come. He delivered us by his blood, and obtained the kingdom of heaven for us, and hath promised that he would go and prepare our places, and come again and fetch us thither. "And if I go and prepare a place for you, I will come again and receive you unto myself, that where I am, there ye may be also." (John xiv. 3.) This, then, is the cause that we wait for him ; we look for the reward of the inheritance at his coming, who have served the Lord Christ in this world.

3. "For our conversation is in heaven, from whence we look for the Saviour, the Lord Jesus Christ." (Phil. iii. 20.) We look for him to come, yet as a Saviour ; a Saviour he was at his first coming, and a Saviour he will be at his second coming. At his first coming, he bought and paid for us ; at his second coming, he will fetch us to himself. At his first coming, he gave us promise of the kingdom ; at his second coming, he will give us possession of the kingdom. At his first coming, he also showed us how we should be, by his own transfiguration ; at his second coming, "he will change our vile body, that it may be fashioned like unto his glorious body." (Phil. iii. 21.)

4. Hence, therefore, it is that his coming is called our blessed hope : " Looking for the blessed hope, and the glorious appearing of the great God, and our Saviour Jesus Christ." (Tit. ii. 13.) A blessed hope indeed, if he hath bought our persons with his blood, and an eternal inheritance for us in the heavens ; a blessed hope indeed, if also at his coming we be certainly carried thither. No marvel, then, if saints be bid to wait for it, and if saints themselves long for it. But what a disappointment would these waiting believers have should all their expectations be rewarded with a fable ! And the result of their blessed hope can amount to no more, if our Saviour, the Lord Jesus Christ, either denieth to come, or coming, bringeth not with him the hope, the blessed hope that is laid up for us in heaven, whereof we have certainly been informed by " the word of the truth of the gospel." (Col. i. 5.)

5. " For Christ was once offered to bear the sins of many ; and unto them that look for him shall he appear the second time without sin unto salvation." (Heb. ix. 28.) Here we have it promised that he shall come, that he shall appear the second time, but not with sin, as he did before, to wit, with, and in the sin of his people, when he bare them in his own body ; but now without sin, for he before did put them away by the sacrifice of himself. Now then let the saints look for him, not to die for the purchasing of their persons by blood, but to bring to them, and to bring them also to that salvation, that before, when he died, he obtained of God for them by his death.

These thing are to be expected, therefore, by them that believe in and love Jesus Christ, and that from faith and love serve him in this world ; they are to be expected by them, being obtained for them by Jesus Christ : " And he shall give the crown," saith Paul, "not only to me, but to them that love his appearing." (2 Tim. iv. 8, 9.)

Now forasmuch as this inheritance in the heavens is the price, purchase, and reward of his blood, how evidently doth it appear that he hath paid full price to God for sinners ! Would God else have given him the heaven to dispose of to us that believe, and would he else have told us so ? Yea, and what comfort could we have to look for his coming, and kingdom, and glory, as the fruits of his death, if his death had not for that purpose been sufficiently efficacious ? Oh, " the sufferings of Christ, and the glory that shall follow ! " (1 Pet. i. 11.)

The Ninth Demonstration.

That Jesus Christ, by what he hath done, hath paid full price to God for sinners, and obtained eternal redemption for sinners, is evident, because of the threatenings wherewith God hath threatened, and the punishments wherewith he punished those that shall refuse to be saved by Christ, or seek to make insignificant the doctrine of righteousness by faith in him.

This demonstration consisteth of three parts : First. It suggesteth that some refuse to be justified or saved by Christ, and also seek to make insignificant the doctrine of righteousness by faith in him. Second. That God does threaten these. Third. That God will punish these.

First. That some refuse to be saved by Christ, is evident from many texts. He is the stone which the builders have rejected ; he is also disallowed of men ; the Jews stumble at him, and to the Greeks he is foolishness ; both saying, This man shall not rule over us ; or, How can this man save us ? (Ps. cxviii. 22. Matt. xxi. 24. 1 Pet. ii. 4. 1 Cor. i. 23. Luke xix. 14.)

The causes of men's refusing Christ are many : 1. Their love to sin. 2. Their ignorance of his excellency. 3. Their unbelief. 4. Their deferring to come to him in the acceptable time. 5. Their leaning to their own righteousness. 6. Their entertaining damnable doctrines. 7. Their loving the praise of men. 8. The meanness of his ways, his people, &c. 9. The just judgment of God upon them. 10. The kingdom is given to others.

Now these, as they all refuse him, so they seek more or less, some practically, others in practice and judgment also, to make insignificant the doctrine of righteousness by faith in him. 1. One does it by preferring his sins before him. 2. Another does it by preferring his righteousness before him. 3. Another does it by preferring his delusions before him. 4. Another does it by preferring the world before him. Now these God threateneth, these God punisheth.

1. God threateneth them. Whosoever shall "not receive that prophet, shall be cut off from amongst his people." (Acts iii. 23.) The prophet is Jesus Christ; the doctrine that he preached was, that he would lay down his life for us, that he would give us his flesh to eat, and his blood to drink by faith; and promised, that if we did eat his flesh, and drink his blood, we should have eternal life. He, therefore, that seeth not, or is afraid to venture his soul for salvation on the flesh and blood of Christ by faith, he refuseth this prophet; he heareth not this prophet; and him God hath purposed to cut off. But would God thus have threatened, if Christ by his blood, and the merits of the same, had not paid full price to God for sinners, and obtained eternal redemption for them?

2. "Sit thou on my right hand, until I make thine enemies thy footstool." (Ps. cx. 1.) The honour of sitting at God's right hand was given him because he died, and offered his body once for all. "This man, when he had offered up one sacrifice for sins for ever, sat down on the right hand of God, from henceforth expecting till his enemies be made his footstool." (Heb. x. 12, 13.) Expecting, since God accepted his offering, that those that refused him should be trodden under foot, that is, sunk by him into and under endless and unsupportable vengeance. But would God have given the world such an account of his sufferings, that by one offering he did perfect for ever them that are sanctified; yea, and would he have threatened to make those foes his footstool, that shall refuse to venture themselves upon his offering (for they are indeed his foes), had not his eternal Majesty been well pleased with the price he paid to God for sinners; had he not obtained eternal redemption for them?

3. He shall come "from heaven with his mighty angels, in flaming fire, taking vengeance on them that know not God, and that obey not the gospel of our Lord Jesus Christ." (2 Thess. i. 7, 8.) Here he expressly telleth us wherefore they shall be punished; because "they know not God, and obey not the gospel of our Lord Jesus Christ;" where also is notably intimated, that he that obeyeth not the gospel of Christ, knoweth not God, neither in his justice or mercy. But what is the gospel of our Lord Jesus Christ, but good tidings of good things; to wit, forgiveness of sins by faith in his blood, an inheritance in heaven by faith in his blood, as the whole of all the foregoing discourse hath manifested? Now, I say, can it be imagined that God would threaten to come upon the world with this flaming, fiery vengeance, to punish them for their non-subjection to his Son's gospel, if there had not been by himself paid to God full price for the souls of sinners, if he had not obtained eternal redemption by his blood for sinners?

4. "And Enoch, the seventh from Adam, also prophesied of these, saying, Behold, the Lord cometh with ten thousands of his saints, to execute judgment upon all, and to convince all that are ungodly among them of all their ungodly deeds which they have ungodlily committed, and of all their hard speeches which ungodly sinners have spoken against him." (Jude 14, 15.) The Lord that is here said to come with ten thousands of his saints, is Jesus Christ himself; and they that come with him are called his saints, because given to him by the Father, for the sake of the shedding of his blood. Now in that he is come to execute judgment upon all, and especially those that speak hard speeches against him, it is evident that the Father tendereth his name, which is Jesus, a Saviour, and his undertaking, for our redemption; and as evident that the hard speeches, intended by the text, are such as vilify him as Saviour, counting the blood of the covenant unholy, and trampling him that is Prince of the covenant under the feet of their reproachful language; this is counted a putting of him to open shame, and a despising the riches of his goodness. (Heb. vi. 10. Rom. ii.) Time would fail to give you a view of the revilings, despiteful sayings, and of the ungodly speeches which these abominable children of hell let fall in their pamphlets, doctrines, and discourses, against this Lord the King. But the threatening is, he shall "execute judgment upon them for all their ungodly deeds, and for all the hard speeches that ungodly sinners have spoken against him."

5. Take heed, therefore, lest that come upon you which is spoken of in the prophets: "Behold, ye despisers, and wonder, and perish: for I work a work in your days, a work which ye shall in no wise believe, though a man declare it unto you." (Acts xiii. 40, 41.) This work is the same we have been all this while treating of, to wit, redemption by the blood of Christ for sinners, or that Christ hath paid full price to God for sinners, and obtained eternal redemption for them. This is manifest from verses 23—29 of this chapter. Now, observe, there are and will be despisers of this doctrine, and they are threatened with the wrath of God: "Behold, ye despisers, and wonder, and perish." But would God so carefully have cautioned sinners to take heed of despising this blessed doctrine, and have backed his caution with a threatening that they shall perish, if they persist, had not himself received by the blood of Christ full price for the souls of sinners?

Third. As God threateneth, so he punisheth those that refuse his Son, or that seek to vilify or make insignificant the doctrine of righteousness by faith in him.

1. He punisheth them with the abidings of his wrath: "He that believeth not the Son shall not see life, but the wrath of God abideth on him."

(John iii. 36.) The wrath of God for men, for sin stands already condemned by the law; and the judgment is, that they who refuse the Lord Jesus Christ shall have this wrath of God for ever lie and abide upon them; for they want a sacrifice to pacify wrath for the sin they have committed, having resisted and refused the sacrifice of the body of Christ. Therefore it cannot be that they should get from under their present condition, who have refused to accept of the undertaking of Christ for them.

Besides; God, to show that he taketh it ill at the hands of sinners that they should refuse the sacrifice of Christ, hath resolved that there shall be no more sacrifice for sin. "If, therefore, we sin wilfully after we have received the knowledge of the truth, there remaineth no more sacrifice for sin?" (Heb. x. 26.) God doth neither appoint another, neither will he accept another, whoever brings it. And here those sayings are of their own natural force: "How shall we escape if we neglect so great salvation!" And again, "See that ye refuse not him that speaketh; for if they escaped not who refused him that spake on earth (Moses), how shall we escape if we turn away from him (Christ) that speaketh from heaven!" (Heb. ii. 3; xii. 25.)

This, therefore, is a mighty demonstration, that Christ by what he hath done hath paid full price to God for the souls of sinners, because God so severely threateneth, and also punisheth them that refuse to be justified by his blood: he threateneth, as you have heard, and punisheth, by leaving such men in their sins, under his heavy and unsupportable vengeance here.

2. "He that believeth not shall be damned, damned in hell-fire." (Mark xvi. 16.) "He that believeth not." But what should he believe? Why,

(1.) That Jesus is the Saviour. "If," saith he, "ye believe not that I am he, ye shall die in your sins."

(2.) He that believeth not that he hath undertaken and completely perfected righteousness for us, shall die in his sins, shall be damned, and perish in hell-fire; for such have no cloak for their sin, but must stand naked to the show of their shame before the judgment of God, that fearful judgment. Therefore, after he had said, "there remains" for such "no more sacrifice for sin," he adds, "but a certain fearful looking for of judgment;" there is for them left nothing but the judgment of God, and his fiery indignation, which shall devour the adversaries. "He that despised Moses' law died without mercy under two or three witnesses; of how much sorer punishment, suppose ye, shall he be thought worthy, who hath trodden under foot the Son of God, and counted the blood of the covenant wherewith he was sanctified an unholy thing, and done despite to the Spirit of grace?" (Heb. x. 28, 29.)

See here, if fury comes not up now into the face of God: now is mention made of his fearful judgment and fiery indignation. Now, I say, is mention made thereof, when it is suggested that some have light thoughts of him, count his blood unholy, and trample his sacrificed body under the feet of their reproaches: now is he a consuming fire, and will burn to the lowest hell. "For we know him that hath said, Vengeance belongeth unto me; I will recompence, saith the Lord." And again, "The Lord shall judge his people." (Heb. x. 30.) These words are urged by the Holy Ghost on purpose to beget in the hearts of the rebellious reverent thoughts, and a high esteem of the sacrifice which our Lord Jesus offered once for all upon Mount Calvary unto God the Father for our sins; for that is the very argument of the whole epistle.

It is said to this purpose in one of Paul's Epistles to the Thessalonians, that because men receive not the love of the truth, that they might be saved, "For this cause God shall send them strong delusions, that they should believe a lie, and be damned." (2 Thess. ii. 11, 12.)

"The truth" mentioned in the place is Jesus Christ: "I am the truth," saith he. (John xiv. 6.) The love of the truth is none else but the love and compassion of Jesus Christ in shedding his blood for man's redemption. "Greater love than this hath no man, that a man lay down his life for his friend." (John xv. 13.) This, then, is the love of the truth (of Jesus), that he hath laid down his life for us. Now, that the rejecters of this love should, by this their rejecting, procure such wrath of God against them, that rather than they shall miss of damnation, himself will choose their delusions for them, and also give them up to the effectual workings of these delusions; what doth this manifest, but that God is displeased with them that accept not of Jesus Christ for righteousness, and will certainly order that their end shall be everlasting damnation? Therefore, Jesus Christ hath paid full price to God for sinners, and obtained eternal redemption for them.

THE USE OF THE DOCTRINE.

I come now to make some use of, and to apply this blessed doctrine of the undertaking of Jesus Christ, and of his paying full price to God for sinners, and of his obtaining eternal redemption for them.

The First Use.

By this doctrine we come to understand many things which otherwise abide obscure and utterly unknown, because this doctrine is accompanied with the Holy Ghost, that revealer of secrets, and searcher of the deep things of God. (1 Pet. i. 2. Eph. i. 17. 1 Cor. ii.) The Holy Ghost comes down with this doctrine, as that in which it alone delighteth: therefore, is it called "the Spirit of wisdom and revelation in the knowledge" of Jesus Christ. He giveth also "the light of the knowledge of the glory of God in the face of Jesus

Christ." (2 Cor. iv. 6.) Little of God is known in the world where the gospel is rejected : the religious Jew and the wise Gentile may see more of God in a crucified Christ than in heaven and earth besides. For in him " are hid all the treasures of wisdom and knowledge," not only in his person as God, but also in his undertakings as Mediator. (Col. ii. 3.) Hence Paul telleth us, That he " determined not to know anything " among the Corinthians, but " Jesus Christ, and him crucified." (1 Cor. ii. 2.) I say, more of God is revealed in this doctrine to us, than we can see of him in heaven and earth without it.

First. Here is more of his *wisdom* seen than in his making and upholding all the creatures. His wisdom, I say, in devising means to reconcile sinners to a holy and infinite Majesty ; to be a just God, and yet a Saviour ; to be just to his law, just to his threatening, just to himself, and yet save sinners, can no way be understood till thou understandest why Jesus Christ did hang on the tree ; for here only is the riddle unfolded, " Christ died for our sins," and therefore can God in justice save us. (Isa. xlv. 21.) And hence is Christ called the Wisdom of God, not only because he is so essentially, but because by him is the greatest revelation of his wisdom towards man. In redemption, therefore, by the blood of Christ, God is said to abound towards us in all wisdom. Here we see the highest contradictions reconciled, here justice kisseth the sinner, here a man stands just in the sight of God, while confounded at his own pollutions ; and here he that hath done no good, hath yet a sufficient righteousness, even the righteousness of God which is by faith of Jesus Christ.

Second. The *justice* of God is here more seen than in punishing all the damned. " He spared not his own Son," is a sentence which more revealeth the nature of the justice of God than if it had said, He spared not all the world. True, he cast angels from heaven, and drowned the old world ; he turned Sodom and Gomorrha into ashes, with many more of like nature ; but what were all these to the cursing of his Son ? Yea, what were ten thousand such manifestations of his ireful indignation against sin, to that of striking, afflicting, chastising, and making the darling of his bosom the object of his wrath and judgment ? Here it is seen he respecteth not persons, but judgeth sin, and condemneth him on whom it is found ; yea, although on Jesus Christ his wellbeloved. (Rom. viii. 32. Gal. iii. 13.)

Third. The mystery of God's *will* is here more seen than in hanging the earth upon nothing, while he condemneth Christ, though righteous, and justifieth us, though sinners, while he maketh him to be sin for us, and us the righteousness of God in him. (1 Pet. iii. 18. 2 Cor. v. 20.)

Fourth. The *power* of God is here more seen than in making of heaven and earth ; for, for one to bear, and get the victory over sin, when charged by the justice of an infinite Majesty, in so doing he showeth the height of the highest power ; for where sin by the law is charged, and that by God immediately, there an infinite Majesty opposeth, and that with the whole of his justice, holiness, and power. So, then, he that is thus charged and engaged for the sin of the world, must not only be equal with God, but show it, by overcoming that curse and judgment that by infinite justice is charged upon him for sin.

When angels and men had sinned, how did they fall and crumble before the anger of God ! they had not power to withstand the terror, nor could there be worth found in their persons or doings to appease displeased justice. But behold here stands the Son of God before him in the sin of the world ; his Father finding him there, curseth and condemns him to death ; but he, by the power of his Godhead, and the worthiness of his person and doings, vanquisheth sin, satisfieth God's justice, and so becomes the Saviour of the world. Here, then, is power seen : sin is a mighty thing, it crusheth all in pieces save Him whose Spirit is eternal. (Heb. ix. 14.) Set Christ and his sufferings aside, and you neither see the evil of sin, nor the displeasure of God against it ; you see them not in their utmost. Hadst thou a view of all the legions that are now in the pains of hell, yea, couldst thou hear their shrieks and groans together at once, and feel the whole of all their burden, much of the evil of sin, and of the justice of God against it, would be yet unknown by thee ; for thou wouldst want power to feel and bear the utmost. A giant shows not his power by killing of a little child, nor yet is his might seen by the resistance that such a little one makes ; but then he showeth his power when he dealeth with one like himself ; yea, and the power also of the other is then made manifest, in saving himself from being swallowed up with his wrath. Jesus Christ also made manifest his eternal power and Godhead, more by bearing and overcoming our sins, than in making or upholding the whole world : hence Christ crucified, is called " the power of God." (1 Cor. i. 23, 24.)

Fifth. The love and mercy of God is more seen in and by this doctrine than any other way. Mercy and love are seen in that God gives us rain and fruitful seasons, and in that he filleth our hearts with food and gladness ; from that bounty he bestoweth upon us as men, as his creatures. Oh ! but herein is love made manifest, in that " Christ laid down his life for us." " And God commended his love toward us, in that while we were yet sinners, Christ died for us." (1 John iii. 16. Rom. v. 8.)

Never love like this, nor did God ever give such discovery of his love from the beginning to this day. " Herein is love, not that we loved God, but that he loved us, and sent his Son to be the propitiation for our sins." (1 John iv. 10.)

Here is love, that God sent his Son, his darling, his Son that never offended, his Son that was always his delight ! Herein is love, that he sent him to save sinners, to save them by bearing their sins, by bearing their curse, by dying their death, and by carrying their sorrows! Here is love, in that while we were yet enemies Christ died for us; yea, here is love, in that while "we were yet without strength, Christ died for the ungodly." (Rom. v. 6.)

The Second Use.

But, as this doctrine giveth us the best discovery of God, so also it giveth us the best discovery of ourselves and our own things.

First. It giveth us the best discovery of ourselves. Wouldst thou know, sinner, what thou art? Look up to the cross, and behold a weeping, bleeding, dying Jesus: nothing could do but that, nothing could save thee but his blood; angels could not, saints could not, God could not, because he could not lie, because he could not deny himself. What a thing is sin, that it should sink all that bear its burden; yea, it sunk the Son of God himself into death and the grave, and had also sunk him into hell-fire for ever, had he not been the Son of God; had he not been able to take it on his back, and bear it away! Oh this Lamb of God! Sinners were going to hell; Christ was the delight of his Father, and had a whole heaven to himself; but that did not content him, heaven could not hold him; he must come into the world to save sinners. Ay, and had he not come, thy sins had sunk thee, thy sins had provoked the wrath of God against thee, to thy perdition and destruction for ever. There is no man but is a sinner, there is no sin but would damn an angel, should God lay it to his charge. Sinner, the doctrine of Christ crucified crieth therefore aloud unto thee, that sin hath made thy condition dreadful. See yourselves, your sin, and, consequently, the condition that your souls are in, by the death and blood of Christ; Christ's death giveth us the most clear discovery of the dreadful nature of our sins. I say again, if sin be so dreadful a thing as to break the heart of the Son of God, for so he saith it did, how shall a poor, wretched, impenitent, damned sinner wrestle with the wrath of God? Awake, sinners, you are lost, you are undone, you perish, you are damned; hell-fire is your portion for ever, if you abide in your sins, and be found without a Saviour in the dreadful day of judgment.

Second. For your good deeds cannot help you; the blood of Christ tells you so. For by this doctrine, "Christ died for our sins," God damneth to death and hell the righteousness of the world. Christ must die, or man be damned. Where is now any room for the righteousness of men? room, I say, for man's righteousness, as to his acceptance and justification? Bring, then, thy righteousness to the cross of Jesus Christ, and in his blood behold the demands of justice; behold them, I say, in the cries and tears, in the blood and death of Jesus Christ. Look again, and behold the person dying; such an one as never

sinned, nor offended at any time, yet he dies. Could a holy life, an innocent, harmless conversation, have saved one from death, Jesus had not died. But he must die; sin was charged, therefore Christ must die.

Men, therefore, need to go no further to prove the worth of their own righteousness, than to the death of Christ; they need not be waiting to seek in that matter till they stand before the judgment-seat.

Quest. But how should I prove the goodness of mine own righteousness by the death and blood of Christ?

Ans. Thus: if Christ must die for sin, then all thy righteousness cannot save thee. "If righteousness comes by the law, then Christ is dead in vain." (Gal. ii. 21.) By this text it is manifest that either Christ died in vain, or thy righteousness is vain. If thy righteousness can save thee, then Christ died in vain; if nothing below or besides the death of Christ could save thee, then thy righteousness is in vain; one of the two must be cast away, either Christ's or thine. Christ crucified to save the world, discovereth two great evils in man's own righteousness; I mean, when brought for justification and life. 1. It opposeth the righteousness of Christ. 2. It condemneth God of foolishness.

1. It opposeth the righteousness of Christ, in that it seeketh itself to stand where should the righteousness of Christ; to wit, in God's affection for the justification of thy person; and this is one of the highest affronts to Christ that poor man is capable to give him: right worthily, therefore, doth the doctrine of the gospel damn the righteousness of men, and promiseth the kingdom of God to publicans and harlots rather.

2. It condemneth God of foolishness: for if works of righteousness which we can do can justify from the curse of the law in the sight of God, then are not all the treasures of wisdom found in the heart of God and Christ; for this dolt-headed sinner hath now found out a way of his own, unawares to God, to secure his soul from wrath and vengeance. I say, unawares to God, for he never imagined that such a thing could be; for had he, he would never have purposed before the world began, to send his Son to die for sinners. Christ is the wisdom of God, as you have heard, and that as he is our justifying righteousness. God was manifest in the flesh to save us, is the great mystery of godliness. But wherein lieth the depth of this wisdom of God in our salvation, if man's righteousness can save him?

Yea, wherefore hath God also given it out, that there is none other name given to men under heaven, whereby we must be saved? I say again, why is it affirmed, "without shedding of blood is no remission," if man's good deeds can save him?

This doctrine, therefore, of the righteousness of

Christ being rightly preached, and truly believed, arraigneth and condemneth man's righteousness to hell; it casteth it out, as Abraham cast out Ishmael. *Blood, blood,* the sound of blood abaseth all the glory of it. When men have said all, and showed us what they can, they have no blood to present God's justice with; yet it is blood that maketh an atonement for the soul, and nothing but blood can wash us away from our sins. (Lev. xvii. 11. Rev. i. 5. Heb. ix.)

Justice calls for blood, sins call for blood, the righteous law calls for blood; yea, the devil himself must be overcome by blood. Sinner, where is now thy righteousness? Bring it before a consuming fire; "for our God is a consuming fire;" bring it before the justice of the law; yea, try if aught but the blood of Christ can save thee from thy sins, and devils; try it, I say, by this doctrine; go not one step further before thou hast tried it.

Third. By this doctrine we are made to see the worth of souls. It cannot be but that the soul is of wonderful price, when the Son of God will not stick to spill his blood for it. Oh, sinners, you that will venture your souls for a little pleasure, surely you know not the worth of your souls. Now, if you would know what your souls are worth, and the price which God sets them at, read that price by the blood of Christ. The blood of Christ was spilt to save souls. "For ye are bought with a price," and that price none other than the blood of Christ; "wherefore glorify God in your bodies and in your spirits, which are God's." (1 Cor. vi. 20.) Sinners, you have souls, can you behold a crucified Christ and not bleed, and not mourn, and not fall in love with him?

The Third Use.

By this doctrine, sinners, as sinners, are encouraged to come to God for mercy, for the curse due to sin is taken out of the way. I speak now to sinners that are awake, and see themselves sinners.

There are two things in special, when men begin to be awakened, that kill their thoughts of being saved. 1. A sense of sin. 2. The wages due thereto. These kill the heart, for who can bear up under the guilt of sin? "If our sins be upon us, and we pine away in them, how should we then live?" (Ezek. xxxiii. 10.) How indeed! it is impossible. So, neither can man grapple with the justice of God. "Can thine heart endure, or can thine hands be strong?" (ch. xxii. 14.) They cannot. "A wounded spirit who can bear?" (Prov. xviii. 14.) Men cannot, angels cannot: wherefore, if now Christ be hid, and the blessing of faith in his blood denied, woe be to them; such go after Saul and Judas, one to the sword, and the other to the halter, and so miserably end their days; for come to God they dare not, the thoughts of that eternal Majesty strikes them through.

But now, present such poor dejected sinners with a crucified Christ, and persuade them that the sins under which thay shake and tremble were long ago laid upon the back of Christ, and the noise, and sense, and fear of damning begins to cease, depart, and fly away; dolours and terrors fade and vanish, and that soul conceiveth hopes of life; for thus the soul argueth, Is this indeed the truth of God, that Christ was made to be sin for me? was made the curse of God for me! Hath he indeed borne all my sins, and spilt his blood for my redemption? Oh, blessed tidings! oh, welcome grace! "Bless the Lord, O my soul, and all that is within me, bless his holy name." Now is peace come; now the face of heaven is altered: "Behold, all things are become new." Now the sinner can abide God's presence, yea, sees unutterable glory and beauty in him; for here he sees justice smite. While Jacob was afraid of Esau, how heavily did he drive even towards the promised land? but when killing thoughts were turned into kissing, and the fears of the sword's point turned into brotherly embraces, what says he?—"I have seen thy face, as though it had been the face of God; and thou wast pleased with me." (Gen. xxxiii. 10.)

So and far better is it with a poor distressed sinner, at the revelation of the grace of God through Jesus Christ. "God was in Christ, reconciling the world unto himself, not imputing their trespasses to them." Oh, what work will such a word make upon a wounded conscience, especially when the next words follow: "For he hath made him to be sin for us, who knew no sin, that we might be made the righteousness of God in him!"

Now, the soul sees qualifications able to set him quit in the sight of God; qualifications prepared already. Prepared, I say, already; and that by God through Christ; even such as can perfectly answer the law. What doth the law require? If obedience, here it is; if bloody sacrifice, here it is; if infinite righteousness, here it is! Now, then, the law condemns him that believes before God no more; for all its demands are answered, all its curses are swallowed up in the death and curse Christ underwent.

Obj. But reason saith, since personal sin brought the death, surely personal obedience must bring us life and glory.

Ans. True; reason saith so, and so doth the law itself, (Rom. x. 5;) but God, we know, is above them both, and he in the covenant of grace, saith otherwise; to wit, that "If thou shalt confess with thy mouth the Lord Jesus, and shalt believe in thine heart that God hath raised him from the dead, thou shalt be saved." (Rom. x. 9.)

Let reason, then, hold its tongue: yea, let the law, with all its wisdom, subject itself to him that made it; let it look for sin where God hath laid it; let it approve the righteousness· which God approveth; yea, though it be not that of the law, but that by faith of Jesus Christ.

God hath made him our righteousness; God hath made him our sin; God hath made him our curse; God hath made him our blessing; methinks this word, God hath made it so, should silence all the world.

The Fourth Use.

By this doctrine, sufficiency of argument is ministered to the tempted to withstand thereby the assaults of the devil.

When souls begin to seek after the Lord Jesus, then Satan begins to afflict and distress, as the Canaanites did the Gibeonites, for making peace with Joshua. (Jos. x. 1—6.)

There are three things that do usually afflict the soul that is earnestly looking after Jesus Christ. 1. Dreadful accusations from Satan. 2. Grievous defiling and infectious thoughts. 3. A strange readiness in our nature to fall in with both.

1. By the first of these, the heart is made continually to tremble. Hence his temptations are compared to the roaring of a lion, (1 Pet. v. 8;) for as the lion, by roaring, killeth the heart of his prey, so doth Satan kill the spirit of these that hearken to him: for when he tempteth, especially by way of accusation, he doth to us as Rabshakeh did to the Jews: he speaks to us in our own language; he speaks our sin at every word, our guilty conscience knows it; he speaks our death at every word, our doubting conscience feels it.

2. Besides this, there doth now arise, even in the heart, such defiling and foul infectious thoughts, as put the tempted to their wits' end; for now it seems to the soul that the very flood-gates of the flesh are opened, and that to sin there is no stop at all; now the air seems to be covered with darkness, and the man is as if he was changed into the nature of a devil; now if ignorance and unbelief prevail, he concludeth that he is reprobate, made to be taken and destroyed.

3. Now also he feeleth in him a readiness to fall in with every temptation; a readiness, I say, continually present. (Rom. vii. 21.) This throws all down. Now despair begins to swallow him up; now he can neither pray, nor read, nor hear, nor meditate on God, but fire and smoke continually bursteth forth of the heart against him. Now sin and great confusion puts forth itself in all; yea, the more the sinner desireth to do a duty sincerely, the further off it always finds itself: for by how much the soul struggleth under these distresses, by so much the more doth Satan put forth himself to resist, still infusing more poison, that, if possible, it might never struggle more—for strugglings are also as poison to Satan. The fly in the spider's web is an emblem of the soul in such a condition: the fly is entangled in the web; at this the spider shows himself; if the fly stir again, down comes the spider to her, and claps a foot upon her; if yet the fly makes a noise, then with poisoned mouth the spider lays hold upon her; if the fly struggle still, then he poisons her more and more. What shall the fly do now? Why, she dies, if somebody does not quickly release her. This is the case of the tempted; they are entangled in the web; their feet and wings are entangled; now Satan shows himself; if the soul now struggleth, Satan laboureth to hold it down; if it now shall make a noise, then he bites with blasphemous mouth, more poisonous than the gall of a serpent. If it struggle again, then he poisoneth more and more, insomuch that it needs at last must die in the net, if the man, the Lord Jesus, helps not out.

The afflicted conscience understands my words.

Further; though the fly in the web is altogether incapable of looking for relief, yet this awakened tempted Christian is not. What must he do, therefore? How should he contain hopes of life? If he look to his heart, there is blasphemy; if he look to his duties, there is sin; if he strive to mourn and lament, perhaps he cannot; unbelief and hardness hinder. Shall this man lie down and despair? No. Shall he trust to his duties? No. Shall he stay from Christ till his heart is better? No. What then? Let him *now* look to Jesus Christ crucified, then shall he see his sins answered for, then shall he see death dying, then shall he see guilt borne by another, and there shall he see the devil overcome. This sight destroys the power of the first temptation, purifies the heart, and inclines the mind to all good things.

And to encourage thee, tempted creature, to this most gospel-duty, consider, that when Jesus Christ read his commission upon the entering into his ministry, he proclaimed, "The Spirit of the Lord is upon me, because he hath anointed me to preach the gospel to the poor; he hath sent me to heal the broken-hearted, to preach deliverance to the captives, and recovering of sight to the blind; to set at liberty them that are bruised, to preach the acceptable year of the Lord." (Luke iv. 18, 19.)

These things, therefore, should the tempted believe; but believing is now sweating work; for Satan will hold as long as possible, and only stedfast faith can make him fly: but oh, the toil of a truly gracious heart in this combat! If faith be weak, he can scarce get higher than his knees: Lord, help! Lord, save! and then down again till an arm from heaven takes him up; until Jesus Christ be evidently set forth crucified for him, and cursed for his sin; for then, and not till then, the temptation rightly ceaseth, at leastwise for a season. Now the soul can tend to look about it, and thus consider with itself: If Christ hath borne my sin and curse, then it is taken away from me; and seeing thus to take away sin was the contrivance of the God of heaven, I will bless his name, hope in his mercy, and look upon death and hell with comfort. "Thine heart shall meditate terror," thou shalt see the land that is very far off. (Isa. xxxiii. 16—18.)

The Fifth Use.

This doctrine makes Christ precious to the believer. "Unto you, therefore, which believe he is precious." (1 Pet. ii. 7.) This head might be greatly enlarged upon, and branched out into a thousand particulars, and each one full of weight and glory. 1. By considering what sin is. 2. By considering what hell is. 3. By considering what wrath is. 4. By considering what eternity is. 5. By considering what the loss of a soul is. 6. What the loss of God is. 7. What the loss of heaven is. 8. And what it is to be in utter darkness with devils and damned souls for ever and ever. And after all to conclude, from all these miseries the Lord Jesus delivered me.

Further, this makes Christ precious, if I consider in the next place,

1. How he did deliver me: it was with his life, his blood; it cost him tears, groans, agony, separation from God; to do it he endured his Father's wrath, bare his Father's curse, and died thousands of deaths at once.

2. He did this while I was his enemy, without my desires, without my knowledge, without my deserts; he did it unawares to me.

3. He did it freely, cheerfully, yea, he longed to die for me; yea, heaven would not hold him for the love he had to my salvation, which also he hath effectually accomplished for me at Jerusalem. Honourable Jesus! precious Jesus! loving Jesus! Jonathan's kindness captivated David, and made him precious in his eyes for ever. "I am distressed for thee, my brother Jonathan," said he, " very pleasant hast thou been to me; thy love to me was wonderful, passing the love of women." (2 Sam. i. 26.) Why, what had Jonathan done? Oh, he had delivered David from the wrath of Saul. But how much more should he be precious to me who hath saved me from death and hell! who hath delivered me from the wrath of God! "The love of Christ constraineth us." Nothing will so edge the spirit of a Christian as, "Thou wast slain, and hast redeemed us to God by thy blood." This makes the heavens themselves ring with joy and shouting. Mark the words, "Thou wast slain, and hast redeemed us to God with thy blood, out of every kindred, and tongue, and people, and nation; and hast made us unto our God, kings and priests, and we shall reign on the earth." What follows now? "And I beheld, and I heard the voice of many angels round about the throne, and the beasts, and the elders; and the number of them was ten thousand times ten thousand, and thousands of thousands; saying with a loud voice, Worthy is the Lamb that was slain, to receive power, and riches, and wisdom, and strength, and honour, and glory, and blessing. And every creature which is in heaven, and on the earth, and such as are in the sea, and all that are therein, heard I, saying, Blessing, honour, glory and power, be unto them that sitteth upon the throne, and to the Lamb for ever and ever." (Rev. ix. 9—14.)

Thus also is the song, that new song that is said to be sung by the hundred forty and four thousand which stand with the Lamb upon Mount Zion, with his Father's name written in their foreheads. These are also called harpers, harping with their harps. "And they sang as it were a new song before the throne, and before the four beasts, and the elders; and none could learn that song but the hundred and forty and four thousand, which were redeemed from the earth." (Rev. xiv. 1—3.)

But why could they not learn that song? Because they were not redeemed; none can sing of this song but the redeemed; they can give glory to the Lamb, the Lamb that was slain, and that redeemed them to God by his blood. It is faith in his blood on earth that will make us sing this song in heaven. These shoutings and heavenly songs must needs come from love put into a flame by the sufferings of Christ.

The last Use.

If all these things be true, what follows but a demonstration of the accursed condition of those among the religious in these nations, whose notions put them far off from Jesus, and from venturing their souls upon his bloody death. I have observed such a spirit as this in the world, that careth not for knowing of Jesus; the possessed therewith do think, that it is not material to salvation to venture upon a crucified Christ, neither do they trouble their heads or hearts with enquiring whether Christ Jesus be risen, and ascended into heaven, or whether they see him again or no, but rather are for. concluding, that there will be no such thing. These men speak not by the Holy Ghost, for in the sum they call Jesus accursed; but I doubt not to say that many of them are anathematised of God, and shall stand so, till the coming of the Lord Jesus, to whom be glory for ever and ever. Amen.

PREFATORY REMARKS

ON

THE GREATNESS OF THE SOUL.

THE aspects in which this subject may be viewed are very manifold. A human soul is great, because of its wonderful capacity : it is great because of its value, viewed in respect to its salvation, or its loss ; and great from what has been done for it in the way of redemption, and is done in it by the inscrutable mystery of its sanctification. Sublime, indeed, must be the nature of that being to whom this character belongs, and in whom all these processes close and concentrate when it reoccupies the place designed it in creation.

Life and soul, both in Scriptural and ordinary language, are often spoken of as identical. There would be little necessity for caution, in this respect, were life and soul to bear uniformly the same meaning. But in each case there is a higher and a lower signification. Life, as physical and temporal, is a very humble possession as compared with that which exists by other laws than those of earth and time. The soul, as quickened only by the properties which it enjoys in common with other animated creatures of this world, has little more claim to be priceless than the rest. Could reason, with all its mysterious attendant powers, be considered as belonging to the natural soul, independent of a higher essence, this would render it worthy of admiration above all other earthly beings : but nothing could overcome the check which would be given to that feeling of reverence by the discovery that this soul is mortal ; that though, for a time, it may unite in itself the tenderest grace and the most majestic energy, it will ultimately pass away into thin air ; and become as nothing,—like the melody which, whatever its power to charm, exists no longer than the vibration which produces it. Attribute, then, to the soul the noblest power of reason, and all that is sweet and sublime in the affections, but show that it can perish by an accident, or grow infirm and die, and, thus degraded from the ranks of the immortals, its very glories are a painful mystery. Let us imagine, for an instant, that two spirits stand before us. Each is invested with the beauty proper to a heavenly origin. But one exceeds the other both in the splendour of this beauty, and in all the signs of power and varied wisdom. We naturally feel a greater veneration for this apparently superior being. But suddenly we learn, that it is one of an order of spirits which rapidly attain to the maturity of their powers, and then suddenly perish, like an extinguished flame. The other, on the contrary, has been endowed with a deathless nature. It is now of comparatively low degree in the ranks of spiritual life ; but it has before it the line of an endless progress : it may be millions of years before it attain to the power and glory exhibited by its companion ; but when that bright subject of mortality shall have long passed into nothingness, this heir of hope and eternity shall be still ascending from height to height of limitless perfection.

Thus the human soul, if supposed to be mortal, could not bear comparison with the humblest of created beings inhabiting a sphere out of the reach of death. It is not to the animal soul, therefore, any more than to the animal life, that we can properly attach the idea of an invaluable possession. The entire superstructure of an edifice may present the finest combinations of architectural genius, with the most successful efforts of masonry, but if the building itself rests upon a shifting quicksand, who would purchase it ? The certainty that it will fall, and the uncertainty as to when, are equally opposed to the feeling of safety.

Such reflections lead inevitably to the conclusion, that both the dignity and the happiness of the human race depend upon the immortality of the soul. Progress, to which there is a limit, is especially unsatisfactory and discouraging. Mankind at large, and each individual man, have the same interest in this fact. No number of souls, however wonderful their united energy, can even accomplish the designs proper to their own allotment of time, without the strength and the hopes of immortal being. It is from the instincts of an imperishable nature, from the ardour of an unextinguishable flame, that man is urged on to attempts utterly disproportioned to the length of his earthly existence, or to the value of anything which it can give. Deprive him of the mysterious impulses to which he is thus happily subject, and slow and fluctuating as the progress of mankind even now is, it would then cease altogether, or become retrograde. The dull weight of mere earthly existence would grind us to dust. Ignorant as most men are of this great truth, they owe to the fact itself all that has ever been gained of the good, the beautiful, and the precious, by the doings or sufferings of successive generations.

With immortality as a basis, there need be no boundary in human apprehension to the increasing grandeur of the soul. Starting with a just view of its proper attributes and capabilities, we may contemplate its growth in wisdom and power as the intended result of its lengthened existence. There being no waste of life, the life within it will itself become more and more intense, and the light and glory beaming from it will have a greater radiance. Then if, having traced the course of its wonderful ascent, as far as our thoughts will allow, we return to consider its present actual state, the contrast may startle us, without dispossessing us of a single hope. Weak as the soul now is, burdened as we feel it to be with unholiness and guilt, it is still great, and its greatness is plainly discernible through the dark veil of its sorrows and infirmities. Capability not exercised, the powers of a great life dormant but unabridged, are subjects for melancholy reflection; but in the case of the human soul, the sadness of the sentiment is relieved by the sublimity of the truths with which it is connected. There is a witness to the greatness of the soul in its own instincts: there is another in the subordination of all earthly things to its will: another speaks in the works it has achieved: another in the surpassing grandeur of its designs. But immeasurably in worth above all these, or any other that can be conceived, is the witness of the mystery, that God has redeemed it from self-destruction by the blood of his Son, and reanimates it by the breath of his own Spirit.

H. S.

THE GREATNESS OF THE SOUL,

AND

UNSPEAKABLENESS OF THE LOSS THEREOF;

WITH THE CAUSES OF THE LOSING IT.

" Or what shall a man give in Exchange for his Soul ?"—MARK viii. 37.

I HAVE chosen at this time to handle these words among you, and that for several reasons:— 1. Because the soul, and the salvation of it, are such great, such wonderful great things, nothing is a matter of that concern as is, and should be, the soul of each one of you. House and land, trades and honours, places and preferments, what are they to salvation? to the salvation of the soul? 2. Because I perceive that this, so great a thing, and about which persons should be so much concerned, is neglected to amazement, and that by the most of men; yea, who is there of the many thousands that sit daily under the sound of the gospel, that are concerned, heartily concerned, about the salvation of their souls?—that is, concerned, I say, as the nature of the thing requireth. If ever a lamentation was fit to be taken up in this age about, for, or concerning anything, it is about, for, and concerning the horrid neglect, that everywhere puts forth itself with reference to eternal salvation. Where is one man of a thousand—yea, where is there two of ten thousand, that do show by their conversation, public and private, that the soul, their own souls, are considered by them, and that they are taking that care for the salvation of them as becomes them? to wit, as the weight of the work, and the nature of salvation requireth. 3. I have, therefore, pitched upon this text at this time, to see, if peradventure the discourse which God shall help me to make upon it, will awaken you, rouse you off of your beds of ease, security, and pleasure, and fetch you down upon your knees before him, to beg of him grace to be concerned about the salvation of your souls. And then, in the last place, I have taken upon me to do this, that I may deliver if not you, yet myself; and that I may be clear of your blood, and stand quit, as to you, before God, when you shall, for neglect, be damned, and wail to consider that you have lost your souls. "When I say," saith God to the wicked, "thou shalt surely die; and thou," the prophet or preacher, "givest him not warning, nor speakest to warn the wicked from his wicked way, to save his life; the same wicked man shall die in his iniquity; but his blood will I require at thine hand. Yet if thou warn the wicked, and he turn not from his wickedness, nor from his wicked way, he shall die in his iniquity, but thou hast delivered thy soul." (Ezek. iii. 18, 19.)

"Or what shall a man give in exchange for his soul?"

In my handling of these words, I shall first speak to the occasion of them, and then to the words themselves.

The occasion of the words was, for that the people that now were auditors to the Lord Jesus, and that followed him, did it without that consideration as becomes so great a work; that is, the generality of them that followed him, were not for considering first with themselves, what it was to profess Christ, and what that profession might cost them.

"And when he had called the people unto him," the great multitude that went with him, (Luke xiv. 25,) "with his disciples also, he said unto them, whosoever will come after me, let him deny himself, and take up his cross and follow me," (Mark viii. 34.) Let him first sit down, and count up the cost, and the charge he is like to be at, if he follows me. For following of me is not like following of some other masters. The winds sit always on my face, and the foaming rage of the sea of this world, and the proud and lofty waves thereof, do continually beat upon the sides of the bark or ship that myself, my cause, and my followers are in: he therefore that will not run hazards, and that is afraid to venture a drowning, let him not set foot into this vessel: so "whosoever doth not bear his cross, and come after me, he cannot be my disciple. For which of you intending to build a tower, sitteth not down first and counteth the cost, whether he have sufficient to finish it?" (Luke xiv. 27, 28.)

True, to reason, this kind of language tends to cast water upon weak and beginning desires; but to faith it makes the things set before us, and the greatness, and the glory of them, more apparently excellent and desirable. Reason will say, Then who will profess Christ that hath such coarse entertainment at the beginning? but Faith will say, Then surely the things that are at the end of a Christian's race in this world, must needs be unspeakably glorious; since whoever hath had but the knowledge and due consideration of them, have not stuck to run hazards, hazards of every kind, that they might embrace and enjoy them. Yea, saith Faith, it must needs be so, since the Son himself, that best knew what they were, even, " For the joy that was set before him, endured the cross, despising the shame, and is set down at the right hand of the throne of God," (Heb: xii. 2.)

But, I say, there is not in every man this knowledge of things, and so by consequence not such consideration as can make the cross and self-denial acceptable to them for the sake of Christ, and of the things that are where he now sitteth at the right hand of God, (Col. iii. 2—4.) Therefore our Lord Jesus doth even at the beginning give to his followers this instruction. And lest any of them should take distaste at his saying, he presenteth them with the consideration of three things together, namely, the cross, the loss of life, and the soul; and then reasoneth with them for the same, saying, Here is the cross, the life, and the soul. 1. The cross, and that you must take up, if you will follow me. 2. The life, and that you may save for a time, if you cast me off. 3. And the soul, which will everlastingly perish if you come not to me, and abide not with me. Now consider what is best to be done, will you take up the cross, come after me, and so preserve your souls from perishing? or will you shun the cross to save your lives, and so run the danger of eternal damnation? or, as you have it in John, will you love your life till you lose it? or will you hate your life and save it? "He that loveth his life shall lose it, and he that hateth his life in this world, shall keep it unto life eternal," (John xii. 25.) As who should say, He that loveth a temporal life, he that so loveth it as to shun the profession of Christ to save it, shall lose it upon a worse account, than if he had lost it for Christ and the gospel; but he that will set light by it, for the love that he hath to Christ, shall keep it unto life eternal.

Christ having thus discoursed with his followers about their denying of themselves, their taking up their cross and following of him, doth, in the next place, put the question to them, and so leaveth it upon them for ever, saying, " For what shall it profit a man, if he shall gain the whole world, and lose his own soul?" (Mark viii. 36.) As who should say, I have bid you take heed that you do not lightly, and without due consideration, enter into a profession of me and of my gospel; for he that without due consideration shall begin to profess Christ, will also without it, forsake him, turn from him, and cast him behind his back; and since I have, even at the beginning, laid the consideration of the cross before you, it is because you should not be surprised and overtaken by it unawares, and because you should know that to draw back from me, after you have laid your hand to my plough, will make you unfit for the kingdom of heaven. (Luke ix. 62.) Now, since this is so, there is no less lies at stake than salvation, and salvation is worth all the world, yea, worth ten thousand worlds, if there should be so many. And since this is so also, it will be your wisdom to begin to profess the gospel with expectation of the cross and tribulation, for to that are my gospellers in this world appointed. (1 Thess. iii. 3.) And if you begin thus, and hold it, the kingdom and crown shall be yours; for as God counteth it a righteous thing to recompense tribulation to them that trouble you, so to you who are troubled and endure it—" for we count them happy," says James, " that endure " (James i. 12; v. 11)— rest with saints, when the Lord Jesus shall be revealed from heaven with his mighty angels in flaming fire, to take vengeance on them that know not God, and that obey not the gospel, &c. And if no less lies at stake than salvation, then is a man's soul and his all at the stake; and if it be so, what will it profit a man if, by forsaking of me, he should get the whole world? " For what shall it profit a man, if he shall gain the whole world, and lose his own soul?"

Having thus laid the soul in one balance, and the world in the other, and affirmed that the soul outbids the whole world, and is incomparably for value and worth beyond it; in the next place, he descends to a second question, which is that I have chosen at this time for my text, saying, " Or what shall a man give in exchange for his soul?"

In these words, we have first a supposition, and such an one as standeth upon a double bottom.

The supposition is this, That the soul is capable of being lost; or thus, It is possible for a man to lose his soul. The double bottom that this supposition is grounded upon, is, first, man's ignorance of the worth of his soul, and of the danger that it is in; and the second is, for that men commonly do set a higher price upon present ease and enjoyments than they do upon eternal salvation. The last of these doth naturally follow upon the first; for if men be ignorant of the value and worth of their souls, as by Christ in the verse before is implied, what should hinder but that men should set an higher esteem upon that with which their carnal desires are taken than upon that about which they are not concerned, and of which they know not the worth?

But again, as this by the text is clearly supposed, so there is also something implied, namely, That it is impossible to possess some men with the worth of their souls, until they are utterly and everlastingly lost. " What shall a man give in exchange for his soul ? " That is, men, when their souls are lost, and shut down under the hatches in the pits and hells in endless perdition and destruction, then they will see the worth of their souls, then they will consider what they have lost, and truly not till then. This is plain, not only to sense, but by the natural scope of the words, " What shall a man give in exchange for his soul ? " Or what would not those that are now for sin made to see themselves lost, by the light of hell-fire—for some will never be convinced that they are lost, till, with rich Dives, they see it in the light of hell-flames, (Luke xvi. 22, 23 ;) I say, what would not such, if they had it, give in exchange for their immortal souls, or to recover them again from that place and torment ?

I shall observe two truths in the words.

The first is, That the loss of the soul is the highest, the greatest loss—a loss that can never be repaired or made up. " What shall a man give in exchange for his soul ? " that is, to recover or redeem his lost soul to liberty.

The second truth is this, That how unconcerned and careless soever some now be about the loss or salvation of their souls, yet the day is coming—but it will then be too late—when men will be willing, had they never so much, to give it all in exchange for their souls. For so the question implies, " What shall a man give in exchange for his soul ? " What would he not give ? What would he not part with at that day—the day in which he shall see himself damned—if he had it, in exchange for his soul ?

The first observation, or truth, drawn from the words, is cleared by the text, " What shall a man give in exchange for his soul ? " That is, there is not anything, nor all the things under heaven, were they all in one man's hand, and all at his disposal, that would go in exchange for the soul, that would be of value to fetch back one lost soul, or that would certainly recover it from the confines of hell. " The redemption of their soul is precious, and it ceaseth for ever." (Ps. xlix. 8.) And what saith the words before the text but the same : " For what shall it profit a man, if he shall gain the whole world, and lose his own soul ? " What shall profit a man that has lost his soul ? Nothing at all, though he hath by that loss gained the whole world ; for all the world is not worth a soul, not worth a soul in the eye of God, and judgment of the law. And it is from this consideration, that good Elihu cautioneth Job to take heed, " Because there is wrath," saith he, " beware lest he take thee away with his stroke : then a great ransom cannot deliver thee. Will he esteem thy riches ? no, not gold, nor all the forces of strength." (Job xxxvi. 18, 19.) Riches and power, what is there

more in the world : for money answereth all things —that is, all but soul-concerns ; it can neither be a price for souls while here, nor can that, with all the forces of strength, recover one out of hell-fire.

Doctrine First.

So then the first truth drawn from the words stands firm, namely, That the loss of the soul is the highest, the greatest loss, a loss that can never be repaired or made up.

In my discourse upon this subject, I shall observe this method :—

First. I shall show you what the soul is.

Second. I shall show you the greatness of it.

Third. I shall show you what it is to lose the soul.

Fourth. I shall show you the cause for which men lose their souls ; and by this time the greatness of the loss will be manifest.

First. I shall show you what the soul is, both as to the various names it goes under, as also by describing of it by its powers and properties, though in all I shall be but brief, for I intend no long discourse.

1. The soul is often called the heart of man, or that in and by which things, to either good or evil, have their rise : thus desires are of the heart or soul ; yea, before desires, the first conception of good or evil is in the soul, the heart. The heart understands, wills, affects, reasons, judges, but these are the faculties of the soul ; wherefore, heart and soul are often taken for one and the same. " My son, give me thy heart." (Prov. xxiii. 26.) " Out of the heart proceedeth evil thoughts," &c. (Matt. xv. 19. 1 Pet. iii. 15. Ps. xxvi. 2.)

2. The soul of man is often called the spirit of a man ; because it not only giveth being, but life to all things and actions in, and done by, him. Hence soul and spirit are put together, as to the same action. " With my soul have I desired thee in the night ; yea, with my spirit within me will I seek thee early." (Isa. xxvi. 9.) When he saith, " Yea, with my spirit I will seek thee," he explaineth not only with what kind of desires he desired God, but with what principal matter his desires were brought forth. It was with my soul, saith he ; to wit, with my spirit within me. So that of Mary, " My soul," saith she, " doth magnify the Lord, and my spirit hath rejoiced in God my Saviour." (Luke i. 46, 47.) Not that soul and spirit are, in this place, to be taken for two superior powers in man ; but the same great soul is here put under two names or terms, to show that it was the principal part in Mary, to wit, her soul, that magnified God, even that part that could spirit, and put life into her whole self to do it. Indeed, sometimes spirit is not taken so largely, but is confined to some one power or faculty of the soul, as

"the spirit of my understanding," (Job xx. 3;) and "be renewed in the spirit of your mind;" and sometimes by spirit we are to understand other things, but many times by spirit we must understand the soul, and also by soul the spirit.

3. Therefore, by soul we understand the spiritual, the best, and the most noble part of man, as distinct from the body, even that by which we understand, imagine, reason, and discourse. And, indeed, as I shall further show you presently, the body is but a poor empty vessel, without this great thing called the soul. "The body without the spirit," or soul, "is dead," (James ii. 26;) or nothing but a clod of dust (her soul departed from her, for she died). It is, therefore, the chief and most noble part of man.

4. The soul is often called the life of man, not a life of the same stamp and nature of the brute; for the life of man—that is, of the rational creature—is that, as he is such, wherein consisteth and abideth the understanding and conscience, &c. Wherefore, then, a man dieth, or the body ceaseth to act, or live in the exercise of the thoughts, which formerly used to be in him, when the soul departeth, as I hinted even now—her soul departed from her, for she died; and, as another good man saith, "In that very day his thoughts perish," &c. (Ps. cxlvi. 4.) The first text is more emphatical: "Her soul was in departing," for she died. There is the soul of a beast, a bird, &c., but the soul of a man is another thing: it is his understanding, and reason, and conscience, &c. And this soul, when it departs, he dies. Nor is this life, when gone out of the body, annihilate, as is the life of a beast; no, this in itself is immortal, and has yet a place and being when gone out of the body it dwelt in; yea, as quick, as lively is it in its senses, if not far more abundant, than when it was in the body; but I call it the life, because so long as that remains in the body, the body is not dead. And in this sense it is to be taken, where he saith, "He that loseth his life for my sake shall find it unto life eternal;" and this is the soul that is intended in the text, and not the breath, as in some other places is meant. And this is evident, because the man has a being, a sensible being after he has lost the soul: I mean not, by the man, a man in this world, nor yet in the body, or in the grave; but by man we must understand either the soul in hell, or body and soul there, after the judgment is over. And for this the text, also, is plain, for therein we are presented with a man sensible of the damage that he has sustained by losing of his soul: "What shall a man give in exchange for his soul?" But,

5. The whole man goeth under this denomination: man, consisting of body and soul, is yet called by that part of himself that is most chief and principal. "Let every soul," that is, let every man "be subject to the higher powers," (Rom. xiii. 1;) "then sent Joseph, and called his father Jacob

to him, and all his kindred, threescore and fifteen souls," (Acts vii. 14.) By both these, and several other places, the whole man is meant, and is also so to be taken in the text; for whereas here he saith, "What shall it profit a man, if he shall gain the whole world, and lose his own soul?" It is said elsewhere, "For what is a man advantaged, if he shall gain the whole world, and lose himself?" (Luke ix. 25;) and so, consequently, or, "What shall a man give in exchange (for himself) for his soul?" his soul when he dies, and body and soul in and after judgment.

6. The soul is called good man's darling: "Deliver," Lord, saith David, "my soul from the sword; my darling from the power of the dog:" (Ps. xxii. 20.) So, again, in another place, he saith, "Lord, how long wilt thou look on? rescue my soul from destruction, my darling from the (power of the) lions?" (Ps. xxxv. 17.) My darling, this sentence must not be applied universally, but only to those in whose eyes their souls, and the redemption thereof, is precious. My darling, most men do, by their actions, say of their soul—My drudge, my slave; nay, thou slave to the devil and sin; for what sin, what lust, what sensual and beastly lust is there in the world, that some do not cause their souls to bow before and yield unto? But David here, as you see, calls it his darling, or his choice and most excellent thing; for, indeed, the soul is a choice thing in itself, and should, were all wise, be every man's darling, or chief treasure. And that it might be so with us, therefore, our Lord Jesus hath thus expressed the worth of the soul, saying, "What shall a man give in exchange for his soul?" But if this is true, one may see already what misery he is like to sustain that has, or shall lose his soul; he has lost his heart, his spirit, his best part, his life, his darling, himself, his whole self, and so, in every sense, his all. And now "what shall a man," what would a man, but what can a man that has thus lost his soul, himself, and his all, "give in exchange for his soul?" Yea, what shall the man that has sustained this loss do to recover all again, since this man, or the man put under this question, must needs be a man that is gone from hence, a man that is cast in the judgment, and one that is gone down the throat of hell?

But to pass this, and to proceed.

I come next to describe the soul unto you, by such things as it is set out by in the Holy Scriptures, and they are in, general, three:—

First, The powers of the soul. Second, The senses, the spiritual senses of the soul. Third, The passions of the soul. First, We will discourse of the powers, I may call them the members of the soul; for as the members of the body, being many, do all go to the making up of the body, so these do go to the completing of the soul.

1. There is the understanding, which may be termed the head, because in that is placed the eye of the soul; and this is that which, or by which

the soul, discerneth things that are presented to it, and that either by God or Satan ; this is that by which a man conceiveth and apprehendeth things so deep and great that cannot, by mouth, or tongue, or pen be expressed.

2. There is, also, belonging to the soul, the conscience, in which, I may say, is placed the seat of judgment ; for, as by the understanding things are let into the soul, so by the conscience the evil or good of such things are tried ; especially when, in the

3. Third place, the judgment, which is another part of this noble creature, has passed, by the light of the understanding, his verdict upon what is let into the soul.

4. There is, also, the fancy or imagination, another part of this great thing, the soul ; and a most curious thing this great fancy is : it is that which presenteth to the man the idea, form, or figure of that, or any of those things wherewith a man is frighted or taken, pleased or displeased. And,

5. The mind, another part of the soul, is that unto which this fancy presenteth its things to be considered of ; because, without the mind, nothing is entertained in the soul.

6. There is the memory, too, another part of the soul ; and that may be called the register of the soul ; for it is the memory that receiveth and keepeth in remembrance what has passed, or has been done by the man, or attempted to be done unto him : and in this part of the soul, or from it, will be fed the worm that dieth not, when men are cast into hell ; also, from this memory will flow that peace at the day of judgment, that saints shall have in their service for Christ in the world.

7. There are the affections too, which are, as I may call them, the hands and arms of the soul ; for they are they that take hold of, receive, and embrace what is liked by the soul ; and it is a hard thing to make the soul of a man cast from it what its affections cleave to and have embraced. Hence the affections are called for, when the Apostle bids men " seek the things above ; set your affections upon them," saith he, (Col. iii. 2 ;) or, as you have it in another place, " lay hold " of them ; for the affections are as hands to the soul, and they by which it fasteneth upon things.

8. There is the will, which may be called the foot of the soul, because by that soul, yea, the whole man, is carried hither and thither, or else held back, and kept from moving.

These are the golden things of the soul ; though, in carnal men, they are every one of them made use of in the service of sin and Satan. For the unbelieving are throughout impure, as is manifest, because their " mind and conscience, (two of the masterpieces of the soul) is defiled," (Tit. i. 15 :) for if the most potent parts of the soul are engaged in their service, what, think you, do the more inferior do ? But I say, so it is ; the more is the

pity ; nor can any help it. " This work ceaseth for ever," unless the great God, who is over all, and can save souls, shall himself take upon him to sanctify the soul, and to recover it, and persuade it to fall in love with another master.

But, I say, what is man without this soul, or wherein lieth his pre-eminence over a beast ? (Eccles. iii. 19—21.) Nowhere that I know of : for both (as to man's body) go to one place, only the spirit or soul of a man goes upward, to wit, to God that gave it, to be by him disposed of with respect to things to come, as they have been, and have done in this life. But,

Second, I come, in the next place, to describe the soul by its senses, its spiritual senses, for so I call them : for as the body hath senses pertaining to it, and as it can see, hear, smell, feel, and taste, so can the soul ; I call, therefore, these the senses of the soul, in opposition to the senses of the body, and because the soul is the seat of all spiritual sense, where supernatural things are known and enjoyed ; not that the soul of a natural man is spiritual in the Apostle's sense, for so none are, but those that are born from above, (1 Cor. iii. 1—3,) nor they so always neither. But to go forward.

1. Can the body see ? hath it eyes ? so hath the soul. " The eyes of your understanding being enlightened." (Eph. i. 18.) As, then, the body can see beasts, trees, men, and all visible things, so the soul can see God, Christ, angels, heaven, devils, hell, and other things that are invisible ; nor is this property only peculiar to the souls that are illuminated by the Holy Ghost, for the most carnal soul in the world shall have a time to see these things, but not to its comfort, but not to its joy, but to its endless woe and misery, it dying in that condition. Wherefore, sinner, say not thou, " I shall not see him, for judgment is before him," (Job xxxv. 14,) and he will make thee see him.

2. Can the body hear ? hath it ears ? so hath the soul : (see Job iv. 12, 13.) It is the soul, not the body, that hears the language of things invisible. It is the soul that hears God when he speaks in and by his Word and Spirit ; and it is the soul that hears the devil when he speaks by his illusions and temptations. True, there is such an union between the soul and the body, that ofttimes, if not always, that which is heard by the ears of the body doth influence the soul, and that which is heard by the soul doth also influence the body ; but yet, as to the organ of hearing, the body hath one of his own, distinct from that of the soul, and the soul can hear and regard even then, when the body doth not nor cannot : as in time of sleep, deep sleep and trances, when the body lieth by as a thing that is useless. " For God speaks once, yea twice, yet man (as to his body) perceiveth it not. In a dream, in a vision of the night, when deep sleep falleth upon men in slumberings upon the bed ; then openeth he the ears of men, and sealeth their instruction," &c. (Job xxxiii.

14—16.) This must be meant of the ears of the soul, not of the body; for that at this time is said to be in deep sleep; moreover, this hearing, it is a hearing of dreams, and the visions of the night. Jeremiah also tells us that he had the rare and blessed visions of God in his sleep, (Jer. xxxi. 26;) and so doth Daniel too, by the which they were greatly comforted and refreshed; but that could not be, was not the soul also capable of hearing. "I heard the voice of his words," said Daniel, "and when I heard the voice of his words, then was I in a deep sleep on my face, and my face toward the ground." (Dan. x. 9.)

3. As the soul can see and hear, so it can taste and relish, even as really as doth the palate belonging to the body. But then the thing so tasted must be that which is suited to the temper and palate of the soul. The soul's taste lieth not in, nor is exercised about meats, the meats that are for the body. Yet the soul of a saint can taste and relish God's Word, (Heb. vi. 5:) and doth ofttimes find it sweeter than honey, (Ps. xix. 10,) nourishing as milk, (1 Pet. ii. 2,) and strengthening like to strong meat, (Heb. v. 12—14.) The soul also of sinners, and of those that are unsanctified, can taste and relish, though not the things now mentioned, yet things that agree with their fleshly minds, and with their polluted, and defiled, and vile affections. They can relish and taste that which delighteth them; yea, they can find soul-delight in an alehouse, a whorehouse, a playhouse. Ay, they find pleasure in the vilest things, in the things most offensive to God, and that are most destructive to themselves. This is evident to sense, and is proved by the daily practice of sinners. Nor is the Word barren as to this: "They feed on ashes," (Isa. xliv. 20:) "They spend their money for that which is not bread," (Isa. lv. 2;) Yea, they eat and suck sweetness out of sin. "They eat up the sin of my people" as they eat bread. (Hos. iv. 8.)

4. As the soul can see, hear, and taste, so it can smell, and bring refreshment to itself that way. Hence the church saith, "My fingers dropped with sweet-smelling myrrh," and again, she saith of her beloved, that "his lips dropped sweet-smelling myrrh." (Cant. v. 5—13.) But how came the church to understand this, but because her soul did smell that in it that was to be smelled in it, even in his word and gracious visits? The poor world, indeed, cannot smell, or savour anything of the good and fragrant scent and sweet that is in Christ; but to them that believe, "Thy name is as ointment poured forth, therefore do the virgins love thee." (Cant. i. 3.)

5. As the soul can see, hear, taste, and smell, so it hath the sense of feeling, as quick and as sensible as the body. He knows nothing that knows not this: he whose soul is "past feeling," (Eph. iv. 19;) has his "conscience seared with a hot iron." (1 Tim. iv. 2.) Nothing so sensible as the soul, nor feeleth so quickly the love and mercy, or the anger and wrath of God. Ask the awakened man, or the man that is under the convictions of the law, if he doth not feel? and he will quickly tell you, that he faints and dies away by reason of God's hand, and his wrath that lieth upon him. Read the first eight verses of the 38th Psalm, (if thou knowest nothing of what I have told thee by experience,) and there thou shalt hear the complaints of one whose soul lay at present under the burden of guilt, and that cried out that without help from heaven, he could by no means bear the same. They also that know what the peace of God means, and what an eternal weight there is in glory, know well that the soul has the sense of feeling, as well as the sense of seeing, hearing, tasting, and smelling. But thus much for the senses of the soul.

Third. I come, in the next place, to describe the soul by the passions of the soul. The passions of the soul, I reckon, are these, and such like, to wit, love, hatred, joy, fear, grief, anger, &c. And these passions of the soul are not therefore good, nor therefore evil, because they are the passions of the soul; but are made so by two things, to wit, principle and object. The principle I count that from whence they flow, and the object that upon which they are pitched. To explain myself.

1. For that of love. This is a strong passion; the Holy Ghost saith "it is strong as death, and cruel as the grave," (Cant. viii. 6, 7.) And it is then good, when it flows from faith, and pitches itself upon God in Christ as the object; and when it extendeth itself to all that is good, whether it be the good Word, the good work of grace, or the good men that have it, and also to their good lives. But all soul-love floweth not from this principle, neither hath these for its object. How many are there that make the object of their love the most vile of men, the most base of things, because it flows from vile affections, and from the lusts of the flesh? God and Christ, good laws and good men, and their holy lives, they cannot abide, because their love wanteth a principle that should sanctify it in its first motion, and that should steer it to a goodly object. But that is the first.

2. There is hatred, which I count another passion of the soul; and this, as the other, is good or evil, as the principle from whence it flows, and the object of it are. "Ye that love the Lord, hate evil," (Ps. xcvii. 10.) Then, therefore, is this passion good, when it singleth out from the many of things that are in the world, that one filthy thing called sin; and when it setteth itself, the soul, and the whole man, against it, and engageth all the powers of the soul to seek and invent its ruin. But, alas, where shall this hatred be found? What man is there whose soul is filled with this passion, thus sanctified by the love of God, and that makes sin, which is God's enemy, the only object of its indignation? How many be there, I say, whose hatred is turned another way, because of the malignity of their minds.

M 2

They hate knowledge, (Prov. i. 22.) They hate God, (Deut. vii. 10. 2 Chron. xix. 2.) They hate the righteous, (Ps. xxxiv. 21. Prov. xxix. 10.) They hate God's ways, (Job xxi. 14. Mal. iii. 14. Prov. viii. 12.) And all is, because the grace of final fear is not the root and principle from whence their hatred flows. " For the fear of the Lord is to hate evil;" wherefore, where this grace is wanting for a root in the soul, there it must of necessity swerve in the letting out of this passion; because the soul, where grace is wanting, is not at liberty to act simply, but is biassed by the power of sin, that, while grace is absent, is present in the soul. And hence it is that this passion, which, when acted well, is a virtue, is so abused, and made to exercise its force against that for which God never ordained it, nor gave it licence to act.

3. Another passion of the soul is joy: when the soul " rejoiceth not in iniquity, but rejoiceth in the truth," (1 Cor. xiii. 6.) This joy is a very strong passion, and will carry a man through a world of difficulties: it is a passion that beareth up, that supporteth and strengtheneth a man, let the object of his joy be what it will. It is this that maketh the soul fat in goodness, if it have its object accordingly; and that which makes the soul bold in wickedness, if it indeed doth rejoice in iniquity.

4. Another passion of the soul is fear, natural fear; for so you must understand me of all the passions of the soul, as they are considered simply, and in their own nature. And, as it is with the other passions, so it is with this, it is made good or evil in its acts, as its principle and objects are: when this passion of the soul is good, then it springs from sense of the greatness, and goodness, and majesty of God; also, God himself is the object of this fear: " I will forewarn you," says Christ, " whom ye shall fear. Fear him that can destroy both body and soul in hell; yea, I say unto you, Fear him:" (Matt. x. 28. Luke xii. 5.) But in all men this passion is not regulated and governed by these principles and objects; but is abused and turned, through the policy of Satan, quite into another channel. It is made to fear men: (Numb. xiv. 9;) to fear idols, (2 Kings xvii. 7—38;) to fear devils and witches; yea, it is made to fear all the foolish, ridiculous, and apish fables, that every old woman, or atheistical fortune-teller, has the face to drop before the soul. But fear is another passion of the soul.

5. Another passion of the soul is grief, and it, as those afore-named, acteth even according as it is governed. When holiness is lovely and beautiful to the soul, and when the name of Christ is more precious than life, then will the soul sit down and be afflicted, because men keep not God's law. " I beheld the transgressors, and was grieved; because they kept not thy words." (Ps. cxix. 158.) So Christ; he looked round about with anger, " Being grieved for the hardness of their hearts." (Mark iii. 5.) But it is rarely seen that this passion of the soul is thus exercised: almost everybody has other things for the spending of the heat of this passion upon. Men are grieved that they thrive no more in the world; grieved that they have no more carnal, sensual, and worldly honour; grieved that they are suffered no more to range in the lusts and vanities of this life; but all this is because the soul is unacquainted with God, sees no beauty in holiness, but is sensual, and wrapped up in clouds and thick darkness.

6. And lastly, There is anger, which is another passion of the soul; and that, as the rest, is extended by the soul, according to the nature of the principle by which it is acted, and from whence it flows. And, in a word, to speak nothing of the fierceness and power of this passion, it is then cursed when it breaketh out beyond the bounds that God hath set it, the which to be sure it doth, when it shall by its fierceness or irregular motion, run the soul into sin. " Be ye angry, and sin not," (Eph. iv. 26,) is the limitation wherewith God hath bounded this passion; and whatever is more than this is a giving place to the devil. And one reason, among others, why the Lord doth so strictly set this bound and these limits to anger, is, for that it is so furious a passion, and for that it will so quickly swell up the soul with sin, as they say a toad swells with its poison. Yea, it will in a moment so transport the spirit of a man, that he shall quickly forget himself, his God, his friend, and all good rule. But my business is not now to make a comment upon the passions of the soul, only to show you that there are such, and also which they are.

And now, from this description of the soul, what follows but to put you in mind what a noble, powerful, lively, sensible thing the soul is, that by the text is supposed may be lost, through the heedlessness, or carelessness, or slavish fear of him whose soul it is; and also to stir you up to that care of, and labour after, the salvation of your soul, as becomes the weight of the matter. If the soul were a trivial thing, or if a man, though he lost it, might yet himself be happy, it were another matter; but the loss of the soul is no small loss, nor can that man that has lost his soul, had he all the world, yea, the whole kingdom of heaven in his own power, be but in a most fearful and miserable condition. But of these things more in their place.

Second. Having thus given you a description of the soul, what it is, I shall in the next place, show you the greatness of it.

First, And the first thing that I shall take occasion to make this manifest by, will be by showing you the disproportion that is betwixt that and the body; and I shall do it in these following particulars :—

1. The body is called the house of the soul, a house for the soul to dwell in. Now, everybody

knows that the house is much inferior to him that, by God's ordinance, is appointed to dwell therein; that it is called the house of the soul you find in Paul to the Corinthians: "For we know," saith he, "that if our earthly house of this tabernacle were dissolved, we have a building of God, a house not made with hands, eternal in the heavens." (2 Cor. v. 1.) We have, then, a house for our soul in this world, and this house is the body, for the Apostle can mean nothing else; therefore, he calls it an earthly house. "If our earthly house—" our house. But who doth he personate, if he says, This is a house for the soul? for the body is part of him that says, Our house.

In this manner of language he personates his soul with the souls of the rest that are saved; and thus to do, is common with the Apostles, as will be easily discerned by them that give attendance to reading. Our earthly houses; or as Job saith, "houses of clay," for our bodies are bodies of clay: "Your remembrances are like unto ashes, your bodies to bodies of clay." (Job iv. 19; xiii. 12.) Indeed, he after maketh mention of a house in heaven, but that is not it about which he now speaks; now he speaks of this earthly house which we have—we, our souls—to dwell in, while on this side glory, where the other house stands, as ready prepared for us when we shall flit from this to that; or in case this should sooner or later be dissolved. But that is the first; the body is compared to the house, but the soul to him that inhabiteth the house; therefore, as the man is more noble than the house he dwells in, so is the soul more noble than the body. And yet, alas! with grief be it spoken, how common is it for men to spend all their care, all their time, all their strength, all their wit, and parts for the body, and its honour and preferment, even as if the soul were some poor, pitiful, sorry, inconsiderable, and under thing, not worth the thinking of, or not worth the caring for. But,

2. The body is called the clothing, and the soul that which is clothed therewith. Now, everybody knows that "the body is more than raiment," even carnal sense will teach us this. But read that pregnant place: "For we that are in this tabernacle do groan, being burdened (that is, with mortal flesh); not for that we would be unclothed, but clothed upon, that mortality might be swallowed up of life." (2 Cor. v. 4.) Thus the greatness of the soul appears in the preference that it hath to the body—the body is its raiment. We see that, above all creatures, man, because he is the most noble among all visible ones, has, for the adoring of his body, that more abundant comeliness; it is the body of man, not of beast, that is clothed with the richest ornaments. But, now, what a thing is the soul, that the body itself must be its clothing! No suit of apparel is by God thought good enough for the soul but that which is made by God himself, and that is that curious thing the body. But oh! how little is this con-

sidered, namely, the greatness of the soul. It is the body, the clothes, the suit of apparel, that our foolish fancies are taken with; not at all considering the richness and excellency of that great and more noble part, the soul, for which the body is made a mantle to wrap it up in; a garment to clothe it withal. If a man gets a rent in his clothes, it is little in comparison of a rent in his flesh; yea, he comforts himself when he looks on that rent, saying, Thanks be to God, it is not a rent in my flesh. But ah! on the contrary, how many are there in the world that are more troubled for that they have a rent, a wound, or a disease in the body, than for that they have souls that will be lost and cast away. A little rent in the body dejecteth and casteth such down, but they are not at all concerned, though their soul is now, and will yet further be, torn in pieces. "Now consider this, ye that forget God, lest he tear you in pieces, and there be none to deliver." (Ps. l. 22.) But this is the second thing whereby, or by which, the greatness of the soul appears, to wit, in that the body, that excellent piece of God's workmanship, is but a garment, or clothing for the soul. But,

3. The body is called a vessel, or a case, for the soul to be put and kept in. "That every one of you should know how to possess his vessel in sanctification and honour." (1 Thess. iv. 4.) The apostle here doth exhort the people to abstain from fornication, which, in another place, he saith, "is a sin against the body." (1 Cor. vi. 18.) And here again he saith, "This is the will of God, your sanctification, that you should abstain from fornication;" that the body be not defiled; "that every one of you should know how to possess his vessel in sanctification and honour." His vessel, his earthen vessel, as he calls it in another place, for "we have this treasure in earthen vessels." Thus, then, the body is called a vessel; yea, every man's body is his vessel. But what has God prepared this vessel for, and what has he put into it? Why, many things this body is to be a vessel for, but at present God has put into it that curious thing, the soul. Cabinets, that are very rich and costly things of themselves, are not made nor designed to be vessels to be stuffed or filled with trumpery, and things of no value; no, these are prepared for rings and jewels, for pearls, for rubies, and things that are choice. And if so, what shall we then think of the soul for which it is prepared, and that of God, the most rich and excellent vessel in the world? Surely it must be a thing of worth, yea, of more worth than is the whole world besides. But, alas! who believes this talk? Do not even the most of men so set their minds upon, and so admire the glory of the case or vessel, that they forget once with seriousness to think, and, therefore, must of necessity be a great way off, of those suitable esteems that becomes them to have of their souls. But oh, since this vessel, this cabinet, this body is so curiously made, and that to receive and contain what

thing is that for which God has made this vessel, and what is that soul that he hath put into it? Wherefore thus, in the third place, is the greatness of the soul made manifest, even by the excellency of the vessel, the body, that God has made to put it in.

4. The body is called a tabernacle for the soul. "Knowing that shortly I must put off this my tabernacle," (2 Pet. i. 14,) that is, my body, "my death." (John xxi. 18, 19.) So again, "For we know that if our earthly house of this tabernacle were dissolved, we have a building of God," &c. (2 Cor. v. 1.) In both these places, by tabernacle, can be meant nothing but the body; wherefore both the Apostles, in these sentences, do personate their souls, and speak as if the soul was the all of a man; yea, they plainly tell us, that the body is but the house, clothes, vessel, and tabernacle for the soul. But what a famous thing therefore is the soul!

The tabernacle of old was a place erected for worship, but the worshippers were far more excellent than the place; so our body is a tabernacle for the soul to worship God in, but must needs be accounted much inferior to the soul, forasmuch as the worshippers are always of more honour than the place they worship in; as he that dwelleth in the tabernacle hath more honour than the tabernacle. "I serve," says Paul, God and Christ Jesus "with my spirit (or soul) in the gospel," (Rom. i. 9,) but not with his spirit out of, but in, this tabernacle. The tabernacle had instruments of worship for the worshippers; so has the body for the soul, and we are bid to "yield our members as instruments of righteousness unto God." (Rom. vi. 13.) The hands, feet, ears, eyes, and tongue, (which last is our glory when used right,) are all of them instruments of this tabernacle, and to be made use of by the soul, the inhabiter of this tabernacle, for the soul's performance of the service of God. I thus discourse, to show you the greatness of the soul. And, in mine opinion, there is something, if not very much, in what I say. For all men admire the body, both for its manner of building, and the curious way of its being compacted together. Yea, the further men, wise men, do pry into the wonderful work of God, that is put forth in framing the body, the more still they are made to admire; and yet, as I said, this body is but a house, a mantle, a vessel, a tabernacle for the soul. What, then, is the soul itself? But thus much for the first particular.

Second. We will now come to other things that show us the greatness of the soul. And,

1. It is called God's breath of life. "And the Lord God formed man," that is the body, "of the dust of the ground, and breathed into his nostrils the breath of life, and man became a living soul." (Gen. ii. 7.) Do but compare these two together, the body and the soul; the body is made of dust, the soul is the breath of God. Now, if God hath made this body so famous, as indeed he has, and

yet it is made but of the dust of the ground, and we all do know what inferior matter that is, what is the soul, since the body is not only its house and garment, but since itself is made of the breath of God? But, further, it is not only said, that the soul is of the breath of the Lord, but that the Lord breathed into him the breath of life, to wit, a living spirit, for so the next words infer: "And man became a living soul." Man, that is, the more excellent part of him, which, for that it is principal, is called man, that bearing the denomination of the whole; or man, the spirit and natural power, by which, as a reasonable creature, the whole of him is acted, "became a living soul." But I stand not here upon definition, but upon demonstration. The body, that noble part of man, had its original from the dust; for so says the Word, "Dust thou art (as to thy body), and unto dust shalt thou return." (Gen. iii. 19.) But as to thy more noble part, thou art from the breath of God, God putting forth in that a mighty work of creating power, and man "was made a living soul." (1 Cor. xv. 45.) Mark my reason. There is as great a disparity betwixt the body and the soul, as is between the dust of the ground, and that here called the breath of life of the Lord. And, note further, that, as the dust of the ground did not lose, but gain glory by being formed into the body of a man, so this breath of the Lord lost nothing neither by being made a living soul. O man! dost thou know what thou art?

2. As the soul is said to be of the breath of God, so it is said to be made after God's own image, even after the similitude of God. "And God said, Let us make man in our image, after our likeness. So God created man in his own image, in the image of God created he him." (Gen. i. 20, 27.) Mark, in his own image, in the image of God created he him; or, as James hath it, it is "made after the similitude of God," (James iii. 9;) like him, having in it that which beareth semblance with him. I do not read of anything in heaven, or earth, or under the earth, that is said to be made after this manner, or that is at all so termed, save only the Son of God himself. The angels are noble creatures, and for present employ are made a little higher than man himself; (Heb. ii.;) but that any of them are said to be made "after God's own image," after his own image, even after the similitude of God, that I find not. This character the Holy Ghost, in the Scriptures of truth, giveth only of man, of the soul of man; for it must not be thought that the body is here intended in whole or in part. For though it be said, "that Christ was made after the similitude of sinful flesh," (Phil. ii.,) yet it is not said that sinful flesh is made after the similitude of God; but I will not dispute: I only bring these things to show how great a thing, how noble a thing the soul is, in that, at its creation, God thought it worthy to be made, not like the earth, or the heavens, or the angels, seraphims, seraphins,

or archangels, but like himself, his own self, saying, "Let us make man in our own likeness. So he made man in his own image." This, I say, is a character above all angels; for, as the Apostle said, "To which of the angels said he, any time, Thou art my Son?" so of which of them hath he at any time said, This is, or shall be, made in or after mine image, mine own image? Oh, what a thing is the soul of man! that, above all the creatures in heaven or earth, being made in the image and similitude of God.

3. Another thing by which the greatness of the soul is made manifest is this: it is that (and that only, and to say this is more than to say, it is that above all the creatures) that the great God desires communion with: he "hath set apart him that is godly for himself," (Ps. iv. 3;) that is, for communion with his soul; therefore the spouse saith concerning him, "His desire is toward me," (Cant. vii. 10;) and, therefore, he saith, again, "I will dwell in them, and walk in them," (2 Cor. vi. 16.) To dwell in them, and walk with, are terms that intimate communion and fellowship; as John saith, "Our fellowship, truly our fellowship is with the Father, and with his Son Jesus Christ, (1 John i. 3:) that is, our soul-fellowship; for it must not be understood of the body, though I believe that the body is much influenced when the soul has communion with God; but it is the soul, and that only, that at present is capable of having and maintaining of this blessed communion. But, I say, what a thing is this, that God, the great God, should choose to have fellowship and communion with the soul above all. We read, indeed, of the greatness of the angels, and how near also they are unto God; but yet there are not such terms that bespeak such familiar acts between God and angels, as to demonstrate that they have such communion with God as has, or as the souls of his people may have. Where has he called them his love, his dove, his fair one? and where, when he speaketh of them, doth he express a communion that they have with him by the similitude of conjugal love? I speak of what is revealed; the secret things belong to the Lord our God. Now, by all this is manifest the greatness of the soul. Men of greatness and honour, if they have respect for their own glory, will not choose for their familiars the base and rascally crew of this world; but will single out for their fellows, fellowship, and communion, those that are most like themselves. True, the king has not an equal; yet he is for being familiar only with the nobles of the land: so God, with him none can compare; yet, since the soul is by him singled out for his walking mate and companion, it is a sign it is the highest born, and that upon which the blessed majesty looks, as upon that which is most meet to be singled out for communion with himself. Should we see a man familiar with the king, we would, even of ourselves, conclude he is one of the nobles of the land; but this is not the lot of every soul, (some have fellowship with devils, yet, not because they have a more base original than those that lie in God's bosom, but they, through sin, are degenerate, and have chosen to be great with his enemy,) but all these things show the greatness of the soul.

4. The souls of men are such as God counts worthy to be the vessels to hold his grace, the graces of the Spirit, in. The graces of the Spirit, what like them, or where here are they to be found, save in the souls of men only? "Of his fulness have all we received, and grace for grace," (John i. 16;) received, into what? into "the hidden part," as David calls it. (Ps. li. 6.) Hence the king's daughter is said to be "all glorious within," (Ps. xlv. 13,) because adorned and beautified with the graces of the Spirit. For that which David calls the hidden part is the inmost part of the soul; and it is, therefore, called the hidden part, because the soul is invisible, nor can any one living infallibly know what is in the soul but God himself. But, I say, the soul is the vessel into which this golden oil is poured, and that which holds, and is accounted worthy to exercise and improve the same. Therefore the soul is it which is said to love God: "Saw ye him whom my soul loveth?" (Cant. iii. 3;) and, therefore, the soul is that which exerciseth the spirit of prayer, "With my soul have I desired thee in the night; yea, with my spirit within me will I seek thee early." (Isa. xxvi. 9.) With the soul, also, men are said to believe, and into the soul God is said to put his fear. This is the vessel into which the wise virgins got oil, and out of which their lamps were supplied by the same. But what a thing, what a great thing therefore is the soul, that that above all things that God hath created, should be the chosen vessel to put his grace in. The body is the vessel for the soul, and the soul is the vessel for the grace of God. But,

5. The greatness of the soul is manifest by the greatness of the price that Christ paid for it, to make it an heir of glory; and that was his precious blood. (1 Cor. vi. 20. 1 Pet. i. 18, 19.) We do use to esteem of things according to the price that is given for them, especially when we are convinced that the purchase has not been made by the estimation of a fool. Now the soul is purchased by a price, that the Son, the wisdom of God, thought fit to pay for the redemption thereof; what a thing, then, is the soul? Judge of the soul by the price that is paid for it, and you must needs confess—unless you count the blood that hath bought it an unholy thing—that it cannot but be of great worth and value. Suppose a prince, or some great man, should on a sudden descend from his throne or chair of state, to take up, that he might put in his bosom, something that he had espied lying trampled under the feet of those that stand by; would you think that he would do this for an old horse-shoe, or for so trivial a thing as a pin or a point? nay, would you not even of yourselves conclude, that that thing for which the prince, so

great a man, should make such a stoop, must needs be a thing of very great worth? Why, this is the case of Christ and the soul. Christ is the prince, his throne was in heaven, and as he sat there, he espied the souls of sinners trampled under the foot of the law and death for sin. Now what doth he, but comes down from his throne, stoops down to the earth, and there, since he could not have the trodden-down souls without price, he lays down his life and blood for them. (1 Cor. viii. 9.) But would he have done this for inconsiderable things? No, nor for the soul of sinners neither, had he not valued them higher than he valued heaven and earth besides. This, therefore, is another thing by which the greatness of the soul is known.

6. The soul is immortal, it will have a sensible being for ever, none can kill the soul. (Luke xii. 4. Matt. x. 28.) If all the angels in heaven, and all the men on earth, should lay all their strength together, they cannot kill or annihilate one soul. No, I will speak without fear, if it may be said, God cannot do what he will not do; then he will not annihilate the soul; but, notwithstanding all his wrath, and the vengeance that he will inflict on sinful souls, they yet shall abide with sensible beings, yet to endure, yet to bear punishment. If anything could kill the soul, it would be death; but death cannot do it, neither first nor second; the first cannot, for when Dives was slain, as to his body by death, his soul was found alive in hell: "He lifted up his eyes in hell, being in torment." (Luke xvi. 22, 23. Mark ix. 44.) The second death cannot do it, because it is said, their worm never dies, but is always torturing them with his gnawing: but that could not be, if time, or lying in hell fire for ever, could annihilate the soul. Now, this also shows the greatness of the soul, that it is that which has an endless life, and that will, therefore, have a being endlessly. Oh, what a thing is the soul!

The soul, then, is immortal, though not eternal. That is eternal that has neither beginning nor end, and, therefore, eternal is properly applicable to none but God; hence he is called "the eternal God." (Deut. xxxiii. 27.) Immortal is that which, though it hath a beginning, yet hath no end, it cannot die, or cease to be; and this is the soul. It cannot cease to have a being when it is once created; I mean a living, sensible being. For I mean by living, only such a being as distinguishes it from annihilation or incapableness of sense and feeling. Hence, as the rich man is after death, said to "lift up his eyes in hell," (Luke xvi. 22, 23;) so the beggar is said, when he died, to be "carried by the angels into Abraham's bosom." And both these sayings must have respect to the souls of these men; for, as for their bodies, we know at present it is otherwise with them. The grave is their house, and so must be till the trumpet shall sound, and the heavens pass away like a scroll. Now, I say, the immortality of the soul shows the greatness of it, as the eternity of God shows the greatness of God. It cannot be said of any angel but that he is immortal, and so it is, and ought to be said of the soul. This, therefore, shows the greatness of the soul, in that it is as to abiding so like unto him.

7. But a word or two more, and so to conclude this head. The soul! why, it is the soul that acteth the body in all these things, good or bad, that seem good and reasonable, or amazingly wicked. True, the acts and motions of the soul are only seen and heard in and by the members and motions of the body, but the body is but a poor instrument, the soul is the great agitator and actor: "The body without the spirit is dead." (James ii. 26.) All those famous arts, and works, and inventions of works that are done by men under heaven, they are all the inventions of the soul, and the body as acting and labouring therein, doth it but as a tool that the soul maketh use of, to bring his invention unto maturity. (Eccles. vii. 29.) How many things have men found out to the amazing of one another, to the wonderment of one another, to the begetting of endless commendations of one another in the world, while, in the meantime, the soul, which indeed is the true inventor of all, is overlooked, not regarded, but dragged up and down by every lust, and prostrate, and made a slave to every silly and beastly thing. Oh the amazing darkness that hath covered the face of the hearts of the children of men, that they cannot deliver their soul, nor say, "Is there not a lie in my right hand?" (Isa. xliv. 20.)—though they are so cunning in all other matters. Take man in matters that are abroad, and far from home, and he is the mirror of all the world; but take him at home, and put him upon things that are near him, I mean, that have respect to the things that concern his soul, and then you will find him the greatest fool that ever God made. But this must not be applied to the soul simply, as it is God's creature, but to the soul sinful, as it has willingly apostatized from God, and so suffered itself to be darkened, and that with such thick and stupefying darkness, that it is bound up and cannot—it hath a napkin of sin bound so close before its eyes that it is not able, of itself, to look to, and after, those things which should be its chiefest concern, and without which it will be most miserable for ever.

8. Further, as the soul is thus curious about arts and sciences, and about every excellent thing of this life, so it is capable of having to do with invisibles, with angels good or bad; yea, with the Highest and Supreme Being, even with the holy God of heaven. I told you before, that God sought the soul of man to have it for his companion; and now I tell you, that the soul is capable of communion with him, when the darkness that sin hath spread over its face is removed. The soul is an intelligent power, it can be made to know and understand depths, and heights, and lengths, and breadths, in those high, sublime, and

spiritual mysteries, that only God can reveal and teach; yea, it is capable of diving unutterably into them. And here is God, the God of glory, much delighted and pleased, to wit, that he hath made himself a creature that is capable of hearing, of knowing, and of understanding of his mind, when opened and revealed to it. I think I may say, without offence to God or man, that one reason why God made the world was, that he might manifest himself, not only by, but to the works which he made; but (I speak with reverence) how could that be, if he did not also make some of his creatures capable of apprehending of him in those most high mysteries and methods in which he purposed to reveal himself? But, then, what are those creatures which he hath made, (unto whom, when these things are shown,) that are able to take them in and understand them, and so to improve them to God's glory, as he hath ordained and purposed they should, but souls? for none else in the visible world are capable of doing this but they. And hence it is, that to them, and them only, he beginneth to reveal himself in this world. And hence it is that they, and they only, are gathered up to him, where he is, for they are they that are called " the spirits of just men made perfect," (Heb. xii. 23;) the spirit of a beast goeth downward to the earth, it is the spirit of a man that goes upwards to God that gave it. (Eccles. iii. 21; xii. 7.) For that, and that only, is capable of beholding and understanding the glorious visions of heaven, as Christ said, " Father, I will that those whom thou hast given me be with me where I am; that they may behold my glory, which thou hast given me; for thou lovedst me before the foundation of the world." (John xvii. 24.) And thus the greatness of the soul is manifest. True, the body is also gathered up into glory, but not simply for its own sake, or because that is capable of itself to know and understand the glories of its Maker; but that has been a companion with the soul in this world, has also been its house, its mantle, its cabinet and tabernacle here; it has also been it by which the soul hath acted, in which it hath wrought, and by which its excellent appearances have been manifested; and it shall also there be its co-partner and sharer in its glory. Wherefore, as the body here did partake of soul excellencies, and was also conformed to its spiritual and regenerate principles, so it shall be hereafter a partaker of that glory with which the soul shall be filled; and also be made suitable by that glory, to become a partaker and co-partner with it of the eternal excellencies which heaven will put upon it. In this world it is a gracious soul, (I speak now of the regenerate,) and in that world it shall be a glorious one. In this world the body was conformable to the soul, as it was gracious, and in that world it shall be conformable to it, as it is glorious; conformable, I say, by partaking of that glory that then the soul shall partake of; yea, it

shall also have an additional glory to adorn, and make it yet the more capable of being serviceable to it, and with it in its great acts before God in eternal glory. Oh, what great things are the souls of the sons of men!

9. But again, as the soul is thus capable of enjoying God in glory, and of prying into these mysteries that are in him, so it is capable, with great profundity, to dive into the mysterious depths of hell. Hell is a place and state utterly unknown to any in this visible world, excepting the souls of men; nor shall any for ever be capable of understanding the miseries thereof, save souls and fallen angels. Now, I think, as the joys of heaven stand not only in speculation, or in beholding of glory, but in a sensible enjoyment and unspeakable pleasure, which these glories will yield to the soul, (Ps. xv. 11;) so the torments of hell will not stand in the present lashes and strokes which by the flames of eternal fire God will scourge the ungodly with; but the torments of hell stand much, if not in the greatest part of them, in those deep thoughts and apprehensions, which souls in the next world will have of the nature and occasions of sin, of God, and separation from him; of the eternity of those miseries, and of the utter impossibility of their help, ease, or deliverance for ever. Oh, damned souls will have thoughts that will clash with glory, clash with justice, clash with law, clash with itself, clash with hell, and with the everlastingness of misery; but the point, the edge, and the poison of all these thoughts will still be galling, and, dropping, and spewing out their stings into the sore, grieved, wounded, and fretted place, which is the conscience, though not the conscience only; for I may say of the souls in hell, that they all over are but one wound, one sore. Miseries as well as mercies sharpen and make quick the apprehensions of the soul. Behold Spira in his book, Cain in his guilt, and Saul with the witch of Endor, and you shall see men ripened, men enlarged and greatened in their fancies, imaginations, and apprehensions, though not about God, and heaven and glory, yet about their loss, their misery, and their woe, and their hells. (Isa. xxxiii. 14. Ps. l. 3. Rev. xiv. 10. Mark ix. 44, 46.)

10. Nor doth their ability to bear (if it be proper to say they bear those dolours which there for ever they shall endure) a little demonstrate their greatness. Everlasting burning, devouring fire, perpetual pains, gnawing worms, utter darkness, and the ireful words, face, and strokes of Divine and infinite justice will not, cannot, make this soul extinct, as I said before. I think it is not so proper to say, the soul that is damned for sin doth bear these things, as to say it doth ever sink under them; and, therefore, their place of torment is called the bottomless pit, because they are ever sinking, and shall never come there where they will find any stay. Yet they live under wrath but yet only so as to be sensible of it, as to smart and

be in perpetual anguish by reason of the intolerableness of their burden. But doth not their thus living, abiding, and retaining a being, (or what you will call it,) demonstrate the greatness and might of the soul? Alas! heaven and earth are short of this greatness, for these, though under less judgment by far, do fade and wax old like a moth-eaten garment, and, in their time, will vanish away to nothing. (Heb. i.)

Also, we see how quickly the body, when the soul is under a fear of the rebukes of justice, how soon, I say, it wastes, moulders away, and crumbleth into the grave; but the soul is yet strong, and abides sensible to be dealt withal for sin, by everlasting burnings.

11. The soul, by God's ordinance, while this world lasts, has a time appointed it to forsake and leave the body, to be turned again to the dust, as it was, (Heb. ix. 27,) and this separation is made by death; therefore, the body must cease for a time to have sense, or life, or motion; and a little thing brings it now into this state; but in the next world, the wicked shall partake of none of this; for the body and the soul being at the resurrection rejoined, this death, that once did rend them asunder, is for ever overcome and extinct; so that these two which lived in sin must for ever be yoked together in hell. Now, there the soul being joined to the body, and death, which before did separate them, being utterly taken away, the soul retains not only its own being, but also continueth the body to be, and to suffer sensibly the pains of hell, without those decays that it used to sustain.

And the reason why this death shall then be taken away is, because justice, in its bestowing its rewards for transgressions, may not be interrupted, (Matt. x. 28,) but that body and soul, as they lived and acted in sin together, might be destroyed for sin in hell together, (Luke xii. 5.) Destroyed, I say, but with such a destruction, which, though it is everlasting, will not put a period to their sensible suffering the vengeance of eternal fire, (2 Thess. i. 8, 9.)

This death, therefore, though that also be the wages of sin, would now, were it suffered to continue, be a hindrance to the making known of the wrath of God, and also of the created power and might of the soul. (1.) It would hinder the making known of the wrath of God, for it would take the body out of the way, and make it uncapable of sensible suffering for sin, and so removing one of the objects of vengeance, the power of God's wrath would be so far undiscovered. (2.) It would also hinder the manifestation of the power and might of the soul, which is discovered much by its abiding to retain its own being while the wrath of God is grappling with it, and more by its continuing to the body a sensible being with itself.

Death, therefore, must now be removed, that the soul may be made the object of wrath without molestation or interruption. That the soul, did I say? yea, that soul and body both might be so.

Death would now be a favour, though once the fruit of sin, and also the wages thereof, might it now be suffered to continue, because it would ease the soul of some of its burden: for a tormented body cannot but be a burden to a spirit, and so the wise man insinuates when he says, "The spirit of a man will sustain his infirmity;" that is, bear up under it, but yet so as that it feels it a burden. We see that because of the sympathy that is between body and soul, how one is burthened if the other be grieved. A sick body is a burden to the soul, and a wounded spirit is a burden to the body; "a wounded spirit who can bear?" (Prov. xviii. 14.) But death must not remove this burden, but the soul must have the body for a burden, and the body must have the soul for a burden, and both must have the wrath of God for a burden. Oh, therefore, here will be burden upon burden, and all upon the soul, for the soul will be the chief seat of this burden. But thus much to show you the greatness of the soul.

Third, I shall now come to the third thing which was propounded to be spoken to; and that is, to show you what we are to understand by losing of the soul or what the loss of the soul is, "What shall a man give in exchange for his soul?"

First, The loss of the soul is a loss, in the nature of it, peculiar to itself. There is no such loss, as to the nature of loss, as is the loss of the soul; for that he that hath lost his soul has lost himself. In all other losses, it is possible for a man to save himself, but he that loseth his soul loseth himself: "For what is a man advantaged, if he gain the whole world, and lose himself?" (Luke ix. 25.) Wherefore, the loss of the soul is a loss that cannot be paralleled. He that loseth himself loseth his all, his lasting all; for himself is his all, his all in the most comprehensive sense. What mattereth it what a man gets, if by the getting thereof he loseth himself? Suppose a man goeth to the Indies for gold, and he loadeth his ship therewith, but at his return, that sea that carried him thither swallows him up—now what has he got? But this is but a lean similitude with reference to the matter in hand, to wit, to set forth the loss of the soul. Suppose a man that has been at the Indies for gold should, at his return, himself be taken by them of Algiers, and there made a slave of, and there be hunger-bit, and beaten till his bones are broken, what has he got? what is he advantaged by his rich adventure? Perhaps, you will say, he has got gold enough to obtain his ransom. Indeed this may be; and therefore no similitude can be found that can fully amplify the matter, "For what shall a man give in exchange for his soul?" It is a loss that standeth by itself, there is not another like it, or unto which it may be compared: it is only like itself, it is singular, it is the chief of all losses, the highest, the greatest loss. "For what shall a man give in exchange for his soul?" A man may lose his wife, his children, his estate, his liberty, and his life, and have all made up again, and have all restored with advantage, and may, therefore, nothwithstanding all these losses, be far enough off from losing of himself. (Luke xiv. 26. Mark viii. 35.) For he may lose his life, and save it; yea, sometimes the only way to save that, is to lose it; but when a man has lost himself, his soul, then all is gone to all intents and purposes. There is no word says, " he that loses his soul shall save it;" but contrariwise, the text supposeth that a man has lost his soul, and then demands if any can answer it, " What shall a man give in exchange for his soul?" All, then, that he gains that loseth his soul is only this, he has gained a loss, he has purchased the loss of losses, he has nothing left him now but his loss, but the loss of himself, of his whole self. He that loseth his life for Christ, shall save it; but he that loseth himself for sin, and for the world, shall lose himself to perfection of loss; he has lost himself and there is the full point.

There are several things fall under this first head, upon which I would touch a little.

1. He that has lost his soul has lost himself. Now, he that has lost himself is no more at his own dispose. While a man enjoys himself, he is at his own dispose. A single man, a free man, a rich man, a poor man, any man that enjoys himself, is at his own dispose. I speak after the manner of men. But he that has lost himself, is not at his own dispose. He is, as I may say, now out of his own hands; he has lost himself, his soul-self, his own self, his whole self by sin, and wrath and hell hath found him : he is, therefore, now no more at his own dispose, but at the dispose of justice, of wrath, and hell; he is committed to prison, to hell prison, there to abide, not at pleasure, not as long and as little time as he will, but the term appointed by his judge : nor may he there choose his own affliction, neither for manner, measure, or continuance. It is God that will spread the fire and brimstone under him, it is God that will pile up wrath upon him, and it is God himself that will blow the fire. And "the breath of the Lord, like a stream of brimstone, doth kindle it." (Isa. xxx. 33.) And thus it is manifest that he that has lost himself, his soul, is no more at his own dispose, but at the dispose of them that find him.

2. Again, as he that has lost himself is not at his own dispose, so neither is he at liberty to dispose of what he has; for the man that has lost himself, has something yet of his own. The text implies that his soul is his when lost, yea, when that and his all, himself, is lost; but as he cannot dispose of himself, so he cannot dispose of what he hath. Let me take leave to make out my meaning. If he that is lost, that has lost himself, has not, notwithstanding, something that in some sense may be called his own, then he that is lost is nothing. The man that is in hell has yet the powers, the senses, and passions of his soul; for not he nor his soul must be thought to be stripped of these; for then he would be lower than the brute ; but yet all these, since he is there, are by God improved against himself; or, if you will, the point of this man's sword is turned against his own heart, and made to pierce his own liver.

The soul by being in hell loseth nothing of its aptness to think, its quickness to pierce, to pry, and to understand ; nay, hell has ripened it in all these things; but, I say, the soul with its improvements as to these, or anything else, is not in the hand of him that hath lost himself to manage for his own advantage, but in the hand, and in the power, and to be disposed as is thought meet by him into whose revenging hand by sin he has delivered himself, to wit, in the hand of God. So, then, God now has the victory, and disposeth of all the powers, senses, and passions of the soul for the chastising of him that has lost himself. Now, the understanding is only employed and improved in and about the apprehending of such things as will be like daggers at the heart, to wit, about justice, sin, hell, and eternity, to grieve and break the spirit of the damned ; yea, to break, to wound, and to tear the soul in pieces. The depths of sin which the man has loved, the good nature of God whom the man has hated, the blessings of eternity which the soul has despised, shall now be understood by him more than ever, but yet so only as to increase grief and sorrow, by improving of the good and of the evil of the things understood, to the greater wounding of the spirit; wherefore now, every touch that the understanding shall give to the memory will be as a touch of a red-hot iron, or like a draught of scalding lead poured down the throat. The memory also letteth these things down upon the conscience with no less terror and perplexity. And now the fancy or imagination doth start and stare like a man by fears bereft of wits, and doth exercise itself, or rather is exercised by the hand of revenging justice, so about the breadth and depth of present and future punishments, as to lay the soul as on a burning rack. Now also the judgment, as with a mighty maul, driveth down the soul in the sense and pangs of everlasting misery, into that pit that has no bottom; yea, it turneth again, and, as with a hammer it riveteth every fearful thought and apprehension of the soul so fast that it can never be loosed again for ever and ever. Alas! now the conscience can sleep, be dull, be misled, or flatter, no longer : no, it must now cry out; understanding will make it, memory will make it, fancy or imagination will make it. Now, I say, it will cry out of sin, of justice, and of the terribleness of the punishment that hath swallowed him up that has lost himself. Here will be no forgetfulness, yet nothing shall be thought on but that which will wound and kill; here will be no time, cause, or means for diversion; all will stick and gnaw like a viper. Now the memory will go out to where sin was heretofore committed, it will also go out to the word that did forbid it. The understanding also, and the judgment too, will now consider of the pretended necessity that the man had to break the commandments of God and of the seasonableness of the cautions and of the convictions which were given him to forbear, by all which more load will be laid upon him that has lost himself; for here all the powers, senses, and passions of the soul must be made self-burners, self-tormentors, self-executioners, by the just judgment of God; also all that the will shall do in this place shall be but to wish for ease, but the wish shall only be such as shall only seem to lift up, for the cable rope of despair shall with violence pull him down again. The will indeed will wish for ease, and so will the mind, &c., but all these wishers will by wishing arrive to no more advantage but to make despair, which is the most twinging stripe of hell, to cut yet deeper into the whole soul of him that has lost himself; wherefore, after all that can be wished for, they return again to their burning chair, where they sit and bewail their misery. Thus will all the powers, senses, and passions of the soul of him that has lost himself be out of his own power to dispose for his advantage, and will be only in the hand and under the management of the revenging justice of God. And herein will that state of the damned be worse than it is now with the fallen angels; for though the fallen angels are now cast down to hell, in chains, and sure in themselves at last to partake of eternal judgment, yet at present they are not so bound up as the damned sinners shall be; for notwithstanding their chains, and their being the prisoners of the horrible hells, yet they have a kind of liberty granted them, and that liberty will last till the time appointed, to tempt, to plot, to contrive, and invent their mischiefs against the Son of God and his. (Job i. 7; ii. 2.) And though Satan knows that this at last will work for his future condemnation, yet at present he finds it some diversion to his trembling mind, and obtains, through his being so busily employing of himself against the gospel and its professors, something to sport and refresh himself withal; yea, and doth procure to himself some small crumbs of minutes of forgetfulness of his own present misery, and of the judgment that is yet to pass upon him; but this privilege will then be denied to him that has lost himself; there will be no cause nor matter for diversion; there it will, as in the old world, rain day and night, fire and brimstone from the Lord out of heaven upon them. (Rev. xiv. 10, 11.) Misery is fixed, the worm will be always sucking at, and gnawing of, their soul; also, as I have said afore, all the powers, senses, and passions of the soul will throw their darts inwards, yea, of God will be made to do it to the utter, unspeakable, and endless torment of him that has lost himself. Again,

3. All, therefore, that he that has lost himself can do, is to sit down by the loss. Do I say he can do this? Oh! if that could be, it would be to such a mercy; I must, therefore, here correct myself: that they cannot do; for to sit down by the loss implies a patient enduring; but there will be no such grace as patience in hell with him that has lost himself; here will also want a bottom for patience, to wit, the providence of God; for a providence of God, though never so dismal, is a bottom for patience to the afflicted; but men go not to hell by providence, but by sin. Now, sin being the cause, other effects are wrought; for they that go to hell, and that there miserably perish, shall never say it was God by his providence that brought them hither, and so shall not have that on which to lean and stay themselves.

They shall justify God, and lay the fault upon themselves, concluding that it was sin with which their souls did voluntarily work, yea, which their souls did suck in as sweet milk, that is the cause of this their torment. Now this will work after another manner, and will produce quite another thing than patience, or a patient enduring of their torment; for their seeing that they are not only lost, but have lost themselves, and that against the ordinary means that of God was provided to prevent that loss; yea, when they shall see what a base thing sin is, how that it is the very worst of things, and that which also makes all things bad, and that for the sake of that they have lost themselves, this will make them fret, and gnash, and gnaw with anger themselves; this will set all the passions of the soul, save love, (for that I think will be stark dead,) all in a rage, all in a self-tormenting fire. You know there is nothing that will sooner put a man into, and manage his rage against himself, than will a full conviction in his conscience, that by his own folly, and that against caution, and counsel, and reason to the contrary, he hath brought himself into extreme distress and misery. But how much more will it make this fire burn, when he shall see all this is come upon him for a toy, for a bauble, for a thing that is worse than nothing!

Why, this is the case with him that has lost himself; and therefore he cannot sit down by the loss, cannot be at quiet under the sense of his loss. For sharply and wonderful piercingly, considering the loss of himself, and the cause thereof, which is sin, he falls to a tearing of himself in pieces with thoughts as hot as the coals of juniper, and to a gnashing upon himself for this; also the divine wisdom and justice of God helpeth on this self-tormentor in his self-tormenting work, by holding the justice of the law against which he has offended, and the unreasonableness of such offence, continually before his face. For if, to an enlightened man who is in the door of hope, the sight of all past evil practices will work in him "vexation of spirit," to see what fools we were, (Eccles. i. 14,) how can it but be to them that go to hell a vexation, only to understand the report, the report that God did give them of sin, of his grace, of hell, and of everlasting damnation, and yet that they should be such fools to go thither. (Isa. xxviii. 19.) But to pursue this head no further, I will come now to the next thing.

Secondly, As the loss of the soul is, in the nature of the loss, a loss peculiar to itself, so the loss of the soul is a double loss; it is, I say, a loss that is double, lost both by man and God: man has lost it, and by that loss has lost himself; God has lost it, and by that loss it is cast away. And to make this a little plainer unto you: I suppose it will be readily granted that men do lose their souls; but now how doth God lose it? The soul is God's as well as man's: man's because it is of themselves; God's because it is his creature: God has made us this soul, and hence it is that all souls are his. (Jer. xxxviii. 16. Ezek. xviii. 4.)

Now the loss of the soul doth not only stand in the sin of man, but in the justice of God. Hence he says, "What is a man advantaged if he gain the whole world, and lose himself, or be cast away." (Luke ix. 25.) Now this last clause, "or be cast away," is not spoken to show what he that has lost his soul has done, though a man may also be said to cast away himself; but to show what God will do to those who have lost themselves, what God will add to that loss. God will not cast away a righteous man, (Job viii. 20,) but God will cast away the wicked, (Matt. xiii. 50,) such a wicked one as by the text is under our consideration. This, then, is that which God will add, and so make the sad state of them that lose themselves double. The man for sin has lost himself, and God by justice will cast him away; according to that of Abigail to David, "The soul of my Lord," said she, "shall be bound in the bundle of life with the Lord thy God; and the souls of thine enemies, them shall he sling out, as out of the midst of a sling." (1 Sam. xxv. 29.) So that here is God's hand as well as man's; man's by sin, and God's by justice. "God shall cast them away;" wherefore in the text above-mentioned he doth not say, or cast away himself, as meaning the act of the man whose soul is lost; but, "or be cast away;" supposing a second person joining with the man himself in the making up of the greatness of the loss of the soul, to wit, God himself, who will verily cast away that man who has lost himself. God shall cast them away; that is, exclude them his favour or protection, and deliver them up to the due reward of their deeds! He shall shut them out of his heaven, and deliver them up to their hell; he shall deny them a share in his glory, and shall leave them to their own shame; he shall deny them a portion in his peace, and shall deliver them up to the torments of the devil, and of their own guilty consciences; he shall cast them out of his affection, pity, and compassion, and shall leave them to the flames that they by sin have kindled, and to the worm, or biting cockatrice, that they themselves have hatched, nursed, and nourished in their bosoms. And this will make their loss double, and so a loss that is loss to the uttermost, a loss above every loss. A man may cast away himself, and not be cast away of God; a man may be cast away by others, and not be cast away of God; yea, what way soever a man be cast away, if he be not cast away for sin, he is safe, he is yet sound, and in a sure hand. But for a man so to lose himself, as by that loss to provoke God to cast him away too, this is fearful!

The casting away, then, mentioned in Luke, is a casting away by the hand of God, by the revenging hand of God; and it supposeth two things, 1. God's abhorrence of such a soul. 2. God's just repaying of it for its wickedness, by way of retaliation.

1. It supposeth God's abhorrence of the soul. That which we abhor, that we cast from us, and put out of our favour and respect with disdain, and a loathing thereof. So, when God teacheth Israel to loathe and abhor their idols, he bids them "to cast away their very covering as a stinking and menstruous cloth, and to say unto it, Get you hence." (Isa. xxx. 22.) "He shall gather the good into vessels, and cast the bad away." (Matt. xiii. 48; xxv. 41.) Cast them out of my presence. Well, but whither must they go? The answer is, Into hell, into utter darkness, into the fire that is prepared for the devil and his angels. Wherefore, to be cast away of God, it showeth unto us God's abhorrence of such souls, and how vile and loathsome such are in his divine eyes. And the similitude of Abigail's sling, mentioned before, doth yet further show us the greatness of this abhorrence. "The souls of thine enemies," said she, "God shall sling out as out of the middle of a sling." When a man casts a stone away with a sling, then he casteth it farthest from him, for with a sling he can cast a stone farther than by his hand: "And he," saith the text, "shall cast them away as with a sling." But that is not all, neither; for it is not only said, that he shall sling away their souls, but that he shall sling them away as "out of the middle of a sling." When a stone is placed to be cast away, just in the middle of a sling, then doth the slinger cast it furthest of all. Now, God is the slinger, abhorrence is his sling, the lost soul is the stone, and it is placed in the very middle of the sling, and is from thence cast away. And therefore it is said again, that "such shall go into utter, outer darkness," that is, furthest off of all. This, therefore, shows us how God abhors that man that for sin has lost himself. And well he may: for such an one has not only polluted and defiled himself with sin, (and that is the most offensive thing to God under heaven,) but he has abused the handiwork of God. The soul, as I said before, is the workmanship of God, yea, the top-piece that he hath made in all the visible world; also he made it for to be delighted with it, and to admit it into communion with himself. Now for man thus to abuse God; for a man to take his soul, which is God's,

and prostrate it to sin, to the world, to the devil, and every beastly lust, flat against the command of God, and notwithstanding the soul was also his: this is horrible, and calls aloud upon that God, whose soul this is, to abhor, and to show, by all means possible, his abhorrence of such an one.

2. As this casting of them away supposeth God's abhorrence of them, so it supposeth God's just repaying of them for their wickedness by way of retaliation.

God all the time of the exercise of his long-suffering and forbearance towards them, did call upon them, wait upon them, send after them by his messengers, to turn them from their evil ways; but they despised at, they mocked, the messengers of the Lord. Also they shut their eyes, and would not see; they stopped their ears, and would not understand; and did harden themselves against the beseeching of their God. (Hos. xi. 2.) Yea, all that day long he did stretch out his hand towards them, but they chose to be a rebellious and gainsaying people; yea, they said unto God, "Depart from us;" and "what is the Almighty" that we should pray unto him? (Rev. xvi. 21. Job xxi. 14, 15. Mal. iii. 14.)

And of all these things God takes notice, writes them down, and seals them up for the time to come, and will bring them out and spread them before them, saying, I have called, and you have refused; I have stretched out mine hand, and no man regarded; I have exercised patience and gentleness, and long-suffering towards you, and in all that time you despised me, and cast me behind your back; and now the time, and the exercise of my patience, when I waited upon you, and suffered your manners, and did bear your contempts and scorns, is at an end; wherefore I will now arise, and come forth to the judgment that I have appointed.

But, Lord, saith the sinner, we turn now.

But now, saith God, turning is out of season; the day of my patience is ended.

But, Lord, says the sinner, behold our cries.

But you did not, says God, behold nor regard my cries.

But, Lord, saith the sinner, let our beseeching find place in thy compassions.

But, saith God, I also beseeched, and I was not heard.

But, Lord, saith the sinner, our sins lie hard upon us.

But I offered you pardon when time was, saith God, and then you did utterly reject it.

But, Lord, says the sinner, let us therefore have it now.

But now the door is shut, saith God.

And what then? Why, then, by way of retaliation, God will serve them as they have served him; and so the wind-up of the whole will be this, they shall have like for like. Time was when they would have none of him, and now will God have none of them. Time was when they

cast God behind their back, and now he will cast away their soul. Time was when they would not heed his calls, and now he will not heed their cries. Time was when they abhorred him, and now his soul also loatheth them. (Zech. xi. 8.) This is now by way of retaliation, like for like, scorn for scorn, repulse for repulse, contempt for contempt; according to that which is written, "Therefore it is come to pass, that as he cried, and they would not hear; so they cried, and I would not hear, saith the Lord." (Zech. vii. 13.) And thus I have also showed you that the loss of the soul is double—lost by man, lost by God.

But oh! who thinks of this? who, I say, that now makes light of God, of his Word, his servants and ways, once dreams of such retaliation, though God to warn them hath even, in the day of his patience, threatened to do it in the day of his wrath, saying, "Because I called, and ye refused; I have stretched out my hand, and no man regarded; but ye have set at nought all my counsel, and would none of my reproof: I also will laugh at your calamity, I will mock when your fear cometh; when your fear cometh as desolation, and your destruction cometh as a whirlwind; when distress and anguish cometh upon you. Then shall they call upon me, but I will not answer; they shall seek me early, but they shall not find me." (Ps. i. 24—28.) I will do unto them as they have done unto me; and what unrighteousness is in all this? But,

Thirdly, As the loss of the soul is a loss peculiar to itself, and a loss double, so, in the third place, it is a loss most fearful, because it is a loss attended with the most heavy curse of God. This is manifest both in the giving of the rule of life, and also in, and at the time of execution for, the breach of that rule. It is manifest at the giving of the rule, "Cursed be he that confirmeth not all the words of this law to do them. And all the people shall say, Amen." (Deut. xxvii. 26. Gal. iii. 10.) It is also manifest that it shall be so at the time of execution: "Depart from me, ye cursed, into everlasting fire, prepared for the devil and his angels." (Matt. xxv. 41.) What this curse is, none do know so well as God that giveth it, and as the fallen angels, and the spirit of damned men that are now shut up in the prison of hell, and bear it. But certainly it is the chief and highest of all kind of curses. To be cursed in the basket and in the the store, in the womb and in the barn, in my cattle and in my body, are but flea-bitings to this, though they are also insupportable in themselves; only in general it may be described thus. But to touch upon this curse, it lieth in a deprivation of all good, and in a being swallowed up of all the the most fearful miseries that a holy, and just, and eternal God can righteously inflict, or lay upon the soul of a sinful man. Now let reason here come in, and exercise itself in the most exquisite manner; yea, let him now count up all, and all manner of curses and torments that a reasonable and an immortal soul is, or can be made capable of, and able to suffer under, and when he has done, he shall come infinitely short of this great anathema, this master curse which God has reserved amongst his treasuries, and intends to bring out in that day of battle and war, which he purposeth to make upon damned souls in that day. And this God will do, partly as a retaliation, as the former, and partly by way of revenge. 1. By way of retaliation : " As he loved cursing, so let it come unto him : as he delighted not in blessing, so let it be far from him." Again, " As he clothed himself with cursing like as with his garment, so let it come into his bowels like water, and like oil into his bones. Let it be unto him as the garment which covereth him, and for a girdle wherewith he is girded continually," (Ps. cix. 17—19.) " Let this," saith Christ, " be the reward of mine adversaries from the Lord," &c. 2. As this curse comes by way of retaliation, so it cometh by way of revenge. God will right the wrongs that sinners have done him, will repay vengeance for the despite and reproach wherewith they have affronted him, and will revenge the quarrel of his covenant. And the beginning of revenges are terrible, what, then, will the whole execution be, when he shall come in flaming fire, taking vengeance on them that know not God, and that obey not the gospel of Jesus Christ ? And, therefore, this curse is executed in wrath, in jealousy, in anger, in fury ; yea, the heavens and the earth shall be burned up with the fire of that jealousy in which the great God will come, when he cometh to curse the souls of sinners, and when he cometh to defy the ungodly. (2 Thess. i. 7—9.)

It is little thought of, but the manner of the coming of God to judge the world declares what the souls of impenitent sinners must look for then. It is common among men, when we see the form of a man's countenance changed, when we see fire sparkle out of his eyes, when we read rage and fury in every cast of his face, even before he says aught, or doth aught either, to conclude that some fearful thing is now to be done. (Dan. iii. 19—23.) Why, it is said of Christ when he cometh to judgment, that the heavens and the earth fly away, (as not being able to endure his looks,) (Rev. xx. 11, 12 ;) that his angels are clad in flaming fire, and that the elements melt with fervent heat; and all this is, that the perdition of ungodly men might be completed, from the presence of the Lord, in the heat of his anger, from the glory of his power. (2 Pet. iii. 7. 2 Thess. i. 8, 9.) Therefore, God will now be revenged, and so ease himself of his enemies, when he shall cause curses like millstones to fall as thick as hail on " the hairy scalp of such a one as goeth on still in his trespasses." (Ps. lxviii. 21.) But,

Fourthly, As the loss of the soul is a loss peculiar to itself, a loss double, and a loss most fearful, so it is a loss everlasting. The soul that is lost is never to be found again, never to be recovered again, never to be redeemed again. Its banishment from God is everlasting; the fire in which it burns, and by which it must be tormented, is a fire that is ever, everlasting fire, everlasting burnings ; the adder, the snake, the stinging-worm, dieth not, nor is the fire quenched; and this is a fearful thing. A man may endure to touch the fire with a short touch, and away, but to dwell with everlasting burnings, that is fearful. Oh, then, what is dwelling with them, and in them, for ever and ever ! We use to say, light burdens far carried are heavy; what, then, will it be to bear that burden, that guilt, that the law and the justice and wrath of God will lay upon the lost soul for ever ? Now tell the stars, now tell the drops of the sea, and now tell the blades of grass that are spread upon the face of all the earth, if thou canst ; and yet sooner mayest thou do this than count the thousands of millions of thousands of years that a damned soul shall lie in hell. Suppose every star that is now in the firmament was to burn, by himself, one by one, a thousand years apiece, would it not be a long while before the last of them was burned out ? and yet sooner might that be done than the damned soul be at the end of punishment.

There are three things couched under this last head that will fill up the punishment of a sinner. 1. The first is, that it is everlasting. 2. The second is, that, therefore, it will be impossible for the souls in hell ever to say, Now we are got half way through our sorrows. 3. The third is, and yet every moment they shall endure eternal punishment.

1. The first I have touched upon already, and, therefore, shall not enlarge ; only I would ask the wanton or unthinking sinner, whether twenty, or thirty, or forty years of the deceitful pleasures of sin is so rich a prize, as that a man may well venture the ruins that everlasting burnings will make upon his soul for the obtaining of them, and living a few moments in them. Sinner, consider this before I go any further, or before thou readest one line more. If thou hast a soul, it concerns thee ; if there be a hell, it concerns thee ; and if there be a God that can and will punish the soul for sin everlastingly in hell, it concerns thee ; because,

2. In the second place, it will be impossible for the damned soul ever to say, I am now got half way through my sorrows. That which has no end, has no middle. Sinner, make a round circle, or ring, upon the ground, of what bigness thou wilt ; this done, go thy way upon that circle, or ring, until thou comest to the end thereof; but that, sayest thou, I can never do, because it has no end. I answer, but thou mayest as soon do that, as wade half way through the lake of fire that is prepared for impenitent souls. Sinner, what wilt thou take to make a mountain of sand that will reach as high as the sun is at noon ? I know thou wilt not be engaged in such a work,

because it is impossible thou shouldst ever perform it. But I dare say the task is greater when the sinner has let out himself to sin for a servant, because the wages is everlasting burnings. I know thou mayest perform thy service, but the wages, the judgment, the punishment is so endless, that thou, when thou hast been in it more millions of years than can be numbered, art not, nor never yet shalt be, able to say, I am half way through it. And yet,

3. That soul shall partake of (every moment) that punishment that is eternal. "Even as Sodom and Gomorrah, and the cities about them in like manner, giving themselves over to fornication, and going after strange flesh, are set forth for an example, suffering the vengeance of eternal fire." (Jude vii.)

(1.) They shall endure eternal punishment in the nature of punishment. There is no punishment here wherewith one man can chastise another that can deserve a greater title than that of transient, or temporary punishment; but the punishment there is eternal, even in every stripe that is given, and in every moment that it grappleth with the soul; even every twinge, every gripe, and every stroke that justice inflicteth, leaveth anguish that, in the nature of punishment, is eternal behind it. It is eternal, because it comes from God, and lasts for ever and ever. The justice that inflicts it has not a beginning, and it is this justice in the operations of it that is always dealing with the soul.

(2.) All the workings of the soul under this punishment are such as cause it, in its sufferings, to endure that which is eternal. It can have no thought of the end of punishment, but it is presently recalled by the decreed gulf that bindeth them under perpetual punishment. The great fixed gulf, they know, will keep them in their present place, and not suffer them to go to heaven. (Luke xvi. 26.) And now there is no other place but heaven or hell to be in; for then the earth, and the works that are therein, will be burned up. Read the text, " But the day of the Lord will come as a thief in the night; in the which the heavens shall pass away with a great noise, and the elements shall melt with fervent heat; the earth also, and the works that are therein, shall be burnt up." (2 Pet. iii. 10.) If, then, there will be no third place, it standeth in their minds, as well as in God's decree, that their punishments will be eternal: so, then, sorrows, anguish, tribulation, grief, woe, and pain, will, in every moment of its abiding upon the soul, not only flow from thoughts of what has been, and what is, but also from what will be, and that for ever and ever. Thus every thought that is truly grounded in the cause and nature of their state will roll, toss, and tumble them up and down in the cogitations and fearful apprehensions of the lastingness of their damnation. For, I say, their minds, their memories, their understandings, and consciences, will all, and always, be swallowed up with for ever: yea, they themselves will, by the means of these things, be their own tormentors for ever.

(3.) There will not be spaces, as days, months, years, and the like, as now; though we make bold so to speak, the better to present our thoughts to each other's capacities; for then there shall be time no longer; also, day and night shall then be come to an end. "He hath compassed the waters with bounds, until the day and night come to an end;" (Job xxvi. 10;) until the end of light with darkness. Now, when time, and day, and night, are come to an end, then there comes in eternity, as there was before the day, and night, or time, was created; and when this is come, punishment nor glory must none of them be measured by days, or months, or years, but by eternity itself. Nor shall those concerned either in misery or glory reckon of their new state as they used to reckon of things in this world; but they shall be suited in their capacities, in their understandings and apprehensions, to judge and count of their condition, according as will best stand with their state in eternity.

Could we but come to an understanding of things done in heaven and hell, as we understand how things are done in this world, we should be strangely amazed to see how the change of places and of conditions has made a change in the understandings of men, and in the manner of their enjoyment of things. But this we must let alone till the next world, and until our launching into it; and then, whether we be of the right or left hand ones, we shall know the state and condition of both kingdoms. In the meantime, let us addict ourselves to the belief of the Scriptures of truth, for therein is revealed the way to that of eternal life, and how to escape the damnation of the soul. (Matt. xxv. 33.) But thus much for the loss of the soul, unto which let me add, for a conclusion, these verses following:

These cry, alas! but all in vain;
   They stick fast in the mire;
They would be rid of present pain,
   Yet set themselves on fire.

Darkness is their perplexity,
   Yet do they hate the light;
They always see their misery,
   Yet are themselves all night.

They are all dead, yet live they do,
   Yet neither live nor die;
They die to weal, and live to woe—
   This is their misery.

Now will confusion so possess
   These monuments of ire,
And so confound them with distress,
   And trouble their desire,

That what to think, or what to do,
   Or where to lay their head,
They know not: 'tis the damned's woe
   To live, and yet be dead.

These castaways would fain have life,
   But know they never shall;
They would forget their dreadful plight,
   But that sticks fast'st of all.

God, Christ, and heav'n, they know are best,
Yet dare not on them think;
They know the saints enjoy their rest,
While they their tears do drink.

Fourth, And now I come to the fourth thing, that is, to show you the cause of the loss of the soul. That men have souls, that souls are great things, that souls may be lost, this I have showed you already; wherefore I now proceed to show you the cause of this loss. The cause is laid down in the 18th chapter of Ezekiel, in these words, "Behold all souls," says God, "are mine; as the soul of the father, so also the soul of the son is mine; the soul that sinneth, it shall die." (ver. 4.)

First. It is sin, then, or sinning against God, that is the cause of dying, of damning in hell-fire, for that must be meant by dying; otherwise, to die, according to our ordinary acceptation of the notion, the soul is not capable of, it being indeed immortal, as hath been afore asserted. So, then, the soul that sinneth—that is, and persevering in the same—that soul shall die, be cast away, or damned; yea, to ascertain us of the undoubted truth of this, the Holy Ghost doth repeat it again, and that in this very chapter, saying, "The soul that sinneth, it shall die." (ver. 20.) Now, the soul may divers ways be said to sin against God; as,

1. In its receiving of sin into its bosom, and in its retaining and entertaining it there. Sin must first be received before it can act in, or be acted by, the soul. Our first parents first received it in the suggest, or motion, and then acted it. Now, it is not here to be disputed when sin was received by the soul, so much as whether ever the soul received sin; for if the soul has indeed received sin into itself, then it has sinned, and by doing so, has made itself an object of the wrath of God, and a firebrand of hell. I say, I will not here dispute when sin was received by the soul, but it is apparent enough that it received it betimes, because in old time every child that was brought unto the Lord was to be redeemed, and that at a month old, (Ex. xiii. 13; xxxiv. 20; Numb. xviii. 15, 16;) which, to be sure, was very early, and implied that then, even then, the soul in God's judgment stood before him as defiled and polluted with sin. But although I said I will not dispute at what time the soul may be said to receive sin, yet it is evident that it was precedent to the redemption made mention of just before, and so before the person redeemed had attained to the age of a month. And that God might, in the language of Moses, give us to see cause of the necessity of this redemption, he first distinguisheth, and saith, "The firstling of a cow, or the firstling of a sheep, or the firstling of a goat," did not need this redemption, for they were clean, or holy. But the firstborn of men, who was taken in lieu of the rest of the children, and the "firstling of unclean beasts, thou shalt surely redeem," saith he. But why was the firstborn of men coupled with unclean beasts, but because

they were both unclean? But how? I answer, The beast was unclean by God's ordination, but the other was unclean by sin. Now, then, it will be demanded, how a soul, before it was a month old, could receive sin to the making of itself unclean? I answer, there are two ways of receiving, one active, the other passive; this last is the way by which the soul at first receiveth sin, and by so receiving, becometh culpable, because polluted and defiled by it. And this passive way of receiving is often mentioned in scripture. Thus the pans received the ashes; (Ex. xxvii. 3;) thus the molten sea received three thousand baths; (2 Chron. iv. 5;) thus the ground receiveth the seed; (Matt. xiii. 20—22;) and this receiving is like that of the wool which receiveth the dye, either black, white, or red; and as the fire that receiveth the water till it be all quenched therewith; or as the water receiveth such stinking and poisonous matter into it, as for the sake of it, it is poured out and spilt upon the ground. But whence should the soul thus receive sin? I answer, from the body, while it is in the mother's belly, (Ps. li. 5;) the body comes from polluted man, and therefore is polluted. "Who can bring a clean thing out of an unclean." (Job xiv. 4.) The soul comes from God's hand, and therefore, as so, is pure and clean; but being put into this body, it is tainted, polluted, and defiled with the taint, stench, and filth of sin; nor can this stench and filth be by man purged out, when once from the body got into the soul; sooner may the blackamoor change his skin, or the leopard his spots, than the soul, were it willing, might purge itself of this pollution. "Though thou wash thee with nitre, and take thee much soap, yet thine iniquity is marked before me, saith the Lord God." (Jer. ii. 22.)

2. But as I said, the soul has not only received sin, but retains it, holds it, and shows no kind of resistance. It is enough that the soul is polluted and defiled, for that is sufficient to provoke God to cast it away; for which of you would take a cloth annoyed with stinking, ulcerous sores, to wipe your mouth withal, or to thrust it into your bosoms? and the soul is polluted with far worse pollution than any such can be. But this is not all; it retains sin as the wool retains the dye, or as the infected water receives the stench or poisonous scent. I say, it retains it willingly; for all the power of the soul is not only captivated by a seizure of sin upon the soul, but it willingly, heartily, unanimously, universally falleth in with the natural filth and pollution that is in sin, to the estranging of itself from God, and an obtaining of an intimacy and compliance with the devil.

Now this being the state and condition of the soul from the belly, yea, from before it sees the light of this world, what can be concluded, but that God is offended with it? For how can it otherwise be, since there is holiness and justice in God? Hence those that are born of a woman, whose original is by carnal conception with man, are said to be as serpents so soon as born: "The wicked," and all at first are so, "go astray as soon as they be born, speaking lies. Their poison is like the poison of a serpent: they are like the deaf adder that stoppeth her ear." (Ps. lviii. 3, 4.) They go astray from the belly; but that they would not do if aught of the powers of their soul was unpolluted. "But their poison is like the poison of a serpent." Their poison, what is that? Their pollution, their original pollution, that is as the poison of a serpent; to wit, not only deadly, for so poison is, but hereditary. It comes from the old one, from the sire and dam; yea, it is also now become connatural to and with them, and is of the same date with the child as born into the world. The serpent has not her poison in the original of it, either from imitation or from other infective things abroad, though it may by such things be helped forward and increased; but she brings it with her in her bowels, in her nature, and it is to her as suitable in her present condition as is that which is most sweet and wholesome to other of the creatures. So, then, every soul comes into the world as poisoned with sin; nay, as such which have poison connatural to them; for it has not only received sin, as the wool has received the dye, but it retaineth it. The infection is got so deep, it has taken the black so effectually, that the fire, the very fire from hell, can never purge the soul therefrom.

And that the soul has received this infection thus early, and that it retains it so surely, is not only signified by children coming into the world besmeared in their mothers' blood, and by the firstborn being redeemed at a month old, but also by the first inclinations and actions of children when they are so come into the world. (Ezek. xvi.) Who sees not that lying, pride, disobedience to parents, and hypocrisy, do put forth themselves in children before they know that they do either well or ill in so doing, or before they are capable to learn either of these arts by imitation, or seeing understandingly the same thing done first by others? He that sees not that they do it naturally from a principle, from an inherent principle, is either blinded, and has retained his darkness by the same sin as they, or has suffered himself to be swayed by a delusion from him who at first infused this spawn of sin into man's nature.

Nor doth the averseness of children to morality a little demonstrate what has been said; for as it would make a serpent sick, should one give it a strong antidote against his poison, so then are children, and never more than then, disturbed in their minds, when a strict hand and a stiff rein by moral discipline is maintained over and upon them. True, sometimes restraining grace corrects them, but that is not of themselves; but more oft hypocrisy is the great and first moving wheel to all their seeming compliances and admonitions, which indulgent parents are apt to overlook; yea, and sometimes, through unadvisedness, to commit for the principles of grace. I speak now of that which comes before conversion. But as I said before, I would not now dispute, only I have thought good thus to urge these things to make my assertion manifest, and to show what is the cause of the damnation of the soul.

3. Again; as the soul receives sin, and retains it, so it also doth entertain it; that is, countenance, smile upon, and like its complexion and nature well. A man may detain—that is, hold fast—a thing which yet he doth not regard; but when he entertains, then he countenances, likes, and delights in the company. Sin, then, is first received by the soul, as has been afore explained, and by that reception is polluted and defiled. This makes it hateful in the eyes of justice; it is now polluted. Then, secondly, this sin is not only received, but retained; that is, it sticks so fast, abides so fixedly in the soul, that it cannot be gotten out; this is the cause of the continuation of abhorrence: for if God abhors, because there is a being of sin there, it must needs be that he should continue to abhor, since sin continues to have a being there. But then, in the third place, sin is not only received, detained, but entertained by the now defiled and polluted soul; wherefore this must needs be a cause of the continuance of anger, and that with aggravation. When I say, entertained, I do not mean as men entertain their enemies, with small and great shot; but as they entertain those whom they like, and those that have got into their affections. And therefore the wrath of God must certainly be let out upon the soul, to the everlasting damnation of it.

Now that the soul doth thus entertain sin, is manifest by these several particulars:—

1. It hath admitted it with complacence and delight into every chamber of the soul; I mean, it has been delightfully admitted to an entertainment by all the powers or faculties of the soul. The soul hath chose it rather than God; it also, at God's command refuseth to let it go; yea, it chooseth that doctrine, and loveth it best, since it must have a doctrine that has most of sin and baseness in it. (Isa. lxv. 12; lxvi. 3.) They "say to the seers, See not; and to the prophets, Prophesy not unto us right things, speak unto us smooth things, prophesy deceits." (Isa. xxx. 10.) These are signs that the soul with liking hath entertained sin; and if there be any time, as indeed there is, a warrant issued out from the mouth of God to apprehend, to condemn, and mortify sin, why then,

2. These shifts the souls of sinners do presently make for the saving of sin from those things that by the Word men are commanded to do unto it:—

(1.) They will, if possible, hide it, and not suffer it to be discovered, "He that hideth his sins shall not prosper." (Prov. xxviii. 13.) And again, they hide it, and refuse to let it go. (Job xx. 12, 13.)

This is an evident sign that the soul has a savour for sin, and that with liking it, entertains it.

(2.) As it will hide it, so it will excuse it, and plead that this and that piece of wickedness is no such evil thing; men need not be so nice, and make such a pother about it; calling those that cry out so hotly against it, men more nice than wise: hence the prophets of old used to be called madmen; and the world would reply against their doctrine. Wherein have we been so wearisome to God, and what have we spoken so much against him? (Mal. i. 6, 7; iii. 8, 13.)

(3.) As the soul will do this, so to save sin, it will cover it with names of virtue, either moral or civil; and of this God greatly complains, yea, breaks out into anger for this, saying, "Woe unto them that call evil good, and good evil; that put darkness for light, and light for darkness; and put bitter for sweet, and sweet for bitter." (Isa. v. 20.)

(4.) If convictions and discovery of sin be so strong and so plain, that the soul cannot deny but that it is sin, and that God is offended therewith, then it will give flattering promises to God that it will indeed put it away; but yet it will prefix a time that shall be long first; if it also then at all performs it, saying, Yet a little sleep, yet a little slumber, yet a little folding of sin in mine arms, till I am older, till I am richer, till I have had more of the sweetness and the delights of sin. Thus, "Their soul delighteth in their abominations." (Isa. lxvi. 3.)

(5.) If God yet pursues, and will see whether this promise of putting sin out of doors shall be fulfilled by the soul, why then it will be partial in God's law; it will put away some, and keep some; put away the grossest and keep the finest; put away those that can best be spared, and keep the most profitable for a help at a pinch. (Mal. ii. 9.)

(6.) Yea, if all sin must be abandoned, or the soul shall have no rest, why then the soul and sin will part, (with such a parting as it is,) even as Phaltiel parted with David's wife, with an ill will and a sorrowful mind; or as Orpha left her mother, with a kiss. (2 Sam. iii. 16. Ruth i. 14.)

(7.) And if at any time they can, or shall meet with each other again, and nobody never the wiser, oh what courting shall be betwixt sin and the soul! And this is called doing of things in the dark. (Ezek. viii. 12.)

By all these, and many more things that might be instanced, it is manifest that sin has a friendly entertainment by the soul, and that therefore the soul is guilty of damnation; for what do all these things argue, but that God, his Word, his ways, and graces, are out of favour with the soul, and that sin and Satan are its only pleasant companions? But,

Secondly, That I may yet show you what a great thing sin is with the soul that is to be damned, I will show how sin, by the help of the soul, is managed from the motion of sin, even till it comes to the very act; for sin cannot come to an act without the help of the soul. The body doth little here, as I shall further show you anon.

There is then a motion of sin presented to the soul, (and whether presented by sin itself, or the devil, we will not at this time dispute;) motions of sin, and motions to sin there are, and always the end of the motions of sin are to prevail with the soul to help that motion into an act. But, I say, there is a motion to sin moved to the soul; or, as James calls it, a conception. Now behold how the soul deals with this motion, in order to the finishing of sin, that death might follow. (Rom. vii. 5.)

1. This motion is taken notice of by the soul, but is not resisted or striven against, only the soul lifts up its eyes upon it, and sees that there is present a motion to sin, a motion of sin presented to the soul, that the soul might midwife it from the conception into the world.

2. Well, notice being taken that a motion to sin is present, what follows but that the fancy or imagination of the soul taketh it home to it, and doth not only look upon it and behold it more narrowly, but begins to trick and trim up the sin to the pleasing of itself and of all the powers of the soul. That this is true, is evident, because God findeth fault with the imagination as with that which lendeth to sin the first hand, and that giveth it the first lift towards its being helped forward to act. "And God saw that the wickedness of man was great in the earth," (Gen. vi. 5, 12, 13;) that is, many abominable actions were done; for all flesh had corrupted God's way upon the earth. But how came this to be so? Why, every imagination of the thoughts, or of the motions that were in the heart to sin, was evil, only evil, and that continually. The imagination of the thoughts was evil; that is, such as tended not to deaden or stifle, but such as tended to animate and forward the motions or thoughts of sin into action. Every imagination of the thoughts; that which is here called a thought, is by Paul to the Romans called a motion. Now the imagination should, and would, had it been on God's side, so have conceived of this motion of and to sins, as to have presented it in all its features so ugly, so ill favoured, and so unreasonable a thing to the soul, that the soul should forthwith have let down the sluice, and pulled up the drawbridge, put a stop, with greatest defiance, to the motion now under consideration; but the imagination being defiled, it presently, at the very first view or noise of the motion of sin, so acted as to forward the bringing the said motion or thought into act. So, then, the thought of sin, or motion thereto, is first of all entertained by the imagination and fancy of the soul, and thence conveyed to the rest of the powers of the soul to be condemned, if the imagination be good; but to be helped forward to act, if the

N 2

imagination be evil. And thus the evil imagination helpeth the motion of, and to, sin towards the act, even by dressing of it up in that guise and habit that may best delude the understanding, judgment, and conscience; and that is done after this manner: suppose a motion of sin to commit fornication, to swear, to steal, to act covetously, or the like, be propounded to the fancy and imagination; the imagination, if evil, presently dresseth up this motion in that garb that best suiteth with the nature of the sin. As, if the lust of uncleanness, then is the motion to sin dressed up in all imaginable pleasurableness of that sin; if to covetousness, then is the sin drest up in the profits and honours that attend that sin; and so of theft and the like; but if the motion be to swear, hector, or the like, then is that motion dressed up with valour and manliness; and so you may count of the rest of sinful motions; and thus being trimmed up like a Bartholomew baby, it is presented to all the rest of the powers of the soul, where with joint consent it is admired and embraced, to the firing and inflaming of all the powers of the soul.

And hence it is that men are said to inflame themselves with their idols under every green tree, (Isa. lvii. 5;) "and to be as fed horses, neighing after their neighbour's wife," (Jer. v. 8:) for the imagination is such a forcible power, that if it putteth forth itself to dress up and present a thing to the soul, whether that thing be evil or good, the rest of the faculties cannot withstand it. Therefore, when David prayed for the children of Israel, he said, "I have seen with joy thy people, which are present here, to offer willingly unto thee;" that is, for preparations to build the temple. "O Lord God," saith he, "keep this for ever in the imagination of the thoughts of the heart of thy people, and prepare their hearts unto thee." (1 Chron. xxix. 18.) He knew that as the imagination was prepared, so would the soul be moved, whether by evil or good; therefore, as to this he prays that their imagination might be engaged always with apprehensions of the beauteousness of the temple, that they might always, as now, offer willingly for its building.

But, as I said, when the imagination hath thus set forth sin to the rest of the faculties of the soul, they are presently entangled, and fall into a flame of love thereto: this being done, it follows that a purpose to pursue this motion, till it be brought unto act, is the next thing that is resolved on. Thus Esau, after he had conceived of that profit that would accrue to him by murdering of his brother, fell the next way into a resolve to spill Jacob's blood. And Rebecca sent for Jacob, and said unto him, "Behold, thy brother Esau, as touching thee, doth comfort himself, purposing to kill thee." (Gen. xxvii. 42. Jer. xlix. 30.) Nor is this purpose to do an evil without its fruit, for he comforted himself in his evil purpose: "Esau, as touching thee, doth comfort himself, purposing to kill thee."

The purpose, therefore, being concluded, in the next place the invention is diligently set to work to find out what means, methods, and ways, will be thought best to bring this purpose into practice, and this motion to sin into action. Esau invented the death of his brother when his father was to be carried to his grave. (Gen. xxvii. 42.) David purposed to make Uriah father his bastard child by making of him drunk. (2 Sam. xi. 13.) Amnon purposed to ravish Tamar, and the means that he invented to do it were by feigning himself sick. Absalom purposed to kill Amnon, and invented to do it at a feast. (2 Sam. xiii. 32.) Judas purposed to sell Christ, and invented to betray him in the absence of the people. (Luke xxii. 3—6.) The Jews purposed to kill Paul, and invented to entreat the judge of a blandation to send for him, that they might murder him as he went. (Acts xxiii. 12—15.)

Thus you see how sin is, in the motion of it, handed through the soul; first, it comes into the fancy or imagination, by which it is so presented to the soul, as to inflame it with desire to bring it into act; so from this desire the soul proceedeth to a purpose of enjoying, and from a purpose of enjoying to inventing how, or by what means, it had best to attempt the accomplishing of it.

But, further, when the soul has thus far, by its wickedness, pursued the motion of sin to bring it into action, then to the last thing—to wit, to endeavours, to take the opportunity, which, by the invention, is judged most convenient; so to endeavours it goes, till it has finished sin, and finished, in finishing of that, its own fearful damnation. "Then when lust hath conceived, it bringeth forth sin; and sin, when it is finished, bringeth forth death." (James i. 15.)

And who knows, but God and the soul, how many lets, hindrances, convictions, fears, frights, misgivings, and thoughts of the judgment of God, all this while are passing and repassing, turning and returning, over the face of the soul? how many times the soul is made to start, look back, and tremble, while it is pursuing the pleasure, profit, applause, or preferment that sin, when finished, promiseth to yield unto the soul? for God is such a lover of the soul, that he seldom lets it go on in sin, but he cries to it by his Word and providences, "Oh, do not this abominable thing that I hate!" (Jer. xliv. 4;) especially at first, until it shall have hardened itself, and so provoked him to give it up in sin-revenging judgment to its own ways and doings, which is the terriblest judgment under heaven; and this brings me to the third thing, the which I now will speak to.

3. As the soul receives, detains, entertains, and wilily worketh to bring sin from the motion into act, so it abhorreth to be controlled and taken off of this work: "My soul loathed them," says God, "and their soul also abhorred me." (Zech. xi. 8.) My soul loathed them, because they were so bad; and their souls abhorred me, because I am so good.

Sin, then, is the cause of the loss of the soul; because it hath set the soul, or rather, because the soul of love to sin hath set itself against God. "Woe unto their soul, for they have rewarded evil unto themselves." (Isa. iii. 9.)

Thirdly, That you may the better perceive that the soul, through sin, has set itself against God, I will propose, and speak briefly to, these two things :—I. The law. II. The gospel.

I. *For the law.* God has given it for a rule of life, either as written in their natures, or as inserted in the holy Scriptures ; I say, for a rule of life to all the children of men. But what have men done, or how have they carried it to this law of their Creator ? let us see, and that from the mouth of God himself. 1. "They have not hearkened unto my law." (Jer. vi. 19.) 2. "They have forsaken my law." (Jer. ix. 13.) 3. "They have forsaken me, and not kept my law." (Jer. xvi. 11.) 4. "They have not walked in my law, nor in my statutes." (Jer. xliv. 4.) 5. "Her priests have violated my law." (Ezek. xxii. 26.) 6. And saith God, "I have written to him the great things of my law, but they were counted as a strange-thing." (Hos. viii. 12.)

Now, whence should all this disobedience arise? Not from the unreasonableness of the commandment, but from the opposition that is lodged in the soul against God, and the enmity that it entertains against goodness. Hence the apostle speaks of the enmity, and says, that men are enemies in their minds, their souls, as is manifest by wicked works, (Col. i. 21.) This, if men went no further, must needs be highly provoking to a just and holy God ; yea, so highly offensive is it, that, to show the heat of his anger, he saith, " Indignation and wrath, tribulation and anguish, upon every soul of man that doth evil," and this is evil with a witness, " of the Jew first, and also of the Gentiles," that doth evil, (Rom. ii. 8, 9:) that breaketh the law, for that evil he is crying out against now. But,

II. *To speak of the gospel,* and of the carriage of sinful souls toward God under that dispensation.

The gospel is a revelation of a sovereign remedy, provided by God, through Christ, for the health and salvation of those that have made themselves objects of wrath by the breach of the law of works ; this is manifest by all the Scripture. But how doth the soul carry it towards God, when he offereth to deal with it under and by this dispensation of grace ? Why, just as it carried it under the law of works ; they oppose, they contradict, they blaspheme, and forbid that this gospel be mentioned. (Acts xiii. 45 ; xvii. 6.) What higher affront or contempt can be offered to God, and what greater disdain can be shown against the gospel ? (2 Tim. ii. 25. 1 Thess. ii. 4—16.) Yet all this the poor soul, to its own wrong, offereth against the way of its own salvation ; as it is said in the Word of truth, ".He that sinneth against me wrongeth his own soul ; all that hate me love death." (Prov. viii. 36.)

But, further, the soul despiseth not the gospel in that revelation of it only, but the great and chief bringer thereof, with the manner, also, of his bringing of it. The Bringer, the great Bringer of the gospel, is the good Lord Jesus Christ himself ; he came and preached peace to them that the law proclaimed war against ; he " came and preached peace to them that were far off, and to them that were nigh." (Eph. ii. 17.) And it is worth your observation to take notice how he came, and that was, and still is, as he is set forth in the word of the gospel, to wit, first, as making peace himself to God for us in and by the blood of his cross ; and then as bearing (as set out by the gospel) the very characters of his sufferings before our faces in every tender of the gospel of his grace unto us. And to touch a little upon the dress in which, by the gospel, Christ presenteth himself unto us, while he offereth unto sinful souls his peace, by the tenders thereof.

1. He is set forth as born for us, to save our souls. (Isa. ix. 6. Luke ii. 9—12.) 2. He is set forth before us as bearing of our sins for us, and suffering God's wrath for us. (1 Cor. xv. 3. Gal. iii. 13.) 3. He is set forth before us as fulfilling the law for us, and as bringing of everlasting righteousness to us for our covering. (Rom. x. 4. Dan. ix. 24.)

Again, as to the manner of his working out the salvation of sinners for them, that they might have peace and joy, and heaven and glory, for ever. 1. He is set forth as sweating of blood while he was in his agony, wrestling with the thoughts of death, which he was to suffer for our sins, that he might save the soul. (Luke xxii. 44.) 2. He is set forth as crying, weeping, and mourning under the lashes of justice that he put himself under, and was willing to bear for our sins. (Heb. iii. 7.) 3. He is set forth as betrayed, apprehended, condemned, spit on, scourged, buffeted, mocked, crowned with thorns, crucified, pierced with nails and a spear, to save the soul from being betrayed by the devil and sin ; to save it from being apprehended by justice, and condemned by the law ; to save it from being spit on in a way of contempt by holiness ; to save it from being scourged with guilt of sins, as with scorpions ; to save it from being continually buffeted by its own conscience ; to save it from being mocked at by God ; to save it from being crowned with ignominy and shame for ever ; to save it from dying the second death ; to save it from wounds and grief for ever.

Dost thou understand me, sinful soul? He wrestled with justice, that thou mightest have rest ; he wept and mourned, that thou mightest laugh and rejoice ; he was betrayed, that thou mightest go free ; was apprehended, that thou mightest escape ; he was condemned, that thou mightest be justified ; and was killed, that thou mightest live ; he wore a crown of thorns, that thou mightest wear a crown of glory ; and was nailed to the cross, with his arms wide open, to show with what freeness all his merits shall be bestowed on the coming soul, and how heartily he will receive it into his bosom.

Further, all this he did of mere good will, and offereth the benefit thereof unto thee freely; yea, he cometh unto thee, in the word of the gospel, with the blood running down from his head upon his face, with his tears abiding upon his cheeks, with his holes as fresh in his hands and his feet, and as with the blood still bubbling out of his side, to pray thee to accept of the benefit, and to be reconciled to God thereby. (2 Cor. v.) But what saith the sinful soul to this? I do not ask what he saith with his lips, for he will assuredly flatter God with his mouth; but what doth his actions and carriages declare as to his acceptance of this incomparable benefit? For "a wicked man speaketh with his feet, and teacheth with his fingers." (Prov. vi. 12, 13.) With his feet—that is, by the way he goeth; and with his fingers—that is, by his acts and doings. So, then, what saith he by his goings, by his acts and doings, unto his incomparable benefit, thus brought unto him from the Father, by his only Son Jesus Christ? What saith he? Why, he saith, that he doth not at all regard this Christ, nor value the grace thus tendered unto him in the gospel.

1. He saith, that he regardeth not this Christ, that he seeth nothing in him why he should admit him to be entertained in his affections. Therefore the prophet, speaking in the person of sinners, says, "He (Christ) hath no form nor comeliness, and when we shall see him, there is no beauty that we should desire him;" and then adds, to show what he meaneth by his thus speaking, saying, "He is despised and rejected of men." (Isa. liii. 2, 3.) All this is spoken with reference to his person, and it was eminently fulfilled upon him in the days of his flesh, when he was hated, maligned, and persecuted to death, by sinners: and is still fulfilled in the souls of sinners, in that they cannot abide to think of him what thoughts that have a tendency in them to separate them and their lusts asunder, and to the making of them to embrace him for their darling, and the taking up of their cross to follow him. All this sinners speak out with loud voices, in that they stop their ears and shut their eyes as to him, but open them wide and hearken diligently to anything that pleaseth the flesh, and that is a nursery to sin. But,

2. As they despise, and reject, and do not regard his person, so they do not value the grace that he tendereth unto them by the gospel; this is plain by that indifferency of spirit that always attends them when, at any time, they hear thereof, or when it is presented unto them.

I may safely say, that the most of men who are concerned in a trade, will be more vigilant in dealing with a twelvepenny customer than they will be with Christ when he comes to make unto them, by the gospel, a tender of the incomparable

grace of God. Hence they are called fools, because a price is put into their hands to get wisdom, and they have no heart unto it. (Prov. xvii. 16.) And hence, again, it is, that that bitter complaint is made, "But my people would not hearken to my voice; and Israel would none of me." (Ps. lxxxi. 11.) Now, these things being found, as practised by the souls of sinners, must needs, after a wonderful manner, provoke; wherefore, no marvel that the heavens are bid to be astonished at this, and that damnation shall seize upon the soul for this. (Jer. ii.)

And, indeed, the soul that doth thus by practice, though with his mouth, (as who doth not?) he shall show much love, he doth, interpretatively, say these things:—

1. That he loveth sin better than grace, and darkness better than light, even as our Lord Jesus Christ hath showed: "And this is the condemnation, that light is come into the world, and men loved darkness more than light (as is manifest) because their deeds were evil." (John iii. 19.)

2. They do, also, by their thus rejecting of Christ and grace, say, that for what the law can do to them, they value it not; they regard not its thundering, threatenings, nor will they shrink when they come to endure the execution thereof; wherefore God, to deter them from such bold and desperate ways, that do, interpretatively, fully declare that they make such desperate conclusions, insinuates that the burden of the curse thereof is intolerable, saying, "Can thy heart endure, or can thy hands be strong, in the days that I shall deal with thee? I, the Lord, have spoken it, I will do it." (Ezek. xxii. 14.)

3. Yea, by their thus doing, they do as good as say that they will run the hazard of a sentence of death at the day of judgment, and that they will, in the meantime, join issue, and stand a trial at that day with the great and terrible God. What else means their not hearkening to him, their despising of his Son, and the rejecting of his grace; yea, I say again, what else means their slighting of the curse of the law, and their choosing to abide in their sins till the day of death and judgment? And thus I have showed you the causes of the loss of the soul; and, assuredly, these things are no fables.

Objection. But some may object, and say, But you denounce all against the soul, as if the body were in no fault at all; or, as if there were no punishment assigned for the body.

Answer 1. The soul must be the part punished, because the soul is that which sins. "Every sin that a man doeth is without the body;" fornication or adultery excepted. (1 Cor. vi. 18.) "Is without the body;" that is, as to the wilily inventing, contriving, and finding out ways to bring the motions of sin into action. For, alas! what can the body do as to these? It is in a manner wholly passive; yea, altogether as to the lusting and purposing to do the wickedness, excepting the sin before excepted; ay, and not excepting that, as to the rise of that sin; for even that, with all the rest, ariseth and proceedeth out of the heart, the soul: " For from within, out of the heart of men, proceed evil thoughts, adulteries, fornications, murders, thefts, covetousness, wickedness, deceit, lasciviousness, an evil eye, blasphemy, pride, foolishness: all these evil things come from within, and defile the man :" (Mark vii. 21—23 ;) that is, the outward man. But a difference must always be put betwixt defiling and being defiled, that which defileth being the worst; not but that the body shall have its share of judgment, for body and soul must be destroyed in hell, (Luke xii. 4, 5. Matt. x. 28;) the body as the instrument, the soul as the actor; but oh ! the soul, the soul, the soul is the sinner; and, therefore, the soul, as the principal, must be punished.

And that God's indignation burneth most against the soul appears in that death hath seized upon every soul already; for the Scripture saith, that every natural or unconverted man is dead. (Eph. ii. 1—3.) Dead! How? Is his body dead? No, verily; his body liveth, but his soul is dead. (1 Tim. v. 6.) Dead! But with what death? Dead to God, and to all things gospelly good, by reason of that benumbing, stupefying, and senselessness, that, by God's just judgment for and by sin, hath swallowed up the soul. Yea, if you observe, you shall see, that the soul goeth first, or before, in punishment, not only by what has been said already, in that the soul is first made a partaker of death, but in that God first deals with the soul by convictions, yea, and terrors, perhaps, while the body is well; or, in that he giveth up the soul to judicial hardness and further blindness, while he leaveth the body to do his office in the world; yea, and also when the day of death and dissolution is come, the body is spared, while the soul is tormented in unutterable torment in hell. And, so I say, it shall be spared, and the clods of the valley shall be sweet unto it, while the soul mourneth in hell for sin. It is true, at the day of judgment, because that is the last and final judgment of God on men, then the body and soul shall be re-united, or joined together again, and shall then, together, partake of that recompense for their wickedness which is meet. When I say, the body is spared, and the soul tormented, I mean not that the body is not then, at death, made to partake of the wages of sin, " For the wages of sin is death," (Rom. vi. 23 ;) but I mean the body partakes then but of temporal death, which, as to sense and feeling, is sometimes over presently, and then resteth in the grave, while the soul is tormenting in hell. Yea, and why is death suffered to stay the body ? I dare say, not chiefly for that the indignation of God most burneth against the body; but the body being the house for the soul in this world, God even pulls down this body, that the soul may be stript naked; and being stript, may be carried to prison, to the place where damned souls are, there to suffer in the beginning of suffering, that punishment that will be endless.

Ans. 2. Therefore, the soul must be the part most sorely punished, because justice must be distributed with equity. God is a God of knowledge and judgment ; by him actions are weighed; actions in order to judgment. (1 Sam. ii.) Now, by weighing of actions, since he finds the soul to have the deepest hand in sin, and he says that he hath so, of equity the soul is to bear the burden of punishment: " Shall not the Judge of all the earth do right," in his famous distributing of judgment? (Gen. xviii. 25.) " He will not lay upon man more than right, that he should enter into judgment with God." (Job. xxxiv. 23.) The soul, since deepest in sin, shall also be deepest in punishment. " Shall one man sin," said Moses, " and wilt thou be wrath with all the congregation?" (Numb. xvi. 22.) He pleads here for equity in God's distributing of judgment ; yea, and so exact is God in the distribution thereof, that he will not punish heathens so as he will punish Jews ; wherefore he saith, " Of the Jew first," or chiefly, " and also of the Gentile." (Rom. ii. 9.) Yea, in hell he has prepared several degrees of punishment for the several sorts or degrees of offenders: and some " shall receive greater damnation." (Luke xx. 47.) And will it not be unmeet for us to think, since God is so exact in all his doings, that he will, without his weights and measures, give to soul and body, as I may say, carelessly, not severally, their punishments, according to the desert and merit of each ?

Ans. 3. The punishment of the soul in hell must needs, to be sure, as to degree, differ from the punishment of the body there. When I say, differ, I mean, must needs be greater, whether the body be punished with the same fire with the soul, or fire of another nature. If it be punished with the same fire, yet not in the same way ; for the fire of guilt, with the apprehensions of indignation and wrath, are most properly felt and apprehended by the soul, and by the body by virtue of its union with the soul; and so felt by the body, if not only, yet, I think, mostly, by way of sympathy with the soul; and the cause, we say, is worse than the disease; and if the wrath of God, and the apprehensions of it, as discharging itself for sin, and the breach of the law, be that with which the soul is punished, as sure it is; then the body is punished by the effects, or by those influences that the soul, in its torments, has upon the body, by virtue of the great oneness and union that is between them.

But if there be a punishment prepared for the body distinct in kind from that which is prepared for the soul, yet it must be a punishment inferior to that which is prepared for the soul; not that the soul and body shall be severed, but being made of things distinct, their punishments will be by that which is most suitable to each. I say, it must be inferior, because nothing can be so hot, so tormenting, so intolerably unsupportable, as the quickest apprehensions of, and the immediate sinking under, that guilt and indignation that is proportionable to the offence. Should all the wood, and brimstone, and combustible matter on earth be gathered together for the tormenting of one body, yet that cannot yield that torment to that which the sense of guilt and burning-hot application of the mighty indignation of God will do to the soul; yea, suppose the fire wherewith the body is tormented in hell should be seven times hotter than any of our fire; yea, suppose it, again, to be seven times hotter than that which is seven times hotter than ours, yet it must, suppose it be but created fire, be infinitely short, as to tormenting operations, of the unspeakable wrath of God, when in the heat thereof he applieth it to, and doth punish, the soul for sin in hell therewith. So, then, whether the body be tormented with the same fire wherewith the soul is tormented, or whether the fire be of another kind, yet it is not possible that it should bear the same punishment as to degree, because, or for the causes that I have showed. Nor, indeed, is it meet it should, because the body has not sinned so, so grievously as the soul has done; and God proportioneth the punishment suitable to the offence.

Ans. 4. With the soul by itself are the most quick and suitable apprehensions of God and his wrath; wherefore, that must needs be made partaker of the sorest punishment in hell; it is the soul that is now most subtle at discerning, and it is the soul that will be so; then conscience, memory, understanding, and mind, these will be the seat of torment, since the understanding will let wrath immediately upon these, from what it apprehends of that wrath: conscience will let in the wrath of God immediately upon these, from what it fearfully feels of that wrath; the memory will then, as a vessel, receive and retain up to the brim of this wrath, even as it receiveth by the understanding and conscience the cause of this wrath, and considers of the durableness of it: so, then, the soul is the seat and the receiver of wrath, even as it was the receiver and seat of sin; here, then, is sin and wrath upon the soul, the soul in the body, and so soul and body tormented in hell fire.

Ans. 5. The soul will be most tormented, because strongest; the biggest burden must lie upon the strongest part, especially since, also, it is made capable of it by its sin. The soul must bear its own punishment, and a great part of the body's too, forasmuch as, so far as apprehension goes, the soul will be quicker at that work than the body. The body will have its punishment to lie most in feeling, but the soul in feeling and apprehending both. True, the body, by the help of the soul, will see too, but the soul will see yet abundantly further. And good reason that the soul should bear part of the punishment of the body, because it was through its allurements that the body yielded to help the soul to sin. The devil presented sin, the soul took it by the body, and now devil, and soul, and body, and all must be lost, cast away; that is, damned in hell for sin; but the soul must be the burden-bearer.

Objection. But you may say, Doth not this give encouragement to sinners to give away to the body to be in all its members loose, and vain, and wicked, as instruments to sin?

Answer. No; forasmuch as the body shall also have his share in punishment. For though I have said, the soul shall have more punishment than the body, yet I have not said that the body shall at all be eased by that; no, the body will have its due. And for the better making out of my answer further, consider of these following particulars :—

1. The body will be the vessel to hold a tormented soul in; this will be something; therefore, man, damned man, is called a vessel of wrath, a vessel, and that in both body and soul. (Rom. ix. 22.) The soul receiveth wrath into itself, and the body holdeth that soul that has thus received, and is tormented with, this wrath of God. Now, the body being a vessel to hold this soul that is thus possessed with the wrath of God, must needs itself be afflicted and tormented with that torment, because of its union with the body; therefore the Holy Ghost saith, " His flesh upon him shall have pain, and his soul within him shall mourn." (Job xiv. 22.) Both shall have their torment and misery, for that both joined hand in hand in sin, the soul to bring it to the birth, and the body to midwife it into the world; therefore it saith again, with reference to the body, let the curse " come into his bowels like water, and like oil into his bones. Let it be unto him as a garment which covereth him, and for a girdle," &c. (Ps. cix. 17—19.) The body, then, will be tormented as well as the soul, by being a vessel to hold that soul in, that is now possessed and distressed with the unspeakable wrath and indignation of the Almighty God, and this will be a great deal, if you consider,

2. That the body, as a body, will, by reason of its union with the soul, be as sensible, and so as capable in its kind, to receive correction and torment as ever, nay, I think more; for if the quickness of the soul giveth quickness of sense to the body, as in some case, at least, I am apt to think it doth, then forasmuch as the soul will now be most quick, most sharp in apprehension, so the body, by reason of union and sympathy with the soul, will be most quick, and most sharp as to sense. Indeed, if the body should not receive and retain sense, yea, all its senses, by reason of its being a vessel to hold the soul, the torment of the soul could not, as torment, be ministered to the body, no more than the fire' tormented the King of Babylon's furnace, (Dan. iii. ;) or than the King of Moab's limekiln was afflicted, because the King of Elom's bones were burnt to lime

therein. (Amos ii. 1.) But now the body has received again its senses, now therefore it must, yea, it cannot choose but must feel that wrath of God that is let out, yea, poured out like floods of water into the soul. Remember also, that besides what the body receiveth from the soul by reason of its union and sympathy therewith, there is a punishment, and instruments of punishment, though I will not pretend to tell you exactly what it is, prepared for the body for its joining with the soul in sin, therewith to be punished; a punishment, I say, that shall fall immediately upon the body, and that such an one, as will most fitly suit with the nature of the body, as wrath and guilt do most fitly suit the nature of the soul.

3. Add to these, the durable condition that the body in this state is now in with the soul. Time was when the soul died, and the body lived, and that the soul was tormented while the body slept and rested in the dust; but now these things are past; for at the day of judgment, as I said, these two shall be re-united, and that which once did separate them, be destroyed; then of necessity they must abide together, and, as together, abide the punishment prepared for them; and this will greaten the torment of the body.

Death was once the wages of sin, and a grievous curse; but might the damned meet with it in hell, they would count it a mercy, because it would separate soul and body, and not only so, but take away all sense from the body, and make it incapable of suffering torment; yea, I will add, and by that means give the soul some ease; for without doubt, as the torments of the soul extend themselves to the body, so the torments of the body extend themselves to the soul; nor can it be otherwise, because of union and sympathy. But death, natural death, shall be destroyed, and there shall be no more natural death, no, not in hell. (1 Cor. xv. 26.) And now it shall happen to men, as it hath done in less and inferior judgments, " They shall seek death, and desire to die, and death shall not be found by them." (Job ix. 21. Rev. ix. 6.) Thus, therefore, they must abide together; death that used to separate them asunder is now slain—1. Because it was an enemy in keeping Christ's body in the grave; and 2. Because a friend to carnal men in that, though it was a punishment in itself, yet while it lasted and had dominion over the body of the wicked, it hindered them of that great and just judgment, which for sin was due unto them; and this is the third discovery of the manner and way of punishing of the body. But,

4. There will then be such things to be seen and heard, which the eye and the ear (to say no more than has been said of the sense of feeling) will see and hear, that will greatly aggravate the punishment of the body in hell: for though the eye is the window, and the ear a door for the soul to look out at, and also to receive in by, yet whatever goeth in at the ear, or the eye, leaves influence upon the body, whether it be that which the soul delighteth in, or that which the soul abhorreth, for as the eye affecteth the heart, or soul, (Lam. iii. 51,) so the eye and ear, by hearing and beholding, both ofttimes afflict the body. " When I heard, my belly trembled, rottenness entered into my bones." (Hab. iii. 16.)

Now, I say, as the body after the resurrection, to damnation, to everlasting shame and contempt, (Dan. xii. 2. John v. 29,) will receive all its senses again, so it will have matter to exercise them upon, not only to the letting into the soul those aggravations which they by hearing, feeling, and seeing, are capable to let in thither, but, I say, they will have matter and things to exercise themselves upon for the helping forward of the torment of the body. Under temporal judgments of old, the body as well as the soul had no ease, day nor night, and that not only by reason of what was felt, but by reason of what was heard and seen. " In the morning thou shalt say, Would God it were even! and at even thou shalt say, Would God it were morning!" (Deut. xxviii. 67.) 1. " For the fear of thine heart, wherewith thou shalt fear." 2. " And for the sight of thine eyes, which thou shalt see." Nay, he tells them a little before, that they should be mad for the sight of their eyes which they should see. (Deut. xxviii. 34.)

See! why, what shall they see? Why, themselves in hell, with others like them; and this will be a torment to their body. There is bodily torment, as I said, ministered to the body by the senses of the body. What think you? If a man saw himself in prison, in irons, upon the ladder, with the rope about his neck, would not this be distress to the body, as well as to the mind? To the body, doubtless. Witness the heavy looks, the shaking legs, trembling knees, pale face, and beating and aching heart; how much more, then, when men shall see themselves in the most dreadful place; it is a fearful place, doubtless, to all to behold themselves in that shall come thither. (Luke xvi. 28.)

Again; They shall see others there, and shall by them see themselves. There is an art by which a man may make his neighbour look so ghastly, that he shall fright himself by looking on him, especially when he thinks of himself, that he is of the same show also. It is said concerning men at the downfall of Babylon, that they shall be amazed one at another, for " their faces shall be as flames." (Isa. xiii. 8.) And what if one should say, that even as it is with an house set on fire within, where the flame ascends out at the chimneys, out at the windows, and the smoke out at every chink and crevice that I can find, so it will be with the damned in hell. That soul will breathe hell-fire and smoke, and coals will seem to hang upon its burning lips; yea, the face, eyes, and ears will seem all to be chimneys and vents for the flame and smoke of the burning which God by his breath hath kindled therein, and upon them, which will be beheld one in another, to the great torment and distress of each other.

What shall I say? Here will be seen devils, and here will be heard howlings and mournings; here will the soul see itself at an infinite distance from God; yea, the body will see it too. In a word, who knows the power of God's wrath, the weight of sin, the torments of hell, and the length of eternity? If none, then none can tell, when they have said what they can, the intolerableness of the torments that will swallow up the soul, the lost soul, when it is cast away by God, and from him, into outer darkness for sin. But thus much for the cause of the loss of the soul.

DOCTRINE SECOND.

I now come to the second doctrine that I gathered from the words, namely, that how unconcerned and careless soever some now be about the loss or salvation of their souls, the day is coming, but it will then be too late, when men will be willing, had they never so much, to give it all in exchange for their souls. There are four things in the words that do prove this doctrine.

1. There is an intimation of life and sense in the man that has lost, and that after he has lost, his soul in hell. "Or what shall a man give in exchange for his soul?" These words are by no means applicable to the man that has no life or sense; for he that is dead according to our common acceptation of death, that is, deprived of life and sense, would not give twopence to change his state; therefore the words do intimate that the man is yet alive and sensible. Now, were a man alive and sensible, though he was in none other place than the grave, there to be confined, while others are at liberty, what would he give in exchange for his place, and to be rid of that for a better! but how much more to be delivered from hell, the present place and state of his soul!

2. There is in the text an intimation of a sense of torment: "Or what shall a man give in exchange for his soul?" I am tormented in this flame. Torment, then, the soul is sensible of, and that there is a place of ease and peace. And from the sense and feeling of torment, he would give, yea, what would he not give in exchange for his soul?

3. There is in the text an intimation of the intolerableness of the torment, because that it supposeth that the man whose soul is swallowed up therewith would give all, were his all never so great, in exchange for his soul.

4. There is yet in the text an intimation that the soul is sensible of the lastingness of the punishment, or else the question rather argues a man unwary than considerate in his offering, as is supposed by Christ, so largely, his all in exchange for his soul.

But we will, in this manner, proceed no further, but take it for granted that the doctrine is good;

wherefore I shall next inquire after what is contained in this truth. And,

First, That God has undertaken, and will accomplish, the breaking of the spirits of all the world, either by his grace and mercy to salvation, or by his justice and severity to damnation.

The damned soul under consideration is certainly supposed, as by the doctrine, so by the text, to be utterly careless, and without regard of salvation, so long as the acceptable time did last, and as the white flag, that signifies terms of peace, did hang out; and, therefore, it is said to be lost; but, behold, now it is careful, but now it is solicitous, but now, "What shall a man give in exchange for his soul?" He of whom you read in the gospel, that could tend to do nothing in the days of the gospel, but to find out how to be clothed in purple and fine linen, and to fare sumptuously every day, was by God brought so down, and laid so low at last, that he could crouch, and cringe, and beg for one small drop of water to cool his tongue—a thing that but a little before he would have thought scorn to have done, when he also thought scorn to stoop to the grace and mercy of the gospel. (Luke xvi. 19, 24.) But God was resolved to break his spirit, and the pride of his heart, and to humble his lofty looks, if not by his mercy, yet by his justice; if not by his grace, yet by hell-fire.

This he also threatens to bring upon the fool in the Proverbs: "They shall call, they shall seek, they shall cry." (Prov. i. 22—32.) Who shall do so? the answer is, They that sometimes scorned either to seek, or call, or cry; they that stopped their ears, that pulled away their shoulders, and that refused to seek, or call, or cry to God for mercy. (Zech. vii. 11—13.)

Sinner, careless sinner, didst thou take notice of this first inference that I have drawn from my second doctrine? If thou didst, yet read it again; it is this, "God has undertaken, and will accomplish, the breaking of the spirits of all the world, either by his grace and mercy unto salvation, or by his justice and severity to damnation." The reason for this is this, God is resolved to have the mystery, he is resolved to have the victory. "Who will set the briers and thorns against me in battle? I would go through them, I would burn them together." (Isa. xxvii. 4.) I will march against them. God is merciful, and is come forth into the world by his Son, tendering of grace unto sinners by the gospel, and would willingly make a conquest over them for their good by his mercy. Now he being come out, sinners, like briers and thorns, do set themselves against him, and will have none of his mercy. Well, but what says God? Saith he, Then I will march on: I will go through them, and burn them together. I am resolved to have the mastery one way or another; if they will not bend to me, and accept of my mercy in the gospel, I will bend them and break them by my justice in hell-fire. They say they will not bend; I say they shall; now they "shall know whose words shall stand, mine or theirs." (Jer. xliv. 25—28.) Wherefore the Apostle, when he saw that some of the Corinthians began to be unruly, and to do those things that did begin to hazard them, saith, "Do we provoke the Lord to jealousy? are we stronger than he?" (1 Cor. x. 22.) As who should say, My brethren, are you aware what you do? do you not understand that God is resolved to have the mastery one way or another? and are you stronger than he? If not, tremble before him, or he will certainly have you under his feet: "I will tread them in mine anger, and trample them in my fury." (Isa. lxiii. 3.) Thus he speaks of them that set themselves against him; therefore, beware. Now, the reason of this resolution of God, it flows from a determination in him to make all his sayings good, and to verify them on the consciences of sinners. And since the incredulous world will not believe now, and fly from wrath, they shall shortly believe and cry under it; since they will not now credit the Word, before they see, unto salvation, they shall be made to credit it by sense and feeling unto damnation.

Second, The second inference that I draw from my second doctrine is this, "That it is, and will be the lot of some to bow and break before God, too late, or when it is too late."

God is resolved, as I said, to have the mastery, and that not only in a way of dominion and lordship in general, for that he has now; but he is resolved to master, that is, to break the spirit of the world, to make all men crouch and cringe unto him, even those that now say, "There is no God," (Ps. xiv. 1;) or if there be, yet, "What is the Almighty, that we should serve him?" (Job xxi. 15. Mal. iii. 14.)

This is little thought of by those that now harden their hearts in wickedness, and that turn their spirit against God; but this they shall think of, this they must think of, this God will make them think of, in that day, at which day they also now do mock and deride, that the Scripture might be fulfilled upon them. (2 Pet. iii. 3, 4.) And, I say, they shall think then of those things, and break at heart, and melt under the hand, and power, and majesty of the Almighty; for, "As I live, saith the Lord, every knee shall bow to me; and every tongue shall confess to God." (Isa. xlv. 23. Rom. xiv. 11.) And again, "The nations shall see, and be confounded at all their might; they shall lay their hand upon their mouth, their ears shall be deaf. They shall lick the dust like a serpent, they shall move out of their holes like worms," or creeping things, "of the earth; they shall be afraid of the Lord our God, and shall fear because of thee." (Mic. vii. 16, 17.)

For then they, will they nill they, shall have to do with God, though not with him as merciful, or as one that may be entreated; yet with him as just, and as devouring fire, (Heb. xii. 29;) yea, they shall see that face, and hear that voice, from whom and from which the heavens and the earth will fly away, and find no place of stay. And by this appearance, and by such words of his mouth as he then will speak to them, they shall begin to tremble, and call for the rocks to fall upon them and cover them; for if these things will happen at the execution of inferior judgment, what will be done; what effects will the last, most dreadful, and eternal judgment have upon men's souls?

Hence you find, that at the very first appearance of Jesus Christ, the whole world begins to mourn and lament, "Every eye shall see him, and they also which pierced him, and all kindreds of the earth shall wail because of him." (Rev. i. 7.) And, therefore, you shall also find them to stand at the door and knock, saying, "Lord, Lord, open unto us." (Luke xiii. 25. Matt. xxv. 11.) Moreover, you find them also desiring, yea, also so humble in their desires as to be content with the least degree of mercy, one drop, one drop upon the tip of one's finger: what stooping, what condescension, what humility is here! All and every one of those passages declare, that the hand of God is upon them, and that the Almighty has got the mastery of them, has conquered them, broke the pride of their power, and laid them low, and made them cringe and crouch unto him, bending the knee, and craving of kindness.

Thus, then, will God bow, and bend, and break them; yea, make them bow and bend, and break before him. And hence also it is that they will weep, and mourn, and gnash their teeth, and cry, and repent that ever they have been so foolish, so wicked, so traitorous to their souls, and such enemies of their own eternal happiness, as to stand out in the day of their visitation in a way of rebellion against the Lord.

But here is their hard hap, their dismal lot and portion—that all these things must be when it is too late. It is, and will be the lot and hap of these to bow, bend, and break too late. (Matt. xxv.) You read, they come weeping and mourning, and with tears; they knock and cry for mercy; but what did tears avail? Why, nothing; for the door was shut. He answered and said, "I know you not whence ye are." (Luke xiii. 26, 27.) But they repeat and renew their suit, saying, "We have eaten and drunk in thy presence, and thou hast taught in our streets." What now? Why, he returns upon them his first answer the second time, saying, "I tell you, I know you not whence ye are; depart from me, all ye workers of iniquity;" then he concludes, "There shall be weeping and gnashing of teeth, when you shall see Abraham, and Isaac, and Jacob, and all the prophets, in the kingdom of God, and yourselves thrust out." (Luke xiii. 26—28.) They come weeping, and go weeping away. They came to him weeping, for they saw that he had conquered them; but they departed weeping, for they saw that he would damn them; yet, as we read in another place, they were very loth to go from him, by the reasoning and expostulating with him, "Lord, when saw we thee an hungered, or athirst, or a stranger, or naked, or sick, or in prison, and did not minister unto thee?" But all would not do; here is no place for change of mind, "These shall go away into everlasting punishment; but the righteous into life eternal." (Matt. xxv. 44—46.) And now what would a man give in exchange for his soul? So that, as I said before, all is too late; they mourn too late, they repent too late, they pray too late, and seek to make an exchange for their soul too late.

"Or what shall a man give in exchange for his soul?" Two or three things there may yet be gathered from these words; I mean, as to the desires of them that have lost their souls, to make for them an exchange. "What shall a man give in exchange?" What shall? what would? yea, what would not a man, if he had it, give in exchange for his soul?

First, What would not a man—I mean, a man in the condition that is by the text supposed some men are, and will be in—give in exchange to have another man's virtues instead of their own vices? "Let me die the death of the righteous," let my soul be in the state of the soul of the righteous, that is, with reference to his virtues, when I die, "and let my last end be like his." (Numb. xxiii. 10.) It is a sport now to some to taunt, and squib, and deride at other men's virtues; but the day is coming when their minds will be changed, and when they shall be made to count those that have done those righteous actions and duties which they have scoffed at, the only blessed men; yea, they shall wish their soul in the blessed possession of those graces and virtues, that those whom they hated were accompanied with, and would, if they had it, give a whole world for this change; but it will not now do; it is now too late. What then shall a man give in exchange for his soul? And this is more than intimated in that 25th of Matthew, named before; for you find by that text how loth they were, or will be, to be counted for unrighteous people: "Lord," say they, "when did we see thee an hungered, or athirst, naked, or sick, and did not minister unto thee?" Now they are not willing to be of the number of the wicked, though heretofore the ways of the righteous were an abomination to them. But, alas! they are before a just God, a just judge, a judge that will give every one according to their ways; therefore, "Woe unto (the soul of) the wicked! it shall be ill with him; for the reward of his hands shall be given him," (Isa. iii. 11;) thus, therefore, he is locked up as to this; he cannot now change his vices for virtues, nor put himself, or his soul, in the stead of the soul of the saved; so that it still, and will, for ever abide a question unresolved, "Or what shall a man give in exchange for his soul?" I do not doubt but that a man's state may be such in this world, that if he had it, he would give thousands of gold, to be as innocent and guiltless in the judgment of the law of the land as is the state of such or such, heartily

wishing that himself was not that he, that he is; how much more then will men wish thus when they stand ready to receive the last, their eternal judgment! "But what shall a man give in exchange for his soul?"

Second, As they would, for the salvation of their souls, be glad to change away their vices for the virtues, their sins for the good deeds of others, so what would they not give to change places now, or to remove from where now they are, into paradise, into Abraham's bosom! But neither shall this be admitted; the righteous must have their inheritance to themselves: "Neither," said Abraham, "can they pass to us, that would come from thence," (Luke xvi. 26;) neither can they dwell in heaven that would come from hell.

They, then, that have lost, or shall lose, their souls, are bound to their place, as well as to their sins. When Judas went to hell, he went to his home, "to his own place," (Acts i. 25:) and when the righteous go hence, they also go home to their house, to their own place; for the kingdom of heaven is prepared for them. (Matt. xxv. 34.) Between heaven and hell "there is a great gulf fixed," (Luke xvi. 26;) that is, a strong passage. "There is a great gulf fixed." What this gulf is, and how impassable, they that shall lose their souls will know to their woe; because it is fixed there where it is, on purpose to keep them in their tormenting place, so that they that would pass from hell to heaven cannot. But, I say, "Would they not change places? would they not have a more comfortable house and home for their souls?" Yes, verily, the text supposes it, and the 16th of Luke affirms it; yea, and could they purchase for their soul a habitation among the righteous, would they not? Yes, they would give all the world for such a change. What shall, what shall not, a man, if he had it, if it would answer his design, give in exchange for his soul?

Third, As the damned would change their own vices for virtues, and the place where they are for that into which they shall not come, so, what would they give for a change of condition? Yea, if an absolute change may not be obtained, yet what would they give for the least degree of mitigation of that torment, which now they know will without any intermission be, and that for ever and ever. "Tribulation and anguish, indignation and wrath," (Rom. ii. 8, 9,) the gnawing worm, and everlasting destruction from the presence of the Lord, and from the glory of his power, cannot be borne but with great horror and grief. (2 Thess. i. 7—10.) No marvel, then, if these poor creatures would, for ease for their souls, be glad to change their conditions. Change! with whom? with an angel, with a saint? ay, with a dog or a toad; for they mourn not, they weep not, nor do they bear indignation of wrath; they are as if they had not been; only the sinful soul abides in its sins, in the place designed for lost souls, and in the condition that wrath and indignation for sin and transgression hath decreed them to abide for ever. And this brings me to the conclusion, which is, "That seeing the ungodly do seek good things too late," therefore, notwithstanding their seeking, they must still abide in their place, their sins, and their torment; "For what can a man give in exchange for his soul?" Therefore, God saith, that they there must still abide and dwell, no exchange can be made: "This shall ye have of mine hand, ye shall lie down in sorrow;" they shall lie down in it, they shall make their bed there, there they shall lie. (Isa. l. 11. Ezek. xxxii. 25—27.) And this is the bitter pill that they must swallow down at last; for, after all their tears, their sorrows, their mournings, their repentings, their wishings and wouldings, and all their inventings, and desires to change their state for a better, they must "lie down in sorrow." The poor condemned man that is upon the ladder or scaffold has, if one knew them, many a long wish and long desire that he might come down again alive, or that his condition was as one of the spectators that are not condemned and brought thither to be executed as he. How carefully also doth he look with his failing eyes, to see if some comes not from the king with a pardon for him, all the while endeavouring to fumble away, as well as he can, and to prolong the minute of his execution! But at last, when he has looked, when he has wished, when he has desired, and done whatever he can, the blow with the axe, or turn with the ladder, is his lot, so he goes off the scaffold, so he goes from among men: and thus it will be with those that we have under consideration; when all comes to all, and they have said, and wished, and done what they can, the judgment must not be reversed—they must "lie down in sorrow."

They must, or shall lie down. Of old, when a man was to be chastised for his fault, he was to lie down to receive his stripes; so here, saith the Lord, they shall lie down: "And it shall be, if the wicked man be worthy to be beaten, the judge shall cause him to lie down, and to be beaten before his face." (Deut. xxv. 2.) And this lying down was to be his lot after he had pleaded for himself what he could; and the judge shall cause him to be beaten before his face, while he is present to behold the execution of judgment: and thus it shall be at the end of the world; the wicked shall lie down, and shall be beaten with many stripes in the presence of Christ, "and in the presence of the holy angels." (2 Thess. i. Rev. xiv. 10.) For there will be his presence, not only at the trial as judge, but to see execution done, nay, to do it himself by the pouring out, like a river, his wrath as burning brimstone upon the soul of the lost and cast away sinner.

He shall lie down. These words imply that, at last, the damned soul shall submit; for to lie down is an act that signifies submission, especially to lie down to be beaten. "The wicked shall be silent in darkness." (1 Sam. ii. 9.) When the malefactor has said and wished all that he can, yet at last he submits, is silent, and, as it were, helps to put his head into the halter, or doth lay down his neck upon the block; so here it is said of the damned, "They shall lie down in sorrow." There is also a place that saith, "These shall go away into everlasting punishment." (Matt. xxv. 46.) To go, to go to punishment, is also an act of submission. Now, submission to punishment doth, or should, flow from full conviction of the merit of punishment; and I think it is so to be understood here: for "every mouth shall be stopped, and all the world (of soul-losers) become guilty before God." (Rom. iii. 4, 19. Luke xiii. 25—28. Matt. xxv. 46.) Every mouth shall be stopped, not at the beginning of the judgment; for then they plead, and pray, and also object against the judge; but at the end, after that by a judicial proceeding he shall have justified against them his sayings, and have overcome these his judges, then they shall submit, and also lie down in sorrow; yea, they shall go away to their punishment as those who know they deserve it; yea, they shall go away with silence.

How they shall behave themselves in hell, I will not here dispute; whether in a way of rage and blasphemy, and in rending and tearing of the name and just actions of God towards them, or whether by way of submission there; I say, though this is none of this task, yet a word or two, if you please.

Doubtless, they will not be mute there; they will cry, and wail, and gnash their teeth, and perhaps, too, sometimes at God; but I do not think but that the justice they have deserved, and the equal administration of it upon them, will, for the most part, prevail with them to rend and tear themselves, to acquit and justify God, and to add fuel to their fire, by concluding themselves in all the fault, and that they have sufficiently merited this just damnation; for it would seem strange to me that just judgment among men shall terminate in this issue, if God should not justify himself in the conscience of all the damned. But as here on earth, so he will let them know that go to hell, that he hath not done without a cause, a sufficient cause, all that he hath done in damning of them. (Ezek. xiv. 23.)

I come now to make some use and application of the whole. And,

First Use.—If the soul be so excellent a thing as we have made it appear to be, and if the loss thereof be so great a loss, then here you may see who they are that are those extravagant ones; I mean, those that are such in the highest degree. Solomon tells us of "a great waster," and saith also, that he that is slothful in his business, is "brother" to such an one. (Prov. xviii. 9.) Who Solomon had his eye upon, or who it was that he counted so great a waster, I cannot tell; but I will challenge all the world to show me one, that for wasting, and destroying, may be compared to him that for the lusts and pleasures of this life will hazard the loss of his soul. Many men will be so profuse, and will spend at that prodigal rate, that they will bring a thousand pound a year to five hundred, and five hundred to fifty, and some also will bring that fifty to less than ninepence; but what is this to him that shall never leave losing until he has lost his soul? I have heard of some who would throw away a farm, a good estate, upon the trundling of one single bowl; but what is this to the casting away the soul? I say, what is this to the loss of the soul, and that for less than the trundling of a bowl? Nothing can for badness be compared to sin; it is the vile thing, it cannot have a worse name than its own; it is worse than the vilest man, than the vilest of beasts; yea, sin is worse than the devil himself, for it is sin, and sin only, that hath made the devils devils: and yet for this, for this vile, this abominable thing, some men, yea, most men, will venture the loss of their soul; yea, they will mortgage, pawn, and set their souls to sale for it. (Jer. xliv. 4.) Is not this a great waster? doth not this man deserve to be ranked among the extravagant ones? What think you of him who, when he tempted the wench to uncleanness, said to her, If thou wilt venture thy body, I will venture my soul? Was not here like to be a fine bargain, think you? or was not this man like to be a gainer by so doing? This is he that prizes sin at a higher rate than he doth his immortal soul; yea, this is he that esteems a quarter of an hour's pleasure more than he fears everlasting damnation. What shall I say? This man is minded to give more to be damned, than God requires he should give to be saved; is not this an extravagant one? "Be astonished, O ye heavens! at this, and be ye horribly afraid!" (Jer. ii. 9—12.) Yea, let all the angels stand amazed at the unaccountable prodigality of such an one.

Objection 1. But some may say, I cannot believe that God will be so severe as to cast away into hell-fire an immortal soul for a little sin.

Answer. I know thou canst not believe it, for if thou couldst, thou wouldst sooner eat fire than run this hazard; and hence all they that go down to the lake of fire are called the unbelievers; and the Lord shall cut thee, that makest this objection, asunder, and shall appoint thee thy portion with such, except thou believe the gospel, and repent. (Luke xii. 46.)

Obj. 2. But surely, though God should be so angry at the beginning, it cannot in time but grieve him to see and hear souls roaring in hell, and that for a little sin.

Ans. Whatsoever God doeth, it abideth for ever. (Eccles. iii. 14.) He doeth nothing in a passion, or in an angry fit; he proceedeth with sinners by the most perfect rules of justice; wherefore it would be injustice to deliver them whom the law condemneth; yea, he would falsify his word, if after a time he should deliver them from hell, concerning whom he hath solemnly testified, that they shall be there for ever.

Obj. 3. O but, as he is just, so he is merciful; and mercy is pitiful, and very compassionate to the afflicted.

Ans. O but mercy abused becomes most fearful in tormenting. Did you never read that the Lamb turned lion, and that the world will tremble at the wrath of the Lamb, and be afflicted more at the thoughts of that, than at the thoughts of anything that shall happen to them in the day when God shall call them to an account for their sins? (Rev. vi. 16, 17.) The time of mercy will be then past, for now is that acceptable time, behold now is the day of salvation; the gate of mercy will then be shut, and must not be opened again; for now is that gate open, now it is open for a door of hope. (2 Cor. vi. 2. Matt. xxv. 10. Luke xiii. 25.) The time of showing pity and compassion will then be at an end; for that as to acting towards sinners will last but till the glass of the world is run, and when that day is past, mark what God saith shall follow, "I will laugh at your calamity; I will mock when your fear cometh; when your fear cometh as desolation, and your destruction cometh as a whirlwind; when distress and anguish cometh upon you." (Prov. i. 26, 27.) Mark you how many pinching expressions the Lord Jesus Christ doth threaten the refusing sinner with, that refuseth him now: I will laugh at him, I will mock at him. But when, Lord, wilt thou laugh at, and mock at, the impenitent? The answer is, "I will laugh at their calamities, and mock when their fear cometh; when their fear cometh as desolation, and their destruction like a whirlwind; when distress and anguish cometh upon them."

Obj. 4. But if God Almighty be at this point, and there be no moving of him to mercy at that day, yet we can but lie in hell till we are burnt out, as the log doth at the back of the fire.

Ans. Poor besotted sinner, is this thy last shift? wilt thou comfort thyself with this? Are thy sins so dear, so sweet, so desirable, so profitable to thee, that thou wilt venture a burning in hell-fire for them till thou art burnt out? Is there nothing else to be done but to make a covenant with death, and to maintain thy agreement with hell? (Isa. xxviii. 15.) Is it not better to say now unto God, Do not condemn me? and to say now, Lord, be merciful to me, a sinner? Would not tears, and prayers, and cries, in this acceptable time, to God for mercy, yield thee more benefit in the next world than to lie and burn out in hell will do?

But to come more close to thee. Have not I told thee already that there is no such thing as a ceasing to be? that the damned shall never be burned out in hell? there shall be no more such death, or cause of dissolution for ever. This one thing, well considered, breaks not only the neck of that wild conceit on which thy foolish objection is built, but will break thy stubborn heart in pieces. For then it follows, that unless thou canst conquer God, or with ease endure to conflict with his sin-revenging wrath, thou wilt be made to mourn while under his everlasting wrath and indignation; and to know that there is not such a thing as a burning out in hell-fire.

Obj. 5. But if this must be my case, I shall have more fellows; I shall not go to hell, nor yet burn there, alone.

Ans. What, again, is there no breaking of the league that is betwixt sin and thy soul? What, resolved to be a self-murderer, a soul-murderer? what, resolved to murder thine own soul? But is there any comfort in being hanged with company? in sinking into the bottom of the sea with company? or in going to hell, in burning in hell, and in enduring the everlasting pains of hell, with company? O besotted wretch! But I tell thee, the more company, the more sorrow; the more fuel, the more fire. Hence the damned man that we read of in Luke desired that his brethren might be so warned, and prevailed with, as to be kept out of that place of torment. (Luke xvi. 27, 28.)

But to hasten; I come now to the second use.

Second Use.—Is it so? Is the soul such an excellent thing, and the loss thereof so unspeakably great? Then here you may see who are the greatest fools in the world, to wit, those who, to get the world and its preferments, will neglect God till they lose their souls. The rich man in the gospel was one of these great fools, for that he was more concerned about what he should do with his goods, than how his soul should be saved. (Luke xii. 16—21.) Some are for venturing their souls for pleasures, and some for venturing their souls for profits: they that venture their souls for pleasures have but little excuse for their doings; but they that venture their soul for profit seem to have much. "And they all with one consent began to make excuse;" excuse for what? why, for the neglect of the salvation of their souls. But what was the cause of their making this excuse? Why their profits came tumbling in. "I have bought a piece of ground;" "I have bought five yoke of oxen;" and "I have married a wife, and therefore I cannot come." (Luke xiv. 15—20.)

Thus also it was with the fool first mentioned; his ground did bring forth plentifully, wherefore, he must of necessity forget his soul, and as he thought, all the reason of the world he should. Wherefore he falls to crying out, What shall I do? Now, had one said, Mind the good of thy soul, man; the answer would have been ready, But where shall I bestow my goods? If it had been replied, Stay till harvest; he returns again, But I have no room where to bestow my goods. Now, tell him of praying, and he answers, he must go to building. Tell him he should frequent sermons, and he replies, he must mind his workmen. "He cannot deliver his soul, nor say, Is there not a lie in my right hand? (Isa. xliv. 20.)

And see if, in the end, he did not become a fool; for though he accomplished the building of his barns, and put in there all his fruits and his goods, yet even till now his soul was empty, and

void of all that was good; nor did he, in singing of that requiem which he sung to his soul at last, saying, "Soul, take thine ease, eat, drink, and be merry," show himself ever the wiser; for, in all his labours, he had rejected to get that food that indeed is meat and drink for the soul. Nay, in singing this song he did but provoke God to hasten to send to fetch his soul to hell; for so begins the conclusion of the parable, "Thou fool, this night shall thy soul be required of thee; then whose shall those things be which thou hast provided?" So that, I say, it is the greatest folly in the world for a man, upon any pretence whatever, to neglect to make good the salvation of his soul.

There are six signs of a fool, and they do all meet in that same man that concerns not himself, and that to good purpose, for the salvation of his soul. 1. "A fool has not an heart, when the price is in his hand, to get wisdom." (Prov. xvii. 16.) 2. "It is a sport to a fool to do mischief," and to set light by the commission of sin. (Prov. x. 23.) 3. "Fools despise wisdom;" "fools hate knowledge." (Prov. i. 7, 22.) 4. "A fool," after restraint, "returneth to his folly." (Prov. xxvi. 11.) 5. "The way of a fool is right in his own eyes." (Prov. xii. 15.) 6. The fool goes merrily "to the correction of the stocks." (Prov. vii. 22.)

I might add many more, but these six shall suffice at this time, by which it appears that the fool has no heart for the heavenly prize, yet he has to sport himself in sin; and when he despises wisdom, the way is yet right before him; yea, if he be for some time restrained from vice, he greedily turneth again thereto, and will, when he has finished his course of folly and sin in this world, go as heedlessly, as carelessly, as unconcernedly, and quietly, down the steps to hell, as the ox goeth to the slaughter-house. This is a soul-fool, a fool of the biggest size; and so is every one also that layeth up treasure for himself on earth, "and is not rich towards God." (Luke xii. 21.)

Objection 1. But would you not have us mind our worldly concerns?

Answer. Mind them, but mind them in their place; mind thy soul first and most; the soul is more than the body, and eternal life better than temporal; first seek the kingdom of God, and prosper in thy health and thy estate as thy soul prospers. (Matt. vi. 33. 3 John ii.) But as it is rare to see this command obeyed, for the kingdom of God shall be thought of last, so if John's wish was to light upon, or happen to some people, they would neither have health nor wealth in this world. To prosper and be in health, as their soul prospers; what, to thrive and mend in outwards no faster? then we should have them have consumptive bodies and low estates; for are not the souls of most as unthrifty, for grace and spiritual health, as is the tree without fruit, that is pulled up by the roots?

Obj. 2. But would you have us sit still and do nothing?

Ans. And must you needs be upon the extreme? must you mind this world to the damning of your souls, or will you not mind your callings at all? Is there not a middle way? may you not, must you not, get your bread in a way of honest industry; that is, caring most for the next world, and so using of this as not abusing the same? (1 Cor. vii. 29—31.) And then a man doth so, and never but then, when he sets this world and the next in their proper places, in his thoughts, in his esteem, and judgment, and dealeth with both accordingly, (2 Cor. iv. 18.) And is there not all the reason in the world for this? are not the things that are eternal best? Will temporal things make thy soul to live? or art thou none of those that should look after the salvation of their soul? (Deut. viii. 3. Matt. iv. 4. Heb. x. 39.)

Obj. 3. But the most of men do that which you forbid, and why may not we?

Ans. God says, "Thou shalt not follow a multitude to do evil." (Exod. xxiii. 2.) It is not what men do, but what God commands; it is not what doth present itself unto us, but what is best, that we should choose. (Matt. vi. 33. Luke x. 41, 42.) Now, "He that refuseth instruction, despiseth his own soul;" and "he that keepeth the commandment, keepeth his own soul." (Prov. xvi. 32; xix. 16.) Make not, therefore, these foolish objections. But what saith the Word? how readest thou? That tells thee, that the pleasures of sin are but for a season, that the things that are seen are but temporal; that he is a fool that is rich in this world, and is not so towards God; "and what shall it profit a man, if he shall gain the whole world, and lose his own soul?"

Obj. 4. But may one not be equally engaged for both?

Ans. A divided heart is a faulty one. (Hos. x. 2.) "You cannot serve God and mammon." (Matt. vi. 24. Luke xvi. 13.) "If any man love the world, the love of the Father is not in him," (1 John ii. 15.) And yet this objection bespeaks that thy heart is divided, that thou art a mammonist, or that thou lovest the world. But will riches profit in the day of wrath? (Prov. xi. 4.) Yea, are they not hurtful in the day of grace? do they not tend to surfeit the heart, and to alienate a man and his mind from things that are better? (Luke xxi. 34.) Why, then, wilt thou set thy heart upon that which is not? yea, then what will become of them that are so far off of minding of their souls, that they, for whole days, whole weeks, whole months, and years together, scarce consider whether they have souls to save?

Third Use.—But thirdly, Is it so? Is the soul such an excellent thing, and is the loss thereof so unspeakably great? Then this should teach people to be very careful to whom they commit the teaching and guidance of their souls.

This is a business of the greatest concern; men will be careful to whom they commit their children, who they make the executors of their will, in whose hand they trust the writing and **evidences of their** lands; but how much more careful should we be, and yet the most are the least of all careful, unto whom they commit the teaching and guidance of their souls. · There are several sorts of soul shepherds in the world:—1. There are idol shepherds, (Zech. xi. 17.) 2. There are foolish shepherds, (Zech. xi. 15.) 3. There are shepherds that feed themselves, and not their flock, (Ezek. xxxiv. 2.) 4. There are hard-hearted and pitiless shepherds, (Zech. xi. 3.) 5. There are shepherds that, instead of healing, smite, push, and wound the diseased. (Ezek. xxxiv. 4, 21.) 6. There are shepherds that "cause their flocks to go astray," (Jer. i. 6.) 7. And there are shepherds that feed their flock; these are the shepherds to whom thou shouldst commit thy soul for teaching and for guidance.

Question. You may ask, How should I know those shepherds?

Answer. First, surrender up thy soul unto God by Christ, and choose Christ to be the chief shepherd of thy soul; and he will direct thee to his shepherds, and he will, of his mercy, set such shepherds over thee, "as shall feed thee with knowledge and understanding." (1 Pet. ii. 25; iv. 19. John x. 4, 5. Cant. i. 7, 8. Jer. iii. 15; xxiii. 4.) Before thou hast surrendered up thy soul to Christ, that he may be thy chief shepherd, thou canst not find out, nor choose to put thy soul under the teaching and guidance of his under shepherds, for thou canst not love them; besides, they are so set forth by false shepherds, in so many ugly guises, and under so many false and scandalous dresses, that, should I direct thee to them, while thou art a stranger to Christ, thou wilt count them deceivers, devourers, and wolves in sheeps' clothing, rather than the shepherds that belong to the great and chief Shepherd, who is also the Bishop of the soul.

Yet this I will say unto thee, take heed of that shepherd that careth not for his own soul, that walketh in ways, and doth such things, as have a direct tendency to damn his own soul; I say, take heed of such an one, come not near him, let him have nothing to do with thy soul; for if he be not faithful to that which is his own soul, be sure he will not be faithful to that which is another man's. He that feeds his own soul with ashes, (Isa. xliv. 20,) will scarce feed thine with the bread of life; wherefore, take heed of such an one; and many such there are in the world, "By their fruits you shall know them;" they are for flattering of the worst, and frowning upon the best; they are for promising of life to the profane, and for slaying the souls that God would have live; they are also men that hunt souls that fear God, but for sewing pillows under those arm-holes, which God would have to lean upon that which would afflict them. These be them that "with lies do make the heart of the righteous sad, whom I have not made sad," saith God; and that have "strengthened the hands of the wicked, that he should not return from his wicked way, by promising him life." (Ezek. xiii. 18—22.)

And as thou shouldst, for thy soul's sake, choose for thyself good soul-shepherds, so also, for the same reason, you should choose for yourselves a good wife, a good husband, a good master, a good servant; for in all these things, the soul is concerned. Abraham would not suffer Isaac to take a wife of the daughters of Canaan, (Gen. xxiv. 3,) nor would David suffer a wicked servant to come into his house, or to tarry in his sight. (Ps. ci. 7.) Bad company is, also, very destructive to the soul, and so is evil communication; wherefore be diligent to shun all these things, that thou mayst persevere in that way, the end of which will be the saving of thy soul. (Prov. xiii. 20. 1 Cor. xv. 33.)

And since, under this head, I am fallen upon cautions, let me add these to those which I have presented to thee already :—

1. Take heed, take heed of learning to do evil of any that are good. It is possible for a good man to do things that are bad; but let not his bad action imbolden thee to run upon sin. Seest thou a good man that stumbleth at a stone, or that slippeth into the dirt—let that warn thee to take heed; let his stumble make thee wary; let his fall make thee look well to thy goings; " Ever follow that which is good." (1 Thess. v. 15.) Thy soul is at stake.

2. Take heed of the good things of bad men, for in them there lies a snare also; their " good words and fair speeches" tend to deceive. (Rom. xvi. 17, 18.) Learn to be good, by the Word of God and by the holy lives of them that be good; envy not the wicked, "nor desire to be with them;" "choose none of his ways." (Prov. iii. 31; xxiv. 1.) Thy soul lies at stake.

3. Take heed of playing the hypocrite in religion. What of God and his Word thou knowest, profess it honestly, confirm to it heartily, serve him faithfully; for what is the hypocrite bettered by all his profession, " when God taketh away his soul ?" (Job xxvii. 8.)

4. Take heed of delays to turn to God, and of choosing his ways for the delight of thy heart; " For the Lord's eye is upon them that fear him, to deliver their souls." (Ps. xxxiii. 18, 19.)

5. Boast not thyself of thy flocks and thy herds, of thy gold and thy silver, of thy sons and of thy daughters. What is a house full of treasures, and all the delights of this world, if thou be empty of grace, " if thy soul be not filled with good ?" (Eccles. vi. 3.) But,

Fourth Use.—Is it so ? Is the soul such an excellent thing, and is the loss thereof so unspeakably great ? Then, I pray thee, let me inquire a little of thee, what provision hast thou made for thy soul ? There be many that, through their eagerness after the things of this life, do bereave their soul of good, even of that good the which if they had it would be a good to them for ever. (Eccles. iv. 8.)

But I ask not concerning this; it is not what provision thou hast made for this life, but what for the life, and the world to come. " Lord, gather not my soul with sinners," saith David, (Ps. xxvi. 9 ;) not with men of this world; Lord, not with them that have their portion in this life, whose belly thou fillest with thy hid treasures. Thus you see how Solomon laments some, and how his father prays to be delivered from their lot who have their portion in this life, and that have not made provision for their soul. Well, then, let me inquire of thee about this matter. What provision hast thou made for thy soul ? And,

1. What hast thou thought of thy soul ? what ponderous thoughts hast thou had of the greatness and of the immortality of thy soul ? This must be the first inquiry; for he that hath not had his thoughts truly exercised, ponderously exercised, about the greatness and the immortality of his soul, will not be careful, after an effectual manner, to make provision for his soul, for the life and world to come. The soul is a man's all, whether he knows it or no, as I have already showed you. Now, a man will be concerned about what he thinks is his all. We read of the poor servant that " setteth his heart upon" his wages, (Deut. xxiv. 14, 15 :) but it is because it is his all, his treasure, and that wherein his worldly worth lieth. Why, thy soul is thy all; it is strange if thou dost not think so; and more strange if thou dost think so, and yet hast light, seldom, and trivial thoughts about it. These two seem to be inconsistent, therefore, let thy conscience speak; either thou hast very great and weighty thoughts about the excellent greatness of thy soul, or else thou dost not count that thy soul is so great a thing as it is, else thou dost not count it thy all.

2. What judgment hast thou made of the present state of thy soul ? I speak now to the unconverted. Thy soul is under sin, under the curse, and an object of wrath; this is that sentence that by the Word is passed upon it, " Woe unto their souls," saith God, " for they have rewarded evil unto themselves." (Isa. iii. 9.) This is the sentence of God. Well, but what judgment hast thou passed upon it while thou livest in thy debaucheries ? Is it not that which thy fellows have passed on theirs before thee, saying, "I shall have peace, though I walk in the imagination of my heart, to add drunkenness to thirst." (Deut. xxix. 19.) If so, know thy judgment is gross, thy soul is miserable, and turn, or in little time thine eyes will behold all this.

3. What care hast thou had of securing of thy soul, and that it might be delivered from the danger that by sin it is brought into ? If a man has a horse, a cow, or a swine that is sick, or in danger by reason of this or that casualty, he will take care for his beast, that it may not perish; he will pull it out of the ditch on the Sabbath day. But, oh ! that is the day on which many men do put their soul into the ditch of sin; that is the day that they

set apart to pursue wickedness in. But, I say, what care hast thou taken to get thy soul out of this ditch? a ditch out of which thou canst never get it without the aid of an omnipotent arm. In things pertaining to this life, when a man feels his own strength fail, he will implore the help and aid of another; and no man can, by any means, deliver by his own arm his soul from the power of hell, which thou also wilt confess, if thou beest not a very brute; but what hast thou done with God for help? hast thou cried? hast thou cried out? yea, dost thou still cry out, and that day and night before him—" Deliver my soul," (Ps. xvii. 13;) " Save my soul, preserve my soul," (Ps. xxv. 20;) " Heal my soul," (Ps. xli. 4;) and " I pour out my soul unto thee?" (Ps. lxii. 5;) yea, canst thou say, My soul, my soul waiteth upon God, my soul thirsteth for him, my soul followeth hard after him? (Ps. lxiii. 1, 8.) I say, dost thou this, or dost thou hunt thine own soul to destroy it? The soul, with some, is the game, their lusts are the dogs, and they themselves are the huntsmen, and never do they more halloo, and lure, and laugh, and sing, than when they have delivered up their soul, their darling, to these dogs; a thing that David trembled to think of, when he cried, " Dogs have compassed me. Deliver my darling," my soul, " from the power of the dog." (Ps. xxii. 16—20.) Thus, I say, he cried, and yet these dogs were but wicked men. But, oh! how much is a sin, a lust, worse than a man to do us hurt; yea, worse than is a dog, a lion, to hurt a lamb!

4. What are the signs and tokens that thou bearest about thee concerning how it will go with thy soul at last? There are signs and tokens of a good, and signs and tokens of a bad end that the souls of sinners will have: there are signs of the salvation of the soul; (Heb. vi. 9;) evident tokens of salvation; and there are signs of the damnation of the soul, evident signs of damnation. (Phil. i. 27, 28. Job. xxi. 29, 30. Isa. iii. 9.) Now, which of these hast thou? I cannot stand here to show thee which are which; but thy soul and its salvation lieth before thee, and thou hast the book of signs about these matters by thee; thou hast also men of God to go to, and their assemblies to frequent. Look to thyself; heaven and hell are hard by, and one of them will swallow thee up; heaven, into unspeakable and endless glory; or hell, into unspeakable and endless torment. Yet,

5. What are the pleasures and delights of thy soul now? Are they things divine, or things natural? Are they things heavenly, or things earthly? Are they things holy, or things unholy? For look what things thou delightest in now, to those things the great God doth count thee a servant, and for and of those thou shalt receive thy wages at the day of judgment: " His servants ye are to whom ye obey; whether of sin unto death, or of obedience unto righteousness." (Rom. vi. 16.)

Wicked men talk of heaven, and say they hope and desire to go to heaven, even while they con-tinue wicked men; but, I say, what would they do there? If all that desire to go to heaven should come thither, verily they would make a hell of heaven; for, I say, what would they do there? why, just as they do here, scatter their filthiness quite over the face of heaven, and make it as vile as the pit that the devils dwell in. Take holiness away out of heaven, and what is heaven? I had rather be in hell, were there none but holy ones there, than be in heaven itself with the children of iniquity. If heaven should be filled with wicked men, God would quickly drive them out, or forsake the place for their sakes. It is true, they have been sinners, and none but sinners, that go to heaven; but they are washed: " Such were some of you; but ye are washed, but ye are sanctified, but you are justified, in the name of the Lord Jesus, and by the Spirit of our God." (1 Cor. vi. 10, 11.) When the maidens were gathered together for the great king Ahasuerus, before they were brought to him into his royal presence, they were to be had to the house of the women, there to be purified with things for purification, and that for twelve months together, to wit, six months with oil of myrrh, and six months with sweet odours, and other things, and so came every maiden to the king. (Esther ii. 3, 9, 12, 13.) God also hath appointed that those that come into his royal presence should first go to the house of the women, the church, and there receive of the eunuchs things for purification, things to make us " meet to be partakers of the inheritance of the saints in light." (Col. i. 12.) None can go from a state of nature to glory but by a state of grace, the Lord gives grace and glory; hence he that goeth to heaven is said to be wrought for it, fitted, prepared for it. (1 Cor. v. 5. Rom. ix. 23.)

Fifth Use. Again fifthly, Is it so? is the soul such an excellent thing, and is the loss thereof so unspeakably great? Then this doctrine commends those for the wise ones, and above all business concern themselves with the salvation of their souls; those that make all other matters but things by the by, and the salvation of their souls the one thing needful. But, but few comparatively will be concerned with this use; for where is he that doth this? Solomon speaks of one man of a thousand. (Eccles. vii. 28.) However, some there be, and blessed be God for some; but they are they that are wise, yea, wise in the wisdom of God.

1. Because they reject what God hath rejected, and that is sin. 2. Because they esteem but little of that which, by the Word, is counted but of little esteem, and that is the world. 3. Because they choose for a portion that which God commendeth unto us for that which is the most excellent thing, viz., himself, his Christ, his heaven, his Word, his grace, and holiness; these are the great and most excellent things, and the things that he hath chosen that is truly wise for his soul, (and all other wise men are fools in God's account, and in the judg-ment of his Word;) and if it be so, glory and bliss

must needs be their portion, though others shall miss thereof: "The wise shall inherit glory, but shame shall be the promotion of fools." (Prov. iii. 35.)

Let me, then, encourage those that are of this mind to be strong, and hold on their way. Soul, thou hast pitched right; I will say of thy choice, as David said of Goliath's sword, "There is none like that; give it me;" "Hold that fast which thou hast, that no man take thy crown." (Rev. iii. 11.) Oh! I admire this wisdom; this is by the direction of the Law-giver; this is by the teaching of the blessed Spirit of God; not the wisdom which this world teacheth, nor the wisdom which the world doth choose, which comes to nought. (1 Cor. ii. 6.) Surely thou hast seen something of the world to come, and of the glory of it, through faith; surely God has made thee see emptiness in that wherein others find a fulness, and vanity in that which by others is counted for a darling. Blessed are thine eyes, for they see; and thine ears, for they hear.

But who told thee that thy soul was such an excellent thing, as by thy practice thou declarest thou believest it to be? What! set more by thy soul than by all the world? What! cast a world behind thy back for the welfare of a soul? Is not this to play the fool, in the account of sinners, while angels wonder at and rejoice for thy wisdom? What a thing is this, that thy soul and its welfare should be more in thy esteem than all those glories wherewith the eyes of the world are dazzled! Surely thou hast looked upon the sun, and that makes gold look like a clod of clay in thine eyesight.

But who put the thoughts of the excellencies of the things that are eternal? I say, who put the thoughts of the excellency of those things into thy mind in this wanton age?—in an age wherein the thoughts of eternal life, and the salvation of the soul, are with and to many like the Morocco ambassador and his men, of strange faces, in strange habits, with strange gestures and behaviours, monsters to behold.

But where hadst thou that heart that gives entertainment to these thoughts, these heavenly thoughts? These thoughts are like the French Protestants, banished thence where they willingly would have harbour. How came they to thy house, to thy heart, and to find entertainment in thy soul? The Lord keep them in every imagination of the thoughts of thy heart for ever, and incline thine heart to seek him more and more.

And since the whole world have slighted and despised, and counted foolish the cogitations wherewith thy soul is exercised, what strong and mighty supporter is it upon and with which thou bearest up thy spirit, and takest encouragement in this thy forlorn, unoccupied and singular way? for so, I dare say, it is with the most; but certainly it is something above thyself, and that is more mighty to uphold thee than is the power, rage, and malice of all the world to cast thee down, or else

thou couldst not bear up, now the stream and the force thereof are against thee.

Objection 1. "I know my soul is an excellent thing, and that the world to come and its glories, even in the smallest glimpse thereof, do swallow up all the world that is here; my heart also doth greatly desire to be exercised about the thoughts of eternity, and I count myself never better than when my poor heart is filled with them; as for the rage and fury of this world, it swayeth very little with me, for my heart is come to a point; but yet, for all that, I meet with many discouragements, and such things that indeed do weaken my strength in the way."

But, brave soul, pray tell me what the things are that discourage thee, and that weaken thy strength in the way?

" Why, the amazing greatness of this my enterprise, that is one thing. I am now pursuing things of the highest, the greatest, the most enriching nature, even eternal things; and the thoughts of the greatness of them drowned me; for when the heat of my spirit in the pursuit after them is a little returned and abated, methinks I hear myself talking thus to myself: Fond fool! canst thou imagine that such a gnat, a flea, a pismire as thou art, can take and possess the heavens, and mantle thyself up in the eternal glories? If thou makest first a trial of the successfulness of thy endeavours upon things far lower, more base, but much more easier to obtain, as crowns, kingdoms, earldoms, dukedoms, gold, silver, or the like, how vain are these attempts of thine; and yet thou thinkest to possess thy soul of heaven! Away, away! by the heighth thereof thou mayest well conclude that it is far above, out of thy reach; and by the breadth thereof it is too large for thee to grasp and by the nature of the excellent glories thereof, too good for thee to possess. These are the thoughts that sometimes discourage me, and that weaken my strength in the way."

Answer. The greatness of thy undertaking does but show the nobleness of thy soul, in that it cannot, will not, be content with such low and dry things as the baseborn spirits that are of the world can and do content themselves withal. And as to the greatness of the things thou aimest at, though they be, as they are indeed, things that have not their like, yet they are not too big for God to give, and he has promised to give them to the soul that seeketh him; yea, he hath prepared the kingdom, given the kingdom, and laid up in the kingdom of heaven the things that thy soul longeth for, presseth after, and cannot be content without. (Luke xii. 32. Matt. xxv. 14. Col. i. 5. 1 Pet. i. 4.) As for thy making a trial of the successfulness of thy endeavours upon things more inferior and base, that is but a trick of the old deceiver. God has refused to give his children the great, the brave, and glorious things of this world, a few only excepted, because he has prepared some better thing for them, (1 Cor. i. 27. Heb. xi. 36—40;)

wherefore faint not, but let thy hand be strong, for thy work shall be rewarded. (Gal. vi. 9.) And since thy soul is at work for soul-things, for divine and eternal things, God will give them to thee; thou art not of the number of them that draw back unto perdition, but of them that believe to the saving of the soul; thou shalt receive the end of thy faith, the salvation of thy soul. (Heb. x. 39. 1 Pet. i. 8, 9.)

Obj. 2. But all my discouragements doth not lie in this. I see so much of the sinful vileness of my nature, and feel how ready it is to thrust itself forth at all occasions, to the defiling of my whole man, and more. Now this, added to the former, adds to my discouragement greatly.

Ans. This should be cause of humiliation and of self-abasement, but not of discouragement; for the best of saints have their weaknesses, these their weaknesses. The ladies as well as she that grinds at the mill, know what doth attend that sex; and the giants in grace, as well as the weak and shrubs, are sensible of the same things, which thou layest in against thy exercising of hope, or as matter of thy discouragement. Poor David says, (Ps. lxxvii. 2,) "My soul refused to be comforted," upon this very account; and Paul cries out under sense of this, "O wretched man that I am!" and comes as it were to the borders of a doubt, saying, "Who shall deliver me?" (Rom. vii. 24;) only he was quick at remembering that Christ was his righteousness and price of redemption, and there he relieved himself.

Again: This should drive us to faith in Christ; for therefore are corruptions by Divine permission still left in us; they are not left in us to drive us to unbelief, but to faith; that is, to look to the perfect righteousness of Christ for life. And for further help, consider, that therefore Christ liveth in heaven, making intercession, that thou mightest be saved by his life, not by thine, and by his intercessions, not by thy perfections. (Rom. v. 6—9. Col. i. 20.) Let not therefore thy weaknesses be thy discouragements; only let them put thee upon the duties required of thee by the gospel, to wit, faith, hope, repentance, humility, watchfulness, diligence, &c. (1 Pet. i. 13; v. 5. 2 Cor. vii. 11. Mark xiii. 37. 2 Pet. i. 10.)

Obj. 3. "But I find, together with these things, weakness and faintness as to my graces; my faith, my hope, my love, and desires to these and all other Christian duties are weak: I am like the man in the dream, that would have run, but could not; that would have fought but could not; and that would have fled, but could not."

Ans. 1. Weak graces are graces, weak graces may grow stronger; but if the iron be blunt, put to the more strength. (Eccles. x. 10.) 2. Christ seems to be most tender of the weak; "He shall gather the lambs with his arm, and carry them in his bosom, and shall gently lead those that are with young," (Isa. xl. 11;) and again, "I will seek that which was lost, and bring again that which

was driven away, and will bind up that which was broken, and will strengthen that which was sick." (Ezek. xxxiv. 16.) Only here will thy wisdom be manifested, to wit, that thou grow in grace, and that thou use lawfully and diligently the means to do it. (2 Pet. iii. 18. Phil. iii. 10, 11. 1 Thess. iii. 11—13.)

Sixth Use.—I come, in the next place, to a use of terror, and so I shall conclude. Is it so? is the soul such an excellent thing, and is the loss thereof so unspeakably great? Then this showeth the sad state of those that lose their souls. We used to count those in a deplorable condition, that by one only stroke are stript of their whole estate: the fire swept away all that he had; or all that he had was in such a ship, and that ship sunk into the bottom of the sea; this is sad news, this is heavy tidings, this is bewailed of all, especially if such were great in the world, and were brought by their loss from a high to a low, to a very low condition; but alas! what is this to the loss about which we have been speaking all this while? The loss of an estate may be repaired, or if not, a man may find friends in his present deplorable condition to his support, though not recovery; but far will this be from him that shall lose his soul. Ah! he has lost his soul, and can never be recovered again, unless hell-fire can comfort him; unless he can solace himself in the fiery indignation of God; terrors will be upon him, anguish and sorrow will swallow him up, because of present misery; slighted and set at nought by God and his angels, he will also be in this his miserable state, and this will add to sorrow, sorrow, and to his vexation of spirit, howling.

To present you with emblems of tormented spirits, or to draw before your eyes the picture of hell, are things too light for so ponderous a subject as this; nor can any man frame or invent words, be they never so deep and profound, sufficient to the life to set out the torments of hell. All those expressions of fire, brimstone, the lake of fire, a fiery furnace, the bottomless pit, and a hundred more to boot, are all too short to set forth the miseries of those that shall be damned souls: "Who knoweth the power of God's anger?" (Ps. xc. 11;) none at all; and unless the power of that can be known, it must abide as unspeakable as the love of Christ, which passeth knowledge.

We hear it thunder, we see it lighten; yea, eclipses, comets and blazing stars, are all subject to smite us with terror; the thought of a ghost, of the appearing of a dead wife, a dead husband, or the like, how terrible are these things! But alas, what are these? mere flea-bitings, nay not so bad, when compared with the torments of hell. Guilt and despair, what are they? Who understands them unto perfection? The ireful looks of an infinite Majesty, what mortal in the land of the living can tell us to the full, how dismal and breaking to the soul of man it is, when it comes as from "the power of His anger," and arises from the utmost indignation? Besides, who knows of all the ways by which the Almighty will inflict his just revenges upon the souls of damned sinners? when Paul was caught up to the third heaven, he heard words that were unspeakable; and he that goes down to hell shall hear groans that are unutterable. Hear, did I say? they shall feel them, they shall feel them burst from their wounded spirits as thunder claps do from the clouds. Once I dreamed that I saw two (whom I knew) in hell, and methought I saw a continual dropping from heaven, as of great drops of fire lighting upon them, to their sore distress. Oh! words are wanting, thoughts are wanting, imagination and fancy are poor things here; hell is another kind of place and state than any alive can think; and since I am upon this subject, I will here treat a little of hell as the Scriptures will give me leave, and the rather because I am upon the use of terror, and because hell is the place of torment. (Luke xvi.)

1. Hell is said to be beneath, as heaven is said to be above; because as above signifieth the utmost joy, triumph, and felicity, so beneath is a term most fit to describe the place of hell by, because of the utmost opposition that is between these two; hell being the place of the utmost sorrow, despair, and misery, there are the underlings ever trampled under the feet of God; they are beneath, below, under. (Prov. xv. 24.)

2. Hell is said to be darkness, and heaven is said to be light; light to show the pleasureableness and the desirableness of heaven; and darkness to show the dolesome and wearisomeness of hell; and how weary, oh! how weary and wearisomely, as I may say, will damned souls turn themselves from side to side, from place to place, in hell, while swallowed up in the thickest darkness, and griped with the burning thoughts of the endlessness of that most unutterable misery! (Matt. xxii. 13.)

3. Men are said to go up to heaven, but they are said to go down to hell, (Ezek. xxxii. 18;) up, because of exaltation, and because they must abound in beauty and glory that go to heaven; down, because of those sad dejections, that great deformity and evil contempt that sin hath brought them to that go to hell.

4. Heaven is called a hill or mount, (Heb. xii.;) hell is called a pit or hole, (Rev. ix. 2;) heaven, a mount, the mount Zion, (Rev. xiv.;) to show how God has and will exalt them that loved him in the world; hell, a pit or hole, to show how all the ungodly shall be buried in the yawning paunch and belly of hell, as in a hollow cave.

5. Heaven! It is said of heaven, the height of heaven, (Job xxi. 12,) and of hell, the bottomless pit, (Rev. ix. 2; xx. 3.) The height of heaven, to show that the exaltation of them that do ascend up thither is both perfect and unsearchable; and hell, the bottomless pit, to show that the downfall of them that descend in thither will never be at an end—down, down, down they go, and nothing but down, down still.

6. Heaven! It is called the paradise of God, (Rev. ii. 7;) but hell, the burning lake. (Rev. xx. 15.) A paradise, to show how quiet, harmless, sweet, and beautiful heaven shall be to them that possess it, as the garden was at the beginning of the creation; hell, the burning lake, to allude to Sodom, that since its destruction is turned into a stinking lake and to show that as their distress was unutterable, and to the highest amazement, full of confusion and horror, when that tempestuous storm of fire and brimstone was rained from the Lord out of heaven upon them, so, to the utmost degree, shall it be with the souls that are lost and cast into hell.

7. It is said that there are dwelling-houses or places in the kingdom of heaven, (John xiv. 1—3. Zech. iii. 7. Isa. lvii. 1, 2;) and also that there are the cells or the chambers of death in hell, (Prov. vii. 27.) There are mansions or dwelling-places in heaven, to show that every one of them that go thither might have his reward, according to his work, and that there is hell, and the lowest hell, (Deut. xxxii. 22. Ps. lxxxvi. 13,) and the chambers of death in hell, to show there are places and states in hell too, for sinners to be imprisoned in, according to their faults: hence it is said of some, These shall receive greater damnation, (Luke xx. 47;) and of others, That it shall be more tolerable for Sodom and Gomorrah in the judgment, than for them, &c. (Luke x. 12—14.)

The lowest hell. How many hells there are above that, or more tolerable tormenting places than the most exquisite torments there, God, and they that are there, know best; but degrees without doubt there are; and the term "lowest" shows the utmost and most exquisite distress: so the chambers of death, the second death in hell, for so I think the words should be understood, "Her house is the way to hell, going down to the chambers of death," (Prov. vii. 27.) These are the chambers that the chambers in the temple, or that the dwelling-places in the house in heaven, are opposed to; and this opposition shows that as there will be degrees of glory in heaven, so there will of torments in hell; and there is all reason for it, since the punishment must be inflicted by God, the infinitely just. Why should a poor, silly, ignorant man, though damned, be punished with the same degree of torment that he that has lived a thousand times worse shall be punished with? It cannot be; justice will not admit it; guilt and the quality of the transgression, will not admit it; yea, the tormenting fire of hell itself will not admit it; for if hell-fire can kindle upon nothing but sin, and the sinner for the sake of it, and if sin be as oil to that fire, as the Holy Ghost seems to intimate, saying, "Let it come into his bowels like water, and like oil into his bones," (Ps. cix. 18,) then as the quantity of the oil is, so will the fire burn, and so will the flaming flame ascend and the smoke of their torment, for ever and ever. Suppose a piece of timber a little bedaubed with oil, and another that hath been soaking in it many a year, which of these two, think you, would burn fiercest? and whence would the flaming flame ascend highest, and make the most roaring noise? Suppose two vessels filled with oil, one containing the quantity of a pint, the other containing the quantity of a hogshead, and suppose that in one place they were both set on fire, yet so that they might not intermix flames; nay, though they did, yet all would conclude that the most amazing, roaring flame would be upon the biggest vessel, and would be the effect of the greatest quantity of oil; so it will be with the wicked in hell. The lowest hell is for the biggest sinners, and theirs will be the greater damnation, and the more intolerable torment, though he that has least of this oil of sin in his bones, and of the kindlings of hell-fire upon him, will find he has hell enough, and will be weary enough thereof, for still he must struggle with flames that are everlasting; for sin is such a thing, that it can never be burned out of the soul and body of a damned sinner.

But again; having treated thus of hell, we will now speak a word or two of sin, for that is it upon which hell-fire seizes, and so on the soul by that. Sin! it is the sting of hell—the sting of death is sin. (1 Cor. xv. 56.) By death in this place we must not understand that which is natural, but that which is in hell, the second death, even everlasting damnation; for natural death the saints die, yea, and also many sinners, without the least touch of a sting from that; but here is a death that has a sting to hurt, to twinge, and wound the sinner with, even then when it has the utmost mastery of him. And this is the death that the saved are delivered from; not that which is natural, for that is the end of them as of others. (1 Cor. xv. 55. Eccles. ii. 15, 16.) But the second death, the death in hell, for that is the portion of the damned, and it is from that that the saints have a promise of deliverance—" He that overcometh shall not be hurt of the second death," (Rev. ii. 11;) and again, " Blessed and holy is he that hath part in the first resurrection : on such the second death hath no power." (Rev. xx. 6.) It is this death, then, that hath the chambers to hold each damned soul in; and sin is the twining, winding, biting, poisoning sting of this death, or of these chambers of hell, for sinners to be stricken, stung, and pierced with. " The sting of death is sin." Sin, in the general of it, is the sting of hell, for there would be no such thing as torment, even there, were it not that sin is there with sinners; for, as I have hinted already, the fire of hell, the indignation and wrath of God, can fasten and kindle upon nothing but for or because of sin; sin, then, as sin, is the sting, and the hell of hells, of the lowest and upmost hells. Sin, I say, in the nature of it, simply as it is concluded both by God and the damned to be a breach of his holy law, so it is the sting of the second death, which is the worm of hell. But then, as sin is such a sting in itself, so it is heightened, sharp-ened, and made more keen and sharp by those circumstances that, as concomitants, attend it in every act; for there is not a sin at any time committed by man, but there is some circumstance or other attends it, that makes it, when charged home by God's law, bigger and sharper, and more venom and poisonous to the soul, than if it could be committed without them; and this is the sting of the hornet, the great sting. I sinned without a cause, to please a base lust, to gratify the devil; here is the sting. Again, I preferred sin before holiness, death before life, hell before heaven, the devil before God, and damnation before a Saviour; here is the sting. Again, I preferred moments before everlastings, temporals before eternals, to be racked and always slaying, before the life that is blessed and endless; here is the sting. Also, this I did against light, against convictions, against conscience, against persuasion of friends, ministers, and the godly lives which I beheld in others; here is the sting. Also, this I did against warnings, forewarnings, yea, though I saw others fall before my face by the mighty hand of God for committing of the same; here is the sting.

Sinners, would I could persuade you to hear me out. A man cannot commit a sin, but, by the commission of it, he doth, by some circumstance or other, sharpen the sting of hell, and that to pierce himself through and through, and through, with many sorrows. (1 Tim. vi. 10.) Also, the sting of hell to some will be, that the damnation of others stand upon their score, for that by imitating of them, by being deluded by them, persuaded by them, drawn in by them, they perish in hell for ever; and hence it is that these principal sinners must die all these deaths in themselves, that those damned ones that they have drawn into hell, are also to bear in their own souls for ever. And this God threatened to the Prince of Tyrus, that capital sinner, because by his pride, power, practice, and policy, he cast down others into the pit; therefore saith God to him, " They shall bring thee down to the pit, and thou shalt die the deaths of them that are slain in the midst of the seas;" and again, " Thou shalt die the deaths of the uncircumcised by the hand of strangers : for I have spoken it, saith the Lord God." (Ezek. xxviii. 8, 10.) Ah! this will be the sting of them, of those that are principal, chief, and, as I may call them, the captain and ringleading sinners. Vipers will come out of other men's fire and flames, and settle upon, seize upon, and for ever abide upon their consciences; and this will be the sting of hell, the great sting of hell to them.

I will yet add to this : how will the fairness of some for heaven, even the thoughts of that, sting them when they come to hell! It will not be so much their fall into the pit, as from whence they fell into it, that will be to them the buzzing noise and sharpened sting of the great and terrible hornet. " How art thou fallen from heaven, O Lucifer!" there is the sting. (Isa. xiv. 12.) Thou that art exalted up to heaven shalt be thrust down to hell, though thou hast made "thy nest among the stars," from thence will I fetch thee down; there is a sting. (Matt. xi. 23. Obad. iv.) To be pulled, for and through love to some vain lust, from the everlasting gates of glory, and caused to be swallowed up for it in the belly of hell, and made to lodge for ever in the darksome chambers of death; there is the piercing sting.

But again, as there is the sting of hell, so there is the strength of that sting; for a sting, though never so sharp, or venom, yet if it wanteth strength to force it to the designed execution, it doth but little hurt. But this sting has strength to cause it to pierce into the soul; "the sting of death is sin; and the strength of sin is the law." (1 Cor. xv. 56.) Here, then, is the strength of the sting of hell; it is the law in the perfect penalty of it; " for without the law, sin is dead," (Rom. vii. 8:) yea, again he saith, " where no law is, there is no transgression." (Rom. iv. 15.) The law then followeth, in the executive part of it, the soul into hell, and there strengtheneth sin, that sting of hell, to pierce by its unutterable charging of it on the conscience, the soul for ever and ever; nor can the soul justly murmur or repine at God or at his law, for that then the sharply apprehensive soul will well discern the justness, righteousness, reasonableness, and goodness of the law, and that nothing is done by the law under it but that which is just and equal.

This, therefore, will put great strength and force into sin to sting the soul, and to strike it with the lashes of a scorpion. Add yet to these the abiding life of God, the Judge and God of this law, will never die. When princes die, the law may be altered by the which at present transgressors are bound in chains; but, oh! here is also that which will make this sting so sharp and keen—the God that executes it will never die. " It is a fearful thing to fall into the hands of the living God." (Heb. x. 30, 31.)

PREFATORY REMARKS

ON

THE WATER OF LIFE.

"The Water of Life." This beautiful expression conveys refreshment to the mind by numberless delightful associations. It connects itself with the imagery of places and seasons, rich in the fulness of the Creator's blessing; and affording the surest marks of his united power and will to connect with the gift and the means of life those which minister to high and pure enjoyment. When Paradise was planted, there went a river out of Eden to water the garden; the fruits and flowers, and grassy glades of man's first and happiest home, being no longer left to the mists which rose out of the ground, but confessing by endless successions of growth the supply of perennial life. The beauty of these things—the enjoyment and nourishment which they ministered, as connected with the flowing of the river, must have early led the contemplative understanding of man to regard it as an emblem of still higher blessings. In after periods, he was again and again recalled to the thought of this first association of the running stream with the renovation, the delights and adornments of his life. When the waste desert howled around him, as the very contrast of Paradise, and its rocky boundaries as the gloomiest of all opposites to Eden, a miracle brought the two extremes together. The rock poured out its bright, affluent waters, like the river of Eden, and the wilderness became, for the time, to the fainting wanderers, beautiful as Paradise. As they approached the termination of their weary journey, and the longed-for home lay in prospect before them, their fainting spirits leaped with joy at the description which proclaimed that the promised land was "a land of brooks of water; of fountains and depths that spring out of valleys and hills."

Recollections of Paradise, of the rock pouring out its living waters in the wilderness, of the first passage of the Jordan, so grand in mysterious suggestions for all after ages, were to the ancient religious mind a general consecration of streams and fountains. This feeling was further cherished when prophets spoke of " drawing water out of wells of salvation;" of water and divine grace as combined in the language of heavenly consolation,—" I will pour water upon him that is thirsty, and floods upon the dry ground: I will pour my Spirit upon thy seed, and my blessing upon thine offspring." Even the highest of all delights were similarly typified. Of God's goodness to his children it is said, " Thou shalt make them drink of the river of thy pleasures;" and of God himself— " with Thee is the fountain of life."

In the majestic outlines of a regenerate world, no part of the picture excites a sublimer feeling of hope than that which shadows forth the " Baptism of Nations." Hordes of a prostrate race are seen grovelling in the dust. The heavens open: a hand is stretched forth; copious showers of living water fall on the fevered, dying multitudes. They breathe again; and, baptized to a new existence, live to rejoice in this second act of creation.

Amid these grander events and prophecies, indicative of the symbolic sacredness of water, are some incidents of only partial importance, but of very beautiful significance. Gideon's fleece was heavy with dew, as a sign that the people should be saved by his hand: and when the fleece was dry, all the ground about it was wet with showers. Nor less full of meaning, in its way, is the record of Rizpah's sorrowful watch by the bodies of her sons: " And Rizpah, the daughter of Aiah, took sackcloth, and spread it for her upon the rock, from the beginning of harvest, until water dropped upon them out of heaven." The dry bones of the gaunt skeletons may have seemed to the heart of the poor mother to be prepared, by that water out of heaven, for a new vesture of immortality.

It is easy to perceive how readily the minds of men who had been thus instructed, would pass to the contemplation of the " pure river of water of life;" understanding by the expression, that fathomless source of grace and renovation existing in the love of God. They had been taught both by types and prophecies to unite, in their thoughts, the running stream and fresh dews of heaven, with a sense of refreshment and blessing. Now, in contemplating the dispensation of the fulness of time, they heard a voice inviting them to the very fountain-head of all those waters—to the very river of life itself.

Naturally beautiful as is the language derived from this imagery of water-springs, it is rendered still more so, in its religious use, by its admirable fitness to make the highest truths intelligible and precious to the soul. A conviction of unholiness, with all its attendant impurities, gives unspeakable value to the means by which they may be utterly removed. And what means so fitting? what of such ready use, as the fountain which has been opened for the purpose by divine grace? That fountain may be reached; its purifying waters applied, as readily as the stream running through some neighbouring meadow may be found by the traveller who has asked his way to its banks. The faintness of the soul, sick with the mortal disease of sin, how can it be overcome unless by the water of life? But faintness and thirst need not be suffered any longer, when that call is heard, " Let him that is athirst come : and whosoever will, let him take of the water of life freely." A mountain spring known to have healing virtues, cannot be more open to the sick man than is this water of life to the soul.

Both the copiousness of water and the glorious freedom with which it permeates all the depths of nature, the purity and health which attend upon its courses, the added beauty and freshness which it continually gives to the life dependent upon it, leave no room for questioning why this benignant element was selected above all others to represent the power and the freeness of divine grace.

The soul, exalted to a high degree of faith and hope, will naturally be unwilling to lower or restrict its expectations of approaching joy by mere earthly similitudes ; yet even in its grandest mood of contemplation, the " river of God's pleasures," the " river of water of life," will suggest to it images of delight in harmony with its aspirations. Thus, from the hour when that word is first understood, " Except a man be born of water and of the Spirit, he cannot enter the kingdom of God," to the hour when his salvation is perfected, it is the water of life which sustains both his being and his hope.

H. S.

THE WATER OF LIFE;

OR,

A DISCOURSE

SHOWING THE RICHNESS AND GLORY OF THE GRACE AND SPIRIT OF THE GOSPEL, AS SET FORTH IN SCRIPTURE BY THIS TERM,

"THE WATER OF LIFE."

" And whosoever will, let him take the water of life freely."—REV. xxii. 17.

THE EPISTLE TO THE READER.

COURTEOUS READER,—I have now presented thee with something of a discourse of the water of life and its virtues, therefore thou mayest, if thou wilt, call this book, "Bunyan's bill of his master's water of life." True, I have not set forth at large the excellent nature and quality thereof, nor can that so be done by the pen or tongue of men or angels. Yet this I have said, and so saying, said truly, that whosoever shall drink of this water, shall find it in him a well of water; and not only so, but a well springing up in him to everlasting life, let his disease be what it will. And as men in their bills, for conviction to readers, do give an account to the country of the persons cured, and the diseases that have been removed by liquors and preparations they have made for that end, so could I, were it not already (by holy writ) done by an infallible pen to my hand, give you accounts of numberless numbers that have not only been made to live, but to live for ever, by drinking of this water, this pure water of life. Many of them indeed are removed from hence, and live where they cannot be spoken with as yet, but abundance of them do still remain here, and have their abode yet with men.

Only, if thou wouldest drink it, drink it by itself, and that thou mayest not be deceived by that which is counterfeit, know it is as it comes from the hand of our Lord, without mixture, pure and clear as crystal. I know there are many mountebanks in the world, and every of them pretend they have this water to sell. But my advice is, that thou go directly to the throne thyself, or as thou art bidden, come to the waters, and there thou shalt be sure to have that which is right and good, and that which will certainly make thee well, let thy disease, or trouble, or pain, or malady, be what it will. For the price, care not for that, it is cheap enough, this is to be had without money or price. "I will give," saith God and the Lamb, "to him that is athirst, of the fountain of the water of life freely." (Rev. xxi. 6.) "Hence," he says again, "whosoever will, let him take the water of life freely," (chap. xxii. 17,) so that thou hast no ground to keep back because of thy poverty: nay, for the poor it is prepared, and set open, to the poor it is offered, the poor and needy may have it of free cost. (Isa. xli. 17, 18.)

But let it not be slighted because it is offered to thee upon terms so full, so free. For thou art sick, and sick unto death if thou drinkest not of it, nor is there any other than this that can heal thee and make thee well. Farewell. The Lord be thy physician: so prays thy friend,

JOHN BUNYAN.

THE WATER OF LIFE.

" And he showed me a pure river of water of life, clear as crystal, proceeding out of the throne of God, and of the Lamb."—REV. xxii. 1.

THESE words are part of that description that one of the seven angels, which had the seven vials full of the seven last plagues, gave unto John of the New Jerusalem, or of the state of that gospel church that shall be in the latter days. (Rev. xxi. 1.) Wherefore he saith, "And he showed me; He, the angel showed me it."

In the text we have these things to consider of:—

I. The matter, the subject matter of the text,

and that is, the water of life. " He showed me the water of life."

II. We have also here the quantity of this water showed to him, and that is, under the notion of a river. " He showed me a river of water of life."

III. He shows him also the head, or well-spring from whence this river of water of life proceeds, and that is, " the throne of God, and of the Lamb." " He showed me a river of water of life, proceeding out of the throne of God, and of the Lamb."

IV. We have also here the nature and quality of this water, it is pure, it is clear as crystal. " And he showed me a pure river of water of life, clear as crystal, proceeding out of the throne of God, and of the Lamb."

I. We will begin with the first of these, to wit, with the matter, the subject matter of the text, which is, " the water of life." These words, " water of life," are metaphorical, or words by which a thing most excellent is presented to, and amplified before our faces: and that thing is the Spirit of grace, the Spirit and grace of God. And the words, " water of life," are words most apt to present it to us by ; for what is more free than water, and what more beneficial and more desirable than life? Therefore, I say, it is compared to, or called, the " water of life." He showed me the water of life.

That it is the Spirit of grace, or the Spirit and grace of God, that is here intended. Consider,

First. The Spirit of grace is in other places compared to water ; and,

Second. It is also called, the Spirit of life. Just as here it is presented unto us, " He showed me the water of life."

First, The Spirit of grace is compared to water. " Whosoever," saith the Lamb, " drinketh of the water that I shall give him, shall never thirst. But the water that I shall give him shall be in him a well of water, springing up into everlasting life." (John iv. 14.) What can here by water be intended, but the Spirit of grace, that this poor harlot, the woman of Samaria, wanted, although she was ignorant of her want, as also of the excellency thereof? which water also is here said to be such as will spring up in them that have it, as a well into everlasting life.

Again, " In the last day, that great day of the feast, Jesus stood and cried, saying, If any man thirst, let him come unto me and drink." (John vii. 37—39.) But of what? why, of his rivers of living waters. But what are they? why, he answers, " This he spake of the Spirit, which they that believe on him should receive."

Yea, the prophets and servants of God in the Old Testament did take this water of life for the Spirit of grace that should in the latter days be poured out into the church. Hence Isaiah calls water God's Spirit and blessing, and Zechariah, the Spirit of grace. " I will pour water upon him that is thirsty, and floods upon the dry ground.

I will pour my Spirit upon thy seed, and my blessing upon thy offspring." (Isa. xliv. 3.) And Zacharias saith, " I will pour upon the house of David, and upon the inhabitants of Jerusalem, the Spirit of grace and supplication, and they shall mourn," &c. (Zech. xii. 10.) Behold, in all these places the Spirit of grace is intended, and for our better understanding it is compared to water, to a well of water, to springs of water, and to floods of water.

Second, It is also called the spirit of life. (1.) More closely. (2.) More openly.

(1.) More closely, where it is called " living water," " that living water," and " water springing up to everlasting life." (John iv. 10, 11, 14 ; vii. 38.)

(2.) Then more openly or expressly it is called " the Spirit of life." " And after three days and a half, the Spirit of life from God entered into them, and they stood upon their feet." (Rev. xi. 11.)

From hence therefore I conclude, that by these terms, " water of life," is meant the Spirit of grace, or the Spirit and grace of the gospel. And the terms are such as are most apt to set forth the Spirit and grace of the gospel by. For,

1. By this term "water," an opposition to sin is presented unto us. Sin is compared to water, to deadly waters, and man is said to drink it, as one that drinketh waters. " How much more abominable and filthy is man, which drinketh iniquity like water!" (Job xv. 16.) So then that grace and the Spirit of grace is compared to water, it is to show what an antidote grace is against sin, (Zech. xiii. 1;) it is, as I may call it, counterpoison to it. It is that only thing by the virtue of which sin can be forgiven, vanquished, and overcome.

2. By this term " water," you have an opposition also to the curse that is due to sin presented unto you. The curse is compared to water, the remedy is compared to water. " Let the curse come into the bowels of the damned," saith the Psalmist, " like water." (Ps. cix. 18.) The grace of God also, as you see, is compared to water. The curse is burning, water is cooling ; the curse doth burn with hell-fire, cooling is by the grace of the holy gospel: but they that over-stand the day of grace, shall not obtain to cool their tongues so much of this water as will hang on the tip of one's finger. (Luke xvi. 24, 25.)

3. Water is also of a spreading nature, and so is sin ; wherefore sin may, for this, be also compared to water. It overspreads the whole man, and infects every member ; it covereth all, as doth water. Grace for this cause may be also compared to water, for that it is of a spreading nature, and can, if God will, cover the face of the whole earth ; of body and soul.

4. Sin is of a fouling, defiling nature, and grace is of a washing, cleansing nature : therefore grace, and the Spirit of grace, is compared to water. " I will," saith God, " sprinkle clean water upon

you," (my Spirit, ver. 27,) "and ye shall be clean; and from all your filthiness, and from all your idols will I cleanse you." (Ezek. xxxvi. 25.)

5. Water: the element of water naturally descends to, and abides in low places, in valleys and places which are undermost; and the grace of God, and the Spirit of grace, is of that nature also; the hills and lofty mountains have not the rivers running over the tops of them; no, though they may run among them: but they run among the valleys; and "God resisteth the proud, but giveth grace to the humble," "to the lowly." (Prov. iii. 34. James iv. 6. 1 Pet. v. 5.)

6. The grace of God is compared to water, for that it is it which causeth fruitfulness. Water causeth fruitfulness, want of water is the cause of barrenness; and this is the reason why the whole world is so empty of fruit to God-ward, even because so few of the children of men have the Spirit of grace in their hearts.

But, as there is a special signification in this term "water," so there is also in this term "life;" water of life. "He showed me the water of life." In that, therefore, there is added to this word Water, that of life, it is, in the general, to show what excellent virtue and operation there is in this water. It is *aquæ vitæ*, water of life, or water that hath a health and life in it. And this term shows us,

1. That the world of graceless men are dead, (John v. 21, 25. Eph. ii. 1. Colos. ii. 13,) dead in trespasses and sins. Dead, that is, without life and motion God-ward, in the way of the testament of his Son.

2. It also shows us that there is not anything in the world, or in the doctrine of the world, the law, that can make them live. Life is only in this water, death is in all other things. The law, I say, which is that that would, if anything in the whole world, give life unto the world, but that yet killeth, condemneth, and was added that the offence might abound; wherefore there is no life, either in the world, or in the doctrine of the world: it is only in this water, in this grace of God, which is here called the water of life, or God's *aquæ vitæ*.

3. It is also called the water of life, to show, that by the grace of God men may live, how dead soever their sins have made them. When God will say to a sinner, "Live;" though he be dead in his sins, "he shall live." "When thou wast in thy blood, I said unto thee, Live; yea, when thou wast in thy blood, I said, Live." (Ezek. xvi. 6.) And again, "The dead shall hear the voice of the Son of God, and they that hear shall live." (John v. 25.) That is, when he speaks words of grace, and mixeth those words with the Spirit and grace of the gospel, then men shall live; for such words, so attended, and such words only, are spirit and life. "The words that I speak unto you," saith Christ, "they are spirit, and they are life." (John vi. 63.)

4. In that this grace of God is here presented unto us under the terms of water of life, it is to show, that some are sick of that disease, that nothing can cure but that. There are many diseases in the world, and there are also remedies for those diseases; but there is a disease that nothing will, can, or shall cure, but a dram of this bottle, a draught of this *aquæ vitæ*, this water of life. This is intimated by the invitation, "Let him take the water of life freely." (Rev. xxii. 17.) And again, "I will give to him that is athirst of the fountain of the water of life freely." (Rev. xxi. 6.) This is spoken to the sick, to them that are sick of the disease that only Christ as a physician with his water of life can cure. (Mark ii. 17.) But few are sick of this disease, but few know what it is to be made sick of this disease. There is nothing can make sick of this disease but the law and sin, and nothing can cure but the grace of God by the gospel, called here the water of life.

II. We come now to discourse of the second thing with which we are presented by the text: and that is, the quantity that there is of this water of life. It is a river. "He showed me a river of water of life." Waters that are cordial, and that have in them a faculty to give life to them that want it, and to maintain life where it is, are rare and scarce, and to be found only in close places, and little quantities; but here, you see, there is abundance; a great deal, a river, a river of water of life. In my handling of this point, I will show you,

First, What a river of water of life this is.

Second, And then draw some inferences therefrom.

First, What a river this is; this river of water of life.

1. It is a deep river. It is a river that is not shallow, but deep with an, "O the depth!" (Rom. xi. 33.) "I will make their waters deep," saith God. (Ezek. xxxii. 14.) And again, "They have drunk of the deep waters." (Ezek. xxxiv. 18.) A river of water of life is much; but a deep river is more. Why, soul-sick sinner, sin-sick sinner, thou that art sick of that disease that nothing can cure but a portion of this river of the water of life, here is a river for thee, a deep river for thee. Those that at first are coming to God by Christ for life are of nothing so inquisitive, as of whether there is grace enough in him to save them. But for their comfort, here is abundance, abundance of grace; a river, a deep river of the water of life for them to drink of.

2. As this river is deep, so it is wide and broad. (Eph. iii. 18. Job xi. 9.) Wherefore as thou art to know the depth, that is, that it is deep, so thou art to know its breadth, that is, that it is broad. It is broader than the sea: "A river that cannot be passed over." (Ezek. xlvii. 5.) Never did man yet go from one side of this river to the other, when the waters indeed were risen; and now they are risen, even now they proceed out of the

throne of God and of the Lamb too. Hence this grace is called "the unsearchable riches of Christ." (Eph. iii. 8.) Sinner, sick sinner, what sayest thou to this? Wouldst thou wade, wouldst thou swim? here thou mayest wade, here thou mayest swim; it is deep, yet fordable at first entrance. And when thou thinkest that thou hast gone through and through it, yet turn again and try once more, and thou shalt find it deeper than hell, and a river that cannot be passed over. If thou canst swim, here thou mayest roll up and down, as the fishes do in the sea. Nor needest thou fear drowning in this river; it will bear thee up, and carry thee over the highest hills, as Noah's waters did carry the ark. But,

3. As this river of water of life is deep and large, so it is a river that is full of waters. A river may be deep, and not full. A river may be broad, and not deep; ay, but here is a river deep, and broad, and full too. "Thou waterest it; thou greatly enrichest it with the river of God, which is full of water." (Ps. lxv. 9.) Full of grace and truth. Fill the water-pots, saith Christ, up to the brim. "The waters of a full cup" the wicked shall have, and a river full of the water of life is provided for those who indeed have a desire thereto.

4. As this river is deep, broad, and full, so it still aboundeth with water. "The waters," says the prophet, "were risen." (Ezek. xlvii. 4.) Hence the Holy Ghost saith, God causeth the waters to flow. (Ps. cxlvii. 18.) And again, "And it shall come to pass in that day," the day of the gospel, "the mountains shall drop with new wine, and the hills shall flow with milk, and all the rivers of Judah shall flow with waters, and a fountain shall come forth of the house of the Lord, and shall water the valley of Shittim." (Joel iii. 18.) When a river overflows, it has more water than its banks can bound; it has water. "Behold, he smote the rock that the waters gushed out, and the streams overflowed." (Ps. lxxviii. 20.) This river of water of life, which is also signified by these waters, is a river that abounds, and that overflows its banks in an infinite and unspeakable manner. Thus much for the river, to wit, what a river of water of life it is. It is a river deep, broad, full, and abounding with this water, with this Spirit and grace of the gospel.

Second, Now I shall come to draw some inferences from it, that is from this term, a river. A river of water of life.

1. First then, a river is water that is common, common in the streams, though otherways in the head. This river proceeds out of the throne, and so, as to its rise, it is special; it is also called the water of life; and as it is such, it is special; but as it is a river it is common, and of common use, and for common good. Hence the grace of God is called the common salvation, (Jude 3;) for that by the word there is no restraint, no denial to, or forbidding of any that will from receiving thereof.

"And whosoever will, let him take the water of life freely." (Rev. xxii. 17.) What can more fully declare the commonness of a thing. Yea, this river is called at the very head of it, an "open fountain;" a fountain opened to the house of Judah, and the inhabitants of Jerusalem. (Zech. xiii. 1.) And by David or Judah and Jerusalem is comprehended every soul that would drink of the water of life, or living water. And hence it is that this river is said to "go down to the desert and to the sea," where all kind of fishes are. (Ezek. xlvii. 8.) By sea is meant the world, and by fish the people, and thither shall run this river of water of life. But,

2. Though a river, in the streams of it, is common, yet a river, as it passes through a country or province, will choose its own way. It will run in the valleys, in the plains, not over steeples and hills. It will also fetch its compasses and circuits; it will go about and reach hither and thither; and according to its courses, it will miss, by its turning, what places and people it lists; yet it is common, for that it lies open; yet it is common for all the beasts of the field. There is therefore a difference to be put betwixt the commonness of a thing and its presence. A thing may be common yet far enough off of thee. Epsom, Tunbridge waters, and the Bath, may be common, but yet a great way off of some that have need thereof. The same may be said of this river; it is common in the streams, but it runs its own circuit, and keeps its own water-courses. "He sendeth the springs into the valleys, which run among the hills." (Ps. civ. 10.) Indeed he openeth his river in high places, in his throne, and of the Lamb, but still they run in the midst of the valleys to water the humble and the lowly. Wherefore, they that thirst, and would drink, are bid to come down to the waters: "Ho, every one that thirsteth, come ye to the waters; and he that hath no money, come ye, buy," &c. (Isa. lv. 1.) And again, "If any man thirst, let him come unto me and drink." (John vii. 37.) The waters are common, but you must come to them, to them where they are, or you will be nothing the better for them. "Come ye to the waters."

3. This water of life is called a river, to intimate to you by what store of the same it is supplied. All rivers have the sea for their original: "All the rivers run into the sea, yet the sea is not full: unto the place from whence the rivers came, thither they return again." (Eccles. i. 7.) And so this river of water of life is said to proceed out of the throne, as out of a place where it breaketh out, but the original is the sea, the ocean of grace, which is in an infinite deity. "Thou wilt cast all our sins into the depths of the sea," (Mic. vii. 19;) "into the depth of the sea of thy grace." Rivers, when they are broken up, do with their gliding streams carry away a great deal of the filth, which from all parts of the countries through which they run is conveyed into them; and they carry it away

into the sea, where it is everlastingly swallowed up. And, oh, the filth that is cast into this river of God! and, oh, how many dirty sinners are washed white therein! for by its continual gliding away, it carrieth that filth into the midst of the sea. A river will take away the very stink of a dead dog; nor doth all the soil and draught that is cast into rivers cause that those that can should be afraid to make use thereof. All that have need do betake themselves to this river notwithstanding. But how much more virtue is there in this sweet river of grace, that is designed, yea, opened on purpose to wash away sin and uncleanness in, to carry away all our filth, and to remain as virtuous still?

4. It is called a river, to show that it yields a continual supply, as I may call it, of new and fresh grace. Rivers yield continually fresh and new water. For though the channel or water-course in which the water runs is the same, yet the waters themselves are always new. That water that but one minute since stood in this place or that of the river, is now gone, and new and fresh is come in its place. And thus it is with the river of God, which is full of water; it yieldeth continually fresh supplies, fresh and new supplies of grace to those that have business in those waters. And this is the reason that when sin is pardoned, it seems as if it were carried away. Those waters have with their continual streams carried away the filth of the sinner from before his face. It is not so with ponds, pools, and cisterns; they will be foul and stink if they be not often emptied, and filled again with fresh water. We must then put a difference between the grace that dwelleth in us, and this river of water of life. We are but as ponds, pools, and cisterns, that can hold but little, and shall also soon stink notwithstanding the grace of God is in us, if we be not often emptied from vessel to vessel, and filled with fresh grace from this river. (Jer. xlviii. 11.) But the river is always sweet, nor can all the filth that it washed out of the world make it stink or infect it; its water runs with a continual gliding stream, and so carries away all annoyance, as was said, into the depth of the sea.

5. The grace of God is called a river, to show that it is only suited to those who are capable of living therein. Water, though it is that which every creature desireth, yet it is not an element in which every creature can live. Who is it that would not have the benefit of grace, of a throne of grace? but who is it that can live by grace? even none but those whose temper and constitution is suited to grace. Hence, as the grace of God is compared to a river, so those that live by grace are compared to fish, for that, as water is that element in which the fish liveth, so grace is that which is the life of the saint. "And there shall be a very great multitude of fish, because these waters shall come thither; for they shall be healed, and everything shall live whither the river cometh." (Ezek. xlvii. 9.) Art thou a fish, man, art thou a fish?

canst thou live in the water? canst thou live always, and nowhere else, but in the water? is grace thy proper element? The fish dieth if she be taken out of the water, unless she be timely put in again; the saint dieth if he be not in this river. Take him from this river, and nothing can make him live: let him have water, water of life enough, and nothing can make him die.

I know that there are some things besides fish that can make a shift to live in the water; but the water is not their proper, their only proper element. The frog can live in the water, but not in the water only; the otter can live in the water, but not in the water only. Give some men grace and the world, grace and sin; admit them to make use of their lusts for pleasure, and of grace to remove their guilt, and they will make a pretty good shift, as we say: they will finely scrabble on in a profession; but hold them to grace only, confine their life to grace, put them into the river, and let them have nothing but river, and they die; the word, and way, and nature of grace is to them as light bread, and their soul can do no other but loathe it; for they are not suited and tempered for that element. They are fish, not frogs, that can live in the river as in their only proper element; wherefore the grace of God, and Spirit of grace is compared to a river, to show that none but those can live thereby, whose souls and spirits are suited and fitted thereto.

6. The grace and Spirit of grace of God is called or compared to a river, to answer those unsatiable desires, and to wash away those mountainous doubts that attend those that indeed do thirst for that drink. The man that thirsteth with spiritual thirst fears nothing more than that there is not enough to quench his thirst; all the promises and sayings of God's ministers to such a man seem but as thimbles instead of bowls. (Ps. lxiii. 1; cxliii. 6.) I mean, so long as his thirst and doubts walk hand in hand together. There is not enough in this promise; I find not enough in that promise to quench the drought of my thirsting soul. He that thirsteth aright, nothing but God can quench his thirst: "My soul thirsteth for God, for the living God." (Ps. xlii. 2.) Well, what shall be done for this man? will his God humour him, and answer his desires? Mark what follows: "When the poor and needy seek water, and there is none," (and they can find none, when all the promises seem to be dry, and like clouds that return after the rain,) "and their tongue fails for thirst, I the Lord will hear them, I the God of Israel will not forsake them." Ay, but Lord, what wilt thou do to quench their thirst? "I will open rivers," saith he, "in high places, and fountains in the midst of the valleys. I will make the wilderness a pool of water, and the dry land springs of water." (Isa. xli. 17, 18.) Behold! here are rivers and fountains, a pool, and springs, and all to quench the thirst of them that thirst for God.

Wherefore, as I said, such provision for the

thirsty, intimates their fears of want, and the craving appetite of their souls after God. Right spiritual thirst is not to be satisfied without abundance of grace. And " they shall be abundantly satisfied with the fatness of thy house, and thou shalt make them drink of the river of thy pleasures." (Ps. xxxvi. 8.)

7. The grace of God is compared to a river, to show the greatness of the family of God. He has a family, a great family, and therefore it is not a little that must be provided for them. When Israel went out of Egypt, and thirsted by the way, God provided for them a river, he made it gush out of a rock. (Ps. lxxviii. 20.) For, alas! what less than a river could quench the thirst of more than six hundred thousand men, besides women and children?

I say, what less than a river could do it? When the people lusted for flesh, Moses said, " Shall the flocks and herds be slain, for them to suffice them, or shall all the fish of the sea be gathered together for them to suffice them?" (Numb. xi. 22.) Even so could not less than a river sustain and suffice that great people. Now his people in gospel-days are not to be diminished but increased, and if then they had need of a river, surely now of a sea; but the river is deep and broad, full, and abounds, or rises with water, so it will suffice.

8. The grace of God is compared to a river, perhaps to show of what a low esteem it is with the rich and the full. The destitute indeed embrace the rock instead of a shelter, and the poor and needy, they seek water, but they that can drink wine in bowls, that can solace themselves with, as they think, better things, they come not to this river to drink; they never say they shall die if they drink not of this water. It is therefore for the poor and needy; God will lead them to his " living fountains of waters," and will " wipe away all tears from their eyes." (Rev. vii. 17.) And thus I pass the second, and come to the third particular, and that is, to show the head and spring from whence this river proceeds, or springs.

III. Rivers have their heads from whence they rise, out of which they spring; and so, accordingly, we read this river has; wherefore he saith, " He showed me a pure river of water of life, clear as crystal, proceeding out of the throne of God, and of the Lamb."

" God " is here to be taken for the whole Godhead, Father, Son, and Spirit, for that grace proceeds from them all. The grace of the Father, the grace of the Son, and the grace of the Spirit is here included. Hence, as the Father is called " the God of grace," so the Son is said to be full of grace, grace to be communicated; and the Holy Ghost is called " the Spirit of grace." (1 Pet. v. 10. John i. 14—16. Heb. x. 29.) So then by this we perceive whence grace comes. Were all the world gracious, if God were not **gracious, what was man the better?** If the

Father, or the Son, or the Holy Ghost are gracious, if they were not all gracious, what would it profit? but now God is gracious, the three persons in the Godhead are gracious, and so long they that seek grace are provided for; for that there proceeds from them a river, or grace like a flowing stream. Indeed, the original of grace to sinners is the good-will of God; none can imagine how loving God is to sinful man. A little of it is seen, but they that see most see but a little.

But there is added, "And of the Lamb." The Lamb is, Jesus as sacrificed, Jesus as man, and suffering. Hence you have the Lamb, at the first vision of the throne, set forth unto us, that is, as slain: "And I beheld, and lo in the midst of the throne, and of the four beasts, and in the midst of the elders, stood a Lamb as it had been slain." (Rev. v. 6.) Wherefore, by this word " Lamb," we are to understand who, or by what means grace doth now run from the throne of God, like a river to the world. It is because of, or through, the Lamb. We are " justified freely by the grace of God, through the redemption that is in Jesus Christ, whom God hath set forth to be a propitiation through faith in his blood." (Rom. iii. 24.) And again, " We have redemption through his blood," even " the forgiveness of sins, according to the riches of God's grace." (Eph. i. 7.)

Nor doth the Lamb of God, by becoming a means, through death, of the conveyance of grace to us, at all darken the nature or glory of grace, but rather doth set it off the more. For wherein can grace or love more appear than in his laying down his life for us? I speak now of the grace of the Son. And wherein could the nature and glory of grace of the Father more appear than in giving his Son to death for us, that grace might in a way of justice as well as mercy be bestowed upon the world? Wherefore, as he saith here, that the river of water of life proceedeth from God, so he adds, that the Lamb, because he would have us, while we are entangled and overcome with this river of God's pleasure, not forget what it cost the Lamb of God that this grace might come unto us.

For the riches of grace and of wisdom are, that grace comes to us not only in a way of mercy and compassion, but in a way of justice and equity; but that could be by no other means but by redeeming blood; which redeeming blood came not from us, nor yet through our contrivance or advice; wherefore, whatever it is to the Lamb, still all is of grace to us. Yea, the higher, the greater, the richer is grace, by how much the more it cost the Father and the Lamb that we might enjoy it. When a man shall not only design me a purse of gold, but shall venture his life to bring it to me, this is grace indeed! But, alas! what are a thousand such short comparisons to the unsearchable love of Christ!

The Lamb, then, is he from whom, by, or through whom the grace of God doth come to us.

It proceeds from the throne of God and of the Lamb. ...nd it proceeds from him now as a donator; from him, not only as a means of conveyance, but as one that has power to give grace; power as he is the Son of man. For as the Son of man, he is the Lamb; and as he is the Lamb, it cometh from him. " The Son of man hath power on earth to forgive sins," and that before he had actually paid to God the price of our redemption. (Matt. ix. 6. 1 Cor. i. 3. 2 Cor. i. 2. Gal. i. 3.) But how much more now ? Wherefore Paul, in his prayer for grace and peace for saints, supplicates both God and the Lamb. "Grace be to you from God the Father, and from our Lord Jesus Christ." (Eph. i. 2.)

" *Proceeding out of the throne.*"—Formerly this river of waters is said to come from under the threshold of the house of the Lord. (Ezek. xlvii. 1.) And it is said again, they " shall go out from Jerusalem," (Zech. xiv. 8;) that is, the church or house of God still. In that they are said to come out from under the threshold, it may be to intimate that they ran but low formerly, if compared to what they do now : which might also be signified by this, that they issued out; that that issues out ordinarily comes forth but slowly. Also the prophet saith, the first time he went through the waters they were but up to the ankles. (Ezek. xlvii. 3, 4.) But what is ankle-deep to that which followeth after ? It is said also to come out from Jerusalem, where I perceive were no great rivers, to intimate that as long as the first priesthood, first temple, and type were in their splendour, only the shadow of heavenly things were in use, and that then grace ran but slowly, nor would run much faster, because Jesus was not yet glorified. For the Spirit and abundance of grace was to be given, not before, but after his ascension.

Wherefore, now Jesus is ascended, now he is glorified; now grace proceeds from the throne, not from the threshold of the house. "He showed me a pure river of water of life, clear as crystal, proceeding out of the throne of God, and of the Lamb." (Exod. xxv. 17.)

" *The throne.*"—That of which the mercy-seat was a type; that which is called " the throne of grace." (Heb. iv. 16.) And it is called the throne of grace even therefore because it is that from, or out of which proceeds this river of water of life, this overflowing grace of God. Now it may be asked, What is the throne of grace ? And I shall answer, it is the humanity of Christ. (Isa. xxii. 22, 23.) He is the throne; he is the Jacob in which God sitteth. And he shall be for a glorious throne to his Father's house. (Rev. iii. 7.) The fulness of the Godhead dwells in him bodily, and God was in Christ, reconciling the world unto himself, nor can grace come to men but by Christ, nor can God rest as to our salvation but in him. But because I have spoken of this thing more particularly upon that text, " Let us therefore

come boldly to the throne of grace," &c., I shall therefore here say no more. Only methinks it is a glorious title that the Holy Ghost has given to the humanity of Christ, in that he calls it the throne of God; and methinks he gives it the highest preference, in that he saith, out thence proceeds a pure river of water of life. We will a little, therefore, speak something to this word—the throne, the throne of God.

First, A throne is the seat of majesty and greatness; it is not for things of an inferior quality to ascend or assume a throne. Now, then, since this river of water of life proceeds from the throne, it intimates that in grace and mercy there is great majesty; for grace, as it proceeds, has a voice from the throne. And, indeed, there is nothing in heaven or earth that can so awe the heart as the grace of God. (Hos. iii. 5.) It is that which makes a man fear; it is that which makes a man tremble; it is that which makes a man bow and bend, and break to pieces. (Jer. xxxii. 9.) Nothing has that majesty and commanding greatness in and upon the hearts of the sons of men, as has the grace of God.

So that, I say, when he saith, that this river of grace proceeds out of the throne of God, it is to show us what a majesty, what a commanding greatness there is in grace. " The love of Christ constraineth us."

When Moses went up to the mount the first time to receive the law, he did exceedingly fear and quake. Why ? Because of the fire and smoke, thick darkness and thunder, &c.; but when he went up the second time thither, " he made haste, and bowed his head towards the earth, and worshipped." But why ? Because it was before proclaimed, that " the Lord was gracious and merciful, long-suffering, and abundant in goodness and truth : keeping mercy for thousands, forgiving iniquity, transgression, and sin," &c. (Exod. xxxiv. 6—9.)

There is nothing over-mastereth the heart like grace, and so obligeth to sincere and unfeigned obedience as that. " Examine me, O Lord," said David, " and prove me; try my reins and my heart, for thy loving-kindness is before my eyes, and I walked in thy truth." (Ps. xxvi. 2, 3.) Therefore he saith again, O Lord, our Lord, " how excellent is thy loving-kindness " in all the earth ! And that loving-kindness is marvellous, for it has that majesty, and that excellent glory in it, as to command the heart and subdue sin. And, therefore, grace has given to it the title of sovereignty, or of one that reigns. The throne is called, " the throne of grace," that on which it sits and reigns, as well as that from whence it proceeds, (Heb. iv. 16.) " Grace reigns through righteousness to eternal life, by Jesus Christ our Lord." (Rom. v. 21.)

Second, As a throne is a seat of majesty and greatness, and so can awe, so it is the seat of authority and legislative power, and so will awe; this is confirmed from what was said but now, "grace reigns." Wherefore it is expected, that they that hear the word of God's grace should submit thereto, and that at their peril. "He that believes not shall be damned," is a word of power, of law, and of authority, and the contemner shall find it so. Grace proceeds from the throne, from the throne of God and of the Lamb. Wherefore, sinner, here is laid a necessity upon thee; one of the two must be thy lot; either thou must accept of God's grace, and be content to be saved freely thereby, notwithstanding all thy undeservings and unworthiness, or else thou must be damned for thy rebellion, and for thy rejecting of this grace. Wherefore consider with thyself, and think what is best to be done. Is it better that thou submit to the grace and mercy of God, and that thou acceptest of grace to reign for thee, in thee, and over thee, than that thou shouldst run the hazard of eternal damnation, because thou wouldst not be saved by grace? Consider of this, I say, for grace is now in authority, it reigns, and proceeds from the throne. Now, you know, it is dangerous opposing, rejecting, despising, or disowning of them in authority: better speak against twenty, than against one that is in authority. If "the wrath of a king is as messengers of death," (Prov. xvi. 14,) if the wrath of the king "is as the roaring of a lion," (xix. 12,) what is the wrath of God? And you know, to despise grace, to refuse pardon, to be unwilling to be saved from the guilt and punishment due to treasons the king's way, since that also is the best way, how will that provoke? how hot will that make wrath? But to accept of grace, especially when it is free grace, grace that reigns, grace from the throne, how sweet is it? "His favour is as dew upon the grass."

This, therefore, calls for thy most grave and sedate thoughts. Thou art in a strait, wilt thou fly before Moses, or with David fall into the hands of the Lord? Wilt thou go to hell for sin, or to life by grace? One of the two, as was said before, must be thy lot; for grace is king, is upon the throne, and will admit of no other way to glory. In and by it thou must stand, if thou hast any hope, or canst at all "rejoice in hope of the glory of God." (Rom. v. 2.)

Third, As the throne is the seat of majesty and authority, so it is the highest seat of authority. There is none above the throne, there is no appeal from the throne. There are inferior courts of judicature, there are under-governors, and they may sometimes perhaps be faulty; wherefore in some cases an appeal from such may be lawful, or permitted; but from the throne none can appeal. Now grace is upon the throne, reigns upon the throne, proceeds from the throne. A man may appeal from the law to the throne; from Moses to Christ; from him that spake on earth, to him that speaks from heaven; but from heaven to earth, from Christ to Moses, none can appeal. Moses himself has forbid it. For "Moses truly said unto the fathers, A prophet shall the Lord your God raise up unto you, of your brethren, like unto me; him shall you hear in all things whatsoever he shall say unto you; and it shall come to pass, that every soul which will not hear that prophet shall be destroyed from among the people." (Acts iii. 22, 23.)

See here, this new prophet judges in the highest court; he is master of grace, the throne by which grace reigns; and even Moses admits, that from himself an appeal may be made to this prophet, yea, he allows that men may flee from himself to this prophet for refuge; but there must be no appeal from him. Thou must hear him, or die. How shall we escape, "if we turn away from him that speaketh from heaven?" (Heb. xii. 25.)

This, therefore, is to be duly weighed, and deeply considered by us. It is not a saint, nor a minister, nor a prophet, nor an angel that speaks, for all these are but servants, but inferiors; no, it is a voice from the throne, from authority, from the highest authority; it is the Lord from heaven. This grace proceeds from the throne; and therefore men must stand and fall by what shall come from hence. He that comes not hither to drink, shall die for thirst. He that refuses this water now, shall not have so much as will hang upon the tip of his finger, if it would save his soul, hereafter. "How shall we escape, if we neglect so great salvation?" (Heb. ii. 3.)

Apostates will, therefore, from hence find griping pangs and burning coals, for they have turned themselves away from this throne, and from the grace that proceeds therefrom; nor is it to any purpose whatever they plead for themselves. They are fallen from grace, and what can help them? Christ is become of none effect unto such, whosoever is, that is, seeks to be justified by the law, they "are fallen from grace." (Gal. v. 4.)

Fourth, The throne is the seat of glory. "When the Son of man shall come in his glory, and all the holy angels with him; then he shall sit upon the throne of his glory." (Matt. xxv. 31.) And if the throne of judgment is the seat of glory, much more the throne of grace. We will venture then to say, that the throne of grace is the throne of God's glory, as the throne of judgment will be the throne of Christ's glory; and that grace proceedeth from his throne, that both IT and HE might have glory, glory in a way of mercy.

1. That it might have glory; therefore has he designed, that grace shall be effectual in, and to the salvation of some; even "to the praise of the glory of his grace, wherein he hath made us accepted in the Beloved." (Eph. i. 6.) He has designed, not the glory of man's works, but the glory of his own grace; and therefore has put man's works, as to justifications before God, under his feet, and counts them as filthy rags; but hath set his grace up above, has made it a king, given it authority to reign, has provided for it a throne, and called that throne the throne of grace; from whence it also proceeds to its own praise and glory,

in and by the effectual salvation of those that receive it, and receive it not in vain.

2. As grace is exalted, and made to proceed out of the throne to its own praises, to its own glory, so is it also thus exalted and made flow to us like a river, that we should be the praise of the glory of him that hath exalted it. We that receive it, and submit unto the throne whence it proceeds, have thereby " obtained an inheritance, being pre-destinated according to the purpose of him who worketh all things after the counsel of his own will, that we should be to the praise of his glory." (Eph. i. 11, 12.) So that this throne is a throne of glory: "A glorious high throne from the be-ginning is the place of our sanctuary." Now, what follows from this, but that they that accept of this grace give glory to God, to his grace, and to the word of his grace? such, I say, glorify God for his mercy, (Rom. xv. 9;) "they glorify God by their professed subjection to the gospel of Christ," (2 Cor. ix. 13,) which is the gospel, or good tidings "of the grace of God." (Acts xx. 24.) They with Abraham believe and give glory to God, (Rom. iv. 20,) and with the Gentiles they "glorify the word of the Lord." (Acts xiii. 48.)

But to slight grace, to do despite to the Spirit of grace, to prefer our own works to the derogating from grace, what is it, but to contemn God? to contemn him when he is on the throne, when he is on the throne of his glory? I say, it is to spit in his face, even then when he commands thee to bow before him, to subject unto him, and to glorify the grace of his glory, that proceeds from the throne of his glory. If men in old times were damned because they glorified him not as God, shall not they be more than damned, if more than damned can be, who glorify him not for his grace? And, to be sure, none glorify him for his grace but those that close in therewith, and submit themselves thereto. Talkers of grace are but mockers of God, but flatterers of God. Those that only talk highly of grace, and submit not themselves unto it, are but like those that praise a look, or flatter him in his own conceits. Grace God has exalted; has set it upon the throne, and so made it a king, and given it authority to reign; and thou goest by and hearest thereof, but wilt not submit thyself thereto, neither thy soul, nor thy life : why, what is this more than to flatter God with thy lips, and than to lie unto him with thy tongue; what is this but to count him less wise than thyself, while he seeks glory by that by which thou wilt not glorify him; while he displays his grace before thee in the world from the throne, and as thou goest by, with a nod thou callest it a fine thing, but followest that which leadeth therefrom? Tremble, tremble, ye sinners, that have despised the riches of his goodness. The day is coming when ye shall behold, and wonder, and perish, if grace pre-vaileth not with you to be content to be saved by it to the praise of its glory, and to the glory of him who hath set it upon the throne. (Acts xiii. 38—41.)

Fifth, The throne is the seat of wisdom. Hence he is called the Ancient of Days that sits on this throne, the throne of God. (Dan. vii. 9.) Infinite in wisdom, whose garments were white as snow, and the hair of his head like pure wool. By Ancient of Days, and in that it is said the hair of his head is like the pure wool, his wisdom is set forth unto us. Wherefore when we read that out of the throne proceeds a river of grace, when we read this proceedeth out of the throne of God, it is as much as to say, the wise God, who most per-fectly knoweth all ways, counteth in his wisdom that to save men by grace is the best, most safe, and sure way. "Therefore it is of faith, that it might be by grace, to the end the promise might be sure to all the seed." (Rom. iv. 16.) And again, for-giveness is according to the riches of his grace, "Wherein he has abounded towards us, in all wis-dom and prudence." (Eph. i. 7, 8.) Wherefore to set grace upon the throne, to let grace proceed out of the throne as a river, is by the wise God, the only wise God, counted the best way, the safest way, the way that dost best suit the condition of a sinful man, and that tends most to the utter disap-pointment of the devil, and death, and hell. Grace can justify freely, when it will, who it will, from what it will. Grace can continue to pardon, favour, and save from falls, in falls, out of falls. Grace can comfort, relieve, and help those that have hurt themselves. And grace can bring the un-worthy to glory. This the law cannot do, this man cannot do, this angels cannot do, this God cannot do, but only by the riches of his grace, through the redemption that is in Jesus Christ. Wherefore seeing God has set grace on the throne, and ordered that it should proceed from this throne to the world; yea, seeing he has made it king, and granted to it, to it only, the authority and sovereignty of saving souls; he has magnified, not only his love, but his wisdom, and his prudence before the sons of men. (2 Sam. xiv. 14. Prov. viii. 11, 12.) This, then, is his great device, the master-piece of all his witty inventions; and there-fore it is said, as was hinted afore, in this thing he hath proceeded toward us in all wisdom and prudence.

So then, he that comes to, and drinks of this water, glorifies God for his wisdom, praises God for his wisdom. Such an one saith, that God is only wise, and, bowing his head, saith again, "To God only wise, be glory, both now and for ever. Amen." But he that shall contemn this grace, confronts the highest wisdom, even wisdom upon the throne. He saith to himself, I am wiser than Daniel, than the judgment of God. I could have found out a more safe way to heaven myself, and had I been of God's counsel, I would have told him so. All this so horrible blasphemy naturally proceeds from him that liketh not that grace should be king on the throne, and should proceed out of the throne to the world. But "shall he that contendeth with the Almighty instruct him?" he that reproveth God, let him answer it. (Job xl. 2.)

The text says, that this very doctrine to the Greeks, to the wise, is foolishness, and the preaching of it a foolish thing to them. (1 Cor. i. 21—25.) But it will appear even then, when the conclusion of all things is come, and when these wise ones by their wisdom have fooled themselves to hell, that this "foolishness of God is wiser than men, and the weakness of God is stronger than men."

Christ Jesus, because he was low in the world, is trampled upon by some, but he is a glorious throne to his Father's house. For since his humility was the lowest of all, now he is exalted to be the throne of God; yea, is made the fountain whence grace continually flows, like the rivers, and comes down to us like a mighty stream. Wherefore, I will conclude this with both comfort and caution; with comfort, and that because of the security that they are under, that indeed have submitted themselves to grace. "Sin shall not have dominion over you, for you are not under the law, but under grace." And let it be a caution to those that despise. Take heed! it is dangerous affronting of the wisdom of God. Now, here is the wisdom of God, even wisdom upon the throne. It pleased God, for the glory of his wisdom, to make this the way; to wit, to set up grace to reign. I have often thought, and sometimes said, if God will be pleased with any way, surely he will be pleased with his own. Now this is the way of his own devising, the fruit and effect of his own wisdom. Wherefore, sinner, please him, please him in that wherein he is well-pleased. Come to the waters, cast thyself into them, and fear not drowning; let God alone to cause them to carry thee into his paradise, that thou mayest see his throne.

Sixth, The throne is the seat of faithfulness, the place of performing of engagements and promises. "When I shall receive the congregation," saith Christ, "I will judge uprightly," (Ps. lxxv. 2;) that is, faithfully. And now he has received it, and is made head over all things to it; and for this cause is he upon the throne, yea, is the throne from whence proceeds all this grace, that like a river doth flow and glide from heaven into the world. (Eph. i. 22, 23.) This river, then, is nothing else but the fulfilling of promises, the faithful fulfilling of promises. "If I go not away the Comforter will not come unto you; but if I depart I will send him unto you." (John xvi. 7.) "This is that which was spoken by the prophet Joel: And it shall come to pass in the last days, saith God, I will pour out of my Spirit upon all flesh," &c. (Acts ii. 16—18.) Now this river is the Spirit, the Spirit and grace of God, which was promised by the Father and the Son, and now it comes running from the throne of God and of the Lamb. For "being by the right hand of God exalted, and having received of the Father the promise of the Spirit, he hath shed forth that which ye now see and hear." (Acts ii. 33.)

Behold then how mindful, how careful, how faithful our Father and the Lamb of God is! It is not exaltation, nor glory, nor a crown, nor a kingdom, nor a throne, that shall make him neglect his poor ones on earth. Yea, therefore, even because he is exalted and on the throne, therefore it is that such a river with its golden streams proceeds from the throne to come unto us. And it shall proceed to be far higher than ever was the swellings of Jordan. True, it runs not so high now as in former days, because of the curse of God upon antichrist, by whose means the land of God's people is full of briers and thorns, (Isa. xxxii. 13—17;) but when the tide is at the lowest, then it is nearest the rising; and this river will rise, and in little time be no more so low as but ankle-deep. It will be up to the knees, to the loins, and be a broad river to swim in. (Ezek. xlvii.) For "there the glorious Lord shall be unto us a place of broad rivers and streams." (Isa. xxxiii. 21.) And "there shall be no more curse" in the church, "but the throne of God and of the Lamb shall be in it, and his servants shall serve him" without molestation. (Rev. xxii. 3—6.)

"These sayings are faithful and true," and in faithfulness shall they, from the throne of God and of the Lamb, be performed to the church. Faithfulness in him that rules, is that which makes Sion rejoice; because thereby the promises yield milk and honey. For now the faithful God, that keepeth covenant, performs to his church that which he told her he would. Wherefore our rivers shall run, and our brooks yield honey and butter. (Job. xx. 17.) Let this teach all God's people to expect, to look, and wait for good things from the throne. But oh! methinks, this throne out of which good comes like a river, who would not but be a subject to it? who would not but worship before it? But,

Seventh, A throne is "the seat of justice." "Justice and judgment are the habitation of thy throne." (Ps. lxxxix. 14.) And it is also from justice that this river of grace flows to us—justice to Christ, and justice to those that are found in him. (Rom. iii. 24.) God declares that he can justly justify, and justly forgive. Now if he can justly justify, and justly forgive, then can he give grace, and cause that it should proceed to, yea, flow after us as a river. (1 Cor. x. 4.) The river that gushed out of the rock in the wilderness ran after the people there, wherever they wandered therein. They drank of the rock that followed them; the rock was not removed out of his place; but the flood followed them whither they went. "He opened the rock, and the waters gushed out, they ran in the dry places like a river." (Ps. cv. 41.) This rock, saith he, was Christ, that is, figuratively; and this throne is Christ really. And the water gushing out of the rock, and following of them in the wilderness, was to show how, when

Christ became a throne, grace and goodness should follow us in the wilderness from thence so long as here we abide. Wherefore David considering this, said, " Surely goodness and mercy shall follow me all the days of my life, and I will dwell in the house of the Lord for ever." (Ps. xxiii. 6.) But whence must this come ? The text says, from the throne ; from the throne, the seat of justice ; for from thence, by reason of what He hath found in Christ for us, he in a way of righteousness and justice lets out to us rivers of his pleasures ; whose original is that great and wide sea of mercy, that flows in his infinite heart beyond thought.

All is paid for both us and grace. (John vii. 39.) "We are bought with a price." (1 Cor. vi. 20.) He has obtained eternal redemption for us. (Heb. ix. 12.) Yea, and as we are made his, and heaven made ours thus, so this river of grace has been also obtained by him for us. Wherefore all comes to us in a way of justice and righteousness. Hence we are said to obtain " faith through the righteousness of God," (2 Pet. i. 1 ;) that is, through the justice of God, and of Jesus our Lord. Mark, here is the justice of God, and the justice of Jesus our Lord ; and we have our faith from the justice of God, because of the righteousness of Jesus our Lord. That is, Jesus answered with works of justice the demands of justice ; and therefore, in a way of justice, grace reigns and comes to us like a river, as is signified for that it is said to come to us out of the throne.

Again ; grace is said to "reign through righteousness unto eternal life." (Rom. v. 21.) Through what righteousness ? The righteousness or justice of God by Jesus Christ our Lord. By Jesus Christ, or for his sake. For, for his sake, as I said, we are forgiven, and for his sake have all things pertaining to life and godliness. Which all things come to us, through, or down the stream of this river in a way of justice, and therefore it is said to come from the throne.

Eighth. This throne is the seat of grace and mercy ; and therefore it is called the mercy-seat, and throne of grace. This throne turns all into grace, all into mercy! This throne makes all things work together for good. It is said of Saul's sons, they were not buried after they were hanged until water dropped upon them out of heaven. (2 Sam. xxi. 10, 14.) And it may be said of us, there is nothing suffered to come near us until it is washed in that water that proceeds from the throne of grace. Hence afflictions flow from grace; persecutions flow from grace ; poverty, sickness, yea, death itself is now made ours by the grace of God through Christ. (Ps. cxix. 67. 1 Cor. iii. 22. Rev. iii. 19. Heb. xii. 5—7.) O grace ! O happy church of God ! all things that happen to thee are for Christ's sake turned into grace. They talk of the philosopher's stone, and how, if one had it, it would turn all things into gold. Oh ! but can it turn all things into grace ? can it make all things work together for good ? No, no, this quality,

virtue, excellency, what shall I call it ? nothing has in it, but the grace that reigns on the throne of grace ; the river that proceeds from the throne of God. This, this turns majesty, authority, the highest authority, glory, wisdom, faithfulness, justice, and all into grace. Here is a throne ! God, let us see it. John had the honour to see it, and to see the streams proceeding from it. Oh, sweet sight! Oh, heart-ravishing sight! " He showed me a pure river of water of life, proceeding out of the throne of God."

Indeed, as was hinted before, in the days of the reign of antichrist there are not those visions of this throne, nor of the river that proceedeth therefrom ; now he holdeth back the face of his throne, and spreadeth a cloud upon it; but the preserving, saving benefits thereof, we have, as also have all the saints in the most cloudy and dark day. And since we can see so little we must believe the more; and by believing, give glory to God. We must also labour for more clear scripture knowledge of this throne; for the holy word of God is the perspective-glass by which we may, and the magnifying-glass that will cause us to behold " with open face the glory of this Lord." (2 Cor iii. 18.)

But, methinks, I have yet said nothing of this throne, which is indeed none other but the spotless and glorified humanity of the Son of God. This throne is the Lord Jesus, this grace comes from the Divine Majesty as dwelling bodily in the Lord Jesus. Wherefore let us fall down before the throne, and cast our crowns at the foot of the throne, and give thanks to him that sits upon the throne, and to the Lamb for ever and ever.

Oh how should Jesus be esteemed of ! The throne of the king is a royal seat. (1 Kings x. 20.) It is said of Solomon's, there was not its like in any kingdom ; but of this it may be said, there is not its like in heaven and earth. (Rev. iv. 1—8.) At the setting up of this throne the angels flocked round about it, and the beasts and the elders gathered together to see it. When this throne was set in heaven, there was silence, all the heavenly host had no leisure to talk; they were surprised with sight and wonder. When this throne was set in heaven, what talk there was! it was as the music of the trumpet. " And behold," says John, " a door was open in heaven ; and the first voice that I heard, was as it were of a trumpet talking with me, which said, Come up hither, and I will show thee things which must be hereafter. And immediately I was in the spirit, and behold a throne was set in heaven, and one sat upon the throne."

This throne was Jesus Christ exalted; set, that is, lifted up, not as upon the cross, to the contempt and scorn of his person ; but, as I said, to the wonderment of the four beasts, and the elders, and all the angels in heaven. " A throne was set in heaven, and one sat upon the throne ;" that is, God. And this intimates his desirable rest for ever ; for to sit is to rest, and Christ is his rest for ever. Was it not, therefore, well worth the seeing ? yea, if John had taken the pains to go up thither upon his hands and knees ; I say, to see the Lord Jesus as a throne set in heaven, and the glory of God resting and abiding upon him, and giving out by him all things, not only his Word, but all his dispensations and providences to the end of the world ; and this blessed thing among the rest, even "a pure river of water of life, clear as crystal."

IV. But I leave this, and proceed to the fourth and last thing; namely, to the nature and quality of this water. It is said to be pure and clear, pure and clear as crystal ; "And he showed me a pure river of water of life, clear as crystal." I know that there is a twofold quality in a thing, one with respect to its nature, and the other with respect to its operation. The first of these is inherent, and remaineth in the subject being as such, and so for the most part useless. The other is put forth then when it meeteth with fit matter on which it may freely work. As to instance, *aquæ vitæ*, the very metaphor here made use of, hath a quality inherent in it, but keep it stopped up in a bottle, and then who will may faint notwithstanding ; but apply it, apply it fitly, and to such as have need thereof, and then you may see its quality by the operation. This water, or river of grace, is called, I say, "the water of life," and so, consequently, has a most blessed inherent quality; but its operation is seen by its working, the which it doth only then, when it is administered, and received for those ends for which it is administered; for then it revives where life is, and gives life where it is not. And thus far in the general have we spoken to it already. We will therefore in this place more particularly, though briefly, speak a few words unto it.

First, then. This water of life is the very groundwork of life *in* us, though not the groundwork of life *for* us. The groundwork of life *for* us, is the passion and merits of Christ ; this is that for the sake of which grace is given unto us, as it is intimated by the text ; it proceeds from the throne of God, who is Christ. Christ then having obtained grace for us, must needs be precedent, as to his merit, to that grace he hath so obtained. Besides, it is clear that the Spirit and grace come from God through him ; therefore as to the communications of grace to us, it is the fruit of his merit and purchase. But, I say, in us, grace is the groundwork of life ; for though we may be said before to live virtually in the person of Christ before God, yet we are dead in ourselves, and so must be until the Spirit be poured upon us from on high ; for the Spirit is life, and its graces are life, and when that is infused by God from the throne, then we live, and not till then. And hence it is called, as before, living water, the water of life springing up in us to everlasting life. The Spirit then, and graces of the Spirit, which is the river here spoken of, is that, and that only, which can cause us to

live ; that being life to the soul, as the soul is life to the body. All men, therefore, as was said afore, though elect, though purchased by the blood of Christ, are dead, and must be dead until the Spirit of life from God and his throne shall enter into them ; until they shall drink it in by vehement thirst, as the parched ground drinks in the rain.

Now when this living water is received, it takes up its seat in the heart, whence it spreads itself to the awakening of all the powers of the soul. For as in the first creation the Spirit of God moved upon the face of the waters, in order to putting of that creature into that excellent fashion and harmony which now we behold with our eyes ; even so the new creation, to wit, the making of us new to God, is done by the overspreading of the same Spirit also. For the Spirit, as I may so say, sitteth and broodeth upon the powers of the soul, as the hen doth on cold eggs, till they wax warm and receive life. The Spirit then warmeth us, and bringeth the dead and benumbed soul, for so it is before conversion, to a godly sense and understanding of states, of states both natural and spiritual. And this is the beginning of the work of the Spirit, by which the soul is made capable of understanding what God and himself is.

And this drinking in of the Spirit is rather as the ground drinks in rain, than as a rational soul does through sense of the want thereof.

The Spirit also garnisheth the soul with such things as are proper for it to the making of it live that life that by the word of God is called for. It implanteth light, repentance, faith, fear, love, desires after God, hope, sincerity, and what else is necessary for the making the man a saint. These things, I say, are the fruits and effects of this Spirit, which, as a river of water of life, proceedeth forth of the throne of God and of the Lamb. Hence the Spirit is called the Spirit of faith, the Spirit of love, and the Spirit of a sound mind ; for that the Spirit is the root and original of all these things by his operations in, and upon the face of, the soul. (2 Cor. iv. 13. Gal. v. 22. 2 Tim. i. 7.)

But, again, as this living water, this Spirit, and the grace thereof, doth thus, so it also maintains these things once planted in the soul, by its continual waterings of them in the soul. Hence he saith, (Isa. xxvii. 3,) "I will water it every moment." Water *it* ; his vineyard, the soul of the church, the graces of the church ; and so the soul and graces of every godly man. And because it so happeneth sometimes, that some of those things wherewith the Holy Ghost has beautified the soul, may languish to a being, if not quite dead, yet ready to die, (Rev. iii. 2,) therefore he doth not only refresh and water our souls, but renews the face thereof, by either quickening to life that which remains, or by supplying of us with that which is new, to our godly perseverance and everlasting life. Thus "thou visitest the earth, and waterest it ; thou greatly enrichest it with the river of God." (Ps. lxv. 9.) For this must be remembered, that as the herb that is planted, or seed sown, needs watering with continual showers of the mountains, so our graces implanted in us by the Spirit of grace, must also be watered by the rain of heaven. "Thou waterest the ridges thereof abundantly, thou settlest the furrows thereof; thou makest it soft with showers, thou blessest the springing thereof." (ver. 10.) Hence he says that our graces shall grow. But how?—"I will be as the dew unto Israel; he shall grow as the lily, and cast forth his roots as Lebanon. His branches shall spread, and his beauty shall be as the olive-tree, and his smell as Lebanon. They that dwell under his shadow shall return; they shall revive as the corn, and grow as the vine; the scent thereof shall be as the wine of Lebanon." (Hos. xiv. 5—7.) Or, as he saith in another place, "The Lord shall guide thee continually, and satisfy thy soul in drought, and make fat thy bones; and thou shalt be like a watered garden, and like a spring of water whose waters fail not." (Isa. lviii. 11.)

There is, besides this, another blessing that comes to us by this living water, and that is the blessing of communion. All the warmth that we have in our communion, it is the warmth of the Spirit. When a company of saints are gathered together in the name of Christ, to perform any spiritual exercise, and their souls be edified, warmed, and made glad therein, it is because this water, this river of water of life, has, in some of the streams thereof, run into that assembly. (Jer. xxxi. 12, 13.) Then are Christians like those that drink wine in bowls, merry and glad; for that they have drank into the Spirit, and had their souls refreshed with the sweet gales, and strong wine thereof. This is the feast that Isaiah speaks of, when he saith, "In this mountain shall the Lord of hosts make unto all people a feast of fat things, a feast of wines on the lees, of fat things full of marrow, of wines on the lees well refined." (Isa. xxv. 6.) This is called in another place, "The communion of the Holy Ghost." (2 Cor. xiii. 14.) Now he warmeth spirits, uniteth spirits, enlighteneth spirits, revives, cherisheth, quickeneth, strengtheneth graces; renews assurances, brings old comforts to mind, weakens lusts, emboldeneth and raiseth a spirit of faith, of love, of hope, of prayer, and makes the Word a blessing, conference a blessing, meditation a blessing, and duty very delightful to the soul. Without this water of life, communion is weak, flat, cold, dead, fruitless, lifeless; there is nothing seen, felt, heard, or understood in a spiritual and heart-quickening way. Now ordinances are burdensome, sins strong, faith weak, hearts hard; and the faces of our souls dry, like the dry and parched ground.

This drink also revives us, when tempted, when sick, when persecuted, when in the dark, and when we faint for thirst. The life of religion is this water of life; where that runs, where that is received, and where things are done in this spirit,

there all things are well; the church thrifty, the soul thrifty, graces thrifty, and all is well. And this hint I thought convenient to be given of this precious water of life, that is, with reference to the operative quality of it.

Second, I shall come, in the next place, to speak of it as to the other descriptions which John doth give us of it. He says it is, 1. Pure. 2. Clear. 3. Clear to a comparison. "And he showed me a pure river of water of life, clear as crystal."

1. You read here, (1.) that this water of life is *pure*, that is, alone without mixture, for so sometimes that word "pure" is to be understood. As where it saith pure, pure oil olive, pure frankincense, pure gold, pure blood of the grape, and the like. (Exod. xxvii. 20; xxx. 34; xxv. 11, 17. Deut. xxxii. 14.) So, then, when he saith, "He showed me a pure river of water of life," it is as if he had said, he showed me a river of water that was all living, all life, and that had nothing in it but life. There was no death, or deadness, or flatness in it: or as he saith a little after, "And there shall be no more curse." A pure river. There is not so much as a grudge, or a piece of an upbraiding speech found therein. There is in it nothing but heart, nothing but love, nothing but grace, nothing but life. "The gifts and calling of God are without repentance." (Rom. xi. 29.)

(2.) "Pure" is sometimes set in opposition to show or appearance: as where he says, "The stars are not pure," (Job xv. 5;) that is, not so without mixture of darkness as they seem to be. So again, "If thou wert pure and upright," (Job viii. 6,) that is, as thou seemest to be, or as thou wouldst have us believe thou art. Now take "pure" in this sense here, and then the meaning is, it is grace without deceit, without guile; its show and its substance are the same; it has nothing but substance in it; it is indeed what it seems to be in bulk; it is a river in show, and a river indeed. It comes from God and from his throne in appearance, and really it comes from his very heart. The great fear of the tempted is, that there is not so much grace in God, and that he is not so free of it, as some scriptures seem to import. But this word "pure" is levelled against such objections and objectors, for the destroying of their doubts, and the relieving of their souls. There is no fraud, nor guile, nor fable in the business; for though God is pleased to present us with his grace, under the notion of a river, it is not to delude our fancies thereby; but to give us some small illustration of the exceeding riches of his grace, which as far, for quantity, outstrips the biggest rivers as the most mighty mountain doth the least ant's egg, or atom in the world.

(3.) But again, this word "pure" is set in opposition to that which is hurtful and destructive. "I am pure from the blood of all men;" that is, I have hurt nobody. "The wisdom that is from above is first pure," it is not hurtful. Do you count them pure with the wicked balances? how can that be, since they are hurtful? (Acts xx. 26. James iii. 17. Micah vi. 11.) Now take "pure" in this sense here, and then it intimates that the grace of God, and the doctrine of grace, is not a hurtful thing. (Eph. v. 18.) It is not as wine of an intoxicating nature. If a man be filled with it, it will do him no harm. The best of the things that are of this world are some way hurtful. Honey is hurtful, wine is hurtful, silver and gold are hurtful; but grace is not hurtful. (Prov. xxv. 16; xx. 1. 1 Tim. vi. 10.) Never did man yet catch harm by the enjoyment and fulness of the grace of God. There is no fear of excess, or of surfeiting here. Grace makes no man proud, no man wanton, no man haughty, no man careless, or negligent as to his duty that is incumbent upon him, either from God or man; no, grace keeps a man low in his own eyes, humble, self-denying, penitent, watchful, savory in good things, charitable; and makes him kindly affectionated to the brethren, pitiful and courteous to all men.

True, there are men in the world that abuse the grace of God, as some are said "to turn it into wantonness, and into lasciviousness." (Jude 4.) But this is, not because grace has any such tendency, or for that it worketh any such effect; but because such men are themselves empty of grace, and have only done as death and hell hath done with wisdom, "heard the fame thereof with their ears." (Job xxviii. 22.) It is a dangerous thing for a man to have the notions of grace while his heart is void of the spirit and holy principles of grace; for such a man can do no other than abuse the grace of God. Alas! what can be expected of him that has nothing in him to teach him to manage that knowledge of grace which he has, but his flesh, his lusts, and lustful passions? Can these teach him to manage his knowledge well? Will they not rather put him upon all tricks, evasions, irreligious consequences and conclusions, such as will serve to cherish sin? What Judas did with Christ, that a graceless man will do with grace, even make it a stalking-horse to his fleshly and vile designs; and rather than fail, betray both it, and the profession of it, to the greatest enemies it has in the world.

And here, I may say, though grace is pure, and not hurtful at all, yet one altogether carnal, sinful, and graceless, having to do with the doctrine of it, by the force of his lusts, which tamper with it, he will unavoidably bring himself into the highest ruin thereby. An unwary man may destroy himself by the best of things, not because there is in such things an aptness to destroy, but because of the abuse and misuse of them. Some know the way of life, the water of life, by knowledge that is naked and speculative only; and it had been better for such if they had not known, than to know and turn from what they know; than to know and make that knowledge subservient to their lusts. (2 Pet. ii. 20—22.) Some

receive the rain of God, and the droppings of his clouds, because they continually sit under the means of his grace. But, alas! they receive it as stones receive showers, or as dunghills receive the rain; they either abide as hard stones still, or else return nothing to heaven for his mercy, but as the dunghills do, a company of stinking fumes. These are they that drink in the rain that comes often upon them, and that instead of bringing forth herbs meet for the dresser, bring forth briers and thorns; and these are they who are nigh unto cursing, whose end is to be burned. (Heb. vi. 7, 8.)

(4.) By this word "pure" I understand sometimes the chiefest good, the highest good. There are many things that may be called good, but none of them are good, "as grace is good." All things indeed are pure, that is, all creatures in themselves are good and serviceable to man, but they are not so good as grace. (Rom. xiv. 20. Gen. i. 31.) "There is a generation that are pure," that are good in their own eyes. (Prov. xxx. 12.) There are good men, good consciences, good works, good days, good angels, &c.; but none so good as grace, for it is grace that has made them so. Grace, this water of life, therefore, is good, superlatively good, good in the highest degree; for that it makes all things good, and preserveth them good. And whatever it be that this water of life washeth not, it is evil and given to the curse, as the prophet intimates where he saith, "But the miry places thereof, and the marshes thereof, shall not be healed, they shall be given to salt." (Ezek. xlvii. 11.)

But who understands this, who believes it? Its goodness is kept close from the fowls of the air; men, most men are ignorant of the goodness of it, nor do they care to inquire after the enjoyment of this pure, this good water of life. The reason is, because though it is good in itself, good in the highest degree, and that which makes all things good, yet it is not such a good as is suited to a carnal appetite. There is good, and there is suitable good; now suitable good is of two sorts, either such as is spiritual or such as is temporal. That which is spiritual is desired only of them that are spiritual; for temporal good will satisfy a carnal mind. Now grace is a spiritual good; this river of grace is the goodness of spiritual good. It is the original life of all the grace in our souls. No marvel then if it be so little set by of those that are carnally-minded. Hay will serve a horse, and mire will serve a sow; so things of this life suit best with the men of this world, for their appetite is gross and carnal, and they savour not the things that be of the Spirit of God. "The natural man receiveth not the things that be of the Spirit of God," (the things that be of this river of God,) "for they are foolishness unto him; neither can he know them, because they are spiritually discerned." (1 Cor. ii. 14.) This is the river of oil which the prophet speaks of, the river of spirit. Were it a river of gold and silver there would be old fishing on the banks thereof. But it is a river that runs " like oil, saith the Lord God." This rock pours us out rivers of oil, fresh oil, soft oil, sweet oil, the oil of joy, the oil of gladness, oil to anoint the head withal, oil to make the face to shine, oil by which thou wilt be made able to honour both God and man in some good measure as becomes thee. (Job xxix. 6. Ps. xcii. 10; lv. 21. Isa. lxi. 3. Ps. xlv. 7. Eccles. ix. 8. Ps. civ. 15. Judges ix. 9.)

I might have enlarged upon this head, and have showed you many more particulars wherein this term of "pure" might serve for the better setting forth of the excellency of this water of life, but I shall proceed no further upon this, but will come to that which remains.

Second. As this river of water of life is said to be pure, so it is said to be *clear*. "He showed me a pure river of water of life, clear." This term has also its particular signification, and therefore ought to be heeded.

(1.) "Clear" is set in opposition to "dark;" therefore some are said to be "clear as the sun," (Sol. Song vi. 10.) And again, "The light shall not be clear nor dark." (Zech. xiv. 6.) In both these places "clear" is to be taken for light, daylight, sunlight; for indeed it is never day nor sunshine with the soul until the streams of this river of water of life come gliding to our doors, into our houses, into our hearts. Hence the beginning of conversion is called illumination, (Heb. x. 32;) yea, the coming of this river of water of life unto us is called the day-spring from on high, through the tender mercy of our God. (Luke i. 78.) It is also called the "dawning of the day." (2 Pet. i. 19.) And hence again, these men unto whom this river of water of life comes not, are said to be dark, darkness: "Ye were sometimes darkness, but now are ye light in the Lord." (Eph. v. 8.) Wherefore this water is like Jonathan's honey, it hath a faculty to open the eyes, to make them that sit in darkness see a great light, (1 Sam. xiv. 27,) the light of the knowledge of the glory of God in the face of Jesus Christ; (Matt. iv. 16;) " God who commanded the light to shine out of darkness, hath shined in our hearts, to give the light," (the Spirit that enlighteneth and giveth the light,) " of the knowledge of the glory of God in the face of Jesus Christ." (2 Cor. iv. 6.) This river casteth beams where it goes, like the beams of the sun; it shines, it casts out rays of glory unto those that drink thereof. The streams of this grace were they that overtook Saul when he was going to Damascus; they were the waters of this flood that compassed him round about. And if you will believe him, he saith, this light from heaven was a great light, a light above the brightness of the sun, a light that did, by the glory of it, make dark to him all the things in the world. (Acts ix. 3; xxii. 6; xxvi. 13.)

(2.) "Clear" is set in opposition to that which is not pleasing: For to be "clear" is to be plea-

sant. Hence it is said, "Truly the light is sweet, and a pleasant thing it is for the eyes to behold the clear sun." (Eccles. xi. 7.) I read of rivers that looked red as blood, that stank like the blood of a dead man; but this is no such river. (2 Kings iii. 22, 23. Exod. vii. 19, 20.) I read of rivers whose streams are like streams of brimstone, fiery streams, streams of burning pitch, but this is none of them. (Isa. xxx. 27—33. Dan. vii. 9—11. Isa. xxxiv. 9.) "There is a river," besides all these, clear and pleasant, "the streams whereof shall make glad the city of God." (Ps. xlvi. 4.) These are the waters that the doves love to sit by, because by the clearness of these streams, they can see their pretty selves as in a glass. (Sol. Song v. 12.) These are the streams where the doves wash their eyes, and by which they solace themselves and take great content. These streams are instead, as I said, of a looking-glass; their clearness presents us with an opportunity of seeing our own features. As in fair waters a man may see the body of the sun, and of the moon, and of the stars, and the very body of heaven; so he that stands upon the bank of this river, and that washeth his eyes with this water, may see the Son of God, the stars of God, the glory of God, and the habitation that God has prepared for his people. And are not these pleasant sights? is not this excellent water? has not this river pleasant streams?

(3.) "Clear" is set in opposition to dirty water and muddiness. I read of some waters that are fouled with the feet of beasts, and with the feet of men, yea, and deep waters too. Yea, saith God to some, ye "have drunken of the deep waters," and have fouled "the residue with your feet;" and again, "As for my flock, they eat that which ye have trodden with your feet, and they drink that which ye have fouled with your feet." (Ezek. xxxiv. 18, 19.) These waters are doctrines contained in the text, muddied and dirtied by the false glosses and sluttish opinions of erroneous judgments; of which the poor sheep have been made to drink. And verily this is apparent enough, by the very colour and hue of those poor souls; for though the truth of God was in them, yet the very stain of tradition and superstition might be also seen in their scales. For as the fish of the river receive, by being there, the changeable colours of the waters, so professors, what doctrine they hear and drink, do look like that. If their doctrines are muddy, their notions are muddy; if their doctrines are bloody, their notions and tempers are bloody: but if their doctrines are clear, so are their notions, for their doctrine has given them a clear understanding of things.

Now here we have a river of water of life, that is clear, clear without dirt and mud. Clear without the human inventions and muddy conceptions of unsanctified and uninstructed judgments; yea, here you have a river, the streams whereof lie

THE WATER OF LIFE.

open to all in the church, so that they need not those instruments of conveyance that are foul, and that use to make water stink if they receive it, to bring it to them that have need.

(4.) By "clear" we sometimes understand purgation; or that a thing has purged itself, or is purged from those soils and imputations of evil wherewith sometimes they have been charged. "Then shalt thou be clear from this my oath;" or, "How shall we clear ourselves?" (Gen. xxiv. 8—14; xliv. 16.) Something of this sense may be in the text, for if men are not afraid to charge God with folly, which is intimated by Ps. li. 4: "That thou mightest be clear when thou judgest;" will they, think you, be afraid to impute evil to his word, and grace, and Spirit? No, verily; they are bold enough at this work. Nay, more than this, even from the foundation of the world men have cast slanders upon, and imputed base things unto the blessed grace of the gospel. But not to look so far back, Paul was one of the pipes through which God conveyed this grace to the world; and what was he counted for his so doing, but "a pestilent fellow, and a mover of sedition throughout the whole world?" (Acts xxiv. 5, 6.)

But behold no imputation can stick on the grace of God, not stick long, for that, like honey, will purge itself of what filth is put into it, and of all bad imputations of evil men. Springs and rivers are of a self-purging quality: now here we have to do with a river, a river of water of life, (2 Kings x. 10—12;) but a river more slandered than ever did Naaman, the Syrian, slander the waters of Israel, in preferring those of Abana and Pharpar, rivers of Damascus, beyond them. But behold now, at last, when all the world have done what they can, and have cast what reproaches and slanders upon it they are able, it is a river pure and clear. It has purged itself before kings, it has purged itself before princes and judges, and all the Naamans in the world. It is still a river, a river of water of life, a river of water of life clear.

(5.) By "clear" we sometimes understand purity manifest, or innocency and goodness made known. "In all things you have approved yourselves to be clear in this matter." (2 Cor. vii. 11.) That is you have made it appear, and stand upon your justification, and are willing to be searched and sounded to the bottom by those that have a desire to undertake that work. So this river of water of life in the fountain, and in the streams thereof, offer themselves to the consideration and conscience of all men. To this end, how often doth God, the head of this river, and he out of whose throne it proceeds, call upon men to challenge him, if they can, with any evil or misdoing towards them, either by presence or doctrine; hence he says, "Put me in remembrance, let us plead together; declare thou," if thou canst, "that thou mayest be justified," (Isa. xliii. 26,) and I con-

demned. So again, "What iniquity have your fathers found in me, that they are gone far from me, and have walked after vanity, and are become vain?" (Jer. ii. 5.) So Christ: "Which of you convinceth me of sin?" And, "If I have spoke evil, bear witness of the evil." (John viii. 46; xviii. 23.) So Paul: "We have renounced the hidden things of dishonesty, not walking in craftiness, nor handling the word of God deceitfully; but by the manifestation of the truth commending ourselves to every man's conscience in the sight of God." (2 Cor. iv. 2.) All these sentences are chiefly to be applied to doctrine, and so are, as it were, an offer to any, if they can, to find a speck, or a spot, or a wrinkle, or any such thing in this river of water of life.

Some men fly from it as from a bear; and some are afraid to drink of it, for fear it should be poison unto them. Some, again, dare not take it, because it is not mixed, and as they, poor souls, imagine, qualified and made toothsome by a little of that which is called the wisdom of this world. Thus one shucks, another shrinks, and another will none of God. Meanwhile, whoso shall please to look into this river, shall find it harmless and clear; yea, offering itself to the consciences of all men to make trial, if it be not the only chief good, the only necessary waters, the only profitable for the health of the soul, of all the things that are in the world, and as clear of mischief as is the sun of spots.

Third. As John saw this river pure and clear, so he saw it clear to a comparison. Clear, to the best of comparisons, *clear as crystal.* Crystal is a very clear stone, as clear as the clearest glass, if not clearer; one may see far into it, yea through it; it is without those spots, and streaks, and smirches that are in other precious stones. Wherefore when he saith, that this river is clear as crystal, it is as if God should say, Look, sinners, look to the bottom of these my crystal streams. I have heard of some seas, that are so pure and clear that a man may see to the bottom though they may be forty feet deep. I know this river of water of life is a deep river; but though it is said to be deep, it is not said we can see no bottom. Indeed as to the wideness of it, it is said to be such as that it cannot be passed over. But I say, it is no where said that we cannot see to the bottom; nay, the comparison implies, that a man with good eyes may see to the bottom. It is clear, as clear as crystal. So, then, we will a little look down to the bottom, and see through these crystal streams, what is at the bottom of all.

1. Then, the bottom of all is, "that we might be saved." (John v. 34.) "These things I say," saith Christ, "that you might be saved;" and again, "I am come that ye might have life, and that you might have it more abundantly." (John x. 10.) This is the bottom of this great river of water of life; and of its proceeding from the throne of God and of the Lamb, it is, that we might be

saved; it is, that we might live. What a good bottom is here! what a sound bottom is here! but few deep rivers have a good bottom. Mud is at the bottom of most waters in the world; even the sea itself when it worketh, casts up mire and dirt, and so do the hearts of sinners: but the bottom of this grace of God, and of the Spirit, and word thereof, is that we might be saved; consequently a very good bottom.

2. As the bottom of all is, "that we may be saved;" so that we may be saved by grace, and this is a bottom sounder and sounder. Our salvation might have been laid upon a more difficult bottom than this. It might have been laid on our works; God might have laid it there, and have been just, or he might have left us to have laid it where we would, and then to be sure we had laid it there, and so had made but a muddy bottom to have gone upon to life. But now, this river of water of life, it has a better bottom; the water of life is as clear as crystal; look down to the bottom and see. "We are justified freely by his grace." (Rom. iii. 24.) "By grace are ye saved." (Eph. ii. 5, 8.) There is the bottom.

Now grace, as I have showed you, is a firm bottom to stand on, it is of grace, that life might be sure. (Rom. iv. 16.) Surely David was not here, or surely this was not the river that he spake of when he said, "I sink in deep waters, where there is no standing; I am come into deep waters, where the floods overflow me: deliver me out of the mire, and let me not sink." (Ps. lxix. 2, 14.) I say, to be sure this could not be the river. No, David was now straggled out of the way, was tumbled into some pit, or into some muddy and dirty hole; for as for this river, it has a good bottom, a bottom of salvation by grace; and a man needs not cry out when he is here, that he sinks, or that he is in danger of being drowned in mud or mire.

3. The bottom of all is, as I said, that we might be saved, saved by grace, and I will add, "through the redemption that is in Christ." This is still better and better. We read that when Israel came over Jordan, the feet of the priests that did bear the ark stood on firm ground in the bottom, and that they set up great stones for a memorial thereof. (Josh. iii. 17.) But had Jordan so good a bottom as has this most blessed river of water of life, or were the stones that Israel took out thence like this "tried stone," this "sure foundation?" (Isa. xxviii. 16.) Oh the throne! this river comes out of the throne, and we are saved by grace through the redemption that is in him." We read that there is a city that has foundations; grace is one, Christ another, and the truth of all the prophets and apostles, as to their true doctrine another, &c. (Heb. xi. 10.) And, again, all these are the very bottom of this goodly river of the water of life. (Eph. ii. 19, 20.)

4. There is another thing to be seen at the bottom of this holy river, and that is the glory of God; we are saved, saved by grace, saved by grace through the redemption that is in Christ, to the praise and glory of God. And what a good bottom here! Grace will not fail, Christ has been sufficiently tried, and God will not lose his glory; therefore they that drink of this river shall doubtless be saved, to wit, they that drink of it of a spiritual appetite to it: and thus much for the explication of the text.

I now come to make some use of the whole.

You know our discourse has been at this time of the water of life, of its quantity, head-spring and quality: and I have showed you that its nature is excellent, its quantity abundant, its head-spring glorious, and its quality singularly good.

First. Let this then, in the first place, be a provocation to us to be more free in making use of this water. There are many now-a-days, that are for inventing of waters to drink for the health of the body; and to allure those that are ill to buy, they will praise their waters beyond their worth. Yea, and if they be helpful to one person in a hundred, they make as if they could cure every one. Well, here you have the great Physician himself with his water, and he calls it the water of life, water of life for the soul; this water is *probatum est*. It has been proved times without number! it never fails, but where it is not taken. (Acts xxvi. 18. Isa. v. 4, 5.) No disease comes amiss to it; it cures blindness, deadness, deafness, dumbness. It makes "the lips of them that are asleep to speak." (Sol. Song vii. 9.) This is the right *holy water*, all other is counterfeit; it will drive away devils and spirits, it will cure enchantments and witchcrafts, it will heal the mad and lunatic. (Gal. iii. 1—3. Mark xvi. 17, 18.) It will cure the most desperate melancholy; it will dissolve doubts and mistrusts, though they are grown as hard as stone in the heart. (Ezek. xxxvi. 26.) It will make you speak well. (Col. iv. 6.) It will make you have a white soul, and that is better than to have a white skin. (Ezek. xxxvi. 25.) It will make you taste well, it will make you disrelish all hurtful meats, (Isa. xxx. 22;) it will beget in you a good appetite to that which is good; it will remove obstructions in the stomach and liver; it will cause that what you receive of God's bread shall turn to good nourishment, and make good blood. In a word, it preserveth life. (John iv. 14.) They that take this water shall live longer than did old Methuselah; and yet he lived a great while. (Gen. v. 27.)

Wherefore let me continue my exhortation to you. Be more free in making use of this water; it is the wholesomest water in the world; you may take it at the third, sixth, ninth, or eleventh hour, but to take it in the morning of your age is best, (Matt. xx. 3—6;) for then diseases have not got so great a head as when they are of long continuance, consequently they will be removed with far more ease: besides, those that thus do, will receive endless life and the comfort of it betimes, and that you know is a double life to one. (Eccles. xi. 1—4.)

This water gently purges, and yet more effectually than any others. True, where bad humours are more tough and churlish, it will show itself stronger of operation, for there is no disease can be too hard for it. It will, as we say, throw the house out of the windows, but it will rid us of the plague of those most deadly infections that otherwise will be sure to make us sleep in death, and bring us with the multitude down to hell. But it will do no hurt; it only breaks our sleep in security, and brings us to a more quick apprehension of the plague of our heart and flesh. It will, as I said before, provoke to appetite, but make us only long after that which is wholesome. If any ask why I thus allegorize, I answer, the text doth lead me to it.

Second. I advise therefore, in the next place, that thou get thee a dwelling-place by these waters. "The beloved of the Lord shall dwell in safety by him, and the Lord shall cover him all the day long." (Deut. xxxiii. 12.) If thou ask where that dwelling is, I answer, in the city of God, in and among the tabernacles of the Most High. This river comes from the throne, to water the city of God; and to that end it is said to run "in the midst of the street of it." (Rev. xxii. 2.) If ye will inquire, inquire, return, come. "The seed also of his servants shall inherit it, and they that love his name shall dwell therein." (Ps. lxix. 36.) Get thee a dwelling in Jerusalem, in the midst of Jerusalem, and then thou wilt be seated by this river.

In old times the ancients had their habitations by the rivers; yea, we read of Aroer, that stood upon the brink of the river Arnon. (Josh. xiii. 9.) Balaam also had his dwelling in his city Pethor, "by the river of the land of the children of his people." Oh, by a river side is the pleasantest dwelling in the world, and of all rivers, the river of the water of life is the best. They that dwell there "shall not hunger nor thirst, neither shall the heat or sun smite them, for he that hath mercy on them shall lead them, even by the springs of water shall he guide them." (Isa. xlix. 10.) Trees planted by the rivers, and that spread out their roots by the rivers, they are the flourishing trees, they bring forth their fruit in the season. (Ps. i. 3. Jer. xvii. 8.) And the promise is that men that take up their dwellings by this river of water of life shall be fruitful as such trees.

If thou art a Christian, thou hast more than an ordinary call and occasion to abide by these waters; thy things will not grow but by these waters. Weeds, and the excellencies of most men, we may find in the barren wilderness; they grow under every hedge; but thine are garden, and so choice things, and will not thrive without much water, no, without the water of God's river. Dwell, therefore, here, that thy soul may be as a watered garden. (Jer. xxxi. 12. Isa. xii. 1—3.) And when thou

seeth how those that are loth to die make provision at Tunbridge, Epsom, the Bath, and other places, and what houses they get that they may have their dwellings by those waters, then do thou consider of thy spiritual disease, and how nothing can cure thee but this blessed water of life. Be also much of desires to have a dwelling-place in Jerusalem, that thou mayest always be nigh to these waters. Be often also in watering thy plants with these waters. I mean, the blessed graces of God in thy soul; then shalt thou grow and retain thy greenness, and prove thyself to be a disciple indeed. And herein is God and thy Father glorified, that thou bear much fruit. (John xv. 8.)

Third. My third word is, Bless God for providing for man such waters. These only can make us live; all others come out of the Dead Sea, and do kill: there is no living water but this. I say, show thy acceptation of it with thanksgiving; if we are not to receive our bread and cheese but with thankfulness, how should we bless God for this unspeakable gift? (2 Cor. ix. 15.) This is soul life, life against sin, life from sin; life against the curse, life from the curse; life beyond hell, beyond desert, beyond thought, beyond desires. Life that is pleasing, life that is profitable, life everlasting. Oh, my brethren, bless God! who doth good, and gives us such rain, filling our hearts with food and gladness! When Moses would take the heart of Israel, and took in hand to raise up their spirits to thankfulness, he used to tell them that the land they were to go to was a land that God cared for, and that was watered with the dew of heaven. Yea, "a land of brooks of water, of fountains and depths that spring out of valleys and hills: a land that flowed with milk and honey, which is the glory of all lands." (Deut. viii. 7. Exod. iii. 8; xiii. 5. Lev. xx. 24. Numb. xiv. 8.) But yet in his description he makes no mention of a river of water of life; a river the streams whereof make glad the city of God.

This river is the running out of God's heart, the letting out of his very bowels, for God is the living God. This is his heart and soul. "Yea, I will rejoice over them to do them good, and I will plant them in this land assuredly, with my whole heart, and with my whole soul." (Jer. xxii. 41.) I say, if ever God's heart and soul appeared, it showed itself in giving this water of life, and the throne from whence it proceeds. Wherefore, all the reason of the world that in the reception of it thy heart and soul should run out and flow after him in thanksgivings. See how David words it in the hundred and third psalm, all the five first verses; and do likewise.

Fourth. By the characters that are given of this water of life, thou art capacitated to judge when a notion, a doctrine, an opinion, comes to thine ears, whether it is right good and wholesome, or how. This river is pure, is clear, is pure and clear as crystal. Is the doctrine offered unto thee so? or is it muddy, and mixed with the doctrines of men? Look, man, and see if the foot of the worshippers of Bel be not there; and if the waters be not fouled thereby. What water is fouled, is not the water of life, or at least not the water of life in its clearness. Wherefore, if thou findest it not right, go up higher to the spring-head; for always the nearer to the spring, the more pure and clear is the water. Fetch then thy doctrine from afar, if thou canst not have it good nearer hand. (Job xxxvi. 3.) Thy life lies at stake, the counterfeit of things is dangerous; everybody that is aware, is afraid thereof. Now a counterfeit here is most dangerous, is most destructive; wherefore take heed how you hear, what you hear, for, as I said before of the fish, by your colour it will be seen what waters you swim in; wherefore look you well to yourselves.

Fifth. Doth this water of life run like a river? like a broad, full, and deep river? Then let no man, be his transgressions never so many, fear at all, but there is enough to save his soul, and to spare. Nothing has been more common to many, than to doubt of the grace of God; a thing most unbecoming a sinner of anything in the world. To break the law is a fact foul enough; but to question the sufficiency of the grace of God to save therefrom, is worse than sin, if worse can be. Wherefore, despairing soul, for it is to thee I speak, forbear thy mistrusts, cast off thy slavish fears, hang thy misgivings as to this upon the hedge; and believe thou hast an invitation sufficient thereto, a river is before thy face. And as for thy want of goodness and works, let that by no means daunt thee: this is a river of water of life; streams of grace and mercy. There is, as I said, enough therein to help thee, for grace brings all that is wanting to the soul. Thou, therefore, hast nothing to do, I mean as to the curing of thy soul of its doubts, and fears, and despairing thoughts, but to drink and live for ever.

Sixth. But what is all this to the dead world; to them that love to be dead? They toss their vanities about as the boys toss their shuttlecocks in the air, till their foot slips, and themselves descend into the pit.

Let this suffice for this time.

PREFATORY REMARKS

ON

SOLOMON'S TEMPLE SPIRITUALIZED.

An active mind is generally disposed to discover in outward things, if invested with more than ordinary beauty, or grandeur, the type of things, still more worthy of admiration, not yet revealed. This tendency, remarkable in men of genius, is sanctified by the uses to which it may be put in making the highest order of truths more intelligible and practical. But the observation of such a natural property in the human mind, leads to another. If the objects presented in material creation, the mere transitory forms even of daily life, can excite ideas of a higher existence, much more may such intimations be looked for in the records of divine government. And yet further : is it to be supposed that nature has been arranged with reference to such teaching and revelations, and that when men most needed aid in the study of heavenly mysteries, the systems divinely given them were wanting in provisions so likely to be profitable ?

The fact answers to the supposition. In the system which was intended both to embody the sublimest mysteries, and to convey them to mankind, its divine Author employed a connected series of symbols and types. Of these, some were calculated to secure attention by their exceeding beauty ; some had in them an awfulness which bowed the most wanton spirit ; others stimulated to inquiry by their wide, but as yet, indefinite significance. None could present a greater number of such points for the exercise of a devout curiosity, than the plan and furniture of the Temple. In that wonderful structure were comprehended, as in a massive volume, all the elements of holy science. Every part of the edifice was a distinct chapter, conveying, if studied aright, some animating truth : every object on which the eye could rest was a word, or expression, grandly suggestive of divine power.

An interpreter of any species of types, or symbols, requires a twofold qualification for the office. He must have a ready sensibility to perceive that the objects before him have a meaning ; are intended, that is, to teach something. This is not identical with the knowledge, or ability, by which the meaning is discovered, but it is an essential preparative to the exercise of such gifts. The wisdom, which forms the other part of the qualification, is equally constituted of acquired learning, and ability cherished by divine grace. Without this twofold endowment, an interpreter, in either of the wide-stretching provinces of nature and revelation, will prove a hazardous, or defective guide. Quick sensibility ; a loving and earnest disposition, may give beauty, and sometimes an accidental truth, to his suggestions, but there can be no certainty in them ; and the inquirer, who has some painful doubt to settle, will quickly feel that an instructor of this kind can only sow the seeds of future perplexity.

The mode in which nature is observed by different minds affords a sufficient illustration of this principle. When the evening sky, red and lowering, teaches the mariner what weather he is to expect on the morrow, both the readiness to observe and the knowledge conferred by experience have led to the right conclusion. One of the constituted symbols of nature has been studied and interpreted. With more of sensibility, perhaps, another observer may have watched the appearance of the heavens. He may be deeply affected with the threatening gloom. It will excite in him thoughts of a far more distant future than the morrow. The weather and everything else of which the dark red clouds are the practical sign, is no concern of his. He employs the symbol of nature for another purpose. His feelings may have carried him into the very track of truth ; but whether they have or not is uncertain. We may take a contrary instance. Skilled as the mariner may be in the observation of winds and clouds, there may be a student of natural science, whose exact and profound knowledge renders him incomparably superior in the interpretation of all atmospheric phenomena. But suppose him to have no present interest in observing them. Let his mind have been long engaged in speculations which leave him indifferent to these things. His want of all wakeful attention to what is passing in the changeful sky, will deprive the best of his attainments of any practical importance.

When we turn to Scripture, and the manifold objects which it offers to our contemplation, the same rule holds good. Learning, suited to the purpose, enables the observer to give at once the true meaning of the mystery symbolically represented. In proportion to the variety, the greatness of the interests, here concerned, ought to be the exactness and comprehensiveness of the knowledge employed to interpret the sign. Damage might attend the frequent mistakes of a seaman wrongly viewing the signs of the sky : but it is certain, that utter loss would be the consequence of his erring as to the points of the compass. Thus also much harm may arise from a disposition to colour the narrative of Scripture with tints supplied by ardent sentiment or fancy. Injury is done to faith by every kind of pleasing conceit, which, vanishing at the sound of some simple question, leaves the mind with more than its ordinary amount of perplexity. This is commonly the condition of those readers of Scripture who have not attained to adequate ideas of its proper and intrinsic grandeur. Undisciplined to rejoice in truth itself, they pause too long among the symbols by which it is transmitted, and will often rather add to them meanings of their own, than let their understanding pass on as readily as it might to its proper object.

Hence the twofold difficulty of finding among the numerous interpreters of Scripture, men exactly fitted to comment upon the parts symbolical, or typical. If they be wanting in sensibility, they will give heed to nothing but that which is most obvious and palpable. Intimations full of sweet and soothing meanings, will be left unnoticed. If, on the contrary, they be under the influence of a lively imagination, and ardent temperament, the weightier matters of divine revelation will appear to occupy a subordinate place by the disproportionable splendour shed on those of inferior concernment. The first principles of interpretation are violated when this is the case ; and it is always likely to be so, when the solid learning, the spiritual-mindedness, and wise discretion of the interpreter, do not more than counterbalance the temptations of a subtle fancy.

" What is the mind of the Spirit ?" is a question of peculiar significance for the commentator. There is also another which he cannot with safety neglect to consider, or answer : " In what channels, by what means, has the Spirit chiefly made known his mind ?" Without a clear understanding of this matter, an interpreter of Scripture may commit the dangerous mistake of looking for revelations where none are meant, and of converting things described in Scripture to uses for which they were never intended. " THE WORD," stands in such eminent superiority to every other medium employed by the divine Spirit for communicating truth, that when truth is looked for through any other channel, it must be with the firm conviction, first, that the object, the building, the mountain, or whatever else it may be, is really intended by the Spirit to convey a special truth ; and next, that the method of interpretation chosen is not adopted to force a meaning, but to search for it as a treasure, the reality of which, if actually found, no one can dispute.

H. S.

SOLOMON'S TEMPLE SPIRITUALIZED;

OR,

GOSPEL-LIGHT FETCHED OUT OF THE TEMPLE AT JERUSALEM, TO LET US MORE EASILY INTO

THE GLORY OF NEW TESTAMENT TRUTHS.

" Thou son of man, show the house to the house of Israel; show them the form of the house, and the fashion thereof, and the goings out thereof, and the comings in thereof, and all the forms thereof, and all the ordinances thereof, and all the forms thereof, and all the laws thereof."—EZEK. xliii. 10, 11.

TO THE CHRISTIAN READER.

COURTEOUS CHRISTIAN READER,—I have, as thou by this little book mayest see, adventured at this time to do my endeavour to show thee something of the gospel glory of Solomon's temple; that is, of what it, with its utensils, was a type of, and, as such, how instructing it was to our fathers, and also is to us their children. The which, that I might do the more distinctly, I have handled particulars one by one, to the number of threescore and ten; namely, all of them I could call to mind, because, as I believe, there was not one of them but had its signification, and so something profitable for us to know.

For, though we are not now to worship God in those methods, or by such ordinances as once the old church did; yet to know their methods, and to understand the nature and signification of their ordinances, when compared with the gospel, may, even now, when themselves, as to what they once enjoined on others, are dead, may minister light to us. And hence the New Testament ministers, as the apostles, made much use of Old Testament language, and ceremonial institutions, as to their signification, to help the faith of the godly in their preaching of the gospel of Christ.

I may say, that God did in a manner tie up the church of the Jews to types, figures, and similitudes, I mean, to be butted and bounded by them in all external parts of worship. Yea, not only the Levitical law and temple, but, as it seems to me, the whole land of Canaan, the place of their lot to dwell in, was to them a ceremonial, or a figure. Their land was a type of heaven, their passage over Jordan into it, a similitude of our going to heaven by death. The fruit of their land was said to be uncircumcised, as being at their first entrance thither unclean, in which their land was also a figure of another thing, even as heaven was a type of grace and glory.

Again; the very land itself was said to keep Sabbath, and so to rest a holy rest, even then

when she lay desolate, and not possessed of those to whom she was given for them to dwell in.

Yea, many of the features of the then church of God were set forth, as in figures and shadows, so by places and things in that land. 1. In general, she is said to be beautiful as Tirzah, (Sol. Song vi. 4;) and to be comely as Jerusalem. 2. In particular, her neck is compared to the tower of David, building for an armoury. (ch. iv. 4.) Her eyes to the fish-pools of Heshbon, by the gate of Bethrabbim. (ch. vii. 4.) Her nose is compared to the tower of Lebanon, which looketh towards Damascus. (ch. iv. 1.) Yea, the hair of her head is compared to a flock of goats, which come up from Mount Gilead; and the smell of her garments to the smell of Lebanon. (ver. 11.)

Nor was this land altogether void of shadows, even of her Lord and Saviour. Hence, he says of himself, " I am the rose of Sharon, and the lily of the valleys." (ch. ii. 1.) Also she, his beloved, saith of him, " His countenance is as Lebanon, excellent as the cedars." (ch. v. 15.) What shall I say? The two cities, Sion and Jerusalem, were such as sometimes set forth the two churches, (Gal. iv.,) the true and the false, and their seed Isaac and Ishmael.

I might also here show you, that even the gifts and graces of the true church were set forth by the spices, nuts, grapes, and pomegranates that the land of Canaan brought forth. Yea, that hell itself was set forth by the valley of the sons of Hinnom, and Tophet, places in this country. Indeed the whole, in a manner, was a typical and a figurative thing.

But I have, in the ensuing discourse, confined myself to the temple, that immediate place of God's worship; of whose utensils in particular, as I have said, I have spoken, though to each with what brevity I could; for that none of them are without a spiritual, and so a profitable signification to us.

And here we may behold much of the richness

of the wisdom and grace of God; namely, that he, even in the very place of worship of old, should ordain visible forms and representations for the worshippers to learn to worship him by. Yea, the temple itself was, as to this, to them a good instruction.

But in my thus saying, I give no encouragement to any now, to fetch out of their own fancies figures of similitudes to worship God by. What God provided to be a help to the weakness of his people of old, was one thing, and what they invented without his commandment was another. For though they had his blessing when they worshipped him with such types, shadows, and figures, which he had enjoined them for that purpose, yet he sorely punished and plagued them when they would add to these, inventions of their own. Yea, he in the very act of instituting their way of worshipping him, forbad their giving, in anything, way to their own humours or fancies, and bound them strictly to the orders of heaven. "Look," said God to Moses, their first great legislator, "that thou make all things according to the pattern showed thee in the mount." (Exod. xxv. 40. Heb. viii. 5.) Nor doth our Apostle but take the same measures, when he saith, "If any man thinketh himself a prophet, or spiritual, let him acknowledge that the things that I write unto you, are the commandments of the Lord." (1 Cor. xiv. 37.)

When Solomon, also, was to build this temple for the worship of God, though he was wiser than all men, yet God neither trusted to his wisdom nor memory, nor to any immediate dictates from heaven to him, as to how he would have him build it. No, he was to receive the whole platform thereof, in writing, by the inspiration of God. Nor would God give this platform of the temple, and of its utensils, immediately to this wise man, lest perhaps by others his wisdom should be idolized, or that some should object, that the whole fashion thereof proceeded of his fancy, only he made pretensions of divine revelation, as a cover for his doings.

Therefore, I say, not to him, but to his father David, was the whole pattern of it given from heaven, and so by David to Solomon his son, in writing: "Then David, says the text, "gave to Solomon, his son, the pattern of the porch, and of the houses thereof, and of the treasuries thereof, and of the upper chambers thereof, and of the inner parlours thereof, and of the place of the mercy-seat." (1 Chron. xxviii. 11.) "And the pattern of all that he had by the Spirit, of the courts of the house of the Lord, and of all the chambers round about, and of the treasuries of the house of God, and of the treasuries of the dedicated things." (ver. 12.) "Also for the courses of the priests and Levites, and for all the work of the service of the house of the Lord, and for all the vessels of service in the house of the Lord." (ver. 13.)

Yea, moreover, he had from heaven, or by divine revelation, what the candlesticks must be made of, and also how much was to go to each; the same order and commandment he also gave for the making of the tables, fleshhooks, cups, basins, altar of incense, with the pattern for the chariot of the cherubims, &c. (ver. xiv. 19.) "All this," said David, "the Lord made me understand by writing by his hand upon me, even all the work of this pattern." (ver. xx.) So, I say, he gave David the pattern of the temple, so David gave Solomon the pattern of the temple, and according to that pattern did Solomon build the temple, and no otherwise.

True, all these were but figures, patterns, and shadows of things in the heavens, and not the very image of the things; but, as was said before, if God was so circumspect and exact in these, as not to leave anything to the dictates of the godly and wisest of men, what! can we suppose he will now admit of the wisdom and contrivance of men in those things that are, in comparison to them, the heavenly things themselves!

It is also to be concluded, that since those shadows of things in the heavens are already committed by God to sacred story; and since that sacred story is said to be able to make the man of God perfect in all things, (2 Tim. iii. 15—17,) it is duty to us to leave off to lean to common understandings, and to inquire and search out by that very holy writ, and nought else, by what, and how we should worship God. David was for inquiring in his temple. (Ps. xxvii. 4.)

And although the old church way of worship is laid aside as to us in New Testament times, yet since those very ordinances were figures of things and methods of worship now, we may, yea, we ought to search out the spiritual meaning of them, because they serve to confirm and illustrate matters to our understandings. Yea, they show us the more exactly how the New and Old Testament, as to the spiritualness of the worship, was as one and the same; only the old was clouded with shadows, but ours is with more open face.

Features to the life, as we say, set out by a picture, do excellently show the skill of the artist. The Old Testament had the shadow, nor have we but the very image; both, then, are but emblems of what is yet behind. We may find our gospel clouded in their ceremonies, and our spiritual worship set out somewhat by their carnal ordinances.

Now because, as I said, there lies, as wrapt up in a mantle, much of the glory of our gospel-matters in this temple which Solomon builded; therefore I have made, as well as I could, by comparing spiritual things with spiritual, this book upon this subject.

I dare not presume to say, that I know I have hit right in everything, but this I can say, I have endeavoured so to do. True, I have not for these things fished in other men's waters; my Bible and Concordance are my only library in my writings. Wherefore, courteous reader, if thou findest anything, either in word or matter, that thou shalt judge doth vary from God's truth, let it be counted no man's else but mine; pray God also to pardon my fault. Do thou also lovingly pass it by, and receive what thou findest will do thee good.

Thy Servant in the Gospel,

JOHN BUNYAN.

SOLOMON'S TEMPLE SPIRITUALIZED;

OR, GOSPEL-LIGHT FETCHED OUT OF THE TEMPLE AT JERUSALEM.

I. *Where the Temple was built.*

THE temple was built at Jerusalem, on Mount Moriah, in the threshing-floor of Arnon the Jebusite; whereabout Abraham offered up Isaac; there where David met the angel of the Lord, when he came with his drawn sword in his hand to cut off the people at Jerusalem, for the sin which David committed in his disorderly numbering the people. (Gen. xxii. 3—5. 1 Chron. xxi. 15; xxi. 12; iii. 1.)

There Abraham received his Isaac from the dead; there the Lord was entreated by David to take away the plague, and to return to Israel again in mercy; from whence, also, David gathered that there God's temple must be built. "This," said he, "is the house of the Lord God, and this is the altar of the burnt-offering for Israel." (1 Chron. xxi. 28; xxii. 1; iii. 1.)

This Mount Moriah, therefore, was a type of the Son of God, the mountain of the Lord's house, the rock against which the gates of hell cannot prevail.

II. *Who built the Temple.*

The temple was built by Solomon, a man peaceable and quiet; and that in name, by nature, and in governing. For so God had before told David, namely, that such a one the builder of the temple should be. "Behold," saith he, "a son shall be born unto thee, who shall be a man of rest; and I will give him rest from all his enemies round about; for his name shall be called Solomon, and I will give peace and quietness to Israel in his days. He shall build an house for my name, and he shall be my son, I will be his Father." (1 Chron. xxii. 9, 10. Ps. lxxii. 1—4.)

As, therefore, Mount Moriah was a type of Christ, as the foundation, so Solomon was a type of him, as the builder of his church. The mount was signal, for that thereon the Lord God, before Abraham and David, did display his mercy. And as Solomon built this temple, so Christ doth build his house; yea, "He shall build the everlasting temple, and he shall bear the glory." (Heb. iii. 3, 4. Zech. vi. 12, 13.) And in that Solomon was called peaceable, it was to show with what peaceable doctrine and ways Christ's house and church should be built. (Isa. ix. 6. Mich. vii. 2—4.)

III. *How the Temple was built.*

The temple was built, not merely by the dictates of Solomon, though he was wiser than Ethan, and Heman, and Chalcol, and Darda, and all men, (1 Kings iv. 31,) but it was built by rules, prescribed by, or in a written word; and as so delivered to him by his father David.

For when David gave to Solomon his son a charge to build the temple of God, with that charge he gave him also the pattern of all in writing; even a pattern of the porch, house, chambers, treasuries, parlours, &c., and of the place for the mercy-seat, which pattern David had of God; nor would God trust his memory with it. "The Lord made me," said he, "understand in writing, by his hand upon me, even all the works of this pattern." Thus, therefore, David gave to Solomon his son the pattern of all; and thus Solomon his son built the house of God. (See 1 Chron. xxviii. 9—20.)

And answerable to this, Christ Jesus, the builder of his own house, whose house are we, doth build his holy habitation for him to dwell in; even according to the commandment of God the Father. For, saith he, "I have not spoken of myself, but the Father which sent me. He gave me a commandment, what I should speak." And hence it is said, God gave him the revelation; and again, that he took the book out of the hand of him that sat on the throne, and so acted, as to the building up of his church. (John xii. 49, 50. Rev. i. 1; v. 5.)

IV. *Of what the Temple was built.*

The materials with which the temple was built were such as were in their own nature common to that which was left behind; things that naturally were not fit, without art, to be laid on so holy a house. And this shows that those of whom Christ Jesus designs to build his church, are by nature no better than others. But as the trees and stones of which the temple was built, were first hewed and squared before they were fit to be laid in that house; so sinners, of which the church is to be built, must first be fitted by the Word and doctrine, and then fitly laid in their place in the church.

For though, as to nature, there is no difference betwixt those made use of to build God's house with, yet by grace they differ from others; even as those trees and stones that are hewed and squared for building, by art are made to differ from those which abide in the wood or pit.

The Lord Jesus, therefore, while he seeketh materials wherewith to build his house, he findeth them, the clay of the same lump that he rejecteth and leaves behind. "Are we better than they? No, in no wise." (Rom. iii. 9.) Nay, I think if any be best it is they which are left behind: "He came not to call the righteous, but sinners to repentance." (Mark ii. 17.) And indeed in this he doth show both the greatness of his grace and workmanship; his grace in taking such, and his workmanship in that he makes them meet for his holy habitation.

This the current of Scripture maketh manifest; wherefore it is needless now to cite particulars: only we must remember, that none are laid in this building as they come out of the wood or pit; but as they first pass under the hand and rule of this great builder of the temple of God.

V. *Who was to fell those trees, and to dig those stones, with which Solomon built the Temple.*

As the trees were to be felled, and stones to be digged, so there was for that matter select workmen appointed.

These were not of the sons of Jacob nor of the house of Israel; they were the servants of Hiram, king of Tyre, and the Gibeonites; namely, their children that made a league with Joshua, in the day that God gave the land of Canaan to his people. (Josh. ix. 21, 22. 1 Kings v. 1. 1 Chron. xxviii.; xxix.)

And these were types of our gospel ministers, who are the men appointed by Jesus Christ to make sinners, by their preaching, meet for the house of God. Wherefore, as he was famous of old who was strong to lift up his axe upon the thick boughs, to square wood for the building of the temple, so a minister of the gospel now is also famous, if much used by Christ for the converting of sinners to himself, that he may build him a temple with them. (Ps. vii. 4—6. Rom. xvi. 7.)

But why, may some say, do you make so homely a comparison? I answer, because I believe it is true; for it is grace, not gifts, that makes us sons, and the beloved of God. Gifts make a minister; and as a minister, one is but a servant to hew wood and draw water for the house of my God. Yea Paul, though a son, yet counted himself not a son but a servant, purely as he was a minister: a servant of God, a servant of Christ, a servant of the church, and your servant for Jesus' sake. (Tit. i. 1. Rom. i. 1. 2 Cor. iv. 5.)

A man then is a son, as he is begotten and born of God to himself, and a servant as he is gifted for work in the house of his Father; and though it is truth, the servant may be a son, yet he is not a son, because he is a servant. Nor doth it follow, that because all sons may be servants, therefore all

servants are sons; no, all the servants of God are not sons; and therefore when time shall come, he that is only a servant here, shall certainly be put out of the house, even out of that house himself did help to build. "The servant abideth not in the house for ever," the servant, that is, he that is only so. (Ezek. xlvi. 16, 17. John viii. 35.)

So then, as a son, thou art an Israelite; as a servant, a Gibeonite. The consideration of this made Paul start; he knew that gifts made him not a son. (1 Cor. xii. 28—31; xiii. 1, 2.)

The sum then is, a man may be a servant and a son; a servant, as he is employed by Christ in his house for the good of others; and a son, as he is a partaker of the grace of adoption. But all servants are not sons, and let this be for a caution, and a call to ministers, to do all acts of service for God, and in his house, with reverence and godly fear: and with all humility let us desire to be partakers ourselves of that grace we preach to others. (1 Cor. ix. 25.)

This is a great saying, and written perhaps to keep ministers humble: "And strangers shall stand and feed your flocks, and the sons of the alien shall be your ploughmen and your vinedressers." (Isa. lxi. 5.) To be a ploughman here, is to be a preacher; and to be a vinedresser here, is to be a preacher. (Luke ix. 59—62. 1 Cor. ix. 27. Matt. xx. 1—8; xxi. 28. 1 Cor. ix. 7.) And if he does this work willingly, he has a reward; if not, a dispensation of the gospel was committed to him, and that is all. (1 Cor. ix. 17.)

VI. *In what condition the timber and stones were, when brought to be laid in the building of the Temple.*

The timber and stones with which the temple was built were squared and hewed at the wood or pit; and so there made every way fit for that work, even before they were brought to the place where the house should be set up: "So that neither hammer, nor axe, nor any tool of iron was heard in the house while it was in building." (1 Kings vi. 7.)

And this shows, as was said before, that the materials of which the house was built, were, before the hand of the workman touched them, as unfit to be laid in the building as was those that were left behind; consequently that themselves, none otherwise but by the art of others, were made fit to be laid in this building.

To this our New Testament temple answers. For those of the sons of Adam who are counted worthy to be laid in this building, are not by nature but by grace made meet for it; not by their own wisdom, but by the word of God. Hence he saith, "I have hewed them by the prophets." And again, ministers are called God's builders and labourers, even as to this work. (Hos. vi. 5. 1 Cor. iii. 10. 2 Cor. vi. 1. Col. i. 28.)

No man will lay trees, as they come from the

wood, for beams and rafters in his house; nor stones, as digged, in the walls. No; the trees must be hewed and squared, and the stones sawn and made fit, and so be laid in the house. Yea, they must be so sawn and so squared, that in coupling they may be joined exactly; else the building will not be good, nor the workmen have credit of his doings.

Hence our gospel-church, of which the temple was a type, is said to be fitly formed, and that there is a fit supply of every joint for the securing of the whole. (1 Pet. ii. 5. Eph. ii. 20, 21; iv. 16. Col. ii. 19.) As they therefore build like children, that build with wood, as it comes from the wood or forest, and with stones as they come from the pit, even so do they who pretend to build God a house of unconverted sinners, unhewed, unsquared, unpolished. Wherefore God's workmen, according to God's advice, prepare their work without, and make it fit for themselves in the field, and afterwards build the house. (Prov. xxiv. 27.)

Let ministers, therefore, look to this, and take heed, lest, instead of making their notions stoop to the Word, they make the Scriptures stoop to their notions.

VII. *Of the foundation of the Temple.*

The foundation of the temple is that upon which it stood, and it was twofold: First, the hill Moriah, and then those great stones upon which it was erected. This hill Moriah, as was said before, did more properly typify Christ. Hence Moriah is called "The Mountain of the house," it being the rock on which it was built. Those great stones called foundation stones were types of the prophets and apostles, (Matt. xvi. 18. Eph. ii. 20, 21. Heb. xi. 10;) wherefore these stones were stones of the biggest size, stones of eight cubits, and stones of ten cubits. (1 Kings vii. 10.)

Now, as the temple had this double foundation, so we must consider it respectively and distinctly. For Christ is the foundation one way, the prophets and apostles a foundation another; Christ is the foundation personally and meritoriously, but the prophets and apostles by doctrine ministerially. The church, then, which is God's New Testament temple, is said to be built on Christ the foundation; so none other is the foundation but he. (1 Cor. iii. 11, 12.) But as it is said to be built upon the apostles, so it is said to have twelve foundations, and must have none but they. (Rev. xxi. 14.)

What is it, then? Why we must be builded upon Christ, as he is our priest, sacrifice, prophet, king, and advocate; and upon the other, as they are infallible instructors and preachers of him; not that any may be an apostle that shall so esteem of himself, nor that any other doctrine be administered but what is the doctrine of the twelve, for they are set forth as the chief and last. These are also they, as Moses, which are to look over all the

building, and to see that all in this house be done according to the pattern showed to them in the mount. (Exod. xxxix. 43. John xx. 21—23. 1 Cor. iii. 9; iv. 9.)

Let us, then, keep these distinctions clear, and not put an apostle in the room of Christ, nor Christ in the place of one of those apostles. Let none but Christ be the high-priest and sacrifice for your souls to God; and none but that doctrine which is apostolical be to you as the mouth of Christ for instruction to prepare you, and to prepare materials for this temple of God, and to build them upon this foundation.

VIII. *Of the richness of the stones which were laid for the foundations of the Temple.*

These foundation stones, as they were great, so they were costly stones; though, as I said, of themselves, of no more worth than they of their nature that were left behind. Their costliness, therefore, lay in those additions which they received from the king's charge.

First. In that labour which was bestowed upon them in sawing, squaring, and carving. For the servants, as they were cunning at this work, so they bestowed much of their art and labour upon them, by which they put them into excellent form, and added to their bigness, glory, and beauty, fit for stones upon which so goodly a fabric was to be built.

Second. These stones, as they were thus wrought within and without, so, as it seems to me, they were inlaid with other stones, more precious than themselves: inlaid, I say, with stones of divers colours; according as it is written, "I will lay thy foundations with sapphires." (Isa. liv. 11.) Not that the foundations were sapphires, but they were laid, inlaid with them; or, as he saith in another place: "They were adorned with goodly stones and gifts." (Luke xxi. 5.)

This is still more amplified, where it is written of the New Jerusalem, which is still the New Testament church on earth, and so the same in substance with what is now. "The foundations of the wall of the city," saith he, "were garnished with all manner of precious stones." (Rev. xxi. 19.) True, these there are called, "the foundations of the wall of the city," but it has respect to the matter in hand, for that which is before called a temple, for its comparative smallness, is here called a city, for or because of its great increase: and both the foundations of the wall of the city, as well as of the temple, are "the twelve apostles of the Lamb." (Rev. xxi. 14.) For these carvings and inlayings, with all other beautifications, were types of the extraordinary gifts and graces of the apostles. Hence the Apostle calls such gifts signs of apostleship. (Rom. xv. 19. 2 Cor. xii. 21. Heb. ii. 4.) For as the foundation stones of the temple were thus garnished, so were the apostles beautified with a call, gifts, and graces peculiar to themselves. Hence he says, "First apostles," for that they were first and chief in the church of Christ. (1 Cor. xii. 28.)

Nor were these stones only laid for a foundation for the temple; for the great court, the inner court, as also the porch of the temple, had round about them three rows of these stones for their foundation, (1 Kings vii. 12;) signifying, as seems to me, that the more outward and external part, as well as that more internal worship to be performed to God, should be grounded upon apostolical doctrine and appointments. (1 Cor. iii. 10—12. 2 Thess. ii. 15; iii. 6. Heb. vi. 1—5.)

IX. *Which way the face or front of the Temple stood.*

The temple was built with its face or front towards the east, and that, perhaps, because the glory of the God of Israel was to come from the way of the east unto it, (Ezek. xliii. 1—5; xlvii. 1;) wherefore, in that its front stood towards the east, it may be to show that the true gospel church would have its eye to, and expectation from the Lord. We look, said Paul, but whither? "We have our conversation," said he, "in heaven, from whence our expectation is." (2 Cor. iv. 18. Phil. iii. 20, 21. Ps. lxii. 5.)

2. It was set also with its face towards the east, to keep the people of God from committing of idolatry; to wit, from worshipping the host of heaven, and the sun, whose rising is from the east. For since the face of the temple stood towards the east, and since the worshippers were to worship at, or with their faces towards the temple, it follows, that both in their going to and worshipping God towards that place, their faces must be from, and their backs towards, the sun. The thus building of the temple, therefore, was a snare to idolatry, and a proof of the zeal of those that were the true worshippers; as also to this day the true gospel instituted worship of Jesus Christ is. Hence he is said to idolaters to be a snare and trap, but to the godly a glory. (Isa. viii. 14; lx. 19.)

3. Do but see how God catched the idolatrous Jews by this means in their naughtiness: "And he brought me," said the prophet, "into the inner court of the Lord's house, and behold at the door of the temple of the Lord, even between the porch and the altar, were about five and twenty men, with their backs towards the temple of the Lord, and their faces towards the east." (Ezek. viii. 16.) It was, therefore, as I said, set with its face towards the east to prevent false worships, and detect idolaters.

4. From the east also came the most blasting winds, winds that are destructive to man and beasts, to fruit and trees, and ships at sea. (Exod. x. 13. Job xxvii. 21. Ezek. xvii. 10; xix. 12. Ps. xlviii. 7. Ezek. xxvii. 26.) I say, the east wind, or that which comes from thence, is the most hurtful; yet, you see, the temple hath set her face against it, to show that the true church cannot be blasted or made turn back by any affliction. It is not east winds, nor none of their blastings, that can make the temple turn about. Hence he saith that Jacob's face will not wax pale. And again, "I have made thy face strong against their faces," and that "the gates of hell shall not prevail against it." (Isa. xxix. 22. Ezek. iii. 8. Matt. xvi. 18.)

5. It might be also built with its face towards the east, to show that the true church looketh, as afore I hinted, for her Lord and King from heaven, knowing that at his coming he will bring healing in his wings: for from the east he will appear when he comes the second time without sin unto salvation, of which the sun gives us a memento in his rising there every morning: "For as the lightning cometh out of the east, and shineth unto the west, so shall also the coming of the Son of man be." (Mal. iv. 2. Heb. ix. 28. Col. iii. 3. 2 Pet. iii. 11—14. Matt. xxiv. 27.)

6. Christ, as the north pole, draws those touched with the loadstone of his word, with the face of their souls towards him, to look for, and hasten to his coming. And this also is signified by the temple standing with its face towards the east.

X. *Of the courts of the Temple.*

I perceive that there were two courts belonging to the temple. The first was called the outward court. (Ezek. xl. 17; xlvi. 21.)

1. This was that into which the people of necessity first entered, when they went to worship in the temple; consequently that was it, in and by which the people did first show their desires to be the worshippers of God. And this answer to those badges and signs of love to religion that people have in face or outward appearance. (Matt. xxv. 27. 2 Cor. x. 7.)

2. In this, though here may sometimes be truth, yet oftener lies and dissimulation; wherefore commonly an outward appearance is set in opposition to faith and truth, as the outward is in opposition to the inner court, and outward to the inner man; and that is, when it is by itself, for then it profits nothing. (Rom. ii. 28. 1 Cor. xiii. 1—3. 2 Cor. v. 12.)

3. Hence, though the outward court was something to the Jews, because by outward bodies they were distinguished from the Gentiles, yet to us it is little, for now he is not a Jew who is one only outwardly. Therefore all the time of the beast's reign, this court is given to be trodden under foot; for, as I said, outward show will avail nothing when the beast comes to turn and toss up professors with his horns. (Rev. xi. 10—12.)

4. But as there was an outward, so there was an inner court, a court that stood nearer to the temple, and so to the true practical part of worship, than that outward court did. (Ezek. x. 13; xlvi. 1. 1 Kings vi. 36.)

5. This inner court is that which is called "the court of the priests," because it was it in which they boiled the trespass-offerings, and in which they prepared the sin-offering for the people. (2 Cor. iv. 9. Ezek. xlvi. 20.)

6. This court, therefore, was the place of practice and of preparation to appear before God, which is the first true token of a sincere and honest mind. Wherefore here, and not in the outward court, stood the great brazen altar, which was a type of Christ, by whom alone true worshippers make their approach with acceptance unto God. Also here stood the great brazen scaffold, on which the king kneeled when he prayed for the people, a type of Christ's prayers for his when he was in the world. (2 Chron. vi. 13. John xvii.)

7. Wherefore this court was a type of practical worship, and so of our praying, hearing, and eating before God. There belonged to this court several gates, an east, a south, and a north gate; and when the people of the land went into this court to worship, they were not to go out at the gate by which they came in, but out of the gate over against it, to show that true Christians should persevere right on, and not turn back, whatever they meet with in the way. "He that entereth in by the way of the north gate to worship, shall go out by the way of the south gate: and he that entereth in by the way of the north gate, he shall not return by the way of the gate whereby he came in, but shall go forth over against it." (Ezek. xlvi. 9.)

8. These courts were places of great delight to the Jews, as both feigned and sincere profession is to those that practise therein. Wherefore when the Jews did enter into these, they did use to do it with praise and pipe, as do both hypocrites and sincere ones. So then, when a man shall tread in both these courts, and shall turn what he seems to be into what he should be in reality, then, and not till then, he treads them as he should. For then he makes the outward court, and his treading there, but a passage to that which is more inward and sincere. But he that stays in the outward one, is but such an one as pleases not God, for that he wants the practice of what he professes with his mouth.

XI. *Of the great brazen altar that stood in the inner court of the Temple.*

In the inner court stood the great brazen altar which Solomon made. This is evident, for that when he kneeled upon the scaffold there to pray, he kneeled before this altar. (See Exod. xl. 6, 29. 2 Chron. vi. 13. 2 Kings xvi. 14. Joel ii. 17.)

2. This altar seems to be placed about the middle of this court, over against the porch of the house; and between it and the temple was the place where Zechariah was slain. This altar was called the altar of burnt-offering, and therefore it was a type of Christ in his dignity. For Christ's body was our true burnt-offering, of which the bodies of the sacrificed beasts were a type: now that altar upon which his body was offered was his divinity or Godhead; for that, and that only, could bear up that offering in the whole of its sufferings, and that therefore, and that only, was to receive the fat, the glory. Hence it is said, He "through the Eternal Spirit, offered himself without spot to God." (Heb. ix. 14.)

3. For Christ is priest, and sacrifice, and altar, and all. And as a priest he offered, as a sacrifice he suffered, and as God he supported his humanity, in that suffering of all the pains it underwent. (Gal. i. 4; ii. 20. 1 Pet. iii. 18. Heb. ix. 14.)

4. It was then Christ's godhead, not the tree, that was the altar of burnt-offering, or that by which Christ offered himself an offering and a sacrifice to God for a sweet-smelling savour.

5. That it was not the tree, is evident, for that could not sanctify the gift, to wit, his body; but Christ affirmeth, that "the altar sanctifieth the gift." And by so saying, he affirmeth that the altar on which he offered his offering was greater than the offering itself. (Matt. xxiii. 19.) Now the body of Christ was the gift, for so he saith, "I give my flesh for the life of the world." (John 6.) But now, what thing is that which is greater than his body, save the altar, his divinity, on which it was offered. The tree, then, was not the altar which sanctified this gift, to make it of virtue enough to make reconciliation for iniquity. (John vi. 51; xvii. 19. Heb. ix. 14. Col. i. 19—21.) Now, since this altar of burnt-offering was thus placed in the inner court, it teaches us several things:

First. That those that come only into the outward court, or that rest in a bare appearance of Christianity, do not, by so doing, come to Jesus Christ; for this altar stands not there. Hence John takes notice only of the temple and this altar, and them that worship therein, and leaves out the outward court, and so them that come no further. (Rev. xi. 1, 2.)

Second. This teaches us, also, that we are to enter into that temple of God by blood. The altar, this altar of burnt-offering, stood as men went into the temple: they must go by it, yea, there they must leave their offering, and so go in and worship, even as a token that they came thither by sacrifice and by blood.

Third. Upon this altar Solomon at the dedication of the temple offered thousands, both of oxen and of sheep; to signify surely the abundant worth and richness that would be in the blood of Christ to save when it should be shed for us. For his blood is spoken of with an "how much more?" "For if the blood of bulls and goats, and the ashes of an heifer sprinkling the unclean, sanctifieth to the purifying of the flesh, how much more shall the blood of Christ, who through the eternal Spirit offered himself without spot to God, purge your conscience from dead works, to serve the living God!" (Heb. ix. 14. 2 Chron. vii. 5—8 Heb. x. 1, 12.)

Let us, then, not dare to stop or stay in the outward court, for there is not this altar. Nor let us dare, when we come into this court, to be careless whether we look to this altar or no. For it is by blood we must enter; "for without shedding of blood is no remission." Let us always, then, when we come hither, wash our hands in innocency, and so compass this holy altar; for that by Christ, who is the altar indeed, we are reconciled to God. This is looking to Jesus; this is coming to God by him, of whom this altar and the sacrifice thereon was a type.

XII. *Of the pillars that were before the porch of the Temple.*

There were divers pillars belonging to the temple; but in this place we are confined to speak of only two; namely, those which stood before the temple.

These pillars stood before the porch, or entrance into the temple, looking towards the altar, the court, and them that were the worshippers there; also they were a grace and a beauty to the front of the house.

1. These pillars stood, one on the right hand, and the other on the left, at the door of the porch of the temple, and they had names given them, you may be sure, to signify something. The name of that on the right hand was called Jachin, " God shall establish ;" and the name of that on the left hand was Boaz, " in it is strength." (1 Kings vii. 21. 2 Chron. iii. 17.)

2. These two pillars were types of Christ's apostles, of the apostles of circumcision and of the uncircumcision. Therefore, the Apostle Paul also calleth them pillars, (Gal. ii.,) and saith that that pillar on the right hand was a type of himself and his companions, who were to go to the uncircumcised, and teach the Gentiles the way of life. When James, Cephas, and John, saith he, " who seemed to be pillars, perceived the grace that was given unto me, they gave unto me and Barnabas the right hand of fellowship, that we should go unto the heathen, and they unto the circumcision." (Gal. ii. 9.) So then, these two pillars were types of these two orders of the apostles in this their divers service for God.

3. And that Paul and Barnabas were signified by those on the right hand, to wit, to be the apostles of the Gentiles, he showeth again, where he saith, I am " the minister of Christ to the Gentiles, ministering the grace of God, that the offering up of the Gentiles might be acceptable, being sanctified by the Holy Ghost." (Rom. xi. 13; xv. 16.)

4. And since the name of this pillar was Jachin, (God shall establish), as it showeth that opposition shall attend it, so also, that God would bless his Word preached by them to the Gentiles, to the conversion of numbers of them, maugre all the opposition of the enemy.

5. This is further implied. for that they were made of brass; as he saith of the prophet, I have made thee a fenced brazen wall, an iron pillar: and their fighting against thee shall nothing at all prevail. Wherefore Paul says of himself, " I am set for the defence of the gospel," " that the truth thereof might continue with you." (Phil. i. 17. Gal. ii. 5.)

XIII. *Of the height of these pillars, that thus stood before the porch of the door of the Temple.*

The pillars were eighteen cubits high apiece, and that is as high, yea, as high again, as the highest giant that ever we read of in the Word; for the highest of which we read, was but six cubits and a span. True, the bedstead of Og was nine cubits long, but I trow, the giant himself was shorter. (Deut. iii. 11. 2 Chron. iii. 15.) But put the longest to the longest, and set the one upon the shoulders of the other, and yet each pillar was higher than they.

We have now, as I know of, but few that remain of the remnant of the giants, and though they boast, as if they were higher than Agag, yet these pillars are higher than they. These pillars are the highest, you may equal them; and an inch above, is worth an ell below. The height, therefore, of these pillars is, to show us what high dignity God did put upon those of his saints, whom he did call to be apostles of the Lamb; for their office and call thereto is the highest in the church of God. These men, I say, were made thus high by their being cast in such a mould. Of that which added yet further to their height, we will speak anon ; we only speak now of the high call by which they, and only they, were made capable of apostolical authority. The apostles were sent immediately, their call was extraordinary, their office was universal, they had alike power in all churches, and their doctrine was infallible. (Acts xxvi. 16. 1 Cor. ix. 1. Gal. i. 1. 1 John i. 1—3. John ii. 23.)

And what can our pretended giants do or say in comparison of these ? The truth is, all other men to these are dwarfs, are low, dark, weak, and beneath them, not only as to call and office, but also as to gifts and grace. This sentence, " Paul, an apostle of Jesus Christ," drowneth all. What now are all other titles of grandeur and greatness, when compared with this one sentence ?

True, the men were but mean in themselves, for what is Paul or Apollos, or what was James or John ? Yet by their call to that office they were made highest of all in the church. Christ did raise them eighteen cubits high, not in conceit, for so there are many higher than they, but in office, and calling, and divine authority.

And observe it, these stand at the door at the entering into the temple of God, at which they enter that go in thither to worship God. to show that all right worship, and that which will be acceptable to God, is by, or according to, their doctrine.

XIV. *Of the chapiters of the pillars of the Temple.*

There were also two chapiters made for the pillars of the temple; for each, one; and they were five cubits high apiece. These were for the adorning of the pillars, and therefore were types and shadows of that abundance of grace which God did put upon the apostles after the resurrection of our Lord. Wherefore, as he saith here, the chapiters were upon the pillars; so it saith, that great grace was upon all the apostles. (Acts iv. 33.)

These chapiters had belonging to them a bowl made pumil-fashion, and it was placed upon the head of them, perhaps to signify their aptness to receive, and largeness to contain of the dew of heaven, that shadow of the doctrine of the gospel, which doctrine the apostles, as the chief, were to receive and hold forth to the world for their conversion. Hence, as the bowls were capable to receive the dew of heaven, these are said to receive "grace and apostleship for obedience to the faith among all nations, for his name." (Rom. i. 5. 1 Kings vii. 16, 42. 2 Chron. iv. 13. Deut. xxxii. 10. Rom. xv. 29.)

There was also upon these chapiters a network, or nets like unto chequer-work, which still added to their lustre. These nets were they which showed for what intent the apostolical office was ordained; namely, that by their preaching they might bring many souls to God. And hence Christ calls them fishermen, saying, "Ye shall catch men." (Matt. iv. 19. Mark i. 17. Luke v. 10. 2 Cor. xii. 16.) The world is compared to a sea, men to fishes, and the gospel to a net. (Ezek. xlvii. 10—14. Matt. xiii. 47—50.) As, therefore, men catch fish with a net, so the apostles caught men by their word, which word, as I told you, to me is signified by this net-work upon the top of these pillars. See, therefore, the mystery of God in these things.

XV. *Of the pomegranates adjoined to these nets on the chapiters.*

There were also joined to these nets upon the top of the pillars, pomegranates in abundance, four hundred for the net-work. Pomegranates, you know, are beautiful to look on, pleasant to the palate, comfortable to the stomach, and cheering by their juice. (1 Kings vii. 42. Sol. Song iv. 3; viii. 2; iv. 13; vi. 11; vii. 12.) There were to be two rows of these pomegranates for one net-work, and so two rows of them for the other.

And this was to show that the net of the gospel is not an empty thing; but is sufficiently baited with such varieties as are apt to allure the world

to be caught by them. The law is but a sound of words, but the gospel is not so; that is baited with pomegranates, with variety of excellent things. Hence it is called "the gospel of the kingdom," and "the gospel of the grace of God;" because it is, as it were, baited with grace and glory, that sinners may be allured, and may be taken with it to their eternal salvation. (Matt. xxiv. 14. Acts xx. 24.)

Grace and glory! grace and glory! these are the pomegranates with which the word of the gospel is baited, that sinners may be taken and saved thereby. The argument of old was, "milk and honey," that was, I say, the alluring bait, with which Moses drew six hundred thousand out of Egypt into the wilderness of old. (Exod. iii. 8.) But behold we have pomegranates, two rows of pomegranates; grace and a kingdom, as the bait of the holy gospel; no wonder, then if when men of skill did cast this net into the sea, such numbers of fish have been caught, even by one sermon. (Acts ii.) They baited their nets with taking things, things taking to the eye and taste.

Nets are truly instruments of death, but the net of the gospel doth catch to draw from death, wherefore this net is contrary, life and immortality is brought to light through this. No marvel, then, if men are so glad, and that for gladness they leap like fishes in a net, when they see themselves caught in this drag of the holy gospel of the Son of God. They are caught from death and hell, caught to live with God in glory.

XVI. *Of the chains that were upon these pillars that stood before the Temple.*

As there were nets to catch, and pomegranates to bait, so there were chains belonging to these chapiters on these pillars. "And he made chains, as in the oracle, and put them upon the head of the chapiters." (2 Chron. iii. 16.)

But what were these chains a type of? I answer, they were, perhaps, a type of those bonds which attend the gospel, by which souls are taken, and tied fast to the horns of the altar. Gospel grace, and gospel obligations, are ties and binding things; they can hold those that are entangled by the word. "Love is strong as death;" bands of love, and the cords of a man, and chains take hold on them that are taken by the gospel. (Hos. xi. Sol. Song viii. 6.)

But this strength to bind lieth not in outward force, but in a sweet constraint, by virtue of the displays of undeserved love. "The love of Christ constraineth us." (2 Cor. v. 14.) Wherefore as you find the nets, so the chains had pomegranates on them: "And he made an hundred pomegranates, and put them upon the chains." (2 Chron. iii. 16.) The chains then had baits, as well as the nets, to show that the bands of the gospel are unresistible goodnesses; such with which men love to be bound, and such as they pray they may hold fast by. He binds his foal to the vine, his saint unto this Saviour. (Gen. xlix. 11.)

By these chains there is therefore showed what strength there is in gospel-charms, if once the adder doth but hear them ; never man yet was able to resist them that well did know the meaning of them ; they are mighty to make poor men obedient, and that in word and deed. These chains were such as were in the oracle, to show that gospel-bonds are strong as the joys of heaven, and as the glories there ; can make them chains as in the oracle, as in the most holy place. It is heaven that binds sinners on earth to the faith and hope of the gospel of Christ.

XVII. *Of the lily-work which was upon the chapiters, that were upon these pillars of the Temple.*

These pillars were also adorned with lily-work, as well as with pomegranates and chains : " The chapiters also which were upon the top of the pillars were of lily-work ;" " so was the work of the pillars finished." (1 Kings vii. 19, 20, 22.)

This lily-work is here put in on no purpose, even to show us how far off those that were to be the true apostles of the Lamb should be from seeking carnal things, or of making their preaching a stalking-horse to worldly greatness, and that preferment. There was lily-work upon them ; that is, they lived upon the bounty and care of God, and were content with that glory which he had put upon them. " The lilies," saith Christ, " they toil not, neither do they spin ; and yet Solomon in all his glory was not arrayed like one of these." (Matt. vi. 28, 29. Luke xii. 28, 29.) Thus, therefore, these pillars show, that as the apostles should be fitted and qualified for their work, they should be also freed from cares and worldly cumber ; they should be content with God's providing for them, even as the goodly lilies are. And as thus prepared, they were set in the front of the house, for all ministers to see and learn, and take example of them how to behave themselves as to this world in the performing of their office.

And that which gives us further light in this is, that this lily-work is said, by divine institution, to be placed " over against the belly," the belly of the pillars, a type of ours. (1 Kings vii. 20.) The belly is a craving thing ; and these things, saith the text, were placed over against the belly, to teach that they should not humour, but put check unto the desires and cravings of the belly ; or to show that they need not do it, for that he that calls to his work will himself provide for the belly. It is said of the church, that " her belly is as a heap of wheat set about with lilies," (Sol. Song vii. 2 ;) to show that she should without covetousness have sufficient, if she would cast all her care upon God, her great provider. This the apostles did, and this is their glory to this day.

" So was the work of the pillars finished." To live lily-lives, it seems, is the glory of an apostle, and the completing of their office and service for God. But this is directly opposite to the belly, over against the belly, and this makes it the harder work. But yet so living is the way to make all that is done sweet-scented to those that be under this care. Covetousness makes a minister smell frowish, and look more like a greedy dog than an apostle of Jesus Christ. Judas had none of this lily-work, so his name stinks to this day. " He that grows like the lily shall cast forth his scent like Lebanon, his branches shall spread, and his beauty shall be as the olive-tree, and his smell as Lebanon." (Hos. xiv. 6.) Thus lived Christ, first ; and thus the apostles, next ; nor can any other, as to this, live like or be compared to them. They coveted no man's silver or gold, or apparel. They lived like lilies in the world, and did send forth their scent as Lebanon.

Thus you see of whom these pillars were a shadow, and what their height, their chapiters, their bowls, their nets, their chains, their pomegranates, and their lily-work did signify, and how all was most sweetly answered in the antitype. These were men of the first rate ; the apostles, I mean, were such.

XVIII. *Of the fashion of the Temple.*

1. Of the length and the breadth of the temple, I shall say nothing : but as to the height thereof, there methinks I see something. The temple was higher than the pillars, and so is the church than her officers ; I say, consider them singly as officers, though inferior as to gifts and office : for, as I said before of ministers in general, so now I say the same of the apostles, though as to office they were the highest, yet the temple is above them. Gifts and office make no men sons of God ; as so, they are but servants, though these were servants of the highest form. It is the church, as such, that is the lady, a queen, the bride, the Lamb's wife ; and prophets, apostles, and ministers, &c., are but servants, stewards, labourers, for her good. (Ps. xlv. 9. Rev. xix. 7. 1 Cor. iii. 5 ; iv. 1, 2.) As therefore the lady is above the servant, the queen above the steward, or the wife above all her husband's officers, so is the church, as such, above these officers. The temple was higher than the pillars.

2. Again ; as the temple was highest, so it enlarged itself still upward ; for as it ascended in height, so it still was wider and wider ; even from the lowest chambers to the top.

The first chambers were but five cubits broad, the middle ones were six, but the highest were seven cubits. (1 Kings vi. 5, 6.) The temple, therefore, was round about above, some cubits wider than it was below ; for " there was an enlarging and ascending about still upwards to the side chambers, for the winding about was still upward round about the house; therefore the breadth of the house was still upwards, and so increased from the lowest chambers to the highest, by the midst." (Ezek. xli. 7.)

And this was to show us that God's true gospel temple, which is his church, should have its enlargedness of heart still upward, or most for spiritual and eternal things; wherefore he saith, " Thy heart shall fear and be enlarged;" that is, be most affected with things above, " where Christ sitteth on the right hand of God." (Isa. lx. 5. Col. iii. 2, 3.) Indeed, it is the nature of grace to enlarge itself still upwards, and to make the heart widest for the things that are above. The temple, therefore, was narrowest downwards, to show that a little of earth, or this world, should serve the church of God. And having food and raiment, let us be therewith content.

But now, upwards, and as to heavenly things, we are commanded to be covetous, as to them, and after them to enlarge ourselves, both by the fashion of the temple, as by express words. (1 Kings iv. 29. Isa. lx. 5. Phil. iii. 14. 1 Cor. xii. 31. 1 Tim. vi. 8. Ps. cxix. 32.)

Since, then, the temple was widest upwards, let us imitate it, and have our conversation in heaven. Let our eyes, our ears, our hands, and hearts, our prayers, and groans be most for things above. Let us open our mouths, as the ground that is chapt doth for the latter rain, for the things that are eternal. (Job. xxix. 23. Ps. lxxxi. 10.)

Observe again, that the lowest parts of the temple were the narrowest parts of the temple; so those in the church who are nearest, or most concerned with earth, are the most narrow spirited as to the things of God. But now let even such an one be taken up higher, to above, to the uppermost parts of the temple, and there he will be enlarged, and have his heart stretched out. For the temple, you see, was widest upwards; the higher, the more it is enlarged. Paul being once caught up into paradise, could not but be there enlarged. (2 Cor. xii.)

One may say of the fashion of the temple, as some say of a lively picture, it speaks. I say, its form and fashion speaks; it says to all saints, to all the churches of Christ, Open your hearts for heaven; be ye enlarged upwards.

I read not in Scripture of any house but this that was thus enlarged upwards, nor is there anywhere, save only in the church of God, that which doth answer this similitude. All other are widest downward, and have the largest heart for earthly things. The church only is widest upwards, and has its greatest enlargements towards heaven.

XIX. *Of the outward glory of the Temple.*

I do also think, that as to this, there was a great expression in it; I mean, a voice of God, a voice that teacheth the New Testament church to carry even conviction in her outward usages that, I say,

might give conviction to the world. And besides this of its enlarging upwards, there was such an outward beauty and glory put upon it as was alluring to beholders. The stones were curiously carved, and excellently joined together; its outward show was white and glittering to the dazzling of the eyes of the beholders; yea, the disciples themselves were taken with it, it was so admirable to behold. Hence it is said, they came to Christ to show him the building of the temple: " Master," said they, " see what manner of stones, and what buildings are here." (Matt. xxiv. 1. Mark xiii. 1. Luke xxi. 5.) And hence it is said that kings, and the mighty of the earth, were taken with the glory of it : " Because of thy temple at Jerusalem, shall kings bring presents unto thee;" as it is Ps. lxviii. 29, 31. Kings, Gentile kings, they shall be so taken with the sight of the outward glory of it, for they were not suffered to go into it; no uncircumcised were admitted in thither. It was therefore the outward glory of it with which the beholders were thus taken.

Her enlarging upward, as that was to show us what the inward affections of Christians should be, (Col. iii. 1—3,) so her curious outward adorning and beauty was a figure of the beauteous and holy conversation of the godly. And it is brave when the world are made to say of the lives and conversations of saints, as they were made to say of the stones and outward buildings of the temple, Behold what Christians, and goodly conversations are here ! I say, it is brave, when our light so shines before men, that they seeing our good works shall be forced to glorify our Father which is in heaven. (Matt. v. 16.)

Hence this is called our adorning wherewith we adorn the gospel, and that by which we beautify it. (Tit. ii. 10.) This, I say, is taking to beholders, as was this goodly outside of the temple. And without this, what is to be seen in the church of God ? Her inside cannot be seen by the world, but her outside may. Now, her outside is very homely, and without all beauty save that of the holy life; this only is her visible godliness. This puts to silence the ignorance of foolish men. This allureth others to fall in love with their own salvation, and makes them fall in with Christ against the devil and his kingdom.

XX. *Of the porch of the Temple.*

We come next to the porch of the temple, that is commonly called Solomon's. 1. This porch was in the front of the house, and so became the common way into the temple. (1 Kings vi. 3. 2 Chron. iii. 4.) 2. This porch, therefore, was the place of reception in common for all, whether Jews or religious proselytes, who came to Jerusalem to worship. (Acts iii. 11; v. 12.) 3. This porch had a door or gate belonging to it, but such as was seldom shut except in declining times, or when men put themselves into a rage against those better than themselves. (2 Chron. xxix. 7. Acts

xxi. 28—30.) 4. This gate of this porch was called Beautiful, even the Beautiful gate of the temple, and was that at which the lame lay, to beg for an alms of them that went in thither to worship. (Acts iii. 1, 2, 10.)

Now, then, since this porch was the common place of reception for all worshippers, and the place also where they laid the beggars, it looks as if it were to be a type of the church's bosom for charity. Here the proselytes were entertained, here the beggars were relieved, and received alms. These gates were seldom shut; and the houses of Christian compassion should be always open. This, therefore, beautified this gate, as charity beautifies any of the churches. Largeness of heart, and tender compassion at the church-door, is excellent. It is the bond of perfectness. (1 Cor. xii. 31; xiii. 1—4. Heb. xiii. 1—3. 3 John 5—7. Col. iii. 14.)

The church-porch to this day is a place for beggars, and perhaps this practice at first was borrowed from the beggars lying at the temple-gate. This porch was large, and so should the charity of the churches be. It was for length the breadth of the temple, and of the same size with the holiest of all. (1 Kings vi. 3. 2 Chron. iii. 4—8.) The first might be to teach us, in charity we should not be niggardly, but according to the breadth of our ability we should extend it to all the house, and that in our so doing the very emblem of heaven is upon us, of which the holiest was a figure. "As therefore we have opportunity, let us do good to all," &c. (Gal. vi. 10.)

It is a fine ornament to a true church to have a large church-porch, or a wide bosom for reception of all that come thither to worship. This was commanded to the Jews, and their glory shone when they did accordingly: "And it shall come to pass, in what place the stranger sojourneth, there shall ye give him his inheritance, saith the Lord God." (Ezek. xlvii. 23.)

This porch was, as I said, not only for length the breadth of the temple, and so the length and breadth of the holiest, but it was, if I mistake not, for height, far higher than them both. For the holy place was but thirty cubits high, and the most holy but twenty; but the porch was in height an hundred and twenty cubits. This beautiful porch, therefore, was four times as high as was the temple itself. (1 Kings vi. 2, 20. 2 Chron. iii. 4.)

One excellent ornament, therefore, of this temple was, for that it had a porch so high, that is, so famous for height: hence he says, "This house that is so high," that is, so famous for height,—so high as to be seen afar off. Charity, if it be rich, runs up from the church like a steeple, and will be seen afar off; I say, if it be rich, large, and abounds. Christ's charity was blazed abroad, it was so high no man could hide it, and the charity of the churches will be seen from church to church, yea, and will be spoken of

to their commendations in every place, if it be warm, fervent, and high. (Mark vii. 36. 2 Cor. viii. 24; ix. 2, 13, 14.)

XXI. *Of the ornaments of the porch of the Temple.*

There were three things belonging to the porch, besides its height that was an ornament unto it. 1. It was overlaid within with gold. 2. It had the pillars adjoined unto it. 3. It was the inlet into the temple.

1. It was overlaid with gold. Gold ofttimes was a type of grace, and particularly of the grace of love. That in Solomon's chariot called gold, is yet again mentioned by the name, Love. (Sol. Song iii. 9, 10.) As it is in the church, the grace of love is as gold: it is the greatest, the richest of graces, and that which abides for ever. Hence they that show much love to saints are said to be rich. (1 Tim. vi. 17—19.) And hence charity is called a treasure, a treasure in the heavens. (Luke xii. 33, 34.) Love is a golden grace; let then the churches, as the porch of the temple was, be inlaid with love, as gold.

2. It had the pillars adjoined to it, the which, besides their stateliness, seem to be there typically to teach example. For there was seen, by the space of four cubits, their lily-work in the porch. (1 Kings vii. 19.) Of their lily-work I spake before. Now that they were so placed, that they might be seen in the porch of the house, it seems to be for example to teach the church that she should live without worldly care, as did the apostles, the first planters of the church. And let ministers do this; they are now the pillars of the churches, and they stand before the porch of the house; let them also show their lily-work to the house, that the church may learn of them to be without carefulness as to worldly things, and also to be rich in love and charity towards the brethren. A covetous minister is a base thing, a pillar more symbolizing Lot's wife than an holy apostle of Jesus Christ; let them, since they stand at the door, and since the eyes of all in the porch are upon them, be patterns and examples of good works. (1 Tim. vi. 10—12. Tit. ii. 7.)

3. Another ornament unto this porch was, that it was an inlet into the temple. Charity is it which receiveth orphans, that receiveth the poor and afflicted into the church; worldly love, or that which is carnal, shuts up bowels, yea, and the church-doors too, against the poor of the flock; wherefore look that this kind of love be never countenanced by you. Crave that rather which is a fruit of the Spirit. Oh churches, let your ministers be beautified with your love, that they may beautify you with their love; and also be an ornament unto you, and to that gospel they minister to you, for Jesus Christ's sake.

XXII. *Of the ascent by which they went up into the porch of the Temple.*

1. This porch also had certain steps by which they went up into the house of the Lord. I know not directly the number of them, though Ezekiel speaks something about it. (Ezek. xl. 38, 39.) Hence, when men went to worship in the temple, they were said to go up into the house of the Lord. (Isa. xxxviii. 22.)

These steps, which were the ascent to the temple, were so curiously set, and also so finely wrought, that they were amazing to behold. Wherefore, when the Queen of Sheba, who came to prove Solomon's wisdom, saw the house which he had built, and his ascent by which he went up into the house of the Lord, she had no more spirit in her. She was by that sight quite drowned and overcome. (1 Kings x. 4, 5.)

2. These steps, whether cedar, gold, or stone, yet that which added to their adornment was the wonderment of a queen. And whatever they were made of, to be sure they were a shadow of those steps which we should take to and in the house of God : steps of God. (Ps. lxxxv. 13.) Steps ordered by him. (Ps. xxxvii. 23.) Steps ordered in his Word. (Ps. cxix. 133.) Steps of faith. (Rom. iv. 12.) Steps of the Spirit. (1 Cor. xii. 18.) Steps of truth. (3 John 4.) Steps washed with butter. (Job xxix. 6.) Steps taken before, or in the presence of God. Steps butted and bounded by a divine rule. These are steps indeed !

3. There are therefore no such steps as these to be found anywhere in the world. A step to honour, a step to riches, a step to worldly glory, these are everywhere ; but what are these to the steps by which men do ascend or go up to the house of the Lord ?

He then that entereth into the house of the Lord is an ascending man ; as it is said of Moses, he went up into the Mount of God. It is ascending to go into the house of God. The world believe not this ; they think it is going downward to go up to the house of God, but they are in a horrible mistake.

The steps, then, by which men went up into the temple are, and ought to be, opposed to those which men take to their lusts and empty glories. Hence such steps are said not only to decline from God, but to take hold of the path to death and hell. (Ps. xliv. 18. Prov. ii. 18 ; v. 5 ; vii. 25—27.)

The steps, then, by which men went up to the house of the Lord were significative of those steps which men take when they go to God, to heaven, and glory ; for these steps were the way to God, to God in his holy temple.

But how few are there that, as the Queen of the South, are taken with these goodly steps ! Do not most rather seek to push away our feet from taking hold of the path of life, or else lay snares for us in the way ? But all these, notwithstanding, the Lord guides us in the way of his steps ; they are goodly steps, they are the best.

XXIII. *Of the gate of the porch of the Temple.*

1. The porch, at which was an ascent to the temple, had a gate belonging to it. This gate, according to the Prophet Ezekiel, was six cubits wide. The leaves of this gate were double, one folding this way, the other folding that. (Ezek. xl. 48.)

Now here some may object, and say, Since the way to God by these doors were so wide, why doth Christ say the way and gate is narrow ?

Ans. The straitness, the narrowness, must not be understood of the gate simply, but because of that cumber that some men carry with them, that pretend to be going to heaven. Six cubits ! what is sixteen cubits to him who would enter in here with all the world on his back ? The young man in the gospel, who made such a noise for heaven, might have gone in easy enough ; for in six cubits' breadth there is room : but, poor man, he was not for going in thither unless he might carry in his houses upon his shoulder too, and so the gate was strait. (Mark x. 17—23.) Wherefore he that will enter in at the gate of heaven, of which this gate into the temple was a type, must go in by himself, and not with his bundles of trash on his back ; and if he will go in thus, he need not fear there is room,—" The righteous nation that keepeth the truth, they shall enter in." (Isa. xxvi. 2.)

2. They that enter in at the gate of the inner court must be clothed in fine linen ; how then shall they go into the temple that carry the clogs of the dirt of this world at their heels ?—" Thus saith the Lord, No stranger uncircumcised in heart, or uncircumcised in flesh, shall enter into my sanctuary." (Ezek. xliv. 9.)

3. The wideness, therefore, of this gate is for this cause here made mention of, to wit, to encourage them that would gladly enter thereat, according to the mind of God, and not to flatter them that are not for leaving of all for God.

4. Wherefore let such as would go in remember that here is room, even a gate to enter in at six cubits wide. We have been all this while but on the outside of the temple, even in the courts of the house of the Lord, to see the beauty and glory that is there. The beauty hereof made men cry out, and say, " How amiable are thy tabernacles, O Lord of hosts ! my soul longeth, yea, fainteth for the courts of the Lord ;" and to say, " A day in thy courts is better than a thousand." (Ps. lxxxiv. 1, 2, &c.)

XXIV. *Of the pinnacles of the Temple.*

1. There were also several pinnacles belonging to the temple. These pinnacles stood on the top aloft in the air, and were sharp, and so difficult to

stand upon: what men say of their number and length I wave, and come directly to their signification.

2. I therefore take those pinnacles to be types of those lofty, airy notions with which some men delight themselves, while they hover like birds above the solid and godly truths of Christ. Satan attempted to entertain Christ Jesus with this type and antitype at once, when he set him on one of the pinnacles of the temple, and offered to thrust him upon a false confidence in God, by a false and unsound interpretation of a text. (Matt. iv. 5, 6. Luke iv. 9—11.)

3. You have some men cannot be content to worship in the temple, but must be aloft; no place will serve them but pinnacles, pinnacles; that they may be speaking in and to the air, that they may be promoting their heady notions, instead of solid truth; not considering that now they are where the devil would have them be, they strut upon their points, their pinnacles; but let them look to it, there is difficult standing upon pinnacles, their neck, their soul is in danger. We read, God is in his temple, not upon these pinnacles. (Ps. xi. 4. Hab. ii. 20.)

4. It is true, Christ was once upon one of these, but the devil set him there, with intent to have dashed him in pieces by a fall, and yet even then told him, if he would venture to tumble down, he should be kept from dashing his foot against a stone. To be there, therefore, was one of Christ's temptations, consequently one of Satan's stratagems; nor went he thither of his own accord, for he knew that there was danger; he loved not to clamber pinnacles.

5. This should teach Christians to be low and little in their own eyes, and to forbear to intrude into airy and vain speculations, and to take heed of being puffed up with a foul and empty mind.

XXV. *Of the porters of the Temple.*

1. There were porters belonging to the temple. In David's time their number was four thousand men. (1 Chron. xxiii. 5.)

2. The porters were of the Levites, and their work was to watch at every gate of the house of the Lord. At the gate of the outer court, at the gates of the inner court, and at the door of the temple of the Lord. (2 Chron. xxxv. 15.)

3. The work of the porters, or rather the reason of their watching, was to look that none not duly qualified entered into the house of the Lord. "He set," saith the text, "porters at the gates of the house of the Lord, that none which was unclean in anything should enter in." (2 Chron. xxiii. 19.)

4. The excellency of the porters lay in these three things: their watchfulness, diligence, and valour, to make resistance to those that, as unfit, would attempt to enter those courts and the house of God. (1 Chron. xxvi. 6. Mark xiii. 34.)

5. These porters were types of our gospel-ministers, as they are set to be watchmen in and over the church, and the holy things of God. Therefore as Christ gives to every man in the church his work, "So he commands the porter to watch." (Isa. xxi. 11. Ezek. iii. 17; xxxiii. 7. Acts xx. 27—31. 2 Tim. iv. 5. Rev. ii. 2, 3.)

6. Sometimes every awakened Christian is said to be a porter, and such at Christ's first knock open unto him immediately. (Luke xii. 36—39.)

7. The heart of a Christian is also sometimes called the porter, for that when the true Shepherd comes to it, to him this porter openeth also. (John x. 3.)

8. This last has the body for his watchhouse, the eyes and ears for his port-holes; the tongue therewith to cry, Who comes there? as also to call for aid, when any thing unclean shall attempt with force and violence to enter in, to defile the house.

XXVI. *Of the charge of the porters of the Temple more particularly.*

1. The charge of the porters was to keep their watch, in four-square, even round about the temple of God. Thus it was ordained by David, before him by Moses, and after him by Solomon his son. (1 Chron. ix. 24. Numb. iii. 2 Chron. xxiii. 19; xxxv. 15.)

2. The porters had, some of them, the charge of the treasure-chambers, some of them had the charge of the ministering-vessels, even to bring them in and out by tale; also the opening and shutting of the gates of the house of the Lord was a part of their calling and office.

3. I told you the porters were types of our gospel-ministers, as they are watchmen in and over the house of God; and therefore in that they were thus to watch round about the temple, what is it but to show how diligent Satan is, to see if he may get in somewhere, by some means, to defile the church of God. He goes round and round, and round us, to see if he can find a hog-hole for that purpose.

4. This also showeth that the church of itself, without its watchmen, is a weak, feeble, and very helpless thing. What can the lady or mistress do to defend herself against thieves and sturdy villains if there be none but she at home? It is said, when the shepherd is smitten, the sheep will be scattered. What could the temple do without its watchmen?

5. Again; in that the porters had charge of the treasure-chambers (as it is, 1 Chron. ix. 26), it is to intimate that the treasures of the gospel are with the ministers of our God; and that the church, next to Christ, should seek them at their mouth. "We have this treasure in earthen vessels," saith Paul, and they are stewards of the "manifold mysteries of God." (1 Cor. iv. 1. 2 Cor. iv. 7. 1 Pet. iv. 10. Eph. iv. 11—13.)

6. These are God's true scribes, and bring out of their treasury things new and old ; or, as he saith in another place, " At our gates," that is, where our porters watch, " are all manner of pleasant fruit, which I have laid up for thee, O my beloved." (Matt. xiii. 52. Sol. Song vii. 13.)

7. Further ; some of them had charge of the ministering vessels, and they were to bring them in and out by tale. (1 Chron. ix. 18.) (1.) If, by ministering vessels you understand gospel-ordinances, then you see who has the charge of them, to wit, the watchmen and ministers of the Word. (Luke i. 12. 2 Thess. ii. 15. 2 Tim. ii. 2.) (2.) If by ministering vessels you mean the members of the church—for they are also ministering vessels—then you see who has the care of them, to wit, the pastors, the gospel-ministers. Therefore " obey them that have the rule over you, for they watch for your souls as they that must give an account, that they may do it with joy, and not with grief, for that is unprofitable for you." (Heb. xiii. 17.)

8. The opening of the gates did also belong to the porters, to show that the power of the keys, to wit, of opening and shutting, of letting in and keeping out of the church, doth ministerially belong to these watchmen. (Matt. xvi. 19. Heb. xii. 15.)

9. The conclusion is, then let the churches love their pastors, hear their pastors, be ruled by their pastors, and suffer themselves to be watched over, and to be exhorted, counselled, and if need be, reproved and rebuked by their pastors. And let the ministers not sleep, but be watchful, and look to the ordinances, to the souls of the saints, and the gates of the churches. Watchman, watchman, watch !

XXVII. *Of the doors of the Temple.*

Now we come to the gate of the temple ; namely, to that which let out of the porch into the holy place.

1. These doors or gates were folding, and they opened by degrees. First, a quarter, then a half, after that three quarters, and last of all the whole. These doors also hanged upon hinges of gold, and upon posts made of the goodly *olive-tree.* (1 Kings vi. 33, 34. Ezek. xli. 23, 24.)

2. These doors did represent Christ, as he is the way to the Father, as also did the door of the tabernacle at which the people were wont to stand when they went to inquire of God. " Wherefore Christ saith, I am the door," alluding to this, " by me if any man enter he shall be saved, and shall go in and out, and find pasture." (Exod. xxxiii. 9, 10 ; xxxviii. 8 ; xl. 12. Levit. i. 3, 4 ; viii. 3, 4, 33 ; xv. 14. Numb. vi. 13, 18 ; x. 3 ; xxv. 6 ; xxvii. 2. 1 Sam. ii. 22. John x. 9.) (1.) " I am the door." The door into the court, the door into the porch, the door into the temple, the door into the holiest, the door to the Father. But now we are at the door of the temple. (2.) And observe it, this door by Solomon was not measured as the door of the porch was ; for though the door into the court, and the door into the porch were measured, to show that the right to ordinances, and the inlet into the church is to be according to a prescript rule, yet this door was not measured ; to show that Christ, as he is the inlet to saving grace, is beyond all measure, and unsearchable. Hence his grace is called " unsearchable riches," and that above all we can ask or think, for that it passeth knowledge. (Eph. iii. 8, 19, 20.) (3.) It is therefore convenient that we put a note upon this, that we may distinguish rule and duty from grace and pardoning mercy ; for as I said, though Christ, as the door to outward privileges, is set forth by rule and measure ; yet, as he is the door to grace and favour, never a creature, as yet, did see the length and breadth of him. (Eph. iii. 17—19.) (4.) Therefore, I say, this gate was not measured ; for what should a rule do here, where things are beyond all measure ? (5.) This gate being also to open by degrees, is of signification to us, for it will be opening first by one fold, then by another, and yet will never be set wide, wide open, until the day of judgment. For then, and not till then, will the whole of the matter be open. " For now we see through a glass darkly, but then face to face ; now we know in part, but then shall we know even as we are known." (1 Cor. xiii. 12.)

XXVIII. *Of the leaves of this gate of the Temple.*

The leaves of this gate or door, as I told you before, were folding, and so, as was hinted, has something of signification in them. For by this means a man, especially a young disciple, may easily be mistaken ; thinking that the whole passage, when yet but a part was open, whereas three parts might yet be kept undiscovered to him. For these doors, as I said before, were never yet so wide open, I mean, in the antitype ; never man yet saw all the riches and fulness which is in Christ. So that I say, a new comer, if he judged by present sight, especially if he saw but little, might easily be mistaken ; wherefore such, for the most part, are most horribly afraid that they shall never get in thereat.

How sayest thou, young comer, is not this the case with thy soul ? So it seems to thee that thou art too big, being so great, so tun-bellied a sinner. But, O thou sinner, fear not, the doors are folding-doors, and may be opened wider, and wider again after that ; wherefore when thou comest to this gate, and imaginest there is not space enough for thee to enter, knock, and it shall be wider opened unto thee ; and thou shalt be received. (Luke xi. 9. John vi. 37.) So, then, whoever thou art that art come to the door, of which the temple door was a type, trust not to thy first conceptions of things, but believe there is grace abundant. Thou knowest not yet what Christ can do, the doors are folding-doors. He can do exceedingly abundantly above all that we can ask or think. (Eph. iii. 20.)

The hinges on which these doors do hang, were, as I told you, gold, to signify that they both turned upon motives, and motions of love, and also that the openings thereof were rich. Golden hinges the gate to God do turn upon.

The posts on which these doors did hang were of the olive-tree, that fat and oily tree, to show that they do never open with lothness or sluggishness, as doors do whose hinges want oil. They are always oily, and so open easily and quickly to those who knock at them. Hence you read, that he that dwells in this house gives freely, loves freely, and doth us good with all his heart. Yea, saith he, "I will rejoice over them to do them good, and I will plant them in this land assuredly with my whole heart, and with my whole soul." (Jer. iii. 12, 14, 22; xxxii. 41. Rev. xxi. 6; xxii. 17.) Wherefore the oil of grace, signified by this oily tree, or these olive-posts, on which these doors do hang, cause that they open glibly or frankly to the soul.

XXIX. *What the doors of the Temple were made of.*

1. The doors of the temple were made of fir, that is so sweet scented, and pleasant to the smell. (1 Kings vi. 34.)

2. Mankind is also often compared to the fir-tree, as Isa. xli. 19; lv. 13; lx. 17; xiv. 8.

3. Now, since the doors of the temple were made of the same, doth it not show that the way into God's house, and into his favour, is by the same nature which they are of that thither enter, even through the veil, his flesh? (Heb. x. 20.) For this door, I mean the antitype, doth he even say of himself, " I am as a green fir-tree; from me is thy fruit found." (Hos. xiv. 8.)

4. This fir-tree is Christ; Christ as man, and so as the way to the Father. The doors of the temple are also, as you see here, made of the fir-tree; even of that tree which was a type of the humanity of Jesus Christ. Consider Heb. ii. 14.

5. The fir-tree is also the house of the stork, that unclean bird, even as Christ is a harbour and shelter for sinners. As for the stork, saith the text, the fir-tree is her house; and Christ saith to the sinners, that see their want of shelter, " Come unto me, and I will give you rest." He is a refuge for the oppressed, a refuge in time of trouble. (Deut. xiv. 18. Lev. xi. 19. Ps. civ. 17; lxxxiv. 2, 3. Matt. xi. 27, 28. Heb. vi. 17—21.) He is, as the doors of fir of the temple, the inlet to God's house, to God's presence, and to a partaking of his glory. Thus God did of old, by similitudes, teach his people his way.

XXX. *How the doors of the Temple were adorned.*

And Solomon carved upon the doors " cherubims, palm-trees, and open flowers, and overlaid them all with gold." (1 Kings vi. 35. Ezek. xli. 15.)

First. He carved cherubims thereon. These cherubims were figures, or types of angels; and forasmuch as they were carved here upon the door, it was to show,

1. What delight the angels take in waiting upon the Lord, and in going at his bidding, at his beck. They are always waiting servants at the door of their Lord's house.

2. It may be also to show how much pleased they are to be where they may see sinners come to God. For " there is joy in the presence of the angels of God over one sinner that repenteth, and comes to God by Christ for mercy." (Luke xv. 10.)

3. They may also be placed here to behold with what reverence or irreverence those that come hither to worship do behave themselves. Hence Solomon cautions those that come to God's house to worship, that they take heed to their feet, because of the angels. Paul also says, Women must take heed that they behave themselves in the church as they should, and that because of the angels. (Eccles. v. 1, 2, 6. 1 Cor. xi. 5.)

4. They may also be carved upon the temple doors, to show us how ready they are, so soon as any poor creature comes to Christ for life, to take the care and charge of its conduct through this miserable world: " Are they not all ministering spirits, sent forth to minister for those which shall be heirs of salvation?" (Heb. i. 14.)

5. They may also be carved here, to show that they are ready at Christ's command, to take vengeance for him upon those that despise his people, and hate his person. Hence he bids the world take heed what they do to his " little ones," for " their angels behold the face of their Father which is in heaven," and are ready at the door to run at his bidding. (Matt. xviii. 10.)

6. Lastly. They may be carved upon these doors, to show that Christ Jesus is the very supporter and upholder of angels, as well as the Saviour of sinful man: for as he is before all things, so by him all things consist; angels stand by Christ, men are saved by Christ, and therefore the very cherubims themselves were carved upon these doors to show they are upheld and subsist by him. (1 Cor. viii. 6. Col. i. 17. Heb. i. 3.)

Second. Again; as the cherubims are carved here, so there were palm-trees carved here also. The palm-tree is upright, it twisteth not itself awry. (Jer. x. 5.)

1. Apply this to Christ, and then it shows us the uprightness of his heart, word, and ways with sinners. " Good and upright is the Lord, therefore will he teach sinners in the way," in at the door to life. (Ps. xxv. 8; xcii. 15.)

2. The palm or palm-tree is also a token of victory; and as placed here, it betokeneth the conquest that Christ, the door, should get over sin, death, the devil, and hell for us. (Rom. vii. 24; viii. 37. 1 Cor. xv. 54—56. Rev. vii. 9—11.)

3. If we apply the palm-tree to the church, as
we may, for she also is compared thereto, (Sol.
Song vii. 8—10,) then the palm-tree may be
carved here to show, that none but such as are
upright of heart and life shall dwell in the presence
of God. "The hypocrite," says Job, "shall not
come before him." "The upright," says David,
"shall dwell in thy presence." (Job xiii. 16. Ps.
cxi. 13.) They are they that are clothed in
white robes, which signifies uprightness of life,
that stand before the Lamb with palms in their
hands. (Rev. vii. 9.)

Third. There was also carved upon these doors
open flowers; and that to teach us that here is the
sweet scent and fragrant smell, and that the coming
soul will find it so in Christ, this door. "I am,"
saith he, "the rose of Sharon, and the lily of the
valleys." And again, "His cheeks are as beds of
spices and sweet flowers; his lips like lilies drop
sweet smelling-myrrh. (Sol. Song ii. 1; v. 13.)
"Open flowers." Open flowers are the sweetest,
because full grown, and because, as such, they
yield their fragrancy most freely. Wherefore,
when he saith upon the doors are open flowers, he
setteth Christ Jesus forth in his good favours, as
high as by such similitudes he could; and that
both in name and office. For open flowers lay,
by their thus opening themselves before us, all
their beauty also most plainly before our faces.
There are varieties of beauty in open flowers, the
which they also commend to all observers. Now
upon these doors, you see are open flowers, flowers
ripe and spread before us, to show that his name
and offices are savoury to them that by him do
enter his house to God his Father. (Sol. Song i.
1—4.)

"All these were overlaid with fine gold." Gold
is the most rich of all metals; and here it is said
the doors, the cherubims, the palm-trees, and open
flowers were overlaid therewith. And this shows
that as these things are rich in themselves, even
so they should be to us. We have a golden door
to go to God by, and golden angels to conduct us
through the world; we have golden palm-trees, as
tokens of our victory, and golden flowers to smell
on all the way to heaven.

XXXI. *Of the wall of the Temple.*

The wall of the temple was "ceiled with fir,
which he overlaid with fine gold; and set thereon
palm-trees and chains." (2 Chron. iii. 5—7.)

The walls were as the body of the house, unto
which Christ alluded when he said, "Destroy this
temple, and in three days I will raise it up."
(John ii. 19, 21.) Hence to be, and worship in
the temple, was a type of being in Christ, and
worshipping God by him. For Christ, as was
said, is the great temple of God, in the which all
the elect meet, and in whom they do service to
and for his Father.

Hence, again, the true worshippers are said to

be in him, to speak in him, to walk in him, to
obey in him. (2 Cor. ii. 14; xii. 19. Col. ii. 6.)
For as of old all true worship was to be found at
the temple, so now it is only found with Christ,
and with them that are in him. The promise of
old was made to them that worshipped within
these walls. "I will give," saith he, "to them in
my house, and within my walls," to them that
worship there in truth, "a place, and a name,
better than that of sons and of daughters."
(Isa. lvi. 5.)

But now, in New Testament times, "all the
promises in him are yea, and in him amen, to the
glory of God by us." (2 Cor. i. 20.) This is yet
further hinted to us, in that it is said these walls
are ceiled with fir; which, as was showed before,
was a figure of the humanity of Jesus Christ.

A wall is for defence, and so is the humanity of
Jesus Christ. It is, was, and will be our defence
for ever. For it was that which underwent and
overcame the curse of the law, and that in which
our everlasting righteousness is found. Had he
not in that interposed, we had perished for ever.
Hence we are said to be reconciled to God in
the body of his flesh through death. (Col. i. 19, 20.
Rom. v. 8—10.)

Now, this wall was overlaid with fine gold.
Gold here is a figure of the righteousness of
Christ, by which we are justified in the sight of
God. Therefore you read, that his church, as
justified, is said to stand at his right hand in
cloth of gold: "Upon thy right hand did stand
the queen in gold of Ophir." And again, "Her
clothing is of wrought gold." (Ps. xlv. 9, 13.)
This the wall was overlaid with, this the body
of Christ was filled with. Men while in the
temple were clothed with gold, even with the
gold of the temple: and men in Christ are clothed
with righteousness, the righteousness of Christ.
Wherefore this consideration doth yet more illustrate the matter. In that the palm-trees were
set on this wall, it may be to show that the
elect are fixed in Jesus, and so shall abide for
ever.

Chains were also carved on these walls, yea,
and they were golden chains; there were chains
on the pillars, and now also we find chains upon
the walls. (Phil. i. 12, 13.) 1. Chains were used
to hold captives, and such Paul did wear at Rome,
but he calls them his bands in Christ. 2. Chains
sometimes signify great afflictions, which God lays
on us for our sins. (Ps. cvii. 9—11. Lam. i. 14;
iii. 7.) 3. Chains also may be more mystically
understood, as of those obligations which the love
of God lays upon us, to do and suffer for him.
(Acts xx. 22.) 4. Chains do sometimes signify
beauty and comely ornaments: "Thy neck," saith
Christ to his spouse, "is comely with chains of
gold." And again, "I put bracelets upon thy
hands, a chain about thy neck." (Sol. Song i. 10.
Ezek. xvi. 8—11. Prov. i. 9.) 5. Chains also do
sometimes denote greatness and honour, such as

Daniel had when the king made him the third ruler in the kingdom. (Dan. v. 7, 16, 29.)

Now all these are temple-chains, and are put upon us for good; some to prevent our ruin, some to dispose our minds the better, and some to dignify, and to make us noble. Temple-chains are brave chains. None but temple-worshippers must wear temple-chains.

XXXII. *Of the garnishing the Temple with precious stones.*

"And he garnished the house with precious stones for beauty." (2 Chron. iii. 6, 7.) 1. This is another ornament to the temple of the Lord; wherefore, as he saith, it was garnished with them; he saith, it was garnished with them for beauty. The line saith, "garnished," the margin saith, "covered." 2. Wherefore I think they were fixed as stars, or as the stars in the firmament, so they were set in the ceiling of the house as in the heaven of the holy temple. 3. And thus fixed, they do the more aptly tell us of what they were a figure—namely, of the ministerial gifts and officers in the church. For ministers, as to their gifts and office, are called stars of God, and are said to be in the hand of Christ. (Rev. i. 20.) 4. Wherefore, as the stars glitter and twinkle in the firmament of heaven, so do true ministers in the firmament of his church. (1 Chron. xxix. 2. John v. 35. Dan. xii. 3.) 5. So that it is said again, these gifts come down from above, as signifying they distil their dew from above. And hence, again, the ministers are said to be set over us in the Lord, as placed in the firmament of his heaven, to give a light upon his earth. "There is gold, and a multitude of rubies, but the lips of knowledge are a precious jewel." (Prov. xx. 15.)

Verily, it is enough to make a man in this house look always upward; since the ceiling above head doth thus glitter with precious stones. Precious stones, all manner of precious stones, stones of all colours: "For there are divers gifts, differences of administrations, and diversities of operations: but it is the same God which worketh all in all." (1 Cor. xii. 4—6.) Thus had the ceiling of this house a pearl here, and there a diamond; here a jasper, and there a sapphire; here a sardius, and there a jacinth; here a sardonyx, and there an amethyst. "For to one is given by the Spirit the word of wisdom, to another the word of knowledge; to one the gift of healing, to another faith; to this man to work miracles, to that a spirit of prophecy; to another the discerning of spirits, to another divers kinds of tongues." (1 Cor. xii. 8—11.)

He also overlaid the house, beams, posts, walls, doors, &c., and all with gold. Oh, what a beautiful house the temple was; how full of glory was it! And yet all was but a shadow, a shadow of things to come, and which was to be answered in the church of the living God, the pillar and ground of truth, by better things than these.

XXXIII. *Of the windows of the Temple.*

"And for the house, he made windows of narrow lights." (1 Kings vi. 4.) There were windows for this house, windows for the chambers, and windows round about. (Ezek. iv. 16, 22—25, 29, 33, 36.) These windows were of several sizes, but all narrow, narrow without, but wide within; they also were finely wrought, and beautified with goodly stones. (Isa. liv. 14.)

1. Windows, as they are to a house an ornament, so also to it they are a benefit. "Truly the light is good, and a pleasant thing it is for the eye to behold the sun." (Eccles. xi. 7.) The window is that which Christ looks forth at, the window is that which the sun looks in at. (Sol. Song ii. 9.)

2. By the light which shines in at the window we also see to make and keep the house clean, and also to do what business is necessary there to be done. "In thy light we see light;" light to do our duty, and that both to God and man.

3. These windows, therefore, were figures of the written Word, by and through which Christ shows himself to his, and by which we also apprehend him. And hence the word of God is compared to a glass through which the light doth come, and by which we see not only the beams of the sun, but our own smutches also. (2 Chron. xxx. 18. James i. 23—25.)

4. The lights, indeed, were narrow, wherefore we see also through their antitype but darkly and imperfectly. "Now we see through a glass darkly," or as in a riddle, "now we know but in part." (1 Cor. xiii. 12.)

5. Their windows and their lights are but of little service to those that are without; the word sees but little of the beauty of the church by the light of the written Word, though the church by that light can see the dismal state of the world, and also how to avoid it.

XXXIV. *Of the chambers of the Temple.*

In the temple Solomon made chambers. (1 Kings vi. 5.)

First. The chambers were of several sizes; some little, some large; some higher, some lower; some more inward, and some outward.

Second. These chambers were for several services: some were for rest, some to hide in, some to lay up treasure in, and some for solace and delight. (2 Chron. iii. 9. Ezek. xl. 7; xli. 5, 9—11. 2 Chron. xxxi. 11, 12. 2 Kings xi. 1—3. Ezra viii. 29.) 1. They were for resting-places. Here the priests and porters were wont to lodge. 2. They were for hiding-places. Here Jehoshebah hid Joash from Athaliah the term of six years. 3. They were also to lay the temple-treasure, or dedicated things, in, that they might be safely kept there for the worshippers. 4. And some of them were for solace and delight; and, I must add, some for durable habitation. Wherefore in some of them some dwelt always; yea, their names dwelt there when they were dead.

(1.) Those of them which were for rest, were types of that rest which by faith we have in the Son of God, (Matt. xi. 28,) and of that eternal rest which we shall have in heaven by him. (Heb. iv. 3.) (2.) Those chambers which were for hiding and security were types of that safety which we have in Christ from the rage of the world. (Isa. xxvi. 20.) (3.) Those chambers which were for the reception of the treasures and dedicated things were types of Christ, as he is the common storehouse of believers. "For it pleased the Father that in him should all fulness dwell;" "and of his fulness we all receive, and grace for grace." (John i. 16. Col. i. 19.) (4.) Those chambers that were for solace and delight were types of those retirements and secret meetings of Christ with the soul, where he gives it his embraces, and delights her with his bosom and ravishing delight. "He brought me," said she, "into his chambers," "into the chamber of her which conceived me;" and there he gave her his love. (Sol. Song i. 4; iii. 4.)

The chambers which were for durable dwelling-places were types of those eternal dwelling-places which are in the heavens, prepared of Christ and the Father for them that shall be saved. (John xiv. 1—4. 2 Cor. v. 1—4.) This it is to "dwell on high," and to be safe from fear of evil. Here, therefore, you see, are chambers for rest, chambers for safety, chambers for treasure, chambers for solace, and chambers for durable habitations. Oh the rest and peace that the chambers of God's high house will yield to its inhabitants in another world! Here they will rest from their labours, rest upon their beds, rest with God, rest from sin, temptation, and all sorrow. (Rev. xiv. 13. Isa. lvii. 1, 2. 2 Thess. i. 7.) God, therefore, then shall wipe all tears from our eyes, even when he comes out of his chambers as a bridegroom, to fetch his bride, his wife, unto him thither, to the end they may have eternal solace together. Oh these are far better than the chambers of the south!

XXXV. *Of the stairs, by which they went up into the chambers of the Temple.*

There were stairs, by which men went up into these chambers of the temple, and they were but one pair, and they went from below to the first, and so to the middle, and thence to the highest chambers in the temple. (1 Kings vi. 8. Ezek. xli. 7.)

1. These stairs were winding, so that they turned about that did go up them. So, then, he that essayed to go into these chambers must turn

with the stairs, or he could not go up—no, not into the lowest chambers.

2. These stairs, therefore, were a type of a twofold repentance. That by which we turn from nature to grace, and by which we turn from the imperfections which attend a state of grace to glory. Hence true repentance, or the right going up these turning stairs, is called repentance to salvation; for true repentance stoppeth not at the reception of grace, for that is but a going up these stairs to the middle chambers. (2 Cor. vii. 10.)

Thus, therefore, the soul, at its going up these stairs, turns and turns, till it enters the doors of the highest chambers. It groans, though in a state of grace, because that is not the state of glory. I count, then, that from the first to the middle chambers may be a type of turning from nature to grace. But from the middle to the highest, these stairs may signify a turning still from the imperfections and temptations that attend a state of grace, to that of immortality and glory. (2 Cor. v. 1—10.)

For as there are turning stairs from the lowest to the middle chambers, so the stairs from thence still turn, and so will do, till you come to the highest chambers. I do not say that they that have received grace do repent they have received grace, but I say, they that have received grace are yet sorry that grace is not consummate in glory; and hence they are for going up thither still by these turning stairs; yea, they cannot rest below, as they would, till they ascend to the highest chambers. "Oh wretched man that I am!" And "in this we groan earnestly," is the language of gracious souls. (Rom. vii. 24. 2 Cor. v. 1—3.) True, every one doth not do thus that comes into the temple of God; many rest below stairs, they like not to go turning upward. Nor do I believe that all that bid fair for ascending to the middle chambers get up to the highest stories, to his stories in the heavens. Many in churches, who seem to be turned from nature to grace, have not the grace to go up turning still; but rest in that show of things, and so die below a share in the highest chambers.

All these things are true in the antitype, and, as I think, prefigured by these turning stairs to the chambers of the temple. But this turning, and turning still, displeases some much; they say it makes them giddy; but I say there is no way like this to make a man stand steady; steadfast in the faith, and with boldness in the day of judgment. For he has this seated in his heart: I went up the turning stairs, till I came to the highest chambers. A strait pair of stairs are like that ladder by which men ascend to the gallows; they are the turning ones, that lead us to the heavenly mansion-houses. Look, therefore, you that come into the temple of God to worship, that you stay not at the foot of these turning stairs, but go up thence; yea, up them, and up them, and up them, till you come to the view of the heavens; yea, till you are possessed of the highest chambers. How many times has God, by the Scripture, called upon you to *turn*, and told you, you must turn or die! and now here he has added to his call a figure, by placing a pair of turning stairs in his temple, to convict your very senses that you must *turn*, if you mean to go up into his holy chambers, and so into his eternal mansion-houses: and look that you turn to purpose; for every turning will not serve. Some turn, but not to the Most High, and so turn to no purpose.

XXXVI. *Of the molten sea that was in the Temple.*

There was also a molten sea in the temple; it was made of brass, and contained three thousand baths. (2 Chron. iv. 2—9.) This sea was for the priests to wash in, when they came into the temple to accomplish the service of God: to wash their hands and feet at, that they might not, when they came thither, die for their unpreparableness. The laver also which was in the wilderness was of the same use there. (Exod. xxx.)

1. It was, as may be supposed, called a sea, for that it was large to contain; and a sea of brass, for that it was made thereof. It is called in Revelations a sea of glass, alluding to that in the wilderness, which was made of the brazen looking-glasses of the women that came to worship at the door of the tabernacle. (Rev. iv. 6; xv. 2. Exod. xxviii. 8.)

2. It was also said to be molten, because it was made of that fashion by fire, and its antitype, therefore, said to be a sea of glass mingled with fire. (Rev. xv. 2.) (1.) This sea was a figure of the word of the gospel, in the cleansing virtue of it; which virtue then it has when mingled with the fire of the Holy Ghost. And to this Christ alludes, when he saith, "Now ye are clean through the word which I have spoken unto you." (John xv. 3.)

(2.) It was a figure of the word, without mixture of men's inventions; hence it is called "pure water." Having your "bodies washed with pure water." And again, he sanctifies and cleanseth his church "with the washing of water by the word." (Eph. v. 25. Tit. iii. 5.) All these places are an allusion to the molten sea, at which of old they washed, when they went into the temple to worship. "Therefore," saith he, "being washed, let us draw near to God." (Heb. x. 22.)

3. This sea from brim to brim was complete ten cubits; perhaps to show there is as much in the word of the gospel to save as there is in the ten words to condemn.

4. From under this sea round about appeared oxen, ten in a cubit did compass it round about. (2 Chron. iv. 3.) Understand by these oxen, *ministers*, for to them they are compared in

1 Cor. ix. 9. And then we are taught whence true ministers come, to wit, from under the power of the gospel, for this sea breeds gospel ministers, as the waters breed fish.

5. It is also said in the text, that these oxen were cast when the sea was cast; insinuating that when God ordained a word of grace to save us, he also in his decree provided ministers to preach it to us to that end. Paul tells us that he was made a minister of the gospel, "according to God's eternal purpose, which he purposed in Christ Jesus our Lord." (Eph. iii. 9—11. Col. i. 25.)

6. This sea is said to have a brim like the brim of a cup: to invite us as well to drink of its grace, as to wash in its water. For the word and Spirit, when mixed, has not only a cleansing, but a saving quality in it. (2 Chron. iv. 1—5. 1 Cor. xv. 1, 2.)

7. This brim was wrought with lilies; or was like a lily-flower; to show how they should grow and flourish, and with what beautiful robes they should be adorned, who were washed, and did drink of this holy water. Yea, that God would take care of them, as he also did of lilies, and would not fail to bestow upon them what was necessary for the body as well as for the soul. (Matt. vi. 28—34.)

XXXVII. *Upon what the molten sea stood in the Temple.*

1. This molten sea stood upon the backs of twelve brazen bulls, or oxen. (2 Chron. iv. 4.)

2. These oxen, as they thus stood, looked three towards the north, three towards the west, three towards the east, and three towards the south.

3. These twelve oxen were types of the twelve apostles of the Lamb, who, as these beasts, stood looking into the four corners of the earth, and were bid to go preach the gospel in all the world.

4. They were compared to oxen, because they were clean, for the ox was a clean beast. Hence the apostles are called holy. They were compared to oxen, because the ox is strong; and they also were mighty in the word. (Prov. xiv. 4. 2 Cor. xii. 12.)

5. The ox will not lose what he has got by drawing; he will not let the wheels go back: so the apostles were set to defend, and not let that doctrine go back, which they had preached to others; nor did they, they delivered it pure to us.

6. One of the cherubs of which you read in the vision had a face like an ox, to show that the apostles, these men of the first order, are most like the angels of God. (Ezek. i. 10.)

7. In that they stood with their faces every way, it was, as I said, to show how the apostles should carry the gospel into all the world. (Matt. xxviii. 19. Mark xvi.)

8. And observe, just as these oxen were placed looking in the temple every way, even so stand open the gates of the New Jerusalem, to receive

those that by their doctrine should be brought into it. "And they shall come from the east, and from the west, and from the north, and from the south, and shall sit down in the kingdom of God." (Rev. xxi. 13, 14. Luke xiii. 29.)

9. These oxen bear this molten sea upon their backs, to show that they should be the foundation workmen of the gospel, and that it ought not to be removed, as was the molten sea of old from that basis to another.

10. It is also said concerning these oxen, that thus did bear this molten sea, that all their hinder parts were inwards, that is, covered by that sea that was set upon their backs. Their hinder parts, or as the Apostle has it, "our uncomely parts." (1 Cor. xii. 23, 24.)

11. And, indeed, it becomes a gospel minister to have his uncomely parts covered with that grace which by the gospel he preacheth unto others; as Paul exhorts Timothy to take heed unto himself, and to his doctrine. (1 Tim. iv. 6.)

12. But, alas, there are too many who, can they but have their heads covered with a few gospel notions, care not though their hinder parts are seen of all the world! But such are false ministers; the prophet calls them "the tail." "The prophet that speaketh lies, either by word or with his feet, he is the tail." (Isa. ix. 15. Prov. vi. 12, 13.)

13. But what a shame is it to hide his head under this molten sea, while his hinder parts hang out! Such an one is none of Christ's oxen, for they, with honour to their Master, show their heads before all the world, for that their hinder parts are inward covered.

14. Look to thy hinder parts, ministers; lest, while thy mouth doth preach the gospel, thy nakedness and shame be seen of those which hear thee. For they that do not observe to learn this lesson themselves, will not teach others to believe the word, nor to live a holy life: they will learn of them to show their shame, instead of learning to be holy.

XXXVIII. *Of the lavers of the Temple.*

Besides this molten sea, there were ten lavers in the temple; five of which were put on the right side, and five also on the left. (2 Chron. iv. 6.)

1. Of their fashion and their furniture, you may see 1 Kings vii. These lavers, as the molten sea, were vessels which contained water, but they were not of the same use with it. True, they were both to wash in; the sea to wash the worshippers, but the lavers to wash the sacrifice! "He made the ten lavers to wash in them such things as they offered for burnt-offering, but the sea was for the priest to wash in." (2 Chron. iv. 6.) 2. The burnt-offering was a type of the body of Christ, which he once offered for our sins; and the fire on which the sacrifice was burned, a type of the curse of

the law which seized on Christ when he gave himself a ransom for us. For, therefore, that under the law was called the burnt-offering, because of the burning upon the altar. (Lev. vi. 9.)

But what, then, must we understand by these lavers, and by this sacrifice being washed in them in order to its being burned upon the altar?

I answer, Verily, I think, that the ten lavers were a figure of the Ten Commandments; in the purity and perfection of Christ's obedience to which, he became capable of being made a burnt-offering, acceptable to God for the sins of the people. Christ was made under the law, and all his acts of obedience to God for us were legal, and his living thus a perfect legal life was his washing his offering in these ten lavers, in order to his presenting it upon the altar for our sins. The lavers went upon wheels, to signify walking feet; and Christ walked in the law, and so became a clean offering to God for us. The wheels were of the very same as were the lavers, to show that Christ's obedience to the law was of the same, as to length and breadth, with its commands and demands to their utmost tittle and extent. The inwards and legs of the burnt-offering were to be washed in these lavers, (Lev. i. 9, 13. 2 Chron. iv. 6,) to show that Christ should be pure and clean in heart and life.

We know that obedience, whether Christ's or ours, is called "a walking in the way," typified by the lavers walking upon their wheels. But I mean not by Christ, his washing of his offering, that he had any filthiness cleaving to his nature or obedience; yet this I say, that so far as our guilt laid upon him could impede, so far he wiped it off by washing in these lavers. For his offering was to be without blemish, and without spot, to God. Hence it is said, he sanctified himself in order to his suffering. "And being made perfect, he became the author of eternal salvation to all them that obey him." (John xvii. 19. Heb. v. 6—10.)

For albeit he came holy into the world, yet that holiness was but preparatory to that by which he sanctified himself, in order to his suffering for sin. That, then, which was his immediate preparation for his suffering, was his obedience to the law, his washing in these lavers. He, then, first yielded complete obedience to the law on our behalf, and then, as so qualified, offered his washed sacrifice for our sins without spot to God. Thus, therefore, he was our burnt-offering washed in the ten lavers, that he might, according to law, be accepted of the Lord.

"And he set five of the lavers on the right side of the house, and five of them on the left." Thus was the ten divided, as the tables of the law, one showing our duty towards our God, the other our duty towards our neighbour; in both which the burnt-offering was washed, that it might be clean in both respects. They might also be thus placed, the better to put the people in mind of the necessity of the sanction of Christ according to the law, in order to his offering of himself an offering to God for us.

XXXIX. *Of the tables in the Temple.*

"He made also ten tables, and placed them in the temple, five on the right hand, and five on the left." (2 Chron. iv. 8.)

Some, if not all of these tables, so far as I can see, were they on which the burnt-offering was to be cut in pieces, in order to its burning.

These tables were made of stone, of hewn stones, on which this work was done. (Ezek. xl. 40—44.) Now, since the burnt-offering was a figure of the body of Christ, the tables on which this sacrifice was slain must needs, I think, be a type of the heart, the stony heart of the Jews. For had they not had hearts hard as adamant, they could not have done that thing. Upon these tables, therefore, was the death of Christ contrived, and this horrid murder acted, even upon these tables of stone.

In that they are called tables of hewn stone, it may be to show that all this cruelty was acted under smooth pretences, for hewn stones are smooth. The tables were finely wrought with tools, even as the hearts of the Jews were with hypocrisy. But, alas! they were stone still, that is, hard and cruel, else they could not have been an anvil for Satan to forge such horrid barbarisms upon. The tables were in number the same with the lavers, and were set by them, to show what are the fruits of being devoted to the law, as the Jews were, in opposition to Christ and his holy gospel. There flows nothing but hardness, and a stony heart from thence. This was showed in its first writing; it was writ on tables of stone, figures of the heart of man; and on the same tables or hearts was the death of Jesus Christ compassed.

One would think that the meekness, gentleness, or good deeds of Jesus Christ, might have procured in them some relentings, when they were about to take away his life; but, alas, their hearts were tables of stone! What feeling or compassion can a stone be sensible of? Here were stony hearts, stony thoughts, stony counsels, stony contrivances, a stony law, and stony hands; and what could be expected hence, but barbarous cruelty indeed! If I ask you," said Christ, "you will not answer me, neither will you let me see." (Luke xxii. 68.)

In that the stony tables were placed about the temple, it supposeth that they were temple-men, priests, scribes, rulers, lawyers, &c., that were to be the chief on whose hearts this murder was to be designed, and by them enacted to their own damnation, without repentance.

XL. *Of the instruments wherewith this sacrifice was slain, and of the four tables they were laid on in the Temple.*

The instruments that were laid upon the tables in the temple were not instruments of music, but those with which the burnt-offering was slain: "and the four tables were of hewn stone for the burnt-offering: whereon also they laid the instruments wherewith they slew the burnt-offering and the sacrifice." (Ezek. xl. 42, 43.)

Here we are to take notice, that the tables are the same, and some of them of which we spake before. That the instruments with which they slew the sacrifice were laid upon these tables. The instruments with which they slew the sacrifices, what were they, but a bloody axe, bloody knives, bloody hooks, and bloody hands? For these we need no proof; matter of fact declares it. But what were those instruments the type of?

Ans. Doubtless they were a type of our sins. They were the bloody axe, the knife, and bloody hands, that shed his precious blood. They were the meritorious ones, without which he could not have died. When I say ours, I mean the sins of the world. Though, then, the hearts of the Jews were the immediate contrivers, yet they were our sins that were the bloody tools or instruments which slew the son of God. "He was wounded for our transgressions, he died for our sins." (Isa. liii. 1 Cor. xv. Gal. i.)

Oh the instruments of us churls, by which this poor man was taken from off the earth! (Isa. xxxii. 7. Prov. xxx. 14.) The whip, the buffetings, the crown of thorns, the nails, the cross, the spear, with the vinegar and gall, were all nothing in comparison of our sins. "For the transgressions of my people was he stricken." (Isa. liii. 8.) Nor were the flouts, taunts, mocks, scorns, derisions, &c., with which they followed him from the garden to the cross, such cruel instruments as these. They were our sins, then, our cursed sins, by, with, and for the sake of which, the Lord Jesus became a bloody sacrifice.

But why must the instruments be laid upon the tables?

1. Take the tables for the hearts of the murderers, and the instruments for their sins, and what place more fit for such instruments to be laid upon? It is God's command, that these things should be laid to heart, and he complains of those that do not do it. (Isa. xlii. 25; lvii. 11.)

2. Nor are men ever like to come to good, until these instruments with which the Son of God was slain indeed be laid to heart. And they were eminently laid to heart even by them soon after; the effect of which was, the conversion of thousands of them. (Acts ii. 36, 37.)

3. Wherefore when it says these instruments must be laid upon the stony tables, he insinuates, that God would take a time to charge the murder of his Son home upon the consciences of them

that did that murder, either to conversion or condemnation. And is it not reason that they who did this horrid villany should have their doings laid before their faces upon the tables of their heart? " That they may look upon him, whom they have pierced, and mourn." (Zech. xii. 10. Rev. i. 7.)

4. But these instruments were laid but upon some of the tables, and not upon all the ten, to show that not all, but some of those, so horrid, should find mercy of the Lord.

5. But we must not confine these tables only to the hearts of the bloody Jews; they were our sins for the which he died. Wherefore these instruments should be laid upon our tables too; and the Lord lay them there for good, that we also may see our horrid doings, and come bending to him for forgiveness!

6. These instruments thus lying on the tables in the temple, became a continual motive to God's people to repentance, for so oft as they saw these bloody and cruel instruments, they were put in mind how their sins should be the cause of the death of Christ.

7. It would be well also, if these instruments were at all times laid upon our tables, for our more humbling for our sins in everything we do, especially upon the Lord's table, when we come to eat and drink before him. I am sure the Lord Jesus doth more than intimate, that he expects that we should do so, where he saith, When ye eat that bread, and drink that cup, " Do this in remembrance of me;" in remembrance that I died for your sins, and, consequently, that they were the meritorious cause of the shedding of my blood.

To conclude. Let all men remember, that these cruel instruments are laid upon the table of their hearts, whether they see them there or no. " The sin of Judah is written with a pen of iron, and with the point of a diamond, upon the tables of their heart." (Jer. xvii. 1.) A pen of iron will make letters upon a table made of stone, and the point of a diamond will make letters upon glass. Wherefore in this saying, God informs us that if we shall forbear to read these lines to our conversion, God will one day read them against us unto our condemnation.

XLI. Of the candlesticks of the Temple.

" And he made ten candlesticks of gold, according to the form, and he set them in the temple, five on the right hand, and five on the left." (2 Chron. iv. 7.)

1. These candlesticks were made of gold, to show the worth and value of them. 2. They were made after the form, or exact, according to rule, like those that were made in the tabernacle, or according to the pattern which David gave to Solomon to make them by. Observe, there was great exactness in these, and need there was of this

hint, that men might see that everything will not pass for a right ordered candlestick with God. (Exod. xxv. 31—37. 1 Chron. xxviii. 15, 16.)

These candlesticks are said sometimes to be ten, sometimes seven, and sometimes one; ten here; seven Rev. i. and one in Zech. iv. Ten is a note of multitude, and seven a note of perfection, and one a note of unity. Now as the precious stones with which the house was garnished were a type of ministerial gifts, so these candlesticks were a type of those that were to be the churches of the New Testament; wherefore he says, " The candlesticks which thou sawest are the seven churches." (Rev. i. 12, 13—20.)

1. The candlesticks were here in number ten, to show that Christ under the New Testament would have a many gospel-churches. " And I, if I be lifted up from the earth," saith he, " will draw all men unto me;" that is, abundance. " For the children of the desolate," that is, of the New Testament church, " shall be many more than they of the Jews were." (John xii. 32. Gal. iv. 27.)

2. In that the candlesticks were set by the lavers and stony tables, it might be to show us, that Christ's churches should be much in considering, that Christ, though he was righteous, yet died for our sins; though his life was according to the holy law, yet our stony hearts caused him to die. Yea, and that the candlesticks are placed there, it is to show us also that we should be much in looking on the sins by which we caused him to die, for the candlesticks were set by those tables whereon they laid the instruments with which they slew the sacrifice.

3. These candlesticks being made according to form, seem not only to be exact as to fashion, but also as to work. For that in Exodus, with its furniture, was made precisely of one talent of gold, perhaps to show, that Christ's true spouse is not to be a grain more, nor a dram less, but just the number of God's elect. This is Christ's completeness, his fulness: one more, one less, would make his body a monster.

4. The candlestick was to hold the lights, and to show it to all the house, and the church is to let her light so shine that they without may see the light. (Matt. v. 15, 16. Luke viii. 16; xi. 33; xii. 35.)

5. To this end the candlesticks were supplied with oil-olive, a type of the supply that the church hath, that her light may shine, even of the Spirit of grace.

XLII. Of the lamps belonging to the candlesticks of the Temple.

To these candlesticks belonged several lamps, with their flowers, and their knops. (2 Chron. iv. 21.)

1. These lamps were types of that profession that the members of the church do make of Christ. whether such members have saving grace or not (Matt. xxv. 1—7.)

2. These lamps were beautified with knops and flowers, to show how comely and beautiful that professor is that adorns his profession with a suitable life and conversation.

3. We read that the candlestick in Zechariah had seven lamps belonging to it, and a bowl of golden oil on the top; and that by golden pipes this golden oil emptied itself into the lamps, and all, doubtless, that the lamps might shine. (Zech. iv.)

4. Christ, therefore, who is the high-priest, and to whom it belongs to dress the lamps, doth dress them accordingly. But now there are lamp-carriers of two sorts; such as have only oil in their lamps, and such as have oil in their lamps and vessels too, and both these belong to the church, and in both these Christ will be glorified. And they should have their proper places at last: they that have the oil of grace in their hearts, as well as a profession of Christ in their hands, they shall go in with him to the wedding; but they who only make a profession, and have not oil in their vessels, will surely miscarry at last. (Matt. xxv.)

5. Wherefore, O thou professor, thou lamp-carrier! have a care and look to thyself; content not thyself with that only that will maintain thee in a profession, for that may be done without saving grace. But I advise thee to go to Aaron, to Christ, the trimmer of our lamps, and beg thy vessel full of oil of him (that is, grace), for the seasoning of thy heart, that thou mayest have wherewith, not only to bear thee up now, but at the day of the bridegroom's coming, when many a lamp will go out, and many a professor be left in the dark, for that will to such be a woful day. (Lev. xxiv. 2. Matt. xxv.)

Some there are that are neither for lamps nor oil for themselves, neither are they pleased if they think they see it in others. But they that have lamps, and they that have none, and they which would blow out other folks' light, must shortly appear to give an account of all their doings to God. And then they shall see what it is to have oil in their vessels and lamps; and what it is to be without it in their vessels, though it is in their lamps; and what a dismal thing it is to be a malignant to either; but at present let this suffice.

XLIII. *Of the shew-bread on the golden table in the Temple.*

There was also shew-bread set upon a golden table in the temple. (1 Kings vii. 48.) The shew-bread consisted of twelve cakes made of fine flour; "Two tenth deals were to go to one cake, and they were to be set in order in two rows upon the pure table." (Exod. xxix. 33. Lev. viii. 31; xxiv. 5—9.)

1. These twelve loaves to me do seem to be a type of the twelve tribes under the law, and of the children of God under the gospel, as they present themselves before God, in and by his ordinances through Christ. Hence the Apostle says, "For we being many are one bread," &c. (1 Cor. x. 17.) For so were the twelve cakes, though twelve, and so are the gospel saints, though many. "For we being many are one body in Christ." (Rom. xii. 5.)

2. But they were a type of the true church, not of the false. For Ephraim, who was the head of the ten tribes in their apostacy, is rejected, as "a cake not turned." Indeed he is called a cake, as a false church may be called a church; but he is called "a cake not turned," as a false church is not prepared for God, nor fit to be set on the golden table before him. (Hos. vii. 8.)

3. These cakes or shew-bread were to have frankincense strewed upon them, as they stood upon the golden table, which was a type of the sweet perfumes of the sanctifications of the Holy Ghost. To which, I think, Paul alludes, when he says, "The offering up of the Gentiles is acceptable to God, being sanctified by the Holy Ghost." (Rom. xv. 16.)

4. They were to be set upon the pure table, new and hot; to show that God delighteth in the company of new and warm believers. "I remember thee, the kindness of thy youth:" "When Israel was a child, I loved him." Men at first conversion are like to a cake well baked, and new taken from the oven; they are warm, and cast forth a very fragrant scent, especially when as warm sweet incense is strewed upon them. (Jer. ii. Hos. xi. 1.)

5. When the shew-bread was old and stale, it was to be taken away, and new and warm put in its place, to show that God has but little delight in the service of his own people when their duties grow stale and mouldy. Therefore he removed his old, stale, mouldy church of the Jews from before him, and set in their rooms upon the golden table the warm church of the Gentiles.

6. The shew-bread, by an often remove and renewing, was continually to stand before the Lord in his house, to show us, that always, as long as ordinances shall be of use, God will have a new, warm, and sanctified people to worship him.

7. Aaron and his sons were to eat the old shew-bread, to show that when saints have lived in the world as long as living is good for them, and when they can do no more service for God in the world, they shall yet be accepted of Jesus Christ; and that it shall be as meat and drink to him to save them from all their unworthinesses.

8. The new shew-bread was to be set even on the Sabbath before the Lord, to show with what warmth of love and affections God's servants should approach his presence upon his holy day.

XLIV. *Of the snuffers belonging to the candlesticks and lamps of the Temple.*

As there were candlesticks and lamps, so there were snuffers also prepared for these in the temple of the Lord: "And the snuffers were snuffers of gold." (1 Kings vi. 50.) 1. Snuffers. The use of snuffers is to trim the lamps and candles, that their lights may shine the brighter. 2. Snuffers, you know, are biting, pinching things; but use them well, and they will prove not only beneficial to those within the house, but profitable to the lights.

Snuffers, you may say, of what were they a type?

Ans. If our snuffs are our superfluities of naughtiness, our snuffers then are those righteous reproofs, rebukes, and admonitions which Christ has ordained to be in his house for good, or, as the Apostle hath it, for our edification; and perhaps Paul alludes to these when he bids Titus to rebuke the Cretians sharply, that they might be sound in the faith. (Tit. i. 12, 13.) As who should say, they must use the snuffers of the temple to trim their lights withal, if they burn not well. These snuffers, therefore, are of great use in the temple of God, only, as I said, they must be used wisely. It is not for every fool to handle snuffers at or about the candles, lest perhaps, instead of mending the light, they put the candle out; and therefore Paul bids them that are spiritual to do it. (Gal. vi. 1.) My reason tells me, that if I use these snuffers as I should, I must not only endeavour to take the superfluous snuff away, but so to do it that the light thereby may be mended; which then is done if, as the Apostle saith, "I use sharpness to edification, and not for destruction. (1 Cor. v. 4, 5. 2 Cor. xiii. 10.)

Are not the seven churches in Asia called by the name of candlesticks? And why candlesticks, if they were not to hold the candles? And candles must have snuffers therewith to trim the lights. And Christ, who is our true Aaron, in those rebukes which he gave those churches, alluding to these snuffers, did it that their lights might shine the brighter. (Rev. ii. iii.) Wherefore as he used them, he did it still with caution to their light, that it might not be impaired. For as he still thus trimmed these lamps, he yet encouraged what he saw would shine if helped. He only nipped the snuff away.

Thus, therefore, he came to them with these snuffers in his hand, and trimmed their lamps and candlesticks. (Rev. ii. iv. 20; iii. 2, 15.) This should teach ministers, to whom it belongs under Christ to use these snuffers well. Strike at the snuff, not at the light, in all your rebukes and admonitions; snuff not your lamps of a private revenge, but of a design to nourish grace and gifts in churches. Thus our Lord himself says he did, in his using of these snuffers about these candlesticks. "As many," saith he, "as I love, I rebuke and chasten; be zealous, therefore, and repent." (Rev. iii. 19.)

To conclude; Watchmen, watch, and let not your snuffs be too long, nor pull them off with your fingers, or carnal reasonings, but with godly ad-

monitions, &c. Use your snuffers graciously, curb vice, nourish virtue; so you will use them well, and so your light will shine to the glory of God.

XLV. *Of the snuff-dishes that were with the snuffers in the Temple.*

As there were snuffers, so there were also snuff-dishes in the temple: "And they were also made of gold." (Exod. xxv. 28; xxxvii. 23. Numb. iv. 9.) The snuff-dishes were those in which the snuffs were put when snuffed off, and by which they were carried forth of the temple. They therefore, as the snuffers are, are of great use in the temple of God. 1. By them the golden floor of the temple is kept from being daubed by the snuffs. 2. By them, also, the clean hands of those that worship there are kept from being defiled. 3. By them, also, the stinks of the snuffs are soonest suppressed in the temple, and consequently the tender noses of them that worship there preserved from being offended.

Snuffs, you know, are daubing things, stinking things, nauseous things; therefore we must take heed that they touch not this floor on which we walk, nor defile the hands which we lift up to God, when we come to worship him. But how must this be done, but as we take them off with the snuffers, and put them in these snuff-dishes? Some are for being at the snuffs with their fingers, and will also cast them at their feet, and daub the floor of God's holy house; but usually such do burn as well as defile themselves. But is it not a shame for a man to defile himself with that vice which he rebuketh in another? Let us then, while we are taking away the snuffs of others, hate even the garment spotted by the flesh, and labour to carry such stink with the snuff-dishes out of the temple of God.

Snuff-dishes, you may say, what are they?

I answer, If sins are the snuffs, and rebukes and admonitions the snuffers; then, methinks, repentance, or, in case that be wanting, the censures of the church should be the snuff-dishes. Hence repentance is called a church-cleansing grace, and the censures of the church a purging out of the old leaven, and making it a new lump. (1 Cor. v. 2. 2 Cor. vii. 11.)

Ah! were these snuff-dishes more of use in the churches, we should not have this man's snuff defile that man's fingers as it doth. Nor would the temple of God be so besmeared with these snuffs, and bedaubed as it is.

Ah! snuffs pulled off lie still in the temple-floor, and there stink, and defile both feet and fingers; both the callings and conversations of temple-worshippers, to the disparaging of religion, and the making of religious worship but of low esteem with men; and all, I say, for want of the due use of these snuffers and these snuff-dishes, there. Nay, are not whole churches now defiled with those very snuffs that long since were plucked off, and all for want of the use of these snuff-dishes, according to the Lord's commandment? For you must know, that reproofs and admonitions are but of small use where repentance, or church censures, are not thereto annexed. When ministers use the snuffers, the people should hold the snuff-dishes.

Round reproofs for sin, when they light upon penitent hearts, then brave work is in the church; then the snuff is not only pulled away, but carried out of the temple of God aright, &c. And now the worship and worshipper shine like gold. "As an earring of gold, and an ornament of fine gold; so is a wise reprover upon an obedient ear." (Prov. xxv. 12.)

Ministers, it appertains to you to use the snuffers, and to teach the people to hold the snuff-dishes right. (Acts xx. 20, 21. 1 Tim. iv. 2.) We must often be snuffed with these snuffers, or our light will burn but dimly, our candle will also waste: Pray, therefore, O men of God, look diligently to your people. Snuff them as you see there is need; but touch not their snuff with your white fingers; a little smutch on you will be seen a great way. Remember, also, that you leave them nowhere, but with these snuff-dishes that the temple may be cleared of them. Do with the snuff, as the neat housewife doth with the toad which she finds in her garden. She takes the fork, or a pair of tongs, and therewith doth throw it over the pales. Cast them away, I say, with fear, zeal, care, revenge, and with great indignation, (2 Cor. vii. 11;) and then your church, your conversation, your fingers, and all will be kept white and clean.

XLVI. *Of the golden tongs belonging to the Temple.*

There were also tongs of gold used in the temple of old. (1 Kings vii. 49.) 1. These tongs were used about the altar, to order the fire there. 2. They were used too about the candlestick, and therefore called His tongs. 3. Perhaps there were tongs for both these services, but of that the Word is silent.

But what were they used about the candlestick to do?

Ans. To take holy fire from off the altar to light the lamps withal. For the fire of the temple was holy fire, such as at first was kindled from heaven, and when kindled, maintained by the priests, and of that the lamps were lighted. (Lev. ix. 24. 2 Chron. vii. 1.) Nor was there, upon pain of death, any other fire to be used there. (Lev. x. 1.) These tongs, therefore, were used to take fire from off the altar, to light the lamps and candlesticks withal; for to trim the lights, and to dress the lamps, was Aaron's work day by day. (Exod. xl. 24, 25. Lev. xxiv. 2, 3. Numb. viii. 3.) "He shall light and order the lamps upon the pure candlestick before the Lord, and Aaron did so: he lighted the seven lamps thereof, as the Lord commanded Moses." What is a lamp or candlestick to us, if there be not light thereon; and how lighted without fire, and how shall we take up coals to light the lamps withal, if we have not tongs prepared for that purpose? With these tongs fire also was taken from off the altar, and put into the censers to burn sweet incense with, before the Lord. The tongs then were of great use in the temple of the Lord.

But what were the tongs a type of?

The altar was a type of Christ; the fire, of the Holy Ghost; and these tongs were a type of that holy hand of God's grace, by which the coals, or several dispensations and gifts of this Holy Ghost, are taken and given to the church, and to her members, for her work and profit in this world.

Tongs, we know, are used instead of fingers, wherefore Aaron's golden tongs were a type of Christ's golden fingers. (Sol. Song v. 14.) Isaiah saith that one of the seraphims flew to him with a live coal in his hand, which he had taken with the tongs from off the altar. Here the type and antitype, to wit, tongs and hand, are put together. (Isa. vi.) But the Prophet Ezekiel, treating of like matters, quite waves the type, the tongs, and speaketh only of this holy hand: "And he spake to the man clothed with linen, and said, Go in between the wheels under the cherub," where the mercy-seat stood, where God dwelt, (Exod. ii. Ps. lxxx. 1,) "and fill thy hand with coals of fire from between the cherubims." (Ezek. x. 2.)

Thus you see our golden tongs are now turned into a gold hand; into the golden hand of the man clothed in linen, which is Jesus Christ, who at his ascension received of God the Father the Spirit in all fulness, to give, as his divine wisdom knew was best, the several coals or dispensations thereof unto this church, for his praise and her edification. (Matt. iii. 11. Acts ii.) It is by this hand, also, that this holy fire is put into our censers. It is this hand, also, that takes this coal, therewith to touch the lips of ministers, that their words may warm like fire; and it is by this hand that the Spirit is given to the churches, as returns of their holy prayers. (Luke xi. 1, 2. Rom. viii. 26. Rev. viii. 5.)

It was convenient that fire in the temple should be disposed of by golden tongs; but the Holy Ghost, by the golden hand of Christ's grace, for that can wittingly dispose of it, according as men and things are placed, and to do and be done in the churches: wherefore he adds, "And one cherub stretched forth his hand from between the cherubims, unto the fire that was between the cherubims, and took thereof, and put it into the hands of him that was clothed with linen, who took it and went out." (Ezek. x. 7.)

By this hand, then, by this man's hand, the coals of the altar are disposed of, both to the lamps, the candlesticks, the censers, and the lips of ministers, according to his own good pleasure. And of all this were the tongs in the temple a type.

XLVII. *Of the altar of incense in the Temple.*

The altar of incense was first made for the tabernacle, and that of shittim-wood; but it was made for the temple of cedar, and it was to be set before the veil, that is, by the ark of the testimony, before the mercy-seat; that is, at the entering of the holiest, but not within. And the priest was to approach it every morning, which as to the holiest he might not do. Besides, when he went in to make an atonement, he was to take fire from off that altar, to burn his incense within the holy place. (Exod. xxx. 1—10. Lev. xvi. 18.)

1. It was called the golden altar, because it was overlaid with pure gold. This altar was not for burnt-offering, as the brazen altar was; nor for the meat-offering, nor the drink-offering, but to burn incense thereon, (Lev. xvi. 7;) which sweet incense was a type of the grace of prayer. (Ps. cxli. 2.)

2. Incense, or that called incense here, was not a simple, but a compound, made up of sweet spices, called *stacte, onycha,* and *galbanum.* These three may answer to these three parts of this duty, to wit, prayer, supplication, and intercession. (Exod. xxx. 34—37; xxxvi. 29. 1 Tim. ii. 1.)

3. This incense was to be burned upon the altar every morning, upon that altar which was called the altar of incense, which was before the veil; to show, that it is our duty every morning to make our prayer to God by Jesus Christ before the veil; that is, before the door of heaven, and there to seek, knock, and ask for what we need, according to the Word. (Luke xi. 9—12.)

4. This incense was to be kindled every morning, to show how he continueth interceding for us, and also that all true praise of men to God is by the work, the renewed work of the Holy Ghost upon our hearts. (Rom. viii. 26.)

5. Incense, as you see, was made of sweet spices, such as were gummy, and so apt to burn with a smoke, to show that not cold and flat, but hot and fervent, is the prayer that flows from the spirit of faith and grace. (Zech. xii. 10. Jer. v. 16.)

6. The smoke of this incense was very sweet and savoury, like pleasant perfume; to show how delightful and acceptable the very sound and noise of right prayer is unto the nostrils of the living God, because it comes from a broken heart. (Ps. li. 17. Sol. Song ii. 14.)

7. This incense was to be offered upon the golden altar to show us that no prayer is accepted but what is directed to God, in the name of his holy and blessed Son our Saviour. (1 Pet. ii. 5. Heb. xiii. 15.)

8. They were commanded to burn incense every morning upon this altar to show that God is never weary of the godly prayers of his people. It also showeth that we need every day to go to God for fresh supplies of grace to carry us through this evil world.

9. This altar, though it stood without the veil to teach us to live by faith, and to make use of the name of Christ, as we find it recorded in the first temple; yet was placed so nigh unto the holiest that the smell of the smoke might go in thither to show that it is not distance of place that can keep the voice of true prayer from our God, the God of heaven; but that he will be taken with what we ask for according to his Word. It stood, I say, nigh the veil, nigh the holiest, and he that burnt incense there did make his approach to God. Hence the Psalmist, when he spake of praying, saith, "It is good for me to draw nigh unto God." (Ps. lxxiii. 28. Heb. x. 22.)

10. This altar thus placed did front the ark within the veil; to put us in mind that the law is kept therein from hurting us; to let us know, also, that the mercy-seat is above, upon the ark, and that God doth sit thereon, with his pardon in his hand to save us. Oh, what speaking things are types, shadows, and parables, had we but eyes to see, had we but ears to hear! He that did approach the altar with incense of old, aright (and then he did so when he approached it by Aaron, his high priest) pleased God; how much more shall we have both person and prayers accepted, and a grant of what we need, if indeed we come as we should to God by Jesus Christ! But take heed you approach not to a wrong altar; take heed also that you come not with strange fire; for they are dangerous things, and cause the worshippers to miss of what they would enjoy. But more of this in the next particular.

XLVIII. *Of the golden censers belonging to the Temple.*

There were also golden censers belonging to the temple; and they were either such as belonged to the sons of Levi in general, or that were for Aaron and his sons in special, as Numbers xvi. 16—18. The censers of the Levites were a type of ours, but the censer of Aaron was a type of Christ's. The censers, as was hinted before, were for this use in the temple, namely, to hold the holy fire in, on which incense was to be burned before the Lord. (Lev. x. 1.)

These censers, then, were types of hearts. Aaron's golden one was a type of Christ's golden heart, and the censers of the Levites were types of other worshippers' hearts. The fire, also, which was put therein, was a type of that spirit by which we pray, and the incense that burnt thereon, a type of our desires. Of Christ's censer we read, Revelations the eighth, which is always filled with much incense, that is, with continual intercessions, which he offereth to God for us; and from whence also there always goes a cloud of sweet savour, covering the mercy-seat. (Lev. xvi. 13. Heb. vii. 25. Rev. viii. 3, 4.)

But to speak of the censers, and fire, and incense of the worshippers; for albeit they were all put under one rule, that is, to be according to law, yet oftentimes, as were the worshippers, such were the censers, fire, and incense. 1. Hence the two hundred and fifty censers with which Corah and his company offered, are called the censers of sinners; for they came with wicked hearts then to burn incense before the Lord. (Numb. xvi. 17, 37.) 2. Again, as the censers of these men were called the censers of sinners, showing they came at that time to God with naughty hearts, so the fire that was in Nadab and Abihu's censers is called strange fire, which the Lord commanded them not. (Lev. x. 1.) This strange fire was a type of that strange spirit, opposed to the Spirit of God, in and by which, notwithstanding, some adventure to perform worship to God. 4. Again, as these censers are called the censers of sinners, and this fire called strange fire, so the incense of such is also called strange, and is said to be an abomination unto God. (Exod. xxx. 9. Isa. i. 13; lxvi. 3.)

Thus you see that both the censers, fire, and incense of some, are rejected, even as the heart, spirit, and prayer of sinners are an abomination unto God. (Hos. vii. 14; iv. 12; v. 4. Prov. xxviii. 9.)

But there were besides these true censers, holy fire, and sweet incense among the worshippers in the temple, and their service was accepted by Aaron their high priest; for that was through the faith of Christ, and these were a type of our true gospel-worshippers, who come with holy hearts, the Holy Spirit, and holy desires before their God, by their Redeemer. These are a perfume in his nose. "The prayer of the upright is his delight." "David's prayers went up like incense, and the lifting up of his hands, as the evening sacrifice." (Prov. xv. 8. Ps. cxli. 2.)

Let them, then, that pretend to worship before God in his holy temple, look to it that both their censers, fire, and incense, heart, spirit, and desires, be such as the Word requires; lest instead of receiving of gracious returns from the God of heaven, their censers be laid up against them; lest the fire of God devours them, and their incense becomes an abomination to him, as it happened to those made mention of before.

But it is said the censers of Corah and his company were hallowed.

Ans. So is God's worship, which is so his by his ordination, yet even that very worship may be spoiled by man's transgressions. Prayer is God's ordinance, but all prayer is not accepted of God. We must then distinguish between the thing commanded, and our using of that thing. The temple was God's house, but was abused by the irreverence of those that worshipped there, even to the demolishing of it.

A golden censer is a gracious heart, heavenly fire is the Holy Ghost, and sweet incense the effectual fervent prayer of faith. Have you these? These God expects, and these you must have, if ever your persons or performances be of God accepted.

XLIX. *Of the golden spoons of the Temple.*

1. The golden spoons belonging to the temple were in number, according to Moses, twelve; answering to the twelve tribes. But when the temple was built, I suppose they were more, because of the number of the basins. (Numb. vii. 14, 20, 26, 32, 38, 44, 50, 56, 62, 68, 74, 80, 86.)

2. The spoons, as I suppose, were for the worshippers in the temple to eat that broth withal, wherein the trespass-offerings were boiled: for which purpose there were several cauldrons hanged in the corners of that court called the priests', to boil them in. (2 Sam. ii. 13, 14. Ezek. xlvi. 19, 20.)

3. Now in that he saith here were spoons, what is it, but that there are also babes in the temple of the Lord. There was broth for babes, as well as meat for men, and spoons to eat the broth withal.

4. True, the gospel being more excellent than the law, doth change the term, and instead of broth, saith, There is milk for babes. But in that he saith milk, he insinuates there are spoons for children in the church.

5. "I could not," saith Paul to them at Corinth, "speak to you as unto spiritual, but as unto carnal, even as unto babes in Christ. I have fed you with milk and not with meat, for hitherto ye were not able to bear it, neither yet now are ye able." (1 Cor. iii. 1, 2.)

6. See, here were need of spoons, milk is spoon-meat; for here were those which could not feed themselves with milk, let them then that are men eat the strong meat. "For every one that useth milk is unskilful in the word of righteousness, for he is a babe. For strong meat belongeth to them that are full of age, who by reason of use have their senses exercised to discern both good and evil." (Heb. vi. 13, 14.)

7. Spoons, you know are to feed us with weak and thin food, even with that which best suiteth with weak stomachs, or with a babyish temper. Hence as the strong man is opposed to the weak, so the milk is opposed to the strong meat.

8. So then, though the babe in Christ is weaker than the man in Christ, yet is he not by Christ left unprovided for; for here is milk for babes, and spoons to eat it with. All this is taught us by the spoons, for what need is there of spoons, where there is nothing to eat but strong meat?

9. Babes, you know, have not only babyish stomachs, but also babyish tricks, and must be dealt withal as babes; their childish talk and froward carriages must be borne withal.

10. Sometimes they cry for nothing, yea, and count them for their foes which rebuke their childish toys and ways. All which the church must bear, because they are God's babes; yea, they must feed them too; for if he has found them milk and spoons, it is that they may be fed therewith and live: yea, grown ministers are God's nurses, wherefore they must have a lap to

lay them in, and knees to dandle them upon, and spoons to feed them with.

11. Nor are the babes without their use in the church of God, for he commands that they be brought to cry with the congregation before the Lord, for mercy for the land. (Joel ii. 16.)

12. Incense, I told you, was a type of prayers, and the spoons in the time of Moses, were presented at the temple full of it; perhaps to show that God's will, with the milk which he provided for them, give it to them as a return of their crying to him, even as the nurse gives the child the teat and milk.

13. You know the milk is called for, when the child is crying, as we say, to stop its mouth with it. O babes! did you but cry soundly, God would give you yet more milk.

14. But what were these golden spoons a type of? I answer, if the milk is the juice and consolations of the Word, then the spoons must be those soft sentences, and golden conclusions, with which the ministers feed their souls by it. "I have fed you," said Paul, "with the milk of the word:" saith Peter, "even as you have been able to bear it." Compare these two or three texts—1 Pet. ii. 1—3. 1 Cor. iii. 2. 1 Thess. ii. 7.

15. And this is the way to strengthen the weak hands, and to confirm the feeble knees. This is the way to make them grow to be men, who now are but as infants of days. "Thus a little one may become a thousand, and a small one a strong nation." Yea, thus in time you may make a little child to jostle it with a leopard, yea, to take a lion by the head; yea, thus you may embolden him to put his hand to the hole of the asp, and to play before the den of the cockatrice. (Isa. xi. 6—8; lx. 22.)

Who is most stout, was once a babe; he that can now eat meat, was sometimes glad of milk, and to be fed with the spoon. Babes in Christ therefore must not be despised, nor overlooked; God has provided them milk, and spoons to eat it with, that they may grow up to be men before him.

L. *Of the bowls and basins belonging to the Temple.*

As there were spoons, so there were bowls and basins belonging to the temple. Some of these were of gold, and some of silver; and when they were put together, their number was four hundred and forty. These you read of, Ezra. i. 10. The bowls or basins were not to wash in, as was the sea and lavers of the temple; they were rather to hold the messes in, which the priests at their holy feasts did use to set before the people. This being so, they were types of that proportion of faith, by which, or by the measure of which, every man received of the holy food, for the nourishment of his soul. For, as a man, had he a thousand messes set before him, he eating for his health, cannot go beyond what his stomach will bear; so neither can the child of God, when

he comes to worship in the temple of God, receive the good things that are there beyond the "proportion of his faith," or, as it is in another place, "according to the ability which God giveth." (Rom. xii. 6. 1 Pet. iv. 11.) And hence it is at the selfsame ordinance some receive three times as much as others do; for that their bowl, I mean their faith, is able to receive it. Yea, Benjamin's mess was five times as big as was the mess of any of his brethren; and so it is with some saints while they eat with their brother Joseph in the house of the living God.

There are three go to the same ordinance, and are all of them believers, who when they come and compare notes, do find their receivings are not of the same quantity. One says, I got but little; the other says, It was a pretty good ordinance to me; the third says, I was exceeding well there. Why, to be sure, he that had but little there, had there but little faith, but great faith in him would have received more. He had it then according to the largeness of his bowl, even "according to his faith, even as God hath dealt to every man the measure of faith." (Rom. xii. 3.) Mark, faith is a certain measure, and that not only as to its degree, but for that it can receive, retain, or hold what is put into it.

So then, here it is no matter how much milk or holy broth there is, but how big is thy bowl, thy faith. Little bowls hold but little, nor canst thou receive, but as thy faith will bear—I speak now of God's ordinary dealing with his people; for so he said in his Word, "According to thy faith be it unto thee." (Matt. ix. 29.) If a man goeth to the ocean for water, let him carry but an egg-shell with him, and with that he shall not bring a gallon home. I know indeed that our little pots have a promise of being made like the bowls of the altar; but still our mess must be according to our measure, be that small or be it great. The same prophet saith again, the saints shall be "filled like bowls, as the corners of the altar:" which, though it supposes an enlargement, yet it must be confined to that measure of faith which is provided for its reception. (Zech. ix. 15; xiv. 2.) And suppose these bowls should signify the promises, though the saints, not the promises, are compared to them, because they, not promises, are the subjects of faith; yet it is the promise by our measure of faith in that, that is nourishing to our souls.

When Ahasuerus made a feast to his subjects, they drank their wine in bowls. They did not drink it by the largeness of the vessel, whence they drew it, but according to their health, and as their stomachs would so receive it. (Esth. i. 7.) Thy faith, then, is one of the bowls or basins of the temple, by, or according to which, thou receivedst thy mess when sitting feasting at the table of God. And observe, all the bowls were not made of gold, as all faith is not of a saving sort. It is the golden faith that is right; the silver bowls were of an inferior sort. (Rev. iii. 18.)

Some, I say, have golden faith; all faith is not so. Wherefore look to it, soul, that thy bowl, thy faith, be golden faith, or of the best kind. Look, I say, after a good faith, and great, for a great faith receives a great mess. Of old, beggars did use to carry their bowls in their laps when they went to a door for an alms; consequently, if their bowls were but little, they ofttimes came off by the loss, though the charity of the giver was large. Yea, the greater the charity, the larger the loss, because the beggar's bowl was too little. Mark it well, it is ofttimes thus in the matters of our God. Art thou a beggar, a beggar at God's door? be sure thou gettest a great bowl, for as thy bowl is, so will be thy mess. "According to thy faith," saith he, "be it unto thee." (Matt. ix. 29.)

LI. *Of the flagons and cups of the Temple.*

The next things to be considered are the flagons and cups of the temple; of these we read, 1 Chron. xxviii. 17. Jer. lii. 19. These were of great use among the Jews, especially on their feasting-days; as of their sabbaths, new-moons, and the like. (Lev. xxiii. 13. Numb. xxviii. 7. 1 Chron. xvi. 3. Isa. xxv. 6; lxii. 8, 9.)

For instance, the day that David danced before the ark, he dealt among all the people, even to the whole multitude of Israel, as well to the women as to men, to every man a cake of bread, a good piece of flesh, and a flagon of wine. (2 Sam. vi. 19. 1 Chron. xvi. 3.) "In this mountain," that is, in the temple typically, saith the prophet, "shall the Lord of hosts make unto all people a feast of fat things, a feast of wine on the lees, of fat things full of marrow, of wine on the lees well refined." (Isa. xxv. 6.)

These are feasting-times; the times in which our Lord used to have his spouse into his wine-cellar, and in which he used to display with delight his banner over her head in love. (Sol. Song ii. 5.) The church of Christ, alas! is of herself a very sickly, puely thing, a woman, a weaker vessel; but how much more must she needs be so weak, when she is sick of love! Then she indeed has need of a draught, for she now sinks, and will not else be supported; "stay me with flagons," saith she, "and comfort me with apples, for I am sick of love." (Sol. Song ii. 4, 5.)

These flagons, therefore, were types of those feastings, and of those large draughts of divine love, that the Lord Jesus draweth for, and giveth to his spouse in those days that he feasteth with them. For then he saith, "Drink, yea, drink abundantly, O beloved." This he does to cheer her up under her hours of sadness and dejection; for now "new corn makes the young men cheerful, and new wine the maids." (Prov. xxxi. 6, 7. Ps. cxvi. 13. Jer. xvi. 7. Sol. Song v. Zech. ix. 17.)

As there were flagons, so there were cups, and they are called cups of consolation, and cups of salvation, because, as I said, they were they by which God at his feastings with his people, or when he suppeth with them, giveth out the more large draughts of his love unto his saints, to revive the spirits of the humble, and to revive the hearts of the contrite ones. At these times God made David's cup run over. For we are now admitted, if our faith will bear it, to drink freely into this grace, and to be merry with him. (Ps. xxiii. 5. Luke xv. 22—24. Sol. Song v. 1; vii. 11, 12. John xiv. 23. Rev. iii. 20.) This is that to which the Apostle alludeth, when he saith, "Be not drunk with wine, wherein is excess, but be ye filled with the Spirit; speaking to yourselves in psalms, and hymns, and spiritual songs, singing and making melody in your hearts unto the Lord." (Eph. v. 18.)

For the cups, as to their use in the general, understand them as of the bowls made mention of before. For assurances are the blooms and flowers of faith, not always on it, though usually on feasting days it is so. So the degree of the one is still according to the measure of the other. (James v. Rom. xv. 13.)

LII. *Of the chargers of the Temple.*

In the tabernacle they had but twelve of them, and they were made of silver, but in the temple they had in all a thousand and thirty. The thirty were made of gold, the rest were made of silver. (Numb. vii. 84.) These chargers were not for uses common or profane, but, as I take it, they were those in which the passover and other meat-offerings were dressed up, when the people came to eat before God in his holy temple. The meat, you know, I told you was opposite to milk, and so are these chargers to the bowls, and cups, and flagons of the temple.

The meat was of two sorts, roast or boiled. Of that which was roast was the passover, and of that which was boiled was the trespass-offerings. Wherefore, concerning the passover, he saith, "Eat not of it raw, nor sodden at all in water, but roast with fire; his head, with his legs, and with the purtenance thereof." (Exod. xii. 9.) This roast meat was a type of the body of Christ, as suffering for our sins, the which when it was roast was, and is, as dressed up in chargers, and set before the congregations of the saints.

But what were the chargers a type of? I also ask, in what chargers our gospel-passover is now dressed up, and set before the people? Is it not in the evangelists, the prophets, and epistles of the apostles? They therefore are the chargers, and the ordinance of the supper; in these also are the trespass-offerings, with what is fried in pans, mystically prepared for the children of the Highest.

And why might they not be a type of gospel-sermons? I answer, I think not so fitly; for, alas! the best of sermons in the world are but as thir. slices cut out of those large dishes. Our ministers are the carvers, good doctrine is the meat, and the chargers in which this meat is found are the holy canonical Scriptures, &c., though, as I said, most properly the New Testament of our Lord and Saviour Jesus Christ. In these is Christ most truly, lively, and amply set before us as crucified, or roast at the fire of God's law for our sins, that we might live by him through faith, feeding upon him. (2 Cor. iii. 12. Gal. iii. 12. Acts iii. 18—22; xiii. 2—5; xxvi. 22. 1 Pet. i. 10. Acts vii. 52; xv. 15; xxviii. 23. Rom. xvi. 26. Rev. x. 7.)

There is in these chargers not only meat, but sauce, if you like it, to eat the meat withal; for the passover there is bitter herbs, or sound repentance; and for other, as the thank-offerings, there is holy cheerfulness and prayers to God for grace. All these are set forth before in the Holy Scriptures, and presented to us thereby, as in the golden chargers of the temple. He that will scoff at this, let him scoff. The chargers were a type of something, and he that can show a fitter antitype than is here proposed to consideration, let him do it, and I will be thankful to him.

Christians, here is your meat before you, and get your carvers to slice it out for you; and this know, the deeper you dip it in the sauce, the better it will relish. But let not unbelief teach you such manners, as to make you leave the best bits behind you; for your liberty is to eat freely of the best, of the fat, and of the sweet.

LIII. *Of the goings out of the Temple.*

As to the comings into the temple, of them we have spoken already; namely of the outer and inner court, as also of the doors of the porch and temple. The coming in was but one straight course, and that a type of Jesus Christ, but the goings out were many. (John x. 9; xiv. 6.)

Now, as I said, it is insinuated that the goings out are many, answerable to the many ways which the children of men have invented to apostatize in from God. Christ is the way into, but sin the way out of the temple of God. True, I read not of a description of the goings out of this house, as I read of the comings in; only when they had Athaliah out thence, she is said to go out by the way by which the horses come into the king's stables, and there she was slain; as it were upon the horse-dunghill. (2 Kings xi. 16. 2 Chron. xxiii. 15.) When Uzziah also went out of this house for his transgression, he was cast out of all society, and made to dwell in a kind of a pest-house, even to the day of his death. (2 Chron. xxvi. 21.)

Thus, therefore, though these goings out are not particularly described, the judgments that followed them, that have for their transgressions been thrust out thence, have been both remarkable and tre-mendous; for to die upon a dunghill, or in a pest-house, and that for wicked actions, is a shameful, a disgraceful thing: and God will still be spreading dung upon the faces of such; no greatness shall prevent it: "Yea, and will take them away with it." (Mal. ii. 3.) "I will drive them out of my house," says he, "I will love them no more." (Hos. ix. 15.)

But what are we to understand in gospel days, by going out of the house of the Lord for or by sin? I answer, If it be done voluntarily, then sin leads you out; if it be done by the holy compulsion of the church, then it is done by the judicial judgment of God; that is, they are cut off, and cast out from thence, as a just reward for their transgressions. (Lev. xx. 18; xxii. 3. Ezek. xiv. 8. 1 Cor. v. 13.)

Well, but whither do they go, that are thus gone out of the temple or church of God? I answer, Not to the dunghill with Athaliah, nor to the pest-house with Uzziah, but to the devil, that is the first step, and so to hell, without repentance. But if their sin be not unpardonable, they may by repentance be recovered, and in mercy tread these courts again. Now the way to this recovery is to think seriously what they have done, or by what way they went out from the house of God. Hence the prophet is bid to show to the rebellious house, first the goings out of the house, and then the comings in. But, I say, first he bids show them the goings out thereof. (Ezek. xliii. 10, 11.) And this is of absolute necessity for the recovering of the sinner; for until he that has sinned himself out of God's house shall see what danger he has incurred to himself by this his wicked going out, he will not unfeignedly desire to come in thither again.

There is another thing as to this point to be taken notice of. There is a way by which God also doth depart from this house, and that also is by sin as the occasion. The sin of man will thrust him out, and the sin of men will drive God out of his own house. Of this you read, Ezek. xi. 22, 23. For this, he saith, "I have forsaken mine house, I have left mine heritage, I have given the dearly beloved of my soul into the hand of her enemies." (Jer. xii. 7.) And this also is dreadful. The great sentence of Christ upon the Jews lay much in these words, "Your house is left unto you desolate;" that is, God has left you to bare walls, and to lifeless traditions. Consider, therefore, of this going out also. Alas, a church, a true church, is but a poor thing, if God leaves, if God forsakes it! By a true church, I mean one that is congregated according to outward rule, that has sinned God away, as she had almost quite done that was of Laodicea. (Rev. iii.)

He that sins himself out, can find no good in the world, and they that have sinned God out can find no good in the church. A church that has sinned God away from it, is a sad lump indeed. You, therefore, that are in God's church, take heed of sinning yourselves out thence; also take heed that while you keep in, you sin not God away, for thenceforth no good is there. "Yea, woe unto them, when I depart from them," saith God. (Hos. ix. 12.)

LIV. *Of the singers belonging to the Temple.*

Having thus far passed through the temple, I come now to the singers there. The singers were many, but all of the church, either Jews or proselytes. Nor was there any, as I know of, under the Old Testament-worship, admitted to sing the songs of the church, and to celebrate that part of worship with the saints, but they who, at least in appearance, were so. The song of Moses, of Deborah, and of those that danced before David, with others that you read of, they were all performed either by Jews by nature, or by such as were proselyted to their religion. (Exod. xv. 1. Judges v. 1, 2. 1 Sam. xviii. 6.) And such worship then was occasioned by God's great appearance for them, against the power of the Gentiles their enemies.

But we are confined to the songs of the temple, a more distinct type of ours in the church under the gospel. 1. The singers then were many, but the chief of them, in the days of David, were David himself, Asaph, Jeduthan, and Heman, and their sons. 2. In David's time the chief of these singers were two hundred fourscore and eight. (1 Chron. xxv.) These singers of old were to sing their songs over the burnt-offering, which were types of the sacrificed body of Christ, a memorial of which offering we have at the Lord's table, the consummation of which Christ and his disciples celebrated with a hymn. (Matt. xxvi. 30.) And as of old they were the church that did sing in the temple, according to institution, to God, so also they are by God's appointment to be sung by the church in the new. Hence,

1. They are said to be the redeemed that sing. 2. The songs that they sing are said to be the "songs of their redemption." (Rev. v. 9, 10.) 3. They were and are songs that no man can learn but they.

But let us run a little in the parallel.

1. They were of old appointed to sing, that were cunning and skilful in songs. And answerable to that, it is said, that no man could learn our New Testament-songs but the hundred and forty and four thousand which were redeemed from the earth. (1 Chron. xv. 22. Rev. xiv. 3.)

2. These songs were sung with harps, psalteries, cymbals, and trumpets; a type of our singing with spiritual joy, from grace in our hearts. (1 Chron. xxv. 26. 2 Chron. xxix. 26—28. Col. iii. 16.)

3. The singers of old were to be clothed in fine linen, which fine linen was a type of innocency, and an upright conversation. Hence the singers under the New Testament are said to be virgins, such in whose mouth was no guile, and that were

without "fault before the throne of God." (1 Chron. xv. 27. Rev. xvii. 1—5. See also vii. 9—16. Ps. xxxiii. 1.)

4. The songs sung in the temple were new, or such as were compiled after the manner of repeated mercies that the church of God had received, or were to receive; and answerable to this is the church to sing now new songs, with new hearts, for new mercies. (Ps. xxxiii. 3; xl. 3; xcvi.; cxliv. 9. Rev. xiv. 3.) New songs, I say, are grounded on new matter, new occasions, new mercies, new deliverances, new discoveries of God to the soul, or for new frames of heart; and are such as are most taking, most pleasing, and most refreshing to the soul.

5. These songs of old, to distinguish them from heathenish ones, were called God's songs, the Lord's songs; because taught by him, and learned of him, and enjoined to them to be sung to his praise. Hence David said, "God had put a new song in his mouth, even praises to our God." (1 Chron. xxv. 7. Ps. xlvii. 6, 7; cxxxvii. 4; xl. 3.)

6. These songs also were called the "songs of Zion," and "the songs of the temple." (Ps. cxxxvii. 3. Amos viii. 3.) And they are so called as they were theirs to sing there, I say, of them of Zion, and the worshippers in the temple: I say, to sing in the church, by the church, to him who is the God of the church, for the mercies, benefits, and blessings which she has received from him. Zion-songs, temple-songs must be sung by Zion's sons, and temple-worshippers.

"The redeemed of the Lord shall return, and come to Zion with songs and everlasting joy upon their heads; they shall obtain joy and gladness, and sorrow and sighing shall fly away. Therefore they shall come and sing in the height, or upon the mountain of Zion; and shall flow together thither, to the goodness of the Lord." "Break forth into singing, ye mountains, and let the inhabitants of the rock sing." (Isa. xliv. 23; xlii. 11.)

To sing to God is the highest worship we are capable of performing in heaven; and it is much if sinners on earth, without grace, should be capable of performing it, according to his institution, acceptably. I pray God it be done by all those that now-a-days get into churches in spirit, and with understanding.

LV. *Of the union of the holy and most holy Temple.*

That commonly called the temple of God at Jerusalem, considered as standing of two parts, was called the outward and inward temple, or the holy and most holy place. They were built upon one and the same foundation, neither could one go into the holiest, but as through the holy place. (1 Kings iii. 1; vi. 1. 2 Chron. v. 1, 13; vii. 2.)

The first house, namely, that which we have been speaking of, was a type of the church militant, and the place most holy a type of the church triumphant. I say, of the church triumphant, as it is now.

So, then, the house standing of these two parts, was a shadow of the church both in heaven and earth. And for that they are joined together by one and the same foundation, it was to show, that they above, and we below, are yet one and the selfsame house of God. Hence they, and we together, are called, " The whole family in heaven and earth." (Eph. iii. 14, 15.)

And hence it is said again, that we who believe on earth, " are come to Mount Zion, to the city of the living God, the heavenly Jerusalem, and to an innumerable company of angels, to the general assembly, and church of the first-born, which are written in heaven, and to the spirits of just men made perfect, and to God the judge of all, and to Jesus the mediator of the new covenant, and to the blood of sprinkling, that speaketh better things than that of Abel." (Heb. xii. 22—24.)

The difference, then, betwixt us and them, is, not that we are really two, but one body in Christ, in divers places. True, we are below stairs, and they above ; they in their holiday, and we in our working-day clothes ; they in harbour, but we in the storm; they at rest, and we in the wilderness ; they singing, as crowned with joy, we crying, as crowned with thorns. But, I say, we are all of one house, one family, and are all the children of one Father. This, therefore, we must not forget, lest we debar ourselves of much of that which otherwise, while here, we have a right unto. Let us, therefore, I say, remember, that the temple of God is but one, though divided, as one may say, into kitchen and hall, above stairs and below ; or holy and most holy place. For it stands upon the same foundation, and is called but one, the temple of God; which is built upon the Lord our Saviour.

I told you before, that none of old could go into the most holy, but by the holy place, even by the veil that made the partition between. (Exod. xxvi. 33. Lev. xvi. 2, 12, 15. Heb. ix. 7, 8 ; x. 19.) Wherefore, they are deceived that think to go into the holiest, which is heaven, when they die, who yet abandon and hate the holy place while they live. Nay, sirs, the way into the holiest is through the holy place ; the way into heaven is through the church on earth ; for that Christ is there by his word to be received by faith, before he can by us in person be received in the beatifical vision. The church on earth is as the house of the women spoken of in the Book of Esther, where we must be dieted, perfumed, and made fit to go into the bridegroom's chamber ; or, as Paul says, "made meet to be partakers of the inheritance of the saints in light." (Esth. ii. Col. i. 12.)

LVI. *Of the holiest or inner Temple.*

The most holy place was, as I said, a figure of heaven itself, consequently, a type of that where the most special presence of God is, and where his face is most clearly seen, and the gladness of his countenance most enjoyed. (Heb. ix. 23, 24. Exod. xxv. 22. Numb. vii. 89.)

The most holy place was dark : it had no windows in it, though there was such round the chambers ; the more special presence of God, too, on Mount Sinai, was in the thick darkness there. (1 Kings viii. 12. 2 Chron. vii. 1. Exod. xix. 9; xx. 21.)

1. This holiest, therefore, being thus made, was to show that God, as in heaven, to us on earth is altogether invisible, and not to be reached otherwise than by faith. For I say, in that this house had no windows, nothing therein could be seen by the highest light of this world. Things there were only seen by the light of the fire of the altar, which was a type of the shinings of the Holy Ghost. (1 Cor. ii.) And hence it is said, notwithstanding this darkness, " He dwelleth in the light, which no man can approach unto ;" none but the high priest, Christ. (1 Tim. vi. 16. 1 Pet. iii. 21, 22.)

2. The holiest, therefore, was thus built to show how different our state in heaven will be from this our state on earth. We walk here by one light, by the light of a written Word; for that is now a light to our feet, and a lanthorn to our path. But that place, where there will be no written Word, nor ordinances as here, will yet to us shine more light and clear than if all the lights that are in the world were put together to light one man : " For God is light, and in him is no darkness at all." (1 John i. 5.) And in his light, and in the light of the Lamb immediately we shall live, and walk, and rejoice all the days of eternity.

3. This also was ordained thus to show that we, while in the first temple, should live by faith as to what there was, or as to what was done in the second. Hence it is said, as to that, " We walk by faith, not by sight." (2 Cor. v. 9.) The things that are there we are told of, even of the ark of the testimony, and mercy-seat, and the cherubims of glory, and the presence of Christ and of God ; we are, I say, told of them by the Word, and believe, and are taken therewith, and hope to go to them hereafter; but otherwise we see them not. Therefore we are said to "look, not at the things that are seen, but at the things that are not seen ; for the things that are seen are temporal, but the things that are not seen are eternal." (2 Cor. iv. 18.)

4. The people of old were not to look into the holiest, lest they die, (Numb. xvii. 13,) save only their high-priest, he might go into it: to show that we, while here, must have a care of vain speculations, for there is nothing to be seen by us while here, in heaven, otherwise than by faith in God's eternal testament. True, we may now come to the holiest, even as nigh as the first temple will admit us to come ; but it must be by blood and faith, not by vain imagination, sense, or carnal reason.

5. This holiest of all was four square every way, both as to height, length, and breadth. To be thus, is a note of perfection, as I have showed elsewhere; wherefore it was on purpose thus built, to show us, that all fulness of blessedness is there, both as to the nature, degree, and duration. So "when that which is perfect is come, that which is in part shall be done away." (1 Cor. xiii. 8—10. Heb. x. 19—22.)

LVII. *Of the veil of the Temple.*

The veil of the temple was a hanging, made of "blue, and purple, and crimson, and fine linen, and there were cherubims wrought thereon." (Exod. xxvi. 31, 32.)

1. This veil was one partition betwixt the holy and most holy place. And I take it, it was to keep from the sight of the worshippers the things most holy, when the high-priest went in thither to accomplish the service of God. (Exod. xxvi. 33. 2 Chron. iii. 14. Heb. ix. 8.)

2. The veil was a type of two things.

(1.) Of these visible heavens, through which Christ passed when he went to make intercession for us. And as by the veil, the priest went out of the sight of the people when he went into the holiest of all, so Jesus Christ when he ascended, was by the heavens, that great and stretched out curtain, received out of the sight of his people here. Also by the same curtain, since it is become as a tent for him to dwell in, he is still received, and still kept out of our sight: for now we see him not, nor shall, until these heavens be rolled together as a scroll, and pass away like a thing rolled together. (Isa. xl. 22. Acts i. 9—11; iii. 19—21. 1 Pet. i. 8.)

(2.) This is that veil through which the Apostle saith Jesus, as a forerunner for us, entered into the presence of God. For by veil here also must be meant the heavens, or outspread firmament thereof; as both Mark and Peter says, "He is gone into heaven, and is on the right hand of God." (Mark xvi. 19. 1 Pet. iii. 22.)

(3.) The veil of the temple was made of blue, the very colour of the heavens. Of purple, and crimson, and scarlet also, which are the colour of many of the clouds: because of the reflections of the sun. But again,

(4.) The veil was also a type of the body of Christ. For as the veil of the temple, when whole, kept the view of the things of the holiest from us, but when rent, gave place to man to look in unto them; even so the body of Christ, while whole, kept the things of the holiest from that view we, since he was pierced, have of them. Hence we are said to enter into the holiest, by faith, through the veil, that is to say, his flesh. (Heb. x. 19—22.) But yet, I say, all is by faith; and indeed the rending of the veil that day that Christ was crucified, did loudly preach this to us. For no sooner was the body of Christ pierced, but the veil of the temple rent in twain from the top

to the bottom: and so a way was made for a clearer sight of what was there beyond it, both in the type and antitype. (Matt. xxvii. 50—53. Heb. x. 19, 20.)

Thus you see that the veil of the temple was a type of these visible heavens, and also of the body of Christ; of the first, because he passed through it unto the Father; of the second, because we by it have boldness to come to the Father.

I read also of two other veils: as of that spread over the face of Moses, to the end the children of Israel should not steadfastly behold, and of the first veil of the tabernacle. But of these I shall not in this place speak.

Upon the veil of the temple there were also the figures of cherubims wrought, that is, of angels; to show that as the angels are with us *here*, and wait upon us all the days of our pilgrimage in this world: so, when we die, they stand ready, even at the veil, at the door of these heavens, to come when bid, to fetch us, and carry us away into *Abraham's bosom.* (Luke xvi. 22.)

The veil, then, thus understood, teaches us first where Jesus is, namely, not here, but gone into heaven, from whence we should wait for him. It also teaches us, that if we would even now discern the glories that are in the holiest of all, we must look through Jesus to them, even through the veil, "that is to say, his flesh." Yea, it teaches us that we may, by faith through him, attain to a kind of a presence, at least of the beauty and sweetness of them.

LVIII. *Of the doors of the inner Temple.*

1. Besides the veil, there was a door to the inner temple, and that door was made of olive-tree; "and for the entering in of the oracle, he made doors of olive-tree. The two doors also of olive-tree, and he carved upon them cherubims, and palm-trees, and open flowers, and overlaid them with gold, and spread gold upon the cherubims, and upon the palm-trees." (1 Kings vi. 31.)

2. These doors were a type of the gate of heaven, even of that which lets into the eternal mansion-house that is beyond that veil. I told you before, that the veil was a type of the visible heavens, which God has spread out as a curtain, and through which Christ went, when he ascended to the right hand of the Father.

3. Now beyond this veil, as I said, I find a door, a gate opening with two leaves, as afore we found at the door of the outward temple. These are they which the Psalmist calls to, when he saith, "Lift up your heads, O ye gates, even lift them up ye everlasting doors, and the king of glory shall come in." (Ps. xxiv. 7, 9.)

4. The doors of the temple were made of fir, but these, as you see, were made of olive: to show us by that fat tree, that rich type, with what glory we shall meet, who shall be counted worthy to enter at these gates. The olive-tree has its name

from the oil and fatness of its nature, and the doors that let into the holiest were made of this olive-tree.

5. Cherubims were also carved upon these doors, to show, that as the angels met us at the temple-door, and as they wait upon us in the temple, and stand also ready at the veil, so even at the gate of the mansion-house, they will be also ready to give us a welcome thither, and to attend us into the presence-chamber.

6. Palm-trees also, as they were carved upon the temple-doors, so we also find them here before the oracle, upon the doors that let in thither. To show that as Christ gave us the victory at our first entering into faith, so he will finish that victory, by giving of us eternal salvation. Thus is he the author and finisher of our faith. For as sure as at first we received the palm-branch by faith, so surely shall we wear it in our hands, as a token of his faithfulness in the heaven of heavens, for ever. (Rev. vii. 9.)

7. Open flowers are also carved here, to show that Christ, who is the door to glory, as well as the door to grace, will be precious to us at our entering in thither, as well as at the first step we took thitherward in a sinful miserable world. Christ will never lose his sweet scent in the nostrils of his church. He is most sweet now, will be so at death, and sweetest of all, when by him we shall enter into that mansion-house prepared for us in heaven.

8. The palm-trees and open flowers may also be a type of the precious ones of God, who shall be counted worthy of his kingdom: the one, of the uprightness of their hearts; the other, of the good savour of their lives. "The upright shall dwell in thy presence; and to him that ordereth his conversation aright, I will show the salvation of God." (Ps. cxl. 13 ; l. 23.)

9. Thus sweet on earth, sweet in heaven; and he that yields the fruit of the gospel here, shall find it for himself, and his eternal comfort, at the gates of glory.

10. All these were overlaid with gold, as you may say, and so they were at the door of the first house. True, but observe here we have an addition. Here is gold upon gold. Gold laid on them, and then gold spread upon that. He overlaid them with gold, and then spread gold upon them. The Lord gives grace and glory. (Ps. lxxxiv. 11.) Gold and gold. Gold spread upon gold. Grace is gold in the leaf, and glory is gold in plates. Grace is thin gold, Glory is gold that is thick. Here is gold laid on, and gold spread upon that. And that both upon the palm-trees and the cherubims. Gold upon the palm-trees, that is, on the saints ; Gold upon the cherubims, that is, upon the angels. For I doubt not but that the angels themselves shall receive additional glory for the service which they have served Christ and his church on earth.

11. The angels are God's harvest men, and

doubtless he will give them good wages, even glory upon their glory then. (Matt. xiii. 38, 39 ; xxiv. 31. John iv. 36.)

12. You know harvest-men use to be paid well for gathering in the corn, and I doubt not but so shall these, when the great ingathering is over. But what an entrance into life is here ? Here is gold upon gold at the door, at our first step into the kingdom.

LIX. *Of the golden nails of the inner Temple.*

I shall not concern myself with all the nails of the temple, as of those made with iron, &c. (1 Chron. xxii. 3,) but only with the golden ones, of which you read, 2 Chron. iii. 4, where he saith, "And the weight of the nails was fifty shekels of gold." These nails, as I conceive, were all fastened to the place most holy, and of form most apt to that of which they were a figure.

1. Some of them represented Christ Jesus our Lord, as fixed in his mediatory office in the heavens ; wherefore in one place, when the Holy Ghost speaks of Christ, as he sprang from Judah to be a Mediator, saith, "Out of him came the corner," the corner-stone, "out of him the nails." (Zech. x. 4.) Now, since he is here compared to a nail, a golden nail, it is to show, that as a nail, by driving, is fixed in his place, so Christ by God's oath is made an everlasting priest. (Heb. vii. 25.) Therefore, as he saith again, the nail, the Aaronical priesthood, that was fastened in a sure place, should be removed, be cut down, and fall ; so he who has the key of David, which is Christ, (Rev. iii. 7,) shall by God, as a nail, be fastened in a sure place, and abide ; therefore he says again, "And he shall be for a glorious throne," or mercy-seat, "to his Father's house." And moreover, that "they shall hang on him," as on a nail, "all the glory of his Father's house, the offspring, and the issue, all vessels of small quantity, from the vessels of cups, even to the vessels of flagons." According to that which is written, "And they sang a new song" to the Lamb that was slain, "saying, Thou art worthy," &c. (Isa. xxii. 20—25. Rev. v. 9—12.)

And therefore it is again that Christ under the similitude of a nail, is accounted by saints indeed their great pledge or hope, as he is in heaven, of their certain coming thither. Hence they said of old, "God has given us a nail in his holy place ;" "A nail," says the line, "a pin, a constant and sure abode," says the margin. (Ezra ix. 8.) Now this nail in his holy place, as was showed before, is Christ ; Christ, as possessed of heaven, and as abiding and ever living therein for us. Hence he is called, as there, our head, our life, and our salvation ; and also we are said there to be set down together in him. (Eph. i. 23. Col. iii. 3. Eph. ii. 5, 6.)

2. Some of these nails were types of the holy words of God, which for ever are settled in heaven.

Types, I say, of their yea, and amen. Hence Solomon in another place compares the words of the wise God " to goads and nails, fastened by the masters of the assemblies, which are given from one shepherd." (Eccles. xii. 11.)

They are called goads, because, as such prick the oxen on in their drawing, so God's words prick Christians on in their holy duties. They are called nails, to show that as nails, when fastened well in a sure place, are not easily removed ; so God's words, by his will, stand firm for ever. The masters of the assemblies are, first the apostles. The one shepherd is Jesus Christ. Hence the gospel of Christ is said to be everlasting, to abide for ever, and to be more steadfast than heaven and earth. (Isa. xl. 6—8. 1 Pet. i. 24, 25. Heb. xviii. 20. Rev. xiv. 6. Matt. xxiv. 35.) The Lord Jesus, then, and his holy words, are the golden nails of the temple, and the fixing of these nails in the temple was to show that Christ is the same to-day, yesterday, and for ever ; and that his words abide, and remain the same for ever and ever. He then that hath Christ, has a nail in the holiest ; he that hath a promise of salvation hath also a nail in heaven, a golden nail in heaven.

LX. *Of the floor and walls of the inner Temple.*

1. The floor of the oracle was overlaid with cedar, and so also were the walls of this house. " He built twenty cubits on the sides of the house, both the floor and the walls with boards of cedar. He even built for it within, for the oracle, for the most holy place." (1 Kings xvi. 16.)

2. In that he doth tell us with what it was ceiled, and doth also thus repeat, saying, " for the oracle, for it within, even for the most holy place ;" it is because he would have it noted, that this only is the place that thus was done.

3. Twenty cubits, that was the length, and breadth, and height of the house ; so that by his thus saying, he teacheth that thus it was builded round about.

4. The cedar is, if I mistake not, the highest of the trees. (Ezek. xxxi. 3—8.) Now in that it is said the house, the oracle, was ceiled round about therewith, it may be to show that in heaven, and nowhere else, is the height of all perfections. Perfection is in the church on earth, but not such as is in heaven.

(1.) There is a natural perfection, and so a penny is as natural silver as is a shilling. (2.) There is a comparative perfection, and so one thing may be perfect and imperfect at the same time ; as a half-crown is more than a shilling, yet less than a crown. (3.) There is also that which we call the utmost perfection, and that is it which cannot be added to, or taken from him ; and so God only is perfect. Now, heavenly glory is that which goes beyond all perfection on the earth, as the cedar goes beyond all trees for height. Hence God, when he speaks of his own excellency, sets it

forth by its height. The high God, the most high, and the high and lofty One ; and the highest. (Ps. xcvii. 9 ; cxxxviii. 6. Gen. xiv. 19—21. Dan. iii. 26 ; v. 18. Ps. xviii. 13 ; lxxxv. 7. Luke i. 32 ; vi. 35. Ps. ix. 2 ; lvi. 2 ; xcii. 1. Isa. xiv. 14.) These terms also are ascribed to this house, for that it was the place where utmost perfection dwelt.

I take, therefore, the cedar in this place to be a note of perfection, even the cedar with which this house was ceiled. For since it is the wisdom of God to speak to us ofttimes by trees, gold, silver, stones, beasts, fowls, fishes, spiders, ants, frogs, flies, lice, dust, &c., and here by wood ; how should we by them understand his voice, if we count there is no meaning in them ? "And the cedar of the house within was carved with knops and flowers ; all was cedar ; there was no stone seen." (1 Kings vi. 18.)

Knops and flowers were they with which the golden candlestick was adorned, as you read, Exod. xxv. 33, 35 ; xxxvii. 10, 21. The candlestick was a type of the church, and the knops and flowers a type of her ornaments. But what ! must heaven be hanged round about with the ornaments of saints ! with the fruits of their graces ! Well, it is certain that something more than ordinary must be done with them, since they are admitted to follow them into the holy place. (Rev. xiv. 13 ;) and since it is said they shall have a far more exceeding and eternal weight of glory bestowed on them, for them in the heavens. (2 Cor. iv. 16, 17.)

" All was cedar ; there was no stone seen." Take stone in the type for that which was really so, and in the antitype, for that which is so mystically, and then it may import to us, that in heaven, the antitype of this holiest, there shall never be anything of hardness of heart in them that possess it for ever. All imperfection ariseth from the badness of the heart, but there will be no bad hearts in glory. No shortness in knowledge, no crossness of disposition, no workings of lusts or corruptions will be there, no not throughout the whole heavens. Here, alas ! they are seen, and that in the best of saints, because here our light is mixed with darkness, but there will be no night there, nor any stone seen.

"And the floor of the house was overlaid with gold." (1 Kings vi. 30.) This is like that of which we read of the New Jerusalem that is to come from God out of heaven ; says the text, " The street of the city was pure gold ;" and like that of which you read in Exodus : " They saw under the feet of the God of Israel, as it were a paved work of a sapphire stone, and as it were the body of heaven in its clearness." (Rev. xxi. 21. Exod. xxiv. 10.) All the visions were rich, but this the richest, that the floor of the house should be covered, or overlaid with gold. The floor and street are walking places, and how rich will our steps be then ! Alas ! here we sometimes step into the mire, and then again stumble upon blocks and stones. Here we sometimes fall into holes, and have our heel often catched in a snare; but there will be none of these. Gold! gold! all will be gold, and golden perfections when we come into the holy place. Job at best took but his steps in butter, but we then shall take all our steps in the gold of the sanctuary.

LXI. *Of the ark of the covenant, which was placed in the inner Temple.*

In the Word I read of three arks; to wit, Noah's ark, that in which Moses was hid, and the ark of the covenant of God. (Gen. vi. 14. Exod. ii. 3, 5.) But it is the ark of the covenant of which I shall now speak.

"The ark was made of shittim-wood; two cubits and a-half was the length thereof, and one cubit and a-half the breadth thereof, and a cubit and a-half the height thereof. It was overlaid with pure gold within and without, and a crown of gold was made for it round about." (Exod. xxv. 10, 11.)

1. This ark was called the ark of the covenant, as the first that you read of was called Noah's, because, as he in that was kept from being drowned, so the tables of the covenant were kept in this from breaking.

2. This ark, in this, was a type of Christ; for that in him only, and not in the hand of Moses, these tables were kept whole. Moses brake them, the ark keeps them.

3. Not only that wrote on two tables of stone, but that also called the ceremonial, was put into the ark to be kept. The two tables were put into the midst of the ark, to answer to this: thy law is within my heart to do it. But the ceremonial was put into the side of the ark, to show, that out of the side of Christ must come that which must answer that. For out thence came blood and water; blood, to answer the blood of the ceremonies, and water, to answer the purifyings and rinsings of that law. The ceremonies, therefore, were lodged in the side of the ark, to show that they should be answered out of the side of Jesus Christ. (Exod. xxv. 16, 17. Deut. x. 5; xxxi. 26. Ps. xl. 8. John xix. 34. Heb. x. 7.)

4. The ark had the name of God put upon it; yea, it was called the strength of God, and his glory, though made of wood. And Christ is God both in name and nature, though made flesh; yea more, made to be sin for us. (2 Sam. vi. 2. 1 Chron. xiii. 6. 2 Chron. vi. 1. John i. 14. Rom. ix. 5. 2 Cor. v. 21.)

5. The ark was carried upon men's shoulders this way and that, to show how Christ should be carried and preached by his apostles and ministers into all parts of the world. (Exod. xxv. 14. 1 Chron. xv. 15. Matt. xxvii. 19, 20. Luke xxiv. 46, 47.)

6. The ark had those testimonies of God's presence accompanying it, as had no other cere-

mony of the law; and Christ had those signs and tokens of his presence with him, as never had man either in law or gospel. This is so apparent it needs no proof. And now for a few comparisons more.

(1.) It was at that that God answered the people, when they were wont to come to inquire of him; and in these last days God has spoken to us by his Son. (1 Chron. xiii. 3. 1 Sam. xiv. 18. Heb. i. 2. John xvi. 23, 24.)

(2.) At the presence of the ark the waters of Jordan stood still, till Israel, the ransomed of the Lord, passed over from the wilderness to Canaan; and it is by the power and presence of Christ that we pass over death, Jordan's antitype, from the wilderness of this world to heaven. (Josh. iii. 15—17. John xi. 25. Rom. viii. 37—39. 1 Cor. xv. 54—57.)

(3.) Before the ark the walls of Jericho fell down; and at the presence of Christ shall all high towers, and strongholds, and hiding-places for sinners be razed, and dissolved at his coming. (Josh. vi. 20. Isa. xxx. 25; ii. 10, 16. 2 Pet. iii. 10. Rev. xx. 11—13.)

(4.) Before the ark Dagon fell, that idol of the Philistines; and before Christ Jesus devils fell, those gods of all those idols. "And he must reign till all his enemies be put under his feet; and until they be made his footstool." (1 Sam. v. 1—4. Mark v. 12. 1 Cor. xv. 25. Heb. x. 13.)

(5.) The Philistines were also plagued for meddling with the ark, while they abode uncircumcised; and the wicked will one day be most severely plagued for their meddling with Christ, with their uncircumcised hearts. (1 Sam. v. 6—13. Ps. l. 6. Matt. xxiv. 51; xxv. 11, 12. Luke xiii. 25—29.)

(6.) God's blessing was upon those that entertained the ark as they should; and much more is, and will his blessing be upon those that so embrace and entertain his Christ, and profess his name sincerely. (2 Sam. vi. 11. Acts iii. 26. Gal. iii. 13, 14. Matt. xix. 27—29. Luke xxii. 28, 29.)

(7.) When Uzzah put forth his hand to stay the ark, when the oxen shook it, as despairing of God's protecting of it without a human help, he died before the Lord; even so will all those do, without repentance, who use unlawful means to promote Christ's religion, and to support it in the world. (1 Chron. xiii. 9, 10. Matt. xxvi. 52. Rev. xiii. 10.)

(8.) The ark, though thus dignified, was of itself, but low; but a cubit and a half high; also Christ, though he was the glory of heaven and of God, yet made himself of no reputation, and was found in the likeness of a man. (Exod. xxv. 11, 12. Phil. ii. 6—11.)

(9.) The ark had a crown of gold round about it, to show how Christ is crowned by his saints by faith, and shall be crowned by them in glory, for all the good he hath done for them, as also how all crowns shall one day stoop to him, and be set upon his head. This is showed in the type. (Zech. vi

11—14,) and in the antitype. (Rev. iv. 10; xix. 12.)

(10.) The ark was overlaid with gold within and without, to show that Christ was perfect in inward grace and outward life, in spirit and in righteousness. (John i. 14. 1 Pet. ii. 22.)

(11.) The ark was placed under the mercy-seat, to show that Jesus Christ, as Redeemer, brings and bears, as it were upon his shoulders, the mercy of God to us, even in the body of his flesh, through death. (Exod. xxv. 21. Eph. iv. 22; v. 1, 2.)

(12.) When the ark was removed far from the people, the godly went mourning after it; and when Christ is hid, or taken from us, then we mourn in those days. (2 Sam. vii. 2. Mark ii. 19, 20. Luke v. 34, 35. John xvi. 20—22.)

(13.) All Israel had the ark again, after their mourning-time was over; and Christ, after his people have sorrowed for him awhile, will see them again, "and their hearts shall rejoice." (John xvi. 1—3, 20—22.)

By all these things, and many more that might be mentioned, it is most evident that the ark of the testimony was a type of Jesus Christ; and take notice a little of that which follows, namely, that the ark at last arrived to the place most holy. (Heb. ix. 3, 4.) That is, after its wanderings; for the ark was first made to wander, like a non-inhabitant, from place to place; now hither, and then thither; now in the hands of enemies, and then abused by friends; yea, it was caused to rove from place to place, as that of which the world was weary. I need instance to you for proof, none other place than the 5th, 6th, and 7th chapters of the first book of Samuel; and, answerable to this, was our dear Lord Jesus posted backwards and forwards, hither and thither, by the force of the rage of his enemies. 1. He was hunted into Egypt so soon as he was born. (Matt. ii.) (2.) Then he was driven to live in Galilee the space of many years. 3. Also, when he showed himself to Israel, they drove him sometimes into the wilderness, sometimes into the desert, sometimes into the sea, and sometimes into the mountains, and still in every one of these places he was either haunted or hunted by new enemies.

And last of all, the Pharisees plot for his life, Judas sells him, the priests buy him, Peter denies him, his enemies mock, scourge, buffet, and much abuse him. In fine, they get him condemned, and crucified, and buried; but at last God commanded, and took him to his place, even within the veil, and sets him to bear up the mercy-seat, where he is to this very day, being our ark to save us, as Noah's did him, as Moses' did him; yea, better, as none but Christ doth save his own.

LXII. *Of the placing of the ark in the holiest, or inner Temple.*

1. The ark, as we have said, and as the text declares, when carried to its rest, was placed in the inner temple, or in the most holy place, "even under the wings of the cherubims." "And the priests brought in the ark of the covenant of the Lord unto his place, to the oracle of the house, unto the most holy place, even under the wings of the cherubims." (Exod. xxvi. 33; xxxix. 35. 1 Kings viii. 3. 2 Chron. v. 7.)

2. Before this, as was said afore, the ark was carried from place to place, and caused to dwell in a tent under curtains, as all our fathers did; to show that Christ, as we, was made for a time to wander in the world, in order to his being possessed of glory. (2 Sam. vii. 1—6. Heb. xi. 9. John i. 10; xvi. 28; iii. 13.)

3. But now, when the ark was brought into the holiest, it is said to be brought into its place. This world then was not Christ's place, he was not from beneath, he came from his Father's house; wherefore while here, he was not at his place, nor could until he ascended up where he was before. (John viii. 23; xvi. 28; vi. 62; iii. 13.)

4. Christ's proper place, therefore, is the holiest. His proper place, as God, as priest, as prophet, as king, and as the advocate of his people. Here with us he has no more to do, in person, as mediator. If he were on earth, he should not be a priest, &c. His place and work is now above with his Father, and before the angels. (Acts v. 31. 1 Pet. iii. 22. Heb. iv. 14; viii. 4; ix. 24. 1 John ii. 1, 2. Rev. i. 4, 5.)

5. It is said, the ark was brought to the oracle of the house. Solomon was not content to say, it was brought into the holiest; but he saith, his place was the oracle, the holy oracle, that is, the place of hearing. For he, when he ascended, had somewhat to say to God on the behalf of his people. To the oracle, that is, to the place of revealing: for he also was there to receive, and from thence to reveal to his church on earth something that could not be made manifest but from this holy oracle. There therefore he is with the two tables of testimony in his heart, as perfectly kept; he also is there with the whole fulfilling of the ceremonial law in his side, showing and pleading the perfection of his righteousness, and the merit of his blood with his Father, and to receive and to do us good, who believe in him, how well pleased the Father is, with what he has done in our behalf.

6. "Into the most holy place." By these words is showed, whither also the ark went, when it went to take up its rest. And in that this ark was a type of Christ in this, it is to show or further manifest, that what Christ doth now in heaven, he doth it before his Father's face. Yea, it intimates that Christ even there makes his appeals to God concerning the worth of what he did on earth; to God the judge of all, I say, whether he ought not for his suffering sake, to have granted to him his whole desire, as priest and advocate for his people.

"Wilt thou," said Festus to Paul, "go up to Jerusalem, and there be judged of these things before me?" (Acts xxv. 9.) Why, this our blessed Jesus was willing, when here, to go up to Jerusalem to be judged; and being misjudged of there, he made his appeal to God, and is now gone thither, even into the holy place, even to him that is judge of all, for his verdict upon his doing; and whether the souls for whom he became undertaker, to bring them to glory, have not by him a right to the kingdom of heaven.

7. "Under the wings of the cherubims." This doth further confirm our words; for having appealed from earth to heaven, as the ark was set under the wings of the cherubims, so he in his interceding with God, and pleading his merits for us, doth it in the presence and hearing of all the angels of heaven.

And thus much of the ark of the covenant, and of its antitype. We come next to speak of the mercy-seat.

LXIII. *Of the mercy-seat, and how it was placed in the holy Temple.*

The mercy-seat was made in the wilderness, but brought up by Solomon, after the temple was built, with the rest of the holy things. (2 Chron. v. 2—10.)

The mercy-seat, as I have showed of the ark, was but low: "Two cubits and a half was the length, and a cubit and a half the breadth thereof;" but the height thereof "was without measure."

1. The length and breadth of the mercy-seat is the same with that of the ark; perhaps to show us that the length and breadth of the mercy of God to his elect, is the same with the length and breadth of the merits of Christ. (Exod. xxv. 10—17.) Therefore we are said to be justified in him, blessed in him, even according to the purpose which God purposed in him.

2. But in that the mercy-seat is without measure, as to the height, it is to show, that, would God extend it, it is able to reach even them that fall from heaven, and to save all that ever lived on earth, even all that are now in hell. For there is not only breadth enough for them that shall be saved, but "bread enough and to spare." (Luke xv. 17.) "And thou shalt," says God, "put the mercy-seat above upon the ark." Thus he said to Moses, and this was the place which David assigned for it. (Exod. xxv. 21. 1 Chron. xxviii. 11.) Now, its being by God's ordinance placed thus, doth teach us many things.

(1.) That mercy's foundation to us is Christ. The mercy-seat was set upon the ark of the testimony, and there it rested to usward. Justice would not, could not have suffered us to have had any benefit by mercy, had it not found an ark, a Christ to rest upon. "Deliver him," saith God, "from going down into the pit; I have found a ransom." (Job xxxiii. 24.)

(2.) In that it was placed above, it doth show also that Christ was, of mercies, ordaining a fruit

of mercy. Mercy is above, is the ordainer; God is love, and sent of love his Son to be the Saviour, and propitiation for our sins. (John iii. 16. 1 John iv. 10.)

(3.) In that the mercy-seat and ark were thus joined together, it also shows, that without Christ mercy doth not act. Hence, when the priest came of old to God for mercy, he did use to come into the holy place with blood; yea, and did use to sprinkle it upon the mercy-seat, and before it seven times. Take away the ark, and the mercy-seat will fall, or come greatly down at least. So take away Christ, and the flood-gate of mercy is let down, and the current of mercy stopped. This is true, for so soon as Christ shall leave off to mediate, will come the eternal judgment.

(4.) Again: in that the mercy-seat was set above upon the ark, it teacheth us to know, that mercy can look down from heaven, though the law stand by, and looks on; but then it must be in Christ, as kept there and fulfilled by him for us. The law out of Christ is terrible as a lion, the law in him is meek as a lamb. The reason is, for that it finds in him enough to answer for all their faults, that come to God for mercy by him. "Christ is the end of the law for righteousness;" and if that be true, the law for that can look no further upon whoever comes to God by him. The law did use to sentence terribly, until it was put into the ark to be kept: but after it was said, "It is there to be kept, we read not of it as afore." (1 Kings viii. 9. 2 Chron. v. 10. Rom. x. 4.)

(5.) Let them then that come to God for mercy, be sure to come to him by the ark, Christ. For grace, as it descends to us from above the mercy-seat, so that mercy-seat doth rest upon the ark. Wherefore, sinner, come thou for mercy that way; for there, if thou meetest with the law, it can do thee no harm; nor can mercy, shouldst thou elsewhere meet it, do thee good. Come, therefore, and come boldly, to the throne of grace, this mercy-seat, thus borne up by the ark, and "obtain mercy, and find grace to help in time of need." (Heb. iv. 16.)

Wherefore the thus placing of things in the holiest, is admirable to behold in the word of God. For that indeed is the glass, by and through which we must behold this glory of the Lord. Here we see the reason of things; here we see how a just God can have to do, and that in a way of mercy, with one that has sinned against him. It is because the law has been kept by the Lord Jesus Christ; for as you see, the mercy-seat stands upon the ark of the covenant, and there God acts in a way of grace towards us. (Exod. xxv. 17—23.)

LXIV. *Of the living waters of the inner Temple.*

Although in the holy relation of the building of the temple no mention is made of these waters, but only of the mount on which, and the materials with which the king did build it, yet it seems to me, that in that mount, and there too, where the temple was built, there was a spring of living water. This seems more than probable by Ezek. xlvii. 1, where he saith, "He brought me to the door of the house, and behold, waters issued out from under the threshold of the house eastward, for the fore-front of the house stood toward the east, and the waters came down from under, from the right side of the house, at the south side of the altar." So again, Joel iii. 18 : "And a fountain shall come forth of the house of the Lord, and shall water the valley of Shittim. Nor was the spring, wherever was the first appearance of these holy waters, but in the sanctuary, which is the holiest of all, (Ezek. xlvii. 12,) where the mercy-seat stood, which in Revelations is called, "The throne of God, and of the Lamb." (Ezek. xxii. 1, 2.)

This also is that which the prophet Zechariah means, when he says, "Living waters shall go forth from Jerusalem, half of them toward the former sea, and half of them toward the hinder sea," &c. (Zech. xiv. 8.) They are said to go forth from Jerusalem, because they came down to the city from out of the sanctuary which stood in Jerusalem. This is that which in another place is called a river of water of life, because it comes forth from the throne, and because it was at the head of it, as I supposed, used in and about temple worship. It was with this, I think, that the molten sea and the ten lavers were filled, and in which the priests washed their hands and feet when they went into the temple to do service; and that also in which they washed the sacrifices before they offered them to God. Yea, I presume, all the washings and rinsings about their worship was with this water.

This water is said in Ezekiel and Revelations to have the tree of life grow on the banks of it, (Ezek. xlvii. Rev. xxii.;) and was a type of the word and Spirit of God, by which both Christ himself sanctified himself, in order to his worship as high priest; and also this water is that which heals all those that shall be saved; and by which they, being sanctified thereby, also do all their works of worship and service acceptably, through Jesus Christ our Lord.

This water, therefore, is said to go forth into the sea, the world, and to heal its fish, the sinners therein; yea, this is that water of which Christ Jesus our Lord saith, "Whosoever shall drink thereof shall live for ever." (Ezek. xlvii. 8—10. Zech. xiv. 8.)

LXV. *Of the chains which were in the oracle or inner Temple.*

As there were chains on the pillars that stood before the porch of the temple, and in the first house; so, like unto them, there were chains in the holiest, here called the oracle.

These chains were not chains in show, or as carved on wood, &c., but chains indeed; and that of gold; and they were prepared to make a partition "before the oracle within." (1 Kings vi. 21. 2 Chron. iii. 16.)

I told you before that the holiest was called the oracle, not because in a strict sense the whole of it was so, but because such answer of God was there as was not in the outward temple; but I think that the ark and mercy-seat were indeed more specially that called the oracle; "for there will I meet with thee," saith God, "and from above that will I commune with thee." When David said, "I lift my hands toward thy holy oracle," he meant not so much towards the holiest house, as toward the mercy-seat that was therein; or, as he saith in the margin, "toward the oracle of thy sanctuary." (Ps. xxviii. 2.)

When, therefore, he saith, "before the oracle," he means, these chains were put in the most holy place, before the ark and mercy-seat, to give to Aaron and his sons to understand, that an additional glory was there; for the ark and mercy-seat were preferred before that holy house itself, even as Christ and the grace of God are preferred before the highest heavens. "The Lord is high above all nations, and his glory is above the heavens." (Ps. cxiii. 4.)

So, then, the partition that was made in this house by these chains, these golden chains, was not so much to divide the holy from the place most holy, as to show that there is in the holiest house that which is yet more worthy than it.

The holiest was a type of heaven, but the ark and mercy-seat were a type of Christ, and of the mercy of God to us by him; and I trow any man will conclude, if he knows what he says, that the God and Christ of heaven are more excellent than the house they dwell in. Hence David said again, "Whom have I in heaven but thee?" For thou art more excellent than they. (Ps. lxxiii. 25.) For though that which is called heaven would serve some, yea, though God himself was out on it, yet none but the God of heaven will satisfy a truly gracious man : it is God that the soul of this man thirsteth for; it is God that is his exceeding joy. (Ps. xlii. 2; lxiii. 1; cxliii. 6; xvii. 15; xliii. 4.)

These chains, then, as they made this partition in the most holy place, may teach us, that when we shall be glorified in heaven, we shall yet, even then, and there, know that there will continue an infinite disproportion between God and us. The golden chains that are there will then distinguish the Creator from the creature. For we, even we which shall be saved, shall yet retain our own nature, and shall still continue finite beings; yea, and shall there also see a disproportion between our Lord, our head, and us; for though now we are, and also then shall be like him, as to his manhood; yea, and shall be like him also as being glorified with his glory; yet he shall transcend and go beyond us, as to degree and splendour, as far as ever the highest king on earth did shine above the meanest subject that dwelt in his kingdom.

Chains have of old been made use of as notes of distinction, to show us who are bondmen, and who free: yea, they shall at the day of judgment be a note of distinction of bad and good; even as here they will distinguish the heavens from God, and the creature from the Creator. (2 Pet. ii. 4. Jude 6. Matt. xxii. 13.)

True, they are chains of sin and wrath, but these chains of gold; yet these chains, even these also will keep creatures in their place, that the Creator may have his glory, and receive those acknowledgments there from them, which are due unto his Majesty. (Rev. iv.; v. 11—15.)

LXVI. *Of the high-priest, and of his office in the inner Temple.*

When things were thus ordained in the house most holy, then went the high-priest in thither, according as he was appointed, to do his office, which was to burn incense in his golden censer, and to sprinkle with his finger the blood of his sacrifice, for the people, upon and above the mercy-seat. (Exod. xxx. 7—10. Lev. xvi. 11—14.)

Now for this special work of his he had peculiar preparations. 1. He was to be washed in water. 2. Then he was to put on his holy garments. 3. After that he was to be anointed with holy oil. 4. Then an offering was to be offered for him, for the further fitting of him for his office. 5. The blood of this sacrifice must be put, some of it upon his right ear, some on the thumb of his right hand, and some on the great toe of his right foot. This done, some more of the blood, with the anointing-oil, must be sprinkled upon him and upon his garment; for after this manner must he be consecrated to his work as high-priest. (Exod. xxix.)

His being washed in water was to show the purity of Christ's humanity. His curious robes were a type of all the perfections of Christ's righteousness. The holy oil that was poured on his head was to show how Christ was anointed with the Holy Ghost unto his work as priest. The sacrifice of his consecration was a type of that offering Christ offered in the garden, when he mixed his sweat with his own blood, and tears, and cries, when " he prayed to him that was able to save him ; and was heard in that he feared ;" for with his blood, as was Aaron with the blood of the bullock that was slain for him, was this blessed one besmeared from head to foot, when his sweat, as great drops or clodders of blood, fell down from head and face, and whole body, to the ground. (Luke xxii. 44. Heb. x. 20.)

When Aaron was thus prepared, then he offered his offering for the people, and carried the blood within the veil. (Lev. xvi.) The which Christ Jesus also answered when he offered his own body without the gate, and then carried his blood into the heavens, and sprinkled it before the mercy-seat. (Heb. xiii. 11, 12; ix. 11, 12, 24.) For Aaron was a type of Christ; his offering a type of Christ's offering his body; the blood of the sacrifice a type of the blood of Christ; his garments a type of Christ's righteousness; the mercy-seat a type of the throne of grace; the incense a type of Christ's praise; and the sprinkling of the blood of the sacrifice upon the mercy-seat a type of Christ's pleading the virtue of his sufferings for us in the presence of God in heaven.

" Wherefore, holy brethren, partakers of the heavenly calling, consider the apostle and high-priest of our profession, Christ Jesus. And seeing we have a great high-priest that is passed into the heavens, Jesus the Son of God, let us hold fast our profession. For we have not an high-priest which cannot be touched with the feeling of our infirmities; but was in all points tempted as we are, yet without sin. Let us therefore come boldly to the throne of grace, that we may obtain mercy, and find grace to help in time of need. For every high-priest taken from among men is ordained for men, in things pertaining to God, that he may offer both gifts and sacrifices for sin, who can have compassion on the ignorant, and on them that are out of the way, for that he himself also is compassed with infirmity.

" This then is our high-priest; and he was made so, not after the law of a carnal commandment, but after the power of an endless life. For Aaron and his sons were made priests without an oath, but this with an oath by him that said unto him, The Lord sware, and will not repent. Thou art a priest for ever, after the order of Melchisedec.

" By so much was Jesus made the surety of a better testament; and they truly were many priests, because they were not suffered to continue by reason of death; but this man, because he continueth ever, hath an unchangeable priesthood. Wherefore he is able to save them to the uttermost that come to God by him, seeing he ever liveth to make intercession for them. For such an high-priest became us, who is holy, harmless, undefiled, separate from sinners, and made higher than the heavens; who needeth not daily, as those high-priests, to offer up sacrifice, first for his own sins, and then for the sins of the people : for this he did once, when he offered up himself. For the law maketh men high-priests which have infirmities; but the word of an oath, which was since the law, maketh the Son, who is consecrated for evermore.

" Now of the things which we have spoken, this is the sum : We have such an high-priest who is set down on the right hand of the throne of the majesty in the heavens. A minister of the sanctuary, and of the new tabernacle, which the Lord pitched, and not man. For every high-priest is ordained to offer sacrifices, wherefore it is of necessity that this man have somewhat also to offer. For if he were on earth, he should not be a high-priest, seeing that there are priests that offer gifts according to the law, who serve unto the example and shadow of heavenly things; as Moses was admonished when he was about to make the tabernacle: for see, saith he, that thou make all things according to the pattern showed to thee in the mount.

"But Christ being come an high-priest of good things to come; by a greater and more perfect tabernacle, that is to say, not of this building: neither by the blood of bulls and calves, but by his own blood he entered in once into the holy place, having obtained eternal redemption for us. For if the blood of goats, bulls, and ashes of an heifer, sprinkling the unclean, sanctifieth to the purifying of the flesh; how much more shall the blood of Christ, who through the eternal Spirit offered himself without spot to God, purge your consciences from dead works, to serve the living God.

"For Christ is not entered into the holy places made with hands, which are the figures of the true; but into heaven itself, now to appear in the presence of God for us. Nor yet that he should offer himself often, as the high-priest entered into the holiest every year with the blood of others, for then must he often have suffered since the foundation of the world. But now once in the end of the world hath he appeared to put away sin by the sacrifice of himself. And as it is appointed unto men once to die, and after this the judgment: so Christ was once offered to bear the sins of many. And to them that look for him, shall he appear the second time without sin, unto salvation." (Heb. iii. 1, 2; iv. 14, 15; v. 1, 2; vii. 16—29; viii. 1—5; ix. 10—29.)

LXVII. *Of the high-priest's going into the holiest alone*

As it was the privilege of the high-priest to go into the holiest alone, so there was something of mystery also; to which I shall speak a little. "There shall," says God, "be no man in the tabernacle of the congregation when Aaron goeth in to make an atonement in the holy place until he comes out, and have made an atonement for himself, and for his household, and for all the congregation of Israel." (Lev. xvi. 17, &c.) The reason is, for that Christ is mediator alone; he trod the wine-press alone, and of the people there was none with him to help him there. (Isa. lxiii. 3. 1 Tim. ii. 5.)

Of the people, there was none to help him to bear his cross, or in the management of the first part of his priestly office; why then should there be any to share with him in his executing of the second part thereof? Besides, he that helps an intercessor must himself be innocent, or in favour, upon some grounds not depending on the worth of the intercessor. But as to the intercession of

Christ, who can come in to help upon the account of such innocency or worth? Not the highest angel; for there is none such but one, wherefore he must do that alone. Hence it is said, he went in alone, is there alone, and there intercedes alone. And this is manifest, not only in the type, Aaron, but in the antitype, Christ Jesus. (Heb. vi. 19, 20; ix. 7—12, 23, 24.)

I do not say that there is no man in heaven but Jesus Christ; but I say, he is there to make intercession for us alone. Yea, the holy text says more: "I go," saith Christ, "to prepare a place for you; and if I go to prepare a place for you, I will come again and take you to myself, that where I am there ye may be also." (John xiv. 1—4.)

This text seems to insinuate that Christ is in the holiest, or highest heavens alone; and that he there alone must be until he has finished his work of intercession; for not till then he comes again to take us to himself. Let us grant Christ the pre-eminency in this, as also in all other things; for he is intercessor for his church, and makes it for them in the holiest alone. It is said he is the light that no man can approach unto.

LXVIII. *Of the high-priest's going in thither but once a year.*

As the high-priest went into the holiest, when he went thither alone; so to do that work, he went in thither but once a year. "Thou shalt not come at all times," said God to him, "into the holy place, within the veil, before the mercy-seat, which is upon the ark, that thou die not." (Lev. xvi. 2.)

And as he was to go in thither but once a year, so not then neither, unless clothed and adorned with his Aaronical holy robes. Then he was to be clothed, as I hinted before, with the holy robes, the frontlet of gold upon his forehead, the names of the twelve tribes upon his breast, and the jingling bells upon the skirts of his garment; nor would all this do, unless he went in thither with blood. (Exod xxviii. Lev. xvi.)

Now, this once a year the Apostle taketh special notice of, and makes great use of it. "Once a year," saith he, this high-priest went in thither; once a year, that is, to show that Christ should once in the end of the world go into heaven itself, to make intercession there for us. For by this word, "year," he shows the term and time of the world is meant; and by "once" in that year, he means once in the end of the world.

"Not," saith he, "that he should offer himself often; as the high-priest entered into the holy place every year with the blood of others: for then must he often have suffered since the foundation of the world. But now once in the end of the world hath he appeared to put away sin by the sacrifice of himself." (Heb. ix.)

And having thus once offered his sacrifice without the veil, he is now gone into the holiest, to perfect his work of mediation for us. Not into the holy places made with hands, which are the figures of the true, but into heaven itself, now to appear in the presence of God for us.

Now if our Lord Jesus is gone indeed, now to appear in the presence of God for us; and if this now be the once a-year that the type speaks of; the once in the end of the world, as our Apostle says; then it follows, that the people of God should all stand waiting for his benediction that to them he shall bring with him, when he shall return from thence. Wherefore he adds, "Christ was once offered to bear the sins of many; and to them that look for him shall he appear the second time without sin unto salvation."

This therefore shows us the greatness of the work that Christ has to do at the right hand of God, for that he stays there so long. He accomplished all the first part of his priesthood in less than forty years, if you take in the making of his holy garments and all; but about this second part thereof, he has been above in heaven above sixteen hundred years, and yet has not done. This therefore calls for faith and patience in saints, and by this he also tries the world; so that they in mocking manner begin to say already, "Where is the promise of his coming?" (2 Pet. iii. 4 ;) but I say again, "We must look and wait."

If the people waited for Zacharias, and wondered that he stayed so long, because he stayed in the holy place somewhat longer than they expected, no marvel if the faith of the world about Christ's coming is fled and gone long ago, yea, and that the children also are put to wait, since a scripture "little while" doth prove so long. For that which the Apostle saith, "Yet a little while," doth prove to some to be a very long little. (John xvi. Heb. x. 37.)

True, Zacharias had then to do with angels, and that made him stay so long. Oh, but Jesus is with God, before him, in his presence, talking with him, swallowed up in him and with his glory, and that is one cause he stays so long. He is there also pleading his blood for his tempted ones, and interceding for all his elect, and waits there till all his be fitted for, and ready to enter into glory, I say, he is there, and there must be till then; and this is another reason why he doth stay the time we count so long.

And indeed, it is a wonder to me, that Jesus Christ our Lord should once think, now he is there, of returning hither again, considering the ill-treatment he met with here before. But what will not love do? Surely he would never touch the ground again, had he not a people here that cannot be made perfect but by his coming to them. He also is made judge of quick and dead, and will get him glory in the ruin of them that hate him.

His people are as himself to him. Can a loving husband abide to be always from a beloved spouse? Besides, as I said, he is to pay the wicked off for all their wickedness, and that in that very plat

where they have committed it. Wherefore the day appointed for this is set, and he will and shall come quickly to do it. For however the time may seem long to us, yet, according to the reckoning of God, it is but a little while since he went into the holiest to intercede. "A thousand years with the Lord is but as one day;" and after this manner of counting he has not been gone yet full two days into the holiest. "The Lord is not slack concerning his promise, as some men count slackness; he will come quickly, and will not tarry." (2 Pet. iii. Heb. x. 37.)

LXIX. *Of the cherubims, and of their being placed over the mercy-seat in the inner Temple.*

There were also cherubims in the most holy place, which were set on high above the mercy-seat. (See 1 Kings vi. 23—28.)

1. These are called by the apostles, "The cherubims of glory covering the mercy-seat." (Heb. ix. 5.)

2. These cherubims were figures of the angels of God, as in other places we have proved.

3. It is said these cherubims were made of image-work, and that in such manner as that they could, as some think, move their wings by art; wherefore it is said "they stretched forth their wings;" the wings of the "cherubims spread themselves;" and that the "cherubims spread forth their wings over the place of the ark, and the staves thereof above." (1 Kings vi. 27. 2 Chron. iii. 13 ; v. 8.)

4. I read also of these cherubims, that they had chariots and wheels; by which is taught us how ready and willing the angels are to fetch us when commanded unto the paradise of God; for these chariots were types of the bosoms of the angels; and these wheels, of the quickness of their motion to come for us when sent. "The chariots of God are twenty thousand, even thousands of angels; the Lord is among them, as in Sinai, in the holy place." (1 Chron. xxviii. 18. Ezek. x. 9, 15, 16, 18, 19, 20. 2 Kings vi. 17. Ps. lxviii. 17. 2 Kings ii. 11. Dan. ix. 20.)

5. What difference, if any, there is between cherubims and seraphims, into that I shall not now inquire; though I believe that there is divers orders and degrees of angels in the heavens, as there are degrees and divers orders among men in the world. But that these cherubims were figures of the holy angels, their being thus placed in the holy oracle doth declare; for their dwelling-place is heaven, though they, for our sakes, are conversant in the world. (Heb. i.)

6. It is said that these cherubims, in this holy place, did stand upon their feet. To show—(1.) That the angels of heaven are not fallen from their station, as the other angels are. (2.) To show also that they are always ready, at God's bidding, to run with swiftness to do his pleasure. (3.) To show also that they shall continue in their

station, being therein confirmed by Jesus Christ, "by whom all things consist." (Col. i.)

7. It is said, "their faces were inward," looking one to another, yet withal somewhat ascending, to show that the angels both behold and wonder at the mysteries of grace, as it is displayed to us-ward from off the mercy-seat. "The faces of the cherubims shall look one to another; toward the mercy-seat shall the faces of the cherubims be." (Exod. xxv. 20. 2 Chron. iii. 13. 1 Pet. i. 12. Eph. iii. 10.)

(1.) "Towards the mercy-seat." They are de-sirous to see it, and how from hence, I say, mercy doth look towards us.

(2.) "They look one towards another," to show that they agree to rejoice in the salvation of our souls. (Luke xv. 10.)

(3.) They are said to stand above the mercy-seat, perhaps, to show that the angels have not need of those acts of mercy and forgiveness as we have, who stand below, and are sinners. They stand above it, they are holy. I do not say, they have no need that the goodness of God should be extended to them, for it is by that they have been and are preserved; but they need not to be for-given, for they have committed no iniquity.

(4.) They stand there also with wings stretched out, to show how ready, if need be, the angels are to come from heaven to preach this gospel to the world. (Luke ii. 9—14.)

(5.) It is said in this, that thus standing, their wings did reach from wall to wall; from one side of this holy house to the other, to show that all the angels within the boundaries of the heavens, with one consent and one mind, are ready to come down to help, and serve, and do for God's elect at his command.

It is said, also, that their wings are stretched on high, to show that they are only delighted in those duties which are enjoined them by the high and lofty one, and not inclined, no not to serve the saints in their sensual or fleshly designs. It may be also to show that they are willing to take their flight from one end of heaven to the other, to serve God and his church for good. (Matt. xiii. 41, 49; xxiv. 31; xxv. 31. 2 Thess. i. 7, 8.)

LXX. *Of the figures that were upon the walls of the inner Temple.*

The wall of the inner temple, which was a type of heaven, was, as I have already told you, ceiled with cedar from the bottom to the top. Now by the vision of Ezekiel, it is said this wall was carved with cherubims and palm-trees. "So that a palm-tree was between a cherub and a cherub, and every cherub had two faces; so that the face of a man was toward the palm-tree on the one side, and the face of a young lion toward the palm-tree on the other side: it was made through all the house round about. From the ground to above the door

were cherubims and palm-trees made." (Ezek. xli. 18—20.)

1. As to these cherubims and palm-trees, I have already told you what I think them to be figures of. The cherubims are figures of the holy angels, and the palm-trees of upright ones; we therefore here are to discourse only of the placing of them in the heavens.

2. Now you see the palm-trees in the holiest are placed between a cherub and a cherub, round about the house, which methinks should be to sig-nify that the saints shall not there live by faith and hope, as here, but in the immediate enjoyment of God; for to be placed between the cherubims is to be placed where God dwells; for holy writ says plainly, He dwells between the cherubims, even where here it is said these palm-trees, or upright ones, are placed. (1 Sam. iv. 4. 2 Kings xix. 15. 1 Chron. xiii. 6. Ps. lxxx. 1. Isa. xxxvii. 16.) The church on earth is called God's house, and he will dwell in it for ever; and heaven itself is called God's house, and we shall dwell in it for ever, and that between the cherubims. This is more than grace, this is grace and glory, glory indeed.

3. To dwell between the cherubims may also be to show that there we shall be equal to the angels. Mark, here is a palm-tree and a cherub, a palm-tree and a cherub. Here we are a little lower, but there we shall not be a whit behind the very chief of them. A palm-tree and a cherub, an upright one between the cherubs, will then be round about the house; we shall be placed in the same rank, "neither can they die any more, for they are equal to the angels." (Luke xx. 36.)

4. The palm-trees thus placed may be also to show us that the elect of God shall there take up the vacancies of the fallen angels; they for sin were cast down from the holy heavens, and we by grace shall be caught up thither, and be placed between a cherub and a cherub. When I say their places, I do not mean the fickleness of that state, that they for want of electing love did stand in while in glory; for the heavens, by the blood of Christ, is now to us become a purchased possession; wherefore, as we shall have their place in the heavenly kingdom, so by virtue of redeeming blood we shall there abide, and go no more out; for by that means that kingdom will stand to us unshaken. (Heb. ix. 12; xii. 22—24, 28. Rev. iii. 12.)

5. These palm-trees, I say, seem to take their places who for sin were cast from thence. The elect therefore take that place in possession, but a better crown for ever. Thus "Israel possessed that of the Canaanites;" and David, Saul's king-dom; and Matthias, the apostleship of Judas. (Acts i. 20—26.)

6. Nor were the habitations which the fallen angels lost, excepting that which was excepted before, at all inferior to theirs that stood; for their captain and prince is called son of the morning, for he was the antitype thereof. (Isa. xiv. 12.)

7. Thus, you see, they were placed from the

ground, up to above the door; that is, from the lowest to the highest angel there. For as there are great saints and small ones in the church on earth, so there are angels of divers degrees in heaven, some greater than some; but the smallest saint, when he gets to heaven, shall have an angel's dignity, an angel's place. From the ground you find a palm-tree, between a cherub and a cherub.

8. And every cherub had two faces, so here; but I read in chap. x. that they had four faces apiece. The first was the face of a cherubim; the second, the face of a man; the third, the face of a lion; and the fourth, the face of an eagle.

9. They had two faces apiece, not to show that they were of a double heart, for their appearance and themselves was the same, "and they went every one straight forward." (Ezek. x. 22.) These two faces, then, were to show here the quickness of their apprehension, and their terribleness to execute the mind of God. The face of a man, signifies them masters of reason; the face of a lion, the terribleness of their presence. (1 Cor. xiii. 12. Judges xiii. 6.)

In another place I read of their wheels; yea, that themselves, their whole bodies, their backs, their hands, their wings, and their wheels, were full of eyes round about. (Ezek. i. 18; x. 12.) And this is to show us how knowing and quick-sighted they are in all providences and dark dispensations, and how nimble in apprehending the mischievous designs of the enemies of God's church, and so how able they are to undermine them; and forasmuch also as they have the face of a lion, we by that are showed how full of power they are to kill and to destroy, when God says go forth and do so. Now with these we must dwell and cohabit, a palm-tree and a cherub; a palm-tree and a cherub must be from the ground to above the door, round about the house, the heavens.

"So that the face of a man was toward the palm-tree on the one side, and the face of a young lion toward the palm-tree on the other side." By these two faces may be also showed, that we in the heavens shall have glory sufficient to familiarise us to the angels. Their lion-like looks, with which they used to fright the biggest saint on earth, as you have it, (Gen. xxxii. 30. Judges xiii. 15—22,) shall then be accompanied with the familiar looks of a man. Then angels and men shall be fellows, and have to do with each as such.

Thus, you see something of that little I have found in the temple of God.

PREFATORY REMARKS

ON

REPROBATION ASSERTED.

THE subject of reprobation should be approached with a twofold caution. We must remember, in the first place, that there is no doctrine the personal application of which involves a more perilous responsibility; and, in the next, that it is only as a revealed, and not as a metaphysical truth, it can be made intelligible.

Writers on reprobation generally acknowledge, that no man can in this life safely point to another and pronounce him doomed to eternal wrath. That there are many so doomed—that they form a large class of mankind—is pre-supposed by the doctrine : its very substance consists of this terrible fact. It is only in proportion to the belief that there are reprobates, that the decree of reprobation can be regarded as a reality. But, certain as it is that, if the doctrine be true, there are many persons in this doleful state of hopeless ruin, it is equally certain that not one of them can be confidently named. The most ordinary experience of Christian societies tends to prove that a human soul may be recovered from the lowest depths of depravity. It is utterly impossible for the keenest observer to discover the line which, in the state of probation, separates the probably from the certainly lost. Probabilities have, in this case, been utterly set at nought by the omnipotence of divine grace. He who should dare to say "such or such a man is reprobate," would be guilty of an affront to the divine Spirit, who might that very hour visit the heart of the wretched sinner, and turn it in humble penitence to God.

There is something very awful, therefore, in the temptation to which a severe judge of mankind may be exposed, if he view the doctrine of reprobation as entitling him to pass sentence according to his own opinion. That such a temptation is far from uncommon the history of churches and sects affords abundant proofs. Excommunications, the burning of heretics, the invention of insulting titles, are all but varied modes of expressing the belief of one party that some other party should be considered reprobate. In the judgment passed upon individuals there is the same danger, the same frequent yielding to an erring severity. God has not opened his books for the inspection of any man. The human heart is itself inscrutable. Its movements are determined by innumerable springs. The Holy Spirit works by ways, at times, and through agents, many of which are absolutely hidden from the eye, and even the understanding of man. But these must all come within the scope of our reasoning, if we would say this man will, and that man will not be saved.

But to warn is not to judge. The doctrine of reprobation is, therefore, to be viewed under a different light when considered as furnishing an argument to repentance, rather than the test of a state beyond repentance. Still, even here, there is need of caution. The appeal to the horrors of reprobation may be made in two cases. If a fear be entertained that the man who knows the gospel is gradually receding further and further from the mark of his high calling, he may be warned of his peril; reprobation, like a black precipice or huge gulf of fire, lying straight across his downward path. Suppose, on the other hand, that the person to be warned is a man who has never regarded salvation as worth a serious thought. To him reprobation may be described as the proper fate of all such reckless sinners. Its terrific developments and accompaniments will, at least, furnish a lesson calculated, if any be, to rouse him from his torpor.

In neither instance, however, should the reference to reprobation be made without earnest consideration. In the case of an alarmed, conscious-stricken offender, it frequently depends very much upon individual character, whether fear or hope will operate most powerfully to foster repentance. A mistake in the application of the means may prove fatal. Thus, if, instead of persuasives to hope, reprobation comes into view just as the agonized spirit is quivering doubtfully on the verge of despair, it will resign itself helplessly to ruin. Where there are no terrors of conscience, and the idea of reprobation is suggested to compel alarm, it is not impossible that the very thought of this awful state may act like a fiery stimulant on the perverted intellect, and confirm the sinner in his daring instead of breaking down his obduracy. This is certain : that whatever the importance assigned, the doctrine of reprobation in the Christian system, its uses, in the way of practical application, depend upon very careful distinctions.

In the next place : for proofs of the doctrine, a sober and cautious inquirer will be content with the statements of Scripture, be they few or many ; more or less explicit. Arguments drawn from views of the divine attributes are often based on the assumption of knowledge not possessed. What God has decreed we may know by his publishing the decree ; but as we could not have known it had he withheld the revelation, so neither can we increase the certainty of its truth, or better understand it, by any study of his attributes, the contemplation of which would not originally have enabled us to discover it.

It requires little effort of thought to convince us that ideas and objects cannot have the same relation to an infinite Being which they have to creatures limited and erring. The decrees of God, therefore, are not to be referred to any standard with which we are acquainted. Their justice is impeachable, but it is not to be proved so by particular cases of its application. We acknowledge its perfection from the very nature of God. If He have consigned some beings to a state of reprobation, no reason for impugning his righteousness can be drawn from this act. We are absolutely unable to determine the relation which it holds to other proceedings in the vast dispensation of his kingdom : could we see them all, it is certain that this particular judgment would not have the same aspect which it has when isolated, in our weak apprehensions, from all the rest. But neither the counsels of God, nor the original or eternal principles of his government, can be so contemplated as to bring this, or any other mystery, within the scope of human reasoning. It is on revelation only that our faith must rest. Reason exercises her highest functions in transmitting the burden of proof from herself to the word of God. If a doctrine be but obscurely stated, there is an intention in the obscurity. What light there is upon it is light from heaven, and the degree of light measures the greater or less importance of the doctrine to us.

H. S.

REPROBATION ASSERTED;

OR,

THE DOCTRINE OF ETERNAL ELECTION AND REPROBATION PROMISCUOUSLY HANDLED, IN ELEVEN CHAPTERS.

WHEREIN THE MOST MATERIAL OBJECTIONS MADE BY THE OPPOSERS OF THIS DOCTRINE ARE FULLY ANSWERED, SEVERAL DOUBTS REMOVED, AND SUNDRY CASES OF CONSCIENCE RESOLVED.

" What then ? Israel hath not obtained that which he seeketh for ; but the Election hath obtained it, and the rest were blinded."
—ROM. xi. 7.

CHAPTER I.

That there is a Reprobation.

IN my discourse upon this subject, I shall study as much brevity as clearness and edification will allow me ; not adding words to make the volume swell, but contracting myself within the bounds of few lines, for the profit and commodity of those that shall take the pains to read my labours. And though I might abundantly multiply arguments for the evincing and vindicating this conclusion, yet I shall content myself with some few scripture demonstrations: the first of which I shall gather out of the ninth of the Romans, from that discourse of the Apostle's, touching the children of the flesh, and the children of the promise.

1. At the beginning of this chapter, we find the Apostle grievously lamenting and bemoaning of the Jews, at the consideration of their miserable state : " I say the truth in Christ," saith he ; " I lie not, my conscience also bearing me witness in the Holy Ghost, that I have great heaviness, and continual sorrow in my heart. For I could wish myself accursed from Christ, for my brethren, my kinsmen according to the flesh." Poor hearts, saith he, they will perish ; they are a miserable, sad, and helpless people ; their eyes are darkened that they may not see, and their back is bowed down alway. (Rom. xi. 10.) Wherefore ? have they not the means of grace ? Yes, verily, and that in goodly measure : first they are Israelites, to whom pertaineth the adoption, and the glory, and the covenants, and the giving of the law, and the service of God, and the promises ; whose are the Father's, and of whom, as concerning the flesh, Christ came, who is over all, God blessed for ever. Amen. What then should be the reason ? " Why," saith he, " though they be the children of Abraham according to the flesh, yet they are the children of Abraham but according to the flesh : for they are not all Israel (in the best sense) that are of Israel ; neither because they are the seed of Abraham, are they children ; but in Isaac shall thy seed be called." That is, they that are the children of the flesh, they are not the children of God ; but the children of the promise shall be counted for the seed. So, then, here you see that they are only the children of the flesh, as the greatest part of Israel were, they are those that are neither counted for the seed, the children of promise, nor the children of God ; but are rejected, and of the reprobation. This, therefore, shall at this time serve for the first scripture-demonstration.

2. Another scripture you have in the eleventh chapter of this epistle, from these words, " The election hath obtained it, and the rest were blinded." (Rom. xi. 7.) These words are shedding words, they sever between men and men ; the election, the rest ; the chosen, the left ; the embraced, the refused : " The election have obtained it, and the rest were blinded." By rest here, must needs be understood those not elect, because set one in opposition to the other ; and if not elect, what then but reprobate ?

3. A third scripture is that in the Acts of the Apostles, " And as many as were ordained to eternal life, believed." (Acts xiii. 48.) " And as many ;" by these words, as by the former, you may see how the Holy Ghost distinguisheth or divideth between men and men ; the sons, and the sons of Adam. " As many as were ordained to eternal life, believed :" if by many here, we are to understand every individual, then not only the whole world must at least believe the gospel, of which we see the most fall short, but they must be ordained to eternal life ; which other scriptures contradict : for there is the rest, besides the elect ; the stubble and chaff, as well as wheat : many therefore must here include but some ; " for though

Israel be as the sand of the sea, a remnant shall be saved." (Isa. i. 9; x. 22, 23. Rom. ix. 27.)

I might here multiply many other texts, but in the mouth of two or three witnesses shall every word be established. Let these therefore for this, suffice to prove that there is a reprobation. For this I say, though the children of the flesh, the rest besides the election, and the like, were not mentioned in the Word; yet seeing there is such a thing as the children of the promise, the seed, the children of God, and the like, and that too under several other phrases, as predestinated, foreknown, chosen in Christ, and written in the book of life, and appointed unto life, with many others; I say, seeing these things are thus apparent, it is without doubt, that there is such a thing as a reprobation also. (Rom. viii. Eph. i. 3, 4. 1 Thess. v. 9.)

Nay, further, from the very word election, it followeth unavoidably; for whether you take it as relating to this, of distinguishing between persons as touching the world to come, or with reference to God's acts of choosing this or that man to this or that office, work, or employment in this world, it still signifieth such a choosing, as that but some are therein concerned, and that therefore some are thence excluded. Are all the elect, the seed, the saved, the vessels of mercy, the chosen and peculiar? are not some, yea the most, the children of the flesh, the rest, the lost, the vessels of wrath, of dishonour, and the children of perdition? (Rom. xi. 9. 1 Pet. ii. 8, 9. Matt. x. 16. 2 Sam. vi. 21. Ps. lxxviii. 67, 68. John xv. 16. 2 Cor. iv. 3. Rom. ix. 21. 22. John xvii. 12.)

CHAPTER II.

What Reprobation is.

Having thus showed you that there is such a thing as a reprobation, I come now to show what it is: which that I may do to your edification, I shall first show you what this word reprobation signifieth in the general, as it concerneth persons temporarily and visibly reprobate: secondly, more particularly, as it concerneth persons that are eternally and invisibly reprobate.

First, generally, as it concerneth persons temporarily and visibly reprobate, thus: to be reprobate is to be disapproved, void of judgment, and rejected, &c. To be disapproved, that is, when the Word condemns them, either as touching the faith or the holiness of the gospel; the which they must needs be that are void of spiritual and heavenly judgment in the mysteries of the kingdom, a manifest token they are rejected. And hence it is that they are said to be reprobate or void of judgment concerning the faith; reprobate or void of judgment touching every good work; having a reprobate mind to do those things that are not convenient, either as to faith or manners. And hence it is again, that they are also said to

be rejected of God, cast away, and the like. (2 Cor. xiii. 6, 7. 2 Tim. iii. 8. Tit. i. 16. Rom. i. 28. Jer. vi. 30. 1 Cor. ix. 27.)

I call this temporary visible reprobation, because these appear, and are detected by the Word as such that are found under the above-named errors, and so adjudged without the grace of God. Yet it is possible for some of these, however for the present disapproved, through the blessed acts and dispensations of grace, not only to become visible saints, but also saved for ever. Who doubts but that he who now by examining himself, concerning faith, doth find himself, though under profession, graceless, may after that, he seeing his woeful state, not only cry to God for mercy, but find grace, and obtain mercy to help in time of need? though it is true that for the most part the contrary is fulfilled on them.

Second. But to pass this, and more particularly to touch the eternal invisible reprobation, which I shall thus hold forth: it is to be passed by in, or left out of, God's election; yet so, as considered upright: in which position you have these four things considerable: 1. The act of God's election. 2. The negative of that act. 3. The persons reached by that negative. And 4. Their qualification when thus reached by it.

For the first. This act of God in electing, it is a choosing or fore-appointing of some infallibly unto eternal life, which he also hath determined shall be brought to pass by the means that should be made manifest and efficacious to that very end. (Eph. i. 3—5. 1 Pet. i. 2.)

Second. Now the negative of this act is, a passing by, or a leaving of those not concerned in this act; a leaving of them, I say, without the bounds, and so the saving privileges of this act; as it followeth by natural consequence, that because a man chooseth but some, therefore he chooseth not all, but leaveth, as the negative of that act, all others whatsoever. Wherefore, as I said before, those not contained within this blessed act, are called the rest besides the election. "The election hath obtained it, and the rest were blinded."

Third. The persons, then, that are contained under the negative of this act, they are those, and those only, that pass through this wicked world without the saving grace of God's elect; those, I say, that miss the most holy faith, which they in time are blessed withal, who are fore-appointed unto glory.

Fourth. And now for the qualification they were considered under, when this act of reprobation laid hold upon them; to wit, they were considered upright.

This is evident, First, From this consideration, that reprobation is God's act, even the negative of his choosing or electing, and none of the acts of God make any man a sinner. Second. It is further evident by the similitude that is taken from the carriage of the potter in his making of his pots; for by this comparison the God of heaven is pleased to show unto us the nature of his determining in the act of reprobation : "Hath not the potter power over the clay of the same lump ?" &c. (Rom. ix. 21.)   Consider a little, and you shall see that these three things do necessarily fall in, to complete the potter's action in every pot he makes.

1. A determination in his own mind what pot to make of this or that piece of clay ; a determination, I say, precedent to the fashion of the pot ; the which is true, in the highest degree, in him that is excellent in working ; he determines the end before the beginning is perfected. (Isa. xli. 22 ; xlvi. 10.)   "For this very purpose have I raised thee up." (Exod. ix. 16.)

2. The next thing considerable in the potter ; it is the so making of the pot, even as he determined ; a vessel to honour, or a vessel to dishonour.   There is no confusion or disappointment under the hand of this eternal God, his work is perfect, and every way doth answer to what he hath determined. (Deut. xxxii. 4.)

3. Observe again, that whether the vessel be to honour or to dishonour, yet the potter makes it good, sound, and fit for service ; his fore-determining to make this a vessel to dishonour, hath no persuasion at all with him to break or mar the pot : which very thing doth well resemble the state of man as under the act of eternal reprobation, for " God made man upright." (Eccles. vii. 29.)

From these conclusions, then, consider—

1. That the simple act of reprobation, it is a leaving or passing by, not a cursing of the creature.

2. Neither doth this act alienate the heart of God from the reprobate, nor tie him up from loving, favouring, or blessing of him ; no, not from blessing of him with the gift of Christ, of faith, of hope, and many other benefits : it only denieth them that benefit that will infallibly bring them to eternal life, and that in despite of all opposition ; it only denieth so to bless them as the elect themselves are blessed.   Abraham loved all the children he had by all his wives, and gave them portions also ; but his choice blessing, as the fruit of his chiefest love, he reserved for chosen Isaac. (Gen. xxv. 5, 6.)

Lastly. The act of reprobation doth harm to no man, neither means him any ; nay, it rather decrees him upright, lets him be made upright, and so be turned into the world.

CHAPTER III.

Of the Antiquity of Reprobation.

Having now proceeded so far as to show you what reprobation is, it will not be amiss in this place, if I briefly show you its antiquity, even when it began its rise ; the which you may gather by these following particulars.

First. Reprobation is before the person cometh into the world, or hath done good or evil. This is evident by that of Paul to the Romans : " For the children being not yet born, neither having done any good or evil, that the purpose of God, according to election, might stand, not of works, but of him that calleth ; it was said unto Rebecca, the elder shall serve the younger." (Rom. ix. 11.) Here you find twain in their mother's womb, and both receiving their destiny, not only before they had done good or evil, but before they were in a capacity to do it, they being yet unborn ; their destiny, I say, the one unto, the other not unto, the blessing of eternal life ; the one chose, the other refused ; the one elect, the other reprobate.   The same also might be said of Ishmael and his brother Isaac, both which did also receive their destiny before they came into the world : for the promise that this Isaac should be the heir, it was also before Ishmael was born, though he was elder by fourteen years, or more, than his brother. (Gen. xv. 4, 5 ; xvi. 4, 5, 16 ; xvii. 25 ; xxi. 5.)   And it is yet further evident,

1. Because election is an act of grace ; " There is a remnant, according to the election of grace." (Rom. xi. 5.)   Which act of grace saw no way so fit to discover its purity and independency, as by fastening on the object before it came into the world ; that being the state in which at least no good were done, either to procure good from God, or to eclipse and darken this precious act of grace. For though it is true that no good thing that we have done before conversion, can obtain the grace of election ; yet the grace of election then appeareth most, when it prevents our doing good, that we might be loved therefore. Wherefore he saith again, " That the purpose of God according to election, might stand, not of works, but of him that calleth ; it was said unto her, the elder shall serve the younger."

2. This is most agreeable to the nature of the promise of giving seed to Abraham ; which promise, as it was made before the child was conceived, so it was fulfilled at the best time, for the discovery of the act of grace, that could have been pitched upon : " At this time will I come (saith God) and Sarah shall have a son ;" (Gen. xviii. 14 ;) which promise, because it carried in its bowels the very grace of electing love, therefore it left out Ishmael, with the children of Keturah : " For in Isaac shall thy seed be called." (Rom. iv. 16—19; ix. 7.)

3. This was the best and fittest way for the decrees to receive sound bottom, even for God both to choose and refuse, before the creature had done good or evil, and so before they came into the world.   " That the purpose of God, according to election, might stand," saith he, therefore before the children were yet born, or had done any good or evil, " it was said unto her," &c.   God's decree would for ever want foundation, should it depend at all upon the goodness and holiness either of men

or angels; especially if it were to stand upon that good that is wrought before conversion, yea, or after conversion either. We find, by daily experience, how hard and difficult it is, for even the holiest in the world, to bear up and maintain their faith and love to God; yea, so hard, as not at all to do it without continual supplies from heaven. How then is it possible for any so to carry it before God, as to lay, by this his holiness, a foundation for election, as to maintain that foundation, and thereby to procure all those graces that infallibly saveth the sinner? But now the choice, I say, being a choice of grace, as is manifest, it being acted before the creature's birth; here grace hath laid the corner-stone, and determined the means to bring the work to perfection. Thus "the foundation of God standeth sure, having this seal, the Lord knoweth them that are his." (2 Tim. ii. 19.) That is, who he hath chosen, having excluded works, both good and bad, and founded all in an unchangeable act of grace; the negative whereof, is this harmless reprobation.

Second. But secondly, To step a little backward, and so to make all sure; this act of reprobation was before the world began; which, therefore, must needs confirm that which was said but now, that they were, before they were born, both destinated before they had done good or evil. This is manifest by that of Paul to the Ephesians, at the beginning of his epistle; where, speaking of Election, whose negative is reprobation, he saith, "God hath chosen us in Christ before the foundation of the world." Nay further, if you please, consider, that as Christ was ordained to suffer before the foundation of the world, and as we that are elected were chosen in him before the foundation of the world; so it was also ordained we should know him, before the foundation of the world; ordained that we should be holy before him in love, before the foundation of the world; and that we in time should be created in him to good works, and ordained before that we should walk in them. Wherefore reprobation also, it being the negative of electing love; that is, because God elected but some, therefore he left the rest: these rest, therefore, must needs be of as ancient standing under reprobation, as the chosen are under election; both which, it is also evident, was before the world began. Which serveth yet further to prove that reprobation could not be with respect to this or the other sin, it being only a leaving them, and that before the world, out of that free choice which he was pleased to bless the other with. Even as the clay with which the dishonourable vessel is made, did not provoke the potter, for the sake of this or that impediment, therefore to make it so; but the potter of his own will, of the clay of the same lump, of the clay that is full as good as that of which he hath made the vessel to honour, did make this and the other a vessel of dishonour, &c. (1 Pet. i. 20, 21. 1 Cor. ii. 6, 7. Eph. i. 3, 4; ii. 10.)

CHAPTER IV.
Of the causes of Reprobation.

Having thus in a word or two showed the antiquity of Reprobation, I now come in this place to show you the cause thereof; for doubtless this must stand a truth, that whatever God doth, there is sufficient ground therefore, whether by us apprehended, or else without our reach.

First then, It is caused from the very nature of God. There are two things in God, from which, or by the virtue of which, all things have their rise, to wit, the eternity of God in general, and the eternal perfection of every one of his attributes in particular: for as by the first, he must needs be before all things; so by virtue of the second, must all things consist. And as he is before all things, they having consistence by him; so also is he before all states, or their causes, be they either good or bad, of continuance or otherwise, he being the first without beginning, &c., whereas all other things, with their causes, have rise, dependence, or toleration of being from him. (Col. i. 17.)

Hence it follows, that nothing, either person, or cause, &c., can by any means have a being, but first he knows thereof, allows thereof, and decrees it shall be so: "Who is he that saith, and it cometh to pass, when the Lord commandeth it not?" (Lam. iii. 37.) Now then, because that reprobation, as well as election, are subordinate to God; his will also, which is eternally perfect, being most immediately herein concerned; it was impossible that any should be reprobate, before God had both willed and decreed it should be so. It is not the being of a thing that administers matter of knowledge of foresight thereof to God, but the perfection of his knowledge, wisdom, and power, &c., that giveth the thing its being: God did not fore-decree there should be a world, because he foresaw there would be one; but there must be one, because he had before decreed there should be one. The same is true as touching the case in hand: "For this very purpose have I raised thee up, that I might show in thee my power." (Exod. ix. 16. Rom. ix. 17.)

Second. A second cause of eternal reprobation, is the exercise of God's sovereignty; for if this is true, that there is nothing either visible or invisible, whether in heaven or earth, but hath its being from him, then it must most reasonably follow, that he is therefore sovereign Lord, &c., and may also according to his own will, as he pleaseth himself, both exercise and manifest the same; being every whit absolute; and can do and may do whatsoever his soul desireth: and indeed, good reason, for he hath not only made them all, but for his pleasure they both were and are created. (Rev. iv. 11.)

Now the very exercise of this sovereignty produceth reprobation: "Therefore hath he mercy on whom he will have mercy, and whom he will he hardeneth:" (Rom. ix. 18.) "Hath not the potter power over the clay of the same lump?" and doth he not make his pots according to his pleasure? here therefore the mercy, justice, wisdom and power of God, take liberty to do what they will; saying, "my counsel shall stand, and I will do all my pleasure." (Job xxiii. 13. Dan. iv. 35. Rev. iv. 11. Isa. xliii. 13; xlvi. 10.)

Third. Another cause of eternal reprobation, is the act and working of distinguishing love, and everlasting grace. God hath universal love, and particular love; general love, and distinguishing love; and so accordingly doth decree, purpose, and determine: from general love, the extension of general grace and mercy; but from that love that is distinguishing, peculiar grace and mercy. "Was not Esau Jacob's brother?" saith the Lord, "yet I loved Jacob;" (Mal. i. 2;) yet I loved Jacob, that is, with a better love, or a love that is more distinguishing: as he farther makes appear in his answer to our father Abraham, when he prayed to God for Ishmael—"as for Ishmael," saith he, "I have heard thee; behold I have blessed him, and will make him fruitful: but my covenant will I establish with Isaac, which Sarah shall bear unto thee." (Gen. xvii. 20, 21.) Touching which words, there are these things observable,

1. That God had better love for Isaac, than he had for his brother Ishmael. Yet,

2. Not because Isaac had done more worthy and goodly deeds, for Isaac was yet unborn.

3. This choice blessing could not be denied to Ishmael, because he had disinherited himself by sin; for this blessing was entailed to Isaac, before Ishmael had a being also. (Rom. iv. 16—19. Gen. xv. 4, 5; xvi.)

4. These things, therefore, must needs fall out through the working of distinguishing love and mercy, which had so cast the business, "that the purpose of God according to election might stand."

Further, Should not God decree to show distinguishing love and mercy, as well as that which is general and common, he must not discover his best love at all to the sons of men. Again, if he should reveal and extend his best love to all the world in general, then there would not be such a thing as love that doth distinguish; for distinguishing love appeareth in separating between Isaac and Ishmael, Jacob and Esau, the many called, and the few chosen. Thus by virtue of distinguishing love, some must be reprobate: for distinguishing love must leave some, both of the angels in heaven, and the inhabitants of the earth; wherefore the decree also that doth establish it, must needs leave some.

Fourth. Another cause of reprobation is God's willingness to show his wrath, and to make his power known. This is one of those arguments that the holy Apostle setteth against the most knotty and strong objection that ever was framed against the doctrine of eternal reprobation: "Thou wilt say then unto me," saith he, "Why doth he yet find fault?" For if it be his will that some should be rejected, hardened, and perish, why then is he offended that any sin against him; "for who hath resisted his will?" Hold, saith the Apostle; stay a little here; first remember this, Is it meet to say unto God, what doest thou? "Shall the thing formed say to him that formed it, why hast thou made me thus? Hath not the potter power over the clay of the same lump," &c. Besides, when you have thought your worst, to wit, that the effects of reprobation must needs be consummate in the eternal perdition of the creature; yet again consider, "What if God be willing to show his wrath," as well as grace and mercy? And what if he, that he may so do, exclude some from having share in that grace that would infallibly, against all resistance, bring us safe unto eternal life? What then? Is he therefore the author of your perishing, or his eternal reprobation either? Do you not know that he may refuse to elect who he will, without abusing of them? Also that he may deny to give them that grace that would preserve them from sin, without being guilty of their damnation? May he not, to show his wrath, suffer "with much long-suffering" all that are "the vessels of wrath," by their own voluntary will, to fit themselves for wrath and for destruction? (Rom. ix. 19—22.) Yea, might he not even in the act of reprobation, conclude also to suffer them thus left, to fall from the state he left them in, that is, as they were considered upright; and when fallen, to bind them fast in chains of darkness unto the judgment of the great day, but he must needs be charged foolishly? You shall see in that day what a harmony and what a glory there will be found in all God's judgments in the overthrow of the sinner; also how clear the Lord will show himself of having any working hand in that which causeth eternal ruin; notwithstanding he hath reprobated such, doth suffer them to sin, and that too that he might show his wrath on the vessels of his wrath; the which I also after this next chapter, shall further clear up to you. As "the Lord knoweth how to deliver the godly out of temptations," without approving of their miscarriages; so he also knoweth how "to reserve the unjust unto the day of judgment to be punished," (2 Pet. ii. 9,) yet never to deserve the least of blame for his so reserving of them; though none herein can see his way, for he alone knows how to do it.

CHAPTER V.

Of the unchangeableness of eternal Reprobation.

Many opinions have passed through the hearts of the sons of men concerning reprobation; most of them endeavouring so to hold it forth, as therewith they might, if not heal their conscience slightly, yet maintain their own opinion, in their judgment, of other things; still wringing, now the Word this way, and anon again that, for their purpose; also framing within their soul such an imagination of God and his acts in eternity, as would suit with such opinions, and so present all to the world. And the rather they have with greatest labour strained unweariedly at this above many other truths, because of the grim and dreadful face it carrieth in most men's apprehensions. But none of these things, however they may please the creature, can by any means in any measure, either cause God to undo, unsay, or undetermine what he hath concerning this decreed and established.

First. Because they suit not with his nature, especially in these foundation-acts : " The foundation of God standeth sure," (2 Tim. ii. 19,) even touching reprobation, " that the purpose of God according to election might stand." (Rom. ix. 11.) " I know," saith Solomon, " that whatsoever God doeth, it shall be for ever ; nothing can be put to it, nor anything taken from it," &c. (Eccles. iii. 14.) " Hath he said, and shall he not do it ? or hath he spoken, and shall he not make it good ? " (Numb. xxiii. 19.) His decrees are composed according to his eternal wisdom, established upon his unchangeable will, governed by his knowledge, prudence, power, justice, and mercy, and are brought to conclusion, on his part, in perfect holiness, through the abiding of his most blessed truth and faithfulness : " He is a Rock, his work is perfect, for all his ways are judgment : a God of truth, and without iniquity, just and right is he." (Deut. xxxii. 4.)

Second. This decree is made sure by the number, measure, and bounds of election ; for election and rebrobation do inclose all reasonable creatures ; that is, either the one or the other ; election, those that are set apart for glory ; and reprobation, those left out of this choice.

Now as touching the elect, they are by this decree confined to that limited number of persons that must amount to the complete making up the fulness of the mystical body of Christ ; yea, so confined by this eternal purpose, that nothing can be diminished from or added thereunto : and hence it is that they are called his body and members in particular, " the fulness of him that filleth all in all," (Eph. i. 23,) and " the measure of the stature of the fulness of Christ ;" (Eph. iv. 13 ;) which body, considering him as the head thereof, in conclusion maketh up one perfect man, and holy temple for the Lord. These are called Christ's substance, inheritance, and lot, (Ps. xvi.,) and are said to be booked, marked, and sealed with God's most excellent knowledge, approbation, and liking. (2 Tim. ii. 19.) As Christ said to his Father, " Thine eyes did see my substance, yet being unperfect, and in thy book are all my members written, which in continuance were fashioned, when as yet there was none of them." (Ps. cxxxix. 16.) This being thus, I say, it is, in the first place, impossible that any of those members should miscarry, for " Who shall lay anything to the charge of God's elect ? " (Rom. viii. 33.) And because they are as to number every way suffi-

cient, being his body, and so by their completing to be made a perfect man ; therefore all others are rejected, that the " purpose of God according to election might stand." (Rom. ix. 11. Besides, it would not only argue weakness in the decree, but monstrousness in the body, if, after this, any appointed should miscarry, or any besides them be added to them. (Matt. xxiv. 24.)

Third. Nay, further, that all may see how punctual, exact, and, to a tittle, this decree of election is, God hath not only as to number and quantity confined the persons, but also determined and measured, and that before the world, the number of the gifts and graces that are to be bestowed on these members in general ; and also what graces and gifts to be bestowed on this or that member in particular : " He hath blessed us with all spiritual blessings in Christ, according as he hath chosen us in him before the foundation of the world ;" (Eph. i. 3, 4 ;) and bestoweth them in time upon us, " according to the eternal purpose which he purposed in Christ Jesus our Lord." (Eph. iii. 11.) He hath given to the eye, the grace that belongeth to the eye ; and to the hand that which he also hath appointed for it. And so to every other member of the body elect, he doth deal out to them their determined measure of grace and gifts most fit for their place and office. Thus is the decree established, both of the saved, and also the non-elect. (Rom. xii. 3. Eph. iv. 16. Col. ii. 19. Eph. iv. 12, 13.)

Fourth. But again, another thing that doth establish this decree of eternal reprobation, is the weakness that sin in the fall, and since, hath brought all reprobates into : for though it be most true, that sin is no cause of eternal reprobation ; yet seeing sin hath seized on the reprobate, it cannot be but thereby the decree must needs be the faster fixed. If the king, for this or the other weighty reason, doth decree not to give this or that man (who yet did never offend him) a place in his privy chamber ; if this man after this shall be infected with the plague, this rather fastens than loosens the king's decree. As the angels that were left out of God's election, by reason of the sin they committed after, are so far off from being by that received into God's decree, that they are therefore bound for it in chains of everlasting darkness to the judgment of the great day.

CHAPTER VI.

Whether to be reprobated be the same with being appointed beforehand unto eternal condemnation? If not, how do they differ ? Also, whether reprobation be the cause of condemnation ?

It hath been the custom of ignorant men much to quarrel at eternal reprobation, concluding, for want of knowledge in the mystery of God's will, that if he reprobate any from eternity, he had as good have said, I will make this man to damn him; I will decree this man, without any consideration, to the everlasting pains of hell. When in very deed, for God to reprobate, and to appoint beforehand to eternal condemnation, are two distinct things, properly relating to two distinct attributes, arising from two distinct causes.

First. They are two distinct things: reprobation, a simple leaving of the creature out of the bounds of God's election; but to appoint to condemnation is to bind them over to everlasting punishment. Now there is a great difference between my refusing to make of such a tree a pillar in my house, and of condemning it unto the fire to be burned.

Second. As to the attributes; reprobation respects God's sovereignty; but to appoint to condemnation, his justice. (Rom. ix. 18. Gen. xviii. 25.)

Third. As to the causes; sovereignty being according to the will of God, but justice according to the sin of man. For God, though he be the only sovereign Lord, and that to the height of perfection; yet he appointeth no man to the pains of everlasting fire, merely from sovereignty, but by the rule of justice: God damneth not the man because he is a man, but a sinner; and fore-appoints him to that place and state, by foreseeing of him wicked. (Rom. i. 18, 19. Col. iii. 6.)

Again, as reprobation is not the same with fore-appointing to eternal condemnation, so neither is it the cause thereof.

If it be the cause, then it must either, 1. Leave him infirm. Or, 2. Infuse sin into him. Or, 3. Take from him something that otherwise would keep him upright. 4. Or both license Satan to tempt, and the reprobate to close in with the temptation. But it doth none of these; therefore it is not the cause of the condemnation of the creature.

That it is not the cause of sin, it is evident,

1. Because the elect are as much involved therein as those that are passed by.

2. It leaveth him not infirm; for he is by an after-act, to wit, of creation, formed perfectly upright.

3. That reprobation infuseth no sin, appeareth, because it is the act of God.

4. That it taketh nothing, that good is, from him, is also manifest, it being only a leaving of him.

5. And that it is not by this act that Satan is permitted to tempt, or the reprobate to sin, is manifest; because as Christ was tempted, so the elect fall as much into the temptation, at least many of them, as many of those that are reprobate: whereas if these things came by reprobation, then the reprobate would be only concerned therein. All which will be further handled in these questions yet behind.

Obj. From what hath been said, there is concluded this at least, that God hath infallibly determined, and that before the world, the infallible damnation of some of his creatures: for if God hath before the world bound some over to eternal punishment, and that as you say, for sin; then this determination must either be fallible or infallible; not fallible, for then your other position of the certainty of the number of God's elect is shaken; unless you hold that there may be a number that shall neither go to heaven nor hell. Well then, if God hath indeed determined, fore-determined, that some must infallibly perish, doth not this his determination lay a necessity on the reprobate to sin, that he may be damned? for, no sin, no damnation: that is your own argument.

Ans. That God hath ordained (Jude 4) the damnation of some of his creatures, it is evident; but whether this his determination be positive and absolute, there is the question: for the better understanding whereof, I shall open unto you the variety of God's determinations, and their nature, as also rise.

The determinations of God touching the destruction of the creature, they are either ordinary or extraordinary: those I count ordinary that were commonly pronounced by the prophets and apostles, &c., in their ordinary way of preaching, to the end men might be affected with the love of their own salvation: now these either bound or loosed, but as the condition or qualification was answered by the creature under sentence, and no otherwise. (1 Sam. xii. 25. Isa. i. 20. Matt. xviii. 3. Luke xiii. 1—3. Rom. ii. 8, 9; viii. 13; xi. 23. 1 Cor. vi. 9—11.)

Again, these extraordinary, though they respect the same conditions, yet they are not grounded immediately upon them, but upon the infallible fore-knowledge and fore-sight of God, and are thus distinguished. First, the ordinary determination, it stands but at best upon a supposition that the creature may continue in sin, and admits of a possibility that it may not; but the extraordinary stands upon an infallible fore-sight that the creature will continue in sin; wherefore this must needs be positive, and as infallible as God himself.

Again, these two determinations are also distinguished thus: the ordinary is applicable to the elect as well as to the reprobate, but the other to the reprobate only. It is proper to say even to the elect themselves, "He that believeth shall be saved, and he that believeth not shall be damned;" but not to say to them, These are appointed to *utter* destruction, or that they shall utterly perish in their own corruptions; or that for them is reserved the blackness of darkness for ever. (1 Kings xx. 42. 2 Pet. ii. 12. Jude 13.)

So, then, though God, by these determinations, doth not lay some under irrecoverable condemnation, yet by one of them he doth; as is further made out thus:—

1. God most perfectly foreseeth the final impenitency of those that so die, from the beginning to the end of the world. (Prov. xv. 11. Ps. cxxxix. 2. Isa. xlvi. 10.)

2. Now from this infallible foresight, it is most easy and rational to conclude, and that positively, the infallible overthrow of every such creature. Did I infallibly foresee that this or that man would cut out his heart in the morning, I might infallibly determine his death before night.

Object. But still the question is, Whether God by this his determination doth not lay a necessity on the creature to sin? for, no sin, no condemnation: this is true by your own assertion.

Ans. No, by no means: for,

1. Though it be true, that sin must of absolute necessity go before the infallible condemnation and overthrow of the sinner; and that it must also be pre-considered by God; yet it needs not lay a necessity upon him to sin: for let him but alone to do what he will, and the determination cannot be more infallible than the sin, which is the cause of its execution.

2. As it needs not, so it doth not: for this positive determination is not grounded upon what God will effect, but on what the creature will; and that not through the instigation of God, but the instigation of the devil. What, might not I, if I most undoubtedly foresaw that such a tree in my garden would only cumber the ground, notwithstanding reasonable means, might not I, I say, from hence determine, seven years before, to cut it down, and burn it in the fire, but I must, by so determining, necessitate this tree to be fruitless? the case in hand is the very same. God, therefore, may most positively determine the infallible damnation of his creature, and yet not at all necessitate the creature to sin, that he might be damned.

Object. But how is this similitude pertinent? For God did not only foresee sin would be the destruction of the creature, but let it come into the world, and so destroy the creature. If you, as you foresee the fruitlessness of your tree, should withal see that which makes it so, and that too before it makes it so, and yet let the impediment come and make it so; are not you now the cause of the unfruitfulness of that tree which you have before condemned to the fire to be burned? for God might have chose whether he would have let Adam sin, and so sin to have got into the world by him.

Ans. Similitudes never answer every way; if they be pertinent to that for which they are intended, it is enough; and to that it answereth well, being brought to prove no more but the natural consequence of a true and infallible foresight. And now as to what is objected further, as that God might have chose whether sin should have come into the world by Adam, to the destruction of so many: to that I shall answer,

1. That sin could not have come into the world without God's permission, it is evident, both from the perfection of his foresight and power.

2. Therefore all the means, motives, and inducements thereunto, must also by him be not only foreseen, but permitted.

3. Yet so, that God will have the timing, proceeding, bounding, and ordering thereof, at his dispose: "Surely the wrath of man shall praise thee, and the remainder of wrath shalt thou restrain." (1 Kings xxii. 20—22. John viii. 20. Luke xxii. 51, 52. Ps. lxxvi. 10.)

4. Therefore it must needs come into the world, not without, but by the knowledge of God; not in despite of him, but by his suffering of it.

Object. But how then is he clear from having a hand in the death of him that perisheth?

Ans. Nothing is more sure than that God could have kept sin out of the world, if it had been his will; and this is also as true, that it never came into the world with his liking and compliance; and for this, you must consider that sin came into the world by two steps:

1. By being offered. 2. By prevailing.

Touching the first of these, God without the least injury to any creature in heaven or earth, might not only suffer it, but so far countenance the same: that is, so far forth as for trial only; as it is said of Abraham; God tempted Abraham to slay his only son, (Gen. xxii. 1, 2,) and led Christ by the Spirit into the wilderness to be tempted of the devil. (Mark i. 12. Luke iv. 1.) This is done without any harm at all; nay, it rather produceth good; for it tends to discover sincerity, to exercise faith in, and love to his Creator; also to put him in mind of the continual need he hath of depending on his God for the continuation of help and strength, and to provoke to prayers to God, whenever so engaged. (Deut. viii. 1—3. 1 Pet. i. 7. Heb. v. 7. Matt. xxvi. 22, 41.)

Object. But God did not only admit that sin should be offered for trial, and there to stay; but did suffer it to prevail, and overcome the world.

Ans. Well, this is granted; but yet consider,

1. God did neither suffer it, nor yet consent it should, but under this consideration; if Adam, upright Adam, gave way thereto, by forsaking his command, "in the day thou eatest thereof thou shalt surely die." (Gen. ii. 17; iii. 3.) Which Adam did, not because God did compel him or persuade him to it, but voluntarily of his own mind, contrary to his God's command: so then God by suffering sin to break into the world, did it rather in judgment, as disliking Adam's act, and as a punishment to man for listening to the tempter; and as a discovery of his anger at man's disobedience; than to prove that he is guilty of the misery of his creature.

2. Consider also, that when God permitted sin for trial, it was, when offered first, to them only who were upright, and had sufficient strength to resist it.

3. They were by God's command to the contrary, driven to no strait to tempt them to incline to Satan: "Of every tree of the garden thou mayest freely eat," saith God; only let this alone.

4. As touching the beauty and goodness that was in the object unto which they were allured;

What was it? Was it better than God? Yea, was it better than the tree of life? For from that they were not exempted till after they had sinned. Did not God know best what was best to do them good?

5. Touching him that persuaded them to do this wicked act; was his word more to be valued for truth, more to be ventured on for safety, or more to be honoured for the worthiness of him that spake, than was his that had forbad it? The one being the devil, with a lie, and to kill them; the other being God, with his truth, and to preserve them safe.

Quest. But was not Adam unexpectedly surprised? Had he notice beforehand, and warning of the danger? For God foresaw the business.

Ans. Doubtless God was fair and faithful to his creature in this thing also; as clearly doth appear from these considerations:

1. The very commandment that God gave him, fore-bespake him well to look about him; and did indeed insinuate that he was likely to be tempted.

2. It is yet more evident, because God doth even tell him of the danger; "In the day thou eatest thereof, thou shalt surely die."

3. Nay God by speaking to him of the very tree that was to be forborn, telling him also where it stood, that he might the better know it; did in effect expressly say unto him, "Adam, if thou be tempted, it will be about that tree, and the fruit thereof: wherefore if thou findest the tempter there, then beware thy life."

To conclude then: though sin did not come into the world without God's sufferance, yet it did without his liking: God suffered also Cain to kill his brother, and Ishmael to mock at Isaac, but he did not like the same. (Gen. iv. 9—11. Gal. iv. 30.)

Secondly. Therefore though God was first in concluding sin should be offered to the world; yet man was the first that consented to a being overcome thereby.

Thirdly then. Though God did fore-determine that sin should enter, yet it was not but with respect to certain terms and conditions, which yet was not to be enforced by virtue of the determination, but permitted to be completed by the voluntary inclination of a perfect and upright man. And in that the determination was most perfectly infallible, it was through the foresight of the undoubted inclination of this good and upright person.

Quest. But might not God have kept Adam from inclining, if he would?

Ans. What more certain? but yet consider,

1. Adam being now an upright man, he was able to have kept himself, had he but looked to it as he should and might.

2. This being so, if God had here stepped in, he had either added that which had been needless, and so had not obtained thankfulness; or else had made the strength of Adam useless, yea his own workmanship in so creating him, superfluous; or else by consequence imperfect.

3. If he had done so, he had taken Adam from his duty, which was to trust and believe his Maker; he had also made void the end of the commandment, which was to persuade to watchfulness, diligence, sobriety, and contentedness; yea, and by so doing would not only himself have tempted Adam to transgression, even to lay aside the exercise of that strength that God had already given him; but should have become the pattern, or the first father to all looseness, idleness, and neglect of duty. Which would also not only have been an ill example to Adam to continue to neglect so reasonable and wholesome duties, but would have been to himself an argument of defence to retort upon his God, when he had come at another time to reckon with him for his misdemeanors.

Many other weighty reasons might here be further added for God's vindication in this particular, but at this time let these suffice.

CHAPTER VII.

Whether any under Eternal Reprobation have just cause to quarrel with God for not electing of them?

That the answer to this question may be to edification, recall again what I have before asserted; to wit, that for a man to be left out of God's election, and to be made a sinner, is two things; and again, for a man to be not elect, and to be condemned to hell-fire, is two things also. Now I say, if non-election makes no man a sinner, and if it appoints no man to condemnation neither, then what ground hath any reprobate to quarrel with God for not electing of him? nay, further, reprobation considereth him upright, leaveth him upright, and so turneth him into the world; what wrong doth God do him, though he hath not elected him? what reason hath he that is left in this case to quarrel against his Maker?

If thou say, because God hath not chosen them, as well as chosen others: I answer, "Nay but, O man, who art thou that repliest against God? shall the thing formed, say to him that formed it, why hast thou made me thus?" (Rom. ix. 20.) "Behold, as the clay is in the potter's hand, so are ye in mine hand, O house of Israel," saith the Lord God. (Jer. xviii. 6.) So then, if I should say no more but that God is the only Lord and Creator, and that by his sovereignty he hath power to dispose of them according to his pleasure, either to choose or to refuse, according to the counsel of his own will, who could object against him and be guiltless? "He giveth not account of any of his matters." (Job xxxiii. 13.) "And what his soul desireth, that doth he." (Job xxiii. 13.)

Again, God is wiser than man, and therefore can show a reason for what he acts and does, both when and where at present thou seest none. Shall God, the only wise, be arraigned at the bar of thy blind reason, and there be judged and condemned for his acts done in eternity? Who hath directed the Spirit of the Lord, "or who hath been his counsellor?" (Rom. xi. 34.) Do you not know that he is far more above us, than we are above our horse or mule that is without understanding? "Great things doth he, that we cannot comprehend?" (Job xxxvii. 5.) "Great things and unsearchable, and marvellous things without number." (Job v. 9.)

But, I say, should we take it well if our beast should call us to account for this and the other righteous act, and judge us unrighteous, and our acts ridiculous, and all because it sees no reason for our so doing? Why, we are as beasts before God. (Ps. lxxiii. 22.)

But again, to come yet more close to the point: the reprobate quarrels with God, because he hath not elected him; well, but is not God the master of his own love? And is not his will the only rule of his mercy? And may he not, without he give offence to thee, lay hold by electing love and mercy on whom himself pleaseth? Must thy reason, nay, thy lust, be the ruler, orderer, and disposer of his grace? "Is it not lawful for me to do what I will with mine own?" saith he; "Is thine eye evil, because mine is good?" (Matt. xx. 15.)

Further, What harm doth God to any reprobate, by not electing of him; he was, as hath been said, considered upright, so formed in the act of creation, and so turned into the world: indeed he was not elected, but hath that taken anything from him? No, verily, but leaveth him in good condition: there is good, and better, and best of all; he that is in a good estate, though others through free grace are in a far better, hath not any cause to murmur either with him that gave him such a place, or at him that is placed above him. In a word, reprobation maketh no man personally a sinner, neither doth election make any man personally righteous. It is the consenting to sin that makes a man a sinner; and the imputation of grace and righteousness that makes gospelly and personally just and holy.

But again, seeing it is God's act to leave some out of the bounds of his election, it must needs be, therefore, positively good: is that then which is good in itself made sin unto thee? God forbid: God doth not evil by leaving this or that man out of his electing grace, though he choose others to eternal life, through Jesus Christ our Lord. Wherefore there is not a reprobate that hath any cause, and therefore no just cause, to quarrel with his Maker for not electing of him.

And that, besides what hath been spoken, if you consider,

1. For God to elect, is an act of sovereign grace; but to pass by, or to refuse so to do, is an act of sovereign power, not of injustice.

2. God might therefore have chosen whether he would have elected any, or so many or few; and also which and where he would.

3. Seeing then that all things are at his dispose, he may fasten electing mercy where he pleaseth; and other mercy, if he will, to whom and when he will.

4. Seeing also that the least of mercies are not deserved by the best of sinners; men, instead of quarrelling against the God of grace, because they have not what they list, should acknowledge they are unworthy of their breath; and also should confess that God may give mercy where he pleaseth, and that too, both which or what, as also to whom and when he will; and yet be good, and just, and very gracious still. Nay, Job saith, "He taketh away, who can hinder him?" or "Who will say unto him, What doest thou?" (Job ix. 12.)

The will of God is the rule of all righteousness, neither knoweth he any other way by which he governeth and ordereth any of his actions. Whatsoever God doth, it is good because he doth it: whether it be to give grace, or to detain it; whether in choosing or refusing. The consideration of this, made the holy men of old ascribe righteousness to their Maker, even then when yet they could not see the reason of his actions. They would rather stand amazed, and wonder at the heights and depths of his unsearchable judgments, than quarrel at the strange and most obscure of them. (Job xxxiv. 10—12; xxxvi. 3. Jer. xii. 1. Job xxxvii. 23. Rom. xi. 33.)

God did not intend that all that ever he would do should be known to every man, no nor yet to the wise and prudent. It is as much a duty sometimes to stay ourselves and wonder, and to confess our ignorance in many things of God, as it is to do other things that are duty without dispute. So then, let poor dust and ashes forbear to condemn the Lord, because he goeth beyond them; and also they should beware they speak not wickedly for him, though it be, as they think, to justify his actions. "The Lord is righteous in all his ways, and holy in all his works." (Matt. xi. 25. 1 Cor. ii. 8. Job xiii. 6—8. Ps. cxlv. 17.)

CHAPTER VIII.

Whether Eternal Reprobation in itself, or in its doctrine, be in very deed an hindrance to any man in seeking the salvation of his soul.

In my discourse upon this question, I must entreat the reader to mind well what is promised in the beginning of the former chapter, which is, that reprobation makes no man a sinner, appoints no man to condemnation, but leaveth him upright after all. So then, though God doth leave the most of men without the bounds of his election, his so doing is neither in itself, nor yet its doctrine, in very deed, an hindrance to any man in seeking the salvation of his soul.

First. It hindereth not in itself, as is clear by the ensuing considerations:—

1. That which hindereth him is the weakness

that came upon him by reason of sin. Now God only made the man, but man's listening to Satan made him a sinner, which is the cause of all his weakness: this therefore is it that hindereth him, and that also disenableth him in seeking the salvation of his soul. "Let no man say when he is tempted, I am tempted of God; for God cannot be tempted of evil, neither tempteth he any man." (James i. 13. Eccles. vii. 29. Hos. xiii. 9; xiv. 1. Gen. iii. 8—11.) "God made man upright, but he hath sought out many inventions." (Ezek. xvi. 30.)

2. It hindereth not in itself, for it taketh not anything from a man that would help him, might it continue with him; it takes not away the least part of his strength, wisdom, courage, innocency, or will to good; all these were lost by the fall, in that day when he died the death. Nay, reprobation under some consideration did rather establish all these upon the reprobate; for as it decrees him left, so left upright. Wherefore man's hindrance cometh on him from other means, even by the fall, and not by the simple act of eternal reprobation. (Gen. iii.)

3. As reprobation hindereth not either of these two ways, so neither is it from this simple act that Satan is permitted either to tempt them, that they might be tried, or that they might be overthrown.

(1.) It is not by this act that Satan is permitted to tempt them that they might be tried, because then the Son of God himself must be reached by this reprobation, he being tempted by the devil as much, if not more than any. Yea, and then must every one of the elect be under eternal reprobation; for they also, and that after their conversion, are greatly assaulted by him. "Many are the troubles of the righteous," &c. (Matt. iv. 1, 2. Mark i. 12. Heb. ii. 17; iv. 15.)

(2.) Neither is it from the act of reprobation that sin hath entered the world, no more than from election, because those under the power of election did not only fall at first, but do still generally as foully, before conversion, as the reprobate himself. Whereas, if either the temptation, or the fall, were by virtue of reprobation, then the reprobates, and they only, should have been tempted, and have fallen. The temptation then, and the fall, doth come from other means, and so the hindrance of the reprobate, than from eternal reprobation. For the temptation, the fall and hindrance being universal, but the act of reprobation particular, the hindrance must needs come from such a cause as taketh hold on all men, which indeed is the fall; the cause of which was neither election nor reprobation, but man's voluntary listening to the tempter. (Rom. iii. 9.)

(3.) It is yet far more evident that reprobation hindereth no man from seeking the salvation of his soul: because notwithstanding all that reprobation doth, yet God giveth to divers of the reprobates great encouragements thereto; to wit, the tenders of the gospel in general, not excluding any; great light also to understand it, with many a sweet taste of the good Word of God, and the powers of the world to come; he maketh them sometimes also to be partakers of the Holy Ghost, and admitteth many of them into fellowship with his elect; yea, some of them to be rulers, teachers, and governors in his house; all which, without doubt, both are and ought to be great encouragements even to the reprobates themselves, to seek the salvation of their souls. (Matt. xi. 28. Rev. xxii. 17. Heb. vi. 4, 5. Matt. xxv. 1, 2. Acts i. 16, 17.)

Second. As it hindereth not in itself, so it hindereth not by its doctrine: for, all that this doctrine saith, is, that some are left out of God's election, as considered upright. Now this doctrine cannot hinder any man: for,

1. No man still stands upright.

2. Though it saith some are left, yet it points at no man, it nameth no man, it binds all faces in secret: so, then, if it hinder, it hindereth all, even the elect as well as reprobate; for the reprobate hath as much ground to judge himself elect, as the very elect himself hath, before he be converted, being both alike in a state of nature and unbelief, and both alike visibly liable to the curse, for the breach of the commandment. Again, as they are equals here, so also have they ground alike to close in with Christ and live; even the open, free, and full invitation of the gospel, and promise of life and salvation, by the faith of Jesus Christ. (Eph. ii. 1, 2. Rom. iii. 9. John iii. 16. 2 Cor. v. 19—21. Rev. xxi. 6; xxii. 17.)

3. It is evident also by experience, that this doctrine doth not, indeed, neither can it, hinder any (this doctrine, I mean, when both rightly stated and rightly used), because many who have been greatly afflicted about this matter have yet at last had comfort; which comfort, when they have received it, hath been to them as an argument that the thing they feared before was not because of reprobation rightly stated, but its doctrine much abused was the cause of their affliction: and had they had the same light at first they received afterwards, their troubles then would soon have fled, as also now they do. Wherefore discouragement comes from want of light, because they are not skilful in the word of righteousness: for had the discouragement at first been true, which yet it could not be, unless the person knew by name himself under eternal reprobation, which is indeed impossible, then his light would have pinched him harder; light would rather have fastened this his fear than at all have rid him of it. (Heb. v. 12—14.)

Indeed the Scripture saith, the Word is to some the savour of death unto death, when to others the savour of life unto life. But mark, it is not this doctrine in particular, if so much as some other, that doth destroy the reprobate. It was respite at which Pharaoh hardened his heart, and the grace of God that the reprobates of old did turn into lasciviousness. Yea, Christ the Saviour of the world is a stumblingblock unto some, and a rock of offence unto others. But yet again, consider that neither he, nor any of God's doctrines, are so simply, and in their own true natural force and drift; for they beget no unbelief, they provoke to no wantonness, neither do they in the least encourage to impenitency: all this comes from that ignorance and wickedness that came by the fall: wherefore it is by reason of that also, that they stumble, and fall, and grow weak, and are discouraged, and split themselves, either at the doctrine of reprobation, or at any other truth of God. (Exod. viii. 15. Jude 4. 1 Pet. ii. 8.)

Lastly. To conclude as I began, there is no man while in this world, that doth certainly know that he is left out of the electing love of the great God; neither hath he any word in the whole Bible, to persuade him so to conclude and believe; for the Scriptures hold forth salvation to the greatest of sinners: wherefore, though the act of reprobation were far more harsh, and its doctrine also more sharp and severe, yet it cannot properly be said to hinder any. It is a foolish thing, in any to be troubled, with those things which they have no ground to believe concerns themselves; especially when the latitude of their discouragement is touching their own persons only. "The secret things belong unto the Lord our God." (Deut. xxix. 29.) Indeed, every one of the words of God ought to put us upon examination, and into a serious inquiry of our present state and condition, and how we now do stand for eternity; to wit, whether we are ready to meet the Lord, or how it is with us: yet, when search is fully made, and the worst come unto the worst, the party can find himself no more than the chief of sinners, not excluded from the grace of God tendered in the gospel; not from an invitation, nay, a promise, to be embraced and blessed, if he comes to Jesus Christ. Wherefore he hath no ground to be discouraged by the doctrine of reprobation. (1 Tim. i. 15. Acts iii. 19. 2 Chron. xxxiii. John vi. 37; vii. 37: Mark ii. 17.)

CHAPTER IX.

Whether God would, indeed and in truth, that the gospel, with the grace thereof, should be tendered to those that yet he hath bound up under Eternal Reprobation?

To this question I shall answer,

First. In the language of our Lord, "Go preach the gospel unto every creature." (Mark xvi. 15.) And again, "Look unto me, all ye ends of the earth, and be ye saved." (Isa. xlv. 22.) "And whosoever will, let him take the water of life freely." (Rev. xxii. 17.) And the reason is, because Christ died for all, "tasted death for every man," (Heb. ii. 9. 2 Cor. v. 15,) is "the Saviour of the world," (1 John ii. 1—3; iv. 14,) and the propitiation for the sins of the whole world.

Second. I gather it from those several censures that even every one goeth under, that doth not receive Christ, when offered in the general tenders of the gospel; "He that believeth not shall be damned." (Mark xvi. 16.) "He that believeth not God hath made him a liar, makes God a liar, because he believeth not the record that God gave of his Son," (1 John v. 10;) and, Woe unto thee, Capernaum! "Woe unto thee, Corazin! woe unto thee, Bethsaida!" (Matt. xi. 21,) with many other sayings, all which words, with many other of the same nature, carry in them a very great argument to this very purpose; for if those that perish in the days of the gospel, shall have at least their damnation heightened, because they have neglected and refused to receive the gospel, it must needs be that the gospel was with all faithfulness to be tendered unto them; the which it could not be, unless the death of Christ did extend itself unto them, (John iii. 16. Heb. ii. 3;) for the offer of the gospel cannot, with God's allowance, be offered any further than the death of Jesus Christ doth go; because if that be taken away, there is indeed no gospel, nor grace to be extended. Besides, if by every creature, and the like, should be meant only the elect, then are all the persuasions of the gospel to no effect at all; for still the unconverted, who are here condemned for refusing of it, they return it as fast again: I do not know I am elect, and therefore dare not come to Jesus Christ; for if the death of Jesus Christ, and so the general tender of the gospel, concern the elect alone, I, not knowing myself to be one of that number, am at a mighty plunge; nor know I whether is the greater sin, to believe, or to despair; for I say again, if Christ died only for the elect, &c., then I, not knowing myself to be one of that number, dare not believe the gospel, that holds forth his blood to save me; nay, I think with safety may not, until I first do know I am elect of God, and appointed thereunto.

Third. God the Father, and Jesus Christ his Son, would have all men whatever, invited by the gospel to lay hold of life by Christ, whether elect or reprobate; for though it be true, that there is such a thing as election and reprobation, yet God, by the tenders of the gospel in the ministry of his Word, looks upon men under another consideration, to wit, as sinners; and as sinners invites them to believe, lay hold of, and embrace the same. He saith not to his ministers, "Go preach to the elect, because they are elect; and shut out others, because they are not so:" but, "Go preach the gospel to sinners as sinners; and as they are such, go bid them come to me and live." And it must needs be so, otherwise the preacher could neither speak in faith, nor the people hear in faith. First, the preacher could not speak in faith, because he knoweth not the elect from the reprobate; nor they again hear in faith, because, as unconverted, they would be always ignorant of that also. So then, the minister neither knowing whom he should offer life unto, nor yet the people which of them are to receive it, how could the Word now be preached in faith with power? And how could the people believe and embrace it? But now the preacher offering mercy in the gospel to sinners, as they are sinners, here is way made for the Word to be spoke in faith, because his hearers are sinners; yea, and encouragement also for the people to receive and close therewith, they understanding they are sinners: "Christ Jesus came into the world to save sinners." (Luke xxiv. 46, 47.)

Fourth. The gospel must be preached to sinners as they are sinners, without distinction of elect or reprobate; because neither the one nor yet the other, as considered under these simple acts, are fit subjects to embrace the gospel: for neither the one act, nor yet the other, doth make either of them sinners; but the gospel is to be tendered to men as they are sinners, and personally under the curse of God for sin; wherefore, to proffer grace to the elect because they are elect, it is to proffer grace and mercy to them, as not considering them as sinners. And, I say, to deny it to the reprobate, because he is not elected, it is not only a denial of grace to them that have no need thereof, but also before occasion is given on their part, for such a dispensation. And I say again, therefore, to offer Christ and grace to man elect, as simply so considered, this administers to him no comfort at all, he being here no sinner; and so engageth not the heart at all to Jesus Christ; for that comes in, and is effected on them as they are sinners. Yea, to deny the gospel also to the reprobate, because he is not elect, it will not trouble him at all; for, saith he, "So I am not a sinner, and so do not need a Saviour." But now, because the elect have no need of grace in Christ by the gospel, but as they are sinners; nor the reprobates cause to refuse it as they are sinners; therefore Christ by the word of the gospel is to be proffered to both, without considering elect or reprobate, even as they are sinners. "The whole have no need of the physician, but those that are sick. I came not to call the righteous, but sinners to repentance." (Mark ii. 17. 2 Cor. v. 14, 15. Luke vii. 46, 47.)

Thus you see the gospel is to be tendered to all in general, as well to the reprobate as to the elect, to sinners as sinners; and so are they to receive it, and to close with the tenders thereof.

CHAPTER X.

Seeing then that the grace of God in the gospel, is by that to be proffered to sinners, as sinners; as well to the reprobate as the elect; is it possible for those who indeed are not elect, to receive it, and be saved?

To this question I shall answer several things: but first I shall show you what that grace is, that is tendered in the gospel; and secondly, what it is to receive it and be saved.

First, then, The grace that is offered to sinners as sinners, without respect to this or that person, it is a sufficiency of righteousness, pardoning grace, and life, laid up in the person of Christ, held forth in the exhortation and word of the gospel, and promised to be theirs that receive it; yea, I say, in so universal a tender, that not one is by it excluded or checked in the least, but rather encouraged, if he hath the least desire to life; yea, it is held forth to beget both desires and longings after the life thus laid up in Christ, and held forth by the gospel. (John i. 16. Col. i. 19, 23. 1 John v. 11, 12. Acts xiii. 38, 39. Rom. x. 12—14; xvi. 25, 26.)

Second. To receive this grace thus tendered by the gospel, it is,

1. To believe it is true.

2. To receive it heartily and unfeignedly through faith. And,

3. To let it have its natural sway, course, and authority in the soul, and that in that measure, as to bring forth the fruits of good living in heart, word, and life, both before God and man.

Now, then, to the question:

Is it possible that this tender, thus offered to the reprobate, should by him be thus received and embraced, and he live thereby?

To which I answer in the negative. Nor yet for the elect themselves, I mean as considered dead in trespasses and sin, which is the state of all men, elect as well as reprobate. So, then, though there be a sufficiency of life and righteousness laid up in Christ for all men, and this tendered by the gospel to them without exception, yet sin coming in between the soul and the tender of this grace, it hath in truth disabled all men, and so, notwithstanding this tender, they continue to be dead. For the gospel, I say, coming in word only, saveth no man, because of man's impediment; wherefore those that indeed are saved by this gospel, the Word comes not to them in word only, but also in power, and in the Holy Ghost is mixed with faith, even with the faith of the operation of God, by whose exceeding great and mighty power they are raised from this death of sin, and enabled to embrace the gospel. Doubtless, all men being dead in trespasses and sins, and so captivated under the power of the devil, the curse of the law, and shut up in unbelief, it must be the power of God, yea, the exceeding greatness of that power, that raiseth the soul from this condition, to receive the holy gospel. (Eph. ii. 1—3. 1 Thess. i. 5, 6. Col. ii. 12. Heb. iv. 1, 2. Eph. i. 18, 19, &c.)

For man by nature (consider him at best) can see no more, nor do no more, than what the principles of nature understands and helps to do; which nature being below the discerning of things truly, spiritually, and savingly good, it must needs fall short of receiving, loving, and delighting in them. "The natural man receiveth not the things of the Spirit of God, for they are foolishness unto him; neither can he know them, because they are spiritually discerned." (1 Cor. ii. 14.) Now, I say, if the natural man at best (for the elect before conversion are no more, if quite so much) cannot do this, how shall they attain thereto, being now not only corrupted and infected, but depraved, bewitched, and dead; swallowed up of unbelief, ignorance, confusion, hardness of heart, hatred of God, and the like? When a thorn by nature beareth grapes, and a thistle beareth figs, then may this thing be. (Matt. vii. 16—18.) To lay hold of and receive the gospel by a true and saving faith, it is an act of the soul as made a new creature, which is the workmanship of God: "Now he that hath wrought us for the selfsame thing is God." (2 Cor. v. 5.) "For a corrupt tree cannot bring forth good fruit." (Luke vi. 43—45.) "Can the Ethiopian change his skin?" (Jer. xiii. 23.)

But yet the cause of this impossibility—

1. Lieth not in reprobation, the elect themselves being as much unable to receive it as the other.

2. Neither is it because the reprobate is excluded in the tender, for that is universal.

3. Neither is it because there wanteth arguments in the tenders of the gospel, for there is not only plenty, but such as be persuasive, clear, and full of rationality.

4. Neither is it because these creatures have no need thereof, for they have broke the law.

5. Wherefore it is, because indeed they are by sin dead, captivated, mad, self-opposers, blind, alienated in their minds, and haters of the Lord. Behold the ruins that sin hath made!

Wherefore, whoever receiveth the grace that is tendered in the gospel, they must be quickened by the power of God, their eyes must be opened, their understandings illuminated, their ears unstopped, their hearts circumcised, their wills also rectified, and the Son of God revealed in them. Yet, as I said, not because there wanteth argument in these tenders, but because men are dead, and blind, and cannot hear the Word. "Why do you not understand my speech?" saith Christ: "even because you cannot hear my word." (John viii. 43. Acts ix. 15; xxvi. 9, 10. Ps. cx. 3. Gal. i. 15. Matt. xi. 27.)

For otherwise, as I said but now, there is, 1. Rationality enough in the tenders of the gospel. 2. Persuasions of weight enough to provoke to faith. And, 3. Arguments enough to persuade to continue therein.

First. Is it not reasonable that man should believe God in the proffer of the gospel, and life by it?

Second. Is there not reason, I say, both from the truth and faithfulness of God, from the sufficiency of the merits of Christ, as also from the freeness and fulness of the promise? What unreasonable thing doth the gospel bid thee credit? Or what falsehood doth it command thee to receive for truth? Indeed, in many points, the gospel is above reason, but yet in never a one against it; especially in those things wherein it beginneth with the sinner, in order to eternal life.

Again. Touching its persuasions to provoke to faith:

First. With how many signs and wonders, miracles, and mighty deeds hath it been once and again confirmed, and that to this very end? (Heb. i. 1—3. 1 Cor. xiv. 22.)

Second. With how many oaths, declarations, attestations, and proclamations is it avouched, confirmed, and established? (Heb. vi. 18. Acts xiii. 32. Jer. iii. 12. Gal. iii. 15.)

Third. And why should not credence be given to that gospel that is confirmed by blood, the blood of the Son of God himself? yea, that gospel that did never yet fail any that in truth have cast themselves upon it, since the foundation of the world. (Heb. ix. 16—18; xii. 1—3.)

Again. As there is rationality enough, and persuasions sufficient, so there is also argument most prevalent to persuade to continue therein, and that too heartily, cheerfully, and unfeignedly, unto the end: did not, as I have said, blindness, madness, deadness, and wilful rebellion, carry them away in the vanity of their minds, and overcome them. (Eph. iv. 17—19.)

1. For, first, if they could but consider how they have sinned, how they have provoked God, &c., if they could but consider what a dismal state the state of the damned is, and also, that in a moment their condition is like to be the same, would they not cleave to the gospel and live?

2. The enjoyment of God, and Christ, and saints, and angels, being the sweetest, the pleasures of heaven the most comfortable, and to live always in the greatest height of light, life, joy, and gladness imaginable, one would think were enough to persuade the very damned now in hell.

There is no man, then, perisheth for want of sufficient reason in the tenders of the gospel, nor any for want of persuasions to faith; nor yet because there wanteth arguments to provoke to continue therein. But the truth is, the gospel in this hath to do with unreasonable creatures; with such as will not believe it, and that because it is truth. "And because I tell you the truth," saith Christ, "(therefore) ye believe me not." (John viii. 45.)

Quest. Well, but if this in truth be thus, how then comes it to pass that some receive it and live for ever? For you have said before, that the elect are as dead as the reprobate, and full as unable as they, as men, to close with these tenders, and live.

Ans. Doubtless, this is true, and were the elect left to themselves, they, through the wickedness of their hearts, would perish as do others. Neither could all the reasonable, persuasive, prevalent arguments of the gospel of God in Christ prevail to make any receive it, and live. Wherefore here you must consider, that as there is mercy proclaimed in the general tenders of the gospel, so there is also the grace of election; which grace kindly overruleth and winneth the spirit of the chosen, working in them that unfeigned closing therewith, that makes it effectual to their undoubted salvation; which indeed is the cause that not only in other ages, but also to this day, there is a remnant that receive this grace; they being appointed, I say, thereto, before the world began; preserved in time from that which would undo them, and enabled to embrace the glorious gospel of grace, and peace, and life. (1 Kings xix. 18. Rom. xi. 5. 1 Thess. v. 9.)

Now there is a great difference between the grace of election, and of the grace that is wrapped up in the general tenders of the gospel; a difference, I say, and that both as to its timing, latituding, and working.

1. Touching its timing; it is before, yea, long before, there was either tender of the grace wrapped up in the gospel to any, or any need of such a tender. (Eph. i. 4, 5.)

2. They also differ in latitude; the tenders of grace in the gospel are common and universal to all, but the extension of that of election special and peculiar to some. "There is a remnant according to the election of grace." (Rom. xi. 5.)

3. Touching the working of the grace of election; it differs much in some things from the working of the grace that is offered in the general tenders of the gospel. As is manifest in these particulars :—

(1.) The grace that is offered in the general tenders of the gospel calleth for faith to lay hold upon and accept thereof, but the special grace of election worketh that faith which doth lay hold thereof. (Acts xiii. 48: xvi. 31. Phil. i. 29. 2 Thess. i. 11.)

(2.) The grace that is offered in the general tenders of the gospel calleth for faith as a condition in us without which there is no life; but the special grace of election worketh faith in us without any such condition. (Mark xvi. 15, 16. Rom. xi. 5, 6.)

(3.) The grace that is offered in the general tenders of the gospel promiseth happiness upon the condition of persevering in the faith only, but the special grace of election causeth this perseverance. (Col. i. 23. Eph. ii. 10. Rom. xi. 7. 1 Pet. i. 5—7.)

(4.) The grace offered in the general tenders of the gospel, when it sparkleth most, leaveth the greatest part of men behind it; but the special grace of election, when it shineth least, doth infallibly bring every soul therein concerned to everlasting life. (Rom. x. 16; viii. 33—35.)

(5.) A man may overcome and put out all the light and life that is begotten in him by the general tenders of the gospel; but none shall overcome, or make void, or frustrate the grace of election. (Jude 4. 2 Pet. ii. 20—22. Matt. xxiv. 24. Rom. xi. 1—3, &c.)

(6.) The general tenders of the gospel, considered without a concurrence of the grace of election, helps not the elect himself, when sadly fallen. Wherefore, when I say the grace that is offered in the general tenders of the gospel, I mean that grace when offered, as not being accompanied with a special operation of God's eternal love, by way of conjunction therewith. Otherwise the grace that is tendered in the general offers of the gospel, is that which saveth the sinner now, and that brings him to everlasting life; that is, when conjoined with that grace that blesseth and maketh this general tender effectually efficacious. The grace of election worketh not without, but by these tenders generally; neither doth the grace thus tendered, effectually work, but by and with the grace of election: "As many as were ordained to eternal life, believed." (Acts xiii. 48.) The Word being, then, effectual to life, when the hand of the Lord is effectually therewith to that end. (Mark xvi. 20.) They " spake," saith the text, " unto the Grecians, preaching the Lord Jesus; and the hand of the Lord was with them, and a great number believed, and turned unto the Lord." (Acts xi. 21.)

We must always put difference between the Word of the gospel and the power that manageth that Word; we must put difference between the common and more special operations of that power also; even as there is evidently a difference to be put between those words of Christ that were effectual to do what was said, and of those words of his which were but words only, or, at least, not so accompanied with power. As, for instance: that same Jesus that said to the leper, " Say nothing to any man," said also to Lazarus, "Come forth;" yet the one obeyed, the other did not; though he that obeyed was least in a capacity to do it, he being now dead, and stunk in his grave. Indeed, unbelief hath hindered Christ much, yet not when he putteth forth himself as Almighty, but when he doth suffer himself by them to be abused who are to be dealt with by ordinary means: otherwise legions of devils, with ten thousand impediments, must fall down before him, and give way unto him. There is a speaking, and a so-speaking: " They so spake, that a great multitude, both of the Jews, and also of the Greeks, believed." (Acts xiv. 1.) Even as I have hinted already, there is a difference between the coming of the Word when it is in power, (1 Thess. i. 5,) and when it is in word only. So, then, the blessed grace of election chooseth this man to good, not because he is good; it chooseth him to believe, not because he doth believe; it chooseth him to persevere, not because he doth so; it foreordains that this man shall be created in Christ Jesus unto good works, (Eph. i. 4—6,) not if a man will create himself thereto. (1 Pet. i. 2. Eph. ii. 10.)

What shall we say, then ? Is the fault in God, if any perish ? Doubtless, no ; nor yet in his act of eternal reprobation neither : it is grace that saveth the elect, but sin that damns the rest : it is superabundant grace that causeth the elect to close with the tenders of life, and live ; and it is the aboundings of sin that holds off the reprobate from the rational, necessary, and absolute tenders of grace. To conclude, then ; the gospel calleth for credence as a condition, and that both from the elect and reprobate ; but because none of them both, as dead in sin, will close therewith, and live ; therefore grace, by virtue of electing love, puts forth itself to work and do for some beyond reason ; and justice cuts off others, for slighting so good, so gracious, and necessary a means of salvation, so full both of kindness, mercy, and reason.

CHAPTER XI.

Seeing it is not possible that the reprobate should receive this grace and live, and also seeing this is infallibly foreseen of God ; and again, seeing God hath fore-determined to suffer it so to be ; why doth he yet will and command that the gospel, and so grace in the general tenders thereof, should be proffered unto them ?

Why, then, is the gospel offered them ? Well, that there is such a thing as eternal reprobation, I have showed you ; also what this eternal reprobation is, I have opened unto you : and shall now show you also, that though these reprobates will infallibly perish, which God not only foresaw, but fore-determined to suffer them most assuredly so to do ; yet there is reason, great reason, why the gospel, and so the grace of God thereby, should be tendered, and that in general terms, to them as well as others.

But before I come to lay the reasons before you, I must mind you afresh of these particulars :

1. That eternal reprobation makes no man a sinner.

2. That the fore-knowledge of God that the reprobate would perish, makes no man a sinner.

3. That God's infallibly determining upon the damnation of him that perisheth, makes no man a sinner.

4. God's patience, and long-suffering, and for-bearance, until the reprobate fits himself for eternal destruction, makes no man a sinner.

So, then, God may reprobate, may suffer the reprobate to sin, may fore-determine his infallible damnation, through the pre-consideration of him in sin, and may also forbear to work that effectual work in his soul that would infallibly bring him out of this condition, and yet neither be the author, contriver, nor means of man's sin and misery.

Again, God may infallibly foresee that this reprobate, when he hath sinned, will be an un-reasonable opposer of his own salvation ; and may also determine to suffer him to sin, and be thus unreasonable to the end, yet be gracious, yea, very gracious, if he offer him life, and that only upon reasonable terms, which yet he denieth to close with. (Isa. i. 18 ; lv. 12.)

The reasons are—

1. Because not God, but sin, hath made him unreasonable ; without which, reasonable terms had done his work for him : for reasonable terms are the most equal and righteous terms that can be propounded between parties at difference ; yea, the terms that most suiteth and agreeth with a reasonable creature, such as man ; nay, reasonable terms are, for terms, the most apt to work with that man whose reason is brought into and held captive by very sense itself. (Ezek. xviii. ; xxxiii.)

2. God goeth yet further, he addeth promises of mercy, as those that are inseparable to the terms he offereth, even to pour forth his Spirit unto them ; " Turn at my reproof : and behold I will pour forth of my Spirit unto you, and incline your ear : come unto me, hear, and your soul shall live." (Prov. i. 23—27.)

Now, then, to the question itself, to wit, that seeing it is impossible the reprobate should be saved ; seeing also this is infallibly foreseen of God, and seeing also that God hath beforehand determined to suffer it so to be ; yet I shall show you it is requisite, yea, very requisite, that he should both will and command that the gospel, and so grace in the general tenders thereof, should be proffered unto them.

FIRST REASON.—And that, first, to show that this reprobation doth not in itself make any man absolutely incapable of salvation : for if God had intended that by the act of reprobation, the persons therein concerned should also by that only act have been made incapable of everlasting life, then this act must also have tied up all the means from them, that tendeth to that end ; or, at least, have debarred the gospels being offered to them by God's command, for that intent ; otherwise who is there but would have charged the Holy One as guilty of guile, and worthy of blame, for commanding that the gospel of grace and salvation should be offered unto this or that man, whom yet he hath made incapable to receive it, by his act of reprobation. Wherefore, this very thing, to wit, that the gospel is yet to be tendered to those eternally reprobated, showeth that it is not simply the act of God's reprobation, but sin, that incapacitateth the creature of life everlasting. Which sin is no branch of this reprobation, as is evident, because the elect and reprobate are both alike defiled therewith.

SECOND REASON.—God also showeth by this, that the reprobate doth not perish for want of the offers of salvation, though he hath offended God, and that upon most righteous terms ; according to what is written, " As I live, saith the Lord God,

I have no pleasure in the death of him that dieth, but that the wicked turn from his way, and live." (Ezek. xxxiii. 11; xviii. 31, 32.) "Turn unto me, saith the Lord of hosts: and I will turn unto you, saith the Lord of hosts." (Zech. i. 3.) So, then, here lieth the point between God and the reprobate (I mean the reprobate since he hath sinned), God is willing to save him upon reasonable terms, but not upon terms above reason; but no reasonable terms will down with the reprobate, therefore he must perish for his unreasonableness.

That God is willing to save even those that perish for ever, is apparent, both from the consideration of the goodness of his nature, (Ps. cxlv. 9,) of man's being his creature, and indeed in a miserable state. (Job xiv. 15; iii. 16.) But I say, as I have also said already, there is a great difference between his being willing to save them, through their complying with these his reasonable terms, and his being resolved to save them, whether they, as men, will close therewith, or no; so only he saveth the elect themselves, even "according to the riches of his grace." (Eph. i. 7.) Even "according to his riches in glory, by Christ Jesus." (Phil. iv. 19.) Working effectually in them, what the gospel, as a condition, calleth for from them. And hence it is that he is said to give faith, (Phil. i. 29,) yea, the most holy faith, for that is the faith of God's elect, to give repentance, (Acts v. 31,) to give a new heart, to give his fear, even that fear that may keep them for ever from everlasting ruin; still engaging his mercy and goodness to follow them all the days of their lives, (Ezek. xxxvi. 26, 27. Jer. xxxii. 40,) that they may dwell in the house of the Lord for ever; (Ps. xxiii. 6;) and as another scripture saith, "Now he that hath wrought us for the selfsame thing, is God." (2 Cor. v. 5, &c. Rom. viii. 26, &c.)

But I say, his denying to do thus for every man in the world cannot properly be said to be because he is not heartily willing they should close with the tenders of the grace held forth in the gospel, and live. Wherefore you must consider that there is a distinction to be put between God's denying grace on reasonable terms, and denying it absolutely; and also that there is a difference between his withholding further grace, and of hindering men from closing with the grace at present offered; also that God may withhold much, when he taketh away nothing; yea, take away much, when once abused, and yet be just and righteous still. Further, God may deny to do this or that absolutely, when yet he hath promised to do, not only that, but more, conditionally. Which things considered, you may with ease conclude, that he may be willing to save those not elect, upon reasonable terms, though not without them.

It is no unrighteousness in God to offer grace unto the world, though but on these terms only, that they are also foreseen by him infallibly to reject; both because to reject it is unreasonable, especially the terms being so reasonable as to believe the truth and live; and also because it is grace and mercy in God, so much as once to offer means of reconciliation to a sinner, he being the offender; but the Lord, the God offended; they being but dust and ashes, he the heavenly Majesty. If God, when man had broke the law, had yet with all severity kept the world to the utmost condition of it, had he then been unjust? Had he injured man at all? Was not every tittle of the law reasonable, both in the first and second table? How much more then is he merciful and gracious, even in but mentioning terms of reconciliation? especially seeing he is also willing so to condescend, if they will believe his Word, and receive the love of the truth. Though the reprobate then doth voluntarily, and against all strength of reason, run himself upon the rocks of eternal misery, and split himself thereon, he perisheth in his own corruption, by rejecting terms of life. (2 Thess. ii. 10. 2 Pet. ii. 12, 13.)

Obj. But the reprobate is not now in a capacity to fulfil these reasonable terms.

Ans. But I say, suppose it should be granted, is it because reprobation made him incapable, or sin? Not reprobation, but sin: if sin, then before he quarrel, let him consider the case aright, where, in the result, he will find sin, being consented to by his voluntary mind, hath thus disabled him: and because, I say, it was sin by his voluntary consent that he did it, let him quarrel with himself for consenting, so as to make himself incapable to close with reasonable terms; yea, with those terms because reasonable, therefore, most suitable (as terms) for him, notwithstanding his wickedness. And I say again, forasmuch as these reasonable terms have annexed unto them, as their inseparable companions, such wonderful mercy and grace as indeed there is, let even them that perish, yet justify God; yea, cry, "His goodness endureth for ever;" though they, through the wretchedness of their hearts, get no benefit by it.

THIRD REASON.—God may will and command that his gospel, and so the grace thereof, be tendered to those that shall never be saved (besides what hath been said), to show to all spectators what an enemy sin, being once embraced, is to the salvation of man: sin, without the tenders of the grace of the gospel, could never have appeared so exceeding sinful, as by that it both hath and doth: "If I had not come and spoken unto them," saith Christ, "they had not had sin; but now they have no cloak for their sin." (John xv. 22.) As sins that oppose the law, are discovered by the law, that is, by the goodness, and justness, and holiness of the law; (Rom. vii. ;) so the sins that oppose the gospel, are made manifest by that, even by the love, and mercy, and forgiveness of the gospel: If " he that despised Moses' law died without mercy, of how much sorer punishment, suppose ye, shall he be thought worthy, who hath trodden under foot the Son of God?" (Heb. x. 28, 29.) Who could have thought that sin would have opposed that which is just, but especially mercy and grace, had we not seen it with our eyes? And how could we have seen it to purpose, had not God left some to themselves? Here indeed is sin made manifest: "For all he had done so many miracles amongst them" (to wit, to persuade them to mercy), "yet they believed him not." (John xii. 37.) Sin, where it reigneth, is a mortal enemy to the soul; it blinds the eyes, holds the hands, ties the legs, and stops the ears, and makes the heart implacable to resist the Saviour of souls. That man will neither obey the law nor the gospel, who is left unto his sin: which also God is willing should be discovered and made manifest, though it cost the damnation of some: "For this very purpose," saith God to Pharaoh, "have I raised thee up, for to show in thee my power, and that my name may be declared throughout all the earth." (Rom. ix. 17.) For God, by raising up Pharaoh to his kingdom, and suffering him to walk to the height, according as his sin did prompt him forward, showed unto all beholders what a dreadful thing sin is; and that without the special assistance of his Holy Spirit, sin would neither be charmed by law nor gospel. This reason, though it be no profit unto those that are damned; yet it is for the honour of God, and the good of those he hath chosen. (Exod. ix. 16.)

It is for the honour of God, even for the honour of his power and mercy: for his power is now discovered indeed, when nothing can tame sin but that; and his mercy is here seen indeed; because that doth engage him to do it. (Read Rom. ix. 22, 23.)

FOURTH REASON.—God commandeth that the tender of the gospel, and the grace thereof, be in general offered to all, that means thereby might be sufficiently provided for the elect, both to beget them to faith, and to maintain it in them to the end, in what place, or state, or condition soever they are. (Eph. i.) God, through the operation of his manifold wisdom, hath an end and an end in his acts and doings amongst the children of men: and, so in that he commandeth that his gospel be tendered to all, an end, I say, to leave the damned without excuse, and to provide sufficiency of means for the gathering all his elect. "O that God would speak," saith Jophar, "and open his mouth against thee, and show thee the secrets of wisdom, that they are double to that which is." (Job xi. 5, 6.) For though God worketh with and upon the elect, otherwise than with and upon the reprobate; yet he worketh with and upon the elect, with and by the same word he commandeth should be held forth and offered to the reprobate. Now the text thus running in most free and universal terms, the elect then hearing thereof, do through the mighty power of God close in with the tenders therein held forth, and are saved. Thus that Word that was offered to the reprobate Jews, and by them most fiercely rejected, even that Word became yet effectual to the chosen, and they were saved thereby. They gladly received the Word, "and as many as were ordained to eternal life, believed." (Acts xiii. 48.) "Not as though the word of God had taken none effect." (Rom. ix. 6.) "God hath not cast away his people whom he foreknew." (Rom. xi. 12.) The Word shall accomplish the thing for which God hath sent it, even the salvation of the few that are chosen, when tendered to all; though rejected by most, through the rebellion of their hearts. (Acts xxviii. 28. Heb. iv. 1—3.)

Object. But if God hath elected, as you have said, what need he lay a foundation so general for the begetting faith in his chosen particulars, seeing the same Spirit that worketh in them by such means, could also work in them by other, even by a word, excluding the most in the first tenders thereof, amongst men?

Ans. I told you before, that though this be a principal reason of the general tenders of the grace of the gospel, yet it is not all the reason why the tender should be so general, as the three former reasons show.

But again, in the bowels of God's decree of election, is contained the means that are also ordained for the effectual bringing of those elected to that glory for which they were fore-appointed; even to gather together in one, all the children of God. (John xi. 51.) "Whereunto he called you," saith Paul, "by our gospel, to the obtaining of the glory of our Lord Jesus Christ." (2 Thess. ii. 14.) God's decree of election then, destroyeth not the means which his wisdom hath prepared, it rather establisheth, yea ordains and establisheth it; and maketh that means which in the outward sound is indefinite and general, effectual to this and that man, through a special and particular application: (Gal. ii. 20, 21:) thus that Christ that in general was offered to all, is by a special act of faith applied to Paul in particular; "He loved me, and and gave himself for me."

Further, As the design of the Heavenly Majesty is to bring his elect to glory by means, so by the means thus universal and general, as most behoveful and fit; if we consider not only the way it doth please him to work with some of his chosen, in order to this their glory, but also the trials, temptations, and other calamities they must go through thereto.

1. Touching his working with some, how invisible is it to those in whose souls it is yet begun? How is the word buried under the clods of their hearts for months, yea years together? Only thus much is discovered thereof, it showeth the soul its sin, the which it doth also so aggravate and apply to the conscience (Jesus still refraining, like Joseph to make himself known to his brethren) that were there not general tenders of mercy, and that to the worst of sinners, they would soon miscarry and perish, as do the sons of perdition. But by these the Lord upholdeth and helpeth them, that they stand, when others fall for ever. (Ps. cxix. 49.)

2. And so likewise for their trials, temptations, and other calamities, because God will not bring them to heaven without, but by them; therefore he hath also provided a word so large, as to lie fair for the support of the soul in all conditions, that it may not die for thirst.

3. I might add also in this place, their imperfect state after grace received, doth call for such a word; yea, many other things which might be named: which God, only wise, hath thought fit should accompany us to the ship, yea in the sea, to our desired haven.

FIFTH REASON.—God willeth and commandeth the gospel should be offered to all, that thereby distinguishing love, as to an inward and spiritual work, might the more appear to be indeed the fruit of special and peculiar love. For in that the gospel is tendered to all in general, when yet but some do receive it; yea, and seeing these some are as unable, unwilling, and by nature, as much averse thereto, as those that refuse it, and perish; it is evident that something more of heaven and the operation of the Spirit of God doth accompany the word thus tendered for their life and salvation that enjoy it. (1 Thess. i. 4—7.) Not now as a word barely tendered, but backed by the strength of heaven: "Behold what manner of love the Father hath bestowed upon us, that we should be called the sons of God!" (1 John iii. 1;) even we who believe "according to the working of his mighty power which he wrought in Christ, when he raised him from the dead." (Eph. i. 19, 20.) This provoketh to distinguishing admiration, yea, and also to a love like that which hath fastened on the called, the preserved, and the glorified: "He hath not dealt so with any nation; and as for his judgments, they have not known them. Praise ye the Lord." (Ps. cxlvii. 20.) Now are the sacrifices bound even to the horns of the altar, with a "Lord, how is it, that thou wilt manifest thyself to us, and not unto the world?" (John xiv. 22.) "He sent from above, he took me, he drew me out of many waters, he delivered me from my strong enemy, and from them that hated me, for they were too strong for me." (2 Sam. xxii. 17, 18. Ps. xviii. 16.)

For thus the elect considereth: though we all came alike into the world, and are the children of wrath by nature; (Eph. ii. 1—3;) yea, though we have alike so weakened ourselves by sin, (Rom. iii. 9,) that the whole head is sick, and the whole heart faint, (Isa. i. 5,) being altogether gone out of the way, and every one become altogether unprofitable, both to God and ourselves; (Rom. iii. 12;) yet that God should open mine eyes, convert my soul, give me faith, forgive my sins; raise me, when I fall; fetch me again, when I am gone astray; this is wonderful! (Ps. xxxvii. 23.) Yea, that he should prepare eternal mansions for me, (Ps. xxiii. 6,) and also keep me by his blessed and mighty power for that; and that in a way of believing, which, without his assistance, I am no

way able to perform! (2 Cor. v. 5.) That he should do this notwithstanding my sins, though I had no righteousness! (Deut. ix. 5—7.) Yea, that he should do it according to the riches of his grace, through the redemption that is in Jesus Christ our Lord! Even according to an everlasting covenant of grace, which yet the greatest part of the world are void of, and will for ever miss and fall short of! (Ezek. xvi. 60—63.) Besides, that he should mollify my heart! break it, and then delight in it; (Ps. li. 17;) put his fear in it, and then look to me, (Isa. lxvi. 2. Ps. cxxxviii. 6,) and keep me as the apple of his eye; (Deut. xxxii. 10;) yea, resolve to guide me with his counsel, and then receive me to glory! Further, that all this should be the effect of unthought of, undeserved, and undesired love! (Deut. vii. 7, 8. Mal. i. 2.) That the Lord should think on this before he made the world, (Jer. xxxi. 3,) and sufficiently ordain the means before he had laid the foundation of the hills! for this he is worthy to be praised; yea, "Let everything that hath breath praise the Lord; praise ye the Lord." (1 Cor. ii. 2. Jer. xxxii. 4.)

Obj. But you have said before, that the reprobate is also blessed with many gospel-mercies, as with the knowledge of Christ, faith, light, the gift of the Holy Ghost, and the tastes or relish of the powers of the world to come: if so, then what should be the reason that yet he perisheth? Is it because the grace that he receiveth differeth from the grace that the elect are saved by? If they differ, where lieth the difference? Whether in the nature, or in the degree, or in the management thereof?

Ans. To this objection I might answer many things; but, for brevity, take this reply:—That the non-elect may travel very far both in the knowledge, faith, light, and sweetness of Jesus Christ, and may also attain to the partaking of the Holy Ghost; yea, and by the very operation of these things also, escape the pollutions of the world, and become a visible saint, join in church-communion, and be as chief amongst the very elect themselves. This the Scriptures everywhere do show us.

The question, then, is, whether the elect and reprobate receive a differing grace? To which I answer, yes, in some respects, both as to the nature thereof, and also the degree.

First. To begin, then, with the nature of it:

1. The faith that the chosen are blessed with, it goeth under another name than any faith besides, even the faith of God's elect, (Tit. i. 1,) as of a faith belonging to them only, of which none others do partake; which faith also, for the nature of it, is called faith most holy; (Jude 20;) to show it goes beyond all other, and can be fitly matched nowhere else, but with their most blessed faith who infallibly attain eternal glory: even "like precious faith with us," saith Peter, (2 Pet. i. 1,) with his elect companions. And so of other things.

For if this be true, that they differ in their faith, they must needs therewith differ in other things : for faith being the mother grace, produceth all the rest according to its own nature, to wit, love that abounds, that never fails, and that is never contented till it attain the resurrection of the dead, &c. (2 Thess. i. 3. 1 Cor. xiii. 8. Phil. iii.)

2. They differ as to the nature, in this ; the faith, and hope, and love, that the chosen receive, it is that which floweth from election itself ; he hath blessed us according as he hath chosen us, (Eph. i. 4, 5,) even with those graces he set apart for us, when he in eternity did appoint us to life before the foundation of the world : which graces, because the decree in itself is most absolute and infallible, they also, that they may completely answer the end, will do the work infallibly likewise, still through the management of Christ : " I have prayed that thy faith fail not." (Luke ii. 32.)

But second. As they differ in nature, they differ also in degree : for though it be true that the reprobate is blessed with grace, yet this is also as true, that the elect are blessed with more grace : it is the privilege only of those that are chosen, to be blessed with [all] spiritual blessings, and to have [all] the good pleasure of the goodness of God fulfilled in and upon them. Those who are blessed with [all] spiritual blessings must needs be blessed with eternal life ; and those in whom the Lord, not only works all his good pleasure, but fulfilleth all the good pleasure of his goodness upon them, they must needs be preserved to his heavenly kingdom ; (Eph. i. 4, 5. 1 Thess. i. 10 ;) but none of the non-elect have these things conferred upon them ; therefore the grace bestowed upon the one, doth differ both in nature and degree from the other.

Third. There is a difference as to the management also : the reprobate is principal for the management of the grace he receiveth, but Jesus Christ is principal for the management of the grace the elect receiveth. When I say principal, I mean chief ; for though the reprobate is to have the greatest hand in the management of what mercy and goodness the Lord bestoweth on him, yet not so as that the Lord will not help him at all ; nay, contrariwise, he will, if first the reprobate do truly the duty that lieth on him : "If thou do well, shalt thou not be accepted ? but if not well, behold sin lieth at the door." (Gen. iv. 7.) Thus it was also with Saul, who was rejected of God upon this account. (1 Sam. xiii. 11—14 ; xv. 26.) And I say, as to the elect themselves, though Jesus Christ our blessed Saviour be chief, as to the management of the grace bestowed on his chosen, yet not so as that he quite excludeth them from " striving according to his working, which worketh in me mightily." (Col. i. 29.) Nay, contrariwise, if those who in truth are elect, shall yet be remiss, and do wickedly, they shall feel the stroke of God's rod, it may be till their bones do break ! But because the work doth not lie at their door to manage as chief, but as Christ's, therefore though he may perform his work with much bitterness and grief to them ; yet he being engaged as the principal, will perform that which concerneth them, even until the day (the coming) of Jesus Christ. (Ps. cxxxviii. 8. Phil. i. 6.)

From what hath been said, there ariseth this conclusion :

The elect are always under eternal mercy, but those not elect always under eternal justice ; for you must consider this : there is eternal mercy and eternal justice, and there is present mercy and present justice. So then, for a man to be in a state of mercy, it may be either a state of mercy present, or both present and eternal also. And so again for a man to be in a state under justice, it may be understood either of present justice only, or of both present and eternal also.

That this may yet further be opened, I shall somewhat enlarge.

I begin with present mercy and present justice. That which I call present mercy, is that faith, light, knowledge, and taste of the good Word of God, that a man may have, and perish. This is called in Scripture, believing for a while, during for a while, and rejoicing in the light for a season. (Heb. vi. 4, 5. 2 Pet. ii. 20. Matt. xiii. 22. Luke viii. 13.) Now, I call this mercy, both because none, as men, can deserve it, and also because the proper end thereof is to do good to those that have it. But I call it present mercy, because those that are only blessed with that, may sin it away, and perish ; as did some of the Galatians, Hebrews, Alexandrians, with the Asians, and others. (Gal. v. 4. Heb. xii. 15, 16. 1 Tim. i. 20. 2 Tim. ii. 18 ; i. 15. Heb. xii. 25.) But yet observe again, I do not call this present mercy, because God hath determined it shall last but a while absolutely ; but because it is possible for man to lose it, yea, determined he shall, conditionally. (John v. 35. 1 Cor. xii. 7.)

Again. As to present justice, it is that which lasteth but a while also ; and as present mercy is properly the portion of those left out of God's election, so present justice chiefly hath to do with God's beloved ; who yet at that time are also under eternal mercy. This is that justice that afflicted Job, (Job vi. 4,) David, (Ps. lxxxviii ; xxxviii. 3,) Heman, and the godly, who, notwithstanding, do infallibly attain, by virtue of this mercy, eternal life and glory. (Amos iii. 2. 1 Cor. xi. 30, 31. Ps. xxx. 5 ; ciii. 9. 1 Pet. i. 6.) I call this justice, because in some sense God dealeth with his children according to the quality of their transgressions ; and I call it also present justice, because though the hand of God for the present be never so heavy on those that are his by election, yet it lasteth but a while ; wherefore, though this indeed be called wrath, yet is but a little wrath, wrath for a moment, time, or season. " In a little wrath I hid my face from thee for a moment, but with everlasting kindness will I have mercy on thee, saith the Lord thy Redeemer." (Isa. liv. 8.)

Thus you see there is present mercy and present justice; also that the elect may be under present justice, when the rest may be under present mercy.

Again. As there is present mercy and present justice, so there is eternal mercy and eternal justice; and I say, as the elect may be under present justice, when the non-elect may be under present mercy, so the elect at that time are also under eternal mercy, but the other under eternal justice.

That the elect are under eternal mercy, and that when under present justice, is evident from what hath been said before, namely, from their being chosen in Christ before the foundation of the world; as also from the consideration of their sound conversion, and safe preservation quite through this wicked world, even safe unto eternal life; as he also saith by the Prophet Jeremiah: "Yea, I have loved thee with an everlasting love, therefore with loving-kindness have I drawn thee." (Jer. xxxi. 3.) And hence it is that he calleth the elect his sheep, (John x. 16,) his children, (John xi. 52,) and people, (Acts xviii. 9, 10,) and that before conversion; for though none of them as yet were his children by calling, yet were they his according to election.

Now the elect being under this eternal grace and mercy, they must needs be under it both before present justice seizeth upon them, while it seizeth them, and also continueth with them longer than present justice can, it being from everlasting to everlasting. This being so, here is the reason why no sin, nor yet temptation of the enemy, with any other evil, can hurt or destroy those thus elect of God: yea, this is that which maketh even those things that in themselves are the very bane of men, yet prove very much for good to those within this purpose; (Rom. viii. 28;) and as David saith, "It is good for me that I have been afflicted." (Ps. cxix. 71.) And again, "But when we are judged, we are chastened of the Lord, that we should not be condemned with the world." (1 Cor. xi. 32.) Now afflictions, &c., in themselves are not only fruitless and unprofitable, but being unsanctified, are destructive. "I smote him, and he went on frowardly." (Isa. lvii. 17.) But now eternal mercy working with this or that affliction, makes it profitable to the chosen. "I have seen his ways, and will heal him, and will restore comforts to him and to his mourners." (Isa. lvii. 18.) As he saith in another place, "Blessed is the man whom thou chastisest, and teachest out of thy law." (Ps. xciv. 12.) For eternal mercy doth not look on those who are the elect and chosen of God, as poor sinful creatures only, but also as the generation whom the Lord hath blessed, in whom he hath designed to magnify his mercy to the utmost, by pardoning the trans-

gressions of the remnant of his heritage. (1 Pet. ii. 9. Mic. vii. 18, 19.) "Having predestinated us to the adoption of children by Jesus Christ to himself, wherein also he hath made us accepted in the beloved." (Eph. i. 5, 6.) Wherefore, I say, the elect, as they do also receive that grace and mercy that may be sinned away, so they have that grace and mercy which cannot be lost, and that sin cannot deprive them of, even mercy that abounds, and goeth beyond all sin; such mercy as hath engaged the power of God, the intercession of Christ, and the communication of the blessed Spirit of adoption, which Spirit also engageth the heart, directs it into the love of God, that it may not depart from God after that rate as the reprobates do. (Eph. v. 29, 30.) "I will make an everlasting covenant with them," saith God, "that I will not turn away from them to do them good, but will put my fear in their hearts, that they shall not depart from me." (Jer. xxxii. 40.)

But now I say, God's dealing with the non-elect, is far otherwise, they being under the consideration of eternal justice, even then when in the enjoyment of present grace and mercy. And hence it is that as to their standing before the God of heaven, they are counted dogs, and sows, and devils, even then when before the elect of God themselves they are counted saints and brethren: "the dog is returned to his own vomit again, and the sow that was washed, to her wallowing in the mire." (2 Pet. ii. 22.) And the reason is because notwithstanding all their show before the world, their old nature and corruptions do still bear sway within, which in time also, according to the ordinary judgment of God, is suffered so to show itself, that they are visible to saints that are elect, as was the case of Simon Magus, and that wicked apostate Judas, who "went out from us, but they were not of us, for if they had been of us, they would no doubt have continued with us; but they went out from us, that they might be manifest they were not all of us." (1 John ii. 19.) They were not elect as we, nor were they sanctified as the elect of God themselves; wherefore eternal justice counts them the sons of perdition, when under their profession. And I say they being under this eternal justice, it must needs have to do with them in the midst of their profession; and because also it is much offended with them for conniving with their lusts, it taketh away from them, and that most righteously, those gifts and graces, and benefits and privileges that present mercy gave them; and not only so, but cuts them off for their iniquity, and layeth them under wrath for ever. "They have forsaken the right way," saith God, "they have followed the way of Balaam the son of Bosor; these are wells without water, clouds that are carried with a tempest," trees whose fruit withereth, without fruit, twice dead, plucked up by the roots, "to whom the mist of darkness is reserved for ever."

(2 Pet. ii. 15, 17. John xvii. 12. Matt. xiii. 12; xxv. 29. Mark iv. 25. Luke viii. 18. Jude 11, 12, 13.)

These things thus considered, you see,

1. That there is present grace and present mercy, eternal grace and eternal mercy.

2. That the elect are under eternal mercy, and that when under present justice; and that the reprobate is under eternal justice and that when under present mercy.

3. Thus you see again, that the non-elect perish by reason of sin, notwithstanding present mercy, because of eternal justice; and that the elect are preserved from the death, though they sin, and are obnoxious to the strokes of present justice, by reason of eternal mercy. What shall we say then? Is there unrighteousness with God? God forbid: "He hath mercy on whom he will have mercy, and compassion on whom he will have compassion."

NOTE.

Note 1. p. 270—"*That there is a reprobation.*"]—Under whatever form Bunyan treats of subjects involving some deep mystery, we detect the native force and subtlety of his mind in painful conflict with his humble, simple faith. By the latter he felt that truth, as plainly revealed in the word of God, was his sufficient support: by the former he was impelled to find reasons for the goodness, explanations of the mercy, which lay at the root of his salvation. This engaged him imperceptibly in metaphysical difficulties. For these he was not prepared; and when he grapples with them, we cannot help discovering that the superiority of his spiritual attainments gave him, in struggles of this kind, but little advantage over the most ordinary reasoner. In the plain, direct statement, "there is a reprobation," he has stated nothing but what is familiar to us as the known confession of many eminent theologians, and of the churches which they taught. Calvin, who only slightly modified the language of Augustine, sets forth the entire doctrine of election in terms sufficiently intelligible. "Predestination," he says, "we call the eternal decree of God, by which he hath determined in himself what he would have to become of every individual of mankind. For they are not all created with a similar destiny; but eternal life is foreordained for some, and eternal damnation for others. Every man, therefore, being created for one or other of these ends, we say, he is predestinated either to life or to death." Again: "In conformity, therefore, to the clear doctrine of the Scripture, we assert, that by an eternal and immutable counsel, God hath, once for all, determined, both whom He would admit to salvation, and whom He would condemn to destruction. We affirm that this counsel, as far as concerns the elect, is founded on his gratuitous mercy, totally irrespective of human merit: but that to those whom He devotes to condemnation, the gate of life is closed by a just and irreprehensible, but incomprehensible, judgment."—*Institutes*, b. iii. c. xxi.

The first article of the Synod of Dort is to this purport: "God, by an absolute decree, hath elected to salvation a very small number of men, without any regard to their faith or obedience whatsoever; and secluded from saving grace all the rest of mankind, and appointed them by the same decree to eternal damnation, without any regard to their infidelity or impenitency."—Heylin's *Quinquarticular History*, p. i. c. vi. sec. 7. The Lambeth Articles, which were so near being adopted by authority as the doctrine of the Established Church, are equally distinct on this awful theme. Thus the first of the nine articles states that, "God from all eternity has predestinated some persons to life; and some he has reprobated, or doomed to death and destruction." The fourth, that, "Those who are not predestinated to salvation shall necessarily be damned for their sins," and the ninth, that, "It is not in every one's will and power to be saved."—Collier's *Eccles. Hist.* vol. vii. b. vii. p. 185.

A distinction, regarded as of great importance by some writers, is supposed to exist between the view of reprobation given, as we have quoted it, in Heylin's History, and that conveyed by the real language of the Synod of Dort. "Moreover, Holy Scripture doth illustrate and commend to us this eternal and free grace of our election, in this more especially, that it doth also testify all men not to be elected, but that some are non-elect, or passed by in the eternal election of God, whom truly God, from most free, just, irreprehensible, and immutable good pleasure, decreed to leave in the common misery, into which they had, by their own fault, cast themselves; and not to bestow on them living faith, and the grace of conversion; but having been left in their own ways, and under just judgment, at length, not only on account of their unbelief, but also of all their other sins, to condemn and eternally punish them to the manifestation of his own justice. And this is the decree of Reprobation, which determines that God is, in no wise, the Author of sin, which to be thought of is blasphemy, but a tremendous, irreprehensible, just Judge and Avenger."—*Articles of the Synod of Dort*, by the Rev. Thos. Scott, p. 118.

Mr. Scott complains that a great injustice is done the Synod by the abstract, originally given by Tilenus, and adopted by Heylin. There is a vast difference, he intimates, between a decree of reprobation, nakedly considered, and a judgment which merely leaves to their fate the sinners who deserved to perish. A large amount of argument has been expended on this subtle distinction; whether to any purpose, is differently determined according to the different tempers of those who study the subject.

A HOLY LIFE THE BEAUTY OF CHRISTIANITY.

THE state of manners and religion at the period when Bunyan wrote this discourse, gave a necessary prominence to the topics of which it treats. There will always be two classes of professing Christians needing especial warning and reproof on the subject of practical piety. With the varying conditions of society, and the external state of the church, the features of their character will be more or less startling. In favourable times, there is a respectable morality—a public sense of propriety and decency—and its influence is very powerful in lessening the contrast between the personalities of national character and national religion. Princes and their courts exercise a vast control, by the mere force of example, over public manners. Between the outward conduct of the English people in the reign of Charles I., and in that of Charles II., the opposition was sufficiently great to give them the appearance of being a different race. While Cromwell held sway, the doctrines of the gospel were so continuously and energetically preached—its morality was enforced by sanctions so stern and yet so encouraging—that, had the same labour been continued, England would at length have exhibited the most striking lineaments of Christian character in full relief. But, even in this case, there would still have existed the two classes who might be profitably warned and instructed by the following discourse; a class, that is, consisting of persons whose morals were obviously more in accordance with the loose principles of the world than with the rule of holiness; and another class, whose numbers were made up of professedly earnest believers in the gospel, but who honoured it neither in spirit nor conduct.

The error of both these descriptions of people has one main support. They refuse no ceremonial homage to Christianity; they do not question the worth of its doctrines, or the authority of its precepts; on the contrary, they pride themselves on their knowledge of its excellency, and when it can be defended without danger, and zeal on its behalf is but the indulgence of natural temper, or may create some opinion in their favour, they rarely fail to appear as its advocates. The notion is soon established that there is sufficient merit in this acknowledgment of Christianity to give a title to its graces and rewards. An imaginary garb is woven of the supposed virtues thus acquired: the self-satisfied believer goes freely and fearlessly into the world with this cloak about him; its ample folds are sufficient to conceal the real features of his character, both from himself and others. Instinctively cautious not to become involved in any of the peculiar obligations of Christian life, he regards the most ordinary fulfilment of duty as proofs of piety. The fashions of the world are followed as a matter of necessity; and the sins to which they may lead lie lightly on the conscience, because they are the sins of custom and society. Christianity, in fact, exercises no control over either the hearts or manners of such men: it is the world, more or less moral, more or less enlightened, by which they are governed. Their temper and conduct reflect the ruling passions of the age, but no characteristic of the gospel. Many of them are ignorant, no less of the inconsistency, than of the danger of their course. They have a dim perception of the truth, that a religion by which men hope to be saved must necessarily have some claim upon them; but the claim is, in their eyes, of the most indefinite kind: and a vague, occasional dream of some future in which it may become more palpable, and then be answered, silences inquiry.

By far the larger number of professed believers will, in ordinary times, be found to correspond with this description. If riches and luxury increase, the quiet, complacent hypocrisy, into which Christian nations are so easily betrayed, will gain greater triumphs. If, on the other hand, some revolution occur by which zeal and sanctity are found in high places, and the interests of holiness are promoted anew by active agents, the real advancement of religion will be attended with an apparent advancement; and the believer in earnest will be closely imitated by the formalist. Thus another species of self-deceit—another kind of hypocrisy will grow up. Men who will now acquire any credit for Christianity must be skilled in its phraseology, familiar with all public acts of devotion, ready to take the foremost part in the punishment of gainsayers. If all this be attained, the want of pure inward holiness—the absence of those powerful graces which are known by their fruits, will be studiously, and often successfully concealed. The effort made to hide the want of religion will be in proportion to the danger of discovery, or the value of the prize dependent upon effective imitation. Hence hypocrisy, in this case, is far graver than in the former. Men of the world, not willing to lose their hold of Christianity, little as they understand its actual worth, are hypocrites only in so far as they assume a name signifying more virtue than they are willing to practise. The men of a religious age and nation, not absolutely yielding to the spirit of revival, but wishing to imitate its operations, are tempted to hypocrisy of the worst kind. It is necessary to every species of deception that there should be an excess in the imitation: the mask must have exaggerated features; in scene-painting, the colours must be much more vivid than those of nature. So with affected virtues: imitative sincerity is extravagantly candid; calculating purity is prudery; reform, looking for gain, is destruction; piety, aspiring to worldly notice, is fiery zeal.

But in all these cases there is a large mixture of self-deception with the deceit practised on the world. The men who wish society to regard them as holy, believe in themselves that they really have some holiness. With those whose hypocrisy is so much less repulsive, they err in this: it is supposed possible to supply by profession, by form, by occasional or superficial acts of duty, the want of a positive religion, and provide a substitute for its absent principle.

To the vices engendered by this wilful and fatal error, no effectual opposition can be offered without the fullest and clearest exposition of what Christianity demands of its professors. It has in itself an intrinsic beauty. Its holiness is that beauty; and, as a living power, acting on human character, it impresses an image of that holiness on every thought and action which it influences.

H. S.

A HOLY LIFE THE BEAUTY OF CHRISTIANITY:

OR,

AN EXHORTATION TO CHRISTIANS TO BE HOLY.

" Holiness becometh thine house, O Lord, for ever."—Ps. xciii. 5.

AN INTRODUCTION TO THE FOLLOWING DISCOURSE.

When I write of justification before God, from the dreadful curse of the law; then I must speak of nothing but grace, Christ, the promise, and faith. But when I speak of our justification before men, then I must join to these, good works. For grace, Christ, and faith, are things invisible, and so not to be seen by another, otherwise than through a life that becomes so blessed a gospel as has declared unto us the remission of our sins for the sake of Jesus Christ. He then that would have forgiveness of sins, and so be delivered from the curse of God, must believe in the righteousness and blood of Christ: but he that would show to his neighbours that he hath truly received this mercy of God, must do it by good works; for all things else to them, is but talk: as for example; a tree is known to be what it is, to wit, whether of this or that kind, by its fruit. A tree it is without fruit, but so long as it so abideth, there is ministered occasion to doubt what manner of tree it is.

A professor is a professor, though he hath no good works; but that, as such, he is truly godly; he is foolish that so concludeth. (Matt. vii. 17, 18. James ii. 18.) Not that works make a man good; for the fruit maketh not a good tree, it is the principle, to wit, faith, that makes a man good, and his works that show him to be so. (Matt. vii. 16. Luke vi. 44.)

What then? why, all professors that have not good works flowing from their faith, are naught; are bramble bushes; are " nigh unto cursing, whose end is to be burned." (Heb. vi. 8.) For professors by their fruitlessness declare that they are not of the planting of God; nor the wheat: " but tares and children of the wicked one." (Matt. xiii. 37, 38.)

Not that faith needeth good works as an help to justification before God. For in this matter faith will be ignorant of all good works, except those done by the person of Christ. Here then the good man " worketh not, but believeth," (Rom.

iv. 5,) for he is not now to carry to God, but to receive at his hand the matter of his justification by faith; nor is the matter of his justification before God aught else but the good deeds of another man, to wit, Christ Jesus.

But is there, therefore, no need at all of good works, because a man is justified before God without them? or can that be called a justifying faith that has not for its fruit, good works? (Job xxii. 2, 3. James ii. 20, 26.) Verily good works are necessary, though God need them not, nor is that faith, as to justification with God, worth a rush, that abideth alone, or without them.

There is, therefore, a twofold faith of Christ in the world, and as to the notion of justifying righteousness, they both concur and agree, but as to the manner of application, there they vastly differ.

The one, to wit, the non-saving faith, standeth in speculation and naked knowledge of Christ, and so abideth idle: but the other truly seeth, and receives him, and so becometh fruitful. (John i. 12. Heb. xi. 13. Rom. vi. 16.) And hence the true justifying faith, is said to receive, to embrace, to obey the Son of God as tendered in the gospel: by which expressions is showed both the nature of justifying faith, in its actings in point of justification, and also the cause of its being full of good works in the world. A gift is not made mine by my seeing of it, or because I know the nature of the thing so given; but then it is mine if I receive and embrace it, yea, and as to the point in hand, if I yield myself up to stand and fall by it. Now he that shall not only see, but receive, not only know, but embrace the Son of God, to be justified by him, cannot but bring forth good works, because Christ who is now received and embraced by faith, leavens and seasons the spirit of this sinner, through his faith, to the making of him capable so to be. (Acts xv. 9.) Faith made Sarah receive strength to conceive seed, (Heb. xi. 11,) and we are sanctified through faith, which is in Christ. For faith hath joined Christ and the soul together, and being so joined, the soul is one spirit with him: not essentially, but in agreement, and oneness of design. Besides, when Christ is truly received and embraced to the justifying of the sinner, in that man's heart he dwells by his word and Spirit through the same faith also. Now Christ by his Spirit and word must needs season the soul he thus dwells in: so then the soul being seasoned, it seasoneth the body, and body and soul, the life and conversation.

We know it is not the seeing, but taking of a portion that maketh it work as it should, nor is the blood of Christ a purge to this or that conscience, except received by faith. (Heb. ix. 14.)

Shall that then be counted right believing in Christ unto justification, that amounts to no more than to an idle speculation, or naked knowledge of him? shall that knowledge of him, I say, be counted such, as only causes the soul to behold, but moveth it not to good works? No, verily, for the true beholding of Jesus to justification and life, changes from glory to glory. (2 Cor. iii. 18.)

Nor can that man that hath so believed, as that by his faith he hath received and embraced Christ for life before God, be destitute of good works: for, as I said, the word and Spirit comes also by this faith, and dwells in the heart and conscience: now, shall a soul where the word and Spirit of Christ dwells, be a soul without good works? Yea, shall a soul that has received the love, the mercy, the kindness, grace, and salvation of God through the sorrows, tears, groans, cross, and cruel death of Christ, be yet a fruitless tree! God forbid. The faith is as the salt which the prophet cast into the spring of bitter water, it makes the soul good and serviceable for ever. (2 Kings ii. 19—22.)

If the receiving of a temporal gift naturally tends to the making of us to move our cap and knee, and binds us to be the servant of the giver, shall we think that faith will leave him who by it has received Christ, to be as unconcerned as a stock or stone, or that its utmost excellency is to provoke the soul to a lip-labour, and to give Christ a few fair words for his pains and grace, and so wrap up the business? No, no; "the love of Christ constraineth us" thus to judge that it is but reasonable, since he gave his all for us, that we should give our some for him. (2 Cor. v. 14.)

Let no man then deceive himself, as he may and will if he takes not heed with true notions, but examine himself concerning his faith, to wit; whether he hath any? and if some, whether of that kind that will turn to account in the day when God shall judge the world?

I told you before that there is a twofold faith, and now I will tell you that there are two sorts of good works; and a man may be shrewdly guessed at with reference to his faith, even by the works that he chooseth to be conversant in.

There are works that cost nothing, and works that are chargeable: and observe it, the unsound faith will choose to itself the most easy works it can find. For example, there is reading, praying, hearing of sermons, baptism, breaking of bread, church fellowship, preaching, and the like; and there is mortification of lusts, charity, simplicity, open-heartedness, with a liberal hand to the poor, and their like also. Now the unsound faith picks and chooses, and takes and leaves, but the true faith does not so.

There are a great many professors now in England that have nothing to distinguish them from the worst of men, but their praying, reading, hearing of sermons, baptism, church-fellowship, and breaking of bread. Separate them but from these, and everywhere else they are as black as others, even in their whole life and conversation. Thus they have chosen to them the most easy things to do them, but love not to be conscionably found in the practice of the other; a certain sign their faith is nought, and that these things, even the things they are conversant in, are things attended to of them, not for the ends for which God has appointed them, but to beguile and undo themselves withal.

Praying, hearing, reading; for what are these things ordained, but that we might by the godly use of them, attain to more of the knowledge of God, and be strengthened by his grace to serve him better according to his moral law? Baptism, fellowship, and the Lord's supper, are ordained for these ends also. But there is a vast difference between using of these things, and a using of them for these ends. A man may pray, yea pray for such things, had he them, as would make him better in morals, without desire to be better in morals, or love to the thing he prays for. A man may read and hear, not to learn to do, though to know; yea he may be dead to doing moral goodness, and yet be great for reading and hearing all his days. The people then among all professors that are zealous of good works are the peculiar ones to Christ. (Tit. ii. 14.) What has a man done that is baptized, if he pursues not the ends for which that appointment was ordained? The like I say of fellowship, of breaking of bread, &c. For all these things we should use to support our faith, to mortify the flesh, and strengthen us to walk in newness of life by the rule of the moral law. Nor can that man be esteemed holy, whose life is tainted with immoralities, let him be what he can in all things else. I am of that man's mind as to practical righteousness, who said to Christ upon this very question, "Well, master, thou hast said the truth; for to love the Lord our God with all the heart, and with all the understanding, and with all the soul, and with all the strength,—and to love his neighbour as himself, is more than all whole burnt-offerings and sacrifices." (Mark xii. 28—33.) To love my neighbour as myself, to do as I would be done unto, this is the law and the prophets. And he that is altogether a stranger to these things, how dwelleth the love of God in him; or how will he manifest to another that his faith will save him?

Satan is afraid that men should hear of justification by Christ, lest they should embrace it. But yet, if he can prevail with them to keep fingers off, though they do hear and look on, and practice lesser things, he can the better bear it; yea, he will labour to make such professors bold to conclude they shall by that kind of faith enjoy him, though by that they cannot embrace him, nor lay hold of him. For he knows that how far soever a man engages in a profession of Christ with a faith that looks on, but cannot receive nor embrace him, that faith will leave him to nothing but mistakes and disappointments at last.

The gospel comes to some in word only, and the faith of such stands but in a verbal sound; but the apostle was resolved not to know or take notice of such a faith. (1 Thess. i. 4, 5.) "For the kingdom of God," saith he, " is not in word but in power." (1 Cor. iv. 18—20.) He whose faith stands only in a saying, I believe, has his works in bare words also, and as virtual is the one as the other, and both insignificant enough. "If a brother or sister be naked, and destitute of daily food, and one of you say unto them, depart in peace, be ye warmed and filled; notwithstanding ye give them not those things which are needful to the body, what doth it profit? Even so faith, if it hath not works, is dead, being alone." (James ii. 16, 17.) This faith, therefore, Satan can allow, because it is somewhat of kin to his own. (James ii. 19.)

Besides, what greater contempt can be cast upon Christ than by such wordy professors is cast upon him? These are the men that by practice say, the gospel is but an empty sound. Yea, the more they profess, the louder they proclaim it thus to be his disgrace, while they, notwithstanding their profession of faith, hold and maintain their league with the devil and sin.

The Son of God was manifest that he might destroy the works of the devil, but these men profess his faith and keep these works alive in the world. (1 John iii.) Shall these pass for such as believe to the saving of the soul. For a man to be content with this kind of faith, and to look to go to salvation by it, what to God is a greater provocation?

The devil laugheth here, for he knows he has not lost his vassal by such a faith as this, but that rather he hath made use of the gospel, that glorious word of life, to secure his captive, through his presumption of the right faith, the faster in his shackles.

It is marvellous to me to see sin so high amidst the swarms of professors that are found in every corner of this land. Nor can any other reason be given for it, but because the gospel has lost its wonted virtue, or because professors want faith therein. But do you think it is because of the first? no, the word of our God shall stand in its strength

for ever; the faith of such therefore is not right; they have for shields of gold, made themselves shields of brass; or instead of the primitive faith, which was of the operation of God, they have got to themselves a faith that stands by the power and in the wisdom of man. (2 Chron. xii. 9, 10, Col. ii. 12. 1 Cor. ii. 4, 5.)

And, to say no more to this, for what is God so angry with this land, but for the sin of the professors that dwell therein, while they have polluted his name with their gifts, and with their idols? God, I say, has been provoked most bitterly by us, while we have profaned his name, making use of his name, his word, and ordinances to serve ourselves, " O Lord, what wilt thou do to this land!" We are every one looking for something; even for something that carrieth terror and dread in the sound of its wings as it comes, though we know not the form nor visage thereof. One cries out, another has his hands upon his loins, and a third is made mad with the sight of his eyes, and with what his ears do hear; and as their faith hath served them about justification, so it now serves them about repentance and reformation: it can do nothing here neither; for though, as was said, men cry out, and are with their hands upon their loins for fear; yet, where is the church, the house, the man that stands in the gap for the land, to turn away this wrath by repentance and amendment of life. Behold the Lord cometh forth out of his place, and will come down and tread upon the places of the earth, and the mountains shall be molten under him, and the valleys shall be cleft, as wax before the fire, and as the waters that are poured down a steep place. But what is the cause of all this?—For the transgression of Jacob is all this, and for the sins of the house of Israel. (Mich. i.)

It is that that is observed by them that can make observation, that all that God has done to us already has been ineffectual as to cause that humility and reformation, by which his judgments must be turned away. Repentance is rare this day, and yet without doubt, that without which things will grow worse and worse. As for them that hope that God will save his people, though but from temporal judgments, whether they repent and reform, or do otherwise, I must leave them and their opinions together: this I have found, that sometimes the repentance, even of the godly, has come too late to divert such judgments. And how some of the godly should be so indulged as to be saved from punishment without repentance, when the true and unfeigned repentance of others will not deliver them, leaves me, I confess, in a wilderness.

But that which is most of all to be lamented is, that sin, through custom, is become no sin. The superfluity of naughtiness is at this day become no sin with many.

Surely this was the case with Israel, else how could they say when the prophets so bitterly denounced God's judgments against them, "Because we are innocent, surely his anger shall turn from us." (Jer. ii. 35.) When custom or bad example has taken away the conscience of sin, it is a sign that the soul is in a dangerous lethargy; and yet this is the condition of the most that profess amongst us this day. But to leave this and to proceed.

As there is a twofold faith, two sorts of good works, and the like, so there is also a twofold love to Christ; the one standing or stopping in some passions of the mind and affections; the other is that which breaks through all difficulties to the holy commandment to do it. Of both these there is mention made in the scripture; and though all true love begins at the heart, yet that love is but little set by that breaks not through to practice. How many are there in the world that seem to have the first, but how few show the second. (Mark x. 17.) The young man in the gospel did by his running, kneeling, crying, inquiring, and entreating of Christ, to show him the way to life, show that he had inward love to Christ and his own salvation, but yet it was not a love that was strong as death, cruel as the grave, and hotter than the coals of juniper. (Cant. viii. 6.) It was a love that stopped in mind and affection, but could not break out into practice. This kind of love, if it be let alone, and not pressed to proceed till it comes into a labouring practising of the commandment, will love as long as you will, to wit, as long as mouth and tongue can wag; but yet you shall not by all your skill drive this love farther than the mouth; "for with their mouth they show much love, but their heart goeth after their covetousness." (Ezek. xxxiii. 31.)

Nor may this love be counted for that of the right kind, because it is in the heart, for the heart knows how to dissemble about love, as much as about other matters. This is feigned love, or love that pretends to dear affections for Christ, but can bestow no cost upon him. Of this kind of love the world is full at this day, especially the professors of this age, but as I said, of this the Lord Jesus makes little or no account, for that it hath in it an essential defectiveness. Thus, therefore, Christ and his servants describe the love that is true and of the right kind, and that with reference to himself and church.

First, with reference to himself. "If a man loves me," saith he, "he will keep my words." (John xiv. 23.) And again, "He that hath my commandments and keepeth them, he it is that loveth me." (John xiv. 21.) And, "He that loveth me not, keepeth not my sayings." (John xiv. 24.) And, "The word which you hear is not mine, but the Father's which sent me." (John xiv. 24.) Behold you now where Christ placeth a sign of love, it is not in word nor in tongue, not in great and seemingly affectionate gestures, but in a practical walking in the law of the Lord. Hence such, and such only, are called the undefiled in the

way. You know who says, "I am the way." "Blessed," saith David, "are the undefiled in the way, who walk in the law of the Lord." (Ps. cxix. 1.)

But here again the hypocrite will give us the slip by betaking himself to exterior matters, as to his "mint, anise, and cummin." (Matt. xxiii. 23.) Still neglecting the more weighty matters of the law, to wit, judgment, mercy, faith; or else to the significative ordinances, still neglecting to do to all men as he would they should do to him. But let such know that God never ordained significative ordinances, such as baptism, the Lord's supper, or the like, for the sake of water, or of bread and wine; nor yet because he takes any delight that we are dipped in water, or eat that bread; but they were ordained to minister to us by the aptness of the elements, through our sincere partaking of them, further knowledge of the death, burial, and resurrection of Christ, and of our death and resurrection by him to newness of life. Wherefore, he that eateth and believeth not, and he that is baptized, and is not dead to sin, and walketh not in newness of life, neither keepeth these ordinances nor pleaseth God. Now to be dead to sin is to be dead to those things forbidden in the moral law. For sin is the transgression of that, and it availeth not to vaunt that I am a saint and under this or that significative ordinance, if I live in "the transgression of the law." (1 John iii. 4.) For I am convicted of the law as a transgressor, and so concluded to be one that loveth not Christ, though I make a noise of my obedience to Christ, and of my partaking of his significative ordinances. The Jews of old made a great noise with their significative ordinances, while they lived in the breach of the moral law, but their practice of significative ordinances could not save them from the judgment and displeasure of their God. They could frequent the temple, keep their feasts, slay their sacrifices, and be mighty apt about all their significative things. But they loved idols, and lived in the breach of the second table of the law: wherefore God cast them out of his presence: hark what the prophet saith of them, (Amos iv. 4, 5:) "Come to Bethel, and transgress; at Gilgal multiply transgression; and bring your sacrifices every morning, and your tithes after three years: And offer a sacrifice of thanksgiving with leaven, and proclaim and publish the free-will offerings: for this liketh you, O ye children of Israel, saith the Lord God." Thus, as I said, the hypocrite gives us the slip; for when he heareth that love is in the keeping of the commandments of God, then he betakes him to the more external parts of worship, and neglecteth the more weighty matters to the provoking of the God of Israel.

Second. As love to God is showed by keeping of his commandments; so love to my neighbour, is the keeping of the commandments of God likewise. "By this we know that we love the children of God, when we love God, and keep his commandments. For this is the love of God (in us, both to God and man), that we keep his commandments, and his commandments are not grievous." (1 John v. 2, 3.) He that keepeth not God's commandments, loves neither God nor men.

Thus, then, we must learn to love one another. He that keepeth God's commandment, doth to his brother what is right, for that is God's commandment. He that keeps God's commandment, doth to his brother even as he would be done unto himself, for that is God's commandment. He that keeps God's commandment, shutteth not up his bowels of compassion from him, for the contrary is his commandment. Further, he that keepeth God's commandment, showeth his brother what he must do to honour the Christ, that he professeth, aright : therefore, he that keeps the commandment, loves his brother. Yea, the keeping of the commandment is loving the brethren.

But if all love, which we pretend to have one to another, were tried by this one text, how much of that that we call so, would be found to be nothing less ? Preposterous are our spirits in all things, nor can they be guided right, but by the word and Spirit of God ; the which, the good Lord grant unto us plentifully, that we may do that which is well-pleasing in his sight, through Jesus Christ our Lord. Yea, and that there may, by them, be wrought sound repentance in us for all that hath been done by us amiss, lest he give Jacob to the spoil, and Israel to the robbers ; for that they have sinned against him by not walking in his ways, and by not being obedient to his law. (Isa. xlii. 24.)

Let me add, lest God doth not only punish us in the sight, and by the hand of the wicked ; but embolden them to say, it was God that set them on ; yea, lest they make these sins of ours, which we have not repented of, not only their bye-word against us to after generations, but the argument, one to another, of their justification for all the evil that they shall be suffered to do unto us : saying, when men shall ask them, " Wherefore hath the Lord done thus unto this land ? what meaneth the heat of this great anger ? Even because they have forsaken the covenant of the Lord God of their fathers," (Deut. xxix. 24, 25. 1 Kings ix. 8. Jer. xxii. 8,) and walked not in his ways.

JOHN BUNYAN.

A HOLY LIFE THE BEAUTY OF CHRISTIANITY.

" And let every one that nameth the name of Christ, depart from iniquity."—2 TIM. ii. 19.

TIMOTHY, unto whom this epistle was writ, was an evangelist, that is, inferior to apostles and extraordinary prophets, and above ordinary pastors and teachers. (2 Tim. iv. 5. Eph. iv. 1.) And he, with the rest of those under his circumstances, was to go with the apostles hither and thither, to be disposed of by them as they saw need, for the further edification of those who by the apostolical ministry were converted to the faith : and hence it is, that Titus was left at Crete, and that this Timothy was left at Ephesus. (1 Tim. i. 2.) For they were to do a work for Christ in the world, which the apostles were to begin, and leave upon their hands to finish. Now when the apostles departed from places, and had left these evangelists in their stead, usually there did arise some bad spirits among those people, where these were left for the furtherance of the faith. This is manifest by both the Epistles to Timothy, and also by that to Titus : wherefore Paul, upon whom these two evangelists waited for the fulfilling of their ministry, writeth unto them while they abode where he left them, concerning those turbulent spirits which they met with, and to teach them how yet further they ought to behave themselves in the house of God, which is the church of the living God, the pillar and ground of truth. And to this purpose he gives them, severally, divers instructions, as the judicious reader may easily understand, by which he encourageth them to the prosecution of that service which for Christ they had to do for those people where he had left them, and also instructeth them how to carry it towards their disturbers, which last he doth, not only doctrinally, but also by showing them, by his example and practice, what he would have them do.

This done, he laboured to comfort Timothy with the remembrance of the steadfastness of God's eternal decree of election, because grounded on his fore-knowledge ; saying, though Hymeneus and Philetus have erred from the faith, and, by their fall, have overthrown the faith of some, " Yet the foundation of God standeth sure, having this seal, the Lord knoweth them that are his." Now, lest this last hint should still encourage some to be remiss and carnally secure, and foolish, as I suppose this doctrine abused, had encouraged them to be before ; therefore the apostle immediately conjoineth to it this exhortation: " And let every one that nameth the name of Christ, depart from iniquity." Two truths strangely, but necessarily joined together, because so apt to be severed by the children of men; for many, under the pretence of their being elected, neglect to pursue holiness; and many of them again that pretend to be for holiness, quite exclude the doctrine, and motives that election gives thereto. Wherefore the apostle, that he might set men's notions as to these things right, he joins these two together, signifying thereby, that as electing love doth instate a man in the blessing of eternal life, so holiness is the path thereto; and, that he that refuseth to depart from iniquity shall be damned, notwithstanding he may think himself secured from hell by the act of God's electing love. For election designeth men not only to eternal glory, but to holiness of life, a means, thereto. (Eph. i. 4, 5.) And the manner of this connection of truth is the more to be noted by us, because the apostle seems to conjoin them in an holy heat of spirit, saying, "The foundation of God standeth sure, having this seal, the Lord knoweth them that are his." "And let every one that shall but so much as name the name of Christ, depart from iniquity;" or, as who would say, God will be revenged upon them for all, or notwithstanding they appropriate unto themselves the benefits of election.

In the text we have, *First*, An exhortation. *Second*, The extension of that exhortation. 1. The exhortation is, That men depart from iniquity. 2. The extension of it is, to them, all of them, every one of them that name the name of Christ. "And let every one that nameth the name of Christ, depart from iniquity."

In the exhortation there are several things to be taken notice of, because insinuated by the apostle. The first is, that iniquity is a very dangerous and hurtful thing, as to the souls of sinners in general, so to them that name the name of Christ.

It is a very dangerous and hurtful thing to men in general; for it is that which did captivate the world at the beginning, and that made it a bond-slave to the devil. It has also done great hurt to mankind ever since, to instance a few things:

1. It is that which hath stupified and besotted the powers of men's souls, and made them even next to a beast and brute in all matters supernatural and heavenly. (2 Pet. ii. 12.) For as the beast minds nothing but his lusts and his belly, by nature, so man minds nothing but things earthly, sensual, and devilish, by reason of iniquity.

2. It has blinded and darkened the powers of the soul, so that it can neither see where it is, nor which is the way out of this besotted condition. (Eph. iv. 18.)

3. It has hardened the heart against God, and against all admonition and counsel in the things of the gospel of Christ. (Rom. ii. 5.)

4. It has alienated the will, the mind, and affections, from the choice of the things that should save it, and wrought them over to an hearty delight in those things, that naturally tend to drown it in perdition and destruction. (Col. i. 21.)

5. It has made man odious in God's eyes, it has provoked the justice of God against him, and made him obnoxious to hell-fire. (Ezek. xvi. 5.)

6. Yea, it so holds him, so binds him, so reserves him to this, that not he himself, nor yet all the angels of heaven, can deliver him from this deplorable condition. (Prov. v. 22.)

7. To say nothing of the pleasure and delight that it makes him take in that way to hell in which he walketh. (Isa. lxvi. 3. Prov. vii. 22—25.) Never went fat ox so gamesomely to the shambles, nor fool so merrily to the correction of the stocks, nor silly bird so wantonly to the hidden net, as iniquity makes men go down her steps to the pit of hell and damnation.

O it is amazing, it is astonishing to consider what hurt sin has done to man, and into how many dangers it has brought him; but let these few hints at this time suffice as to this.

I will now speak a word to the other particular, namely: that as iniquity is dangerous and hurtful to the souls of men in general, so it is to them that name the name of Christ. As to the so-and-so naming of him, to that I shall speak by and by, but at this time take it thus: That religiously name his name. And I say iniquity is hurtful to them.

1. It plucks many a one of them from Christ and the religious profession of him. I have even seen, that men who have devoutly and religiously professed Jesus Christ, have been prevailed withal, by iniquity, to cast him and the profession of his name quite off, and to turn their backs upon him. "Israel," saith the prophet, "has cast off the thing that is good." (Hos. viii. 3.) But why? "Of their silver and their gold they have made idols." The sin of idolatry drew their hearts from God; their love to that iniquity made them turn their backs upon him. Wherefore God complains, that of forwardness to their iniquity, and through the prevalence thereof, they had cast him behind their back. (Ezek. xxiii. 35.)

2. As it plucks many a professor from Christ, so it keeps many a one from an effectual closing with him. How many are there that religiously profess and make mention of the name of Christ, that yet of love to, and by the interest that iniquity hath in their affections, never close with him unto salvation, but are like to them, of whom you read in Paul to Timothy, that they are ever learning and never come to the knowledge of the truth. (2 Tim. iii. 1—7.)

3. And concerning those that have indeed come to him, and that have effectually closed with him, and that name his name to good purpose; yet how hath iniquity hurt and abused many of them. 1. It has prevailed with God to hide his face from them, a thing more bitter than death. 2. It has prevailed with God to chastise, and to afflict them sorely, a thing in which he taketh no pleasure. (Lam. iii. 33.) 3. It has provoked God to give them over to the hand of the enemy, and to deliver them to the tormentors. (Jer. xii. 7. Matt. xviii.

31.) 4. It hath brought them to question their interest in Christ, and whether they ever had grace in their souls. (Ps. xxxi. 22.) 5. And for those that have yet believed they were in his favour, this iniquity has driven them to fear that God would cast them away, and take all his good things from them. (Ps. li.)

Yea, he that would know the hurt that iniquity hath done to them that name the name of Christ, let him consider the cries, the sighs, the tears, the bemoanings, the bewailings, the lamentations, the sorrows, the confessions, the repentings and griefs wherewith they have been attended, while they have complained that they have been put in the stocks, laid in the dungeon, had their bones broken, suffered the terrors of God, been distressed almost to destruction, and have been fed with gravel, gall, wormwood, and with the water of astonishment, for days, yea, years together. (Ps. xxxviii. 8; xxxi. 10; vi. 6. Jer. xxxi. 18. 2 Cor. xii. 21. Ps. cxvi. 3; xxxi. 3, 4. Job xiii. 27. Ps. lxxxviii. Lam. iii. 4; iii. 16. Jer. viii. 14; xxiii. 15. Ps. lx. 3. Ezek. iv. 16.) By all which, and many more which might be mentioned, it appears that iniquity is a dangerous and hurtful thing.

But I proceed, and come in the next place to the extension of the exhortation, namely : that it reacheth to all those that name the name of Christ. "And let every one that nameth the name of Christ, depart from iniquity." To handle this a little, and, First, to show you what the apostle here means by naming of the name of Christ : he meaneth not an irreligious naming of that worthy name, nor those that name it irreligiously. This is evident, because he passed by their manner of naming it without the least reproof, the which he would not have done had the fault been in their manner of naming of the name of Christ. Now I say, if he intendeth not those that name the name of Christ irreligiously, then, though the exhortation "let every one" seems to extend itself to all, and all manner of persons, that any ways name the name of Christ, yet it is limited by this, to wit, that rightly, religiously, or according to the way of the professors of Christ, name his worthy name. And it must needs be so taken, and that for these reasons :

First. For that, as I said before, the apostle taketh no notice of their manner of naming of his name, so as to reprove any indecency or unseemliness in the naming of him ; wherefore he alloweth of the manner of their naming of him.

Second. Because, the apostle's design in this exhortation, was, and is, that the naming of the name of Christ might be accompanied with such a life of holiness as might put an additional lustre upon that name whenever named in a religious way ; but this cannot be applied to every manner of naming the name of our Lord Jesus Christ. For if a man shall name the name of Christ unduly, or irreligiously, though he shall never so much therewithal depart from iniquity, and be circumspect to the utmost in all civility and morality, yet he answers not the apostle's end which he seeks by this his exhortation. For,

1. Suppose a man should name the name of Christ vainly, idly, in vain mirth, wantonness, false or vain swearing, or the like, and shall back this his manner of naming the name of Christ, with all all manner of justness and uprightness of life, would this answer the apostle's end in this his exhortation ? Verily no ; for this manner of naming the name is worthy reprehension ; "Thou shalt not take my name in vain," or vainly make use thereof ; and moral goodness attending the so naming of the name of Christ, will do more hurt than good. (Exod. xx.)

2. There is a reproachful and scandalous naming of the name of Christ, such as the Jews and Pharisees did accustom themselves unto, as to call him Jesus the deceiver ; and Christ in a way of scorn and contempt. Nor were these men quite destitute of that which put a lustre upon their opinions ; for said the Lord Christ himself unto them, "Ye indeed appear beautiful outward." (Matt. xxiii. 27.)

3. There is such a naming of the name of Christ, as to make it a cloak for false and dangerous errors ; that men, by the use of that name, and the putting of it upon such errors and delusions, may put off their errors to others the better. "Many shall come in my name," to wit, with their delusions, presenting them, in my name, to the world, and shall put them off, in my name, to the destruction of the soul. (Matt. xxiv. 5.) Now can any imagine that the apostle should extend his exhortation to such, that they, thus continuing to name the name of Christ, should depart from iniquity. To what end should such be comprehended in this exhortation of his ? to no purpose at all : for the more an erroneous person, or a deceiver of souls, shall back his errors with a life that is morally good, the more mischievous, dangerous, and damnable, is that man and his delusions ; wherefore such a one is not concerned in this exhortation.

4. There is a naming of the name of Christ magically, and after the manner of exorcism, or conjuration ; as we read in the Acts of the apostles. The vagabond Jews, the exorcists, there say, "We adjure you by Jesus whom Paul preacheth." (Acts xix. 13—15.) Thus they called over them that had evil spirits, the name of the Lord Jesus. But what if these should clothe this their devilish art, and devilish way, of using or naming of the name of the Lord Jesus, with departing from iniquity, so as to commend their whole life to bystanders, for such as is morally good ; what advantage would Christ, or Paul, or the gospel get thereby ? verily none at all, but rather damage and reproach, as will soon appear to any man's reason, if it be considered that goodness of life, joined to badness of principles, is like the devil clothed in white, or Satan transformed into an angel of light. And

Paul was grieved in his spirit, when the wench that had a spirit of divination did acknowledge him to be the servant of the most high God, for he knew it would nothing further, or help forward, the Lord's design, but be rather an hindrance thereto. For when witches and devils come once to commend, or make use of the name of Christ, Christ and Paul like it not; therefore Paul's exhortation, which here we are presented with by the text, is not extended to any of the four sorts aforenamed, but,

1. To those upon whom his name is called, they should depart from iniquity. I say those whom God has so far dignified, as to put the name of Christ upon them, (Acts xv. 17,) and I will add that apply that name to themselves. And the reason is, because God is now concerned. (Acts xi. 26.) God has changed thy name from Pagan to Christian, and thou choosest to call thyself by that name, saying, "I belong to Christ." Now thou must depart from iniquity, for that notice is taken of thee both by heaven and earth, that thou art become a disciple, and let every one that (so) nameth the name of Christ, or, that nameth it (being himself by God and himself put under such circumstances as these) "depart from iniquity." (1 Pet. iv. 16.)

2. It is spoken to those that name the name of Christ either in the public or private worship of God, being themselves professed worshippers of him : and the reason is, for that the ordinances as well as the name of God is holy, and "he will be sanctified in them that come nigh him." (Lev. x. 3.) He, therefore, that approacheth the presence of Christ in prayer or any other divine appointment, must take heed of "regarding iniquity in his heart," (Ps. lxvi. 18,) else the Lord will stop his ears to his prayers, and will shut his eyes, and not take notice of such kind of worship or worshippers.

3. Those that the apostle in this place exhorts to depart from iniquity, are such as have taken unto themselves the boldness to say, that they are in him, abide in him, and consequently are made partakers of the benefits that are in him. "He that saith he abideth in him, ought himself also to walk even as he walked." (1 John ii. 6.) And the reason is, because Christ is a fruitful root, and a free conveyer of sap into the branches; hence it is written, "that the trees of the Lord are full of sap." (Ps. civ. 16.) So then, he that nameth the name of Christ by way of applying to himself his benefits, and as counting that he is found of God in him and so abideth, ought himself to walk even as he walked, that he may give proof of what he saith to be true, by bearing forth before men that similitude of righteousness that is in his root and stem : for such as the stock or tree is, such let the branches be, but that cannot be known but by the fruit : "by their fruit ye shall know them." (Matt. vii. 16.) So then, he that thus shall name the name of Christ, let him depart from iniquity: yea, let every such man do so.

4. This exhortation is spoken to them that name Christ as their Sovereign Lord and King; let them depart from iniquity. "The Lord is our judge, the Lord is our Lawgiver, the Lord is our King ; he will save us," (Isa. xxxiii. 21,) are great words : and as they cannot be spoken by every one ; so they ought not to be spoken lightly by them that can. Nor may he that claims so high a privilege, be but obedient, submissive, apt to learn, conscientiously to put in practice what he hath learnt of his judge, his Lawgiver, and his King. Lest when some shall hear him say that Christ by name is his Lawgiver, and his King, and shall yet observe him to do things evil, and to walk in ways that are not good, they should think evil and speak so of his King; saying, Learnt you this of Christ your King, or doth your King countenance you in ways that are so bad? or do you by thus and thus doing, submit to the laws of your King? yea, your King, his name and gospel shall bear the burden of the evil, together with the shame thereof, if thou that namest the name of Christ, shalt not depart from iniquity.

Lastly, Whatever man he be that by his naming of the name of Christ, shall intimate that he hath any reverence of love to, or delight in that Christ, whose name he nameth, that man should depart from iniquity, not only for the reasons that are above mentioned, but for those that may be named afterwards. But having thus far opened the word, and showed who, and what manner of man the apostle had in his eye, in this his exhortation, I shall come in the next place to make some observations upon the text. As,

First. "That it is incident to men to name the name of Christ religiously, that is, rightly as to words and notions, and not to depart from iniquity." This was the occasion of this exhortation, for Paul saw that there were some that did so : to wit, that named the name of Christ well, as to words, but did not depart from iniquity. Some such he also found among them at Corinth, which made him say, "Awake to righteousness, and sin not." (1 Cor. xv. 34.) He found such at Ephesus, and cries out to them most earnestly, saying, "Awake thou that sleepest, and arise from the dead," (Eph. v. 14,) for albeit they were professors of Christ, yet they lived too much like those that were dead in trespasses and sins. This he also found among the Hebrews, wherefore he saith to them, "Let us lay aside every weight, and the sin that doth so easily beset us, and let us run with patience the race that is set before us." (Heb. xii. 1.) These professors were easily beset with sin, yea, it did hang upon them as weights to hinder them from making of that profession of Christ, whose name they named, so beautiful as did become both him and them.

In my discourse upon this subject, I must endeavour to show you two things.

First. What Paul means when he saith, "depart from iniquity."

Second. Why some that as to words, rightly name the name of Christ, do not "depart from iniquity."

The first of those doth need some explanation, because in some sense even the best of saints cannot depart from sin, or iniquity.

1. Because as to the being of it, it is seated and rooted in their flesh, and hath its dwelling there. Yea, it hath, and so will have an abiding there, so long as man is on this side that state of perfection which is not to be enjoyed while we are in the flesh: "for in me (that is, in my flesh,) sin dwells," (Rom. vii.) nor doth any thing else but sin dwell there: "for in me, (that is, in my flesh,)" said Paul, "dwelleth no good thing;" therefore the apostle must not be understood as if he intended to insinuate that there was a possibility that the nature and being of sin could be plucked up by the roots, and so cast clean away from us, as to the very nature thereof: no, that will abide with us, for it hath its dwelling in us.

2. And as they cannot depart from the nature of it as such, that is, as they cannot be rid of the being of sin, so neither can they depart from the motions and stirrings of sin, no more than they can stir from the motions or stirrings of their natural senses, or of their natural reasons: the motions of sin, which Paul also calls the lusts thereof, will be where the nature and being of sin is, because it is not dead; for that which liveth, what manner of life soever it hath, will have motion according to the manner of life which it hath; and sin being one of the most quick and brisk things that are, it will also have its motions and lusts accordingly. Hence Paul says, (Rom. vi. 12. Gal. v. 17,) it lusts and will lust, where it is, and dwells; though the very Spirit of God, and the utmost diligence of a Christian be also there to oppose it.

3. Again, as the being and motions of sin will be with us, so also will it in its endeavours. It will endeavour to overcome us, and to make us captives to itself, and to Satan; and these endeavours will be with us. (Eph. vi. 12. 2 Cor. x. 5. Heb. xii. 4.) Nor can we so depart from iniquity, as to be utterly rid of all sense and feeling of what endeavours there are in sin and iniquity to be master and lord, and reign. Sin will endeavour to defile the mind, to defile the conscience, to defile the life and conversation; and this endeavour, as endeavour, we cannot depart from; that is, cause that it should not be in our flesh; for there it will be, since sin in its being is there.

4. As the being, motions, and endeavours of sin will still abide in our flesh, so consequently will its polluting times be upon us; nor doth the apostle mean, when he bids us depart from iniquity, that we should think that we can so be, or so do, in this life, as that our being or doing should not smell of the strong scent of sin. "Who can bring a clean thing out of an unclean? not one." (Job xiv. 4.) We are all as an unclean thing, and therefore "all our righteousnesses are as filthy rags." (Isa. lxiv. 6.) The scent, the smell, the rank and odious stink of sins abides upon, yea, and will abide upon us, when most spiritual here, and upon our most spiritual actions too, until they be taken away by Christ. Thus far, therefore, we cannot be concerned in the exhortation. For should Paul exhort us to depart from the being, motion, endeavour, and polluting fumes and scent of sin—I mean so to depart from them, as that there shall no such thing have place, or motion, or striving, or scent in, or upon us—he would exhort us to that which is altogether impossible for us to perform, yea, to perform through that working of the Spirit of God which is to be with us, and in us here. Yea, he must exhort us to that which he could not perform himself. But such exhortations did not stand with the wisdom of an apostle. Wherefore there is a certain meaning in this exhortation, from the which if we swerve, we shall both wrong the apostle and ourselves.

Let us inquire then what Paul should mean when he bids them, "that name the name of Christ depart from iniquity." And for our better understanding of him we must consider that there is an iniquity that is inherent in us, and an iniquity that is apart, and at a distance from us. Now if he means, as certainly he doth, that they that name the name of Christ should depart from that sin and iniquity that is in themselves; then, though he cannot mean that we should separate that from our persons, for that is impossible, yet he would have us take off and withdraw our minds and affections therefrom. And he tells us that they that are Christ's do so. "And they that are Christ's have crucified the flesh with the affections and lusts." (Gal. v. 24.) Sinful lusts and sinful motions, our minds and affections should depart from them. There are the affections and lusts of sin; and there are the affections and lusts, or desires of the soul; and again, there are the affections and lusts of the new man in saints. Now this is that that the apostle would have, to wit, that the affections and passions of our souls should not choose but depart from the affections and lusts of our old man, and should be renewed and made willing to be led by the Holy Ghost from them. "This I say," says he, "Walk in the Spirit, and ye shall not fulfil the lusts of the flesh." (Gal. v. 16.)

Wherefore, when he saith, depart from iniquity; if he means from our own inherent iniquity, then he must mean thus, take your mind and your affections off, carry your minds away from them, set your minds and affections upon other objects, and let your minds and affections be yielded up to the conduct of the word and Spirit of God, "Let not sin therefore reign in your mortal body, that ye should obey it in the lust thereof." (Rom. vi. 12.)

Now a man, in mind and affections, may depart from that which yet will not depart from him; yea, a man in mind may depart from that which yet will dwell in him as long as he lives.

For instance, there are many diseases that cleave to men, from which, in their minds, they willingly depart. Yea, their greatest disquietment is, that so bad a distemper will abide by them, and might they but have their desire accomplished, they would be as far therefrom as the ends of the earth are asunder, and while they are found to continue together, the mind departs therefrom, and is gone either to God or to physicians for help and deliverance from it.

And thus it is with the saint, and should be with every one that by way of profession nameth the name of Christ, he should depart from his indwelling sin, with his mind. With his mind he should serve the law of God. (Rom. vii. 25.)

And this is an excellent thing to do, and can be done by none but such as are possessed with an excellent spirit. Ah! to find a man that really departs from himself, and that draweth the affections of the soul, from the affections and lusts of his flesh, is a rare thing. (Ezek. xi. 21.) The heart of the most of professors go after the heart of their detestable lusts, and after their inward abominations. But such shall " of the flesh reap corruption," notwithstanding they name the name of Christ. (Gal. vi. 8.)

Sin is sweet to him that is nothing but flesh, or that can savour nothing but what is of the flesh. (Job xx. 12.) Nor can it be that he that is such should depart from himself, his sweet self. (Rom. viii. 5—8.) No, they that are after the flesh do mind the things of the flesh; wherefore they that are in the flesh, though they profess religion and name the name of Christ, cannot please God; for such, instead of walking in and after the Spirit, have put the stumbling-block of their iniquity before their faces, to hinder their departing therefrom. (Ezek. xiv. 7, 8.) Nor will all their inquiring of God, nor their seeking and praying to him, keep them from stumbling and falling, and splitting themselves in sunder upon the rocks and ruins that are provided for them, as a reward of the evil of their doings. (Job xiv. 16.) Yea, they shall suck the poison of asps, and the viper's tongue shall slay them, notwithstanding all their profession?

Quest. But some may say, how shall I know that I do depart from the iniquity of my flesh, from the iniquity that is in me.

Ans. I shall answer this question briefly thus:

1. How is iniquity in thine eye, when severed from the guilt and punishment that attends it? Is it, as separate from these, beauteous, or illfavoured? I ask thee how it looks, and how thou likest it, suppose there were no guilt or punishment to attend thy love to, or commission of it? For if in its own nature it be desirable to thy mind, and only therefore shunned for fear of the punishment that attends the commission of it, without doubt thou art none of them that do depart from it; all that thou dost is, thou shunnest the sin, not of abhorrence of the sin, but for fear of the punishment that attends it. Like the thief that yet refuseth to take away his neighbour's horse, not of hatred of theft, but for fear of the gallows.

2. How dost thou like thyself, as considered possessed with a body of sin, and as feeling and finding that sin worketh in thy members? doth this yield thee inward pleasedness of mind, and a kind of secret sweetness, or how? for to be sure, where a sanctified mind is, there is nothing more odious in itself, nor that makes a man so in his own eyes, as doth this sight, the sight of sin in him, of the working of lust in him. (Job xlii. 6; Ezek. xvi. 63; Rom. vi. 12.) It is this that makes the good man ashamed, that makes him blush, and that makes him abhor himself.

3. How looks thy duties in thine eyes, I mean thy duties which thou doest in the service of God? I say, how look the best of these, the most warm and spiritual of these, since not one of them can be performed, but they do catch the stain of sin, as coming from thee? or art thou through the ignorance that is in thee as unacquainted with these things?

4. Why wouldst thou go to heaven? Is it because thou wouldst be saved from hell, or because thou wouldst be freed from sin? I say, wouldst thou go to heaven, because it is a place that is holy, or because it is a place remote from the pains of hell? I ask again, wherein dost thou think the blessedness of heaven consists? Is it in the holiness that is there, or in the freedom that is there from hell? There is not a man alive but would go to heaven, that he may be saved from hell: but how many would go thither that they might be saved from the pleasures of sin, from the inward pleasure of sin; of that I will be silent, though surely they are those that are out of love with sin, and that do depart from iniquity.

Verily, my brethren, it is a great thing to depart from iniquity; it is a great thing to have my will, my mind, and my affections departing from it.

But secondly, As they that depart from iniquity withdraw their minds and affections from the lusts and motions of it, so they depart also from the occasions of it; there are occasions by which sin worketh to bring forth the fruits thereof, and some seek those occasions. (Rom. xiv. 13. 1 Tim. v. 4. Exod. xxiii. 7. Prov. v. 8. 2 Tim. ii. 16.) But he that hath set himself to depart from sin in himself will not seek occasions from abroad to do it. Such a man as will keep far from an evil matter will not company with a person that pollutes and defiles, nor will he come near the door of the adulteress's house; he will shun profane and vain babbling, for fear of the ungodliness that attends it; he will walk with wise men that he may be wise, knowing that " a companion of fools shall be destroyed." (Prov. xiii. 20.)

Now there are occasions given and occasions taken to sin against the Lord Jesus; but he that departeth from iniquity departeth from them both. He is not for giving any occasion to others to sin; he had rather wrong himself and put up with injuries done, than give occasion to others to do iniquity, and as he is for giving none, so neither is he for taking any: he is for partaking of no man's sins, but for keeping of himself pure. (1 Tim. v. 22.)

Third. To depart from iniquity, is to depart from it in those examples that are set before us thereto. Occasions and examples are sometimes the same, but there may be occasions to sin where there are no examples thereto, and therefore in that they differ. And to depart from iniquity is to shun and depart from those examples, those beastly examples, that in every corner of the country present themselves to men.

Examples to drunkenness; examples to whoredom; examples to swearing, to lying, to stealing, to sabbath-breaking, to pride, to covetousness, to deceit, to hypocrisy, and to what not, are now-a-days common among men, and he that is to seek in this matter, and that knows not how to be expertly base, may have patterns and examples thereto in every hole. But to depart from iniquity is to depart from sinful examples, to shut the eyes at them, to turn the back upon them, and to cry out to heaven for grace, to be kept in the path of life. And, "Let every one that nameth the name of Christ depart from iniquity."

Fourth. To depart from iniquity, is to depart from the enticings to iniquity. There is that in iniquity that is of an enticing nature. Its pleasures, profits, honours, delights, and sweetnesses are enticing, and he that hankers after these is not departed, nor departing from iniquity. A man must be weaned from these things, and must find some things somewhere else, that are better than these, else he cannot depart from iniquity.

Quest. But some may say, I go from it and it follows me; I reject it and it returns upon me; I have said it, nay a thousand times, and yet it offereth itself and its deceits to me again, what would you have me do?

Ans. I would answer thus: Departing from iniquity is not a work of an hour, or a day, or a week, or a month, or a year; but it is a work that will last thee thy lifetime, and there is the greatness and difficulty of it. Were it to be done presently, or were the work to be quickly over, how many are there that would be found to have departed from iniquity? but for that it is a work of continuance, and not worth anything, unless men hold out to the end, therefore it is that so few are found actors, or overcomers therein. Departing from iniquity, with many, is but like the falling out of two neighbours, they hate one another for awhile, and then renew their old friendship again.

But again, since to depart from iniquity is a work of time—of all thy time—no wonder if it dogs thee, and offereth to return upon thee again and again; for that is mischievous, and seeks

nothing less than thy ruin: wherefore thou must, in the first place, take it for granted that thus it will be, and so cry the harder to God for the continuing of his presence and grace upon thee in this blessed work, that as thou hast begun to call upon the name of the Lord Jesus, and begun to depart from iniquity, so thou mayest have strength to do it to the last gasp of thy life.

And further, for that departing from iniquity is a kind of a warfare with it, for iniquity will hang in thy flesh what it can, and will not be easily kept under, therefore no marvel if thou find it wearisome work, and that the thing that thou wouldest get rid of is so unwilling to let thee depart from it.

And since the work is so weighty, and that it makes thee to go groaning on, I will for thy help give thee here a few things to consider of: And

1. Remember that God sees thee, and has his eyes open upon thee, even then when sin and temptation is lying at thee to give it some entertainment. This was that that made Joseph depart from it, when solicited to embrace it by a very powerful argument. (Gen. xxxix. 6, 7.)

2. Remember that God's wrath burns against it, and that he will surely be revenged on it, and on all that give it entertainment. This made Job afraid to countenance it, and put him upon departing from it; for destruction from God was a terror to me, and by reason of his highness I could not endure. (Job xxxi. 23.)

3. Remember the mischiefs that it has done to those that have embraced it, and what distress it has brought upon others. This made the whole congregation of Israel tremble to think that any of their brethren should give countenance to it. (Josh. xxii. 16—18.)

4. Remember what Christ hath suffered by it, that he might deliver us from the power of it. This made Paul so heartily to depart from it, and wish all Christians to do so as well as he. (2 Cor. v 14.)

5. Remember that those that are now in hell-fire went thither for that they loved iniquity, and would not depart from it. (Ps. ix. 17; xi. 6.)

6. Remember that a profession is not worth a pin, if they that make it do not depart from iniquity. (James ii. 16, 17.)

7. Remember that thy death-bed will be very uneasy to thee, if thy conscience at that day shall be clogged with the guilt of thy iniquity. (Hos. vii. 13, 14.)

8. Remember that at the judgment-day Christ will say to those, depart from me, that have not here departed from their sin and iniquity. (Luke xiii. 27. Matt. xxv. 41.)

Lastly, Remember well, and think much upon what a blessed reward the Son of God will give unto them at that day that have joined to their profession of faith in him a holy and blessed conversation.

Having thus briefly showed you these things, I shall come in the next place to show you,

Why some, that as to words rightly name the name of Christ, do not depart from iniquity. That it is incident to men to name the name of Christ religiously, and not to depart from iniquity, I have proved already, and now I must show you why it is so, and the reasons are of three sorts:

First. Some profess him, yet have not saving faith in him, nor yet received grace from him. That some profess him that have not faith in him, nor received grace from him, I will make appear first; and then that they do not depart from iniquity, shall be shown afterwards.

That the first is true consider, Christ says to his disciples, "There are some of you that believe not." And again, "For Jesus knew from the beginning who they were that believed not, and who should betray him." (John vi. 64.) Now if they believe not, they have none of his grace in them; for faith is the first and head grace, the beginning and leading grace; he, therefore, that is destitute of that is empty of all the rest. Besides, other scriptures also confirm this truth. James calls some of the professors of Christ that were in his day vain or empty men, (James ii. 20,) that is, men void of grace. And the apostle suggesteth in the very words below the text, that as in God's house there are golden and silver saints, so there are also earthy and wooden ones. For "in a great house," as God's is, "are not only vessels of gold and silver, but also of wood and of earth; and some to honour and some to dishonour," (2 Tim. ii. 20;) that is, some for heaven and some for hell. (Rom. ix. 20—23.)

Now they are these wooden and earthy professors that he aimeth at in the text; to wit, that they should depart from iniquity, or else their profession would do them no good, and these also that he despaireth of in the next words, saying, "But in this great house of God there will not only be golden and silver Christians, but wooden and earthly ones: And if any man purge himself from these, from these men's companies, and from these men's vices, he shall be a vessel to honour, sanctified and meet for the master's use, and prepared to every good work."

From all which it is gathered that there are some that name the name of Christ in a way of profession, that have neither faith nor grace in them, and so consequently that do not depart from iniquity. For,

I. These want that principle, that holy and blessed principle, that should induce them thereunto; to wit, the great and principal graces of the Spirit, and they are four. 1. As I have said, they want faith, that heart-purifying grace, for the heart is purified by faith. (Acts xv. 9.) I have showed you already that departing from iniquity must be with the mind and affections, or with the heart. But how can that be, where the heart is not sanctified and made holy? For an unsanctified mind cannot depart from iniquity no more than the Ethiopian can change his skin, (Jer. xiii. 23,)

but nothing can purify the heart but faith. Therefore nothing can make a professor depart from iniquity where faith is wanting. So then, when men professedly name the name of Christ without having holy faith in him, they still abide by their iniquity; they depart not from their iniquity, but rather make of their profession a cloak for their iniquity, for their malice, and for their covetousness, and the like. (1 Thess. ii. 15. 1 Pet. ii. 16.) It is not profession, but faith, that bringeth God and the soul together; and as long as God and the soul are at a distance, whatever profession is made there is not a departing, not an heart-departing from iniquity. Wherefore to these professors James writeth thus, "Draw nigh to God and he will draw nigh to you, cleanse your hands, ye sinners, and purify your hearts, ye double-minded." Men, far from God cannot think reverently of him, nor so speak and profess him, as standeth with the nature of gospel religion; wherefore God saith, "draw near hither," that is by faith; and again, "let them come near, then let them speak," then let them profess. (Isa. xl. 1.) Without faith a man cannot please God, because he cannot without it stand before him in the spotless righteousness of Christ, nor yet depart from iniquity and live a holy life. (Heb. xi. 6.)

There are three things in faith that directly tend to make a man depart from iniquity. (1.) It apprehendeth the truth of the being, and greatness of God, and so it aweth the spirit of a man. (2.) It apprehendeth the love of this God in Christ, and so it conquereth and overcometh the spirit of a man. (3.) It apprehendeth the sweetness and blessedness of the nature of the godhead, and thence persuadeth the soul to desire here communion with him, that it may be holy, and the enjoyment of him when this world is ended, that it may be happy in and by him for ever.

But without faith these things cannot be apprehended, and therefore those that want it, whatever their profession is, they will not depart from iniquity.

II. Repentance is another of the great and principal graces, which the Holy Ghost worketh in the heart. Wherefore, without this also there can be no departing from iniquity. It is in vain to expect it of any man, let his profession be never so stately and great, if he is a stranger to sound repentance. How many are there in our day, since the gospel is grown so common, that catch up a notion of good things, and from that notion make a profession of the name of Christ, get into churches, and obtain the title of a brother, a saint, a member of a gospel congregation, that have clean escaped repentance. I say they have catched up a notion of good things, and have through that adventured to name the name of Christ, quite forgetting to take repentance with them. Repentance should be, and is one of the first steps into true gospel profession. (Mark i. 15. Prov. iii. 7; xvi. 6.) But some know nothing of it, until they come to the end of all, and their repentance will do them no good. Repentance is not but where the true fear of God is; yea, the fear of God is one ground of repentance. Repentance is the scouring grace, it is that which purges. Repentance is, as I may call it, that bitter pill without the taking, and sound working of which, base and sinful humours will rest unstirred, unpurged, undriven out of the soul. Can repentance be where godly sorrow is not? or can repentance be where the fruits of repentance are not? O the fruits of repentance, thick sown by preachers, but it comes up but thinly! (Mark i. 4, 5. Rom. vi. 21. Jer. vii. 3—5.) Where shall the fruits of repentance be found? Confession of sin is one fruit of repentance; shame for sin is another fruit of repentance; amendment of life is another fruit of repentance; restitution for cozening, cheating, defrauding, beguiling thy neighbour, is another fruit of repentance. (Luke xix. 5—8.) Yea, if you would see the fruits of repentance as described by the Holy Ghost, and put together for the further conviction and shame of the impenitent professor, look into the second epistle to the Corinthians. (2 Cor. vii. 9—11.)

But this is a day that was never read of, a day wherein conversion is frequent without repentance; such a conversion as it is, and therefore doth the church of God now swarm with them that religiously name the name of Christ, and yet depart not from iniquity.

Alas! all houses, all tables, all shops, have hanging up in them the sign of the want of repentance. (Eccles. vii. 27, 28.) To say nothing of the talk, of the beds and the backs of most that profess, by which of these is it that one of a thousand for men; and for women one of ten thousand do show that they have repentance? No marvel then that the name of Christ is so frequently mentioned there, where iniquity dwells, yea reigns, and that with the consent of the mind.

I would not be austere, but were wearing of gold, putting on of apparel, dressing up houses, decking of children, learning of compliments, boldness in women, lechery in men, wanton behaviour, lascivious words, and tempting carriages, signs of repentance; then I must say, the fruits of repentance swarm in our land: but if these be none of the fruits of repentance then, O, the multitude of professors, that religiously name the name of Christ, and do not depart from iniquity. But,

III. Love is another of those great and principal graces, which the Holy Ghost worketh in the heart: wherefore let profession be never so high, yet if love be wanting there, to be sure such professors "depart not from iniquity." (1 Cor. xiii.) Hence all profession, and subjecting to profession are counted nothing, where love is not. Love is counted a most infallible sign that a man is in a state of salvation. "He that loveth dwells in God, is born of God, and knoweth him." (1 John iv. 7, 16, 21.) Love divideth itself, to God, and

to my neighbour. Love to God, is, that we keep his sayings, his commandments, his laws. "If a man love me," saith Christ, "he will keep my words; and he that loveth me not, keepeth not my sayings." (John xiv. 23, 24.) "For this is the love of God, that we keep his commandments: and his commandments are not grievous." (1 John v. 3.) So then, that professor that hath not love, cannot depart from iniquity.

1. Where no love is, men cannot be tender of the name of God, they are not afflicted because men keep not God's law. (Ps. cxix. 136. 1 Cor. xiii. 5.) 2. Where no love is, men cannot deny themselves of that, which otherwise they might lawfully do, lest the weak should fall, and the world be destroyed. (Rom. xiv. 15.) 3. Where love to God is, there is hatred against iniquity; "ye that love the Lord, hate evil." (Ps. xcvii. 10.)

A man cannot love God, that loves not holiness; he loves not holiness, that loves not God's word; he loves not God's word, that doth not do it. It is a common thing to find men partial in God's law, setting much by small things, and neglecting the weightier matters, paying tithe of mint, and anise, and cummin, and neglecting the weightier matters. These turn the tables of God's book upside down; making little laws of great ones; and great ones of little ones; counting half an hour's bodily service, better than a moral life. Love! love is gone out of the country: love to the doctrine of the first table, love to the doctrine of the second table. O how many professors, in God's eyes, are accounted of no more than sounding brass for want of this ornament, love. (1 Cor. xiii.)

To speak nothing of the first table, where is he that hath his love manifested by the second? where are they that feed the hungry, and clothe the naked, and send portions to them, for whom nothing is prepared? Where is Paul that would not eat meat while the world standeth, lest he made his brother offend? (1 Cor. viii. 13.) Where is Dorcas, with her garments she used to make for the widow, and for the fatherless? (Acts ix. 36—39.) Yea, where is that rich man that, to his power, durst say as Job does, as recorded, in Job xxx. 25; xxxi. 13, 32. Love! love is gone, and now coveting, pinching, griping, and such things are in fashion: now iniquity abounds, instead of grace, in many that name the name of Christ. They want love, and therefore cannot depart from iniquity.

IV. Hope is another of those great and principal graces, which the Holy Ghost worketh in the heart, and without which, let a man be never so high in profession, and so open in naming the name of Christ, he cannot depart from iniquity. As was said before of faith, so we say now of hope. "And every one that hath this hope in him, purifieth himself even as he is pure." (1 John iii. 3.) Here is that excellent office, or rather effect of hope made manifest, it purifieth, it cleanseth a man; it makes him make the Lord

Jesus his example, as well as his Saviour. He purifieth himself even as he is pure; to wit, in soul, in body, in spirit, in life and conversation. Hope of life eternal by Christ, makes a man purify himself in obeying the truth through the Spirit. Hope to be with Christ hereafter, will make me strive to believe him here. Hope of being with angels then, will make a man strive to live like an angel here. Alas! alas! there is a company of half-priests in the world, and they cannot, they dare not teach the people the whole counsel of God, because in so doing they will condemn themselves and their manner of living in the world: where is that minister now to be found that dare say to his people, Look on me, and walk as you have me for an example? or that dare say, What you see and hear to be in me, do, "and the God of peace shall be with you." (Phil. iii. 17; iv. 9.) These men had hope, and hope purified them to an example, till they became patterns to others. Is not this now far off from some professors in the world? Are they purified, are they clean that name the name of Christ? are they weaned from that milk, and drawn from the breasts? No, nor their profession is not attended with grace; they name the name of Christ; well, but they do not depart from iniquity. Let a man believe a lie, and according to the reality of his belief, such will his obedience be; let a man hope for that for which he hath no ground to hope, yet his hope will work with him according to the power thereof; and yet we have a generation of men that profess the blessed gospel, which yieldeth the most substantial ground for faith and hope; yea, we have a company of men that will be naming the name of Christ, which is the sweetest, the most taking, and desirable name that is named among the sons of men, and for all that, this gospel, this worthy name, nor yet their naming of it, doth make them depart from iniquity. But what is the reason? Why, they have taken up a profession, but want the grace of Christ; the faith, the repentance, the love and hope of the gospel. No marvel then, if they abide among the wooden sort of professors: no marvel then, though the iniquity of their heels still follows them, and that it droppeth from them wherever they go. But so much for the first reason, why men do name the name of Christ, and yet do not depart from iniquity.

Second. The second reason, why some that name the name of Christ, depart not from iniquity, is, for that, though they rest not in bare notions, as those forementioned, yet they take up as they, short of the saving grace of God. There are bare notions, there are common workings, and there is a work that is saving, and that will do the soul good to eternity.

1. There are bare notions, and they that have them, are such unto whom the gospel comes in word only. (1 Thess. i. 5. 1 Cor. iv. 19, 20.) Such whose religion stands in word only, and is not attended with a power suitable; that is, there goeth not along with the word, a power sufficient to subdue, and work over the heart to a cordial and gracious close with that word that comes to them. Yet such is the noise and sound of the word, that they are willing to become professors thereof; there is some kind of musicalness in it, especially, when well handled and fingered by a skilful preacher. And lo, saith God unto such preachers, when their auditory is made up of such kind of hearers, "And lo, thou art unto them as a very lovely song (or as one that sings a song of loves) of one that hath a pleasant voice, and can play well on an instrument: for they hear thy words but they do them not." (Ezek. xxxiii. 30—32.)

2. But then, besides these, there is another sort, and they go further than these. For to them the word came, not in word only, but also in power: though not in that or in such a power, as is sufficient, absolutely against all attempts whatsoever, to bring the soul to glory. Of these we read in several places; to wit, that they have tasted of the powers of the world to come; but not so as to bring them safe to glory. Yet thus far they go: 1. They attain light or illumination, to see much of their state by nature with. (Heb. vi. 4.) 2. This light standeth not in bare speculation, but lets fall upon the conscience, convincing arguments to the bowing and humbling of the spirit. (1 Kings xxi. 27—29.) 3. They submit to these convictions, and reform, and may, for a time, not only come out from them that live in error, but escape the pollutions of the world, by the knowledge of our Lord and Saviour Jesus Christ. (2 Pet. ii. 18—20. Gal. iii. 4; iv. 20.) 4. Yea, so powerful will this dispensation be, that it will prevail with them, to do and suffer many things for the vindication of the truth of that gospel which they profess. For,

1. The word will be sweet unto them.

2. Christ, the gift of God, will be relished by them. (Heb. vi. 4, 5.)

3. The powers of the world to come will be in them.

4. Some workings of the Holy Ghost will be in them.

5. And joy, which is as oil to the wheels, will be with their souls. (Luke viii. 13.)

Thus, I say, it is with some professors, who yet cannot be said to depart from iniquity, that is, for all ado, because the things that now are upon them, abide with them but awhile. "For awhile, they believe: they rejoice in the light for a season." (Luke viii. 13. John v. 35. 2 Pet. ii. 21.) So they clean escape from them, who live in error for a little, or awhile; and after that return to their old course, and are again entangled with their iniquities, and overcome. This is called "a turning with the dog to his own vomit again, and with the sow that was washed, to her wallowing in the mire." And some of these are set forth by this and such like sayings, "When the unclean spirit is gone out of a man, he walketh through dry places seeking rest, and finding none,

x 2

Then he saith I will return into my house, from whence I came out; and when he is come, he findeth it empty, swept, and garnished. Then goeth he, and taketh with himself seven other spirits more wicked than himself, and they enter in and dwell there, and the last state of that man is worse than the first." (Matt. xii. 43—45.)

Now the causes of this declension, returning, or falling away again unto iniquity, are many.

First. One is for that this work, this work of power that they have been made partakers of, has not been thorough enough upon all the powers of their souls. Their understandings, their judgments and consciences have been dealt with, but the power of God has not been upon their wills and minds, and affections rightly to subdue them to the grace of the gospel. (Ps. cx. 3.) Indeed, there seems to be a subjection of the will, and an overruling of the mind, and affections also, else they could not for a time lay aside their iniquity, come off from the pollutions of the world, and for a season rejoice in the word, and be pleased with the light thereof. But we may consider, that this may be, not for that a sound work of God hath passed upon these powers of the soul, but that rather this was by reason of those reflex acts, that the understanding now enlightened, the judgment now informed, and the conscience now convinced, had upon these other powers of the soul. And I the rather think it so, because willingness, mindfulness of, and affection for this gospel, lasted no longer than the light shined in their understandings, or than the things were relished by their judgment and conscience. So that when the light of their candle went out, and when the taste of this sugar-plum was out of their mouth, their wills and affections, not being possessed with the fear of God, they returned again to their course, and went away as before with iniquity.

Nor do I by anything here discoursed, lay blame or fault at the door of God. For,

1. He is a free agent to do what he pleaseth, and may, if he please, refuse to give anything, or if he gives something, why may he not give what he pleases also? He may give special grace to one, and that which is not so to another: he may open Balaam's eyes, (Num. xxiv. 3,) and open Lydia's heart; (Acts xvi. 14;) he may give some but a taste, and cause some to eat abundantly. (Heb. vi. Cant. v. 1.) He may suffer some to fall away, and keep others by his power, through faith unto salvation.

2. Besides, God's withdrawing, to wit, of those common workings, if they were withdrawn without a cause given (which yet I question), yet why may they not be withdrawn from these, as well as from his own peculiar ones. He knows but little, that doth not know that God ofttimes hides his face from his own, and also withdraws from them the light and great influences of the Holy Ghost: and turns them over, at least in their own apprehensions, to the ungodly, and to fallen angels for their chastisement, or trial, or instruction, &c.

3. And why may not God, since these rebels had such working with them, as that their minds, by their understandings, their wills and affections, by their judgment and consciences were somewhat taken and allured, cause a withdrawing of these for trial, and to see if they would cry after him to return.

But we will let these things pass, and call you again to remembrance of what is in hand; we are now showing that there be them that name the name of Christ, " that yet depart not from iniquity," and in showing the cause of their not so doing, one was for that the gospel came to them in word only; and the other was, for that though it came to others in power, yet not in power, or in that power, that effectually keepeth some to salvation. Upon this second reason I now am, and am showing how it comes to pass that they that are under the power of the things that we have afore discoursed, should, notwithstanding that, return to their vomit again. One cause of this declension, or going back to iniquity, I have just now touched upon, and we have some more behind.

Second. Therefore such persons upon the withdrawing of those influences that at present are mighty upon them, do forthwith forget, both what they had, and what work it made upon them. Straightway they forget what manner of men they were. It is said of Israel, they sang his praises, they soon forgot his word. So these they forget.

1. They forget what light and what conviction they had.

2. They forget what sorrow for sin they had.

3. They forget what tastes of Christ and his word they had.

4. They forget what joy and comfort they had.

5. They forget how fair for heaven they were.

6. And they forget how cleansed once they were.

"They have forgotten that they were purged from their old sins." (2 Pet. i. 9.) Now forgetfulness makes things that are past as nothings; and if so, then it can lay no obligations upon the mind, to engage it to the delight of them, and to the enjoying of them, no not in the thoughts of them, as if they were remembered by us. Forgetfulness is a very dangerous thing; it makes preaching vain, profession vain, faith vain, and all to no purpose. (1 Cor. xv. 1, 2.) Such profession is but a dream, and the professors but as dreamers; all vanishes in the morning. This made Paul so caution the Corinthians, that they forgot not the preaching; and the author to the Hebrews, so earnestly calls them, in their backsliding, back to the remembrance of former days, and to the recollecting of what it was that then had made them so willingly endure their great fight of affliction. (Heb. x. 32, 33.)

Forgetfulness, I say, makes things nothings; it makes us as if things had never been; and so takes away from the soul one great means of stay, support, and encouragement; when choice David was dejected, the remembrance of the hill Hermon was his stay; when he was to go out against Goliah, the remembrance of the lion and the bear was his support; so when those that have had the power of the things of God upon them, can think of this; when they are withdrawn, it will, even the thinking of it, will have some kind of operation upon the soul. And therefore you shall find, that the recovering of a backslider, usually begins at the remembrance of former things. "Remember therefore from whence thou art fallen, and repent, and do the first works." (Rev. ii. 5.)

It is marvellous to see how some men are captivated with this forgetfulness. Those that sometimes have prayed, cried, groaned, and sighed, for eternal life; those that sometimes thought no pains too much, no way too far, no hazards too great to run, for eternal life; those who sometimes were captivated with the word, and with the comforts and joy thereof, and that, had it been possible, could have pulled out their eyes, and have given them to a gospel minister, so dear and sweet were the good tidings which they brought to such. (Gal. iv. 14, 15.)

I say, it is marvellous to see how such men are captivated with the forgetfulness of this. They are as if they never had been those men; they are as if they never had had such things; or, as if they never had thought about them. Yea, they are strange, and carry it strangely to all those that still are under the power of that word, and of that mighty hand, by which sometimes themselves were guided.

Should one say to some, Art not thou the man that I once saw crying under a sermon, that I once heard cry out, What must I do to be saved? and, that some time ago, I heard speak well of the holy word of God? how askew will they look upon one; or if they will acknowledge that such things were with them once, they do it more like images and rejected ghosts, than men. They look as if they were blasted, withered, cast out and dried to powder, and now fit for nothing, but to be cast into the fire, and burned. (John xv. 6.) The godliness from which they are departed, and the iniquity into which again they have joined themselves, has so altered, so metamorphosed and changed their heart, and mind, and ways. This therefore is the second thing which shows why some that have been under something of the power of things, are again with iniquity, entangled and overcome.

Thirdly. Another thing that makes these enlightened ones, that they continue not to depart from iniquity, is the persecution that always attends the word: for persecution always attends the word, that of the tongue, or that of the sword. Now these men that were once enlightened, though they cannot remember what they were themselves, yet Satan helps them to think that their neighbours remember what they were; and having now lost the savour, the sense of what they once had, and sinned away that Spirit that brought it to them, they grow weak; ye are above all men the most unable to stand up, to abide the shock and trial that for their profession is coming upon them. Wherefore, by and by they are offended; to wit, with their own profession, and call themselves an hundred fools, for being so heedless, so witless, and unwary, to mind God's holy things in such a time and day. (Matt. iv. 16, 17. Luke viii. 13.) Then they bethink with themselves, how to make an honourable retreat, which they suppose they usually do, by finding fault, first with their own unadvisedness, and of the over-persuasiveness of others; they also now begin to say farewell conscience, yea, God and heaven and all, and join in confederacy with the world again. Thus are they in fear, where no fear is; and the sound of a shaken leaf doth chase them. And there are four things that are the cause of this.

1. For that, notwithstanding the former power that attended the word to their hearts, their hearts did still abide as hard as a rock, there was no true and sound breaking, nor softening in that: wherefore there the word wanted depth of earth, as our Lord is pleased to call it; and anon when the sun was up, that which remained was presently scorched, and so withered away.

2. Notwithstanding what they had sometimes enjoyed, yet the grace of the fear of God was wanting in them. (Eccles. vii. 16—18.) So wanting that, what should hinder but that they should return to go as they came, and leave Christ, the gospel, and the people of God to shift as well as they can for themselves.

3. All that they enjoyed did not estrange their hearts from their lusts, though, when they were in the power of things, they were deader to them than formerly; I say than formerly. (Ps. lxxviii. 30, 36, 37.) And it is even with such, as with them, who are for a time taken off from what yet they love, by some new employ in which they are engaged. Saul went out to look for David to kill him, but when he came at Naioth, in Ramah, the Spirit of God came upon him, and he prophesied. (1 Sam. xix. 18—24.) But this lasted but for a while, Saul soon returned to his old envy against the holy man again.

4. It comes upon them even of judgment and wrath, for since they so soon give way to sin, and forget, God suffereth them to fall into the fear of men, and to force their hearts to comply with bad things, even as Judas and Demas did; till they are swallowed up of that gulph, into which the ungodly descend. "As for such as turn aside unto their own crooked ways, the Lord shall lead them forth with the workers of iniquity." (Ps. cxxv. 5.)

When once God is angry with a people, he can

deal with them, he can give them up to those lusts in judgment, that they will not be separated from by mercy. Yea, he can make a way for his anger to overtake them that have made a way, by the deceits of their hearts, to go a whoring from under him.

And these are the causes why those that were once enlightened, and have tasted the good word of God, and the powers of the world to come, return with the dog to his own vomit again; and so, though they have or do name the name of Christ, yet depart not from iniquity.

Third. A third reason why they that name the name of Christ do not depart from iniquity may be, because grace is weak, and corruption strong. I speak now of them that are truly gracious: for as those that never had nothing but notion, did never at all depart from iniquity; and as those that never had saving grace, though common workings were with them, do but a little depart from iniquity; so those that yet have the grace of God in them, in truth, do not, as they should, depart from iniquity: wherefore the exhortation is as much to them as it is to anybody else; and let them that name the name of Christ, with gracious lips, depart from iniquity. For though there is a great difference betwixt these, and the two sorts that I mentioned before, these having the true principles of holiness in them, but the other nothing thereof; yet they, even they, also have need of this exhortation; for they do not, as they should, depart from iniquity. Their graces, as I said, are weak, and that is the reason thereof.

That these do not depart from iniquity as they should, is clear.

1. For that their highest acts of holiness, are tainted therewith, and made imperfect thereby. (Isa. lxiv. 6. Ps. cxliii. 2. Heb. xii. 15. Matt. vi. 23.) This is manifest, because they still are afraid to show themselves before God in their own works, and because they betake them for acceptation with God, to the priestly office of Christ, and pray by him, "forgive us our trespasses."

2. This is clear also, because we are, while in this world, nowhere by the word, said to have attained to the mark and point of absolute perfection; but are bid to grow, to follow on, to press forward, and to perfect holiness in the fear of God. (2 Pet. iii. 18. Heb. vi. 12. Phil. iii. 12—14. 2 Cor. vii. 1.) Yea, the best of us all, even the apostles and prophets, have not only made it manifest by their imperfections, that as yet they have not departed from iniquity as they should; but they have confessed, and denied not, that they were yet in the pursuit of righteousness, and had not already attained.

3. This is clear also, for that the righteousness, by the which the best of saints are justified in the sight of God, is a righteousness of another, not their own; the righteousness of another man, for that there is not any upon earth that doth good

and sins not. And what need we pray, "forgive us our trespasses," approach God in the perfections of another, and be hid to perfect holiness, if we had already attained, or were already perfect, or were so departed from iniquity as we should.

4. Alas, the complaints of God concerning this matter, doth sufficiently testify the truth of what I say. When God came to his people in Egypt, and bid them forsake the idols of Egypt, they did not. But they rebelled against me, says he, and would not hearken unto me; they did not, every man, cast away the abominations of his eyes, neither did they forsake the idols of Egypt. Well, he saved them out of Egypt, and brought them into the wilderness, and said to them there, Obey my laws, and my commandments; but the house of Israel rebelled against me in the wilderness, they walked not in my statutes, they despised my judgments. Well, then he had them from the wilderness to Canaan, and then said to them, Keep my laws. (Ezek. xx.) But when he had brought them into the land, then they also polluted themselves, and sinned against him as before.

Again, when God brought them out of captivity, both they, and everything that they did, was unclean. (Hag. ii. 14.)

To be short, what says Paul in the seventh to the Romans? what says James in the third chapter of his epistle? (chap. iii. 2.) And what says John in his first epistle, and first chapter? (1 John i. 9.) Do they not all confess, though themselves were apostles, and so for grace and gifts beyond any that breathe in this world, that sin and iniquity was yet with them; and so consequently, that there was not as yet that departing by them therefrom, as there should.

And the reason, as I have said, is, because grace is weak, weak in the best and most strong of the saints of God. Hence the greatest saints use to complain, when much assaulted with corruptions, or attended with very hard service for God, of their weakness and insufficiency, as to a completeness of doing the will of God.

(1.) Moses, when God did but bid him nourish and succour Israel in the wilderness, and carry them in his bosom, as the nursing-father beareth the sucking child, was stricken with such fear of miscarrying, through the weakness of his graces and the power of his corruptions, that he cried to God, saying, "I am not able to bear all this people alone, because it is too heavy for me. And if thou deal thus with me, kill me, I pray thee, out of hand, and let me not see my wretchedness." (Num. xi. 11—15.)

(2.) Job, when he was, for a proof of his integrity, to be exercised a while with some of the judgments of God, cries out, in a sense of his weakness to bear them, and to go through as he should, "Is my strength the strength of stones, or is my flesh of brass?" And again, "Am I a sea, or a whale, that thou settest a watch over me? Wilt thou break a leaf driven to and fro? And wilt thou pursue the dry stubble?" (Job vi. 12; vii. 12; xiii. 25.)

(3.) So Daniel, when he was but to stand and talk with the angel, how weak did he find himself: "There remained," saith he, "no strength in me;" and, "O my Lord, by the vision my sorrows are turned upon me, and I have retained no strength. For how can the servant of this my Lord, talk with this my Lord? for as for me, straightway there remained no strength in me, neither is breath left in me." (Dan. x.) Some may say, but this is natural weakness. But I ask, how came nature to be so weak, but through sin? the remains whereof abiding still upon the best of saints, make them, notwithstanding their graces, incapable to do anything as they should.

(4.) Paul, a man of men, who had so much grace, revelation of grace and communion with Christ, that sometimes he knew not whether he was in or out of the body, and yet you find him making bitter complaint of the weakness of his grace, and of the power of his corruptions. "I am carnal," saith he, "and what I hate, that do I. How to perform that which is good I find not; when I would do good, evil is present with me. But I see another law in my members, warring against the law of my mind, and bringing me into captivity to the law of sin, which is in my members. O wretched man that I am." &c. What complaints, what confessions, what bewailings of weakness is here? And what need was there of any of this, if Paul could, as he would, have departed from iniquity?

I have instanced in these four men, because as to failings and miscarriages they are as free (by what the holy record saith) as any four of whose lives you shall read in all the Bible; but you see they were too weak to do good, and depart from iniquity as they would.

Grace may be said to be weak, either when a lower or less degree thereof is compared with a higher and greater degree of the same; or it may be said to be weak when, in what degree of it you will, it shall be engaged by, or engage itself against sin, &c.

1. There are degrees of grace in the world, some have less, and some bigger measures thereof, and according to the measure of grace received, so is a Christian capable of action. He that has little, acts but weakly; he that has much, acts more strongly; and he of the saints that has most, acteth best of all: but yet none of these three can act so as they should and would, and, consequently, so depart from iniquity as is their duty. Witness those four that I mentioned but now, for they are among the first rate of saints, yet you see what they did, and hear what they said.

Sin is a mighty tyrant; it is also installed in our flesh, and has moreover, that in it which suiteth with whatever is sensual in us. The flesh relisheth it well, though the spirit of the Christian is against it.

Sin is an active beast, and will not admit that the soul should attempt to put forth itself in any good thing, without opposition and contradiction. "When I should do good, evil is present with me."

Sin is of a polluting and defiling nature, and what grace soever it toucheth it staineth, and in staining makes it weaker than, were it not so defiled, it would be. Besides, not a grace, nor an act of grace in the soul can escape untouched.

Unbelief stands ready to annoy faith in the grace, as well as in the act of faith.

Hardness of heart will not let love so affectionately and sympathisingly act as it should.

Sense and reason being polluted will not let hope be so steadfastly fixed upon unseen things as it should.

Pride will not let us be so humble as we ought, nor self so self-denying. Passion often interrupts our patience, and angry motions our meekness. By these, and more that might be named, it appears, that sin is in us, opposeth our graces, and letteth them from acting as they should; and because this sin has part of ourself in its possession, therefore, though our more noble part be utterly against it, yet we depart not from it as we should.

God chargeth Moses with rash and unadvised words, and so he doth Job also. Daniel did wear the name of an idol-god, and Paul freely confesseth himself unfirm. (Num. xx. 12. Ps. cvi. 32. Job xxxviii. 2; xlii. 6. Dan. iv. 8. Rom. vii. 24.)

Nor may what hath now been said be applied to those that are weak in faith, and so in every other grace; for the strongest grace when acted as well as we can, cannot cause that we depart from iniquity as we should. I. Because the strongest grace cannot act without opposition. II. Because we that are the actors are lame, infirm, and made weak by sin that dwells in us. III. Because grace and a state of grace, is not that wherein the perfection designed for us doth lie, for that is in another world. 1. This is a place to act faith in. 2. This is a place to labour and travel in. 3. This is a place to fight and wrestle in. 4. This is a place to be tried in.

And therefore this is no place of perfection, and consequently no place where God's people can depart from iniquity as they should.

Now there is a twofold way of departing from iniquity. I. One is when the mind is set against it, and withdrawn from the love and liking of it. II. The other is when the practice of it is shunned by the whole man.

The first of these ways, the saints though they truly do depart from iniquity yet depart not from it as they should. 1. Their understanding sees not the utmost baseness that is in it. 2. Their judgment is not informed about the vileness of it to perfection. 3. The conscience has not yet been convinced of all the evil that is in it.

Then, (1.) How should the soul abhor it as it should? (2.) How should the desires depart from it with that fervency as they should? (3.) And the will and affections so turn away from it as they should?

Second. As to the shunning of the acts of sin, there we also come wonderful short.

We shun not the sins of others as we should. This is made appear, 1. For that we shun not the company of base men as we should. 2. Nor shun or refuse to imitate them in their evil as we should. How easily are good men persuaded to comply with bad men's ways. Yea, Jehoshaphat himself said to Ahab, that base one,—"Behold, I am as thou art, my people as thy people, my horses as thy horses." (1 Kings xxii. 4.) Joseph could learn in Pharaoh's court, to swear by Pharaoh's life. (Gen. xlii. 15, 16.) Peter also, when dissembling was in fashion among the people, could learn to dissemble likewise. (Gal. ii. 11—14.)

We shun not our own sins, or the sins of our own company as we should. Christians learn to be proud one of another, to be covetous one of another, to be treacherous and false one of another, to be cowardly in God's matters one of another, to be remiss and negligent in Christian duties one of another.

Besides, if I should go about to show here, how Christians will hide iniquity, as David, (2 Sam. xii. 12,) how they will excuse it, as did Aaron, (Exod. xxxii. 22—24,) how they will plead for it, as did the men of the city of Joash for Baal, (Judges vi. 29—31,) and the like, I might soon make it abundantly appear, that Christians do not depart from iniquity as they should; and therefore the exhortation stands good, and of use to the best of saints on earth, "that they and every of them should depart from iniquity." Yea, the observation also that they do not do it as they should, doth still stand good against us.

Wherefore, as it is true in those that have nothing but notion, and that it is true in those that are wrought upon, but not effectually, so it is true, upon those that are truly gracious; observation proves it, fears of damnation prove it, the outcry of the world proves it, and the confession of the best men proves it.

I come now to another observation with which I will present you, and that is this, namely, " that every one that in way of profession and religion names the name of Christ, should depart from iniquity." I say, that every one that in a way of profession and religion, nameth the name of Christ, should depart from iniquity. This truth needs more practice than proof: for I think there are none that have either scripture or reason by them, but will freely consent to this.

Nor is there anything ambiguous in the observation that we need now to stand upon the explaining of. For,

What iniquity is, who knows not?

That it cleaves to the best, who knows not?

That it is disgraceful to profession, who knows not? and therefore that it ought to be departed from, who knows not?

But because the motives in particular may not be so much considered as they ought, and because it is Satan's design to tempt us to be unholy, and to keep iniquity and the professing man together; therefore I will in this place spend some arguments upon you that profess, and in a way of profession do name the name of Christ, that you depart from iniquity; to wit, both in the inward thought, and in the outward practice of it. And those arguments shall be of four sorts, some respecting Christ, some his Father, some ourselves, and some the world.

First. The Christ, whom you profess, whose name you name, and whose disciples you pretend to be, is holy. "Be ye holy, for I am holy." (1 Pet. i. 16.) This is natural to our discourse : for if Christ be holy, and if we profess him, and in professing of him, declare that we are his disciples, we ought therefore to depart from iniquity, that we may show the truth of our profession to the world.

Second. They that thus name the name of Christ should depart from iniquity, because this Christ, whose name we name is loving. Those that have a loving master, a master that is continually extending his love unto his servants, should be forward in doing of his will, that thereby they may show their sense, and acceptation of the love of their master. Why, this is his will, " that we depart from iniquity, that we throw sin away ; that we fly every appearance of evil." (1 Thess. v. 22.)

Third. They that thus name the name of Christ should depart from iniquity, because of the honour and reputation of the Lord. It is a disparagement to Christ, that any of his servants, and that any that name his name, should yet abide by, and continue with iniquity. " A son honoureth his father, and a servant his master : if then I be a Father, where is mine honour? and if I be a Master, where is my fear? saith the Lord of Hosts, unto you, O priests, that despise my name; and ye say, Wherein have we despised thy name?" (Mal. i. 6.)

Fourth. They that name the name of Christ should depart from iniquity, because of his name, that his name may not be evil spoken of by men ; for our holiness puts a lustre and a beauty upon the name of Christ, and our not departing from iniquity draws a cloud upon it. Wherefore we ought to depart from iniquity, that the name of the Lord Jesus may be glorified, and not reproached through us.

Fifth. They that name the name of Christ should depart from iniquity, because of the gospel of the Lord Jesus Christ. That the gospel of our Lord Jesus Christ, which they profess, may not be evil spoken of by our neighbours. " The gospel is called holy, therefore let them be holy that profess it." (2 Pet. ii. 21.) The which they can by no means be, if they depart not from iniquity. Men cannot serve the designs of the gospel, and their own worldly and fleshly designs. But they that profess the name of Christ, they should be tender of his gospel, that they keep that in good esteem and reputation in the world. The which they can by no means do, unless they depart from iniquity.

Sixth. They that name the name of Christ should depart from iniquity, because the very profession of that name is holy. The profession is an holy profession. Be ye clean that bear the vessels of the Lord; the vessels, that is, the profession, for by that is, as it were, carried about the name and gospel of Jesus Christ. We must, therefore, lay aside all iniquity, and superfluity of naughtiness, and do as persons professing godliness, as professing a profession, that Christ is the priest of, the high-priest of. (1 Tim. ii. 10. Heb. iii. 1.) It is a reproach to any man to be but a bungler at his profession, to be but a sloven in his profession. And it is the honour of a man to be excellent in the managing of his profession. Christians should be excellent in the management of their profession, and should make that which is good in itself, good to the church and to the world, by a sweet and cleanly managing of it.

Seventh. They that profess the name of Christ, or that name it religiously, should to their utmost depart from iniquity, because of the church of Christ which is holy. He that religiously professeth the name of Christ, has put himself into the church of Christ, though not into a particular one, yet, into the universal one. Now that is holy. What agreement then hath the temple of God with idols? or any pillar, or post, or pin, or member of that temple? (2 Cor. vi. 16.) One black sheep is quickly espied among five hundred white ones, and one mangy one will soon infect many. One also among the saints, that is not clean, is a blemish to the rest, and, as Solomon says, " one sinner destroyeth much good." (Eccles. ix. 18.)

Eighth. They that profess the name of Christ, or that name that name religiously, should depart from iniquity, because of the ordinances of Christ, for they are holy. (Exod. xxx. 17—21.) Men of old, before they went in to meddle with holy things, were to wash their hands and their feet in a vessel prepared for that purpose. Now since they that name that name religiously do also meddle with Christ's appointments, they must also wash and be clean; cleanse your hands ye sinners if you mean to meddle with Christ in his appointments; wash, lest God cut you off for your not departing from iniquity.

Ninth. They that name the name of Christ religiously, should depart from iniquity, because of Christ's observers. There are many that keep their eye upon Christ, and that watch for an opportunity to speak against him, even through the sides of those that profess him. " Behold, this child is set for the fall and rising again of many in Israel: and for a sign that shall be spoken against." (Luke ii. 34.) Some take occasion to

speak against him, because of the meanness of his person; here some again speak against him, because of the plainness of his doctrine; also some speak against him, because of the meanness of his followers; and some speak against him, because of the evil deeds of some that profess him. But if he that gives just occasion of offence to the least of saints had better be drowned in the sea with a millstone about his neck; what, think you, shall his judgment be, who, through his mingling of his profession of Christ's name with a wicked life, shall tempt or provoke men to speak against Christ?

I come now to those arguments that respect God the Father.

First. Then, they that profess the name of Christ should depart from iniquity; because of God the Father, because God the Father has made Christ to be to us what he is; to wit, the apostle and high-priest of our profession. " He that honoureth not the Son, honoureth not the Father, which hath sent him." (1 Cor. i. 30. John v. 23; xv. 8.) Nor can the Father be honoured by us, but by our departing from iniquity. All our talk and profession of Christ adds no glory to his Father, who has made him our King, and Priest, and Prophet, if it be not joined to an holy conversation. Wherefore, if you profess the name of Christ, and would hold the word in hand, that you have believed in him, depart from iniquity, for the Father's sake that hath sent him.

Second. As it is the Father which hath made Christ to us what he is; so it is the Father, who hath called us to partake of Christ and all his benefits. (1 Cor. i. 9.) " Wherefore we must depart from iniquity, that profess the name of Christ, that we may glorify him for his call." (Heb. iii. 1.) He has called us to the fellowship of his Son Jesus Christ; that is, to partake of all that good that is in him, as Mediator, and to be done by him for those that trust in him. Nor had we ever come out of a cursed and condemned condition, to Christ for life and blessedness, but by the call of the Father; for it is " not of works, but of him that calleth." (Rom. ix. 11.) Now since he has called us to this privilege (even us whom he has called) and left others in their sins to perish by his judgments, it is meet, we should depart from iniquity. (Heb. iii. 1. 2 Pet. i. 2, 3.) Especially since the call by which he called us, is heavenly, and holy, and because he has not only called us to glory, but to virtue.

Third. We that religiously name the name of Christ, should depart from iniquity, because God the Father of our Lord Jesus Christ has commanded us so to do. Wherefore gird up the loins of your minds, be sober, and hope to the end, for the grace that is to be brought unto you at the revelation of Jesus Christ. As obedient children, not fashioning yourselves according to your former lusts in your ignorance; but as he that has called you is holy, so be ye holy in all manner of conversation: because it is written, "Be ye holy, as I am holy."

Fourth. They that religiously name the name of Christ, should depart from iniquity, that they may answer the end for which they are called to profess his name. The Father has therefore called them to profess his name, that they might be trees of righteousness, the planting of the Lord, that he might be glorified. Dost thou then profess the name of Christ; bring forth those fruits that become that holy profession, that you may be called trees of righteousness, and that God may be glorified for, and by your professed subjection to the gospel of his son. (Isa. lxi. 3.)

Fifth. They that name, as afore, the name of the Lord Jesus Christ, should depart from iniquity, that they may show to the world the nature and power of those graces, which God the Father has bestowed upon them that do religiously name the name of Christ. And the rather, because, he that religiously nameth that name, declareth even by his so naming of him, that he has received grace of the Father, to enable him so to do. Now he cannot declare this by deeds, unless he depart from iniquity; and his declaring of it by words alone, signifies little to God or man. (Tit. i. 16.)

Sixth. We, therefore, that religiously name the name of Christ, should also depart from iniquity, because the Spirit of the Father will else be grieved. (Eph. iv. 30.) The countenancing of iniquity, the not departing therefrom, will grieve the holy Spirit of God, by which you are sealed to the day of redemption; and that is a sin of an higher nature than men commonly are aware of. He that grieveth the Spirit of God shall smart for it here, or in hell, or both. And that Spirit that sometimes did illuminate, teach and instruct them, can keep silence, can cause darkness, can withdraw itself, and suffer the soul to sin more and more; and this last is the very judgment of judgments. He that grieves the Spirit, quenches it; and he that quenches it, vexes it; and he that vexes it, sets it against himself, and tempts it to hasten destruction upon himself. (1 Thess. v. 19.) Wherefore take heed, professors, I say take heed, you that religiously name the name of Christ, that you meddle not with iniquity, that you tempt not the Spirit of the Lord to do such things against you, whose beginnings are dreadful, and whose end in working of judgments is unsearchable. (Isa. lxiii. 10. Acts v. 9.) A man knows not whither he is going, nor where he shall stop, that is but entering into temptation; nor whether he shall ever turn back, or go out at the gap that is right before him. He that has begun to grieve the Holy Ghost, may be suffered to go on until he has sinned that sin which is called the sin against the Holy Ghost. And if God shall once give thee up to that, then thou art in the iron cage, out of which there is neither deliverance nor redemption. Let every one therefore that nameth the name of Christ, depart from iniquity, upon this second consideration.

In the next place, I come now to those arguments that do respect thyself.

First. Those that religiously name the name of Christ should, must, depart from iniquity, because else our profession of him is but a lie. "If we say we have fellowship with him, and walk in darkness, we lie." (1 John i. 6.) "And walk in darkness;" that is, and walk in iniquity, and depart not from a life that is according to the course of this world. "He that saith, I know him, and keepeth not his commandments, is a liar, and the truth is not in him." (1 John ii. 4.) The truth that he professes to know, and that he saith he hath experience of, is not in him. Every man that nameth the name of Christ, is not therefore a man of God, nor is the word in every man's mouth, truth; though he makes profession of that worthy name. (1 Kings xvii. 24.) It is then truth in him, and to others with reference to him, when his mouth and his life shall agree. (Rev. ii. 2, 9; iii. 9.) Men may say they are apostles, and be liars: they may say they are Jews, that is, Christians, and lie, and be liars, and lie in so saying. Now this is the highest kind of lying, and certainly must therefore work the saddest sort of effects. Thus man's best things are lies. His very saying, I know him, I have fellowship with him, I am a Jew, a Christian, is a lie. His life giveth his mouth the lie: and all knowing men are sure he lies. 1. He lies unto God: he speaks lies in the presence, and to the very face of God. Now this is a daring thing: I know their lies, saith he: and shall he not recompense for this? (See Acts v. 4. Rev. xxi. 8, 27; xxii. 15, and take heed.) I speak to you that religiously name the name of Christ, and yet do not depart from iniquity. 2. He lies unto men; every knowing man; every man that is able to judge of the tree by the fruit, knows that that man is a liar, and that his whole profession as to himself is a lie, if he doth not depart from iniquity. Thus Paul called the slow bellies, the unsound professors among the Cretians, liars. They were so in his eyes, for that their profession of the name of Christ was not seconded with such a life as became a people professing godliness. (Tit. i. 12—16.) They did not depart from iniquity. But again, 3. Such a man is a liar to his own soul. Whatever such an one promiseth to himself, his soul will find it a lie. There be many in the world that profess the name of Christ, and consequently promise their soul the enjoyment of that good that indeed is wrapt up in him, but they will certainly be mistaken hereabout, and with the greatest terror, will find it so, when they shall hear that direful sentence, "Depart from me, all ye workers of iniquity." (Luke xiii. 27.) Christ is resolved that the loose-lived professor shall not stand in the judgment, nor any such sinners in the congregation of the righteous. They have lied to

God, to men, and to themselves; but Jesus then will not lie unto them: he will plainly tell them that he hath not known them, and that they shall not abide in his presence. But,

Second. Those that religiously name the name of Christ should depart from iniquity, else, as they are liars in their profession, so they are self-deceivers. I told you but now such lie to themselves, and so, consequently, they deceive themselves. "But be ye doers of the word, not hearers only, deceiving your ownselves." (James i. 22.) It is a sad thing for a man, in, and about eternal things, to prove a deceiver of others; but for a man to deceive himself, his ownself of eternal life, this is saddest of all: yet there is in man a propenseness so to do. Hence the apostle says, "be not deceived, and let no man deceive himself." And again (ver. 26), "If any man among you seem to be religious, and bridleth not his tongue, but deceiveth his own heart, this man's religion is vain." These words "but deceiveth his own heart" I have much mused about: for they seem to me to be spoken to show how bold and prodigiously desperate some men are, who yet religiously name the name of Christ: desperate I say at self-deceiving. He deceiveth his own heart; he otherwise persuadeth it, than of its ownself it would go: ordinarily, men are said to be deceived by their hearts, but here is a man that is said to deceive his own heart, flattering it off from the scent and dread of those convictions, that by the word sometimes it hath been under: persuading of it that there needs no such strictness of life be added to a profession of faith in Christ, as by the gospel is called for: or that since Christ has died for us, and rose again, and since salvation is alone in him, we need not be so concerned, or be so strict to matter how we live. This man is a self deceiver; he deceives his own heart. Self-deceiving and that about spiritual and eternal things, especially when men do it willingly, is one of the most unnatural, unreasonable, and unaccountable actions in the world. 1. It is one of the most unnatural actions. For here a man seeks his own ruin, and privily lurks for his own life. (Prov. i. 18.) We all cry out against him that murders his children, his wife, or his own body, and condemn him to be one of those that has forgot the rules and love of nature. But behold the man under consideration is engaged in such designs as will terminate in his own destruction: he deceiveth his own soul. 2. This is also the most unreasonable act; there can no cause, nor crumb of cause that has the least spark or dram of reason, or of anything that looks like reason, be shown why a man should deceive himself, and bereave his soul of eternal life. Therefore, 3. Such men are usually passed over with astonishment and silence. "Be astonished, O ye heavens at this, and be horribly afraid, for my people have committed two evils; they have forsaken me the fountain of living waters, and hewed them out cisterns, broken cisterns that can hold no water." (Jer. ii. 12, 13.)

But above all this, as to this head, is the most amazing place, where it is said, that the self-deceiver makes his self-deceiving his sport: "Sporting themselves with their own deceivings." (2 Pet. ii. 13.) These are a people far gone to be sure, that are arrived to such a height of negligence, carelessness, wantonness, and desperateness of spirit, as to take pleasure in, and make a sport of, that which will assuredly deceive them for ever. But this is the fruit of professing of Christ, and of not departing from iniquity. The wisdom and judgment of God is such, as to give such over to the sporting of themselves in their own deceivings.

Third. Those that religiously name the name of Christ, should depart from iniquity, because of the scandal that will else assuredly come upon religion, and the things of religion through them. Upon this head I may begin to write, with a sigh; for never more of this kind than now. There is no place where the professors of religion are, that is clean and free from offence and scandal. Iniquity is so entailed to religion, and baseness of life to the naming of the name of Christ, that one may say of the professors of this age, as it was said of them of old, "All tables are full of vomit and filthiness, so that there is no place clean." (Isa. xxviii. 8.) Where are they, even amongst those that strive for the rule, that mind it at all, when it pinches upon their lusts, their pride, avarice, and wantonness? Are not now-a-days, the bulk of professors like those that strain at a gnat and swallow a camel? (Matt. xxiii. 24.) Yea, do not professors teach the wicked ones to be wicked? (Jer. ii. 33.) Ah! Lord God, this is a lamentation, and will be for a lamentation. What a sore disease is now got into the church of God, that the generality of professors should walk with scandal!

No fashion, no vanity, no profuseness, and yet no niggardliness, but is found amongst professors. They pinch the poor, and nip from them their due, to maintain their own pride and vanity. I shall not need to instance particulars, for from the rich to the poor, from the pastor to the people, from the master to his man, and from the mistress to her maiden, all are guilty of scandal, and of reproaching, by their lives, the name of the Lord. For they profess, and name that worthy name of Christ, but are not, as they should be, departed from iniquity.

1. Hence the name of God is polluted and reproached, even till God is weary and cries out, "Pollute ye my name no more with your gifts, and with your idols." (Ezek. xx. 39.) O do not pollute my name, says God; rather leave off profession, and go every one to his wickedness. Tell the world, if you will not depart from iniquity, that Christ and you are parted, and that you have left him, to be embraced by them to whom iniquity is an abomination. It would far better secure the name of God from scandal and reproach, than for you to name the name of Christ, and yet not to depart from iniquity. Then, though you sin as

now you do, the poor world would not cry out, Ay, this is your religion! Then they would not have occasion to vilify religion because of you, since you tell them that Christ and you are parted. But,

2. If you will not leave off to name the name of Christ, nor yet depart from iniquity, you also scandal the sincere professors of religion; and that is a grievous thing. There are a people in the world that have made it their business ever since they knew Christ, to cleanse themselves from all filthiness of flesh and spirit, and that desire to perfect holiness in the fear of God; and you scandalous professors mixing yourselves with them, "make their gold look dim." You are spots and blemishes to them, you are an evil mixing itself with their good, and a scandal to their holy profession. (2 Pet. ii. 13. Jude 12.) You are they that make the heart of the righteous sad, whom God would not have sad. You are they that offend his little ones. Oh! the millstone that God will shortly hang about your necks, when the time is come that you must be drowned in the sea and deluge of God's wrath.

3. If you will not leave off to name the name of Christ, nor yet depart from iniquity, you continue to extend your scandal also to the word and doctrine of God. They that name the name of Jesus religiously, should so carry it in the world, that they might adorn the doctrine of God their Saviour; but thou that professest and yet departest not from iniquity, thou causest the name and doctrine which thou professest to be blasphemed and reproached by the men of this world; and that is a sad thing, a thing that will bring so heavy a load upon thee, when God shall open thine eyes, and he will open them either here or in hell-fire, that thou wilt repent it with great bitterness of soul. (1 Tim. vi. 1. Tit. ii. 5, 10.) The Lord smite thee to the making of thee sensible to thy shame and conversion, if it be his blessed will. Amen. But,

4. If thou wilt not leave off to name the name of Christ, nor yet depart from iniquity, thou wilt bring reproach, scorn, and contempt upon thyself. For "sin is a reproach to any people." (Prov. xiv. 34.) 1. These are they that God will hold in great contempt and scorn: (see the first of Isaiah.) 2. These are they that his people shall have in great contempt. "Therefore," saith he, "have I also made you contemptible and base before all the people, according as you have not kept my ways, but have lifted up the face against my law." (Mal. ii. 9. Jer. xxv. 9, 18.) 3. Such shall also be contemned, and had in derision of the men of this world. They shall be an hissing, a bye-word, a taunt, and a reproach among all people. "For he that honoureth me," saith God, "I will honour, but he that despiseth me shall be lightly esteemed." (1 Sam. ii. 30.) I remember that Philpot used to tell the papists that they danced bare-buttocked in a net, because of the evil of their ways; and

the Lord bids professors have a care, "that the shame of their nakedness does not appear," or lest they walk naked, and their shame be discovered. For those professors that depart not from iniquity, however they think of themselves, their nakedness is seen of others. And if it be a shame to the modest to have their nakedness seen of others, what bold and brazen brows have they who are not ashamed to show their nakedness, yea, the very shame of it, to all that dwell about them? And yet thus doth every one that religiously names the name of Christ, and yet doth not depart from iniquity.

Fourth. Those that religiously name the name of Christ, and do not depart from iniquity; "they are the cause of the perishing of many." "Woe," saith Christ, "to the world because of offences." (Matt. xviii. 7.) And again, "woe to that man by whom the offence cometh." These are they that cause many to stumble at sin, and fall into hell. Hark, you that are such, what God says to you. "You have caused many to stumble at the law, and at religion." (Mal. ii. 8.) Men that are for taking of occasion, you give it them; men that would enter into the kingdom, you puzzle and confound them with your iniquity, while you name the name of Christ, and do not depart therefrom. One sinner destroyeth much good; these are the men that encourage the vile to be yet more vile; these be the men that quench weak desires in others; and these be the men that tempt the ignorant to harden themselves against their own salvation. A professor that hath not forsaken his iniquity is like one that comes out of the pest-house, among the whole, with his plaguey sores running upon him. This is the man that hath the breath of a dragon, he poisons the air round about him. This is the man that slays his children, his kinsmen, his friend, and himself. What shall I say? A man that nameth the name of Christ, and that departeth not from iniquity; to whom may he be compared? The Pharisees, for that they professed religion, but walked not answerable thereto, unto what doth Christ compare them, but to serpents and vipers? what does he call them, but hypocrites, whited walls, painted sepulchres, fools, and blind? and tells them that they made men more the children of hell than they were before. (Matt. xxiii.) Wherefore such an one cannot go out of the world by himself: for as he gave occasion of scandal when he was in the world, so is he the cause of the damnation of many. "The fruit of the righteous is a tree of life." (Prov. xi. 30.) But what is the fruit of the wicked, of the professors that are wicked? why, not to perish alone in their iniquity. (Job xxii. 20.) These, as the dragon, draw many of the stars of heaven, and cast them to the earth with their most stinking tail; (Rev. xii. 4;) cast many a professor into earthly and carnal delights, with their most filthy conversations.

The apostle did use to weep when he spake of these professors, such offence they knew he were and would be in the world. (Acts xx. 30. Phil. iii. 18, 19.)

These are the chief of the engines of Satan, with these he worketh wonders. One Balaam, one Jeroboam, one Ahab, O how many fish bring such to Satan's net! These are the tares that he strives to sow among the wheat, for he knows they are mischief to it. "Wherefore let every one that nameth the name of Christ depart from iniquity."

Fifth. Those that religiously name the name of Christ, and do not depart from iniquity; how will they die, and how will they look that man in the face, unto the profession of whose name they have entailed an unrighteous conversation? or do they think that he doth not know what they have done, or that they may take him off with a few cries and wringing of hands, when he is on the throne to do judgment against transgressors? Oh! it had been better they had not known, had not professed: yea, better they had never been born. For as Christ said of Judas, so may it be said of these; it had been good for that man if he had never been born. And as Christ says it had been good, so Peter says it had been better. (Mark xiv. 22. 2 Pet. ii. 20, 21.) Good they had not been born, and better they had not known and made profession of the name of Christ.

But perhaps some may ask me, what iniquity they must depart from, that religiously name the name of Christ?

I answer first, in general, those that religiously profess the name of Christ, must depart from all iniquity. They should "lay aside every weight;" (Heb. xii. 2;) they should fly "all appearance of evil." (1 Thess. v. 22.) Many there be that are willing to part with some sins, some pleasures, some unjust profits, if they may be saved; but this selling of all, parting with all, forsaking of all, is a very hard chapter.

And yet the Lord Jesus lays it there, saying so likewise, "whosoever he be of you (of any of you that professeth my name) that forsaketh not all that he hath, he cannot be my disciple." (Luke xiv. 33.) Christ by this text requireth more of them that are his than to forsake all iniquity. Wherefore, to be sure, every sin is included. No less than universal obedience will prove a man sincere. (Hos. x. 2.) A divided heart is a faulty one. He that forsaketh not every sin is partial in the law, nor can he have respect to all God's commandments. (Job xx. 13. John xiv. 21—24.) There can be no true love to Christ where there are reserves; he that will hide any one sin in his bosom, or that will keep it, as the phrase is, under his tongue, is a secret enemy to Jesus Christ. He loveth not Christ that keepeth not his sayings. To halt between two is nought, and no man can serve two masters. Christ is a master, and sin is a master; yea and masters are they so opposite,

that he that at all shall cleave to the one shall by the other be counted his enemy. If sin at all be countenanced, Christ counts himself despised. What man would count himself beloved of his wife that knows she hath a bosom for another? "Thou shalt not be for another man," saith he, "so will I be for thee." (Hos. iii. 3.) Would the king count him a loyal subject who would hide in his house, nourish in his bed, and feed at his table, one that implacably hateth and seeketh to murder his majesty? Why, sin is such an enemy to the Lord Jesus Christ; therefore, as kings command that traitors be delivered up to justice, so Christ commands that we depart from iniquity. "Take away all iniquity," is a good prayer, and to "resist unto blood, striving against sin" is a good warfare, and he that brings "every thought to the obedience of Christ" gets a brave victory. (Hos. xiv. 2. Heb. xii. 4, 2. 2 Cor. x. 5.) Grace leaveneth the whole soul, and so, consequently, all the parts thereof. Now where the whole is leavened, the taste must needs be the same throughout. Grace leaves no power, faculty, or passion of the soul unsanctified, wherefore there is no corner in a sanctified soul where sin may hide his head, to find rest and abode without control. Consequently, he that has harbour for this or that sin, and that can find a hiding-place, and an abode for it in his heart, is no Christian man. Let them then that christianly name the name of Christ, make it manifest that they do not do it feignedly by departing from iniquity. But,

Second. And more particularly, they that name the name of Christ, as above, let them depart from their constitution-sin, or if you will, the sin that their temper most inclines them to. Every man is not alike inclined to the same sin, but some to one and some to another. Now let the man that professes the name of Christ religiously, consider with himself, unto what sin or vanity am I most inclined: is it pride? is it covetousness? is it fleshly lust? And let him labour, by all means, to leave off and depart from that. This is that which David called his own iniquity, and saith, "I was also upright before him, and I kept myself from mine iniquity." (Ps. xviii. 23.) Rightly are these two put together, for it is not possible that he should be an upright man that indulgeth or countenanceth his constitution-sin; but on the contrary, he that keeps himself from that will be upright as to all the rest; and the reason is, because if a man has that grace, as to trample upon, and mortify his darling, his bosom, his only sin, he will more easily and more heartily abhor and fly the rest.

And indeed, if a man will depart from iniquity, he must depart from his darling sin first; for as long as that is entertained, the other; at least those that are most suiting with that darling, will always be haunting of him. There is a man that has such and such haunt his house, and spend his substance, and would be rid of them, but cannot;

but now, let him rid himself of that, for the sake of which they haunt his house, and then he shall with ease be rid of them. Thus it is with sin. There is a man that is plagued with many sins, perhaps because he embraceth one; well, let him turn that one out of doors, and that is the way to be rid of the rest. Keep thee from thy darling, thy bosom, thy constitution-sin.

Motives to prevail with thee to fall in with this exhortation, are several.

1. There can no great change appear in thee, make what profession of Christ thou wilt, unless thou cast away thy bosom sin. A man's constitution-sin is, as I may call it, his visible sin; it is that by which his neighbours know him and describe him; whether it be pride, covetousness, lightness, or the like; now if these abide with thee, though thou shouldest be much reformed in thy notions, and in other parts of thy life, yet say thy neighbours, he is the same man still; his faith has not saved him from his darling; he was proud afore, and is proud still; was covetous afore, and is covetous still; was light and wanton afore, and is so still. He is the same man, though he has got a new mouth. But now, if thy constitution-sin be parted with, if thy darling be cast away, thy conversion is apparent, it is seen of all, for the casting away of that is death to the rest, and ordinarily makes a change throughout.

2. So long as thy constitution-sin remains, as winked at by thee, so long thou art an hypocrite before God, let thy profession be what it will; also when conscience shall awake and be commanded to speak to thee plainly, what thou art, it will tell thee so, to thy no little vexation and perplexity.

3. Besides, do what thou canst, so long as thou remainest thus thou wilt be of a scandalous life. No honour is brought to religion by such. But,

Again, As they that name the name of Christ should depart from their constitution-sin, so they should depart from the sins of other men's tempers also. Much harm among professors is done by each other's sins. There is a man that has clean escaped from those who live in error, has shaken off the carnal world and the men thereof, and is come among professors; but behold, there also he meeteth with wicked men, with men that have not departed from iniquity, and there he is entangled; this is a sad thing, and yet so it is. I doubt there are some in the world, I mean professors, that will curse the day that ever they were acquainted with some professors. There are professors that are defilers, professors that are wicked men, professors of whom a wicked man may learn to sin. (Jer. v. 26; ii. 33.) Take heed of these, lest having fled from thine own sins, thou shouldest be taken with the sins of others. "Be not partakers of other men's sins," is the counsel and caution that Paul giveth to Timothy, if he would keep himself pure. (1 Tim. v. 22.)

4. Dost thou profess the name of Christ, and dost thou pretend to be a man departing from ini-

quity? Then take heed thou dost not deceive thyself, by changing one bad way of sinning for another bad way of sinning. This was a trick that Israel played of old; for when God's prophets followed them hard with demands of repentance and reformation, then they would "gad about to change their ways." (Jer. ii. 36.) But behold, they would not change a bad way for a good, but one bad way for another, hopping as the squirrel, from bough to bough, but not willing to forsake the tree. Hence they were said to return, but not to the Most High. Take heed, I say, of this. Many leave off to be drunkards, and fall in with covetousness. Many fall off from covetousness to pride and lasciviousness. Take heed of this. (Hos. vii. 16.) This is a grand deceit, and a common one too, a deceit of a long standing, and almost a disease epidemical among professors.

Many times men change their darling sins, as some change their wives and servants; that which would serve for such an one this year may not serve to be so for the year ensuing. Hypocrisy would do awhile ago, but now debauchery. Profaneness would do when profaneness was in fashion, but now a deceitful profession. Take heed, professor, that thou dost not throw away thy old darling sin for a new one. Men's tempers alter. Youth is for pride and wantonness; middle age for cunning and craft; old age for the world and covetousness. Take heed, therefore, of deceit in this thing.

5. Dost thou profess the name of Christ, and dost thou pretend to be a man departing from iniquity? take heed, lest thy departing from iniquity should be but for a time. Some do depart from iniquity, as persons in wrangling fits depart from one another; to wit, for a time, but when the quarrel is over, by means of some intercessor, they are reconciled again. O! Satan is the intercessor between the soul and sin, and though the breach between these two may seem to be irreconcileable; yea, though the soul has sworn it will never give countenance to so vile a thing as sin is more: yet he can tell how to make up this difference, and to fetch them back to their vomit again, who, one would have thought, had quite escaped his sins, and been gone. (2 Pet. ii. 18—22.) Take heed, therefore, O professor. For there is danger of this, and the height of danger lies in it; and I think that Satan, to do this thing, makes use of those sins again, to begin this rejoinder, which he findeth most suitable to the temper and constitution of the sinner. These are, as I may call them, the master sins; they suit, they jump with the temper of the soul. These, as the little end of the wedge, enter with ease, and so make way for those that come after, with which Satan knows he can rend the soul in pieces. Wherefore,

6. To help this, take heed of parleying with thy sins again, when once thou hast departed from them. Sin has a smooth tongue; if thou hearken to its enchanting language, ten thousand

to one but thou art entangled. See the saying of the wise man, "with her much fair speech she caused him to yield, with the flattering of her lips she forced him. He goeth after her straightway, as an ox goeth to the slaughter, or as a fool to the correction of the stocks." (Prov. vii. 21, 22.) He heard her charm, and by hearing, is noosed, and led away to her house, which is the way to hell, "going down to the chambers of death." Take heed therefore of listening to the charms wherewith sin enchanteth the soul. In this, be like the deaf adder; stop thine ear, plug it up with sin, and let it only be open to hear the words of God.

Third. Let them that name the name of Christ, depart from the iniquity of the times. There are sins that may be called the iniquity of the day. It was thus in Noah's day, it was thus in Lot's day, and it was thus in Christ's day—I mean in the days of his flesh: and it is a famous thing for professors to keep themselves from the iniquities of the times. Here lay Noah's excellency, here lay Lot's excellency, and here will lie thy excellency, if thou keep thyself from the iniquity of this day. Keep or "save yourselves from this untoward generation," is seasonable counsel, (Acts ii. 40,) but taken of but few; the sin of the time or day, being as a strong current or stream that drives all before it. Hence Noah and Lot were found, as it were, alone, in the practice of this excellent piece of righteousness in their generation. Hence it is said of Noah that he "was a just man, and perfect in his generations." (Gen. vi. 9.) And again, the Lord said unto Noah, "Come thou and all thy house into the ark; for thee have I seen righteous before me in this generation." (Gen. vii. 1.) The meaning is, he kept himself clear of the sin of his day, or of the generation among which he lived.

The same I say of Lot, he kept himself from the sin of Sodom; and hence Peter cries him up for such a righteous man. "Just Lot," saith he, "that righteous man whose righteous soul was vexed with the filthy conversation of the wicked." (2 Pet. ii. 7, 8) Mark, "a just man, a righteous man, his righteous soul," &c. But how obtained he this character? Why, he abhorred the sin of his time, he fell not in with the sin of the people, but was afflicted and vexed thereabout: yea, it was to him a daily burden. "For that righteous man dwelling among them, in seeing and hearing, vexed his righteous soul from day to day, with their unlawful deeds." So David, "I beheld," saith he, "the transgressors, and was grieved because they kept not thy word." (Ps. cxix. 158.) The sin of the times, is to God the worst of sins; and to fall in with the sin of the times is counted as the highest of transgressions. Consequently, to keep from them, though a man should, through infirmity, be guilty of others, yet he is accounted upright. And hence it is, I think, that David was called a man after God's own heart; to wit, because he served his own generation, by the will of God, or as in Acts xiii. after he had, in his own

age, served the will of God. By the sin of the times Satan, as it were, set up his standard in defiance to God; seeking then to cause his name in a signal way to be dishonoured, and that by the professors of that age. And hence it is that the Lord doth manifest such wrath against his people that are guilty of the common sin of their day, and that he shows such special favour to them that abstain therefrom. Was there no more, think you, but Noah, in his generation that feared God? Yes, several, no doubt; but he was the man that kept clear of the sin of his day, therefore he and his family must be partakers of God's deliverance; the other must die before, and not be permitted to the mercy of the ark, nor to see the new world with Noah. Unbelief was the sin of the day, when Israel was going from Egypt to Canaan; therefore all that were guilty of that transgression must be denied to go in to see that good land, yea, though it were Moses himself. "And the Lord said to Moses and Aaron, Because ye believed me not, to sanctify me in the eyes of the children of Israel, therefore ye shall not bring this congregation into the land which I have given them." (Numb. xx. 12.)

The sin of the day, is a high transgression; from the which, because Caleb and Joshua kept themselves, God kept them from all the blasting plagues that overtook all the rest, and gave them the land which he had promised to their fathers. "But my servant Caleb, because he had another spirit with him, and hath followed me fully, him will I bring into the land, whereinto he went, and his seed shall possess it." (Numb. xiv. 24.) Idolatry was the sin of the day, just before Israel was carried captive into Babylon. Now those of the priests that went astray then, even they say, God shall bear their iniquity. "But the priests, the Levites, the sons of Zadok, that kept the charge of my sanctuary, when the children of Israel went astray from me, they shall come near unto me, to minister unto me; and they shall stand before me, to offer unto me the fat and the blood, saith the Lord God. They shall enter into my sanctuary, and they shall come near to my table, to minister unto me, and they shall keep my charge." (Ezek. xliv. 15, 16.)

Great complaints have we now among professors, of deadness in duties, barrenness of the ministry, and of the withdrawing of God from his people; but I can tell you a cause of all this, namely, the sin of the day is got into the church of God, and has defiled that holy place. This is the ground and cause of all these things; nor is it like to be otherwise, till the cause shall be removed. If any should ask me what are the sins of our day, I would say they are conspicuous, they are open, they are declared as Sodom's were. (Isa. iii. 9.) They that have embraced them, are not ashamed of them: yea, they have got the boldness to plead for them, and to count them their enemies that seek to reform them. All tables are full of vomit and filthiness. And for pride and covetousness, for loathing of the gospel and contemning holiness, as these have covered the face of the nation, so they have infected most of them, that now name the name of Christ.

And I say again, when you find out a professor that is not horribly tainted with some of these things (I exclude not the ministers nor their families), let him be as a beacon upon a hill, or as an ensign in our land. But says one, Would you have us singular? and says another, Would you have us make ourselves ridiculous? and says a third, Such and such, more godly-wise than we, do so. But I answer, if God has made you singular, and called you to grace, that is singular; and bid you walk in ways that are singular, and diverse from the ways of all others. Yea, if to depart from iniquity will make you ridiculous, if to be holy in all manner of conversation will make you ridiculous, then be contented to be counted so. As for the godly-wise you speak of, let them manifest themselves to be such by departing from iniquity. I am sure that their being tainted with sins of the day, will not prove them godly-wise. "Behold, I have taught you," said Moses, "statutes and judgments, even as the Lord my God commanded me; that ye should do so in the land whither you go to possess it. Keep therefore and do them; for this is your wisdom, and your understanding in the sight of the nations, which shall hear of all these statutes, and say, Surely, this great nation is a wise and understanding people." (Deut. iv. 5, 6.) Here then is wisdom, and this is that that manifesteth a people to be understanding, and godly-wise, even the keeping of the commandments of God. And why follow the apish fashions of the world? Hath the God of wisdom set them on foot among us? or is it because the devil and wicked men, the inventors of these vain toys, have outwitted the law of God? "What nation is there so great, who hath God so nigh unto them as his people have, and as he is in all things that we call upon him for? and what nation is there so great, that hath statutes and judgments so righteous, as all this law," said Moses, "which I set before you this day." (Deut. iv. 7, 8.) This then is that which declareth us to be godly-wise, when we keep our soul diligently to the holy words of God; and fit not only our tongues and lips, but also our lives thereto.

Fourth. But again, let them that name the name of Christ depart from iniquity, that is, as I may call it, from family iniquity. There is a house iniquity; an iniquity that loves not to walk abroad, but to harbour within doors. This the holy man David was aware of, therefore he said that he would behave himself wisely, in a perfect way; yea, saith he, "I will walk within my house, with a perfect heart." (Ps. ci. 2.)

Now this house iniquity standeth in these things. 1. In domestic broils and quarrels. 2. In domestic chamberings, and wantonness. 3. In domestic misorders of children and servants.

First. For house broils and quarrels, it is an iniquity to be departed from whether it be betwixt husband and wife, or otherwise. This, as I said, is an iniquity that loves not to walk abroad, but yet it is a horrible plague within doors. And many that show like saints abroad, yet act the part of devils when they are at home, by giving way to this house iniquity; by cherishing of this house iniquity. This iniquity meeteth the man and his wife at the very threshold of the door, and will not suffer them to enter, no not with one foot, into the house in peace, but how far this is from walking together as heirs of the grace of life, is easy to be determined. Men should carry it in love to their wives, as Christ doth to his church; and wives should carry it to their husbands, as the church ought to carry it to her Saviour. (Eph v. 21—28. 1 Pet. iii. 7.) And until each relation be managed with respect to these things, this house iniquity will be cherished there. O! God sees within doors as well as without, and will judge too for the iniquity of the house as well as for that more open.

Second. As house iniquity standeth in domestic broils and contentions, so it also standeth in "chamberings and wantonness." (Rom. xiii. 13.) Wherefore the apostle putteth them both together, saying, "not in chambering and wantonness, not in strife and envying." This chambering and wantonness is of a more general extent, being entertained by all, insomuch that sometimes from the head to the foot all are horribly guilty. But, "it is a shame even to speak of those things that are done of them in secret," (Eph. v. 12;) for "through the lusts of their own hearts, they dishonour their own bodies between themselves, working that which is unseemly," (Rom. i. 24, 27;) to their ignominy and contempt, if not with their fellows, yet with God who sees them; "for the darkness hideth not from him." (Ps. cxxxix. 12.) It was for this kind of iniquity with other, that God told Eli that he would "judge his house for ever," (1 Sam. iii. 13;) also the words that follow are to be trembled at, that say, "The iniquity of Eli's house shall not be purged with sacrifice nor offering for ever." (ver. 14.) Such an evil thing is house iniquity in the eyes of the God that is above.

Third. As domestic iniquity standeth in these, so also in the disorders of children and servants. Children's unlawful carriages to their parents, is a great house iniquity, yea, and a common one too. (2 Tim. iii. 2, 3.) Disobedience to parents is one of the sins of the last days. O! it is horrible to behold how irreverently, how irrespectively, how saucily and malapertly, children, yea, professing children, at this day, carry it to their parents; snapping and checking, curbing and rebuking of them, as if they had never received their beings by them, or had never been beholden to them for bringing of them up: yea, as if the relation was lost, or as if they had received a dispensation from God to dishonour, and disobey parents.

I will add, that this sin reigns in little and great, for not only the small and young, but men are disobedient to their parents; and indeed, this is the sin with a shame, that men shall be disobedient to parents; the sin of the last times, that men shall be disobedient to parents, and without natural affection. Where now-a-days shall we see children that are come to men and women's estate, carry it as by the word they are bound, to their aged and worn-out parents? I say, where is the honour they should put upon them? who speaks to their aged parents with that due regard to that relation, to their age, to their worn-out condition, as becomes them? Is it not common now-a-days, for parents to be brought into bondage and servitude by their children? For parents to be under, and children above; for parents to be debased, and children to lord it over them. Nor doth this sin go alone in the families where it is; no, those men are "lovers of their ownselves, covetous, boasters, proud, blasphemers, that are disobedient to their parents." (2 Tim. iii. 2.) This is that the prophet means, when he saith, "The child shall behave himself proudly against the ancient, and the base against the honourable." (Isa. iii. 5.) This is a common sin, and a crying sin, and to their shame be it spoken that are guilty; a sin that makes men vile to an high degree, and yet it is the sin of professors. But behold how the apostle brands them; he saith, such have but "a form of godliness, but denying the power thereof," and bids the godly shut them out of their fellowship. (2 Tim. iii. 5.) This sin also is, I fear, grown to such a height in some, as to make them weary of their parents, and of doing their duty to them. Yea, I wish that some are not murderers of fathers and mothers, by their thoughts, while they secretly long after, and desire their death; that the inheritance may be theirs, and that they may be delivered from obedience to their parents. (1 Tim. i. 9.) This is a sin in the house, in the family, a sin that is kept in hugger-mugger, close; but God sees it, and hath declared his dislike against it, by an explicit threatening, to cut them off that are guilty of it. (Eph. v. 1, 2, 3.) Let them then that name the name of Christ, depart from this iniquity.

Disorders of servants is also a house iniquity, and to be departed from by the godly. "He that worketh deceit shall not dwell within my house," said David; "and" he "that telleth lies shall not tarry in my sight." (Ps. ci. 7.) One of the rarities in Solomon's house, and which the queen of Sheba was so taken with, was the goodly order of his servants. (2 Chron. ix. 4.)

Some of the disorders of servants are to be imputed to the governors of families, and some to the servants themselves. Those that are to be imputed to the governors of families, are such as

these: 1. When the servant learns his vileness of his master, or of her mistress. 2. When servants are countenanced by the master against the mistress; or by the mistress against the master; or when in opposition to either, they shall be made equals in things. 3. When the extravagancies of servants are not discountenanced, and rebuked by their superiors, and the contrary taught them by word and life.

Those to be imputed to the servants themselves are: 1. Their want of reverence to their superiors. 2. Their backbiting and slandering of them. 3. Their unfaithfulness in serving of them. 4. Their murmuring at their lawful commands, &c.

From all these domestic iniquities, let every one depart that religiously nameth the name of Christ. And before I leave this head, let me, to enforce my exhortation, urge upon you a few considerations to work with you, yet further to depart from these house iniquities.

First. A man's house, and his carriage there, doth more bespeak the nature and temper of his mind, than all public profession. If I were to judge of a man for my life, I would not judge of him by his open profession, but by his domestic behaviours. Open profession is like a man's best cloak, the which is worn by him when he walketh abroad, and with many is made but little use of at home. But now what a man is at home, that he is indeed. There is abroad, my behaviour to my friends, and customers, my outward honesty in dealing and avoiding gross sins. There is at home, my house, my closet, my heart; and my house, my closet, show most what I am; though not to the world, yet to my family, and to angels. And a good report from those most near, and most capable of advantage to judge, is like to be truer than to have it only from that which is gotten by my observers abroad. The outside of the platter and cup may look well, when within they may be full of excess. (Matt. xxiii. 25—28.) The outward show and profession may be tolerable, when within doors may be bad enough. "I and my house will serve the Lord," is the character of a godly man. (Josh. xxiv. 15.)

Second. As the best judgment is made upon a man from his house; so that man is like to have the approbation of God for good, that is faithful in all his house. "I know Abraham" says God, "that he will command his children and his household after him, and they shall keep the way of the Lord." (Gen. xviii. 19.) To make religion, and the power of godliness the chief of my designs at home, among those among whom God by a special hand has placed me, is that which is pleasing to God, and that obtaineth a good report of him. But to pass these, and to come to other things,

1. A master of a family, and mistress of the same, are those that are entrusted of God, with those under their tuition and care, to be brought up for him, be they children or servants. This is plain

from the text last mentioned; wherefore here is a charge committed to thee of God. Look to it, and consider with thyself whether thou hast done such duty and service for God in this matter, as, setting common frailties aside, thou canst with good conscience lift up thy face unto God; the which to be sure thou canst by no means do, if iniquity, to the utmost, be not banished out of thy house.

2. And will it not be a sad complaint that thy servant shall take up against thee, before the Judge at the last day, that he learnt the way to destruction in thy house, who art a professor? Servants, though themselves be carnal, expect, when they come into the house of professors, that there they shall see religion in its spangling colours; but behold, when he enters thy door, he finds sin and wickedness there. There is pride instead of humility, and height and raillery instead of meekness and holiness of mind. He looked for a house full of virtue, and behold nothing but spider-webs; fair and plausible abroad, but like the sow in the mire at home. Bless me, saith such a servant, are these the religious people! Are these the servants of God, where iniquity is made so much of, and is so highly entertained! And now is his heart filled with prejudice against all religion, or else he turns hypocrite like his master and his mistress, wearing, as they, a cloak of religion to cover all abroad, while all naked and shameful at home. But perhaps thy heart is so hard, and thy mind so united to the pleasing of thy vile affections, that thou wilt say, "What care I for my servant. I took him to do my work, not to train him up in religion." Well, suppose the soul of thy servant be thus little worth in thine eyes; yet what wilt thou say for thy children, who behold all thy ways, and are as capable of drinking up the poison of thy footsteps, as the swine is of drinking up swill: I say, what wilt thou do for them? Children will learn to be naught of parents, of professing parents soonest of all. They will be tempted to think all that they do is right. I say, what wilt thou say to this? Or art thou like the ostrich, whom God hath deprived of wisdom, and has hardened her heart against her young? (Job xxxix. 13—17.) Will it please thee when thou shalt see that thou hast brought forth children to the murderer? or when thou shalt hear them cry, I learnt to go on in the paths of sin by the carriages of professing parents. (Hos. ix. 13.) If it was counted of old a sad thing for a man to bring forth children to the sword, as Ephraim did, what will it be for a man to bring up children for hell and damnation? But,

Fifth. Let those that name the name of Christ depart from the iniquity of their closet. This may be called part of the iniquity of the house; but because it is not public, but as a retired part, therefore I put it here by itself. There are many closet sins that professors may be guilty of, and from which they have need to depart: As,

1. There is the pride of a library, that is, the study or closet, and I doubt this sin and iniquity to this day is with many great professors, and in my judgment it is thus manifested : 1. When men secretly please themselves to think it is known what a stock of books they have, or when they take more pleasure in the number of, than the matter contained in their books. 2. When they buy books rather to make up a number than to learn to be good and godly men thereby. 3. When, though they own their books to be good and godly, yet they will not conform thereto.

This is an iniquity now on foot in this land, and ought to be departed from. It is better to have no books, and depart from iniquity, than to have a thousand, and not to be bettered in my soul thereby.

II. There is an iniquity that attends the closet, which I may call by the name of vacancy. When men have a closet to talk of, not to pray in; a closet to look upon, not to bow before God in; a closet to lay up gold in, but not to mourn in for the sins of my life; a closet that, could it speak, would say, my owner is seldom here upon his knees before the God of heaven; seldom here humbling himself for the iniquity of his heart, or to thank God for the mercies of his life.

III. Then also a man is guilty of closet iniquity, when though he doth not utterly live in the neglect of duty, he formally, carnally, and without reverence, and godly fear, performs it. Also when he asketh God for that which he cannot abide should be given him, or when he prayeth for that in his closet, that he cannot abide in his house, nor his life.

IV. Then also a man is guilty of closet iniquity, when he desireth that the sound of the devotion he doth there may be heard by them without in the house, the street, or of those that dwell by; for a closet is only for the man and God to do things in secretly. (Matt. vi. 6.)

These things let the professor beware of, lest he add to his iniquity sin, until he and it comes to be loathsome. The closet is by God appointed for men to wait upon him in, and to do it without hypocrisy; to wait there for his mind and his will, and also for grace to perform it. And how can a man that went last time out of his closet to be naught, have the face to come thither again? If I regard iniquity in my heart, the Lord will not hear my prayer; and if so, then he will not meet me in my closet; and if so, then I shall quickly be weary thereof, being left to myself, and the vanity of my mind.

It is a great thing to be a closet Christian, and to hold it; he must be a close Christian that will be a closet Christian. When I say a close Christian, I mean one that is so in the hidden part, and that also walks with God. Many there be that profess Christ, who do oftener, in London, frequent the coffee-house than their closet; and that sooner in a morning run to make bargains than to pray unto God, and begin the day with him. But for thee, who professest the name of Christ, do thou depart from all these things; do thou make conscience of reading and practising; do thou follow after righteousness; do thou make conscience of beginning the day with God; for he that begins it not with him will hardly end it with him; he that runs from God in the morning will hardly find him at the close of the day; nor will he that begins with the world and the vanities thereof, in the first place, be very capable of walking with God all the day after. It is he that finds God in his closet that will carry the savour of him into his house, his shop, and his more open conversation. When Moses had been with God in the Mount his face shone, he brought of that glory into the camp. (Exod. xxxiv.)

Sixth. I add again, let those that name the name of Christ depart from the iniquity that cleaveth to opinions. This is a sad age for that; let opinions in themselves be never so good, never so necessary, never so innocent, yet there are spirits in the world that will entail iniquity to them, and will make the vanity so inseparable with the opinion, that it is almost impossible with some to take in the opinion and leave out the iniquity, that by the craft and subtilty of Satan is joined thereto. Nor is this a thing new, and of yesterday; it has been thus almost in all ages of the church of God, and that not only in things small and indifferent, but in things fundamental and most substantial. I need instance in none other for proof hereof but the doctrine of faith and holiness. If faith be preached as that which is absolutely necessary to justification, then faith fantastical, and looseness and remissness in life, with some, are joined therewith. If holiness of life be preached as necessary to salvation, then faith is undervalued, and set below its place, and works as to justification with God set up and made co-partners with Christ's merits in the remission of sins. Thus iniquity joineth itself with the great and most substantials of the gospel, and it is hard to receive any good opinion whatever, but iniquity will join itself thereto. (Eph. v. 12, 13.) Wicked spirits do not only tempt men to transgress the moral law, but do present themselves in heavenly things, working there, and labouring in them, to wrest the judgment, and turn the understanding and conscience awry in those high and most important things. Wherefore, I say, we must be the more watchful and careful lest we be abused in our notions and best principles, by the iniquities that join themselves thereto.

It is strange to see at this day how, notwithstanding all the threatenings of God, men are wedded to their own opinions, beyond what the law of grace and love will admit. Here is a Presbyter, here is an Independent, an Anabaptist, so joined each man to his own opinion, that they cannot have that communion one with another, as by the testament of the Lord Jesus they are commanded and enjoined. What is the cause? Is the truth?

No! God is the author of no confusion in the church of God. (1 Cor. xiv. 33.) It is then because every man makes too much of his own opinion, abounds too much in his own sense, and takes not care to separate his opinion from the iniquity that cleaveth thereto. That this confusion is in the church of Christ, I am of Paul, I of Apollo, I of Cephas, and I of Christ, is too manifest. But what unbecoming language is this for the children of the same father, members of the same body, and heirs of the same glory, to be accustomed to? whether it is pride, or hypocrisy, or ignorance, or self, or the devil, or the jesuit, or all these jointly working with the church, that makes and maintains these names of distinction. This distance, and want of love, this contempt of one another, these base and undervaluing thoughts of brethren will be better seen, to the shame and confusion of some in the judgment.

In the meantime, I advise thee with whom I am at this time concerned, to take heed of this mixture, this sinful mixture of truth and iniquity together; and to help thee in this thing, keep thine eye much upon thine own base self, labour also to be sensible of the imperfections that cleave to thy best performances, be clothed with humility, and prefer thy brother before thyself; and know that Christianity lieth not in small matters, neither before God, nor understanding men. And it would be well if those that so stickle by their private and unscriptural notions, which only is iniquity cleaving to truth; I say, it would be well if such were more sound in faith and morals, and if by their lives they gave better conviction to the world that the truth and grace of Christ is in them.

Sometimes so much iniquity is mixed with good opinions. that it prevails, not only to hurt men in this world, but to drown them in misery everlasting. It was good that the Jews did own and allow the ceremonies of the law, but since the iniquity that joined itself thereto, did prevail with them to make those ceremonies copartners with Christ in those matters that pertained to Christ alone, therefore they perished in them. The Galatians, also, together with many of the Corinthians, had like to have been overthrown by these things. Take heed, therefore, of that iniquity that seeketh to steal with the truth into thy heart, thy judgment, and understanding.

Nor doth one iniquity come without another; they are linked together, and come by companies, and therefore, usually, they that are superstitious in one thing, are corrupted in several other. The more a man stands upon his points to justify himself, and to condemn his holy brethren, the more danger he is in of being overcome of divers evils. And it is the wisdom of God to let it be so, that flesh might not glory in his presence. "His soul, which is lifted up," (Hab. ii. 4;) to wit, with his good doings, with his order and methods in religion, "his soul is not upright in him." I have often said in my heart, What is the reason that some of the brethren should be so shy of holding communion with those every whit as good, if not better than themselves? Is it because they think themselves unworthy of their holy fellowship? No, verily; it is because they exalt themselves, they are leavened with some iniquity that hath mixed itself with some good opinions that they hold, and therefore it is that they say to others, "Stand by thyself, come not near me, for I am holier than thou." (Isa. lxv. 5.) But what is the sentence of God concerning those? Why, these are a smoke in my nose, a fire that burneth all the day. Wherefore, as I said before, so I say now again, take heed of the iniquity that cleaveth to good opinions; the which thou wilt in no wise be able to shun, unless thou beest clothed with humility. But,

Seventh. Let them that name the name of Christ, depart from hypocrisies. This exhortation is as the first, general; for hypocrisies are of that nature, that they spread themselves (as the leprosy of the body) all over; not the faculties of the soul only, but all the duties of a man. So that here is a great iniquity to be parted from, an over-spreading iniquity. This sin will get into all thy profession, into every whit of it, and will make the whole of it a loathsome stink in the nostrils of God. Hypocrisy will be in the pulpit, in conference, in closets, in communion of saints, in faith, in love, in repentance, in zeal, in humility, in alms, in the prison, and in all duties. (Matt. vi. 2; vii. 20, 21; xxiii. 15. Luke xii. 1, 2; xx. 19, 20. Ezek. viii. 12. 2 Tim. i. 5. 1 Cor. xiii. 3. 2 Cor. vi. 6. Mal. ii. 23. Col. ii. 23.) So that here is, for the keeping of thy soul upright and sincere, more than ordinary diligence to be used. Hypocrisy is one of the most abominable of iniquities. It is a sin that dares it with God. It is a sin that saith God is ignorant, or that he delighteth in iniquity. It is a sin that flattereth, that dissembleth, that offereth to hold God, as it were, fair in hand, about that which is neither purposed nor intended. It is also a sin that puts a man upon studying and contriving to beguile and deceive his neighbour, as to the bent and intent of the heart, and also as to the cause and end of actions. It is a sin that persuadeth a man to make a show of civility, morality, or Christian religion, as a cloak, a pretence, a guise to deceive withal. It will make a man preach for a place and praise, rather than to glorify God and save souls; it will put a man upon talking that he may be commended; it will make a man, when he is at prayer in his closet, strive to be heard without door; it will make a man ask for that he desireth not, and show zeal in duties, when his heart is as cold, as senseless, and as much without savour as a clod; it will make a man pray to be seen and heard of men, rather than to be heard of God; it will make a man strive to weep when he repenteth not, and to pretend much friendship when he doth not love; it will make a man pretend to experience, and sanctifi-

cation when he has none, and to faith and sincerity when he knows not what they are. There is opposed to this sin, simplicity, innocence, and godly sincerity, without which three graces thou wilt be a hypocrite, let thy notions, thy knowledge, thy profession, and commendations from others, be what they will. Helps against this sin there are many, some of which I shall now present thee with. (Prov. xvi. 2; xxi. 2. Luke xvi. 15.)

1. Believe that God's eye is always upon thy heart, to observe all the ways, all the turnings and windings of it.

2. Believe that he observeth all thy ways, and marks thy actions. "The ways of man are before the eyes of the Lord, and he pondereth all his goings." (Prov. v. 21.)

3. Believe that there is a day of judgment a-coming, and that then, all things shall be revealed and discovered as they are. "For there is nothing covered that shall not be revealed, nor hid that shall not be known. Therefore, whatsoever ye have spoken in darkness, shall be heard in light, and that which ye have spoken in the ear in closets, shall be proclaimed upon the house-tops." (Luke xii. 2, 3.)

4. Believe that a hypocrite, with the cunning and shrouds for his hypocrisy, can go unseen no farther than the grave, nor can he longer flatter himself with thoughts of life. For "the triumphing of the wicked is short, and the joy of the hypocrite but for a moment. Though his excellency mount up to the heavens, and his head reach unto the clouds; yet he shall perish for ever, like his own dung: they which have seen him shall say, Where is he? He shall fly away as a dream, and shall not be found; yea, he shall be chased away as a vision of the night." (Job xx. 5—8.)

5. Believe that God will not spare a hypocrite in the judgment, no, nor punish him neither with ordinary damnation; but as they have here sinned in a way by themselves, so there they "shall receive greater damnation." (Luke xx. 47.)

Of all sins, the sin of hypocrisy bespeaks a man most in love with some lust, because he dissembleth both with God and man to keep it.

For a conclusion upon this sevenfold answer to the question above propounded; let me advise those that are tender of the name of Christ, to have regard to these things :—

First. Be well acquainted with the word, and with the general rules of holiness; to wit, with the moral law; the want of this is the cause of much unholiness of conversation. These licentious and evil times, wherein we live, are full of iniquity; nor can we, though we never so much love God, do our duty as we are enjoined, if we do not know it. The law is cast behind the back of many, when it should be carried in the hand and heart, that we might do it to the end the gospel which we profess might be glorified in the world. Let, then, the law be with thee to love it.

and do it in the spirit of the gospel, that thou be not unfruitful in thy life. Let the law, I say, be with thee, not as it comes from Moses, but from Christ; for though thou art set free from the law, as a covenant for life, yet thou still art under the law to Christ; and it is to be received by thee, as out of his hand, to be a rule for thy conversation in the world. (1 Cor. ix. 18.) What, then, thou art about to do, do it or leave it undone, as thou shalt find it approved or forbidden by the law. And when aught shall come into thy mind to be done, and thou art at a stand, and at a loss about the lawfulness or unlawfulness thereof, then betake thyself to the law of thy God, which is in thy hand, and ask if this thing be good, or to be avoided.

If this were practised by professors, there would not be so much iniquity found in their beds, their houses, their shops, and their conversations, as there is.

Second. As thou must be careful to find out the lawfulness or unlawfulness of a thing before thou puttest forth thy hand thereto, so thou must also consider again, whether that which is lawful is expedient. A thing may be lawful in itself, and may yet be unlawful to thee; to wit, if there be an inconveniency, or an inexpediency attending the doing of it. "All things are lawful for me," says the apostle, "but all things are not expedient: all things are lawful for me, but all things edify not." (1 Cor. x. 23.) This then thou must consider, and this also thou must practise.

But this is a hard lesson, and impossible to be done, except thou art addicted to self-denial. For this text, and so the practice of what is contained therein, has respect chiefly to another; to wit, to thy neighbour, and his advantage and edification; and it supposeth, yea, enjoineth thee, if thou wilt depart from iniquity, to forbear also some things that are lawful, and consequently profitable to thee, for the sake of, and of love to, thy neighbour. But how little of this is found among men! Where is the man that will forbear some lawful things, for fear of hurting the weak thereby? Alas! how many are there that this day profess, that will not forbear palpable wickedness; no, though the salvation of their own souls are endangered thereby; and how then should these forbear things that are lawful, even of godly tenderness to the weakness of their neighbour?

Thus much have I thought good to speak in answer to this question, What iniquity should we depart from that religiously name the name of Christ? And now we will make some use of what hath been spoken.

First. And the first shall be a use of examination. Art thou a professor? Dost thou religiously name the name of Christ? If so, I ask, dost thou according to the exhortation here, "Depart from iniquity?" I say, examine thyself about this matter, and be thou faithful in this work; for the deceit in this will fall upon thine own pate.

Deceive thyself thou mayest, but beguile God thou shalt not. "Be not deceived, God is not mocked: for what a man soweth, that shall he reap." (Gal. vi. 7.) Wherefore let no man deceive himself, either in professing while he lives viciously, or in examining whether his profession of this name, and his life, and conversation, do answer one another. What departing from iniquity is, I have already showed in the former part of this book; wherefore I shall not here handle that point farther, only press upon thee the necessity of this exhortation, and the danger of the not doing of it faithfully. The necessity of it is urged—

1. From the deceitfulness of man's heart, which will flatter him with promises of peace and life, both now and hereafter, though he live in iniquity, while he professeth the name of Christ. For there are that say in their hearts, or that have their hearts say unto them, "I shall have peace, though I walk in the imagination of my heart, to add drunkenness to thirst." (Deut. xxix. 19.) And what will become of them that so do, you may see by that which followeth in the text. The heart, therefore, is not to be trusted; for it will promise a man peace in the way of death and damnation. I doubt not but many are under this fearful judgment to this day. What means else their quietness of mind, their peace and boasts of heaven, and glory, though every step they take, as to life and conversation, is an apparent step to hell and damnation. These sayings—"The heart is deceitful," (Jer. xvii. 9,) and, "He that trusteth in his own heart is a fool," (Prov. xxviii. 26,) were not written without a cause. Let as many, therefore, as would examine themselves about this matter have a jealous eye over their own heart, and take heed of being beguiled thereby; let them mix hearty prayer with this matter unto God, that he will help them to be faithful to themselves in this so great a matter, yea, let them compare their lives with the holy commandment, and judge by that rather than by the fleshly fondness, that men naturally are apt to have for, and of, their own actions. For by the verdict of the word thou must stand and fall, both now, at death, and in the day of judgment. Take heed, therefore, of thy heart, thy carnal heart, when thou goest into thy life, to make a search for iniquity. Take the word with thee, and by the word do thou examine thyself. (John xii. 48.)

2. It is urged from the cunning of Satan. Wouldest thou examine thyself faithfully as to this thing, then take heed of the flatteries of the devil: can he help it, thou shalt never find out the iniquity of thy heels. He will labour to blind thy mind, to harden thy heart, to put such virtuous names upon thy foulest vices, that thou shalt never, unless thou stoppest thine ear to him, after a godly sort, truly examine and try thy ways, according as thou art commanded. (Lam. iii. 40. 2 Cor. xiii. 5.) Wherefore take heed of him, for

he will be ready at thy side when thou goest about this work. Now for thy help in this matter set God, the holy God, the all-seeing God, the sin-revenging God, before thine eyes; "for our God is a consuming fire." (Heb. xii. 29.) And believe that he hath pitched his eyes upon thy heart; also that he pondereth all thy goings, and that thy judgment, as to thy faithfulness or unfaithfulness in this work, must proceed out of the mouth of God. (Prov. v. 21; xxi. 2.) This will be thy help in this thing, that is, if thou usest it faithfully; also this will be thy hindrance if thou shalt neglect it, and suffer thyself to be abused by the devil.

3. It is urged from the dangerousness of the latter days. Wouldst thou examine thyself, then make not the lives of others any rule to thee in this matter. It is prophesied long ago, by Christ and by Paul, concerning the latter times, "that iniquity shall abound, and be very high among professors." (Matt. xxiv. 12. 2 Tim. iii. 1—8.) Therefore it will be a rare thing to find an exemplary life among professors. Wherefore cease from man, and learn of the word, try thyself by the word, receive conviction from the word; and to take off thyself from taking of encouragement from others, set the judgment before thine eyes, and that account that God will demand of thee then; and know that it will be but a poor excuse of thee to say, "Lord, such a one doth so, did so, would do so; and they professed," &c. Whether thou wilt hear me, or not, I know not, yet this I know, "If thou be wise, thou shalt be wise for thyself: but if thou scornest, thou alone shalt bear it." (Prov. ix. 12.)

Let me then, to press this use farther upon thee, show thee in a few particulars the danger of not doing of it, that is, of not departing from iniquity, since thou professest.

1. The iniquity that cleaveth to men that profess, if they cast it not away, but countenance it, will all prove nettles and briars to them: and I will assure thee, nay, thou knowest, that nettles and thorns will sting and scratch but ill-favouredly. "I went," saith Solomon, "by the field of the slothful, and by the vineyard of the man void of understanding. And, lo! it was all grown over with thorns, and nettles had covered the face thereof, and the stone wall thereof was broken down." (Prov. xxiv. 30, 31.)

Suppose a man were, after work all day, to be turned into a bed of nettles at night; or, after a man had been about such a business, should be rewarded with chastisements of briars and thorns: this would for work be but little help, relief, or comfort to him; why this is the reward of a wicked man, of a wicked professor from God; nettles and thorns are to cover over the face of his vineyard, his field, his profession, and that at the last of all; for this covering over the face of his vineyard with nettles and thorns is to show what fruit the slovenly, slothful, careless professor will reap out of his profession when reaping time shall come.

Nor can he whose vineyard, whose profession is covered over with these nettles and thorns of iniquity, escape being afflicted with them in his conscience: for look, as they cover the face of his vineyard through his sloth now, so will they cover the face of his conscience in the day of judgment. For profession and conscience cannot be separated long: if a man, then, shall make profession without conscience of God's honour in his conversation, his profession and conscience will meet in the day of his visitation. Nor will he, whose condition this shall be, be able to ward off the guilt and sting of a slothful and bad conversation, from covering the face of his conscience, by retaining in his profession the name of Jesus Christ: for naming, and professing of the name of Christ, will, instead of salving such a conscience, put venom, sting, and keenness into those nettles, and thorns, that then shall be spread over the face of such consciences. This will be worse than was that cold wet cloth that Hazael took and spread over the face of Benhadad, that he died. (2 Kings viii. 15.) This will sting worse, tear worse, torment worse, kill worse. Therefore look to it.

2. Nor may men shift this danger by their own neglect of inquiring into the truth of their separation from iniquity, for that God himself will search them. "I search the reins and the heart," saith he, "to give unto every one of you according to your works." (Rev. ii. 23.)

There are many that wear the name of Christ for a cloak, and so make their advantages by their iniquity; but Christ at death and judgment will rend this cloak from off such shoulders, then shall they walk naked, yea, the shame of their nakedness shall then appear. Now, since no man can escape the search of God, and so, not his judgment, it will be thy wisdom to search thine own ways, and to prevent judgment by judging of thyself.

3. Christ will deny those to be his that do not depart from iniquity, though they shall name his name among the rest of his people. "Depart from me," saith he, "all you that departed not from iniquity." (Luke xiii. 25—27.) Yea, they that shall name his name religiously, and not depart from iniquity, are denied by him all along.

(1.) He alloweth them not now to call him Lord. "And why call ye me Lord, Lord," saith he, "and do not the things which I say?" (Luke vi. 46.) He cannot abide to be reputed the Lord of those that presume to profess his name, and do not depart from iniquity. (Ezek. xx. 39.) The reason is, for that such do but profane his name, and stave others off from falling in love with him and his ways. Hence he says again: "Behold I have sworn by my great name, saith the Lord, that my name shall no more be named in the mouth of any man of Judah." (Rom. ii. 24. Jer. xliv. 26.)

(2.) He regardeth not their prayers. "If I regard iniquity in my heart, the Lord will not hear my prayer." (Ps. lxvi. 18.) And if so, then whatever thou hast at the hand of God, thou hast it, not in mercy, but in judgment, and to work out farther thine everlasting misery.

(3.) He will not regard their soul, but at the last day will cast it from him, as a thing abhorred by him. As is evidently seen by that thirteenth of Luke but now noted above.

Wherefore, from these few hints, thou, whoever thou art, mayest well perceive what a horrible thing it is to make a profession of the name of Christ, and not to depart from iniquity. Therefore let me exhort thee again to examine thyself, if thou hast, and dost—since thou professest that name—depart from iniquity.

And here I would distinguish, for there is two parts in iniquity, to wit, the guilt and filth. As for the guilt that is contracted by iniquity, I persuade myself, no man who knows it needs to be bid to desire to depart from that; nay, I do believe that the worst devil in hell would depart from his guilt, if he could, and might: but this is it, to wit, to depart from the sweet, the pleasure and profit of iniquity. There are that call evil good, iniquity good, and that of professors, too: this is that to be departed from, and these are they that are exhorted to forsake it upon the pains and penalties before threatened. Therefore, as I said, let such look to it, that they examine themselves if they depart from iniquity. And come, now thou art going about this work, let me help thee in this matter:—1. Ask thy heart, what evil dost thou see in sin? 2. How sick art thou of sin? 3. What means dost thou use to mortify thy sins? 4. How much hast thou been grieved to see others break God's law, and to find temptations in thyself to do it?

For the first: 1. There is a soul-polluting evil in iniquity. 2. There is a God-provoking evil in iniquity. 3. There is a soul-damning evil in iniquity. And until thou comest experimentally to know these things, thou wilt have neither list, nor will, to depart from iniquity.

For the second: I mean not sick with guilt, for so the damned in hell are sick; but I mean sick of the filth and polluting nature of it. Thus was Moses sick of sin, thus Jabez was sick of sin, and thus was Paul sick of sin. (Numb. xi. 14, 15. 1 Chron. iv. 9, 10. Rom. vii. 14. 2 Cor. v. 1—3. Phil. iii. 10—14.)

For the third: You know that those that are sensible of a sickness will look out after the means to be recovered; there is a means also for this disease, and dost thou know what that means is, and hast thou indeed a desire to it? yea, couldest thou be willing even now to partake of the means that would help thee to that means, that can cure thee of this disease? There are no means can cure a man that is sick of sin, but glory; and the means to come by that is Christ, and to go out of this world by the faith of him. There is no grace can cure this disease; yea, grace doth rather increase it: for the more grace any man has, the more is he sick of sin; the greater an offence is iniquity to him. So then, there is nothing can cure this disease, but glory; but immortal glory. And dost thou desire this medicine? and doth God testify that thy desire is true, not feigned? (2 Cor. v. 4.) I know that there are many things that do make some even wish to die: but the question is not whether thou dost wish to die, for death can cure many diseases: but is this that that moveth thee to desire to depart; to wit, that thou mightest be rid, quite rid, and stripped of a body of death, because nothing on this side the grave can rid thee and strip thee of it. And is hope that this day is approaching, a reviving cordial to thee? and doth the hope of this strike arrows into the heart of thy lusts, and draw off thy mind and affections yet farther from iniquity.

To the fourth: How much hast thou been grieved to see others break God's law, and to find temptations in thyself to do it? "I beheld the transgressors and was grieved," said David, "because men kept not thy word." (Ps. cxix. 158.) The same also had Paul, because of that body of sin and death which was in him. Professor, I beseech thee, be thou serious about this thing, because it will be found, when God comes to judge, that those that profess Christ, and yet abide with their iniquity, are but wooden, earthy professors, and none of the silver or golden ones: and so, consequently, such as shall be vessels, not to honour, but to dishonour; not to glory, but to shame.

Second. My next shall be a use of terror. Has God commanded, by the mouth of his holy apostles and prophets, that those that name the name of Christ should depart from iniquity; then what will become of those that rebel against his word? Where the word of a king is, there is power: and if the wrath of a king be as the roaring of a lion, what is, and what will be the wrath of God, when with violence it falls upon the head of the wicked?

Sirs, I beseech you consider this, namely, that the man that professeth the name of Christ, and yet leadeth a wicked life, is the greatest enemy that God has in the world, and consequently, one that God, in a way most eminent, will set his face against. Hence he threateneth such so hotly, saying, "And the destruction of the transgressors, and of the sinners shall be together; and that they that forsake the Lord shall be consumed." (Isa. i. 28; xxxiii. 14.) But what sinners are these? why, the sinners in Zion, the hypocrites in the church. So again, the Lord shall "purge out from among you the rebels, and them that transgress against him." (Ezek. xx. 38.) "All the sinners of my people shall die with the sword, which say, The evil shall not overtake nor prevent us." (Amos ix. 10.) For though such do think that by professing of the name of Christ, they shall prevent their going down to hell, yet they shall go down thither with those that have lived openly wicked and profane. Egypt and Judah, the circumcised with them that are not, for it is not a profession of faith that can save them. (Jer. ix. 26.) "Whom dost thou pass in beauty? saith God: wherein art thou bettered by the profession, than the wicked? Go down, and be thou laid with the uncircumcised." (Ezek. xxxii. 19.)

This in general; but more particularly, the wrath of God manifesteth itself against such kind of professors.

In that the gospel and means of salvation shall not be effectual for their salvation, but that it shall work rather quite contrary effects. It shall bring forth, as I said, quite contrary effects. (2 Cor. ii. 15, 16.) As,

1. The preaching of the word shall be to such, the savour of death unto death, and that is a fearful thing.

2. Yea, Christ Jesus himself shall be so far off from being a savour unto them, that he shall be a snare, a trap and a gin to catch them by the heel withal; "that they may go and fall backward," and be broken, and snared, and taken. (Isa. viii. 15; xxviii. 13.)

3. The Lord also will choose out such delusions, or such as will best suit with the workings of their flesh, as will effectually bring them down with the bullocks and with the bulls to the slaughter: yea, he will lead such forth with the workers of iniquity. (Isa. lxvi. 3, 4. Ps. cxxv. 5.)

4. Such, above all, lie open to the sin against the Holy Ghost, that unpardonable sin, that must never be forgiven. For, alas! it is not the poor ignorant world, but the enlightened professor that committeth the sin that shall never be forgiven.

I say, it is one enlightened, one that has tasted the good word of God, and something of the powers of the world to come. (Heb. vi. 3. 1 John v. 16.) It is one that was counted a brother, that was with us in our profession: it is such an one that is in danger of committing of that most black and bloody sin. But yet all and every one of those that are such, are not in danger of this; but those among these that take pleasure in unrighteousness, and that rather than they will lose that pleasure, will commit it presumptuously. Presumptuously, that is, against light, against convictions, against warnings, against mercies. Or thus, a presumptuous sin is such an one as is committed in the face of the command, in a desperate venturing to run the hazard, or in a presuming upon the mercy of God, through Christ to be saved notwithstanding: this is a leading sin to that which is unpardonable, and will be found with such professors that do hanker after iniquity. I say, it is designed by the devil, and suffered by the just judgment of God, to catch and overthrow the loose and carnal gospellers. And hence it is that David cries unto God, that he

would hold him back from these sort of sins, "Cleanse thou me from my secret faults," says he; and then adds, "keep back thy servant also from presumptuous sins; let them not have dominion over me; then shall I be upright, and I shall be innocent from the great transgression." (Ps. xix. 12, 13.)

If there were any dread of God, or of his word, in the hearts of the men of this generation, the consideration of this one text is enough to shake them in pieces: I speak of those that name the name of Christ, but do not depart from iniquity. But the word of God must be fulfilled; in the last days, iniquity must abound; wherefore these days will be perilous and dangerous to professors. "In the last days perilous times shall come, for men shall be lovers of their ownselves, covetous, boasters, proud, blasphemers, disobedient to parents, unthankful, unholy." (2 Tim. iii. 1, 2. Matt. xxiv. 12.) I do the oftener harp upon this text at this time, because it is a prediction of what shall be in the latter days, to wit, what a sea and deluge of iniquity shall in the latter days overspread and drown those that then shall have a form of godliness and of religion. So that this day is more dangerous than were the days that have been before us. Now iniquity, even immorality, shall with professors be in fashion, be pleaded for, be loved and more esteemed than holiness itself. Now godliness, and self-denial, shall be little set by; even those very men that have a form of godliness hate the life and power thereof; yea, they shall despise them that are good. Now, therefore, ministers must not think that what they say of the doctrine of self-denial among professors, will be much, if at all regarded. I say, regarded, so as to be loved and put in practice by them that name the name of Christ. For the strong hold that iniquity shall have of their affections, will cause that but little effectualness to this end will be found to attend the preaching of the word unto them.

But what will these kind of men do, when God that is just, God that is holy, and God that is strong to execute his word, shall call them to an account for these things?

Now some may say, but what shall we do to depart from iniquity?

I answer—1. Labour to see the odiousness and unprofitableness thereof, which thou mayest do by the true knowledge of the excellent nature of the holiness of God. For until thou seest a beauty in holiness, thou canst not see odiousness in sin and iniquity. Danger thou mayest see in sin before, but odiousness thou canst not.

2. Be much in the consideration of the power, justice, and faithfulness of God to revenge himself on the workers of iniquity.

3. Be much in the consideration of the greatness and worth of thy soul.

4. Be often asking of thyself, What true profit did I ever get by the commission of any sin?

5. Bring thy last day often to thy bedside.

6. Be often thinking of the cries and roarings of the damned in hell.

7. Be often considering the lastingness of the torments of hell.

8. Be often thinking what would those that are now in hell give, that they might live their lives over again.

9. Consider often of the frailty of thy life, and that there is no repentance to be found in the grave, whither thou goest.

10. Consider that hell is a doleful place, and that the devils are but uncomfortable companions.

11. Again, consider together with these how the patience of God has been abused by thee : yea, how all his attributes have been despised by thee, who art a professor, that does not depart from iniquity.

12. Moreover, I would ask with what face thou canst look the Lord Jesus in the face, whose name thou hast profaned by thine iniquity ?

13. Also, how thou wilt look on those that are truly godly, whose hearts thou hast grieved, while they have beheld the dirt and dung that hath cloven to thee and to thy profession.

14. But especially consider with thyself how thou wilt bear, together with thine own, the guilt of the damnation of others. For as I have often said, a professor, if he perishes, seldom perishes alone, but casteth others down to hell with himself. The reason is, because others, both weak professors and carnal men, are spectators and observers of his ways ; yea, and will presume also to follow him especially in evil courses, concluding that he is right. We read that the tail of the dragon, or that the dragon by his tail, did draw and cast down abundance of the stars of heaven to the earth. (Rev. xii. 4.) The tail. "The prophet that teacheth lies, he is the tail." (Isa. ix. 14, 15.) The prophet that speaketh lies, either by opinion or practice, he is the tail, the dragon's tail, the serpentine tail of the devil. And so in his order, every professor that by his iniquity draweth both himself and others to hell, he is the tail. The tail, says the Holy Ghost, draws them down ; draws down even the stars of heaven ; but whither doth he draw them ? The answer is, from heaven, the throne of God, to earth, the seat of the dragon ; for he is the God of this world. The professor then that is dishonourable in his profession, he is the tail. "The ancient and honourable, he is the head ; and the prophet that teacheth lies, he is the tail." Nor can Satan work such exploits by any, as he can by unrighteous professors. These he useth in his hand, as the giant useth his club ; he, as it were, drives all before him with it. It is said of Behemoth, that "he moveth his tail like a cedar." (Job xl. 17.) Behemoth is a type of the devil, but behold how he handleth his tail, even as if a man should swing about a cedar. (Rev. ix.) This is spoken to show the hurtfulness of the tail, as it is also said in another place. Better no professor than a wicked professor. Better open profane, than a hypocritical namer of the name of

Christ ; and less hurt shall such an one do to his own soul, to the poor ignorant world, to the name of Christ, and to the church of God.

Let professors, therefore, take heed to themselves, that they join to their naming of the name of Christ, a holy and godly conversation ; for away they must go else with the workers of iniquity to the pit, with more guilt, and bigger load, and more torment by far than others. But,

Third. My next word shall be to those that desire to be true, sincere professors of the name of Christ.

First. Do you bless God, for that he has put not only his name into your lips, but grace into your hearts, that thereby that profession· which thou makest of him, may be seasoned with that salt. "Every sacrifice shall be salted with salt." (Mark ix. 49.) Now naming of the name of Christ is a sacrifice, and a sacrifice acceptable, when the salt of the covenant of thy God is not lacking, but mixed therewith. (Heb. xiii. 15. Lev. ii. 13.) Therefore I say, since God has put his name into thy mouth to profess the same, and grace into thy heart to season that profession with such carriage, such behaviour, such life, and such conversation, as doth become the same, thou hast great cause to thank God. A man into whose mouth God has put the name of Christ to profess it, is as a man that is to act his part upon the stage in the market-place ; if he doth it well, he brings praise both to his master and himself ; but if he doth it ill, both are brought into contempt. No greater praise can by man be brought to God, than by joining to the profession of the name of Christ a fruitful life and conversation. "Herein," saith Christ, "is my Father glorified, that ye bear much fruit, so shall ye be my disciples." (Job xv. 8.) Fruitful lives God expecteth of all that profess the name of Christ. And let every one that nameth the name of Christ depart from iniquity. Bless God, therefore, if he hath kept thee from blotting and blemishing of thy profession ; if thy conversation has not been stained with the blots and evils of the times. What thou feelest, fightest with, and groanest under, by reason of the working of thine inward corruptions, with that I meddle not, nor is thy conversation the worse for that, if thou keepest them from breaking out. Thou also shall be counted holy unto God through Christ, if thou be of an upright conversation ; though plagued every day with the working of thine own corruption.

As God's grace is the salt of saints, so saints are the salt of God. The one is the salt of God in the heart, and the other is the salt of God in the world. "Ye are the salt of the earth," (Matt. v. 13,) that is, the salt of God in the earth. For the earth would be wholly corrupt, and would altogether stink, if professors were not in it. But now if the professor, which is the salt, shall indeed lose his savour, and hath nothing in his conversation to season that part of the earth, in which God has placed him, wherewith shall it be seasoned ? The place where he dwells, as well as his profession, will both stink odiously in the nostrils of the Lord, and so both come to ruin and desolation.

Indeed, as I have showed, the professor will come to the worst of it; for that God doth deny further to give him salt. "If the salt has lost its savour, wherewith shall it be salted?" (Luke xiv. 35.) Wherewith shall the salt be salted? with nothing. Therefore it is thenceforth good for nothing. No, not for the dunghill, but to be cast out, and trodden under foot of men. "He that hath ears to hear, let him hear."

How much, therefore, is the tender-hearted, and he that laboureth to beautify his profession with a gospel conversation, bound to bless God for the salt of his grace, by the which his heart is seasoned, and from his heart, his conversation.

Second. As such Christians should bless God, so let them watch, let them still watch, let them still watch and pray, watch against Satan, and pray yet for more grace, that they may yet more and more beautify their profession of the worthy name of Christ with a suitable conversation. Blessed is he that watcheth and keepeth his garment; that is, his conversation clean, nor is there anything, save the overthrowing of our faith, that Satan seeketh more to destroy. He knows holiness in them that rightly, as to doctrine, name the name of Christ, is a maul and destruction to his kingdom, an allurement to the ignorant, and a cutting off those occasions to stumble, that by the dirty life of a professor is laid in the way of the blind. (Lev. xix. 14.) He knows that holiness of lives, when they shine in those that profess the name of Christ, doth cut off his lies that he seeketh to make the world believe, and slanders that he seeketh to fasten upon the professors of the gospel. Wherefore, as you have begun to glorify God in your body and in your spirit, which are God's, so I beseech you to do it more and more.

Third. To this end, shun those professors that are loose of life and conversation. "From such withdraw thyself," saith Paul, "and follow righteousness, faith, charity, peace with them that call on the Lord out of a pure heart." (1 Tim. vi. 5. 2 Tim. ii. 22.) If a man, if a good man takes not good heed to himself, he shall soon bring his soul into a snare. Loose professors are defilers and corrupters; a man shall get nothing but a blot by having company with them. (Isa. i. 4.) Besides, as a man shall get a blot by having much to do with such; so, let him beware that his heart learn none of their ways. Let thy company be the excellent in the earth; even those that are excellent for knowledge and conversation. "He that walketh with wise men shall be wise; but a companion of fools shall be destroyed."

Be content to be counted singular, for so thou shalt, if thou shalt follow after righteousness, &c., in good earnest; for holiness is a rare thing now in the world. I told thee before that it is foretold by the word, that in the last days perilous times shall come,

and that men shall walk after their own lusts, yea, professors, to their destruction. Nor will it be easy to keep thyself therefrom. But even as when the pestilence is come into a place, it infecteth, and casteth down the healthful; so the iniquity of the last times will infect and pollute the godly. I mean the generality of them. Were but our times duly compared with those that went before, we should see that which now we are ignorant of. Did we but look back to the Puritans, but especially to those that but a little before them suffered for the word of God in the Marian days, we should see another life than is now among men, another manner of conversation than now is among professors. But I say, predictions and prophecies must be fulfilled; and since the word says plainly, that "in the last days there shall come scoffers, walking after their own lusts." (2 Pet. iii. 3, 17.) And since the Christians shall be endangered thereby, let us look to it, that we acquit ourselves like men, seeing we know these things before; lest we, being led away with the error of the wicked, fall from our own steadfastness.

Singularity in godliness, if it be in godliness, no man should be ashamed of. For that is no more than to be more godly, than to walk more humbly with God than others; and for my part, I had rather be a pattern and example of piety. I had rather that my life should be instructing to the saints, and condemning to the world, with Noah and Lot, than to hazard myself among the multitude of the drossy.

I know that many professors will fall short of eternal life, and my judgment tells me, that they will be of the slovenly sort of professors, that so do. And for my part, I had rather run with the foremost and win the prize, than come behind, and lose that and my labour and all. If a man also strive for masteries, yet is he not crowned, except he strive lawfully. And when men have said all they can, they are the truly redeemed, "that are zealous of good works." (1 Cor. ix. 24. 2 Tim. ii. 4, 5. Tit. ii. 14.)

Not that works do save us, but faith, which layeth hold on Christ's righteousness for justification, sanctifies the heart, and makes men desirous to live in this world, to the glory of that Christ, who died in this world to save us from death.

For my part, I doubt of the faith of many, and fear that it will prove no better at the day of God than will the faith of devils. For that it standeth in bare speculation, and is without life and soul to that which is good. Where is the man that walketh with his cross upon his shoulder? Where is the man that is zealous of moral holiness? Indeed, for those things that have nothing of the cross of the purse, or of the cross of the belly, or of the cross of the back, or of the cross of the vanity of household affairs; for those things, I find we have many, and those, very busy sticklers; but otherwise, the cross, self-denial, charity, purity in life and conversation, is almost quite out-of-doors among professors. But, man of God, do thou be singular as to these, and as to their conversation. "Be not ye therefore partakers with them" (Eph. v. 7) in any of their ways, but keep thy soul diligently, for if damage happeneth to thee, thou alone must bear it.

But he that will depart from iniquity, must be well fortified with faith, and patience, and the love of God, for iniquity has its beauty-spots, and its advantages attending on it: hence it is compared to a woman, (Zech. v. 7,) for it allureth greatly. Wherefore, I say, he that will depart therefrom had need have faith, that being it which will help him to see beyond it, and that will show him more in things that are invisible, than can be found in sin, were it ten thousand times more entangling than it is. (2 Cor. iv. 18.) He has need of patience also to hold out in this work of departing from iniquity. For indeed to depart from that, is to draw my mind off from that, which will follow me with continual solicitations. Samson withstood his Delilah for a while, but she got the mastery of him at the last; why so? Because he wanted patience, he grew angry and was vexed, and could withstand her solicitation no longer. (Judges xvi. 15—17.) Many there be also, that can well enough be contented to shut sin out-of-doors for a while; but because sin has much fair speech, therefore it overcomes at last. (Prov. vii. 21.) For sin and iniquity will not be easily said nay; it is like her of whom you read, she has a whore's forehead, and refuses to be ashamed. (Jer. iii. 3.) Wherefore, departing from iniquity is a work for length, as long as life shall last. A work did I say? it is a war; a continual combat; wherefore, he that will adventure to set upon this work must needs be armed with faith and patience, a daily exercise he will find himself put upon by the continual attempts of iniquity to be putting forth itself. (Matt. xxiv. 13. Rev. iii. 10.) This is called an enduring to the end, a continuing in the word of Christ, and also a keeping of the word of his patience. But what man in the world can do this, whose heart is not seasoned with the love of God, and the love of Christ? Therefore, he that will exercise himself in this work must be often considering of the love of God to him in Christ; for the more sense or apprehension a man shall have of that, the more easy and pleasant will this work be to him; yea, though the doing thereof should cost him his heart's blood. "Thy loving-kindness is before mine eyes," says David, "and I have walked in thy truth." (Ps. xxvi. 3.) Nothing like the sense, sight, or belief of that, to the man of God, to make him depart from iniquity.

But what shall I do, I cannot depart therefrom as I should?

Keep thine eye upon all thy shortnesses, or upon all thy failures, for that is profitable for thee. 1. The sight of this will make thee base in thine own eyes. 2. It will give thee occasion to see the need and excellency of repentance. 3. It will put

thee upon prayer to God for help and pardon. 4. It will make thee weary of this world. 5. It will make grace to persevere the more desirable in thine eyes.

Also, it will help thee in the things which follow:—1. It will make thee see the need of Christ's righteousness. 2. It will make thee see the need of Christ's intercession. 3. It will make thee see thy need of Christ's advocateship. 4. It will make thee see the riches of God's patience. 5. And it will make heaven and eternal life the sweeter to thee when thou comest there.

But to the question. Get more grace, for the more grace thou hast, the further is thine heart set off of iniquity, the more also set against it, and the better able to depart from it, when it cometh to thee, tempteth thee, and entreats thee for entertainment. Now the way to have more grace, is to have more knowledge of Christ, and to pray more fervently in his name; also to subject thy soul and thy lusts with all thy power to the authority of that grace thou hast, and to judge and condemn thyself most heartily before God, for every secret inclination that thou findest in thy flesh to sin-ward.

The improvement of what thou hast, is that, as I may say, by which God judges how thou wouldest use, if thou hadst it more; and according to that, so shalt thou have, or not have, a further measure. He that is faithful in that which is least, is faithful, and will be so, also in much, and he that is unjust in the least, is, and will be, unjust also in much. I know Christ speaks here about the unrighteous mammon, but the same may be applied also unto the thing in hand. (Luke xvi. 10—12.)

And if ye have not been faithful in that which is another man's, who will commit unto you that which is your own? that is a remarkable place to this purpose in the Revelations: " Behold," saith he, " I have set before thee an open door (that thou mayest have what thou wilt, as was also said to the improving woman of Canaan), and no man can shut it: for thou hast a little strength, and hast held fast my word, and hast not denied my name." (Rev. iii. 8. Matt. xv. 28.)

A good improvement of what we have of the grace of God at present pleases God, and engages him to give us more; but an ill improvement of what we at present have will not do so. " To him that hath (that hath an heart to improve what he hath) to him shall be given; but to him that hath not, from him shall be taken even that which he hath." (Matt. xxv. 24—30.) Well, weigh the place and you shall find it so.

I know that to depart from iniquity so as is required, that is to the utmost degree of the requirement, no man can; for it is a copy too fair for mortal flesh exactly to imitate while we are in this world. But with good paper, good ink, and a good pen, a skilful and willing man may go far. And it is well for thee if thy complaint be sincere, to wit, that thou art troubled that thou canst not forsake iniquity, as thou shouldest; for God accepteth of thy design and desire, and it is counted by him as thy kindness. (Prov. xix. 22.) But if thy complaint in this matter be true, thou wilt not rest, nor content thyself in thy complaints, but wilt, as he that is truly hungry, or greatly burdened, useth all lawful means to satisfy his hunger, and to ease himself of his burden, use all thy skill and power to mortify and keep them under by the word of God. Nor can it otherwise be but that such a man must be a growing man. "Every branch that beareth fruit, he purgeth it, that it may bring forth more fruit." (John xv. 2.) Such a man shall not be stumbling in religion, nor a scandal to it in his calling; but shall, according to God's ordinary way with his people, be a fruitful and flourishing bough.

And I would to God this were the sickness of all them that profess in this nation. For then should we soon have a new leaf turned over in most corners of this nation; then would graciousness of heart, and life, and conversation, be more prized, more sought after, and better improved and practised than it is. Yea, then would the throats of ungodly men be better stopped, and their mouths faster shut up, as to their reproaching of religion than they are. A Christian man must be the object of the envy of the world; but it is better, if the will of God be so, that we be reproached for well-doing than for evil. (1 Pet. ii.; iii.) If we be reproached for evil-doing, it is our shame; but if for well-doing, it is our glory. If we be reproached for our sins, God cannot vindicate us; but if we be reproached for a virtuous life, God himself is concerned, will espouse our quarrel, and in his good time will show our foes our righteousness, and put them to shame and silence. Briefly, a godly life annexed to faith in Christ, is so necessary, that a man that professes the name of Christ is worse than a beast without it.

But thou wilt say unto me, Why do men profess the name of Christ, that love not to depart from iniquity?

I answer, There are many reasons for it.

1. The preaching of the gospel, and so, the publication of the name of Christ, is musical and very taking to the children of men. A Saviour! a Redeemer! a loving sin-pardoning Jesus! what better words can come from man? what better melody can be heard? "Son of man," said God to the prophet, "Lo! thou art to them as a very lovely song," or as a song of loves, "of one that hath a pleasant voice, and can play well on an instrument." (Ezek. xxxiii. 32.) The gospel is a most melodious note, and sweet tune to any that are not prepossessed with slander, reproach, and enmity against the professors of it. Now its melodious notes being so sweet, no marvel if it entangle some, even of them that yet will not depart from iniquity to take up and profess so lovely a profession. But,

2. There are a generation of men that are and have been frightened with the law, and terrified with fears of perishing for their sins, but yet have not grace to leave them. Now, when the sound of the gospel shall reach such men's ears, because there is by that made public the willingness of Christ to die for sin, and of God to forgive them for his sake; therefore, they presently receive and profess those notions as the only ones that can rid them from their frights and terrors, falsely resting themselves content with that faith thereof which standeth in naked knowledge; yea, liking of that faith best that will stand with their pride, covetousness, and lechery, never desiring to hear of practical holiness, because it will disturb them; wherefore they usually cast dirt at such, calling them legal preachers.

3. Here also is a design of Satan set on foot. For these carnal gospelers are his tares, the children of the wicked one; those that he hath sowed among the wheat of purpose, if possible, that that might be rooted up by beholding and learning to be vile and filthy of them. (Matt. xiii. 36—42.)

4. Another cause hereof is this, the hypocrites that begin to profess find as bad as themselves already in a profession of this worthy name; and, think they, these do so and so, and therefore so will I.

5. This comes to pass also through the righteous judgment of God, who, through the anger that he has conceived against some men for their sins, will lift them up to heaven before he casts them down to hell, that their fall may be the greater and their punishment the more intolerable. (Matt. xi. 20—24.) I have now done, when I have read to you my text over again: "And let every one that nameth the name of Christ depart from iniquity."

PREFATORY REMARKS

ON

THE ACCEPTABLE SACRIFICE.

By whatever words, or title, the process be described, some great change, or breaking up of the human heart has generally preceded the grander displays of its power and affections. In the records of history and biography we meet perpetually with cases illustrating this truth. Some affliction piercing it as with a sword; some event shaking it with awe and astonishment; or even the burst of light, following on the discovery of a new truth, has often been found to open springs of fresh life in the heart, and so prepare it for a more vigorous existence. The process thus indicated is analogous to the change which the seed undergoes before it germinates into apparent and fruitful life. Its death, as it is termed, is but the breaking up of the outward folds, which form a barrier to its hidden virtues. Without the bursting of these coverings, it would never fulfil the objects of its creation. The human heart, sensitive and trembling, shrinks from the suffering involved in any change so accomplished. It is not, therefore, left to itself to choose the way in which it shall be effected. Divine Providence and the Holy Spirit are the sole efficient agents in this work. They alone possess the varied means, the wisdom and the power, by which human hearts may be broken, and then remoulded, with unspeakable additions to their worth.

That which is commonly spoken of in the world as moral discipline, aims continually at this object, but with inadequate means. It is well understood that the heart, in its natural state of pride and wilfulness, can never rightly work out what seems to be its proper destiny. Sacrifices are asked of it, which it obstinately refuses to render. It is expected to bear burdens which it indignantly casts off. Truths are proposed for its acceptance; but instead of them, it fosters prejudices and errors. Kindly affections and sympathies soothe it for a season, and in a narrow circle; but change the scene, and it is maddened with passions as selfish as they are turbulent.

Reason and experience are amply sufficient to convince mankind that some vast change must be wrought in the heart before it can be made cheerfully obedient to all the calls of duty. It is this conviction which has urged civilized nations to make so many experiments with systems of education. Whether spoken of or not, the first object of these systems is to overcome the multiplied resistances, which every congregation of human beings offers to general improvement. The greater or less success of the effort made, is determined by the conquests over individual obstinacy, or the supply of energy in some essential but defective personal virtue. Every human heart, when fairly studied, exhibits some disorder, either retarding its proper movements, or accelerating them into unequal and unhealthy action. Whether a watch gain or lose, it is equally certain that there is something wrong with its works, and to correct the evil they must be taken to pieces.

It is on the improvement of social character that the happiness of the world depends; but no improvement of this kind has ever been accomplished without the employment of a powerful corrective influence. In some cases the change has only followed on the terrible explosions of revolution. In others, it has sprung from the beneficent energies of peace, and the grave control of advancing science. But in both instances, force has been exercised on the hearts of men. They have suffered violence, more or less, according to circumstances; the breaking up of old prejudices, evil customs, base and sensual superstitions, being, in reality, the breaking of the hearts which fostered them, and thus preparing those same hearts to receive the seeds of truth and virtue.

The grander capabilities and mysteries of spiritual nature involve profounder necessities. To sow the seeds of eternal life in a human heart must be the work of God only: to prepare it to receive the seed must be equally his work; but if really subjected to the operation of his grace, it is with no superficial or partial change that it will leave his hand. Broken as to its wilfulness, cleansed as to its impurity, the fire of the divine Spirit burning up all the dross of evil memories, it now possesses the capabilities of an emancipated and purified nature, and awaits the gift of the wonderful life for which it is thus prepared.

Hence there is an excellency in the humbled and broken heart to which the proudest can make no pretension. Let the latter be endowed with the best dispositions attainable by unassisted nature, there will be hindrances to their working, perceptible to itself, and felt, not merely as occasional interruptions to a free choice of good, but as an insurmountable obstacle both to action and resolve.

And this is a necessary condition of that imperfect moral state, with which the best of men, unreached by the power of God's Spirit, must remain content. But it happily ceases to be a condition in our moral state immediately on the accomplishment of the design meditated by divine grace. Weakness, imperfection, irresolution, there may still be, and that with their manifold complications; but all these together do not constitute a necessity. They are conquerable. Not so the moral disease of the natural heart. Against this the will strives only to be, again and again, evaded or overcome. However admirable the personal character, looking at it from any standing place in the world, and on the outside,—however attractive of love and sympathy the fruits of kindly and generous dispositions, the subtle poison of innate sin will sooner or later betray its virulence, and render all the promises of virtue and happiness abortive.

When the struggles of a man, humbled and sanctified by God, are compared with the uncertain efforts of one dependent still upon his mere natural vigour, it only requires freedom from irreligious prejudice to let us discover, with startling clearness, the excellency of a broken heart. There is a beauty in the gentle, unselfish spirit, manifested in such a heart which no worldly temper can possess. There is a force and energy in it which show how wisely it has forgone all its own pretensions to goodness or merit for the honour which comes from God only; from God who when he humbles by his grace, always exalts and dignifies by his love.

H. S.

THE ACCEPTABLE SACRIFICE;

OR,

THE EXCELLENCY OF A BROKEN HEART:

SHOWING THE NATURE, SIGNS, AND PROPER EFFECTS OF A CONTRITE SPIRIT.

WITH A PREFACE PREFIXED THEREUNTO BY AN EMINENT MINISTER OF THE GOSPEL IN LONDON.

A PREFACE TO THE READER.

THE author of the ensuing discourse, now with God, reaping the fruit of all his labour, diligence, and success in his Master's service, did experience in himself, through the grace of God, the nature, excellency, and comfort of a truly broken and contrite spirit; so that what is here written is but a transcript out of his own heart: for God, who had much work for him to do, was still hewing and hammering him by his word, and sometimes also by more than ordinary temptations and desertions. The design, and also the issue thereof, through God's goodness, was the humbling and keeping of him low in his own eyes. The truth is, as himself sometimes acknowledged, he always needed the thorn in the flesh, and God in mercy sent it him, lest under his extraordinary circumstances, he should be exalted above measure; which perhaps was the evil that did more easily beset him than any other. But the Lord was pleased to overrule it, to work for his good, and to keep him in that broken frame which is so acceptable unto him, and concerning which it is said, that "he healeth the broken in heart, and bindeth up their wounds." (Ps. cxlvii. 3.) And indeed it is a most necessary qualification that should always be found in the disciples of Christ, who are most eminent, and as stars of the first magnitude in the firmament of the church. Disciples in the highest form of profession need to be thus qualified in the exercise of every grace, and the performance of every duty. It is that which God doth principally and more especially look after, in all our approaches and accesses to him. It is to him that God will look, and with him God will dwell, who is poor and of a contrite spirit. (Isa. lvii. 15; lxvi. 2.) And the reason why God will manifest so much respect to one so qualified, is, because he carries it so becomingly towards him. He comes and lies at his feet, and discovers a quickness of sense, and apprehensiveness of whatever may be dishonourable and distasteful to God. (Ps. xxxviii. 4.) And if the Lord doth at any time but shake his rod over him, he comes trembling, and kisses the rod, and says, "It is the Lord, let him do what seemeth him good." (1 Sam. iii. 18.) He is sensible he hath sinned and gone astray like a lost sheep, and therefore will justify God in his severest proceedings against him. This broken heart is also a pliable and flexible heart, and prepared to receive whatsoever impressions God shall make upon it, and is ready to be moulded into any frame that should best please the Lord. He says with Samuel, "Speak, Lord, for thy servant heareth." (1 Sam. iii. 10.) And with David, "When thou sayest, seek ye my face; my heart said unto thee, Thy face, Lord, will I seek." (Ps. xxvii. 8.) And so with Paul, who tremblingly said, "Lord, what wilt thou have me to do?" (Acts ix. 6.)

Now, therefore, surely such a heart as this must needs be very delightful to God. He says to us, "My son, give me thy heart." (Prov. xxiii. 15.) But, doubtless he means there a broken heart: an unbroken heart we may keep to ourselves; it is the broken heart which God will have us to give him; for, indeed, it is all the amends that the best of us are capable of making, for all the injury we have done to God in sinning against him. We are not able to give better satisfaction for breaking God's laws, than by breaking our own hearts; this is all we can do of that kind, for the blood of Christ only must give the due and full satisfaction to the justice of God for what provocations we are at any time guilty of; but all that we can do, is to accompany the acknowledgments we make of miscarriages with a broken and contrite spirit. Therefore we find that when David had committed those two foul sins of adultery and murder against God, he saw that all his sacrifices signified nothing to the expiating of his guilt; therefore he brings to God a broken heart, which carried in it the best expression of indignation against himself, as of the highest respect he could show to God. (2 Cor. vii. 11.)

The day in which we live, and the present circumstances which the people of God and these nations are under, do loudly proclaim a very great necessity of being in this broken and tender frame; for who can foresee what will be the issue of these violent fermentations that are amongst us? Who knows what will become of the ark of God? Therefore it is a seasonable duty, with old Eli, to sit trembling for it. Do we not also hear the sound of the trumpet, the alarm of wars; and ought we not with the prophet to cry out, " My bowels, my bowels! I am pained at my very heart; my heart maketh a noise in me, I cannot hold my peace," &c.? (Jer. iv. 19.) Thus was that holy man affected with the consideration of what might befall Jerusalem, the temple, and ordinance of God, &c., as the consequence of the present dark dispensations they were under. Will not a humble posture best become us when we have humbling providences in prospect? Mercy and judgment seem to be struggling in the same womb of Providence; and which will come first out we know not; but neither of them can we comfortably meet, but with a broken and a contrite spirit. If judgment comes, Josiah's posture of tenderness will be the best we can be found in; and also to say with David, " My flesh trembleth for fear of thee, and I am afraid of thy judgments." (Ps. cxix. 120.) It is very sad when God smites, and we are not grieved; which the prophet complains of, " Thou hast stricken them, but they have not grieved," &c. " They have made their faces harder than a rock, they have refused to return." (Jer. v. 3.)

But such as know the power of his anger will have a deep awe of God upon their hearts, and, observing him in all his motions, will have the greatest apprehensions of his displeasure. So that when he is coming forth in any terrible dispensation, they will, according to their duty, prepare to meet him with a humbled and broken heart. But if he should appear to us in his goodness, and further lengthen out the day of our peace and liberty, yet still the contrite frame will be most seasonable; then will be a proper time, with Job, to abhor ourselves in dust and ashes, (Job xlii. 6,) and to say with David, " Who are we, that thou hast brought us hitherto?" (2 Sam. vii. 18.)

But we must still know that this broken tender heart is not a plant that grows in our own soil, but is the peculiar gift of God himself. He that made the heart must break the heart. We may be under heart-breaking providences, and yet the heart remain altogether unbroken; as it was with Pharaoh, whose heart, though it was under the hammers of ten terrible judgments, immediately succeeding one another, yet continued hardened against God. The heart of man is harder than hardness itself, till God softeneth and breaks it. Men move not, they relent not, let God thunder never so terribly; let God in the greatest earnest cast abroad his firebrands, arrows, and death, in the most dreadful representations of wrath and judgment, yet still man trembles not, nor is any more astonished than if in all this God were but in jest, till he comes and falls to work with him, and forces him to cry out, What have I done? What shall I do?

Therefore, let us have recourse to him, who, as he gives the new heart, so also therewith the broken heart. And let men's hearts be never so hard, if God comes once to deal effectually with them, they shall become mollified and tender; as it was with those hardened Jews who, by wicked and cruel hands, murdered the Lord of life, though they shouted it out a great while; yet how suddenly, when God brought them under the hammer of his word and Spirit, in Peter's powerful ministry, were they broken, and, being pricked in their hearts, cried out, " Men and brethren, what shall we do?" (Acts ii. 37.)

And the like instance we have in the jailer, who was a most barbarous hard-hearted wretch; yet when God came to deal with him, he was soon tamed, and his heart became exceeding soft and tender. (Acts xvi. 29, 30.)

Men may speak long enough, and the heart not at all be moved; but, " The voice of the Lord is powerful, the voice of the Lord is full of majesty, and breaketh the rocks and cedars." " He turns the rock into a standing water, the flint into a fountain of waters." And this is a glorious work indeed, that hearts of stone should be dissolved and melted into waters of godly sorrow, working repentance not to be repented of. (2 Cor. vii. 10.)

When God speaks effectually, the stoutest heart must melt and yield. Wait upon God, then, for the softening thy heart, and avoid whatsoever may be a means of hardening it; as the Apostle cautions the Hebrews, " Take heed, lest you be hardened through the deceitfulness of sin." (Heb. iii. 23.)

Sin is deceitful, and will harden all those that indulge it; the more tender any man is to his lust, the more will he be hardened by it. There is a native hardness in every man's heart; and though it may be softened by gospel means, yet if those means be afterwards neglected, the heart will fall to its native hardness again; as it is with the wax and the clay. Therefore, how much doth it behove us to keep close to God, in the use of all gospel means whereby our hearts, being once softened, may be always kept so; which is best done by repeating the use of those means which were at first blessed for the softening of them.

The following treatise may be of great use to the people of God, through his blessing accompanying it, to keep their hearts tender and broken, when so many, after their hardness and impenitent heart, are treasuring up wrath against the day of wrath. (Rom. ii. 5.)

Oh let none who peruse this book herd with that generation of hardened ones, but be a companion of all those that mourn in Zion, and whose hearts are broken for their own, the church's, and the nation's provocations; who, indeed, are the only likely ones that will stand in the gap to divert judgments. When Shishak, King of Egypt, with a great host, came up against Judah, and having taken their frontier fenced cities, they sat down before Jerusalem, which put them all under a great consternation; but the king and princes, upon this, humbled themselves; the Lord sends a gracious message to them, by Shemaiah the prophet, the import whereof was, That because they humbled themselves, the Lord would not destroy them, nor pour out his wrath upon them by the hand of Shishak. (2 Chron. xii. 5—7.)

The greater the party is of mourning Christians the more hope we have that the storm impending may be blown over, and the blessings enjoyed may yet be continued. As long as there is a sighing party, we may hope to be yet preserved; as least such will have the mark set upon themselves, which shall distinguish them from those whom the slaughtermen shall receive commission to destroy. (Ezek. ix. 4.)

But I shall not further enlarge the porch, as designing to make way for the reader's entrance into the house, where I doubt not but he will be pleased with the furniture and provision he finds in it. And I shall only further assure him, that this whole book was not only prepared for, but also put into the press by the author himself, whom the Lord was pleased to remove, to the great loss and inexpressible grief of many precious souls, before the sheets could be all wrought off.

And now, as I hinted in the beginning, that what was transcribed out of the author's heart into the book, may be transcribed out of the book into the hearts of all who shall peruse it, is the desire and prayer of

A lover and honourer of all saints as such,

GEORGE COKEYN.

Sept. 21, 1688.

THE ACCEPTABLE SACRIFICE.

" The sacrifices of God are a broken spirit : a broken and a contrite heart, O God, thou wilt not despise."—Ps. li. 17.

THIS psalm is David's penitential psalm. It may be fitly so called, because it is a psalm by which is manifest the unfeigned sorrow which he had for his horrible sin, in defiling of Bathsheba, and slaying Uriah her husband; a relation at large of which you have in the 11th and 12th of the Second of Samuel. Many workings of heart, as this psalm showeth, this poor man had, so soon as conviction did fall upon his spirit; one while he cries for mercy, then he confesses his heinous offences, then he bewails the depravity of his nature; sometimes he cries out to be washed and sanctified, and then, again, he is afraid that God will cast him away from his presence, and take his Holy Spirit utterly from him. And thus he goes on till he comes to the text, and there he stayeth his mind, finding in himself that heart and spirit which God did not dislike: " The sacrifices of God," says he, " are a broken spirit;" as if he should say, I thank God I have that. "A broken and a contrite heart," saith he, " O God, thou wilt not despise:" as if he should say, I thank God I have that.

The words consist of two parts :—I. An assertion. II. A demonstration of that assertion.

The assertion is this, " The sacrifices of God are a broken spirit." The demonstration is this, " Because a broken and a contrite heart God will not despise."

In the assertion, we have two things present themselves to our consideration :—First. That a broken spirit is to God a sacrifice. Second. That it is to God, as that which answereth to, or goeth beyond all sacrifices : " The sacrifices of God are a broken spirit."

The demonstration of this is plain; for that heart God will not despise it, " A broken and a contrite heart, O God, thou wilt not despise." Whence I draw this conclusion: That a spirit rightly broken, an heart truly contrite, is to God an excellent thing; that is, a thing that goeth beyond all external duties whatever; for that is intended by this saying, The sacrifices, because it answereth to all sacrifices which we can offer to God; it serveth in the room of all: all our sacrifices without this are nothing, this alone is all.

There are four things that are very acceptable to God. The

First is: The sacrifice of the body of Christ for our sins; of this you read, Heb. x.; for there you have it preferred to all burnt-offerings and sacrifices: it is this that pleaseth God, it is this that sanctifieth and so setteth the people acceptable in the sight of God.

Second: Unfeigned love to God is counted better than all sacrifices, or external parts of worship: " And to love the Lord thy God with all thy heart, with all the understanding, and with all the soul, and with all the strength; and to love his neighbour as himself, is better than all whole burnt-offerings and sacrifices." (Mark xii. 33.)

Third: To walk holily and humbly, and obediently, towards and before God, is another: " Hath the Lord as great delight in burnt-offerings and sacrifices, as in obeying the voice of the Lord?" " Behold, to obey is better than sacrifice; and to hearken, than the fat of rams." (Mich. vi. 6—8. 1 Sam. xv. 22.)

Fourth: And this in our text is the fourth, " The sacrifices of God are a broken spirit: a broken and a contrite heart, O God, thou wilt not despise."

But note by the way that this broken, this broken and contrite heart, is thus excellent only to God: " O God," saith he, " thou wilt not despise it;" by which is implied, the world have not this esteem or respect for such a heart, or for one that is of a broken and a contrite spirit. No, no; a man, a woman, that is blessed with a broken heart, is so far off from getting by that esteem with the world, that they are but burdens, and trouble houses wherever they are or go; such people carry with them molestation and disquietment; they are in carnal families, as David was to the king of Gath, " troublers of the house." (1 Sam. xxi.)

Their sighs, their tears, their day and night groans, their cries and prayers and solitary carriages, put all the carnal family out of order; hence you have them browbeaten by some, contemned by others; yea, and their company fled from and deserted by others. But mark the text, " A broken and a contrite heart, O God, thou wilt not despise," but rather accept; for not to despise, is with God to esteem and set a high price upon.

But we will demonstrate by several particulars, that a broken spirit, a spirit rightly broken, a heart truly contrite, is to God an excellent thing.

First. This is evident from the comparison, " Thou desirest not sacrifice, else would I give it; thou delightest not in burnt-offerings: the sacrifices of God are a broken spirit," &c. Mark, he rejecteth sacrifices, offerings, and sacrifices; that is, all levitical ceremonies under the law, and all external performances under the gospel—but accepteth a broken heart. It is therefore manifest by this, were there nothing else to be said, that proves that a heart rightly broken, truly contrite,

is to God an excellent thing; for, as you see, such a heart is set before all sacrifice; and yet they were the ordinances of God, and things that he commanded; but lo, a broken spirit is above them all, a contrite heart goes beyond them, yea, beyond them, when all put together. Thou wilt not have the one, thou wilt not despise the other. O brethren, a broken and a contrite heart is an excellent thing. Have I said a broken heart, a broken and a contrite heart is esteemed above all sacrifices? I will add,

Secondly. It is of greater esteem with God than is either heaven or earth, and that is more than to be set before external duties. " Thus, saith the Lord, heaven is my throne, and the earth is my footstool: where is the house that ye built me, or where is the place of my rest? For all these things hath mine hands made, and all these things have been, saith the Lord. But to this man will I look, even to him that is poor and of a contrite spirit, and that trembleth at my word." (Isa. lxvi. 1, 2.)

Mark, God saith he hath made all these things, but he doth not say that he will look to them, that is, take complacency and delight in them. No, there is that wanting in all that he hath made that should take up and delight his heart. But now, let a broken-hearted sinner come before him; yea, he ranges the world throughout to find out such an one, and having found him, " To this man," saith he, " will I look." I say again, that such a man to him is of more value than is either heaven or earth; " They," saith he, " shall wax old," they shall perish and vanish away; but this man, he continues; he, as is presented to us in another place, under another character, " he shall abide for ever." (Heb. i. 10—12. 1 John ii. 17.)

" To this man will I look," with this man will I be delighted; for so to look doth sometimes signify, " Thou hast ravished my heart, my sister, my spouse," saith Christ to his humble-hearted, " thou hast ravished my heart with one of thine eyes." While it is as a conduit to let the rivers out of thy broken heart. " I am taken," saith he, " with one chain of thy neck." (Sol. Song iv. 9.) Here, you see, he looks and is ravished, he looks and is taken, as it saith in another place, " The king is held in the galleries," (Sol. Song vii. 5,) that is, is taken with his beloved, with the dove's eyes of his beloved, (Sol. Song i. 15,) with the contrite spirit of his people. But it is not thus reported of him with respect to heaven or earth; them he sets more lightly by, them he " reserves unto fire against the day of judgment and perdition of ungodly men." (2 Pet. iii. 7.) But the broken in heart are his beloved, his jewels.

Wherefore, what I have said as to this must go for the truth of God, to wit, that a broken-hearted sinner, a sinner with a contrite spirit, is of more esteem with God than is either heaven or earth. He saith he hath made them, but he doth not say he will look to them; he saith they are his throne and footstool, but he doth not say they have taken or ravished his heart; no, it is those that are of a contrite spirit do this. But there is yet more in the words, "To this man will I look;" that is, For this man will I care, about this man will I camp, I will put this man under my protection; for so to look to one doth sometimes signify; and I take the meaning in this place to be such. (Prov. xxvii. 23. Jer. xxxix. 12; xl. 4.) "The Lord upholdeth all that fall, and raiseth up all that are bowed down." (Ps. cxlv. 14.) And the broken-hearted are of this number, wherefore he careth for, campeth about, and hath set his eyes upon such an one for good. This, therefore, is a second demonstration to prove that the man that hath his spirit rightly broken, his heart truly contrite, is of great esteem with God.

Third. Yet further, God doth not only prefer such an one, as has been said, before heaven and earth, but he loveth, he desireth to have that man for an intimate, for a companion; he must dwell, he must cohabit with him that is of a broken heart, with such as are of a contrite spirit. "For thus saith the high and lofty One, that inhabiteth eternity, whose name is Holy, I dwell in the high and holy place, with him also that is of a contrite and humble spirit," &c. (Isa. lvii. 15.)

Behold here both the majesty and condescension of the high and lofty One; his majesty, in that he is high, and the inhabiter of eternity; "I am the high and lofty One," saith he, "I inhabit eternity." Verily this consideration is enough to make the broken-hearted man creep into a mouse-hole, to hide himself from such a majesty! But behold his heart, his condescending mind; I am for dwelling also with him that hath a broken heart, with him that is of a contrite spirit; that is the man that I would converse with, that is the man with whom I will cohabit; that is, he, saith God, "I will choose for my companion." For to desire to dwell with one supposeth all these things; and verily, of all the men in the world, none have acquaintance with God, none understand what communion with him, and what his teachings mean, but such as are of a broken and contrite heart. "He is nigh to them that are of a broken spirit." (Ps. xxxiv. 18.) These are intended in the 14th Psalm, where it is said, "The Lord looked down from heaven, to see if any did understand and seek God," that he might find somebody in the world with whom he might converse; for indeed there is none else that either understand or that can tend to hearken to him. God, as I may say, is forced to break men's hearts, before he can make them willing to cry to him, or be willing that he should have any concerns with them; the rest shut their eyes, stop their ears, withdraw their hearts, or say unto God, Begone (Job xxi.) But now, the broken in heart can tend it; he has leisure, yea, leisure, and will, and understanding, and all; and therefore is a fit man to have to do with God. There is also room in this man's house, in this man's heart, in this man's spirit, for God to dwell, for God to walk, for God to set up a kingdom.

Here, therefore, is suitableness. "Can two walk together," saith God, "except they are agreed?" (Amos iii. 3.) The broken-hearted desireth God's company: When wilt thou come unto me? saith he. The broken-hearted loveth to hear God speak and talk to him. Here is a suitableness, "Cause me," saith he, "to hear joy and gladness, that the bones which thou hast broken may rejoice." (Ps. li. 8.) But here lies the glory, in that the high and lofty One, the God that inhabiteth eternity, and that has a high and holy place for his habitation, should choose to dwell with, and to be a companion of the broken in heart, and of them that are of a contrite spirit. Yea, and here is also great comfort for such.

Fourth. God doth not only prefer such a heart before all sacrifices, nor esteems such a man above heaven and earth, nor yet only desire to be of his acquaintance, but he reserveth for him his chief comforts, his heart-reviving, and soul-cherishing cordials. "I dwell," saith he, "with such, to revive them, and to support and comfort them; to revive the spirit of the humble, and to revive the heart of the contrite ones." (Isa. lvii. 15.) The broken-hearted man is a fainting man; he has his qualms, his sinking fits; he ofttimes dies away with pain and fear; he must be stayed with flagons, and comforted with apples, or else he cannot tell what to do: he pines, he pines away in his iniquity; nor can anything keep him alive and make him well, but the comforts and cordials of Almighty God. Wherefore with such an one God will dwell, to revive the heart, to revive the spirit: "To revive the spirit of the humble, and to revive the heart of the contrite ones." (Ezek. xxxiii. 10, 11.)

God has cordials, but they are to comfort them that are cast down, (2 Cor. vii. 6;) and such are the broken-hearted: as for them that are whole, they need not the physician. (Mark ii. 17.) They are the broken in spirit that stand in need of cordials. Physicians are men of no esteem, but with them that feel their sickness; and this is one reason why God is so little accounted of in the world, even because they have not been made sick by the wounding stroke of God. But when a man is wounded, has his bones broken, or is made sick, and laid at the grave's mouth, who is of that esteem with him as is an able physician? What is so much desired as are the cordials, comforts, and suitable supplies of the skilful physician in those matters? And thus it is with the broken-hearted; he needs, and God has prepared for him, plenty of the comforts and cordials of heaven, to succour and relieve his sinking soul.

Wherefore such a one lieth under all the promises that have succour in them, and consolation for men, sick and desponding under the sense of sin, and heavy wrath of God; and they, says God, shall be refreshed and revived with them. Yea, they are designed for them; he hath therefore broken their hearts, he hath therefore wounded their spirits, that he might make them apt to relish his reviving cordials, that he might minister to them his reviving comforts. For indeed, so soon as he hath broken them, his bowels yearn, and his compassions roll up and down within him, and will not suffer him to abide afflicting. Ephraim was one of these; but so soon as God had smitten him, behold his heart, how it works towards him! "Is Ephraim," saith he, "my dear son?" that is, he is so, "Is he a pleasant child?" that is, he is so, "for since I spake against him, I do earnestly remember him still, therefore my bowels are troubled for him; I will surely have mercy upon him, saith the Lord God." (Jer. xxxi. 18—20.) This therefore is another demonstration.

Fifth. As God prefers such a heart, and esteems the man that has it above heaven and earth; as he covets intimacy with such an one, and prepares for him his cordials; so when he sent his Son Jesus into the world to be a Saviour, he gave in special a charge to take care of such; yea, that was one of the main reasons, he sent him down from heaven, anointed for his work on earth. "The Spirit of the Lord God is upon me," saith he, "because he hath anointed me to preach the gospel to the poor, he hath sent me to bind up the broken-hearted," &c. (Isa. lxi. 1.) Now that this is meant of Christ, is confirmed by his own lips; for in the days of his flesh he takes this book in his hand, when he was in the synagogue at Nazareth, and read this very place unto the people, and then tells them, that that very day that scripture was fulfilled in their ears. (Luke iv. 16—18.)

But see, these are the souls whose welfare is contrived in the heavens. God consulted their salvation, their deliverance, their health, before his Son came down from thence. Doth not therefore this demonstrate, that a broken-hearted man, that a man of a contrite spirit, is of great esteem with God? I have often wondered at David, that he should give Joab and the men of war a charge, that they take heed that they carry it tenderly to that young rebel Absalom his son. (2 Sam. xviii. 5.) But that God, the high God, the God against whom we have sinned, should, so soon as he has smitten, give his son a command, a charge, a commission, to take care of, to bind up, and heal the broken in heart; this is that which can never be sufficiently admired, or wondered at, by men or angels.

And as this was his commission, so he acted; as is set forth by the parable of the man who fell among thieves. He went to him, poured into his wounds wine and oil; he bound him up, took him, set him upon his own beast, had him to an inn, gave the host a charge to look well to him, with money in hand, and a promise at his return to recompense him in what further he should be expensive while he was under his care. (Luke

x. 30—35.) Behold, therefore, the care of God which he has for the broken in heart; he has given a charge to Christ his son, to look well to them, and to bind up and heal their wounds. Behold also the faithfulness of Christ, who doth not hide, but read his commission as soon as he entereth upon his ministry, and also falls into the practical part thereof: "He healeth the broken in heart, and bindeth up their wounds." (Ps. cxlvii. 3.)

And behold again into whose care a broken heart and a contrite spirit hath put this poor creature; he is under the care of God, the care and cure of Christ. If a man was sure that his disease had put him under the special care of the king and the queen, yet could he not be sure of life, he might die under their sovereign hands. Ay, but here is a man in the favour of God; and under the hand of Christ to be healed; under whose hand none yet ever died for want of skill and power in him to save their life; wherefore this man must live; Christ has in commission not only to bind up his wounds but to heal him; he has of himself so expounded it in reading his commission: wherefore he that has his heart broken, and that is of a contrite spirit; must not only be taken in hand, but healed; healed of his pain, grief, sorrow, sin, and fears of death and hell-fire. Wherefore he adds, that he must give unto such "Beauty for ashes, the oil of joy for mourning, the garment of praise for the spirit of heaviness, and must comfort all that mourn." (Isa. lxi. 2, 3.) This, I say, he has in the commission; the broken-hearted are put into his hand, and he has said himself he will heal him. Hence he says of that same man, "I have seen his ways and will heal him; I will lead him also, and restore comforts unto him and to his mourners; and I will heal him. (Isa. lvii. 18, 19.) And this is a fifth demonstration.

Sixth. As God prefers such a heart, and so esteems the man that has it; as he desires his company, has provided for him his cordials, and given a charge to Christ to heal him: so he has promised in conclusion to save him. "He saveth such as be of a contrite spirit;" or, as the margin has it, that be "contrite of spirit." (Ps. xxxiv. 18.)

And this is the conclusion of all; for to save a man is the end of all special mercy. "He saveth such as be of a contrite spirit." To save is to forgive; for without forgiveness of sins we cannot be saved. To save is to preserve one in this miserable world; and to deliver one from all those devils, temptations, snares, and destructions that would were we not kept, were we not preserved of God, destroy us body and soul for ever. To save, is to bring a man body and soul to glory; and to give him an eternal mansion-house in heaven, that he may dwell in the presence of this good God, and the Lord Jesus, and to sing to them the songs of his redemption for ever and ever. This it is to be saved; nor can anything less than this complete the salvation of the sinner. Now this is to be the lot of him that is of a broken heart, and the end that God will make with him that is of a contrite spirit. "He saveth such as be contrite of spirit. He saveth such! This is excellent!

But, do the broken in heart believe this? Can they imagine that this is to be the end that God has designed them to, and that he intended to make with them in the day in which he began to break their hearts? No, no; they, alas! think quite the contrary. They are afraid that this is but the beginning of death, and a token that they shall never see the face of God with comfort, either to this world or that which is to come. Hence they cry, "Cast me not away from thy presence;" or, "Now I am free among the dead, whom God remembers no more." (Ps. li. 11; lxxxviii. 4, 5.) For indeed there goes to the breaking of the heart a visible appearance of the wrath of God, and a home-charge from heaven of the guilt of sin to the conscience. This to reason is very dreadful; for it cuts the soul down to the ground: "For a wounded spirit none can bear." (Prov. xviii. 14.)

It seems also now to this man, that this is but the beginning of hell, but as it were the first step down to the pit; when, indeed, all these are but the beginnings of love, and but that which makes way for life. The Lord kills before he makes alive, he wounds before his hands make whole. Yea, he does the one, in order to, or because he would do the other; he wounds, because his purpose is to heal. "He maketh sore, and bindeth up; he woundeth, and his hands make whole." (Deut. xxxii. 39. 1 Sam. ii. 6. Job v. 18.) His design, I say, is the salvation of the soul. He scourgeth, he breaketh the heart of every son whom he receiveth, and woe be to him whose heart God breaketh not.

And thus have I proved what at first I asserted, namely, that a spirit rightly broken, a heart truly contrite, is to God an excellent thing. "A broken and a contrite heart, O God, thou wilt not despise." For thus say I: 1. This is evident, for that it is better than sacrifices, than all sacrifice. 2. The man that has it is of more esteem with God than heaven and earth. 3. God coveteth such a man, for his intimate and house companion. 4. He reserveth for him his cordials and spiritual comforts. 5. He has given his Son a charge, a commandment, to take care that the broken-hearted be healed, and he is resolved to heal them. 6. And concluded that the broken-hearted, and they that are of a contrite spirit, shall be saved, that is possessed of the heavens.

I come now in order to show you what a broken heart and what a contrite spirit is. This must be done, because in the discovery of this lies both the comfort of them that have it, and the conviction of them that have it not. Now, that I may do this the better, I must propound and speak to these four things: I. I must show you what an one that heart is that is not broken, that is not contrite. II. I must show you how or with what the heart is broken and made contrite.

III. Show you how and what it is when broken and made contrite. And, IV. I shall, last of all, give you some signs of a broken and contrite heart.

I. For the first of these, to wit, What an one that heart is that is not a broken, that is not a contrite heart.

1. The heart, before it is broken, is hard and stubborn, and obstinate against God and the salvation of the soul. (Zech. vii. 12. Deut. ii. 30; ix. 27.)

2. It is a heart full of evil imaginations and darkness. (Gen. viii. 12. Rom. i. 21.)

3. It is a heart deceitful and subject to be deceived, especially about the things of an eternal concernment. (Isa. xliv. 20. Deut. xi. 16.)

4. It is a heart that rather gathereth iniquity and vanity to itself, than anything that is good for the soul. (Ps. xli. 6; xciv. 11.)

5. It is an unbelieving heart, and one that will turn away from God to sin. (Heb. iii. 12. Deut. xvii. 17.)

6. It is a heart not prepared for God, being uncircumcised, nor for the reception of his holy word. (2 Chron. xii. 14. Ps. lxviii. 8. Acts vii. 51.)

7. It is a heart not single, but double; it will pretend to serve God, but will withal lean to the devil and sin. (Ps. xii. 2. Ezek. xxxiii. 31.)

8. It is a heart proud and stout; it loves not to be controlled, though the controller be God himself. (Ps. ci. 5. Prov. xvi. 5. Mal. iii.)

9. It is a heart that will give place to Satan, but will resist the Holy Ghost. (Acts v. 3; vii. 51.)

10. In a word, "It is deceitful above all things, and desperately wicked; so wicked that none can know it." (Jer. xvii. 9.)

That the heart before it is broken is such, and worse than I have described it to be, is sufficiently seen by the whole course of the world. Where is the man, whose heart has not been broken, and whose spirit is not contrite, that according to the word of God deals honestly with his own soul? it is one character of a right heart, that it is found in God's statutes, and honest. (Ps. cxix. 18. Luke viii. 15.) Now, an honest heart will not put off itself, nor be put off with that which will not go for current money with the merchants; I mean, with that which will not go for saving grace at the day of judgment. But, alas, alas! but few men, how honest soever they are to others, have honesty towards themselves; though he is the worst of deceivers who deceiveth his own soul, as James has it, about the things of his own soul. (James i. 22, 26.) But,

II. I now come to show you with what, and how the heart is broken, and the spirit made contrite.

First. The instrument with which the heart is broken, and with which the spirit is made contrite, is the word, "Is not my word," says God, "like a fire, and like a hammer, that breaketh the rock in pieces?" (Jer. xxiii. 29.) The rock, in this text, is the heart, which in another place is compared to an adamant, which adamant is harder than flint. (Zech. vii. 11, 12. Ezek. iii. 9.) This rock, this adamant, this stony heart, is broken and made contrite by the word. But it only is so when the word is as a fire, and as a hammer to break and melt it. And then, and then only it is as a fire, and a hammer to the heart to break it, when it is managed by the arm of God. No man can break the heart with the word; no angel can break the heart with the word; that is, if God forbears to second it by mighty power from heaven. This made Balaam go without a heart rightly broken and truly contrite, though he was rebuked by an angel; and the Pharisees die in their sins, though rebuked for them, and admonished to turn from them, by the Saviour of the world. Wherefore, though the word is the instrument with which the heart is broken, yet it is not broken with the word, till that word is managed by the might and power of God.

This made the prophet Isaiah, after long preaching, cry out, that he had laboured for nought, and in vain; and this made him cry to God, "to rend the heavens and come down;" that the mountains, or rocky hills, or hearts, might be broken, and melt at his presence. (Isa. xlix. 4; lxvi. 1, 2.) For he found by experience, that as to this no effectual work could be done, unless the Lord put to his hand. This also is often intimated in the Scriptures, where it saith, "When the preachers preached effectually to the breaking of men's hearts, the Lord wrought with them; the hand of the Lord was with them;" and the like. (Mark xvi. 20. Acts xi. 21.)

Now when the hand of the Lord is with the word, then it is mighty; it is "mighty through God to the pulling down of strongholds." It is sharp, then, as a sword in the soul and spirit; it sticks like an arrow in the hearts of sinners, to the causing of the people to fall at his foot for mercy. Then it is, as was said afore, as a fire, and as a hammer to break this rock in pieces. (2 Cor. x. 4. Heb. iv. 12. Ps. cx. 3.) And hence the word is made mention of, under a double consideration. 1. As it stands by itself. 2. As attended with power from heaven.

1. As it stands by itself, and is not seconded with saving operation from heaven, it is called the word only, the word barely, or as if it was only the word of men. (1 Thess. i. 5—7. 1 Cor. iv. 19, 20. 1 Thess. ii. 13.) Because, then, it is only as managed by men, who are not able to make it accomplish that work. The word of God, when in a man's hand only, is like the father's sword in the hand of the sucking child; which sword, though never so well pointed, and though never so sharp on the edges, is not now able to conquer a foe, and to make an enemy fall and cry out for mercy, because it is but in the hand of the child. But now, let the same word be put into the hand of a skilful father (and God is both skilful and able to manage his word), and then the sinner, and

then the proud helpers too, are both made to stoop and submit themselves. Wherefore, I say, though the word be the instrument, yet of itself doth do no saving good to the soul, the heart is not broken, nor the spirit made contrite thereby; it only worketh death, and leaveth men in the chains of their sins, still faster bound over to eternal condemnation. (2 Cor. ii. 15, 16.)

2. But when seconded by mighty power, then the same word is as the roaring of a lion, as the piercing of a sword, as a burning fire in the bones, as thunder, and as a hammer that dashes all to pieces. (Jer. xxv. 30. Amos i. 2; iii. 8. Acts ii. 37. Jer. xx. 9. Ps. xxix. 3—10.) Wherefore, from hence it is to be concluded, that whoever has heard the word preached, and has not heard the voice of the living God therein, has not as yet had their hearts broken, nor their spirits made contrite for their sins.

Second. And this leads me to the second thing, to wit, to show how the heart is broken and the spirit made contrite by the word; and verily it is when the word comes home with power. But this is but general; wherefore, more particularly,

1. Then the word works effectually to this purpose, when it findeth out the sinner and his sin, and shall convince him that it has found him out. Thus it was with our first father; when he had sinned, he sought to hide himself from God; he gets among the trees of the garden, and there he shrouds himself; but yet, not thinking himself secure, he covers himself with fig-leaves, and now he lieth quiet. Now God shall not find me, thinks he, nor know what I have done; but lo, by and by, he hears the voice of the Lord God walking in the garden. And now Adam, what do you mean to do? Why as yet he skulketh, and hides his head, and seeks yet to lie undiscovered; but behold, the voice cries out, "Adam!" And now he begins to tremble. "Adam, where art thou?" says God; and now Adam is made to answer. But the voice of the Lord God doth not leave him here. No, it now begins to search, and to inquire after his doings, and to unravel what he had wrapt together and covered, until it had made him bare and naked in his own sight before the face of God. (Gen. iii. 7—12.) Thus, therefore, doth the word, when managed by the arm of God. It findeth out, it singleth out the sinner; the sinner finds it so; it finds out the sins of the sinner, it unravels his whole life, it strips him, and lays him naked in his own sight before the face of God; neither can the sinner nor his wickedness be longer hid and covered; and now begins the sinner to see what he never saw before.

2. Another instance for this is David, the man of our text; he sins, he sins grossly, he sins and hides it; yea, and seeks to hide it from the face of God and man. Well, Nathan is sent to preach a preaching to him, and that in common, and that in special: in common, by a parable; in special, by a particular application of it to him. While

Nathan only preached in common, or in general, David was fish-whole, and stood as right in his own eyes as if he had been as innocent and as harmless as any man alive. But God had a love for David, and therefore commands his servant Nathan to go home, not only to David's ears, but to David's conscience.

Well, David now must fall, says Nathan, "Thou art the man;" says David, "I have sinned," (2 Sam. xii. 13;) and then his heart was broken, and his spirit made contrite, as this psalm and our text doth show.

3. A third instance is that of Saul; he had heard many a sermon, and was become a great professor, yea, he was more zealous than were many of his equals; but his heart was never broken, nor his spirit never made contrite, till he heard one preach from heaven, till he heard God, in the word of God, making inquiry after his sins: "Saul, Saul, why persecutest thou me?" says Jesus; and then he can stand no longer; for then his heart brake, then he falls to the ground, then he trembles, then he cries out, "Who art thou, Lord?" And, "Lord, what wilt thou have me to do?" (Acts ix.) Wherefore, as I said, then the word works effectually to this purpose, when it findeth out the sinner and his sin, and also when it shall convince him that it has found him out. Only I must join here a caution, for every operation of the word upon the conscience is not saving; nor doth all conviction end in the saving conversion of the sinner. It is then only such an operation of the word that is intended, namely, that shows the sinner not only the evil of his ways, but brings the heart unfeignedly over to God by Christ. And this brings me to the third thing.

III. I am therefore come to show you, how, and what the heart is, when broken and made contrite. And this I must do, by opening unto you the two chief expressions in the text. First. What is meant by this word broken. Second. What is meant by this word contrite.

First. For this word "broken," Tindal renders it a troubled heart, but I think there is more in it. I take it therefore to be a heart disabled, as to former actions; even as a man whose bones are broken is disabled, as to his way of running, leaping, wrestling, or aught else, which vainly he was wont to do: wherefore that which was called a broken heart in the text, he calls his broken bones in verse the eighth. "Cause me," saith he, " to hear joy and gladness, that the bones that thou hast broken may rejoice." And why is the breaking of the heart compared to the breaking of the bones? but because, as when the bones are broken the outward man is disabled as to what it was wont to do; so when the spirit is broken, the inward man is disabled as to what vanity and folly it before delighted in. Hence feebleness is joined with his brokenness of heart. "I am feeble," saith he, "and sore broken;" I have lost my strength

and former vigour, as to vain and sinful courses. (Ps. xxxviii. 8.)

This, then, it is to have the heart broken; namely, to have it lamed, disabled, and taken off, by sense of God's wrath due to sin, from that course of life it formerly was conversant in ; and to show that this work is no fancy, nor done but with great trouble to the soul, it is compared to the putting the bones out of joint, the breaking of the bones, the burning of the bones with fire ; or as the taking the natural moisture from the bones ; the vexing of the bones, &c. (Ps. xxxii. 14 Jer. xx. 9. Lam. i. 13. Ps. vi. 2. Prov. xvii. 22.) All which are expressions adorned with such similitudes as do undeniably declare that to sense and feeling a broken heart is a grievous thing.

Second. What is meant by the word contrite? A contrite spirit is a penitent one; one sorely grieved, and deeply sorrowful for the sins it has committed against God, and to the damage of the soul; and so it is to be taken in all those places where a contrite spirit is made mention of; as in Ps. xxxiv. 18. Isa. lvii. 15; lxvi. 2.

As a man that has by his folly procured a broken leg or arm, is heartily sorry that ever he was so foolish as to be engaged in such foolish ways of idleness and vanity ; so he whose heart is broken with a sense of God's wrath due to his sin, hath deep sorrow in his soul, and greatly repents that ever he should be such a fool, as by rebellious doings to bring himself and his soul to so much sharp affliction. Hence, while others are sporting themselves in vanity, such a one doth call his sin his greatest folly. "My wounds stink, and are corrupt," saith David, "because of my foolishness." And again, "O God, thou knowest my foolishness, and my sins are not hid from thee." (Ps. xxxviii. 5; lxix. 5.)

Men, whatever they say with their lips, cannot conclude, if yet their hearts want breaking, that sin is a foolish thing. Hence it says, " The foolishness of fools is their folly." (Prov. xiv. 24.) That is, the foolishness of some men is, that they take pleasure in their sins; for their sins are their foolishness, and the folly of their soul lies in their countenancing of this foolishness. But the man whose heart is broken, he is none of these, he cannot be one of these, no more than he that has his bones broken can rejoice that he is desired to play a match at football. Hence to hear others talk foolishly, is to the grief of those whom God has wounded ; or, as it is in another place, "Their words are like the piercings of a sword." (Ps. lxix. 26. Prov. xii. 18.) This, therefore, I take to be the meaning of these two words, a broken and a contrite spirit.

IV. Lastly. As to this I now come more particularly, to give you some signs of a broken heart, of a broken and a contrite spirit.

First. A broken-hearted man, such as is intended in the text, is a sensible man; he is brought to the exercise of all the senses of his soul. All others are dead, senseless, and without true feeling of what the broken-hearted man is sensible of.

1. He sees himself to be what others are ignorant of ; that is, he sees himself to be not only a sinful man, but a man by nature in the gall and bond of sin. "In the gall of sin ;" it is Peter's expression to Simon, and it is a saying common to all men. For every man in a state of nature is in the gall of sin. He was shapen in it, conceived in it ; it has also possession of, and by that possession, infected the whole of his soul and body. (Ps. li. 5. Acts viii. 23.) This he sees, this he understands ; every professor sees not this, because the blessing of a broken heart is not bestowed on every one. David says, "There is no soundness in my flesh." And Solomon suggests that a plague or running sore is in the very heart. But every one perceives not this. (Ps. xxxviii. 3. 1 Kings viii. 38.) He saith, again, that his "wounds stank, and were corrupted ;" that his "sore ran, and ceased not." (Ps. xxxviii. 5 ; lxxvii. 2.) But these things the brutish man, the man whose heart was never broken, has no understanding of. But the broken-hearted, the man that has a broken spirit, he sees, as the prophet has it, he sees his sickness. he sees his wound. "When Ephraim saw his sickness, and Judah saw his wound." (Hos. v. 13.) He sees it to his grief, he sees it to his sorrow.

2. He feels what others have no sense of. He feels the arrows of the Almighty, and that they stick fast in him. He feels how sore and sick, by the smiting of God's hammer upon his heart to break it, his poor soul is made. He feels a burden intolerably lying upon his spirit. "Mine iniquities,' saith he, "are gone over my head ; as a heavy burden, they are too heavy for me." He feels also the heavy hand of God upon his soul, a thing unknown to carnal men. (Ps. xxxviii. 2. Hos. vi. 13. Ps. xxxviii. 4.) He feels pain, being wounded, even such pains as others cannot understand, because they are not broken. "My heart," says David, " is sore pained within me." Why so ? Why, "the terrors of death are fallen upon me." The terrors of death cause pain ; yea, pain of the highest nature. Hence that which is here called pains, is in another place called pangs. (Ps. lv. 4. Isa. xxi. 3.)

You know broken bones occasion pain, strong pain ; yea, pain that will make a man or woman groan, "with the groaning of a deadly wounded man." (Ezek. xxx. 24.) Soul pain is the sorest pain, in comparison to which the pain of the body is a very tolerable thing. (Prov. xviii. 14.) Now, here is soul pain, here is heart pain ; here we are discoursing of a wounded, of a broken spirit. Wherefore this pain is to be felt to the sinking of the whole man ; neither can any support this but God. Here is death in this pain, death for ever, without God's special mercy ; and this the broken-hearted man doth feel. "The sorrows of death," said David, "compassed me about, and the pains of hell got hold upon me, and I found trouble and sorrow." (Ps. cxvi.) Aye, I'll warrant thee, poor man, thou foundest trouble and sorrow indeed. For the pains of hell and sorrows of death are pains and sorrow the most intolerable. But this the man is acquainted with that has his heart broken.

3. As he sees and feels, so he hears that which augments his woe and sorrow. You know, if a man has his bones broken, he does not only see and feel, but ofttimes also hears what increases his grief ; as that his wounds are incurable ; that his bone is not rightly set ; that there is danger of a gangrene ; that he may be lost for want of looking to. These are the voices, the sayings, that haunt the house of one that has his bones broken. And a broken-hearted man knows what I mean by this ; he hears that which makes his lips quiver, and at the noise of which he seems to feel rottenness enter into his bones ; he trembleth in himself, and wishes that he may hear joy and gladness, that the bones, the heart and spirit which God has broken, may rejoice. (Hab. iii. 16. Ps. li. 8.) He thinks he hears God say, the devil say, his conscience say, and all good men to whisper among themselves, saying, There is no help for him from God. Job heard this, David heard this, Haman heard this ; and this is a common sound in the ears of the broken-hearted.

4. The broken-hearted smell what others cannot scent. Alas ! sin never smelled so to any man alive, as it smells to the broken-hearted. You know, wounds will stink ; but no stink like that of sin, to the broken-hearted man. His own sins stink, and so do the sins of all the world to him. Sin is like carrion, it is of a stinking nature ; yea, it has the worst of smells ; however, some men like it. (Ps. xxxviii. 5.) But none are offended with the scent thereof but God, and the broken-hearted sinner. "My wounds stink, and are corrupt," saith he, both in God's nostrils, and mine own. But, alas ! who smells the stink of sin ? None of the carnal world ; they, like carrion crows, seek it, love it, and eat it as the child eats bread. "They eat up the sins of my people," saith God, " and set their heart on their iniquity." (Hos. iv. 8.) This, I say, they do, because they do not smell the nauseous scent of sin. You know, that what is nauseous to the smell cannot be palatable to the taste. The broken-hearted man doth find that sin is nauseous, and therefore cries out it stinketh. They also think at times the smell of fire, of fire and brimstone, is upon them, they are so sensible of the wages due to sin.

5. The broken-hearted is also a tasting-man. Wounds, if sore, and full of pains, of great pains, do sometimes alter the taste of a man ; they make him think his meat, his drink, yea, that cordials have a bitter taste in them. How many times doth the poor people of God, that are the only men that know what a broken heart doth mean, cry out that gravel, wormwood, gall, and vinegar, was made their meat ! (Lam. iii. 15, 16, 19.) This gravel, gall, and wormwood, is the true temporal taste of sin ; and God, to make them loathe it for ever, doth feed them with it till their hearts

both ache and break therewith. Wickedness is pleasant of taste to the world; hence it is said, they feed on ashes, they feed on wind. (Isa. xliv. 20. Hos. xii. 1.) Lusts, or anything that is vile and refuse, the carnal world think relishes well; as is set out most notably in the parable of the prodigal son: "He would fain have filled his belly," saith our Lord, "with the husks that swine did eat." But the broken-hearted man has a relish that is true as to these things; though, by reason of the anguish of his soul, it also abhors all manner of dainty meat. (Job xxxiii. 19, 20. Ps. cvii. 17—19.) Thus I have showed you one sign of a broken-hearted man; he is a sensible man, he has all the senses of his soul awakened, he can see, hear, feel, taste, smell, and that as none but himself can do. I come now to another sign of a broken and contrite man.

Second. And that is, he is a very sorrowful man. This, as the other, is natural; it is natural to one that is in pain, and that has his bones broken, to be a grieved and sorrowful man. He is none of the jolly ones of the times; nor can he, for his bones, his heart, his heart is broken.

1. He is sorry that he feels and finds in himself a pravity of nature: I told you before he is sensible of it, he sees it, he feels it; and here I say he is sorry for it. It is this that makes him call himself a wretched man; it is this that makes him loathe and abhor himself: it is this that makes him blush, blush before God and be ashamed. (Rom. vii. 24. Job xlii. 5, 6. Ezek. xxxvi. 31.) He finds by nature no form nor comeliness in himself; but the more he looks in the glass of the word, the more unhandsome, the more deformed he perceiveth sin has made him. Everybody sees not this, therefore everybody is not sorry for it; but the broken in heart sees that he is by sin corrupted, marred, full of lewdness and naughtiness; he sees that in him, that is, in his flesh, dwells no good thing; and this makes him sorry, yea, it makes him sorry at heart. A man that has his bones broken, finds he is spoiled, marred, disabled from doing as he would and should, at which he is grieved and made sorry.

Many are sorry for actual transgressions, because they do oft bring them to shame before men; but few are sorry for the defects that sin has made in nature, because they see not those defects themselves. A man cannot be sorry for the sinful defects of nature till he sees they have rendered him contemptible to God; nor is it anything but a sight of God that can make him truly see what he is, and so be heartily sorry for being so. Now "mine eyes see thee," said Job, "now I abhor myself." "Woe is me, I am undone," said the prophet, "for mine eyes have seen the Lord the King." And it was this that made Daniel say, his "comeliness in him was turned into corruption;" for he had now the vision of the Holy One. (Job xlii. 6. Isa. vi. 1—5. Dan. x. 8.) Visions of God break the heart, because by the sight the soul then has of his perfections, it sees its own infinite and unspeakable disproportion, because of the vileness of its nature.

Suppose a company of ugly, uncomely, deformed persons dwelt together in one house; and suppose that they never yet saw any man or woman more than themselves, or that were arrayed with the splendours and perfections of nature; these would not be capable of comparing themselves with any but themselves, and consequently would not be affected, and made sorry, for their uncomely natural defections. But now bring them out of their cells and holes of darkness, where they have been shut up by themselves, and let them take a view of the splendour and perfections of beauty that are in others; and then, if at all, they will be sorry and dejected at the view of their own defects.

This is the case; men by sin are marred, spoiled, corrupted, depraved, but they dwell by themselves in the dark; they see neither God, nor angels, nor saints, in their excellent nature and beauty; and therefore they are apt to count their own uncomely parts, their ornaments, and their glory. But now let such, as I said, see God, see saints, or the ornaments of the Holy Ghost, and themselves as they are without them; and then they cannot but must be affected with, and sorry for their own deformity. When the Lord Christ put forth but a little of his excellency before his servant Peter's face, it raised up the depravity of Peter's nature before him to his great confusion and shame, and made him cry out to him in the midst of all his fellows, "Depart from me, for I am a sinful man, O Lord." (Luke v. 4—8.)

This therefore is the cause of a broken heart, even a sight of divine excellencies, and a sense that I am a poor, depraved, spoiled, defiled wretch; and this sight having broken the heart, begets sorrow in the broken-hearted.

2. The broken-hearted is a sorrowful man, for that he finds his depravity of nature strong in him, to the putting forth itself to oppose and overthrow what his changed mind doth prompt him to. "When I would do good," said Paul, "evil is present with me." (Rom. vii. 21.) Evil is present to oppose, to resist, and make head against the desires of my soul. The man that has his bones broken, may have yet a mind to be industriously occupied in a lawful and honest calling, but he finds by experience that an infirmity attends his present condition, that strongly resists his good endeavours; and at this he shakes his head, makes complaints, and with sorrow of heart he sighs, and says, "I cannot do the thing that I would." (Rom. vii. 15. Gal. v. 17.) I am weak, I am feeble; I am not only depraved, but by that depravity deprived of ability to put good motions, good intentions and desires into execution, to completeness: Oh, says he, I am ready to halt, my sorrow is continually before me!

You must know, the broken-hearted loves God, loves his soul, loves good, and hates evil. Now, for such an one to find in himself an opposition and continual contradiction to this holy passion, it must needs cause sorrow; godly sorrow, as the apostle Paul calls it. For such are made sorry after a godly sort. To be sorry, for that thy nature is with sin depraved, and that through this depravity thou art deprived of ability to do what the word and thy holy mind doth prompt thee to, is to be sorry after a godly sort. For this sorrow worketh that in thee, of which thou wilt never have cause to repent; no, not to eternity. (2 Cor. vii. 9—11.)

3. The broken-hearted man is sorry for those breaches that, by reason of the depravity of his nature, is made in his life and conversation. And this was the case of the man in our text. The vileness of his nature had broken out to the defiling of his life, and to the making of him at this time base in conversation. This, this was it, that all to [altogether] broke his heart. He saw in this he had dishonoured God, and that cut him. "Against thee, thee only, have I sinned, and done this evil in thy sight." (Ps. li. 4.) He saw in this he had caused the enemies of God to open their mouths and blaspheme; and this cut him to the heart. This made him cry, "I have sinned against thee, Lord." This made him say, "I will declare mine iniquity, I will be sorry for my sin." (Ps. xxxviii. 18.)

When a man is designed to do a matter, when his heart is set upon it, and the broken-hearted doth design to glorify God, an obstruction to that design, the spoiling of this work, makes him sorrowful. Hannah coveted children, but could not have them, and this made her "a woman of a sorrowful spirit." (1 Sam. i. 15.) A broken-hearted man would be well inwardly, and do that which is well outwardly; but he feels, he finds, he sees, he is prevented, prevented at least in part. This makes him sorrowful, in this he groans, groans earnestly, being burdened with his imperfection. (2 Cor. v. 1—3.) You know one with broken bones has imperfections many, and is more sensible of them too, as was said afore, than any other man; and this makes him sorrowful, yea, and makes him conclude that he shall go softly all his his days, in the bitterness of his soul. (Isa. lvii. 15.)

Third. The man with a broken heart is a very humble man; or, true humility is a sign of a broken heart. Hence, brokenness of heart, contrition of spirit, and humbleness of mind, are put together, "To revive the heart of the humble, and to revive the spirit of the contrite ones." (Isa. lvii. 15.)

To follow our similitude. Suppose a man while in bodily health, stout and strong, and one that fears and cares for no man; yet let this man have but a leg or an arm broken, and his courage is quelled; he is now so far off from hectoring of it with a man, that he is afraid of every little child that doth but offer to touch him. Now he will court the most feeble that has aught to do with him, to use him and handle him gently. Now he is become a child in courage, a child in fear, and humbleth himself as a little child.

Why, thus it is with that man that is of a broken and contrite spirit. Time was, indeed, he could hector, even hector it with God himself, saying, "What is the Almighty, that we should serve him?" or, "What profit shall I have if I keep his commandments?" (Job xxi. 15. Mal. iii. 13, 14.) Ay! But now his heart is broken; God has wrestled with him, and given him a fall, to the breaking of his bones, his heart; and now he crouches, now he cringes, now he begs of God that he will not only do him good, but do it with tender hands. "Have mercy upon me, O God," said David; yea, "according to the multitude of thy tender mercies, blot out my transgressions." (Ps. li. 1.)

He stands, as he sees, not only in need of mercy, but of the tenderest mercies. God has several sorts of mercies; some more rough, some more tender. God can save a man, and yet have him a dreadful way to heaven! This the broken-hearted sees, and this the broken-hearted dreads, and therefore pleads for the tenderest sort of mercies; and here we read of his gentle dealing, and that he is very pitiful, and that he deals tenderly with his. But the reason of such expressions no man knows but he that is broken-hearted; he has his sores, his running sores, his stinking sores; wherefore he is pained, and therefore covets to be handled tenderly. Thus God has broken the pride of his spirit, and humbled the loftiness of man. And his humility yet appears,

1. In his thankfulness for natural life. He reckoneth at night, when he goes to bed, that like as a lion, so God will tear him to pieces before the morning light. (Isa. xxxviii. 13.) There is no judgment that has fallen upon others, but he counts of right he should be swallowed up by it. "My flesh trembleth for fear of thee, and I am afraid of thy judgments." (Ps. cxix. 120.) But perceiving a day added to his life, and that he in the morning is still on this side hell, he cannot choose but take notice of it, and acknowledge it as a special favour; saying, God be thanked, for holding my soul in life till now, and for keeping my life back from the destroyer. (Compare Job xxxiii. 22. Ps. lvi. 13; lxxxvi. 13.)

Man, before his heart is broken, counts time his own, and therefore he spends it lavishingly upon every idle thing. His soul is far from fear, because the rod of God is not upon him; but when he sees himself under the wounding hand of God, or when God, like a lion, is breaking all his bones, then he humbleth himself before him, and falleth at his foot. Now he has learned to count every moment a mercy, and every small morsel a mercy.

2. Now also the least hopes of mercy for his soul, oh, how precious is it! He that was wont to make orts of the gospel, and that valued promises

but as stubble, and the words of God but as rotten wood; now, with what an eye doth he look on the promise? Yea, he counted a peradventure of mercy more rich, more worth than the whole world. Now, as we say, he is glad to leap at a crust; now, to be a dog in God's house is counted better by him than to " dwell in the tents of the wicked." (Matt. xv. 16, 27. Luke xv. 17—19.)

3. Now he that was wont to look scornfully upon the people of God, yea, that used to scorn to show them a gentle cast of his countenance; now he admires and bows before them, and is ready to lick the dust of their feet, and would count it his greatest, the highest honour, to be as one of the least of them. " Make me as one of thy hired servants," says he. (Luke xv. 19.)

4. Now he is, in his own eyes, the greatest fool in nature, for that he sees he has been so mistaken in his ways, and has not yet but little, if any true knowledge of God. " Every one now," says he, " has more knowledge of God than I; every one serves him better than I." (Ps. lxxiii. 21, 22. Prov. xxx. 2, 3.)

5. Now may he be but one, though the least in the kingdom of heaven! Now may he be but one, though the least in the church on earth! Now may he be but beloved, though the least loved of saints! How high an account doth he set thereon?

6. Now, when he talketh with God or men, how doth he debase himself before them! If with God, how does he accuse himself, and load himself with the acknowledgments of his own villanies, which he committed in the days wherein he was the enemy of God? " Lord," said Paul, that contrite one, " I imprisoned and did beat in every synagogue them that believe on thee. And when the blood of thy martyr Stephen was shed, I also was standing by, and consenting unto his death, and kept the raiment of them that slew him." (Acts xxii. 19, 20.) Yea, I punished thy saints " oft in every synagogue, and compelled them to blaspheme; and being exceeding mad against them, I persecuted them even unto strange cities." (Acts xxvi. 9—11.)

Also when he comes to speak to saints, how doth he make himself vile before them? " I am," saith he, " the least of the apostles; I am not meet to be called an apostle; I am less than the least of all saints: I was a blasphemer, I was a persecutor, and injurious," &c. (1 Cor. xv. 9. Eph. iii. 8. 1 Tim. i. 13.) What humility, what self-abasing thoughts, doth a broken heart produce! When David danced before the ark of God also, how did he discover his nakedness to the disliking of his wife? And when she taunted him for his doings, says he, " It was before the Lord," &c. " And I will be yet more vile than thus, and will be base in mine own sight." (2 Sam. vi. 20—22.) Oh, the man that is, or that has been kindly broken in his spirit, and that is of a contrite heart, is a lowly, a humble man!

Fourth. The broken-hearted man is a man that sees himself in spirituals to be poor; therefore, as humble and contrite, so poor and contrite are put together in the word: " But to this man will I look, even to him that is poor and of a contrite spirit." (Isa. lxvi. 1, 2.) And here we still pursue our metaphor. A wounded man, a man with broken bones, concludes his condition to be but poor, very poor. Ask him how he does, and he answers, Truly, neighbour, in a very poor condition. Also you have the spiritual poverty of such as have, or have had their hearts broken, and that have been of contrite spirits, much made mention of in the word. And they go by two names to distinguish them from others. They are called thy poor—that is, God's poor; they are also called " The poor in spirit." (Ps. lxxii. 2; lxxiv. 9. Matt. v. 3.) Now, the man that is poor in his own eyes for of him we now discourse, and the broken-hearted is such an one, is sensible of his wants. He knows he cannot help himself, and therefore is forced to be content to live by the charity of others. Thus it is in nature, thus it is in grace.

1. The broken-hearted now knows his wants, and he knew it not till now. As he that has a broken bone knew no want of a bone-setter till he knew his bone was broken: his broken bone makes him know it, his pain and anguish make him know it. And thus it is in spirituals. Now he sees, to be poor indeed is to want the sense of the favour of God; for his great pain is sense of wrath, as hath been shown before. " And the voice of joy would heal his broken bones." (Ps. li. 8.) Two things he thinks would make him rich:—1. A right and title to Jesus Christ, and all his benefits. 2. And saving faith therein. They that are spiritually rich are rich in him, and in the faith of him. (2 Cor. viii. 9. James ii. 5.)

The first of these giveth us a right to the kingdom of heaven; and the second yields the soul the comfort of it; and the broken-hearted man wants the sense and knowledge of his interest in these. That he knows he wants them is plain; but that he knows he has them, is what as yet he wants the attainment of. Hence he says, " The poor and needy seek water, and there is none, and their tongue fails for thirst;" there is none in their view, none in their view for them. (Isa. xli. 17.) Hence David, when he had his broken heart, felt he wanted washing, he wanted purging, he wanted to be made white. He knew that spiritual riches lay there, but he did not so well perceive that God had washed and purged him; yea, he rather was afraid that all was going, that he was in danger of being cast out of God's presence, and that the Spirit of grace would be utterly taken from him. (Ps. li.) That is the first thing: the broken-hearted is poor, because he knows his wants.

2. The broken-hearted is poor, because he knows he cannot help himself to what he knows he wants.

The man that has a broken arm, as he knows it, so he knows of himself he cannot set it. This therefore is a second thing that declares a man is poor, otherwise he is not so : for suppose a man wants never so much, yet if he can but help himself, if he can furnish himself, if he can support his own wants out of what he has, he cannot be a poor man. Yea, the more he wants, the greater is his riches, if he can supply his own wants out of his own purse.

He then is the poor man that knows his spiritual want, and also knows he cannot supply, or help himself. But this the broken-hearted knows, therefore he in his own eyes is the only poor man. True, he may have something of his own, but that will not supply his want, and therefore he is a poor man still. I have sacrifices, says David, but thou dost not desire them, therefore my poverty remains. (Ps. li. 16.) Lead is not gold, lead is not current money with the merchant. There is none has spiritual gold to sell but Christ. (Rev. iii. 18.) What can a man do to procure Christ, or procure faith or love ? Yea, had he never so much of his own carnal excellencies, no not one penny of it will go for pay in that market where grace is to be had. " If a man will give all the substance of his house for love, it would be utterly contemned." (Sol. Song viii. 7.)

This the broken-hearted man perceives, and therefore he sees himself to be spiritually poor. True, he has a broken heart, and that is of great esteem with God : but that is not of nature's goodness ; that is a gift, a work of God, that is the sacrifices of God. Besides, a man cannot remain content and at rest with that ; for that, in the nature of it, does but show him he is poor, and that his wants are such as himself cannot supply. Besides, there is but little ease in a broken heart.

3. The broken-hearted man is poor, and sees it ; because he finds he is now disabled to live any way else but by begging. This David betook himself to, though he was a king ; for he knew, as to his soul's health, he could live no way else : " This poor man cried," saith he, " and the Lord heard him, and saved him out of all his troubles." (Ps. xxxiv. 6.) And this leads me to the fifth sign.

Fifth. Another sign of a broken heart is a crying, a crying out. Pain, you know, will make one cry. Go to them that have upon them the anguish of broken bones, and see if they do not cry ; anguish makes them cry. This, this is that which quickly follows, if once thy heart be broken, and thy spirit indeed made contrite.

1. I say, anguish will make thee cry. " Trouble and anguish," saith David, " have taken hold upon me." (Ps. cxix. 143.) Anguish, you know, doth naturally provoke to crying ; now, as a broken bone has anguish, a broken heart has anguish : hence the pains of one that has a broken heart are compared to the pangs of a woman in travail. (John xvi. 20—22.)

1. Anguish will make one cry alone, cry to one's self ; and this is called a bemoaning of one's self. " I have surely heard Ephraim bemoaning himself," saith God ; (Jer. xxxi. 18 ;) that is, being at present under the breaking, chastising hand of God : " Thou hast chastised me," saith he, " and I was chastised, as a bullock unaccustomed to the yoke." This is his meaning also, who said, " I mourn in my complaint, and make a noise." And why ? Why ? " My heart is pained within me." (Ps. liii. 2—4.)

This is a self-bemoaning, a bemoaning themselves in secret and retired places. You know, it is common with them who are distressed with anguish, though all alone, to cry out to themselves of their present pains, saying, Oh, my leg ! Oh, my arm ! Oh, my bowels ! or, as the son of the Shunamite, " My head, my head." (2 Kings iv. 19.) Oh, the groans, the sighs, the cries, that the broken-hearted have when by themselves, or alone ! Oh, say they, my sins ! my sins ! my soul ! my soul ! How am I loaden with guilt ! How am I surrounded with fear ! Oh, this hard, this desperate, this unbelieving heart ! Oh, how sin defileth my will, my mind, my conscience ! " I am afflicted, and ready to die." (Ps. lxxxviii. 15.)

Could some of you carnal people but get behind the chamber-door, to hear Ephraim when he is at the work of self-bemoaning, it would make you stand amazed to hear him bewail that sin in himself in which you take delight ; and to hear him bemoan his misspending of time, while you spend all in pursuing your filthy lusts ; and to hear him offended with his heart, because it will not better comply with God's holy will, while you are afraid of his word and ways, and never think yourselves better than when farthest off from God. The unruliness of the passions and lusts of the broken-hearted make them often get into a corner, and thus bemoan themselves.

2. As they thus cry out in a bemoaning manner of and to themselves, so they have their outcries of and against themselves to others : as she said in another case, " Behold, and see if there be any sorrow like my sorrow." (Lam. i. 12.) Oh, the bitter cries and complaints that the broken-hearted have and make to one another ! Still every one imagining that his own wounds are deepest, and his own sores fullest of anguish, and hardest to be cured. Say they, " If our iniquities be upon us, and we pine away in them, how can we then live ?" (Ezek. xxxiii. 10.) Once being at an honest woman's house, I after some pause asked her how she did ? She said, Very badly : I asked her if she was sick ; she answered, No. What then ? said I ; are any of your children ill ? She told me, No : What, said I, is your husband amiss, or do you go back in the world ? No, no, said she, but I am afraid I shall not be saved ; and broke out with heavy heart, saying, Ah, goodman Bunyan ! Christ and a pitcher ! if I had Christ, though I went and begged my bread with a pitcher, it would be better with me than I think it is now.

This woman had her heart broken, this woman wanted Christ, this woman was concerned for her soul. There are but few women, rich women, that count Christ and a pitcher better than the world, their pride, and pleasures. This woman's cries are worthy to be recorded; it was a cry that carried in it not only a sense of the want, but also of the worth of Christ. This cry, "Christ and a pitcher!" made a melodious noise in the ears of the very angels.

But I say, few women cry out thus; few women are so in love with their own eternal salvation, as to be willing to part with all their lusts and vanities, for Jesus Christ and a pitcher. Good Jacob also was thus. "If the Lord," said he, "will give me bread to eat, and raiment to put on, then he shall be my God." Yea, he vowed it should be so. "And Jacob vowed a vow, saying, If God will be with me, and keep me in this way that I go, and will give me bread to eat, and raiment to put on; so that I come again to my father's house in peace: then shall the Lord be my God." (Gen. xxviii. 20.)

3. As they bemoan themselves, and make their complaints to one and another, so they cry to God. "O God," said Heman, "I have cried day and night to thee." But when? Why, when his soul was full of trouble, and his life drew near to the grave. (Ps. lxxxviii. 1—3.) Or, as it says in another place, "Out of the deep, out of the belly of hell cried I;" by such words expressing what painful condition they were in when they cried. (Ps. cxxx. 1. Jonah ii. 2.)

See how God himself words it: "My pleasant portion," says he, "is become a desolate wilderness, and being desolate, it mourneth unto me." (Jer. xii. 11.) And this also is natural to those whose hearts are broken. Whither goes the ·child, when it catcheth harm, but to its father, to its mother? Where doth it lay its head, but in their laps? Into whose bosom doth it pour out its complaint, more especially, but into the bosom of the father, of a mother; because there are bowels, there is pity, there are relief and succour? And thus it is with them whose bones, whose hearts are broken; it is natural to them, they must cry, they cannot but cry to him. "Lord, heal me," said David, "for my bones are vexed; Lord, heal me, for my soul is vexed." (Ps. vi. 1—3.) He that cannot cry, feels no pain, sees no want, fears no danger, or else is dead.

Sixth. Another sign of a broken heart and of a contrite spirit is, it trembleth at God's word. "To him that is poor, and of a contrite spirit, and trembleth at my word." (Isa. lxvi. 2.)

The word of God is an awful word to a broken-hearted man. Solomon says, "The word of a king is as the roaring of a lion;" and if so, what is the word of God? for by the wrath and fear is meant the authoritative word of a king. We have a proverb, "The burnt child dreads the fire: the whipped child fears the rod;" even so the broken-hearted fears the word of God. Hence you have a remark set upon them that tremble at God's word; to wit, they are they that keep among the godly; they are they that keep within compass; they are they that are aptest to mourn, and to stand in the gap, when God is angry; and to turn away his wrath from a people.

It is a sign the word of God has had place, and wrought powerfully, when the heart trembleth at it, is afraid, and stands in awe of it. When Joseph's mistress tempted him to lie with her, he was afraid of the word of God; "How shall I do this great wickedness," said he, "and sin against God?" He stood in awe of God's word, durst not do it, because he kept in remembrance what a dreadful thing it was to rebel against God's word. When old Eli heard that the ark was taken, his very heart trembled within him; for he read by that sad loss that God was angry with Israel, and he knew the anger of God was a great and terrible thing. When Samuel went to Bethlehem, the elders of the town trembled; for they feared that he came to them with some sad message from God, and they had had experience of the dread of such things before. (Gen. xxxix. 7—9. 1 Sam. iv. 13; xvi. 1—4.) When Ezra would have a mourning in Israel for the sins of the land, he sent, and there came to him "every one that trembled at the words of the God of Isaac, because of the transgressions of those that had been carried away." (Ezra ix. 4.)

There are, I say, a sort of people that tremble at the words of God, and that are afraid of doing aught that is contrary to them; but they are only such with whose souls and spirits the word has had to do. For the rest, they are resolved to go on their course, let God say what he will. "As for the word of the Lord," said rebellious Israel to Jeremiah, "which thou hast spoken to us in the name of the Lord, we will not hearken unto it. But we will do whatsoever thing goeth out of our own mouth." (Jer. xliv. 16, 17.) But do you think that these people did ever feel the power and majesty of the word of God, to break their hearts? No, verily; had that been so, they would have trembled at the words of God, they would have been afraid of the words of God. God may command some people what he will, they will do what they list. What care they for God? What care they for his word? Neither threats nor promises, neither punishments nor favours, will make them obedient to the word of God; and all because they have not felt the power of it, their hearts have not been broken with it. When king Josias did but read in God's book what punishment God had threatened against rebellious Israel, though he himself was a holy and good man, he rent his clothes, and wept before the Lord, and was afraid of the judgment threatened. (2 Kings xxii. 2 Chron. xxxiv.) For he knew what a dreadful thing the word of God is. Some men, as I said before, dare do anything, let the word of

God be never so much against it; but they that tremble at the word dare not do so. No, they must make the word their rule for all they do; they must go to the holy Bible, and there inquire what may or may not be done; for they tremble at the word. This then is another sign, a true sign that the heart has been broken, namely, when the heart is made afraid of, and trembleth at the word. (Acts ix. 4—6; xvi. 29—31.) Trembling at the word is caused by a belief of what is deserved, threatened, and of what will come, if not prevented by repentance; and therefore the heart melts, and breaks before the Lord.

I come in the next place to speak to this question. But what necessity is there that the heart must be broken? Cannot a man be saved unless his heart be broken?

I answer, avoiding secret things, which only belong to God, there is a necessity of breaking the heart, in order to salvation; because a man will not sincerely comply with the means conducing thereunto until his heart is broken. For,

First. Man, take him as he comes into the world, as to spirituals, as to evangelical things, in which mainly lie man's eternal felicity, and there he is as one dead, and so stupified, and wholly in himself, as unconcerned with it. Nor can any call or admonition, that has not a heart-breaking power attending of it, bring him to a due consideration of his present state, and so unto an effectual desire to be saved.

Many ways God has manifested this. He has threatened men with temporal judgments; yea, sent such judgments upon them, once and again, over and over, but they will not do. What! says he, "I have given you cleanness of teeth in all your cities; I have withholden the rain from you; I have smitten you with blasting and mildew; I have sent among you the pestilence; I have overthrown some of you, as God overthrew Sodom and Gomorrah: yet have ye not returned unto me, saith the Lord." (Amos iv. 6—12.) See here! Here is judgment upon judgment, stroke after stroke, punishment after punishment, but all will not do unless the heart is broken! Yea, another prophet seems to say, that such things instead of converting the soul, sets it further off. If heart-breaking work attend not such strokes, "Why should ye be stricken any more?" says he, "ye will revolt more and more." (Isa. i. 5.)

Man's heart is fenced, it is grown gross, there is a skin that, like a coat of mail, has wrapped it up, and enclosed it on every side. This skin, this coat of mail, unless it be cut off and taken away, the heart remains untouched, whole; and so as unconcerned, whatever judgments or afflictions light upon the body. (Matt. xiii. 15. Acts xxviii. 27.) This which I call the coat of mail, the fence of the heart, has two great names in Scripture. It is called "the foreskin of the heart," and the

"armour in which the devil trusteth." (Deut. x. 16. Luke xi. 22.)

Because these shield and fence the heart from all gospel doctrine, and from all legal punishments, nothing can come at it till these are removed. Therefore, in order unto conversion, the heart is said to be circumcised; that is, this foreskin is taken away, and this coat of mail is spoiled. "I will circumcise thy heart," saith he, "to love the Lord thy God with all thy heart," (and then the devil's goods are spoiled,) "that thou mayest live." (Deut. xxx. 6. Luke xi. 22.)

And now the heart lies open, now the word will prick, cut, and pierce it; and it being cut, pricked, and pierced, it bleeds, it faints, it falls and dies at the foot of God, unless it is supported by the grace and love of God in Jesus Christ. Conversion, you know, begins at the heart; but if the heart be so secured by sin and Satan, as I have said, all judgments are, while that is so, in vain. Hence, Moses, after he had made a long relation of mercy and judgment unto the children of Israel, suggests, that yet the great thing was wanting to them; and that thing was, an heart to perceive, and eyes to see, and ears to hear unto that day. (Deut. xxix. 2, 3.) Their hearts were as yet not touched to the quick, were not awakened, and wounded by the holy word of God, and made to tremble at its truth and terror.

But I say, before the heart be touched, pricked, made smart, &c., how can it be thought, be the danger never so great, that it should repent, cry, bow, and break at the foot of God, and supplicate there for mercy? And yet thus it must do? for thus God has ordained, and thus God has appointed it; nor can men be saved without it. But, I say, can a man spiritually dead, a stupid man, whose heart is past feeling, do this, before he has his dead and stupid heart awakened to see and feel its state and misery without it? But,

Second. Man, take him as he comes into the world, (and how wise soever he is in worldly and temporal things,) he is yet a fool as to that which is spiritual and heavenly. Hence he says, "The natural man receiveth not the things that are of the Spirit of God; for they are foolishness to him," because he is indeed a fool to them; "neither," says the text, "can he know them, for they are spiritually discerned." (1 Cor. ii. 14.) But, how now? must this fool be made wise? Why wisdom must be put into his heart. (Job xxxviii. 36.) Now none can put it there but God; and how doth he put it there, but by making room there for it, by taking away the thing which hinders, which is that folly and madness which naturally dwelleth there? But how does he take that away but by a severe chastising of his soul for it, until he has made him weary of it? The whip and stripes are provided for the natural fool, and so it is for him that is spiritually so. (Prov. xix. 29.)

Solomon intimates, that it is a hard thing to make a fool become wise. "Though thou shouldest bray a fool in a mortar among wheat with a pestle, yet will not his foolishness depart from him." (Prov. xxvii. 22.)

By this it appears that it is a hard thing to make a fool a wise man. To bray one in a mortar is a dreadful thing, to bray one there with a pestle; and yet it seems a whip, a mortar, and a pestle is the way. And if this is the way to make one wise in this world; and if all this will hardly do, how must the fool that is so in spirituals be whipped, and beaten, and stripped, before he is made wise therein! Yea, his heart must be put into God's mortar, and must be beaten: yea, brayed there with the pestle of the law, before it loves to hearken unto heavenly things. It is a great word in Jeremiah, "Through deceit," that is, folly, "they refuse to know me, saith the Lord." And what follows? Why, "Therefore thus saith the Lord, Behold I will melt them, and try them," (that is, with fire,) "for how shall I do for the daughter of my people?" (Jer. ix. 6, 7.)

I will melt them; I will put them into my furnace, and there will I try them; and there I will make them know me, saith the Lord. When David was under spiritual chastisement for his sin, and had his heart under the breaking hand of God; then he said, "God should make him know wisdom." (Ps. li. 6.) Now he was in the mortar, now he was in the furnace, now he was bruised and melted; yea, now his bones, his heart was breaking; and now his folly was departing. Now, says he, thou shalt make me to know wisdom. If I know anything of the way of God with us fools, there is nothing else will make us wise men: yea, a thousand breakings will not make us so wise as we should be.

We say, wisdom is not good till it is bought; and he that buys it, according to the intention of that proverb, usually smarts for it. The fool is wise in his own conceit; wherefore there is a double difficulty attends him before he can be wise indeed. Not only his folly, but his wisdom must be removed from him; and how shall that be, but by a ripping up of his heart, by some sore conviction, that may show him plainly that his wisdom is his folly, and that which will undo him. A fool loves his folly; that is, as treasure, so much is he in love with it. Now then it must be a great thing that must make a fool forsake his folly. The foolish will not weigh, nor consider, nor compare wisdom with their folly. "Folly is joy to him that is destitute of wisdom." "As a dog returneth to his vomit, so a fool returneth to his folly." So loth are they when driven from it, to let it go, to let it depart from them. (Prov. xv. 21; xxvi. 11.)

Wherefore, there must go a great deal to the making of a man a Christian: for as to that, every man is a fool; yea, the greatest fool, the most unconcerned fool, the most self-willed fool of all fools; yea, one that will not be turned from his folly, but by the breaking of his heart. David

was one of these fools; Manasseh was one of these fools; Saul, otherwise called Paul, was one of these fools; and so was I, and that the biggest of all.

Third. Man, take him as he comes into the world, and he is not only a dead man, and a fool, but a proud man also. Pride is one of those sins that first showeth itself in children; yea, and it grows up with them, and mixeth itself with all they do: but it lies most hid, most deep in man as to his soul concerns. For the nature of sin, as sin, is not only to be vile, but to hide its vileness from the soul. Hence many think they do well when they sin. Jonah thought he did well to be angry with God. The Pharisees thought they did well, when they said, Christ had a devil; and Paul thought verily that he ought to do many things against, or contrary to the name of Jesus; which he also did with great madness. (Jonah iv. 9. John viii. 48. Acts xxvi. 9, 10.) And thus sin puffs up men with pride and a conceit of themselves, that they are a thousand times better than they are. Hence they think they are the children of God, when they are the children of the devil; and that they are something as to Christianity, when they neither are such, nor know what it is that they must have to make them such. (John viii. 41—44. Gal. vi. 3.)

Now, whence flows this, but from pride, and a self-conceit of themselves, and that their state is good for another world, when they are yet in their sins, and under the curse of God? Yea, and this pride is so strong and high, and yet so hid in them, that all the ministers in the world cannot persuade them that this is pride, not grace, in which they are so confident. Hence they slight all reproofs, rebukes, threatenings, or admonitions that are pressed upon them, to prevail with them to take heed, that they be not herein deceived. "Hear ye," saith the prophet, "and give ear; be not proud, for the Lord hath spoken." (Jer. xiii. 15.) "And if ye will not hear it, my soul shall weep in secret for your pride." (ver. 17.) And what was the conclusion? Why, all the proud men stood out still, and maintained their resistance of God and his holy prophet. (Jer. xliii. 2.)

Nor is there anything that will prevail with these to the saving of their souls, until their hearts are broken. David, after he had defiled Bathsheba, and slain her husband, yet boasted himself in his justice and holiness, and would by all means have the man put to death that had but taken the poor man's lamb, (2 Sam. xii.1—6;) when, alas, poor soul! himself was the great transgressor. But would he believe it? No, no, he stood upon the vindicating of himself to be a just doer; nor would he be made to fall, until Nathan, by authority from God, did tell him, that he was the man whom himself had condemned; "Thou art the man," said he: at which word his conscience was awakened, his heart wounded, and so his soul made to fall under the burden of his guilt, at the feet of the God of heaven for mercy. (ver. 7—13.)

Ah, pride, pride! thou art that which holds many a man in the chains of his sins; thou art it, thou cursed self-conceit, that keepest them from believing that their state is damnable. "The wicked through the pride of his countenance will not seek after God." (Ps. x. 4.) And if there is so much in the pride of countenance, what is there, think you, in the pride of his heart? Therefore Job says, it is to hide pride from man, and so to save his soul from hell, that God chasteneth him with pain upon his bed, until the multitude of his bones stick out, and until his life draws nigh to the destroyer. (Job xxxiii. 17—22.)

It is a hard thing to take a man off his pride, and make him, instead of trusting in, and boasting of his goodness, wisdom, honesty, and the like, to see himself a sinner, a fool, yea, a man that is cruel as to his own immortal soul. Pride of heart has a power in it, and is therefore compared to an iron sinew, and an iron chain, by which they are made stout, and with which they are held in that stoutness, to oppose the Lord, and drive his word from their hearts. (Lev. xxvi. 19. Ps. lxxiii. 6.)

This was the sin of devils, and it is the sin of man; and the sin, I say, from which no man can be delivered until his heart is broken; and then his pride is spoiled, then he will be glad to yield. If a man be proud of his strength or manhood, a broken leg will maul him; and if a man be proud of his goodness a broken heart will maul him; because, as has been said, a broken heart comes by the discovery and charge of sin, by the power of God upon the conscience.

Fourth. Man, take him as he comes into the world, and he is not only a dead man, a fool, and proud, but also self-willed and headstrong. (2 Pet. ii. 10.) A stubborn ungain creature is man before his heart is broken. Hence they are so often called rebels, rebellious and disobedient; they will only do what they list. "All day long," says God, "have I stretched out my hand to a disobedient and gainsaying people." And hence, again, they are compared to a self-willed or head-strong horse, that will, in spite of his rider, rush into the battle. "Every one," says God, "turneth to his course, as the horse rusheth into the battle." (Jer. viii. 6.) They say, "With our tongues we will prevail, our lips are our own; who is lord over us?" (Ps. xii. 4.)

Hence they are said to stop their ears, to pull away their shoulder, to shut their eyes, and harden their hearts " against the words of God, and to contemn the counsel of the most High." (Zech. vii. 10—12. Ps. cvii. 11.) They are fitly compared to the rebellious son, who would not be ruled by his parents; or to the prodigal, who would have all in his own hand, and remove himself far away from father, and father's house. (Deut. xxi. 20. Luke xv. 13.) Now for such creatures nothing will do but violence. The stubborn son must be stoned till he dies; and the prodigal must be famished out of all; nothing else, I say, will do. Their self-willed stubborn heart will not comply with the will of God before it is broken. (Deut. xxi. 21. Luke xv. 14—17.)

These are they that are called the stout-hearted; these are said to be far from righteousness, and so will remain until their hearts are broken; for so they must be made to know themselves. (Isa. ix. 9—11.)

Fifth. Man as he comes into the world is not only a dead man, a fool, proud, and self-willed, but also a fearless creature. "There is," saith the text, "no fear of God before their eyes." (Rom. iii. 18.) No fear of God! There is fear of man, fear of losing his favour, his love his goodwill, his help, his friendship: this is seen everywhere. How do the poor fear the rich; the weak fear the strong; and those that are threatened, them that threaten? But come now to God; why, none fears him; that is, by nature, none reverence him; they neither fear his frowns, nor seek his favour, nor inquire how they may escape his revenging hand that is lifted up against their sins and their souls because of sin. Little things, they fear the losing of them; but the soul they are not afraid to lose. "They fear not me, saith the Lord." (Mal. iii. 5.)

How many times are some men put in mind of death, by sickness upon themselves, by graves, by the death of others? How many times are they put in mind of hell, by reading the word, by lashes of conscience, and by some that go roaring in despair out of this world? How many times are they put in mind of the day of judgment? As, 1. By God's binding the fallen angels over to judgment. 2. By the drowning of the old world. (2 Pet. ii. 4, 5. Jude 6, 7.) 3. By the burning of Sodom and Gomorrah with fire from heaven. (2 Pet. ii. 6. Jude 7.) 4. By appointing a day. (Acts xvii. 29—31.) 5. By appointing a judge. (Acts x. 40—42.) 6. By reserving their crimes in records. (Isa. xxx. 8. Rev. xx. 12.) 7. By appointing and preparing of witnesses. (Rom. ii. 15.) 8. And by promising, yea, threatening, yea, resolving to call the whole world to his bar, there to be judged for all which they have done and said, and for every secret thing. (Matt. xxv. 31—33; xii. 36. Eccles. xi. 9; xii. 14.)

And yet they fear not God: alas! they believe not these things. These things, to carnal men, are like Lot's preaching to his sons and daughters that were in Sodom. When he told them that God would destroy that place, he seemed unto them as one that mocked; and his words to them were as idle tales. (Gen. xix. 14.) Fearless men are not won by words; blows, wounds, and killings are the things that must bring them under fear. How many struggling fits had Israel with God in the wilderness? How many times did they declare, that there they feared him not? And observe, they were seldom, if ever, brought to fear and dread his glorious name, unless he beset them round with death and the grave. Nothing, nothing but a severe hand will make the fearless fear. Hence, to speak after the manner of men, God is put upon it to go this way with sinners, when he would save their souls; even bring them, and lay them at the mouth, and within sight of hell and everlasting damnation; and there also charge them with sin and guilt, to the breaking of their hearts, before they will fear his name.

Sixth. Man as he comes into the world is not only a dead man, a fool, proud, self-willed, and fearless, but he is a false believer concerning God. Let God report of himself never so plainly, man by nature will not believe this report of him. No; they are become vain in their imaginations, and their foolish heart is darkened; wherefore, they turn the glory of God, which is his truth, into a lie. (Rom. i. 21—25.) God says, He sees; they say, He seeth not: God saith, He knows; they say, He doth not know: God saith, None is like himself; yet they say, He is altogether like to them: God saith, None shall keep his door for nought; they say, It is in vain, and to no profit to serve him: he saith, He will do good; they say, He will neither do good nor evil. (Job xxii. 13, 14. Ps. l. 21. Job xxi. 14, 15. Mal. iii. 14. Zeph. i. 12.) Thus they falsely believe concerning God; yea, as to the word of his grace, and the revelation of his mercy in Christ, they stick not to say by their practice,—for a wicked man " speaketh with his feet," (Prov. vi. 13,)—that that is a stark lie, and not to be trusted to. (1 John v. 10.)

Now, what shall God do to save these men? If he hides himself, and conceals his glory, they perish: if he sends to them by his messengers, and forbears to come to them himself, they perish: if he comes to them, and forbears to work upon them by his word, they perish: if he worketh on them, but not effectually, they perish: if he works effectually, he must break their hearts, and make them, as men wounded to death, fall at his feet for mercy, or there can be no good done on them; they will not rightly believe, until he fires them out of their misbelief; and makes them to know, by the breaking of their bones for their false faith, that he is and will be what he has said of himself in his holy word. The heart, therefore, must be broken before the man can come to God.

Seventh. Man as he comes into the world is not only a dead man, a fool, proud, self-willed, fearless, and a false believer, but a great lover of sin. He is captivated, ravished, drowned in the delights of it. Hence it says, they love sin, delight in lies, do take pleasure in iniquity, and in them that do it; that they sport themselves in their own deceivings, and glory in their shame. (John iii. 19. Ps. lxii. 4. Rom. i. 32. 2 Pet. ii. 13. Phil. iii. 19.)

This is the temper of man by nature, for sin is mixed with and has the mastery of all the powers of his soul. Hence they are said to be captives to it, and to be led captive into the pleasures of it, at the will of the devil. (2 Tim. ii. 26.) And you know, it is not an easy thing to break love, or to take the affections off of that object on which they are so deeply set, in which they are so deeply rooted, as man's heart is in his sins. Alas! how many are there that contemn all the allurements of heaven, and that trample upon all the threatenings of God, and that say, Tush! at all the flames of hell, whenever they are propounded as motives to work them off their sinful delights? So fixed are they, so mad are they, upon these beastly idols! Yea, he that shall take in hand to stop their course in this their way, is as he that shall attempt to prevent the raging waves of the sea from their course, when driven by the mighty winds.

When men are somewhat put to it, when reason and conscience shall begin a little to hearken to a preacher, or a judgment that shall begin to hunt for iniquity, how many tricks, evasions, excuses, demurs, delays, and hiding-holes will they make, invent, find, to hide and preserve their sweet sins with themselves and their souls, in the delights of them, to their own eternal perdition. Hence they endeavour to stifle conscience, to choke convictions, to forget God, to make themselves atheists, to contradict preachers that are plain and honest, and to heap to themselves such of them only as are like themselves, that speak unto them smooth things, and prophesy deceits; yea, they say themselves to such preachers, " Get ye out of the way; turn aside out of the path; cause the Holy One of Israel to cease from before us." (Isa. xxx. 8—11.) If they be followed still, and conscience and guilt shall, like bloodhounds, find them out in their secret places, and roar against them for their wicked lives, then they will flatter, cog, dissemble, and lie against their souls, promising to mend, to turn, to repent, and grow better shortly; and all to daff off convictions and molestations in their wicked ways, that they may yet pursue their lusts, their pleasures, and sinful delights in quiet, and without control.

Yea, further, I have known some that have been made to roar like bears, to yell like dragons, and to howl like dogs, by reason of the weight of guilt and the lashes of hell upon their conscience for their evil deeds; who have, so soon as their present torments and fears were gone, returned again with the " dog to his vomit; or as the sow that was washed, to her wallowing in the mire." (Hos. vii. 14. 2 Pet. ii. 20—22.)

Once again; some have been made to taste of the good word of God, of the joy of heaven, and of the powers of the world to come; and yet could not by any one, nay, by all of these, be made to break their league for ever with their lusts and sins. (Heb. vi. 4, 5. Luke viii. 13. John v. 33—35.) O Lord! what is man, that thou art mindful of him? Wherein is he to be accounted of? He has sinned against thee, he loves his sins more than thee. He is a lover of pleasures more than he is a lover of God.

But now, how shall this man be reclaimed from this sin? How shall he be brought, wrought, and made to be out of love with it? Doubtless it can be by no other means, by what we can see in the word, but by the wounding, breaking, and disabling of the heart that loves it; and by that means making it a plague and gall unto it. Sin may be made an affliction, and as gall and worm-wood to them that love it; but the making of it so bitter a thing to such a man, will not be done but by great and sore means. I remember we had in our town, some time since, a little girl that loved to eat the heads of foul tobacco-pipes, and neither rod nor good words could reclaim her, and make her leave them. So her father takes advice of a doctor, to wean her from them, and it was this: Take, saith he, a great many of the foulest tobacco-pipe heads you can get, and boil them in milk, and make a posset of that milk, and make your daughter drink the posset-drink up. He did so, and gave his girl it, and made her drink it up; the which become so irksome and nauseous to her stomach, and made her so sick, that she could never abide to meddle with tobacco-pipe heads any more, and so was cured of that disease.

Thou lovest thy sin, and neither rod nor good words will as yet reclaim thee. Well, take heed; if thou wilt not be reclaimed, God will make thee a posset of them, which shall be so bitter to thy soul, so irksome to thy taste, so loathsome to thy mind, and so afflicting to thy heart, that it shall break it with sickness and grief, till it be loathsome to thee. I say, thus he will do, if he loves thee; if not, he will suffer thee to take thy course, and will let thee go on with thy tobacco-pipe heads.

The children of Israel will have flesh, must have flesh; they weep, cry, and murmur because they have not flesh. The bread of heaven, that is but light and sorry stuff in their esteem. (Numb. xi. 1—6.) Moses goes and tells God how the people despised his heavenly bread, and how they longed, lusted, and desired to be fed with flesh. Well, says God, they shall have flesh, they shall have their fill of flesh: I will feed them with it; they shall have to the full; and that "Not for a day, or two days, or five days, neither ten days, nor twenty days; but even a whole month, until it come out at their nostrils, and it be loathsome unto them; because they have despised the Lord." (Numb. xi. 11—20.) He can tell how to make that loathsome to thee on which thou most dost set thine evil heart. And he will do so, if he loves thee; else, as I said, he will not make thee sick by smiting of thee, nor punish thee for or when thou committest whoredom, but will let thee alone till the judgment-day, and call thee to a reckoning for all thy sins then. But to pass this.

Eighth. Man as he comes into the world is not only a dead man, a fool, proud, self-willed, fearless, a false believer, and a lover of sin, but a wild man. He is of the wild olive-tree, of that which is wild by nature. (Rom. xi. 17, 24.) So in another place man by nature is compared to the ass, to a wild ass: " For vain or empty man would be wise, though man be born as a wild ass's colt." (Job xi. 12.) Isaac was a figure of Christ, and of all converted men. (Gal. iv. 28.) But Ishmael was a figure of man by nature; and the Holy Ghost, as to that, saith this of him, " And he will be a wild man." (Gen. xvi. 12.) This man, I say, was a figure of all carnal men in their wildness or estrangedness from God. Hence it is said of the prodigal at his conversion, that he came to himself then; implying that he was mad, wild, or out of his wits before. (Luke xv. 17.) I know there is a difference sometimes betwixt one's being wild and mad; yet sometimes wildness arriveth to that degree as to give one rightly the denomination of being mad. And it is always true in spirituals; namely, that he that is wild as to God, is mad, or beside himself; and so not capable, before he is tamed, of minding his own eternal good as he should. There are these several things that are tokens of one wild or mad; and they all meet in a carnal man.

1. A wild or mad man gives no heed to good counsel; the frenzy of his head shuts all out, and by its force leads him away from men that are wise and sober; and thus it is with carnal men. Good counsel is to them as pearls are, that are cast afore swine; it is trampled under foot of them, and the man is despised that brings it. " The poor man's wisdom is despised, and his words are not heard." (Matt. vii. 6. Eccles. ix. 16.)

2. A wild or mad man, let him alone, and he will greatly busy himself all his life to accomplish that which, when it is completed, amounts to nothing. The work, the toil, the travail of such a one comes to nothing, save to declare that he was out of his wits that did it. David, imitating of such a one, scrabbled upon the gate of the king, as fools do with chalk; and like to this is all the work of all carnal men in the world. (1 Sam. xxi. 12, 13.) Hence such a one is said to labour for the wind, or for what will amount to no more than if he filled his belly with the east wind. (Eccles. v. 16. Job xv. 2.)

3. A wild or mad man, if you set him to do anything, and he does it, he will yet do it, not by or according to your bidding, but after the folly of his own wild fancy, even as Jehu executed the commandment of the Lord; he did it in his own madness, taking no heed to the commandment of the Lord. (2 Kings ix. 20; x. 31.) And thus do carnal men do when they meddle with any of God's matters, as hearing, praying, reading, professing; they do all according to their own wild fancy; they take no heed to do these after the commandment of the Lord.

4. Wild or mad men, if they deck or array

themselves with aught, as many times they do, why the spirit of their wildness or frenzy appears even in the mode and way in which they do it. Either the things themselves which they make use of for that purpose are very toys and trifles, or if they seem to be better, they are put on after an antic manner, rather to the rendering of them ridiculous than to bespeak them sober, judicious, or wise: and so do natural men array themselves with what they would be accepted in with God. Would one in his wits think to make himself fine or acceptable to men, by arraying himself in menstruous cloths, or by painting his face with dross and dung? And yet, this is the finery of carnal men when they approach for acceptance into the presence of God. (Isa. lxiv. 6. Phil. iii. 7, 8.)

Oh, the wildness, the frenzy, the madness, that possess the heart and mind of carnal men! They walk according to the course of this world, according to or after that spirit which is in truth the spirit of the devil, which worketh in the children of disobedience. (Eph. ii. 1, 3.) But do they believe that thus it is with them? No, they are, in their own account as other madmen are, the only ones in the world. Hence they are so taken and tickled with their own frantic notions, and deride all else that dwell in the world.

But which is the way to make one that is wild, or a madman, sober? To let him alone will not do it; to give him good words only will not do it. No, he must be tamed; means must be used to tame him. "He brought down their hearts with labour," or with continual molestation; as you have it. (Ps. cvii. 10—12.) He speaketh there of madmen that are kept up in darkness, and bound in afflictions and irons, because they rebelled against the words of God, and contemned the counsel of the Most High.

This, therefore, is the way to deal with such, and none but God can so deal with them. They must be taken, they must be separated from men; they must be laid in chains, in darkness, afflictions, and irons; they must be blooded, half-starved, whipped, purged, and be dealt with as mad people are dealt with. And thus they must be dealt with till they come to themselves, and cry out in their distresses. And then they cry to the Lord in their troubles, and he saveth them out of their distresses; then he brings them out of darkness and the shadow of death, and breaks their bands in sunder. (Ps. cvii. 13—15.)

Thus, I say, God tames the wild, and brings mad prodigals to themselves, and so to him for mercy.

Ninth. Man as he comes into the world is not only a dead man, a fool, proud, self-willed, fearless, a false believer, a lover of sin, and a wild man; but a man that disrelishes the things of the kingdom of God. I told you before that unconverted man is such as did not taste things; but now I add that he disrelishes things; he calls bitter things sweet, and sweet bitter; he judges quite amiss. These are they that God threateneth with a woe: "Woe to them that call evil good, and good evil; that put darkness for light, and light for darkness; that put bitter for sweet, and sweet for bitter." (Isa. v. 20.)

This latter part of this text shows us evidently that the things of God are disrelished by some. They call his sweet things bitter, and the devil's bitter things sweet; and all this is for want of a broken heart. A broken heart relishes otherwise than an whole or unbroken one doth. A man that has no pain or bodily distress cannot find, or feel virtue or good in the most sovereign plaister, were it applied to arm or leg; no, he rather says, Away with these stinking daubing things. Oh, but lay the same plaisters where there is need, and the patient will relish, and taste, and savour the goodness of them; yea, will prize and commend them to others. Thus it is in spirituals. The world, they know not what the anguish or pain of a broken heart means; they say, "Who will show us any good?" that is, better than we find in our sports, pleasures, estates, and preferments? "There may be many," says the Psalmist, "speak after this sort;" but what says the distressed man? Why, "Lord, lift thou up the light of thy countenance upon us." And then adds, "Thou hast put gladness in our heart;" namely, by the light of thy countenance, for that is the plaister for a broken heart. "Thou hast put gladness in our hearts, more than in the time that their corn and their wine increaseth." (Ps. iv. 1, 6, 7.)

Oh, a broken heart can savour pardon, can savour the consolations of the Holy Ghost! Yea, as a hungry or thirsty man prizes bread and water in the want thereof, so do the broken in heart prize and set a high esteem on the things of the Lord Jesus. His flesh, his blood, his promise, and the light of his countenance, are the only sweet things both to scent and taste, to those that are of a wounded spirit. The full soul loatheth the honeycomb; the whole despise the gospel, they savour not the things that are of God.

If twenty men were to hear a pardon read, and but one of those twenty were condemned to die, and the pardon was for none but such; which of these men, think you, would taste the sweetness of that pardon—they who were not, or he that was condemned? The condemned man, doubtless. This is the case in hand. The broken in heart is a condemned man; yea, it is sense of condemnation, with other things, that has, indeed, broken his heart; nor is there anything but sense of forgiveness that can bind it up or heal it. But could that heal it, could he not taste, truly taste, or rightly relish this forgiveness? No: forgiveness would be to him as it is to him that has not sense of the want of it.

But, I say, what is the reason some so prize what others so despise, since they both stand in need of the same grace and mercy of God in Christ? Why the one sees, and the other sees nothing, of this woful miserable state. And thus have I shown you the necessity of a broken heart. 1. Man is dead, and must be quickened. 2. Man is a fool, and must be made wise. 3. Man is proud, and must be humbled. 4. Man is self-willed, and must be broken. 5. Man is fearless, and must be made to consider. 6. Man is a false believer, and must be rectified. 7. Man is a lover of sin, and must be weaned from it. 8. Man is wild, and must be tamed. 9. Man disrelishes the things of God, and can take no savour in them until his heart is broken.

And thus have I done with this, and shall come next to the reasons of the point ; namely, to show you why or how it comes to pass, that a broken heart, a heart truly contrite, is to God such an excellent thing.

That to him it is so, we have proved by six demonstrations ; what it is, we have showed by the six signs thereof ; that it must be, is manifest by those nine reasons but now urged ; and why it is with God or in his esteem an excellent thing, that is shown by that which follows.

First. A broken heart is the handiwork of God ; a heart of his own preparing, for his own service ; it is a sacrifice of his own providing, of his providing for himself. As Abraham said in another case, " God will provide himself a lamb." (Gen. xxii. 8.) Hence it is said, "The preparation of the heart of man, &c., is from the Lord." And again, " God maketh my heart soft, and the Almighty troubleth me." (Job xxiii. 16.) The heart, as it is by nature hard, stupid, and impenetrable, so it remains, and so will remain, until God, as was said, " bruiseth it with his hammer and melts it with his fire." The stony nature of it is, therefore, said to be taken away of God. " I will take away the stony heart out of your flesh and will give you," saith he, " a heart of flesh." (Ezek. xxxvi. 26.)

I will take away the stony heart, or the stoniness, or the hardness of your heart, and I will give you a heart of flesh ; that is, I will make your heart sensible, soft, yielding, governable, and penitent. Sometimes he bids men to rend their hearts, not because they can, but to convince them, rather, that though it must be so, they cannot do it ; so he bids them make themselves a new heart and a new spirit, for the same purpose also ; for if God doth not rend it, it remains unrent ; if God makes it not new, it abides an old one still.

This is that that is meant by his bending of men for himself, and of his working in them that which is pleasing in his sight. (Zech. ix. 13.) The heart, soul, or spirit, as in itself, as it came from God's fingers, is a precious thing, a thing in God's account worth more than all the world ; this heart, soul, or spirit, sin has hardened, the devil has bewitched, the world has deceived. This heart thus beguiled God coveteth and desireth. " My son," saith he, " give me thy heart, and let thine eyes observe my ways." (Prov. xxiii. 26.)

This man cannot do this thing, for that his heart has the mastery of him, and will not but carry him after all manner of vanity. What now must be done ? Why, God must take the heart by storm, by power and bring it to a compliance with the word : but the heart of itself will not ; it is deluded, carried away to another than God. Wherefore God now betakes him to his sword, and brings down the heart with labour ; opens it and drives out the strong man armed, that did keep it ; wounds it and makes it smart for its rebellion, that it may cry ; so he rectifies it for himself. " He maketh sore, and bindeth up ; he woundeth and his hands make whole." (Job v. 18.) Thus having wrought it for himself, it becomes his habitation, his dwelling-place. " That Christ may dwell in your hearts by faith." (Eph. iii. 17.)

But I would not swerve from the thing in hand. I have told you a broken heart is the handiwork of God ; a sacrifice of his own preparing, a material fitted for himself.

1. By breaking of the heart he openeth it, and makes it a receptacle for the graces of his Spirit ; that is the cabinet, when unlocked, where God lays up the jewels of the gospel. There he puts his fear, " I will put my fear in their heart ;" there he writes his law, " I will write my law in their heart ;" there he puts his Spirit, " I will put my Spirit within you." (Jer. xxxi. 31—33 ; xxxii. 39—41. Ezek. xxxvi. 26, 27.) The heart, I say, God chooses for his cabinet ; there he hides his treasure, there is the seat of justice, mercy, and of every grace of God : I mean, when it is broken, made contrite, and so regulated by the holy word.

2. The heart, when broken, is like sweet gums and spices when beaten ; for as such cast their fragrant scent into the nostrils of men, so the heart when broken casts its sweet smell in the nostrils of God. The incense, which was a type of prayer of old, was to be beaten or bruised, and so to be burned in the censer. The heart must be beaten or bruised, and then the sweet scent will come out ; even groans, and cries, and sighs, for the mercy of God ; which cries, &c., to him are a very excellent thing, and pleasing in his nostrils.

Second. A broken heart is in the sight of God an excellent thing ; because a broken heart is submissive, it falleth before God, and giveth to him his glory. All this is true from a multitude of scriptures, which I need not here mention. Hence such a heart is called an honest heart, a good heart, a perfect heart, a heart fearing God, and such as is sound in God's statutes.

Now this cannot but be an excellent thing, if we consider that by such a heart unfeigned obedience is yielded unto him that calleth for it " You have obeyed from the heart," says Paul to them at Rome, " that form of doctrine which was delivered unto you." (Rom. vi. 17.) Alas ! the heart, before it is broken and made contrite, is quite of another temper ; " It is not subject to the law of God, neither indeed can be." The great stir before the heart is broken is about who shall be Lord God or the sinner. True, the right of dominion is the Lord's, but the sinner will not suffer it, but will be all himself, saying, " Who is Lord over us ;" and again, say they to God, " We are lords, we will come no more unto thee." (Ps. xii. 4. Jer. ii. 31.)

This also is evident, by their practice; God may say what he will, but they will do what they list. Keep my sabbath, says God; I will not says the sinner. Leave your whoring, says God; I will not, says the sinner. Do not tell lies, nor swear, nor curse, nor blaspheme my holy name, says God; Oh but I will, says the sinner. Turn to me, says God; I will not, says the sinner. The right of dominion is mine, says God; but (like that young rebel, 1 Kings, i. 5,) I will be king, says the sinner. Now this is intolerable, this is unsufferable, and yet every sinner by practice says thus; for they have not submitted themselves unto the righteousness of God. Here can be no concord, no communion, no agreement, no fellowship. Here, here is enmity on the one side, and flaming justice on the other. (2 Cor. vi. 14—16. Zech. xi. 8.)

And what delight, what content, what pleasure can God take in such men? None at all; no, though they should be mingled with the best of saints of God; yea, though the best of saints should supplicate for them. "Thus," says Jeremiah, "said the Lord unto me, Though Moses and Samuel stood before me," that is, to pray for them, "yet my mind could not be toward this people; cast them out of my sight and let them go forth." (Jer. xv. 1.)

Here is nought but open war, acts of hostility, and shameful rebellion on the sinner's side; and what delight can God take in that? Wherefore, if God will bend and buckle the spirit of such an one, he must shoot an arrow at him, a bearded arrow, such as may not be plucked out of the wound; an arrow, that will stick fast, (Ps. xxxiii. 1, 2,) and cause that the sinner falls down as dead at God's foot: then will the sinner deliver up his arms, and surrender up himself as one conquered into the hand of, and beg for the Lord's pardon, and not till then; I mean, not sincerely.

And now God has overcome, and his right hand and his holy arm has gotten him the victory. Now he rides in triumph with his captive at his chariot-wheel; now he glories; now the bells in heaven do ring, now the angels shout for joy; yea, are bid to do so, " Rejoice with me, for I have found my sheep which was lost." (Luke xv. 1—11.) Now also the sinner, as a token of being overcome, lies grovelling at his foot, saying, " Thine arrows are sharp in the heart of the king's enemies, whereby the people fall under thee." (Ps. xlv. 3—5.)

Now the sinner submits, now he follows his conqueror in chains, now he seeks peace, and would give all the world, were it his own, to be in the favour of God, and to have hopes by Christ

of being saved. Now this must be pleasing, this cannot but be a thing acceptable in God's sight : "A broken and a contrite heart, O God, thou wilt not despise." For it is the desire of his own heart, the work of his own hands.

Third. Another reason why a broken heart is to God such an excellent thing, is this: a broken heart prizes Christ, and has a high esteem for him. The whole have no need of a physician, but the sick; this sick man is the broken-hearted in the text; for God makes men sick by smiting of them, by breaking of their hearts. Hence sickness and wounds are put together, for that the one is a true effect of the other. (Mark ii. 17. Micah vi. 13. Hos. v. 13.) Can any think that God should be pleased when men despise his Son, saying, he hath no form nor comeliness; and when we shall see him, there is no beauty that we should desire him? And yet so say they of him whose hearts God has not mollified; yea, the elect themselves confess, that before their hearts were broken, they set light by him also. He is, say they, "despised and rejected of men, and we hid as it were our faces from him; he was despised, and we esteemed him not." (Isa. liii. 2, 3.)

He is indeed the great deliverer; but what is a deliverer to them that never saw themselves in bondage, as was said before. Hence it is said of him that delivered the city, "No man remembered that same poor man." (Eccles. ix. 15.) He has sorely suffered, and been bruised for the transgression of man, that they might not receive the smart, and hell, which by their sins they have procured to themselves. But what is that to them that never saw aught but beauty, and that never tasted anything but sweetness in sin? It is he that holdeth by his intercession the hands of God; and that causes him to forbear to cut off the drunkard, the liar, and unclean person, even when they are in the very act and work of their abomination; but their hard heart, their stupified heart, has no sense of such kindness as this, and therefore they take no notice of it. How many times has God said to this dresser of the vineyard, " Cut down the barren fig-tree ;" while he yet, by his intercession, has prevailed for a reprieve for another year? But no notice is taken of this, no thanks is from them returned to him for such kindness of Christ. Wherefore such ungrateful, inconsiderate wretches as these must needs be a continual eye-sore, as I may say, and great provocation to God. And yet thus men will do before their hearts are broken. (Luke xiii. 6—9.)

Christ, as I said, is called a physician; yea, he is the only soul-physician. He heals, how desperate soever the disease be; yea, and heals whom he undertakes for ever. " I give unto them eternal life," (John x. 27, 28,) and doth all of free cost, of mere mercy and compassion. But what is all this to one that neither sees his sickness, that sees nothing of a wound? What is the best physician alive, or all the physicians in the world, put all together, to him that knows no sickness, that is sensible of no disease? Physicians, as was said, may go a-begging for all the healthful; physicians are of no esteem, save only to the sick, or upon a supposition of being so now, or at any other time.

Why, this is the cause Christ is so little set by in the world. God has not made them sick by smiting of them; his sword has not given them the wound, his dart has not been struck through their liver, they have not been broken with his hammer, nor melted with his fire. So they have no regard to his physician; so they slight all the provision which God has made for the salvation of the soul. But now, let such a soul be wounded; let such a man's heart be broken; let such a man be made sick through the sting of guilt, and be made to wallow himself in ashes under the burden of his transgressions; and then who but Christ, as has been showed afore, then the physician? then, wash me, Lord; supple my wounds; then, pour thy wine and oil into my sore; then, Lord Jesus, cause me to hear the voice of joy and gladness, that the bones which thou hast broken may rejoice. Nothing now so welcome as healing; and so nothing, no man, so desirable now as Christ. His name to such is the best of names; his love to such is the best of love; himself being now, not only in himself, but also to such a soul, the chiefest of ten thousand. (Sol. Song v. 10.)

As bread to the hungry, as water to the thirsty, as light to the blind, and liberty to the imprisoned; so, and a thousand times more, is Jesus Christ to the wounded, and to them that are broken-hearted. Now, as was said, this must be excellent in God's eyes, since Christ Jesus is so glorious in his eyes. To contemn what a man counts excellent is an offence to him; but to value, esteem, or think highly of that which is of esteem with me, this is pleasing to me, such an opinion is excellent in my sight. What says Christ? "My Father loveth you, because ye loved me." Who hath an high esteem for Christ, the Father hath an high esteem for them. Hence it is said, "He that hath the Son, hath the Father;" the Father will be his, and will do for him as a Father, who receiveth and sets an honourable esteem on his Son. (John xvi. 27.) But none will, none can do this, but the broken-hearted; because they, and they only, are sensible of the want and worth of an interest in him.

I dare appeal to all the world as to the truth of this; and do say again, that these, and none but these, have hearts of esteem in the sight of God. Alas! "the heart of the wicked is little worth," (Prov. x. 20,) for it is destitute of a precious esteem of Christ, and cannot but be destitute, because it is not wounded, broken, and made sensible of the want of mercy by him.

Fourth. A broken heart is of great esteem with God, because it is a thankful heart for that sense of sin and of grace it has received. The broken heart is a sensible heart. This we touched upon before. It is sensible of the dangers which sin leadeth to; yea, and has cause to be sensible thereof, because it has seen and felt what sin is, both in the guilt and punishment that by law is due thereto. As a broken heart is sensible of sin, in the evil nature and consequences of it, so it is also sensible of the way of God's delivering the soul from the day of judgment; consequently, it must be a thankful heart. Now he that praises me, glorifies me, saith God; and God loves to be glorified. God's glory is dear unto him, he will not part with that. (Ps. l. 23. Isa. xlii. 8.)

The broken-hearted, say I, forasmuch as he is the sensible soul, it follows that he is the thankful soul. "Bless the Lord, O my soul," said David, "and all that is within me bless his holy name." Behold what blessing of God is here! And yet not content herewith, he goes on with it again, saying, "Bless the Lord, O my soul, and forget not all his benefits." (Ps. ciii. 1, 2.) But what is the matter? Oh, he has "forgiven all thine iniquities, and healed all thy diseases. He has redeemed thy life from destruction, and crowneth thee with loving-kindness and tender mercies." (Ps. ciii. 3, 4.) But how came he to be affected with this? Why, he knew what it was to hang over the mouth of hell for sin; yea, he knew what it was for death and hell to beset and compass him about; yea, they took hold of him, as we have said, and were pulling of him down into the deep; this he saw to the breaking of his heart. He saw also the way of life, and had his soul relieved with faith and sense of that, and that made him a thankful man. If a man who has had a broken leg is but made to understand that by the breaking of that he was kept from breaking of his neck, he will be thankful to God for a broken leg. "It is good for me," said David, "that I have been afflicted;" I was by that preserved from a great danger, for before that I went astray. (Ps. cxix. 67, 71.)

And who can be thankful for a mercy that is not sensible that they want it, have it, and have it of mercy? Now this the broken-hearted, this the man that is of a contrite spirit, is sensible of, and that with reference to mercies of the best sort; and therefore must needs be a thankful man, and so have a heart of esteem with God, because it is a thankful heart.

Fifth. A broken heart is of great esteem with, or an excellent thing in the sight of God, because it is a heart that desires now to become a receptacle or habitation for the spirit and graces of the Spirit of God. It was the devil's hold before, and was contented so to be. But now it is for entertaining of, for being possessed with, the Holy Spirit of God. "Create in me a clean heart," said David, "and renew a right spirit within me. Take not thy Holy Spirit from me; uphold me with thy free Spirit." (Ps. li. 10—12.) Now he was for a clean heart, and a right spirit; now he was for the sanctifying of the blessed Spirit of grace; a thing which the uncircumcised in heart resist, and do despite unto. (Acts vii. 51. Heb. x. 29.)

A broken heart, therefore, suiteth with the heart of God, a contrite spirit is one spirit with him. God, as I told you before, covets to dwell with the broken in heart, and the broken in heart desireth communion with him. Now here is an agreement, a oneness of mind; now the same mind is in thee which was also in Christ Jesus. This must needs be an excellent spirit; this must needs be better with God, and in his sight, than thousands of rams, or ten thousand rivers of oil. But does the carnal world covet this, this spirit, and the blessed graces of it? No, they despise it, as I said before, they mock at it, they prefer and countenance any sorry dirty lust rather; and the reason is, because they want a broken heart, that heart so highly in esteem with God; and remain for want thereof, in their enmity to God.

The broken-hearted know, that the sanctifying of the Spirit is a good means to keep from that relapse, out of which a man cannot come unless his heart be wounded a second time. Doubtless David had a broken heart at first conversion, and if that brokenness had remained, that is, had he not given way to hardness of heart again, he had never fallen into that sin out of which he could not be recovered but by the breaking of his bones a second time. Therefore, I say, a broken heart is of great esteem with God; for it—and I will add, so long as it retains its tenderness—covets none but God, and the things of his Holy Spirit; sin is an abomination to it.

And here, as in a fit place, before I go any further, I will show you some of the advantages that a Christian gets by keeping of his heart tender. For, as to have a broken heart is to have an excellent thing, so to keep this broken heart tender is also very advantageous.

First. This is the way to maintain in thy soul always a fear of sinning against God. Christians do not wink at, or give way to sin, until their hearts begin to lose their tenderness. A tender heart will be afflicted at the sin of another, much more it will be afraid of committing sin itself. (2 Kings xxii. 19.)

Second. A tender heart quickly yieldeth to prayer; yea, prompteth to it, puts an edge and fire into it. We never are backward to prayer until our heart has lost its tenderness, though then it grows cold, flat, and formal, and so carnal to and in that holy duty.

Third. A tender heart has always repentance at hand for the least fault, or slip, or sinful thought that the soul is guilty of. In many things the best offend; but if a Christian loseth his tenderness, if he says he has his repentance to seek, his heart is grown hard—has lost that spirit, that kind spirit of repentance it was wont to have. Thus it was with the Corinthians; they were decayed, and lost their tenderness; wherefore their sin, yea, great sins, remain unrepented of. (2 Cor. xii. 20, 21.)

Fourth. A tender heart is for receiving often its communion with God, when he that is hardened, though the seed of grace is in him, will be content to eat, drink, sleep, wake, and go days without number without him. (Isa. xvii. 10, 18. Jer. ii. 32.)

Fifth. A tender heart is a wakeful, watchful heart. It watches against sin in the soul, sin in the family, sin in the calling, sin in spiritual duties and performances, &c. It watches against Satan, against the world, against the flesh, &c. But now, when the heart is not tender, there is sleepiness, unwatchfulness, idleness, a suffering the heart, the family, and calling to be much defiled, spotted and blemished with sin; for a hard heart departs from God, and turns aside in all these things.

Sixth. A tender heart will deny itself, and that in lawful things, and will forbear even that which may be done, for some Jew, or Gentile, or the church of God, or any member of it should be offended, or made weak thereby; whereas the Christian that is not tender, that has lost his tenderness, is so far off of denying himself in lawful things, that he will even adventure to meddle in things utterly forbidden, whoever is offended, grieved, or made weak thereby. For an instance of this, we need go no further than to the man in the text who, while he was tender trembled at little things, but when his heart was hardened, he could take Bathsheba to satisfy his lust, and kill her husband to cover his wickedness.

Seventh. A tender heart, I mean the heart kept tender, preserves from many a blow, lash, and fatherly chastisement; because it shuns the causes, which is sin, of the scourging hand of God. "With the upright thou wilt show thyself upright, but with the froward thou wilt show thyself unsavoury." (2 Sam. xxii. 27. Ps. xviii. 25—27.)

Many a needless rebuke and wound doth happen to the saints of God through their unwise behaviour; when I say needless, I mean, they are not necessary, but to reclaim us from our vanities; for we should not feel the smart of them were it not for our follies. Hence the afflicted is called a fool, because his folly brings his affliction upon him. "Fools," says David, "because of their transgressions, and because of their iniquities, are afflicted." (Ps. cvii. 17.) And therefore it is, as was said before, that he calls his sin his foolishness. And again, "God will speak peace to his people, and his saints, but let not them return again to folly." (Ps. xxxviii. 5; lxxxv. 8.) "If his children transgress my laws, I will visit their transgressions with a rod, and their iniquities with stripes." (Ps. lxxxiv. 30—32.)

Quest. But what should a Christian do, when God has broke his heart, to keep it tender?

Ans. To this I will speak briefly. And, 1. Give you several cautions. 2. Several directions.

For *cautions* :—

1. Take heed that you choke not those convictions that at present do break your hearts, by labouring to put those things out of your minds which were the cause of such convictions, but rather nourish and cherish those things in a deep and sober remembrance of them. Think therefore with thyself thus, What was it that at first did wound my heart? And let that still be there, until, by the grace of God, and the redeemed blood of Christ, it is removed.

2. Shun vain company. The keeping of vain company has stifled many a conviction, killed many a desire, and made many a soul fall into hell, that once was hot in looking after heaven. A companion that is not profitable to the soul, is hurtful. " He that walketh with wise men shall be wise, but a companion of fools shall be destroyed." (Prov. xiii. 20.)

3. Take heed of idle talk, that thou neither hear nor join with it. " Go from the presence of a foolish man, when thou perceivest not in him the lips of knowledge." (Prov. xiv. 7.) " Evil communications corrupt good manners. And a fool's lips are a snare to his soul." Wherefore take heed of these things. (Prov. xviii. 7. 1 Cor. xv. 33.)

4. Beware of the least motion to sin, that it be not countenanced, lest the countenancing of that makes way for a bigger. David's eye took his heart, and so his heart, nourishing the thought, made way for the woman's company, the act of adultery, and bloody murder. "Take heed, therefore, brethren, lest any of you be hardened through the deceitfulness of sin." (Heb. iii. 12, 13.) And remember, that he that will rend the block, puts the thin end of the wedge first thereto, and so by driving does his work.

5. Take heed of evil examples among the godly; learn of no man to do that which the word of God forbids. Sometimes Satan makes use of a good man's bad ways to spoil and harden the heart of them that come after; Peter's false doing had like to have spoiled Barnabas, yea, and several others more. Wherefore take heed of men, of good men's ways, and measure both theirs and thine own by no other rule but the holy word of God. (Gal. ii. 11—13.)

6. Take heed of unbelief, or atheistical thoughts; make no question of the truth and reality of heavenly things : for know, unbelief is the worst of evils; nor can the heart be tender that nourisheth or gives place unto it. " Take heed, therefore, lest there be in any of you an evil heart of unbelief, in departing from the living God." (Heb. iii. 12.)

These cautions are necessary to be observed with all diligence, of all them that would, when their heart is made tender, keep it so.

And now to come to the *directions* :—

1. Labour after a deep knowledge of God, to keep it warm upon thy heart; knowledge of his presence, that is everywhere. " Do not I fill heaven and earth? saith the Lord." (Jer. xxiii. 24.) Knowledge of his piercing eye; that it runneth to and fro through the earth, beholding in every place the evil and the good; that his eyes behold, and his eyelids try the children of men. (Prov. xv. 3.) The knowledge of his power, that he is able to turn and dissolve heaven and earth into dust and ashes; and that they are in his hand but as a scroll or vesture. (Heb. i. 11, 12.) The knowledge of his justice, that the rebukes of it are as devouring fire. (Heb. xii. 19.) The knowledge of his faithfulness, in fulfilling promises to them to whom they are made, and of his threatenings on the impenitent. (Matt. v. 18; xxiv. 35. Mark xiii. 31.)

2. Labour to get and keep a deep sense of sin, in its evil nature, and in its soul-destroying effects upon thy heart; be persuaded, that it is the only enemy of God, and that none hate, or are hated of God, but through that. Remember, it turned angels into devils, thrust them down from heaven to hell. That it is the chain in which they are held and bound over to judgment. (2 Pet. ii. Jude 6.) That it was for that that Adam was turned out of Paradise; that for which the old world was drowned; that for which Sodom and Gomorrah were burned with fire from heaven; and that which cost Christ his blood to redeem thee from the curse it has brought upon thee; and that, if anything, will keep thee out of heaven for ever and ever. Consider the pains of hell. Christ makes use of that as an argument to keep the heart tender; yea, to that end repeats and repeats both the nature and durableness of the burning flame thereof, and of the gnawing of the never-dying worm that dwells there. (Mark ix. 43—48.)

3. Consider of death, both as to the certainty of thy dying, and uncertainty of the time when. We must die, we must needs die, our days are determined, the number of our months are with God, though not with us; nor can we pass them, would we, had we them, give a thousand worlds to do it. (2 Sam. xiv. 14. Job vii. 1; xiv. 1—5.) Consider thou must die but once, I mean but once as to this world; for if thou, when thou goest hence, dost not die well, thou canst not come back again and die better. " It is appointed unto all men once to die, and after this the judgment." (Heb. ix. 27.)

4. Consider also of the certainty and terribleness of the day of judgment, when Christ shall sit upon his great white throne, when the dead shall, by the sound of the trump of God, be raised up; when the elements, with heaven and earth, shall be on a burning flame; when Christ shall separate men one from another, as a shepherd divideth his sheep from the goats; when the books shall be opened, the witnesses produced, and every man

be judged according to his works; when heaven's gate shall stand open to them that shall be saved, and the jaws of hell stand gaping for them that shall be damned. (Acts v. 30, 31; x. 42. Matt. xxv. 30, 31, 34, 41. Rev. ii. 11. 1 Cor. xv. 51. Rev. xx. 12. 2 Pet. iii. 7, 10, 12. Matt. xxv. 32. Rom. ii. 2, 15, 16. Rev. xxii. 12, 15.)

5. Consider, Christ Jesus did use no means to harden his heart against doing and suffering those sorrows which were necessary for the redemption of thy soul. No; though he could have hardened his heart against thee, in the way of justice and righteousness, because thou hadst sinned against him, he rather awakened himself, and put on all pity, bowels, and compassion; yea, tender mercies, and did it. In his love, and in his pity he saved us. His tender mercy from on high hath visited us. He loved us, and gave himself for us.

Learn, then, of Christ, to be tender of thyself, and to endeavour to keep thy heart tender to Godward, and to the salvation of thy soul. But to draw to a conclusion.

The Use.

Let us now, then, make some use of this doctrine: as—

I. From the truth of the matter, namely, that the man who is truly come to God has had his heart broken—his heart broken in order to his coming to him. And this shows us what to judge of the league that is between sin and the soul; to wit, that it is so firm, so strong, so inviolable, as that nothing can break, disannul, or make it void, unless the heart be broken for it. It was so with David; yea, his new league with it could not be broken until his heart was broken.

It is amazing to consider what hold sin has on some men's souls, spirits, will, and affections. It is to them better than heaven, better than God, than the soul, ay, than salvation; as is evident, because, though all these are offered them upon this condition, if they will but leave their sins; yet they will choose rather to abide in them, to stand and fall by them. How sayest thou, sinner? Is not this a truth? How many times hast thou had heaven and salvation offered to thee freely, wouldst thou but break thy league with this great enemy of God?—of God, do I say; if thou wouldst but break this league with this great enemy of thy soul? but couldst never yet be brought unto it; no, neither by threatening, nor by promise couldst thou ever yet be brought unto it.

It is said of Ahab, he sold himself to work wickedness: and in another place, "Yea, for your iniquities have ye sold yourselves." (1 Kings xxi. 25. Isa. l. 1.) But what is this iniquity? Why, a thing of nought; nay, worse than nought a thousand times; but because nought is as we say nought, therefore it goes under that term, where God saith again to the people. "Ye have sold yourselves for nought." (Isa. lii. 3.) But, I say, what an amazing thing is this, that a rational creature should make no better a bargain; that one that is so wise in all terrene things, should be such a fool in the thing that is most weighty. And yet such a fool he is, and he tells every one that goes by the way that he is such an one, because he will not break his league with sin until his heart is broken for it. Men love darkness rather than light. Ay, they make it manifest they love it, since so great a professor will not prevail with them to leave it.

II. Is this a truth, that the man that truly comes to God in order thereto has had his heart broken? Then this shows us a reason why some men's hearts are broken; even a reason why God breaks some men's hearts for sin; namely, because he would not have them die in it, but rather come to God that they might be saved. Behold, therefore, in this, how God resolved as to the saving of some men's souls! He will have them, he will save them, he will break their hearts but he will save them; he will kill them, that they may live; he will wound them, that he may heal them. And it seems by our discourse, that now there is no way left but this; fair means, as we say, will not do; good words, a glorious gospel, entreatings, beseeching with blood and tears will not do. Men are resolved to put God to the utmost of it; if he will have them he must fetch them, follow them, catch them, lame them; yea, break their bones, or else he shall not save them.

Some men think an invitation, an outward call, a rational discourse will do; but they are much deceived. There must a power, an exceeding great and mighty power attend the word, or it worketh not effectually to the salvation of the soul. I know these things are enough to leave men without excuse; but yet they are not enough to bring men home to God. Sin has hold of them, they have sold themselves to it; the power of the devil has hold of them; they are his captives at his will; yea, and more than all this, their will is one with sin, and with the devil, to be held captive thereby. And if God gives not contrition, repentance, or a broken heart for sin, there will not be, no, not so much as a mind in man to forsake this so horrible a confederacy and plot against his soul. (2 Tim. ii. 24, 25.)

Hence men are said to be drawn from these breasts, that come, or that are brought to him. (Isa. xxvi. 9. John vi. 44.) Wherefore John might well say, "Behold what manner of love the Father hath bestowed upon us!" Here is cost bestowed, pains bestowed, labour bestowed, repentance bestowed; yea, and an heart made sore, wounded, broken, and filled with pain and sorrow, in order to the salvation of the soul.

III. This then may teach us what estimation to set upon a broken heart. A broken heart is such as God esteems; yea, as God counts better than all external service. A broken heart is that which is in order to salvation, in order to thy coming to Christ for life. The world know not what to make of it, not what to say to one that has a broken heart, and therefore do despise it, and count that man that carries it in his bosom a moping fool, a miserable wretch, an undone soul. "But a broken and a contrite spirit, O God, thou wilt not despise;" a broken heart takes thine eye, thy heart; thou choosest it for thy companion; yea, hast given thy Son a charge to look well to such a man, and hast promised him thy salvation, as has afore been proved.

Sinner, hast thou obtained a broken heart? has God bestowed a contrite spirit upon thee? He has given thee what himself is pleased with; he has given thee a cabinet to hold his grace in, he has given thee a heart that can heartily desire his salvation; a heart after his own heart; that is such as suits his mind. True, it is painful now, sorrowful now, penitent now, grieved now; now it is broken, now it bleeds, now, now it sobs, now it sighs, now it mourns and crieth unto God. Well, very well. All this is because he has a mind to make thee laugh; he has made thee sorry on earth, that thou mightest rejoice in heaven. "Blessed are ye that mourn, for ye shall be comforted, Blessed are ye that weep now, for ye shall laugh." (Matt. v. 4. Luke vi. 21.)

But, soul, be sure thou hast this broken heart; all hearts are not broken hearts, nor is every heart that seems to have a wound a heart that is truly broken. A man may be cut to, yet not into the heart; a man may have another, yet not a broken heart. (Acts vii. 54. 1 Sam. x. 9.) We know there is a difference betwixt a wound in the flesh and a wound in the spirit; yea, a man's sin may be wounded, and yet his heart not broken; so was Pharaoh's, so was Saul's, so was Ahab's; but they had none of them the mercy of a broken heart. Therefore, I say, take heed; every scratch with a pin, every prick with a thorn, nay, every blow that God giveth with his word upon the heart of sinners, doth not therefore break them. God gave Ahab such a blow, that he made him stoop, fast, humble himself, gird himself with and lie in sackcloth, which was a great matter for a king; and go softly, and yet he never had a broken heart. (1 Kings xxi. 27—29.)

What shall I say? Pharaoh and Saul confessed their sin, Judas repented himself of his doings, Esau sought the blessing, and that carefully with tears, and yet none of these had a heart rightly broken, or a spirit truly contrite: Pharaoh, Saul, and Judas, were Pharaoh, Saul, and Judas still; Esau was Esau still: there was no gracious change, no thorough turn to God, no unfeigned parting with their sins; no hearty flight for refuge to lay hold on the hope of glory, though they indeed had thus been touched. (Exod. x. 16. 1 Sam. xxvi. 21. Matt. xxvii. 3. Heb. xii. 14—17.)

The consideration of these things calls aloud to us to take heed, that we take not that for a broken and a contrite spirit, that will not go for one at the day of death and judgment. Wherefore, seeking soul, let me advise thee, that thou mayest not be deceived as to this thing of so great weight.

First. To go back towards the beginning of this book, and compare thyself with those six or seven signs of a broken and a contrite heart which there I have, according to the word of God, given to thee for that end; and deal with thy soul impartially about them.

Second. Or, which may and will be great help to thee if thou shalt be sincere therein, namely, to betake thyself to the search of the word, especially where thou readest of the conversion of men, and try if thy conversion be like, or has a good resemblance or oneness with theirs. But in this have a care that thou dost not compare thyself with those good folk, of whose conversion thou readest not, or of the breaking of whose heart there is no mention made in Scripture; for all that are recorded in the Scripture for saints, have not their conversion, as to the manner or nature of it, recorded in the Scripture.

Third. Or else, do thou consider truly of the true signs of repentance, which are laid down in Scripture, for that is the true effect of a broken heart and of a wounded spirit. And for this see Matt. iii. 5, 6. Luke xviii. 13; xix. 8. Acts ii 37—41, &c.; xvi. 29, 30: xix. 18, 19. 2 Cor. vii. 8—11.

Fourth. Or else, take into consideration how God has said they shall be in their spirits, that he intends to save. And for this, read these scriptures:—1. That in the one and thirtieth of Jeremiah, "They shall come with weeping, and with supplications will I lead them," &c. (ver. 9.) 2. Read Jer. l. 4, 5: "In those days, and at that time, the children of Israel shall come, they and the children of Judah together, going and weeping: they shall go, and seek the Lord their God. They shall ask the way to Zion, with their faces thitherward; saying, Come, and let us join ourselves to the Lord, in a perpetual covenant that shall not be forgotten." 3. Read Ezek. vi. 9: "And they that escape of you shall remember me among the nations whither they shall be carried captives, because I am broken with their whorish heart, which has departed from me, and with their eyes, which go a-whoring after their idols; and they shall loath themselves for the evils which they have committed in all their abominations." 4. Read Ezek. vii. 16: "But they that escape of them shall escape, and shall be on the mountains like doves of the valleys, all of them mourning, every one for his iniquity." 5. Read Ezek. xx. 43: "And there shall ye remember your ways, and all your doings, wherein ye have been defiled; and ye shall loath yourselves in your own sight, for all your evils that ye have committed." 6. Read Ezek. xxxvi. 31: "Then shall ye remember your own evil ways, and your doings that were not good, and shall loath yourselves in your sight, for your iniquities, and for your abominations. 7. Read Zech. xii. 10: "And I will pour upon the house of David, and upon the inhabitants of Jerusalem, the spirit of grace and of supplications: and they shall look upon me whom they have pierced, and they shall mourn for him, as one mourneth for his only son, and shall be in bitterness for him as one that is in bitterness for his first-born."

Now all these are the fruits of the Spirit of God, and of the heart, when it is broken: wherefore, soul, take notice of them, and because these are texts by which God promiseth that those whom he saveth shall have this heart, this spirit, and these holy effects in them; therefore consider, again, and examine thyself, whether this is the state and condition of thy soul. And that thou mayest do it fully, consider again, and do thou,

1. Remember that here is such a sense of sin, and of the irksomeness thereof, as maketh the man not only to abhor that, but himself because of that; this is worth the noting by thee.

2. Remember, again, that here is not only a self-abhorrence, but a sorrowful mourning unto God, at the consideration that the soul by sin has affronted, contemned, disregarded, and set at nought both God and his holy word.

3. Remember, also, that here are prayers and tears for mercy, with desires to be now out of love with sin for ever, and to be in heart and soul firmly joined and knit unto God.

4. Remember, also, that this people here spoken of have all the way from Satan to God, from sin to grace, from death to life, scattered with tears and prayers, with weeping and supplication: they shall go weeping, and seeking the Lord their God.

5. Remember that these people, as strangers and pilgrims do, are not ashamed to ask the way of those they meet with to Zion, or the heavenly country; whereby they confess their ignorance, as became them, and their desire to know the way of life; yea, thereby they declare that there is nothing in this world under the sun, or this side heaven, that can satisfy the longings, the desires, and cravings of a broken and a contrite spirit. Reader, be advised, and consider of these things seriously, and compare thy soul with them, and with what else thou shalt find here written for thy conviction and instruction.

IV. If a broken heart and a contrite spirit be of such esteem with God, then this should encourage them that have it, to come to God with it. I know the great encouragement for men to come to God is, for that there "is a mediator between God and man, the man Christ Jesus." (1 Tim. ii. 5.) This, I say, is the great encouragement, and in its place there is none but that; but there are other engagements subordinate to that, and a broken and a contrite spirit is one of them: this is evident from several places of Scripture.

Wherefore, thou that canst carry a broken heart and a sorrowful spirit with thee, when thou goest to God, tell him thy heart is wounded within thee, that thou hast sorrow in thy heart, and art sorry for thy sins; but take heed of lying. Confess also thy sins unto him, and tell him they are continually before thee. David made an argument of these things, when he went to God by prayer. "O Lord," saith he, "rebuke me not in thine anger, neither chasten me in thy sore displeasure." But why so? "Oh," says he, "thine arrows stick fast in me, and thy hand presseth me sore. There is no soundness in my flesh, because of thine anger, neither is there any rest in my bones because of my sin. For mine iniquities are gone over mine head; as a heavy burden, they are too heavy for me. My wounds stink and are corrupt, because of my foolishness. I am troubled, I am bowed down greatly; I go mourning all the day long. For my loins are filled with a loathsome disease; and there is no soundness in my flesh. I am feeble and sore broken: I have roared by reason of the disquietness of my heart. Lord, all my desire is before thee; and my groaning is not hid from thee. My heart panteth, my strength faileth me: as for the light of mine eyes, it also is gone from me. My lovers and friends stand aloof from my sore." And so he goes on. (Ps. xxxviii. 1—4, &c.)

These are the words, sighs, complaints, prayers, and arguments of a broken heart to God for mercy; and so are they—"Have mercy upon me, O God, according to thy loving-kindness; according to the multitude of thy tender mercies, blot out my transgressions. Wash me thoroughly from mine iniquity, and cleanse me from my sin. For I acknowledge my transgressions, and my sins are ever before me." (Ps. li. 1—3.)

God alloweth poor creatures that can, without lying, thus to plead and argue with him. "I am poor and sorrowful," said the good man to him, "let thy salvation set me on high." (Ps. lxix. 29.) Wherefore, thou that hast a broken heart, take courage, God bids thee take courage; say therefore to thy soul, "Why art thou cast down, O my soul?" (as usually the broken-hearted are:) "and why art thou disquieted within me? Hope thou in God. I had fainted if I had not been of good courage; therefore be of good courage, and he shall strengthen thine heart." (Ps. xlii. 11; xliii. 5; xxvii. 12—14.)

But, alas! the broken-hearted are far off from this; they faint; they reckon themselves among the dead; they think God will remember them no more; the thoughts of the greatness of God, and his holiness, and their own sins and vilenesses, will certainly consume them. They feel guilt and anguish of soul; they go mourning all the day long; their mouth is full of gravel and gall, and they are made to drink draughts of wormwood and gall; so that he must be an artist indeed at believing, who can come to God under his guilt and horror, and plead in faith that the sacrifices of God are a broken heart, such as he had, and that "a broken and a contrite spirit God will not despise."

V. If a broken heart, if a broken and contrite spirit, is of such esteem with God; then why should some be, as they are, so afraid of a broken heart, and so shy of a contrite spirit.

I have observed that some men are as afraid of a broken heart, or that they for their sins would have their hearts broken, as the dog is of the whip. Oh, they cannot away with such books, with such sermons, with such preachers, or with such talk, as tends to make a man sensible of, and to break his heart, and to make him contrite for his sins! Hence they heap to themselves such teachers, get such books, love such company, and delight in such discourse, as rather tends to harden than soften; to make desperate in, than sorrowful for their sins. They say to such sermons, books, and preachers, as Amaziah said to Amos, "O thou seer, go, flee thou away into the land of Judah, and there eat bread, and prophecy there, but prophecy not again any more at Bethel," &c. (Amos vii. 12, 13.)

But do these people know what they do? Yes, think they, for such preachers, such books, such discourses tend to make one melancholy or mad; they make us, that we cannot take pleasure in ourselves, in our concerns, in our lives.

But, O fool in grain! let me speak unto thee, is it a time to take pleasure, and to recreate thyself in anything, before thou hast mourned and been sorry for thy sins? That mirth that is before repentance for sin, will certainly end in heaviness. Wherefore the wise man, putting both together, saith, that mourning must be first: "There is a time to weep, and a time to laugh; a time to mourn, and a time to dance." (Eccles. iii. 4.) What, an unconverted man, and laugh! Shouldst thou see one singing merry songs that is riding up Holborn to Tyburn, to be hanged for felony, wouldst thou not count him besides himself, if not worse? and yet thus it is with him that is for mirth, while he standeth condemned by the book of God for his trespasses. Man! man! thou hast cause to mourn; yea, thou must mourn, if ever thou art saved. Wherefore my advice is, that instead of shunning, thou covet both such books, such preachers, and such discourses as have a tendency to make a man sensible of, and to break his heart for sin; and the reason is, because thou wilt never be as thou shouldst, concerned about, nor seek the salvation of thine own soul, before thou hast a broken heart, a broken and a contrite spirit. Wherefore be not afraid of a broken heart, be not shy of a contrite spirit. It is one of the greatest mercies that God bestows upon a man or a woman. The heart rightly broken at the sense of, and made truly contrite for transgression, is a certain forerunner of salvation. This is evident from those six demonstrations, which were laid down to prove the point in hand at first.

And for thy awaking in this matter, let me tell thee, and thou wilt find it so, thou must have thy heart broken whether thou wilt or no. God is resolved to break all hearts for sin some time or other.

Can it be imagined, sin being what it is, and God what he is—to wit, a revenger of disobedience—but that one time or other man must smart for sin; smart, I say, either to repentance or to condemnation. He that mourns not now, while the door of mercy is open, must mourn for sin when the door of mercy is shut.

Shall men despise God, break his law, contemn his threats, abuse his grace; yea, shut their eyes when he says, See; and stop their ears when he says, Hear; and shall they so escape? No, no, because he called, and they refused; he stretched out his hand, and they regarded it not; therefore shall calamity come upon them as upon one in travail, and they shall cry in their destruction, and then God will laugh at their destruction, and mock when their fear cometh. Then, saith he, "they shall cry." (Prov. i. 24—26, &c.) I have often observed, that this threatening is repeated at least seven times in the New Testament, saying, "There shall be weeping and gnashing of teeth;" "There shall be wailing and gnashing of teeth," as Matt. viii. 12; xiii. 42, 50; xii. 13; xxiv. 51; xxv. 30. Luke xiii. 28.

There, Where? In hell, and at the bar of Christ's tribunal, when he comes to judge the world, and shall have shut to the door to keep them out of glory, that have here despised the offer of his grace, and overlooked the day of his patience: "There shall be wailing and gnashing of teeth." They shall weep and wail for this.

There are but two scriptures that I shall use more, and then I shall draw towards a conclusion. One is that in Proverbs, where Solomon is counselling of young men to beware of strange, that is, of wanton, light, and ensnaring women. Take heed of such, said he, "Lest thou mourn at last," that is, in hell, when thou art dead, "when thy flesh and thy body are consumed, and say, How have I hated instruction, and despised reproof, and have not obeyed the voice of my teachers, nor inclined mine ears to them that instructed me!" (Prov. v. 11—13, &c.)

The other scripture is that in Isaiah, where he says, "Because when I called, ye did not answer; when I spake, ye did not hear, but did evil before mine eyes, and did choose that wherein I delighted not: therefore, thus saith the Lord God, Behold, my servants shall eat, but ye shall be hungry; behold, my servants shall drink, but ye shall be thirsty; behold, my servants shall rejoice, but ye shall be ashamed; behold, my servants shall sing for joy of heart, but ye shall cry for sorrow of heart, and howl for vexation of spirit." (Isa. lxv. 12—14.)

How many "beholds" are here? And every behold is not only a call to careless ones to consider, but as a declaration from heaven, that thus at last it shall be with all impenitent sinners; that is, when others sing for joy in the kingdom of heaven, they, they shall sorrow in hell, and howl for vexation of spirit there.

Wherefore, let me advise that you be not afraid of, but that ye rather covet a broken heart, and prize a contrite spirit; I say, covet it now, now the white flag is hung out, now the golden sceptre of grace is held forth to you. Better mourn now God inclines to mercy and pardon, than mourn when the door is quite shut up. And take notice, that this is not the first time that I have given you this advice.

Lastly. If a broken heart be a thing of so great esteem with God, as has been said, and if duties cannot be rightly performed by a heart that has not been broken, then this shows the vanity of those people's minds, and also the invalidity of their pretended divine services, who worship God with an heart that was never broken, and without a contrite spirit. There have, indeed, at all times been great flocks of such professors in the world in every age; but to little purpose, unless to deceive themselves, to mock God, and lay stumbling-blocks in the way of others; for a man whose heart was never truly broken, and whose spirit was never contrite, cannot profess Christ in earnest, cannot love his own soul in earnest; I mean, he cannot do these things in truth, and seek his own good the right way, for he wants a bottom for it, to wit, a broken heart for sin, and a contrite spirit.

That which makes a man a hearty, an unfeigned, a sincere seeker after the good of his own soul, is sense of sin, and a godly fear of being overtaken with the danger which it brings a man into. This makes him contrite, or repentant, and puts him upon seeking of Christ the Saviour, with heart-aching and heart-breaking considerations. But this cannot be, where this sense, this godly fear, and this holy contrition is wanting. Profess men may, and make a noise, as the empty barrel maketh the biggest sound; but prove them, and they are full of air, full of emptiness, and that's all.

Nor are such professors tender of God's name, nor of the credit of that gospel which they profess; nor can they, for they want that which should oblige them thereunto, which is a sense of pardon and forgiveness; by the which their broken hearts have been replenished, succoured, and made to hope in God. Paul said, " the love of Christ constrained him;" but what was Paul, but a broken-hearted and a contrite sinner? (See Acts ix. 3—6. 2 Cor. v. 14.) When God shows a man the sin he has committed, the hell he has deserved, the heaven he has lost; and yet that Christ, and grace, and pardon may be had; this will make him serious, this will make him melt, this will break his heart, this will show him that there is more than air, than a noise, than an empty sound in religion; and this is the man whose heart, whose life, whose conversation and all, will be engaged in the matters of the eternal salvation of his precious and immortal soul.

Obj. But some may object, that in this saying I seem too rigid and censorious; and will, if I moderate not these lines with something milder afterward, discourage many an honest soul.

Ans. I answer, Not a jot; not an honest soul in all the world will be offended at my words, for not one can be an honest soul, I mean, with reference to its concerns in another world, that has not had a broken heart, that never had a contrite spirit. This I will say, because I would be understood aright, that all attain not to the same degree of trouble, nor lie so long thereunder, as some of their brethren do : but to go to heaven without a broken heart, or to be forgiven sin without a contrite spirit, is no article of my belief. We speak not now of what is secret; revealed things belong to us and our children; nor must we venture to go further in our faith. Doth not Christ say, " The whole have no need of a physician?" that is, they see no need, but Christ will make them see their need before he ministers his sovereign grace unto them; and good reason, otherwise he will have but little thanks for his kindness.

Obj. But there are those that are godly educated from their childhood, and so drink in the principles of Christianity they know not how.

Ans. I count it one thing to receive the faith of Christ from men only, and another to receive it from God by the means. If thou art taught by an angel, yet if not taught of God, thou wilt never come to Christ; I do not say thou wilt never profess him. But if God speaks, and thou shalt hear and understand him, that voice will make such work within thee as was never made before. The voice of God is a voice by itself, and is so distinguished by them that are taught thereby (John vi. 44, 45. Ps. xxix. Hab. iii. 15, 16. Eph. iv. 20, 21. 1 Pet. ii. 2, 3.)

Obj. But some men are not so debauched and profane as some, and so need not to be so hammered and fired as others; so broken and wounded as others.

Ans. God knows best what we need. Paul was as righteous before conversion as any that can pretend to civility now, I suppose; and yet, that notwithstanding, he was made to shake, and was astonished at himself at his conversion. And truly, I think, the more righteous any is in his own eyes before conversion, the more need he has of heart-breaking work in order to his salvation; because a man is not by nature so easily convinced that his righteousness is to God abominable, as he is that his debauchery and profaneness is.

A man's goodness is that which blinds him most, is dearest to him, and hardly parted with; and, therefore, when such an one is converted, that thinks he has goodness of his own enough to commend him in whole, or in part, to God—though but few such are converted—there is required a great deal of breaking work upon his heart to make him come to Paul's conclusion, " What!

are we better than they? No; in no wise." (Rom. iii. 9.) I say, before he can be brought to see his glorious robes are filthy rags, and his gainful things but loss and dung. (Isa. lxiv. Phil. iii.)

This is also gathered from these words:— "Publicans and harlots enter into the kingdom of God before the Pharisees." (Matt. xxi. 31.) Why before them, but because they lie fairer for the word, are easier convinced of their need of Christ, and so are brought home to him without, as I may say, all that ado that the Holy Ghost doth make to bring home one of these to him.

True; nothing is hard or difficult to God. But I speak after the manner of men. And let who will take to task a man debauched in this life, and one that is not so, and he shall see, if he laboureth to convince them both that they are in a state of condemnation by nature, that the Pharisee will make his appeals to God, with a great many "God, I thank thees;" while the publican hangs his head, shakes at heart, and smites upon his breast, saying, "God be merciful to me a sinner." (Luke xviii. 11—13.)

Wherefore a self-righteous man is but a painted Satan, or a devil in fine clothes; but thinks he so of himself? No, no! He saith to others, Stand back, come not near me, I am holier than thou. It is almost impossible that a self-righteous man should be saved. But he that can drive a camel through the eye of a needle, can cause that even such a one shall see his lost condition, and that he needeth the righteousness of God, which is by faith of Jesus Christ. He can make him see, I say, that his own goodness did stand more in his way to the kingdom of heaven than he was aware of; and can make him feel, too, that his leaning to that is as great iniquity as any immorality that men commit. The sum then is, that men that are converted to God by Christ, through the word and Spirit (for all this must go to effectual conversion), must have their hearts broken, and spirits made contrite; I say, it must be so, for the reasons showed before. Yea, and all decayed, apostatized, and backslidden Christians must, in order to their recovery again to God, have their hearts broken, their souls wounded, their spirits made contrite, and sorry for their sins.

Come, come, conversion to God is not so easy and so smooth a thing as some would have men believe it is. Why is man's heart compared to fallow ground, God's word to a plough, and his ministers to ploughmen, if the heart indeed has no need of breaking, in order to the receiving of the seed of God unto eternal life? (Jer. iv. 3.

Luke ix. 62. 1 Cor. ix. 10.) Who knows not that fallow ground must be ploughed, and ploughed too before the husbandman will venture his seed; yea, and after that oft soundly harrowed, or else he will have but a slender harvest?

Why is the conversion of the soul compared to the grafting of a tree, if that be done without cutting? The word is the graft, the soul is the tree, and the word, as the scion, must be let in by a wound; for to stick on the outside, or to be tied on with a string, will do no good here. Heart must be set to heart, and back to back, or your pretended ingrafting will come to nothing. (Rom. xi. 17, 24. James i. 21.) I say, heart must be set to heart, and back to back, or the sap will not be conveyed from the root to the branch. And I say, this must be done by a wound. The Lord opened the heart of Lydia, as a man openeth the stock to graft in the scions, and so the word was let into her soul, and so the word and her heart cemented, and became one. (Acts xvi. 14.)

Why is Christ bid to gird his sword upon his thigh? and why must he make his arrows sharp, and all, that the heart may with this sword and these arrows be shot, wounded, and made to bleed? Yea, why is he commanded to let it be so, if the people would bow and fall kindly under him, and heartily implore his grace without it? (Ps. xlv. 55; iii. 4.) Alas! men are too lofty, too proud, too wild, too devilishly resolved in the ways of their own destruction; in their occasions they are like the wild asses upon the wild mountains; nothing can break them of their purposes, or hinder them from ruining of their own precious and immortal souls, but the breaking of their hearts.

Why is the broken heart put in the room of all sacrifices which we can offer to God; and a contrite spirit put in the room of all offerings, as they are, and you may see it so, if you compare the text with that verse which goes before it; I say, why is it counted better than all, were they all put together, if any one part, or if all external parts of worship, were they put together, could be able to render the man a sound and a rightly-made new creature without it? "A broken heart, a contrite spirit, God will not despise;" but both thou, and all thy service, he will certainly slight and reject; if, when thou comest to him, a broken heart be wanting. Wherefore, here is the point, Come broken, come contrite, come sensible of and sorry for thy sins, or thy coming will be counted no coming to God aright; and if so, consequently thou wilt get no benefit thereby.

PREFATORY REMARKS

ON

AN EXPOSITION OF FIRST TEN CHAPTERS OF GENESIS.

THE qualifications of a commentator, in Bunyan's time, were less easily attainable than in ours, but they were not less understood. A diligent and thoughtful reading of the text of Scripture will speedily make an earnest man perceive what is needed for its explication. If the obscurity lies in the phraseology, it will at once occur to him that a further examination of the original is required. Let the difficulty arise from allusion to things remote in age or country, and he will look to the oriental antiquary, or traveller, for assistance. We have many more helps, in these ways, than a commentator could have obtained in the seventeenth century. Such, however, were not wanting even then. The Buxtorfs, the Pococks, and Lightfoots, were of the highest class of auxiliaries to students of Scripture. It may be questioned whether any of their successors have exceeded them in the grand qualities of patience and earnestness.

It is not improbable that Bunyan availed himself, if not directly, yet indirectly, of these masters in Biblical illustration. There are portions of the following commentary which show traces of study and research. For an exposition that should rest upon learning and scientific criticism, he was clearly unfitted, unless the traditions of his life be accounted a fable. But, acute and diligent as he was, he might, without any great difficulty, acquire some degree of skill in the use of the Biblical apparatus prepared to his hand. He was even bound to make an attempt in this direction. His name gave authority to his writings; and an expositor of the Bible is, of all other writers, self-invested with the most awful species of professorship. Even the humblest interpreter of Scripture, one who assuming, that is, no higher character than that of an instructor, seeking rather to apply what is easy than expound what is difficult, must look warily at his words, speaking only from himself. But the professed commentator takes loftier ground than a preacher: it is the object of his labours to bring what lies dark and obscure into light; and to give, as far as possible, not barely the true, but the whole meaning of passages only partially understood without his aid.

The works of celebrated commentators afford an equally grand and affecting instance of patient devotion to the cause of truth. In the most valuable of their writings, no trace can be discovered of a feeling not wholly absorbed in the one simple design of explaining difficulties. Other writers scarcely attempt to conceal the pride and excitement which attend their labours; but the genuine commentator has a stern task in hand, and he fulfils it in a stern spirit.

Few men are fitted both by acquirements and disposition for undertakings of this kind: they form a literature by itself; and a very skilful essayist, or experienced preacher, may be far from proving a useful commentator. We are not sufficiently acquainted with the particular circumstances under which Bunyan began this new branch of literary labour: they may have had great influence in determining him to such an attempt. He probably saw that the love of inquiry was daily increasing; and that it would soon be difficult for him, or any other pastor, to answer verbally the numberless questions asked on certain portions of Scripture. A commentary written by himself, in his own style and manner, and just meeting the necessities of his people, would appear to him as a very valuable instrument of instruction. His ardent mind wanted no other suggestion to set him to work as an expositor; and it is not unlikely that it was really in this way that he was induced to begin a Commentary.

But as there is little to show us why he commenced this work, we know as little why he so abruptly discontinued it. Here then again some degree of conjecture must be allowed. Few readers, perhaps, will set so high a value upon this specimen of an Exposition, as upon many of Bunyan's other works. It is not improbable that he soon found himself either unequal to such a labour, or not sufficiently prepared for it. The difficulties which it involved were not of a kind to appear on the surface. It was natural for a mind like his to grasp at the idea of bringing out into full relief the wonderful scenes and characters of Mosaic history; and then to pass on, in triumphant progress, through lines of prophets and evangelists. Many a student of Scripture, excited by some incidental discovery of a fuller or a deeper meaning than others look for, has been tempted to believe himself a commentator: but it is not a fitful illumination, throwing light here and there on some page of Scripture, which marks the mental characteristics proper to a good and sound expositor. The patient study of opinion; great freedom from the affectation of originality; a willingness to spend any length of time and labour in the work,—these are the qualities which a man should find in himself before he determines to sit down, and become a writer of commentaries.

It is evident that few men, however spiritual, and though worthy of all admiration in other departments of literature, are imbued with this special fitness for Biblical exposition. Nor is it to be forgotten that there is another very necessary condition to the successful pursuit of such a labour. Learning, zeal, and patience, all combined, will scarcely suffice to make a man worthy of confidence as a commentator, if his circumstances fail to afford him an ample share of leisure and independence. The instances of heroic struggles, by which all the difficulties of an adverse condition have been overcome, and laborious ministers have proved valuable commentators, are exceptional cases: they do not alter the fact that to be a safe commentator, a man should have great command of his time; should be free to shut himself up against all intrusion; and be able to say, at the end of every note which he has written, that it is the result of long inquiry, and uninterrupted, quiet reflection.

When Bunyan first sat down to the great undertaking here commenced, his hopefulness and energy gave him quite sufficient support for a beginning. But he could not have gone beyond the third or fourth chapter, before some misgiving must have occurred to him. It is almost impossible that he should have failed to discover his want of ancient learning; or to perceive that the riches of his experience, so abundantly helpful to him in other respects, could not in this case be used as a substitute for skill in grammar and criticism. He was far too wise not thus to make an early discovery of his insufficiency for the task he had attempted. The perpetual inroads upon his quiet, a necessary consequence of his usefulness and popularity as a pastor, would add tenfold weight to the doubts which might arise from any other cause. It is no wonder, therefore, that we possess a commentary on only ten chapters of Genesis from the pen of Bunyan. Had he begun with some portion of the New Testament, his store of doctrinal and practical theology might have carried him much farther. The difficulties in his way would have been less insuperable; and even when he did not remove them, the reader would not have been left without some sweet and noble lesson to compensate him for the want of more erudite instruction.

But though no great importance can be attached to this portion of Bunyan's writings, it is not without its value and interest. It shows us the ever laborious activity of his mind; it proves the anxious watchfulness with which he looked on all sides, to see what ways of profitable labour were open to him; and it thus affords an additional mark of his powerful intellect, its readiness to make great experiments, and to turn from them, if found unfitted to its capacity, to others more practicable and useful.

H. S.

AN EXPOSITION

ON

THE FIRST TEN CHAPTERS OF GENESIS,

AND PART OF THE ELEVENTH.

CHAPTER I.

Of God.

GOD is a Spirit, eternal, infinite, incomprehensible, perfect, and unspeakably glorious in his being, attributes, and works : the eternal God. "Do not I fill heaven and earth? saith the Lord." (Jer. xxiii. 24.) "Neither is there any creature that is not manifest in his sight." (Heb. iv. 13.)

In his attributes of wisdom, power, justice, holiness, mercy, &c., he is also inconceivably perfect and infinite, not to be comprehended by things in earth, or things in heaven ; known in the perfection of his being only to himself. The seraphims cannot behold him but through a veil ; no man can see him in his perfection, and live.

His attributes, though apart laid down in the word of God, that we, being weak, might the better conceive of his eternal power and godhead ; yet in him they are without division—one glorious and eternal being. Again, though sometimes this, as of wisdom, or that, as of justice and mercy, is most manifest in his works and wonders before men ; yet every such work is begun and completed by the joint concurrence of all his attributes. No act of justice is without his will, power, and wisdom ; no act of mercy is against his justice, holiness, and purity.

Besides, no man must conceive of God as if he consisted of these attributes, as our body doth of its members—one standing here, another there, for the completing personal subsistence. For though by the word we may distinguish, yet may we not divide them, or presume to appoint them their places in the Godhead. Wisdom is in his justice, holiness is in his power, justice is in his mercy, holiness is in his love, power is in his goodness.

Wherefore, he is in all his attributes almighty, all-wise, holy, and powerful. Glory is in his wisdom, glory is in his holiness, glory is in his mercy, justice, and strength ; and God is love.

Of the Persons or Subsistences in the Godhead.

The Godhead is but one, yet in the Godhead there are three. "There are three that can bear record in heaven." (1 John v. 7.) These three are called the Father, the Son, and the Holy Spirit ; each of which is really, naturally and eternally God : yet there is but one God. But again, because the Father is of himself, the Son by the Father, and the Spirit from them both, therefore to each, the Scripture not only applieth, and that truly, the whole nature of the Deity, but again distinguisheth the Father from the Son, and the Spirit from them both ; calling the Father HE, by himself ; the Son HE, by himself ; the Spirit HE, by himself. Yea, the Three of themselves, in their manifesting to the church what she should believe concerning this matter, hath thus expressed the thing : "Let us make man in our image, after our likeness." (Gen. i. 26.) Again, "The man is become as one of us." (Gen. iii. 22.) Again, "Let us go down and there confound their language." (Gen. xi. 7.) And again, "Whom shall I send, and who will go for us?" (Isa. vi. 8.) To these general expressions might be added, That Adam heard the voice of the Lord God walking in the midst of the garden : Which voice John will have to be one of the Three, calling that which Moses here saith is the voice, the word of God : "In the beginning," saith he, "was the word :" the voice which Adam heard walking in the midst of the garden. This "word," saith John, "was with God," this "word was God ; the same was in the beginning with God." (John i. 1, 2.) Marvellous language ! Once asserting the unity of essence, but twice insinuating a distinction of substances therein. "The word was with God, the word was God, the same was in the beginning with God." Then follows, "All things were made by him," the word, the second of the three.

Now the godly in former ages have called these three, thus in the Godhead, Persons or Subsistences ;

the which, though I condemn not, yet choose rather to abide by Scripture phrase, knowing, though the other may be good and sound, yet the adversary must needs more shamelessly spurn and reject, when he d..th it against the evident text.

To proceed then:—First. There are three. Second. These three are distinct.

First. By this word Three is intimated the Father, the Word, and the Holy Ghost, and they are said to be three. 1. Because those appellations that are given them in Scripture, demonstrate them so to be, to wit, Father, Son, and Holy Ghost. 2. Because their acts one towards another discover them so to be.

Second. These three are distinct. 1. So distinct as to be more than one only: there are three. 2. So distinct as to subsist without depending. The Father is true God, the Son is true God, the Spirit is true God. Yet the Father is one, the Son is one, the Spirit is one: the Father is one of himself, the Son is one by the Father, the Spirit is one from them both. Yet the Father is not above the Son, nor the Spirit inferior to either: the Father is God, the Son is God, the Spirit is God.

Among the three then there is not superiority. 1. Not as to time: the Father is from everlasting, so is the Son, so is the Spirit. 2. Not as to nature: the Son being of the substance of the Father, and the Spirit of the substance of them both. 3. The fulness of the Godhead is in the Father, is in the Son, and is in the Holy Ghost.

The Godhead then, though it can admit of a Trinity, yet it admitteth not of inferiority in that Trinity: if otherwise, then less or more must be there, and so either plurality of gods, or something that is not God: so then, Father, Son, and Spirit are in the Godhead, yet but one God; each of these is God over all, yet no Trinity of Gods, but one God in the Trinity.

The Godhead then is common to the three, but the three themselves abide distinct in that Godhead: distinct I say, as Father, and Son, and Holy Spirit. This is manifest further by these several positions.

First. Father and Son are relatives, and must needs therefore have their relation as such: a Father begetteth, a Son is begotten.

Proof.—"Who hath ascended up into heaven, or descended? who hath gathered the wind in his fists? who hath bound the waters in a garment? What is his name, and what is his Son's name, if thou canst tell?" (Prov. xxx. 4.)

"God so loved the world, that he gave his only begotten Son," &c. (John iii. 16.)

"The Father sent the Son to be the Saviour of the world." (1 John iv. 14.)

Second. The Father then cannot be that Son he begat, nor the Son that Father that begat him, but must be distinct as such.

Proof.—"I am one that beareth witness of my-self, and the Father that sent me beareth witness of me." (John viii. 18.)

"I came forth from the Father, and am come into the world: again, I leave the world, and go to the Father." (John xvi. 28.)

"The Father judgeth no man, but hath committed all judgment unto the Son, that all men should honour the Son, even as they honour the Father." (John v. 22, 23.)

Third. The Father must have worship as a Father, and the Son as a Son.

Proof.—They that worship the Father must worship him "in Spirit and in truth, for the Father seeketh such to worship him." (John iv. 24.)

And of the Son he saith, "And when he bringeth his first-begotten into the world, he saith, And let all the angels of God worship him." (Heb. i. 6.)

Fourth. The Father and Son have really those distinct, but heavenly, relative properties, that discover them, as such, to be two as well as one.

Proof.—"The Father loveth the Son, and showeth him all things." (John v. 20.)

"Therefore doth my Father love me, because I lay down my life, that I might take it again." (John xi. 17.) The Father sent the Son; the Father commanded the Son; the Son prayed to the Father, and did always the things that pleased him.

The absurdities that flow from the denial of this are divers, some of which hereunder follow.

1 Absurdity.—It maketh void all those scriptures that do affirm the doctrine; some of which you have before.

2 Absurdity.—If in the Godhead there be but one, not three, then the Father, Son, or the Spirit, must needs be that one, if any one only: so then the other two are nothing. Again, If the reality of a being be neither in the Father, Son, nor Spirit, as such, but in the eternal Deity, without consideration of Father, Son, and Spirit as three; then neither of the three are anything but notions in us, or manifestations of the Godhead, or nominal distinctions, so related by the word; but if so, then when the Father sent the Son, and the Father and Son the Spirit, one notion sent another, one manifestation sent another. This being granted, this unavoidably follows, there was no Father to beget a Son, no Son to be sent to save us, no Holy Ghost to be sent to comfort us, and to guide us into all the truth of the Father and Son, &c. The most amounts but to this, a notion sent a notion, a distinction sent a distinction, or one manifestation sent another. Of this error these are the consequences, we are only to believe in notions and distinctions, when we believe in the Father and the Son; and so shall have no other heaven and glory, than notions and nominal distinctions can furnish us withal.

3 *Absurdity.* If Father and Son, &c., be no otherwise three, than as notions, names, or nominal distinctions, then to worship these distinctly, or together, as such, is to commit most gross and horrible idolatry: For albeit we are commanded to fear that great and dreadful name, The Lord our God; yet to worship a Father, a Son, and Holy Spirit in the Godhead, as three, as really three as one, is by this doctrine to imagine falsely of God, and so to break the second commandment: but to worship God under the consideration of Father, and Son, and Holy Ghost, and to believe them as really three as one when I worship, being the sum and substance of the doctrine of the scriptures of God, there is really substantially three in the eternal Godhead.

But to help thee a little in thy study on this deep.

1. Thou must take heed when thou readest, there is in the Godhead, Father, and Son, &c., that thou do not imagine about them according to thine own carnal and foolish fancy; for no man can apprehend this doctrine but in the light of the word and Spirit of God. "No man knoweth the Son but the Father; neither knoweth any man the Father save the Son; and he to whomsoever the Son will reveal him." (Matt. xi. 27.) If therefore thou be destitute of the Spirit of God, thou canst not apprehend the truth of this mystery as it is in itself, but will either by thy darkness be driven to a denial thereof; or if thou own it, thou wilt (that thy acknowledgment notwithstanding) falsely imagine about it.

2. If thou feel thy thoughts begin to wrestle about this truth, and to struggle concerning this one against another; take heed of admitting of such a question, How can this thing be? For here is no room for reason to make it out, here is only room to believe it is a truth. You find not one of the prophets propounding an argument to prove it; but asserting it, they let it lie, for faith to take it up and embrace it.

"The grace of our Lord Jesus Christ, and the love of God, and the communion of the Holy Ghost be with you all. Amen." (2 Cor. xiii. 14.)

Of the Creation of the World.

The Apostle saith, that "to us there is but one God, the Father, of whom are all things; and we in him; and one Lord Jesus Christ, by whom are all things, and we by him." (1 Cor. viii. 6.) "God that made the world." (Acts xvii. 24.) "All things were made by him, and without him was not anything made that was made." (John i. 3.) This world therefore had a beginning, and was created by the God of heaven. Which work, because it is wonderful, and discovereth much of the greatness, of the wisdom and power of the eternal Godhead, it behoveth such poor mortals as we to behold these works of the mighty God, that thereby we may see how great he is, and be made to cry out, "What is man!" (Ps. viii. 4.)

Now in the creation of the world we may consider several things; as, What was the order of God in this work? And, whether there was a secret or mystery in this work containing the truth of some higher thing? For the first of these:

Of the Order of God in Making the World.

Although God be indeed omnipotent, and not only can, but doth do whatsoever he will; and though to do his works he needeth not length of time; yet it pleased him best, in the creation of the world (though he could, had it pleased him, have done all by one only word) to proceed by degrees from one thing to another, to the completing of six days' work in the making thereof.

And forasmuch as this work went on by degrees, now this thing, and then another, it may not be amiss, if in our discourse on this wonderful work, we begin where God began; and if we can, go wondering after him who hath thus wrought.

1. The first thing that God made, was time; I say, it was time. All the plain in which he would build this beautiful world; he made nothing before, but in the beginning. "In the beginning God created the heaven and the earth," (Gen. i. 1:) in the beginning of time. "For in six days the Lord made heaven and earth, the sea, and all that in them is." (Exod. xx. 11.) Therefore the first day must first have a beginning to be. Whatsoever was before time, was eternal; but nothing but God himself is eternal, therefore no creature was before time. Time, therefore, which was indeed the beginning, was the first of the creatures of God.

2. I think, the second of creatures that the Lord created, were the holy angels of God, they being called the morning stars, as created and shining in the morning of the world; and therefore they are said to be by, when the corner-stone of the universe was laid; that is, when he laid the foundation of the world: Then "the morning stars sang together, and all the sons of God shouted for joy." (Job xxxviii. 7.)

3. I think the third thing that the Lord created, was these large and copious heavens; for they are mentioned with respect to their being before the earth, or any visible creature. "In the beginning God created the heavens, &c." (Gen. i. 1.) Neither do I think that the heavens were made of that confused chaos that afterwards we read of. It is said, he stretched out the heavens as a curtain, and with his hand he hath spanned the heavens, (Ps. civ. 2. Isa. xl. 22; xlviii. 13;) intimating, that they were not taken out of that formless heap, but were immediately formed by his power. Besides, the Holy Ghost, treating of the creating of heaven and earth, he only saith, The earth was void, and without form; but no such thing of the heavens.

4. The fourth thing that God created, it was (in mine opinion) that chaos, or first matter, with which he in the six days framed this earth, with its appurtenances; for the visible things that are here below, seem to me to be otherwise put into being and order, than time, the angels, and the heavens, they being created in their own simple essence by themselves: But the things that are visibly here below, whatever their essence and nature be, they were formed of that first deformed chaos. "In the beginning God created the heaven and the earth, and the earth was without form, and void." (Gen. i. 1, 2.) He saith not so of the heavens; they, as I said, were at first stretched forth as a curtain; indeed they were afterwards garnished with the beauty which we now behold; but otherwise they had, at their first instant of being, that form which now they have. This seems clear by the antithesis which the Holy Ghost put between them, " God created the heaven and the earth, but the earth was without form, and void." (Gen. i. 1, 2.) The earth was without form, &c., without order; things were together on a confused heap; the waters were not divided from the earth, neither did those things appear which are now upon the face of the earth, as man, and beast, fish, fowls, trees, and herbs; all these did afterwards show themselves, as the word of God gave them being, by commanding their appearance, in what form, order, place, and time he in himself had before determined; but all, I say, took their matter and substance of that first chaos, which he in the first day of the world had commanded to appear, and had given being to. And therefore 'tis said, God said, Let the earth bring forth grass, herbs, trees, &c., (Gen. i. 11,) and that the waters brought forth the fish, and fowl, yea, even to the mighty whales. (ver. 21.) Also the earth brought forth cattle, and creeping things. (ver. 24.) And that God made man of the dust of the ground. (Gen. ii. 7.) All these things therefore were made of, or caused by his word distinctly to appear, and be after its kind, of that first matter which he had before created by his word. Observe therefore, That the matter of all earthly things was made at the same instant, but their forming, &c., was according to the day in which God gave them their being, in their own order and kind. And hence it is said, that after that first matter was created, and found without form, and void, that the Spirit of God moved upon the face of the waters; that is to work, and cause those things to appear in their own essence and form, which, as to matter and substance, was before created. Wherefore it follows, And God said, Let there be light; and God divided the light from the darkness, &c. Now he set to putting in frame that which before lay in disorder and confusion. And this was a great part of the six days' work; I say, a great part, but not all; for (as I said) before that, time, the angels, and the heavens were made; yea, after the beginning of the morning of the first day. I am of the belief, that other things also, that were formed after, were not made of that first chaos, as the sun, the moon, the stars, the light, the souls of men, and possibly the air, &c. The sun, and moon, and stars are said to be made the fourth day, yet not of the body of heaven itself, much less, in my opinion, of any earthly matter: God made them, and set them in the firmament of heaven. (Gen. i. 16, 17.) So the light that was made before, it seems to be a thing created after the heavens and the earth were created: Created, I say, as a thing that wanted a being before, any otherwise than in the decree of God: and God said, Let there be light, (Gen. i. 3;) Let it have a being. And so, though the body of man was made of the substance of earth, yet as to his soul, it is said, God breathed into his nostrils the breath of life, and man became a living soul. (Gen. ii. 7.)

Whether there was a secret or mystery in this work, containing the truth of some higher thing.

Though God in very deed, by his eternal power, created heaven and earth of things that do not appear, we that are Christians believe: yet in this his wonderful work, neither his will nor understanding did here terminate, or make a stop; but being infinite in wisdom, he made them, that both as to matter and manner, they might present unto us, as in a mystery, some higher and more excellent thing; in this wisdom he made them all. And hence it is that other things are also called a creation: As, 1. The essential conversion of a sinner. (2 Cor. ix. 7.)

2. The recovery of the church from a degenerate state. (Rev. xxi. 5.)

And therefore, as Moses begins with the creation of the world, so John begins with the gospel of salvation. (Gen. i. 1. John i. 1.) There is also besides many excellent things in the manner and order of the creation of the world, held forth to those that have understanding; some of which I may touch upon by way of observation. But to begin with the first:

The first appearance of this earthy part of the world, is recorded to be but a formless and void heap or chaos; and such is man before a new creation: formless, I mean, as to the order of the Testament of Christ, and void of the holy order thereof. And hence Jeremiah, when he would set forth the condition of a wicked people, he doth it under this metaphor: "I beheld," saith he, "the earth, and it was without form, and void." (Jer. iv. 23.) Indeed, the world would make this a type of Christ; to wit, a man of no form or comeliness. But 'tis only true of themselves; they are without a New Testament impression upon them; they are void of the sovereign grace of God. So then the power of God gave the world a being, but by his word he set it in form and beauty; even as by his power he gives a being to man, but by his word he giveth him New Testament framing and glory. This is still followed by that which follows:

Verse 2. "And darkness was upon the face of the deep."

The Deep here might be a type of the heart of man before conversion; and so Solomon seems to intimate. Now as the darkness of this world did cover the face of this first chaos; so spiritual darkness the heart of the sons of men: and hence they are said to be darkened, to be in darkness, yea, to be very darkness itself.

"And the Spirit of God moved upon the face of the waters."

A blessed emblem of the word of God in the matter of regeneration: for as the first chaos remained without form, and void, until the Spirit of God moved to work upon it, and by working, to put this world into frame and order; so man as he comes into the world, abides a confused lump, an unclean thing; a creature without New Testament order, until by the Spirit of the Lord he is transformed into the image of Jesus Christ.

"And the Spirit of God moved upon the face."

Solomon compares the heart to a man's face; because as in the face may be discerned whether there is anger or otherwise; so by the inclinations of the heart is discovered the truth of the condition of the man, as to his state either for heaven or hell. And besides as the "Spirit of God moved upon the face of the waters;" so in the work of our conversion, the Spirit of God beginneth with the heart of the sons of men; because the heart is the main fort. Now if the main fort be not taken, the adversary is still capable of making continual resistance. Therefore God first conquers the heart; therefore the Spirit of God moveth upon the face of our heart, when he cometh to convert us from Satan to God.

Verse 3. "And God said, Let there be light."

This is the first thing with which God began the order of the creation; to wit, light, "Let there be light." From which many profitable notes may be gathered, as to the order of God in the salvation of the soul. As,

1. When the Holy Ghost worketh upon us, and in us, in order to a new creation; he first toucheth our understanding, that great piece of the heart, with his spiritual illumination. His first word in order to our conversion, is, "Let there be light," light, to see their state by nature; light, to see the fruits and effects of sin; light, to see the truth and worth of the merits of Jesus Christ; light to see the truth and faithfulness of God, in keeping promise and covenant with them that embrace salvation upon the blessed terms of the gospel of peace. Now that this word, "Let there be light," was a semblance of the first work of the Holy Ghost upon the heart, compare it with that of Paul to the Corinthians: "For God who commanded the light to shine out of darkness," that is, at the beginning of the world, "hath shined in our hearts

to give the light of the knowledge of the glory of God in the face of Jesus Christ." (2 Cor. iv. 6

2. "And God said, Let there be light." As here, the light of this world; so in conversion, the light of the New Testament of Christ, it comes by the word of God. No word, no light: therefore the apostle saith, He "hath brought life and immortality to light through the gospel." (2 Tim. i. 10.) And therefore Paul saith again, That salvation is manifest through preaching, through the expounding or opening of the word of faith.

3. And God said, "Let there be light; and there was light:" He spake the word, and it was done; all that darkness that before did cover the face of the deep, could not now hinder the being of light. So neither can all the blindness and ignorance that is in the heart of man, hinder the light of the knowledge of the glory of God in the face of Jesus Christ. When it pleaseth God to reveal, it is revealed; when he openeth, none can shut: he said, "Let there be light, and there was light."

And God saw that the light was good. "Truly the light is good," saith Solomon, "and a pleasant thing it is for the eye to behold the sun." It was good, because it was God's creature; and so in the work of grace that is wrought in our hearts, that light of the new covenant, it is good, because it is God's work, the work of his good pleasure; that good work which he hath not only begun, but promised to fulfil until the day of Jesus Christ.

God saw that the light was good. The darkness that before did cover the face of the waters, was not a creature of God, but a privation, or that which was caused by reason that light was not as yet in the world; so sin, that darkness that might be felt, is not the workmanship of God in the soul, but that which is the work of the devil; and that taketh occasion to be, by reason that the true light, as yet, doth not shine in the soul.

"And God divided the light from the darkness." As Paul saith, "What communion hath light with darkness?" they cannot agree to dwell together. We see the night still flies before the day, and dareth not come upon us again, but as the light diminisheth and conveyeth itself away. So it is in the new creation; before the light of the glorious gospel of Christ appears, there is night, all night in the soul; but when that indeed doth shine in the soul, then for night there is day in the soul. "Ye were darkness," saith Paul, "but now ye are light in the Lord." (Eph. v. 8.) And, "The darkness is past," saith John, "and the true light now shineth." (1 John ii. 8.)

Verse 1. "And God divided the light from the darkness."

God took part with the light, and preserved it from the darkness. By these words, it seems that darkness and light began the quarrel, before that bloody bout of Cain and Abel. The light and the darkness struggled together, and nothing could divide or part them but God. Darkness is at implacable enmity with light in the creation of the world; and so it is in that rare work of regeneration, the flesh lusteth against the spirit, and the spirit against the flesh; as Peter saith, "Fleshly lusts, they war against the soul." (1 Pet. ii. 11.) This every Christian feels, and also that which I mentioned before, namely, that before he be capable of opposing antichrist, with Abel, in the world, he findeth a struggling in his own soul between the light and the darkness that is there.

Verse 5. "And God called the light Day, and the darkness he called Night."

God doth not only distinguish by separating, but also by certain characters; that things which are distinguished and separate, may to us be the better known: he did so here in the work of creating the world, and doth so also in the great concern of man's eternal happiness. The place of felicity is called heaven. The place of torment is called hell; that which leads to hell is called sin, transgression, iniquity, and wickedness; that which leads to heaven, righteousness, holiness, goodness, and uprightness; even as in these types God called the light day, of which the godly are the children; but the darkness he called night, of which all ungodly men are the inhabiters and children also. Thus after the Spirit of God had moved upon the face of the waters; after God had commanded the light to shine, and had divided between the light and the darkness, and had characterised them by their proper names, he concludes the first day's work, "And the evening and the morning was the first day." (Gen. i. 5.) In which conclusion there is wrapped up a blessed gospel-mystery; for God, by concluding the first day here, doth show us how we ought to determine that one is made indeed a Christian. Even then when the Spirit of God, hath moved upon the face of the heart, when he hath commanded that light should be there, when he divideth between, or setteth the light at variance with the darkness; and when the soul doth receive the characters of both, to observe them, and carry it to each according to the mouth of God.

Verse 6. "And God said, Let there be a firmament."

This firmament he calleth heaven. (ver. 8.) Now this firmament, or heaven, was to make a separation, or to divide between the waters and the waters; to separate, I say, the waters from the waters; the waters which were under the firmament, from the waters which were above the firmament. (ver. 7.) Now by waters is signified in the scriptures many things, as afflictions, worldly people, and particularly the saints; but in this place is figured forth, all the people in the world, but so as consisting of two parts, the children of God, and the children of the wicked one: They under the heaven, figure out the world, or ungodly: they above the firmament, the elect and chosen of God. And hence in scripture the one is called heaven, and the other is called earth, to signify the separa-

tion and difference that there is between the one and the other.

"And God made the firmament, and divided the waters from the waters."

Indeed the world think that this separation comes, or is made, through the captiousness of the preacher: but in truth it is the handy work of God; "And God made the firmament, and God divided," &c. "I," saith he, "will put enmity between thee and the woman, and between thy seed and her seed." (Gen. iii. 15.) The good seed are the children of the kingdom of God, but the bad are the children of the wicked one. (Matt. xiii. 8.)

Verse 7. "And God made the firmament, and divided the waters which were under the firmament from the waters which were above the firmament: and it was so." (Gen. i. 7.)

Whatsoever the Lord doth, it abideth for ever. (Eccles. iii. 14.) And again, What he hath made crooked, who can make straight? (Eccles. i. 15.) He said it in the beginning, and behold how it hath continued! Yea, though there hath been endeavours on Satan's part, to mingle his children with the seed of men; yet it hath not been possible they should "ever cleave one to another, even as iron is not mixed with clay." (Dan. ii. 43.) Yea, let me add further, What laws have been made, what blood hath been shed, what cruelty hath been used, and what flatteries and lies invented, and all to make these two waters and people one? And yet all hath failed, and fallen short of producing the desired effect; for the Lord hath made a firmament, even heaven itself hath divided between them.

Verse 8. "And God called the firmament heaven. And the evening and the morning were the second day."

After the waters were divided from the waters, God called the cause of dividing, heaven; and so concluded the second day's work. And indeed it was a very great work, as in the antitype we feel it to this very day. Dividing work is difficult work, and he that can, according to God, completely end and finish it, he need do no more that day of his life.

Verse 9. "And God said, Let the waters under the heaven be gathered together unto one place, and let the dry land appear: and it was so."

Although in the second day's work, the waters above the firmament, and those that be under, are the two peoples, or great families of the world; yet because God would show us by things on earth, the flourishing state of those that are his, therefore he here doth express his mind by another kind of representation of things: And God said, "Let the waters under the heaven be gathered together unto one place; and let the dry land appear." The waters here signifying the world; but the fruitful earth, the thrifty church of God. That the fruitful earth is a figure of the thriving church of God in this world, is evident from many scriptures, (and there was nothing but thriftiness till the curse came.) And hence it is said of the church, that he should break the clods of the ground; that she should sow righteousness, and reap it; that she should not sow among thorns; that if this be done, the heart is circumcised, and spiritual fruit shall flow forth, and grow abundantly. And hence again it is that the officers and eminent ones in the church, are called vines, trees, and other fruitful plants. And hence it is said again, When the Lord reigneth, let the earth (that is, the church) rejoice. The earth which bringeth forth fruit meet for him by whom it is dressed, receiveth blessing from God. In all which places, and many more that might be named, the earth is made a figure of the church of God; and so I count it here in this place.

"And God said, Let the waters under the heaven be gathered into one place."

Let them be together: It is not thus of all waters, but of the sea, which is still here a type of the world. Let them be so together, that the earth may appear; that the church may be rid of their rage and tumult, and then she will be fruitful, as it follows in this first book of Genesis. The church is then in a flourishing state, when the world is farthest off from her, and when the roaring of their waves are far away. Now therefore let all the wicked men be far from thence. (Ezra vi. 6.) The Lord gather these waters, which in another place are called the doleful creatures, and birds of prey; Let these, O Lord, be gathered together to their own places, and be settled in the land of Shinar, upon their own base. (Zech. v. 11.) "Then the wilderness and the solitary place shall be glad for them;" that is, for that they are departed thence, "the desert shall rejoice and blossom as a rose." (Isa. xxxv. 1.)

Verse 10. "And God called the dry land Earth; and the gathering together of the waters called he Seas; and God saw that it was good."

God saw, that to separate the waters from the earth was good: And so it is, for then have the churches rest. Then doth this earth bring forth her fruit, as in the 11th and 12th verses may here be seen.

Verse 14. "And God said, Let there be lights in the firmament of the heaven."

The wisdom of God, is there to make use of figures and shadows, even where most fit things, the things under consideration, may be most fitly demonstrated. The dividing the waters from the waters, most fitly doth show the work of God in choosing and refusing; by dividing the waters from the earth, doth show how fruitful God's earth, the church is, when persecutors are made to be far from thence.

Wherefore he speaketh not of garnishing of his church until he comes to this fourth day's work: By his Spirit he hath garnished the heavens, that most fitly showing the glory of the church.

"Let there be lights;" to wit, the sun, the moon, and the stars.

The sun is in this place a type of Christ, the Sun of Righteousness: The moon is a type of the church, in her uncertain condition in this world: The stars are types of the several saints and officers in this church. And hence it is that the sun is said not only to rule, but it, with the moon and stars, to be set for signs, and for seasons, and for days and for years, &c. But if we take the heaven for the church, then how is she beautified, when the Son of God is placed in the midst of her! And how plainly is her condition made out, even by the changing, increasing, and diminishing of the moon! And how excellent is that congregation of men, that for light and glory are figured by the stars!

From this day's work much might be observed.

1. That forasmuch as the sun was not made before the fourth day, it is evident there was light in the world before the sun was created; for in the first day God said, "Let there be light, and there was light." This may also teach us thus much, That before Christ came in person, there was spiritual light in the saints of God. And again, That as the sun was not made before the fourth day of the creation, so Christ should not be born before the fourth mystical day of the world; for it is evident, that Christ, the true light of the world, was not born till about four thousand years after the world was made.

2. As to the moon, there are four things attending her, which fitly may hold forth the state of the church. (1.) In that she changeth from an old to a new, we may conceive, that God by making her so, did it to show he would one day make a change of his church, from a Jewish to a Gentile congregation. (2.) In that she increaseth, she showeth the flourishing state of the church. (3.) In her diminishing, the diminishing state of the church. (4.) The moon is also sometimes made to look as red as blood, to show how dreadful and bloody the suffering of the church is at some certain times.

3. By the stars, we understand two things. (1.) How innumerable the saints, those spiritual stars shall be. (2.) How they shall differ each from other in glory.

"And God said, Let there be lights in the firmament of the heaven, to divide the day from the night."

For though before the light was divided from the darkness, yet the day and night was not so kept within their bounds, as now by these lights they were: probably signifying, that nothing should be so clearly distinguished and made appear, as by the sun-light of the gospel of Christ: for by that it is that the "shadows flee away." (Sol. Song ii. 17.) The light of the sun gathers the day to its hours, both longer and shorter, and forceth also the night to keep within his bounds.

Verse 16. "And God made two great lights; the greater light to rule the day, and the lesser light to rule the night."

Signifying, That Christ should be the light and governor of his church, which are the children of the day; but the church, a light to the children of the night, that by them they might learn the mysteries of the kingdom. Saith Christ to his own, "Ye are the light of the world." And, again, "Let your light so shine, that men may see," &c., for though they that only walk in the night, cannot see to walk by the sun, yet by the moon they may. Thus the heaven is a type of the church, the moon a type of her uncertain state in this world; the stars are types of her immovable converts; and their glory, of the differing degrees of theirs, both here, and in the other world. Much more might be said, but I pass this.

Verse 20. "And God said, Let the waters bring forth abundantly the moving creature that hath life."

The sea, as I said, is a figure of the world; wherefore the creatures that are in it, of the men of the world. This sea bringeth forth small and great beasts, even as the world doth yield both small and great persecutors, who, like the fishes of prey, eat up and devour what they can of those fish that are of another condition. Now also out of the world that mystical sea, as fishers do out of the natural, both Christ and his servants catch mystical fish, even fish as of the great sea.

In the sea God created great whales, he made them to play therein.

Which whales in the sea are types of the devils in the world: therefore as the devil is called, the Prince of this world; so the whale is called, King over all the children of pride.

Verse 24. "And God said, Let the earth bring forth the living creature after his kind."

Of the beginning of this sixth day's work that may be said which is said of the fishes, and the rest of the sea; for as there is variety of fish in the one, so of beasts and cattle in the other, who also make a prey of their fellows, as the fishes do; a most apt representation of the nature and actions of bloody and deceitful men. Hence persecutors are called bulls, bears, lions, wolves, tigers, dragons, dogs, foxes, leopards, and the like.

Verse 26. "And God said, Let us make man."

I observe, that in the creation of the world God goeth gradually on, from things less, to things more abundantly glorious; I mean, as to the creation of this earth, and the things that thereto appertain. First he bringeth forth a confused chaos, then he commands matter to appear distinct, then the earth bringeth forth trees, and herbs, and grass; after that beasts; and the sea, fowls; and last of all, Let us make man. Now passing by the doctrine of the Trinity, because spoken to before, I come to make some observation upon this wonderful piece of the workmanship of God.

"Let us make man." Man, in whom is also included the woman, who was made the last of the creatures. From whence we may gather,

First. God's respect to this excellent creature, in that he first provideth for him, before he giveth him his being: he bringeth him not to an empty house, but to one well furnished with all kind of necessaries, having beautified the heaven and the earth with glory, and all sorts of nourishment for his pleasure and sustenance.

"Let us make man in our image, after our likeness."

An image, or the likeness of anything, is not the thing of which it is a figure; so here, Adam is an image, or made in the likeness of God. Now as Adam is the image of God, it must either respect him, as he consisteth of the soul, as a part, or as he consists of a body and soul together. If as he is made a reasonable soul, then he is an excellent image of the eternal Godhead, the attributes of the one being shadowed out by the qualities and passions of the other; for as there is in the Godhead power, knowledge, love, and righteousness; so a likeness of these is in the soul of man, especially of man before he had sinned: and as there is passions of pity, compassion, affections, and bowels in man; so there are these in a far more infinite way in God.

Again, If this image respect the whole man, then Adam was a figure of God, as incarnate; or of God, as he was to be made afterwards man. And hence it is, that as Adam is called the image of God; so also is Christ himself called and reckoned as the answering antitype of such an image.

But again, though Adam be here called the image or similitude of God; yet but so as that he was the shadow of a more excellent image. Adam was a type of Christ, who only is the express image of his Father's person, and the likeness of his excellent glory; (Heb. i. 3;) for those things that were in Adam, were but of a humane, but of a created substance; but those that were in Christ, of the same divine and eternal excellency with the Father.

Is Christ then the image of the Father, simply, as considered of the same divine and eternal excellency with him? Certainly, no; for an image is doubtless inferior to that of which it is a figure. Understand, then, that Christ is the image of the Father's glory, as born of the Virgin Mary, yet so, as being very God also: not that his Godhead in itself was a shadow or image, but by the acts and doing of that man, every act being infinitely perfect by virtue of his Godhead, the Father's perfections were made manifest to flesh. An image is to be looked upon, and by being looked upon, another thing is seen; so by the persons and doings of the Lord Jesus, they that indeed could see him as he was, discovered the perfection and glory of the Father.—"Philip, he that hath seen me, hath seen the Father, and how sayest thou then, Show us the Father?" (John xiv. 9.) Neither the Father nor the Son can by us at all be seen, as they are simply and entirely in their own essence.

Therefore the person of the Father must be seen by us, through the Son, as consisting of God and man; the Godhead, by working effectually in the manhood, showing clearly there through the infinite perfection and glory of the Father: the word was made flesh, and (then) we beheld his glory, the glory of the only begotten of his Father, (he being in his personal excellencies, infinitely and perfectly, what is recorded of his Father,) full of grace and truth. (John i. 14.) So again, he "is the image of the invisible God." (Col. i. 15.) The Godhead is indeed invisible; how then is Christ the image of it? Not by being invisible also; for so is he as much hid as the Father; but being clothed with flesh, that the works of the Son might by us be seen, he thereby presenteth to us, as in a figure, the eternal excellency of the Father. And hence as he is called "an image," he is also called the "first-born of every creature" (Col. i. 15): his being a creature, respecting his manhood, and his birth, his rising again from the dead. Therefore a little after, he is called, "the first-born from the dead;" (Col. i. 18;) and in another place "the first-begotten of the dead" (Rev. i. 5): and "the first-fruits of them that slept." (1 Cor. xv. 20.) So then, though Adam was the image of God, yet God's image but as a mere creature: but Christ though a creature as touching his manhood, yet being also God, as the Father, he showed forth expressly, in capital characters, by all his works and doings in the world, the beauty and glory of the Father. The light of the knowledge of the glory of God, is given in the face of Jesus Christ. (2 Cor. iv. 6.) Where, by face, we must understand that which is visible, that being open when all else is covered, and that by which most principally we are discovered to others, and known. Now, as to the case in hand, this face must signify to us the personal virtues and doings of Christ, by which the glory of the Father is exposed; the glory of his justice by Christ's exactness of life; the glory of his love, by Christ's compassion to sinners, &c.

Verse 26. "And God said, Let us make man in our image, after our likeness: and let them have dominion over the fish of the sea, and over the fowl of the air, and over the cattle, and over all the earth, and over every creeping thing that creepeth upon the earth."

As Adam was a type of Christ, as the image and glory of God; so by these words he further showeth, that he was a type of his sovereign power, for to him be dominion and power everlasting, "to whom be praise and dominion for ever." (1 Pet. iv. 11.) Now, by the fish of the sea, the beast of the earth, the fowls of the air, and every creeping thing, we may understand all creatures, visible and invisible, whether they be men, angels, or devils, in heaven, earth, or under the earth: also all thrones, authorities, and powers, whether in heaven, in earth, or hell: Christ is made head over all; He hath also a name above every

name, "not only in this world, but in that which is to come." (Eph. i. 21.)

Verse 28. "And God blessed them; and God said unto them (that is, to the man and his wife), Be fruitful, and multiply, and replenish the earth, and subdue it," &c.

This in the type doth show in the antitype how fruitful Christ and his church shall be; and how he at last shall, all over the earth, have a seed to replenish and subdue it by the power of the immortal seed of the word of God: how his name shall be reverenced from one end of the earth to the other: how the kingdoms of the earth shall all at last become the kingdoms of our Lord, and of his Christ.

"And subdue it." God did put that majesty and dread upon Adam, at his creation, that all the beasts of the field submitted themselves unto him. As God also said to Noah, "The fear of you, and the dread of you, shall be upon every beast of the earth, and upon every fowl of the air; upon all that moveth upon the earth, and upon all the fishes of the sea; into your hand are they delivered." (Gen. ix. 2.)

Verse 29. "And God said, Behold I have given you every herb bearing seed, which is upon the face of all the earth; and every tree, in the which is the fruit of a tree yielding seed, to you it shall be for meat."

These herbs and trees are types of the wholesome words of the gospel, on which both Christ, his church, and unconverted sinners, ought to feed and be refreshed; and without which there is no subsisting either of one or the other: "He causeth the grass to grow for the cattle, and herb for the service of man, that he may bring forth food out of the earth; and wine, that maketh glad the heart of man, and oil, to make his face to shine, and bread, which strengtheneth man's heart." (Ps. civ. 13, 14.)

Verse 31. "And God saw everything that he had made, and, behold, it was very good."

All things have their natural goodness by creation. Things are not good, because they have a being only, but because God gave them such a being; neither did God make them, because he saw they would attract a goodness to themselves; but he made them in such kind, as to bring forth that goodness he before determined they should. "And the evening and the morning were the sixth day."

CHAPTER II.

Verse 3. "And God blessed the seventh day, and sanctified it; because that in it he had rested from all his work which God created and made."

The seventh day did signify two things:—

First. Christ Jesus, who is as well the rest of the justice of God, as a rest for sinful man.

Second. It was also a type of that glorious rest

that saints shall have when the six days of this world are fully ended.

For the First. The apostle makes the sabbath a shadow of Jesus Christ, a shadow of things to come, but the body or substance, " is Christ." (Col. ii. 17.) And hence it is that he is so often said to be "a rest" to the Gentiles, a glorious rest, and that he promiseth rest to such as cast their burthen upon him.

The Second also the apostle asserteth in that fourth chapter to the Hebrews, " There remaineth therefore a rest," or the keeping of a sabbath, " to the people of God:" (ver. 9:) which sabbath, as I conceive, will be the seventh thousand of years, which are to follow immediately after the world hath stood six thousand first: for as God was six days in the works of creation, and rested the seventh; so in six thousand years he will perfect his works and providences that concern this world. As also he will finish the toil and travail of his saints, with the burthen of the beasts, and the curse of the ground; and bring all into rest for a thousand years. A day with the Lord, is as a thousand years: wherefore this blessed and desirable time is also called a day, a great day, " that great and notable day of the Lord," (Acts ii. 20,) which shall end in the eternal judgment of the world. God hath held forth this by several other shadows, as the sabbath of weeks, the sabbath of years, and the great jubilee, which is to be the year after forty-nine years are expired. (Lev. xxv. 1—13.) Of all which, more in their place, if God permit.

Verse 4. " These are the generations of the heavens, and of the earth, when they were created; in the day that the Lord God created the earth and the heavens."

Moses seems, by these words, " In the day," to insist principally upon them in their first and primitive state, before there was sin or curse in the world; for in the day that they were created, there was a far more glorious lustre and beauty than now can be seen; the heaven, for sin, is, as it were, turned into brass; and the rain into powder and dust, in comparison of what it was as it came from the fingers of God. The earth hath also from that time a curse upon it; yea, the whole creation, by sin, is even made subject to vanity, is in travail, and groans under the burthen that sin hath brought upon it. (Rom. viii. 20—23.)

Verse 5. " And every plant of the field before it was in the earth, and every herb of the field before it grew."

Thus it was in the first creation; they therefore became neither herbs nor trees, by the course of nature, but by the creation of God. And even so it is in the new creation, men spring not up by nature to be saints. No, not in the church of God, but first they are created in Christ Jesus, and made meet to be partakers of the benefit, and then planted in the church of God; planted, I say, as plants before prepared. Indeed, hypocrites, and

formal professors, may spring up in the church, by virtue of her forms, and outward services, as thorns and thistles spring up in the earth, by virtue of her moisture and heartiness. But these are but the fruits of the curse, and are determined to be burned at last in the fire : " Every plant," saith Christ, " which my heavenly Father hath not planted, shall be rooted up." (Matt. xv. 13.)

" For the Lord God had not caused it to rain upon the earth." This is the reason that they came not up by nature first, but were first created, then planted, then made to grow. So the reason why men by nature grow not in the church, is because the Lord doth not cause it to rain upon them, they still abiding and doing according to the course of this world; but he plants them in his house by the mighty power of his word and Spirit, by which they are created saints, and then they afterwards grow in grace, and in the knowledge of our Lord and Saviour Jesus Christ.

" And there was not a man to till the ground." It seems by this there was a kind of necessity why God should make man, yea, a multitude of men; for otherwise he had made what before he made in vain; that is, his end in making so glorious a creature as this world, which was to show forth his glory by, had been void, and without effect; for although it was glorious, as it came out of the hand of God; yet it was not of power so to preserve itself, but would, without men to look after and dress it, be turned into a wilderness.

Thus it is with the world of men, if there was not the second Adam to plough them and sow them, they could none of them become saints; no, not the elect themselves; because the means are determined, as well as the end.

By this we may likewise see what a woful condition that people is in, that have no ministers of the word of the gospel : " My people are destroyed for lack of knowledge." (Hos. iv. 6.) And again, " Where there is no vision, the people perish." (Prov. xxix. 18.) Pray therefore to the Lord of the harvest, that he would send out his ploughers to plough, and his labourers into his harvest.

Verse 6. " But there went up a mist from the earth, and watered the whole face of the ground."

Although as yet there was no ploughman nor rain, yet a mist arose from the earth; so where there is not the word of the gospel, there is yet sufficiency of light, to teach men how to govern themselves in civil and natural society. But this is only a mist, men cannot gospelly grow by this; therefore, as in the next verse, of necessity man must be formed.

But again, I have sometimes thought by this mist, might be held forth that nourishment men had by the doctrine of faith, before the gospel was divulged by Moses, the prophets, or Christ, &c. for before these, that nourishment the church received, was but slender and short, even as short as the nourishing of the mist is to sober and moderate showers of rain ; to which both the law and the gospel is compared.

Again, I have also sometimes thought, that by this mist might be typified those excellent proverbs and holy sayings of the men of old, before there was a written word ; for it cannot be but the godly did contain in proverbs, and certain sayings, the doctrine of salvation hereafter, and of good living here ; of which we have a touch in Genesis, but more at large by that blessed book of Job ; which book, in my opinion, is a holy collection of those proverbs and sayings of the ancients, occasioned by the temptation of that good man. But whatever this mist did signify (in other men's judgment), certain it is, it was for present necessity, till a man should be made to till the ground, and the fruits thereof watered with the bottles of heaven : which, so far as I see yet, most aptly presents us with some of all these.

Verse 7. " And the Lord God formed man of the dust of the ground," &c.

In the creation of man, God began with his outside ; but in the work of regeneration, he first begins within, at the heart. He made him ; that is, his body, of the dust of the ground ; but he abides a lifeless lump, till the Lord puts forth a second act. " And he breathed into his nostrils the breath of life, and man became a living soul." Now he lives, now he acts : so it is in the kingdom of Christ, no man can be a living soul in that kingdom by his first creation, he must have life breathed into him, life and spirit from Jesus Christ.

Now therefore is Adam a type, yet but an earthly one, of things more high and heavenly ; " And as we have borne the image of the earthy, we shall also bear the image of the heavenly." (1 Cor. xv. 49.)

Verse 8. " And the Lord God planted a garden eastward in Eden ; and there he put the man whom he had formed."

" And the Lord God planted a garden." Thus the Holy Ghost speaks clearer and clearer ; for now he presents the church to us under the similitude of a garden, which is taken out of the wide and open field, and inclosed ; " A garden inclosed is my sister, my spouse ;" a garden inclosed, " a spring shut up, a fountain sealed ;" (Sol. Song iv. 12 ;) and there he put the man whom he had formed. An excellent type of the presence of Christ with his church.

Verse 9. " And out of the ground made the Lord God to grow every tree that is pleasant to the sight," &c.

These trees, and their pleasurableness, do show us the beauty of the truly godly, whom the Lord hath beautified with salvation. And hence it is said, the glory of Lebanon, of Sharon, and of Carmel, is given to the church : that is, she is more beautified with gifts and graces than can by types and shadows be expressed. " The tree of life also in the midst of the garden, and the tree of the knowledge of good and evil."

This " tree of life" was another type of Christ, as the bread and healing medicine of the church, that stands " in the midst of the paradise of God." (Rev. ii. 7.)

The tree of the knowledge of good and evil was a type of the law, or covenant of works, as the sequel of the story clearly manifesteth ; for had not Adam eaten thereof, he had enjoyed for ever his first blessedness. As Moses saith, " It shall be our righteousness, if we observe to do all these commandments before the Lord our God, as he hath commanded us." (Deut. vi. 25.) But both Adam and we have touched, that is, broken the boughs and fruit of this tree, and therefore now for ever, by the law, no man can stand just before God.

Verse 10. " And a river went out of Eden, to water the garden ; and from thence it was parted, and became into four heads."

This river while it abided in Eden, in the garden, it was the river of God ; that is, serviceable to the trees and fruit of the garden, and was herein a type of those watering ministers that water the plants of the Lord. But observe, when it had passed the garden, had gotten without the bound of the garden, from thence it was parted, and became into four heads ; from thence it was transformed, or turned into another manner of thing : it now became into four heads ; a type of the four great monarchies of the world, of which Babylon, though the first in order of being, yet the last in a gospel or mysterious sense. The fourth is the river Euphrates, that which was the face of the kingdom of Babel of old. Hence note, That how eminent and serviceable soever men are while they abide in the garden of Eden—the church ; yet when they come out from thence, they evilly seek the great things of the world : one is for compassing the whole land of Havilah, where is gold ; another is for compassing this, a third that, and a fourth another thing, according as you see these four heads did. Observe again, That while men abide in the church of God, there is not by them a seeking after the monarchies of this world ; but when they depart from thence, then they seek and strive to be heads : as that cursed monster the pope, forsaking the garden of God, became in a manner the prince of all the earth : Of whom Tyrus, mentioned by Ezekiel, was a very lively type, " Thou hast been in Eden, the garden of God ; every precious stone, (that is, doctrine,) was thy covering, the sardius, topaz, diamond," &c., " till iniquity was found in thee," (Ezek. xxviii. 13—15 ;) till thou leftest thy station, and place appointed of God, and then thou wast cast as profane out of the mountain of God, yea, though a covering cherub. See it again in Cain, who while he continued in the church, he was a busy sacrificer, as busy as Abel his brother ; but when he left off to fear the Lord, and had bloodily butchered his holy brother, then he seeks to be a head, or monarch ; then he goeth and buildeth a city to preserve his name and posterity for ever.

Verse 15. " And the Lord God took the man, and put him into the garden of Eden, to dress it, and to keep it."

In this also Adam was a figure of our Lord Jesus Christ, as pastor and chief bishop of his church. I the Lord, saith Christ, do keep it; I will water it night and day. (Isa. xxvii. 3.)

" And the Lord God took the man." No man taketh this honour upon him, but he that is called of God, as was Aaron. Blessed is he also that can say as the prophet Amos; " And the Lord took me," said he, " as I followed the flock ; and the Lord said unto me, Go prophesy unto my people Israel." (Amos vii. 15.)

" To dress it, and to keep it." He that is not dressed, is not kept : That is a sad judgment, That which dieth, let it die ; That which is diseased, let it not be dressed, let it die of that disease. By dressing therefore I understand, pruning, manuring, and the like, which the dresser of the vineyard was commanded to do, without which all is overrun with briers and nettles, and is fit for nothing but cursing, and to be burned. (Luke xiii. 6—9. Prov. xxiv. 30—34. Heb. vi. 7, 8.)

Verse 16. " And the Lord God commanded the man, saying, Of every tree of the garden thou mayest freely eat."

It is God's word that giveth us power to eat, to drink, and do other our works, and without the word we may do nothing. The command gave Adam leave : " Every creature of God is good, and nothing to be refused, if it be received with thanksgiving ; for it is sanctified by the word of God (by the command of the word, and by receiving of it according to the limits thereof,) and prayer." (1 Tim. iv. 4, 5.)

Verse 17. " But of the tree of the knowledge of good and evil, thou shalt not eat of it." I said before, What God's word prohibits, we must take care to shun.

This " tree of knowledge," as I said before, was a type of the covenant of works, the which had not Adam touched, (for by touching it he broke that covenant,) he then had lived ever, but touching it he dies.

Adam going into the garden under these conditions and penalties, was therein a type of the humiliation of Christ; who, at his coming into the world, was made under the law, under its command and penalty, even as other men, but without sin.

" For in the day that thou eatest thereof thou shalt surely die."

" For in the day." Adam lived to God no longer than while he kept himself from eating forbidden fruit ; in that very day he died ; first a spiritual death in his soul ; his body also was then made capable of mortality, and all diseases, which two great impediments in time brought him down to dust again.

Verse 18. " And the Lord God said, It is not good that the man should be alone ; I will make him an help meet for him."

By these words, Adam's state, even in innocency, seems to crave for help ; wherefore it is manifest that that state is short of that we attain by the resurrection from the dead ; yea, forasmuch as his need required earthly help, it is apparent his condition was not heavenly : " The first man is of the earth, earthy ; the second man is the Lord from heaven." (1 Cor. xv. 47.) Adam in his first estate was not spiritual : " That was not first which is spiritual, but that which is natural ; and afterwards that which is spiritual." (1 Cor. xv. 46.) Wherefore those that think it enough to attain to the state of Adam in innocency, think it sufficient to be mere naturalists ; think themselves well, without being made spiritual : yea, let me add, they think it safe standing by a covenant of works ; they think themselves happy, though not concerned in a covenant of grace ; they think they know enough, though ignorant of a mediator, and count they have no need of the intercession of Christ.

Adam stood by a covenant of works : Adam's kingdom was an earthly paradise ; Adam's excellency was, that he had no need of a Saviour ; and Adam's knowledge was ignorant of Jesus Christ : Adam in his greatest glory, wanted earthly comforts ; Adam in his innocency, was a mere natural man.

Verse 19. " And out of the ground the Lord God formed every beast of the field, and every fowl of the air."

This proveth further what I said at first, That in the first chaos was contained all that was made upon the earth.

" And brought them to Adam, to see what he would call them ; and whatsoever Adam called every living creature, that was the name thereof."

In this Adam was a lively type of the Lord Christ's sovereign and glorious power over all flesh : " Thou hast given him power over all flesh, that he should give eternal life to as many as thou hast given him." (John xvii. 2.)

" And he brought them to Adam, to see what he would call them."

So Christ nameth the world ; whom he will he calleth saints ; and whom he will he calleth the world, ungodly, serpents, vipers, and the like. " I pray for them ; I pray not for the world." (John xvii. 9.)

" And whatsoever Adam called every living creature, that was the name thereof." Even as Christ passes sentence, so shall their judgment be.

Verse 20. " And Adam gave names to all cattle, and to the fowl of the air, and to every beast of the field." So Christ judgeth of angels, devils, and men.

" But for Adam, there was not found an help meet for him." All the glory of this world, had not Adam had a wife, could not have completed this man's blessedness ; he would yet have been wanting : so all the glory of heaven, considering Christ as mediator, could not, without his church, have made him up complete. The church, I say, which is his body, the fulness of him that filleth all in all.

Verses 21, 22. "And the Lord God caused a deep sleep to fall upon Adam, and he slept; and he took one of his ribs, and closed up the flesh instead thereof. And the rib which the Lord God had taken from man made he a woman, and brought her unto the man."

In these words we find a help provided for Adam; also, whence it came. The help was a wife: she came out of his side; she was taken thence while Adam slept. A blessed figure of a further mystery. Adam's wife was a type of the church of Christ; for that she was taken out of his side, it signifies we are flesh of Christ's flesh, and bone of Christ's bone. And in that she was taken thence while Adam slept, it signifies, the church is Christ's, by virtue of his death and blood: "Feed the church of God, which he purchased with his own blood." (Acts xx. 28.)

"And he brought her to the man." That is, And God brought her to the man. By which he clearly intimates, That as the church is the workmanship of God, and the purchase of the blood of Christ; so yet she cannot come to Christ, unless brought to him of God: "No man can come to me," saith Christ, "except the Father which hath sent me draw him." (John vi. 44.)

Verse 23. "And Adam said, This is bone of my bones, and flesh of my flesh: she shall be called Woman, because she was taken out of Man."

In that Adam doth thus acknowledge his wife to be bone and flesh of his substance, it shows us, that Christ will acknowledge those that are his: "He is not ashamed to call them brethren, saying, I will declare thy name unto my brethren; in the midst of the church will I sing praise unto thee." (Heb. ii. 11, 12.)

And observe it, He said, "She is bone of my bone," &c., before that God that brought her to him; intimating, that Christ both owns us now at his Father's right hand, and will not be ashamed of us, even in the day of judgment.

Verse 24. "Therefore shall a man leave his father and his mother, and shall cleave unto his wife: and they shall be one flesh."

This ought to be truly performed in our married estate in this world. But here endeth not the mystery.

"Therefore shall a man leave his father." Thus did Christ when he came into the world to save sinners: He came forth from the Father; "I came forth from the Father, and am come into the world." (John xvi. 28.)

"Therefore shall a man leave his father and his mother." The Jewish church may, in a mystical sense, be called the mother of Christ; for she was indeed God's wife, and of her came his Son Jesus Christ: yet his mother he left and forsook, to be joined to his Gentile spouse, which is now his only wife.

Verse 25. "And they were both naked, the man and his wife, and were not ashamed."

No sin, no shame: Let men stand where God hath set them, and there is no cause of shame, though they be exposed in outward appearance to never so much contempt.

"And they were both naked." Apparel is the fruits of sin; wherefore let such as pride themselves therein, remember, that they cover one shame with another. But let them that are truly godly have their apparel modest and sober, and with shamefacedness put them on, remembering always the first cause of our covering our nakedness, was the sin and shame of our first parents.

CHAPTER III.

Verse 1. "Now the serpent was more subtil than any beast of the field which the Lord God had made. And he said unto the woman, Yea, hath God said, Ye shall not eat of every tree of the garden?"

In these words we have an entrance of the first great spiritual conflict that was fought between the devil and flesh; and it is worth the observing, how the enemy attempted, engaged, and overcame the world.

1. He tempts by means; he appeareth not in his own shape and hue, but assumeth the body of one of the creatures, the body of the serpent, and so begins the combat. And from hence it is, that in after ages he is spoken of under the name of that creature, "the dragon, that old serpent which is the devil, and Satan;" (Rev. xx. 2;) because, as the Holy Ghost would have us beware of the devil, so of the means and engines which he useth; for where one is overcome by his own fearful appearance, ten thousand are overcome by the means and engines that he useth.

2. "The serpent was more subtil." The devil, in his attempts after our destruction, maketh use of the most suitable means. "The serpent was more subtil;" therefore the cunning of the devil was least of all discerned. Had he made use of some of the most foolish of the creatures, Adam had luckily started back, for he knew the nature of all the creatures, and gave them names accordingly; wherefore the serpent, Adam knew, was subtil; therefore Satan useth him, thereby to catch this goodly creature. Hereby the devil least appeared; and least appearing, the temptation soonest took the tinder.

"Now the serpent was more subtil." More subtil. Hence the devil is called "the serpent with heads," [with great cunning;] "the crooked serpent," [with knotty objections;] "the piercing serpent," [for he often wounds;] and his ways are called "devices," "temptations," "delusions," "wiles," "power," and "the gates of hell;" because of their mighty prevalency. This is he that undertook our first parents.

But how did he undertake them?

1. He labours to make them question the simplicity of the word of God, bearing Adam's wife in hand, that there must needs be some meaning that palliates the text; Hath God said ye shall not eat of the tree? Which interrogatory suggested them with a strong doubt that this word would not appear a truth, if you compare it with the fourth verse.

Hence learn, that so long as we retain the simplicity of the word, we have Satan at the end of the staff; for unless we give way to a doubt about that, about the truth and simplicity of it, he gets no ground upon us. And hence the apostle says, He feared lest by some means, as the serpent beguiled Eve through his subtilty, so our minds should be corrupted from the simplicity that is in Christ; (2 Cor. xi. 3;) that is, lest our minds should be drawn off from the simplicity of the word of the gospel by some devilish and delusive arguments: For mark, Satan doth not first of all deny, but makes a doubt upon the word, whether it is to be taken in this or another sense; and so first corrupting the mind with a doubt about the simplicity of the true sense, he after brings them to a denial thereof; "Hath God said, Ye shall not eat of every tree of the garden?"

Verse 2. "And the woman said unto the serpent, We may eat of the fruit of the trees of the garden."

"And the woman said." Indeed, the question was put to her, but the command was not so immediately delivered to her: "The Lord commanded the man." (Gen. ii. 16.) This, therefore, I reckon a great fault in the woman, an usurpation, to undertake so mighty an adversary, when she was not the principal that was concerned therein; nay, when her husband, who was more able than she, was at hand, to whom also the law was given as chief. But for this act, I think it is, that they are now commanded silence, and also commanded to learn of their husbands: (1 Cor. xiv. 34, 35. 1 Tim. ii. 9—15:) A command that is necessary enough for that simple and weak sex. Though they see it was by them that sin came into the world, yet how hardly are some of them to this day dissuaded from attempting unwarrantably to meddle with potent enemies, about the great and weighty matters that concern eternity.

Hence note, That often they who are least able, will first adventure to put in their head to defend that, from whence they return with shame.

"And the woman said unto the serpent, We may eat of the fruit of the trees of the garden."

This was her prologue to her defence, but that also for which she had no warrant. In time of temptation, it is our wisdom and duty to keep close to the word, that prohibits and forbids the sin; and not to reason with Satan, of how far our outward and worldly privileges go, especially of those privileges that border upon the temptation, as she here did: We may eat of all but one. By this she goeth to the outside of her liberty, and sets herself upon the brink of the danger. Christ might have told the tempter, when he assaulted him, That he could have made stones bread; and that he could have descended from the pinnacle of the temple, as afterwards he did; but that would have admitted of other questions. Wherefore he chooseth to lay aside such needless and unwarrantable reasonings, and resisteth him with a direct word of God, most pertinent to quash the tempter, and also to preserve himself in the way. To go to the outside of privileges, especially when tempted of the devil, is often, if not always, very dangerous and hazardous.

By these words therefore, in mine opinion, she spoke at this time too much in favour of the flesh; and made way for what after came upon her, We may eat of all but one.

Verse 3. "But of the fruit of the tree which is in the midst of the garden, God hath said, Ye shall not eat of it, neither shall ye touch it, lest ye die."

Now, too late, she urgeth that which should have been her only stay and weapon; to wit, the express word of God. That she should, if she would have disputed with the tempter, having urged at the first that only, and have thought of nothing else. Thus did the Lord himself: but she looking first into those worthy privileges which God had given her, and dilating delightfully of them before the devil, she lost the dread of the command from off her heart, and retained now but the notion of it: which Satan perceiving, and taking heart therefrom to make his best advantage, he now adds to his former forged doubt, a plain and flat denial, "Ye shall not surely die."

Verse 4. "And the serpent said unto the woman, Ye shall not surely die."

When people dally with the devil, and sit too near their outward advantages; when they are tempted to break the command of God, it is usual for them, even by setting their hearts upon things that in themselves are honest and lawful, to fall into temptation. To see a piece of ground, to prove a yoke of oxen, to marry a wife, are doubtless lawful things; (Luke xiv. 18—20;) but upon the borders of these privileges lay the temptation of the devil; therefore by the love of these, which yet were lawful in themselves, the devil hardened the heart, and so at last made way for, and perfectly produced in them, flatly to deny, as then, to embrace the words of God's salvation. The like befel our first mother; wherefore though at last she freely objected the word; yet because before she had so much reasoned to the pleasing of the flesh, she lost the dread and savour of the command, and having nought but notion left, she found not wherewith to rebuke so plain a lie of the devil, but hearkened to his further reasoning.

"Ye shall not surely die." Not surely; in the word there is some slight meaning, of which you need not be so afraid. And besides,

Verse 5. "God doth know, that in the day ye eat thereof, then your eyes shall be opened, and ye shall be as gods, knowing good and evil."

In these words two privileges are asserted: one, That their eyes shall be opened; the other, That they should be as gods, knowing good and evil. The first is very desirable, and was not at all abridged by them; the second, as to their knowing good and evil, was absolutely forbidden; because they could not attain to the knowledge of that which was evil, but by transgressing, or by eating of that forbidden tree.

Hence observe, That it is usual with the devil, in his tempting of poor creatures, to put a good and bad together, that by show of the good, the tempted might be drawn to do what which in truth is evil. Thus he served Saul; he spared the best of the herd and flock, under pretence of sacrificing to God, and so transgressed the plain command. (1 Sam. xix. 23.) But this the apostle saw was dangerous, and therefore censureth such, as in a state of condemnation. Thus he served Adam; he put the desirableness of sight, and a plain transgression of God's law together, that by the loveliness of the one, they might the easier be brought to do the other. O poor Eve! Do we wonder at thy folly! Doubtless we had done as bad with half the argument of thy temptation.

"Ye shall be as gods." In these words he attempts to beget in them a desire to be greater than God had made them. He knew this was a likely way, for by this means he fell himself; for being puffed up with pride, they left their own estate, or habitation, and so became devils, and were tumbled down to hell, where they are "reserved in chains, under darkness, unto the judgment of the great day." (Jude 6.)

"Ye shall be as gods." When souls have begun to hearken to the tempter, that hearkening hath made way for, and given way to so much darkness of mind, and hardness of heart, that now they can listen to anything: as to hear God charged with folly, "Ye shall not surely die;" as to hear him made the author of ignorance, and that he delights to have it so, by seeking by a command to prohibit them from knowing what they could; for God doth know, that in the day ye eat thereof, then your eyes shall be opened; and therefore he forbids to touch it.

"Ye shall be as gods." Here is also a pretence of holiness, which he knew they were prone unto; "Ye shall be as gods," as knowing and perfect as God. Oh! Thousands are, even to this day, by such temptations overcome! Thus he wraps his temptations up in such kind of words and suggestions as will carry it either way. But mark his holiness, or the way that he prescribes for holiness; it is, if not point blank against, yet without and besides the word, not by doing what God commands, and abhorring what he forbids, but by following the delusion of the devil, and their own roving fancies; as Eve here does.

Verse 6. "And when the woman saw that the tree was good for food, and that it was pleasant to the eyes, and a tree to be desired to make one wise, she took of the fruit thereof," &c.

This verse presents us with the use that Eve made of the reasonings of the serpent; and that was, to take them into consideration; not by the word of God, but as her flesh and blood did sense them: A way very dangerous and devouring to the soul, from which Paul fled, as from the devil himself: "Immediately I conferred not with flesh and blood." (Gal. i. 17.) Wherefore, pausing upon them, they entangled her as with a threefold cord. 1. "The lust of the flesh;" she saw it was good for food. 2. "The lust of the eye;" she saw it was pleasant to the eye. 3. "The pride of life;" a tree to be desired, to make one wise. Being taken, I say, with these three snares of the adversary, which are not of the Father, but of the world, and the devil the prince thereof, forthwith she falls before him: "And when the woman saw" this, "she took of the fruit thereof, and did eat."

"And when the woman saw." This seeing, as I said, is to be understood of her considering what Satan presented to her, and of her sensing or tasting of his doctrine; not by the word, which ought to be the touchstone of all, but by and according to her own natural reason without it. Now this makes her forget that very command that but now she had urged against the tempter: this makes her also to consent to that very reason, as an inducement to transgress; which, because it was the nature of the tree, was by God suggested as a reason why they should forbear; it was the tree of the knowledge of good and evil, therefore they should not touch it; it was the tree, that would by touching it, make them know good and evil; therefore she toucheth, and also eateth thereof. See therefore what specious pretences the devil, and those that are under the power of temptation, will have to transgress the command of God. That which God makes a reason of the prohibition, even that the devil will make a reason of their transgression.

God commands to self-denial, but the world makes that a reason of their standing off from the very grace of God in the gospel. God also commands, That we be sober, chaste, humble, just, and the like; but the devil, and carnal hearts, make these very things the argument that keeps sinners from the word of salvation. Or rather take it thus; God forbids wickedness, because it is delightful to the flesh, and draws the heart from God, but therefore carnal men love wickedness and sin: therefore they go on in sin, and "therefore they say unto God, Depart from us, for we desire not the knowledge of thy ways." (Job xxi. 14.)

She "did eat, and gave also unto her husband with her, and he did eat."

The great design of the devil, as he supposed, was now accomplished; for he had both in the snare, both the man and his wife, and in them, the whole world that should be after. And indeed the chief design of Satan was at the head at first, only he made the weakest the conveyance for his mischief. Hence note again, That Satan by tempting one, may chiefly intend the destruction of another. By tempting the wife, he may aim at the destruction of the husband; by tempting the father, he may design the destruction of the children; and by tempting the king, he may design the ruin of the subjects. Even as in the case of David: "Satan stood up against Israel, and provoked David to number the people." (1 Chron. xxi. 1.) He had a mind to destroy seventy thousand, therefore he tempted David to sin.

She "gave also to her husband, and he did eat." Sin seldom or never terminates in one person; but the pernicious example of one, doth animate and embolden another; or thus, the beholding of evil in another, doth often allure a stander-by. Adam was the looker-on, he was not in the action as from the serpent: "Adam was not deceived," that is, by having to do with the devil, but the woman, "the woman being deceived, was in the transgression." (1 Tim. ii. 14.) This should exhort all men that they take heed of so much as beholding evil done by others, lest also they should be allured. When Israel went into Canaan, God did command them not so much as to ask, "How those nations served their gods?" (Deut. xii. 30,) lest by so doing, Satan should get an advantage of their minds, to incline them to do the like. Evil acts, as well as evil words, will eat as doth a canker. This then is the reason of that evil-favouredness that you see attending some men's lives and professions; they have been corrupted, as Adam was, either by evil words, or bad examples, even till the very face of their lives and professions are disfigured as with the pox or canker.

Thus have we led you through that woful tragedy that was acted between the woman and the serpent; and have also showed, how it happened that the serpent went away as victor.

1. The woman admitted of a doubt about the truth of the word that forbad her to eat; for unbelief was the first sin that entered the world.

2. She preferred the privileges of the flesh, before the argument to self-denial; by which means her heart became hardened, and grew senseless of the dread and terror of the words of God.

3. She took Satan's arguments into consideration, and sensed, or tasted them; not by the word of God, but her own natural, or rather sore-deluded fancy.

4. She had a mind to gratify the lusts of the flesh, the lusts of the eyes, and the pride of life.

Now to speak of the evil consequences that followed this sinful act: That is not in the wisdom of mortal man to do; partly, because we know but in part even the evil and destructive nature of sin;

and partly, because much of the evil that will follow this action, is yet to be committed by persons unborn. Yet enough might be said to astonish the heavens, and to make them horribly afraid. (Jer. ii. 12.) 1. By this act of these two, the whole world became guilty of condemnation and eternal judgment. 2. By this came all the blindness, atheism, ignorance of God, enmity and malice against him, pride, covetousness, adultery, idolatry, and implacableness, &c., that is found in all the world. By this, I say, came all the wars, blood, treachery, tyranny, persecution, with all manner of rapine and outrage that is found among the sons of men. 3. Besides, all the plagues, judgments, and evils that befall us in this world, with those everlasting burnings that will swallow up millions for ever and ever; all and every whit of these ..me into the world as the portion of mankind, for that first transgression of our first parents. (Rom. v.)

Verse 7. "And the eyes of them both were opened, and they knew that they were naked; and they sewed fig-leaves together, and made themselves aprons."

That their eyes might be opened, was one branch of the temptation, and one of the reasons that prevailed with the woman to forsake the word of God: but she little thought of seeing after this manner, or such things as now she was made to behold. She expected some sweet and pleasant sight, that might tickle and delight her deluded fancy; but behold, sin and the wrath of God appears, to the shaking of their hearts! And thus, even to this very day, doth the devil delude the world: his temptations are gilded with some sweet and fine pretences; either they shall be wiser, richer, more in favour, live merrier, fare better, or something; and that they shall see it, if they will but obey the devil: which the fools easily are, by these and such like things, allured to do. But behold, when their eyes are opened, instead of seeing what the devil falsely told them, they see themselves involved in sin, made guilty of the breach of God's command, and subject to the wrath of God.

"And they knew that they were naked." Not only naked of outward clothing, but even destitute of righteousness; they had lost their innocency, their uprightness, and sinless vail, and had made themselves polluted creatures, both in their hearts, and in their flesh; this is nakedness indeed; such a kind of nakedness as Aaron made Israel naked with, when he set up his idol calf for them to worship: "For Aaron had made them naked unto their shame." (Exod. xxxii. 25.) Naked before the justice of the law.

"And they knew that they were naked." And they knew it: why did they not know it before? the text says, they were naked, and were not ashamed. O! they stood not naked before God! they stood not without righteousness, or uprightness before him, and therefore were not ashamed, but now they knew they were naked as to that.

"And they sewed fig-leaves together, and made themselves aprons." A fit resemblance of what is the inclination of awakened men, who are yet but natural! They neither think of Christ, or of the mercy of God in him for pardon, but presently they betake themselves to their own fig-leaves, to their own inventions, or to the righteousness of the law, and look for healing from means which God did never provide for cure. "When Ephraim saw his sickness, and Judah saw his wound, then went Ephraim to the Assyrian," (Hos. v. 13,) not to God, and sent to King Jareb, not to Christ, yet could they not heal him, nor cure him of his wound.

"And made themselves aprons." Not coats, as God did afterwards. A carnal man thinks himself sufficiently clothed with righteousness, if the nakedness which he sees can be but covered from his own sight: as if God also did see that and only that which they have a sight of by the light of nature ; and as if because fig-leaves would hide their nakedness from their sight, that therefore they would hide it from the sight of God. But alas! No man, without the help of another, can bring all his nakedness to the sight of his own eye ; much is undiscovered to him, that may yet lie open and bare to a stander-by : so it is with the men that stand without Christ. before God, at best they see but some of their nakedness, to wit, their most gross and worst faults, and therefore they seek to cover them ; which when they have hid from their own sight, they think them hid also from the sight of God. Thus did Adam, he saw his own most shameful parts, and therefore them he covered : they made themselves aprons, or things to gird about them, not to cover them all over withal. No man, by all his own doings can hide all his own nakedness from the sight of the justice of God, and yet, but in vain, as busy as Adam to do it.

"And they sewed fig-leaves together, and made themselves aprons." Fig-leaves! A poor apron, but it was the best they could get. But was that a sufficient shelter against either thorn or thistle ? Or was it possible but that after a while these fig-leaves should have become rotten, and turned to dung ? So it will be with all man's own righteousness which is of the law; Paul saw it so, and therefore counted it but loss and dung, that he might win Christ, and be found in him. (Phil. iii. 7, 8.)

Verse 8. "And they heard the voice of the Lord God walking in the garden in the cool of the day, and Adam and his wife hid themselves from the presence of the Lord God, among the trees of the garden."

"And they heard the voice of the Lord God." This voice was not to be understood according, as if it was the effect of a word ; as when we speak, the sound remains with a noise for some time after ; but by voice here, we are to understand the Lord Christ himself ; wherefore this voice is said to walk, not to sound only : "They heard the voice of the Lord God walking." This voice John calls the word, the word that was with the Father before he made the world, and that at this very time was heard to walk in the garden of Adam. Therefore John also saith, this voice was in the beginning ; that is, in the garden with Adam, at the beginning of his conversion, as well as of the beginning of the world. (John i. 1.)

"And they heard the voice of the Lord God walking in the garden in the cool of the day." The gospel of it is, in the season of grace ; for by the cool of the day, he here means, in the patience, gentleness, goodness, and mercy of the gospel ; and it is opposed to the heat, fire, and severity of the law.

"And Adam and his wife hid themselves." Hence observe, that a man's own righteousness will not fortify his conscience from fear and terror, when God begins to come near to him to judgment. Why did Adam hide himself, but because, as he said, he was naked ? But how could he be naked, when before he had made himself an apron ? O! the approach of God consumed and burnt off his apron ! Though his apron would keep him from the sight of a bird, yet it would not from the eye of the incorruptible God.

Let, therefore, all self-righteous men beware, for however they at present please themselves with the worthiness of their glorious fig-leaves ; yet, when God shall come to deal with them for sin, assuredly they will find themselves naked.

"And they hid themselves." A man in a natural state, cannot abide the presence of God ; yea, though a righteous man. Adam, though adorned with his fig-leaves, flies.

Observe again, that a self-righteous man, a man of the law, takes grace and mercy for his greatest enemy. This is apparent from the carriage of the Pharisees to Jesus Christ, who, because they were wedded to the works of their own righteousness, therefore they hated, persecuted, condemned, and crucified the Saviour of the world. As here in the text, though the voice of the Lord God walked in the garden in the cool of the day, in the time of grace and love, yet how Adam with his fig-leaves flies before him.

"And Adam and his wife hid themselves from the presence of the Lord God." These latter words are spoken, not to persuade us that men can hide themselves from God, but that Adam, and those that are his by nature, will seek to do it, because they do not know him aright. These words, therefore, further show us what a bitter thing sin is to the soul; it is only for hiding work, sometimes under its fig-leaves, sometimes among the trees of the garden. O what a shaking, starting, timorous, evil conscience, is a sinful and guilty conscience ! especially when 'tis but a little awakened, it could run its head into every hole, first by one fancy, then by another ; for the power and goodness of a man's own righteousness cannot withstand or answer the demands of the justice of God, and his holy law.

"And Adam and his wife hid themselves from the presence of the Lord God among the trees of the garden." If you take the trees in a mystical sense, as sometimes they may be taken ; then take them here to signify, or to be a type of the saints of God, and then the gospel of it is, that carnal men, when they are indeed awakened, and roused out of their foolish fig-leaf righteousness, then they would be glad of some shelter with them that are saved and justified freely by grace, as they in the gospel of Matthew : "Give us of your oil, for our lamps are gone out." (Matt. xxv. 8.) And again, the man without the wedding garment had crowded himself among the wedding guests. (Matt. xxii. 11.) Had hid themselves among the trees of the garden.

Verse 9. "And the Lord God called unto Adam, saying unto him, Where art thou ?"

Adam having eaten of the forbidden tree, doth now fleet his station, is gone to another than where God left him. Wherefore, if God will find Adam, he must now look him where he had hid himself. And, indeed, so he does with "Adam, Where art thou ?"

"And the Lord God called," &c. Here begins the conversion of Adam, from his sinful state, to God again. But mark, it begins not at Adam's calling upon God, but at God's calling upon him : "And the Lord God called unto Adam." Wherefore, by these words, we are to understand the beginning of Adam's conversion. And, indeed, grace hath gone the same way with the elect, from that time to this day. Thus he dealt with Abraham, Isaac, and Jacob ; he called them from their native country, the country of their kindred. And hence it is that, especially in the New Testament, the saints are said to be the Called ; "Called of God," and "Called of Jesus Christ." And hence again it is that Calling is by Paul made the first demonstration of election, and that saints are admonished to prove their election by their calling ; for as Adam was in a lost, miserable, and perishing condition, until God called him out of those holes into which sin had driven him : so we do lie where sin and the devil hath laid us, until, by the word of God, we are called to the fellowship of his Son Jesus Christ.

By these words, therefore, we have the beginning of the discovery of effectual calling or conversion ; "And the Lord God called :" In which call observe three things—

1. God called so that Adam heard him. And so it is in the conversion of the New Testament saints, as Paul says, " If so be that ye have heard him, and have been taught by him, as the truth is in Jesus." (Eph. iv. 21.) That, therefore, is one discovery of effectual calling, the sinner is made to hear him, even to hear him distinctly, singling out the very person, calling, "Adam, Where art thou ?"

" Saul, Saul, Why persecutest thou me ? " I have called thee by thy name, thou art mine. As he also said to Moses, " I know thee by name, and thou hast also found grace in my sight." (Exod. xxxiii. 12.)

2. God called so as to fasten sin upon his conscience, and as to force a confession from him of his naked and shameful state.

3. God called so as to make him tremble under, and be afraid of the judgment of God.

"And the Lord God called unto Adam, and said unto him, Where art thou ?" Indeed, Where art thou must of necessity be forcibly urged to every man on whose soul God doth work effectual conversion ; for until the person is awakened, as to the state and condition he is in, he will not desire, nay, will not endure to be turned to God ; but when in truth they are made to see what condition sin hath brought them to, namely, that it hath laid them under the power of sin, the tyranny of the devil, the strength of death, and the curse of God by his holy law ; then is mercy sweet.

"Where art thou ?" God knew where he was, but foolish Adam thought otherwise ; he thought to hide himself from the presence of the Lord, but the Lord found him out. Indeed, deluded sinners think that they can hide themselves and sins from God : "How doth God know," say they, "Can he see through the dark cloud ? " (Job xxii. 13.) But such shall know he sees them ; they shall know it, either to their correction, or to their condemnation. "Though they dig into hell," said God, "thence shall mine hand take them ; though they climb up to heaven, thence will I bring them down ; and though they hide themselves in the top of Carmel, I will search and take them out thence," &c. (Amos ix. 2, 3.) " Can any hide themselves in secret places that I shall not see him, saith the Lord ? Do not I fill heaven and earth, saith the Lord ? " (Jer. xxxiii. 24.)

Verse 10. "And he said, I heard thy voice in the garden, and I was afraid, because I was naked, and I hid myself."

This, then, was the cause of his flying, he heard the voice of God. A wicked and evil conscience saith everything is to it as the messenger of death and destruction ; for, as was said before, "the voice of the Lord walked in the garden in the cool of the day," in the time of grace and mercy. But it mattereth not whether he came with grace or vengeance ; guilt was in Adam's heart, therefore he could not endure the presence of God : He "that doeth evil hateth the light." (John iii. 20.) And again, "The wicked flee when no man pursueth." (Prov. xxviii. 1.) Cain thought all that met him would seek his blood and life.

"I heard thy voice." Something by the word of God was spoken, that shook the heart of this poor creature ; something of justice and holiness, even before they fell into this communication : for observe it, Adam went forthwith from the tree of knowledge of good and evil a convinced man, first to his fig-leaves, but they would not do; therefore he seeks to be hid among the trees. And observe again, That the insufficiency of fig-leaves were discovered by this voice of the Lord God, that at this time walked in the garden : " I heard thy voice in the garden, and I was afraid, because I was naked, and I hid myself." So then, there was a first and second voice which Adam heard ; the first he ran away from, " I heard thy voice, and hid myself." The second was this, wherein they commune each with other. The first, therefore, was the word of justice, severity, and of the vengeance of God; like that in the 19th of Exodus, from the pronouncing of which, a trembling, and almost death, did seize six hundred thousand persons.

" I heard thy voice in the garden." It is a word from without that doth it. While Adam listened to his own heart, he thought fig-leaves a sufficient remedy, but the voice that walked in the garden shook him out of all such fancies : "I heard thy voice in the garden, and I was afraid, because I was naked, and I hid myself."

Verse 11. " And he said, Who told thee that thou wast naked ? Hast thou eaten of the tree, whereof I commanded thee that thou shouldest not eat ?"

" Who told thee ?" This, as I said before, supposeth a third person, a preacher, and that was the Son of God ; the voice of the Lord God that walked in the garden.

" Hast thou eaten of the tree ?" That is, If thou hast been showed thy nakedness, thou hast indeed sinned ; for the voice of the Lord God will not charge guilt, but where and when a law hath been transgressed. God, therefore, by these words, driveth Adam to the point, either to confess or deny the truth of the case. If he confess, then he concludes himself under judgment; if he deny, then he added to his sin : therefore he neither denieth nor confesseth, but so as he may lessen and extenuate his sin.

Verse 12. " And the man said, The woman whom thou gavest to be with me, she gave me of the tree, and I did eat."

He had endeavoured with fig-leaves to hide his transgressions before, but that being found too scanty and short, he now trieth what he can do with arguments. Indeed, he acknowledgeth that he did eat of the tree of which he was forbidden ; but mark where he layeth the reason : Not in any infection which was centred in him by reason of his listening to the discourse which was between the woman and the serpent; but because God had given him a woman to be with him : "The woman which thou gavest to be with me, she gave me of the tree." The woman was given for a help, not a hindrance ; but Satan often maketh that to become our snare, which God hath given us as a blessing. Adam, therefore, here mixeth truth with falsehood. It is true, he was beguiled by the woman ; but she was not intended of God, as he

would insinuate, to the end she might be a trap unto him. Here, therefore, Adam sought to lessen and palliate his offence, as man by nature is prone to do ; for if God will needs charge them with the guilt of sin for the breach of the law, they will lay the fault upon anything, even upon God's ordinance, as Adam here doth, rather than they will honestly fall under the guilt, and so the judgment of the law for guilt. It is a rare thing, and it argueth great knowledge of God, and also hope in his mercy, when men shall heartily acknowledge their iniquities, as is evident in the case of David: " Wash me throughly from mine iniquity, and cleanse me from my sin. For I acknowledge my transgressions : and my sin is ever before me." (Ps. li. 2, 3.) But this knowledge is not at first in young converts ; therefore, when God begins to awaken, they begin, as sleepy men, to creep further under their carnal covering ; which yet is too short to hide them, and too narrow to cover their shame. (Isa. xxviii. 20.)

" The woman which thou gavest to be with me, she gave me of the tree." Although, as I said, this sinner seeks to hide, or, at least, to lessen his sin, by laying the cause upon the woman, the gift of God, yet it argueth that his heart was now filled with shame and confusion of face, for that he had broken God's command ; for, indeed, it is the nature of guilt, however men may in appearance ruffle under it, and set the best leg before, for their vindication, yet inwardly to make them blush and fail before their accuser. Indeed, their inward shame is the cause of their excuse; even as Aaron when he had made the golden calf, could not for shame of heart confess in plainness of speech the truth of the fact to his brother Moses, but faulteringly : They gave me their gold, saith he, and " I cast it into the fire, and there came out this calf." (Exod. xxxii. 24.) " And there came out this calf;" a pitiful fumbling speech. The Holy Ghost saith, Aaron had made them naked ; " had made them naked to their shame ;" for he, as also Adam, should, being chief and lord in their place, have stoutly resisted the folly and sin which was to them propounded ; and not as persons of a womanish spirit, have listened to wicked proposals.

Verse 13. " And the Lord God said unto the woman, What is this that thou hast done ?" &c.

Forasmuch as Adam did acknowledge his sin, though with much weakness and infirmity, God accepts thereof ; and now applieth himself to the woman, whom Satan had used as his engine to undo the world.

Hence observe, That when God sets to search out sin, he will follow it from the seduced to the seducer, even till he comes to the rise and first author thereof, as in the following words may more clearly appear. Not that he excuseth or acquitteth the seduced, because the seducer was the first cause, as some do vainly imagine ; but to lay all under guilt who are concerned therein : the woman was concerned as a principal, therefore he taketh her to examination.

"And the Lord God said unto the woman, What is this that thou hast done?" What is this? God seems to speak as if he were astonished at the inundation of the evil which the woman by her sin had overflowed the world withal: "What is this that thou hast done?" Thou hast undone thyself, thou hast undone thy husband, thou hast undone all the world; yea, thou hast brought a curse upon the whole creation, with an overplus of evils, plagues, and distresses.

"What is this that thou hast done!" Thou hast defiled thy body and soul, thou hast disabled the whole world from serving God; yea, moreover, thou hast let in the devil at the door of thy heart, and hast also made him the prince of the world. "What is this that thou hast done!" Ah, little, little do sinners know what they have done, when they have transgressed the law of the Lord. I say, they little know what death, what plagues, what curse, yea, what hell they, by so doing, have prepared for themselves.

"What is this that thou hast done!" God, therefore, by these words, would fasten upon the woman's heart a deep sense of the evil of her doings. And indeed, for the soul to be brought into a deep sense of its sin, to cry out before God, Ah! what have I done! it is with them the first step towards conversion: "Acknowledge thine iniquity," saith God, "that thou hast transgressed against the Lord." (Jer. iii. 13.) And again, "If we confess our sins, he is faithful and just to forgive us our sins, and to cleanse us from all unrighteousness." (1 John. i. 9.) The want of this is the cause of that obdurate and lasting hardness that continueth to possess so many thousands of sinners, they cry not out before God, what have I done? but foolishly they rush into, and continue in sin till their iniquity be found to be hateful, yea, their persons, because of their sin.

"What is this that thou hast done?" By this interrogatory the Lord also implied an admonition to the woman, to plead for herself, as he also did to her husband. He also makes way for the working of his bowels towards her, which (as will be shown anon) he flatly denies to the serpent, the devil: I say he made way for the woman to plead for, or bemoan herself; an evident token that he was unwilling to cast her away for her sin: "I have surely heard Ephraim bemoaning himself; I will surely have mercy upon him, saith the Lord." (Isa. xxxi. 18—20.) Again, by these words, he made way for the working or yearning of his own bowels over her; for when we begin to cry out of our miscarriages, and to bewail and bemoan our condition because of sin, forthwith the bowels of God begin to sound, and to move towards his distressed creature, as by the place before alleged appears. "I have surely heard Ephraim bemoaning himself—therefore my bowels are troubled for him; I will surely have mercy upon

him, saith the Lord." (See also the 11th and 14th chapters of Hosea.)

"And the woman said, the serpent beguiled me, and I did eat." A poor excuse, but a heart-affecting one; for many times want of wit and cunning to defend ourselves, doth affect and turn the heart of a stander-by to pity us. And thus, as I think, it was with the woman; she had to do with one that was too cunning for her, with one that snapt her by his subtilty or wiles; which also the woman most simply confesses, even to the provoking of God to take vengeance for her.

Verse 14. "And the Lord God said unto the serpent, Because thou hast done this, thou art cursed above all cattle, and above every beast of the field."

The serpent was the author of the evil; therefore the thunder rolls till it comes over him, the hot burning thunder-bolt falls upon him.

The Lord, you see, doth not with the serpent, as with the man and his wife; to wit, minister occasion to commune with him, but directly pronounced him cursed above all, "above every beast of the field." This showeth us, that as concerning the angels that fell, with them God is at eternal enmity, reserving them in everlasting chains under darkness. Cursed art thou: By these words, I say, they are prevented of a plea for ever, and also excluded a share in the fruits of a Messiah which should afterwards be born into the world.

"Because thou hast done this, cursed art thou." "Because thou hast done this:" not as though he was blessed before; for had he not before been wicked, he had not attempted so wicked a design. The meaning, then, is, that either by this deed the devil did aggravate his misery, and make himself the faster to hang in the everlasting chains under darkness; or else by this he is manifested to us to be indeed a cursed creature.

Further, "Because thou hast done this," may also signify how great complacency and content God took in Adam and his wife while they continued without transgression; but how much against his mind and workmanship this wicked work was. 1. Against his mind; for sin so sets itself against the nature of God, that, if possible, it would annihilate and turn him into nothing, it being in its nature point blank against him. 2. It is against his workmanship; for had not the power of the Messias stept in, all had again been brought to confusion, and worse than nothing: as Christ himself expresses it: "The earth, and all the inhabitants thereof are dissolved; I bear up the pillars of it." (Ps. lxxv. 3.) And again, He upholdeth all things by the word of his power. (Heb. i. 3.)

Besides, this being done, man, notwithstanding the grace of God, and the merits of Jesus Christ, doth yet live a miserable life in this world; for albeit that Christ hath most certainly secured the elect and chosen of God from perishing by what Satan hath done; yet the very elect themselves are, by reason of the first transgression, so infested and annoyed with inward filth, and so assaulted still by the devil, and his vassals the proper children of hell, that they groan unutterably under their burthen; yea, all creatures, "the whole creation groaneth and travaileth in pain together until now." (Rom. viii. 22.) And that most principally upon the very account of this first sin of Adam; it must needs be therefore, this being so high an affront to the divine majesty, and so directly destructive to the work of his hands; and the aim of the devil most principally also at the most excellent of his creation, (for man was created in God's own image,) that he should hereat be so highly offended, had they not sinned at all before, to bind them over for this very fact to the pains of the eternal judgment of God.

Verse 15. "And I will put enmity between thee and the woman, and between thy seed and her seed; it shall bruise thy head, and thou shalt bruise his heel."

The woman may, in this place, be taken either really or figuratively; if really and naturally, then the threatening is also true, as to the very natures of the creatures here under consideration, to wit, the serpent and the woman, and so all that come of human race; for we find that so great an antipathy is between all such deadly beasts as serpents and human creatures, that they abiding in their own natures, it is not possible they should ever be reconciled: "I will put enmity;" I will put it. This enmity then was not infused in creation, but afterwards; and that as a punishment for the abuse of the subtilty of the serpent; for before the fall, and before the serpent was assumed by the fallen angels, they were, being God's creatures, good, as the rest in their kind; neither was there any jarring or violence put between them; but after the serpent was become the devil's vizor, then was an enmity begot between them.

"I will put enmity between thee and the serpent." If by woman, we here understand the church, (but then we must understand the devil, not the natural serpent simply,) then also the threatening is most true; for between the church of God, and the devil, from the beginning of the world, hath been maintained most mighty wars and conflicts, to which there is not a like in all the bloodshed on the earth. Yea, here there cannot be a reconciliation, (the enmity is still maintained by God:) the reason is, because their natural dispositions and inclinations, together with their ends and purposes, are most repugnant each to other, even full as much as good and evil, righteousness and sin, God's glory, and an endeavour after his utter extirpation.

Indeed, Satan hath tried many ways to be at amity with the church; not because he loves her holiness, but because he hates her welfare, (wherefore such amity must only be dissembled,) and that he might bring about his enterprise, he sometimes hath allured with the dainty delicates of this world, the lust of the flesh, of the eyes, and the pride of life. This being fruitless, he hath attempted to entangle and bewitch her with his glorious appearance, as an angel of light; and to that end hath made his ministers as the ministers of righteousness, preaching up righteousness, and contending for a divine and holy worship: but this failing also, he hath taken in hand at length to fright her into friendship with him, by stirring up the hellish rage of tyrants to threaten and molest her; by finding out strange inventions to torment and afflict her children; by making many bloody examples of her own bowels, before her eyes, if by that means he might at last obtain his purpose. But behold! all hath been in vain, there can be no reconciliation. And why, but because God himself maintains the enmity?

And this is the reason why the endeavours of all the princes and potentates of the earth, that have through ignorance or malice managed his design against the church, have fallen to the ground, and been of none effect.

God hath maintained the enmity: doubtless the mighty wonder, that their laws cannot be obeyed; I mean their laws and statutes, which by the suggestion of the prince of this world they have made against the church: but if they understood but this one sentence, they might a little perceive the reason. God hath put enmity between the devil and the woman; between that old serpent called the Devil and Satan, and the holy, and beloved, and espoused wife of Christ.

"I will put enmity between thee and the woman, and between thy seed and her seed." The seeds here are the children of both, but that of the woman, especially Christ: "God sent forth his Son made of a woman." (Gal. iv. 4.) Whether you take it literally or figuratively; for in a mystery the church is the mother of Jesus Christ, though naturally, or according to his flesh, he was born of the virgin Mary, and proceeded from her womb: but take it either way, the enmity hath been maintained, and most mightily did show itself against the whole kingdom of the devil, and death, and hell, by the undertaking, engaging, and war which the Son of God did maintain against them, from his conception, to his death and exaltation to the right hand of the Father, as is prophesied of, and promised in the text, "It shall bruise thy head."

"It shall bruise thy head." By head, we are to understand the whole power, subtilty, and destroying nature of the devil; for as in the head of the serpent lieth his power, subtilty, and poisonous nature; so in sin, death, hell, and the wisdom of the flesh, lieth the very strength of the devil himself. Take away sin, then, and death is not hurtful: "The sting of death is sin:" and take away the condemning power of the law, and sin doth cease to be charged, or to have any more hurt in it, so as to destroy the soul: "The strength of sin is the law." (1 Cor. xv. 56.) Wherefore the seed,

Jesus Christ, in his bruising the head of the serpent, must take away sin, abolish death, and conquer the power of the grave. But how must this be done? Why, he must remove the curse, which makes sin intolerable, and death destructive. But how must he take away the curse? Why, by taking upon him flesh, as we; by being made under the law, as we; by being made to sin for us, and by being made a curse for us. He standing therefore in our room, under the law and the justice of God, did both bear, and overcome the curse, and so did bruise the power of the devil.

"It shall bruise thy head." To bruise is more than to break; he shall quash thy head to death; so he also quashed the heel of Christ; which would, had not his eternal power and Godhead sustained, have caused that he had perished for ever.

"And thou shalt bruise his heel." By these words, a necessity was laid upon Jesus Christ to assume our flesh, to engage the devil therein; and also because of the curse that was due to us for sin, that he might indeed deliver us therefrom; even for awhile to fall before this curse, and to die that death that the curse inflicteth: "Christ hath redeemed us from the curse of the law, being made a curse for us." Thus therefore did Satan, that is, by the fruits and effects of sin, bruise, or kill, the flesh of Christ: But he being God, as the Father, it was not possible he should be overcome. Therefore his head remaineth untouched. A man's life lieth not in his heel, but in his head and heart; but the Godhead being the head and heart of the manhood, it was not possible Satan should meddle with that; he only could bruise his heel; which yet by the power of the Godhead of this eternal Son of the Father, was raised up again from the dead: He "was delivered for our offences, and was raised again for our justification." (Rom. iv. 25.)

In these words therefore the Lord God gave Adam a promise, That notwithstanding Satan had so far brought his design to pass, as to cause them by falling from the command, to lay themselves open to the justice and wrath of God; yet his enterprise by grace, should be made of none effect. As if the Lord had said, "Adam, thou seest how the devil hath overcome thee; how he, by thy consenting to his temptation, hath made thee a subject of death and hell: but though he hath by this means made thee a spectacle of misery, even an heir of death and damnation: yet I am God, and thy sins have been against me. Now because I have grace and mercy, I will therefore design thy recovery. But how shall I bring it to pass? Why I will give my Son out of my bosom, who shall in your room, and in your nature, encounter this adversary, and overcome him. But how? Why, by fulfilling my law, and by answering the penalties thereof. He shall bring in a righteousness which shall be everlasting, by which I will justify you from sin, and the curse of God due

thereto: But this work will make him smart, he must be made a man of sorrows, for upon him will I lay your iniquities; Satan shall bruise his heel."

Verse 16. "Unto the woman he said, I will greatly multiply thy sorrow, and thy conception; in sorrow thou shalt bring forth children; and thy desire shall be to thy husband, and he shall rule over thee."

"I will greatly multiply thy sorrow," &c. This is true, whether you respect the woman according to the letter of the text, or as she was a figure of the church; for in both senses their sorrows for sin are great, and multiplied upon them. The whole heap of the female sex know the first, the church only knows the second.

"In sorrow thou shalt bring forth children." The more fruitful, the more afflicted is the church in this world; because the rage of hell, and the enmity of the world, are by her righteousness set on fire so much the more.

But again: Forasmuch as the promise is made before this judgment of God for sin is threatened, we must count these afflictions not as coming from the hand of God in a way of vengeance, for want of satisfaction for the breach of the law; but to show and keep us in mind of his holiness, that henceforth we should not, as at first through ignorance, so now from notions of grace and mercy, presume to continue in sin.

I might add, That by these words it is manifest, that a promise of mercy and forgiveness of sin, and great afflictions and rebukes for the same, may and shall attend the same soul: "I will greatly multiply thy sorrows," comes after the promise of grace.

"And thy desire shall be to thy husband, and he shall rule over thee." Doubtless the woman was, in her first creation, made in subordination to her husband, and ought to have been under obedience to him: wherefore, still that had remained a duty, had they never transgressed the commandment of God; but observe, the duty is here again not only enjoined, and imposed, but that as the fruit of the woman's sin; wherefore, that duty that before she might do as her natural right by creation, she must now do as the fruits of her disobedience to God. Women therefore, whenever they would perk it and lord it over their husbands, ought to remember, that both by creation and transgression they are made to be in subjection to their own husbands. This conclusion makes Paul himself: "Let," saith he, "the woman learn in silence, with all subjection. But I suffer not a woman to teach, nor to usurp authority over the man, but to be in silence. For Adam was first formed, then Eve. And Adam was not deceived, but the woman being deceived, was in the transgression." (1 Tim. ii. 11—14.)

Verse 17. "And unto Adam, he said, Because thou hast hearkened unto the voice of thy wife, and hast eaten of the tree of which I commanded thee, saying, Thou shalt not eat of it: cursed is the ground for thy sake, in sorrow shalt thou eat of it all the days of thy life."

God having laid his censure upon the woman, he now proceedeth and cometh to her husband, and also layeth his judgment on him: The judgment is, "Cursed is the ground for thy sake," and in sorrow thou shalt eat thereof. The causes of this judgment are, First, For that he "hearkened to his wife:" And also, For that he had "eaten of the tree."

1. "Because thou hast hearkened to thy wife." Why? Because therein he left his station and headship, the condition which God had appointed him, and gave way to his wife to assume it, contrary to the order of creation, of her relation and of her sex; for God had made Adam lord and chief, who ought to have taught his wife, and not to have become her scholar.

Hence note, That the man that suffereth his wife to take his place, hath already transgressed the order of God.

"Because thou hast hearkened to the voice," &c. Wicked women, such as Eve was now, if hearkened unto, are the snares of death to their husbands; for, because they are weaker built, and because the devil doth easier fasten with them than with men, therefore they are more prone to vanity, and all mis-orders in the matters of God than they; and so, if hearkened unto, more dangerous upon many accounts: "Did not Solomon, king of Israel, sin by these things? yet among many nations was there no king like him, who was beloved of his God, and God made him king over all Israel: nevertheless, even him did outlandish [wicked] women, cause to sin." (Neh. xiii. 26.) "But there was none like unto Ahab, which did sell himself to work wickedness in the sight of the Lord, whom Jezebel his wife stirred up." (1 Kings xxi. 25.)

Hence note further, That if it be thus dangerous for a man to hearken to a wicked wife, how dangerous is it for any to hearken unto wicked whores, who will seldom yield up themselves to the lusts of beastly men, but on condition they will answer their ungodly purposes! What mischief by these things hath come upon souls, countries, and kingdoms, will here be too tedious to relate.

"Because thou hast hearkened to the voice of thy wife, and hast eaten of the tree." That is, From the hand of thy wife; for it was she that gave him to eat: "Therefore," &c., Although the scripture doth lay a great blot upon women, and cautioneth men to beware of these fantastical and unstable spirits, yet it limiteth man in his censure. She is only then to be rejected and rebuked, when she doth things unworthy her place and calling. Such a thing may happen, as that the woman, not the man, may be in the right, (I mean, when both are godly,) but ordinarily it is otherwise. Therefore the conclusion is, Let God's word judge between the man and his wife, as it ought to have done between Adam and his, and neither of them

will do amiss; but contrariwise, they will walk in all the commandments of God without fault.

"Therefore cursed be the ground for thy sake." Behold what arguments are thrust into every corner, thereby to make man remember his sin; for all the toil of man, all the barrenness of the ground, and all the fruitlessness after all; what is it but the fruits of sin? Let not us then find fault with the weed, with the hotness, coldness, or barrenness of the soil; but by seeing these things, remember our sin, "Cursed be the ground for thy sake;" for this God makes our heaven as iron, and our earth as brass: "The Lord shall make the rain of thy land powder and dust; from heaven shall it come down upon thee, until thou be destroyed." (Deut. xxviii. 24.)

"In sorrow shalt thou eat of it all the days of thy life." He then is much deceived, who thinks to fill his body with the delicates of this world, and not therewith to drink the cruel venom of asps: Yea, "He shall suck the poison of asps, the viper's tongue shall slay him." (Job xx. 16.) The reason is, because he that shall give up himself to the lusts and pleasures of this life, he contracts guilt, because he hath sinned; which guilt will curdle all his pleasures, and make the sweetest of them deadly as poison.

"In sorrow shalt thou eat." Even thou that hast received the promise of forgiveness: How then can they do it with pleasure, who eat, and forget the Lord?

Again, Let not the sorrows, crosses, and afflictions, that attend the godly in the things of this life, weaken their faith in the promise of grace, and forgiveness of sins: for such things may befall the dearest Christian.

Verse 18. "Thorns also and thistles shall it bring forth to thee, and thou shalt eat the herb of the field."

This shows us (as I also hinted before), That the thorns and thistles of the ground, are but as the excrements thereof; and the fruits of sin, and the curse for sin. This world, as it dropped from the fingers of God, was far more glorious than it is now: Now it is loaden with a burden of corruption, thorns, thistles, and other annoyances, which Adam knew none of in the days of his innocence. None therefore ever saw this world as it was in its first creation, but only Adam and his wife; neither shall any ever see it, until the manifestation of the children of God: that is, until the redemption or resurrection of the saints: but then it shall be delivered from the bondage of corruption, into the glorious liberty of the children of God.

"And thou shalt eat the herb of the field." These words are for his comfort, under all the sorrow sin should bring upon him; "Thou shalt eat the herb:" The herb was a type of the gospel-comforts which the destroying angels were forbidden to smite. Of these medicinal and healing herbs, therefore, Adam and his seed are admitted to eat, that their soul may be replenished in the midst of their sorrow.

Verse 19. " In the sweat of thy face shalt thou eat bread, till thou return unto the ground; for out of it wast thou taken : for dust thou art, and unto dust shalt thou return."

" In the sweat of thy face." This is true, whether literally or allegorically understood : For as touching the things that pertain to this life, as they become not ours without toil and labour ; so the spiritual comforts of the kingdom of heaven are not obtained without travail and sweat : " Labour," saith Christ, " for the bread and meat which endureth to everlasting life." (John vi. 27.)

" In the sweat of thy face." Those that make conscience of walking in the commandments of God, they shall be blessed with the bread of life, when others shall be hunger-bit. That may also be mystically applied, " On all hills that shall be digged with the mattock, there shall not come thither the fear of briers and thorns : but it shall be for the sending forth of oxen, and for the treading of lesser cattle." (Isa. vii. 25.) The meaning is, Where people are diligent, according to the word of God, especially in spiritual and heavenly things, they shall be fat and flourishing, though sorrow be mixed therewith. When men shall say, There is casting down; then thou shalt say, There is lifting up; and he shall save the humble person. (Job xxii. 29.)

" Till thou return to the ground." A Christian should not leave off sweating labour so long as he is above the ground ; even until he returneth thither, he ought to be diligent in the way and worship of God. Jacob, when sick, would worship God, though so weak as not able to do it, without leaning upon the top of his staff. (Heb. xi. 21.) A blessed example for the diligent, and reproof for those that are slothful.

" For out of it wast thou taken." That is, out of the ground. Behold how the Lord doth mix his doctrine ! Now he tells him of his sin, then he promiseth to give him a Saviour, then again he shows him the fruits of his sin, and immediately after the comforts of the promise ; yet again, he would have him remember that he is but a mortal creature, not to live here for ever ; neither made of silver nor gold, but even of a clod of dust : " For dust thou art." Observe, therefore, that in the midst of all our enjoyments, God would have us consider our frame, that we may know how frail we are.

" For out of it wast thou taken." It is hard for us to believe it, though we daily see it is the way even of all the earth, to return thither again : " For dust thou art, and to dust thou shalt return."

Whether this was spoken to Adam, as a judgment, or a mercy, or both, is not hard to determine, (this first premised, that Adam had received the promise ;) for as it was the fruit of sin, so a judgment and a token of God's displeasure ; " for

the wages of sin is death :" (Rom. vi. 23.) But as it is made, by the wisdom of God, a prevention of further wickedness, and a conveyance through faith in Christ, to a more perfect enjoyment of God in the heavens ; so it is a mercy and blessing of God; for thus " to die is gain." Wherefore thus we may praise the dead, that are already dead, more than the living, which are yet alive. (Eccles. iv. 2.) This made Paul desire to depart; for he knew that through death was the way to have more perfect sight of, and more close and higher communion with the Father, and the Son, and the Spirit in the heavens : I have a desire to depart, and be with Christ, which is far better. (Phil. i. 23.) Thus, therefore, those things that in their own nature are the proper fruits and wages of sin, may yet through the wisdom of God be turned about for our good; but let not this embolden to sin, but rather minister occasion to us to magnify the wisdom of God.

Verse 20. " And Adam called his wife's name Eve ; because she was the mother of all living."

By this act Adam returneth to his first station and authority in which God had placed him, from which he fell when he became a scholar to his wife; for to name the creatures, was in Adam a note of sovereignty and power. This he attained to, as an effect of his receiving the promise ; for before the promise is received, man cannot serve God in his station, because as he wanteth the power of will, so also a good understanding ; but when he hath received the promise, he hath also received the Holy Ghost, which giveth to the godly to know and do his duty in his station : The spiritual man discerneth, and so judgeth all things; but he is not discerned nor judged of any. (1 Cor. ii. 15.)

And he called his wife's name Eve, or Hevah : Because she gave life to, or was the first mother of all mankind. This, then, admits of two positions. First, That the world was created when Adam was created. And, Second, That there were none of the sons of men in the world before Adam, as some have not only vainly, but irreligiously and blasphemously suggested. " Eve is the mother of all living :" Not a man, therefore, that is the son of man, but had his being since the woman was made.

Verse 21. " Unto Adam also, and to his wife, did the Lord God make coats of skins, and clothed them."

By this action the Lord God did preach to Adam, and to his wife, the meaning of that promise that you read of in verse fifteen, namely, That by the means of Jesus Christ, God himself would provide a sufficient clothing for those that accept of his grace by the gospel : the coats here, being a type of that blessed and durable righteousness.

" The Lord God made the coats." Not Adam now, because now he is received into a covenant of grace with God : Indeed, before he entered into this covenant, he made his own clothing, such as it was, but that could not cover his nakedness; but now the Lord will make them: And "unto Adam also, and to his wife, did the Lord God make coats:" " Their righteousness is of me, saith the Lord:" (Isa. liv. 17.) " Of me," that is, of my providing, of my performing. " And this is the name whereby he shall be called, THE LORD OUR RIGHTEOUSNESS." (Jer. xxiii. 6.)

" He made them coats, and clothed them." As the righteousness by which a sinner stands just in the sight of God from the curse, is a righteousness of God's providing; so also it is of his putting on. No man can put on the righteousness of Christ, otherwise than by God's imputation: if God reckon it ours, then it is ours indeed; but if he refuseth to show that mercy, who can impute that righteousness to men? Blessed are they to whom the Lord imputeth righteousness. (Rom. iv. 8.) Cursed, then, must they needs be to whom God hath not imputed the righteousness of his Son. " The Lord clothed them," according to that of Paul, " Christ is made unto us of God wisdom and righteousness," &c. (1 Cor. i. 30.) And of that God who hath made him thus to us, even of him are we in Christ Jesus.

Did the Lord God make coats of skins? The coats were made of the skins of beasts, of the skins of the slain, which were slain either for food only, or for sacrifice also. This being so, the effects of that promise mentioned before were by this action the more clearly expounded unto Adam; to wit, That Christ, " in the fulness of time," should be born of a woman clothed with flesh; and as so considered, should be made a curse, and so die that cursed death which by sin we had brought upon ourselves; the effects and fruits of which should to us be durable clothing; that is, Everlasting righteousness.

Verses 22, 23. " And the Lord God said, Behold, the man is become as one of us, to know good and evil: and now, lest he put forth his hand and take also of the tree of life, and eat, and live for ever: therefore the Lord God sent him forth from the garden of Eden, to till the ground from whence he was taken."

" Behold, the man is become as one of us:" These words respect the temptation of the devil; the argument that prevailed with Adam; and the fruits of their consenting. And therefore I understand them as spoken ironically, or in derision to Adam. As if God had said, " Now, Adam, you see what a god you are become. The serpent told you ' you should be as gods,' as one that was infinite in wisdom: but, behold, your godhead is horrible wickedness, even pollution of body and soul by sin; a thing you little thought of, when you pleased yourself with the thought of that high attainment. And now, if you be not prevented, you will proceed from evil to evil; for, notwithstanding I have made promise of sending a Saviour, you will, through the pollution of your

mind, forget, and set at nought my promise; and seek life and salvation by that tree of life which was never intended for the justification of sinners; therefore I will turn you out of the garden, ' to till the ground whence thou wast taken.' "

1. Hence observe, That it often falls out, after the promised blessing is come, that God yet maketh us to possess our former sins, not that the guilt thereof might be charged to condemnation, but that remembering of them, we might blush before God, and be the more effectually driven to a continual embracing of the mercy promised.

2. Observe again, That as God would have us to remember our former sins, so he would not that we should feed upon aught but the very mercy promised. We must not rest in shadowish sacraments, as the typical tree of life, but must remember it is our duty to live by faith in the promised seed.

3. Observe also, That even our outward and temporal employments, if they be lawful and honest, are so ordered of God, as that we may gather some heavenly mystery from them: " To till the ground from whence he was taken:" Mysteriously intimating two things to Adam. (1.) That seeing he was of the earth, he stood in as much need to be ordered and dressed by God, in order to his future happiness, as the ground, in order to its thrift and fruitfulness. (2.) Again, Seeing he was taken from the ground, he is neither God, nor angel, but a poor earthen vessel, such as God can easily knock in pieces, and cause to return to the ground again. These things therefore Adam was to learn from his calling, that he might neither think too highly of himself, nor forget to live by faith, and depending on the Lord God, to be blessed of him.

Verse 24. " So he drove out the man; and he placed at the east of the garden of Eden Cherubims, and a flaming sword which turned every way, to keep the way of the tree of life."

" So he drove out the man." Adam was loth to forsake this garden of Eden, because there was the tree of life. The promise will hardly satisfy, where faith is weak and low. Had this man with great faith received and retained the gospel preached before, he would not have so hankered after a shadow; but the conscience being awakened, and faith low and weak there, because faith wants the flower or bloom of assurance, the ceremonial or moral law doth with ease engender bondage.

" And he placed at the east of the garden of Eden, Cherubims and a flaming sword." This shows the truth of what I said before; to wit, that Adam was loth to forsake the garden, loth to forsake his doing of something; but God sets a shaking sword against him, a sword to keep that way, or to prevent that Adam should have life by eating of the tree of life.

Observe, this tree of life, though lawful for Adam to feed on before he had transgressed, yet now is wholly forbidden him; intimating, that that which would have nourished him before he brake the law, will now avail him nothing as to life before the justice of God: the tree of life might have maintained his life before he sinned; but having done that, he hath no ways now but to live by faith in the promise; which that he might effectually do, God takes from him the use of all other things, he driveth him out of the garden, and sets to keep him from the tree of life, "Cherubims, and a flaming sword."

"And he placed at the east of the garden Cherubims, and a flaming sword." These cherubims are one sort of the angels of God, at this time made ministers of justice, shaking the flaming sword of God's severity against Adam for sin, threatening to cut him off thereby, if he ever return by the way that he went.

We read, also, that the law was delivered to Israel from Sinai, by the hand and disposition of angels, (Acts vii. 38;) the gospel only, by the Son himself. (Heb. i. 1, 2.)

"To keep the way." Hence the apostle implicitly concludes it a way, that is, to death and damnation; by opposing another against it, even the new and living one; a new, not this the old; a living one, not this the dead one, (Heb. x. 19, 20;) for, for that the cherubims are here placed with a flaming, shaking sword, to keep the tree of life, it is evident that death is threatened to him that shall at any time attempt to come at, or that seeks for life that way.

"A flaming sword, turning every way to keep," &c. This still shows us, that man, though he hath already received the promise, is yet exceeding prone to seek life by another way than free-grace by Jesus Christ; to wit, either by the law he hath broken, or by the law and Christ together; and so hough not directly, yet "as it were by the works of the law." (Rom. ix. 32.) But all is to no purpose, they are every way prevented: for, forsake the simplicity of the promise in the gospel, and thou shalt meet with the stroke of the justice of God; for that flaming sword of his vengeance, it turneth every way, and therefore will, in every way, lay wrath upon thee, if thou seek life by aught but Christ.

CHAPTER IV.

Verse 1. "And Adam knew Eve his wife; and she conceived, and bare Cain, and said, I have gotten a man from the Lord."

Now we are come to the generation of mankind. "Adam knew his wife:" a modest expression; and it should teach us, in all such matters where things are discoursed of, that are either the fruits of sin, or the proper effects of man's natural infirmities, there to endeavour the use of such expressions, as neither to provoke to lust, nor infect us with evil and uncivil communication. "Adam

knew his wife;" Jacob, Samson, David, and others, are said to go in unto them. So as to our natural infirmities of the stool, the scripture expression is, "When thou goest abroad to ease thyself, thou shalt turn again and cover that which cometh from thee:" modest and bashful expressions, and such as become the godly, being those that are furthest off of occasioning evil, and nearest to an intimation, that such infirmities bespeak us infirm and imperfect creatures.

"And she conceived and bare Cain." The first sprout of a disobedient couple, a man in shape, but a devil in conditions. This is he that is called elsewhere, the child of that wicked one. (1 John iii. 12.)

"And she said, I have gotten a man from the Lord." If Eve by these words did only ascribe the blessing of children to be the gift of God, then she spake like a godly woman; but if she supposed that this man Cain was indeed the seed promised, then it shows, that she in this was also deceived, and was therein a figure of all such as make false and strange delusions, signs of the mercy of God towards them; the man she thought she had got from the Lord as a mercy, and to be a Saviour, he proved a man of the devil, a curse, and to be a destroyer.

Verse 2. "And she again bare his brother Abel. And Abel was a keeper of sheep, but Cain was a tiller of the ground."

Observe here, that the good child is not the first-born, but Abel. God often doth as Jacob did, even cross hands, in bestowing blessings, giving that which is best to him that is least esteemed: for Cain was the man in Eve's esteem; she thought, when she had him, she had got an inheritance; but as for Abel, he was little worth; by his name they showed how little they set by him. It is so with the sincere to this day; they bear not the name of glory with the world; Cain with them is the profitable son; Abel is of no credit with them, neither see they form nor comeliness in him; he is the melancholy, or lowering child, whose countenance spoileth the mirth of the world: "The heart of the wise is in the house of mourning, but the heart of fools is in the house of mirth." (Eccles. vii. 4.)

"And Abel was a keeper of sheep, but Cain was a tiller of the ground." By this it seems yet further, that Cain was the man in favour, even him that should, by his Father's intentions, have been heir, and have enjoyed the inheritance: he was nurtured up in his father's employment, but Abel was set in the lower rank.

It was also thus with Isaac and Jacob, Ishmael and Esau, being the eldest, and those that by intention were to be heirs.

Now in the inheritance lay, of old, a great blessing; so that Esau in losing his father's inheritance, lost also the blessing of grace, and moreover the kingdom of heaven. Wherefore Cain had by this the better of Abel, even as the Jews by their privileges had the better of the Gentiles. But mark it, the blessing of grace is not led by outward order, but by electing love; where the person then is under the blessing of election, be he the first or the second son, the highest or lowest in the family, or whether he be more or less loved of his friends, it is he that with Abel hath the everlasting blessing.

Verse 3. "And, in process of time, it came to pass that Cain brought of the fruit of the ground an offering unto the Lord."

Mark here, that the devil can suffer his children, in outward forms of worship, to be godly and righteous men; Cain, a limb of the devil, and yet the first in order that presents himself and his service to God.

Cain brought of the fruit of the ground, as of wheat, oil, honey, or the like; which things were also clean and good. Hence it is intimated, that his offering was excellent; and I conceive, not at all, as to the matter itself, inferior to that of Abel's; for in that it is said that Abel's was more excellent, it is not with respect to the excellency of the matter or things with which they sacrificed, but with respect to Abel's faith, which gave glory and acceptableness to his offering with God, "By faith he offered to God a more excellent sacrifice than Cain." (Heb. xi. 4.)

Verse 4. "And Abel, he also brought of the firstlings of his flock, and of the fat thereof," &c.

Abel, last in appearance, but in truth the first in grace; as it also is at this day; who do so flutter it out as our ruffling formal worshippers? Alas! the good, the sincere and humble, they seem to be least and last; but the conclusion of the tragedy will make manifest that the first is last, and the last first; for the many are but called, the few are chosen.

"And the Lord had respect unto Abel, and to his offering." Herein are the true footsteps of grace discovered; to wit, the person must be the first in favour with God, the person first, the performance afterwards.

"And the Lord had respect to Abel." But how can God respect a man, before he respect his offering! "A man's gift," saith Solomon, "makes way for him:" it should seem therefore that there lies no such stress in the order of words, but that it might as well be read, "The Lord had respect to Abel, because he respected his offering."

Ans. Not so: for though it be true among men, that the gift makes way for the acceptance of the person, yet in the order of grace it is after another manner; for if the person be not first accepted, the offering must be abominable; for it is not a good work that makes a good man, but a good man makes a good work. The fruit doth not make a good tree, but a "good tree bringeth forth good fruit." "Make," saith Christ, "the tree good, and his fruit good; or the tree evil, and his fruit evil. Do men gather grapes of thorns, or figs of thistles?" Had Abel been a thorn, he had not brought forth grapes; had he been a thistle, he had not brought forth figs. So then, Abel's person must be first accepted, and after that his works.

Obj. But God accepteth no man while he remains a sinner, but all men are sinners before they do good works, how then could the person of Abel be accepted first?

Ans. Abel was just before he did offer sacrifice. Just, I say, in the sight of God. This God witnessed by testifying of his gift: "By faith Abel offered unto God a more excellent sacrifice than Cain, by which he obtained witness that he was righteous:" that is, God by accepting of the gift of Abel did testify that Abel was a righteous man; for we know God "heareth not sinners." "The prayers of the wicked are an abomination unto God:" but Abel was accepted, therefore he was righteous first.

Hence observe, that a man must be righteous before he can do any good work.

Quest. Righteous! With what righteousness?

Ans. With the righteousness of faith: and therefore it is said, that Abel had faith before he offered sacrifice: by faith he offered. (Heb. xi. 4.) Where faith is made to precede or go before the work which by faith he offered unto God.

Quest. But are not good works the righteousness of faith?

Ans. They are the fruits of faith: as here in the case of Abel; his faith produced an offering; but before he gave his offering, his faith had made him righteous; for faith respects a promise of grace, not a work of mine. Now the promise of grace, being this, that the seed of woman, which is Christ, should destroy the power of the devil; by this Abel saw that it was Christ that should abolish sin and death by himself, and bring in "everlasting righteousness" for sinners. Thus believing he had accepted of Christ for righteousness, which because he had done, God in truth proclaims him righteous by accepting of his person and performances when offered.

Abel then presented his person and offering, as shrouding both by faith under the righteousness of Christ, which lay wrapped up in the promise; but Cain stands upon his own legs, and so presents his offering. Abel therefore is accepted, both his person and his offering, while Cain remains accursed.

Verse 5. "But unto Cain, and to his offering, he [the Lord] had not respect. And Cain was very wroth, and his countenance fell."

Mark: As first Abel's person is accepted, and then his offering; so first Cain's person is rejected, and afterwards his offering. For God seeth not sin in his own institutions, unless they be defiled by them that worship him; and that they needs must, when persons by themselves offer sacrifice to God, because then they want the righteousness of faith.

This then made the difference betwixt Abel and

his brother; Abel had faith, but Cain had none. Abel's faith covered him with Jesus Christ, therefore he stood righteous in his person before God. This being so, his offering was accepted, because it was the offering of one that was righteous.

"But unto Cain, and to his offering, the Lord had not respect." Hence note, That a Christless man is a wicked man, let him be never so full of actions that be righteous; for righteous actions make not a righteous man, the man himself must first be righteous.

Wherefore, though Cain was the eldest, and first in the worship; yet Abel was the wisest, and the most acceptable therein.

"And Cain was very wroth, and his countenance fell." From these words it may be gathered, that Cain had some evident token from the observation of God's carriage towards both himself and brother; that his brother was smiled upon, but he rejected. He was wroth: wroth with God, and wroth with his brother. And indeed, before the world hate us, they must needs hate Jesus Christ: "It hated me," saith he, "before it hated you." (John xv. 18.) He was wroth: and why? Wroth because his sacrifice was not accepted of God: and yet the fault was not in the Lord, but Cain. He came not before the Lord, as already made righteous with the righteousness of Christ, which indeed had been doing well, but as a cursed wicked wretch, he thought that by his own good works he must be just before the Lord.

The difference therefore that was between these worshippers, it lay not in that they worshipped divers gods, but in that they worshipped the same God after a diverse manner: The one in faith, the other without; the one as righteous, the other as wicked.

And even thus it is between us and our adversaries: We worship not divers gods, but the same God in a diverse manner: We according to faith; and they according to their own inventions.

"And Cain was wroth." This further shows us the force of the law, and the end of those that would be just by the same; namely, That in conclusion they will quarrel with God; for when the soul in its best performances, and acts of righteousness, shall yet be rejected and cast off by God, it will fret and wrangle, and in its spirit let fly against God. For thus it judgeth, That God is austere and exacting; it hath done what it could to please him, and he is not pleased therewith. This again offendeth God, and makes his justice curse and condemn the soul: condemn it, I say, for imagining that the righteousness of a poor, sinful, wretched creature, should be sufficient to appease eternal justice for sin. Thus the law worketh wrath, because it always bindeth our transgression to us, and still reckoneth us sinners, and accursed, when we have done our utmost to answer and fulfil it. (Rom. iv. 15.)

"And his countenance fell." However a hypocrite, while God forbeareth to smite him, may triumph and joy in his goodness, yet when God shall pronounce his judgment according as he approves of his act, he needs must lower and fall in his countenance; for his person and gift are rejected, and he still counted a sinner.

Verse 6. "And the Lord said unto Cain, Why art thou wroth? and why is thy countenance fallen?"

These words are applied to Cain, for a further conviction of his state to be miserable. "Why art thou wroth?" Is it because I have not accepted thy offering? This is without ground, thy person is yet an abomination to me: Must I be made by thy gift, which is polluted, for and by thy person, to justify thee as righteous? Thou hast not yet done well. Wherefore, Cain had no cause to be wroth; for God rejected only that which was sinful, as was both his person, and gift for the sake thereof. Neither had he grounds to lift up his looks on high, when he came to offer his sacrifice; because he came not as a man in a justified state. But "there is a generation that are pure in their own eyes, and yet are not washed from their filthiness. There is a generation, O how lofty are their eyes! and their eyelids are lifted up." (Prov. xxx. 12, 13.) Such an one, or the father of these, was Cain; he counted himself clean, and yet was not washed; he lifted up his looks on high, before he was changed from his iniquity.

Verse 7. "If thou doest well, shalt thou not be accepted? and if thou doest not well, sin lieth at the door. And unto thee shall be his desire, and thou shalt rule over him."

"If thou doest well:" Why, is not worshipping of God, well-doing? It may, and may not, even as the person that worships is found. If he be found righteous at his coming to worship, and if he worship according to rule, then he does well, then he is accepted of God; but if he be not found righteous before, be you sure he cannot do well, let the matter with which he worshippeth be wrong or right. Can a man "bring a clean thing out of an unclean?" (Job xiv. 4.) Let Cain be clean, and his offering will be clean, because brought to God in a vessel that is clean; but if Cain be unclean, all the holy things he toucheth, or layeth up in his skirt, it is made unclean by the uncleanness of his person: "And so is this nation before me, saith God, and so is every work of their hands, and that which they offer there is unclean." (Hag. ii. 14.)

Men therefore ought to distinguish between doing and well-doing, even in the worship of God. All that worship do not do well, though the matter of worship be good in itself. Cain's offering you find not blamed, as if it had been of a superstitious complexion; but he came not aright to worship. Why? he came not as one made righteous before. Wherefore, as I have already touched, the difference that lay between the gifts of Abel and Cain, was not in the gifts themselves, but the qualifica-

Vanderwerf.   Edwards.

DEATH OF ABEL.

tions of the persons. Abel's faith, and Cain's works, made God approve and reject the offering: "By faith Abel offered to God a more excellent sacrifice than Cain." (Heb. xi. 4.) For, as I said, Faith in Christ, as promised to come, made him righteous, because thereby he obtained "the righteousness of God;" for so was Christ in himself, and so to be to him that by faith received and accepted of him: This, I say, Abel did; wherefore now he is righteous or just before God. This being so, his offering is found to be an offering of Abel the just, and is here said to obtain witness even of God, that he was righteous, because he accepted his gift.

Wherefore, he that does well must first be good: He that doth righteousness must first be righteous, (1 John iii. 7:) He is righteous first; he is righteous even as Christ is righteous, because Christ is the righteousness of such a person. And so on the contrary; the reason why some men's good deeds are accursed of God, it is because in truth, and according to the law, the Lord finds sin in them; which sins he cannot pardon, because he finds them not in Christ. Thus they being evil for want of the righteousness of the Son of God, they worship God as sinners, according to that of the apostle, Because they are not good, therefore they do not good, no, not one of them. (Rom. iii. 12.)

The way therefore to do well, it is first to receive the mercy of God in Christ; which act of thine will be more pleasing to the Divine Majesty, than all whole burnt offerings and sacrifices: "I will have mercy," saith God, "I will have mercy, and not sacrifice." (Matt. ix. 13; xii. 7.) This Cain did not understand, therefore he goes to God in his sins, and without faith in the mercy of God through Christ, he offereth his sacrifice. Wherefore because his sacrifice could not take away his sin, therefore it still abode upon him.

But "if thou doest not well, sin lieth at the door." This reasoning therefore was much to Cain's condition; he would be wroth, because God did not accept his offering, and yet he did not well. Now, if he had done well, God, by receiving of his brother's sacrifice, shows, he would have accepted him: for this is evident, they were both alike by nature; their offerings also were in themselves one as holy as the other. How then comes it to pass that both were not accepted, they both offered to God? Why, Abel only sacrificed well, because he first by faith in Christ was righteous: this because Cain wanted, sin abideth at his door.

"And to thee shall be his desire, and thou shalt rule over him." That is, if sin abideth at thy door still, to thee shall be his desire; he shall love, pity, pray for thee, and endeavour thy conversion; but thou shalt be lord over him, and shalt put thy yoke upon his neck. This was Jacob's portion also; for after Esau had got head, he broke Jacob's yoke from off his neck, and reigned by

nineteen or twenty dukes and princes, before there was any king in Israel.

It is the lot of Cain's brood, to be lords and rulers first, while Abel and his generation have their necks under persecution; yet while they lord it, and thus tyrannically afflict and persecute, our very desire is towards them, wishing their salvation. While they curse, we bless; and while they persecute, we pray.

Verse 8. "And Cain talked with Abel his brother: and it came to pass, when they were in the field, that Cain rose up against Abel his brother, and slew him."

When Cain saw that by God's judgment Abel was the better worshipper, and that himself must by no means be admitted for well-doing, his heart began to be more obdurate and hard, and to grow into that height of desperateness, as to endeavour the extirpating of all true religion out of the world; which it seems he did, by killing his brother, mightily accomplish, until the days of Enos; for then began men again to call upon the name of the Lord. (Gen. iv. 27.)

Hence see the spite of the children of hell against God: They have slain thy prophets, and digged down thine altars, (1 Kings xix. 10:) if they may have their wills, God must be content with their religion, or none; other they will not endure should have show within their reach, but with Cain, will rather kill their brother; or with the Pharisees, kill their Lord; and with the evil kings of old, will rather kill their sons and subjects. That the truth, I say, may fall to the ground, and their own inventions stand for acceptable sacrifices, they will not only envy, but endeavour to invalidate all the true worship and worshippers of God in the world; the which if they cannot without blood accomplish, they will slay and kill till their cruelty hath destroyed many ten thousands, even as Cain, who slew his brother Abel.

And Cain talked with his brother. He had not a law whereby to arraign him, but malice enough, and a tongue to set all on fire, of which no doubt, but the goodly replies of his brother, was easily blown up into choler and madness, the end of which was the blood of his brother.

"And Cain talked with Abel," &c. To wit, about the goodness and truth of his religion. For that the New Testament seems to import, he slew him because his works were righteous; (1 John iii. 12;) which Abel, no doubt, had justified before his brother, even then when he most set himself to oppose him. Besides this, the connection of the relation importeth, he talketh with him, he slew him; he talked with him and slew him, purely upon a religious account, because his works were righteous.

Hence note, That when wicked men have the head in the world, professors had need be resolved to hazard the worst, before they do enter debate with ungodly men about the things that pertain to the kingdom of God. For behold here, words did not end in words, but from words came blows, and from blows blood. The counsel therefore is, That you sit down first, and count up the cost, (Luke xiii. 28,) before ye talk with Cain of religion: "They make a man an offender for a word, and lay a snare for him that reproveth in the gate, and turn aside the just for a thing of nought." (Isa. xxix. 21.)

"And Cain talked with Abel his brother." With Abel his only brother, who also was a third part of the world. But tyrants matter nothing, neither nearness of kin, nor how much they destroy: "The brother shall betray the brother to death," &c.

"And it came to pass when they were in the field, that Cain rose up against Abel his brother and slew him." When they were in the field, from home, out of the sight, and far from the help of his father. Subtle persecutors love not to bite, till they can make their teeth to meet; for which they observe their time and place. Joseph was also hated of his brethren, but they durst not meddle till they found him in the field. (Gen. xxxvii. 15.) Here it is also that the holy virgin falleth: "He found her in the field,—and there was none to save her." (Deut. xxii. 27.)

Hence observe again, That be the danger never so imminent, and the advantage of the adversary never so great, the sincere professor of the truth stands his ground against wind and weather. Bloody Cain daunteth not holy Abel; no, though now he have his advantage of him.

"He rose up against Abel his brother, and slew him." "And wherefore slew he him? Because his own works were evil," &c. (1 John iii. 12.) It is therefore hence to be observed, That it is a sign of an evil way, be it covered with the name of the worship of God, when it cannot stand without the shedding of innocent blood. "Wherefore slew he him? Because his own works were evil." Had his works been good, they had been accepted of God: he had also had the joy thereof in his conscience, as doubtless Abel had; which joy and peace would have produced love and pity to his brother, as it was with his brother towards him; but his works being evil, they minister to him no heavenly joy, neither do they beget in him love to his brother; but contrariwise, his heart fills his eye with evil also; which again provoketh (while it beholdeth the godly carriage of Abel) the heart to more desperate resolutions, even to set upon him with all his might, and to cut him off from the earth. Thus the goodness of God's people provoketh to envy the wicked heart of the hypocrite. As it was betwixt Saul and David; for after Saul had seen that God had rejected him for his wickedness, the more he hated the goodness of David: And Saul saw and knew that the Lord was with David, (1 Sam. xii.)—"And Saul was yet the more afraid of David, and Saul became David's enemy continually." (ver. 29.)

Verse 9. "And the Lord said unto Cain, Where is Abel thy brother? And he said, I know not: Am I my brother's keeper?"

Cain thought it had been no more but to kill his brother, and his intentions and desires must needs be accomplished, and that himself should then be the only man: "Come, let us kill him, and the inheritance shall be ours." (Mark xii. 7.) But stay, Abel was beloved of his God, who had also justified his offering, and accepted it as a service more excellent than his brother's! So then, because the quarrel arose between them upon this very account, therefore Abel's God doth reckon himself as engaged (seeing he is not) to take up his servant's cause himself.

"And the Lord God said unto Cain, Where is Abel thy brother?" A question not grounded on uncertainity, but proposed as a beginning of further reasoning; and also to make way to this wicked wretch, to discover the desperate wickedness of his bloody heart the more. For questions that stand at first afar off, do draw out more of the heart of another: and also do minister more occasion for matter, than if they had been placed more near to the matter.

"Where is Abel?" God missed the acceptable sacrifices of Abel; Abel was dead, and his sacrifices ceased, which had wont to be savoury in the nostrils of God. Cain could not supply them; his sacrifices were deficient, they were not of faith. Hence note, that if tyrants should have their will, even to destroying of all the remnant of God, their sacrifices and worship would be yet before God as abominable as they were before.

"And the Lord said unto Cain, Where is Abel?" O dreadful question? the beginning of Cain's hell, for now God entereth into judgment with him. Wherefore, however this wretch endeavoured at first to stifle and choke his conscience, yet this was to him the arrow of death: Abel crieth, but his brother would not hear him while alive, and now being dead God hears the cry of his blood. "When he maketh inquisition for blood, he remembereth them: he forgetteth not the cry of the humble." (Ps. ix. 12.) Blood that is shed for the sake of God's word, shall not be forgotten or disregarded of God: "Precious in his sight is the death of his saints." (Ps. cxiv. 15.) "And precious shall their blood be in his sight." (Ps. lxxii. 14.)

"Where is Abel thy brother?" This word, thy brother, must not be left out, because it doth greatly aggravate his wickedness. He slew his brother; which horrid act the very law and bond of nature forbiddeth. But when a man is given up of God, it is neither this nor another relation that will bind his hands, or make him keep within the bounds of any law. Judas will seek his master's, and Absalom his father's blood. "Where is Abel thy brother?"

"And he said, I know not." He knew full well what he had done, and that by his hands his brother's blood was fallen to the ground, but now being called into question for the same, he endeavoureth to plead ignorance before God : " I know not." When men have once begun to sin, they know not where they shall end ; he slew his brother, and endeavours to cover his fact with a lie. David also little thought his act of adultery would have led him to have spilt the blood of Uriah, and afterwards to have covered all with dissembling lips and a lying tongue.

" I know not : Am I my brother's keeper ? "

This is the way of all ungodly men, they will not abide that guilt should be fastened. Sin they love, and the lusts and delights thereof, but to count for it they cannot abide ; they will put it off with excuses, or denials : even like Saul, who though he had spared the cattle and Agag contrary to the command of God, yet would needs bear Samuel down, that he had kept, yea performed, the commandment of the Lord. But they are denials to no boot, and excuses that will not profit, that are made to hide the sin of the soul from the sight and judgment of God. Lies and falsehood will here do nothing.

Verse 10. "And he said, What hast thou done ? the voice of thy brother's blood crieth unto me from the ground."

Poor Cain, thy feeble shifts help thee nothing, thy excuses are drowned by the cries of the blood which thou hast shed.

" What hast thou done ? " the blood of thy brother cries. Beware, persecutors, you think that when you have slain the godly, you are then rid of them ; but you are far wide, their blood which you have shed, cries in the ears of God against you. O the cries of blood are strong cries, they are cries that reach to heaven ; yea, they are cries that have a continual voice, and that never cease to make a noise, until they have procured vengeance from the hands of the Lord of sabbath. And therefore this is the word of the Lord against all those that are for the practice of Cain : "As I live, saith the Lord God, I will prepare thee unto blood and blood shall pursue thee : sith thou hast not hated blood, (that is, hated to shed it,) blood shall pursue thee." (Ezek. xxx. 6.)

" The voice of thy brother's blood cries unto me." The apostle makes this voice of the blood of Abel, a type of the voice of the justice of the law, and so extends it further than merely to the act of murder ; intimating that he sheds blood, that breaks any of the commands of God, (and indeed so he doth, he layeth wait for his own blood, and privily lurketh for his own life.) (Prov. i. 18.) Wherefore the apostle compareth the blood of Abel and the blood of Christ together ; but so as by the rule of contraries, making betwixt them a contrary voice, even as there is between a broken command and a promise of grace, the one calling for vengeance and damnation ; the other calling for forgiveness and salvation ; " the blood of sprinkling, that speaketh better things than the

blood of Abel," (Heb. xii. 24 ;) that is, it calls to God to forgive the sinner : but Abel's blood, of the breach of the law, that cries damn them, damn them. Christ also sets his own blood in opposition to the blood of all that was shed before him ; concluding that the proper voice of all blood of the godly, is to call for vengeance on the persecutors, even from the blood of Abel to the blood of Zecharias, that was slain between the temple and the altar. (Matt. xxiii. 35.) And let me here take leave to propound my private thoughts : Namely, that the Zecharias that here is mentioned, might not be he that we find in the book of Chronicles ; (2 Chron. xxiii. 20 ;) but one of that name that lived in the days of Christ, possibly John Baptist's father, or some other holy man. My reasons for this conjecture, are, 1. Because the murderers are convict by Christ himself : Zecharias, " whom ye slew between the temple and the altar." 2. Because Christ makes a stop at the blood of Zecharias, not at the blood of John the Baptist : wherefore, if the person here mentioned were not murdered after, but before John the Baptist, then Christ seems to excuse them for killing his servant John ; for the judgment stops at the including of the guilt of the blood of Zecharias. 3. I think such a thing, because the voice of all holy blood that hath been shed before the law by the adversary, excepting only the blood of Jesus, must needs be included here ; the proper voice of his, only being to plead for mercy to the murderers. However, the voice of blood is a very killing voice, and will one day speak with such thunder and terror in the consciences of all the brood of Cain, that their pain and burthen will be for ever insupportable.

Verse 11. "And now art thou cursed from the earth, which hath opened her mouth to receive thy brother's blood from thy hand."

Here begins the sentence of God against this bloody man ; a sentence fearful and terrible, for it containeth a removing of him from all the privileges of grace and mercy, and a binding of him over to the punishment and pains of the damned.

" And now art thou cursed from the earth." Peace on earth, is one branch of that blessed tidings that was brought into the world, at the coming of the Messias. Again, before Christ was come in the flesh, it is said, He rejoiced " in the habitable part of his earth." (Prov. viii. 31.) Wherefore, by the earth in this place, I understand the state that the men are in, to whom, by the mind of God, the gospel and grace of God is to be tendered. Now, whether it respect the state of man by nature, or the state of those that are saints, from both these privileges Cain is separate, as are all whom the Lord has utterly rejected. Not but that yet they may live long in the world, but God hath cut them off from the earth, and all the gospel privileges therein, and set them in the condition of devils ; so that as to grace and mercy they are separate therefrom, and stand as men, though alive, bound over to eternal judgment. And as to their lives, it matters not how long they live, there is " no sacrifice for their sins, but a certain fearful looking for of judgment and fiery indignation, which shall devour the adversaries." (Heb. x. 26, 27.) So that I say, as the devils be bound in hell, so such lie bound in earth ; bound I say in the chains of darkness, and their own obstinate heart, over to the day of wrath and revelation of the righteous judgment of God. Cain therefore by these words is denied the blessing of future means of grace, and stands bound over to answer for his brother's blood, which the ground had received from his cruel hand.

Verse 12. "When thou tillest the ground, it shall not henceforth yield unto thee her strength : a fugitive and a vagabond shalt thou be in the earth."

This is a branch, or the fruits of this wilful murder. Indeed, sins carry in them not only a curse with respect to eternity, but are also the cause of all the miseries of this life. "God turneth a fruitful hand into barrenness, for the wickedness of them that dwell therein." (Ps. cvii. 34.)

"When thou tillest the ground." Sin committed doth not always exclude the sinner from an enjoyment of God's mercies, but yet if unrepented of, bringeth a curse upon them. "I will curse," saith God, "your blessings : yea, I have cursed them already, because ye do not lay it to heart." (Mal. ii. 2.) This also is the reason that the table of some is made their snare, their trap, a stumbling-block and a recompence unto them ; (Rom. xi. 9 ;) men ought not therefore to judge of the goodness of their state, by their enjoyment of God's creatures, but rather should tremble while they enjoy them, lest for sin they should become accursed to them, as were the enjoyments of this wicked man.

"A fugitive and a vagabond shalt thou be in the earth." The meaning is, thou shalt not have rest in the world, but shalt be continually possessed with a guilty conscience, which shall make thy condition restless and void of comfort. For the man that indeed is linked in the chains of guilt and damnation, as Cain here was, he cannot rest, but (as we say) fudge up and down from place to place, because his burthen is insupportable. As David said, " Let their eyes be darkened that they see not, and make their loins continually to shake." (Ps. lxix. 23.) A continual shaking and restlessness doth therefore possess such persons as are given up of God, and swallowed up of guilt.

"A fugitive and vagabond shalt thou be in the earth." Some men certainly know, even while they are in this world, their state to be most miserable, and damnable, as Cain, Saul, and Judas did; which knowledge, as I have hinted, puts them besides the very course of other carnal men ; who while they behold them at quiet under their enjoyments, these cannot but wonder, fear, and be amazed with the deep cogitations which will abide upon them, of their certain misery and everlasting perdition.

Verse 13. "And Cain said unto the Lord, My punishment is greater than I can bear." Or as the margin hath it, "My sin is greater than that it may be forgiven." And both readings are true : for however some men please themselves in lessening sin, and the punishment thereof, yet a burdened conscience judgeth otherwise. And if Cain failed in either, it was in that he counted his sin (if he did so) beyond the reach of God's mercy. But again, when men persecute the worship and people of God, as Cain did his blessed and religious brother, even of spite, and because he envied the goodness of his brother's work, I question whether it be lawful for a minister to urge to such the promise of grace and forgiveness ; and also whether it be the mind of God such persons should hope therein. He that sins the sin unto death, is not to be prayed for, (1 John v. 16,) but contrariwise he is to be taken from God's altar that he may die. (Exod. xxi. 14.) This was Cain's case, and now he knew it; therefore as one excluded of God from his mercy and all the means thereof, he breaks out with roaring under the intolerable burden of the judgment of God upon him, concluding his punishment at present "greater than he could bear," and that yet his sin should remain unpardonable for ever : As saith our Lord Jesus Christ, He hath neither forgiveness here nor in the world to come. (Matt. xii. 32.)

Verse 14. " Behold, thou hast driven me out this day from the face of the earth, and from thy face shall I be hid : And I shall be a fugitive and a vagabond in the earth, and it shall come to pass that every one that findeth me, shall slay me."

By these words is confirmed what was said before, to wit, to be cursed from the earth, was to be separated from the privileges of the gospel. For Cain was not now to die, neither was he driven into any den or cave ; yet driven out from the face of the earth, that is, as I have said, he was excluded from a share in those special mercies that by the gospel were still offered by grace to the others that inhabited the world : The mercies, I say, that are offered by the gospel, as namely, The mercy of eternal life : for as to the blessings of this world, he had yet a notable share thereof. Besides, he groaneth under this judgment, as an unsupportable curse. " Thou hast driven me out this day from the face of the earth." And indeed, if we take it according as I have laid it down, it is a curse that would break the whole world to pieces ; for he that is denied a share in the grace that is now offered, must needs be denied a portion in God's kingdom. And this Cain saw ; wherefore he adds in the process of his complaint, " And from thy face shall I be hid :" " I shall never come into thy kingdom, I shall never see thy face in heaven." This is therefore the highest of all complaints ; namely, for a man from a certain conviction that his condition must without fail be damnable, to condole and bemoan his forlorn condition.

" Thou hast driven me out." O! when God shall bind one over for his sin, to eternal judgment, who then can release him? This was Cain's state, God had bound him over. The blood of his brother was to rest upon him and not to be purged with sacrifices for ever.

" Thou hast driven me out THIS DAY." He knew by the sentence that fell from heaven upon him, even from that very day that he was made companion of, and an associate with devils. This day, or for this day's work, I am made an inhabitant of the pit with the devil and his angels. Hence note, That God doth sometimes smite the reprobate so apparently, that himself from that day may make a certain judgment of the certainty of his damnation. Thus did Balaam: " I shall see him, but not now; I shall behold him, but not nigh." (Numb. xxiv. 17.) Where, by " now," he respects the time of grace; and by " nigh," the time or day of judgment: As who should say, " I, for my sorceries, and wicked divinations, am excluded a portion in the day of grace, and therefore shall not see the Saviour 'now:' I am also rejected, as to a portion in the blessed world to come: and therefore when he judgeth, I shall not see him 'nigh:' Nigh, as a friend, as a favour to my soul." I doubt this is the condition of many now alive, who for their perfidiousness and treachery to Christ, and his church, have already received, even " in themselves, that recompence of their error which was meet." (Rom. i. 27.)

Ishmael also, in the day he laughed at Isaac, and Esau in the day he sold his birthright, might have gathered, the one from God's concurring with the judgment of Sarah, the other, from his father's adhering to his brother; his adhering, I say, in a prophetic spirit; that from thenceforth they both were excluded grace and glory, as the apostle by the Holy Ghost afterwards doth. (Heb. xii. 16, 17.)

" And from thy face shall I be hid." By face here, we are to understand God's favour, and blessed presence, which is enjoyed by the saints both here, and in the world to come: Both which this wicked man, for the murdering of his brother, and his envy to the truth, now knew himself excluded from.

" From thy face shall I be hid." The pit of hell to which the damned go, besides the torment that they met with there, is such a region of darkness, and at such a distance from the heavens, and the glorious comfortable presence of God, that those that shall be found the proper subjects of it, shall for ever be estranged from one glimpse of him: besides, sin shall bind all their faces in secret, and so confound them with horror, shame, and guilt, that they shall not be able from thenceforth for ever, so much as once to think of God with comfort.

" From thy face." As it were all the glory of heaven, it lieth in beholding the face of God: A thing the ungodly little think of; yet the men that have received in themselves already the sentence of eternal damnation, they know it after a wonderful rate; and the thoughts of the loss of his face and presence, doth, do what they can, as much torment them, as the thoughts of all the misery they are like to meet withal besides.

" And a fugitive and a vagabond shall I be in the earth." Even from the present frame of his spirit, Now, having received the sentence, he knew, the judgment past being unrevokable, how it would be with him all his life long; that he should spend his days in trouble and guilt, rolling under the justice of God, being always a terror and burthen to himself, to the day he was to be cut off from the earth, that he might go to the place appointed for him.

" And it shall come to pass, that every one that findeth me shall slay me." Guilt is a strange thing, it makes a man think that every one that seeth him, hath knowledge of his iniquity; it also bringeth such a faintness into the heart, (Lev. xxvi. 36,) that the sound of a shaken leaf doth chase such persons. And above all things, the cries of blood are most fearful in the conscience; the cries of the blood of the poor innocents, which the seed of Cain hath shed on the face of the earth. (Jer. iii. 34; xix. 4.) Thus far of Cain's complaint.

Verse 15. " And the Lord said unto him, Therefore, whosoever slayeth Cain, vengeance shall be taken on him sevenfold. And the Lord set a mark upon Cain, lest any finding him should kill him."

By these words, the judgment is confirmed, which Cain, in the verse before, so mournfully pronounced against his own soul. As if the Lord said, " Cain, thy judgment is as thou hast said, I have driven thee out this day from a share in my special favour; and when thy life is ended, thou shalt be hid from my face, and blessed presence for ever; and seeing it is thus, therefore I will not suffer that thou die before thy time: Alas, thy glass will be quickly run! Besides, thy days, while thou art here, will sufficiently be filled with vexation and distress; for thou shalt always carry in thy conscience the cries of innocent blood, and the fear of the wrath of God: I have said it, and will perform it: I am not a man, that I should repent: So that thus shall thy judgment be: Therefore, he that killeth Cain, I will take vengeance on him."

Hence note, That none need to add to the sorrows of the persecutors. They above all men are prepared unto wrath: " Let them alone," saith Christ, " they will quickly fall into the ditch." Besides, God hath taken the revengement of the blood of his servants into his own hand, and will execute his wrath himself. Therefore he saith to his saints (as to this), " Dearly beloved, avenge not yourselves, but rather give place unto wrath; for it is written, Vengeance is mine; I will repay, saith the Lord." (Rom. xii. 19.) And the reason is, because the quarrel is in special between the prosecutor and God himself. For we are not hated because we are men, nor because we are men of evil and debauched lives; but because we are religious; because we stand to maintain the truth of God. Therefore no man must here intercept, but must leave the enemy in the hand of that God he hath slighted and condemned. This made Moses that he meddled not with Korah and his company, but left them to that new thing which the Lord himself would do unto them, because they had condemned the ordinance of God. (Numb. xvi. 23—35.) This made David also that he meddled not with Saul, but left him to the vengeance of God, though he had opportunity to have destroyed him. (1 Sam. xxiv.) Let us learn, therefore, to be quiet and patient under the hand of wicked and bloodthirsty men. Let us fall before them like holy Abel; it is and will be grief enough to them, that when we are dead, our blood will cry from the ground against them.

" Therefore, he that killeth Cain, vengeance shall be taken," &c. He now that shall, after this admonition, plead for religious blood with the sword, vengeance shall be taken on him, because he giveth not place to the wrath of God, but intercepts with his own, which "worketh not the righteousness of God." (James i. 20.) Say, therefore, with David, when you are vexed with the persecutor, Mine hand shall not be upon him; but " as the Lord liveth, the Lord shall smite him; or, his day shall come to die; or, he shall descend in battle, and perish." (1 Sam. xxiv. 10.)

" Vengeance shall be taken on him sevenfold." It would not be hard to show how little they have prevailed, who have taken upon them to take vengeance for the blood of saints, on them that have been the spillers of it. But my business here is brevity, therefore I shall not launch into that deep, only shall say to such as shall attempt it hereafter, "Put up again thy sword into his place: for all they that take the sword shall perish with the sword!" (Matt. xxvi. 52;) and here " is the patience and faith of the saints." (Rev. xiii. 10.) Let Cain and God alone, and do you mind faith and patience; suffer with Abel, until your righteous blood be spilt; even the work of persecutors is, for the present, punishment enough; the fruits thereof being the provoking God to jealousy, a denying of them the knowledge of the way of life, and a binding of them over to the pains and punishment of hell.

"And the Lord set a mark upon Cain." What the opinion of others is about this mark, I know not; to me it seems like those in Timothy, who had " their conscience seared with an hot iron." (1 Tim. iv. 2.) Which words are an allusion to the way of the magistrates in their dealing with rogues and felons; who, that they may be known to all, are either in the hand, shoulder, or cheek branded with a hot iron. So Cain was marked of God or a reprobate, for one that had murdered a

righteous man, even of envy to the goodness of his work: But the mark (as it was on those in Timothy) was not on any outward or visible part of his body, but (as there the apostle expresseth it) even upon his very conscience; his conscience then had received the fire-mark of the wrath and displeasure of God, which (as a burning iron doth to the flesh) had left such a deep impression therein, that it abode as a scar or brand upon him, in token that good would for ever after hold him for a fugitive rogue or vagabond.

"And the Lord set a mark upon Cain, lest any finding him should kill him." For though the mark was branded with burning upon his conscience, and so inward and invisible; yet the effects of this hot iron might be visible, and seen of all: the effects, I say, which were, or might be, his restlessness in every place, his dejectedness, the sudden and fearful pangs and agonies of his mind, which might break out into dolorous and amazing complaints; besides, his timorous carriage before all he met, lest they should kill him, gave all to understand that God had with a vengeance branded him. And, indeed, this was such a mark as was amazing to all that beheld him, and did ten times more make them afraid of spilling blood, than if any visible mark had been set upon him; for by his trouble and distress of mind, they saw, what was the guilt of blood: and by his continual fear and trembling under the judgment of God, what it was to be in fear of, nay, to have the first fruits of everlasting damnation. Thus, therefore, God reserved Cain to the judgment which he had appointed for him.

Verse 16. " And Cain went out from the presence of the Lord, and dwelt in the land of Nod, on the east of Eden."

The right carriage of a reprobate, and the infallible fruits of final desperation. For a man that hath received in his mind the stroke of the judgment of God, and that is denied all means of saving and sanctifying grace (as the great transgressors are), the presence of God is to such most dreadful; whether we understand the knowledge of him as he is in himself, or as he discovereth himself in his church; for the thought of his being, and eternal majesty, keeps the wound open, and makes terror and guilt revive. To such it would be the best of news, to hear that the Godhead doth cease to be, or that themselves were high above him: But that they are in the hand of the living God, this is the dreadful and fearful thought.

" And Cain went out from the presence of the Lord." These words may be taken many ways.

1. That he separated himself from the church (the place of God's presence) which then consisted of his father and mother, and of those other children they had. And this appears by the text, " He went out from the presence of the Lord, and dwelt in the land of Nod."

2. A man goes out from the presence of God, when he withdraws his thoughts from holy meditations, and employeth the strength of his mind about the things of this life. And thus he also did; he went into the land of Nod, and there fell to building a city, and to recreate himself with the pleasures of the flesh what he might.

3. A man goes out from the presence of God, when he throweth up the worship and way of God; and this he did in departing from the church.

4. Besides, his going out from the presence of the Lord, implieth, that he hardened his heart against him, that he set his spirit against him; that he said to God, Depart from me; that he grew an implacable enemy to him, and to every appearance of good in the world.

"And Cain went out from the presence of the Lord." These words may also respect his being thrust out from God, as one anathematized, accursed, or cut off, in effect the same with excommunication. But be it so, the act was extraordinary, being administered by God himself; even as he served Korah and his company, though in kind there was a difference, the one, even Cain, being yet permitted to live for a while in the world; the other being sent down quick into hell; but both, for their villany against the worship and people of God, stand bound over to answer it at the eternal judgment.

Verse 17. "And Cain knew his wife, and she conceived, and bare Enoch: and he builded a city, and called the name of the city after the name of his son Enoch."

Cain's wife was his sister, or near kinswoman; for she sprang from the same loins with himself; because his mother was the "mother of all living." (Gen. iii. 20.)

This wife bare him a son; for whose sake, as it seems, he built the city. Hence note, That men who are shut out of heaven, will yet use some means to be honourable on earth. Cain being accursed of God, yet builds him a city; the renown of which act, that it might not be forgotten, he calleth it after the name of his son. Much like this was that carnal act, of blasted Absalom; because he had no child, he would erect a pillar, which must forsooth be called Absalom's place, after the name of Absalom, to keep his name in remembrance upon earth. (2 Sam. xviii. 18.)

"And he built a city," &c. Note, That it is the design of Satan, and the deceitful heart of man, to labour to quiet a guilty conscience, not by faith in the blood of Christ, but by over-much business in the things of this world.

"And called the name of the city after the name of his son Enoch." Although Cain had a mind to keep up his name with fame in the world, yet he would not venture to dedicate the city to his own name; that would have been too gross; and perhaps the others would have called it, The City of the Murderer; but he called it after the name of his son, his son Enoch; whom he pretended was a man both taught, and dedicate, as it seems his name imports. Hence note again, That men who themselves are accursed of God, will yet put as fair glosses on their actions, as their hypocritical hearts can invent. Who must this city be dedicated to, but to him whom Cain had dedicated and taught. I will not say that in truth he gave him to God, for that his reprobate heart would not suffer; but being given up of God, yet retaining, with Saul, considerations of honour: therefore, as is the custom of ungodly hypocrites, he would put the best show on his ungodly actions.

Thus Saul, when he had received the sentence of the Lord against him; yet, Turn again with me (saith he to Samuel), yet honour me now before the people and before Israel. (1 Sam. xv. 30.) So the money wherewith the high-priests and scribes had bought the life, and obtained the death of Christ; with that they make some show of godliness, in buying with it a piece of ground to bury strangers in. (Matt. xxvii. 6, 7.)

Verse 18. "And unto Enoch was born Irad; and Irad begat Mehujael; and Mehujael begat Methusael; and Methusael begat Lamech."

These are the offspring of Cain; the English of whose names, if the nature and disposition of the persons were according, they might well be called, with abhorrence, the brood of wicked Cain, even the generation whom the Lord had cursed, notwithstanding Enoch was their father. Enoch begat Irad, a wild ass; Irad begat Mehujael, one presumptuous above measure; his name signifies one teaching God. But "Who hath directed the Spirit of the Lord?" (Isa. xl. 13.) Or "Shall any teach God knowledge?" (Job xx. 22.) The son of this man was Methusael, asking death, the true fruit of all such presumptuous ones. "His confidence shall be rooted out of his tabernacle, and it shall bring him to the king of terrors." (Job xviii. 14.) His son was Lamech, one poor, or smitten: the first that, as we read, did break the order of God in the matter of marriage.

Verse 19. "And Lamech took unto him two wives: the name of the one was Adah, and the name of the other Zillah."

This man was the first that brake the first institution of God concerning marriage. He "took unto him two wives." The New Testament says, "Let every man have his own wife." And so said the law in its first institution: therefore plurality of wives first came into practice by the seed of cursed Cain, and for a time was suffered in the world through the hardness of man's heart.

Verses 20, 21. "And Adah bare Jabal: he was the father of such as dwell in tents, and of such as have cattle. And his brother's name was Jubal; he was the father of all such as handle the harp and organ."

Jabal signifies bringing, or budding; Jubal bringing, or fading. So then in these two sons might be showed unto us the world, as it is in its utmost glory: that is, it brings buds, it brings fading: to-day in the field, to-morrow in the oven: "All flesh is grass, and all the goodliness thereof, as the flower of the field. The grass withereth, the flower fadeth, because the Spirit of the Lord bloweth upon it; surely the people is grass." (Isa. xl. 6, 7).

And observe in these, the last was the musical one. Indeed, the spirit of the world, after things have budded, is so far off from remembering that they again must fade; that then it begins its Requiem; then it saith to itself, "Eat, drink, and be merry;" (Luke xii. 19;) then it is for handling the harp and organ.

Verse 22. "And Zillah, she also bare Tubal-Cain, an instructer of every artificer in brass and iron: and the sister of Tubal-Cain was Naamah."

Tubal-Cain, a worldly possession; and Naamah, one that by her name should be beautiful. Lamech his fruit then was, a budding, fading, worldly possession, with a little deceitful vain beauty, for "Favour is deceitful, and beauty is vain: but a woman that feareth the Lord, she shall be praised." (Prov. xxxi. 30.)

Verse 23. "And Lamech said unto his wives, Adah and Zillah, hear my voice; ye wives of Lamech, hearken unto my speech: for I have slain a man to my wounding, and a young man to my hurt."

He that sticks not to exceed in one point, will not fear to transgress in another. He had hardened his heart by breaking the modest and orderly bounds of marriage, and so fitted himself to shed blood, or do any other wickedness.

"Hearken to me, ye wives." Lustful men break their minds to their fleshly companions, sometimes, sooner than to wiser counsellors. Even as Ahab, in the business of the vineyard of Naboth, breaks his mind to that ungodly Jezebel his wife.

"I have slain a man to my wounding." Who, or what a man this murdered person was, therein the word is silent: yet this Lamech being the son of a bloody murderer, it is possible he was some godly man, one of Adam's other children, or of his grandchildren, the son of Seth: for these sons of Cain, and namely this in special, as it seems, took not heed to the mark wherewith God branded Cain; but, like Belshazzar, he hardened his heart, though he knew it, and would turn murderer also. (Dan. v. 17—24.)

"I have slain a man to my wounding." The guilt of blood who can bear? or who can help himself thereby? It is a wounding thing, it is a hurtful thing, he that sheds man's blood wrongfully, cannot establish himself thereby. The Jews thought to have preserved themselves and country by killing Jesus Christ; but this so provoked the justice of God, that for this thing's sake he sent the Gentiles upon them to burn up their city; who when they were come, if stories be true, slew of them eleven hundred thousand; and those of them

that were taken alive, were sold to who would buy them, Thirty a penny. "Ye shed blood," says God, "and shall you possess the land? Ye stand upon your sword, ye work abomination, and ye defile every one his neighbour's wife, and shall ye possess the land?" (Ezek. xxxiii. 25, 26).

Verse 24. "If Cain shall be avenged sevenfold, truly Lamech seventy and sevenfold."

Though wicked men may be willingly ignorant of that part of the judgments of God, that are to premonish them, that they do not that wicked thing for which the judgment was executed; yet if there be anything like favour mixed with the judgment, of that they will take notice, to encourage themselves to evil: even as this ungodly person, he would not be stopped from blood by the judgment of God upon Cain; but rather, as it seems, because the judgment was not speedily executed, his heart was fully set in him to do evil. (Eccles. viii. 11.) Much like that of the Jews, who because Jehoiakim had slain Uriah the prophet, and yet God spared the land; therefore make that an argument to prevail with Zedekiah to kill Jeremiah also. (Jer. xxvi. 20—23.)

"If Cain shall be avenged sevenfold, truly Lamech seventy and sevenfold." Give wicked men leave to judge of themselves, and they will pass a sentence favourable enough. Though Lamech had not pity when he spilt blood; yea, though the judgment of God upon Cain could not hold his murderous hands: yet now he is guilty, let him but make a law in the case, and woe be to him that killeth Lamech: Vengeance shall be taken of him seventyfold and seven. Joab could with pitiless hands spill the blood of more righteous men than himself, not regarding what became of their souls: but when his blood was by vengeance required for the same, then he would take sanctuary at the horns of the altar. (1 Kings ii. 28.) But judgment is not wholly left to men, the Lord is judge himself; before whom both Cain and Lamech, and all their successors, shall be arraigned, and receive just doom, and that never to be reversed.

Verse 25. "And Adam knew his wife again, and she bare a son, and called his name Seth: for God, said she, hath appointed me another seed instead of Abel, whom Cain slew."

Now we have done, for a while, with Cain, and are come again to the church of God. Cain had slain Abel, and, by that means, for a while, had greatly suppressed the flourishing of religion; in which time his own brood began to be mighty upon earth; so increasing, as if religion was put to an end for ever. But behold their disappointment! "Adam knew his wife again," (for Adam's family was then the true church of God;) or take Adam for a type of Christ, and his wife for a type of the church, and then this observation followeth; namely, That so long as Christ and the church hath to do with one another, it is in vain for Cain to think of suppressing religion.

"Adam knew his wife again." If Eve had now been barren, or Adam had died without further issue, then Cain might have carried the day; but behold another seed! a seed to stand in Abel's place: therefore she called his name Seth; that is, Set or Put, as namely, in the room of Abel, to stand up for, and to defend the truth against all the army and power of Cain: As Paul also saith of himself, "I am set (or put) for the defence of the gospel." (Phil. i. 17.) This man therefore, so far as can be gathered, was the first that put check to the outrage of Cain and his company. But mark some observations about him.

1. He was set in the stead or place of Abel; not an inch behind him, but even at the place where his blood was spilt. So that he that will revive lost religion must avow it as God's Abels have done before him: every talker cannot do this. The blood that was shed before his face must not put check to his godly stomach; yea, he must say to religion, as Ruth said once to her mother, "Where thou diest, will I die, and there will I be buried." (Ruth i. 17.) This is the way to revive and to maintain the ways of God, in despite of bloody Cain.

2. This Seth that was set to put check to Cain, did not do it of his own brain, but the hand of God was principal in the work: "God," said she, "hath appointed me another seed to be set in the place of Abel." And indeed it is otherwise in vain, when religion is once suppressed, to think it should ever revive again. Alas! where is the man, if he want God's spirit, that will care for the flourishing state of religion? and that in truth will make the Lord his delight: "This is Zion, whom no man seeketh (for, or seeketh) after." (Jer. xxx. 17.) All men here say, "See to thine own house, David." (1 Kings xii. 16.) But when Seth comes, then the ground is made good again; then a living saint is found to stand and maintain that truth which but now his brother bled for. When James was killed, Peter stands up, &c. (Acts xii. 1—3.) And therefore Seth is said to be another seed, a man of another spirit: one who was principled with a spirit beyond and above the spirit of the world. "Another seed," one that was spirited for God's word, and God's worship, and that would maintain his brother's cause.

3. Observe, that when Seth maintains his brother's lot, you hear no more of the brood of Cain. And indeed, the way to weary out God's enemies, it is to maintain and make good the front against them: "Resist the devil, and he will fly." (James iv. 7.) Now, if the captain, their king Apollion, be made to yield, how can his followers stand their ground? "The dragon, the devil, Satan, he was cast out into the earth, and his angels were cast out with him." (Rev. xii. 9.) But how? It was by fighting: Michael and his angels fought with the dragon, and overcame him by the blood of the Lamb, by the word of their testimony, and by not loving of their lives unto the death. (Rev. xii. 7—12.)

4. Let this, in the last place, serve for persecutors, That when you have cast down many ten thousands, and also the truth to the ground; there is yet a Seth, another seed behind, that God hath appointed to stand in the stead of his brethren, by whom you will certainly be put to flight, and made to cease from oppressing the truth.

Verse 26. "And to Seth, to him also there was born a son; and he called his name Enos: then began men to call upon the name of the Lord."

The Holy Ghost, in recording the birth of Enos, goeth out of his ordinary style, in that he doubleth the mentioning of his father, with respect to the birth of this son. And indeed it is worth the observing; for it staggereth the faith of some, to think that the man that makes good the ground of a murdered brother, should not leave issue behind him: But "to Seth, to him was born a son." Our faithfulness to the truth, shall be no hindrance to the flourishing state of our offspring, take them either for the fleshly or spiritual seed of God's servants, but sons (especially in the latter sense, if we truly stand by the word of God) shall surely be born unto us.

"And to Seth, to him also there was born a son, and he called his name Enos." Enos, a man; not a devil, like Cain, but a man; or, a man that was miserable in this world, for the sake and cause of God; for it seems, as was his father, so was he, even both given up to maintain God's truth, which cannot be done but with great hazard, so long as Cain or his offspring remain. His father, therefore, by his very name, did offer him up to bear all hardships for the name and cause of God: "Behold I send you forth," saith Christ, "as lambs in the midst of wolves." In effect, he called their name Enos, men to be acquainted with grief and miseries: But mark, "Then began men to call upon the name of the Lord."

"Then," when Seth maintained Abel's ground, and when Enos endured all miseries for the same. For indeed this makes spectators believe that religion is more than a fictitious notion: The hardships, miseries, and blood of the saints, will make men, otherwise heedless, consider and ponder their cause aright.

"Then began." For, as I also before have hinted, the outrage of bloody Cain did put, for a time, a stop to the flourishing state of God's worship; which in all probability was not so little as half a hundred years, even till Seth, and the son of Seth, stood up to maintain the same; but "then, then men began (more men than Seth and Enos) to call upon the name of the Lord."

Note again, That all true religion beginneth with fervent prayer: Or thus, That when men begin to be servants to God, they begin it with calling upon him. Thus did Saul, "Behold he prayeth." (Acts ix. 11.) And, "Lord, have mercy upon me," is the first of the groans of a sanctified heart.

The margin hath it, " They began to call themselves by the name of the Lord :" As God saith in another place, " My name is called on them." The disciples were called Christians (nay, the saints are called the anointed ones, and the church is called Christ.) (1 Cor. xii. 12.) But note, That fervent prayer ends in faith and confidence in God. They called themselves by the name; they counted themselves not from a vain and groundless opinion, but through the faith they had in the mercy of God, The saints and holy people of God.

They began to publish themselves, in contradistinction to the offspring of Cain, the holy people of God, wherefore, a separation from the wicked began betimes; the one going by the name of "the sons of God;" the other, by the sons and "daughters of men." Then began men to call upon the name of the Lord.

CHAPTER V.

Verse 1. " This is the book of the generations of Adam. In the day that God created man, in the likeness of God made he him."

The Holy Ghost having thus largely treated of Cain and his offspring, and of the head made against him by Seth and Enos, and of the good success that followed, he now comes to treat of the church in particular, and of the flourishing state of the same.

" This is the book." The Holy Ghost cuts off the genealogy of Cain, accounting him none of the race of the church, although before he was within the pale thereof. John observing this, calls him, a child of that " wicked one," (John iii. 12,) as our Lord also accounted Judas. Wherefore, he here begins his book again, that this wicked race might be quite excluded : " Let them be blotted out of the book of the living, and not written with the righteous." (Ps. lxix. 28.)

" In the day that God created man, in the likeness of God made he him." Although by this new beginning the Holy Ghost excludeth Cain, yet he fetched the genealogy of the church from the day that man was created; intimating that God, in the very act of creation, had a special intention to plant him a church in the world; and therefore, even before sin was in the world, the image of God was upon man, as a token of his special respect, and of the great delight that he intended to take in that creature above all that he had made.

Verse 2. " Male and female created he them; and blessed them, and called their name Adam, in the day when they were created."

When Adam was created, the Lord created two in one : So when Christ, the head of the church, was chosen, the church was also chosen in him.

" And blessed them." With the blessing of generation : A type of the blessing of regeneration that was to be by Christ in the church, according to that which is written, " So shall thy seed be."

" And called their name Adam, in the day that they were created :" So that in the man the woman is included; " Neither is the man without the woman, nor the woman without the man in the Lord." (1 Cor. xi. 11.) For the Holy Ghost, in the work of the new creation, of which this creation was a type, counteth not by male and female, but " ye are all one in Christ Jesus." (Gal. iii. 28.) Wherefore, women are not to be excluded out of the means of salvation; nay, they have, if they believe, a special right to all the promises of grace that God hath made to his saints in all ages : Yea, she shall be saved, though she bear children, if she continue in the faith, and charity, and holiness with sobriety. (1 Tim. ii. 15.)

Verse 3. " And Adam lived an hundred and thirty years, and begat a son in his own likeness, after his image; and called his name Seth."

Here also by the book of Chronicles, the Holy Ghost carrieth away the genealogy, because Abel had no children, saying " Adam, Sheth," &c. (1 Chron. i. 1.)

" An hundred and thirty years." Behold the rage of hell! for until Seth stood in Abel's place, religion was greatly hindered, and that was after the world had stood an hundred and thirty years. Indeed, Abel, while he had his breath, did hold it up in the world; but Cain, who was of that " wicked one," smote him and religion both to the ground.

" And begat a son in his own likeness." " Who can bring a clean thing out of an unclean? not one." (Job xiv. 4.) If the father be polluted with the inward filth of sin, the son must needs be like him : " I was shapen in iniquity," said David, " and in sin did my mother conceive me." (Ps. li. 5.) Seth then was no better than we by nature, but came into the world in the blood of his mother's filth : " What is man that he should be clean? and he which is born of a woman, that he should be righteous ?" (Job xv. 14.)

This therefore should teach us not to count of our election, and of our effectual calling, but by the word of God. Seth by nature was a sinful man, and yet the chosen servant of God; the first that took up God's quarrel after the death of blessed Abel.

This should also help us to hold up the bucklers against the kingdom of the devil and hell. Seth was subject to like infirmities with us, and yet he got ground of the children of iniquity. I know a sense of our own infirmities is apt to weaken our hand in so mighty an undertaking, but it should not: Although we be like old Adam by nature, yet God is able to make us stand.

Verse 4. " And the days of Adam, after he had begotten Seth, were eight hundred years: and he begat sons and daughters."

Adam therefore, as a type of Christ, reigned in

the church almost a thousand years. The world therefore beginning thus, doth show us how it will end; namely, by the reign of the second Adam, as it began with the reign of the first.

These long-lived men therefore show us the glory that the church shall have in the latter day, even in the seventh thousand years of the world, that sabbath when Christ shall set up his kingdom on earth, according to that which is written, "They lived and reigned with Christ a thousand years." (Rev. xx. 4.) They:—Who? The church of God, according also as it was with Adam. Therefore they are said by John to be holy, as well as blessed : "Blessed and holy is he that hath part in the first resurrection ; on such the second death hath no power—but they shall be priests of God, and of Christ, and shall reign with him a thousand years." (Rev. xx. 6.) In all which time the wicked in the world shall forbear to persecute, as did also the brood of wicked Cain in the days of Adam, Seth, &c. Hence therefore we find in the first place the dragon chained for these thousand years.

Verse 5. "And all the days that Adam lived were nine hundred and thirty years: and he died."

Adam therefore lived to see the translation of Enoch : in whose translation a conquest was got over all the enemies of his soul and body. So Christ shall reign in and among his saints till all his enemies be destroyed. "The last enemy that shall be destroyed is death;" (1 Cor. xv. 26;) which shall be swallowed up when the members of that glorious head have "put on incorruption," and their mortal shall have "put on immortality." Adam's reigning therefore until Enoch's translation, looks like a prophecy of the perfection of Christ's kingdom : For he shall reign till he hath "delivered up the kingdom to God, even the Father." (1 Cor. xv. 24.) As Adam, till his Enoch was translated and took up to God.

Verse 6. "And Seth lived an hundred and five years, and begat Enos."

Seth therefore stood by the truth of God, a long time, without much help or encouragement from man ; which was a great trial to his spirit, and proof of the truth of his faith, and tended much to the perfection of his patience. Somewhat like this was that of Paul, who had no man stood with him when he stood before Nero.

Seth was set in the stead of Abel, to keep the gap against the children of hell ; which, by the grace of God, he faithfully did, even till Enos was sent to his aid and assistance.

Seth therefore was the forlorn hope of the church in those days : so set of God to put check to the enemy, until the church was increased, and more able to defend herself from the outrage.

This therefore should teach the saints of God, especially those that are sent before, against the offspring of Cain, to stand their ground, and not to shrink like Saul, till God shall send others to take part with them. (1 Sam. x. 8 ; xiii. 8—14.)

Thus David stood, as it were, by himself, against the wicked that was in his day ; which made him cry, "Who will rise up for me against the evildoers? or who will stand up for me against the workers of iniquity?" (Ps. xciv. 16.)

Verse 7. "And Seth lived after he begat Enos eight hundred and seven years, and begat sons and daughters."

Hence also we may gather great encouragement who are set in the front of the army of the Lamb, against the army and regiment of Cain. Seth, saith the spirit, was set in the stead of Abel, there as forlorn, to defend religion. Must he not now be swallowed up? Will the bloodhounds let him escape? Behold, therefore his life must be accounted a wonder! (as was also that of Paul,) to stand eight hundred years against such a murderous crew, and yet to have his breath in his nostrils! Our times are in thy hands, and thou, Lord, "holdest our soul in life." (Ps. lxvi. 9.)

Verse 8. "And all the days of Seth were nine hundred and twelve years : and he died."

His life was therefore eighteen years shorter than that of Adam ; he lived fifty-five years after Enoch, and died six hundred and fourteen years before the flood.

Verse 9. "And Enos lived ninety years, and begat Cainan."

Cainan signifieth a buyer, or owner. Let it be with respect to religion, and then the sense may be, that he had this privilege in religion by the hazard of his father and grandfather's life ; they bought it for him, and made him the owner of it. As Paul saith, He gave not place to the false apostles, "that the truth of the gospel might continue with the Galatians." (Gal. ii. 5.) As Jotham also said to Shechem, "My father fought for you, and adventured his life far, and delivered you out of the hand of Midian," (Judges ix. 17;) namely, that they might still be owners of the inheritance that the Lord had given them. This shows us then, that the fruit of a constant standing to the word of God, is, that the generations yet unborn shall be made the possessors and owners of it.

Verse 10. "And Enos lived after he begat Cainan eight hundred and fifteen years, and begat sons and daughters."

He lived then to see his son enjoy the fruits of his own constancy to the truth, so long a time as eight hundred years, &c., as we hope God's people now may do. It is true, they now do own the truth with hazard, and do hold it up by enduring much misery, according to the rage of wicked men ; but, I say, it is hoped others will reap the fruits of our travels, and that some of us shall live to see it, as Enos lived to see his Cainan possess religion eight hundred years.

Verse 11. "And all the days of Enos were nine hundred and five years, and he died."

He lived then one hundred and fifty-three years after Enoch, and died five hundred and sixteen years before the flood.

Verse 12. "And Cainan lived seventy years, and begat Mahalaleel."

Mahalaleel, signifieth praising God. Wherefore he was born in settled times, wherein religion met with little or no molestation. It began to be as hereditary in the days of blessed Cainan; wherefore it was requisite that the very next that should possess the truth should spend their days in praising God. And thus it will be at the downfall of antichrist. "After this," saith John, "I heard a great voice of much people in heaven, saying Allelujah! Salvation, and glory, and honour, and power unto the Lord our God. And a voice came out of the throne, saying, Praise our God, all ye his servants; and ye that fear him, both small and great." (Rev. xix. 1, 5.)

"The whole earth," saith the prophet, "is at rest and quiet, they break forth into singing. Yea, the fir-trees rejoice at thee, (O thou brood of the bloodthirsty Cain,) and the cedars of Lebanon, saying, Since thou wast laid down, no feller is come up against us." (Isa. xiv. 7, 8.)

Verse 13. "And Cainan lived after he begat Mahalaleel eight hundred and forty years, and begat sons and daughters."

God gave him a long possession and enjoyment of the fruits of his father's labours. They sowed (as Christ said) and he was entered into their labours: they sowed in tears, and he reaped in joy. Mahalaleel, or praise our God, was the language of those times.

Verse 14. "And all the days of Cainan were nine hundred and ten years; and he died."

He lived then two hundred and forty-eight years after Enoch, and died four hundred and twenty-one years before the flood.

Verse 15. "And Mahalaleel lived sixty and five years, and begat Jared."

Jared signifies ruling, and showeth us what is the holy fruits of peace and thanksgiving in the church; to wit, government according to the testament of Christ. It is hard to have all things according to rule, in the day of the church's affliction; because of the weakness and fearfulness of some; and because possibly those who have most skill in that matter, may for a time be laid up in chains; but now when the church hath rest and quietness, then as she praiseth God, so she conceiveth and bringeth forth governors, and good government and rule among her members. David, a man of blood, could not build that house to the Lord, which peaceable Solomon, that man of rest, afterwards did. (1 Chron. xxviii. 3—6.) When armies are engaged, and hot in battle, it is harder to keep them in rank and file, than when they have rest, and time for discipline. Jared therefore is the fruits of thanksgiving, as thanksgiving is the fruits of peace and possession.

Verse 16. "And Mahalaleel lived after he begat Jared eight hundred and thirty years, and begat sons and daughters."

He lived not only to give thanks unto God, but to show to all that he gave thanks in truth, by submitting his neck the rest of the hundred years that he lived, to the holy law and word of God.

A good rule to prove people by; for all that pretend to give thanks for liberty, put not their neck under the yoke, but rather use their liberty as an occasion for the flesh, than by love to serve and advantage one another in the things of the kingdom of Christ. (Gal. v. 13.) "But as the bramble said to (the rest of) the trees," so saith Christ to such feigned thanksgivers, "If in truth ye anoint me king over you, then come and put your trust under my shadow," (Judges ix. 15;) submit to my law, and be governed by my testament. Let your thanksgiving bring forth Jared, and walk with God in the days of Jared.

Verse 17. "And all the days of Mahalaleel were eight hundred ninety and five years; and he died."

He lived then three hundred and three years after Enoch, and died three hundred and sixty-six years before the flood.

Verse 18. "And Jared lived an hundred sixty and two years, and he begat Enoch."

Enoch, is taught, or dedicate: the true effect of rule or government, be it good or bad; in Cain's posterity it was bad; for an evil tree cannot bring forth good fruit. By Enoch here, we are to understand, one taught in, and dedicated unto God. This Enoch, therefore, was a son that would hear the rules, and submit to the government of his father Jared. "As an earring of gold, and an ornament of fine gold, so is a wise reprover upon an obedient ear." (Prov. xxv. 12.)

Verse 19. "And Jared lived after he begat Enoch eight hundred years, and begat sons and daughters."

He lived therefore to see the fruit of his good rule and government in the church, even to see his teachable and dedicated son caught up to God, and to his throne. A good encouragement to all rulers in the house of God, and also to all godly parents to teach and rule in the fear of God; for that is the way to part with church members, and children with comfort; yea, that is the way, if we shall outlive them, to send them to heaven, and to God before us.

Verse 20. "And all the days of Jared were nine hundred sixty and two years, and he died."

He lived then three hundred and thirty-five years after Enoch, and died two hundred and thirty-four before the flood.

Verse 21. "And Enoch lived sixty and five years, and begat Methuselah."

Methuselah signifieth, Spoiling his death. This, therefore, is the true fruits of one that is truly taught in, and dedicate to the service of God, as Enoch was; by this means he spoileth his death. Wherefore, he adds, "And Enoch walked with God." Walking with God, spoileth death, or overcomes it, or it shall be prevented, he shall not be hurt therewith. As Christ saith, "If a man keep my sayings, he shall never see death." (John viii. 52.)

Verse 22. "And Enoch walked with God after he begat Methuselah three hundred years, and begat sons and daughters.

These words " after he begat Methuselah " may have respect either to his beginning to walk with God, or to the number of the years that he lived after the birth of Methuselah, or both.

If it respect the first, then it showeth that the only encouragement that a sinner hath to walk with God, it is to see Methuselah, or his death spoiled : for when a man seeth death and all evils, conquered and overcome, then his soul is encouraged in holiness. No encouragement to walking with God like this : " Enoch walked with God after he begat Methuselah." As Paul saith, " Now being made free from sin," which indeed is the sting of death, " ye have your fruit unto holiness, and the end everlasting life." (Rom. vi. 22.)

If it respect the second, then it shows us the invincible nature of true faith, (for by faith Enoch walked with God;) I say, it showeth us the invincible nature of true faith, in that it would hold up a man in close communion with God for the space of three hundred years.

"He walked with God three hundred years." How will the conversation of Enoch rise up in judgment with this generation, that walk not with God at all! Or if they do, do it so by fits, as if walking with God was but a work by the by.

"He walked with God and begat sons and daughters." And kept house, and lived with his wife, according to knowledge. This shows, then, that it is sin, not our lawful and honest employment, that hindereth one's walking with God.

Verses 23, 24. "And all the days of Enoch were three hundred and sixty and five years. And Enoch walked with God, and he was not; for God took him."

The New Testament saith, " By faith Enoch was translated, that he should not see death ; and was not found, because God had translated him ; for before his translation he had this testimony, that he pleased God."

" And all the days of Enoch were three hundred sixty and five years." Enoch therefore lived here but a while ; he was too good to live long in this world, the world was not worthy of him ; neither would he be spared so long out of heaven, " for God took him." The end of walking with God, or the pathway thereof, it leads men to heaven, to the enjoyment of the glory of God. Thus also it was with blessed Elijah, he followed God from place to place, till at length he was caught up into heaven. (2 Kings ii. 1—11.)

A word or two more of Enoch. Jude observes, That he was the seventh from Adam : Closely intimating (as I conceive) that by him God prefigured the resurrection and end of the world : And intimated, That in the seventh great day of

the world this resurrection should be, each generation from Adam being a type of a thousand years : So that Enoch, the seventh from Adam, was a type of the seventh thousand, in which the Lord will reign with his church a thousand years.

There are two things in Enoch that incline me to this opinion. First, he crieth out, " Behold the Lord comes!" and then is translated that he should not see death : The right posture and end of those that shall live at the day of God Almighty ; and that shall, like Enoch, be found walking with God, when the Lord shall come from heaven. (Jude 14, 15.)

Verse 25. "And Methuselah lived an hundred eighty and seven years, and begat Lamech."

Lamech signifieth poor, or smitten ; wherefore I doubt that the apostacy that you read of in the next chapter, began either in the days of, or by, this man : he being, as it seems, more dry and void of grace than those that went before him ; poor, or smitten.

Hence note, That faith and godliness, though often it goeth from the father to the son, as from Seth to Enos, and from him to Cainan, yet it is not tied here, but runs according to electing love, as also do the fruits thereof.

Verse 26, 27. "And Methuselah lived after he begat Lamech seven hundred eighty and two years, and begat sons and daughters. And all the days of Methuselah were nine hundred sixty and nine years : and he died."

Methuselah, the spoiling of death, is the longest liver in the world ; yet he died in the year that the flood was upon the earth ; not by the flood, but by the course of nature, as also did Lamech his son, for the wicked reprobate only was swept away by that, according to the apostle Peter.

Verses 28, 29. "And Lamech lived an hundred eighty and two years, and begat a son: and he called his name Noah, saying, This same shall comfort us concerning our work and toil of our hands, because of the ground which the Lord hath cursed."

" And he called his name Noah." Noah signifieth rest ; his name was therefore according to his work, for he was a preacher of righteousness, which giveth rest to all that embraceth it. Besides, it was he that prepared the ark, the place of rest to the church of God.

" This same shall comfort us concerning our work, and toil of our hands, because of the ground, which the Lord hath cursed." These words seem to carry in them repentance for the apostacy that before was mentioned ; " This same shall comfort us," by restoring the church to her former rest, and by delivering us from the "toil of our hands;" for sin once admitted of in the church, is not without much toil extirpated, and driven forth of the same ; yea, sometimes it getteth such footing and root, that it cannot again be purged and destroyed, but by breaking the very being of the church where it is. Thus it was as to the case in hand, and is signified also by pulling down the house in which the leprosy was, (Lev. xiv. 45;) yea, Ephesus itself was almost thus far infected, had not a threatening prevented. (Rev. ii. 1—3.)

"Because of the ground which the Lord hath cursed." The Lord did curse it for the sin of Adam. He also renewed the curse to Cain, because he was guilty of the blood of his brother. I incline also to think, that the curse here mentioned, is the first, reiterated for the grievous apostacy of this congregation; according to that which is written, If ye walk contrary unto me, "I will punish you seven times more:" "I will bring seven times more plagues upon you, according to your sins." (Lev. xxvi. 18—21.)

Verse 30. "And Lamech lived after he begat Noah, five hundred ninety and five years, and begat sons and daughters." Wherefore Lamech heard the preaching of Noah, who was the only minister of God in those days, to recover the church to repentance from their apostacy, which also he did in some good measure effect, while he condemned the world for their unbelief. (Heb. xi. 17.)

Verse 31. "And all the days of Lamech were seven hundred seventy and seven years: and he died." He died five years before the flood. Methuselah therefore was the longest liver of those godly that fell on the other side the flood, for he died not before the very year the flood came, not by the water, but before. The righteous is taken away from the evil to come; though, as the prophet saith, no man of the wicked laid it to heart.

Verse 32. "And Noah was five hundred years old: and Noah begat Shem, Ham, and Japheth."

CHAPTER VI.

Verse 1. "And it came to pass, when men began to multiply on the face of the earth, and daughters were born unto them."

Moses now leaveth the genealogy for a while, and searcheth into the state and condition of the church now after so long a time as its standing upwards of, or above a thousand years: where he he presently findeth two things. 1. The church declined. 2. And God provoked. Wherefore he maketh inquiry into the nature of the church's sin; which he relateth in this following chapter.

"And it came to pass when men began to multiply." The men here I understand to be the children of Cain, the church and synagogue of Satan, because they are mentioned by way of antithesis to the church and sons of God.

"And daughters were born unto them." A snare that was often used in the hand of the devil, to intangle withal the church of God; yea, and doth so usually speed, that it hath often been counted by him as infallible; so that this is the doctrine of his prophet Balaam, and it prevailed, when all the engines of hell beside were prevented. "The people began to commit whoredom with the daughters of Moab." (Numb. xxv. 1.) It may be this child of hell, in this his advice to Balak looked back to the daughters of Cain, and calling to remembrance how of old they intangled the church, advertised him to put the same in practice again. (Rev. ii. 14.)

Verse 2. "That the sons of God saw the daughters of men, that they were fair; and they took them wives of all which they chose."

This was the way then of the sons of Cain, to let their fair daughters be showed to the sons of God. For it seems all other their wiles and devices were not able to bring the church and the world together, and to make them live as in one communion. These to the church was such, whose hearts were snares and nets, and whose hands were bands to intangle and hold them from observing the laws and judgments of God. (Eccles. vii. 26.)

"And they took them wives." First their eye saw them, and then their heart lusted after them. Thus the devil deceived the woman, and by this means perished cursed Achan. "And Achan answered Joshua, and said, Indeed I have sinned against the Lord God of Israel, and thus and thus have I done: When I saw among the spoils a goodly Babylonish garment," &c., "then I coveted them." (Josh. vii. 20, 21.)

Note therefore, that it is not good to behold with the eye that which God hath forbid us to touch with our hand. "I made a covenant with mine eyes," saith Job. (Job xxxi. 1.) And again, if at unawares a thing was cast before him, the beholding of which was of an intangling nature, the forthwith would hold back his heart as with a bridle, lest the design of hell should be effected upon him.

Crush sin then in the conception, lest it bring forth death in thy soul.

Verse 3. "And the Lord said, My Spirit shall not always strive with man, for that he also is flesh; yet his days shall be an hundred and twenty years."

By these words is aggravated the sin of the church, that she would attempt to close with, and hold a sinful communion, against the dissuasions of the Spirit of God.

"My Spirit shall not always strive." To wit, my Spirit in Noah, for he was the only preacher of righteousness to the church in those backsliding times.

By this then, I find, that the doctrine of Noah was, To declare against a sinful communion, or to command the church, in the name of God, that she still maintain a separation from the cursed children of Cain: As he said to the prophet Jeremiah, If thou separate "the precious from the vile, thou shalt be as my mouth." (Jer. xv. 19.)

Noah therefore had a hard task, when he preached this doctrine among them: for this above all is hard to be borne, for by this he condemned the world.

The first great quarrel therefore that God had with his church it was for their holding unwarrantable communion with others. The church should always "dwell alone, and not be reckoned among the nations." (Numb. xxiii. 9.) The church is "a chosen generation, a royal priesthood, an holy nation, a peculiar people." (1 Pet. ii. 9.) Therefore the work of the church of God, is not to fall in with any sinful fellowship, or receive into their communion the ungodly world, but to show forth the praises and virtues of him who hath called them out from among such communicants into his marvellous light.

"My Spirit shall not always strive." Hence note, that the people that shall continue to grieve the Spirit of God, and to resist the doctrine of Noah, they are appointed for heavy judgments. "Come out of her, my people, that ye be not partakers of her sins, and that ye receive not of her plagues." (Rev. xviii. 4.) This because those (finally impenitent) in Noah's time refused to do, therefore the wrath of God overtook them, and swept them off the face of the earth.

"Yet his days shall be an hundred and twenty years." Noah therefore began his preaching about the four hundred and four-score year of his life, which continuing the space of six-score more, it reached to the day that the flood came.

In which time doubtless his faith was sufficiently tried, both by the hard censures of the hypocrites of the church, and the open profane of the world, against whom he daily pronounced the judgments of God for maintaining their forbidden communion.

"Yet his days shall be an hundred and twenty years." God also would yet have patience with these people, if peradventure they would repent that his hand might not be upon them.

Verse 4. "There were giants in the earth in those days; and also after that, when the sons of God came in unto the daughters of men, and they bare children to them; the same became mighty men, which were of old, men of renown."

"There were giants in the earth in those days." These words seem to be spoken, to show us the hazards that Noah ran, while he preached the truth of God: He incurred the displeasure of the giants, which doubtless made all men tremble, and kept the whole world in awe. But Noah must engage the giants, he must not fear the face of a giant. This way God took also with Moses, and with his people of Israel, they must go to possess the land of the giants, a people high and tall as the cedars, a people of whom went that proverb, "Who can stand before the children of Anak?" (Deut. ix. 2.) They must not be afraid of Og the king of Bashan, though his head be as high as the ridge of an house, and his bedstead a bedstead of iron. (Deut. iii. 11.)

This should teach us, then, not to fear the faces of men: no, not the faces of the mighty, not to fear them, I say, in the matters of God, though they should run upon us like a giant.

These giants, I suppose, were the children of Cain, because mentioned as another sort than those that were the fruit of their forbidden and ungodly communion: For he adds, "And also after that," or besides them, "when the sons of God came in unto the daughters of men, and they bare children unto them; the same," or they also, "became mighty men, which were of old, men of renown."

Then Noah found giants everywhere: Giants in the world, and giants in this confused communion. And thus it is at this day; we do not only meet with giants abroad, among the most ungodly and uncircumcised in heart, but even among those that seem to be of the religious, among them we also meet with giants; men mighty to oppose the truth, and very profound to make slaughter: But mark the advice of the Lord, Fear not their fear, neither be afraid, but sanctify the Lord of hosts himself, (who is stronger than all the giants that are upon the face of the earth,) and let him be your fear, and let him be your dread. (Isa. viii. 12, 13.)

"And when the sons of God came in unto the daughters of men, and they bare children unto them, the same became mighty men;" much like to the giants. The fruit, therefore, of ungodly communion is monstrous, and of a very strange complexion. They are like unto them that worshipped the Lord, and served their own gods also, (2 Kings xvii. 24—41;) or like to those of the church, of whom Nehemiah speaks, that had mixed themselves with the children of Ashdod, Ammon, and Moab, whose children were a monstrous brood, that spake half the language of Ashdod, and could not speak the Jews' language. (Neh. xiii. 23, 24.)

By both these sorts of giants was faithful Noah despised, and his work for God condemned. In David's time also Goliah despised Israel, and so did his brethren also. (1 Sam. xvii. 10.) Giants, the sons of the giant; but David and his servants must engage them, and fight them, though they were giants. (1 Chron. xx. 4—8.)

"Mighty men which were of old." Persecution, therefore, or the appearance of the giants against the servants of God, is no new business; not a thing of yesterday, but of old. Even when Noah did minister for God in the world, "There were giants in the earth in those days," to oppose him.

"Men of renown." Not for faith and holiness, but for some other high achievements, may be, mighty to fight, and to shed man's blood; or to find out arts, and the nature of things; both which did render them famous, and men to be noted in their place. Such kind of men might be Korah, Dathan, and their company also; yet they opposed Moses and Aaron, yea, God, his way and worship, and perished after an unheard-of manner, (Numb. xvi.,) as also did the opposers of righteous Noah, in the day of the flood.

Verse 5. " And God saw that the wickedness of man was great in the earth, and that every imagination of the thoughts of his heart was only evil continually." The margin saith, "not only the imaginations, but also the purposes and desires."

These words are to be understood, as still respecting the apostacy that we read of in the first and second verses, and are (in my thoughts) to be taken as the effect of their degeneracy: for though it be true, that the best of men, in their most holy and godly behaviour, have wicked and sinful hearts; yet so long as they walk sincerely according to the rules prescribed of God, there is no such character upon them; especially as it stands related to the words that immediately follow; to wit, " that it repented the Lord that he made them."

These evil and wicked purposes, then, were, in special, the fruit of their apostacy: for, indeed, when men are once fallen from God, they then, as the judgment of God upon them, are given up to all unrighteousness. Again, Apostatizing persons are counted abhorrers of God. (Zech. xi. 8.) Yet persons in this condition will seek their own justification, turning things upside down, traversing their ways like the dromedaries; bearing us still in hand, that they stand not guilty of sin, but that what they do is allowable, or winked at of God. Besides, they say their hearts are still upright with God, and that they have not forsaken the simplicity of his way, of a wicked and ungodly design, with an hundred more the like pretences; all which are condemned of God, and held by him as abominable and vile. (Jer. ii. 31—37.)

" And God saw," &c. They covered their shame from men, like the adulterous woman in the Proverbs, and would speak with oily mouths, thereby to cozen the world, (Prov. xxx. 20 ;) but God knew their hearts, and had revealed their sin to his servant Noah ; he therefore, in the Spirit of God, as one alone, cried out against their wickedness.

Hence learn to judge of apostates, not by their words, nor pretences, nor ungodly coverings, whereby they may seek to hide themselves from the stroke of a convincing argument, but judge them by the words of God ; for, however they think of themselves, or would be accounted of others, God sees their wickedness is great.

" And that every imagination of the thoughts of his heart, was only evil continually." If they think they have not sinned ; if they think they promote religion ; if they think to find out a medium to make peace between the seed of the woman and the wicked seed of Cain ; all is alike ungodly, they have forsaken the right way, they have dissembled the known truth, they have rejected the word of the Lord : and what wisdom or goodness is in them ?

Verse 6. " And it repented the Lord that he had made man on the earth, and it grieved him at his heart."

Repentance is in us a change of the mind ; but in God a change of his dispensations ; for otherwise he repenteth not, neither can he ; because it standeth not with the perfection of his nature : In him is no variableness, nor shadow of turning. (James i. 17.)

Wherefore, it is man, not God, that turns. When men, therefore, reject the mercy and ways of God, they cast themselves under his wrath and displeasure ; which, because it is executed according to the nature of his justice and the severity of his law, they miss of the mercy promised before. (Numb. xxiii. 19.) Which, that we may know, those shall one day feel that shall continue in final impenitency. Therefore God, speaking to their capacity, he tells them, he hath repented of doing them good : It repented the Lord that he had made Saul king. (1 Sam. xv. 35.) And yet this repentance was only a change of the dispensation, which Saul, by his wickedness, had put himself under ; otherwise, the strength, the eternity of Israel, " will not lie, nor repent." (1 Sam. xv. 29.)

The sum is, therefore, that men had now by their wickedness put themselves under the justice and law of God ; which justice, by reason of its perfection, could not endure they should abide on the earth any longer : and therefore, now, as a just reward of their deed, they must be swept from the face thereof.

" And it grieved him at his heart." This is spoken to show that he did not feign, but was simple and sincere in his promise of remission and forgiveness of sins, had they kept close to his word, according as he had commanded. Wherefore God's heart went not with them in their backsliding, but left them, and was offended with them.

Verse 7. " And the Lord said, I will destroy man, whom I have created, from the face of the earth ; both man and beast, (or from man to beast,) and the creeping thing, and the fowls of the air ; for it repenteth me that I have made them."

This may be either understood as a threatening, or a determination : if as a threatening, then it admitted of time for repentance ; but if it was spoken as a determination, then they had stood out the day of grace, and had laid themselves under unavoidable judgment. If it respected the first, then it was in order to the ministry of Noah, or in order to the effecting the ends of its sending ; which were either to soften or harden, or bring to repentance, or to leave them utterly and altogether inexcusable. But if it respected the second, as it might, then it was pronounced as an effect of God's displeasure, for their abuse of his patience, his minister, and word : as it also was with Israel of old ; " they mocked the messengers of God, and despised his words, and misused his prophets, until the wrath of the Lord arose against his people, till there was no remedy." (2 Chron. xxxvi. 16.)

" And the Lord said, I will destroy man whom

I have created." This word, "created," is added, on purpose to show that the world is under the power of his hand; for who can destroy, but he that can create? Or who can save alive, when the maker of the world is set against them? "There is one lawgiver, who is able to save, and to destroy." (James iv. 12.) And again, "Fear him which is able to destroy both body and soul in hell." (Matt. x. 28.) In both which places power to destroy is insinuated from his power and Godhead: as he saith in another place, "All souls are mine; the soul that sinneth, it shall die." (Ezek. xviii. 4.)

"Both man and beast, and the creeping thing, and the fowls," &c. Thus it was at first the sin of a man brought a curse and judgment upon other the creatures whom God had made: as Paul says, "The whole creation groaneth." (Rom. viii. 22.)

But again, This threatening upon the beasts, the fowls, and creeping things might arise from a double consideration: First, To show that when God intends the destruction of man, he will also destroy the means of his preservation. Or, Second, To show that when he is determined to execute his judgments, he will cut off all that stands in his way. He could not destroy the earth without a flood, and preserve beast, &c., alive; therefore he destroys them also.

"For it repenteth me that I have made them." This seems to fall under the first consideration, to wit, That God repented that he made the beasts and fowls; because now they were used to sustain his implacable enemies.

Verse 8. "But Noah found grace in the eyes of the Lord."

This word "grace" must in special be observed; for grace is it which delivereth from all deserved judgments and destruction.

Noah, by nature was no better than other men: therefore the reason why he perished not with others, it was because he "found grace in the eyes of the Lord." Ye are saved by grace. (Eph. ii. 8.) And thus was Noah, as is evident, because he was saved by faith. (Heb. xi. 7.) For faith respecteth not works, but grace. Ye are saved by grace through faith. As Paul says again, "Therefore it is of faith, that it might be by grace," &c. (Rom. iv. 16.) We must, therefore, in our deliverance from all the judgments of God, sing grace, grace, unto it.

Verse 9. "These are the generations of Noah: Noah was a just man, and perfect in his generations; and Noah walked with God."

The Holy Ghost here makes a short digression from his progress, in his relation of the wickedness of the world; and yet not impertinently; for seeing Noah was the man that escaped the judgment, his escape must be for some reason; which was, because God was gracious to him, and because God had justified him. Besides, Noah being now made righteous, faithfully walked with God.

"He was just and perfect in his generations,"

But why it is said, "Generations?" It might be, because he was faithful to God and man, having the armour of righteousness on the right hand, and on the left. It is said in Isaiah, that Christ made his grave with the wicked, and with the rich in his death. (Isa. liii. 9.) To import, that they only have benefit by him to eternal life, that die by his example, as well as live by his blood; for in his death was both merit and example; and they are like to miss in the first, that are not concerned in the second.

"Perfect in his generations." In his carriage, doctrines and life, before both God and man. And thus ought every preacher to be; he ought to do in the sight of God, what he commands to men; by this means he saveth both himself, and them that hear him. (1 Tim. iii. 16.)

Besides, Noah was a man, as well as a saint, and in either sense had a generation: to both of which grace made him faithful; and he that shall not serve his generation as a man, will hardly serve his generation as a Christian. But Noah was perfect in both, he was "perfect in his generations."

"And Noah walked with God." This shows he was sincere in his work; for a hypocrite may, as to outward show, do as the saint of God; but he doth it with respect to men, not God, and therefore he is a hypocrite. To walk with God, then, is not only to do the duty commanded, but to do it as God requireth it; that is, to do it with faith, and son-like fear, as in God's sight, with singleness of heart.

Verse 10. "And Noah begat three sons, Shem, Ham, and Japheth."

These are the offspring of Noah, and by these was the earth replenished after the flood, as will be further seen hereafter.

Verse 11. "The earth also was corrupt before God, and the earth was filled with violence."

He is now returned to the matter in hand before; to wit, the causes of the flood.

"The earth also was corrupt." By earth, he may here mean, those that are without the church: and if so, then by "corrupt" here, we must understand, wicked after a most high manner; for albeit the world and generation of Cain be always sinners before God, yet the Lord cutteth not off the world in general, nor a nation in particular, but because of the commission of eminent outrage and wickedness. Thus it was with those of Sodom, a little before the Lord with fire devoured them. "The men of Sodom, saith the text, were wicked, and sinners before the Lord exceedingly." (Gen. xiii. 13.)

Again, as by "corrupt," we may understand, corrupt by way of eminency; so again, they were corrupt incurably. This is evident, because they were not brought off from sin by the ministry of Noah, the only appointed means of their conversion.

Hence note, that when men are sinners exceedingly, and when the means of grace appointed of God for their recovery, prove ineffectual, then they are near some signal judgment. Thus back-sliding Jerusalem, because she was wicked with an high hand, and could not be cured by the ministry of the prophets, therefore her sons must go forth of her into captivity, and the city burned to the ground with fire.

"And the earth was filled with violence." First, they had violated the law of God, in making and maintaining ungodly and wicked communion; according to that of the prophet, "Her priests have violated my law, and have profaned my holy things." But how ? "They have put no difference between the holy and profane, neither have they showed difference between the unclean and the clean." (Ezek. xxii. 26.)

They also perverted judgment between a man and his neighbour ; adhering to their own party, in disaffection to the religious. This is supposed, because of the exceeding latitude of the expression, "The earth was filled with violence ;" that is, all manner of violence, outrage, and cruelty was committed by this sort of people. This takes in that saying of Solomon, the oppression of the poor, especially God's poor, is included in a "violent perverting of judgment and justice." (Eccles. v. 8.)

They also showed violence to the lives of good men, as may be gathered by the act of Lamech, one of the sons of Cain. In a word, "The earth was filled with violence ;" violence of every kind ; lust and wickedness was outrageous, there was a world of ungodliness among these ungodly men.

Verse 12. "And God looked upon the earth, and, behold, it was corrupt ; for all flesh had corrupted his way upon the earth."

By these words, therefore, is confirmed the sense of the former verse, "The earth was corrupt ;" for God saw it was so : "The earth was full of violence," for they had corrupted God's way.

"And God looked upon the earth." This shows us, that the Lord doth not with haste, or in a rash inconsiderate way, pour his judgments upon the world ; but that with judgment and knowledge, the wickedness first being certain, and of merit deserving the same. This is seen in his way of dealing with Sodom : "And the Lord said, Because the cry of Sodom and Gomorrah is great, and because their sin is very grievous, I will go down now, and see whether they have done altogether according to the cry of it, which is come unto me ; and if not, I will know." (Gen. xviii. 20, 21.)

"And, behold, it was corrupt ; for all flesh had corrupted his way upon the earth." It proved, as that of Sodom did, according to the cry thereof; for "all flesh had corrupted his way,"—God's way, by violating his law, and perverting of judgment, as was hinted before. All flesh had corrupted it, therefore the evil needed not to be long in search-

ing out : as God saith by the prophet Jeremiah, "I have not found it by secret search, but upon all these." (Isa. ii. 34.) Here upon the whole earth, none exempted but righteous Noah.

Verse 13. "And God said unto Noah, the end of all flesh is come before me ; for the earth is filled with violence through them ; and, behold, I will destroy them with the earth."

"And God said unto Noah," or told Noah his purpose. The same way he went with Abraham : "Shall I hide from Abraham that thing which I do." (Gen. xviii. 17.) "Surely the Lord will do nothing, but he revealeth his secrets unto his servants the prophets." (Amos iii. 7.)

"The end of all flesh is come." The time or expiration of the world is at hand. God speaks before he smites. Thus he did also by the prophet Ezekiel, saying, "An end" is come, "the end is come." (Ezek. vii. 2.) And again, "An end is come, the end is come ; it watcheth for thee ; behold, it is come." (ver. 6.)

"The end of all flesh is come before me." Sin and wickedness doth not put an end to the ungodly before their own face, yet it brings their end before the face of God. It is said of these very people, they knew not of their destruction, until the day the flood came, and took them all away. (Matt. xxiv. 39.) Indeed, the nature of sin is to blind the mind, that the person concerned may neither see mercy nor judgment ; but God sees their end : "The end of all flesh is come before me."

"The end of all flesh." By these words, the souls are left to, and reserved for another judgment ; wherefore, though here we find the flesh consumed ; yet Peter saith, their spirits are still in prison, even the souls that Christ once preached to in the days, and by the ministry of Noah : even the souls "which sometimes were disobedient when once the long suffering of God waited in the days of Noah, while the ark was preparing," &c. (1 Pet. iii. 19, 20.)

Verse 14. "Make thee an ark of gopher wood ; rooms shalt thou make in the ark, and shalt pitch it within and without with pitch."

This is the fruits of the grace of God. He said before, that Noah "found grace in the eyes of the Lord ;" which grace appoints to him the means of his preservation.

"Make thee an ark." He saith not, make one ; or, make one for me ; but, "Make one, make one for thee : make thee an ark of gopher wood."

Noah, therefore, from this word "thee," did gather, that God did intend to preserve him from the judgment which he had appointed in this his work : therein lay his own profit and comfort, not a thought which he had, not a blow that he struck, about the preparing the ark, but he preached, as to others their ruin, to himself, his safeguard, and deliverance : he "prepared an ark to the saving of his house." (Heb. xi. 7.)

This therefore must needs administer much peace and content to his mind, while he preached to others their overthrow. As the prophet saith, "The work of righteousness shall be peace; and the effects of righteousness, quietness, and assurance for ever. And, My people shall dwell in a peaceable habitation." (Isa. xxxii. 17, 18.) Thus did Noah when he dwelt in the ark, and in sure dwellings, and in quiet resting-places.

"Make thee an ark." The ark was a figure of several things. 1. Of Christ, in whom the church is preserved from the wrath of God. 2. It was a figure of the works of the faith of the godly: "by faith he prepared an ark;" by which the followers of Christ are preserved from the rage and tyranny of the world (for the rage of the water was a type of that, as I shall show you hereafter.) So then Noah, by preparing an ark, or by being bid so to do of God, was thereby admonished, first, to live by the faith of Christ, of whom the ark was a type; and hence it is said, that in preparing the ark, he became "heir of the righteousness which is by faith;" because he understood the mind of God therein, and throughout his figure acted faith upon Christ. But, secondly, His faith was not to be idle, and therefore he was bid to work; this begat in him an obediental fear of doing aught which God had forbidden." By faith Noah being warned of God, of things not seen as yet, moved with fear, prepared an ark, to the saving of his house; by the which he condemned the world, and became heir of the righteousness which is by faith." (Heb. xi. 7.)

"Rooms (nests) shalt thou make in the ark." To wit, for himself, and the beasts, and the birds of the field, &c. Implying, that in the Lord Jesus there is room for Jews and Gentiles. Yea, forasmuch as these rooms were prepared for beasts of every sort, and fowls of every wing. It informs us, that for all sorts, ranks and qualities of men, there is preservation in Jesus Christ: "Compel them to come in," drive them (in a gospel sense) as Noah did the beasts of old into the ark, that my house may be full, and yet there is room. (Luke xiv. 23.)

"And thou shalt pitch it within and without with pitch." This was to secure all from the flood, or to keep them that were in the ark from perishing in the waters.

Verse 15. "And this is the fashion which thou shalt make it of: The length of the ark shall be three hundred cubits, the breadth of it fifty cubits, and the height of it thirty cubits."

A vessel fit to swim upon the waters.

"And this is the fashion," &c. God's ordinances must be according to God's order and appointment, not according to our fancies, "This is the fashion," to wit, according to what is after expressed.

By these words therefore Noah was limited and bound up, as to a direction from which he must not vary; according to that of the angel to the prophet, "Son of man," saith he, "behold with thine eyes, and hear with thine ears, and set thine heart upon all that I shall show thee: for to the intent that I might show them unto thee, art thou brought hither." (Ezek. xl. 4.) As the Lord said also to his servant Moses, "In all things that I have said unto you, be circumspect." (Exod. xxiii. 13.) And so again, about making the tabernacle in the wilderness, which the apostle also takes special notice of, saying, "See, saith he, thou make all things according to the pattern showed to thee in the Mount." (Heb. viii. 5.)

Hence note, That God's command must be the rule whereby we order all our actions, especially when we pretend to worship that is divine and religious. If our walks, orders, and observances, have not this inscription upon them, "This is the fashion," or, This is according to the pattern, such works and orders will profit us nothing: Neither have we any promise when all is done, it wanting the order of God, that we should escape those judgments which those shall assuredly escape, that have their eye in their work to the pattern revealed in the word.

Verse 16. "A window shalt thou make to the ark, and in a cubit shalt thou finish it above; and the door of the ark shalt thou set in the side thereof: with lower, second, and third stories shalt thou make it."

I told you before, That the ark was a type of Christ, and also of the works of the faith of the godly. And now he seems to bring in more, and to make it a type of the church of Christ; as indeed the prophet also does, when he calls the church, one afflicted, and tossed with tempests; and compareth her troublers to the waters of Noah, saying, "This is as the waters of Noah." (Isa. liv. 9.)

Now as the ark was a type of the church, so according to the description of this verse she hath three most excellent things attending her. 1. Light. 2. A door. 3. Stories of a lower and higher rank.

1. She hath a window for light, and that when she was to be tossed upon the waters. Hence note, That the church of Christ wanted not light, no, not in the worst of times. This light is the Word and Spirit of God which Christ hath given to them that obey him. (John xii.)

2. She hath a door. This door was a type of Christ; so was also the door of the tabernacle. And hence it is that you read, That Moses, when he went to walk with God, would stand to talk in the door of the tabernacle; also that the cloudy pillar stood at the door. (Exod. xxxiii. 9, 10.) "I," saith Christ, "am the door:" Again, "I am the door of the sheep." (John x. 7.) By this door then, entered all that went into the ark, as by Christ all must enter that enter aright into the church.

3. She had stories in her, of first, second, and third degree: To show that also in the church of Christ there are some higher than some, both as to persons and states: 1. apostles; 2. evangelists;

3. pastors and teachers. And again, there are in the church degrees of states, as also there is in heaven.

Verse 17. And, behold, I, even I, do bring a flood of waters upon the earth, to destroy all flesh, wherein is the breath of life from under heaven; and every thing that is in the earth shall die."

This is the reason of the former commandment, of making an ark: But some time was yet to intervene: the flood was hereafter to overflow the world: wherefore, from this it is that those words are inserted, of things not seen as yet: And that the ark was a work, or the fruit of Noah's faith: "By faith Noah, being warned of God of things not seen as yet," &c. (Heb. xi. 7.)

"And behold, I, even I," &c. These words excuse Noah of treason or rebellion, forasmuch as his preparation for himself, and his warning and threatening the whole world with death and judgment for their transgression, was solely grounded upon the word of God: God bid him prepare, God said he would punish the world for their iniquity.

Hence note, That a man is not to be counted an offender, how contrary soever he lieth, either in doctrine or practice, to men, &c., if both have the command of God, and are surely grounded upon the words of his mouth. This made Jeremiah, though he preached, That the city of Jerusalem should be burnt with fire, the king and people should go into captivity, yet stand upon his own vindication before his enemies, and plead his innocency against them that persecuted him. (Jer. xxvi. 10—16.) Daniel also, though he did openly break the king's decree, and refused to stoop to his idolatrous and devilish demand; yet purged himself of both treason and sedition, and justifies his act as innocent and harmless, even in the sight of God. "My God," saith he, "hath sent his angel, and hath shut the lions' mouths, so that they have not hurt me; forasmuch as before him innocency was found in me; and also before thee, O king, I have done no hurt." (Dan. vi. 22.) Further, Paul also, although by his doctrine he did cry down the ceremonies of the Jews, and the idolatry of the heathen emperor, yet he quits himself of blame from either side: "Neither against the law of the Jews," saith he, "neither against the temple, nor yet against Cæsar, have I offended anything at all." (Acts xxv. 8.) The reason is, because the words of God, how severely soever they threaten sinners, and how sharply soever (the preacher keeping within the bowels of the word) this doctrine be urged on the world, if it destroy, it destroyeth but sin and impenitent sinners, even as the waters of Noah must do.

This then affords us another note worth remarking, to wit, That what God hath said in his word, how offensive soever it be to ungodly men, That we that are Christians ought to observe: whether it direct us to declare against others' enormities, or to provide for ourselves against the judgment to come.

"And behold, I, even I, do bring a flood," &c. Hence note again, Let us preach and practise well and let God alone to execute his judgments. It is said of Samuel, That not one of his words did fall to the ground. (1 Sam. iii. 19.) He preached, and God, according to his blessing or cursing, did either spare and forgive, or execute his judgments.

"And behold, I, even I." Note again, That when sinners have with the utmost contempt slighted and despised the judgment threatened, yet forasmuch as the execution thereof is in the hand of an omnipotent majesty, it must fall with violence upon the head of the wicked. "I, even I," therefore, were words of a strong encouragement to Noah, and the godly with him; but black, and like claps of thunder to the pestilent unbelieving world. As the prophet says, "He is strong that executes his word:" And again, "Not one of his judgments fail."

"And behold I, even I do bring a flood." The flood was a type of three things.

1. A type of the enemies of the church. (Isa. liv.)
2. A type of the water-baptism under the New Testament. (1 Pet. iii. 20, 21.)
3. A type of the last and general overthrow of the world by fire and brimstone. (2 Pet. iii. 6, 7.)

But here, as it simply respecteth the cause, which (as is afore related) was the sin that before you read of; so it precisely was a type of the last of these, and to that end put an end to the world that then was. The world that then was being overflowed with water, perished, to signify, That the heavens and the earth which are now, are reserved unto fire, against the day of judgment, and perdition of ungodly men.

"I bring a flood of waters upon the earth, to destroy all flesh wherein is the breath of life from under heaven, and everything that is in the earth shall die." By these latter words, as the cause, so the extension of this curse is expressed; and that under a threefold denotation.

1. Everything that is in the earth.
2. All flesh wherein is the breath of life.
3. Everything that is under heaven.

So then, this deluge was universal, and extended itself not only to those parts of the world where Noah and that generation lived, which we find repeated before, but even over the face of all the earth; and it took hold of the life of every living thing that was either on all the earth, or in the air, excepting only those in the ark, as will the general judgment do: "And Noah only remained alive, and they that were with him in the ark." (Gen. vii. 23.)

Verse 18. "But with thee will I establish my covenant; and thou shalt come into the ark, thou, and thy sons, and thy wife, and thy sons' wives with thee."

"But with thee," &c. This concerns what was said before concerning the universality of the flood: As he also said above, "But Noah found grace in the eyes of the Lord." This Peter also notes. He "saved Noah, the eighth per⌐, a preacher of righteousness, bringing in the ⌐od upon the world of the ungodly." (2 Pet. ii. 5.)

"With thee will I establish my covenant." My covenant of mercy, or my promise to save thee when I drown the whole world for their iniquity: And therefore he adds, "And thou shalt come into the ark."

"I will establish." Making and establishing of promises are not always the same: He made his promise to Abraham, he seconded it with an oath unto Isaac, and he confirmed, or established it to Jacob, (Ps. cv. 8—10,) for by him he multiplied the seed of Abraham as the stars of heaven for multitude.

"With thee will I establish." Or, unto thee will I perform my promise, "Thou shalt come into the ark."

Hence note again, That we ought to look upon signal and great deliverances from sore and imminent dangers, to be confirmations of the promise or covenant of God. Or thus: When God finds means of deliverance, and instateth our souls in a special share of that means, this we should take as a sign, That with us God hath confirmed, or established, his covenant.

"Thou, and thy sons, and thy wife, and thy sons' wives with thee." Because in that family did now reside the whole of the visibility of the church upon the earth; all the rest were lost, as Peter also intimates, when he calleth Noah the eighth person, or one, and the chief of the eight that made up the visible church, or that maintained the purity of the worship of God upon the face of the whole earth: As he explains it a little after: "For thee have I seen righteous before me in this generation." (Gen. vii. 1.)

Verse 19. "And of every living thing of all flesh, two of every sort shalt thou bring into the ark, to keep them alive with thee; they shall be male and female."

By these words Noah should seem to be, in this action, a figure or semblance of Christ; who, before the Lord shall rain fire and brimstone from heaven, shall gather into his ark, the church, of all kindreds, and tongues, and people, and nations, even as Noah was to gather of all, of everything, of all flesh, of every sort, with him into the ark.

"Two of every sort." This two, in special, respecteth the unclean, (Gen. vii. 2,) which were a type of the Gentiles, and so further confirms the point.

"They shall be male and female." He would not make a full end, he would in judgment remember mercy.

Verse 20. "Of fowls after their kind, and of cattle after their kind, of every creeping thing of the earth after his kind: two of every sort shall come unto thee to keep them alive."

"Of fowls after their kind, of cattle after their kind." This, still respecting the antitype, may show us also, how that God, for proof of the prophecy of the spreading of the gospel, doth not only tell us, that the Gentiles were gathered into his ark, but as here the beasts and birds, according to their kind, are specified: so the Gentiles are also denominated according to their several countries, Galatians, Corinthians, Ephesians, Colossians, Thessalonians, Bereans, &c., these, after their country and nation, were gathered unto Jesus to be preserved from the flood of wrath that at last shall fall from God who dwells in heaven, to the burning up of the sinner and ungodly.

"Two of every sort shall come in to thee to keep them alive." If the emphasis lieth in "come," as I am apt to think, and as the eighth verse of the next chapter fairly allows me to judge, then we must observe still, that Noah was not only first in the ark, as our Lord and Christ is the first from the dead; but that the cattle, the fowls, and the creeping things, did come to him into the ark, by a special instinct from heaven of the fruits of a divine election. Noah, therefore, as a man, did not make choice which of every kind; but he went first into the ark, and then of clean beasts by sevens, and of unclean beasts by twos, went in unto Noah into the ark, as the Lord commanded Noah.

And thus it is in the antitype: "Unto thee shall all flesh come," saith the prophet. (Ps. lxv. 2.) And again, "To him shall the gathering of the people be." (Gen. xlix. 10.) But how? Why, by an instinct from heaven, the fruit of a divine election: "All that the Father hath given me, shall come to me; but no man can come to me," saith Christ, "unless the Father which hath sent me draw him." (John vi. 37, 44.)

The beasts, therefore, which came into the ark, were neither chosen by men, neither came they in by any instinct of nature which was common to them all, but as being by a divine hand singled out and guided thither, so they entered in: the rest were left to the fury of the flood. Like to this also is the antitype, sinners come not to Jesus by any work or choice of flesh and blood, nor yet by any instinct of nature that is common to all the world; but they come, as being by a divine hand singled out from others; and as guided of the Father, so they come to Christ into the ark. The rest are left to the fury of the wrath of God, which, in the day of judgment, shall swallow them up for ever.

"They shall come unto thee to keep them alive." Indeed, they lived not for their own sakes, they being not better than them that perished; but they shall come unto thee to save them: for, for the sake of Noah they were preserved, when many millions were drowned in the waters. Bring this also to the antitype, and you find them look like one another: for the reason why some are saved from the wrath to come, it is not for that they are better in themselves, for both Jews and Gentiles are all under sin; but it is Christ that saveth by his righteousness, as Noah saved the beasts and fowls, &c. Let us, therefore, as the beasts did, go to Jesus Christ, that he may keep us alive from perishing in the day of judgment.

Verse 21. " And take thou unto thee of all food that is eaten, and thou shalt gather it to thee; and it shall be for food for thee and for them."

This, therefore, was for the preservation of the life of those that were in the ark; by which action there is, as in the former, inclosed a gospel-mystery.

" Take thou unto thee of all food." This food was not to be at the will and dispose of unruly beasts, but Noah was, as the Lord of all that was in the ark, to take it into his own custody: and therefore he doubled the command, " Take it unto thee ;" gather it unto thee ; to wit, to dispose of after thy discretion and faithfulness. In this, therefore, he was a type of Christ, whom God hath set as Lord and King in the church, and " to feed his flock as a shepherd ;" for the " bread of God " is in the hand of Christ, for him to communicate unto his spouses, saints, and children ; as Joseph did to Egypt, according to the power committed to him, and trust reposed in him. And hence it is said, as concerning the bread that endureth to everlasting life, " The Son of man shall give unto you ; for him hath God the Father sealed," (John vi. 27,) or appointed thereunto : and therefore that he giveth, we receive, and no more of the bread of God : " That thou givest them, they gather : thou openest thy hand, they are filled with good." (Ps. civ. 28.)

" Take unto thee all food." That is, to be eaten by man and beast ; the fowl also, and the creeping thing. This still followed, and brought in to the gospel, it shows us that, even then, when the church is driven up into a hole, and tossed upon the waves of the rage and fury of the world, as the ark was upon the face of the waters, that even then her Noah hath all food for her, or food of all sorts for her support and refreshment : " Bread shall be given him ; his waters shall be sure." (Isa. xxxiii. 16.)

" Take unto thee." How blessedly was this answered, when the lion of the tribe of Judah took the book out of the hand of him that sat upon the throne ; (Rev. v. 7 ;) for in the book is contained the words of everlasting life ; and the words of God are the food of his church, which this Noah hath received to nourish them withal : " Man doth not live by bread only, but by every word that proceedeth out of the mouth of the Lord, doth man live." (Deut. viii. 3. Matt. iv. 4.)

" And it shall be for food for thee, and for them." That is, each according to their kind. The same is true also under our present consideration ; Christ is the shepherd, we are the sheep, yet he feedeth with us in the ark : " I will come in to him, and will sup with him, and he with me." (Rev. iii. 20.) Again, here Christ transcends this action of Noah ; for he was to have his food of his own, but Christ feedeth on the same with us, even on the words of God. Yet herein again we differ ; he feedeth as a Lord, we as servants ; he as a Saviour, we as the saved ; but in general, respecting the words of God, we feed all but of one dish, but at one table ; the bread, therefore, that he hath provided, gathered, and taken to him, it was food for him, as well as for us.

Verse 22. " Thus did Noah ; according to all that God commanded him, so did he."

These words, therefore, present us with a description of the sincerity and simplicity of the faith of Noah ; who received the word at the mouth of God ; not to hear only, but to do and live in the same.

" Thus did Noah." As it is also said of his servant Moses, " As the Lord commanded Moses, so did he." As the Lord commanded Moses, so did he ; Yea, to show us how pleasant a thing the Holy Ghost accounteth this holy obedience of faith, he is not weary with repeating, and repeating again not less than eight times in one chapter, the punctuality of Moses' conformity with the word of God, in this manner, " Thus did Moses ;" according to all that the Lord commanded Moses, so did he. (Exod. xl. 16, 19, 21, 23, 25, 27, 29, 32.)

" Thus did Noah." This note, therefore, is, as it were, a character or mark by which the Lord's people are known from the world. They have special regard to the word. " All his saints are in thy hand : and they sat down at thy feet ; every one shall receive of thy words." (Deut. xxxiii. 3.) As Christ said, " I have given them thy words, and they have received them." (John xvii. 8.) Yea, " and they have kept thy word." (ver. 6.)

" Thus did Noah." Let this, then, be the discriminating character of the saints from the men of this world. It was so in the days of Noah, when all the world went a whoring from their God, and said, " We desire not the knowledge of thy ways." (Job xxi. 14.) Then Noah kept the words of God. " Thus did Noah ; according to all that God commanded him, so did he."

CHAPTER VII.

Verse 1. " And the Lord said unto Noah, Come thou and all thy house into the ark ; for thee have I seen righteous before me in this generation."

The ark being now prepared, and the day of God's patience come to an end, he now is resolved to execute his threatening upon the world of ungodly men ; but withal, in the first place, to secure his saints, and them that have feared his name. In this, therefore, we have a semblance of the last judgment, and how God will dispose of his friends and enemies.

"Come thou into the ark." God, I say, will take care of, and safely provide for us that have feared him, when he most eminently entereth into judgment with the world. As he also saith by Isaiah the prophet, "Come, my people, enter thou into thy chambers, and shut thy doors about thee: hide thyself, as it were, for a little moment, until the indignation be overpast." (Isa. xxi. 20.) "He shall send his angels with a great sound of a trumpet, and they shall gather together his elect from the four winds, from one end of heaven to another." (Matt. xxiv. 31.)

"Come thou and all thy house." Not a hoof must be left behind. God will not lose the very dust of his people. Of all that thou hast given me have I lost nothing, but will raise it up at the last day. (John vi. 39.) God, therefore, was careful not only of Noah, but of all that were in his house; because they were all of his visible church, they must, therefore, be preserved from the rage and fury of the deluge: "Gather my saints together unto me," saith he, "those that have made a covenant with me by sacrifice." (Ps. l. 5.)

"For thee have I seen righteous before me." This is not to be understood as the meritorious cause, but as the characteristical note that distinguisheth them that are gods, from others that are subjects of his wrath and displeasure: wherefore, those that at this time perished, bear the badge of ungodliness, as that which made them obnoxious to this overflowing judgment. As also we have it in the book of Job, "Hast thou," said Eliphaz, "marked the old way which wicked men have trodden? which were cut down out of time, whose foundation was overflown with a flood?" (Job xxii. 15, 16.)

Righteousness, therefore, is the distinguishing character whereby the good are known from the bad. Thus it was in Ezekiel's time: "Set a mark," saith God, "upon the foreheads of the men that sigh and that cry for all the abominations that be done in the midst of the city." (Ezek. ix. 4.) Which mark was to distinguish them from those that were profane, and that for their wickedness were to be destroyed by the ministers of God's justice.

"For thee have I seen righteous before me." These words "before me" are inserted on purpose to show us, that Noah was no feigned worshipper, but one who did all things in the sight of God. Indeed, there are two things which are of absolute necessity for the obtaining of this approbation of God. 1. All things must be done as to manner according to the word. 2. All things must be done as to the matter of them according to the word. Both which were found in Noah's performances; and therefore he is said to be perfect in his generations, and that he walked with God. Thus it was also with Zacharias and Elisabeth, "they were both righteous before God;" (Luke i. 6;) that is, sincere and unfeigned in their obedience.

"Righteous before me in this generation." By this we see, righteousness, or the truth of God's worship in the world, was now come to a low ebb; the devil, and the children of Cain, had bewitched the church of God, and brought the professors thereof so off from the truth of his way, that had they got Noah also, the church had been quite extinct and gone: wherefore, it now was time for God to work, and to cherish what was left, even by sending a besom of destruction upon all the face of the earth, to sweep away all the workers of iniquity.

Verses 2, 3. "Of every clean beast thou shalt take to thee by sevens, the male and his female; and of beasts that are not clean, by two, the male and his female. Of fowls also of the air, by sevens, the male and the female, to keep seed alive upon the face of all the earth."

Something hath been said to this already; only this I will add further, that by this commandment of God, both Noah, and all that were with him, were pre-admonished to look to their hearts; that they continued unfeigned before him. For if God would save unclean beasts, and fowls, from the present and terrible destruction: why also might not some of them, though they partook of this temporal deliverance, be still reputed as unclean in his sight? As indeed it came to pass, for a cursed Ham was there. Wherefore, read not lightly the commands of God, there may be both doctrine and exhortation; both item, as well as an obligation to a duty contained therein. Circumcision was a duty incumbent as to the letter of the commandment; but there was also doctrine in it, as to a more high and spiritual teaching than the letter simply imported.

Note then from hence, that when you read that unclean beasts, and unclean birds may be in the ark of Noah: that unclean men, and unclean women may be in the church of God; "One of you is a devil," was an admonition to all the rest: let this also of the beasts unclean be an admonition to you.

Verse 4. "For yet seven days, and I will cause it to rain upon the earth forty days and forty nights; and every living substance that I have made, will I destroy, (or, blot out) from off the face of the earth."

Now the judgment is at the door; it is time to make haste, and pack into the ark. God doth not love to have his people have much vacancy from employment while they are in this world. Idle times are dangerous; David found it so in the business of Uriah's wife. Wherefore Noah having finished the ark, he hath another work to do, even to get himself, with his family and household, fitly settled in the vessel that was to save him from the deluge, and that at his peril in seven days' time.

"For yet seven days, and I will bring a flood." Note again, that it hath been the way of God, even when he doth execute the severest judgments, to tell it in the ears of some of his saints some time before he doth execute the same : yea, it seems to me, that it will be so even in the great day of God Almighty ; for I read, that before the bridegroom came, "there was a cry made, behold the bridegroom cometh !" (Matt. xxv. 6.) Which cry doth not seem to me to be the ordinary cry of the ministers of the gospel, but a cry that was effected by some sudden and marvellous wakening, the product of some new and extraordinary revelation. That also seems to look like some fore-word to the church, "Then shall appear the sign of the Son of man in heaven." (Matt. xxiv. 30.) Some strange and unusual revelation of that notable day to be near, which in other ages was not made known to the world ; upon which sign he presently appears. Now whether this sign will be the appearing of the angels first, or whether the opening of the heavens, or the voice of the arch-angel, and the trump of God, or what, I shall not here presume to determine ; but a fore-word there is like to be, yet so immediately followed with the personal presence of Christ, that they who had not grace before, shall not have time nor means to get it then : "And while they went to buy, the bride-groom came ; and they that were ready went in with him, and the door was shut." (Matt. xxv. 10.)

"And I will cause it to rain upon the earth forty days, and forty nights." This length of time doth fore-pronounce the completing of the judgment : as who should say, I will cause it to rain until I have blotted out all the creatures, both of men, beasts, and fowls ; and so the after-words import ; "And every living substance that I have made, will I destroy from off the face of the earth."

Verse 5. "And Noah did according unto all that the Lord commanded him."

This note, as already I have said, doth denote him to be a righteous man ; one that might with honour to his God, escape the judgment now to be executed ; wherefore, the reiterating of this character is much for the vindicating of God's justice, and for the justification of his overthrowing the world of ungodly sinners.

But again : these words seem to respect in special, what Noah did in the last seven days, in order to the commandment laid before him in the three first verses of this chapter ; and so they signify his faithfulness to the word, and his observance of the law of his God, even to the day that the rain began to fall upon the earth : and therefore they preach unto us, not only that he began well, but that he continued in godly and unfeigned perseverance ; which when perfected, is the most effectual proof, that what before he did, he did with uprightness of heart, and therefore now must escape the judgment. As it is said in the gospel of Matthew, "He that shall endure unto the end, the same shall be saved." (Matt. xxiv. 13.)

Verse 6. "And Noah was six hundred years old when the flood of waters was upon the earth."

Four hundred and fourscore of which the world had leisure to study the prophecy that God gave of him by the mouth of his father Lamech ; (Gen. v. 29;) the other hundred and twenty he spent in a more open testifying, both by word, and his preparing the ark, that God would one day overtake them with judgment ; yet to the day that the flood came, the world was ignorant thereof : (Matt. xxiv. 38, 39.) Astonishing is the fruits of sin. So it came to pass, that in the six hundredth year of Noah's life, which was the one thousand six hundred and fifty-sixth year of the world's age, the flood of waters was upon the earth, to the utter destruction of all that was found upon the face thereof, Noah only being left alive, and they that were with him in the ark.

Verse 7. "And Noah went in, and his sons, and his wife, and his sons' wives with him, into the ark, because of the waters of the flood."

They had hardly done their work in the world, by that it began to rain, by that the first drops of the judgment appeared. They went into the ark, says the text, because of the waters of the flood. This should teach Christians diligence, lest they be called for by God's dispensations, either of death or judgment, before they have served completely their generations, by the will of God. Noah had done it, but it seems he had but done it ; his work was ended just as the judgment came : "therefore be ye also ready ; for at such an hour as ye think not, the Son of man cometh." (Matt. xxiv. 44.)

Verses 8, 9. "Of clean beasts, and of beasts that are not clean, and of fowls, and of every thing that creepeth upon the earth, there went in two and two unto Noah into the ark, the male and the female, as God had commanded Noah."

By these words it seems (as I also touched before) that the beasts, and fowls, both clean and unclean, did come in to Noah, into the ark ; not by Noah's choice, nor by any instinct that was common to all, but by an instinct from above, which so had determined the life and death of these creatures, even to a very sparrow ; for not one of them doth fall to the ground without the providence of our heavenly Father.

"They went in unto Noah." And let no man deride, for that I said, by an instinct from above ; for God hath not only wrought wonders in men, but even in the beasts and fowls of the air ; to the making of them act both above and against their own nature. How did Balaam's ass speak, (Numb. xxii. 28—30,) and the cows that drew the ark, have it right to the place which God had appointed, not regarding their sucking calves. (1 Sam. vi. 10—14.) Yea, how did those ravenous creatures, the ravens, bring the prophet bread and flesh twice a day, (1 Kings xvii. 6,) but by immediate instinct from heaven ? Even by the same did these go in to Noah, into the ark.

Verse 10. "And it came to pass, after seven

NOAH AND HIS FAMILY.

days, that the waters of the flood were upon the earth."

Just as the Lord had denounced before. Look, therefore, what God hath said, shall assuredly come to pass, whether it be believed, or counted an idle tale. The confirmation, therefore, of what God hath spoken, depended not upon the credence of man, because it came not by the will of man : "He hath said it, and shall he not make it good?" it will therefore assuredly come to pass, whatever God hath spoken, be it to save his Noahs, or be it to drown his enemies; and the reason is, because to do otherwise is inconsistent with his nature. He is faithful, holy, and true, and cannot deny himself, that is, the word which he hath spoken.

Verse 11. "In the six hundredth year of Noah's life, in the second month, the seventeenth day of the month, the same day were all the fountains of the great deep broken up, and the windows (or flood-gates) of heaven were opened."

As to the month, and the day of the month I have but little to say; though doubtless, had not there been something worthy of knowing therein, it would not so punctually have been left upon record; for I dare not say this scribe wrote this in vain, or that it was needless thus to punctilio it; a mystery is in it, but my darkness sees it not; I must speak according to the proportion of faith.

"The same day were all the fountains of the great deep broken up." By these words, it seems that it did not only rain from heaven, but also the springs and fountains were opened; which, together with the great rain of his strength, did overflow the world the sooner.

This great deep, in mine opinion, was also a type of the bottomless pit, that mouth and gulf of hell, which at the day of judgment shall gape upon the world of ungodly men, to swallow them up from the face of the earth, and to carry them away from the face and presence of God.

"And the windows (or flood-gates) of heaven were opened." That is, that the water might descend without measure or order, even in its own natural force, with violence upon the head of the wicked. It came as "water out of his buckets" (Numb. xxiv. 7,) upon them, judgment without mercy.

This opening of the flood-gates of heaven, was a type of the way that shall be made for the justice of God upon ungodly men, when Christ hath laid aside his mediatorship; for he indeed is the sluice that stoppeth this justice of God from its dealing according to its infinite power and severity with men. He stands, like Moses, and, as it were, holdeth the hands of God. Oh! but when he shall be taken away! When he shall have finished his mediatory work: then will the flood-gates of heaven be opened, and then will the justice and holiness of God deal with men without stint or diminution, even till it hath filled the vessels of wrath with vengeance till they run over: "It is a fearful thing to fall into the hands of the living God."

Verse 12. "And the rain was upon the earth forty days and forty nights."

That is, It rained so long without stop or stint. (ver. 4.)

Verse 13. "In the selfsame day entered Noah, and Shem, and Ham, and Japheth the sons of Noah; and Noah's wife, and the three wives of his sons, with them, into the ark."

This, therefore, more fully approveth of what I said before; to wit, That they had hardly done their work in the world, by that it began to rain; but so soon as they had done, the flood was upon the earth. Much like this is that of Lot; it was not to rain fire and brimstone upon Sodom, till he was got to Zoar : But when Lot was entered, but just entered, "Then the Lord rained upon Sodom, and upon Gomorrah, brimstone and fire from the Lord out of heaven." (Gen. xix. 24.)

Hence note, That the reason why God doth forbear to destroy the world for the wickedness of them that dwell therein, it is for the sake of the elect; because his work upon them is not fully perfected. "The Lord is not slack concerning his promise," (2 Pet. iii. 9;) no, nor as concerning his threatening neither,—but is long-suffering to usward who are the elect; not willing that any of us should perish : But when Christ, head and members, are complete in all things, let the world look for patience and forbearance no longer; for in that selfsame day the trump of God will sound, and the Lord descend with a shout from heaven, to execute his anger with fury, and his rebukes with flames of fire. Behold, he is now "ready to judge the quick and the dead!" (1 Pet. iv. 5;) "ready to be revealed in the last time!" (1 Pet. i. 5.) The judge also stands at the door, (James v. 9;) it is but opening therefore, and his hand is upon you, which most assuredly he will do when his body is full and complete.

Observe again, that providence sometimes so ordereth it, that as touching the command of the Lord, necessity is as it were the great wheel that brings men into the performances of them, as here the flood drove them into the ark; as he said above, they went in because of the waters of the flood : So concerning the ordinance of unleavened bread, the first institution of that law, was, as it were, accompanied with an unavoidable necessity, it was unleavened, saith the text, "because they were thrust out of Egypt, and could not tarry, neither had they prepared for themselves any victual." (Exod. xii. 39.)

It will be thus also at the day of judgment: Israel will be sufficiently weary of this world, they will even as it were unexpressibly groan to be taken up from hence; wherefore the Lord will come, as making use of the weariness and groaning of his people, and will take them up into his chambers of rest, and will wipe away all tears from their eyes, as here Noah and his sons, &c., did enter the ark.

Verse 14. "They and every beast after his kind, and all the cattle after their kind, and every creeping thing that creepeth upon the earth, after his kind, and every fowl after his kind, every bird of every sort" or wing.

Without doubt this careful repetition is not without a cause, and hath also in the bowels of it some comfortable doctrine for the church of God; every beast, all cattle, every creeping thing that creepeth; every fowl and bird of every wing.

First this showeth, that God hath respect to the fulfilling of his word in the midst of all his zeal and anger against sin. He doth not as we, being angry, run headlong upon the offenders, but if there be but three in a kingdom, or one in four cities, he will have respect to them. (Ezek. xiv. 12—20.)

Secondly, It showeth, that how inconsiderable soever the persons are, that are within the compass, and care of the love and mercy of God, that inconsiderableness shall not be a let to their safety and preservation: Yea, though they are but as these creeping things, that creep upon the earth, or as the saying is, but as a flea, a dead dog, or a grasshopper, or one of the least of the grains of wheat, not one of them, nay, not a hair of the head of them shall fall to the ground and perish.

Verses 15, 16. "And they went in unto Noah into the ark, two and two of all flesh, wherein is the breath of life. And they that went in, went in male and female of all flesh, as God had commanded him, and the Lord shut him in."

The Holy Ghost in this relation is wonderfully punctual and exact: every beast, all cattle, every creeping thing, every fowl, and every bird, after their kind went in; and saith he again, they that went in, went in two and two; as if there had been an intelligence among these irrational creatures, that the flood was shortly to be upon the earth. Indeed, many among the sensitives have strange instincts, as appendixes to their nature, by which they do, and leave to do, to the astonishment of them that have reason: But that any instinct in nature should put them upon afore providing for shelter from the flood, by going into the ark (a place to secure them, rather than to save them, had not the occasion and command of God been otherwise,) it cannot be once with reason imagined. Wherefore, as their going into the ark, so their going in two by two, and that too male and female, plainly declares that their motion was ordered and governed by heaven, themselves being utterly ignorant thereof.

"And they that went in went in male and female of all flesh; (both man and beast,) and the Lord shut him in," that is Noah; and those that were with him.

These latter words are of great importance, and do show us the distinguishing grace of God, for by his thus shutting the door of the ark, he not only confirmed his mercy to Noah, but also discovered the bounds and limits thereof. As who should say, Now, Noah, you have your full tale, just thus many I will save from the flood: and with that he shut the door, leaving all other, both man and beast, &c., to the fury of the waters. God therefore by this act hath showed how it will go in the day of judgment with men. Those that (like those beasts, and birds, and creeping things) shall come to Christ, into his ark, before it rain fire and brimstone from heaven, those will God shut up in the ark, and they shall live in that day; but those that shall then be found in the world strangers to Jesus Christ, those will God shut out: "They that were ready went in with him to the marriage, and the door was shut." (Matt. xxv. 10.)

And observe, it is not not said, that Noah shut the door, but the Lord shut him in: If God shuts in or out, who can alter it? I shut, and no man openeth. (Rev. iii. 7.) Doubtless before the flood had carried off the ark, others besides would with gladness have had there a lodging room, though no better than a dog-kennel; but now it was too late, the Lord had shut the door. Besides, had there been now in the heart of Noah, bowels or compassion to those without the ark, or had he had desire to have received them to him, all had been worth nothing, the Lord had shut him in This signifying, that at the day of judgment, neither the bowels of Jesus Christ, neither the misery that damned men shall be in, will any thing at all avail with God to save one sinner more—the door is shut.

Where you read therefore both in Matthew and Luke of the shutting of the door, understand that by such expressions Christ alludeth to the door in Noah's ark, which door was open while Noah, and his attendants were entering into the ark, but they being got in, the Lord shut the door. Then they that stood without and knocked, did weep, and knock, and ask too late. As Christ saith, "When once the master of the house is risen up, and hath shut to the door, and ye begin to stand without, and knock at the door, saying, Lord, Lord, open unto us; and he shall answer and say unto you, I know you not whence ye are: Then shall ye begin to say, We have eaten and drunk in thy presence, and thou hast taught in our streets, (as Noah did of old.) But he shall say, I tell you I know you not whence you are; depart from me all ye workers of iniquity. There shall be weeping and gnashing of teeth, when ye shall see Abraham, and Isaac, and Jacob, and all the prophets in the kingdom of God, and you yourselves thrust out." (Luke xiii. 25—28.)

Verse 17. "And the flood was forty days upon the earth, and the waters increased and bare up the ark, and it was lift up above the earth."

While the ark rested, and abode in his place, no doubt but the ears of Noah were filled with doleful cries from the wretched and miserable people, whom God shut without the ark, one while crying, another while knocking, according to what but now was related; which for aught I know might be many of the forty days, but when the waters much increased, and lift the ark above the earth, this miserable company were soon shaken off.

It will be thus also in the day of judgment; at the beginning of that day the ears of the godly will be sufficiently filled with the cries and tears of the damned and miserable world; but when the ark shall be taken up, that is, when the godly shall ascend into the clouds, and so go hence with Jesus, they will soon lose this company, and be out of the hearing of their lamentable dolours.

"And the waters increased." God's judgments have no ears to receive the cries, nor heart to pity the miseries of the damned. They cry, it rains; they increase their cries, and the Lord does increase his judgment: "Therefore is it come to pass, that as he cried and they would not hear; so they cried, and I would not hear, saith the Lord of hosts." (Zech. vii. 13.)

Again, As the waters were a type of the wrath of God that in the day of judgment shall fall upon ungodly men, so they were also a type of those afflictions and persecutions that attend the church; for that very water that did drown the ungodly, that did also toss and tumble the ark about; wherefore by the increase of the waters, we may also understand, how mighty and numerous sometimes the afflictions and afflictors of the godly be: As David said, "Lord, how are they increased that trouble me! many are they that rise up against me." (Ps. iii. 1.)

"And the waters increased, and bare up the ark." The higher the rage and tyranny of this world groweth against the church of God, the higher is the ark lifted up towards heaven, the most proud wave lifts it highest: The church is also by persecution more purged and purified from earthly and carnal delights; therefore it is added, "the waters bare up the ark, and it was lifted up above the earth."

Verse 18. "And the waters prevailed, and were increased greatly upon the earth, and the ark went upon the face of the waters."

These words are still to be considered under the former double consideration, to wit, both, as they present us with God's wrath at the last judgment, and as they present us with a sign of the rage and malice of ungodly men.

"And the waters prevailed;" that is, over all ungodly sinners; though they were mighty, and stout, and cared for none, yet the waters prevailed against them, as the fire and brimstone will do over all the world at the day and coming of our Lord Jesus Christ. Wherefore, well may it be said to all impenitent sinners, "Can thy heart endure, or can thy hands be strong, in the day that I shall deal with thee," (Ezek. xxii. 14,) saith the Lord God? Oh they cannot, the waters of the wrath of God will prevail against, and increase upon them, until they have utterly swallowed them up.

"And the waters prevailed." Take it now as a type of the nature of persecution, and then it showeth, that as the waters here did swallow up all but the ark, so when persecution is mighty in the world, it prevaileth to swallow up all but the church: for none else can aright withstand or oppose their wickedness. It is said, when the beast had power to work, the whole "world wondered after the beast," (Rev. xiii. 3;) and all men who were not sealed, and that had not the mark of God in their foreheads, fell in with the worship of the beast; as it is said, "And all that dwell upon the earth shall worship him, whose names are not written in the book of life of the Lamb," &c. (Rev. xiii. 8.) So then it might well be said, "The waters prevailed and increased."

"And the ark went upon the face of the waters." It is said that in the beginning the Spirit of God moved upon the face of the waters, and here that the ark went upon the face of them. Indeed the Spirit of God moveth, and the church, as God, walketh in strange and unthought-of stations. It is said, that God hath a "way in the whirlwind, and in the storm," (Neh. i. 3:) So he hath upon the very face of the persecution of the day, but none but the church can follow him here, it is the ark that can follow him upon the face of the waters. Deep things are seen by them that are upon the waters: "They that go down to the sea in ships, that do business in great waters; they see the works of the Lord, and his wonders in the deep." (Ps. cvii. 23, 24.) Indeed it oft falls out, that the church seeth more of God in affliction, than when she is at rest and ease; when she is tumbled to and fro in the waters, then she sees the works of God, and his wonders in the deep.

And this makes persecution so pleasant a thing, this makes the ark go upon the face of the waters, she seeth more in this her state, than in all the treasures of Egypt.

Verse 19. "And the waters prevailed exceedingly upon the earth, and all the high hills, that were under the whole heaven, were covered.

This second repetition of the prevailing of the waters, doth also call for a second consideration.

1. It shows us, that all hope that any ungodly man might have at the beginning of the flood to escape the rage thereof, was now swallowed up in death. Indeed it is natural to the creatures, when floods and inundations are upon the earth, to repair to the high places, as they only that are left for preservation of life; where life may be also continued if the waters do not overflow them: but when it comes to pass as here we read, that all the hills under the heavens are covered, then life takes its farewell, and is gone from the world, as was the effect of the waters of Noah.

The hills therefore were types of the hope of the hypocrite, upon which they clamber till their heads do touch the clouds, thinking thereby to escape the judgment of God; but "though they hide themselves in the top of Carmel, I will search and take them thence," (Amos ix. 3,) saith God: the flood of his wrath will come thither, even over the tops of all the hills. So that safety is only in the ark with Noah, in the church with Christ, all other places must be drowned with the flood.

2. We may also understand by this verse, how God in a time of persecution will cut off the carnal confidence of his people. We are apt to place our hope somewhere else than in God, when persecution ariseth because of the word. We hope that such a man, or that such outward means may prevent our being swept away with this flood. But because this confidence is not after God, but tendeth to weaken our steadfast dependence on him; therefore this flood shall cover all our hills, not one shall be found for us under the whole heaven. When the king of Babylon came up against Jerusalem to war, then Israel, instead of trusting in God, put their confidence in the king of Egypt, but he also was swallowed up by this flood, that Israel might be ashamed of such confidence; and this at last they confessed. "As for us," said they, "our eyes as yet failed for our vain help: in our watching, we have watched for a nation that could not save us." (Lam. iv. 17.)

It was requisite, therefore, that the hills should be covered, that Noah might not have confidence in them; but surely this dispensation of God was a heart-shaking providence to Noah, and they that were with him; for here indeed was his faith tried, there was no hill left in all the world; now were his carnal helpers gone, there was none shut up or left. Now, therefore, if they could rejoice, it must be only in the power of God. As David said, Should I lift mine eyes to the hills, whence should my help come? (Ps. cxxi. 1.) So the margin: "My help cometh from the Lord that made heaven and earth." (Ps. cxxi. 2.)

Verse 20. "Fifteen cubits upward did the waters prevail; and the mountains were covered." The height of Goliah was but "six cubits and a span," (1 Sam. xvii. 4,) neither was Og's bedstead any more than nine. (Deut. iii. 11.) Wherefore this flood prevailed far above the highest of those mighty ones: even fifteen cubits above the highest mountains.

Verses 21, 22, 23. "And all flesh died that moved upon the earth, both of fowl, and of cattle, and of beast, and of every creeping thing that creepeth upon the earth, and every man: All in whose nostrils was the breath of life, of all that was in the dry land, died. And every living substance was destroyed, which was upon the face of the ground, both man and cattle, and the creeping things, and the fowl of the heaven; and they were destroyed from the earth: and Noah only remained alive, and they that were with him in the ark."

In these words you have the effects of the flood, which was punctually according to the judgment threatened. But observe, I pray you, how the

Holy Ghost, by repeating doth amplify the matter. "All flesh," "all in whose nostrils was the breath of life," "all that was in the dry land," "every living substance," "every man;" "and they were destroyed from the earth." By which manner of language doubtless there is insinuated a threatening to them who should afterward live ungodly. And indeed the Holy Ghost affirmeth, that these judgments, with that of Sodom, are but examples set forth before our eyes, to show us that such sins, such punishment. "Making them an ensample," saith Peter, "unto those that after should live ungodly." (2 Pet. ii. 6.) Nay, Jude saith, they are "set forth" in their overthrow, for that very purpose. (Jude 7.) Wherefore this careful repeating of this judgment of God, doth carry threatening in it, assuredly foreshowing the doom and downfall of those that shall continue to tread their steps.

Yea, mind how Peter hath it: For if God "spared not the old world," (2 Pet. ii. 5,) &c. Secretly intimating, that those that then lived, being the first of his workmanship, and far surpassing in magnificence, if he would have spared, he would have spared them; but seeing he so dreadfully swept them away, let no man be so bold to presume that wickedness shall now deliver him that is given to it.

"And Noah only remained alive, and they that were with him in the ark." Noah was that man of God that had set himself against a world of ungodly men. The man that had hazarded life and limb for the word of God committed to him; he "only remained alive," &c. Hence note, That he was the man that outlived the world, that would for God venture life against all the world. Wherefore the saying in the gospel is true. "He that will lose his life for my sake, shall save it unto life eternal." Thus did Noah, and passed the end, and went over the bounds, that God had appointed for every living thing. Behold! he was a man in both worlds, yea, the world then to come was given him for a possession.

Verse 24. "And the waters prevailed upon the earth an hundred and fifty days." About the same time the scorpions mentioned of John, had power to hurt the earth. (Rev. x. 10.) Wherefore, the thus prevailing of the water, might be a type of our persecution now in the New Testament days. All which time doubtless Noah was sufficiently tried, while the waves of the water had no pity for him.

CHAPTER VIII.

Verse 1. "And God remembered Noah, and every living thing, and all the cattle that was with him in the ark; and God made a wind to pass over the earth, and the waters asswaged."

Moses having thus related the judgment of the waters, as they respected the drowning of the world, and so typed forth the last judgment. He now returneth to speak of them more largely, as they were a type of the persecution and afflictions of the church, and so showeth how God delivered Noah from the merciless violence of the waves thereof.

"And God remembered Noah." This word "remembered" is usual in scripture, both when God is about to deliver his people out of affliction, and to grant them the petition which they ask of him. It is said, God remembered Abraham; and sent Lot out of Sodom, (Gen. xix. 29 ;) that he remembered Rachel, and hearkened to her, (Gen xxx. 22 ;) that he also remembered his covenant with Abraham, when he went to bring Israel out of their bondage. (Exod. ii. 24.)

Hence note, that Noah was now both in an afflicted, and a praying condition ; afflicted with the dread of the waters, and prayed for their asswaging. It is a question accompanied with astonishment, How the ark being of no bigger an hull or bulk should contain so many creatures, with sustenance for them ? And verily, I think, that Noah himself was put to it, to believe and wait for so long a time. But God remembered him, and also the beasts, and every living thing, that was with him, and began to put an end to these mighty afflictions, by causing the waters to asswage.

"And God made a wind to pass over the earth." The waters being here a type of persecutors and persecution : this wind was a type of the breath of the Lord's mouth, by which he is said to slay the wicked. "He shall smite the earth with the rod of his mouth, and with the breath of his lips shall he slay the wicked." (Isa. xi. 4.) It was a wind also that blew away the locusts of Egypt, (Exod. x. 19,) which locusts were a type of our graceless clergy, that have covered the ground of our land. Again, the kingdom of Babel was to be destroyed by a destroying wind, which the Lord would send against her, (Jer. li. 1, 2,) which Paul expounds to be by "the breath of the Lord's mouth, and by the brightness of his coming." This wind therefore, as I said, was a type of the breathing of the Spirit of the Lord, by which means these tumultuous waves shall be laid lower, and God's ark in a while made to rest upon the top of his mountain ; for by the breath of the Lord the earth is lightened, and by this lightning coals are kindled ; yea, he sent out his arrows and scattered them, he shot out lightnings and discomforted them. Then the channels of waters were seen, and the foundations of the world were discovered ; at thy rebuke, O Lord, at the blast of the breath of thy nostrils." (Ps. xviii. 14, 15. 1 Sam. xxii. 15, 16.) "And God made a wind to pass over the earth, and the waters asswaged," that is, in New Testament language, the afflictors and afflictions of the church did cease and decay, and come to nought.

"And the waters asswaged :" To wit, by the blowing of this wind, wherefore, as this wind did assault the waters, so it did refresh the spirit of this servant of God, because by it the affliction was driven away. Thus then by the wind of the Lord were these dry bones refreshed, and made to stand upon their feet. (Ezek. xxxvii. 9, 10.)

"And God made a wind to pass over." And God made it ; when God blows, the enemies of his truth shall pass away like waters that fail.

Verse 2. "The fountains also of the deep, and the windows of heaven were stopped, and the rain from heaven was restrained."

By these words we see, that when the church of God is afflicted, both heaven and hell have their hand therein, but so as from a differing consideration, and to a diverse end. From heaven it comes, that we may remember we have sinned, and that we may be made white, and tried, (Dan. xii. 35 ;) but from hell, from the great deep, that we might sin the more, and that we might despair, and be damned. (Job i. 11 ; ii. 5.)

"And the fountains of the great deep." When God begins to slack and abate the afflictions of his church, he rebukes, as it were first, the powers of hell ; for should he take off his own hand, while they have leave to do what they list, the church for this would be worse, not better. But first he rebuketh them : "The Lord rebuke thee, O Satan," that's the first ; and then he clothes them "with change of raiment." (Zech. iii. 2—4.) The fountains of the great deep were stopped, and then the bottles of heaven.

"And the rain from heaven was restrained, or held back, or made to cease." Afflictions are governed by God, both as to time, number, nature, and measure. "In measure, when it shooteth forth, thou wilt debate with it ; he stayeth his rough wind in the day of the east wind." (Isa. xxvii. 8.) Our times therefore, and our conditions in those times, are in the hand of God ; yea, and so are our souls and bodies, to be kept and preserved from the evil, while the rod of God is upon us.

Verse 3. "And the waters returned from off the earth continually : and after the end of an hundred and fifty days the waters were abated."

The verse before doth treat of the original, the fountains of the deep, and the windows of heaven, that they were shut, or stopped ; which being done, the effect beginneth to cease. Hence note, that ease and release from persecution and affliction cometh not by chance, or by the good moods, or gentle dispositions of men, but the Lord doth hold them back from sin, the Lord restraineth them. It is said, the Lord stirred up the adversaries of Solomon. (1 Kings xi. 14—23.) Again, when the Syrians fought against Jehoshaphat, "the Lord helped him, and God moved them to depart from him." (2 Chron. xviii. 31.) The Lord sent the flood, and the Lord took it away

"And the waters returned from off the earth continually." When God ceaseth to be angry, the hearts and dispositions of the adversaries shall be palliated, and made more flexible. It is said, when the afflictions of Israel were ended in Egypt, the hearts of the people were turned to pity them; yea, "he made them also to be pitied of them that carried them captives." (Ps. cvi. 46.)

When you see, therefore, that the hearts of kings and governors begin to be moderated toward the church of God, then acknowledge that this is the hand of God. "I," saith he, "will cause the enemy to entreat thee well in the time of evil, and in the time of affliction." (Jer. xv. 11.) For by waters here are typed out the great and mighty of the world, by the flowing of them, their rage; and by their ebbing and returning, their stillness and moderation.

"And the waters returned." That is, to the sea. "He gathereth the waters of the sea together as an heap; he layeth up the depth in storehouses." (Ps. xxxiii. 7.)

By "gathering up," the persecutors may be understood, his gathering them to their graves, as he did Herod, who stood in the way of Christ, (Matt. ii. 19, 20;) and as he did those in Ezekiel, who hindered the promotion of truth, and the exaltation of the gospel. (Ezek. xxxi. 14.)

"And after the end of an hundred and fifty days the waters were abated." These words then imply, that for so long time, Noah, and the church with him, were to exercise patience. They also show us, That when the waters are up, they do not suddenly fall. They were up four hundred years, from Abraham to Moses, (Gen. xv. 13;) they were up threescore and ten years in the days of the captivity of Babylon, (Jer. xxv. 12. Zech. i. 12;) they were up ten mystical days in the persecution that was in the days of Antipas, (Rev. ii. 10;) and are to be up forty and two months, in the reign, and under the tyranny of antichrist. (Rev. xiii. 5.) But they will abate; the house of Saul will grow weaker; yea, they shall be gathered to their sea, and shall be laid in the pit; yea, they shall not be on the earth, when God shall "set glory in the land of the living." (Ezek. xxvi. 19, 20.)

Verse 4. "And the ark rested in the seventh month, on the seventeenth day of the month, upon the mountains of Ararat."

These instances, therefore, were a type of Christ, the munition of rocks, (Isa. xxxiii. 16,) who is elsewhere called, the mountain of the Lord's house, (Mic. iv. 1;) the rock upon which he will build his "church, and the gates of hell shall not prevail against it." (Matt. xvi. 18.) For after the ark had felt the ground, or had got settlement upon the tops of these mountains, however the waters that came from the great deep did, notwithstanding, for some time, shake and make it stir, yet off from these mountains they could not get it with all their rage and fury. It rested there; these gates of hell could not prevail. But mark, it did rest on these mountains almost a quarter of a year

before any ground appeared to Noah. A right figure of saving faith; for that maketh not outward observation a ground and foundation for faith, but Christ the rock, who as to sense and feeling is at first quite out of sight. Hence the hope of the godly is compared to the anchor of a ship, which resteth on, or taketh hold of the rock that is now invisible under the water, at the bottom of the sea. (Heb. vi. 19.)

This then should learn us to stay on the Lord Jesus, and there to rest when the waters have drowned all the world, and when all the mountains and hills for help are as if they were cast into the midst of the sea.

That is an excellent saying of the prophet, "God is our refuge and strength, a very present help in trouble. Therefore will not we fear, though the earth be removed (as now it seemed), and though the mountains be carried into the midst of the sea; Though the waters thereof roar, and be troubled; though the mountains shake with the swelling thereof. Selah." (Ps. xlvi. 1—3.)

Verse 5. "And the waters decreased continually until the tenth month; in the tenth month, on the first day of the month, were the tops of the mountains seen."

In the third verse we read, that after an hundred and fifty days' flood, the waters returned; that is, began to return, from off the earth: which beginning of their return, was, because that God had mercifully remembered the prayer and affliction of Noah. Again, in this verse we read, that from the day that the ark did rest upon the mountains of Ararat, the waters decreased continually. Now the resting of the ark on the mountain, was a figure of our trusting on Christ. Hence it follows, that the tumults and raging of the mystical waters, are made to decrease by the power of faith. "This is your victory, even our faith." (1 John v. 4.) As it is also said of Moses, By faith he walked through the Red Sea, (Heb. xi. 29;) but, above all, take that as most pertinent, Through faith they subdued kingdoms, stopped the mouths of lions, and turned to flight the armies of aliens. (Heb. xi. 33, 34.) Here you see faith made the waters decrease; it took away the heat and rage of the adversary.

"And the waters decreased continually until the tenth month, (another period of time,) and in the first day of the tenth month were the tops of the mountains seen." These mountains were before the flood, a type of the hope of the hypocrites, and therefore then were swallowed up, fifteen cubits under the waters. But now, methinks, they should be a figure to the church of some visible ground of deliverance from the flood; for almost three months the ark did rest on the invisible mountains of Ararat; but now are the tops of the mountains seen: a further sign that the waters were abated, and a ground that at length they would be quite dried up. Let these mountains then be types of the high and mighty, which God is used to stir up to deliver his church from the heat and rage of tyranny and persecution, as they are often termed and called in scripture, the mountains of Israel, for this very end. So then, from our thus considering the mountains, two things we are taught thereby.

1. That when the great ones of this world begin to discover themselves to the church, by way of encouragement, it is a sign that the waters are now decreasing. Or thus: when God lets us see the tops of the mountains, then we may certainly conclude that the rage of the waters abate.

Doubtless when God made promise of raising up Josiah to Israel, in Canaan, (1 Kings xiii. 2;) and of raising up for them Cyrus, in Babylon, (Isa. xlv.;) the thus appearing of the tops of these mountains, was comfort to the church in her day of affliction.

2. This should teach us while we are in affliction, to look this way and that, if it may be that the tops of the mountains may be seen by us: for though it be too much below a Christian to place his confidence in men, yet when God shall raise up Josiah or a Cyrus, we may take encouragement at this working of God. Therefore is that in the Psalms read both ways, shall I look to the mountains? "I will lift up mine eyes to the hills, from whence cometh my help;" (Ps. cxxi. 1;) yet so as that he would also conclude his help did come from the Lord. So, then, we must take heed that we look not to the mountains. Again, it is our wisdom to look to the mountains: look not to them but when God discovers them: look unto them if God discovereth them; yet then but so as means of God's appointing. But again, God doth not let us see the hills for our help, before we have first of all seen them drowned. Look not to them, therefore, while the water is at the rising; but if they begin to cease their raging, if they begin to fall, and with that the tops of the mountains be seen, you may look upon them with comfort, they are tokens of God's deliverance.

Verse 6. "And it came to pass, at the end of forty days, that Noah opened the window of the ark which he had made."

These forty days seem to commence from the discovery of the tops of the mountains. Wherefore he did not presently go out of the ark, but stayed there above fourteen days, still signifying unto us, that we must not be therefore delivered so soon as the tops of the mountains are seen, but may yet be assaulted with the waters of the flood, days, and weeks, and months, &c.

When Moses was sent to deliver Israel, they came not presently out of Egypt; neither seemed their burdens ever the lighter to sense or feeling, though faith indeed did see the end. Again, when he had brought them forth of Egypt, they came not in a day, or a month, to Canaan; but, saith the Holy Ghost, "He brought them out," (or, forth of affliction,) "after he had showed signs

and wonders in the land of Egypt, and in the Red Sea, and in the wilderness forty years."

Let us therefore take heed of a feverish spirit, while we behold the tops of the mountains; possibly, for all they are visible tokens to us of deliverance, themselves may be yet much under water. We see what work Moses, Gideon, Jephtha, and Samson had to deliver Israel, even after more than their tops were seen. Be content to stay yet forty days; David stayed after he was anointed, till years and times went over him, before he could deliver Israel from the tyranny of its opposers.

"At the end of forty days Noah opened the window of the ark." This opening of the window also was a type that now he was preparing to take possession of the world. It also might be a type of the opening the law and testimony, that light might by that come into the church; for we find not that this window had any other use, but to be a conveyance of light into the ark, and as a passage for the raven and dove, as may be further showed after. Now much like this is that of John: "The temple of God was opened in heaven, and there was seen in his temple the ark of his testament." (Rev. xi. 19.) And again, "I looked, and behold, the temple of the tabernacle of the testimony in heaven was opened." (Rev. xv. 5.) And then, as the raven and the dove came out of the window of the ark; "so the angels," (that is, the Lord's executioners,) "came out of the temple," (Rev. xv. 6,) that was opened in heaven.

Hence note, that though men may be borne with, if they lie in their holes in the height of the tempest; but to do it when the tops of the mountains were seen, if they then shall forbear to open their window, they are worthy of blame indeed. When the lepers saw the Assyrians were fled, and that liberty from heaven was granted to Samaria, then they feared to conceal the thing any further; they feared, I say, that if they went not to the city to declare it, some judgment of God would befall them. (2 Kings vii. 9.)

Verses 7, 8. "And he sent forth a raven, which went forth to and fro until the waters were dried up from off the earth. Also he sent forth a dove from him, to see if the waters were abated from off the face of the ground."

Behold, the raven and dove are now sent out at the window of the ark, as the angels are said to come out of the temple, when it was opened in heaven. This raven, therefore, and the dove, were figures and types of those angels.

But to speak to them both apart. The raven went forth, but returned not again to the ark. This is intimated by these words, "She went to and fro, until the waters were abated, and dried up." This is further evident by that antithesis that the word doth put between the practice of the raven and the dove. The raven went forth, and went to and fro till the waters were dried up. But mark it, "But the dove found no rest for the sole of her foot, and she returned to him into the ark." (Gen. viii. 9.) The raven then did find rest elsewhere, the raven then returned not to him into the ark.

But what did the raven then do? Why, certainly she made a banquet of the carcases of the giants that were drowned by the flood; it fed upon the flesh of the men that had sinned against the Lord.

The raven, therefore, was a type of those messengers that God sends out of his temple against Antichrist; that is, for eating "the flesh of kings, and the flesh of captains, and the flesh of mighty men, and the flesh of horses." (Rev. xix. 18.) He was, I say, a type of those professors that God saith he hath a great sacrifice to sacrifice unto, a sort of professors in his church; as the raven was one that had his being in the ark. These are they which Ezekiel mentions, that were to eat flesh, and drink blood; to eat the fat till they be filled, and to drink blood till they be drunken. (Ezek. xxxix. 17 —20.) These also are the guests that Zephaniah mentions, and saith, God hath bidden to the same feast also. (Zeph. i. 7.)

And let no man be offended that I say these birds are in the church: for one effect of the sixth vial, was that "battle of the great day of God Almighty." (Rev. xvi. 14.) Further, the angel that proclaims this feast, calls to those that are God's guests, by the name of "the fowls that fly in the midst of heaven." (Rev. xix. 17.) That they should come and gather together to the supper of the great God; that they may "eat the flesh of kings, and the flesh of captains, and the flesh of mighty men," &c. Besides, this supper is the effect of the going forth of the King of kings against the Antichristian whore, whose going forth was at the opening of heaven, as the going forth of the raven was at the opening of the window of the ark.

Note, therefore, that God, in the overthrow of the kingdom of Antichrist, and at the asswaging of the rage of her tumultuous waves, will send forth his birds amongst her fat ones, to partake of the banquet that he hath appointed; who, when they shall be tolerated by that angel that standeth in the sun, will come down to their feast with such greediness, that neither king nor captain shall keep them from their prey. They will eat flesh, and fat, till they be full, and drink blood till they be drunk.

"Also he sent forth a dove from him, to see if the waters were abated." This dove was a type of another sort of professors in the church, that are of a more gentle nature; for all the saints are not for such work as the raven; they are not all for feeding upon the carcases, the kingdoms and estates of the Antichristian party, but are for spending their time, and for bending their spirits to a more spiritual and retired work; even as the dove is said to be harmless, and to mourn for communion with her companion, and that is con-

tent she hath her nest in the sides of the rock, Christ. Wherefore he adds—

Verse 9. "But the dove found no rest for the sole of her foot, and she returned unto him into the ark, for the waters were on the face of the whole earth," &c.

The dove could not live as the raven; the raven being content, so long as she found the carcases; but the dove found no rest till she returned again to Noah.

The raven, therefore, though he was in the ark, was not a type of the most spiritual Christian; nay, rather, I think, of the worldly professor, who gets into the church in the time of her affliction, as Ziba did in the army of David, in the day of his trouble; not for love to the grace of David, but that, if time should serve, he might be made the lord of his master's inheritance. (2 Sam. xvi. 1 —4.) But David was content to let him go with him, and that too as under such a consideration. As Christ also lets these ravens to herd with his innocent doves; because he hath flesh to give them which the doves care not for eating.

"But the dove found no rest." It seems the raven did, as it is also with some professors, who, when they, by their profession, have advanced themselves to some worldly honour, they have ease and rest, though, like the raven, they have it by going out of the church.

"But the dove found no rest." Though all the enemies of God lay tumbling in the sea, this could not satisfy a gracious soul: divide her from the ark, and she finds no rest: she is not at ease till she be with Noah.

"And she returned unto him into the ark; and he put forth his hand and took her, and pulled her in unto him into the ark."

Noah here was a type of Christ, who took the dove unto him. And it shows us, that Christ hath a bosom open for the cries and complaints of his people; for the dove returned a-weary with the tidings of this, that the waters still raged. A fit figure of those of the saints that are groaning and weary under the oppression and cruelty of the enemy.

Hence note, that though thou hast no other tidings to Christ but sighs and groans, and weariness, because of the rage of the waters, yet he will not despise thee; yea, he invites thee, as weary, to come.

Verse 10. "And he stayed yet other seven days; and again he sent forth the dove out of the ark."

This staying shows us that he exercised patience, waiting God's leisure till the flood should be taken away. This grace, therefore, had yet seven days' work to do, before he obtained any further testimony that the waters were decreasing. O this staying work is hard work! Alas! sometimes patience is accompanied with so much heat and feverishness, that every hour seems seven until the end of the trial, and the blessing promised be possessed by the waiting soul. It may be Noah might not be altogether herein a stranger: I am sure the psalmist was not, in that he often, under affliction, cries, But how long, O Lord! for ever! Make haste! O Lord, how long!

"And again he sent forth the dove." The first time he sent her, she brought no good news, but came panting and weary home; yet he sends her a second time.

This should teach us, not to make conclusions too suddenly about God's dispensation, saying it must be now or never; for it may be the seven days are not out. The men of David said, This is the day that the Lord will give thee the kingdom of Israel; but David perceived otherwise, and therefore adds yet to his temperance, patience. (2 Sam. xxiv. 1—4; xxvi. 8—10.) Not sullenly saying like that wicked king, Why should I wait on the Lord any longer? (2 Kings vi. 33.) But comforts himself with the truth of the promise, saying, "His day shall come to die," &c. He that believeth, maketh not haste, but waiteth patiently, for the perfecting God's work in God's time. That is excellent in the song: "I charge you," saith the church, "that ye stir not up, nor awake my love until he please." (Sol. Song viii. 4.) Noah was much for this, wherefore he stayed yet other seven days.

"And again he sent forth the dove." Elias did much like this, when his servant, at the first sending, brought him no tidings of rain, he gave him his errand again, saying, Go again; go seven times, (1 Kings xviii. 43;) as Noah here did with the dove, and again he sent her. Seeming delays are no hindrance to faith; they ought to try it and put it into exercise; as here it was with this good man about the waters of the flood; he fainted not, but believed to see the goodness of the Lord. That in the prophet is notable as to this, "The vision is yet for an appointed time, but at the end it shall speak, and not lie; though it tarry, wait for it; because it will surely come, it will not tarry." (Hab. ii. 3.)

Verse 11. "And the dove came in to him in the evening; and lo, in her mouth was an olive leaf plucked off; so Noah knew that the waters were abated from off the earth."

"And the dove came in to him in the evening." Wherefore his patience was tried this day also. All the day he heard nothing of his dove. Surely she could not keep the wing all the day. Is she drowned too? Is she lost? O, no! She comes at last, though she stayed long. Samuel also stayed long before he came to Saul; but Saul could not wait as Noah did, therefore he had not the benefit of the mercy promised.

"The dove came in to him in the evening, and lo, in her mouth was an olive leaf," &c. Now he is recompensed for the exercise of patience: as also was Abraham when God gave him Isaac; for after he had patiently endured, he obtained the promise.

"And lo, an olive leaf." A sign that God was going through with his work of diminishing the waters: a sign, I say, and a good experience of the continued love of God to his servant; according to that of Paul, patience worketh experience; (Rom. v. 3;) that is, it at last obtaineth the blessing promised, and so settleth the soul in a fresh experience of the love and faithfulness of God.

And lo! This word "lo," it is, as it were, an appeal to all readers to judge whether God to Noah was faithful or no. So then, this was not written for his sake only, but for us also that believe in God, that we might now exercise patience, as Noah; and obtain the token of God's goodness, as he; for lo, the dove at last, though 'twas night first, came to Noah into the ark, "and lo, in her mouth was an olive leaf plucked off; so Noah knew that the waters were abated."

"An olive leaf plucked off." These words, "an olive leaf plucked off," do intimate, that Noah was now inquisitive and searching how the dove obtained the leaf: that is, whether she found it as dead, and upon the waters, or whether she plucked it off some tree. But he found by the greenness and freshness of the slip, that she plucked it off from the olive. Wherefore, he had good ground now to be comforted; for if this leaf was plucked from off a tree, then the waters could not be deep; especially, because as the story tells us, the olive used also to stand in the bottoms, or valleys.

This should teach us, that not over highly we conclude messages or tokens to be signs of God's mercy. There are lying visions, and they are causes of banishment; they we should beware of, or else we are not only at present deceived, but our faith is in danger of the rocks: for not a few have cast up all, because the truth of some seeming vision hath failed. Mark how David handleth the messenger that brought him tidings of the death of Saul: says he, How dost thou know that Saul is dead? What proof canst thou make of the truth of this story? (2 Sam. i. 4.) So should we say of all those visions or messengers that come to persuade us that either inward or outward deliverance is for us at the door; prove these stories, look if they be not dead and lifeless fancies; see if you can find that they were plucked off from the tree that is green.

Verse 12. "And he stayed yet other seven days, and sent forth the dove; which returned not again unto him any more."

We read before of forty days' patience, and after that, of seven days' patience; and that after the waters began to return from off the earth; and here again, of seven days more. Whence note, that the best of God's people, in the times of trials, find their patience too short-winded to hold out the whole length of a trial, unless the time be, as it were, cut in pieces. The prophet when he was to lay siege against Jerusalem, he must rest the one side, by turning him upon the other. (Ezek. iv. 4—6.) It was with holy Job exceeding hard, when he might not have time to swallow his spittle, when he might not a little sit down and rest him. And if you observe him, he doth not desire an absolute deliverance as yet, but only time to take wind and breathe a while; and then, if God will, to engage in the combat again. "How long," saith he, "wilt thou not depart from me;" depart! what quite? O! no, saith he, I beg not that absolutely, but only so long as till a man might swallow down his spittle. (Job vii. 19.) This the church in Ezra's time took as an exceeding favour. "And now," say they, "for a little space, grace hath been showed from the Lord our God, to leave us a remnant to escape, and to give us a nail in his holy place, that our God may lighten our eyes, and give us a little reviving in our bondage." (Ezra ix. 8.)

"And he stayed yet other seven days." Note again, that it is not God's way with his people to show them all their troubles at once; but first he shows them a part; first forty days, after that seven other days, and yet again seven days more; that, they coming upon them by piecemeal, they may the better be able to travel through them. While Israel was in affliction in Egypt, they knew not the trials that would meet them at the Red Sea. Again, when they had gone through that, they little thought that yet for forty years they must be tempted and proved in the wilderness.

And thus it was with this blessed Noah; he thought that by the first seven days his trials might be ended. But behold, there is yet seven days more behind: "And he stayed yet other seven days."

Further: there may also be by these words thus much insinuated, that these periods of time might also be of Noah's prefixing: and if so, then note, that the people of God in these days are not the first that have been under mistake, as to the timing of their afflictions. Noah counted it would end many days before it ended indeed, even seven days, and seven days, and seven days to that; for he sent forth his dove about the beginning of the first month, in which month also were his two seven days' trials. Again, after that he had stayed two seven days more, to wit, to the end of that first month. Again, he stayed almost four sevens more; for he came not out of the ark till the twenty-seventh day of the second month.

Hence, therefore, let Christians beware that they set not times for God, lest all men see their folly: "It is not for you to know the times and the seasons, which the Father hath put in his own power:" (Acts i. 7:) yea, I say again, take heed lest that for thy setting of God a seven days' time, he set not thee so many as seven times seven.

"And he sent forth the dove, which returned not again to him any more." This is the third time that the dove was sent to see how the waters were abated on the face of the earth. The first time she, by her restlessness, bespake the waters to be high and mighty: the second time, by her olive leaf, she notifieth that the waters were low and ebbing: but this third time, she seems to be weary of her service, she returned not again to him any more; yet in her so absenting herself, she gives confirmation to Noah, that the waters were even in a manner quite gone: if he will take this for a proof let him, if not, let him hang in suspense with himself. Hence note, that God will not be always testifying, by renewing of his tokens, to that about which we have had sufficient conviction before; for in so doing he should gratify and humour our unbelief. Noah had received already two sufficient testimonies that the waters were decreasing; first, by his seeing the tops of the mountains, and then by the olive leaf; but notwithstanding these two testimonies, his unbelief in part remains; but God will not humour such a groundless mistrust, by giving him any further token, than the very absenting of the dove. Much like this was that of Samson's father; the angel once had told his wife, that she should have a son that should deliver Israel; well, Manoah heard of this, he also desired that he might see that man that had told his wife this happy news. Now God thus far condescends, as to send the angel a second time; but then, this being now a sufficient antidote against their unbelief, the angel after the next departing, was not seen again of them at all; but saith the word, "The angel of the Lord did no more appear to Manoah, and to his wife;" so that now they must live by faith, or not at all. (Judges xiii. 3—21.)

God's dealing with his people with respect to their spiritual condition, is much like this. The Holy Ghost doth not use to confirm us by new revelations of grace and justification, so often as by our fond doubts or mistrust we call for and desire the same. But having confirmed in us the testimony of Christ, it may be twice or thrice, (for the testimony of two men are true,) he then expects we should live by faith. And observe it, if we have after such testimony joyful communion with God, it is either by retreating to former experience, or by arguing according to faith; that because God hath done thus before, he therefore hath given me interest in such and such promises and mercies besides.

I speak now of the first seals of the love of God to the soul, after we have been sufficiently tossed upon the waves of unbelief, as Noah was by the waters of the flood; such seals are few, the Lord gave them to Solomon twice, (1 Kings xi. 9,) and also twice to his servant Paul. (Acts xxii. 6, 18.) It is enough that they have seen the tops of the mountains, and have brought to them the olive leaf. Let them now believe this confirmation of mercy is sufficient, and if they will not believe now, they shall not be established.

Verse 13. "And it came to pass in the six hundredth and first year, in the first month, the first day of the month, the waters were dried up from off the earth: and Noah removed the covering of the ark, and looked, and behold the face of the ground was dry."

"And it came to pass:" That is, by the working of God, that the waters were dried up. This came to pass in God's time, to wit, in "the six hundredth and first year, in the first month, the first day of the month;" not in the times of Noah's prefixing. God's time is the time, the best time, because it is the time appointed by him for the proof and trial of our graces, and that in which so much, and so much of the rage of the enemy, and of the power of God's mercy, may the better be discovered unto us; "I the Lord will hasten it in his time," (Isa. lx. 22,) not before, though we "were the signet upon his right hand," (Jer. xxii. 24.)

Noah the only man with God in that generation, could not be restored before the time; no more could Israel from the thraldom of Egypt. Yea, the Son of God himself must here give place and be content. And when Satan had ended all the temptation, when he "had ended all, then he departed from him for a season." (Luke iv. 13.)

"And Noah removed the covering of the ark, and looked." The failing again of his expected comforter, caused him to be up and doing; probably he had not as yet uncovered the ark, that is, to look round about him, had the dove by returning pleased his humour; but she failing him, he stirs up himself. Thus it should also be with the Christian now: doth the dove forbear to come to thee with a leaf in her bill as before? let not this make thee sullen, and mistrustful, but uncover the ark, and look, and by looking thou shalt see a further testimony of what thou receivest by the first manifestations: "He looked, and behold the earth was dry." Paul tells us, that by looking we have a testimony like, or as that, which at first was given us by the Spirit of the Lord. (2 Cor. iii. 18.) And behold the face of the earth was dry.

Verse 14. "And in the second month, on the seven and twentieth day of the month, was the earth dried."

This prospect was like the rain that we read of in another place, that confirmed God's inheritance when it was weary: It was a comfortable sight to Noah, to see that the face of the earth was dry; and now he could wait upon God with less trial and strain to his patience the remaining days, which were fifty and four, to wit, from the first of the first, to the twenty-seventh of the second month, than he could one of the sevens that he met with before. Indeed the path is narrowest just at entrance, as also our nature is then the most untoward; but after we are in, the walk seems to be wider and easy; the flesh is also then more mortified and conformable. The walk is but a cubit wide at the door, but inward ten times as broad. (Ezek. xlii. 4, 11.)

"And in the second month, on the seven and twentieth day of the month, was the earth dried."

So that from the first day it began to rain, (which was the seventeenth day of the second month in the year before, unto this day, was Noah in the ark,) it was just a year and ten days. That was the time then that God had appointed to try his servant Noah, by the waters of the flood: in which time he was so effectually crucified to the things of this world, that he was as if he was never more to enjoy the same. Wherefore Peter maketh mention of this estate of his, he tells us, it was even like unto our baptism; wherein we profess ourselves dead to the world, and alive to God by Jesus Christ. (1 Pet. iii. 21.)

In the first verse of this chapter, we read that God remembered Noah; but till now we read not, that the face of the earth was dried. Hence note that our being under the rage of the enemy, doth not argue that we are therefore forgotten of God, "he remembereth us in our low estate," (Ps. cxxxvi. 23,) even when tossed to and fro by the waters of a flood of temptations.

Verses 15, 16. "And God spake unto Noah, saying, Go forth of the ark, thou and thy wife, and thy sons, and thy sons' wives with thee."

Now we are come to the end of the trial, and so to the time of Noah's deliverance, and behold as he went in, so he came out: He went into the ark at the commandment of the Lord: "And the Lord said unto Noah, Come thou and all thy house into the ark:" (Gen. vii. 1.) And here again, And "God spake unto Noah, saying, Go forth of the ark." Hence note, that notwithstanding the earth was dry about fifty-four days before, yet Noah waited for the word of God for his commission to bring him forth of the ark. Providence seemed to smile before, in that the earth was dry, to which had but Noah added reason, he must have concluded, the time is come for me to go forth of the ark. But Noah knew, that as well the providences of God, as the waters of the flood might be to try his dependance on the word of the Lord: wherefore, though he saw this, yet because he had no answer of God, he will not take the opportunity.

It is dangerous, or at least very difficult, to make the most smiling providence of God our rule to act by: Had David done it, he had killed Saul before the time, but David respected the word of God. Elisha also would not suffer the king to make that improvement of the providence of God, which reason should be put in execution, when he rebuked the king's desire that he had to have killed the Syrians, and commanded that bread should be set before them, that they might eat, and go home again to their master. (2 Kings vi. 19—23.) Hear the word of the Lord, ye that tremble at his word. "At the commandment of the Lord the children of Israel journeyed, and at the commandment of the Lord they pitched; at the commandment of the Lord they rested in their tents, and at the commandment of the Lord they journeyed; they kept the charge of the Lord, at the commandment of the Lord, by the hand of Moses." (Numb. ix. 18—23.)

"Go forth of the ark, thou and thy wife, and thy sons, and thy sons' wives with thee."

When God delivereth, he delivereth completely. Thus Israel also went out of Egypt, they, their wives, their children, with their flocks and herds, not an hoof was left behind. (Exod. x. 26.) When David's time was come to possess the kingdom, he brought along with him those six hundred men that had been his companions in his suffering state, every man with his household. But I say, he went up to possess it, not simply by the voice of providence, though Saul was dead, but David inquired of the Lord, saying, "Shall I go up to any of the cities of Judah?" Nay, a general answer, even from God, would not satisfy this holy man. The Lord said, Go, but David replied, "Whither shall I go? and he said, Unto Hebron." (2 Sam. ii. 1.) Oh! it is safe to regard the word of the Lord; this makes us all come safe to land. When men wrest themselves from under the hand of God, taking such opportunities for their deliverance, which are laid before them only for trial of obedience to the word: they may, 'tis probable, have a seeming success; the end will be as with Zedekiah king of Judah, affliction with addition. The Jews that were left in the land of Israel, from the hand of the king of Babylon, would flee to the land of Egypt, (Jer. xli. 17,) that they might have quietness there, but they went without the word of God, and therefore their rest brought them to their ruin. (Jer. xlii., xliii.)

Noah therefore chose the safest way, even to stay in the ark, till God's word came. As it is also said of Joseph, "The word of the Lord tried him," (Ps. cv. 19;) till the word of the Lord came to deliver him, and then he had deliverance indeed, as Noah also and David had, safe deliverance for himself and relations.

Verse 17. "Bring forth with thee every living thing that is with thee of all flesh, both of fowl, and of cattle, and of every creeping thing that creepeth upon the earth; that they may breed abundantly in the earth, and be fruitful and multiply upon the earth."

Noah was not only to have in his deliverance, respect to himself and family, but to the good of all the world. Men's spirits are too narrow for the mind of God, when their chief end, or their only design in their enjoying this or the other mercy, is for the sake of their ownselves only. It cannot be according to God, that such desires should be encouraged: none of us liveth to himself, (Rom. xiv. 7;) why then should we desire life only for ourselves?

The church cries thus, "God be merciful unto us, and bless us; and cause his face to shine upon us." Why? "That thy way may be known upon earth, thy saving health among all nations." (Ps. lxvii. 1, 2.)

So David, "Restore unto me the joy of thy salvation, and uphold me with thy free spirit Then will I teach transgressors thy ways; and sinners shall be converted unto thee." (Ps. li. 12, 13.) So then, we must not desire to come out of trials and afflictions alone, or by ourselves, but that in our deliverance the salvation of many may be concerned. It is said, when Israel went up out of Egypt, there went up with them "a mixed multitude," to wit, of Egyptians, and other nations: (Exod. xii. 38.) This going out of captivity was right, they carried out with them the fowls, the beasts, and the creeping things; to wit, the heathens of other lands, and so added increase to the church of God. In Esther's time also, when the Jews came from under the snare of Haman, they brought with them to God many of the people of the provinces. "Many of the people of the land became Jews." (Esth. viii. 17.)

These words, therefore, "bring forth with thee every living thing," &c., are not lightly to be passed over; for they show us, that we ought in our deliverance to have special respect to the deliverance of others. And if our deliverance be with the word and liking of God, it must needs have this effect. "When I shall bring again their captivity, the captivity of Sodom, and her daughters, and the captivity of Samaria, and her daughters, then will I bring again the captivity of thy captives, in the midst of them." (Ezek. xvi. 53.)

And indeed there is reason for this, for in every affliction and persecution, the devil's design is to impair Christ's kingdom. Wherefore no marvel, that God designeth in our deliverance, the impairing and lessening the kingdom of sin and Satan. Wherefore, O thou church of God in England, which art now upon the waves of affliction, and temptation, when thou comest out of the furnace, if thou come out at the bidding of God, there shall come out with thee the fowl, the beast, and abundance of creeping things. "O Judah, he hath set an harvest for thee, when I return the captivity of my people." (Hos. vi. 11.)

"That they may breed abundantly in the earth, and be fruitful and multiply upon the earth."

This was God's end in preserving the creatures from the flood, that again the earth might be replenished therewith. The same end he hath in his suffering of the persecutor, and all manner of adversity to take away but a part, some; some of them they shall kill and crucify, leaving a remnant alive in the world, namely, that they might breed abundantly in the earth, and be fruitful, and multiply upon the earth. As he saith by the prophet Isaiah, "He shall cause them that come of Jacob to take root: Israel shall blossom and bud, and fill the face of the world with fruit." (Isa. xxvii. 6.) And this after their deliverance from persecution: according as he saith again, "the remnant that is escaped of the house of Judah, shall again take root downward, and bear fruit upward: For out of Jerusalem shall go forth a remnant," (Isa. xxxvii. 31, 32,) that is yet to replenish the earth with converts. As Luke observes, that when the churches in Judea, Galilee, and Samaria had rest, they "walking in the fear of the Lord, and in the comforts of the Holy Ghost, were multiplied." (Acts ix. 31.)

Verse 18. "And Noah went forth, and his sons, and his wife, and his sons' wives with him." Obedience is better than sacrifice. Noah is at the beck of God,'what he bid him do, that does he; and, indeed, this is in truth to worship God, yea, this is to know and worship God. It is said of Abraham, when he went at God's command to offer up Isaac, that he counted it going to worship the Lord. (Gen. xxii. 5.) And God saith of Hezekiah, that he did "judgment and justice," judging "the cause of the poor and needy;" and then adds, "Is not this to know me, saith the Lord?" (Jer. xxii. 15, 16.) I bring these to show that obedience to the word of God is the true character of God's people in all ages; and this very text, as also such others before, is on purpose recorded by the Holy Ghost to show you, that Noah was obedient in all things; yea, I may add, these commands were to discover the proof of him, whether he would "be obedient in all things;" (2 Cor. ii. 9;) and this was also his way with New Testament churches. The sincerity of love, and of the uprightness of the heart, is greatly discovered by the commandments of God. "He that hath my commandments, and keepeth them," said Christ, "he it is that loveth me," &c. (John xiv. 21.)

Verse 19. "Every beast, every creeping thing, and every fowl, and whatsoever creepeth upon the earth after their kinds, went forth out of the ark."

These words are yet a further expression of the sincerity of Noah's obedience, for that he at the command of God did carefully search and seek out every little creeping thing that God had brought to him into the ark. Obedience in little things do ofttimes prove us most; for we, through the pride of our hearts, are apt to look over little things, because, though commanded, they are but little. O, but Noah was of another spirit; he carefully looked after little things, even after everything, "whatsoever creepeth upon the earth;" and not only so, but sought diligently that they might go out in order, to wit, male and female, according to their kind. Sometimes God would have men exact to a word, sometimes exact to a tache, or pin, or loop, (Exod. xxxvi. 12, 13,) sometimes to a step. (Ezek. xl. 22, 26, 34, 37.) Be careful, then, in little things, but yet leave not the other undone.

Indeed, the command of God is great; if he, therefore, commands us to worship him, though but with a bird, we must not count such ordinances insignificant, or below a human creature.

Verse 20. "And Noah builded an altar unto the Lord; and took of every clean beast, and of every clean fowl, and offered burnt offerings on the altar."

This is the first work that we read Noah did, when he came forth of the ark, and it shows us, that at this time he had a deep sense of the distinguishing mercy of God. And, indeed, he had sufficient cause to wonder, for the whole world was drowned, save only himself, and they that were with him in the ark.

But, I say, this was the first work, to wit, to worship God. Hence note, that a sense of mercy, of distinguishing mercy, naturally engageth the heart to worship. It is said of Moses, when the name of the Lord was proclaimed before him, as "merciful, gracious," "and abundant in goodness and truth;" and that he pardoned "iniquity, transgression, and sin;" "that he made haste, and bowed his head toward the earth, and worshipped." (Exod. xxxiv. 6—8.)

"And Noah builded an altar." Although this altar be the first that we read of, yet forasmuch as there was before a blessed church, and also an open profession of godliness, together with offering sacrifice, in all probability this was not the first altar that was builded unto the Lord. Besides, we read not of any immediate revelation, from which Noah had light and instruction to build it. The text only saith, he built an altar unto the Lord; which may be aptly expounded, according as he was wont in the other world.

This altar was a type of Christ, as capacitated to bear the sin of the world, (for the altar was it, upon which the sacrifices were burnt,) wherein it, in mine opinion, in special respected his Godhead, by the power of which he offered himself, that is, his flesh. Again, it is said, "The altar sanctifieth the gift." (Matt. xxiii. 19.) So did the Godhead the humanity of Christ, through which "eternal Spirit he offered himself without spot to God." (Heb. ix. 14.) By this altar, then, this blessed man preached to his family the Godhead and eternity of Christ.

"And took of every clean beast, and of every clean fowl." These beasts and fowls were types of the flesh of the Son of God, as Paul, in the ninth and tenth chapters to the Hebrews, affirms; wherefore, by this act he also preached to his family the incarnation of the Lord Christ, how that "in the fulness of time" he should in our flesh offer himself a sacrifice for us; for as all the ordinances of the New Testament ministration preached to us, that Christ is come, so all the ordinances of worship under the Old Testament preached to them that were under it, Christ, as yet to come.

"Of every clean beast, of every clean fowl." This was to show, that when Christ did come, he should not take hold of the Jew, and exclude the Gentile; but that in his flesh he should present unto God every clean beast, and every clean fowl; that is, all the elect, both of Jew and Gentile.

And it was requisite that this by Noah should be preached, because the whole world was yet in his family; from whence, at the multiplication of men, if through their rebellion and idolatry they lost not this doctrine, they might to all their offspring preach the Lord Jesus.

Wherefore, the doctrine of the gospel, had the world been faithful, might have been to this day retained amongst them that now are the most barbarous people.

Verse 21. "And the Lord smelled a sweet savour," (a savour of rest;) "and the Lord said in his heart, I will not again curse the ground any more for man's sake; for the imagination of man's heart is evil from his youth; neither will I again smite any more every thing living, as I have done."

These words more fully show, that this sacrifice of Noah was a type of the offering up of the body of Jesus Christ, he being said to be that blessed sacrifice that is as perfume in the nostrils of God. He gave "himself for us an offering and a sacrifice to God for a sweet-smelling savour." (Eph. v. 2.) Besides, this offering of Noah was a burnt offering to God; which burning signified the curse of God, which Christ was made in his death for us: wherefore, the burnt offerings were all along a type of him; as by reading the Epistle to the Hebrews you may see: "It is the burnt offering," saith God, "because of the burning upon the altar all night unto the morning; and the fire of the altar shall be burning in it." (Lev. vi. 9.) Which was a type of the fire of the law, and the guilt of sin, that Christ, when he offered himself, should undergo for the sins of man.

"And the Lord smelled a sweet savour." This signifies the content and satisfaction that for the sin of the world God should have by the offering up of his Son for us upon the cross. Wherefore he is said to be now "in Christ, reconciling the world unto himself, not imputing their trespasses unto them." (2 Cor. v. 19.)

Now, it is observable, that Noah was a man of faith long before this. Hence note two things—

1. That men, even of eminent faith, have yet need of a continual remembrance of the death and sufferings of Christ; yea, and that in the most plain and easiest manner to understand.

2. They have need also, notwithstanding they have faith before, to present themselves before God, through Jesus Christ our Lord: for as our persons are not accepted, but in and through him, no more are our performances; yea, though they be spiritual services or sacrifices; it is the blood that maketh the atonement, as well for works as persons. (Lev. xvi. 11.) As he saith in another place, "I will accept you with your sweet savour," (Ezek. xx. 41,) but not without it. As he also said to his church in Egypt, "When I see the blood, I will pass over you, and the plague shall not be upon you to destroy you, when I smite the land of Egypt." (Exod. xii. 13.)

"And the Lord said in his heart, I will not again curse," &c. By "heart" here, we may understand two things—

1. That God was altogether unfeigned in this promise. He spake it from his very heart: which we use to count the most sincere expressing of our mind: according to that of the prophet, "Yea, I will rejoice over them to do them good, and I will plant them in this land assuredly, (in truth, in stability,) with my whole heart, and with my whole soul." (Jer. xxxii. 41.) Mark, I will rejoice to do it, I will do it assuredly, I will do it in truth, even with my whole heart, and with my whole soul.

2. By his saying "in his heart" we may understand the secrecy of his purpose; for this doctrine of not cursing again, it is hid from all but those to whom it is revealed by the Spirit of God. For this purpose, in the heart of God, is one of the depths, or of the deep things of God which the spirit of a man cannot understand. "Who hath known the mind of the Lord?" (Rom. xi. 34. 1 Cor. ii. 16.) None of all the sons of men, but those that have the Holy Ghost. Therefore Paul applieth that to himself and fellows as that which is peculiar to them to know, "We have the mind of Christ." (1 Cor. ii. 16.) It is said, that after Christ had, by his parables, preached his gospel to the world, he in private "expounded all things to his disciples." (Mark iv. 34.)

Hence note, that they that will hear God speak this, they must be near his very heart. They that are in his heart may hear it: but to them that are without, in parables. This secret, in revelation of the gospel, is also expressed in other terms: as, that the Lord spake "in mine ears," and "it was revealed in mine ears." (Isa. v. 9; xxii. 14.) And again, "Hear now this word which I speak in thine ears." (Jer. xxviii. 7.)

"I will not again curse the ground any more." These words are also under Moses' veil; for in them is contained the sin of the world, and damnation thereof. He said, when he was to bring the flood, that the "earth was corrupt," and that he would "destroy the earth;" but his great meaning was of the sinners that dwelt therein; as the effect of that flood declared. So he saith again, he will not bring any more a flood to destroy the earth; and that the bow in the cloud should be a sign of peace between him and the earth. By all which is meant in special, the men that dwell on the earth; and they are called the Ground, and the Earth, (Ps. cxiv. 7. Deut. xxxii. 1. Jer. vi. 19; xix. 22,) because they came from thence. So, then, there is, as it were, the foundation of all spiritual blessedness couched under these words, "I will not curse the ground, I will not destroy man." And that this must needs be the meaning thereof, consider, that this promise ariseth from the sweet savour that he smelt before in the burnt offering; which was a figure of Christ, who was "made a curse for us," (Gal. iii. 13,) to deliver us from the curse of the law; that we might through him obtain the blessing of forgiveness of sins; to which the curse stands directly opposite.

"I will not again curse the ground for man's sake; for the imagination of man's heart is evil from his youth." The imagination of man's heart was the ground of this dreadful curse; and the effect of this curse was, to lay them up in chains in hell. Wherefore Peter saith, These men are "now in prison." The curse, therefore, in its most eminent extension, reached the souls of those ungodly ones that were swept away with the flood. But it seems a strange argument, or reason rendered of God, why again he would not curse the ground, if it was because of the evil imagination of man's heart, this being the only argument that prevailed with him to send the flood. The meaning therefore is rather this, that because of the satisfaction that Christ hath given to God for sin, therefore he said in his heart, he would not again curse the ground, for the evil imagination of man; that is, he would not do it, for want of a sacrifice that had in it a sufficient propitiation.

Hence note, That the great cause now of man's condemnation, is not because of his inherent pollution, but because he accepteth not, with Noah, of the satisfaction made by Christ; for to all them that have so accepted thereof, there is now no curse nor condemnation, (Rom. viii. 1,) though still the imagination of their heart be evil. "If any man sin, we have an advocate with the Father, Jesus Christ the righteous." (1 John ii. 1.)

"For the imagination of man's heart is evil from his youth." · These words seem to insinuate the cause of these evil imaginations; and that is, from the corruption of their youth. Now how soon their youth was corrupted, David shows by these words, "I was shapen in iniquity, and in sin did my mother conceive me." (Ps. li. 5.) Ezekiel also shows, we were polluted in the day that we were born. (Ezek. xvi. 1—8.) Further, God to Moses strongly affirms it, in that he commands, That for the firstborn, in whom the rest were included, an offering should be offered, by that they were a month old. (Exod. xiii. 14; xxxiv. 20.) God seems, therefore, by this word, to look back to the transgression of our first parents, by whom sin came into our natures; and by so doing, he not only intimateth, yea, promiseth a pardon to personal miscarriages; but assureth us, That neither them, nor yet our inward pollutions, shall destroy us, because of the rest that he found before in Christ. (Rom. v.)

"Neither will I again smite any more every thing living, as I have done." The creatures therefore also have some kind of benefit by the death and blood of Christ; that is, so as to live, and have a being; for infinite justice is so perfectly just, as that without a sacrifice it could not have suffered the world to stand, after sin was in the world; but must have destroyed, for the sake of sin, the world which he had made.

For although it be foully absurd to say beasts and fowls are defiled with sin, as man; yet doubtless they received detriment thereby: "the creature was made subject to vanity, by reason of him who hath subjected the same," &c. (Rom. viii. 20.) That is, by Adam's sin. Which vanity they also show by divers of their practices; as both in their enmity to man, and one to another, with which they were not created; this came by the sin of man. Now that man lives, yea, that beasts live, it is because of the offering up of Christ. Wherefore it is said in that of the Colossians, The gospel is "preached to every creature;" in every creature under heaven; to wit, in that they live and have a being. (Col. i. 23.)

"Neither will I again smite any more every living thing, as I have done." These words, "as I have done," doth not exempt the creature from every judgment of God, but from this, or such as this; for we know, that other judgments do befall ungodly men now; and if they continue in final impenitence, they shall partake of far greater judgments than to be drowned by the waters of a flood: "The wicked is reserved unto judgment;" (Job xxi. 30;) yea, "the heavens and the earth which are now, are reserved unto fire, and perdition of ungodly men." (2 Pet. iii. 7.)

Verse 22. "While the earth remaineth, seed time and harvest, and cold and heat, and summer and winter, and day and night, shall not cease."

"While the earth remaineth." These words may have respect both to the words before, and to them that follow after. If they respect the words before, then they are as limits to that large promise, of not destroying the world again: not but that the day will come, as I said, in which another general judgment, and that too far more dreadful than this of water, will overflow the world, and every living thing shall again be cut off from the face of all the earth; as now by rain of water, then by rain of fire and brimstone. Which day and sore judgment God showed unto men, when he burned Sodom and Gomorrah with "fire and brimstone from heaven." But,

"While the earth remaineth," this shall not be. But in the end, then indeed both it "and the works that are therein, shall (as Peter saith) be burned up." But so long as it remaineth, that is, until it be overtaken with this second, and that too the beginning of eternal judgment, no universal judgment shall overrun the earth. For albeit that since that flood, the earth hath been smitten with many a curse; yet it hath been· but here and there, not in every place at once. Famines, and earthquakes, and pestilences, have been in divers places, but yet at the same time hath there been seed time and harvest also. (Mark xiii. 8. Luke xxi. 11.)

" Seed time and harvest, and cold and heat, and summer and winter, and day and night, shall not cease." These words were some of the first, with that of " the bow in the cloud," that prevailed with me to believe that the scriptures were the word of God.

For my reason tells me, they are, and have continued a true prophecy, from the day that they were related; otherwise the world could not have subsisted; for take away seed time and harvest, cold and heat, &c., and an end is put to the beginning of the universe.

Besides, if these words be taken in a spiritual sense, they have also stood true from that very day; otherwise the church had ceased to have a being long before this. For take away seed time and harvest from the church, with cold and heat, and day and night, and those ordinances of heaven are taken from her, which were ordained for her begetting and continuation. This head might with much largeness be insisted on; but to pass it, and to come to the next chapter.

CHAPTER IX.

Verse 1. "And God blessed Noah, and his sons, and said unto them, Be fruitful and multiply, and replenish the earth."

Noah having thus waded through these great temptations, and being made also to partake of the mercy of God, in preserving and saving him from the evil thereof, and being brought to partake of the beginning of a new world, while the ungodly that were before the flood were perished for their iniquity : he receiveth now from the mouth of the Lord, before whom he walked before the flood, laws and ordinances, as rules by which he should still govern his life before him. But mark, before he receiveth these rules and commandments, he receiveth blessing from God; blessing, I say, as that which should yet fore-fit him to do his will.

" And God blessed Noah." Blessed him with spiritual and special grace; for without that, no man can walk, with God's acceptance before him: He blessed him with grace suitable to the work he was now to begin; to wit, for the replenishing and governing the new world God had brought him to : so that Noah did not without precedent qualifications take this work upon him. God also gave Caleb and Joshua another spirit, and then they followed him fully. That of David is for this remarkable, " Who am I," said he, " and what is my people, that we should offer so willingly after this sort? for all things come of thee, and of thine own have we given thee." " O Lord our God," saith he, " all this store that we have prepared to build thee an house for thine holy name, cometh of thine hand, and is all thine own." (1 Chron. xxix. 14, 16.) So is faith, love, strength, wisdom, sincerity, and all other good things where-

with and by which we walk with God, worship him, and do his will. All which is comprised in these words, " I will give them an heart to know me, that I am the Lord; and they shall be my people, and I will be their God; for they shall return unto me with their whole heart." (Jer. xxiv. 7.) " A new heart also will I give you." (Ezek. xxxvi. 26.) And again, " I will put my fear in their hearts, that they shall not depart from me." (Jer. xxxii. 40.)

" And God blessed Noah and his sons, and said unto them, Be fruitful, and multiply, and replenish the earth." After he had blessed him, then he tells him what he should do; namely, " Be fruitful, and multiply :" This he spake with respect to the seed that he and his sons should beget, therewith to people the world; which was now the remaining part of his work, and he had three arguments to encourage him thereto. First, He was delivered from the wicked and sinners of the old world; Second, He was made the heir of a new world; and Third, Was to leave it as an heritage to his children.

This, therefore, should teach us, who are brought into the kingdom of Christ, that new world that hath taken its beginning in the word of the gospel, not to be idle, but to be fruitful, and to labour to fill the world with a spiritual seed to God: for as Noah, so are we made heirs of this blessed kingdom; and shall also, as that good man, leave, when we sleep in Jesus, this spiritual seed to possess the kingdom after us.

Verse 2. " And the fear of you, and the dread of you, shall be upon every beast of the earth, and upon every fowl of the air, upon all that moveth upon the earth, and upon all the fishes of the sea; into your hand are they delivered."

These words seem to be a promise of what shall be a consequence of their putting into practice what was commanded in the verse before; namely, of their " being fruitful, and of their multiplying in the earth." Hence note, That the faithful observation of God's word, puts majesty, and dread, and terror upon them that do it: therefore it is said, that when the church is fair as the moon, and clear as the sun, she is terrible as an army with banners. (Sol. Song vi. 10.) The presence of godly Samuel made the elders of Bethlehem tremble; yea, when Elisha was sought for by the king of Syria, he durst not engage him, but with chariots and horses, and a heavy host. (2 Kings vi. 14.) Godliness is a wonderful thing, it commandeth reverence, and the stooping of the spirits, even of the world of ungodly ones.

" And the fear of you, and the dread of you, shall be upon every beast." This is true in the letter; for because there is upon man, as man, more of the image and similitude of God, than there is upon other creatures, therefore the beasts, and all the creatures, are made to stoop and fall before them; yea, though in themselves they are mighty and fierce. " Every kind (or, nature) of beasts, and of birds, and of serpents, and things in the sea, is tamed, and hath been tamed by mankind." (James iii. 7.)

But to allegorize the word, (for by the word, ungodly men are beasts;) then, as I said before, godliness puts such a majesty and dread upon the professors of it, that their enemies are afraid of them; yea, even then when they rage against them, and lay heavy afflictions upon them. It is marvellous to see in what fear the ungodly are, even of godly men, and godliness; in that they stir up the mighty, make edicts against them; yea, and raise up armies, and what else can be imagined, to suppress them; while the persons thus opposed, if you consider them as to their state and capacity in this world, they are most inconsiderable; but as a dead dog, or a flea. (1 Sam. xxiv. 14.) O but they are clothed with godliness! the image and presence of God is upon them! This makes the beasts of the world afraid: one of you shall chase a thousand.

"Into your hand are they delivered." That is, the beasts, birds, and fish of the sea, (as David saith,) to be for the service of man. But again, this is also true in a higher nature; for taking these beasts, &c., for men, even they are delivered into the hand of the church, by whose doctrine, power, and faith, they are smitten with severest judgments; laying all that reject them even in the depth of death, and smiting them "with all plagues as often as they will." (Rev. xi. 6.) The world is therefore in our hand, and disposed of by our doctrine, by our faith and prayers, although they think far otherwise, and shall one day feel their judgments are according.

Verse 3. "Every moving thing that liveth shall be meat for you; even as the green herb have I given you all things."

From these words some would insinuate, that before the flood men lived only upon herbs, not eating flesh; as here they have authority granted to do. But in mine opinion, such should be mistaken, for this reason, if there were no other: because they offered sacrifice before; sacrifices, I say, as types and representatives to the church, of the death and sufferings of Christ. Now, of such sacrifices the offerers used to eat, as is clear by the lamb of the passover, and many other offerings: so that these words seem to be but a renewing of their former privileges, not a granting new liberty to the world.

"Every moving thing." This must be taken with this restriction, that is wholesome and good for food. For by the law of nature, nothing of that is forbidden to man, though for some significations many such creatures were forbidden us to use for a time.

"Even as the green herb." For which they expressly had liberty granted them, in the first chapter of this book. And this liberty might afresh be here repeated, from some scruple that might arise in Noah, &c. He remembering that the world before might, for the abuse of the creatures of God, as well as for the abuse of his worship, be drowned with the flood; for sometimes the abuse of that which is lawful to one, may be a snare, abuse, and stumbling to another. (1 Cor. viii. 9.)

Verse 4. "But flesh with the life thereof, which is the blood thereof, shall ye not eat."

This law seems to be ceremonial, although given long before Moses was, as also some sacrifices and circumcision was. (John vii. 22.) Wherefore we must seek for the reason of this prohibition: "Whatsoever man," saith God, "there be of the house of Israel, that eateth any manner of blood, I will even set my face against that soul that eateth blood, and will cut him off from among his people." Why? "For the life of the flesh is the blood, and I have given it to you upon the altar, to make an atonement for your souls; for it is the blood that maketh the atonement for the soul. Therefore I said unto the children of Israel, No soul of you shall eat blood." (Lev. xvii. 10—12.) Again, as here the prohibition is only concerning blood; so in another place, the word is as well against our eating the fat. "It shall be a perpetual statute for your generations, throughout your dwellings, that you neither eat fat nor blood." (Lev. iii. 17.) And the reason rendered, is, "For all the fat is the Lord's." (Lev. iii. 16.)

So then the meaning, the spiritual meaning, seems to be this. That forasmuch as the blood is the life, and that which maketh the atonement; and the fat, the glory, and the Lord's; therefore they both were to be offered to the Lord. That is, we ought always to offer the merit of our salvation to God, by a continual acknowledgment, that it was through the blood of Christ; and we ought always to give him the glory thereof, and this is the fat of all our performances. (Isa. xxv. 7.) Now this is so blessed a thing, and calleth for that grace, that every professor hath not, every one cannot ascribe to the blood of the Lamb, the whole of his reconciliation to God; nor offer up the fat, the glory, which is God's, to the Lord for so great a benefit: this is the benefit of a peculiar people, even of "the priests, the Levites, the sons of Zadok, (or they that are justified, or just thereby,) that kept the charge of my sanctuary, when the children of Israel went astray from me; they shall come near to me, to minister unto me; and they shall stand before me, to offer unto me the fat, and the blood, saith the Lord God." (Ezek. xliv. 15.)

Wherefore, for men to ascribe to their own works the merit of their salvation, or to take the glory thereof to themselves, it is as eating the blood and the fat themselves, and they shall be cut off from the people of God.

Verse 5. "And surely your blood of your lives will I require; at the hand of every beast will I require it, and at the hand of man; at the hand of every man's brother will I require the life of man."

These words are spoken to the church, which then resided in this family. Not but that God will avenge the blood that is wrongfully shed, though the person murdered be most carnal and irreligious. "A man that doeth violence to the blood of any person shall flee to the pit; let no man stay him." (Prov. xxviii. 17.)

But I say, these words respect the church in a more special and eminent way. "Surely," saith God, "your blood of your lives will I require." Thus also David insinuates the thing: "when he maketh inquisition for blood, he remembereth them, (the saints and godly in special); he forgetteth not the cry of the humble," the afflicted. (Ps. ix. 12.)

"At the hand of every beast will I require it." The beasts are here also to be taken for men, to whom they are frequently likened in scripture; and that because they have cast off human affections; and, like savage creatures, make a prey of those that are better than themselves. Ignorance therefore, or brutishness, O thou wicked man! will not excuse thee in the day of judgment; all the injuries that thou doest to the people of God, shall for certain be required of thee.

"At the hand of man will I require it." By "man" here, we may understand, such as have greater place and show of reason wherewith they manage their cruelty, than those that are as the natural beast. For all persecutors are not brutish alike; some are in words as smooth as oil; others can show a semblance of reason of state, why they should "sell the righteous for silver, and the poor for a pair of shoes." (Amos ii. 6.) These act, to carnal reason, like men, as Saul against David, for the safety of his kingdom; but these must give an account of their cruelty, for blood is in their hands.

"And at the hand of every man's brother will I require the life of man." This word "brother," may reach to all the apostatized hypocrites that forsake or betray the godly, for brother shall betray the brother to death. (Matt. x. 21.) Such are spoken of in Isaiah, "Your brethren that hated you," saith God, "that cast you out for my name's sake, said, Let the Lord be glorified; but he shall appear to your joy, and they shall be ashamed." (Isa. lxvi. 5.) So that let them be as vile as the brute, or as reasonable in appearance as men, or as near in relation as a brother; neither their ignorance, nor their reason, nor their relation to the saints, shall secure them from the stroke of the judgment of God.

Verse 6. "Whoso sheddeth man's blood, by man shall his blood be shed: for in the image of God made he man."

In the words we have both a threatening and a command; and the same words carry both: "By man shall his blood be shed," there is the threatening; "By man shall his blood be shed," there is the command. For as they threaten, so they instruct us, that he is worthy of the loss of his own blood, that doth wickedly shed the blood of another. (Matt. xxvi. 52. Rev. xiii. 10.) Blood for blood, equal measure. As he also saith elsewhere, An eye for an eye, a tooth for a tooth, wound for wound, burning for burning. (Exod. xxi. 24. Lev. xxiv. 20. Deut. xix. 21.)

"For in the image of God made he him." This seems as the reason of this equal law; because no man can slay his neighbour, but he striketh at the image of God. It is counted an heinous crime for a man to run his sword at the picture of a king, how much more to shed the blood of the image of God? He that mocketh, or "oppresseth, the poor, reproacheth his Maker; but he that honoureth him, hath mercy on the poor." (Prov. xiv. 31; xvii. 5.) And if so, how much more do they reproach, yea, despise and abhor their Maker, that slay and murder his image! But most of all those do prove themselves the enemies of God, that make the holiness, the goodness, the religion and sobriety that is found in the people of God, the object of their wrath and hellish cruelty. Hence murder is, in the New Testament, imputed to that man that hated a holy and godly man: "Whosoever hateth his brother, is a murderer; and ye know that no murderer hath eternal life abiding in him." (1 John iii. 15.)

Verse 7. "And you, be ye fruitful, and multiply; bring forth abundantly in the earth, and multiply therein." Thus he doubleth the blessing and command, of multiplying and increasing the church in the earth, for that is the delight of God, and of Christ.

Verses 8, 9. "And God spake unto Noah, and to his sons with him, saying, And I, behold, I establish my covenant with you, and with your seed after you."

God having thus blessed them, and given them laws and judgments to walk by, for the further confirmation of their hope in God, he propoundeth to them the immutability of his mind, by the establishing of his covenant with them; for a covenant is that, which not only concludeth the matter concerned between the persons themselves; but it provideth remedy against after temptations, and fears, and mistrusts, as to the faithful performance of that which is spoken of. As Laban said to Jacob, "Now therefore," said he, "come thou, let us make a covenant, I and thou; and let it be for a witness between me and thee." (Gen. xxxi. 44.) Thus also the apostle insinuates; where making mention of the promise and oath of God, he saith, this promise and oath are both immutable, that "we might have a strong consolation, (or always ground for great rejoicing,) who have fled for refuge to lay hold upon the hope set before us." (Heb. vi. 18.)

This covenant, therefore, it was for the encouragement of Noah and his sons, that they might walk before God without fear: yea, it was to maintain their hope in his promise of forgiveness, though they should find their after performances mixed with infirmities; for so he had told them before, namely, "That he would not again destroy the earth for man's sake, albeit the imagination of man's heart be evil from his youth." "I will establish my covenant with you, and with your seed after you."

Verse 10. "And with every living creature that is with you: of the fowl, of the cattle, and of every beast of the earth with you; from all that go out of the ark, to every beast of the earth." These words respect the whole creation; for all the things in the world, devils only excepted, have a benefit by this covenant of God. And hence it is, that not man only, but "every thing that hath breath" is commanded to "praise the Lord:" but observe it, as for the sin of man, they before were destroyed by the flood, so now by reason of the mercy of God to man, they are spared, and partake of mercy also. This is intimated by these words: "Every creature that is with you; every beast of the earth with you."

Verse 11. "And I will establish my covenant with you, neither shall all flesh be cut off any more by the waters of a flood: neither shall there any more be a flood to destroy the earth."

This is the sum of the covenant, as it respecteth the letter, and the type, and the whole creation in general. But yet as to the spirit and gospel of it, the Holy Ghost must needs have a further reach, an intention of more glorious things, as may further be showed anon.

"And I will establish my covenant with you." For you that are men, and especially the members of the church, have the most peculiar share therein.

"Neither shall all flesh be cut off any more by the waters of a flood." For because of my covenant which I establish with you, I will spare them also, and give them the taste of my mercy and goodness.

"Neither shall there any more be a flood to destroy the earth." This covenant, therefore, is not of that nature as the covenant was which was made with Adam, to wit, a covenant of works, as the only conditions of life; for by that was the ground, for man's sin, accursed, accursed, and accursed again. But now the Lord goeth another way, the way of grace, and forgiveness of sins. Wherefore now, not the curse, but the mercy of God, comes in on the back and neck of sin, still sparing and forgiving man, the great transgressor, and the beast, &c., and the earth, for the sake of him.

Verses 12, 13. "And God said, This is the token of the covenant which I make between me and you, and every living creature that is with you, for perpetual generations. I do set my bow in the cloud, and it shall be for a token of a covenant between me and the earth."

So, then, the way to find out the covenant, what that is, it is to see if we can find out this token of it; to wit, the bow, of which the rainbow is but a type. I find, then, by the scriptures, where this bow is mystically spoken of, that the Lord Jesus Christ himself is encompassed with the bow. The first is this:

"And above the firmament that was over their heads, was the likeness of a throne, as the appearance of a sapphire stone; and upon the likeness of the throne, was the likeness as the appearance of a man upon it. And I saw, as the colour of amber, as the appearance of fire round about within it, from the appearance of his loins even upward, and from the appearance of his loins even downward; I saw as it were the appearance of fire, and it had brightness round about. As the appearance of the bow that is in the cloud in the day of rain, so was the appearance of the brightness round about. This was the appearance of the likeness of the glory of the Lord," the Man, the Lord's Christ, &c. (Ezek. i. 26—28.)

The second scripture is this: "I was in the Spirit; and behold, a throne was set in heaven, and one sat on the throne. And he that sat was to look upon like a jasper and a sardine stone, and there was a rainbow round about the throne, in sight like unto an emerald." (Rev. iv. 2, 3.) In these two texts there is mention of the rainbow, that was, not to be the covenant, but the token or sign thereof. Now then the covenant itself must needs be the man that was set in the midst of the bow upon the throne; for so he saith by the prophet, "I the Lord have called thee in righteousness, and will hold thine hand, and will keep thee, and give thee for a covenant of the people." (Isa. xlii. 6.) The covenant, therefore, is Jesus Christ the Saviour, whom the bow in the cloud was a sign or a token of. So then the sum of the text is this, that God, for the sake of the Lord Jesus Christ, will not again all the days of the earth bring an universal judgment upon the creature, as in the days of Noah, and of the old world he did; for Christ by the worth of his blood and righteousness hath pacified the justice of the law for sin: so then the whole universe standeth not upon a bottom of its own, but by the word and power of Christ. "The earth," said he, "and the inhabitants thereof are dissolved. I bear up the pillars of it." (Ps. lxxv. 3.)

But how must Christ be reckoned of God, when he maketh him the poise against all the sin of the world?

The prophet tells us thus: He shall be the covenant of the people, or he shall be accounted the conditions and worth of the world; He shall be the covenant, or works, or righteousness of the people; for, he as the high-priest under the law, is set for the people to Godward; that is, he standeth always in the presence of God, as the complete obedience of the people. So then, so long as the Lord Christ bears up his mediatorship, God in justice will neither destroy the world, nor the things that are therein.

In this covenant, therefore, the justice as well

as mercy of God is displayed in its perfection, inasmuch as without the perfection of the mediator Christ, the world could not be saved from judgment.

Verse 14. "And it shall come to pass when I bring a cloud over the earth, that the bow shall be seen in the cloud."

By these words the Lord looks back to the flood that before had drowned the earth; for in those clouds there was no bow, no token of Christ, or of the mercy of God. But now, saith God, I will do far otherwise; from henceforth when I bring a cloud, and there be showers of rain on the earth, these clouds shall not be as the other. But my bow shall be therein.

The cloud, then, that here is spoken of, must be understood of the judgment of God for sin, like those before, and at the overthrow of the world; only with this difference, they were clouds, judgments without mercy, but these judgments mixed therewith; and often the clouds are thus to be understood. Job, when he curseth his day, saith, "Let a cloud dwell upon it." (Job iii. 5.) So the judgments of God upon Zion, are called the covering of a cloud. (Lam. ii. 1.) So in Joel also, to the darkness of clouds, are the judgments of the church compared, (Joel ii. 2;) yea, that pillar that went before the children of Israel, it being a judgment to the people of Egypt, goes under this epithet, as a term most fit to express this judgment by, "it was a cloud and darkness to them." (Exod. xix. 20.)

And now to the cloud in hand, the cloud in which is the bow, the cloud of rain, although by the mercy and grace of God it is so great a blessing as it is, yet it sometimes becomes a judgment, it comes for correction, as a rod to afflict the inhabitants of the world withal. Thus it was in the days of Ezra, and very often both before and since. (Ezra x. 14.)

"The bow shall be seen in the cloud." This is the mercy of God to the world, and that by which it hath been hitherto preserved; "The bow shall be seen in the cloud." You know I told you of the bow before, that it was a sign or token of the covenant of God with the world, and that the covenant itself was Christ, as given of God unto us, with all his good conditions, merit, and worth. So then, in that God set this bow in the cloud, and especially in the clouds that he sends for judgment, he would have the world remember, that there comes no judgment as yet on the world, but it is mixed with, or poised by the mercy of God in Christ.

"The bow shall be seen in the cloud." This may respect God, or the world, that is, the seeing of the bow in the cloud; if it respect God, then it tells us he in judgment will remember mercy; if it respect the world, then it admonisheth us not to despond, or sink in despair under the greatest judgment of God, for the bow, the token of his covenant, is seen in the judgments that he executeth.

When the vision of the ruin of Jerusalem was revealed to the prophet Ezekiel, he saw that yet Christ sat under the bow. (Ezek. i. 28.)

When Antichrist was to come against the saints of God, the commission came from Christ, as he sat under the bow. (Rev. iv. 3.) This John did see and relate, of which we should take special notice: for by this token God would have us to know that these clouds, though they come for correction, yet not to destroy the church.

My bow shall be seen in the cloud.

Verse 15. "And I will remember my covenant which is between me and you, and every living creature of all flesh; and the waters shall no more become a flood to destroy all flesh."

"And I will remember my covenant." Much like this is that of the Lord to Israel, when they are under all, or any of those forty judgments mentioned. (Lev. xxvi.) If they shall confess their iniquity, saith he, and the iniquity of their fathers, &c., then will I remember my covenant with Jacob, and also my covenant with Isaac, and also my covenant with Abraham will I remember, and I will remember the land. (Lev. xxvi. 40—42.) His usual way in other sayings, is to begin with Abraham, but here he ends with him; and the reason is, because there, as it were, the great promise of the Messiah to that people began, saying, "In thy seed shall all nations be blessed."

"And I will remember my covenant which is between me and you." We read not here of any compact or agreement between Noah and God Almighty; wherefore such conditions and compacts could not be the terms between him and us: what then? why that covenant that he calls his, which is his gift to us, "I will give thee for a covenant," this is the covenant which is between God and us: "There is one God, and one mediator between God and man, the man Christ Jesus." This then is the reason why all the waters, why all the judgments of God, and why all the sins that have provoked those judgments, cannot become a flood to destroy all flesh.

Verse 16. "And the bow shall be in the cloud, and I will look upon it, that I may remember the everlasting covenant between God and every living creature of all flesh that is upon the earth."

"And the bow shall be in the cloud." This is a kind of a repetition; for this he had told us before, saying, "I do set my bow in the cloud," and "the bow shall be seen in the cloud:" which repetition is very needful, for it is hard for us to believe that Christ and grace are wrapped up in the judgments of God. Wherefore it had need be attested twice and thrice: "To write the same things to you," saith Paul, "to me indeed is not grievous, but for you it is safe." (Phil. iii. 1.)

"And I will look upon." A familiar expression, and suited to our capacity, and spoken to prevent a further ground of mistrust; much like to that of God, when he was to send the plague upon Egypt. "The blood," saith God, (of the lamb,) "shall be to you for a token upon the houses where you are : and when I see the blood, I will pass over you, and the plague shall not be upon you, to destroy you, when I smite the land of Egypt." (Exod. xii. 13.)

"And I will look upon it that I may remember." Not that God is forgetful—"He is ever mindful of his covenant." But such expressions are used to show and persuade us that the whole heart and delight of God is in it.

" That I may remember the everlasting covenant." This word covenant is also the sixth repetition thereof ; my covenant, the covenant, a covenant, and the everlasting covenant. O how fain would God beat it into the heads of the world, that he hath for men a covenant of grace.

" The everlasting covenant." Because the parties on both sides are faithful, perfect, and true ; the Father being the one, and the Son of his love the other ; for this covenant, as I said before, is not a compact and agreement betwixt God and the world, but his Son as his gift to men, is set for them to Godward. (Zech. ix. 11.) So that what conditions there are, they are perfectly found in Christ, by whose blood the covenant is sealed and established, and indeed becomes everlasting, hence it is called "the blood of the everlasting covenant." (Heb. xiii. 20.) And again, the New Testament is said to be in this blood. Besides, the promises are all in Christ—I mean the promises of this covenant—in him they are yea, and in him amen, to the glory of God the Father. Now, they being all in him, and yea and amen nowhere else, the covenant itself must needs be of pure grace and mercy, and the bow in the cloud, not qualifications in us, the proper tokens of this covenant.

Verse 17. " And God said unto Noah, this is the token of the covenant, which I have established between me and all flesh that is upon the earth."

Behold a repetition of all things that were essential either to the covenant itself, or to our faith therein, the making of the covenant, the looking on the covenant, and the token of the covenant ; how often are they mentioned, that we might be more fully convinced of the unchangeable nature of it : as Joseph said unto Pharaoh, " For that the dream was doubled unto Pharaoh twice, it is because the thing is established by God." (Gen. xli. 32.)

"And God said unto Noah." Where God loveth, he delighteth to apply himself to such, in a more than general way ; he singleth out the person, Noah, Abraham, and the like. " I know thee by name," saith he to Moses, " and thou hast found grace in my sight."

This is the token of the covenant. It still wants beating into people's heads. where they should look for the covenant itself, to wit, the throne which the rainbow compasseth round about ; for that is the token of the presence of the Messias, and thither we are to look for salvation from all plagues, and from all the judgments that are due to sin. The Lord for Christ's sake forgave you, this is the token of the covenant.

" Of the covenant which I have established."

This word " I," as also hinted before, doth intimate that this covenant is the covenant of grace and mercy, for a covenant of works cannot be established ; that is, settled between God and men, before both parties have, either by sureties or performance, ratified and confirmed the same. Indeed, it may be so established as that God will appoint no other ; but to be so established as to give us the fruits thereof, that must be the effects of his being well pleased with the conditions of those concerned in the making thereof. But that is not the world, but the Son of God, and therefore it is called his covenant, and he "as given to us of God," is so reckoned our condition and worth. (Zech. ix. 11.)

" Which I have established." To wit, upon better promises than duties purely commanded, or than the obedience of all the angels in heaven. I have established it in the truth and faithfulness, in the merit and worth of the blood of my Son, of whom the rainbow that you see in the cloud is a token.

Verse 18. "And the sons of Noah, that went forth of the ark, were Shem, and Ham, and Japheth : and Ham is the father of Canaan."

By these words Moses is returned again to the history of Noah. " And the sons of Noah that went forth of the ark." If these words, " that went forth of the ark," bear the emphasis of this part of the verse, then it may seem that Noah had more children than these ; but they were not accounted of ; for they being ungodly, as the rest of the world, they perished with them in their ungodliness. These only went in, and came out of the ark with him ; to wit,

" Shem, and Ham, and Japheth." The names thus placed is not according to their birth, for Japheth was the elder, Ham the younger, and Shem the middlemost of the two.

Shem, therefore, takes the place, because of his eminency in godliness ; also, because from him went the line up to Christ ; for which cause also the family of the sons of Judah, though he was but the fourth son of Israel, was reckoned before the family of Reuben, Jacob's firstborn ; or before the rest of the sons of his brethren. (1 Chron. ii. 3.) Sometimes persons take their place in genealogy, from the foresight of the mightiness of their offspring. Thus was Ephraim placed before Manasseh ; for, " truly," said Jacob, " his younger brother shall be greater than he. . . . And he set Ephraim before Manasseh." (Gen. xlviii. 20.)

Ham is the next in order ; not for the sake of his birthright, or because he was much, if anything, now for godliness ; but for that he was the next to be eminent in his offspring, for opposing and fighting against the same.

Shem and Ham, therefore, the two heads, or chief, from whence sprang good and evil men, by way of eminency. Ham is "the father of Canaan," or of the Canaanites, the people of God's curse, whom the sons of Shem, who afterwards sprang from Abraham, Isaac, and Jacob, was to cut off from the earth, for their most high abominations.

Japheth comes in, in the first place, as one that at present was least concerned either in the mercy or displeasure of God; being neither, in his offspring, to be devoutly religious, nor yet incorrigibly wicked, though afterwards he was to be persuaded to dwell in the tents of Shem.

Verse 19. "These are the three sons of Noah: and of them was the whole earth overspread."

Thus, though Noah's beginning was small, his latter end did greatly increase.

Verses 20, 21. "And Noah began to be an husbandman, and he planted a vineyard. And he drank of the wine, and was drunken; and he was uncovered within his tent."

This is the blot in this good man's scutcheon; and a strange blot it is, that such an one as Noah should be thus overtaken with evil! One would have thought that Moses should now have began with a relation of some eminent virtues, and honourable actions of Noah, since now he was saved from the death that overtook the whole world, and was delivered, both he and his children, to possess the whole earth himself. Indeed, he stepped from the ark to the altar; as Israel of old did sing on the shore of the Red Sea. But, as they, he soon forgot; he rendered evil to God for good.

Neither is Noah alone in this matter. Lot also being delivered from that fire from heaven that burnt up Sodom and Gomorrah, falls soon after into lewdness with the children of his body, and begetteth his own two daughters with child. (Gen. xix. 36.)

Gideon also, after he was delivered out of the hands of his enemies, took that very gold which God had given him, as the spoil of them that hated him, and made himself idols therewith. (Judges viii. 24—27.) What shall I say of David? and of Solomon also, who, after he had been twenty years at work for the service of the true God, both in building and preparing for his worship, and in writing of proverbs by divine inspiration, did, after this, make temples for idols; yea, almost for the gods of all countries? Yea, he did it when he was old, when he should have been preparing for his grave, and for eternity. "It came to pass when Solomon was old, that his wives turned away his heart after other gods;" "for Solomon went after Ashtoreth, the goddess of the Zidonians; and after Milcom, the abomination of the Ammonites." He did also "build an high place for Chemosh, the abomination of Moab, in the hill before Jerusalem; and for Molech, the abomination of the children of Ammon. And

likewise did he for all his strange wives, which burnt incense, and sacrificed unto their gods." (1 Kings xi. 4—8.)

All these sins were sins against mercies; yea, and doubtless against covenants, and the most solemn resolutions to the contrary. For who can imagine but that when Noah was tossed with the flood, and Lot within the scent and smell of the fire and brimstone that burned down Sodom, with his sons, and his daughters; and Gideon, when so fiercely engaged with so great an enemy, and delivered by so strange a hand; should in the most solemn manner both promise and vow to God. But behold! now they in truth are delivered and saved, they recompense all with sin. Lord, what is man! "How abominable and filthy is man, who drinketh in iniquity like water." (Job xv. 16.) Let these things learn us to cease "from man, whose breath is in his nostrils; for wherein is he to be accounted of?" (Isa. ii. 22.) Indeed, it is a vain thing to build our faith upon the most godly man in the world, because he is subject to err; yea, far better than he was so. If Noah, and Lot, and Gideon, and David, and Solomon, who wanted not matter from arguments, and that of the strongest kind, (as arguments that are drawn from mercy and goodness be,) to engage to holiness, and the fear of God; yet after all, did so foully fall, as we see: let us admire grace, that any stand; let the strongest fear, lest he fearfully fall; and let no man but Jesus Christ himself be the absolute platform and pattern of faith and holiness. As the prophet saith, "Let us cease from man." But to return.

"And Noah began to be an husbandman." This trade he took up for want of better employment; or rather, in mine opinion, from some liberty he took to himself, to be remiss in his care and work as a preacher. For seeing the church was now at rest, and having the world before them, they still retaining outward sobriety, poor Noah, good man, now might think with himself, "I need not now be so diligent, watchful, and painful in my ministry as formerly; the church is but small, without opposition, and also well settled in the truth; I may now take to myself a little time to tamper with worldly things." So he makes an essay upon husbandry. "He began to be an husbandman." Ha, Noah! it was better with thee when thou wast better employed! Yea, it was better with thee when a world of ungodly men set themselves against thee! Yea, when every day thy life was in danger to be destroyed by the giants, against whom thou wast a preacher above a hundred years! For then thou didst walk with God; then thou wast better than all the world; but now thou art in the relapse!

Hence note, That though the days of affliction, of temptation, and distress are harsh to flesh and blood, yet they are not half so dangerous as are the days of peace and liberty. Wherefore Moses preadmonished Israel, that when they had received the land of Canaan, and had herds, and silver, and gold in abundance, that then their heart be not lifted up to forget the Lord their God. (Deut. viii. 10—20.) Jesurun kicked when he was fat. (xxxii. 15.) O! when provender pricks us, we are apt to be as the horse or mule, that is without understanding.

"He planted a vineyard, and drank of the wine, and was drunken." Although in the course of godliness, many men have but a speculative knowledge of things; yet it is not so in the ways of this world and sin, the practical part of these things are lived in by all the world. They are sinners indeed. "He drank of the wine."

"He drank of the wine, and was drunken." The Holy Ghost, when it hath to do with sin, it loveth to give it its own name: drunkenness must be drunkenness, murder must be murder, and adultery must bear its own name. Nay, it is neither the goodness of the man, nor his being in favour with God, that will cause him to lessen or mince his sin. Noah was drunken; Lot lay with his daughters; David killed Uriah; Peter cursed and swore in the garden, and also dissembled at Antioch. But this is not recorded to the intent that the name of these godly should rot or stink; but to show, that the best men are nothing without grace; and, "That he that standeth should not be high-minded, but fear." (Rom. xi. 20.) Yea, they are also recorded for the support of the tempted, who, when they are fallen, are oft raised up by considering the infirmities of others: "Whatsoever things were written aforetime, were written for our learning, that we, through patience and comfort of the Scriptures, might have hope." (Rom. xv. 4.)

"And he was uncovered within his tent." That is, He lay like a drunken man, that regarded not who saw his shame. Hence note, how beastly a sin drunkenness is; it bereaveth a man of consideration, and civil behaviour; it makes him as brutish and shameless as a beast; yea, it discovereth his nakedness to all that behold.

"And he was uncovered." That is, lay naked. Behold ye now, that a little of the fruit of the vine lays gravity, grey hairs, and a man that for hundreds of years was a lover of faith, holiness, goodness, sobriety, and all righteousness, shamelessly, as the object to the eye of the wicked, with his nakedness in his tent.

"He was uncovered within his tent." The best place of retirement he had; but it could not hide him from the eye of the ungodly; it is not therefore thy secret chamber, nor thy lurking in holes, that will hide thee from the eye of the reproacher: nothing can do this but righteousness, goodness, sobriety, and faithfulness to God; this will hide thee; these are the garments, which, if they be on thee, will keep thee, that the shame of thy nakedness do not appear.

Verse 22. "And Ham, the father of Canaan, saw the nakedness of his father, and told his two brethren without."

Ham was the unsanctified one, the father of the children of the curse of God: he saw the nakedness of his father, and he blazed abroad the matter. Hence note, That the wicked and ungodly man is he that doth watch for the infirmities of the godly: as David says, "They watched for my halting." (Jer. xx. 10.) Indeed, they know not else how to justify their own ungodliness; but this, instead of excusing them of their wickedness, doth but justify the word against them; for by this they prove themselves graceless, and men that watch for iniquity. They said "in their hearts," said David, "Ah! so would we have it." (Ps. xxxv. 25.) Ammon said, "Aha! against the sanctuary when it was profaned, and against the land of Israel when it was desolate, and against the house of Judah when it went into captivity." (Ezek. xxv. 2.) The enmity that is in the hearts of ungodly men will not suffer them to do otherwise; when they see evil befal the saint, they rejoice and skip for joy.

"He saw the nakedness of his father." Hence note, That saints can rarely slip, but the eyes of the Canaanites will see them. This should make us walk in the world with jealous eyes, with eyes that look round about, not only to what we are and do, but also, how what we do is resented in the world. Abraham was good at this, and so was Isaac and Jacob; for they tendered more the honour and glory of God, than they minded their own concerns.

"He saw the nakedness of his father." Who was the nearest and dearest relation he had in the world; yet neither relation nor kin, nor all the good that his father had done him, could keep his polluted lips from declaring his father's follies, but out they must go; the sin of his own defiled heart must take place of the fifth commandment, and must rather solace itself in rejoicing in his father's iniquity, than in covering his father's nakedness. Wicked men regard not kindred; and no marvel, for they love not godliness. He that loveth not God, loveth not his brother, or father: nay, he "wrongeth his own soul." (Prov. viii. 36.)

"And he told his two brethren without." He told them, that is, mockingly, reflecting not only upon Noah, but also upon his brethren; to all of whom himself was far inferior, both as to grace and humanity.

Verse 23. "And Shem and Japheth took a garment, and laid it upon both their shoulders, and went backward, and covered the nakedness of their father; and their faces were backward, and they saw not their father's nakedness."

Shem and Japheth did it: This is recorded for the renown of these, as the action of Ham is for his perpetual infamy.

They "took a garment, and went backward, and covered their father, and saw not his nakedness." Love will attempt to do that with difficulty that it cannot accomplish otherwise. I think it might be from this action that the wise man gathered his proverb from: "Hatred stirreth up strifes; but love covereth all sins." (Prov. x. 12.) Indeed, Ham would fain have made variance between his father and his brethren, by presenting the folly of the one to the shame and provocation of others. But Shem, and his brother Japheth, they took the course to prevent it; they covered their father's nakedness.

Verse 24. "And Noah awoke from his wine, and knew what his younger son had done unto him."

By these words more is implied than expressed; for this awaking of Noah not only informeth us of natural awaking from sleep, but of his spiritual awaking from his sin. He awoke from his wine. As Ely said to Hannah, "How long wilt thou be drunken? Put away thy wine from thee." (1 Sam. i. 14.) By which words he exhorted to repentance. It is said of Nabal, That his wine went from him, as many men's sins forsake them, because they are decayed, and want strength and opportunity to perform them. Now this may be done, where the heart remaineth yet unsanctified: but Noah awoke from his wine, put it away, or, repented him of the evil of his doing. "A just man falleth seven times, and riseth again; but the wicked shall fall into mischief." (Prov. xxiv. 16.) Wherefore they have cause to say to all the Hams in the world, "Rejoice not against me, O thou mine enemy. When I fall, I shall arise," but your fall, is a "fall into mischief." (Mic. vii. 8.)

"He knew what his younger son had done unto him." Whether this was by revelation from heaven, or through the information of Japheth and Shem, I determine not; but so it was, that the good man had understanding thereof: which might be requisite upon a double account; not only that he might now be ashamed thereof; but take notice, that he had caused the enemies of God to reproach; for this sinks deep into a good man's heart, and afflicteth him so much the more.

Verse 25. "And he said, cursed be Canaan; a servant of servants shall he be unto his brethren."

By these words one would think that Canaan, the grand-child of Noah, was the first that discovered his nakedness; but of this I am uncertain: I rather think that Noah, in a spirit of prophecy, determined the destruction of Ham's posterity, from the prodigiousness of his wicked action, and of his name, which signifieth indignation, or heat; for names of old were ofttimes given according to the nature and destiny of the persons concerned. "Is not he rightly called Jacob?" (Gen. xxvii. 36.) And again, "As his name is, so is he." (1 Sam. xxv. 25.) Besides, by this act did Ham declare himself void of the grace of God; for he that rejoiceth in iniquity, or that maketh a mock, as being secretly pleased with or at the infirmities of the godly, is declared already, by the Spirit of God, to be nothing. (1 Cor. xiii. 2, 3.)

"A servant of servants shall he be unto his brethren." This was accomplished when Israel took the land of Canaan, and made the offspring of this same Ham, even so many as escaped the edge of the sword, to be captives and bondsmen, and tributers unto them.

Hence note, that the censures of good men are dreadful, and not lightly to be passed over, whether they prophecy of evil or good; because they speak in judgment, and according to the tenor of the word of God.

Verse 26. "And he said, Blessed be the Lord God of Shem; and Canaan shall be his servant."

Shem seems by this, to be the first in that action of love to his father, and that Japheth did help through his persuasion; for Shem is blessed in a special manner, and Canaan is made his servant.

Hence note, That forwardness in things that are good, is a blessed sign that the Lord is our God: "Blessed be the Lord God of Shem." It is said of Hananiah, That "he was a faithful man, and feared God above many." (Neh. vii. 2.) Now such men are provocations to good, as I doubt not but Shem's was to Japheth. As Paul saith of some, "Your zeal hath provoked very many." (2 Cor. ix. 2.)

Verse 27. "God shall enlarge Japheth, and he shall dwell in the tents of Shem."

In the margin, it is "God shall persuade:" and it looks like a confirmation of what I said before, and is a prophecy of that requital of love that God should one day give his posterity, for his kindness to Noah his father: as if Noah had said, "Well, Japheth, thou wast soon persuaded by Shem to show kindness to me thy father, and the Lord shall hereafter persuade thy posterity to trust in the God of Shem."

"God shall enlarge." This may respect liberty of soul, or how great the church of the Gentiles should be; for Japheth was the father of the Gentiles. (Gen. x. 2—5.)

If it respect the first, then it shows that sin is as fetters and chains that holds souls in captivity and thraldom. And hence, when Christ doth come in the gospel, "it is to preach deliverance to captives," and "to set at liberty them that are bruised." (Luke iv. 18.)

"God shall persuade." That is, God shall enlarge him by persuasion; for the gospel knows no other compulsion, but to force by argumentation. Them therefore that God brings into the tents, or churches of Christ, they by the gospel are enlarged from the bondage and thraldom of the devil, and persuaded also to embrace his grace to salvation.

Verse 28. "And Noah lived after the flood three hundred and fifty years."

He lived therefore to see Abraham fifty and eight years old. He lived also to see the foundation of Babel laid; nay, the top stone thereof: and also the confusion of tongues. He lived to see of the fruit of his loins, mighty kings and princes. But in all this time he lived not to do one work that the Holy Ghost thought worthy to record for the savour of his name, or the edification and benefit of his church, save only, That he died at "nine hundred and fifty years;" so great a breach did this drunkenness make upon his spirit.

Verse 29. "And all the days of Noah were nine hundred and fifty years: and he died."

CHAPTER X.

Verse 1. "Now these are the generations of the sons of Noah, Shem, Ham, and Japheth; and unto them were sons born after the flood."

Having thus passed over the flood, with what Noah and his sons did after, we now come to the second plantation of the world, to wit, by the three sons of Noah; for by these three was the world replenished after the flood. Shem was the father of the Jews; Ham the father of the Canaanites; and Japheth, the father of the Gentiles. So then, of Shem came the then present visible church; of Ham the opposers and enemies of it: but of Japheth came those that should be received into the church afterwards; as also abundance of the haters of the Lord.

Verse 2. "The sons of Japheth; Gomer, and Magog, and Madai, and Javan, and Tubal, and Meshech, and Tiras."

Gomer, a consumer; Magog, covering or melting: Madai, measuring, or judging; Javan, making sad; Tubal, born, brought, or worldly; Meshech, prolonging; Tiras, a destroyer; these are the English of their names.

Gomer, and Magog, and Meshech, and Tubal, are the great persecutors of the church in the latter days: they shall be persecuted then by consumers, melters, and men of this world. Madai, and Javan, (as some say,) were the fathers of the Medes and Greeks. These therefore did sometimes help, and not always hinder the church.

Verses 3, 4. "And the sons of Gomer; Ashkenaz, and Riphath, and Togarmah. And the sons of Javan; Elishah, and Tarshish, Kittim, and Dodanim."

Riphath, medicine, or release; Elishah, the Lamb of God; Dodanim, beloved. Either these names were given them by way of prophecy; implying, that of their seed should arise many Gentile churches; or to show us, that when men, as their fathers, have left or lost the power of godliness, yet something of the notion they may yet retain.

Verse 5. "By these were the isles of the Gentiles divided in their lands; every one after his tongue, after their families, in their nations."

But this must be understood to be after the building of, and confusion at Babel; for before they had all but one tongue; and besides they kept all together.

Verse 6. "And the sons of Ham; Cush, and Mizraim, and Phut, and Canaan."

Cush, black. Of Ham and Mizraim came the Ethiopians, or blackamoor: the land of Ham was the country about Egypt; wherefore Israel was first afflicted by them.

Verse 7. "And the sons of Cush; Seba and Havilah, and Sabtah, and Raamah, and Sabtechah: and the sons of Raamah; Sheba, and Dedan."

Seba and Sheba, sometimes look well upon the church; (Ps. lxxii. 10;) but when they did not, God gave them for her ransom. (Isa. xliii. 3.)

Verse 8. "And Cush begat Nimrod, (or the rebellious one;) he began to be a mighty one in the earth."

The begetting of Nimrod, is accounted a thing that is over and above, and is laid by the Holy Ghost as a blot upon Cush for ever; for when men would vilify, they used to say, Thou art the son of the rebellious, the son of a murderer. So again, He that begetteth Solomon's fool, (or, wicked one) he begetteth him to his own shame. (Prov. xvii. 21.)

"Cush begat Nimrod." So then, the curse came betimes upon the sons of Ham; for he was the father of Cush. For the curse, as it were, begins in rebellion, and a rebellious one was Nimrod, both by name and nature.

"He began to be a mighty one in the earth." I am apt to think he was the first that in this new world sought after absolute monarchy.

"He began to be a mighty one in the earth," (or, among the children of men.) I suppose him to be a giant; not only in person, but in disposition; and so, through the pride of his countenance, did scorn that others, or any, should be his equal; nay, could not be content, till all made obeisance to him. He therefore would needs be the author and master of what religion he pleased; and would also subject the rest of his brethren thereto, by what ways his lusts thought best. Wherefore here began a fresh persecution. That sin, therefore, which the other world was drowned for, was again revived by this cursed man, even to lord it over the sons of God, and to enforce idolatry and superstition upon them; and hence he is called "the mighty hunter."

Verse 9. "He was a mighty hunter before the Lord: wherefore it is said, even as Nimrod the mighty hunter before the Lord."

"He was a mighty hunter." That is, a persecutor: Wherefore Saul's persecuting of David is compared to hunting. (1 Sam. xxvi. 20.) And so is the persecution of others. "They hunt every man his brother with a net." (Mic. vii. 2.) And it may well be compared thereto; for the dog or lion that hunteth, is void of bowels and pity; and if they can but satisfy their doggish and lionish nature, they care neither for innocence, nor goodness, nor life of that they pursue. The life, the blood, the extirpation of the contrary party, is the end of their course of hunting.

"He was a mighty hunter." As it is said of Jabin, "He mightily oppressed Israel twenty years:" that is, he did it exceedingly; he went beyond others; he was more cruel and barbarous; "he was a mighty hunter." Wherefore the children of blessed Shem, by this monster, had sore affliction. (Judges iv. 3.) Noah therefore lived to see Nimrod, the mighty one, make havoc of the children of his bowels, to his no little grief and compunction of spirit.

"He was a mighty hunter before the Lord;" or, in the presence of the Lord; or, in defiance to him. This shows, that the hand of God was stretched forth against his work; as also it was against Jeroboam's, by that man of God that from Judah went down to prophesy against him; (1 Kings xiii. 1—3;) but he abode obdurate and hard; he regarded not the Lord, nor the operation of his hands: as he also saith in another place of the cursed blood of Antichrist, "When they shall fall upon the sword, they shall be wounded:" (Joel ii. 8.) Let them do things never so much against the plain text, they feel not the wounds of conscience; but this is a sore judgment, and that under which this hunter was; and therefore the presence and hand of God would not break him off, nor hinder his hunting of souls. But even before the face of the keeper of the godly, would Nimrod, the rebel, hunt for their precious life to destroy it.

"Wherefore it is said, even as Nimrod, the mighty hunter, before the Lord." These words, as it seems, was the proverb that went of him among the godly in after generations; for he had so left his marks in the sides of the church, that she could not quickly forget him. Wherefore, when at any time there arose another that showed cruelty to the ways of God, he was presently compared to Nimrod, that "hunted before the Lord." Nimrod, therefore, was rebellious to a proverb. And as it is said of Ahab, so might it be said of him, "There was none like unto Nimrod, which did sell himself to work wickedness in the sight of, or, before the Lord." (1 Kings xxi. 25.)

Verse 10. "And the beginning of his kingdom was Babel, and Erech, and Accad, and Calneh, in the land of Shinar."

By these words, as I suppose, are those in the chapter that followeth expounded: Where it says, "Let us build us a city, and a tower;" for this work was chiefly the invention of Nimrod, who, with his wicked council, contrived this work; and as one that had made himself head of the people, be enjoined them to set to the work.

"And the beginning of his kingdom was Babel." Babel therefore was the first great seat of oppressors after the flood; whose situation was in the land of Shinar, in that land which is now called Babylon. By this we may also gather, by whom our mystical Babel was builded; to wit, by those that rebelled (as Nimrod) from the simplicity of the gospel of Christ; for the builders, especially the chief, have a semblance one of another. It was even such as came of the seed of the godly, as these did of blessed Noah; who, in time, apostatizing from the word, and desiring mastership over their brethren; they, as lords, fomented their own conceptions, and then enjoined the people to build. As Rehoboam forsook the counsel of the ancients, that stood before his father Solomon, so these have forsaken the counsel of the old men, the apostles that stood before Jesus Christ; and hearkening to the counsel of a younger sort of wanters of their grace and wisdom, they imagine and build a Babel.

Verses 11, 12. "Out of that land went forth Asshur, and builded Nineveh, and the city Rehoboth, and Calah, and Resen, between Nineveh and Calah: the same is a great city."

Nimrod having began to exalt himself, others, that were big with desires of ostentation, did soon follow his example, making themselves captains and heads of the people, and built them strongholds for the supportation of their glory. But they did it, as I said, by Nimrod's example; wherefore it is said they went "out of the land." Just thus it was at the beginning of mystical Babel: First the tyranny began at Babel itself, where the usurper was seen to sit in his glory, before whose face the world did tremble. Now other inferior persons, inferior, I say, in power, but not in pride, having desire to be lords, as Nimrod himself, they will also go build them cities; by which means Nimrod's invention could not be kept at Rome, but hath spread itself in many and mighty kingdoms.

"Out of that land went forth Asshur, and built Nineveh," &c. Asshur seems to be the second son of Shem, (ver. 22.) A fit resemblance of those persons that have come from mystical Babel, to build their Ninevehs, and Rehoboths, and Calnehs, in all lands. Still they have pretended religion: that they had their orders from the apostolical see: that they were the true sons of Shem, or disciples of Christ. But the seeing Christian should remember, that some of the children of Shem were in Babel with rebellious Nimrod; that instead of learning humility of their father, through the pride and rebellion of their own vain-glorious fancies, they learned wickedness and rebellion of cursed and prodigious Nimrod.

Hence note, that what cities, that is, churches soever have been builded by persons that have come from Romish Babel, those builders and cities are to be suspected for such as had their founder and foundation from Babel itself. Wherefore let Israel say, "Asshur shall not save us," (Hos. xiv. 3,) for he shall not save himself; but as the star of Jacob ariseth, he shall fade and perish for ever. (Numb. xxiv. 24.) So perish all the builders and building that hath had its pattern from mystical Babel, unless a miracle of grace prevents.

It was Asshur that carried away the ten tribes;

(Ezra iv. 2 ;) it is Asshur that joineth with the enemies of the church; (Ps. lxxxiii. 8 ;) it is Asshur that with others upholds the great mart of the nations; (Ezek. xxvii. 23 ;) wherefore Asshur, and all his company, must at last go down into their pit. (Ezek. xxxii. 22, 23.)

So then, let Augustine the monk, come from Rome into England, and let him build his Nineveh here; let others go also into other countries, and build their Resens and Calahs there; these are all but brats of Babel, and their end shall be, that they "perish for ever." John saw it, and the cities, that is, the churches of the nations, or the national churches fell; and "great Babylon," their inventor and founder, "came in remembrance before God, to give unto her the cup of the wine of the fierceness of his wrath." (Rev. xvi. 19.)

Verses 13, 14. "And Mizraim begat Ludim, and Anamim, and Lehabim, and Naphtuhim. And Pahtrusim, and Casluhim, (out of whom came Philistim,) and Caphtorim."

Ludim, as I suppose, may be the same with Lubim that came up with the Egyptians and Ethiopians against Israel, (2 Chron. xii. 3 ; xvi. 8,) of whose cruelty Nahum complains ; where he saith, They also helped Nineveh against the children of God. (Nah. iii. 9.) The rest of them were of the same disposition, especially the Philistine that came of Casluhim ; for they, both in Saul and David's days, were implacable against the church and people of God ; they were a giantish people, and trusted in their strength, and seldom overcome but when Israel went against them in the name of the Lord their God.

Verses 15—18. "And Canaan begat Sidon his firstborn, and Heth, and the Jebusite, and the Amorite, and the Girgasite, and the Hivite, and the Arkite, and the Sinite, and the Arvadite, and the Zemarite, and the Hamathite : and afterward were the families of the Canaanites spread abroad."

These are the children of Canaan, the son of Ham, the accursed of the Lord. These did chiefly possess the land of Canaan before Israel went out of Egypt : they were a mighty giantish people, yet Israel must fight with them, notwithstanding they were, in comparison to these, but as the grasshopper.

Verse 19. "And the border of the Canaanites was from Sidon, as thou comest to Gerar, unto Gaza; as thou goest unto Sodom and Gomorrah, and Admah, and Zeboim, even unto Lasha."

They bordered, therefore upon the Philistines on the one side, for Gerar and Gaza belonged to them, and they touched upon Sodom and Gomorrah, &c., on the other. They were placed, therefore, by the judgment of God, between these two wicked and sinful people, that they might, as a punishment for their former sins, be infected with the sight and infection of their ungodly and monstrous abominations. They that "turn aside unto their crooked ways, the Lord shall lead them forth with the workers of iniquity." (Ps. cxv. 5.)

Verse 20. "These are the sons of Ham, after their families, after their tongues, in their countries, and in their nations."

Ham had a mighty offspring ; but the judgment of God, was, that they should be wicked men, idolaters, persecutors, sinners with a high hand ; such as God was resolved to number to the sword, both in this world, and that to come ; I mean, for the generality of them.

Verse 21. "Unto Shem also, the father of all the children of Eber, the brother of Japheth the elder, even to him were children born."

The manner of style which the Holy Ghost here useth in his preamble to the genealogy of Shem, is worthy to be taken notice of; as that he is called, "the father of all the children of Eber, and the brother of Japheth."

By his being called, "the father of all the children of Eber," we may suppose, that from Eber to Abraham, (by whom the reckoning of the genealogy was cut off from Eber, and entailed to the name of Abraham,) all the children of Eber were, as it were, the disciples of Shem, for he lived awhile after Abraham. His doctrine, therefore, they might profess, though possibly with some mixture of those inventions that came in among men afterwards ; which, I think, were at the greatest about Abraham's time. Besides, he shows by this, that the other children of Shem, as Elam, Asshur, Lud and Aram, with Uz, Hul, Gether and Mash, went away with Nimrod, and the rest of that company, into idolatry, tyranny and other profaneness ; so that only the line from Shem to Eber, and from thence to Abraham, &c., were the visible church in those days.

"The brother of Japheth." So he was of Ham, but because Ham was cut off for his wickedness to his father, therefore both Shem and Japheth did hold him in abomination, and would not own that relation that before was between them, especially in things pertaining to the kingdom of God, and of Christ. Wherefore the Holy Ghost also, in reckoning up the kindred of Shem, excludeth Ham the younger brother, and stops after he had mentioned Japheth : "The brother of Japheth the elder."

"Unto him were children born, unto Shem also. Unto him were children born." The Holy Ghost doth secretly here, as he did before in the generation of Seth, insinuate a wonder. For, considering the godliness of Shem, and the ungodliness of Ham, and the multitude of his tyrannical brood, it is a wonder that there should such a thing as the offspring of Shem be found upon the face of the earth ; for I am apt to think, that Shem, with his posterity, did testify against the actions of Nimrod ; as also against the children of Ham, in their wickedness and rebellion against the way of God ; as may be hinted after. Wherefore he, with his seed, were in jeopardy, among that tumultuous generation. Yet God preserved him and his seed upon the face of the earth. For let the number and wickedness of men be never so great in the world, there must be also a church, by whose actions the ways of the wicked must be condemned.

Verse 22. "The children of Shem; Elam, and Asshur, and Arphaxad, and Lud, and Aram."

These children were born unto Shem. The book of Chronicles mentions four more, as Uz, and Hul, and Gether, Meshech, or Mash; but these were the natural sons of Aram, Shem being only their father's father.

Elam and Asshur, as also Lud and Aram, notwithstanding they were the sons of Shem, struck off, as I think, with Nimrod, and left their father, for the glory of Babel; yea, they had a province there in the days of Daniel. (Dan. viii. 2.) Wherefore great judgments are threatened against Elam; as, That Elam shall drink the cup of God's fury: That their bow shall be broken: That God would bring upon him the four winds: and, That there should be no nation whither the captives of Elam should not come, yet God would save them in the latter days. (Jer. xlix. 34—39.)

As for Lud, although through the wickedness of his heart he forsook his father Shem, and so the true religion; yet a promise is made of his conversion, when God calls home the children of Japheth, and persuadeth them to dwell in the tents of Shem: "I will set a sign among them," saith God, "and I will send to those that escape of them, even to Tarshish, Pul, and Lud—to Tubal and Javan, to the isles afar off that have not heard my fame." (Isa. lxvi. 19.) Yea, thus it shall be, although they were once the soldiers of the adversaries of the church, and bare the shield and helmet against her. (Ezek. xxvii. 10.) Of Asshur I have spoken before. Aram became also an heathen, and dwelt among the mountains of the east: out of him came Balaam, the soothsayer, that Balek sent for, to curse the children of Israel. (Numb. xxiii. 7.)

In Arphaxad, though he was not the eldest, remained the line that went from Abraham to David; and from him to Jesus Christ. (Luke iii. 36.)

Verse 23. "And the children of Aram; Uz, and Hul, and Gether, and Mash."

Uz went also off from Shem, but yet good men came from his loins; for Job himself was of that land. (Job i. 1.) Yet the wrath of God was threatened to go forth against them, because they had a hand in the persecution of the children of Israel, &c. (Jer. xxv. 20. Lam. iv. 21.)

Verses 24, 25. "And Arphaxad begat Salah, and Salah begat Eber. And unto Eber were born two sons; the name of one was Peleg, for in his days was the earth divided; and his brother's name was Joktan."

This Eber was a very godly man, the next after Shem that vigorously stood up to maintain religion. Two things are entailed upon him to his everlasting honour. First, the children of God, even Abraham himself, was not ashamed to own himself one of this man's disciples, or followers; and hence he is called Abraham the Hebrew, or Ebrew. (Gen. xiv. 13.) Joseph also will have it go there: "I was stolen away," said he, "out of the land of the Hebrews." (Gen. xl. 15.) Nay, the Lord God himself, to show how he honoured this man's faith and life, doth style himself the God of his fathers, to wit, the God of the Hebrews, the Lord God of the Hebrews. (Exod. iii. 18; vii. 16; ix. 13.) Secondly, this was the man that kept that language with which Adam was created, and that in which God spake to the fathers of old, from being corrupted and confounded by the confusion of Babel; and therefore it is for ever called his, the Hebrew tongue, the tongue in which Christ spake from heaven to Saul: this man, therefore, was a stiff opposer of Nimrod; neither had he a hand in the building of Babel; for all that had, had their language confounded by that strange judgment of God.

"And unto Eber we. born two sons, the name of the one was Peleg, (or, Division,) for in his days was the earth divided; and his brother's name was Joktan." This division, (in mine opinion,) was not only that division that was made by the confusion of tongues, but a division also that was made among men by the blessed doctrine of God, which most eminently rested in the bosom of Shem and Eber, neither of which had their hands in that monstrous work. Wherefore, as Eber by abstaining kept entire the holy language, so Shem, to show that he was clear from this sin also, is by the Holy Ghost called, "The father of all the children of Eber:" implying, that Eber and Shem did mightily labour to preserve a seed from the tyranny and pollution of Nimrod and Babel; and by that means made a divison in the earth; unto whom because the rebels would not adhere, therefore did God the Lord smite them with confusion of tongues, and scatter them abroad upon the face of all the earth.

Verse 26. "And Joktan begat Almodad, and Sheleph, and Hazarmaveth, and Jerah."

Here again he hath left the holy line, which is from Eber to Abraham, and makes a stop upon Joktan's genealogy, and so comes down to the building of Babel.

Verses 27—31. These therefore begat Joktan: He also begat "Hadoram, and Uzal, and Diklah, and Obal, and Abimael, and Sheba, and Ophir, and Havilah, and Jobab: all these were the sons of Joktan. And their dwelling was from Mesha, as thou goest unto Sephar, a mount of the east. These are the sons of Shem, after their families, after their tongues, in their lands, after their nations."

Moses, as I said, by this relation, respecteth, and handleth chiefly those, or them persons, who were at first the planters of the world after the flood; leaving the church, or a relation of that, and its seed, to be discoursed after the building of Babel, unto the tenth verse of the next chapter.

Hence methinks one might gather, that these above-mentioned, whose genealogies are handled at large, as the families of Japheth, of Ham, and Joktan are, were both in their persons and off-spring engaged (some few only excepted, who might adhere to Noah, Shem, and Eber) in that foul work, the building of Babel. Now that which inclineth me thus to think, it is because immediately after their thus being reckoned by Moses, even before he taketh up the genealogy of Shem, he bringeth in the building thereof; the which he not only mentioneth, but also enlargeth upon; yea, and also telleth of the cause of the stopping of that work, before he returneth to the church, and the line that went from Shem to Abraham.

Verse 32. " These are the families of the sons of Noah after their generations, in their nations : and by these were the nations divided in the earth after the flood."

CHAPTER XI.

Verse 1. " And the whole earth was of one language, and of one speech."

Moses having thus briefly passed through the genealogies of Japheth, Ham, and Joktan ; in the next place he cometh to show us their work which they had by this time engaged to do; and that was, to build a Babel, whose tower might reach to heaven. Now, in order to this their work, or rather to his relation thereof, he maketh a short fore-speech, which consisteth of two branches. The first is, that now they had all one language or lip. The other was, that they yet had kept themselves together, either resting or walking, as an army compact. An excellent resemblance of the state of the church, before she imagined to build her a Babel. For till then, however one might outstrip another in knowledge and love; yet so far as they obtained, their language or lip was but one : having but one heart, and one soul, they with one mouth did glorify God, even the Father.

" And the whole earth was of one language." By these words, therefore, we may conceive the reason why so great a judgment as that great wickedness, Babel, should be contrived, and endeavoured to be accomplished. The multitude was one. Not but that it is a blessed thing for the church to be one : as Christ saith, My beloved is but one. (John xxii. 11.) But here was an oneness, not only in the church, but in her mixing with the world. The whole earth, among which, as I suppose, is included Noah, Shem, and others ; who being over-topped by Nimrod, the mighty hunter, might company with him until he began to build Babel. Therefore it is said in the next verse, that they companied together from the east, to the land of Shinar.

Hence note, That the first and primitive churches were safe and secure, so long as they kept entire by themselves; but when once they admitted of a mixture, great Babel, as a judgment of God, was admitted to come into their mind.

Verse 2. " And it came to pass, as they journeyed from the east, that they found a plain in the land of Shinar, and they dwelt there."

By these words, we gather, that the first rest of Noah, and so the inhabiting of his posterity, was still eastward from Babylon, towards the sun rising.

But to gospelize. They journeyed from the east : and so consequently they turned their backs upon the rising of the sun. So did also the primitive church, in the day when she began to decline from her first and purest state. Indeed, so long as she kept close to the doctrine and discipline of the gospel, according to the word and commandment of the Lord Jesus, then she kept her face still towards the sun rising. According to the type in Ezekiel, who saith of the second and mystical temple, Her fore-front, or face, did stand towards the east. (Ezek. xlvii. 1.) Also he saith, when he saw the glory of God, how it came unto this temple, it came from the way of the east. (Ezek. xliii. 2.) Their journeying, therefore, from the east, was, their turning their backs upon the sun. And to us, in gospel times, it holdeth forth such a mystery as this : That their journey was thus recorded, to show they were now apostatized ; for assuredly they had turned their back upon the glorious Sun of Righteousness, as upon that which shineth in the firmament of heaven.

" They found a plain in the land of Shinar." Shinar is the land of Babylon.

" They found a plain." Or, place of fatness and plenty, as usually the plains are ; and are, upon that account, great content to our flesh. This made Lot separate from Abraham, and choose to dwell with the sinners of Sodom ; why, the country was a plain, and therefore fat and plentiful, even like the garden of the Lord, and the land of Egypt. Here, therefore, they made a stop ; here they dwelt and continued together. A right resemblance of the degenerators' course in the days of general apostacy, from the true apostolical doctrine, to the church of our Romish Babel. So long as the church endured hardship, and affliction, she was greatly preserved from revolts and backslidings ; but after she had turned her face from the sun, and had found the plain of Shinar ; that is, the fleshly contents that the pleasures, and profits, and honours of this world afford ; she, forgetting the world and order of God, was content, with the travellers in the text, to dwell in the land of Babel.

Verse 3. " And they said one to another, Go to, let us make brick, and burn them throughly, (and burn them to a burning.) And they had brick for stone, and slime had they for mortar."

Now they being filled with ease and plenty, they begin to lift up the horn, and to consult one with another what they were best to do. Whereupon, after some time of debate, they came to this conclusion, That they would go to build a Babel.

"And they said one to another, Go to." This manner of phrase is often used in scripture; and is sometimes, as also here, used to show, That the thing intended, must come to pass, what opinion or contradiction to the contrary soever there be. It argueth that a judgment is made in the case, and proceedings shall be accordingly. Thus it is also to be taken in Judges (vii. 3,) Ecclesiastes (ii. 1,) Isaiah (v. 5,) James (v. 1,) &c. Wherefore it shows, that these men had cast off the fear of God, and, like Israel in the days of the prophet Jeremiah, they resolved to follow their own imagination, let God or his judgments speak never so loud to the contrary. And so indeed he says of them at verse the sixth: "And this they have begun to do," saith God, "and nothing will restrain them."

NOTES.

NOTE 1, p. 371.—"*The first thing that God made, was time.*"] —This is an expression without any proper meaning. To speak of time as "a thing," and as "made," is to bewilder the mind which may attempt to form any notion on the subject. It would have been as proper to say, the first thing which God made was "space;" and the same confusion would have followed any effort to comprehend what was meant. There is a great difference between the crude notions which led the commentator thus to speak of time, and the ingenious distinction which he makes between chaos, or the first matter, and the earth created out of it in six days. Writing as he did so long before the investigations of Biblical geologists commenced, it is remarkable that he should have supposed a rudimentary creation existing, how long is not stated, before the creation of the system of nature as we now see it.

NOTE 2, p. 374.—"*They* (the waters) *under the heaven, figure out the world, or ungodly: they above the firmament, the elect and chosen of God.*"]—The reader need scarcely be told that, however pleasant it may be to find allegories in Scripture, allegories do not always exist where a pious fancy busies itself about them. In the present instance, it would be very difficult to give any reason for the assertion, that "the waters under the heaven figure out the world, or ungodly." On the contrary, we have the express statement, that God pronounced the gathering of these waters, as well as the earth which they surrounded, good. Most readers have heard something of the ancient father, the learned, devout Origen. Though reverenced for his genius and his piety, his bold dealing with Scripture in the way of allegory has made sober theologians almost tremble at his name; but Bunyan, with all the credit due to his humility, affords examples of allegorizing, in this short commentary, fully as daring, and certainly as unsubstantial as any to be found in Origen.

NOTE 3, p. 380.—"*This proveth further, that in the first chaos was contained all that was made upon the earth.*"] —Almost any of the theories of modern geology may be adapted to this statement; but still it is very questionable whether it be either theologically or scientifically correct. The remark on verse 24 is painfully presumptuous and indefensible. There is not the remotest analogy between a man's leaving his father and mother for his wife, and the Son of God's coming forth from his Father to save the world.

NOTE 4, p. 382.—"*This was her prologue,*" &c.]— Wherever the subject leads Bunyan to write from the dictates of practical experience, rather than from the temptations of a speculative ingenuity, the lesson taught is valuable, and readily understood. Such is that here given; and such are several others in the course of the commentary.

NOTE 5, p. 400.—"*Behold, thou hast driven me out,*" &c.] —The remarks on the whole of this melancholy narrative of the first fratricide are solemn and edifying. The subject was itself sufficiently interesting to the commentator; and, therefore, he wrote upon it with powerful good sense. Had he been equally contented with the majestic history of creation, as the events recorded are in themselves true and sufficiently sublime, he would have commented on them with corresponding simplicity. But they were of a class not so impressive to his understanding; and he sought for meanings which might make them more so. This is a consideration which may be applied to commentators generally. Wherever they thoroughly comprehend, and feel the importance of a narrative, they are content to illustrate the facts as such. Where the contrary is the case, they have recourse to allegory and speculation.

NOTE 6, p. 415.—"*Rooms (nests)*"]—It is interesting to observe, both from this instance and from numberless others, how anxious Bunyan was to catch at any close interpretation of Scriptural terms. He evidently yearned for a knowledge of the original language; and instead of boasting of his want of such learning, he used every means in his power to overcome the deficiency. This he did, to a great degree, by his assiduous comparing of scripture with scripture; and by treasuring up in his memory every nearer reading of the original which might come before him.

NOTE 7, p. 422.—"*These latter words are of great importance, 'And the Lord shut him in,'*" &c.]—Could Bunyan have written a whole commentary with the same vigour as that displayed in this passage, it would have been of vast value to the world. But he could not always be satisfied with what his natural ability enabled him to do well; when he felt that, with higher artificial attainments, a far wider scope would be open for his labours. The present commentary, brief as it is, has many marks of originality. But it is chiefly interesting, as illustrating some of the most remarkable features of Bunyan's intellectual state and character at the period when it was written. It is evidently not the production of a man passive and unaspiring. It is in the highest degree speculative; and sometimes passes the boundary which most later writers would set to their ingenuity.

PREFATORY REMARKS

on

PAUL'S. DEPARTURE AND CROWN.

PAUL, midway in his course, desiring to depart, and be with the Lord ; Paul checking that desire, and patiently passing through a long series of subsequent labours and afflictions ; Paul grown old, and knowing that his work was done, now again preparing to depart,—Paul, viewed through this train of circumstances, presents as grand a portraiture of man as human history is ever likely to furnish.

No two points in the records of St. Paul's life can be better fixed upon, for marking the progress of his mind, than those here indicated. His state of feeling as expressed in the words, " I desire to depart," and in those which he used some six or seven years later, " I am ready to depart," offers an interesting subject for study. In the former, it is easy to trace indications of weariness—a sense of human infirmity naturally seeking rest. The "desire to be with the Lord" is not expressed as an ardent, triumphant sentiment, but as an emotion which, though strengthened by faith, was largely intermixed with an experience of sadness. Resignation is the predominant witness to the truth and sincerity of any of God's servants in all stages of their course, short of the last. It would still be so ; but resignation ceases to have a meaning when unmixed happiness and glory are its immediate consequence. St. Paul was sick and weary with what he had already endured. He foresaw that if he remained on earth, there was still more to be endured. This he would have avoided, had it been allowed him to pass into a better world, and at once take up his abode with his divine Master ; but he knew that that could not as yet be. He was content, therefore, to remain on earth ; but there was a dignity and grandeur in this submission to necessity, because it arose from the profound assurance that truth and charity might be gainers by his labour and endurance.

A season of toil increasing in severity and peril awaited him ; but this intermediate period was fraught with vast benefits both to himself and mankind. All future ages will rejoice in the records of his knowledge and experience. He had vanquished, at that stage of his course marked by his letter to the Philippians, the most dangerous of all temptations to a spiritual mind—the desire of heavenly rest, a premature yearning for the divine vision. In the patient endurance of all that followed, he acquired that completeness of holiness and wisdom which he doubtless regarded as more than an ample return for continued labour. When the task which had been appointed him was finished, he then again contemplated his departure ; but not, as before, with the mere thought of rest—not as simply with the hope of finding in heaven a refuge from the world. He had now accomplished his course. Profound peace reigned in his heart. His conversation was in heaven : his life hid with Christ in God : his very being complete in Him. Thus perfected, thus enjoying a blessed communion with the Spirit of peace and holiness, his state was characterised rather by an intense tranquillity, than by any of the stirring, agitating emotions of desire. It is deeply interesting, therefore, to observe that his language is not now expressive of a wish to depart, but merely describes his preparedness,—the fit and expectant state of his soul for its great transit from the altar of sacrifice to its mansion in heaven.

A noble and encouraging lesson is taught by the apostle's experience. From the beginning of his labours he enjoyed the assurance, that God had called him to holiness and salvation. He knew that the blessed Spirit was abiding in him, and that he had been ordained to a work which, faithfully performed, would crown him with honour. But though he knew all this, he could not tell whether his course was to be long or short. All that was necessary to support his faith and hope, that he had ; but to let him see when and where his toils were to end, would have interfered with the discipline of his will, and have tempted him to indulge in an impatient looking forward to the future, disjoining it from present duties.

But though left without any direct intimation as to the time of his departure, he became possessed of an inward light which gradually, and in due time, dissipated the darkness which lay on the path before him. By this light he could see opportunities of usefulness still increasing as he advanced, and he knew then that the end was not yet. He could even by the same light discover that his own nature still needed some further working of grace to perfect it in all holiness. Again he had a proof that he was not yet to depart. Weeping friends, weak brethren, churches agitated with rising heresies and schisms, he knew that there would ever be; but he also saw that by his abiding with them for a time, he might lessen both the sorrow and the danger. Here still further was an argument, equivalent to a prophecy, that extended labours were appointed him. He understood all this; and hence that calm and beautiful expression of feeling to his friends—"I know that I shall abide, and continue with you."

Years passed away: more work was done, more abundant grace bestowed; but no trace exists of any special revelation communicating to the apostle the time fixed for his departure. He was left as before to reason by the light given him for general guidance. It was sufficient. His work had been measured out to him by divine wisdom: he had wrought according to its directions. One act only remained for him to perform; and then the work would be ended. He could not doubt that his departure was at hand.

Following the example of the apostle, a humble, thoughtful Christian, however much below him in sublime piety, may form some important conclusions respecting his own duty and condition. If called of God, he may be sure that he has work to do for God. Should he prove a willing servant, but though readily working, grow weary with his toil, and wish for rest, let him remember the case of St. Paul. Seeing that he had more work to do, he cheerfully went on. After a few seasons of further labour and suffering, the light within him grew stronger, and he had an assurance of coming glory. It is not rest merely which awaits the servant of God, working his full time; but the riches of the kingdom of heaven.

H. S.

PAUL'S DEPARTURE AND CROWN;

OR,

AN EXPOSITION UPON 2 TIM. IV. 6—8.

"For I am now ready to be offered, and the time of my departure is at hand. I have fought a good fight, I have finished my course, I have kept the faith: henceforth there is laid up for me a crown of righteousness, which the Lord, the righteous Judge, shall give me at that day: and not to me only, but unto all them also that love his appearing."— 2 Tim. iv. 6—8.

THESE words were, by the Apostle Paul, written to Timothy, whom he had begot to the faith by the preaching of the gospel of Christ; in which are many things of great concernment both for instruction and consolation, something of which I shall open unto you for your profit and edification. But before I come to the words themselves, as they are a relation of Paul's case, I shall take notice of something from them as they depend upon the words going before, being a vehement exhortation to Timothy to be constant and faithful in his work; which in brief may be summed up in these particulars:—1st. A solemn binding charge before God and Jesus Christ our Lord, that he be constant in preaching the word, whether in or out of season, reproving, rebuking, and exhorting with all long-suffering and doctrine; and that because of that ungodly spirit that would possess professors after he was dead: for the time will come, saith he, that they will not endure sound doctrine, neither sound reproof, nor sound trial of their state and condition by the word, but after their own lusts shall they heap to themselves teachers, having itching ears, (the plague that once God threatened to rebellious Israel,) and be turned unto fables. Much like this is that in the Acts of the Apostles: "For I know this, that after my departure shall grievous wolves enter in among you, not sparing the flock. Also of your own selves shall men arise, speaking perverse things to draw away disciples after them. Therefore watch, and remember that by the space of three years I ceased not to warn every one night and day with tears."

This evil, then, is to be prevented; 1. By a diligent watchfulness in ministers; 2. By a diligent preaching the word of the Lord; and, 3. By sound and close rebukes, reproofs, and exhortations to those in whosoever the least there appears any swerving or turning aside from the gospel. The ministers of the gospel have each of them all that authority that belongs to their calling and office, and need not to stay for power from men to put the laws of Christ in his church into due and full execution. This remnant of Jacob should be in the midst of many people as a dew from the Lord, that tarrieth not for man, nor waiteth for the sons of men. (Mic. v. 7.) Therefore, he adds, "Watch thou in all things, endure afflictions, (if thou shouldst be opposed in thy work,) do the work of an evangelist, make full proof of thy ministry." (2 Tim. iv. 5.) How our time-serving and self-saving ministers will salve their conscience from the stroke that God's word will one day give them, and how they will stand before the judgment-seat to render an account of this their doings, let them see to it; surely God will require it of their hand.

But, O Timothy, do thou be diligent, do thou watch in all things, do thou endure affliction, do thou the work of an evangelist, make thou full proof of thy ministry; "for I am now ready to be offered," &c. The words, then, of my text are a reason of this exhortation, of this exhortation to Timothy, that he should continue watchful, and abide faithful in his calling. "For I am now ready to be offered;" that is, to be put to death for the gospel.

Hence, then, learn two things—

First. That the murders and outrage that our brethren suffer at the hands of wicked men should not discourage those that live, from a full and faithful performance of their duty to God and man, whatever may be the consequence thereof. Or thus; when we see our brethren before us fall to the earth by death through the violence of the enemies of God for their holy and Christian profession, we should covet to make good their ground against them, though our turn should be next: we should valiantly do in this matter as is the custom of soldiers in war—take great care that the ground be maintained, and the front kept full and complete. "Thou, therefore," saith Paul, "endure hardness as a good soldier of Jesus Christ." (2 Tim. ii. 3.) And in another place: "We should not be moved by these afflictions," (2 Thess. iii. 3,) but endure by resisting, even unto blood. Wherefore Paul saith again, "Be not thou, therefore, ashamed of the testimony of our Lord, nor of me, his prisoner; but be thou partaker of the affliction of the gospel, according to the power of God." (1 Tim. i. 8.) Thus let the spirit of Moses rest upon Joshua, and the spirit of Elijah rest upon Elisha. (2 Kings ii. 15.) Stand up, therefore, like valiant worthies, as the ministers of my God, and fly not every man to his own, while the cause and ways and brethren of our Lord are buffeted and condemned by the world. And remember that those that keep the charge of the Lord when most go a whoring from under their God, they, when he turns the captivity of his people, shall be counted worthy to come nigh unto him, "to offer the fat and the blood, saith the Lord God." (Ezek. xliv. 15.) But for the rest, though they may yet stand before the people, because they stood before them in a way of idolatry, yet it shall not be to their honour, not to their comfort; but to their shame, as the same scripture saith.

1. Let this, therefore, smite with conviction those that in this day of Jacob's trouble have been false with God, his cause, and people; I say, those first, and especially as the chief ringleaders of this cowardliness, who have done it against light, profession, and resolutions. Behold, thou hast sinned against the Lord, and be sure thy sins will find thee out; and though thou mayest now have, as a judgment of God upon thee, thy right eye darkened that thou mayest not see, (Rom. xi. 10,) yet awakening time will overtake thee, and that, too, between the straits, when he will show thee, to the great confusion of thy face, and the amazement of them that behold thee, how great an affront he counts it to be left by thee, in a day when his truth is cast down to the ground. I have often thought of that prophet that went down from Judah to Bethel, to prophesy against the idolatry that was there set up by the king; who, because he kept not the commandment of God, but did eat and drink in that place, at the persuasion of a lying prophet, was met at last by a lion, who slew him there in the way, where his carcase was made a spectacle of God to passengers. (1 Kings xiii.) If thou be spiritual, judge what I say; and think not to be one of that number that shall have the harps of God, when God appears for Zion, and that shall sing that song of Moses, and also the song of the Lamb, for that is only for those who have fought the godly fight, and gotten the victory over the beast, his image, mark, number, and name.

2. Let this also be an awe to thee, who hast hankerings to do as the other. Beware, and remember Judas, and the end God brought upon him; he will not always bear such things; these times have showed us already that he beholds them with great dislike; why shouldst thou hang up in chains as a fetter to all that know thee? And never object that some have done it, and yet are at peace in their souls; for peace in a sinful course is one of the greatest of curses. And "the man that wandereth out of the way of understanding shall remain in the congregation of the dead." (Prov. xxi. 16.)

The second thing to be learned from these words, as they have relation to them going before, is, encouragement to those that are yet in the storm; and that from three great arguments.

1. Paul's peace and comfort now at the time of his death, which he signifieth to Timothy by these three expressions, "I have fought a good fight; I have finished my course; I have kept the faith." (2 Tim. iv. 7.)

2. By the blessed reward he should have for his labour from Christ in another world, together "with all those that love the appearing of the Lord, at that great and notable day."

3. That now his last act should not be inferior to any act he did for God, while he was alive, and preached in the world; for his body should now be an offering, a sacrifice well pleasing to God. To all which I shall speak something in my discourse upon these words. And therefore to come to them:—

"I am now ready to be offered." (2 Tim. iv. 6.)

In these words we have to inquire into two things—

1. What it is to be "offered?" 2. What it is to be "ready to be offered?" "I am now ready to be offered."

I. For the first of these, Paul, by saying, "he was to be offered," alludeth to some of the sacrifices that of old were under the law, and thereby signifieth to Timothy, that his death and martyrdom for the gospel should be both sweet in the nostrils of God, and of great profit to his church in this world; for so were the sacrifices of old. Paul, therefore, lifts his eyes up higher than simply to look upon death, as it is the common fate of men; and he had good reason to do it, for his death was violent: it was also for Christ, and for his church and truth; and it is usual with Paul thus to set out the suffering of the saints, which they undergo for the name and testimony of Jesus. Yea, he will have our prayers a sacrifice; our praises, thanksgiving, and mortification, sacrifices; (Heb. xiii. 15, 16;) almsdeed, and "the offering up of the Gentiles, sacrifices, being sanctified by the Holy Ghost;" (Rom. xv. 16;) and here his death also must be for a sacrifice, and an acceptable offering to God.

Peter also saith, We are priests "to offer up spiritual sacrifices acceptable to God by Jesus Christ;" (1 Pet. ii. 5;) of which sacrifices, it seems by Paul, the death of a Christian for Jesus' sake must needs be counted one.

Besides, Paul further insinuates this by some other sentences in his epistles. As by that in the epistle to the Colossians, where he saith, " I now rejoice in my sufferings for you, and fill up that which is behind of the affliction of Christ in my flesh for his body's sake, which is the church." (Col. i. 24.) Not by way of merit, for so Christ alone, and that by once being offered himself, " hath perfected for ever them that are sanctified." (Heb. x. 14.) But his meaning is, that as Christ was offered in sacrifice for his church as a Saviour, so Paul would offer himself as a sacrifice for Christ's church, as a saint, as a minister, and one that was counted faithful. " Yea," saith he, " and if I be offered upon the sacrifice and service of your faith, I joy and rejoice with you all." (Phil. ii. 17.) This, then, teacheth us several things worthy our consideration.

First. That the blood of the saints that they lose for his name, is a sweet savour to God. And so saith the Holy Ghost, " Precious in the sight of the Lord is the death of his saints." (Ps. cxvi. 15.) And again, " He shall redeem their soul from deceit and violence, and precious shall their blood be in his sight." (Ps. lxxii. 14.)

Second. Those that suffer for Christ are of great benefit to his church—as the sacrifices of old were confirming and strengthening to Israel—wherefore Paul saith, His bonds encouraged his brethren, and made them much more bold in the way of God to speak his word without fear. (Phil. i. 14.)

Third. The sufferings or offering of the saints in sacrifice, it is of great use and advantage to the gospel; of use, I say, many ways. 1. The blood of the saints defends it; 2. confirmeth it; and 3. redeemeth that thereof that hath been lost in antichristian darkness.

1. They do thereby defend and preserve it from those that would take it from us, or from those that would impose another upon us. " I am set," saith Paul, " for the defence of the gospel," and my sufferings have fallen out for the furtherance of it. (Phil. i. 17.) That is, it hath not only continued to hold its ground, but hath also got more by my contentions, sufferings, and hazards for it.

2. It confirms it; and this is part of the meaning of Paul in those large relations of his sufferings for Christ, saying, "Are they ministers of Christ? I speak as a fool, I am more, in prisons more frequent," &c. As he saith again, and these things " I do for the gospel's sake." And again, that the truth of the " gospel might be continued with you." So again, " I suffer," saith he, in the gospel, " as an evil-doer, even unto bonds, but the word of God is not bound; yea," saith he, " therefore I endure all things for the elect's sake." (2 Tim. ii. 9, 10.) That is, that the gospel may be preserved entire, that the souls that

are yet unborn may have the benefit of it, with eternal glory.

3. The sufferings of the saints are of a redeeming virtue; for, by their patient enduring and losing their blood for the word, they recover the truths of God that have been buried in antichristian rubbish, from that soil and slur that thereby hath for a long time cleaved unto them; wherefore it is said, " they overcame him" (the beast) " by the blood of the Lamb, and by the word of their testimony; and they loved not their lives unto the death." (Rev. xii. 11.) " They overcame him," that is, they recovered the truth from under his aspersion, and delivered it from all its enemies. David saith, "The words of the Lord are as silver tried in a furnace of earth, purified seven times." (Ps. xii. 6.) What is this furnace of earth but the body of the saints of God, in which the word is tried, as by fire, in persecution, yea, " purified seven times;" that is, brought forth at last by the death of the Christians, in its purity before the world? How hath the headship and lordship of Christ, with many other doctrines of God, been taken away from the pope by the sufferings of our brethren before us? While their flesh did fry in the flames the Word of God was cleansed, and by such means purified in these their earthen furnaces, and so delivered to us. The lamps of Gideon were then discovered when his soldiers' pitchers were broken; if our pitchers were broken for the Lord and his gospel's sake, those lamps will then be discovered that before lay hid and unseen. (Judges vii. 15—23.) Much use might be made of this good doctrine. Learn thus much :—

1. The judgment that is made of our sufferings by carnal men, is nothing at all to be heeded; they see not the glory that is wrapped up in our cause, nor the innocence and goodness of our conscience in our enduring of these afflictions; they judge according to the flesh, according to outward appearance. For so, indeed, we seem to lie under contempt, and to be in a disgraceful condition; but all things here are converted to another use and end. That which is contemptible when persons are guilty, is honourable when persons are clear; and that which brings shame when persons are buffeted for their faults, is thankworthy in those that endure grief, suffering wrongfully; though to suffer for sin be the token of God's displeasure, yet to those that suffer for righteousness, it is a token of greatest favour; wherefore matter not how the world doth esteem of thee and thy present distress that thou bearest with patience for God and his word; but believe, that those things that are both shame and dishonour to others, are glory and honour to thee. O for a man to be able to say, " For the hope of Israel I am bound with this chain." (Acts xxviii. 20.) It makes his face to shine like the face of an angel, and his lips to drop like the honeycomb. (Sol. Song iv. 11.)

2. We learn also from hence, the reason why some in days before us have made light of the rage of the world; but they have laughed at destruction when it cometh, (Job v. 21, 22;) and have gone forth to meet the armed men; and with Job's war-horse, mocketh at fear and is not affrighted; neither turneth he back from the sword. The quiver rattleth against him, the glittering spear and the shield, (Job xxxix. 22, 23,) but they have said among the trumpets, ha, ha, (ver. 25,) it hath been their glory to suffer for Christ. As it is said of the saints of old, " they departed from the presence of the council, rejoicing that they were counted worthy to suffer shame for his name." (Acts v. 41.) As Paul also saith, " Most gladly, therefore, will I," mark, "most gladly, rather glory in mine infirmities, that the power of Christ may rest upon me. Therefore I take pleasure in infirmities, in reproaches, in necessities, in persecutions, in distresses for Christ's sake," &c. (2 Cor. xii. 9, 10.) Let those that suffer for theft and murder hang down their heads like a bulrush, and carry it like those that are going to hanging; but let those whose trials are for the word of God, know, by these very things they are dignified.

3. Learn also in this to be confident, that thy sufferings have their sound, and a voice before God and men. First, Before God to provoke him to vengeance, " when he maketh inquisition for blood." (Ps. ix. 12. Gen. iv. 9—11.) The blood of Abel cried until it brought down wrath upon Cain; and so did the blood of Christ and his apostles, till it had laid Jerusalem upon heaps. Second. Thy blood will also have a voice before men, and that possibly for their good. The faithful Christian, in his patient suffering, knows not what work he may do for God; who knows but thy blood may be so remembered by thy children, neighbours, and enemies as to convince them thou wert for the truth? Yea, who knows, but their thoughts of thy resolution for Christ, in thy resisting unto blood, may have so good an effect upon some, as to persuade them to close with his ways? The three children in the fiery furnace made Nebuchadnezzar cry out there was no God like theirs. Indeed, this is hard labour; but be content, the dearer thou payest for it to win the souls of others, the greater will be thy crown when the Lord the righteous judge shall appear; and in the meanwhile thy death shall be as a sacrifice pleasing to God and his saints.

" I am now ready to be offered."

II. The second thing that I would inquire into is this: What it is to be " ready" to be offered? Or how we should understand this word " ready," " I am now ready to be offered." Which I think may be understood three manner of ways.

1. With respect to that readiness that was continually in the heart of those that hated him, to destroy him with his doctrine. 2. Or it may be understood with respect to the readiness of this blessed apostle's mind, his being ready and willing always to embrace the cross for the word's sake: or, 3. We may very well understand it, that he had done his work for God in this world, and therefore was ready to be gone.

I. For the first of these. The enemies of God and his truth they never want will and malice to oppose the word of God; they are also always so far forth in readiness to murder and slaughter the saints, as the prophet cries to Jerusalem, " behold the princes of Israel, every one were in thee to their power to shed blood," (Ezek. xxii. 6,) that is, they had will and malice always at hand to oppose the upright in heart. And therefore our Lord Jesus saith, " they are they that kill the body;" he doth not say they can do it as relating to their power, but that they do it, as relating to their will, and their custom, if let loose: and we may understand thereby that it is no more to them to kill the people of God, than it is to butchers to kill sheep and oxen. For though it be indeed a truth, that God's hand is always safe upon the hilt of their sword, yet by them, " we are killed all the day long, and accounted as sheep for the slaughter." (Ps. xliv. 22. Rom. viii. 26.) That is, in their desires always, as well as by their deeds when they are let loose, as Paul's kinsman said to the captain, " There lie in wait for him of them more than forty men that have bound themselves with an oath, (in a curse,) that they will neither eat nor drink until they have killed him. And now are they ready, looking for a promise from thee." (Acts xxiii. 12, 13, 21.) And hence it is that by the word they are called dragons, lions, bears, wolves, leopards, dogs, and the like: all which are beasts of prey, and delight to live by the death of others. Paul, therefore, seeing and knowing that this readiness was in his enemies, to pour out his bowels to the earth, he cried out to Timothy, saying, " Make thou full proof of thy ministry, for I am now ready to be slain; I am now ready to be offered." (2 Tim. iv. 5, 6.)

These words, thus understood, may be useful many ways.

1. To show us, we live, not because of any good nature or inclination, that is in our enemies towards us; for they, as to their wills, are ready to destroy us; but they are in the hand of God, in whose hand is also our times. (Ps. xxxi. 15.) Wherefore, though by the will of our enemies, we are always delivered to death, yet " behold, we live." (2 Cor. vi. 9.) Therefore in this sense it may be said, " Where is the fury of the oppressor?" It is not in his power to dispose of, therefore here it may be said again, " He is not ready to destroy." (Isa. li. 13.) The cup that God's people in all ages have drank of, even the cup of affliction and persecution, it is not in the hand of the enemy, but in the hand of God; and he, not they, " poureth out of the same." (Ps. lxxv. 8.)

So that they, with all their raging waves, have banks and bounds set to them, by which they are limited within their range, as the bear is by his chain. "Surely the wrath of men shall praise thee : the remainder of wrath shalt thou restrain." (Ps. lxxvi. 10.)

2. This should encourage us, not to forsake the way of our Lord Jesus, when threatened by our adversaries; because they are in his chain. Indeed they are ready in their wills to destroy us, but as to power and liberty to do it, that is not at all with them. Who would fear to go, even by the very nose of a lion, if his chain would not suffer him to hurt us? It is too much below the spirit of a Christian to fear "a man that shall die;" (Isa. li. 12;) and they that have so done have forgotten the Lord their Maker, who preserveth the hairs of our head. (Luke xii. 7.) Yea, let me tell you, he that so doth, he feareth to trust the Lord with his life, estate, and concernments, and chooseth rather to trust to himself, and that too out of God's way; and though such persons may lick themselves whole now, while they are fallen and senseless, they must count for these things again, and then they shall see that fear of men, and to be ashamed of Christ, will load them with no light burden. Also, it is an uncomely thing for any man in his profession to be in and out with the times; and to do this when winked at by men, that they would not do if they frowned. Do such fear God? Nay, they fear the fear of men, when they should sanctify the Lord himself, and let him be their dread, and let him be their fear. (Isa. viii. 13.)

3. Let the readiness that is in the enemies of God to destroy, provoke thee to make ready also, as I said a little before : go out to meet the armed men. David ran to meet Goliath ; (1 Sam. xvii. 48;) rub up man, put on thy harness, "put on the whole armour of God," (Eph. vi. 11,) that thou mayest be ready, as well as thy adversaries, as blessed Paul was here, "I am now ready to be offered, and the time of my departure is at hand." But because this will fall in fittest under the second head, I shall therefore discourse of it there.

II. The second thing considered in the words is this, that to be "ready," might be understood with respect to the blessed apostle's mind, that was graciously brought over into a willingness to embrace the cross for the word's sake, and thus in other places he himself expounds it. "I am ready," saith he, "not to be bound only, but, also to die at Jerusalem for the name of the Lord Jesus." (Acts xxi. 13.) That also implies as much, where he saith, "Neither count I my life dear unto myself, so that I might finish my course with joy, and the ministry, which I have received of the Lord Jesus, to testify the gospel of the grace of God." (Acts xx. 24.) As the enemies, then, were ready and willing in their hearts, so he was ready and willing in his. This man was like

to those mighty men of Solomon, that were ready prepared for the war, and waited on the king, fit to be sent at any time upon the most sharp and pinching service. A thing fitly becoming all the saints, but chiefly those that minister in the word and doctrine.

Understand the words thus, and they also teach us many things both for conviction and for edification.

1. Here we see that a Christian's heart should be unclenched from this world; for he that is ready to be made a sacrifice for Christ and his blessed word, he must be one that is not entangled with the affairs of this life ; how else can he please him who hath chosen him to be a soldier? Thus was it with this blessed man ; he was brought to God's foot with Abraham, and crucified to this world with Christ; he had passed a sentence of death upon all earthly pleasures and profits beforehand, that they might not deaden his spirit when he came to suffer for his profession.

2. This shows us the true effects of unfeigned faith and love, for they were the rise of this most blessed frame of heart; read 2 Cor. iv. 8—14, and compare it with xii. 9, 10. And men may talk what they will of their faith and love to the Lord Jesus, and to his holy gospel, but if they throw up their open professing of his name for fear of those that hate him, it is evident their mouths go before their hearts, and that their words are bigger than their graces. If thou faint in the day of adversity, thy strength is small, (Prov. xxiv. 10 ;) and so thy faith and love. Herein is love, "that a man lay down his life for his friends." (John xv. 13.)

3. This shows us the true effects of a right sight and sense of the sufferings that attend the gospel, that they shall become truly profitable to those that shall bear them aright. What made he ready for? it was for sufferings: and why made he ready for them, but because he saw they wrought out for him "a far more exceeding and eternal weight of glory?" (2 Cor. iv. 17.) This made Moses also spurn at a crown and a kingdom ; to look with a disdainful eye upon all the glory of Egypt. He saw the reward that was laid up in heaven for those that suffered for Christ. Therefore, "he refused to be called the son of Pharaoh's daughter ; choosing rather to suffer affliction with the people of God, than to enjoy the pleasures of sin for a season ; esteeming the reproach of Christ greater riches than the treasures in Egypt: for he had respect unto the recompence of the reward. By faith he forsook Egypt, not fearing the wrath of the king : for he endured, as seeing him who is invisible." (Heb. xi. 24—27.) Every one cannot thus look upon the afflictions and temptations that attend the gospel; no not every one that professeth it, as appears by their shrinking and shirking at the noise of the trumpet, and alarum to war. They can be content, as cowards in a garrison, to lie still under

some smaller pieces of service, as hearing the word, entering in, to follow with loving in word and in tongue, and the like; but to "go forth therefore unto him without the camp, bearing his reproach," (Heb. xiii. 13,) and to be in jeopardy every hour, for the truth of the glorious gospel, that they dare not do. Nay, instead of making ready with Paul to engage the dragon and his angels, they study how to evade, and shun the cross of Christ; secretly rejoicing if they can but delude their conscience, and make it still and quiet while they do yet unworthily.

4. By this readiness we may discern who are unfeignedly willing to find out that they may do the whole will of God; even those that are already made willing to suffer for his sake, they are still inquiring, " Lord, what wouldst thou have me to do ?" not mattering nor regarding the cross and distress that attends it. "The Holy Ghost witnesseth to me," saith Paul, "that in every city, bonds and afflictions abide me. But none of these things move me, neither count I my life dear unto myself, so that I might finish my course with joy," &c., (Acts xx. 23, 24;) counting that to see and be doing of heavenly things, will countervail all the trouble and sorrow that attends them: this, therefore, sharply rebuketh those that can be glad to be ignorant of the knowledge of some truths, especially of them that are persecuted; still answering those that charge them with walking irregularly, that they do but according to their light. Whereas the hearts that be full of love to the name and glory of Christ, will in quiet return and come; yea, and be glad, if they find the words of God, and will eat them with savour and sweet delight, how bitter soever they are to the belly; because of that testimony they bind us up to maintain before peoples, and nations, and kings. (Rev. x. 10, 11.) " I am now ready to be offered."

III. The third thing to be considered in the words is this, that the apostle by saying, "I am now ready," doth signify that now he had done that work that God had appointed him to do in the world. I am now ready, because I have done my work: this is further manifest by the following words of the text—" I am now ready to be offered, and the time of my departure is at hand;" namely, my time to depart this world. The words also that follow, are much to the purpose, " I have fought a good fight, I have finished my course," &c., much like that of our Lord Jesus, " I have finished the work which thou gavest me to do." (John xvii. 4.) Now then, put all these things together, namely, that I am to be offered a sacrifice, and for this my enemies are ready, my heart is also ready; and because I have done my work, I am therefore every way ready. This is a frame and condition that deserveth, not only to stand in the word of God for Paul's everlasting praise, but to be a provoking argument to all that read or hear

thereof, to follow the same steps. I shall therefore, to help it forward according to grace received, draw one conclusion from the words, and speak a few words to it. The conclusion is this: That it is the duty and wisdom of those that fear God, so to manage their time and work that he hath allotted unto them, that they may not have part of the work to do when they should be departing the world.

This truth I might further urge from the very words of the text, they being written on purpose by Paul to stir up Timothy and all the godly to press hard after this very thing. But to pass that, and to mind you of some other scriptures that press it hard as a duty, and then to proceed to some few examples of the wise and most eminent saints. Which when I have done I shall, 1. Show you reason for it. 2. Give you encouragement to it. 3. Press it with several motives. 4. Make some use and application of the whole, and so conclude.

That this is the duty and wisdom of those that fear God, you may see by Christ's exhortation to watchfulness, and to prepare for his second coming: " Therefore be ye also ready; for in such an hour as you think not, the Son of Man cometh." (Matt. xxiv. 44.) These words, as they are spoken to stir up the godly to be ready, to meet their Lord at his coming, so because the godly must meet him as well in his judgments and providences here, as at his personal appearing at the last day; therefore they should be diligent to be fitting themselves to meet him in all such dispensations. " And because," saith God, " I will do this unto thee, prepare to meet thy God, O Israel." (Amos iv. 12.) Now death is one of the most certain of those dispensations; yea, and such, that it leaveth to those no help at all, or means to perform for ever that, which, shouldst thou want it, that is lacking to thy work. Wherefore Solomon also doth press us to this very work, and that from this consideration, " Whatsoever thy hand findeth to do, do it with thy might; for there is no work, nor device, nor knowledge, nor wisdom in the grave whither thou goest." (Eccles. ix. 10.) Baulk nothing of thy duty, neither defer to do it; for thou art in thy way to thy grave, and there thou canst not finish aught that by neglect thou leavest undone; therefore be diligent while life lasts.

Another scripture is that in Peter's epistle to those that were scattered abroad. " Seeing," saith he, " that you look for such things, be diligent, that you may be found of him in peace," &c. (2 Pet. iii. 14.) He is there discoursing of the coming of Christ to judgment, as Christ also was in the other; and from the certainty and dread of that day he doth press them on to a continual diligence, and is to be understood, as that of Paul to Timothy, a diligent watching in all things, that as he saith again, they may stand complete in all the will of God, not lacking this or that of that work which was given them to do of God and this world. Much might be said for the further proof of this duty; but to give you some examples of the godly men of old, whereby it will appear, that as it is our duty to do it, so it is also our wisdom. And hence,

It said of Enoch, that he "walked with God," (Gen. v. 22;) and of Noah, that he was faithful in his generation, and also "walked with God." (Gen. vi. 9.) That is, they kept touch with him, still keeping up to the work and duty that every day required; not doing their duty by fits and by starts, but in a fervent spirit they served the Lord. So again it is said of Abraham, that his work was to walk before God in a way of faith and self-denial, which he with diligence performed. And therefore the Holy Ghost saith, he "died in a good old age," (Gen. xxv. 8;) thereby insinuating, that he made both ends meet together, the end of his work with the end of his days, and so came to his grave in a full age, "as a shock of corn cometh in his season." (Job v. 26.) Jacob, also, when he blessed his sons, as he lay upon his death-bed before them, doth sweetly comfort himself with this, after all his toil and travel, saying, "I have waited for thy salvation, O Lord;" as if he had said, Lord, I have faithfully walked before thee in the days of my pilgrimage through the help and power of thy grace; and now having nothing to do but to die, I lie waiting for thy coming to gather me up to thyself and my fathers: so, when he "had made an end of commanding his sons:" now his bottom was wound, "he gathered up his feet into the bed, and yielded up the ghost, and was gathered unto his people." (Gen. xlix. 18, 33.) Caleb and Joshua are said to be men of excellent spirits, because they were faithful in this their work. (Numb. xiv. 24.) David was eminent this way, and had done his work before his death-day came. "After he had served his own generation by the will of God, fell on sleep." (Acts xiii. 36.) Which in the Old Testament is signified by three passages. 1. By his losing his heat before his death, thereby showing his work for God was done, he now only waited to die. 2. By that passage, "these be the last words of David," (2 Sam. xxiii. 1,) even the winding up of all the doctrines of that sweet psalmist of Israel. 3. That in the Psalms is very significant, "The prayers of David the son of Jesse are ended." (Ps. lxxii. 20.) In the whole, they all do doubtless speak forth this in the main, that David made great conscience of walking with God, by labouring to drive his work before him, that his work and life might meet together; for that indeed is a good man's wisdom. Job had great conscience also as to this very thing, as witness both God's testimony and his own conscience for him. (Job i. 8.) Elijah had brought his work to that issue that he had but to anoint Hazael to be king of Assyria, Jehu to be king of Israel, and Elisha, prophet in his room, and then to be caught up into heaven. (1 Kings xix. 15, 16.) What shall I say? I might come to Hezekiah, Jehoshaphat, Josias; with old Simeon also,

whose days were lengthened chiefly, not because he was behind with God and his conscience as to his work for God in the world, but to see with his eyes now at last, the Lord's Christ: a sweet forefitting for death! Zacharias, with Elisabeth his wife, that good old couple also, how tender and doubtful were they in this matter, to walk "in all the commandments and ordinances of the Lord," (Luke i. 6,) in a blessed, blameless way! Their son also is not to be left out, who, rather than he would be put out of his way, and hindered from fulfilling his course, would venture the loss of the love of a king, and the loss of his head for a word. (Mark vi. 16—19.) All these, with many more, are as so many mighty arguments for the praise of that I asserted before, to wit, that it is the duty and wisdom of those that fear God, so to manage their time and work that he hath here allotted unto them, that they may not have part of their work to do when they should be departing this world. I might urge also many reasons to enforce this truth upon you, as,

1. Otherwise the great and chief design of God in sending us into the world, especially in converting us, and possessing our souls with gifts and graces, and many other benefits, that we might here be to the glory of his grace, is as much as in us lies, frustrate and disappointed. "This people have I formed for myself," saith he, "they shall show forth my praise." (Isa. xliii. 21.) And so again, "ye have not chosen me, but I have chosen you, and ordained you, that ye should go and bring forth fruit, and that your fruit should remain." (John xv. 16.) God never intended, when he covered thy nakedness with the righteousness of his dear son, and delivered thee from the condemning power of sin and the law, that thou shouldst still live as do those who know not God. "This I say therefore," saith Paul, "and testify in the Lord; that ye henceforth walk not as other Gentiles walk, in the vanity of their mind." (Eph. iv. 17.) What, a Christian, and live as does the world? a Christian, and spend thy time, thy strength, and parts, for things that perish in the using? Remember, man, if the grace of God hath taken hold of thy soul, thou art a man of another world, and indeed, a subject of another and more noble kingdom, the kingdom of God, which is the kingdom of the gospel, of grace, of faith and righteousness, and the kingdom of heaven hereafter. In these things thou shouldst exercise thyself: not making heavenly things, which God hath bestowed upon thee, to stoop to things that are of the world; but rather here beat down thy body, to mortify thy members; hoist up thy mind to the things that are above, and practically hold forth before all the world that blessed word of life. This, I say, is God's design; this is the tendency, the natural tendency of every grace of God bestowed upon thee; and herein is our Father glorified, that we bring forth much fruit. (John xv. 8.)

2. A second reason why Christians should so manage their time and the work that God hath appointed them to do for his name in this world, that they may not have part thereof to do when they should be departing this world, it is because, if they do not, dying will be a hard work with them, especially if God awakeneth them about their neglect of their duty. The way of God with his people is to visit their sins in this life; and the worst time for thee to be visited for them, is when thy life is smitten down, as it were, to the dust of death, even when all natural infirmities break in like a flood upon thee; sickness, fainting, pains, wearisomeness, and the like; now I say, to be charged also with the neglect of duty, when in no capacity to do it; yea, when perhaps so feeble, as scarce able to abide to hear thy dearest friend in this life speak to thee; will not this make dying hard? Yea, when thou shalt seem both in thine own eyes, as also in the eyes of others, to fall short of the kingdom of heaven for this and the other transgression; will not this make dying hard? David found it hard, when he cried, "O spare me" a little, "that I may recover strength, before I go hence, and be no more." (Ps. xxxix. 13.) David at this time was chastened for some iniquity; yea, brought for his folly to the doors of the shadow of death. But here he could not enter without great distress of mind; wherefore he cries out for respite, and time to do the will of God, and the work allotted to him. So again, "The sorrows of death compassed me, and the pains of hell gat hold of me: I found trouble and sorrow. Then called I upon the name of the Lord." (Ps. cxvi. 3—5.) Ay, this will make thee cry, though thou be as good as David. Wherefore learn by his sorrow, as he himself also learned, at last to serve his own generation by the will of God, before he fell asleep. God can tell how to pardon thy sins, and yet make them such a bitter thing, and so heavy a burden to thee, that thou wouldst not, if thou wast but once distressed with it, come there again for all this world. Ah! it is easy with him to have this pardon in his bosom, when yet he is breaking all thy bones, and pouring out thy gall upon the ground; yea, to show himself then unto thee in so dreadful a majesty, that heaven and earth shall seem to thee to tremble at his presence. Let then the thoughts of this prevail with thee, as a reason of great weight to provoke thee to study, to manage thy time and work in wisdom while thou art well.

3. Another reason why those that fear God should so manage their time and work for God in this world, that they may not have part to do, when they should be departing this life, it is, because loitering in thy work, doth, as much as in it lieth, defer and hold back the second coming of our Lord and Saviour Jesus Christ. One thing, amongst many, that letteth the appearing of Christ in the clouds of heaven, is, that his body, with the several members thereof, are not yet complete and full; they are not all yet come to the knowledge of the Son of God; "to the measure of the stature of the fulness of Christ." (Eph. iv. 13.) That is, to the complete making up of his body; for, as Peter saith, "The Lord is not slack concerning his promise, as some men count slackness; but is long-suffering to us-ward, not willing that any should perish, but that all should come to repentance." (2 Pet. iii. 9.) And so also to the complete performance of all their duty and work they have for God in this world. And I say, the faster the work of conversion, repentance, faith, self-denial, and the rest of the Christian duties, are performed by the saints in their day, the more they make way for the coming of the Lord from heaven. Wherefore Peter saith again, "Seeing then that" we look for such things, "what manner of persons ought we to be in all holy conversation and godliness, looking for, and hasting unto," or as it is in the margin, "hasting unto the coming of the day of God, wherein the heavens being on fire shall be dissolved, and the elements shall melt with fervent heat?" (2 Pet. iii.; xi. 12.) When the bride hath made herself ready, "the marriage of the Lamb is come." (Rev. xix. 7.) That is, the Lord will then wait upon the world no longer, when his saints are fit to receive him. As he said to Lot when he came to burn down Sodom, "Haste thee" to Zoar, "for I cannot do anything till thou be come thither." (Gen. xix. 20—22.) So concerning the great day of judgment to the world, which shall be also the day of blessedness and rest to the people of God, it cannot come until the Lamb's wife hath made herself ready; until all the saints that belong to glory are ready. And before I go further, what might I yet say to fasten this reason upon the truly gracious soul? What! wilt thou yet loiter in the work of thy day? wilt thou still be unwilling to hasten righteousness? dost thou not know that thou by so doing deferrest the coming of thy dearest Lord? Besides, that is the day of his glory, the day when he shall come in the glory of his Father and of the holy angels; and wilt not thou by thy diligence help it forwards? Must also the general assembly and church of the first-born wait upon thee for their full portions of glory? Wilt thou by thus doing endeavour to keep them wrapt up still in the dust of the earth, there to dwell with the worm and corruption? The Lord awaken thee, that thou mayest see thy loitering doth do this, and doth also hinder thy own soul of the inheritance prepared for thee.

4. Another reason why saints should press hard after a complete performing their work that God hath allotted unto them, is, because so far forth as they fall short, in that they impair their own glory. For as the Lord hath commanded his people to work for him in this world; so also he of grace hath promised to reward whatever they Christianly do. For whatsoever good thing any man doth, the same shall he receive of the Lord,

whether he be bound or free. Yea, he counts it unrighteousness to forget their work of faith and labour of love, but a righteous thing to recompense them for it in the day of our Lord Jesus. (Heb. vi. 10. 2 Thess. i. 6, 7.) This, well considered, is of great force to prevail with those that are covetous of glory, such as Moses and Paul, with the rest of that spirit. As the apostle saith also to the saints at Corinth, "Be ye steadfast, unmoveable, always abounding in the work of the Lord, forasmuch as ye know that your labour is not in vain in the Lord." (1 Cor. xv. 58.)

Having thus given you the reasons why God's people should be diligent in that work that God hath allotted for them to be doing for him in this world, I shall in the next place give you some directions, as helps to further you in this work. And they are such as tend to take away those hindrances that come upon thee either by discouragement, or by reason of hardness and benumbness of spirit. For great hindrances overtake God's people from both these impediments.

First then, If thou wouldst be faithful to do that work that God hath allotted thee to do in this world for his name, labour to live in the savour and sense of thy freedom and liberty by Jesus Christ. That is, keep this, if possible, ever before thee, that thou art a redeemed one, taken out of this world, and from under the curse of the law, out of the power of the devil, &c., and placed in a kingdom of grace, and forgiveness of sins for Christ's sake. This is of absolute use in this matter; yea, so absolute, that it is impossible for any Christian to do his work Christianly without some enjoyment of it. For this in the 1st of Luke is made the very ground of all good works, both as to their nature and our continuance in them; and is also reckoned there an essential part of that covenant, that God made with our fathers; even "that he would grant unto us, that we being delivered out of the hand of our enemies, might serve him without fear, in holiness and righteousness before him all the days of our life." (Luke i. 74, 75.) And, indeed, take this away, and what ground can there be laid for any man to persevere in good works? None at all. For take away grace and remission of sins for Christ's sake, and you leave men nothing to help them but the terrors of the law and judgment of God, which at best can beget but a servile and slavish spirit in that man in whom it dwells; which spirit is so far off from being a help to us in our pursuit of good works, that it makes us we cannot endure that which is commanded, but, Israel-like, it flieth from God even as from the face of a serpent. As Solomon saith, "A servant will not be corrected by words, for though he understand, he will not answer." (Prov. xxix. 19.) Get thou then thy soul possessed with the spirit of the Son, and believe thou art set perfectly free by him from whatsoever thou by sin hast deserved at the hand of revenging justice. This doctrine unlooseth thy bands, takes off thy yoke, and lets thee go upright. This doctrine puts spiritual and heavenly inclinations into thy soul; and the faith of this truth doth show thee that God hath so surprised thee, and gone beyond thee, with his blessed and everlasting love, that thou canst not but reckon thyself his debtor for ever. "Therefore brethren we are debtors, not to the flesh, to live after the flesh." (Rom. viii. 12.) That argument of Paul to Philemon is here true in the highest degree, thou owest to God for his grace to thee, "even thine own self besides." (Philem. 19.) This Paul further testifies both in the 6th and 7th of the Romans: in the one he saith, we are "free from sin," (Rom. vi. 22;) in the other he saith, we are "dead to the law," that our fruit might be unto holiness; "that we might bring forth fruit unto God." (Rom. vii. 4.) For, as I said, if either thy ungodly lusts, or the power and force of the law, have dominion over thy spirit, thou art not in a condition now to be performing thy work to God in this world. I have heretofore marvelled at the quarrelsome spirit that possessed the people that Malachi speaketh of, how they found fault with, in a manner, all things that were commanded them to do; but I have since observed their ungodly disposition was grounded upon this their doubting of the love of God, "Yet ye say, Wherein hast thou loved us?" (Mal. i. 2.) And, indeed, if people once say to God, by way of doubt, "Wherein hast thou loved us?" no marvel though that people be like those in Malachi's time, a discontented, murmuring, backward people about everything that is good. Read that whole book of Malachi.

Second. If thou wouldst be faithful to do that work that God hath allotted thee to do in this world for his name, then labour to see a beauty and glory in holiness, and in every good work: this tends much to the engaging of thy heart. " O worship the Lord in the beauty of holiness: fear before him all the earth." (Ps. xcvi. 9.) And for thy help in this, think much on this in general, that, "Thus saith the Lord," is the wind-up of every command: for, indeed, much of the glory and beauty of duties doth lie in the glory and excellency of the person that doth command them; and hence it is, that " Be it enacted by the king's most excellent majesty " is in the head of every law, because that law should therefore be reverenced by, and be made glorious and beautiful to all. And we see upon this very account, what power and place the precepts of kings do take in the hearts of their subjects, every one loving and reverencing the statute, because there is the name of their king. Will you rebel against the king? is a word that shakes the world. Well, then, turn these things about for an argument to the matter in hand, and let the name of God, seeing he is wiser and better, and of more glory and beauty than kings, beget in thy heart a beauty in all things that are commanded thee of God. And, indeed, if thou do not in this act thus, thou wilt stumble at some of thy duty and work thou hast to do; for some of the commands of God are in themselves so mean and low, that take away the name of God from them, and thou wilt do as Naaman the Syrian, despise instead of obeying. What is there in the Lord's supper, in baptism, yea, in preaching the word and prayer, were they not the appointments of God? His name being entailed to them, makes them every one glorious and beautiful. Wherefore no marvel if he that looks upon them without their title-page goeth away in a rage, like Naaman, preferring others before them. What is Jordan? " Are not Abana and Pharpar, rivers of Damascus, better than all the waters in Israel? may I not wash in them and be clean?" saith he. (2 Kings v. 10—12.) This was because he remembered not that the name of God was in the command. Israel's trumpets of rams' horns, (Josh. vi. 4,) and Isaiah's walking naked, (Isa. xx. 3,) and Ezekiel's wars against a tile, (Ezek. iv. 1—3,) would doubtless have been ignoble acts, but that the name of God was that which gave them reverence, power, glory, and beauty. Set therefore the name of God, and " Thus saith the Lord," against all reasonings, defamings, and reproaches, that either by the world, or thy own heart, thou findest to arise against thy duty, and let his name and authority alone be a sufficient argument with thee, " to behold the beauty" that he hath put upon all his ways, " and to inquire in his temple." (Ps. xxvii. 4.)

Third. Wouldst thou be faithful to do that work that God hath appointed thee to do in this world for his name? then make much of a trembling heart and conscience; for though the word be the line and rule whereby we must order and govern all our actions, yet a trembling heart and tender conscience is of absolute necessity for our so doing. A hard heart can do nothing with the word of Jesus Christ. " Hear the word of the Lord, ye that tremble at his word." (Isa. lxvi. 5.) " Serve the Lord with fear, and rejoice with trembling." (Ps. ii. 11.) I spake before against a servile and slavish frame of spirit, therefore you must not understand me here as if I meant now to cherish such a one; no, it is a heart that trembleth for, or at the grace of God; and a conscience made tender by the sprinkling of the blood of Christ. Such a conscience as is awakened both by wrath and grace, by the terror and the mercy of God, for it stands with the spirit of a son to fear before his father; yea, to fear chastisings, though not to fear damnation. Let, therefore, destruction from God be a terror to thy heart, (Job xxxi. 23,) though not that destruction that attends them that perish by sin for ever. Though this I might add further; it may do thee no harm, but good, to cast an eye over thy shoulder at those that now lie roaring under the vengeance of eternal fire; it may put thee in mind of what thou wast once, and of what

thou must yet assuredly be, if grace by Christ preventeth not. Keep, then, thy conscience awake with wrath and grace, with heaven and hell; but let grace and heaven bear sway. Paul made much of a tender conscience, else he had never done as he did, nor suffered what we read of. " And herein," saith he, " do I exercise myself, to have always a conscience void of offence toward God, and toward men." (Acts xxiv. 16.) But this could not a stony, benumbed, bribed, deluded, or a muzzled conscience do. Paul was like the nightingale with his breast against the thorn. That his heart might still keep waking, he would accustom himself to the meditation of those things that should beget both love and fear; and would always be very chary lest he offended his conscience. " Herein do I exercise myself," &c.

Be diligent, then, in this matter, if thou wouldst be faithful with God. A tender conscience, to some people, is like Solomon's brawling woman, a burden to those that have it. (Prov. xxiv. 24.) But let it be to thee like those that invited David to go up to the house of the Lord. (Ps. cxxii. 1.) Hear it, and cherish it with pleasure and delight.

Fourth. If thou wouldest be faithful to do that work that God hath appointed thee to do in this world for his name, then let religion be the only business to take up thy thoughts and time. " Whatsoever thy hand findeth to do, do it with all thy might," (Eccles. ix. 10,) with all thy heart, with all thy mind, and with all thy strength. Religion, to most men, is but a by-business, with which they use to fill up spare hours; or as a stalking horse, which is used to catch the game. How few are there in the world that have their conversation " only as becomes the gospel!" (Phil. i. 27.) A heart sound in God's statutes, (Ps. cxix. 80,) a heart united to the fear of God, a heart moulded and fashioned by the word of God, is a rare thing. Rare, because it is hard to be found, and rare, because it is indeed the fruit of an excellent spirit, and a token of one saved by the Lord. But this indifferency in religion, this fashioning ourselves in our language, gesture, behaviour, and carriage to the fancies and fopperies of this world, as it is in itself much unbecoming a people that should bear the name of their God in their foreheads, so it cannot but be a very great and sore obstruction to thy faithful walking with God in this world. Gird up, then, thy loins like a man, let God and his Christ, and his word, and his people, and cause, be the chief in thy soul; and as heretofore thou hast afforded this world the most of thy time, and travel, and study, so now convert all these to the use of religion. " As ye have yielded your members servants to uncleanness, and to iniquity unto iniquity; even so now yield your members servants to righteousness unto holiness." (Rom. vi. 19.) Holy things must be in every heart where this is faithfully put in practice.

1. Daily bring thy heart and the word of God together, that thy heart may be levelled by it, and also filled with it. The want of performing this sincerely is a great cause of that unfaithfulness that is in us to God. Bring, then, thy heart to the word daily, to try how thou believest the word to-day, to try how it agrees with the word to-day. This is the way to make clean work daily, to keep thy soul warm and living daily. "Wherewithal shall a young man cleanse his way?" saith David; "by taking heed thereto according to thy word." (Ps. cxix. 9.) So again, "Concerning the works of men, by the word of thy lips, I have kept me from the paths of the destroyer." (Ps. xvii. 4.) And again, "Thy word have I hid in mine heart, that I might not sin against thee." (Ps. cxix. 11.) He that delighteth "in the law of the Lord, and in his law doth meditate day and night, he shall be like a tree planted by the rivers of water, that bringeth forth his fruit in his season; his leaf also shall not wither, and whatsoever he doeth shall prosper." (Ps. i. 2, 3.)

2. A continual remembrance that to every day thou hast thy work allotted thee; and that sufficient for that day are the evils that attend thee. (Matt. vi. 34.) This remembrance set Paul upon his watch daily; made him die to himself and this world daily, and provoked him also daily to wind up the spirit of his mind; transforming himself by the power of the word, from that proneness that was in his flesh to carnal things. (1 Cor. xv. 31.) This will make thee keep the knife at thy throat in all places and business and company. (Prov. xxiii. 2.)

3. Let thy heart be more affected with what concerns the honour of God, and the profit and glory of the gospel, than with what are thy concernments as a man, with all earthly advantages. This will make thee refuse things that are lawful, if they appear to be inexpedient. Yea, this will make thee, like the apostles of old, prefer another man's peace and edification before thine own profit, and to take more pleasure in the increase of the power of godliness in any, than in the increase of thy corn and wine.

4. Reckon with thy own heart every day before thou lie down to sleep, and cast up both what thou hast received from God, done for him, and where thou hast also been wanting. This will beget praise and humility, and put thee upon redeeming the day that is past; whereby thou wilt be able, through the continual supplies of grace, in some good measure, to drive thy work before thee, and to shorten it as thy life doth shorten, and mayst comfortably live in the hope of bringing both ends sweetly together. But to pass this.

Fifth. If thou wouldst be faithful to do that work that God hath appointed thee to do in this world for his name, then beware thou do not stop and stick when hard work comes before thee.

It is with Christians as it is with other scholars, they sometimes meet with hard lessons, but these thou must also learn, or thou canst not do thy work. The word and Spirit of God come sometimes like chain-shot to us, as if it would cut down all; as when Abraham was to offer up Isaac, (Gen. xxii. 1—19,) and the Levites to slay their brethren. (Exod. xxxii. 25—29.) Paul also must go from place to place to preach, though he knew beforehand he was to be afflicted there. (Acts xx. 23.) God may sometimes say to thee, as he said to his servant Moses, "take the serpent by the tail;" (Exod. iv. 4;) or as the Lord Jesus said to Peter, "walk upon the sea." These are hard things, but have not been rejected when God hath called to do them. O how willingly would our flesh and blood escape the cross for Christ! The comforts of the gospel, the sweetness of the promise, how pleasing is it to us! Like Ephraim here, we love to tread out the corn, (Hos. x. 11,) and to hear those pleasant songs and music that gospel sermons make where only grace is preached, and nothing of our duty as to works of self-denial; but as for such, God will tread upon their fair neck, and yoke them with Christ's yoke; for there they have a work to do, even a work of self-denial.

Now this work sometimes lieth in acts that seem to be desperate, as when a man must both leave and hate his life, and all he hath for Christ, or else he cannot serve him nor be counted his disciple. (Luke xiv. 26—33.)

Thus it seemed with Christ himself when he went his fatal journey up to Jerusalem; he went thither, as he knew, to die, and therefore trod every step, as it were, in his own bowels; but yet no doubt with great temptation to shun and avoid that voyage; and therefore it is said he steadfastly set his face to go up, (Luke ix. 51,) scorning to be invited to the contrary, and to prevent the noise of his weak disciples, Master, save thyself. It is said, He ascended before them, (Mark x. 32—34,) insomuch that they were amazed to see his resolution, while they themselves were afraid of that dreadful effect that might follow. Also when he came there, and was to be apprehended, he went to the garden that Judas knew, his old accustomed place: so when they asked him the killing question, he answered, "I am he." (John xviii. 1—8.)

Sometimes in acts that seem to be foolish, as when men deny themselves of those comforts, and pleasures, and friendships, and honours of the world that formerly they used to have, and choose rather to associate themselves with the very abjects of this world; I mean such as carnal men count so; counting their ways and manners of life, though attended with a thousand calamities, more profitable, and pleasing, and delightful, than all former glory. Thus Elisha left his father's house, though to pour water upon the hands of Elijah. (2 Kings iii. 11.) And thus the disciples left their fathers' ships and nets, to live a beggarly life with

Jesus Christ. As Paul did leave the feet of Gamaliel for the whip, and the stocks, and the deaths, that attended the blessed gospel. One would have thought that had been a simple way of Peter, to leave all for Christ, before he knew what Christ would give him, as that 19th of Matthew (ver. 17) seems to import, but Christ will have it so. "He that loveth his life, shall lose it, and he that hateth his life in this world (for Christ,) shall keep it to life eternal." (John xii. 25.) I might add many things of this nature, to show you what hard chapters sometimes God sets his best people; but thy work is, if thou wouldst be faithful, not to stop nor stick at anything. Some, when they come at the cross, they will either there make a stop and go no further, or else, if they can, step over it, if not, they will go round about: do not thou do this; but take it up, and kiss it, and bear it after Jesus. "God forbid," saith Paul, "that I should glory, save in the cross of our Lord Jesus Christ, by whom the world is crucified unto me, and I unto the world." (Gal. vi. 14.) Now for thy better performing this piece of service for our Lord and Saviour Jesus Christ.

O it is hard work to pocket up the reproaches of all the foolish people; as if we had found great spoil, and to suffer all their revilings, lies, and slanders, without cursing them, as Elisha did the children; to answer them with prayers, and blessings for their cursings. It is far more easy to give them taunt for taunt, and reviling for reviling; to give them blow for blow; yea, to call for fire from heaven against them; but to bless them that curse us, and to pray for them that despitefully use and persecute us, (Matt. v. 44. Rom. xii. 14,) even of malice, of old grudge, and on purpose to vex and afflict our mind, and to make us break out into a rage, this is work above us; now our patience should look up to unseen things; now remember Christ's carriage to them that spilt his blood; or all is in danger of bursting, and thou of miscarrying in these things.

I might here also dilate upon Job's case, and the lesson God set him, when at one stroke he did beat down all, only spared his life, (Job i. 13—19,) but made that also so bitter to him, that his soul chose strangling rather than it. (Job vii. 15.) O when every providence of God unto thee is like the messengers of Job, and the last to bring more heavy tidings than all that went before him; when life, estate, wife, children, body and soul, and all at once, seem to be struck at by heaven and earth; here are hard lessons: now to behave myself even as a weaned child, now to say, "The Lord gave, and the Lord hath taken away; blessed be the name of the Lord." (Job i. 21.) Thus with few words Job ascribeth righteousness to his Maker; but though they were but few, they proceeded from so blessed a frame of heart, that caused the penman of the word to stay himself and wonder, saying, "In all this Job sinned not with his lips, nor charged God foolishly, in all this."

(Job i. 22.) What a great deal will the Holy Ghost make of that, which seems but little when it flows from an upright heart, and it indeed may well be so accounted of all that know what is in man, and what he is prone unto.

1. Labour to believe that all these things are tokens of the love of God. (Heb. xii. 6. Rev. iii. 19.) 2. Remember often that thou art not the first that hath met with these things in the world. "It hated me," saith Christ, "before it hated you." (John xv. 18.) 3. Arm thyself with a patient and quiet mind to bear and suffer for his sake. (1 Pet. iv. 1.) 4. Look back upon thy provocations wherewith thou mayest have provoked God; then wilt thou accept of the punishment for thy sins, and confess it was less than thine iniquities deserve. (Ezra ix. 13.) 5. Pray thou mayest hear the voice of the rod, and have an heart to answer the end of God therein. (Mic. vi. 9.) 6. Remember the promise: "All things shall work together for good to them that love God, to them who are the called according to his purpose." (Rom. viii. 28.)

Sixth. If thou wouldst be faithful to do that work that God hath appointed thee to do in this world for his name, then labour alway to possess thy heart with a right understanding, both of the things that this world yieldeth, and of the things that shall be hereafter. I am confident that most, if not all the miscarriages of the saints and people of God, they have their rise from deceivable thoughts here. The things of this world appear to us more, and those that are to come less, than they are; and hence it is that many are so hot and eager for things that be in the world, and so cold and heartless for those that be in heaven. Satan is here a mighty artist, and can show us all earthly things in a multiplying glass; but when we look up to things above, we see them as through sackcloth of hair: but take thou heed, be not ruled by thy sensual appetite, that can only savour fleshly things, neither be thou ruled by carnal reason, which always darkeneth the things of heaven. But go to the word, and as that says, so judge thou. That tells thee all things under the sun are vanity, nay worse, vexation of spirit; (Eccles. i. 2, 14;) that tells thee the world is not, even then when it doth most appear to be: wilt thou set thine heart upon that which is not? "for riches certainly make themselves wings; they fly away as an eagle toward heaven." (Prov. xxiii. 5.) The same may be said for honours, pleasures, and the like, they are poor, low, base things to be entertained by a Christian's heart. The man that hath most of them may, "in the fulness of his sufficiency be in straits." Yea, "when he is about to fill his belly with them, God may cast the fury of his wrath upon him." (Job xx. 22, 23.) So is every one "that layeth up treasure for himself" on earth, and "is not rich towards God." (Luke xii. 21, 22.) A horse that is laden with gold and pearls all day, may have a foul stable and a galled back at night. And woe be to him that increaseth that which is not his, and that ladeth himself with thick clay. O man of God, throw this bone to the dogs, suck not at it, there is no marrow there. Set your affections on things which are above, where Christ sitteth on the right hand of God. (Col. iii. 1—3.) Behold what God hath prepared for them that love him. And if God hath blessed thee with aught, set not thine heart upon it; honour the Lord with thy substance; labour to be rich in good works, ready to distribute, willing to communicate, laying up in store a good foundation for the time to come, that thou mayest lay hold on eternal life. (1 Tim. vi. 17—19.)

Further, to lighten thine eyes a little; and, first, concerning the glory of the world.

1. It is that which God doth mostly give to those that are not his; for the poor receive the gospel, not many rich, "not many mighty, not many noble, are called." (1 Cor. i. 26.)

2. Much of this world and its glory is permitted of God to be disposed of by the devil, and he is called both the prince and god thereof. (John xiv. 30. 2 Cor. iv. 4.) Yea, when Satan told Christ, he could give it to whom he would, Christ did not say "Thou liest;" but answered, by the word, "It is written, Thou shalt worship the Lord thy God, and him only shalt thou serve." (Luke iv. 8.) Implying also, that commonly when men get much of the honours and glory of this world, it is by bending the knee too low to the prince and god thereof.

3. The nature of the best of worldly things, if hankered after, is to deaden the spirit, to estrange the heart from God, to pierce thee through with many sorrows, and to drown thee in perdition and destruction. "O man of God flee these things; and follow after righteousness, godliness, faith, love, patience, meekness;" and "fight the good fight of faith, lay hold on eternal life, whereunto thou art also called," &c. (1 Tim. vi. 9—12.)

Second. As to the things of God, what shall I say? the things of his word, and Spirit, and kingdom, they so far go beyond the conceivings of the heart of man, that none can utter them but by the Holy Spirit; there is no deceit in them, "no lie is of the truth," (1 John ii. 21,) what they promise they will perform with additions of amazing glory. Taste them first, and then thou shalt see them, "O" come "taste and see that the Lord is good; blessed is the man that trusteth in him." (Ps. xxxiv. 8.)

To stoop low is a good work, which is an act of thine, if it be done in faith and love, though but by a cup of cold water, it is really more worth in itself, and of higher esteem with God, than all worldly and perishing glory; there is no comparison, the one perisheth with the using, and for the other is laid up "a far more exceeding and eternal weight of glory." (2 Cor. iv. 17.)

But again, as thou shouldst labour to possess thy heart with a right understanding of the perishing nature of the riches and pleasures of this world,

and of the durable riches and righteousness that is in Christ, and all heavenly things, so thou shouldst labour to keep always in thy eye, what sin is, what hell is, what the wrath of God and everlasting burnings are. Transfer them to thyself, as it were on a finger, that thou mayst learn to think of nothing more highly than is meet, but to give to what thou beholdest their own due weight; then thou wilt fear, where thou shouldst fear, love what is worth thy love, and slight that which is of no worth. These are just weights and even balances; now thou dealest not with deceitful weights; and this is the way to be rich in good works, and to bring thy work, that God hath appointed, to a good issue, against thy dying day.

Seventh. But again, if thou wouldst be faithful to do that work that God hath appointed thee to do in this world for his name, then beware that thou slip not, or let pass by the present opportunity that providence layeth before thee. Work while it is called to-day, "the night comes when no man can work." (John ix. 4.) In that parable of the man that took "a far journey," it is said; "as he gave to every servant his work, so he commanded the porter to watch," that is, for his lord's coming back; and in the meantime, for all opportunities to perform the work he left in their hand, and committed unto their trust. (Mark xiii. 34, 35.) Seest thou the poor? seest thou the fatherless? seest thou thy foe in distress? draw out thy breast, shut not up thy bowels of compassion, deal thy bread to the hungry, bring the poor that are cast out into thine house, hide not thyself from thine own flesh, take the opportunity that presents itself to thee,—either by the eye, or the hearing of the ear, or by some godly motion that passeth over thy heart. (Isa. lviii. 7. Rom. xii. 9—20.) "Say not" to such messengers, "go and come again, and to-morrow, I will give when thou hast it by thee." (Prov. iii. 28,) Now the opportunity is put into thy hand, delay not to do it, and the Lord be with thee. Good opportunities are God's seasons for the doing of thy work; wherefore watch for them and take them as they come. Paul tells us, "He was in watchings often," (2 Cor. xi. 26, 27;) surely it was that he might take the season that God should give him to do this work for him; as he also saith to Timothy, "Watch thou in all things, do the work," &c. Opportunities as to some things come but once in one's lifetime, as in the case of Esther, and of Nicodemus, and holy Joseph; when Esther begged the life of the Jews, and the other the body of Jesus; which once had they let slip or neglected, they could not have recovered it again for ever. Watch then for the opportunity.

1. Because it is God's season; which without doubt is the best season and time for every purpose. 2. Because Satan watches to spoil, by mis-timing as well as by corrupting, whatever thou shalt do for God. "When I would do good," saith Paul, "evil is present," (Rom. vii. 21;) that

is, either to withdraw me from my purpose, or else to infect my work. 3. This is the way to be profitable unto others. "Thy wickedness may hurt a man, as thou art, and thy righteousness may profit the son of man." (Job xxxv. 8.) 4. This is also the way to be doing good to thyself. "He that watereth shall be watered also himself." (Prov. xi. 25.) "Cast thy bread upon the waters: for thou shalt find it after many days." (Eccles. xi. 1.) As God said to Coniah, "Did not thy father eat and drink, and do judgment and justice, and then it was well with him? He judged the cause of the poor and needy, then it was well with him." (Jer. xxii. 15, 16.)

And I say, That the opportunity may not slip thee, either for want of care or provision.

1. Sit always loose from an overmuch affecting thine own concernments, and believe that thou wast not born for thyself; "a brother is born for adversity." (Prov. xvii. 17.) 2. Get thy heart tenderly affected with the welfare and prosperity of all things that bear the stamp and image of God. 3. Study thy own place and capacity that God hath put thee in, in this world; for suitable to thy place, thy work and opportunities are. 4. Make provision beforehand, that when things present themselves, thou mayst come up to a good performance; "be prepared unto every good work." (2 Tim. ii. 21.) 5. Take heed of carnal reasonings, keep thy heart tender; but set thy face like a flint for God. 6. And look well to the manner of every duty.

Eighth. Wouldst thou be faithful to do that work that God hath appointed thee to do, in this world for his name? believe then, that whatever good thing thou dost for him, if done according to the word, it is not only accepted by him now, but recorded to be remembered for thee against the time to come; yea, laid up for thee as treasure in chests and coffers, to be brought out to be rewarded before both men and angels to thy eternal comfort by Jesus Christ our Lord. "Lay not up," saith Christ, "treasures upon earth, where moth and rust doth corrupt, and where thieves break through and steal: but lay up for yourselves treasures in heaven, where neither moth nor rust doth corrupt, and where thieves do not break through nor steal." (Matt. vi. 19, 20.) The treasure that here our Lord commands we should with diligence lay up in heaven, is found both in Luke, and Paul, and Peter, to be meant by doing good works.

1. Luke renders it thus, "Sell that ye have, and give alms; provide yourselves bags which wax not old, a treasure in the heavens that faileth not, where no thief approacheth, neither moth corrupteth," (Luke xii. 33;) the latter part of the verse expounding the former.

2. Paul saith thus, "Charge them that are rich in this world, that they be not highminded, nor trust in uncertain riches, but in the living God, who giveth us all things richly to enjoy; that they do good, that they be RICH IN GOOD WORKS, ready to distribute, willing to communicate; laying up in store for themselves a good foundation against the time to come, that they may lay hold on eternal life." (1 Tim. vi. 17—19.)

3. Peter also acknowledgeth and asserteth this, where, in his exhortation to elders to do their duty faithfully, and with cheerfulness, he affirms, if they do so, they "shall receive a crown of glory that fadeth not away," (1 Pet. v. 2—4;) which Paul also calleth, a reward for cheerful work, (1 Cor. ix. 17;) and that as an act of justice by the hand of a righteous judge, in the day when the Lord shall come to give reward to his servants the prophets, and to his saints, and to all that fear his name, small and great; for "every man shall receive his own reward, according to his own labour." (1 Cor. iii. 8.)

But before I go any further, I must answer three objections that may be made by those that read this book.

First Objection. The first is this, some godly heart may say, I dare not own that what I do shall ever be regarded, much less rewarded by God in another world, because of the unworthiness of my person, and because of the many infirmities and sinful weaknesses that attend me in every duty.

Answer. This objection is built partly upon a bashful modesty, partly upon ignorance, and partly upon unbelief. My answer to it is as followeth.

1. You must remind and look back to what but now hath been proved, namely, That both Christ and his apostles do all agree in this, that there is a reward for the righteous, and that their good deeds are laid up as treasure for them in heaven, and are certainly to be bestowed upon them in the last day with abundance of eternal glory. 2. Now then, to speak to thy case, and to remove the bottom of thy objection, that the unworthiness of thy person, and thy sinful infirmities, that attend thee in every duty, do make thee think thy works shall not be either regarded or rewarded in another world. But consider first, as to the unworthiness of thy person. (1.) They that are in Christ Jesus are always complete before God, in the righteousness that Christ hath obtained, how infirm, and weak, and wicked soever they appear to themselves. Before God, therefore, in this righteousness thou standest all the day long, and that upon a double account; first, by the act of faith, because thou hast believed in him that thou mightest be justified by the righteousness of Christ; but if this fail, I mean the act of believing, still thou standest justified by God's imputing this righteousness to thee, which imputation standeth purely upon the grace and good pleasure of God to thee, that holds thee still as just before God, though thou wantest at present the comfort thereof. Thus, therefore, thy person stands always accepted; and, indeed, no man's works can at all be regarded, if his person, in the

first place, be not respected. The Lord had respect first to Abel, and after to his offering, (Gen. iv. 4. Heb. xi. 4;) but he can have respect to no man before works done, unless he find them in the righteousness of Christ, for they must be accepted through a righteousness, which because they have none of their own, therefore they have one of God's imputing, even that of his Son, which he wrought for us when he was born of the Virgin, &c. (2.) As to thy sinful infirmities that attend thee in every work, they cannot hinder thee from laying up treasure in heaven, thy heart being upright in the way with God; nor will he be unrighteous at all to forget thy good deeds in the day when Christ shall come from heaven.

(1.) Because by the same reason then he must disown all the good works of all his prophets and apostles, for they have all been attended with weaknesses and sinful infirmities; from the beginning hitherto there is not a man, "not a just man upon earth, that doeth good and sinneth not." (Eccles. vii. 20.) The best of our works are accompanied with sin: "When I would do good," saith Paul, "evil is present with me." (Rom. vii. 21.) This, therefore, must not hinder. And for thy further satisfaction in this, consider, as Christ presents thy person before God, acceptable without thy works, freely and alone by his righteousness, so his office is to take away the iniquity of thy holy things, that they also by him may be accepted of God. (Exod. xxviii. 36—38. 1 Pet. ii. 5.) Wherefore it is further said for the encouragement of the weak and feeble, He shall not break a bruised reed, nor quench the smoking flax, but shall bring forth judgment unto victory. (Isa. xlii. 3. Matt. xii. 20.) The bruised reed, you know, is weak; and by bruises we should understand sinful infirmities. And so also concerning the smoking flax, by smoking you must understand sinful weakness; but none of these shall either hinder the justification of thy person, or the acceptation of thy performance, they being done in faith and love, let thy temptations be never so many, because of Jesus Christ his priestly office now at the right hand of God. By him, therefore, let us offer spiritual sacrifices; for they shall be acceptable to God and our Father.

(2.) Because otherwise God and Christ would prove false to their own word, which is horrible blasphemy once to imagine; who hath promised that when the Son of God shall come to judgment, he shall render to every man according to his works, (Rev. xxii. 12. Matt. v. 12; vi. 1; x. 41, 42;) and doth upon this very account encourage his servants to a patient enduring of the hottest persecutions, "For great is your reward in heaven." (Luke vi. 23, 35.) From this also he bindeth his saints and servants to be sincerely liberal and good and kind to all; first, because otherwise they have no reward of their Father which is in heaven; that is, for what they do not; but if they do it, then though it be

but a cup of cold water given to a prophet or righteous man, they shall receive a prophet's reward, a righteous man's reward; yea, they shall receive it in any wise, they shall in no wise lose their reward. (Matt. x. 42.)

(3.) It must be so; otherwise he should deny a reward to the works and operations of his own good grace he hath freely bestowed upon us; but that he will not do. He is not unfaithful to forget your work of faith and labour of love. (Heb. vi. 10.) And so of all other graces, our work shall not be in vain in the Lord. (1 Cor. xv. 58.) And, as I said before, temptations, weaknesses, and sins, shall not hinder the truly gracious of this their blessed reward. Nay, they shall further it, "if need be, ye are in heaviness through manifold temptations; that the trial of your faith being much more precious than of gold that perisheth, might be found unto praise and honour and glory at the appearing of Jesus Christ." (1 Pet. i. 6, 7.) And the reason is, because the truth and sincerity of God's grace in us doth so much the more discover itself, by how much it is opposed and resisted by weakness and sin. It is recorded to the everlasting renown of three of David's mighties, that they would break through a host of giant-like enemies, to fetch water for their longing king, (1 Chron. xi. 11—20;) for it bespake their valour, their love, and goodwill to him; the same also is true concerning thy graces, and every act of them when assaulted with an host of weaknesses.

Second Obj. And now I come to the second objection, and that ariseth from our being completely justified freely by the grace of God through Christ; and by the same means alone brought to glory; and may be framed thus :—But seeing we are freely justified, and brought to glory by free grace, through the redemption that is in Jesus Christ; and seeing the glory that we shall be possessed of upon the account of the Lord Jesus, is both full and complete, both for happiness and continuing therein, what need will there be that our work should be rewarded? Nay, may not the doctrine of reward for good works be here not only needless, but indeed an impairing and lessening the completeness of that glory, to which we are brought, and in which we shall live inconceivably happy for ever, by free grace?

Ans. That we are justified in the sight of the Divine Majesty from the whole lump of our sins— both past, present, and to come—by free grace, through that one offering of the body of Jesus Christ, once for all, I bless God I believe it; and that we shall be brought to glory by the same grace, through the same most blessed Jesus, I thank God by his grace I believe that also. Again, that the glory to which we shall be brought by free grace, through the only merits of Jesus, is unspeakably glorious and complete, I question no more than I question the blessed truths but now confessed. But yet, notwithstanding all this, there is a reward for the righteous, a reward for their works of faith and love, whether in a doing or a suffering way, and that not principally to be enjoyed here, but hereafter, " great is your reward in heaven," as I proved in the answer to the first objection. And now I shall answer further :

1. If this reward had been an impairing or derogation to the free grace of God that saveth us, he would never have mentioned it for our encouragement unto good works, nor have added a promise of reward for them that do them, nor have counted himself unfaithful if he should not do it.

2. The same may be said concerning Jesus Christ, who doubtless loveth and tendereth the honour of his own merits, as much as any who are saved by him can do, whether they be in heaven or earth ; yet he hath promised a reward to a cup of cold water, or giving of any other alms ; and hath further told us, they that do these things they do lay up treasure in heaven, namely, a reward when their Lord doth come, then to be received by them to their eternal comfort.

3. Paul was as great a maintainer of the doctrine of God's free grace, and of justification from sin, by the righteousness of Christ. imputed by grace, as any he that ever lived in Christ's service, from the world's beginning till now : and yet he was for this doctrine ; he expected himself, and encouraged others also to look for such a reward, for doing and suffering for Christ, which he calls, " A far more exceeding and eternal weight of glory." (2 Cor. iv. 17.) Surely, as Christ saith, in a case not far distant from this in hand, If it were not so, he would have told us. (John xiv. 1—3.) Now could I tell what those rewards are that Christ hath prepared, and will one day bestow upon those that do for him in faith and love in this world, I should therein also say more than now I dare or ought ; yet this let me say in general, they are such as should make us leap to think on, and that we should remember with exceeding joy, and never think that it is contrary to the Christian faith, to rejoice and be glad for that which yet we understand not. " Beloved, now are we the sons of God, and it doth not yet appear what we shall be," &c. But every one " that hath this hope in him," namely, that he shall be more than here he can imagine, " purifieth himself, even as he is pure." (1 John iii. 2, 3.) Things promised when not revealed to be known by us while here, are therefore not made known, because too big and wonderful. When Paul was up in paradise, he heard unspeakable words, not possible for man to utter. (2 Cor. xii. 4.) Wherefore, a reward I find, and that laid up in heaven, but what it is I know not, neither is it possible for any here to know it any further, than by certain general words of God, such as these, " praise, honour, glory," (1 Pet. i. 7,) " a crown of righteousness," (2 Tim. iv. 8.) " a crown of glory," (1 Pet. v. 4,)

thrones, judging of angels, (Matt. xxv. 31,) a kingdom, " with a far more exceeding and eternal weight of glory," &c. (2 Cor. iv. 17.)

Wherefore, to both these objections let me yet answer thus in a few words. Though thy modesty or thy opinion will not suffer thee to look for a reward for what thou dost here for thy Lord, by the faith and love of the gospel ; yea, though in the day of judgment thou shouldst there slight all thou didst on earth for thy Lord, saying, When, Lord, when did we do it ? he will answer, Then, even then when ye did it to the least of these my brethren, ye did it unto me. (Matt. xxv. 37—40.)

Third Obj. But is not the reward that God hath promised to his saints for their good works, to be enjoyed only here ?

Ans. 1. For concerning holy walking, according to God's command, yieldeth even here abundance of blessed fruits, as he saith, " in keeping of them there is great reward," and again, " this man shall be blessed in his deed," that is, now, even in this time, as he saith in another place ; for indeed there is so much goodness and blessedness to be found in a holy and godly life, that were a man to have nothing hereafter, the present comfort and glory that lieth as the juice in the grape, in all things rightly done for God, it were sufficient to answer all our travail and self-denial in our work of faith and labour of love to do the will of God.

2. Dost thou love thy friends, dost thou love thine enemies, dost thou love thy family or relations, or the church of God ? then cry for strength from heaven, and for wisdom, and a heart from heaven to walk wisely before them. For if a man be remiss, negligent, and careless in his conversation, not much mattering whom he offends, displeases, or discourages by doing this or that, so he may save himself, please his foolish heart, and get this world, or the like, this man hath lost a good report of them that are without, and is fallen into reproach and the snare of the devil. He is fallen into reproach, and is slighted, disdained, both he, his profession and all he says, either by way of reproof, rebuke, or exhortation. Physician, cure thyself, say all to such a one ; this man is a sayer, but not a doer, say they ; he believeth not what he says ; yea, religion itself is made to stink by this man's ungodly life. This is he that hardens his children, that stumbleth the world, that grieveth the tender and godly Christian ; but I say, he that walketh uprightly, that tenders the name of God, the credit of the gospel, and the welfare of others, seeking with Paul, not his own profit, but the profit of others, that they may be saved ; this man holds forth the word of life, this man is a good savour of Christ amongst them that are saved ; yea, may prove, by so doing, the instrument in God's hand of the salvation of many souls.

3. This is the way to be clear from the blood of all men, the way not to be charged with the ruin and everlasting misery of poor immortal souls. Great is the danger that attends an ungodly life,

or any ungodly action, by them that profess the gospel. When wicked men learn to be wicked of professors, when professors cause the enemies of God to blaspheme, doubtless sad and woeful effects must needs be the fruit of so doing. How many in Israel were destroyed for that which Aaron, Gideon, and Manasseh, unworthily did in their day? A godly man, if he take not heed to himself, may do that in his life that may send many to everlasting burnings, when he himself is in everlasting bliss. But, on the contrary, let men walk with God, and there they shall be excused; the blood of them that perish shall lie at their own door, and thou shalt be clear. "I am pure from the blood of all men," saith Paul. (Acts xx. 26.) And again, "Your blood be upon your own heads; I am clean." (Acts xviii. 6.) Yea, he that doth thus, shall leave in them that perish an accusing conscience, even begotten by his good conversation, and by that they shall be forced to justify God, his people and way, in the day of their visitation; in the day when they are descending into the pit to the damned.

4. This is the way to maintain always the answer, the echoing answer of a good conscience in thy own soul. Godliness is of great use this way; for the man that hath a good conscience to Godward, hath a continual feast in his own soul; while others say there is casting down, he shall say there is lifting up, for he shall save the humble person. (Job xxii. 29.) Some, indeed, in the midst of their profession, are reproached, smitten, and condemned of their own heart, their conscience still biting and stinging of them, because of the uncleanness of their hands, and they cannot lift up their face unto God; they have not the answer of a good conscience toward him, but must walk as persons false to their God, and as traitors to their own eternal welfare; but the godly upright man shall have the light shine upon his ways, and he shall take his steps in butter and honey. "The work of righteousness shall be peace; and the effect of righteousness, quietness and assurance for ever." (Isa. xxii. 17.) "If our heart condemn us, God is greater than our heart, and knoweth all things. Beloved, if our heart condemn us not, then have we confidence toward God." (1 John xx. 21, 22.)

5. The godly man that walketh with God, that chiefly careth to do the work that God hath allotted him to do for his name in this world, he hath not only these advantages, but further, he hath as it were a privilege of power with God, he can sway much with him; as it is said of Jacob, As a prince he had power with God to prevail in times of difficulty. (Gen. xxxii. 28.) And so again, it is said of Judah, Being faithful with the saints, they ruled with God. (Hos. xi. 12.) How many times did that good man, Moses, turn away the wrath of God from the many thousands of Israel? yea, as it were he held the hands of God, and staved off the judgments not once nor twice;

"The effectual fervent prayer of a righteous man availeth much." (James v. 16.) One man that walketh much with God, may work wonders in this very thing, he may be a means of saving whole countries and kingdoms from those judgments their sins deserve. How many times, when Israel provoked the Lord to anger, did he yet defer to destroy them? and the reason of that forbearance, he tells them, it was for David's sake; for my servant David's sake I will not do it. As the Lord said also concerning Paul, "Lo, God hath given thee all them that sail with thee." (Acts xxvii. 23.) That is, to save their lives from the rage of the sea. Yea, when a judgment is not only threatened, but the decree gone forth for its execution, then godly upright men may sometimes cause the very decree itself to cease without bringing forth; or else may so time the judgment that is decreed, that the church shall best be able to bear it.

6. The man that is tender of God's glory in this world, still ruling and governing his affairs by the word, and desirous to be faithful to the work and employment that God hath appointed him to do for his name, that man shall still be let into the secrets of God; he shall know that which God will reserve and hide from many. "Shall I hide from Abraham the thing that I do?" saith the Lord. "For I know him that he will command his children and his household after him, and they shall keep the way of the Lord," &c. (Gen. xviii. 17, 19.) So again, "The secret of the Lord is with them that fear him; and he will show them his covenant." (Ps. xxv. 14.) "And to him that ordereth his conversation aright, shall I show the salvation of God." (Ps. l. 23.) Such a man shall have things new as well as old. His converse with the Father, and the Son, and the Spirit, shall be turned into a kind of familiarity; he shall be led into the word, and shall still increase in knowledge: when others shall be stinted and look with old faces, being black and dry as a stick, he shall be like a fatted calf, like the tree that is planted by the rivers of water, his flesh shall be fresh as the flesh of a child, and God will renew the face of his soul.

7. If any escape public calamities, usually they are such as are very tender of the name of God, and that make it their business to walk before him. They either escape by being mercifully taken away before it, or by being safely preserved in the midst of the judgment, until the indignation be over-past. Therefore God saith in one place, "the righteous are taken away from the evil to come." (Isa. lvii. 1.) But if not so, as all be not, then they shall have their life for a prey. (Jer. xxxix. 18.) Caleb and Joshua escaped all the plagues that befell to Israel in the wilderness, for they followed God. (Numb. xiv. 24.) Somewhat of this you have also in that scripture, "Seek the Lord, all ye meek of the earth, which hath wrought his judgment; seek righteousness, seek

meekness: it may be, ye shall be hid in the day of the Lord's anger." (Zeph. ii. 3.) According to this is that in Luke, "Watch ye, therefore, and pray always, that ye may be accounted worthy to escape all these things that shall come to pass, and to stand before the Son of man." (Luke xxi. 36.) When a man's ways please the Lord he will make his enemies to be at peace with him. Marvellous is the work of God in the preservation of his saints that are faithful with him when dangers and calamities come; as Joseph, David, Jeremiah, and Paul, with many others, may appear. "He shall deliver thee in six troubles: yea, in seven there shall no evil touch thee. In famine he shall redeem thee from death: and in war from the power of the sword. Thou shalt be hid from the scourge of the tongue: neither shalt thou be afraid of destruction when it cometh." (Job v. 19—21.)

8. If afflictions do overtake thee: for whom the Lord loveth he chasteneth, and scourgeth every son whom he receiveth; yet those afflictions shall not befall thee for those causes for which they befall the slothful and backsliding Christian; neither shall they have that pinching and galling operation upon thee, as on those who have left their first love and tenderness for God's glory in the world.

(1.) Upon the faithful upright man, though he also may be corrected and chastised for sin, yet, I say, he abiding close with God, afflictions come rather for trial and for the exercise of grace received, than as rebukes for this or that wickedness; when upon the backsliding, heartless Christian these things shall come from fatherly anger and displeasure, and that for their sins against him. Job did acknowledge himself a sinner, and that God therefore might chastise him; but yet he rather believed it was chiefly for the trial of his grace, as indeed and in truth it was: He is "a perfect man," saith God to Satan, and "one that feareth God, and escheweth evil, and still he holdeth fast his integrity, although thou movedst me against him, to destroy him without cause." (Job ii. 3.) God will not say thus of every one when affliction is laid upon them, though they yet may be his children; but rather declareth and pronounceth that it is for their transgressions, because they have wickedly departed from him.

(2.) Now affliction arising from these two causes, their effects in the manner of their working, though grace turns them both for good, is very different one from the other; he who hath been helped to walk with God, is not assaulted with those turnings and returnings of guilt when he is afflicted, as he who hath basely departed from God; the one can plead his integrity, when the other blusheth for shame. See both these cases in one person, even that goodly, beloved David. When the Lord did rebuke him for sin, then he cries, O blood guiltiness, O "cast me not away from thy presence." (Ps. li. 11.) But when he at another time knew himself guiltless, though then

also sorely afflicted, behold with what boldness he turns his face unto God; "O Lord my God," saith he, "if I have done this; if there be iniquity in my hands; if I have rewarded evil unto him that was at peace with me; (yea, I delivered him that without cause was mine enemy:) let the enemy persecute my soul, and take it; yea, let him tread down my life to the earth, and lay mine honour in the dust. Selah," &c. (Ps. vii. 3—5.)

This, therefore, must needs be a blessed help in distress, for a man to have a good conscience when affliction hath taken hold on him; for a man then in his looking behind and before to return with peace to his own soul, that man must needs find honey in this lion, that can plead his innocency and uprightness. All the people curse me, saith Jeremiah, but that without a cause; for I have neither lent nor taken on usury, (Jer. xv. 10,) which it seems was a sin at that day.

9. When men are faithful with God in this world, to do the work he hath appointed for them, by this means a dying bed is made easier, and that upon a double account. (1.) By reason of that present peace such shall have, even in their time of languishing. (2.) By reason of the good company such shall have at their departure.

1. Such souls usually abound in present peace, they look not back upon the years they have spent with that shame as the idle and slothful Christian does. "Remember now, O Lord, I beseech thee, how I have walked before thee in truth, and with a perfect heart." (Isa. xxxviii. 3.) "Blessed is he that considereth the poor; the Lord will deliver him in the time of trouble. The Lord will preserve him, and keep him alive; and he shall be blessed upon the earth: and thou wilt not deliver him to the will of his enemies. The Lord will strengthen him upon the bed of languishing: thou wilt make all his bed in his sickness." (Ps. xli. 1—3.) Ah! when God makes the bed, he must needs lie easy that weakness hath cast thereon; a blessed pillow hath that man for his head, though to all beholders it is hard as a stone. Jacob, on his death-bed, had two things that made it easy—(1.) The faith of his going to rest, "I am to be gathered unto my people," (Gen. xlix. 29;) that is, to the blessed that have yielded up the ghost before me. (2.) The remembrance of the feelings of the countenance of God upon him, when he walked before him in the days of his pilgrimage: when Joseph came to see him before he left this world, "Israel," saith the word, "strengthened himself and sat upon the bed;" and the first word that dropped out of this good man's mouth, O how full of glory was it! "God Almighty appeared unto me," saith he, "at Luz in the land of Canaan, and blessed me," &c. (Gen. xlviii. 2, 3.) O blessed discourse for a sick bed, when those can talk thus that lie thereon, from as true a ground as Jacob; but thus will God make the bed of those who walk close with him in this world.

2. The dying bed of such a man is made easy by reason also of the good company such shall have at their departure : and that is, (1.) The angels ; (2.) Their good works they have done for God in the world.

1. The angels of heaven shall wait upon them, as they did upon the blessed Lazarus, to carry them " into Abraham's bosom." (Luke xvi. 22.) I know all that go to paradise are by these holy ones conducted thither ; but yet, for all that, such as die under the clouds' for unchristian walking with God, may meet with darkness in that day, may go heavily hence, notwithstanding that ; yea, their bed may be as uncomfortable to them as if they lay upon nothing but the cords, and their departing from it, as to appearance, more uncomfortable by far. But as for those who have been faithful to their God, they shall see before them, shall know their " tabernacle shall be in peace," (Job v. 24,) the everlasting gates shall be opened unto them ; in all which from earth they shall see the glory. I once was told a story of what happened at a good man's death, the which I have often remembered with wonderment and gladness. After he had lain for some time sick, his hour came that he must depart, and behold, while he lay, as we call it, drawing on, to the amazement of the mourners, there was heard about his bed such blessed and ravishing music as they never had heard before ; which also continued till his soul departed, and then began to cease, and grow, as to its sound, as if it was departing the house, and so still seemed to go further and further off, till at last they could hear it no longer. "Eye hath not seen, nor ear heard, neither have entered into the heart of man, the things which God hath prepared for them that love him." (1 Cor. ii. 9.) Behold, then, how God can make thy sick bed easy !

2. A dying bed is made easy by those good works that men have done in their life for the name of God : " Blessed are the dead which die in the Lord from henceforth : Yea, saith the Spirit, that they may rest from their labours, and their works do follow them," (Rev. xiv. 13,) yea, and go before them too. No man need be afraid to be accompanied by good deeds to heaven. Be afraid of sins : they are like bloodhounds at the heels ; and be sure thy sins will find thee out, even thee who hast not been pardoned in the precious blood of Christ ; but as for those who have submitted themselves to the righteousness of God for their justification, and who have through faith and love to his name been frequent in deeds of righteousness, they shall not appear empty before their God, "their works," their good works, " follow them." These shall enter into rest, and walk with Christ in white. I observe when Israel had passed over Jordan, they were to go to possess between Mount Ebal and Mount Gerizim, from whence was to be pronounced the blessing and the cursing : (Deut. xxvii. xviii.) The gospel meaning of which I take to be as followeth :—I take Jordan to be a type of death ; and these two mountains with the cursing and blessing to be a type of the judgment that comes on every man, so soon as he goes from hence, (" and after death the judgment,") so that he that escapes the cursing, he alone goes into blessedness. But he that Mount Ebal smiteth, he falls short of heaven : O ! none knows the noise that doth sound in sinners' souls from Ebal and Gerizim when they are departed hence ; yet it may be they know not what will become of them till they hear these echoings from these two mountains. But here the good man is sure Mount Gerizim doth pronounce him blessed. Blessed, then, are the dead that die in the Lord, for their works will follow them till they are past all danger. These are the Christian's train that follow him to rest ; these are a good man's company that follow him to heaven.

PREFATORY REMARKS

ON

THE DESIRE OF THE RIGHTEOUS GRANTED.

HUMAN nature, in its proper and healthful state, can only desire what is consistent with the divine will; but this limitation is rather the security than the abridgment of liberty. Wishes which contradict some eternal law of right and holiness will either never be fulfilled, even in appearance, or, if partially fulfilled, will lead to such conflicts and disorganizations in the mind which entertains them, that their satisfaction will be purchased at too great an expense. A state of righteousness is essentially a state of freedom; for the only sense in which freedom can be the property of a created being is that in which it signifies the power of an independent will, of a free choice, and while that choice is in harmony with God's supreme wisdom and goodness, there can be no barrier to its liberty but the limits of its own nature. The desire, therefore, of a righteous or holy being, supposing that being to have retained its original perfection, will certainly be fulfilled. Agreeing as it does with the will, the laws, and designs of the Almighty; subject in its length, breadth, intensity, to his Spirit, and growing in strength, if in the direction of his purposes, it ceases to be Desire the moment it can better glorify God as Resignation. Thus it accomplishes itself by the surest of all processes, enjoying on the one hand the satisfaction which follows the attainment of a particular blessing, and, on the other, the far profounder delight of divine communion, felt in the power of looking away from the gifts of God to God himself. It is only in the rare instances of genuine devotion that human desire approaches a state like this. Even in the best cases, it is so disturbed by sudden gusts of passion, or so weakened by infirmities, that it requires a very severe watchfulness to subdue it by considerations of propriety and duty. But neither the rareness of examples, illustrating the harmony of wishes bred in the heart of man with the counsels of heaven, nor the consequent difficulty of showing the effects of such a concord in actual life, ought to create any doubt of its possibility, or of the reality and grandeur of the results wherever it is approached. The principle holds true through every form of man's fluctuating and various desires, that if the desire be conformable to the righteous will of God, it will attain its end, and fill the heart which has cherished it with unspeakable satisfaction.

In this way of viewing the subject, we look at man according to the laws of his nature, and as standing in a proper and recognised relation to his Creator. But a state of sin involves perpetual contradictions to every principle arising from that relation. For any practical purpose, it is of little use to show how certainly desire will be accomplished when, as springing from feelings implanted by God, it seeks but the fulfilment of his own designs. The desire of the righteous is not that of human nature as it at present exists: it is that of the mind and heart which have undergone a mighty transforming process—of man brought into new circumstances by a new covenant with God, and invested with a righteousness which, justifying him from sin, makes his prayers all-powerful at the throne of grace.

Let us suppose, then, that some few individuals of the human race have become aroused to thoughtfulness and inquiry. They find their best plans thwarted, their wishes and desires continually disappointed. Whence arise the obstacles to their success? An answer is given. The plans which they form, the yearnings which they indulge, are irrespective of God. Reason immediately concludes that it is inconsistent with the nature of things to look for good where no regard is had to Him who is its sole fountain. Another step in the argument shows that the hindrance to the fulfilment of human desire, while this state of things continues, is twofold. The laws of God are the laws of nature. They may be broken, trampled upon, as they form a barrier to some present indulgence, but it is impossible really to pass beyond them into a sphere of enjoyment and liberty. There is a stage at which they are fixed, like a wall of adamant, and that reached, desire, beating against it in vain, becomes despair and torment. But besides the resistance which divine law necessarily opposes to the will of an erring creature, every sin is followed by consequences which, of themselves, lessen the means of accomplishing its purpose.

All this becomes evident to the awakened mind. The important discovery is made, that while the most deeply cherished wishes, the dearest hopes of the heart remain unfulfilled, this missing of their aim is not to be ascribed to mere accidents of life, but to their antagonism with the divine government —to some element of evil intermingled with the natural instincts, or to the corruption of those instincts themselves.

There is a truth and solemnity in this discovery which arrogance and blind presumption only can tempt men to neglect. Duly weighed, it will lead to the conclusion, that the broadest, as well as the most solid basis upon which human happiness can rest is holiness of disposition. Desires, subjected to this principle, can indeed pursue their object only along the track left open for them by divine law. But they have a promise to support and speed them on their narrow way—" The desire of the righteous shall be granted." This assurance of final accomplishment is of immeasurably greater worth than the most unrestricted liberty claimed for worldly hope, or the largest choice of earthly means to be gained for its support. Calm in the profound conviction that he is opposing no law of his nature, and gladdened by encouragements that can never fail, happy, beyond all other men, is he who can habitually yield to God the service of an unreluctant will. The wish for ultimate perfection—for a happiness which shall be unmixed and permanent, is the one proper wish of a rational being ; it is the wish instinctively cherished in every human heart, and enters, under various forms, into every desire by which it can be agitated. But it is to the righteous only that its attainment is possible—the righteous who are so because they have been justified by Christ, and are sanctified by his Spirit.

H. S.

THE DESIRE OF THE RIGHTEOUS GRANTED;

OR,

A DISCOURSE OF THE RIGHTEOUS MAN'S DESIRES.

" The desire of the righteous is only good."—PROV. xi. 23.
" The fear of the wicked, it shall come upon him ; but the desire of the righteous shall be granted.—PROV. x. 24.

THIS book of the Proverbs is so called, because it is such as containeth hard, dark, and pithy sentences of wisdom, by which is taught unto young men knowledge and discretion.

Wherefore this book is not such as discloseth truths by words antecedent or subsequent to the text, so as other scriptures generally do, but has its texts or sentences more independent : for usually each verse standeth upon its own bottom, and presenteth by itself some singular thing to the consideration of the reader ; so that I shall not need to bid my reader look back to what went before, nor yet to that which follows, for the better opening of the text, and shall therefore come immediately to the words, and search into them, for what hidden treasures are contained therein.

1. The words, then, in the first place, present us with the general condition of the whole world ; for all men are ranked under one of these conditions—the wicked or the righteous ; for he that is not wicked, is righteous ; and he that is not righteous, is wicked. So again, Lay not wait (O wicked man) against the dwelling of the righteous, spoil not his dwelling-place. I might give you out of this book many such instances, for it flows with such ; but the truth hereof is plain enough.

The world is also divided by other general terms ; as by these : believers, unbelievers ; saints, sinners ; good, bad ; children of God, and children of the wicked one, &c. These, I say, are general terms, and comprehend not this or that sect, or order of each, but the whole. The believer, the saint, the good, and the child of God, is one, to wit, the righteous ; the unbeliever, the sinner, the bad, and the child of the devil, is one, to wit, the wicked ; as also the text expresses it : so that I say, the text, or these two terms in it, comprehend all men : the one, all that shall be saved ; the other, all that shall be damned for ever in hell-fire. (Ps. ix. 17.)

The wicked—who is he but the man that loves not God, nor to do his will ? The righteous—who is he but the man that loveth God, and his holy will, to do it ?

Of the wicked there are several sorts, some more ignorant, some more knowing ; the more ignorant of them are such as go to be executed as the "ox goes to the slaughter, or as a fool to the correction of the stocks," (Prov. vii. 22 ;) that is, as creatures whose ignorance makes them as unconcerned while they are going down the stairs to hell. But, alas ! their ignorance will be no plea for them before the bar of God ; for it is written, " It is a people of no understanding ; therefore he that made them will not have mercy on them, and he that formed them will show them no favour." (Isa. xxvii. 11.)

Though, I must confess, the more knowing the wicked is, or the more light and goodness such a one sins against, the greater will his judgment be ; these shall have greater damnation. (Luke xx. 47.) It shall be more tolerable at the judgment for Sodom than for them. (Matt. xi. 22.)

There is a wicked man that goes blinded, and a wicked man that goes with his eyes open, to hell : there is a wicked man that cannot see, and a wicked man that will not see, the danger he is in ; but hell-fire will open both their eyes.

There are that are wicked, and cover all with a cloak of religion ; and there are that proclaim their profaneness : but they will meet both in the lake that burns with fire and brimstone. " The wicked shall be turned into hell, and all the nations that forget God." (Ps. ix. 17.)

There are also several sorts (if I may so express myself) of those that are truly righteous, as children, young men, fathers, or saints that fear God, both small and great. Some have more grace than some, and some do better improve the grace they have than others of their brethren do ; some also are more valiant for the truth upon the earth than others of their brethren are : yea, some are so swallowed up with God, and love to his word and ways, that they are fit to be a pattern or example in holiness to all that are about them ;

and some again have their light shining so dim, that they render themselves suspicious to their brethren, whether they are of the number of those that have grace or no. But, being gracious, they shall not be lost, although such will at the day of reward suffer loss: for this is the will of the Father that sent the Son to be the Saviour of the world, that of all that he had given him he should lose nothing, but should raise it up at the last day. (John vi. 39.)

2. In the next place, we are here presented with some of the qualities of the wicked and the righteous: the wicked has his fears, the righteous has his desires. The wicked has his fears: "The fear of the wicked, it shall come upon him; but the desire of the righteous shall be granted." (Prov. x. 24.)

Indeed, it seems to the godly, that the wicked feareth not, nor doth he after a godly sort; for he that feareth God aright must not be reputed a wicked man. The wicked, through the pride of his countenance, declareth that he feareth not God aright, because he doth not graciously call upon him; but yet, for all that, the wicked at times are haunted, sorely haunted, and that with the worst of fears. "Terrors," says Bildad, "shall make him afraid on every side." (Job xviii. 11.) And again, "His confidence shall be rooted out of his tabernacle, and it shall bring him to the king of terrors." (Job xviii. 14.)

A wicked man, though he may hector it at times with his proud heart, as though he feared neither God nor hell, yet again, at times, his soul is even drowned with terrors: "The morning is to them even as the shadow of death; if one knew them, they are in the terrors of the shadow of death." (Job xxiv. 17.) At times, I say, it is thus with them, especially when they are under warm convictions that the day of judgment is at hand, or when they feel in themselves as if death was coming as a tempest to steal them away from their enjoyments, and lusts, and delights; then the bed shakes on which they lie, then the proud tongue doth falter in their mouth, and their knees knock one against another; then their conscience stares, and roars, and tears, and arraigns them before God's judgment-seat, or threatens to follow them down to hell, and there to wreak its fury on them, for all the abuses and affronts this wicked wretch offered to it in the day in which it controlled his unlawful deeds.

Oh! none can imagine what fearful plights a wicked man is in sometimes; though God, in his just judgment towards them, suffers them again and again to stifle and choke such awakenings, from a purpose to reserve them unto the day of judgment to be punished. (2 Pet. ii. 9.)

3. In the third place, as the wicked has his fears, so the righteous has his desires; "The desire of the righteous shall be granted:" but this must not be taken exclusively, as if the wicked had nothing but fears, and the righteous

nothing but desires. For, both by Scripture, and experience also, we find that the wicked has his desires, and the righteous man his fears.

(1.) For the wicked, they are not without their desires. "Let me die the death of the righteous, and let my last end be like his," (Numb. xxii. 10,) was the desire of wicked Balaam. And another place saith, "the wicked boasteth of his heart's desire;" that he is for heaven as well as the best of you all, but yet, even then, he blesseth "the covetous, whom the Lord abhorreth." (Ps. x. 3.)

Wicked men have their desires and their hopes too, but the hope and desire of unjust men perisheth, (Prov. xi. 7;) yea, and though they look and long too all the day long, with desires of life and glory, yet their fears, and them only, shall come upon them; for they are the desires of the righteous that shall be granted. (Ps. cxii. 10.)

The desires of the wicked want a good bottom; they flow not from a sanctified mind, nor of love to the God, or the heaven now desired; but only from such a sense as devils have of torments, and so, as they, they cry out, "I beseech thee torment me not." (Luke viii. 28.)

But their fears have a substantial foundation, for they are grounded upon the view of an ill-spent life, the due reward of which is hell-fire: "the unrighteous shall not inherit the kingdom of God," (1 Cor. vi. 9;) their place is without; "for without are dogs and sorcerers, and whoremongers, and murderers, and idolaters, and whosoever loveth and maketh a lie." (Rev. xxii. 15.)

Their fears, therefore, have a strong foundation; they have also matter to work upon, which is guilt and justice, the which they shall never be able to escape without a miracle of grace and mercy. Therefore it saith, and that with emphasis, "The fear of the wicked it shall come upon him;" wherefore his desire must die with him: for the promise of a grant of that which is desired, is only entailed to righteousness: "The desire of the righteous shall be granted:" but "grant not, O Lord, the desire of the wicked," said David. (Ps. cxl. 8.)

(2.) Nor are the righteous without their fears, and that even all their life long. Through fear of death, they (some of them) are all their life-time subject to bondage. (Heb. ii. 15.)

But as the desires of the wicked shall be frustrate, so shall also the fears of the godly; hence you have them admonished, yea, commanded, not to be afraid, neither of devils, death, nor hell; for the fear of the righteous shall not come upon them to eternal damnation: "The desire of the righteous shall be granted." No, they are not to fear what sin can do unto them, nor what all their sins can do unto them; I do not say they should not be afraid of sinning, nor of those temporal judgments that sin shall bring upon them, for of such things they ought to be afraid, as saith the Psalmist, "My flesh trembleth for fear of thee, and I am afraid of thy judgments." (Ps. cxix. 120.)

But of eternal ruin, of that they ought not to be afraid with slavish fear: "Wherefore should I fear," said the prophet, "in the days of evil, when the iniquity of my heels shall compass me about?" (Ps. xlix. 5.) And again, "Ye have done all this wickedness, yet turn not aside from following the Lord; for the Lord will not forsake his people, for his great name's sake." (1 Sam. xii. 20, 22.)

The reason is, because the righteous are secured by their faith in Christ Jesus; also their fears stand upon a mistake of the nature of the covenant, in which they are wrapped up, which is ordered for them in all things, and sure. (2 Sam. xxiii. 5; Isa. lv. 3.) Besides, God is purposed to magnify the riches of his grace in their salvation; therefore goodness and mercy shall to that end follow them all the days of their life, that they may "dwell in the house of the Lord for ever." (Ps. xxiii. 6.) They have also their intercessor and advocate ready with God, to take up matters for them in such a way as may maintain true peace betwixt their God and them; and as may encourage them to be sober, and hope to the end, for the grace that is to be brought unto them at the revelation of Jesus Christ. (1 Pet. i. 13.)

Wherefore, though the godly have their fears, yea, sometimes dreadful fears, and that of perishing for ever and ever; yet the day is coming, when their fears and tears shall be done away, and when their desires only shall be granted: "The fear of the wicked, it shall come upon them; but the desire of the righteous shall be granted."

The words, then, are a prediction or prophecy, and that both concerning the wicked and the righteous, with reference to time and things to come, and shall certainly be fulfilled in their season. Hence it is said concerning the wicked, that their triumphing "is short, and that the joy of the hypocrite is but for a moment." (Job xx. 5.) Oh, their end will be bitter as wormwood, and will cut like a two-edged sword! Of this Solomon admonishes youth, when he saith, "Rejoice, O young man in thy youth, and let thy heart cheer thee in the days of thy youth, and walk in the ways of thine heart, and in the sight of thine eyes; but know thou, that for all these things God will bring thee into judgment." (Eccles. xi. 9.)

This, therefore, showeth the desperate spirit that possesses the children of men, who though they hear and read all this, yet cannot be reclaimed from such courses that are wicked, and that lead to such a condition. I say they will not be reclaimed from such courses as lead to ways that go down to hell, where their soul must mourn, even then when their flesh and body are consumed. Oh, how dear-bought are their pleasures, and how will their laughter be turned into tears and anguish unutterable! and that presently, for it is coming: their "judgment now of a long time lingereth not, and their damnation slumbereth not." (2 Pet.

ii. 3.) But what good will their covenant of death then do them? And will their agreement of hell yield them comfort? (Isa. xxviii. 18.) Is not God as well mighty to punish as to save? Or can these sinners believe God out of the world? or cause that he should not pay them home for their sins, and recompense them for all the evil they have loved, and continued in the commission of? "Can thy heart endure, or can thy hands be strong in the day that God shall deal with thee?" (Ezek. xxii. 14.)

Thou art bold now, I mean bold in a wicked way; thou sayest now, thou wilt keep thy sweet morsels of sin under thy tongue, thou wilt keep them still within thy mouth. Poor wretch! read Job xx. 11. "Thy sins shall lie down in the dust with thee. Thou hast sucked the poison of asps, and the viper's tongue shall slay thee. (Job xx. 16.) Thou shalt not see the rivers, the streaming floods, the brooks of butter and honey. (Job xx. 17.) All darkness shall be hid in thy secret places, a fire not blown shall consume thee, &c. This is the portion of a wicked man from God, and the heritage appointed to him by God." (Job xx. 26—29.)

And as they predict or prophesy what shall become of the wicked; so also they plentifully foretell what shall happen to the righteous, when he saith, "Their desire shall be granted;" of which more anon.

Only here I will drop this short hint, That the righteous have great cause to rejoice; for what more pleasing, what more comfortable to a man, than to be assured, and that from the Spirit of truth, that what he desireth shall be granted? And this the righteous are assured of here; for he saith it in words at length, "The desire of the righteous shall be granted."

This, then, should comfort them against their fears, and the sense of their unworthiness; it should also make them hold up their heads under all their temptations, and the affronts that is usual for them to meet with in the world. The righteous! Who so vilified as the righteous? He, by the wise men of the world, is counted a very Abraham, a fool; like to him who is the father of us all.

But as he left all for the desire that he had of a better country, and at last obtained his desire; for after he had patiently endured, he obtained the promise; so those that walk in the steps of that faith which our father Abraham had, even those also in the end shall find place in Abraham's bosom. Wherefore it is meet that we should cheer up and be glad, because what we desire shall be granted unto us.

But I shall here leave off this short way of paraphrasing upon the text, and shall come distinctly to inquire into the nature of the words; but my subject-matter shall be the last part of the verse, "The desire of the righteous shall be granted." From which words there are these things to be inquired into.

I. What, or who is the righteous man?

II. What are the desires of a righteous man?

III. What is meant or to be understood by the granting of the desires of the righteous. "The desires of the righteous shall be granted."

I. For the first of these—namely,

What or who is the righteous man?

My way of prosecuting this head shall be to show you, first, that I intend a righteous man, not in every sense, but in that which is the best, otherwise I shall miscarry as to the intendment of the Holy Ghost; for it may not be supposed, that these words reach to them that are righteous in general, but in a special sense; such, I mean, that are so in the judgment of God. For, as I hinted, there are several sorts of righteous men, that yet have nothing to do with this blessed promise, or that shall never, as such, have their desires granted.

1. There is one that is righteous in his own eyes, and is yet far enough off from the blessing of the text. "There is a generation that are pure" or righteous "in their own sight, yet are not purged from their filthiness." (Prov. xxx. 12.) These are they that you also read of in the Evangelist Luke, that are said to trust "in themselves that they were righteous, and despised others." (Luke xviii. 9.) These are set so low, by this their foolish confidence, in the eyes of Jesus Christ, that he even preferred a praying publican before them. (Luke xviii. 13, 14.) Wherefore these cannot be the men—I mean those righteous men—to whom this promise is made.

2. There are those that by others are counted righteous: I mean they are so accounted by their neighbours. Thus, Korah and his company are called the people of the Lord, and all the congregation by them also called holy, every one of them. (Numb. xvi. 3, 41.) But as he who commends himself is not approved; so it is no great matter if all the world should count us righteous, if God esteemeth us not for such. "For not he that commendeth himself is approved, but whom the Lord commendeth." (2 Cor. x. 18.)

3. There are those that indeed are righteous when compared with others: "I am not come to call the righteous." (Matt. ix. 13.) For scarcely for a righteous man will one die; and the like, are texts thus to be understood. For such as these, are as to life moral, better than others. But these, if they are none otherwise righteous than by acts and works of righteousness of their own, are not the persons contained in the text that are to have their desires granted.

4. The righteous man therefore in the text is, and ought to be thus described:—(1.) He is one whom God makes righteous, by reckoning him so. (2.) He is one that God makes righteous, by possessing of him with a principle of righteousness. (3.) He is one that is practically righteous.

First. *He is one that God makes righteous.* Now, if God makes him righteous, his righteousness is not his own; I mean this sort of righteousness: "Their righteousness is of me, saith the Lord." (Isa. liv. 17.)

God, then, makes a man righteous by putting righteousness upon him—by putting the righteousness of God upon him. (Phil. iii. 6—9.) Hence, we are said to be made the righteousness of God in Christ. "For he hath made him to be sin for us, who knew no sin, that we might be made the righteousness of God in him." (2 Cor. v. 21.)

Thus God, therefore, reckoneth one righteous, even by imputing that unto us which is able to make us so; he is made unto us of God righteousness. (1 Cor. i. 30.) Wherefore, he saith again, "In the Lord shall all the seed of Israel be justified, and shall glory." (Isa. xlv. 25.)

The righteousness then by which a man is made righteous, with righteousness to justification of life before God (for that is it we are speaking of now), is the righteousness of another than is he who is justified thereby. Hence it is said again, by the soul thus justified and made righteous, "The Lord hath clothed me with the garments of salvation, he hath covered me with the robe of righteousness." (Isa. lxi. 10.) As he also saith in another place, "I spread my skirt over thee, and covered thy nakedness." (Ezek. xvi. 8.) This we call a being made righteous by reckoning, by the reckoning of God; for none is of power to reckon one righteous but God, because none can make one so to be but him.

He that can make me rich, though I am, in myself, the poorest of men, may reckon me rich, if together with his so reckoning, he indeed doth make me rich. This is the case: God makes a man righteous by bestowing of righteousness upon him—by counting the righteousness of his Son for his. He gives him righteousness, a righteousness already performed, and completed by the obedience of his Son. (Rom. v. 19.)

Not that this righteousness, by being bestowed upon us, is severed from Jesus Christ; for it is still his, and in him. How then, may some say, doth it become ours? I answer, by our being put into him; for of God are we in Christ Jesus, who is made unto us, of him, righteousness. And again, we are made "the righteousness of God in him." So, then, the righteousness of Christ covereth his, as a man's garments cover the members of his body, for ye are "the body of Christ, and members in particular." (1 Cor. xii. 27.) The righteousness, therefore, is Christ's; resideth still in him, and covereth us, as the child is lapped up in its father's skirts, (Ezek. xvi. 8,) or as the chicken is covered with the feathers of the hen. (Matt. xxiii. 37.) I make use of all these similitudes, thereby to inform you of my meaning; for by all these things are set forth the way of our being made righteous to justification of law.

Now thus a man is made righteous without any regard to what he has, or to what is of him: for as to him, it is utterly another's. Just as if I should with the skirts of my garment take up and clothe some poor and naked infant that I find cast out into the open field. Now if I cover the person, I cover scabs, and sores, and ulcers, and all blemishes. Hence God, by putting this righteousness upon us, is said to hide and cover our sins. " Blessed is the man whose transgressions are forgiven, and whose sin is covered. Blessed is the man to whom the Lord will not impute sin." (Rom. iv. 7, 8.) For since this righteousness is Christ's, and counted or reckoned ours by the grace of God, it is therefore bestowed upon us, not because we are, but to make us righteous before the face of God. Hence, as I said, it is said to make us righteous, even as gay clothes do make a naked body fine. " He hath made him to be sin for us, who knew no sin, that we might be made the righteousness of God in him." (2 Cor. v. 21.)

This is of absolute necessity to be known, and to be believed. For without this no man can be counted righteous before God; and if we stand not righteous before God, it will benefit us nothing as to life eternal, though we should be counted righteous by all the men on earth. Besides, if God counts me righteous, I am safe, though in and of myself I am nothing but a sinner, and ungodly. The reason is, because God has a right to bestow righteousness upon me, for he has righteousness to spare; he has also a right to forgive, because sin is the transgression of the law. Yea, he has therefore sent his Son into the world to accomplish righteousness for sinners, and God of his mercy bestows it upon those that shall receive it by faith. Now, if God shall count me righteous, who will be so hardy as to conclude I yet shall perish? "It is God that justifieth. Who is he that condemneth? It is Christ that died, yea, rather that is risen again, who is even at the right hand of God, who also maketh intercession for us. Who shall separate us from the love of Christ?" (Rom. viii. 33—35.)

Thus, therefore, is a man made righteous, even of God by Christ, or through his righteousness. Now if, as we said, a man is thus made righteous, then in this sense he is good before God, before he has done anything of that which the law calls good before men; for God maketh not men righteous with this righteousness, because they have been, or have done good, but before they are capable of doing good at all. Hence we are said to be justified while ungodly, even as an infant is clothed with the skirt of another, while naked, as touching itself. (Rom. iv. 5.) Works, therefore, do not precede, but follow after this righteousness; and even thus it is in nature, the tree must be good before it bear good fruit, and so also must a man. It is impossible to make a man bring forth good fruit to God, before he is of God made good,

as it is for a thorn or bramble-bush to bring forth figs or grapes. (Matt. vii. 16.)

But again, a man must be righteous before he can be good; righteous by imputation, before his person, his intellectuals, can be qualified with good, as to the principle of good. For neither faith, the Spirit, nor any grace, is given unto the sinner before God has made him righteous with this righteousness of Christ. Wherefore it is said, that after he had spread his skirt over us, he washed us with water; that is, with the washing of sanctification. (Ezek. xvi. 8, 9.) And to conclude otherwise is as much as to say, that an unjustified man has faith, the spirit and the graces thereof, which to say, is to overthrow the gospel. For what need of Christ's righteousness, if a man may have faith and the Spirit of Christ without it, since the Spirit is said to be the earnest of our inheritance, and that by which we are sealed unto the day of redemption? But the truth is, the Spirit which makes our person good—I mean that which sanctifies our natures—is the fruit of the righteousness which is by Jesus Christ. For as Christ died and rose again before he sent the Holy Ghost from heaven to his; so the benefit of his death and resurrection is by God bestowed upon us, in order to the Spirit's possessing of our souls.

Second. And this leads me to the second thing—namely, *That God makes a man righteous by possessing of him with a principle of righteousness*, even with the spirit of righteousness. (Rom. iv. 6.) For though, as to justification before God from the curse of the law, we are made righteous while we are ungodly and yet sinners; yet being made free from sin thus, we forthwith become, through a change which the Holy Ghost works in our minds, the servants of God. (Rom. v. 7—9.) Hence it is said, " There is therefore now no condemnation to those that are in Christ Jesus, who walk not after the flesh, but after the Spirit." (Rom. viii. 1.) For though, as the apostle also insinuates here, that being in Christ Jesus is antecedent to our walking after the Spirit; yet a man can make no demonstration of his being in Christ Jesus, but by his walking in the Spirit; because the Spirit is an inseparable companion of imputed righteousness, and immediately follows it, to dwell, with whosoever it is bestowed upon.

Now, it dwelling in us, principles us in all the powers of our souls, with that which is righteousness in the habit and nature of it. Hence the fruits of the Spirit are called *the fruits of goodness and righteousness*, as the fruits of a tree are called the fruit of that tree. (Eph. v. 9.)

And again, " He that doth righteousness is righteous," (1 John iii. 7,) not only in our first sense, but even in this also. For who can do righteousness without he be principled so to do? Who can act reason, that hath not reason? So none can bring forth righteousness that hath not in him the root of righteousness, which is the Spirit of God, which comes to us by virtue of our being made sons of God. (Gal. iv. 5—7.) Hence the fruits of the Spirit are called " the fruits of righteousness, which are by Jesus Christ unto the glory and praise of God." (Phil. i. 11.) This, then, is the thing we say, to wit, that he that is made righteous unto justification of life before God, is also habituated with a principle of righteousness, as that which follows that righteousness by which he stands just before : I say, as that which follows it ; for it comes by Jesus Christ, and by our being justified before God, and made righteous through him.

This second, then, also comes to us before we do any act spiritually good. For how can a man act righteousness but from a principle of righteousness ? And seeing this principle is not of or by nature, but of and by grace, through Christ, it follows, that as no man is just before God, that is not covered with the righteousness of Christ, so no man can do righteousness but by the power of the Spirit of God, which must dwell in him. Hence we are said by the Spirit to mortify the deeds of the body, which works are preparatory to fruitful actions. " The husbandman," says Paul, " that laboureth must be first partaker of the fruit," (2 Tim. ii. 6 ;) so he that worketh righteousness must first be blessed with a principle of righteousness.

Men must have eyes before they see, tongues before they speak, and legs before they go : even so must a man be made habitually good and righteous, before he can work righteousness. This then is the second thing. God makes a man righteous by possessing him with a principle of righteousness ; which principle is not of nature, but of grace ; not of man, but of God.

Third. *The man in the text is practically righteous*, or one that declareth himself by works that are good ; a virtuous, a righteous man, even as the tree declares by the apple or plum it beareth what manner of tree it is : " You shall know them by their fruits." (Matt. vii. 16.) Fruits show outwardly what the heart is principled with ; show me then thy faith, which abideth in the heart, by thy works in a well-spent life. Mark how the apostle words it, " But now, being," saith he, " made free from sin, and become servants to God, ye have your fruit unto holiness, and the end everlasting life." (Rom. vi. 22.) Mark his order. First we are made free from sin ; now that is by being justified freely by the grace of God, through the redemption which is in Jesus Christ, (Rom. iii. 24,) whom God has set forth to be a propitiation through faith in his blood. (2 Tim. i. 9.) Now this is God's act, without any regard at all to any good that the sinner has or can accomplish ; " not by works of righteousness which we have done, but according to his mercy," (Tit. iii. 5,) thus he saveth us.

Now, being made free from sin, what follows ?

We become the servants of God—that is, by that turn which the Holy Ghost makes upon our heart, when it reconciles it to the word of God's grace ; for that, as was said afore, is the effect of the indwelling and operation of the Holy Ghost. Now, having our hearts thus changed by God and his word, the fruits of righteousness put forth themselves by us. For as when we were in the flesh, the motions of sin, which is in our members, did bring forth fruit unto death ; so now, if we are in the Spirit—and we are not in the flesh, but in the Spirit, if so be the Spirit of Christ dwells in us —by the motions and workings of that, we have our fruit unto holiness, and the end everlasting life. (Rom. viii. 6—9.)

But now by these fruits we are neither made righteous nor good, for the apple maketh not the tree good, it only declares it so to be. Here therefore all those are mistaken that think to be righteous by doing of righteous actions, or good by doing good. A man must first be righteous, or he cannot do righteousness—to wit, that which is evangelically such. Now, if a man is, and must be righteous, before he acts righteousness, then all his works are born too late to make him just before God ; for his works, if they be right, flow from the heart of a righteous man—of a man that had, before he had any good work, a twofold righteousness bestowed on him : one to make him righteous in the sight of God, the other to principle him to be righteous before the world ; That he might be called a tree of righteousness, " the planting of the Lord, that he might be glorified." (Isa. lxi. 3.)

The want of understanding of this is that which keeps so many in a mist of darkness about the way of salvation ; for they, poor hearts ! when they hear of the need that they have of a righteousness to commend them to God, being ignorant of the righteousness of God,—that is, of that which God imputeth to a man, and that by which he counteth him righteous,—have it not in their thoughts to accept of that unto justification of life, but presently betake themselves to the law of works, and fall to work there for the performing of a righteousness, that they may be accepted of God for the same, and so submit not themselves to the righteousness of God, by which, and by which only, the soul stands just before God. (Rom. x. 3.) Wherefore, I say, it is necessary that this be distinetly laid down : that a man must be righteous first, even before he doth righteousness. The argument is plain from the order of nature—for a corrupt tree cannot bring forth good fruit, (Matt. vii. 18. Luke vi. 43 ;) wherefore make the tree good, and so his fruit good ; or the tree corrupt, and his fruit corrupt.

Reason also says the same, for how can blacks beget white children, when both father and mother are blacks ? How can a man without grace, and the spirit of grace, do good : nature is defiled, even to the mind and conscience, (Tit. i. 15 ;) how then can good fruit come from such a stock ?

Besides, God accepteth not any work of a person which is not first accepted of him : "The Lord had respect unto Abel, and to his offering," (Gen. iv. 4 ;) to Abel first, that is, before that Abel offered. But how could God have respect to Abel, if Abel was not pleasing in his sight? and how could Abel be yet pleasing in his sight, for the sake of his own righteousness, when it is plain that Abel had not yet done good works ? He was therefore first made acceptable in the sight of God, by and for the sake of that righteousness which God of his grace had put upon him to justification of life; through and by which also the Holy Ghost in the graces of it dwelt in Abel's soul; now Abel being justified, and also possessed with this holy principle, he offers his sacrifice to God. Hence it is said, that he "offered by faith"—by the faith which he had precedent to his offering ; for if through faith he offered, he had that faith before he offered—that is, plain. Now his faith looked not for acceptance for the sake of what he offered, but for the sake of that righteousness which it did apprehend God had already put upon him, and by which he was made righteous; wherefore his offering was the offering of a righteous man, of a man made righteous first ; and so the text saith, " By faith Abel offered unto God a more excellent sacrifice than Cain, by which he obtained witness that he was righteous," (Heb. xi. 4,) that is antecedent to his offering ; for he had faith in Christ to come, by which he was made righteous ; he also had the spirit of faith, by which he was possessed with a righteous principle ; and so being in this manner made righteous, righteous before God, and also principled to work, he comes and offereth his more acceptable sacrifice to God. For this all will grant, namely, that the works of a righteous man are more excellent than are even the best works of the wicked. Hence Cain's works came behind, for God had not made him righteous, had no respect unto his person, had not given him the Spirit and faith, whereby alone men are made capable to offer acceptably : " But to Cain and to his offering, he [the Lord] had no respect." From all which it is manifest, that the person must be accepted, before the duty performed can be pleasing unto God ; and if the person must first be accepted, it is evident that the person must first be righteous; but if the person be righteous before he doth good, then it follows that he is made righteous by righteousness that is none of his own, that he hath had no hand in, further than to re- ceive it as the gracious gift of God. Deny this, and it follows that God accepteth men without respect to righteousness ; and then what follows that, but that Christ is dead in vain ?

We must not therefore be deceived, " He that doth righteousness is righteous, even as he [the Lord] is righteous." (1 John iii. 7.) He doth not say, he that doth righteousness shall be righteous; as if his doing works would make him so before God ; but he that doth righteousness *is* righteous,

antecedent to his doing righteousness. And it must be thus understood, else that which follows signifies nothing; for he saith, "He that doth righteousness is righteous, even as he [the Lord his God] is righteous." But how is the Lord righteous? Even antecedent to his works. The Lord was righteous before he wrought righteous- ness in the world; and even so are we, to wit, every child of God. " As he is, so are we, in this world." (1 John iv. 17.)

But we must in this admit of this difference ; the Lord was eternally and essentially righteous before he did any work, but we are imputatively righteous, and also made so by a second work of creation, before we do good works. It holds therefore only as to order ; God was righteous before he made the world, and we are righteous before we do good works.

Thus therefore we have described the righteous man.

(1.) He is one whom God makes righteous, by reckoning or imputation.

(2.) He is one that God makes righteous by pos- sessing of him with a principle of righteousness.

(3.) He is one that is practically righteous.

Nor dare I give a narrower description of a righteous man than this; nor otherwise than thus.

1. I dare not give a narrower description of a righteous man than this, because whoever pretends to justification, if he be not sanctified, pretends to what he is not ; and whoever pretends to sanctifi- cation, if he shows not the fruits thereof by a holy life, he deceiveth his own heart, and pro- fesseth but in vain.

2. Nor dare I give this description otherwise than thus, because there is a real distinction to be put between that righteousness by which we should be just before God, and that which is in us a principle of sanctification ; the first being the obedience of the Son of God without us, the second being the work of the Spirit in our hearts.

3. There is also a difference to be put betwixt the principle by which we work righteousness, and the works themselves ; as a difference is to be put betwixt the cause and the effect, the tree and the apple.

II. I come now to the second thing into which we are to inquire, and that is,

What are the desires of a righteous man?

My way of handling this question shall be, first, to speak of the nature of desire in general, and then to show you more particularly what are the desires of the righteous.

1. For the first; *desires in general* may be thus described :—they are the workings of the heart or mind, after that of which the soul is persuaded that it is good to be enjoyed; this, I say, is so without respect to regulation ; for we speak not now of good desires, but of desires themselves, even as they flow from the heart of a human

creature; I say, desires are, or may be called, the working of the heart after this or that; the strong motions of the mind unto it.

(1.) Hence the love of women to their husbands is called "their desires," (Gen. iii. 16;) and the wife is also called "the desire of thine," [the husband's] "eye." (Ezek. xxiv. 16.) Also love to women, to make her one's wife, is called "by the name of desire." (Deut. xxi. 11.) Now, how strong the motions or passions of love are, who is there that is an utter stranger thereto? (Sol. Song viii. 6, 7.)

(2.) Hunger is also a most vehement thing: and that which is called "hunger" in one place, is called "desire" in another; and he desired "to be fed with the crumbs which fell from the rich man's table." (Luke xvi. 21.)

(3.) Exceeding lustings are called "desires," to show the vehemency of desires. (Ps. cxvi. 14; lxxvii. 27—30.)

(4.) Longings, pantings, thirstings, prayers, &c., if there be any life in them, are all fruits of a desirous soul.

(5.) Desires, therefore, flow from the consideration of the goodness, or profitableness, or pleasureableness of a thing: yea, all desires flow from thence; for a man desires not that about which he has had no consideration, nor that neither on which he has thought, if he doth not judge it will yield him something worth desiring.

When Eve saw that the forbidden fruit was a beautiful tree (though her sight deceived her,) then she desired it, and took thereof herself, and gave to her husband, and he did eat; yea, saith the text, "When she saw that it was a tree to be desired, to make one wise, she took." (Gen. iii. 6.)

(6.) Hence that which is called "coveting" in one place is called "desiring" in another; for desires are craving; and by desires a man seeks to enjoy what is not his. (Exod. xx. 17. Deut. v. 21.)

From all these things, therefore, we see what desire is. It is the working of the heart, after that which the soul is persuaded that it is good to be enjoyed; and of them there are these two effects: One is—on a supposition that the soul is not satisfied with what it has—to cause the soul to range and hunt through the world for something that may fill up that vacancy that yet the soul finds in itself, and would have supplied. Hence desires are said to be wandering, and the soul said to walk by them: "better is the sight of the eyes than the wandering of the desire," (Eccles. vi. 8, 9,) or than the walking of the soul. Desires are hunting things; and how many things do some empty souls seek after, both as to the world, and also as to religion, who have desirous minds! The second effect is, if desires be strong, they carry all away with them. They are like Samson, they will pull down the gates of a city; but they will go out abroad. Nothing can stop the current of desires, but the enjoyment of the thing desired,

or a change of opinion as to the worth or want of worth of the thing that is desired.

2. But we will now come to the thing more particularly intended, which is, to show, *what are the desires of the righteous*. This is that which the text calls us to the consideration of, because it saith, "The desire of the righteous shall be granted."

We have hitherto spoken of desires, as to the nature of them, without respect to them as good or bad; but now we shall speak to them, as they are the effects of a sanctified mind, as they are the breathings, pantings, lusting, hungerings, and thirstings of a righteous man.

The text says, "The desire of the righteous shall be granted;" what then are the desires of the righteous? Now I will, first, speak to their desires in the general, or with reference to them as to their bulk; secondly, I will speak to them, more particularly, as they work this way and that.

First. For their desires in the general: the same Solomon that saith, "The desire of the righteous shall be granted," saith also, "The desire of the righteous is only good." (Prov. xi. 23.)

This text giveth us, in the general, a description of the desires of a righteous man, and a sharp and smart description it is: for where, may some say, is then the righteous man, or the man that hath none but good desires? and if it be answered they are good in the main, or good in the general, yet that will seem to come short of an answer: for in that he saith, "The desires of the righteous are only good," it is as much as to say, that a righteous man has none but good desires, or desireth nothing but things that are good. Wherefore, before we go any further, I must labour to reconcile the experience of good men with this text, which thus gives us a description of the desires of the righteous.

A righteous man, then, is to be considered *more generally*, or *more strictly*.

1. *More generally*, as he consisteth of the whole man, of flesh and spirit, of body and soul, of grace and nature. Now consider him thus, and you can by no means reconcile the text with his experience, nor his experience with the text. For as he is body, flesh, and nature, (for all these are with him, though he is a righteous man,) so he has desires vastly different from those described by this text, vastly differing from what is good; yea, what is it not, that is naught, that the flesh and nature, even of a righteous man, will not desire? "Do ye think that the scripture saith in vain, the spirit that dwelleth in us lusteth to envy?" (James iv. 5.) And again, "In me (that is, in my flesh,) dwelleth no good thing." (Rom. vii. 18.) And again, "The flesh lusteth against the spirit." (Gal. v. 17.) And again, The lusts thereof do "war against the soul." (1 Pet. ii. 11.)

From all these texts we find, that a righteous man has other workings, lusts, and desires, than such only that are good; here then, if we consider of a righteous man thus generally, is no place of agreement betwixt him and this text.

We must then consider of him, in the next place, more strictly, as he may and is to be distinguished from his flesh, his carnal lusts, and sinful nature.

2. *More strictly.* Then a righteous man is taken sometimes as to or for his best part, or as he is *a second creation;* and so, or as so considered, "His desires are only good."

(1.) He is taken sometimes as to or for his best part, or as he is a second creation, as these scriptures declare: "If any man be in Christ, he is a new creature." "All things are become new," (2 Cor. v. 17,) created in Christ Jesus, "born of God," (John iii. 3. 1 John iii. 9,) become "heavenly things," (Heb. ix. 23,) renewed "after the image of him that created them," (Col. iii. 10;) and the like. By all which places, the sinful flesh, the old man, the law of sin, the outward man—all which are corrupt according to the deceitful lusts—are excluded, and so pared off from the man, as he is righteous; for his "delight in the law of God" is "after the inward man." (Rom. vii. 22.) And Paul himself was forced thus to distinguish of himself, before he could come to make a right judgment in this matter; saith he, "For that which I do, I allow not: for what I would, that do I not; but what I hate, that do I." (Rom. vii. 15.) See you not here how he cleaves himself in twain, severing himself as he is spiritual, from himself as he is carnal; and ascribeth his motions to what is good to himself only as he is spiritual, or the new man: "If then I do that which I would not, I consent unto the law that it is good." (Rom. vii. 16.)

But I trow, Sir, your consenting to what is good, is not by that part which doth do what you would not. "No, no," saith he, "that which doth do what I would not, I disown, and count it no part of sanctified Paul." "Now then it is no more I that do it, but sin that dwelleth in me. For I know that in me (that is, in my flesh,) dwelleth no good thing: for to will is present with me; but how to perform that which is good, I find not. For the good that I would, I do not; but the evil which I would not, that I do : Now, if I do that I would not, it is no more I that do it, but sin that dwelleth in me." (Rom. vii. 17—20.) Thus, you see, Paul is forced to make two men of himself, saying, "I and I; I do not; I do, I would not do; what I hate, that I do." Now it cannot be the same I, unto whom these contraries are applied; but his sinful flesh is one I, and his godly mind the other : and, indeed, so he concludes it in this chapter, saying, "So then with the mind I myself serve the law of God, but with the flesh the law of sin." (Rom. vii. 25.)

Thus, therefore, the Christian man must distinguish concerning himself; and doing so, he shall find, though he has flesh, and as he is such, he hath lusts contrary to God; yet as he is a new creature, he allows not, but hates the motions and desires of the flesh, consents to, and wills and delights in the law of God. Yea, as a new creature, he can do nothing else; for the new man, inward man, or hidden man of the heart, being the immediate work of the Holy Ghost, and consisting only of that which is divine and heavenly, cannot breathe, or act, or desire to act, in ways and courses that are carnal. Wherefore, in this sense, or as the righteous man is thus considered, "his desires are only good."

(2.) As the righteous man must here be taken for the best part, for the I that would do good, for the I that hates the evil; so again, we must consider of the desires of this righteous man, as they flow from that fountain of grace, which is the Holy Ghost within him; and as they are immediately mixed with those foul channels, in and through which they must pass, before they can be put forth into acts. For though the desire, as to its birth, and first being, is only good; yet before it comes into much motion, it gathers that from the defilements of the passages through which it comes, as makes it to bear a tang of flesh, and weakness in the skirts of it; and the evil that dwells in us so universal, and also always so ready, that as sure as there is any motions to what is good, so sure evil is present with it; for when or whenever I would do good, says Paul, "evil is present with me." (Rom. vii. 21.) Hence it follows, that all our graces, and so our desires, receive disadvantage by our flesh, that mixing itself with what is good, and so abates the excellency of the good.

There is a spring that yieldeth water good and clear, but the channels through which this water comes to us are muddy, foul, or dirty: now, of the channels the waters receive a disadvantage, and so come to us as savouring of what came not with them from the fountain, but from the channels. This is the cause of the coolness and of the weakness, of the flatness and of the many extravagances, that attend some of our desires. They come warm from the Spirit and grace of God in us; but as hot water running through cold pipes, or as clear water running through dirty conveyances, so our desires gather soil.

You read in Solomon's Ecclesiastes of a time when desires fail, for that man "goeth to his long home." (Eccles. xii. 5.) And as to good desires, there is not one of them, when we are in our prime, but they fail also as to the perfecting of that which a man desires to do. "To will is present with me," says Paul, "but how to perform that which is good I find not." (Rom. vii. 18.)

To will or to desire, that is present with me, but when I have willed or desired to do, to perform is what I cannot attain to. But why not attain to a performance? Why, says he, I find a "law in my members warring against the law of my mind," (Rom. vii. 23;) and this law takes me prisoner, and brings me "into captivity to the law of sin which is in my members." (Rom. vii. 23.) Now, where things willed and desired meet with such obstructions, no marvel if our willing and desiring, though they set out lustily at the beginning, come yet lame home in conclusion.

There is a man, when he first prostrates himself before God, doth it with desires as warm as fire-coals; but erewhile he finds, for all that, that the mettle of those desires, were it not revived with fresh supplies, would be quickly spent and grow cold. But yet the desire is good, and only good, as it comes from the breathing of the Spirit of God within us. We must, therefore, as I said, distinguish betwixt what is good and that which doth annoy it, as gold is to be distinguished from the earth and dross that doth attend it. The man that believed desired to believe better, and so cries out, "Lord, I believe; help thou my unbelief." (Mark ix. 24.) The man that feared God desired to fear him better, saying, I "desire to fear thy name." (Neh. i. 11.)

But these desires failed as to the performance of what was begun, so that they were forced to come off but lamely, as to their faith and fear they had; yet the desires were true, good, and such as was accepted of God by Jesus Christ: not according to what they had not, but as to those good motions which they had. Distinguish then the desires of the righteous in the nature of them, from that corruption and weakness of ours that cleaveth to them, and then again, "they are only good."

(3.) There is another thing to be considered, and that is, the different frames that our inward man is in, while we live as pilgrims in the world. A man, as he is not always well without, so neither is he always well within. Our inward man is subject to transient, though not to utter decays. And as it is when the outward man is sick, strength and stomach, and lust or desire, fails, so it is when our inward man has caught a cold likewise. (Ezek. xxxiv. 4. Isa. i. 5.)

The inward man I call the new creature, of which the Spirit of God is the support, as my soul supports my body. But, I say, this new man is not always well. He knows nothing that knows not this. Now being sick, things fail. As when a man is not in health of body, his pulse beats so as to declare that he is sick, so when a man is not well within, his inward pulse, which are his desires—for I count the desires for the pulse of the inward man—they also declare that the man is not well within. They beat too little after God, weak and faintly after grace; they also have their halts: they beat not evenly, as when the soul is well, but so as to manifest all is not well there.

We read that the church of Sardis was under sore sickness, insomuch that some of her things were quite dead, and they that were not so were yet "ready to die," (Rev. iii. 2;) yet "life is life," we say, and as long as there is a pulse, or breath, though breath scarce able to shake a feather, we cast not away all hope of life. Desires, then, though they be weak, are, notwithstanding, true desires, if they be the desires of the righteous thus described, and therefore are truly good, according to our text.

David says, he "opened his mouth and panted," for he "longed for" God's commandments. (Ps. cxix. 131.) This was a sickness, but not such a one as we have been speaking of. The spouse also cried out that she was "sick of love." (Sol. Song v. 8.) Such sickness would do us good, for in it the pulse beats strongly well.

Obj. 1. But it may be objected, I am yet in doubt of the goodness of my desires, both because my desires run both ways, and because those that run toward sin and the world seem more and stronger than those that run after God, and Christ, and grace.

Ans. There is not a Christian under heaven but has desires run both ways, as is manifest from what hath been said already. Flesh will be flesh; grace shall not make it otherwise. By flesh I mean that body of sin and death that dwelleth in the godly. (Rom. vi. 6.) As grace will act according to its nature, so sin will act according to the nature of sin. (Eph. ii. 3.) Now the flesh has desires, and the desires of the flesh and of the mind are both one in the ungodly; thank God it is not so in thee. The flesh, I say, hath its desires in the godly; hence it is said to lust enviously; it lusts against the Spirit: "The flesh lusteth against the Spirit." (Gal. v. 17.) And if it be so audacious as to fly in the face of the Holy Ghost, wonder that thou art not wholly carried away with it.

Obj. 2. But those desires that run to the world and sin seem most and strongest in me.

Ans. The works of the flesh are manifest, (Gal. v. 19,) that is, more plainly discovered even in the godly, than are the works of the Holy Ghost. And this their manifestation ariseth from these following particulars:—(1.) We know the least appearance of a sin better by its native hue than we know a grace of the Spirit. (2.) Sin is sooner felt in its bitterness to and upon a sanctified soul than is the grace of God. A little aloes will be sooner tasted than will much sweet, though mixed therewith. (3.) Sin is dreadful and murderous in the sight of a sanctified soul: wherefore the apprehending of that makes us often forget, and often question whether we have any grace or no. (4.) Grace lies deep in the hidden part, (Ps. li. 6,) but sin lies high, and floats above in the flesh; wherefore it is easier and oftener seen than is the grace of God. The little fishes swim on the top of the water, but the biggest and best keep down below, and so are seldomer seen. (5.) Grace, as to quantity, seems less than sin. What is leaven, or a grain of mustard-seed, (Matt. xiii. 31—33,) to the bulky lump of a body of death. (6.) Sin is seen by its own darkness, and also in the light of the Spirit; but the Spirit itself neither discovers itself, nor yet its graces, by every glance of its own light. (7.) A man may have the Spirit busily at work in him; he may also have many of his graces in their vigorous acts, and yet may be greatly ignorant of either: wherefore we are not competent judges in this case. There may a thousand acts of grace pass through thy soul, and thou be sensible of few, if any of them. (8.) Do you think that he that repents, believes, loves, fears, or humbles himself, before God, and acts in other graces too, doth always know what he doth? No, no; grace many times, even in a man, is acted by him, unawares unto him? Did Gideon, think you, believe that he was so strong in grace as he was? Nay; was he not ready to give the lie to the angel, when he told him God was with him? (Judges vi. 12, 13.) Or, what do you think of David, when he said he was cast off from God's eyes? (Ps. xxxi. 22;) or of Heman, when he said, he was free among them whom God remembered no more? (Ps. lxxxviii. 5.) Did these, then, see their graces so clear, as they saw themselves by their sins to be unworthy ones? (9.) I tell you it is a rare thing for some Christians to see their graces; but a thing very common for such to see their sins; yea, and to feel them too in their lusts and desires, to the shaking of their souls.

Quest. But since I have lusts and desires both ways, how shall I know to which my soul adheres?

Ans. This may be known thus, (1.) Which wouldst thou have prevail, the desires of the flesh, or the lusts of the Spirit? Whose side art thou of? Doth not thy soul now inwardly say, and that with a strong indignation, O let God, let grace, let my desires that are good, prevail against my flesh, for Jesus Christ his sake? (2.) What kind of secret wishes hast thou in thy soul, when thou feelest the lusts of thy flesh to rage? Dost thou not inwardly, and with indignation against sin, say, "O that I might never, never feel one such motion more! O that my soul were so full of grace, that there might be no longer room for ever the least lust to come into my thoughts!" (3.) What kind of thoughts hast thou of thyself, now thou seest these desires of thine that are good, so briskly opposed by those that are bad? Dost thou not say, "Oh! I am the basest of creatures, I could even spew at myself? There is no man in all the world, in my eyes, so loathsome as myself is. I abhor myself, a toad is not so vile as I am. O Lord, let me be anything but a sinner—anything, so thou subduest mine iniquities for me." (4.) How dost thou like the discovery of that which thou thinkest is grace in other men? Dost thou not cry out, "O, I bless them in my heart! O, methinks grace is the greatest beauty in the world! Yea, I could be content to live and die with those people that have the grace of God in their souls.

A hundred times, and a hundred, when I have been upon my knees before God, I have desired, were it the will of God, that I might be in their condition." (5.) How art thou, when thou thinkest that thou thyself hast grace? "O, then," says the soul, "I am as if I could leap out of myself; joy, joy, joy then is with my heart. It is, methinks, the greatest mercy under heaven to be made a gracious man.

And is it thus with thy soul indeed? Happy man! It is grace that has thy soul, though sin at present works in thy flesh. Yea, all these breathings are the very actings of grace, even of the grace of desire, of love, of humility, and of the fear of God within thee. Be of good courage, thou art on the right side. Thy desires are only good; for that thou hast desired against thy sin, thy sinful self; which indeed is not thyself, but sin that dwells in thee.

Second. I come next to speak of desires more distinctly, or particularly, as they work this way and that. First, then, the desires of the righteous are either such as they would have accomplished here, or else such as they know they cannot come at the enjoyment of, till after death.

For the first of these, *the desires of the righteous are for such good things as they would have accomplished here*—that is, in this world—while they are on this side glory. And they, in general, are comprised under these two general heads: first, communion with their God in spirit, or spiritual communion with him; secondly, the liberty of the enjoyment of his holy ordinances. And indeed this second is that they may both attain to, and have the first maintained with them. But for the first:—

1. *They desire now communion with God.* "With my soul," said she, "have I desired thee in the night, yea, with my spirit within me will I seek thee early." (Isa. xxvi. 9.) The reason of this she renders in the verse foregoing, saying, "the desire of our soul is to thy name, and to the remembrance of thee." (Isa. xxvi. 8.)

Now thus to desire, declares one already made righteous; for herein there appears a mind reconciled to God. Wherefore the wicked are set on the other side, even in that opposition to these; "therefore they say unto God, depart from us, for we desire not the knowledge of thy ways." (Job xxi. 14.) They neither love his presence, nor to be frequenters of his ordinances. "What is the Almighty that we should serve him? and what profit should we have if we pray unto him?" (Job xxi. 15.) So again, speaking of the wicked, he saith, "Ye have said it is in vain to serve God, and what profit is it that we have kept his ordinance?" (Mal. iii. 14.)

This, then, to desire truly to have communion with God, is the property of a righteous man—of a righteous man only; for this desire ariseth from a suitableness which there is in the righteous unto God. "Whom," said the psalmist, "have I in heaven but thee? and there is none upon earth that I desire beside thee." (Ps. lxxiii. 25.) This could never be the desire of a man, were he not a righteous man—a man with a truly sanctified mind. "The carnal mind is enmity against God, for it is not subject to the law of God, neither indeed can be." (Rom. viii. 7.)

When Moses, the man of God, was with the children of Israel in the wilderness, he prayed that God would give them his presence unto Canaan, or else to let them die in that place. It was death to him to think of being in the wilderness without God. And he said unto God, "If thy presence go not with me, carry us not up hence." (Exod. xxxiii. 15.)

Here, then, are the desires of a righteous man, namely, after communion with God. He chooses rather to be a stranger with God in the world, than to be a citizen of the world, and a stranger to God. "For I am," said David, "a stranger with thee, and a sojourner, as all my fathers were." (Ps. xxxix. 12.) Indeed he that walketh with God, is but a stranger to this world. And the righteous man's desires are to, for, and after communion with God, though he be so.

The reason of these desires are many.

(1.) In communion with God is life and favour; yea, the very presence of God with a man is a token of it. (Ps. xxx. 3—5.) For by his presence he helps, succours, relieves, and supports the hearts of his people, and therefore is communion with him desired: "I will" said David, "behave myself wisely in a perfect way. O when wilt thou come unto me?" (Ps. ci. 2.)

(2.) The pleasures that such a soul finds in God that has communion with him, are surpassing all pleasures and delights, yea, infinitely surpassing them: "In thy presence is fulness of joy, and at thy right hand there are pleasures for evermore." (Ps. xvi. 11.) Upon this account he is called the desire of all nations—of all in all nations that know him.

(3.) Job desired God's presence, that he might reason with God. "Surely," said he, "I would speak to the Almighty, and I desire to reason with God." And again, "O that one [God] would hear me! behold, my desire is that the Almighty would answer me." (Job xxxi. 35.) But why doth Job thus desire to be in the presence of God? Oh! he knew that God was good, and that he would speak to him that which would do him good. Will he plead against me with his great power? No; but he would put strength into me. There the righteous might dispute with him; so should I be delivered for ever from my judge. (Job xxiii. 6, 7.)

(4.) God's presence is the safety of a man: If God be with one, who can hurt one? As if he said, "If God be for us, who can be against us?" (Rom. viii. 31.) Now, if so much safety flows from God's being for one, how safe are we when God is with us? "The beloved of the Lord,"

said Moses, "shall dwell in safety by him, and the Lord shall cover him all the day long, and he shall dwell between his shoulders." (Deut. xxxiii. 12.)

(5.) God's presence keeps the heart awake to joy, and will make a man sing in the night. (Job xxxv. 10.) "Can the children of the bridechamber mourn, while the bridegroom is with them?" (Matt. ix. 15.) God's presence is feasting, and feasting is made for mirth. (Eccles. x. 18. Rev. iii. 20.)

(6.) God's presence keeps the heart tender, and makes it ready to fall in with what is made known, as duty or privilege. (Isa. lxiv. 1.) "I will run the way of thy commandments," said the Psalmist, "when thou shalt enlarge my heart." (Ps. cxix. 32.)

(7.) The presence of God makes a man affectionately and sincerely good; yea, makes him willing to be searched and stripped from all the remains of iniquity. (Ps. xxvi. 1—3.)

(8.) What shall I say? God's presence is renewing, transforming, seasoning, sanctifying, commanding, sweetening, and lightening to the soul. Nothing like it in all the world; his presence supplies all wants, heals all maladies, saves from all dangers; is life in death, heaven in hell; all in all. No marvel then if the presence of, and communion with God, is become the desire of a righteous man. (Ps. xxvi. 9.)

(9.) To conclude this, by the presence of God being with us, it is known to ourselves, and to others, what we are. "If thy presence," said Moses, "go not with me, carry us not up hence. For wherein shall it be known here, that I and thy people have found grace in thy sight. Is it not in that thou goest with us? So shall we be separated. I and thy people, from all the people that are upon the face of the earth." (Exod. xxxiii. 15, 16.)

They are then best known to themselves. They know they are his people, because God's presence is with them. Therefore he saith, "My presence shall go with thee, and I will give thee rest," (Exod. xxxiii. 14;) that is, let thee know that thou hast found grace in my sight, and art accepted of me. For if God withdraws himself, or hides his presence from his people, it is hard for them to bear up in the steadfast belief that they belong to him. "Be not silent unto me, O Lord," said David, "lest I be like unto them that go down into the pit." (Ps. xxviii. 1.) "Be not silent unto me," that is, as he has it in another place, "Hide not thy face from me. Hear me speedily, O Lord," saith he, "my spirit faileth; hide not thy face from me, lest I be like unto them that go down into the pit." (Ps. cxliii. 7.) So that God's presence is the desire of the righteous for this cause also, even for that by it they gather, that God delighteth in them: "By this I know that thou favourest me, because mine enemy doth not triumph over me." (Ps. xli. 11.)

And is this all? No: "And as for me, thou upholdest me in mine integrity, and settest me before thy face for ever." (Ps. xli. 12.)

As by the presence of God being with us, we know ourselves to be the people of God, so by this presence of God, the world themselves are sometimes convinced who we are also.

(1.) Thus, Abimelech saw that God was with Abraham. (Gen. xxi. 22.)

(2.) Thus, Abimelech saw that God was with Isaac. (Gen. xxvi. 28, 29.)

(3.) Pharoah knew that God was with Joseph. (Gen. xli. 38.)

(4.) Saul saw and knew that the Lord was with David. (1 Sam. xviii. 28.)

(5.) Saul's servant knew that the Lord was with Samuel. (1 Sam. ix. 6.)

(6.) Belshazzar's queen knew also that God was with Daniel. (Dan. v. 11.)

(7.) Darius knew also that God was with Daniel. (Dan. vi. 16, 26.)

(8.) And when the enemy saw the boldness of Peter and John, they took knowledge of them that they had been with Jesus. (Acts iv. 13.)

(9.) The girl that was a witch, knew that Paul was a servant of the Most High God. (Acts xvi. 17.)

There is a glory upon them that have God with them, a glory that sometimes glances and flashes out into the faces of those that behold the people of God: "And all that sat in the council, looking steadfastly on him, saw his [Stephen's] face, as it had been the face of an angel," (Acts vi. 15;) such rays of divine Majesty did show themselves therein.

The reason is, for that, 1. Such have with them the wisdom of God. (2 Sam. xiv. 17—20.) 2. Such also have special bowels and compassions of God for others. 3. Such have more of his majesty upon them than others. (1 Sam. xvi. 4.) 4. Such, their words and ways, their carriages and doings, are attended with that of God that others are destitute of. (1 Sam. iii. 19, 20.) 5. Such are holier, and of more convincing lives in general, than other people are. (2 Kings iv. 9.) Now there is both comfort and honour in this; for what comfort like that of being a holy man of God? And what honour like that of being a holy man of God? This therefore is the desire of the righteous, to wit, To have communion with God. Indeed none like God, and to be desired as he, in the thoughts of a righteous man.

2. And this leads me to the second thing, namely, *The liberty of the enjoyment of his holy ordinances;* for, next to God himself, nothing is so dear to a righteous man, as the enjoyment of his holy ordinances.

"One thing," said David, "have I desired of the Lord, that will I seek after," namely, "that I may dwell in the house of the Lord all the days of my life, to behold the beauty of the Lord, and to inquire in his temple." (Ps. xxvii. 4.)

The temple of the Lord was the dwelling-house of God; there he recorded his name, and there he made known himself unto his people. (Ps. xi. 4. Hab. ii. 20.) Wherefore this was the cause why David so earnestly desired to dwell there too, "To behold," saith he, "the beauty of the Lord, and to inquire in his temple." (Ps. xxvii. 4.)

There he had promised his presence to his people, yea, and to bring thither a blessing for them: "In all places where I record my name I will come unto thee, and I will bless thee." (Exod. xx. 24.)

For this cause, therefore, as I said, it is why the righteous do so desire that they may enjoy the liberty of the ordinances and appointments of their God; to wit, that they may attain to, and have communion maintained with him.

Alas! the righteous are as it were undone, if God's ordinances be taken from them. "How amiable are thy tabernacles, O Lord of hosts. My soul longeth, yea, even fainteth for the courts of the Lord, my heart and my flesh crieth out for the living God." (Ps. lxxxiv. 1, 2.) Behold what a taking the good man was in, because at this time he could not attain to so frequent a being in the temple of God as his soul desired. It even longed and fainted, yea, and his heart and his flesh cried out for the God that dwelt in the temple at Jerusalem.

Yea, he seems in the next words to envy the very birds that could more commonly frequent the temple than he: "The sparrow," saith he, "hath found her a house, and the swallow a nest for herself, where she may lay her young, even thine altars, O Lord, my King, and my God." (Ps. lxxxiv. 3.) And then blesseth all them that had the liberty of temple worship, saying, "Blessed are they that dwell in thine house, they will be still praising thee." (Ps. lxxxiv. 4.) Then he cries up the happiness of those that in Zion do appear before God. (Ps. lxxxiv. 7.) After this he cries out unto God, that he would grant him to be partaker of this high favour, saying, "O Lord God of hosts, hear my prayer," &c. (Ps. lxxxiv. 8.) "For a day in thy courts is better than a thousand: I had rather be a door-keeper in the house of my God, than to dwell in the tents of wickedness." (Ps. lxxxiv. 10.)

But why is all this? what aileth the man thus to express himself? Why, as I said, the temple was the great ordinance of God; there was his true worship performed, there God appeared, and there his people were to find him. This was, I say, the reason why the psalmist chose out, and desired this one thing, above all the things that were under heaven, even to behold there "the beauty of the Lord, and to inquire in his temple." (Ps. xxvii. 4.)

There were to be seen the shadows of things in the heavens, the candlestick, the table of shew-bread, (the holiest of all, where was the golden censer,) the ark of the covenant, overlaid round about with gold, the golden pot that had manna, Aaron's rod that budded, the tables of the covenant, and the cherubims of glory over-shadowing the mercy-seat, which were all of them then things by which God showed himself merciful to them.

Do you think that love-letters are not desired between lovers? Why these, God's ordinances, they are his love-letters, and his love-tokens too. No marvel then if the righteous do so desire them: "More to be desired are they than gold, yea, than much fine gold; sweeter also than honey and the honey-comb." (Ps. xix. 10.)

Yea, this judgment wisdom itself passes upon these things. "Receive," saith he, "my instruction, and not silver; and knowledge rather than choice gold. For wisdom is better than rubies; and all the things that may be desired are not to be compared to it." (Prov. viii. 10, 11.)

For this cause therefore are the ordinances of God so much desired by the righteous. In them they meet with God; and by them they are builded, and nourished up to eternal life.

"As new-born babes," says Peter, "desire the sincere milk of the word, that ye may grow thereby." (1 Pet. ii. 2.) As milk is nourishing to children, so is the word heard, read, and meditated on, to the righteous. Therefore it is their desire.

He [Christ] made himself known to them in breaking of bread: who would not then, that loves to know him, be present at such an ordinance? (Luke xxiv. 35.) Ofttimes the Holy Ghost, in the comfortable influence of it, has accompanied the baptized in the very act of administering it. Therefore, in the way of thy judgments or appointments, O Lord, thy people have waited for thee; "the desire of their soul is to thy name, and to the remembrance of thee." (Isa. xxvi. 8.)

Church-fellowship, or the communion of saints, is the place where the Son of God loveth to walk; his first walking was in Eden, there he converted our first parents. And "Come, my beloved, says he, let us get up early to the vineyards; let us see if the vine flourish, whether the tender grapes appear, and the pomegranates bud forth: there will I give thee my loves." (Sol. Song vii. 11, 13.)

Church-fellowship, rightly managed, is the glory of all the world. No place, no community, no fellowship, is adorned and bespangled with those beauties as is a church rightly knit together to their head, and lovingly serving one another. "In his temple doth every one speak of his glory." (Ps. xxix. 9.) Hence the church is called the place of God's desire on earth. "This is my rest, here I will dwell for ever, for I have desired it." (Ps. cxxxii. 14.) And again, thus the church confesseth, when she saith, "I am my beloved's, and his desire is toward me." (Sol. Song vii. 10.)

No marvel then if this be the one thing that David desired, and that which he would seek after, namely, "to dwell in the house of the Lord all the days of his life." And this also shows you the reason why God's people of old used to venture so hardly for ordinances, and to get to them "with the peril of their lives, because of the sword of the wilderness." (Lam. v. 9.)

They were their bread, they were their water, they were their milk, they were their honey. Here the sanctuary was called "the desire of their eyes, and that which their soul pitieth," or the pity of their soul. (Ezek. xxiv. 21.) They had rather have died than lost it, or than that it should have been burned down as it was.

When the children of Israel had lost the ark, they counted that the glory was departed from Israel. But when they had lost all, what a complaint made they then! "He hath violently taken away his tabernacle, as if it were of a garden, he hath destroyed the places of the assembly: the Lord hath caused the solemn feasts and sabbaths to be forgotten in Zion, and hath despised in the indignation of his anger the king and the priest." (Lam. ii. 6.) Wherefore, upon this account it was that the church in those days counted the punishment of her iniquity greater than the punishment of Sodom. (Lam. iv. 6.)

By these few hints you may perceive what is the "desire of the righteous." But this is spoken of with reference to things present—to things that the righteous desire to enjoy while they are here: communion with God while here, and his ordinances in their purity while here. I come, therefore, in the second place, to show you, that the righteous have desires that reach further—desires that have so long a neck as to look into the world to come.

Second, then, the desires of the righteous are after that which yet *they know cannot be enjoyed till after death.* And those are comprehended under these two heads: first, they desire that presence of their Lord which is personal; secondly, they desire to be in that country where their Lord personally is—that heavenly country.

1. For the first of these, says Paul, "I have a desire to depart, and to be with Christ." Thus you have it in Phil. i. 23, "I have a desire to be with Christ."

In our first sort of desires, I told you, that the righteous desired spiritual communion with God; and now I tell you they desire to be with Christ's person—"I have a desire to be with Christ;" that is, with his person, that I may enjoy his personal presence, such a presence of his as we are not capable to enjoy while here. Hence he says, "I have a desire to depart, that I might be with him;" "knowing," as he says in another place, "that while we are at home in the body, we are [and cannot but be] absent from the Lord." (2 Cor. v. 6.)

Now this desire, as I said, is a desire that hath a long neck; for it can look over the brazen wall of this, quite into another world; and as it hath a long neck, so it is very forcible and mighty in its operation.

(1.) This desire breeds a divorce—a complete divorce—betwixt the soul and all inordinate love and affections to relations and worldly enjoyments. This desire makes a married man live as if he had no wife, (1 Cor. vii. 29,) a rich man live as if he possessed not what he has, &c. This is a soul-sequestering desire. This desire makes a man willing rather to be absent from all enjoyments, that he may be present with the Lord. This is a famous desire; none hath this desire but a righteous man. There are that profess much love to Christ, that yet never had such a desire in them all their life long. No; the relation that they stand in to the world, together with those many flesh-pleasing accommodations with which they are surrounded, would never yet suffer such a desire to enter into their hearts.

(2.) The strength of this desire is such, that it is ready, so far forth as it can, to dissolve that sweet knot of union that is betwixt body and soul, a knot more dear to a reasonable creature than that can be which is betwixt wife and husband, parent and child, or a man and his estate. For even " all that a man has will he give for his life," and to keep body and soul firmly knit together. But now, when this desire comes, this " silver cord is loosed," is loosed by consent. This desire grants to him that comes to dissolve this union leave to do it delightfully. " We are confident, I say, and willing rather to be absent from the body, and to be present with the Lord." (2 Cor. v. 8.) Yea, this desire makes this flesh, this mortal life, a burden. The man that has this desire, exercises self-denial, while he waits till his desired change comes. For were it not that the will of God is that he should live, and did he not hope that his life might be serviceable to the truth and church of God, he would not have wherewith to cool the heart of this desire, but would rather in a holy passion, with holy Job cry out, " I loathe [or I abhor] it, I would not live alway; let me alone [that I may die] for my days are vanity." (Job vii. 16.)

(3.) The strength of this desire shows itself in this also—namely, in that it is willing to grapple with the king of terrors, rather than to be detained from that sweet communion that the soul looks for when it comes into the place where its Lord is. Death is not to be desired for itself; the apostle chose rather to be " clothed upon" with his house " which is from heaven," " that mortality might be swallowed up of life." (2 Cor. v. 2, 4.) But yet rather than he would be absent from the Lord, he was willing to be absent from the body. Death, in the very thoughts of it, is grievous to flesh and blood; and nothing can so master it in our apprehensions, as that by which we attain to these desires. These desires do deal with death, as Jacob's love to Rachael did deal with the seven long years which he was to serve for her. It

made them seem few, or but a little time; now so I say, doth these desires deal with death itself. They make it seem little—nay, a servant, nay, a privilege; for that by that a man may come to enjoy the presence of his beloved Lord. " I have a desire to depart," to go from the world and relations, to go from my body, that great piece of myself; I have a desire to venture the tugs, and pains, and the harsh handling of the king of terrors, so I may be with Jesus Christ. These are desires of the righteous.

Are not these therefore strong desires? Is there not life and mettle in them? Have they not in them power to loose the bands of nature, and to harden the soul against sorrow? Flow they not, think you, from faith of the finest sort, and are they not bred in the bosom of a truly mortified soul? Are these the effects of a purblind spirit? Are they not rather the fruits of an eagle-eyed confidence? Oh, these desires! they are peculiar to the righteous; they are none others but the desires of the righteous.

Quest. But why do the righteous desire to be with Christ?

Ans. And I ask, why doth the wife—that is, as the loving hind—love to be in the presence of her husband?

(1.) Christ in glory is worth the being with. If the man out of whom the Lord Jesus did cast a legion prayed that he might be with him, notwithstanding all the trials that attended him in this life, how can it be but that a righteous man must desire to be with him now he is in glory?

(2.) What we have heard concerning the excellency of his person, the unspeakableness of his love, the greatness of his sufferings, and the things that he still is doing for us, must needs command our souls into a desire to be with him.

(3.) When we have heard of a man among us that has done for us some excellent thing, the next thing that our hearts doth pitch upon is, I would I could set mine eyes upon him. But was ever heard the like of to what Jesus Christ has done for sinners? Who then that hath the faith of him can do otherwise, but desire to be with him? It was that which some time comforted John, that the time was coming that he should see him. But that consideration made him bray like a hart, (Ps. xlii. 1,) to hasten the time that he might set his eyes upon him quickly. (1 John iii. 2. Rev. xxii. 20.)

To see Jesus Christ then, to see him as he is, to see him as he is in glory, is a sight that is worth going from relations, and out of the body, and through the jaws of death to see; for this is to see him head over all, to see him possessed of heaven for his church, to see him preparing of mansion-houses for those his poor ones that are now by his enemies kicked to and fro, like foot-balls, in the world; and is not this a blessed sight?

2. I have a desire to be with him, to see myself with him; this is more blessed still; for a man to

see himself in glory, this is a sight worth seeing. Sometimes I look upon myself, and say, " Where am I now ?" and do quickly return answer to myself again, " Why, I am in an evil world, a great way from heaven, in a sinful body, among devils and wicked men ; sometimes benighted, sometimes beguiled, sometimes fearing, sometimes hoping, sometimes breathing, sometimes dying, and the like." But then I turn the tables, and say, " But where shall I be shortly ? where shall I see myself anon, after a few times more have passed over me ?" And when I can but answer this question thus—" I shall see myself with Jesus Christ," this yields glory, even glory to one's spirit now. No marvel then if the righteous desire to be with Christ.

3. I have a desire to be with Christ ; there the spirits of the just are perfected ; there the spirits of the righteous are as full as they can hold. (Heb. xii. 23.) A sight of Jesus in the word, some know how it will change them " from glory to glory," (2 Cor. iii. 18 ;) but how then shall we be changed and filled, when we shall see him as he is ? " When he shall appear, we shall be like him, for we shall see him as he is." (1 John iii. 2.)

Moses and Elias appeared to Peter, and James, and John at the transfiguration of Christ in glory. How so ? Why, they had been in the heavens, and came thence with some of the glories of heaven upon them. Gild a bit of wood, yea, gild it seven times over, and it must not compare in difference to wood not gilt, to the soul that but a little while has been dipped in glory.

Glory is a strange thing to men that are on this side of the heavens ; it is that which " eye hath not seen, nor ear heard, neither have entered into the heart of man" (1 Cor. ii. 9) to conceive of ; only the Christian has a Word and Spirit, that at times doth give a little of the glimmering thereof unto him.

But, oh ! when he is in the Spirit, and sees in the Spirit, do you think his tongue can tell ? But I say, if the sight of heaven, at so vast a distance, is so excellent a prospect, what will it look like when one is in it ? No marvel, then, if the desires of the righteous are to be with Christ.

Obj. But if this be the character of a righteous man, to desire to depart and to be with Christ, I am none of them, for I never had such a desire in my heart ; no, my fears of perishing will not suffer me either to desire to die to be with Christ, nor that Christ should come to judge the world.

Ans. Though thine is a case that must be excepted, for that thy desires may not as yet be grown so high, yet, if thou art a righteous man, thy heart has in it the very seeds thereof.

There are therefore desires, and desires to desire, as one child can reach so high, and the other can but desire to do so. Thou, if thou art a righteous man, hast desires, these desires ready to put forth into act, when they are grown a little stronger, or when their impediment is removed.

Many times it is with our desires as it is with saffron, it will bloom, and blossom, and be ripe, and all in a night. Tell me, dost thou not desire to desire ? Yea, dost thou not vehemently desire to desire to depart, and to be with Christ ? I know, if thou art a righteous man, thou dost. There is a man sows his field with wheat, but, as he sows, it is covered with great clods : now, that grows as well as the rest, though it runs not upright as yet ; it grows, and yet is kept down, so do thy desires ; and when one shall remove the clod, the blade will soon point upwards.

I know thy mind—that which keeps thee that thou canst not yet arrive to this—to desire to depart and to be with Christ, is, because some strong doubt or clod of unbelief, as to thy eternal welfare, lies hard upon thy desiring spirit. Now let but Jesus Christ remove this clod, and thy desires will quickly start up to be gone. I say, let but Jesus Christ give thee one kiss, and with his lips, as he kisses thee, whisper to thee the forgiveness of thy sins, and thou wilt quickly break out, and say, " Nay, then, Lord, let me die in peace, since my soul is persuaded of thy salvation."

There is a man upon the bed of languishing ; but, oh ! he dare not die, for all is not as he would have it betwixt God and his poor soul ; and many a night he lies thus in great horror of mind ; but do you think that he doth not desire to desire to depart ? Yes, yes, he also waits and cries to God to set his desires at liberty. At last the visitor comes and sets his soul at ease, by persuading of him that he belongs to God : and what then ? Oh ! now let me die, welcome death.

Now he is like the man in Essex, who, when his neighbour at his bedside prayed for him, that God would restore him to health, started up in his bed, and pulled him by the arm, and cried out, " No, no, pray that God will take me away, for to me it is best to go to Christ."

The desires of some good Christians are pinioned, and cannot stir, especially these sort of desires ; but Christ can and will cut the cord some time or other ; and then thou that wouldst shalt be able to say, " I have a desire to depart, and to be with Jesus Christ."

Meantime, be thou earnest to desire to know thy interest in the grace of God ; for there is nothing short of the knowledge of that can make thee desire to depart, that thou mayest be with Christ. This is that that Paul laid as the ground of his desires to be gone : " We know," says he, " that if our earthly house of this tabernacle were dissolved, we have a building of God, an house not made with hands, eternal in the heavens. For in this we groan earnestly, desiring to be clothed upon with our house, which is from heaven." (2 Cor. v. 1, 2.) And know, that if thy desires be right, they will grow as other graces do—from strength to strength ; only in this they can grow no faster than faith grows as to justification, and than hope grows as to glory.

But we will leave this, and come to the second thing.

2. As the righteous men desire to be present with Jesus Christ, so they desire to be with him in that country where he is. (Heb. xi. 14, 25.) "But now they desire a better country, that is, an heavenly; wherefore God is not ashamed to be called their God, for he hath prepared for them a city." (Heb. xi. 16.)

"But now they desire a better country." Here is a comparison. There was another country, to wit, their native country, the country from whence they came out, that in which they left their friends and their pleasures, for the sake of another world, which indeed is a better country, as is manifest from its character. "It is an heavenly country." As high as heaven is above the earth, so much better is that country which is an heavenly, than is this in which now we are. A "heavenly country," where there is a "heavenly Father," (Matt. vi. 14—16; xv. 13; xviii. 35;) a "heavenly host," (Luke ii. 13;) "heavenly things," (John iii. 12;) "heavenly visions," (Acts xxvi. 19;) "heavenly places," (Eph. i. 3, 20;) a "heavenly kingdom," (2 Tit. iv. 18;) and the "heavenly Jerusalem," (Heb. xii. 22;) for them that are partakers of the "heavenly calling," (Heb. iii. 1;) and that are the "heavenly things" themselves. (Heb. ix. 23.) This is a country to be desired, and therefore no marvel if any, except those that have lost their wits and senses, refuse to choose themselves an habitation here. Here is the "Mount Zion," "the city of the living God," the "heavenly Jerusalem," and "an innumerable company of angels," (Heb. xii. 22;) here is "the general assembly and church of the first-born," and "God the Judge of all," (Heb. xii. 23,) "and Jesus," (Heb. xii. 24,) and "the spirits of just men made perfect." (Heb. xii. 23.) Who would not be here?

This is the country that the righteous desire for a habitation: "but now they desire a better country, that is, an heavenly: wherefore God is not ashamed to be called their God, for he hath prepared for them a city." (Heb. xi. 16.)

Mark! They desire a country, and God prepareth for them a city; he goes beyond their desires, beyond their apprehensions, beyond what their hearts could conceive to ask for.

There is none that are weary of this world from a gracious disposition that they have to an heavenly, but God will take notice of them, will own them, and not be ashamed to own them; yea, such shall not lose their longing. They desire a handful, God gives them a seaful; they desire a country, God prepares for them a city, (Rev. iii. 12;) a city that is a heavenly, "a city that hath foundations," a city "whose builder and maker is God." (Heb. xi. 10.) And all this is, that the promise to them might be fulfilled. "The desire of the righteous shall be granted." And this is the last thing propounded to be spoken to from the text. Therefore,

III. We then, in conclusion, come to inquire into,

What is meant, or to be understood, by the granting of the righteous their desires:

"The desires of the righteous shall be granted."

FIRST. To grant, is to yield to what is desired, to consent that it shall be even so as is requested: "The Lord hear thee in the day of trouble, the name of the God of Jacob defend thee. Send thee help from the sanctuary, and strengthen thee out of Zion. Remember all thy offerings, and accept thy sacrifices. Grant thee according to thine own heart, and fulfil all thy counsel." (Ps. xx. 1—4.)

SECOND. To grant, is to accomplish what is promised; thus God granted to the Gentiles repentance unto life, namely, for that he had promised it by the prophets from the days of old. (Acts xi. 18. Rom. xv. 9—12.)

THIRD. To grant therefore is an act of grace and condescending favour; for if God is said to humble himself when he beholds things in heaven, what condescension is it for him to hearken to a sinful wretch on earth, and to tell him, "Have the thing which thou desirest?" A wretch I call him, if compared to him that hears him, though he is a righteous man, when considered as the new creation of God.

FOURTH. To grant then, is not to part with the thing desired, as if a desire merited, purchased, earned, or deserved it, but of bounty and good-will, to bestow the thing desired upon the humble. Hence God's grants are said to be gracious ones. (Ps. cxix. 29.)

FIFTH. I will add, That to grant is sometimes taken for giving one authority or power to do, or possess, or enjoy such and such privileges. And so it may be taken here; for the righteous has a right to a power, to enjoy the things bestowed on them by their God.

So then, to grant is to give, to accomplish, even of free grace, the desires of the righteous.

(1.) This is acknowledged by David, where he saith to God, "Thou hast given him his heart's desire, and hast not withholden the request of his lips." (Ps. xxi. 2.) (2.) And this is promised to all that delight themselves in God; "Delight thyself also in the Lord, and he shall give thee the desires of thine heart." (Ps. xxxvii. 4.) And again, (3.) "He will fulfil the desire of them that fear him: he also will hear their cry, and will save them." (Ps. cxlv. 19.)

By all these places it is plain, that the promise of granting desires is entailed to the righteous, and also the grant to them is an act of grace and mercy. But it also follows, that though the desires of the righteous are not meritorious, yet they are pleasing in his sight; and this is manifest several ways, besides the promise of a grant of them.

First. In that the desires of God, and the desires of the righteous, jump or agree in one;

they are of one mind in their desires: God's desire is to the work of his hands, and the righteous are for surrendering that up to him.

(1.) In giving up the heart unto him: " My son," says God, " give me thine heart," (Prov. xxiii. 26 ;) " I lift my heart to thee," (Ps. xxv. 1 ; lxxxvi. 4. Lam. iii. 41,) says the righteous man.

Here, therefore, there is an agreement between God and the righteous ; it is, I say, agreed on both sides that God should have the heart: God desires it, the righteous man desires it ; yea, he desires it with a groan, saying, " Incline my heart unto thy testimony." (Ps. cxix. 36.) " Let my heart be found in thy statutes." (Ps. cxix. 80.)

(2.) They are also agreed about the disposing of the whole man : God is for body, and soul, and spirit ; and the righteous desires that God should have it all. Hence they are said to give themselves to the Lord, (2 Cor. viii. 5,) and to addict themselves to his service. (1 Cor. xv. 16.)

(3.) God desireth truth in the inward parts— that is, that truth may be at the bottom of all, (Ps. li. 6 ;) and this is the desire of the righteous man likewise ; " Thy word have I hid in mine heart," said David, " that I might not sin against thee." (Ps. cxix. 11.)

(4.) They agree in the way of justification, in the way of sanctification, in the way of preservation, and in the way of glorification, to wit, which way to come at and enjoy all : wherefore, who should hinder the righteous man, or keep him back from enjoying the desire of his heart ?

(5.) They also agree about the sanctifying of God's name in the world ; saying, " Thy will be done in earth as it is in heaven." (Matt. vi. 10.) There is a great agreement between God and the righteous ; " He that is joined to the Lord is one spirit." (1 Cor. vi. 17.) No marvel, then, if their desires in the general, so far as the righteous man doth know the mind of his God, are one ; consequently, their desires must be granted, or God must deny himself.

Second. The desires of the righteous are the life of all their prayers : and it is said, " The prayer of the upright is God's delight." (Prov. xv. 8.)

(1.) Jesus Christ put a difference betwixt the form and spirit that is in prayer, and intimates, the soul of prayer is in the desires of a man ; " Therefore," saith he, " I say unto you, what things soever ye desire when ye pray, believe that ye receive them, and ye shall have them." (Mark xi. 24.)

(2.) If a man prays never so long, and has never so many brave expressions in prayer, yet God counts it prayer no further than there are warm and fervent desires in it, after those things the mouth maketh mention of. In Ps. xxxviii. 9, saith David, " Lord, all my desire is before thee, and my groaning is not hid from thee."

(3.) Can you say you desire when you pray ? or that your prayers come from the braying, panting, and longing of your hearts ? If not,

they shall not be granted ; for God looks when men are at prayer, to see if their hearts and spirits are in their prayers, (Matt. vi. 7 ;) for he counts all other but vain speaking. Ye shall seek me, and find me, says he, when you shall search for me with all your heart. (Rom. viii. 26, 27. Jer. xxix. 12.) The people that you read of in 2 Chron. xv. are there said to do what they did with all their heart, and with all their soul ; for they sought God with their whole desire. (2 Chron. xv. 11—15.)

When a man's desires put him upon prayer, run along with him in his prayer, break out of his heart, and ascend up to heaven with his prayers, it is a good sign that he is a righteous man, and that his desire shall be granted.

Third. By desire a righteous man shows more of his mind for God than he can by any manner of way besides ; hence it is said, " The desire of a man is his kindness, and a poor man (that is sincere in his desires) is better than he that with his mouth shows much love, if he be a liar." (Prov. xix. 22.)

(1.) Desires, desires, are copious things ; you read that a man may " enlarge his desires as hell," (Hab. ii. 5,) that is, if they be wicked ; yea, and a righteous man may enlarge his desires as heaven. (Ps. lxxiii. 25.)

(2.) No grace is so extensive as desires. Desires out-go all. Who believes as he desires to believe? and loves as he desires to love ? and fears as he desires to fear God's name ? (Neh. i. 11.) Might it be as a righteous man doth sometimes desire it should be, both with God's church, and also with his own soul, stranger things would be than there are ; faith, and love, and holiness would flourish more than it does. Oh! what does a righteous man desire ? What do you think the prophet desired when he said, " O that thou wouldst rend the heavens, and come down ? " (Isa. lxiv. 1.) And Paul, when he said he could wish that himself were accursed from Christ, for the vehement desire that he had that the Jews might be saved ? (Rom. ix. 1—3 ; x. 1.) Yea, what do you think John desired when he cried out to Christ to come quickly ? (Rev. xxii. 20.)

(3.) Love to God, as I said, is more seen in desires than in any Christian act. Do you think that the woman with her two mites cast in all she desired to cast into the treasury of God? Or do you think, when David said that he had prepared for the house of God with all his might, that his desires stinted when his ability was at its utmost ? (1 Chron. xxix.) No, no ; desires go beyond all actions ; therefore I said it is the desires of a man that are reckoned for his kindness.

(4.) Kindness is that which God will not forget —I mean the kindness which his people show to him ; especially in their desires to serve him in the world. When Israel was come out of Egypt, you know how many stumbles they had before they got to Canaan. But forasmuch as they were willing, or desirous to follow God, he passes by all their failures, saying, " I remember thee "—and that almost a thousand years after—" the kindness of thy youth, the love of thine espousals, when thou wentest after me in the wilderness, in a land that was not sown." (Jer. ii. 2.) Israel was holiness to the Lord, and the first fruits of his increase.

(5.) There is nothing that God likes of ours better than he likes our true desires. For, indeed, true desires, they are the smoke of our incense, the flower of our graces, and the very vital part of our new man. They are our desires that ascend, and them that are the sweet of all the sacrifices that we offer to God. The man of desires is the man of kindness.

Fourth. Desires, true and right desires, they are they by which a man is taken up from the ground, and brought away to God, in spite of all opposers. A desire will take a man upon its back, and carry him away to God, if ten thousand men stand by and oppose it. Hence it is said that, " through desire " a man separates himself, to wit, from what is contrary to the mind of God, and so " seeketh and intermeddleth with all wisdom." (Prov. xviii. 1.)

(1.) All convictions, conversions, illuminations, favours, tastes, revelations, knowledge, and mercies will do nothing, if the soul abides without desires. All I say is but like rain upon stones, or favours bestowed upon a dead dog. Oh! but a poor man with desires, a man that sees but little, that knows but little, that finds in himself but little, if he has but strong desires, they will supply all. His desires take him up from his sins, from his companions, from his pleasures, and carry him away to God.

(2.) Suppose thou wast a minister, and wast sent from God with a whip, whose cords were made of the flames of hell, thou mightest lash long enough before thou couldest so much as drive one man that abides without desires, to God, or to his kingdom, by that thy so sore a whip.

(3.) Suppose again that thou wast a minister, and wast sent from God to sinners with a crown of glory in thy hand, to offer to him that first comes to thee for it; yet none can come without desires: but desire takes the man upon its back, and so brings him to thee.

(4.) What is the reason that men will with mouth commend God, and commend Christ, and commend and praise both heaven and glory, and yet all the while fly from him, and from his mercy, as from the worst of enemies? Why, they want good desires; their desires being mischievous, carry them another way. Thou entreatest thy wife, thy husband, and the son of thy womb, to fall in with thy Lord and thy Christ, but they will not. Ask them the reason why they will not, and they know none, only they have no desires: " When we shall see him, there is no beauty that we should desire him." And I am sure if they do not desire him, they can by no means be made to come to him. (Isa. liii. 2.)

But now, desires—desires that are right—will carry a man quite away to God, and to do his will, let the work be never so hard. Take an instance or two for this.

1. You may see it in Abraham, Isaac, and Jacob. The text says plainly, They were not mindful of that country from whence they came out, through their desire of a better. (Heb. xi. 8—16.) God gave them intimation of a better country, and their minds did cleave to it with desires of it. And what then? Why, they went forth, and desired to go, though they did not know whither they went. Yea, they all sojourned in the land of promise, because it was but a shadow of what was designed for them by God, and looked to by their faith, as in a strange country; wherefore they also cast that behind their back, looking for that city that had " foundations," of which mention was made before.

Had not now these men desires that were mighty? They were their desires that thus separated them from their dearest and choicest relations and enjoyments. Their desires were pitched upon the heavenly country, and so they broke through all difficulties for that.

2. You may see it in Moses, who had a kingdom at his feet, and was the alone visible heir thereof; but desire of a better inheritance made him refuse it, and choose rather to take part with the people of God in their afflicted condition, than to enjoy the pleasures of sin for a season.

You may say, " The scripture attributes this to his faith." I answer, so it attributes to Abraham's faith, his leaving of his country. But his faith begat in him these desires after the country that is above. So, indeed, Moses saw these things by faith; and therefore his faith begat in him these desires. For it was because of his desires that he did refuse, and did choose, as you read.

And here we may opportunely take an opportunity to touch upon the vanity of that faith that is not breeding, and that knows not how to bring forth strong desires of enjoying what is pretended to be believed; all such faith is false. Abraham's, Isaac's, Jacob's, and Moses' faith, bred in them desires, strong desires; yea, desires so strong as to take them up, and to carry them after what by their faith was made known unto them. Yea, their desires were so mightily set upon the things made known to them by their faith, that neither difficulties nor dangers, nor yet frowns nor flatteries, could stop them from the use of all lawful attempts of enjoying what they believed was to be had, and what they desired to be possessed of.

3. The women also that you read of, and others that would not, upon unworthy terms, accept of deliverance from torments and sundry trials, that they might (or because they had a desire to) be made partakers of a better resurrection. " And others (saith he) had trial of cruel mockings and scourgings, yea, moreover, of bonds and imprisonment. They were stoned, they were sawn

asunder, were tempted, were slain with the sword; they wandered about in sheep-skins and goat-skins; being destitute, afflicted, tormented; of whom the world was not worthy: they wandered in deserts, and in mountains, and in dens and caves of the earth." (Heb. xi. 36—38.)

4. But we will come to the Lord Jesus himself. Whither did his desires bring him? whither did they carry him? and to what did they make him stoop? For they were his desires after us, and after our good, that made him humble himself to do as he did. (Prov. vii. 10.)

What was it, think you, that made him cry out, " I have a baptism to be baptised with, and how am I straitened till it be accomplished!" (Luke xii. 50.) What was that baptism but his death? and why did he so long for it, but of desire to do us good? Yea, the passover being to be eaten on the eve of his sufferings, with what desires did he desire to eat it with his disciples? (Luke xxii. 15.)

Yea, his desires to suffer for his people, made him go with more strength to lay down his life for them, than they for want of them, had to go to see him suffer. And they were in their way going up to Jerusalem—he to suffer, and they to look on. (Matt. xx. 17—19.) " And Jesus went before them, and they were amazed, and as they followed, they were afraid." (Mark x. 32.)

I tell you, desires are strange things, if they be right; they jump with God's mind; they are the life of prayer; they are a man's kindness to God, and they which will take him up from the ground, and carry him away after God to do his will, let the work be never so hard. Is it any marvel, then, if the desires of the righteous are so pleasing to God as they are? and that God has so graciously promised that the desires of the righteous shall be granted?

But we come now to the use and application.

The first use is a use of information.

You have heard what hath been said of desires, and what pleasing things right desires are unto God. But you must know that they are the desires of his people, of the righteous, that are so. No wicked man's desires are regarded. (Ps. cxii. 10.)

This men must be informed of, lest their desires become a snare to their souls. You read of a man whose desire "killeth him." (Prov. xxi. 25.) And why? but because he rests in desiring, without considering what he is, whether such a one unto whom the promise of granting desires is made: he coveteth greedily all the day long, but to little purpose. The grant of desires, of the fulfilling of desires, is entailed to the righteous man.

There are four sorts of people that desire—that desire the kingdom of heaven; consequently desires have a fourfold root from whence they flow.

First. The natural man desires to be saved, and to go to heaven when he dies. Ask any natural man, and he will tell you so. Besides, we see it is so with them, especially at certain seasons: as when some guilt or conviction for sin takes hold upon them; or when some sudden fear terrifies them; when they are afraid that the plague or pestilence will come upon them, and break up house-keeping for them; or when death has taken them by the throat, and is hauling them down stairs to the grave. Then, O then! Lord, save me! Lord, have mercy upon me! Good people, pray for me! Oh! whither shall I go when I die, if sweet Christ has not pity for my soul? And now the bed shakes, and the poor soul is as loth to go out of the body for fear the devil should catch it, as the poor bird is to go out of the bush, while it sees the hawk waiting there to receive her. But the fears of the wicked, they must come upon the wicked; they are the desires of the righteous that must be granted. Pray, take good notice of this. And to back this with the authority of God, consider that scripture, " The wicked man travaileth with pain all his days, and the number of years is hidden from the oppressor. A dreadful sound is in his ears: in prosperity the destroyer shall come upon him. Trouble and anguish shall make him afraid; they shall prevail against him, as a king ready to the battle." (Job xv. 20, 21, 24.) Can it be imagined, that when the wicked are in this distress, but that they will desire to be saved? Therefore he saith again, " Terrors take hold on him as waters; a tempest stealeth him away in the night. The east wind (that blasting wind) carrieth him away, and he departeth, and as a storm hurleth him out of (the world) his place. For God shall cast upon him, and not spare; (in flying) he would fain flee out of his hand." (Job xxvii. 20—22.) Their terrors and their fears must come upon them; their desires and wishes for salvation must not be granted. (Isa. lxv. 13; lxvi. 4.) " Then shall they call upon me," says God, " but I will not answer; they shall seek me early, but they shall not find me." (Prov. i. 28.)

Second. There is the hypocrite's desire. Now his desire seems to have life and spirit in it. Also he desires, in his youth, his health, and the like; yet it comes to naught. You shall see him drawn to the life in Mark x. 17. He comes running and kneeling, and asking, and that, as I said, in youth and health; and that is more than men merely natural do. But all to no purpose; he went as he came, without the thing desired. The conditions propounded were too hard for this hypocrite to comply withal. (Mark x. 21, 22.)

Some indeed make a great noise with their desires over some again do, but in conclusion all comes to one; they meet together where they go, whose desires are not granted. For what is the hope of the hypocrite, though he has gained to a higher strain of desires, when God taketh away his soul? (Job xxvii. 8.) " Will God hear his cry when trouble cometh upon him ?" (Job xxviii. 9.) Did he not, even when he desired life, yet break with God, in the day when conditions of life were propounded to him ? Did he not, even when he asked what good things were to be done that he might have eternal life, refuse to hear or to comply with what was propounded to him ? How then can his desires be granted, who himself refused to have them answered ? No marvel, then, if he perishes like his own dung, if they that have seen him shall say they miss him among those that are to have their desires granted.

Third. There are the desires of the cold, formal professor ; the desires, I say, of him whose religion lies in a few of the shells of religion ; even as the foolish virgins who were content with their lamps, but gave not heed to take oil in their vessels. (Matt. xxv. 3.) These I take to be those whom the wise man calls the slothful : " The soul of the sluggard desireth and hath nothing ; but the soul of the diligent shall be made fat." (Prov. xiii. 4.) The sluggard is one that comes to poverty through idleness, that contents himself with forms, " That will not plough (in winter) by reason of the cold ; therefore shall he beg in harvest, or at the day of judgment, and have nothing." (Prov. xx. 4.)

Thus you see, that there are many that desire : the natural man, the hypocrite, the formalist, they all desire. For heaven is a brave place, and nobody would go to hell: " Lord, Lord, open to us," (Matt. xxv. 11,) is the cry of many in this world, and will be the cry of more in the day of judgment. Of this, therefore, thou shouldst be informed ; and that for these reasons,

1. Because ignorance of this may keep thee asleep in security, and cause thee to fall under such disappointments as are the worst, and the worst to be borne. For, for a man to think to go to heaven because he desires it, and when all is done to fall into hell, is a frustration of the most dismal complexion. And yet thus it will be when desire shall fail, when "man goeth to his long home, and the mourners go about the streets." (Eccles. xii. 5.)

2. Because, as was said before, else thy desires, and that which should be for thy good, will kill thee.

(1.) They kill thee at death, when thou shalt find them every one empty.

(2.) And at judgment, when thou shalt be convinced, that thou oughtest to go without what thou desirest, because thou wast not the man to whose desires the promise was made, nor the man that didst desire aright.

(3.) To be informed of this is the way to put thee upon such sense and sight of thy case as will make thee in earnest betake thyself in that way to him that is acceptable, who grants the desires of the righteous.

And then shalt thou be happy when thou shunnest to desire as the natural man desireth, as the hypocrite desireth, or as the formalist desireth :

When thou desirest as the righteous do, thy desires shall be granted.

The second use is of examination.

If this be so, then what cause hast thou that art conscious to thyself that thou art a desiring man, to examine thyself whether thou art one whose desires shall be granted ? For to what purpose would a man desire, or what fruits will desire bring him whose desires shall not be granted ? Such a man is but like to her that longs, but loses her longing : or like to him that looks for peace while evil overtakes him.

Thou hast heard it over and over, that the grant of desires belongs to the righteous. Shouldst thou then not inquire into thy condition, and examine thyself whether thou art a righteous man or no ? The apostle said to the Corinthians, " Examine yourselves whether ye be in the faith ; prove your own selves ; know ye not how that Jesus Christ is in you, except ye be reprobates ?" (2 Cor. xiii. 5.) You may be reprobates and not be aware of it, if you do not examine and prove your own selves.

It is, therefore, *for thy life,* wherefore do not deceive thyself.

I have given you before a description of a righteous man, namely, that he is one made so of God by imputation, by an inward principle, and one that brings forth fruit to God. Now, this last thou mayst think thou hast ; for it is easy and common for men to think, when they bring forth fruit to themselves, that they bring it forth to God. Wherefore examine thyself.

First. Art thou righteous ? If thou sayest, Yea, I ask, How comest thou righteous ? If thou thinkest that obedience to the law of righteousness has made thee so, thou art utterly deceived ; for he that thus seeks righteousness, yet is not righteous, because he cannot, by so doing, attain that thing he seeketh for. (Rom. ix. 31, 32.) Did not I tell thee before, that a man must be righteous before he doth one good work, or he can never be righteous ? The tree must be good first, even before it brings forth one good apple.

Second. Art thou righteous ? In whose judgment art thou righteous ? Is it in the judgment of God, or of man ? If not of God, it is no matter though all the men on earth should justify thee ; thou for that art no whit the more righteous.

Third. Art thou righteous in the judgment of God ? Who told thee so ? or dost thou but dream thereof ? Indeed, to be righteous in God's sight, is that, and only that, which can secure a man from wrath to come ; for " if God justifieth, who is he that condemneth ?" (Rom. viii. 33, 34.) And this only is the man whose desires shall be granted.

Fourth. But still I say, is the question, How comest thou to know that thou art righteous in the judgment of God ? Dost thou know by what it is that God makes a man righteous ? Dost thou know where that is, by or with which God makes a man righteous? and also how God doth make a man righteous with it. These are questions in the answer of which thou must have some heavenly skill, or else all that thou sayest about thy being righteous will seem without a bottom.

Fifth. Now, if thou answerest, That that which makes me righteous is the obedience of Christ to his Father's will—that this righteousness is before the throne of God, and that it is made mine by an act of God's free grace, I shall ask thee yet again,

Sixth. How camest thou to see thy need of this righteousness? and by what is this righteousness by thee applied to thyself? For this righteousness is bestowed upon those that see their need thereof. This righteousness is the refuge whereto the guilty fly for succour, that they may be sheltered from the wrath to come. Hast thou then fled, or dost thou indeed fly to it? (Heb. vi. 16—19).

Seventh. None fly to this righteousness for life, but those who feel the sentence of condemnation by God's law upon their conscience; and that in that extremity have sought for righteousness first elsewhere, but cannot find it in all the world.

Eighth. For man, when he findeth himself at first a sinner, doth not straightway betake himself for righteousness to God by Christ, but in the first place, seeks it in the law on earth, by labouring to yield obedience thereto, to the end he may, when he stands before God at death and judgment, have something to commend him to him, and for the sake of which he may at least help forward his acceptance with him.

Ninth. But being wearied out of this—and if God loves him he will weary him out of it—then he looks unto heaven, and cries to God for righteousness; the which God shows him in his own good time, he hath reckoned to him for the sake of Jesus Christ.

Tenth. Now by this very discovery the heart is also principled with the spirit of the gospel; for the spirit comes with the gospel down from heaven to such an one, and fills his soul with good; by which he is capacitated to bring forth fruit, true fruit, which are the fruits of righteousness imputed, and of righteousness infused, to the glory and praise of God.

Eleventh. Nor can anything but faith make a man see himself thus made righteous; for this righteousness is revealed from faith to faith, from the object of faith to the grace of faith, by the Spirit of faith. A faithless man then can see this no more than a blind man can see colours; nor relish this no more than a dead man tasteth victuals. As, therefore, blind men talk of colours, and as dead men relish food, so do carnal men talk of Jesus Christ; to wit, without sense or savour; without sense of the want, or savour of the worth and goodness of him to the soul.

Twelfth. Wherefore, I say, it is of absolute necessity that with thy heart thou deal in this point, and beware of self-deceiving; for if thou fail here, thy desires will fail thee for ever: "For the desire of the righteous," and that only, "must be granted."

The third use is cautionary.

Let me here, therefore, caution thee to beware of some things, by which else, perhaps, thou mayest deceive thyself.

First. Take heed of taking such things for grants of desires, that accidentally fall out; accidentally I mean, as to thy desires; for it is possible that that very thing that thou desirest may come to pass in the current of Providence, not as an answer of thy desires. Now if thou takest such things for a grant of thy desires, and consequently concludest thyself a righteous man, how mayest thou be deceived? The ark of God was delivered into the hands of the Philistines, which they desired; but not for the sake of their desire, but for the sins of the children of Israel.

The land of Canaan was given unto Israel, not for the sake of their desires, but for the sins of those whom God cast out before them; and to fulfil the promise that God, before they were born, had made unto their fathers. (Deut. ix. 5, 6.)

Israel was carred away captive out of their own land, not to fulfil the desires of their enemies, but to punish them for their transgressions. These, with many of smaller importance, and more personal, might be mentioned, to show that many things happen to us, some to our pleasing, and some to the pleasing of our enemies; which, if either we or they should count the returns of our prayer, or the fruits of our desires, and so draw conclusions of our estate to be for the future happy, because in such things we seemed to be answered of God, we might greatly swerve in our judgments, and become the greatest at self-deceiving.

Second. Or shouldest thou take it for granted that what thou enjoyest thou hast it as the fruit of thy desires, yet if the things thou boasteth of are things pertaining to this life, such may be granted thee, as thou art considered of God as his creature, though thyself art far enough off from being a righteous man: "Thou openest thy hand," says the psalmist, "and satisfiest the desire of every living thing." (Ps. cxlv. 16.) Again, he feeds the young ravens that cry to him; and the young lions seek their meat from God. (Ps. cxlvii. 9; civ. 21.) Cain, Ishmael, Ahab too, had in some things their desires granted them of God. (Gen. iv. 14, 15; xxi. 17, 18. 1 Kings xxi. 29.)

For if God will hear the desire of the beasts of the field, the fishes of the sea, and of the fowls of heaven, no marvel if the wicked also may boast him of his heart's desire. (Ps. x. 3.)

Into whose hand, as he saith in another place, "God bringeth abundantly." Take heed, therefore, neither these things, nor the grant of them, are any signs that thou art a righteous man, or that the promise made to the righteous in granting their desires, are accomplished upon thee.

I think a man may say, that the men that know not God have a fuller grant—I mean generally—of their desires of temporal things, than has the child of God himself; for his portion lying in better things, his desires are answered another way.

Third. Take heed, God grants to some men their desires in anger, and to their destruction.

He gave to some their own "desire, but sent leanness into their souls." (Ps. lxxviii. 29; cvi. 15. Jer. xlii. 23.) All that God gives to the sons of men, he gives not in mercy; he gives to some an inferior, and to some a superior portion; and yet so also he answereth them in the joy of their heart.

Some men's hearts are narrow upwards, and wide downwards—narrow as to God, but wide for the world: they gape for the one, but shut themselves up against the other; so as they desire, they have of what they desire. "Whose belly thou fillest with thy hid treasure," (Ps. xvii. 14,) for that they do desire, but as for me, said David, these things will not satisfy; "I shall be satisfied, when I awake, with thy likeness." (Ps. xvii. 15.)

I told you before, that the heart of a wicked man was widest downwards, but it is not so with the righteous: therefore the portion of Jacob is not like them; God has given to him himself. The temple that Ezekiel saw in the vision, was still widest upward; it spread itself toward heaven. (Ezek. xli. 7.) So is the church, and so is the righteous, and so are his desires.

Thy great concern therefore is to consider, since thou art confident that God also heareth thy desires—I say, to consider, whether he answereth thee in his anger; for if he doth so, thy desires come with a woe; therefore I say look to thyself.

A full purse and a lean soul is a sign of a great curse: "He gave them their own desires, but sent leanness into their soul." Take heed of that; many men crave by their desires, as the dropsical man craves drink; his drinking makes his belly swell big, but consumes other parts of his body. Oh! it is a sad grant, when the desire is granted, only to make the belly big, the estate big, the name big; when even by this bigness the soul pines, is made to dwindle, to grow lean, and to look like an anatomy.

I am persuaded that it is thus with many, who, while they were lean in estates, had fat souls; but the fattening of their estates has made their souls, as to good, as lean as a rake. They cannot now breathe after God; they cannot now look to their hearts; they cannot now set watch and ward over their ways; they cannot now spare time to examine who goes out, or who comes in. They have so much their desires in things below, that they have no leisure to concern themselves with, or to look after things above; their hearts are now as fat as grease; their eyes do now too much start out to be turned, and made to look inward. (Ps. cxix. 70; lxxiii. 7.) They are now become as to their best

part, like the garden of the slothful—all grown over with nettles and briars, that cover the face thereof; or, like Saul, removed from a little estate and low condition, to much, even worse and worse.

Men do not know what they do in desiring things of this life, things over and above what are necessary; they desire them, and they have them with a woe. Surely he shall not feel quietness in his belly, (his belly is taken for his conscience) (Prov. xx. 27,) he shall not save of that which he desired, to help him in an evil day. (Job xx. 20. 1 Tim. vi. 17—19.)

I shall not here give my caution to the righteous, but shall reserve that for the next use. But, oh, that men were as wise in judging of the answering of the desires, as they are in judging of the extravagances of their appetites! You shall have a man even from experience reclaim himself from such an excess of eating, drinking, smoking, sleeping, talking, or pleasurable actions, as by his experience he finds is hurtful to him (and yet all this may but hurt the body—at least the body directly); but how blind, how unskilled are they in the evils that attend desires! For, like the man in the dropsy, made mention of before, they desire this world, as he doth drink, till they desire themselves quite down to hell. Look to it therefore, and take heed; God's granting the things pertaining to this life unto thee, doth neither prove that thou art righteous, nor that he acts in mercy towards thee, by giving of thee thy desires.

The fourth use is for encouragement.

Is it so? shall the desire of the righteous be granted? Then this should encourage them that in the first place have sought the kingdom of God and his Son's righteousness, to go on in their desires.

God has given thee his Son's righteousness to justify thee; he has also, because thou art a son, sent forth the spirit of his Son into thy heart to satisfy thee, and to help thee to cry unto him, Father, Father. Wilt thou not cry? wilt thou not desire? thy God has bidden thee open thy mouth; he has bid thee open it wide, and promised, saying, "And I will fill it," (Ps. lxxxi. 10,) and wilt thou not desire?

Oh! thou hast a licence, a leave, a grant to desire; wherefore be not afraid to desire great mercies of the God of heaven: this was Daniel's way, and he set others to do it too. (Dan. ii. 18.)

Obj. But I am an unworthy creature.

Ans. That is true, but God gives to no man for his worthiness, nor rejects any for their sinfulness, that come to him sensible of the want and worth of mercy for them. Besides, I told thee before, that the desires of a righteous man, and the desires of his God, do jump or agree. God has a desire to thee, thou hast a desire to him. (Job xiv. 15.) God desires truth in the inward parts, and so dost thou with all thy heart. (Ps. v. 1—6. Hos. vi. 5.) God desires mercy, and to show it to the needy; that is it thou also wantest, and that which thy soul craves at his hand.

Seek, man, ask, knock, and do not be discouraged, the Lord will grant all thy desires. Thou sayest thou art unworthy to ask the biggest things, things spiritual and heavenly; well, will carnal things serve thee, and answer the desires of thy heart? Canst thou be content to be put off with a belly well filled, and a back well clothed? Oh! better I never had been born.

See, thou wilt not ask the best, and yet canst not make shift without them. Shift, no, no shift without them; I am undone without them, undone for ever, sayest thou. Well then, desire: so I do, sayest thou. Ah! but desire with more strong desires, desire with more large desires; desire spiritual gifts, (1 Cor. xiv. 1,) covet them earnestly, thou hast a licence too to do so. God bids thee do so; and "I," says the apostle, "desire that ye faint not," (Eph. iii. 13,) that is, in the prosecution of your desires, what discouragements soever you may meet with in the way; for he hath said, "The desire of the righteous shall be granted."

Obj. But I find it not so, says one; for though I have desired and desired, a thousand times upon my knees, for something that I want, yet I have not my desire; and, indeed, the consideration of this hath made me question whether I am one of those to whom the promise of granting of desires is made.

Ans. To this objection many things must be replied: first, by way of question; second, then by way of answer.

First. *By way of question;* what are the things thou desirest, are they lawful or unlawful? for a Christian may desire unlawful things, as the mother of Zebedee's children did when she came to Christ (nay, her sons themselves had their hearts therein) saying, "Master, we would that thou shouldst do for us whatsoever we shall desire." (Mark x. 35. Matt. xx. 20.)

They came with a wide mouth, but their desire was unlawful, as is evident, for that Christ would not grant it. James also himself caught those unto whom he wrote, in such a fault as this, where he says, "Ye kill, and desire to have, and cannot obtain." (James iv. 2.)

There are four things that are unlawful to be desired.

(1.) To desire the life of thine enemy is unlawful. (1 Kings iii. 11. Deut. v. 21.)

(2.) To desire anything that is thy neighbour's is unlawful.

(3.) To desire to share in the prosperity of the wicked is unlawful. (Ps. lxxxiii. 3.)

(4.) To desire spiritual things for evil ends is unlawful. (Prov. xxiv. 1, 19. James iv. 2—4.)

Are they lawful things which thou desirest? Yet the question is, Are they absolutely or con-

ditionally promised? If absolutely promised, hold on in desiring; if conditionally promised, then thou must consider whether they are such as are essential to the well-being of thy soul in thy Christian course in this life, or whether they are things that are of a more inferior sort.

If they are such as are essential to the well-being of thy soul in thy Christian course in this world, then hold on in thy desires; and look also for the conditions that that word calls for, that proffereth them to thee; and if it be not possible to find them in thyself, look for them in Christ, and cry to God for them, for the Lord's sake.

But if they be of an inferior sort, and thou canst be a good Christian without them, desire them, and yet be content to go without them; for who knows but it may be better that thou shouldst be denied, than that thou shouldst have now a grant of some things thou desirest? and herein thou hast thy Lord for thy pattern; who, though he desired that his life might be prolonged, yet wound up that prayer with a "nevertheless, not my will, but thine be done." (Matt. xxvi. 42. Mark xiv. 36.)

Second. *By way of answer.* But we will suppose, that the thing thou desirest is good; and that thy heart may be right in asking; as suppose thou desirest more grace; or as David has it, more truth in the inward and hidden part, (Ps. li. 6;) yet there are several things for thy instruction, may be replied to thy objection, as,

1. Thou, though thou desirest more of this, mayest not yet be so sensible of the worth of what thou askest, as perhaps God will have thee be, before he granteth thy desire: sometimes Christians ask for good things without having in themselves an estimate proportionable to the worth of what they desire; and God may hold it therefore back, to learn them to know better the worth and greatness of that thing they ask for. The good disciples asked they knew not what. (Mark x. 38.)

I know they asked what was unlawful, but they were ignorant of the value of that thing; and the same may be thy fault when thou askest for things most lawful and necessary.

2. Hast thou well improved what thou hast received already? Fathers will hold back more money, when the sons have spent that profusely which they had received before. He that is faithful in that which is least, is faithful also in much; and he that is unjust in that which is least, is unjust also in much. "And if ye have not been faithful in that which is another man's, who shall give you that which is your own?" (Luke xvi. 10, 12.)

See here an objection made against a further supply, or rather against such a supply as some would have, because they have misspent, or been unfaithful in what they have already had.

If thou therefore hast been faulty here, go, humble thyself to thy friend, and beg pardon for thy faults that are past, when thou art desiring of him more grace.

3. When God gives to his the grant of their desires, he doth it so as may be best for our advantage; now there are times wherein the giving of grace may be best to our advantage, as, (1.) Just before a temptation comes, then, if it rains grace on thee from heaven, it may be most for thy advantage. This is like God's sending of plenty in Egypt just before the years of famine came. (2.) For God to restrain that which thou desirest, even till the spirit of prayer is in a manner spent, may be further to inform thee, that though prayers and desires are a duty, and such also to which the promise is made, yet God sees those imperfections in both thy prayers and desires, as would utterly bind his hands, did he not act toward thee merely from motives drawn from his own bowels and compassion, rather than from any deserving that he sees in thy prayers. Christians, even righteous men, are apt to lean too much to their own doings; and God, to wean them from them, ofttimes defers to do, what they by doing expect, even until in doing their spirits are spent, and they as to doing can do no longer. When they that cried for water, had cried till their spirits failed, and their tongue clave to the roof of their mouth for thirst; then the Lord did hear, and then the God of Israel did give them their desire. Also when Jonah his soul fainted under the consideration of all the evils that he had brought upon himself, then his prayer came unto God into his holy temple. (Jonah ii. 7.) The righteous would be too light in asking, and would too much overprize their works, if their God should not sometimes deal in this manner with them. (3.) It is also to the advantage of the righteous, that they be kept, and led in that way which will best improve grace already received, and that is, when they spin it out and use it to the utmost; when they do with it, as the prophet did with that meal's meat that he eat under the juniper-tree, " go in the strength of it forty days and forty nights, even to the mount of God." (1 Kings xix. 8.) Or when they do as the widow did, spend upon their handful of flour in the barrel, and upon that little oil in the cruse, until God shall send more plenty. (1 Kings xvii. 9—16.)

The righteous are apt to be like well-fed children, too wanton, if God should not appoint them some fasting days. Or they would be apt to cast away fragments, if God should give them every day a new dish. So then God will grant the desires of the righteous in that way which will be most for their advantage. And that is, when they have made the best of the old store. (1 Kings xix. 4—8.)

If God should give us two or three harvests in a year, we should incline to feed our horse and hogs with wheat; but being as it is, we learn better to husband the matter.

By this means also we are made to see, that there is virtue sufficient in our old store of grace to keep us with God in the way of our duty, longer than we could imagine it would.

I myself have cried out, I can stand no longer, hold out no longer, without a further supply of grace; and yet I have by my old grace been kept even after this, days, and weeks, and months, in a way of waiting on God. A little true grace will go a great way, yea, and do more wonders than we are aware of. If we have but grace enough to keep us groaning after God, it is not all the world that can destroy us.

4. Perhaps thou mayest be mistaken. The grace thou prayest for, may in great measure be come unto thee. Thou hast been desiring of God, thou sayest, more grace; but hast it not.

But how, if whilst thou lookest for it to come to thee at one door, it should come to thee in at another? And that we may a little inquire into the truth of this, let us a little consider what are the effects of grace in its coming to the soul, and then see if it has not been coming unto thee almost ever since thou hast set upon this fresh desire after it.

(1.) Grace, in the general effect of it, is to mend the soul, and to make it better disposed. Hence when it comes it brings convincing light along with it, by which a man sees more of his baseness than at other times. More, I say, of his inward baseness. It is through the shinings of the Spirit of grace, that those cobwebs and stinks that yet remain in thee are discovered: "In thy light we shall see light." And again, whatsoever makes manifest is light. If then thou seest thyself more vile than formerly, grace by its coming to thee has done this for thee.

(2.) Grace, when it comes, breaks and crumbles the heart, in the sense and sight of its vileness. A man stands amazed and confounded in himself; breaks and falls down on his face before God; is ashamed to lift up so much as his face to God, at the sight and apprehension of how wicked he is.

(3.) Grace, when it comes, shows to a man more of the holiness and patience of God; his holiness to make us wonder at his patience, and his patience to make us wonder at his mercy, that yet, even yet, such a vile one as I am, should be admitted to breathe in the land of the living, yea more, suffered to come to the throne of grace.

(4.) Grace is of a heart-humbling nature; it will make a man count himself the most unworthy of anything, of all saints. It will make a man put all others afore him, and be glad too, if he may be one beloved, though least beloved, because most unworthy. It will make him with gladness accept of the lowest room, as counting all saints more worthy of exaltation than himself.

(5.) Grace will make a man prize other men's graces and gracious actions above his own. As he thinks every man's candle burns brighter than his, every man improves grace better than he, every good man does more sincerely his duty than he. And if these be not some of the effects of the renewings of grace, I will confess I have taken my mark amiss.

(6.) Renewings of grace beget renewed self-bemoanings, self-condemnations, self-abhorrences.

And say thou prayest for communion with, and the presence of God. God can have communion with thee, and grant thee his presence, and all this shall, instead of comforting of thee at present, more confound thee, and make thee see thy wickedness. (Isa. vi. 1—5.)

Some people think they never have the presence and renewings of God's grace upon them but when they are comforted, and when they are cheered up; when, alas! God may be richly with them, while they cry out, By these visions my sorrows are multiplied; or, because I have seen God, I shall die. (Dan. x. 8—17. Judges xiii. 22.)

And tell me now, all these things considered, has not grace, even the grace of God, which thou hast so much desired, been coming to thee, and working in thee in all these hidden methods? And so doing, has it not also accommodated thee with all the afore-named conveniencies? The which when thou considerest, I know thou wouldest not be without for all the good of the world. Thus, therefore, thy desire is accomplishing; and when it is accomplished, will be sweet to thy soul. (Prov. xiii. 19.)

5. But we will follow thee a little in the way of thy heart. Thou sayest thou desirest, and desirest grace, yea, hast been a thousand times upon thy knees before God for more grace, and yet thou canst not attain? I answer,

(1.) It may be the grace which thou prayest for, is worth thy being upon thy knees yet a thousand times more. We find, that usually they that go to kings' courts for preferment, are there at great expenses; yea, and wait a great while, even until they have spent their whole estates, and worn out their patience too. Yet they at last prevail, and the thing desired comes. Yea, and when it is come, it sets them up anew, and makes them better men—though they did spend all that they had to obtain it—than ever they were before. Wait, therefore, wait, I say, on the Lord. Wait therefore with David, wait patiently; bid thy soul cheer up, and wait. (Ps. xxxvii. 7; lxii. 5.) "Blessed are all they that wait for him." (Isa. xxx. 18.)

(2.) Thou must consider, that great grace is reserved for great service; thou desirest abundance of grace; thou dost well, and thou shalt have what shall qualify and fit thee for the service that God has for thee to do for him, and for his name in the world. The apostles themselves were to stay for great grace until the time their work was come. (Acts i. 4—8; iv. 33.)

I will not allot thy service, but assure thyself, when thy desire cometh, thou wilt have occasion for it; new work, new trials, new sufferings, or something that will call for the power and virtue of all the grace thou shalt have to keep thy spirit even, and thy feet from slipping, while thou art exercised in new engagements.

Assure thyself, thy God will not give thee straw, but he will expect brick; "For unto whomsoever much is given, of him much shall be required, and to whom men have committed much, of him they will ask the more." (Luke xii. 48.) Wherefore, as thou art busy in desiring more grace, be also desirous that wisdom to manage it with faithfulness may also be granted unto thee. Thou wilt say, "Grace, if I had it, will do all this for me." It will, and it will not. It will, if thou watch and be sober; it will not, if thou be foolish and remiss. Men of great grace may grow consumptive in grace, and idleness may turn him that wears a plush jacket into rags. David was once a man of great grace, but his sin made the grace which he had, to shrink up, and dwindle away, as to make him cry out, O! take not thy Spirit utterly from me (Ps. li. 11; cxix. 8.)

(3.) Or, perhaps God withholds what thou wouldst have, that it may be the more prized by thee when it comes: "Hope deferred maketh the heart sick; but when the desire cometh, it is a tree of life." (Prov. xiii. 12.)

Lastly. But dost thou think that thy more grace will exempt thee from temptations? Alas! the more grace, as was hinted, the greater trials. Thou must be, for all that, like the ship of which thou readest—sometimes high, sometimes low; sometimes steady, sometimes staggering; sometimes in, and sometimes even at the end of thy very wits: for "so he bringeth us to our desired haven." (Ps. cvii. 23—30.)

Yet grace is the gold and preciousness of the righteous man: yea, and herein appears the uprightness of his soul, in that, though all these things attend the grace of God in him, yet he chooseth grace here above all, for that it makes him the more like God and his Christ, and for that it seasons his heart best to his own content; and also for that it capacitates him to glorify God in the world.

THE CONCLUSION.

Is it so? Is this the sum of all—namely, that the fear of the wicked, it shall come upon him, and that "the desire of the righteous shall be granted?" Then this shows us what is determined concerning both: concerning the wicked, that all his hopes shall not bring him to heaven; and concerning the righteous, that all his fears shall not bring him to hell. But what a sad thing it is for one to be a wicked man! Nothing can help him: his wickedness is too strong for him. "His own iniquity shall take the wicked himself, and he shall be holden with the cords of his sins." (Prov. v. 22.)

He may twist and twine, and seek to work himself from under the sentence passed upon him; but all will do him no pleasure. "The wicked is driven away in his wickedness: but the righteous hath hope in his death." (Prov. xiv. 32.)

Loth he is to be righteous now; and as loth he will be to be found in his sins at the dreadful day of doom. But so it must be. "Upon the wicked he [God] shall rain snares, fire, and brimstone, and a horrible (burning) tempest: this shall be the portion of their cup." (Ps. xi. 6.)

"Woe to the wicked," therefore. "It shall be ill with him, for the reward of his hands shall be given him." (Isa. iii. 10.) The just God will recompense both the righteous and the wicked, even according to their works. And yet for all this the wicked will not hear. When I read God's word, and see how the wicked follow their sins,

yea, dance in the ways of their own destruction, it is astonishing to me.

Their actions declare them, though not atheists in principle, yet such in practice. What do all their acts declare but this, that they either know not God, or fear not what he can do unto them?

But oh! how will they change their note when they see what will become of them! How wan will they look! Yea, the hair of their heads will stand on end for fear; for their fear is their portion; nor can their fears, nor their prayers, nor their entreaties, nor their wishes, nor their repentings, help them in this day.

And thus have I showed you what are the "desires of the righteous:" and that "the fear of the wicked shall come upon him, but the desire of the righteous shall be granted."

NOTES.

NOTE 1.—It is greatly to Bunyan's praise that he so carefully analyzed the meaning of the scriptural expressions on which this discourse is founded. Other writers of his age are characterised by the same diligence, but it is peculiarly deserving of notice in an author whose lively fancy and love of allegory, were so likely to divert him from a stricter style. No term in Scripture has been more tried by the severe tests of criticism and etymology than that of "righteous," or "righteousness." Ample reason exists for all the labour which can be employed in bringing out the full meaning of these most important words. An error in their interpretation or application may vitiate the meaning of the most precious passages in Scripture: may even give a false notion of entire covenants and dispensations.

NOTE 2, p. 476.—"*Is counted a very Abraham.*"]—The world may regard the righteous as foolish in their close imitation of Abraham's faith and devotion, and yet not account them either idiots or hypocrites. Bunyan may possibly have had in mind a more insulting allusion to the title of believers, but it is sufficient for his argument that the world generally accounts those whose faith is strong and active, fools for their conduct. "A very Abraham" may simply mean a thorough and unhesitating imitator of the patriarch, and not the same as "Abraham-men." The latter term was applied, it is said, to the vagabonds who, after the dissolution of the monasteries, wandered about the country begging for alms as a substitute for the support no longer to be gained from the doors of a convent. Thus the old play—

"And these, what name or title e'er they bear,
Jarkman, or Patrico, Cranke, or Clapper-dudgeon, ·
Frater, or Abraham-man; I speak to all
That stand in fair election for the title
Of king of beggars."   *Nares* (*Glossary*).

NOTE 3, p. 480.—"*Desires in general may be thus described,*" &c.]—It is interesting to compare Bunyan's account of human wishes and desires with that of the eminent Scotch

metaphysician and moralist, Dr. Brown. "To enumerate the objects of our desire and fear, would be to enumerate almost every object which exists around us on our earth, and almost every relation of these objects, without taking into account the variety of wishes more fantastic, which our wild imagination is capable of forming. A complete enumeration of all the possibilities of human wishes is almost as little to be expected as a complete gratification of all the wishes of man, whose desires are as unlimited as his power is bounded. The most important, however, may be considered as comprehended in the following series:—First, our desire of continued existence without any regard to the pleasure which it may yield; secondly, our desire of pleasure considered directly as mere pleasure; thirdly, our desire of action; fourthly, our desire of society; fifthly, our desire of knowledge; sixthly, our desire of power, direct, as in ambition, or indirect, as in avarice; seventhly, our desire of the affection or esteem of those around us; eighthly, our desire of glory; ninthly, our desire of the happiness of others; and, tenthly, our desire of the unhappiness of those whom we hate."—*Philosophy of the Human Mind,* (*Lecture LXV.*)

NOTE 4, p. 497.—"*A Christian may desire unlawful things,*" &c.]—The instance given is scarcely in point. The mother of Zebedee's children was not yet fully instructed in the nature of Christ's kingdom. It was in mere obedience to motherly affection that she petitioned for her sons. Their own wish was formed in ignorance, and they were admonished, not as desiring unlawful things, but as asking "they knew not what." The object desired was pre-eminently fit for disciples of Jesus to aim at and pray for. It betokened no rebellion of heart to wish for a place at his right hand and his left, but a deficiency of knowledge to be supplied when they should drink of his cup, and be baptized with his baptism. Jesus may refuse many things, even to his most faithful worshippers, not because the things are unlawful, or because they have been asked unlawfully, but for innumerable reasons connected with the dispensations of his grace.

PREFATORY REMARKS

ON

CHRIST A COMPLETE SAVIOUR.

In many of the sorrows and perplexities of human existence men account it a blessing to find even a partial or occasional benefactor. The warmest charity is limited, either by its own defective vision or by the scantiness of the means at its command. In cases of difficulty it often hesitates as to what should be done; and, when the doubt is resolved, sees that the delay has proved fatal to its wishes. Thus the most imperfect works of charity are regarded with admiration. It is well known how many obstacles there are to its success on any large scale; and what gratitude, therefore, ought to attend the names of those who have permanently, though only in some degree, benefited mankind.

The work of Jesus Christ has only to be earnestly considered to show, in this respect, its claim upon our veneration. It consists of numerous parts; each of those parts, separately viewed, is replete with proofs of wisdom and goodness. Even a single miracle wrought by his word displays an amount of power, of power under the guidance of supreme charity, which cannot be contemplated without mingled admiration and thankfulness. Had he possessed only the office of an instructor, teaching as he taught, his right to the gratitude of mankind would have been owned wherever truth and wisdom are respected. Could he have appeared in the character of a mediator, independent of his other offices, even as mediator alone, he would have been to men, wishing to seek God, but perplexed with ignorance and sin, the best of friends. If, on the other hand, he had come but to perform the single act of redemption, that one work of mercy would have constituted him a benefactor infinitely precious to our race.

In each of these characters and offices he has performed countless charities. According to the estimate which men take of the value of their own doings, they would have accounted themselves, or been called, the Saviours of their fellow men, for any act resembling the most unnoticed of his works. It is but in rare cases that even the truest benevolence can do more than alleviate one class of distress, and that only for a time. The amount of misery removed by Jesus Christ in a single answer to prayer is known, in some measure, to those who seek his help, and when it is granted recognise it as his. But the thoughtful and devout mind would be overwhelmed with astonishment were it to make any attempt at calculating the number of his passing mercies; of mercies entering into the common courses of the world, imbuing them with some leaven of good, without which they would be simply and entirely evil; of mercies lessening the weight of every-day cares and distresses, and the increase of which, if not checked by the unacknowledged and unnoticed providence of this Saviour, would at length utterly crush the boasted energies of the world.

These considerations may lead us to more practical views of our Lord's goodness than are commonly entertained. Not to recognise the providence of God is the way to forget him. In the course of his daily manifestations of power and wisdom He speaks to us as a present Father. If we meditate rightly upon the proofs of his care in this respect the feeling created in our minds will open to us far wider prospects of heavenly mercy; and we shall learn to hope in an infinitely greater salvation than that accomplished for us by any temporal deliverance, however striking and important. In the same way, by regarding the intimations which Jesus gave his disciples of his care of them on earth, as applicable to our own condition, the assurance of his goodness, with which we shall thus become impressed, will not let us rest in the first stage of faith. We shall be urged on by the foresight of future days, to look at him as a Saviour in eternity as well as in time. But in both cases there will be this peculiarity,—as long as the divine goodness is contemplated only in particular instances, the gratitude which they create will be as imperfect as the feeling of security. It is when the mind passes from the stage of faith in which it depends upon special manifestations of mercy, to that in which it recognises the all-comprehensive work of grace, that both the devotion and the happiness of the soul are proportionable to the greatness of its deliverance.

It is not difficult to understand, from some such considerations as these, that the idea of salvation, in the fullest sense of the term, or that of a Saviour, complete in all the attributes of so glorious a character, may be formed long before either the mind, or the heart, dare trust itself to believe in the existence of the reality. Wants of every kind, sorrows and trials, may help us to form some notion of what a Saviour should be. When the mysterious alarms of the soul give our higher instincts more than ordinary activity, we have a still stronger feeling of the awful responsibility which would rest on any being whatsoever who should offer himself, without numberless limitations, as a Saviour to so helpless, so distressed, and so perverted a creature as man.

But the nearer men approach the truth in forming a notion of what is needed in salvation, the farther they are likely to be, as far as mere natural understanding is concerned, from the hope that a complete salvation can ever be realized. The man who asks himself earnestly, what he would regard as salvation, finds, to his astonishment, that the whole subject changes its character the farther he proceeds in his inquiry. At the beginning he believed that he should be ready to call any one Saviour who should free him from the cares, or alarms, immediately pressing upon him. Viewing the present trouble as something overcome, and as a thing of the past, he would still feel there was something for a Saviour to do. It might be that the infirmities of his body were bowing him down, and then he would think of a physician who, in the possible range of his imagination, might restore his exhausted vigour. Or he might be trembling at the prospect of lost faculties; of a ruined, or, at least, weakened intellect. Then his desires would be diverted to a Saviour who, by some marvellous spiritual power, could renew his inward life. Nor would a man, in ordinary circumstances, long remain contented with the idea of a Saviour who could accomplish one of these great works, but only one. Human nature covets for itself, as such, a complete salvation. The body falling into the grave, yearns for a resurrection. Mind takes part with it, and thinks not for itself alone. The soul refuses to compromise with death at the expense of the affections and associations formed with the body. Salvation is needed for the whole man. But who is to confer such a boon? who can enter into all the necessities of the case? solving the abstruse problems connected with the life of the soul; and sympathizing with the affections which have been formed on earth, and in time? This can Jesus do: this he has done. He, and he alone, is the complete Saviour of whom we stand in need.

H. S.

CHRIST A COMPLETE SAVIOUR;

THE INTERCESSION OF CHRIST, AND WHO ARE PRIVILEGED IN IT.

" Wherefore he is able also to save them to the uttermost that come unto God by him, seeing he ever liveth to make intercession for them."—HEB. vii. 25.

THE Apostle in this chapter presenteth us with two things; that is, with the greatness of the person, and of the priesthood of our Lord Jesus.

First. He presenteth us with the greatness of his person, in that he preferreth him before Abraham, who is the father of us all: yea, in that he preferreth him before Melchisedec, who was above Abraham, and blessed him who had the promises.

Second. As to his priesthood, he showeth the greatness of that, in that he was made a priest, not by the law of a carnal commandment, but by the power of an endless life. Not without, but with an oath, by him that said, " The Lord sware, and will not repent, thou art a priest for ever after the order of Melchisedec," (Heb. vii. 11, 17, 21; vi. 20;) wherefore this man, because he liveth for ever, hath an unchangeable priesthood. (Heb. vii. 24.) Now my text is drawn from this conclusion, namely, that Christ abideth a priest continually: " Wherefore he is able also to save to the uttermost them that come unto God by him, seeing he ever liveth to make intercession for them."

In the words I take notice of four things:

1. Of the intercession of Christ—" He maketh intercession."

2. Of the benefit of his intercession—" Wherefore he is able also to save to the uttermost," &c.

3. We have also here set before us the persons interested in this intercession of Christ; and they are those " that come unto God by him."

4. We have also here the certainty of their reaping this benefit by him, to wit, seeing he ever liveth to make intercession for them: " Wherefore he is able also to save them to the uttermost that come unto God by him, seeing he ever liveth to make intercession for them."

I. *On the intercession of Christ.*

We will begin with his intercession, and will show you,

1. What that is.

2. For what he intercedes. And,

3. What is also to be inferred from Christ's making intercession for us.

1. I begin, then, with the first, that is, to show you what intercession is. Intercession is prayer; but all prayer is not intercession. Intercession, then, is that prayer that is made by a third person about the concerns that are between two. And it may be made either to set them at further difference, or to make them friends—for intercession may be made against as well as for a person or people. " Know ye not what the Scripture saith of Elias, how he maketh intercession to God against Israel?" (Rom. xi. 2.) But the intercession that we are now to speak of is not an intercession of this kind—not an intercession against, but an intercession for a people. " He ever liveth to make intercession for them." The high priest is ordained for, but not to be against the people. " Every high priest taken from among men is ordained for men in things pertaining to God," to make reconciliation for the sins of the people; or " that he may offer both gifts and sacrifices for sin." (Heb. v. 1.) This, then, is intercession, and the intercession of Christ is to be between two—between God and man, for man's good. And it extendeth itself unto these—

(1.) To pray that the elect may be brought all home to him, that is, to God.

(2.) To pray that their sins committed after conversion may be forgiven them.

(3.) To pray that their graces which they receive at conversion may be maintained and supplied.

(4.) To pray that their persons may be preserved unto his heavenly kingdom.

2. This is the intercession of Christ, or that for which he doth make intercession.

(1.) He prays for all the elect, that they may be brought home to God, and so into the unity of the faith, &c. This is clear, for that he saith,

" Neither pray I for these alone," that is, for those only that are converted, " but for them also that shall believe on me through their word," (John xvii. 20 ;) for all them that shall, that are appointed to believe; or, as you have it a little above, " For all them which thou hast given me." (John xvii. 9.) And the reason is, for that he hath paid a ransom for them. Christ, therefore, when he maketh intercession for the ungodly—and all the unconverted elect are such—doth but petitionarily ask for his own, his purchased ones, those for whom he died before, that they might be saved by his blood.

(2.) When any of them are brought home to God, he yet prays for them—namely, that the sins which through infirmity they after conversion may commit, may also be forgiven them.

This is showed us by the intercession of the high priest under the law, that was to bear away the iniquities of the holy things of the children of Israel; yea, and also by his atonement for them that sinned: for that it saith, " And the priest shall make an atonement for him, for his sin which he hath sinned, and it shall be forgiven him." (Lev. v. 10.)

This also is intimated even where our Lord doth make intercession, saying, " I pray not that thou shouldest take them out of the world, but that thou shouldest keep them from the evil." (John xvii. 15.)

That Christ prayed that the converted should be kept from all manner of commission of sin, must not be supposed; for that is the way to make his intercession, at least in some things, invalid, and to contradict himself; for, saith he, " I knew that thou hearest me always." (John xi. 42.) But the meaning is, I pray that thou wouldest keep them from soul-damning delusions, such as are unavoidably such; also that thou wouldest keep them from the soul-destroying evil of every sin, of every temptation. Now this he doth by his prevailing, and by his pardoning grace.

(3.) In his intercession he prayeth also that those graces which we receive at conversion may be maintained and supplied. This is clear where he saith, " Simon, Simon, behold Satan hath desired to have you, that he might sift you as wheat; but I have prayed for thee, that thy faith fail not." (Luke xxii. 31, 32.) Ay, may some say, he is said to pray here for the support and supply of faith; but doth it therefore follow that he prayed for the maintaining and supply of all our graces? Yes, in that he prayed for the preservation of our faith, he prayed for the preservation of all our graces; for faith is the mother-grace, the root-grace, the grace that hath all others in the bowels of it, and that from the which all others flow; yea, it is that which gives being to all our other graces, and that by which all the rest do live. Let, then, faith be preserved, and all graces continue and live, that is, according to the present

state, health, and degree of faith. So, then, Christ prayed for the preservation of every grace, when he prayed for the preservation of faith. That text also is of the same tendency, where he saith, " Keep through thine own name those whom thou hast given me." (John xvii. 11.) Keep them in thy fear, in the faith, in the true religion, in the way of life by thy grace, by thy power, by thy wisdom, &c. This must be much of the meaning of this place, and he that excludes this sense will make but poor work of another exposition.

(4.) He also in his intercession prayeth that our persons be preserved and brought safe unto his heavenly kingdom. And this he doth—

(a.) By pleading interest in them.

(b.) By pleading that he had given, by promise, glory to them.

(c.) By pleading his own resolution to have it so.

(d.) By pleading the reason why it must be so.

(a.) He prays that their persons may come to glory, for that they are his, and that by the best of titles : " Thine they were, and thou gavest them me." (John xvii. 6.) Father, I will have them : Father, I *will* have them, for they are mine : " Thine they were, and thou gavest them me." What is mine, my wife, or my child, or my jewel, or my joy, sure I may have it with me. Thus therefore he pleads, or cries in his intercession, that our persons might be preserved to glory : They are mine, " and thou gavest them me."

(b.) He also pleads that he had given—given already, that is, in the promise—glory to them, and therefore they must not go without it. " And the glory which thou gavest me, I have given them." (John xvii. 22.) Righteous men, when they give a good thing by promise, they design the performance of that promise ; nay, they more than design it, they purpose, they determine it. As the mad prophet also saith of God, in another case, " Hath he said, and shall he not do it? or hath he spoken, and shall he not make it good?" (Numb. xxiii. 19.) Hath Christ given us glory, and shall we not have it? Yea, hath the truth itself bestowed it upon us, and shall those to whom it is given—even given by scripture of truth—be yet deprived thereof?

(c.) He pleads, in his interceding that they might have glory, his own resolution to have it so : " Father, I will that they also whom thou hast given me, be with me where I am." (John xvii. 24.) Behold ye here, he is resolved to have it so; it must be so; it shall be so; I will have it so. We read of Adonijah, that his father never denied him in anything. He never said to him, Why hast thou done so? (1 Kings i. 6.) Indeed he denied him the kingdom, for his brother was heir of that from the Lord. How much more will our Father let our Lord Jesus have his mind and will in this, since he also is as willing to have it so, as is the Son himself: " Fear not, little flock; for it is your Father's good pleasure to give you the kingdom." (Luke xii. 32.) Resolution will drive things far, especially resolution to do that which none but they that cannot hinder shall oppose. Why, this is the case: the resolution of our Intercessor is, that we be preserved to glory; yea, and this resolution he pleads in his intercession: "Father, I will that they also whom thou hast given me, be with me where I am," &c. (John xvii. 24.) Must it not therefore now be so?

(d.) He also in the last place, in this his intercession, urges a reason why he will have it so, namely, "That they may behold my glory which thou hast given me, for thou lovedst me before the foundation of the world." (John xvii. 24.)

And this is a reason to the purpose. It is as if he had said, Father, these have continued with me in my temptations; these have seen me under all my disadvantages; these have seen me in my poor, low, contemptible condition; these have seen what scorn, reproach, slanders, and disgrace I have borne for thy sake in the world: and now I will have them also be where they shall see me in thy glory. I have told them that I am thy Son, and they have believed that; I have told them that thou lovest me, and they have believed that; I have also told them that thou wouldst take me again to glory, and they have believed that: but they have not seen my glory, nor can they but be like the Queen of Sheba, they will but believe by the halves, unless their own eyes do behold it. Besides, Father, these are they that love me, and it will be an increase of their joy, if they may but see me in glory. It will be as a heaven to their hearts, to see their Saviour in glory. I will therefore that those which "thou hast given me, be with me where I am, that they may behold my glory." This therefore is a reason why Christ Jesus our Lord intercedes to have his people with him in glory.

3. I come now to the third thing, namely, To show you what is to be inferred from Christ's making intercession for us.

(1.) This is to be inferred from hence, that saints—for I will here say nothing of those of the elect uncalled—do ofttimes give occasion of offence to God, even they that have received grace. For intercession is made to continue one in the favour of another, and to make up those breaches that at any time shall happen to be made by one, to the alienating of the affections of the other. And thus he makes reconciliation for iniquity. For reconciliation may be made for iniquity two ways: first, by paying of a price; secondly, by insisting upon the price paid for the offender, by way of intercession. Therefore you read, that as a goat was to be killed, so his blood was by the priest to be brought within the vail, and in a way of intercession to be sprinkled before, and upon the mercy-seat: "Then shall he kill the goat of the sin-offering that is for the people, and bring his blood within the vail, and do with that blood as he did with the blood of the bullock, and

sprinkle it upon the mercy-seat, and before the mercy-seat: and he shall make an atonement for the holy place, because of the uncleannesses of the children of Israel, and because of their transgressions in all their sins: and so shall he do for the tabernacle of the congregation that remaineth among them, in the midst of all their uncleanness." (Lev. xvi. 15, 16.) This was to be done as you see, that the tabernacle, which was the place of God's presence and graces, might yet remain among the children of Israel, notwithstanding their uncleannesses and transgressions. This also is the effect of Christ's intercession; it is that the signs of God's presence and his grace might remain among his people, notwithstanding they have, by their transgressions, so often provoked God to depart from them.

(2.) By Christ's intercession I gather, that awakened men and women, such as the godly are, dare not, after offence given, come in their own names to make unto God an application for mercy. God in himself is a consuming fire, and sin has made the best of us, as stubble is to fire: wherefore they may not, they cannot, they dare not approach God's presence for help, but by and through a mediator and intercessor. When Israel saw the fire, the blackness and darkness, and heard the thunder and lightning and the terrible sound of the trumpet, they said unto Moses, "Speak thou with us, and we will hear: but let not God speak with us, lest we die." (Exod. xx. 19; Deut. xviii. 16.) Guilt, and sense of the disparity that is betwixt God and us, will make us look out for a man that may lay his hand upon us both; and that may set us right in the eyes of our Father again. This, I say, I infer from the intercession of Christ. For, if there had been a possibility of our ability to have approached God with advantage without, what need had there been of the intercession of Christ?

Absalom durst not approach—no not the presence of his father by himself—without a mediator and intercessor; wherefore he sends to Joab to go to the king and make intercession for him. (2 Sam. xiv. 32, 33.) Also, Joab durst not go upon that errand himself, but by the mediation of another. (2 Sam. xiv. 1—11.) Sin is a fearful thing, and it will quash and quell the courage of a man, and make him afraid to approach the presence of him whom he has offended, though the offended is but a man. How much more then shall it discourage a man, when once loaden with guilt and shame, from attempting to approach the presence of a holy, and a sin-revenging God, unless he can come to him through, and in the name of an intercessor? But here now is the help and comfort of the people of God—there is to help them under all their infirmities, an intercessor prepared, and at work: "He ever liveth to make intercession."

(3.) I also infer from hence, that should we, out of an ignorant boldness and presumption, attempt, when we have offended, by ourselves to approach the presence of God, God would not accept us. He told Eliphaz so. What Eliphaz thought, or was about to do, I know not; but God said unto him, "My wrath is kindled against thee, and against thy two friends, for ye have not spoken of me the thing that is right, as my servant Job hath. Therefore take unto you now seven bullocks and seven rams, and go to my servant Job, and offer up for yourselves, (that is, by him) a burnt offering, and my servant Job shall pray for you, for him will I accept, lest I deal with you after your folly, in that ye have not spoken of me the thing which is right, like my servant Job." (Job xlii. 7, 8.) See here, an offence is a bar and an obstruction to acceptance with God, but by a mediator, but by an intercessor. He that comes to God by himself, God will answer him by himself, that is, without an intercessor. And I will tell you such are not like to get any pleasant or comfortable answer—I will answer him that so cometh, according to the multitude of his idols. "And I will set my face against that man, and will make him a sign and a proverb, and I will cut him off from the midst of my people, and ye shall know that I am the Lord." (Ezek. xiv. 8.)

He that intercedes for another, with a holy and just God, had need be clean himself, lest he, with whom he busieth himself, say to him, "First clear thyself, and then come and speak for thy friend." Wherefore this is the very description and qualification of this our high priest and blessed intercessor. "For such an high priest became us, who is holy, harmless, undefiled, separate from sinners, and made higher than the heavens: who needeth not daily, as those high priests, to offer up sacrifice, first for his own sins, and then for the people's: for this he did once, when he offered up himself." (Heb. vii. 26, 27.) Had we not had such an intercessor, we had been but in a very poor case; but we have one that becomes us, one that fits us to the purpose, one against whom our God hath nothing, can object nothing; one in whose mouth no guile could be found.

(4.) Since Christ is an Intercessor, I infer, that he has wherewithal in readiness to answer to any demands that may be propounded by him that hath been by us offended, in order to a renewing of peace, and letting out of that grace to us that we have sinned away, and yet have need of. Ofttimes the offended saith to the intercessor, "Well, thou comest to me about this man: what interest he has in thee is one thing, what offence he has committed against me is another." I speak now after the manner of men. Now, what can an intercessor do, if he is not able to answer this question? But now, if he be able to answer this question—that is, according to law and justice—no question but he may prevail with the offended, for him for whom he makes intercession.

Why this is our case, to be sure thus far it is, we have offended a just and a holy God, and Jesus Christ is become Intercessor. He also knows full well, that for our parts, if it would save us from hell, we cannot produce towards a peace with God, so much as poor two farthings; that is, not anything that can by law and justice be esteemed worth a halfpenny; yet he makes intercession. It follows, therefore, that he hath wherewith of his own, if that question afore is propounded, to answer to every reasonable demand. Hence it is said, that he has gifts as well as sacrifice for sin. "Every high priest is ordained to offer gifts and sacrifices; wherefore it is of necessity, that this man have somewhat also to offer." (Heb. viii. 3.) And observe it, that the apostle speaks here of Christ as in heaven, there ministering in the second part of his office. "For if he were on earth, he should not be a priest." (Heb. viii. 4.) These gifts, therefore, and this sacrifice, he now offereth in heaven by way of intercession, urging and pleading as an Intercessor, the valuableness of his gifts, for the pacifying of that wrath that our Father hath conceived against us for the disobediences that we are guilty of: "A gift in secret pacifieth anger, and a reward in the bosom strong wrath." (Prov. xxi. 14.)

What gifts these are the Scripture everywhere testifies. He gave himself, he gave his life, he gave his all for us. (John vi. Gal. i. 4. 1 Tim. ii. 6. Matt. xx. 28.) These gifts, as he offered them up at the demand of justice, on Mount Calvary for us; so now he is in heaven, he presenteth them continually before God, as gifts and sacrifice valuable for the sins, for all the sins, that we through infirmity do commit, from the day of our conversion to the day of our death. And these gifts are so satisfactory, so prevalent with God, that they always prevail for a continual remission of our sins with him. Yea, they prevail with him for more than for the remission of sins; we have, through their procurement, our graces often renewed, the devil often rebuked, the snare often broken, guilt often taken away from the conscience, and many a blessed smile from God, and love-look from his life-creating countenance. (Eph. iii. 12.)

5. Since Christ is an Intercessor, I infer that believers should not rest at the cross for comfort; justification they should look for there; but, being justified by his blood, they should ascend up after him to the throne. At the cross you will see him in his sorrows and humiliations, in his tears and blood; but follow him to where he is now, and then you shall see him in his robes, in his priestly robes, and with his golden girdle about his paps. Then you shall see him wearing the breast-plate of judgment, and with all your names written upon his heart. Then you shall perceive that the whole family in heaven and earth is named by him, and how he prevaileth with God, the Father of mercies, for you. Stand still awhile, and listen; yea, enter with boldness into the holiest, and see

your Jesus, as he now appears in the presence of God for you; what work he makes against the devil, and sin, and death, and hell, for you. (Heb. x. 9.) Ah, it is brave following of Jesus Christ to the holiest, the vail is rent, you may see with open face, as in a glass, the glory of the Lord. This then is our High Priest, this is intercession, these the benefits of it. It lieth in our part to improve it; and wisdom to do that also comes from the mercy-seat or throne of grace, where he, even our High Priest, ever liveth to make intercession for us: to whom be glory for ever and ever.

And thus have I spoken to the first thing—to wit, of the intercession of Christ.

II. *On the benefits of Christ's Intercession.*

And now I come more particularly to speak to the second, the benefits of his intercession, namely, that we are saved hereby : " Wherefore he is able also to save them, seeing he ever liveth to make intercession for them." "He is able also to save them to the uttermost."

In my handling of this head I must show you,

1. What the apostle means here by save— "wherefore he is able to *save.*"

2. What he means here by saving to the *uttermost* —" He is able to save to the *uttermost.*"

3. And then, thirdly, we shall do as we did in the foregoing—to wit, gather some inferences from the whole, and speak to them.

1. What doth the apostle mean here by save— " he is able to *save* them."

To *save* may be taken two ways. In the general, I know it may be taken many ways; for there are many salvations that we enjoy, yea, that we never knew, nor can know, until we come thither where all secret things shall be seen, and where that which has been done in darkness shall be proclaimed upon the house-tops.

But I say there are two ways that this word may be taken.

(1.) To save in a way of justification.

(2.) Or to save in a way of preservation.

Now Christ saves both these ways : but which of these, or whether both of them are intended in this place, of that I shall tell you my thoughts anon ; meanwhile I will show you,

(1.) What it is to be saved in the first sense.

(2.) And also how that is brought to pass.

(1.) To be saved, is to be delivered from guilt of sin that is by the law, as it is the ministration of death and condemnation ; or to be set free therefrom before God. This is to be saved ; for he that is not set free therefrom, whatever he may think of himself, or whatever others may think concerning him, he is a condemned man. It saith not, he shall be, but he is condemned already. (John iii. 18.) The reason is, for that he has deserved the sentence of the ministration of condemnation, which is the law ; yea, that law has

already arraigned, accused, and condemned him before God, for that it hath found him guilty of sin. Now he that is set free from this, or, as the phrase is, " being made free from sin," (Rom. vi. 22,) that is, from the imputation of guilt, there can to him be no condemnation, no condemnation to hell-fire ; but the person thus made free, may properly be said to be saved. Wherefore, as sometimes it saith, we shall be saved, respecting saving in the second sense, or the utmost completing of salvation, so sometimes it saith we are saved, as respecting our being already secured from guilt, and so from condemnation to hell for sin, and so set safe, and quit from the second death before God. (1 Cor. i. 18. Eph. ii. 5.)

Now, saving thus comes to us by what Christ did for us in this world, by what Christ did for us as suffering for us. I say, it comes to us thus ; that is, it comes to us by grace, through the redemption that is in Christ. And thus to be saved is called justification ; justification to life, because one thus saved is, as I said, acquitted from guilt, and that everlasting damnation to which for sin he had made himself obnoxious by the law. (1 Cor. xv. 1—4. Rom. v. 8—10.)

Hence we are said to be saved by his death, justified by his blood, and reconciled to God by the death of his Son ; all which must respect his offering of himself on the day he died, and not his improving of his so dying in a way of intercession, because in the same place the apostle reserveth a second, or an additional salvation, and applieth that to his intercession, "much more then," being now, or already, "justified by his blood, we shall be saved from wrath through him," that is, through what he will further do for us. For if when we were enemies, we were reconciled to God by the death of his Son, much more being reconciled, (that is, by his death,) " we shall be saved by his life," his intercession, which he ever liveth to complete.

See, here we are said to be justified, reconciled already, and therefore we shall be saved, justified by his blood and death, and saved through him by his life.

(2.) Now, the saving intended in the text is saving in this second sense ; that is, a saving of us by preserving us, by delivering of us from all those hazards that we run betwixt our state of justification and our state of glorification. Yea, such a saving of us as we that are justified need, to bring us into glory. Therefore, when he saith he is able to save, seeing he ever liveth to make intercession, he addeth saving to saving ; saving by his life to saving by his death ; saving by his improving of his blood to saving by his spilling of his blood. He gave himself a ransom for us, and now improves that gift in the presence of God, by way of intercession. For, as I have hinted already, the high priest, under the law, took the blood of the sacrifices that were offered for sin, and brought it within the vail, and there sprinkled it before and upon the mercy-seat, and by it made intercession for the people to an additional way of saving them: the sum of which Paul thus applies to Christ when he saith, "He can save, seeing he ever liveth to make intercession."

That also in the Romans is clear to this purpose, "Who is he that condemneth? It is Christ that died," (Rom. viii. 31—39;) that is, who is he that shall lay anything to the charge of God's elect to condemnation to hell, since Christ has taken away the curse, by his death, from before God? Then he adds, that there is nothing that shall yet happen to us, shall destroy us, since Christ also liveth to make intercession for us: "Who shall condemn? It is Christ that died, yea, rather that is risen again, who even is at the right hand of God, and maketh intercession for us."

Christ, then, by his death saveth us, as we are sinners, enemies, and in a state of condemnation by sin; and Christ by his life saveth us as considered justified, and reconciled to God by his blood. So then we have salvation from that condemnation that sin had brought us unto, and salvation from those ruins that all the enemies of our souls would yet bring us unto, but cannot; for the intercession of Christ preventeth. (Rom. vi. 7—10.)

Christ hath redeemed us from the curse of the law. Whatever the law can take hold of to curse us for, that Christ has redeemed us from, by being made a curse for us. But this curse that Christ was made for us, must be confined to his sufferings, not to his exaltation; and, consequently, not to his intercession, for Christ is made no curse but when he suffered; not in his intercession: so then, as he died he took away the curse, and sin that was the cause thereof, by the sacrifice of himself, and by his life, his intercession, he saveth us from all those things that attempt to bring us into that condemnation again.

The salvation, then, that we have by the intercession of Christ, as was said—I speak now of them that are capable of receiving comfort and relief by this doctrine—is salvation that follows upon, or that comes after, justification. We that are saved as to justification of life, need yet to be saved with that that preserveth to glory. For though by the death of Christ we are saved from the curse of the law, yet attempts are made by many, that we may be kept from the glory that justified persons are designed for; and from these we are saved by his intercession.

A man, then, that must be eternally saved, is to be considered, first, as an heir of wrath; and then as an heir of God. An heir of wrath he is in himself by sin; an heir of God he is by grace through Christ. (Eph. ii. 3. Gal. iv. 7.) Now, as an heir of wrath he is redeemed, and as an heir of God he is preserved: as an heir of wrath he is redeemed by blood, and as an heir of God he is preserved by this intercession.

Christ by his death, then, puts me, I being reconciled to God thereby, into a justified state, and God accepts me to grace and favour through him: but this doth not hinder but that, all this notwithstanding, there are that would frustrate me of the end to which I am designed by this reconciliation to God, by redemption through grace; and from the accomplishing of this design, I am saved by the blessed intercession of our Lord Jesus Christ.

Obj. 1. Perhaps some may say, we are not saved from all punishment of sin by the death of Christ; and if so, so not from all danger of damnation by the intercession of Christ.

Ans. We are saved from all punishment in hell-fire by the death of Christ. Jesus has "delivered us from the wrath to come." (1 Thess. i. 10.) So that as to this great punishment, God for his sake has forgiven us all trespasses. (Col. ii. 13.) But we, being translated from being slaves to Satan to be sons of God, God reserveth yet this liberty in his hand to chastise us if we offend, as a father chastiseth his son. (Deut. viii. 5.) But this chastisement is not in legal wrath, but in fatherly affection—not to destroy us, but that still we might be made to get advantage thereby, even be made partakers of his holiness. This is, that we might not be "condemned with the world." (Heb. xii. 5—11. 1 Cor. xi. 32.) As to the second part of the objection, there do, as we say, many things happen betwixt, or between, the cup and the lip, many things attempt to overthrow the work of God, and to cause that we should perish through our weakness, notwithstanding the price that hath by Christ been paid for us. But what saith the Scripture? "Who shall separate us from the love of Christ? Shall tribulation, or distress, or persecution, or famine, or nakedness, or peril, or sword? As it is written, For thy sake we are killed all the day long; we are accounted as sheep for the slaughter. Nay, in all these things we are more than conquerors, through him that loved us. For I am persuaded, that neither death, nor life, nor angels, nor principalities, nor powers, nor things present, nor things to come, nor height, nor depth, nor any other creature, shall be able to separate us from the love of God, which is in Christ Jesus our Lord." (Rom. vii. 35—39.)

Thus the apostle reckoneth up all the disadvantages that a justified person is incident to in this life, and by way of challenge declares, that not any one of them, nor all together, shall be able to separate us from the love of God, that is, towards us by Christ, his death, and his intercession.

Obj. 2. It may be further objected, that the apostle doth here leave out sin, unto which we know the saints are subject, after justification. And sin of itself—we need no other enemies—is of that nature as to destroy the whole world.

Ans. Sin is sin, in the nature of sin, wherever

it is found. But sin, as to the damning effects thereof, is taken away from them unto whom righteousness is imputed for justification. Nor shall any or all the things afore-mentioned, though there is a tendency in every one of them to drive us into sin, drown us, through it, in perdition and destruction: "I am persuaded (says Paul) they shall never be able to do that." The apostle therefore doth implicitly, though not expressly, challenge sin, yea, sin by all its advantages; and then glorieth in the love of God in Christ Jesus, from which he concludeth it shall never separate the justified. Besides, it would now have been needless to have expressly here put in sin by itself, seeing, before he had argued, that those he speaks of were freely justified therefrom.

One word more before I go to the second head.

The Father, as I told you, has reserved to himself a liberty to chastise his sons, to wit, with temporal chastisements, if they offend. This still abideth to us, notwithstanding God's grace, Christ's death, or blessed intercession. And this punishment is so surely entailed to the transgressions that we who believe shall commit, that it is impossible that we should be utterly freed therefrom; insomuch that the apostle positively concludeth them to be bastards, what pretences to sonship soever they have, if they are not, for sin, partakers of fatherly chastisements.

For the reversing of this punishment it is that we should pray, if perhaps God will remit it, when we are taught to say, "Our Father, forgive us our trespasses." And he that admits of any other sense as to this petition, derogates from the death of Christ, or faith, or both. For either he concludes that for some of his sins Christ did not die, or that he is bound to believe that God, though he did, has not yet, nor will forgive them, till from the petitioner some legal work be done: "Forgive us, as we forgive them that trespass against us." (Matt. vi. 14, 15.) But now apply this to temporal punishments, and then it is true that God has reserved a liberty in his hand to punish even the sins of his people upon them; yea, and will not pardon their sin, as to the remitting of such punishment, unless some good work by them be done: "If you forgive not men their trespasses, neither will your heavenly Father forgive your trespasses." (Matt. vi. 15; xviii. 28—35.)

And this is the cause why some that belong to God are yet so under the afflicting hand of God: they have sinned, and God, who is their Father, punisheth: yea, and this is the reason why some who are dear to God have this kind of punishment never forgiven, but it abides with them to their lives' end, goes with them to the day of their death—yea, is the very cause of their death. By this punishment they are cut off out of the land of the living. But all this is that they might not be "condemned with the world." (1 Cor. xi. 32.)

Christ died not to save from this punishment; Christ intercedes not to save from this punishment. Nothing but a good life will save from this punishment; nor always that either.

The hidings of God's face, the harshness of his providences, the severe and sharp chastisements that ofttimes overtake the very spirits of his people, plainly show that Christ died not to save from temporal punishments, prays not to save from temporal punishments—that is, absolutely. God has reserved a power to punish, with temporal punishments, the best and dearest of his people, if need be. And sometimes he remits them, sometimes not, even as it pleases him.

I come now to the second thing.

Christ saves to the uttermost.

2. I shall now show you something of what it is for Christ by his intercession to save to the *uttermost*—"He is able to save them to the uttermost."

This is a great expression, and carrieth with it much. *Uttermost* signifieth to the outside, to the end, to the last, to the furthest part; and it hath respect both to persons and things. (Gen. xlix. 26. Deut. xxx. 4. Matt. v. 26. Mark xiii. 27. Luke xv.)

1. To persons. Some persons are, in their own apprehensions, even further from Christ than anybody else; afar off, a great way off, yet a-coming, as the prodigal was. Now, these many times are exceedingly afraid; the sight of that distance that they think is betwixt Christ and them makes them afraid. As it is said in another place, "They also that dwell in the uttermost parts, are afraid at thy tokens," (Ps. lxv. 8;) so these are afraid they shall not speed, not obtain that for which they come to God. But the scripture saith, "He is able to save to the uttermost, (to the very hindermost,) them that come to God by him."

Two sorts of men seem to be far, very far from God—the town-sinner and the great backslider. But both these, if they come, he is able to save to the uttermost. (Neh. i. 9.) He is able to save them from all those dangers that they fear will prevent their obtaining of that grace and mercy they would have to help them in time of need. The publicans and harlots enter into the kingdom of heaven.

2. As this scripture respecteth persons, so it respecteth things. There are some things with which some are attended, that are coming to God by Christ, that make their coming hard, and very difficult.

(1.) There is a more than ordinary breaking up of the corruptions of their nature. It seems as if their lusts and the vile passions of the flesh were become masters, and might now do what they will with the soul. Yea, they take this man, and toss and tumble him like a ball in a large place. This man is not a master of himself, of his thoughts, nor of his passions: his iniquities, like the wind, do carry him away. (Isa. lxiv. 6.) He thinks to go forward, but this wind blows him backward; he laboureth against this wind, but cannot find that he getteth ground: he takes what advantage opportunity doth minister to him; but all he gets is to be beat out of heart, out of breath, out of courage: he stands still, and pants, and gapeth as for life: "I opened my mouth, and panted," said David, "for I longed for thy commandments." (Ps. cxix. 131.) He sets forward again, but has nothing but labour and sorrow.

(2.) Nay, to help forward his calamity, Satan and his angels will not be wanting, both to trouble his head with the fumes of their stinking breath, nor to throw up his heels in their dirty places. "And as he was yet a-coming, the devil threw him down and tare him." (Luke ix. 42.) How many strange, hideous, and amazing blasphemies, have those, some of those that are coming to and against Christ, injected and fixed upon their spirits against him! Nothing so common to such, as to have some hellish wish or other against God they are coming to, and against Christ by whom they would come to him. These blasphemies are like those frogs that I have heard of, that will leap up, and catch hold of, and hang by their claws. Now help, Lord; now, Lord Jesus, what shall I do? Now, Son of David, have mercy upon me. I say, to say these words is hard work for such an one. But he is able to save to the uttermost this comer to God by him.

(3.) There are also the oppositions of sense and reason hard at work, for the devil, against the soul. The men of his own house are risen up against him. One's sense and reason, one would think, should not fall in with the devil against ourselves; and yet nothing more common, nothing more natural, than for our own sense and reason to turn the unnatural, and war both against our God and us. And now it is hard coming to God. Better can a man hear, and deal with any objections against himself, than with those that himself doth make against himself. They lie close, stick fast, speak aloud, and will be heard; yea, will haunt and hunt him (as the devil doth some) in every hole and corner. But come, man, come; for he is able to save to the uttermost.

(4.) Now guilt is the consequence and fruit of all this; and what so intolerable a burden as guilt? They talk of the stones and of the sands of the sea, but it is guilt that breaks the heart with its burden. And Satan has the art of making the uttermost of every sin; he can blow it up, make it swell, make every hair of his head as big as a cedar. He can tell how to make it a heinous offence, an unpardonable offence, an offence of that continuance, and committed against so much light, that (says he) it is impossible it should ever be forgiven. But, soul, he [Christ] is able to save to the uttermost, he can "do exceeding abundantly above all that we can ask or think." (Eph. iii. 20.)

(5.) Join to all this the rage and terror of men, which thing of itself is sufficient to quash and break to pieces all desires to come to God by Christ; yea, and it doth do so to thousands that are not willing to go to hell. Yet thou art kept, and made to go panting on; a whole world of men, and devils, and sin, are not able to keep thee from coming. But how comes it to pass that thou art so hearty, that thou settest thy face against so much wind and weather? I dare say it arises not from thyself, not from any of thine enemies: this comes from God, though thou art not aware thereof; and is obtained for thee by the intercession of the blessed Son of God, who is also able to save thee to the uttermost, that comest to God by him.

(6.) And for a conclusion as to this, I will add, that there is much of the honour of the Lord Jesus engaged as to the saving of the coming man to the uttermost: "I am glorified in them," saith he. (John xvii. 10.) He is exalted to be a Saviour. (Acts v. 31.) And if the blessed One doth count it an exaltation to be a Saviour, surely it is an exaltation to be a Saviour, and a great one. "They shall cry unto the Lord because of their oppressors, and he shall send them a Saviour, and a great one, and he shall deliver them." (Isa. xix. 20.) If it is a glory to be a Saviour, a great Saviour, then it is a glory for a Saviour, a great one, to save, and save, and save to the uttermost—to the uttermost man, to the uttermost sin, to the uttermost temptation. And hence it is, that he saith again, speaking of the transgressions, sins, and iniquities that he would pardon, that it should turn to him for a name of joy, a praise, and an honour before all nations. (Jer. xxxiii. 9.) He therefore counts it an honour to be a great Saviour, to save men to the uttermost.

When Moses said, "I beseech thee show me thy glory," the answer was, "I will make all my goodness pass before thee; and I will proclaim the name of the Lord before thee." (Exod. xxxiii. 18, 19.)

And when he came indeed to make proclamation, then he proclaimed, "The Lord, the Lord God, merciful and gracious, long-suffering and abundant in goodness and truth; keeping mercy for thousands, forgiving iniquity, and transgression, and sin, and that will by no means clear the guilty," (Exod. xxxiv. 6, 7;) and that will by no means clear them that will not come to me, that they may be saved. See here, if it is not by himself accounted his glory, to make his goodness—all his goodness—pass before us. And how can that be, if he saveth not to the uttermost all them that come unto God by him? For goodness is by us nowise seen, but by those acts by which it expresseth itself to be so. And I am sure, to save, to save to the uttermost, is one of the most eminent expressions by which we understand it is great goodness. I know goodness has many ways to express itself to be what it is to the world; but then it expresseth its greatness, when it pardons and saves; when it pardons and saves to the uttermost. My goodness, says Christ, extends not itself to my Father, but to my saints. (Ps. xvi. 2, 3.) My Father has no need of my goodness, but my saints have, and therefore it shall reach forth itself for their help, in whom is all my delight. And, "Oh how great is thy goodness which thou hast laid up for them that fear thee; which thou hast wrought for them that trust in thee before the sons of men!" (Ps. xxi. 19.) It is therefore that which tendeth to get Christ a name, fame, and glory, "to be able to save to the uttermost them that come to God by him."

Christ's ability to save, our safety.

But some may say, What is the meaning of this word *able?* "Wherefore he is *able* to save;" "he is able to save to the uttermost." How comes it to pass that his power to save is rather put in than his willingness? For willingness, saith the soul, would better have pleased me.

1. I will speak two or three words to this question. And,

By this word *able* is suggested to us the sufficiency of his merit, the great worthiness of his merit; for as Intercessor, he sticks fast by his merit. All his petitions, prayers, or supplications are grounded upon the worthiness of his person as Mediator, and on the validity of his offering as priest. This is the more clear, if you consider that the reason why those priests and sacrifices under the law could not make the worshippers perfect. It was, I say, because there wanted in them worthiness and merit in their sacrifices. But this man, when he came and offered his sacrifice, he did by that one act perfect for ever them that are sanctified or set apart for glory. Wherefore "this man, after he had offered up one sacrifice for sin, for ever sat down on the right hand of God." (Heb. x. 1—12.)

When Moses prayed for the people of Israel, thus he said, "And now, I beseech thee, let the power of my Lord be great, according as thou hast spoken." (Numb. xiv. 17.) But what had he spoken? "The Lord is long-suffering, and of great mercy, forgiving iniquity and transgression, and by no means clearing the guilty. Pardon, I beseech thee, the iniquity of this people, according unto the greatness of thy mercy, and as thou hast forgiven this people, from Egypt, even until now." (Numb. xiv. 18, 19.)

2. Has he but power, we know he is willing, else he would not have promised; it is also his glory to pardon and save. So then, in his ability lies our safety. What if he were never so willing, if he were not of ability sufficient, what would his willingness do? But he has showed, as I said, his willingness by promising, "Him that cometh to me, I will in no wise cast out," (John vi. 37;) so that now our comfort lies in his power, in that

he is able to make good his word. (Rom. iv. 20, 21.) And this also will then be seen, when he hath saved them that come to God by him, when he hath saved them to the uttermost: not to the uttermost of his ability, but to the uttermost of our necessity. For to the uttermost of his ability, I believe he will never be put to it to save his church; not for that he is loth so to save, but because there is no need so to save; he shall not need to put out all his power, and to press the utmost of his merit for the saving of his church. Alas! there is sufficiency of merit in him to save a thousand times as many more as are like to be saved by him: "He is able to do exceedingly abundantly above all that we ask or think." Measure not therefore what he can do by what he has, doth, or will do; neither do thou interpret this word, *to the uttermost,* as if it related to the uttermost of his ability, but rather as it relateth (for so it doth indeed) to the greatness of thy necessity. For as he is able to save thee, though thy condition be, as it may be supposed to be, the worst that ever man was in that was saved, so he is able to save thee though thy condition were ten times worse than it is.

What! shall not the worthiness of the Son of God be sufficient to save from the sin of man? or shall the sin of the world be of that weight to destroy, that it shall put Christ Jesus to the uttermost of the worth of his person and merit, to save therefrom? I believe it is blasphemy to think so. We can easily imagine that he can save all the world—that is, that he is of ability to do it; but we cannot imagine that he can do more than we can think he can. But our imagination and thoughts set no bounds to his ability—"He is able to do exceeding abundantly above all that we ask or think;" but what that is, I say, no man can think, no man can imagine. So, then, Jesus Christ can do more than ever any man thought he could do as to saving; he can do we know not what.

This, therefore, should encourage comers to come to him, and them that come to hope. This, I say, should encourage them to let out, to lengthen, and heighten their thoughts by the word, "to the uttermost," seeing he can "save to the uttermost them that come to God by him."

The benefits of Christ's intercession.

3. And now I come to the third thing that I told you I should speak to, and that is, to those inferences that may be gathered from these words.

1. Are they that are justified by Christ's blood such as have need yet to be saved by his intercession? Then from hence it follows that justification will stand with imperfection. It doth not, therefore, follow that a justified man is without infirmity, for he that is without infirmity—that is, perfect with absolute perfection—has no need to be yet saved by an act yet to be performed by a mediator, and his mediation.

When I say, justification will stand with imperfection, I do not mean that it will allow, countenance, or approve thereof, but I mean there is no necessity of our perfection, of our personal perfection, as to our justification, and that we are justified without it; yea, that that in justified persons remains.

Again, when I say that justification will stand with imperfection, I do not mean that in our justification we are imperfect; for in that we are complete: we are complete in him who is our justice. (Col. ii. 10.) If otherwise, the imperfection is in the matter that justifieth us, which is the righteousness of Christ; yea, and to say so, would conclude that wrong judgment proceedeth from him that imputeth that righteousness to us to justification, since an imperfect thing is imputed to us for justification. But far be it from any that believe that God is true to imagine such a thing; all his works are perfect: there is nothing wanting in them as to the present design.

Quest. But what, then, do we mean, when we say justification will stand with a state of imperfection?

Ans. Why, I mean, that justified men are yet sinners in themselves, are yet full of imperfections, yea, sinful imperfections. Justified Paul said, " I know that in me," that is, in my flesh, " dwelleth no good thing." (Rom. vii. 18; iv. 5; v. 8, 9.) While we are yet sinners we are justified by the blood of Christ. Hence again it is said, " he justifieth the ungodly." Justification, then, only covereth our sin from the sight of God: it maketh us not perfect with inherent perfection. But God, for the sake of that righteousness which by his grace is imputed to us, declareth us quit and discharged from the curse, and sees sin in us no more to condemnation.

Why the justified need an intercessor.

And this is the reason, or one reason, why they that are justified have need of an intercessor; to wit, to save us from the evil of the sin that remains in our flesh after we are justified by grace through Christ, and set free from the law as to condemnation. Therefore, as it is said, we are saved, so it is said, " He is able to save to the uttermost them that come to God by him, seeing he ever liveth to make intercession for them."

The godly—for now we will call them the godly, though there is yet abundance of sin in them—feel in themselves many things, even after justification, by which they are convinced they are still attended with personal sinful imperfections.

(1.) They feel unbelief, fear, mistrust, doubting, despondings, murmurings, blasphemies, pride, lightness, foolishness, avarice, fleshly lusts, heartlessness to good, wicked desires, low thoughts of Christ, too good thoughts of sin, and, at times, too great an itching after the worst of immoralities.

(2.) They feel in themselves an aptness to incline to errors as to lean to the works of the law for justification; to question the truth of the resurrection and judgment to come; to dissemble and play the hypocrite in profession and in performance of duties; to do religious duties rather to please man than God, who trieth the heart.

(3.) They feel an inclination in them, in times of trial, to faint under the cross, to seek too much to save themselves, to dissemble the known truth, for the obtaining a little favour with men, and to speak things that they ought not that they may sleep in a whole skin.

(4.) They feel wearisomeness in religious duties, but a natural propensity to things of the flesh. They feel a desire to go beyond bounds both at board, and bed, and bodily exercise, and in all lawful recreation.

(5.) They feel in themselves an aptness to take the advantage of using of things that are lawful, as food, raiment, sleep, talk, estates, relations, beauty, wit, parts, and graces, to unlawful ends. These things, with many more of the like kind, the justified man finds and feels in himself to his humbling and often casting down: and to save him from the destroying evil of these, Christ ever liveth to make intercession for him.

Again, the justified man is imperfect in his graces, and therefore needeth to be saved by the intercession of Christ, from the bad fruit that that imperfection yields.

Justifying righteousness is accompanied with graces—the graces of the Spirit. Though these graces are not that matter by and through which we are justified, nor any part thereof, that being only the obedience of Christ imputed to us of mere pleasure and goodwill; but, I say, they come when justification comes, (Rom. ix.,) and though they are not so easily discerned at the first, they show forth themselves afterwards. But, I say, how many soever they are, and how fast soever they grow, their utmost arrivement here is but a state short of perfection.

None of the graces of God's Spirit, in our hearts, can do their work in us without shortness, and that because of their own imperfections, and also because of the opposition that they meet with from our flesh.

(1.) Faith, which is the root-grace, the grand grace, its shortness is sufficiently manifest by its shortness of apprehension of things pertaining to the person, offices, relations, and works of Christ, now in the heavenly place for us. It is also very defective in its fetching of comfort from the word to us, and in continuing of it with us, when, at any time, we attain unto it. In its receiving of strength to subdue sin, and in its purifyings of the heart, (though indeed it doth what it doth in reality,) yet how short is it of doing of it thoroughly? Oftentimes, were it not for supplies, by virtue of the intercession of Christ, faith would fail of performing its office in any measure. (Luke xxii. 31, 32.)

(2.) There is hope, another grace of the Spirit, bestowed upon us; and how often is that also, as to the excellency of working, made to flag! "I shall perish," saith David, "I am cut off from before thine eyes," said he. (Ps. xxxi. 2.) And now, where was his hope in the right gospel discovery of it? Also, all our fear of men, and fears of death, and fears of judgment, they arise from the imperfections of hope. But from all those faults Christ saves us by his intercession.

(3.) There is love, that should be in us as hot as fire. It is compared to fire, to fire of the hottest sort; yea, it is said to be hotter than the coals of juniper. (Sol. Song viii. 6, 7.) But who finds this heat in love, so much as for one poor quarter of an hour together? Some little flashes, perhaps some, at some times, may feel; but where is that constant burning of affection, that the word, the love of God, and the love of Christ, calls for? yea, and that the necessities of the poor and afflicted members of Christ call for also? Ah! love is cold in these frozen days, and short when it is at the highest.

(4.) The grace of humility, where is it? who has a thimbleful thereof? Where is he that is clothed with humility, and that does what he is commanded with all humility of mind? (1 Pet. v. 5. Acts xx. 19.)

(5.) For zeal, where is that also? Zeal for God, against sin, profaneness, superstition, and idolatry. I speak now to the godly, who have this zeal in the root and habit; but, oh, how little of it puts forth itself into actions in such a day as this is!

(6.) There is reverence, fear, and standing in awe of God's word and judgments. Where are the excellent workings thereof to be found? and where it is most, how far short of perfect acts is it?

(7.) Simplicity, and godly sincerity also, with how much dirt is it mixed in the best, especially among those of the saints that are rich, who have got the poor and beggarly art of complimenting? For the more compliment, the less sincerity. Many words will not fill a bushel; but "in the multitude of words there wanteth not sin." (Prov. x. 19.) Plain men are thin come up in this day; to find a mouth without fraud and deceit now, is a rare thing. Thus might one count up all the graces of the Spirit, and show wherein every one of them are scanty and wanting of perfection. Now, look, what they want of perfection is supplied with sin and vanity; for there is a fulness of sin and flesh at hand, to make up all the vacant places in our souls. There is no place in the souls of the godly, but it is filled up with darkness when the light is wanting, and with sin, so far forth as grace is wanting. Satan also diligently waiteth to come in at the door, if Careless has left it a little ajar.

But, oh! the grace of our Lord Jesus Christ, who ever liveth to make intercession for us, and that by so doing, saves us from all the imperfect acts and workings of our graces, and from all the advantages that flesh, and sin, and Satan, getteth upon us thereby.

Further, as Christ Jesus our Lord doth save us, by his intercession, from that hurt that would unavoidably come upon us by these, so also, by that we are saved from the evil that is at any time found in any or all our holy duties and performances, that is our duty daily to be found in. That our duties are imperfect, follows upon what was discoursed before; for if our graces be imperfect, how can our duties but be so too?

(1.) Our prayers, how imperfect are they? with how much unbelief are they mixed! How apt is our tongue to run in prayer before our hearts! With how much earnestness do our lips move, while our hearts lie within as cold as a clod! Yea, and ofttimes it is to be feared, we ask for that with our mouth, that we care not whether we have or no. Where is the man that pursues, with all his might, what but now he seemed to ask for with all his heart? Prayer is become a shell, a piece of formality, a very empty thing, as to the spirit and life of prayer, at this day. I speak now of the prayers of the godly. I once met with a poor woman, that, in the greatest of her distresses, told me she did use to rise in the night, in cold weather, and pray to God, while she sweat with fears of the loss of her prayer and desires that her soul might be saved. I have heard of many that have prayed, but of few that have prayed till they have sweat, by reason of their wrestling with God for mercy in that duty.

(2.) There is the duty of almsgiving, another gospel performance; but how poorly is it done in our days! We have so many foolish ways to lay out money in toys, and fools' baubles for our children, that we can spare none, or very little for the relief of the poor. Also, do not many give that to their dogs, yea, let it lie in their houses until it stinks so vilely that neither dog nor cat will eat it, which, had it been bestowed well in time, might have been a succour and nourishment to some poor member of Christ?

(3.) There is hearing of the word: but, alas! the place of hearing is the place of sleeping with many a fine professor. I have often observed that those that keep shops can briskly attend upon a twopenny customer; but when they come themselves to God's market, they spend their time too much in letting their thoughts to wander from God's commandments, or in a nasty drowsy way The heads, also, and hearts of most hearers, are to the word as the sieve is to water: they can hold no sermon, remember no text, bring home no proof, produce none of the sermon to the edification and profit of others. And do not the best take up too much in hearing, and mind too little, what, by the word, God calls for at their hands, to perform it with a good conscience?

(4.) There is faithfulness in callings, faithfulness to brethren, faithfulness to the world, faithfulness to children, to servants, to all according to our place and capacity. Oh! how little of it is there found in the mouths and lives, to speak nothing of the hearts, of professors.

I will proceed no further in this kind of repetition of things; only thus much give me leave to say over again, even many of the truly godly are very faulty here. But what would they do if there were not one always at the right hand of God, by intercession taking away these kind of iniquities?

2. Are those that are justified by the blood of Christ such, after that, as have need also of saving by Christ's intercession? From hence, then, we may infer, that as sin, so Satan will not give over from assaulting the best of the saints.

It is not justification that can secure us from being assaulted by Satan: "Simon, Simon, behold, Satan hath desired to have you." (Luke xxii. 31.) There are two things that do encourage the devil to set upon the people of God:—

(1.) He knows not who are elect; for all that profess are not, and therefore he will make trial if he can get them into his sieve, whether he can cause them to perish. And great success he hath had this way. Many a brave professor has he overcome: he has cast some of the stars from heaven to earth. He picked one out from among the apostles; and one, as it is thought, from among the seven deacons; and many from Christ's disciples. But how many think you now-a-days doth he utterly destroy with his net?

(2.) If it so happeneth that he cannot destroy because Christ by his intercession prevaileth, yet will he set upon the church to defile and afflict it. For (a), If he can but get us to fall with Peter, then he has obtained that dishonour be brought to God, the weak to be stumbled, the world offended, and the gospel vilified and reproached. Or (b), If he cannot throw up our heels, yet by buffeting of us, he can grieve us, afflict us, put us to pain, fright us, drive us to many doubts, and make our life very uncomfortable unto us, and make us go groaning to our Father's house. But blessed be God for his Christ, and for that "he ever liveth to make intercession for us."

3. Are those that are justified by the blood of Christ, such as, after that, have need to be saved by Christ's intercession? Then hence I infer that it is dangerous going about anything in our own name and strength. If we would have helps from the intercession of Christ, let us have a care that we do what we do according to the word of Christ. Do what he bids us, as well as we can, as he bids us, then we need not doubt but to have help and salvation in those duties, by the intercession of Christ: "Do all," says the apostle, "in the name of the Lord Jesus." (Col. iii. 17.) Oh, but then the devil and the world will be most of all offended. Well, well, but if you do nothing, but as in his fear, by his word, in his name, you may be sure of what help his intercession can afford you; and that can afford you much help, not only to begin, but to go through with your work, in some good measure, as you should: and by that also you shall be secured from those dangers, if not temptations to dangers, that those that go out about business in their own names and strength, shall be sure to meet withal.

4. Are those that are judged by the blood of Christ, such as, after that, have need of being saved by Christ's intercession? Then, hence I infer again, that God has a great dislike of the sins of his own people, and would fall upon them in judgment and anger much more severe than he doth, were it not for Christ's intercession. The gospel is not, as some think, a loose and licentious doctrine, nor God's discipline of his church a negligent and careless discipline, for though those that believe already have also an intercessor, yet God, to show his detestation against sin, doth often make them feel to purpose the weight of his fingers. The sincere, that fain would walk oft with God, have felt what I say, and that to the breaking of their bones full oft. The loose ones, and those that God loves not, may be utter strangers as to this; but those that are his own indeed, do know it is otherwise: "You only have I known of all the families of the earth," says God, "therefore I will punish you for your iniquities." (Amos iii. 2.) God keeps a very strict house among his children. David found it so, Heman found it so, Job found it so; and the church of God found it so. And I know not that this mind is ever the less against sin, notwithstanding we have an Intercessor. True, our Intercessor saves us from damning evils, from damning judgments; but he neither doth nor will secure us from temporal punishment, from spiritual punishment, unless we watch, deny ourselves, and walk in his fear. I would to God that those who are otherwise minded did but feel, for three or four months, something of what I have felt for several years together, for base, sinful thoughts. I wish it, I say, if it might be for their good, and for the better regulating of their understandings. But whether they obtain my wish or no, sure I am that God is no countenancer of sin, no, not in his own people: nay, he will bear it least of all in them. And as for others, however he may for awhile have patience towards them, if perhaps his goodness may lead them to repentance; yet the day is coming, when he will pay the carnal and hypocrites' home, with devouring fire for their offences.

But if our holy God will not let us go altogether unpunished, though we have so able and blessed an Intercessor, that has always to present God with on our behalf, so valuable a price of his own blood, now before the throne of grace, what should we have done, if there had been no day's-man, none to plead for us, or to make intercession on our behalf? Read Jer. xxx. 11: "For I am with thee, saith the Lord, to save thee: though I make a full end of all nations whither I have scattered thee, yet will I not make a full end of thee; but I will correct thee in measure, and will not leave thee altogether unpunished." If it be so, I say, what had become of us, if we had had no intercessor? and what will become of them concerning whom the Lord has said already, " I will not take up their names into my lips?" (Ps. xvi. 4,) "I pray not for the world." (John xvii. 9.)

5. Are those that are already justified by the blood of Christ, yet such as have need of being saved by his intercession? Then hence I infer that Christ is not only the beginner, but the completer of our salvation; or, as the Holy Ghost calls him, "the author and finisher of our faith;" (Heb. xii. 2,) or, as it calls him again, "the author of eternal salvation," (Heb. v. 9,) of salvation throughout, from the beginning to the end, from first to last. His hands have laid the foundation of it in his own blood, and his hands shall finish it by his intercession. (Zech. iv. 9.) As he has laid the beginning fastly, so he shall bring forth the head-stones with shoutings, and we shall cry, Grace, grace at the last, salvation only belongeth to the Lord. (Zech. iv. 7. Ps. iii. 8. Isa. xliii. 11.)

Many there be that begin with grace, and end with works, and think that is the only way. Indeed works will save from temporal punishments, when their imperfections are purged from them by the intercession of Christ; but to be saved and brought to glory, to be carried through this dangerous world, from my first moving after Christ, until I set my foot within the gates of paradise, this is the work of my Mediator, of my High Priest and Intercessor. It is he that fetches us again when we have run away; it is he that lifteth us up when the devil and sin hath thrown us down: it is he that quickeneth us when we grow cold; it is he that comforteth us when we despair; it is he that obtains fresh pardon when we have contracted sin; and it is he that purges our consciences when they are loaden with guilt. (Ezek. xxxiv. 16. Ps. cxlv. 14.)

I know also, that rewards do wait for them in heaven that do believe in Christ, and shall do well on earth; but this is not a reward of merit, but of grace. We are saved by Christ; brought to glory by Christ; and all our works are not otherwise made acceptable to God but by the person and personal excellences and works of Christ: therefore whatever the jewels are, and the bracelets, and the pearls that thou shalt be adorned with as a reward of service done for God in the world, for them thou must thank Christ, and, before all, confess that he was the meritorious cause thereof. (1 Pet. ii. 5. Heb. xiii. 15.) He saves us, and saves our services too, (Rev. v. 9—14.) They would be all cast back as dung in our faces, were they not rinsed and washed in the blood, were they not sweetened and perfumed in the incense, and conveyed to God himself through

the white hand of Jesus Christ: for that is the golden censer, from thence ascends the smoke that is in the nostrils of God of such a sweet savour. (Rev. vii. 12—14; viii. 3, 4.)

6. Are those that are already justified by the blood of Christ, such as do still stand in need of being saved by his intercession? Then hence I infer again, that we that have been saved hitherto, and preserved from the dangers that we have met with since our first conversion to this moment, should ascribe the glory to Jesus Christ, to God by Jesus Christ. "I have prayed that thy faith fail not. I pray that thou wouldst keep them from the evil," is the true cause of our standing, and of our continuing in the faith and holy profession of the gospel to this very day. Wherefore we must give the glory of all to God by Christ: "I will not trust in my bow," said David, "neither shall my sword save me. But thou hast saved us from our enemies, and hast put them to shame that hated us. In God we boast all the day long, and praise thy name for ever. Selah." (Ps. xliv. 6—8.) He "always causeth us to triumph in Christ." (2 Cor. ii. 14.) "We rejoice in Christ Jesus, and have no confidence in the flesh." (Phil. iii. 3.) Thus you see, that both in the Old and New Testament, all the glory is given to the Lord, as well for preservation to heaven as for justification of life. And he that is well acquainted with himself, will do this readily; though light-heads, and such as are not acquainted with the desperate evil that is in their natures, will sacrifice to their own net. But such will so sacrifice but a while. Sir Death is coming, and he will put them into the view of what they see not now, and will feed sweetly upon them, because they made not the Lord their trust. And therefore ascribe thou the glory of the preservation of thy soul in the faith hitherto, to that salvation which Christ Jesus our Lord obtaineth for thee by his intercession.

7. Are those that are already justified by the blood of Christ, such as do still stand in need of being saved by his intercession? Then is this also to be inferred from hence that saints should look to him for that saving that they shall yet have need of betwixt this and the day of their dissolution; yea, from henceforward, even to the day of judgment. I say they should still look to him for the remaining part of their salvation, or for that of their salvation which is yet behind; and let them look for it with confidence, for it is in a faithful hand; and for thy encouragement to look and hope for the completing of thy salvation in glory, let me present thee with a few things—

(1.) The hardest or worst part of the work of thy Saviour is over; his bloody work, his bearing of thy sin and curse, his loss of the light of his Father's face for a time, his dying upon the cursed tree, that was the worst, the sorest, the hardest, and most difficult part of the work of redemption; and yet this he did willingly, cheerfully, and without thy desires; yea, this he did, as considering those for whom he did it, in a state of rebellion and enmity to him.

(2.) Consider, also, that he has made a beginning with thy soul to reconcile thee to God, and to that end has bestowed his justice upon thee, put his Spirit within thee, and began to make the un- weldable mountain and rock, thy heart, to turn towards him, and desire after him, to believe in him, and rejoice in him.

(3.) Consider also that some comfortable pledges of his love thou hast already received—namely, as to feel the sweetness of his love, as to see the light of his countenance ; as to be made to know his power, in raising of thee when thou wast down; and how he has made thee stand, while hell has been pushing at thee, utterly to overthrow thee.

(4.) Thou mayest consider, also, that what re- mains behind of the work of thy salvation in his hands, as it is the most easy part, so the most comfortable, and that part which will more imme- diately issue in his glory ; and therefore he will mind it.

(5.) That which is behind is also more safe in his hand than if it were in thine own. He is wise, he is powerful, he is faithful, and therefore will manage that part that is lacking to our salvation well, until he has completed it. It is his love to thee has made him that he " putteth no trust in thee." He knows that he can himself bring thee to his kingdom most surely, and therefore has not left that work to thee—no, not any part thereof.

Live in hope, then, in a lively hope, that since Christ is risen from the dead, he lives to make in- tercession for thee ; and that thou shalt reap the blessed benefit of this twofold salvation that is wrought, and that is working out for thee, by Jesus Christ our Lord. And thus have we treated of the benefit of his intercession, in that he is able to save to the uttermost. And this leads me to the third particular.

III. *On those interested in Christ's intercession.*

The third particular is to show who are the persons interested in this intercession of Christ, and they are those that come to God by him. The words are very concise, and distinctly laid down; they are they that come, that come to God, that come to God by him. "Wherefore he is able also to save them," to "save to the uttermost them that come to God by him, seeing he ever liveth to make intercession for them."

A little first to comment upon the order of the words, "That come unto God by him."

1. There are that come unto God, but not *by him ;* and these are not included in this text, have not a share in this privilege. Thus the Jews came to God—the unbelieving Jews—who had " a zeal of God, but not according to know- ledge." (Rom. x. 2.) These submitted not to Christ, the righteousness of God, but thought to come to him by works of their own, or at least, as

it were, by them, and so came short of salvation by grace, for that reigns to salvation only in Christ. To these Christ's person and undertakings were a stumbling-stone ; for at him they stumbled, and did split themselves to pieces, though they indeed were such as came to God for life.

2. As there are that come to God, but not by Christ, so there are that come to Christ, but not to God by him. Of this sort are they, who, *hearing* that Christ is Saviour, therefore come to him for pardon, but cannot abide to come to God by him, for that he is holy, and so will snub their lusts, and will change their hearts and natures. Mind me what I say. There are a great many that would be saved by Christ, but love not to be sanctified by God through him. These make a stop at Christ, and will go no further. Might such have pardon, they care not whether ever they went to heaven or no. Of this kind of coming to Christ, I think it is, of which he warneth his disciples, when he saith, " In that day ye shall ask me nothing. Verily, verily, I say unto you, Whatsoever ye shall ask the Father in my name, he will give it you." (John xvi. 23.) As who should say, When you ask for anything, make not a stop at me, but come to my Father by me ; for they that come to me, and not to my Father through me, will have nothing of what they come for. Righteousness shall be imputed to us, "if we believe in him that raised up Jesus our Lord from the dead." (Rom. iv. 24.) To come to Christ for a benefit, and stop there, and not come to God by him, prevaileth nothing. Here the mother of Zebedee's children erred, and about this it was that the Lord Jesus cautioned her. Lord, saith she, " grant that these my two sons may sit, one on thy right hand, and the other on thy left in thy kingdom." (Matt. xx. 21.) But what is the answer of Christ ? " To sit on my right hand and on my left is not mine to give, but to them for whom it is prepared of my Father." (Matt. xx. 23.) As who should say, Woman, of myself I do nothing ; my Father worketh with me. Go, therefore, to him by me, for I am the way to him ; what thou canst obtain of him by me thou shalt have : that is to say, what of the things that per- tain to eternal life, whether pardon or glory.

It is true, the Son has power to give pardon and glory, but he gives it not by himself, but by and according to the will of his Father. (Matt. ix. 6.) They therefore that come to him for an eternal good, and look not to the Father by him, come short thereof: I mean now, pardon and glory.

And hence, though it be said the Son of man hath power on earth to forgive sins—to wit, to show the certainty of his Godhead, and of the excellency of his mediation—yet forgiveness of sin is said to lie more particularly in the hand of the Father, and that God for Christ's sake for- giveth us. (Eph. iv. 32.)

The Father, as we see, will not forgive, unless

we come to him by the Son. Why then should we conceit that the Son will forgive those that come not to the Father by him?

So then, justifying righteousness is in the Son, and with him also is intercession : but forgiveness is with the Father; yea, the gift of the Holy Ghost, yea, and the power of imputing of the righteousness of Christ is yet in the hand of the Father. Hence Christ prays to the Father to forgive, prays to the Father to send the Spirit, and it is God that imputeth righteousness to justification in us. (Luke xxiii. 34. John xiv. 16. Rom. iv. 6.) The Father, then, doth nothing but for the sake of, and through the Son ; the Son also doth nothing derogating from the glory of the Father. But it would be a derogation to the glory of the Father, if the Son should grant to save them that come not to the Father by him; wherefore, you that cry, " Christ, Christ," delighting yourselves in the thoughts of forgiveness, but care not to come by Christ to the Father for it, you are not at all concerned in this blessed text, for he only saves by his intercession them that come to God by him.

There are three sorts of people that may be said to come to Christ, but not to God by him.

1. They whose utmost design in coming is only that guilt and fear of damning may be removed from them. And there are three signs of such a one—

(1.) He that takes up in a belief of pardon, and so goes on in his course of carnality, as he did before.

(2.) He whose comfort in the belief of pardon standeth alone, without other fruits of the Holy Ghost.

(3.) He that having been washed, can be content to tumble in the mire, as the sow again, or as the dog that did spew, to lick up his vomit again.

2. They may be said to come to Christ, but not to God by him, who do pick and choose doctrines, itching only after that which sounds of grace, but secretly abhorring of that which presseth to moral goodness. These did never see God, what notions soever they may have of the Lord Jesus, and of forgiveness from him. (Matt. v. 8.)

3. They surely did never come to God by Christ, however they may boast of the grace of Christ, that will from the freeness of gospel-grace plead an indulgence for sin.

And now to speak a few words of coming to God, of coming as the text intends. And in speaking to this, I must touch upon two things.

1. Concerning God.

2. Concerning the frame of the heart of him that comes to him.

1. *Of God.*—God is the chief good. Good so as nothing is but himself. He is in himself most happy, yea, all good; and all true happiness is only to be found in God, as that which is essential to his nature; nor is there any good, or any happiness in or with any creature or thing, but what is communicated to it by God. God is the only desirable good, nothing without him is worthy of our hearts. Right thoughts of God are able to ravish the heart: how much more happy is the man that has interest in God. God alone is able by himself to put the soul into a more blessed, comfortable, and happy condition than can the whole world; yea, and more than if all the created happiness of all the angels of heaven did dwell in one man's bosom. God is the upholder of all creatures, and whatever they have that is a suitable good to their kind, it is from God; by God all things have their subsistence, and all the good that they enjoy. I cannot tell what to say. I am drowned. The life, the glory, the blessedness, the soul-satisfying goodness that is in God, is beyond all expression.

2. Now there must be in us something of suitableness of spirit to this God before we can be willing to come to him.

Before, therefore, God has been with a man, and has left some impression of his glory upon him, that man cannot be willing to come to him aright. Hence it is said concerning Abraham, that, in order to his coming to God, and following of him aright, the Lord himself did show himself to him. " Men, brethren, and fathers, hearken, The God of glory appeared unto our father Abraham when he was in Mesopotamia, before he dwelt in Charran ; and said unto him, Get thee out of thy country, and from thy kindred, and come into the land which I shall show thee." (Acts vii. 2, 3. Gen. xii. 1.)

It was this God of glory, the sight and visions of this God of glory, that provoked Abraham to leave his country and kindred to come after God. The reason why men are so careless of, and so indifferent about their coming to God, is because they have their eyes blinded, because they do not perceive his glory. God is so blessed a one, that did he not hide himself and his glory, the whole world would be ravished with him; but he has, I will not say reasons of state, but reasons of glory —glorious reasons, why he hideth himself from the world, and appeareth but to particular ones. Now, by his thus appearing to Abraham, down fell Abraham's vanity, and his idolatrous fancies and affections ; and his heart began to turn unto God, for that there was in this appearance an alluring and soul-instructing voice. Hence that which Moses calls here an " appearing," Christ calls a " hearing," and a " teaching," and a " learning." " It is written in the prophets, And they shall be all taught of God. Every man therefore that hath heard, and learned of the Father, cometh unto me," (John vi. 45;) that is, to God by me. But, I say, what must they hear and learn of the Father, but that Christ is the way to glory, the way to the God of glory? This is a drawing doctrine: wherefore that which in this verse is called, *teaching* and *learning*, is called in the verse before, the *drawing* of the Father: "No man can come to me except the Father who hath sent me, draw him," (John vi. 44;) that is, with powerful proposals, and alluring conclusions, and heart-subduing influences.

Having thus touched upon this, we will now proceed to show you what kind of people they are that come to God by Christ; and then shall draw some inferences from this also.

On those who come to God through Christ.

There are therefore three sorts of people that come to God by Christ.

First. Men newly awakened.

Second. Men turned back from backsliding.

Third. The sincere and upright man.

First. *Men newly awakened.*—By awakened I mean awakened thoroughly—so awakened as to be made to see themselves, what they are; the world, what it is; the law, what it is; hell, what it is; death, what it is; Christ, what he is; and God, what he is; and also what judgment is.

A man that will come to God by Christ aright, must needs, precedent to his so coming, have a competent knowledge of things of this kind.

1. He must know himself, what a wretched and miserable sinner he is, before he will take one step forward in order to his coming to God by Christ. This is plain from a great many scriptures. As that of the parable of the prodigal, (Luke xv.,) that of the three thousand, (Acts xi.,) that of the jailer, (Acts xvi.,) and those of many more besides. The whole have no need of the physician. They were not the sound and whole, but the lame and diseased, that came to him to be cured of their infirmities; and it is not the righteous, but the sinners, that do well know themselves to be such, that come to God by Christ.

It is not in the power of all the men on earth to make one man come to God by Christ, because it is not in their power to make men see their state by nature. And what should a man come to God for that can live in the world without him? Reason says so, experience says so, the Scripture beareth witness that so it is of a truth. It is a sight of what I am that must unroost me, that must shake my soul, and make me leave my present rest. No man comes to God by Christ but he that knows himself and what sin hath done to him; that is the first.

2. As he must know himself, and what a wretch he is, so he must know the world, and what an empty thing it is. Cain did see himself, but saw not the emptiness of this world; and therefore, instead of going to God by Christ, he went to the world, and there did take up to his dying-day. (Gen. iv. 16.) The world is a great snare to the soul even to the souls of awakened sinners, by reason of its big looks, and the fair promises that it makes to those that will please to entertain it.

It will also make as though it could do as much to the quieting of the spirit as either sermon, Bible, or preacher. Yea, and it has its followers ready at its heels continually to blow its applause abroad, saying, "Who will show us any (other) good?" (Ps. iv. 6.) And though this their way is their folly, yet their posterity approveth their sayings. (Ps. xlix. 13.) So that unless a man, under some awakenings, sees the emptiness of the world, he will take up in the good things thereof, and not come to God by Christ. Many there be now in hell that can feel to this for truth. It was the world that took awakened Cain, (Gen. iv. 16,) awakened Judas, (Matt. xxvi.,) awakened Demas, (2 Tim. iv. 10.) Yea, Balaam, though he had some kind of visions of God, yet was kept by the world from coming to him aright. (Numb. xxii., xxiii., xxiv.) See with what earnestness the young man in the gospel came to Jesus Christ, and that for eternal life. He ran to him, he kneeled down to him, and asked, and that before a multitude, "Good Master, what shall I do that I may inherit eternal life?" (Mark x. 17.) And yet when he was told he could not come, the world soon stepped betwixt that life and him, and persuaded him to take up in itself; and so, for aught we know, he never looked after life more.

There are four things in the world that have a tendency to lull an awakened man asleep, if God also makes him not afraid of the world.

(1.) There is the bustle and cumber of the world, that will call a man off from looking after the salvation of his soul. This is intimated by the parable of the thorny ground. (Luke viii. 14.) Worldly cumber is a devilish thing: it will hurry a man from his bed without prayer; to a sermon, and from it again, without prayer. It will choke prayer, it will choke the word, it will choke convictions, it will choke the soul, and cause that awakening shall be to no saving purpose.

(2.) There is the friendship of this world, to which, if a man is not mortified, there is no coming for him to God by Christ. And a man can never be mortified to it, unless he shall see the emptiness and vanity of it. Whosoever makes himself a friend of this world, is the enemy of God. And how then can he come to him by Christ? (James iv. 4.)

(3.) There are the terrors of the world; if a man stands in fear of them, he also will not come to God by Christ. The fear of man brings a snare. How many have, in all ages, been kept from coming to God aright, by the terrors of the world? yea, how many are there, to one's thinking, have almost got to the gates of heaven, and have been scared, and driven quite back again, by nothing but the terrors of this world? This is that which Christ so cautioneth his disciples about; for he knew it was a deadly thing. (Luke xii. 4—6.) Peter also bids the saints beware of this, as of a thing very destructive. (1 Pet. iii. 14, 15.)

(4.) There is also the glory of the world, an absolute hindrance to convictions and awakenings, to wit, honours, and greatness, and preferments: "How can ye believe," saith Christ, "who receive honour one of another, and seek not the honour that cometh from God only?" (John v. 44.) If therefore a man is not in his affections crucified to these, it will keep him from coming to God aright.

3. As a man must know himself, how vile he is, and know the world, how empty it is, so he must know the law, how severe it is; else he will not come to God by Jesus Christ our Lord.

A man that is under awakenings, is under a double danger of falling short of coming to God by Christ. If he knows not the severity of the law,

(1.) He is either in danger of slighting its penalty; or,

(2.) Of seeking to make amends to it by doing of good works; and nothing can keep him from splitting his soul upon one of these two rocks, but a sound knowledge of the severity of the law.

(1.) He is in danger of slighting the penalty. This is seen by the practice of all the profane in the world. Do they not know the law? Verily, many of them can say the ten commandments without book. But they do know the severity of law; and therefore when at any time awakenings come upon their consciences, they strive to drive away the guilt of one sin, by wallowing in the filth of another.

But would they do thus if they knew the severity of the law? they would as soon eat fire. The severity of the law would be an intolerable, unsupportable burden to their consciences. It would drive them, and make them fly for refuge to lay hold on the hope set before them.

(2.) Or if he slights not the penalty, he will seek to make amends to it, by doing of good works, for the sins he has committed. This is manifest by the practice of the Jews and Turks, and all that swerve on that hand, to wit, to seek life and happiness by the law. Paul also was here before he met with Jesus in the way. This is natural to consciences that are awakened, unless also they have given to them to see the true severity of the law; the which that thou mayest do, if my mite will help, I will cast in for thy conviction these four things.

(a) The law charges thee with its curse, as well for the pollution of thy nature, as for the defilements of thy life; yea, and if thou hast never committed a sinful act, thy pollution of nature must stand in thy way to life, if thou comest not to God for mercy by Christ.

(b) The law takes notice of, and chargeth thee with its curse, as well for sinful thoughts as for vile and sinful actions. The very "thought of foolishness is sin," (Prov. xxiv. 9,) though it never breaks out into act; and will as surely merit the damnation of the soul, as will the greatest transgression in the world.

(c) If now thou couldst keep all the commandments, that will do thee no good at all, because thou hast sinned first: "The soul that sinneth shall die." Unless, then, thou canst endure the curse, and so in a legal way overcome it for the sins that thou hast committed, thou art gone, if thou comest not to God by Christ for mercy and pardon.

(d) And never think of repentance, thereby to stop the mouth of the law; for the law calleth not for repentance, but life; nor will it accept of any, shouldst thou mourn and weep for thy sins till thou hast made a sea of blood with tears. This, I say, thou must know, or thou wilt not come to God by Christ for life. For the knowledge of this will cause that thou shalt neither slight the severity of the law, nor trust to the works thereof for life. Now, when thou dost neither of these, thou canst not but speed thee to God by Christ for life; for now thou hast no stay—pleasures are gone, all hope in thyself is gone. Thou now diest, and that is the way to live; for this inward death is, or feels like, an hunger-bitten stomach, that cannot but crave and gape for meat and drink. Now it will be as possible for thee to sleep with thy finger in the fire, as to forbear craving of mercy, so long as this knowledge remains.

4. As a man must know himself, the emptiness of this world, and the law, so it is necessary for him to know that there is a hell, and how unsupportable the torments of it are: for all threatenings, curses, and determinations to punish in the next world, will prove but fictions and scarecrows, if there be no woful place, no woful state, for the sinner to receive his wages in for sin, when his days are ended in this world. Wherefore this word *saved*, supposeth such a place and state. He is able to save from hell, from the woful place, from the woful state of hell, them that come unto God by him.

Christ therefore often insinuates the truth of an hell, in his invitations to the sinners of this world to come to him; as where he tells them, they shall be saved if they do; they shall be damned if they do not. As if he had said, there is a hell, a terrible hell, and they that come to me I will save them from it; but they that come not, the law will damn them in it. Therefore, that thou mayst indeed come to God by Christ for mercy, believe there is a hell, a woful terrible place. Hell is God's creature, he hath made it deep and large! the punishments are by the lashes of his wrath, which will issue from his mouth like a stream of burning brimstone, ever kindling itself upon the soul. (Isa. xxx. 33.) Thou must know this by the word, and fly from it, or thou shalt know it by thy sins, and lie and cry in it.

I might enlarge, but if I did I should be swallowed up; for we are, while here, no more able to set forth the torments of hell, than we are (while here) to set forth the joys of heaven: only this may and ought to be said, that God is able.

as to save, so "to cast into hell." (Luke xii. 5.) And as he is able to make heaven sweet, good, pleasurable, and glorious, beyond thought, so he is able to make the torments of hell so exquisite, so hot, so sharp, so intolerable, that no tongue can utter it, no, not the damned in hell themselves. (Isa. lxiv. 4.) If thou lovest thy soul, slight not the knowledge of hell, for that, with the law, are the spurs which Christ useth to prick souls forward to himself withal. What is the cause that sinners can play so delightfully with sin? It is for that they forget that there is a hell for them to descend into for their so doing, when they go out of this world. For here usually he gives our stop to a sinful course; we perceive that hell hath opened her mouth before us. Lest thou shouldst forget, I beseech thee, another time, to retain the knowledge of hell in thine understanding, and apply the burning-hot thoughts thereof to thy conscience; this is one way to make thee gather up thy heels, and mend thy pace in thy coming to Jesus Christ, and to God the Father by him.

5. It is also necessary, that he that cometh to God by the Lord Jesus, should know what death is, and the uncertainty of its approaches upon us. Death is, as I may call it, the feller, the cutter down. Death is that that puts a stop to a further living here, and that which lays man where judgment finds him: if he is in the faith in Jesus, it lays him down there to sleep, till the Lord comes; if he be not in the faith, it lays him down in his sins, until the Lord comes. Again, if thou hast some beginnings that look like good, and death should overtake thee before those beginnings are ripe, thy fruit will wither, and thou wilt fall short of being gathered into God's barn. Some men are cut off like the tops of the ears of corn, and some are even nipped by death in the very bud of their spring: but the safety is, when a man is ripe, and shall be gathered to his grave, as a shock of corn to the barn in its season. (Job xxiv. 20—24; v. 26.)

Now, if death should surprise and seize thee before thou art fit to die, all is lost; for there is no repentance in the grave; or rather, as the wise man has it, "Whatsoever thy hand findeth to do, do it with thy might; for there is no work, no device, nor knowledge, nor wisdom, in the grave, whither thou goest." (Eccles. ix. 10.)

Death is God's sergeant, God's bailiff, and he arrests in God's name when he comes, but seldom gives warning before he clappeth us on the shoulder: and when he arrests us, though he may stay a little while, and give us leave to pant, and tumble, and toss ourselves for a while upon a bed of languishing, yet at last he will prick our bladder, and let out our life, and then our soul will be poured upon the ground, yea, into hell, if we are not ready and prepared for the life everlasting. He that doth not watch for, and is not afraid lest death should prevent him, will not

make haste to God by Christ. What Job said of temporal afflictions, such an one will death be, if thou art not aware: "When I looked for good, then evil came unto me: the days of affliction prevented me." (Job xxx. 26, 27.) If thou lookest, or beginnest to look for good, and the day of death shall cut thee off before thou hast found that good thou lookest for, all is lost, soul, and life, and heaven, and all. Wherefore it is convenient that thou conclude the grave is thy house, and that thou make thy bed once a-day in the grave: also, that thou say "unto corruption, Thou art my father: and to the worm, Thou art my mother and my sister." (Job xvii. 14.) I say, be acquainted with the grave and death. The fool puts the evil day far away, but the wise man brings it nigh. Better be ready to die seven years before death comes, than want one day, one hour, one moment, one tear, one sorrowful sigh, at the remembrance of the ill-spent life that I have lived. This then is that which I admonish thee of—namely, that thou know death, what it is, what it doth, when it comes; also that thou consider well of the danger that death leaves that man in, to whom he comes before he is ready and prepared to be laid by it in the grave.

6. Thou must also be made by thy awakenings to see what Christ *is*. This is of absolute necessity: for how can or shall a man be willing to come to Christ, that knows not what he is, what God has appointed him to do? He is the Saviour, every man will say so; but to sense, smell, and taste, what saving is, and so to understand the nature of the office and work of a Saviour, is a rare thing, kept close from most, known but by some. Jesus of Nazareth is the Saviour, or the reconciler of men to God, in the body of his flesh, through death. (Col. i. 19—21.) This is he whose business in coming from heaven to earth was to save his people from their sins. Now, as was said, to know how he doth this, is that which is needful to be inquired into; for some say he doth it one way, some he doth it another; and it must be remembered, that we are now speaking of the salvation of that man, that from new or first awakenings is coming to God by Christ for life.

(1.) Some say he doth it by giving of us precepts and laws to keep, that we might be justified thereby.

(2.) Some say he doth it by setting himself a pattern for us to follow him.

(3.) Some again hold, that he doth it by our following the light within.

But thou must take heed of all these, for he justifies us by none of these means; and thou dost need to be justified. I say, he justifieth us not, either by giving laws unto us, or by becoming our example, or by our following of him in any sense; but by his blood shed for us. His blood is not laws, nor ordinances, nor commandments, but a price, a redeeming price. (Rom. v. 7—9. Rev.

i. 5.) He justifies us by bestowing upon us, not by expecting from us. He justifies us by his grace, not by our works. (Eph. i. 7.) In a word, thou must be well grounded in the knowledge of what Christ is, and how men are justified by him, or thou wilt not come unto God by him.

As thou must know him, and how men are justified by him, so thou must know the readiness that is in him to receive and to do for those what they need, that come unto God by him. Suppose his merits were never so efficacious, yet if it could be proved that there is a loathness in him that these merits should be bestowed upon the coming ones, there would but few adventure to wait upon him. But now, as he is full, he is free. Nothing pleases him better, than to give what he has away, than to bestow it upon the poor and needy. And it will be convenient that thou, who art a coming soul, should know this for thy comfort to encourage thee to come to God by him. Take two or three sayings of his for the confirming of what is now said : " Come unto me, all ye that labour, and are heavy laden, and I will give you rest." (Matt. xi. 28.) " All that the Father giveth me, shall come to me ; and him that cometh to me, I will in no wise cast out." (John vi. 37.) " I came not to call the righteous, but sinners to repentance." (Mark ii. 17.) " This is a faithful saying, and worthy of all acceptation, that Christ Jesus came into the world to save sinners, of whom I am chief." (1 Tim. i. 15.)

7. As a man that would come to God by Christ, must, antecedent to his so coming, know himself, what he is ; the world, how empty it is ; the law, how severe it is ; death, and what it is ; and Christ, and what he is ; so also he must know God : " He that cometh to God, must believe that he is, and that he is a rewarder of those that diligently seek him." (Heb. xi. 6.) God he must know, else how can the sinner propound him as his end, his ultimate end? For so doth every one that indeed doth come to Christ aright. He comes to Christ, because he is the way ; he comes to God, because he is the end. But, I say, if he knows him not, how can he propound him as the end? The end is that for the sake of which I propound to myself anything, and for the sake of which I use any means. Now then, I would be saved ; but why? Even because I would enjoy God. I use the means to be saved ; and why? Because I would enjoy God. I am sensible that sin has made me come short of the glory of God, and that Christ Jesus is he, the only he, that can put me into a condition of obtaining the glory of God ; and therefore I come to God by him. (Rom. iii. 23 ; v. 1, 2.)

But I say again, who will propound God for his end, that knows him not, that knows him not aright? yea, that knows him not to be worth being propounded as my end, in coming to Jesus Christ? and he that thus knows him, must know him to be above all, best of all. and him in whom

the soul shall find that content, that bliss, that glory and happiness, that can by no means be found elsewhere. And, I say, if this be not found in God, the soul will never propound him to himself as the only highest, and ultimate end in its coming to Jesus Christ ; but it will propound something else, even what it shall imagine to be the best good : perhaps heaven, perhaps ease from guilt, perhaps to be kept out of hell, or the like. I do not say, but a man may propound all these to himself in his coming to Jesus Christ ; but if he propound these as his ultimate end, as the chiefest good that he seeks ; if the presence and enjoyment of God, of God's glorious majesty, be not his chief design, he is not concerned in the salvation that is propounded in our text, " He is able [and so will] to save to the uttermost them that come unto God by him."

What is heaven without God? what is ease without the peace and enjoyment of God? What is deliverance from hell without the enjoyment of God? The propounding, therefore, these, and only these, to thyself for thy happiness, in thy coming to Jesus Christ, is a proposal not a hair's breadth higher than what a man without grace can propound. What or who is he that would not go to heaven? What or who is he that would not also have ease from the guilt of sin? And where is the man that chooseth to go to hell? But many there be that cannot abide God ; no, they like not to go to heaven because God is there. If the devil had a heaven to bestow upon men, a vicious and a beastly heaven, if it be lawful thus to speak, I durst pawn my soul upon it, were it a thousand times better than it is, that upon a bare invitation the foul fiend would have twenty to God's one. They, I say, cannot abide God ; nay, for all the devil has nothing but a hell for them, yet how thick men go to him, but how thinly to God Almighty! The nature of God lieth cross to the lusts of men. A holy God, a glorious holy God, an infinitely holy God ; this spoils all. But to the soul that is awakened, and that is made to see things as they are, to him God is what he is in himself, the blessed, the highest, the only eternal good, and he, without the enjoyment of whom all things would sound but empty in the ears of that soul.

Now, then, I advise thee, that hast a mind to come to God by Christ, that thou seek the knowledge of God. " If thou seekest her [wisdom] as silver, and searchest for her as for hid treasures, then shalt thou understand the fear of the Lord, and find the knowledge of God " (Prov. ii. 4, 5.)

And to encourage thee yet further, he is so desirous of communion with men, that he pardoneth sins for that. Hence he is called, not only loving but love. " God is love ; and he that dwelleth in love, dwelleth in God, and God in him." (1 John iv. 16.)

Methinks, when I consider what glory there is, at times, upon the creatures, and that all their glory is the workmanship of God, O Lord, say I,

What is God himself? He may well be called the God of glory, as well as the glorious Lord; for as all glory is from him, so in him is an inconceivable well-spring of glory, of glory to be communicated to them that come by Christ to him. Wherefore let the glory, and love, and bliss, and eternal happiness that is in God allure thee to come to him by Christ.

8. As thou shouldst, nay, must, have a good knowledge of all these, so thou must have it of judgment to come. They that come to God by Christ are said to fly from the wrath to come, to fly for refuge; "to lay hold on the hope set before them." (Matt. iii. 7. Heb. vi. 18.)

This judgment to come is a warm thing to be thought of, an awakening thing to be thought of: it is called the eternal judgment, because it is, and will be, God's final conclusion with men. This day is called "that great and notable day of the Lord," (Acts ii. 20;) the day that shall "burn as an oven," (Mal. iv. 1;) the day in which the angels shall gather the wicked together as tares into bundles to burn them, but the rest into his kingdom and glory. This day will be it in which all bowels of love and compassion shall be shut up to the wicked, and that in which the flood-gates of wrath shall be opened, by which shall a plentiful reward be given to evil-doers, but glory to the righteous. (Ps. xxxi. 23.) This is the day in which men, if they could, would creep into the ground for fear; but because they cannot, therefore they will call and cry to the mountains to fall upon them, but they shall not; therefore they stand bound to bear their judgment.

This day will be the day of breaking up of closet councils, cabinet councils, secret purposes, hidden thoughts: yea, "God shall bring every work into judgment, with every secret thing." (Eccles. xii. 14.) I say he shall do it then. For he will both "bring to light the hidden things of darkness, and will make manifest the counsels of the heart." (1 Cor. iv. 5.) This is the day that is appointed to put them to shame and contempt in that have, in this world, been bold and audacious in their vile and beastly ways. At this day God will cover all such bold and brazen faces with shame. Now they will blush till the blood is ready to burst through their cheeks. (Dan. xii. 2.) Oh! the confusion and shame that will cover their faces while God is discovering to them what a nasty, what a beastly, what an uncomely, and what an unreasonable life they lived in the world. They shall now see the contemned God that fed them, that clothed them, that gave them life and limb, and that maintained their breath in their nostrils. But, oh! when they see the gulf before them, and all things ready to receive them in thither, then, then they will know what sinning against God means.

And, I say, thou that art for coming to God by Christ must know this, and be well assured of this, or thou wilt never come to God by him.

What of the glory of God shall be put upon them that do indeed come to him will also help in his spiritual journey, if it be well considered by thee; but perhaps terror and unbelief will suffer thee to consider but little of that. However, the things aforementioned will be goads, and will serve to prick thee forward: and if they do so, they will be God's great blessing unto thee, and that for which thou wilt give him thy thanks for ever. (Eccles. xii. 10, 11.)

Thus I have in few words spoken something as to the first sort of comers to God by Christ; namely, of the coming of the newly-awakened man. And I say again, if any of the things aforenamed be wanting, and are not with his heart, it is a question whether, notwithstanding all the noise that he may make about religion, he will ever come to God by Christ.

1. If he knows not himself and the badness of his condition, wherefore should he come?

2. If he knows not the world, and the emptiness and vanity thereof, wherefore should he come?

3. If he knows not the law, and the severity thereof, wherefore should he come?

4. If he knows not hell, and the torments thereof, wherefore should he come?

5. If he knows not what death is, wherefore should he come?

6. And if he knows not the Father and the Son, how can he come?

7. And to know that there is "a judgment to come," is as necessary to his coming, as most of the rest of the things propounded. Coming to God by Christ is for shelter, for safety, for advantage, and everlasting happiness. But he that knows not that, understands not the things aforementioned, sees not his need of taking shelter, of flying for safety, of coming for advantage, to God by Christ. I know there are degrees of this knowledge, and he that has it most warm upon him, in all likelihood, will make most haste; or, as David saith, will hasten his escape from the windy storm and tempest: and he that sees least, is in most danger of being the loiterer, and so of losing the prize. For all that run do not obtain it; all that fight do not win it; and all that strive for it have it not. (Ps. iv. 8. 1 Cor. ix. 24—26 2 Tim. ii. 4, 5.)

The return of the backslider to Christ.

Second. I shall now come to the second man mentioned, to wit, the man that is turned back from his backsliding, and speak something also about his coming again to God by Christ.

There are two things remarkable in the returning of a backslider to God by Christ.

1. The first is, he gives a second testimony to the truth of all things spoken of before.

2. He also gives a second testimony of the necessity of coming to God by Christ.

3. Of the manner of his coming to God by Christ, perhaps I may also speak a word or two. But,

First. The returning again of the backslider gives a second testimony to the truth of man's state being by nature miserable, of the vanity of this world, of the severity of the law, certainty of death, and terribleness of judgment to come. His first coming told them so, but his second coming tells them so with a double confirmation of the truth. It is so, saith his first coming. Oh! it is so, saith his second. The backsliding of a Christian comes through the overmuch persuading of Satan and lust; that the man was mistaken, and that there was no such horror in the things from which he fled, nor so much good in the things to which he hasted. Turn again, fool, says the devil, turn again to thy former course. I wonder what frenzy it was that drove thee to thy heels, and that made thee leave so much good behind thee, as other men find in the lusts of the flesh and the good of the world. As for the law, and death, and an imagination of the day of judgment, they are but mere scarecrows, set up by politic heads, to keep the ignorant in subjection. Well, says the backslider, I will go back again and see: so, fool as he is, he goes back, and has all things ready to entertain him, his conscience sleeps, the world smiles, flesh is sweet, carnal company compliments him, and all that can be got is presented to this backslider to accommodate him. But behold he doth again begin to see his own nakedness, and he perceives that the law is whetting his axe. As for the world, he perceives it is a bubble, he also smells the smell of brimstone, for God hath scattered it upon his tabernacle, and it begins to burn within him. (Job xviii. 15.) Oh! saith he, I am deluded; oh, I am ensnared. My first sight of things was true. I see it is so again. Now he begins to be for flying again to his first refuge; O God, saith he, I am undone, I have turned from thy truth to lies! I believed them such at first, and find them such at last. Have mercy upon me, O God!

This, I say, is a testimony, a second testimony by the same man, as to the miserable state of man, the severity of the law, the emptiness of the world, the certainty of death, and the terribleness of judgment. This man has seen it, and seen it again.

A returning backslider is a great blessing (I mean intended to be so) to two sorts of men.

1. To the elect uncalled.

2. To the elect that are called, and that at present stand their ground.

1. The uncalled are made to hear him and consider; the called are made to hear him, and are afraid of falling. Behold therefore the mystery of God's wisdom, and how willing he is that spectators should be warned, and made take heed. Yea, he will permit, that some of his own shall fall into the fire, to convince the world that hell is hot; and to warn their brethren to take heed that they slip not with their feet. I have often said in my heart, that this was the cause why God suffered so many of the believing Jews to fall, to wit, that the Gentiles might take heed. (Rom. xi. 21.) O brethren, saith the backslider that is returned, did you see how I left my God? did you see how I turned again to those vanities from which some time before I fled? Oh! I was deluded, I was bewitched, I was deceived; for I found all things from which I fled at first, still worse by far when I went to them the second time. Do not backslide, oh! do not backslide. The first ground of your departing from them was good; never tempt God a second time.

2. And as he gives us a second testimony, that the world and himself are so as at first he believed they were, so by this his returning, he testifies that God and Christ are the same, and much more than ever he believed at first they were. This man has made a proof before and a proof after conviction of the evil of the one and good of the other. This man has made a proof by feeling and seeing, and that before and after grace received. This man God has set up to be a witness; this man is two men, has the testimony of two men, must serve in the place of two men. He knows what it is to be fetched from a state of nature by grace; but this all Christians know as well as he. Ay, but he knows what it is to be fetched from the world, from the devil, and hell, the second time; and that but few professors know, for few that fall away return to God again. (Heb. vi. 4—8.) Ay, but this man has come again, wherefore there is news in his mouth, sad news, dreadful news, and news that is to make the standing saint to take heed lest he fall. The returning backslider therefore is a rare man, a man of worth and intelligence, a man to whom the men of the world should flock, and of whom they should learn to fear the Lord God. He also is a man of whom the saints should receive both caution, counsel, and strength, in their present standing: and they should, by his harms, learn to serve the Lord with fear, and to rejoice before him with trembling. (1 Cor. x. 6—13. Ps. li. 11—13. Luke xxii. 32.)

This man has the second time also had a proof of God's goodness in his Christ unto him, a proof which the standing Christian has not—I would not tempt him that stands to fall; but the good that a returning backslider has received at God's hands, and at the hand of Christ, is a double good, he has been converted twice, fetched from the world and from the devil, and from himself twice. Oh grace! and has been made to know the stability of God's covenant, the unchangeableness of God's mind, the sure and lasting truth of his promise in Christ, and of the sufficiency of the merits of Christ over and over.

Of the manner of this man's coming to God by Christ, I shall also speak a word or two.

He comes as the new awakened sinner comes, and that from the same motives, and the knowledge of things, as he hath over and above, (which he had as good have been without,) that which the newly awakened sinner has not, to wit, the guilt of his backsliding, which is a guilt of a worse complexion, of a deeper dye, and of a heavier nature than is any guilt else in the world. He is also attended with fears and doubts that arise from other reasons and considerations than do the doubts and fears of the newly awakened man —doubts built upon the vileness of his backsliding. He has also more dreadful scriptures to consider of, and they will look more wishfully in his face, (yea, and will also make him take notice of their grim physiognomy,) than has the newly awakened man. Besides, as a punishment of his backsliding, God seems to withdraw the sweet influences of his Spirit, and is as if he would not suffer him to pray, nor to repent any more, (Ps. li. 11;) as if he would now take all away from him, and leave him to those lusts and idols that he left his God to follow. Swarms of his new rogueries shall haunt him in every place, and that not only in the guilt, but in the filth and pollution of them. (Prov. xiv. 14.) None know the things that haunt the backslider's mind; his *new* sins are all turned talking devils, threatening devils, roaring devils, within him. Besides he doubts of the truth of his first conversion, consequently he has it lying upon him as a strong suspicion that there was nothing of truth in all his first experience: and this also adds lead to his heels, and makes him come, as to sense and feeling, more heavy and with the greater difficulty to God by Christ. As faithfulness of other men kills him, he can see not an honest, humble, holy, faithful servant of God, but he is pierced and wounded at the heart. Ay, says he, within himself, that man fears God, that man hath faithfully followed God, that man, like the elect angels, has kept his place; but I am fallen from my station like a devil. That man honoureth God, edifieth the saints, convinceth the world, and condemneth them, and is become a heir of the righteousness which is by faith. But I have dishonoured God, stumbled and grieved saints, made the world blaspheme, and, for aught I know, been the cause of the damnation of many. These are the things, I say, together with many more of the same kind, that come with him; yea, they will come with him, yea, and will stare him in the face, will tell him of his baseness, and laugh him to scorn, all the way that he is coming to God by Christ—I know what I say—and this makes his coming to God by Christ hard and difficult to him. Besides, he thinks saints will be aware of him, will be shy of him, will be afraid to trust him, yea, will tell his father of him, and make intercession against him, as Elias did against Israel, (Rom. xi. 2,) or as the men did that were fellow servants with him that took his brother by the throat. (Matt. xviii. 31.) Shame covereth his face all the way he comes. He doth not know what to do; the God he is returning to is the God that he has slighted, the God before whom

he has preferred the vilest lust; and he knows God knows it, and has before him all his ways. The man that has been a backslider, and is returning to God, can tell strange stories, and yet such as are very true. No man was in the whale's belly, and came out again alive, but backsliding and returning Jonah; consequently no man could tell how he was there, what he felt there, what he saw there, and what workings of heart he had when he was there so well as he.

The sincere Christian's coming to God by Christ.

Third. I come now to the third man, to wit, to the sincere and upright man, that cometh to God by Christ. And although this may in some sense be applicable to the two former, for his coming is not worthy to be counted coming to God, that is not in sincerity and uprightness, yet by such an one I now mean one that has been called to the faith, and that has in some good measure of sincerity and uprightness therein abode with God.

This man also comes to God by Christ; but his coming is to be distinguished, I mean in the main of it, from the coming of the other two.

The other comes for the knowledge of forgiveness, a thing that the upright and faithful Christian for the most part has a comfortable faith of, and that for which he is often helped to give thanks to God. I do not say he doubteth not, or that he has not his evidences sometimes clouded. Nor do I say that the knowledge of his reconciliation to God by Christ Jesus is so high, so firm, so fixed, and steadfast, that it cannot be shaken, or that he needs no more. I will then explain myself. He comes not to God as an unconverted sinner comes; he comes not as a backslider comes when he is returning to God from his backslidings; but he comes as a son, as one of the household of God, and he comes as one that has not, after sincere conviction, wickedly departed from his God.

1. He then comes to God with that access and godly boldness that is only proper to such as himself; that is, to them that walk with God. (Rom. v. 2.) Thus every one that shall be saved doth not do; thus every one that shall be saved cannot do—to instance the two spoken of before.

2. He comes to God by Christ constantly by prayer, by meditation, by every ordinance; for therefore he maketh use of ordinances, because by them, through Christ, he getteth into the presence of God. (Ps. xxvii. 4.)

3. He comes to God through Christ, because he judgeth that God only is that good, that blessedness, that happiness that is worth looking after: that good and that blessedness that alone can fill the soul to the brim; that good and that happiness that is worthy of our hearts, and souls, and spirits. Hence David expresseth his coming to God by panting, by thirsting, by tears, saying, "My soul panteth after thee, O God." (Ps. xlii. 1.)

And again, "My soul thirsteth for God, for the living God, when shall I come and appear before God?" (Ps. xlii. 2.) And again, "Then will I go unto the altar of God, unto God, my exceeding joy." (Ps. xliii. 4.) And hence it was that he so envied the swallow and sparrow, even because they could come to the altar of God, where he had promised to give his presence, when he, as I think, by the rage of Saul, was forced to abide remote: "My soul longeth," saith he, "yea, even fainteth for the courts of the Lord: my heart and my flesh crieth out for the living God. Yea, the sparrow hath found an house, and the swallow a nest for herself, where she may lay her young, even thine altars, O Lord of Hosts, my King, and my God. Blessed are they that dwell in thy house, they will be still praising thee." (Ps. lxxxiv. 2—4.) Then after a few more words he saith, "For a day in thy courts is better than a thousand. I had rather be a doorkeeper in the house of my God, (I would choose rather to sit at the threshold of thy house,) than to dwell in the tents of wickedness." (Ps. lxxxiv. 10.) And then renders the reasons—"For the Lord God is a sun and shield; the Lord will give grace and glory," &c. (Ps. lxxxiv. 11.)

The presence of God, and the glory and soul-ravishing goodness of that presence, is a thing that the world understands not, nor can they, *as such*, desire to know what it is.

4. These good men come to God upon other accounts also: for so it is that they have many concerns with God.

(1.) They come to him for a more clear discovery of themselves to themselves; for they desire to know how frail they are, because the more they know that, the more they are engaged in their souls to take heed to their ways, and to fear lest they should tempt their God to leave them. (Ps. xxix. 1—8.)

(2.) They come to God by Christ, for the weakening of their lusts and corruptions: for they are a sore, yea, a plague to a truly sanctified soul. Those, to be rid of which, if it might be, a godly man chooseth rather to die than to live. This David did mean when he cried, "Create in me a clean heart, O God, and renew a right spirit within me." (Ps. li. 10.) And Paul, when he cried out, "O wretched man that I am, who shall deliver me from the body of this death?" (Rom. vii. 24.)

(3.) They come to God by Christ for the renewing and strengthening of their graces. The graces that the godly have received, are, and they feel they are, subject to decay, yea, they cannot live without a continual supply of grace. This is the meaning of that, "Let us have grace," and 'let us therefore come boldly to the throne of grace, that we may obtain mercy, and find grace to help in time of need." (Heb. iv. 16.)

(4.) They come to God by Christ, to be helped against those temptations that they may meet withal. (Matt. vi. 13.) They know that every new temptation has a new snare, and a new evil in it; but what snare, and what evil, that at present they know not: but they know their God knows, and can deliver out of temptation when we are in, and keep us out while we are out. (Ps. cxxxii. 15.)

(5.) They come to God by Christ for a blessing upon that means of grace which God has afforded for the succour of the soul, and the building of it up in the faith; knowing that as the means, so a blessing upon it, is from God. And for this they have encouragement, because God has said, "I will abundantly bless her provision, I will satisfy her poor with bread." (Ps. cxxxii. 15.)

(6.) They come to God by Christ for the forgiveness of daily infirmities, (Ps. xix. 12,) and for the continuing them in the light of his countenance, notwithstanding. Thus he also would always accept them and their services, and grant that an answer of peace may be returned from their father into their bosoms; for this is the life of their souls. There are a great many such things that the sincere and upright man comes to God for, too many here to mention. But again,

(1.) This man also comes to God to beseech him for the flourishing of Christ's kingdom, which he knows will never be until Antichrist is dead, and till the Spirit be more plentifully poured upon us from on high. Therefore he also cries to God for the downfall of the first, and for the pouring out of the other.

(2.) He comes to God for the hastening the gathering in of his elect: for it is an affliction to him to think that so many of those for whom Christ died should be still in a posture of hostility against him. (Ps. cxxii. 6.)

(3.) He comes to God for a spirit of unity to be poured out among believers; for, for the divisions of Reuben he has great thoughts of heart.

(4.) He comes to God to pray for magistrates, and that God would make speed to set them all to that work that is so desirable to his church—that is, to hate the whore, to eat her flesh, to make her desolate, and burn her with fire. (1 Tim. ii. 1. Rev. xvii. 16.)

(5.) He comes to God to beg that he would hasten that great and notable day, the day of the coming of our Lord Jesus; for he knows that Christ will never be exalted as he must be till then; yea, he also knows that God's church will never be as she would, and shall, till then. (Rev. xxii. 20.)

(6.) But the main meaning, if I may so call it, of this high text, is this: that they that come to God by him—that is, by Christ—are those that come by Christ to God to enjoy him by faith and spirit here, and by open vision and unspeakable possession of him in the next world. This is the great design of the soul in its coming to God by Jesus Christ; and it comes to him by Jesus Christ, because it dare not come by itself, and because

God himself has made him the way, the new and living way. Here, as I said, the Father meets with that which pleaseth him, and the soul with that which saveth her. Here is righteousness and merits to spare, even righteousness that can justify the ungodly. Here is always, how empty soever we be, a fulness of merit always presented to God by Christ, for my obtaining of that which at any time I want, whether wisdom, grace, spirit, or any good thing soever. Only since I was upon this subject, I thought a little to touch upon things in this order, for the enlarging of thy thoughts, for the conviction of thy spirit, for the stirring of thee up to God, and for the showing of thee the good signs of grace, where it is, where it is abused, and where any are seeking after it.

Inferences drawn from thus coming to God by Christ.

And now I come to draw some inferences from this point also, as I have already done from these going before it.

You see that I have now been speaking to you of the man that cometh to God, both with respect to the way he comes, as also with respect to the manner of spirit in which he comes: and hence I may well infer,

First, that he is no fool—no fool according to the best judgment—that cometh to God by Christ. The world, indeed, will count him one; for the things that be of the Spirit of God are foolishness to them; but indeed, and in the verdict of true judgment, he is not so.

1. For that he now seeketh and intermeddleth with all wisdom. He has chosen to be concerned with the very head and fountain of wisdom; for Christ is the wisdom of God, and the way to the Father by Christ is the greatest of mysteries, and to choose to walk in that way, the fruits of the most sage advice. Wherefore he is not a fool that thus concerns himself. (Prov. xviii. 1. 1 Cor. i.)

2. It is not a sign of foolishness timely to prevent ruin, is it? They are the prudent men that foresee an evil, and hide themselves; and the fools that go, and are punished. Why, this man foresees an evil, the greatest evil, sin, and the punishment of the soul for sin in hell; and flies to Christ, who is the refuge that God has provided for penitent sinners; and is this a sign of a fool? God make me such a fool, and thee that readest these lines such a fool, and then we shall be wiser than all men that are counted wise by the wisdom of this world. Is it a sign of a fool to agree with one's adversary, while we are in the way with him, even before he delivereth us to the judge? nay, it is a piece of the highest wisdom.

Is he a fool that chooseth for himself long lasters, or he whose best things will rot in a day? Sinners, "before your pots can feel the thorns, (before you can see where you are,) God shall take you away as with a whirlwind, both living and in his wrath." (Ps. lviii. 9.) But this man has provided for

things. Like the tortoise, he has got a shell on his back, so strong and sound that he fears not to suffer a loaden cart to go over him. The Lord is his rock, his defence, his refuge, his high tower, unto which he doth continually resort.

Was the unjust steward a fool in providing for himself for hereafter? for providing friends to receive him to harbour, when others shall turn him out of their doors? (Luke xvi. 8, 9.) No more is he that gets another house for his harbour before death shall turn him out of doors here.

3. As he that cometh to God by Christ is no fool, so he is no little-spirited fellow. There are a generation of men in this world that count themselves men of the largest capacities, when yet the greatness of their desires lift themselves no higher than to things below. If they can, with their net of craft and policy, encompass a bulky lump of earth, oh, what a treasure have they engrossed to themselves! Meanwhile, the man in the text has laid siege to heaven, has found out the way to get into the city, and is resolved, in and by God's help, to make that his own. Earth is a drossy thing in this man's account: earthly greatness and splendours are but like vanishing bubbles in this man's esteem: none but God as the end of his desires, none but Christ as the means to accomplish this end, are things counted great by this man. No company now is acceptable to this man but the Spirit of God: Christ, and angels, and saints, as fellow-heirs with himself. All other men and things he deals with as strangers and pilgrims were wont to do. This man's mind soars higher than the eagle or stork of the heavens. He is for musing about things that are above, and their glory, and for thinking what shall come to pass hereafter.

4. But as I have showed you what he is not, so now let me, by a few words, tell you what he is.

(1.) Then he is a man concerned for his soul, for his immortal soul. The soul is a thing, though of most worth, least minded by most. The souls of most lie waste while all other things are inclosed. But this man has got it by the end, that his soul is of more value than the world; wherefore he is concerned for his soul. Soul-concerns are concerns of the highest nature, and concerns that arise from thoughts most deep and ponderous. He never yet knew what belonged to great and deep thoughts that is a stranger to soul-concerns. Now the man that comes to God by Christ is a man that is engaged in soul-concerns.

(2.) He is a man whose spirit is subjected to a suitableness to spiritual things; for a carnal mind cannot suit with and be delighted in these things. "The carnal mind is enmity against God; for it is not subject to the law of God, neither, indeed, can be." (Rom. viii. 7.) This is the man that God has tamed, and keeps tame by himself, while all other run wild as the asses upon the mountains. If birds could speak, surely they would tell, that those that are kept in the cage have with them another temper than they that range in the air, and fly in the fields and woods. Yea, and could those kept tame express themselves to the rest, they would tell that they have white bread and milk and sugar, while those without make a life out of maggots and worms. They are also in a place where there are better things, and their companions are the children of men. Besides, they learn such notes, and can whistle such tunes, as other birds are strangers to. Oh! the man whose spirit is subjected to God, betwixt whom and God there is a reconciliation, not only as to a difference made up, but also as to a oneness of heart, none knows what lumps of sugar God gives that man, nor what notes and tunes God learns that man. "He hath put a new song in my mouth," saith David, "even praise unto our God; many shall see it, and fear, and shall trust in the Lord." (Ps. xl. 3.)

Second. Is there a man that comes to God by Christ? Thence I infer that there is that believes there is a world to come. No man looks after that which he yet believes is not. Faith must be before coming to Christ will be; coming is the fruit of faith. He that comes must believe, antecedent to his coming: wherefore it is said, " we walk by faith," (2 Cor. v. 7. Heb. xi. 7;) that is, we come to God, through Christ, by faith. And hence I learn two things—

1. That faith is of a strong and forcible quality.

2. That they who come not to God by Christ have no faith.

1. Faith is of a strong and forcible quality, and that whether it be true or false.

(1.) A false faith has done great things; it has made men believe lies, plead for them, and stand to them, to the damnation of their souls. God shall send them strong delusion that they shall believe a lie, (2 Thess. ii. 11,) to their damnation. Hence it is said men make lies their refuge. Why? Because they trust in a lie. (Jer. xxvii. 15.) A lie, if believed, if a man has faith in it, it will do great things, because faith is of a forcible quality. Suppose thyself to be twenty miles from home, and there some man comes and possesses thee that thy house, thy wife and children, are all burned with the fire: if thou believest it, though indeed there should be nothing of truth in what thou hast heard, yet will this lie drink up thy spirit, even as if the tidings were true. How many are there in the world whose heart Satan hath filled with a belief that their state and condition for another world is good? and these are made to live by lying hope, that all should be well with them, and so are kept from seeking for that which will make them happy indeed. Man is naturally apt and willing to be deceived, and therefore a groundless faith is the more taking and forcible. Fancy will help to confirm a false faith, and so will conceit and idleness of spirit. There is also in man a willingness to take things upon trust, without searching into the ground and

reason of them. Nor will Satan be behindhand to prompt and encourage to thy believing of a lie, for that he knows will be a means to bring thee to that end to which he greatly desires thou shouldst come. Wherefore let men beware, and oh, that they could, of a false and lying faith!

(2.) But if a false faith is so forcible, what is a true? What force, I say, is there in a faith that is begotten by truth, managed by truth, fed by truth, and preserved by the truth of God? This faith will make invisible things visible; not fantastically so, but substantially so. "Now, faith is the substance of things hoped for, the evidence of things not seen." (Heb. xi. 1.) True faith carrieth along with it an evidence of the certainty of what it believeth, and that evidence is the infallible word of God. There is a God, a Christ, a heaven, saith the faith that is good; for the word of God doth say so. The way to this God, and this heaven, is by Christ; for the word of God doth say so. If I run not to this God by this Christ, this heaven shall never be my portion; for the word of God doth say so. So, then, thus believing makes the man come to God by him. His thus believing, then, it is that carries him away from this world, that makes him trample upon this world, and that gives him the victory over this world. "For whosoever is born of God overcometh the world: and this is the victory that overcometh the world, even our faith. Who is he that overcometh the world, but he that believeth that Jesus is the Son of God? This is he that cometh by water and blood, even Jesus Christ: not by water only, but by water and blood. And it is the Spirit that beareth witness, because the Spirit is truth." (1 John v. 4—6.)

2. Now, if this be true, that faith, true faith, is so forcible a thing, as to take a man from his seat of ease, and make him come to God by Christ, as afore, then is it not truly inferred from hence that they that come not to God by Christ have no faith? What! is man such a fool as to believe things, and yet not look after them? to believe great things, and yet not to concern himself with them? Who would knowingly go over a pearl, and yet not count it worth stooping for? Believe thou art what thou art; believe hell is what it is; believe death and judgment are coming as they are; and believe that the Father and the Son are, as by the Holy Ghost in the word they are described, and sit still in thy sins, if thou canst. Thou canst not sit still: faith is forcible. Faith is grounded upon the voice of God in the word, upon the teaching of God in the word. And it pleases God by the foolishness of preaching to save them that believe: for believing makes them heartily close in with and embrace what by the word is set before them, because it seeth the reality of them.

Shall God speak to man's soul, and shall not man believe? Shall man believe what God says, and nothing at all regard it? It cannot be.

"Faith comes by hearing, and hearing by the word of God." And we know that when faith is come, it purifies the heart of what is opposite to God, and the salvation of the soul.

So, then, those men that are at ease in a sinful course, or that come not to God by Christ, they are such as have no faith, and must therefore perish with the vile and unbelievers. (Rev. xxi. 8.)

The whole world is divided into two sorts of men, believers and unbelievers. The godly are called believers. And why believers? but because they are they that have given credit to the great things of the gospel of God. These believers are here in the text called also comers, or they that come to God by Christ, because, who so believes, will come; for coming is a fruit of faith in the habit, or, if you will, it is faith in exercise; yet faith must have a being in the soul before the soul can put it into act.

This, therefore, further evidences, that they that come not, have no faith, are not believers, belong not to the household of faith, and must perish; "for he that believes not, shall be damned."

Nor will it be any boot to say, I believe there is a God and a Christ; for still thy sitting still doth demonstrate that either thou liest in what thou sayest, or that thou believest with a worse than a false faith. But the object of my faith is true. I answer, so is the object of the faith of devils: for they believe that there is one God and one Christ, yet their faith, as to the root and exercise of it, that notwithstanding, is no such faith as is that faith that saves, or that is intended in the text, and that by which men come to God through Christ.

Wherefore still, oh thou slothful one, thou deceivest thyself! Thy not coming to God by Christ, declareth to thy face that thy faith is not good, consequently that thou feedest on ashes, and thy deceived heart has turned thee aside, that thou canst not deliver thy soul, nor say, "Is there not a lie in my right hand?" (Isa. xliv. 20.)

Third. Is there a man that comes to God by Christ? Thence I infer, that the world to come is better than this; yea, so much better as to quit cost and bear charges of coming to God, from this, by Christ, to that. Though there is a world to come, yet if it was no better than this, one had as good stay here, as seek that; or if it were better than this, and would bear charges, if a man left this for that, and that was all, still the one would be as good as the other. But the man that comes to God by Christ, has chosen the world that is infinitely good, a world betwixt which and this there can be no comparison. This must be granted, because he that comes to God by Christ, is said to have made the best choice, even chose a city that has foundations. (Heb. xi. 10.) There are several things that make it manifest enough that he that comes to God by Christ has made the best market, or chose the best world.

1. That is the world which God commandeth, but this that that he slighteth and contemneth. Hence that is called the kingdom of God, (2 Thess. i. 5, 6,) but this an "evil world." (Gal. i. 4.) Now let us conclude, that since God made both, he is able to judge which of the two are best: yea, best able to judge thereof. I choose the rather to refer you to the judgment of God in this matter; for should I put you upon asking of him, as to this,—that is, coming to God by Christ, —perhaps you would say, he is as little able to give an account of this matter as yourselves. But I hope you think God knows, and therefore I refer you to the judgment of God, which you have in the Scriptures of truth—"Heaven is his throne, and the earth is his footstool." I hope you will say here is some difference. The Lord is the God of that, the devil the god and prince of this. Thus also it appears there is some difference between them.

2. That world, and those that are counted worthy of it, shall all be everlasting; but so shall not this, nor the inhabitants of it. The earth, with the works thereof, shall be burned up, and the men that are of it shall die in like manner. (2 Pet. iii.) But Israel shall be saved in the Lord with an everlasting salvation: they shall not be ashamed nor confounded, world without end. (Isa. xlv. 17.)

This world, with the lovers of it, will end in a burning hell; but the world to come "fadeth not away." (1 Pet. i. 3, 4.)

3. The world that we are now in, has its best comforts mixed either with crosses or curses; but that to come with neither. There shall be no more curse; and as for crosses, all tears shall be wiped from the eyes of them that dwell there. There will be nothing but ravishing pleasures and holy. There will be no cessation of joys, nor any speck of pollution: "In thy presence is fulness of joy; at thy right hand there are pleasures for evermore." (Ps. xvi. 11.)

4. There men shall be made like angels, "neither can they die any more." (Luke xx. 36.) There shall they behold the face of God and his Son, and swim in the enjoyment of them for ever.

5. There men shall see themselves beyond all misery, and shall know that it will be utterly impossible that either anything like sorrow, or grief, or sickness, or discontent, should touch them more.

6. There men shall be rewarded of God for what they have done and suffered, according to his will for his sake; there they shall eat and drink their comforts, and wear them to their everlasting consolation.

7. They are all kings that go to that world, and so shall be proclaimed there. They shall also be crowned with crowns, and they shall wear crowns of life and glory, crowns of everlasting joy, crowns of loving kindness; yea, "in that day the Lord of hosts himself shall be for a crown of

glory to those that are his people." (Heb. ii. 7. Isa. xxxv. 10. Ps. ciii. 4. Isa. xxviii. 5.) Now if this world, though no more could be said for it than is said in these few lines, is not infinitely far better than what the present world is, I have missed it in my thoughts. But the coming man, the man that comes to God by Christ, is satisfied, knows what he does; and if his way, all his way thither, were strewed with burning coals, he would choose, God helping him, to tread that path rather than to have his portion with them that perish.

Fourth. If there be a world to come, and such a way to it, so safe and good, and if God is there to be enjoyed by them that come to him by Christ, then this shows the great madness of the most of men; madness, I say, of the highest degree; for that they come not to God by Christ that they may be inheritors of the world to come. It is a right character which Solomon gives of them: "The heart," saith he, "of the sons of men are full of evil, and madness is in their hearts while they live, and after that they go to the dead." (Eccles. ix. 3.)

A madman is intent upon his toys, upon anything but that about which he should be intent; and so are they that come not to God by Jesus Christ. A madman has neither ears to hear, nor a heart to do what they that are in their right wits advise him for the best, no more have they that come not to God by Christ. A madman sets more by the straws and cock's feathers by which he decks himself, than he does by all the pearls and jewels in the world. And they that come not to God by Christ, set more by the vanishing bubbles of this life, than they do by that glory that the wise man shall inherit: "The wise shall inherit glory, but shame," says Solomon, "shall be the promotion of fools." What a shame it is to see God's jewels lie unregarded of them that yet think none are wiser than themselves!

I know the wise men of this world will scorn one should think of them that they are mad; but verily it is so: the more wise for this world, the more fool in God's matters, and the more obstinately they stand in their way, the more mad.

When Solomon gave himself to backsliding, he saith, "he gave himself to folly and madness." (Eccles. i. 17; ii. 12.) And when he went about to search out what man is since the fall, he went about to search out foolishness and madness. (Eccles. vii. 25—29.) And is it not said, that when the Jews were angry with Jesus, for that he did good on the Sabbath, that that anger did flow from their being filled with madness? Doth not Paul also, while he opposed himself against Christ, the gospel and professors thereof, plainly tell us, that he did it even from the highest pitch of madness? "And being exceeding mad against them, I persecuted them even unto strange cities." (Acts xxvi. 11.) Now, if it is exceeding madness to do thus, how many at this day must be counted exceeding mad, who yet count themselves the only sober men?

They oppose themselves, they stand in their own light, they are against their own happiness, they cherish and nourish cockatrices in their own bosoms; they choose to themselves those paths which have written upon them, in large characters, "These are the ways of death and damnation." They are offended with them that endeavour to pull them out of their ditch, and choose rather to lie and die there, than to go to God by Christ, that they may be saved from wrath through him : yea, so mad are they, that they count the most sober, the most godly, the most holy man, the mad one, the more earnest for life, the more mad; the more in the Spirit, the more mad; the more desirous to promote the salvation of others, the more mad. But is not this a sign of madness, of madness unto perfection? And yet thus mad are many; and mad are all they, that while it is called to-day, while their door is open, and while the golden sceptre of the golden grace of the blessed God is held forth, stand in their own light, and come not to God by Christ. That is the fourth inference.

Fifth. A fifth inference that I gather from this text, is, that the end that God will make with men will be according as they come or come not to God by Christ. They that come to God by Christ have taken shelter, and have hid themselves, but they that come not to God by Christ lay themselves open to the windy storm and tempest that will be in that day. And the wind then will be high and the tempest strong that will blow upon them that shall be found in themselves. "Our God shall come, and shall not keep silence; a fire shall devour before him, and it shall be very tempestuous round about him : he shall call to the heavens from above, and to the earth, that he may judge his people." (Ps. l. 3, 4.)

And now what will be found in that day to be the portion of them that in this day do not come to God by Christ, none knows but God, with whom the reward of unbelievers is.

But writing and preaching is in vain as to such; let men say what they will, what they can to persuade to come, to dissuade from neglecting to come, they are resolved not to stir. They will try if God will be so faithful to himself and to his word as to dare to condemn them to hell-fire that have refused to hear and comply with the voice of him that speaketh from heaven.

But this is but a desperate venture; several things declare that he is determined to be at a point in this matter.

1. The gallows are built—hell is prepared for the wicked.

2. There are those already in chains, and stand bound over to the judgment of that day, that are, as to creation, higher and greater than men—to wit, the angels that sinned. (2 Pet. ii. 4.) Let sinners then look to themselves.

3. The Judge is prepared and appointed, and it hath fallen out to be he that thou hast refused to come to God by; and that predicts no good to

thee : for then will he say of all such, " Those mine enemies that would not that I should reign over them, bring hither, and slay them before me." (Luke xix. 27.)

But what a surprise will it be to them that now have come to God by Christ to see themselves in heaven indeed, saved indeed, and possessed of everlasting life indeed ? For, alas ! what is faith to possession ? Faith that is mixed with many tears, that is opposed with many assaults, and that seems sometimes to be quite extinguished, I say, what is that to a seeing of myself in heaven ? Hence it is said that he shall then come to be admired in them that now believe, because they did here believe the testimony ; then they shall admire that it was their lot to believe when they were in the world. (2 Thess. i. 10.) They shall also admire to think, to see, and behold what believing has brought them to, while the rest for refusing to come to God by Christ drink their tears mixed with burning brimstone.

Repentance will not be found in heaven among them that come to God by Christ ; no, hell is the place of untimely repentance ; it is there where the tears will be mixed with gnashing of teeth, while they consider how mad, and worse, they were in not coming to God by Jesus Christ.

Then will their hearts and mouths be full of " Lord, Lord, open unto us." But the answer will be, Ye shut me out of doors ; " I was a stranger, and ye took me not in." Besides, you refused to come to my Father by me, wherefore now you must go from my Father by me. (Matt. xxv.)

They that will not be saved by Christ must be damned by Christ. No man can escape one of the two. Refuse the first they may, but shun the second they cannot.

And now they that would not come unto God by Christ will have leisure and time enough (if I may call it time) to consider what they have done in refusing to come to God by Christ. Now they will meditate warmly on this thing, now their thoughts will be burning hot about it, and it is too late, will be in each thought such a sting, that, like a bow of steel, it will continually strike him through.

Now they will bless those whom formerly they have despised, and commend those whom they once contemned. Now, would the rich man willingly change places with poor Lazarus, though he preferred his own condition before his in the world.

The day of judgment will bring the worst to rights, in their opinions ; they will not be capable of misapprehending any more. They will never after that day put bitter for sweet, or darkness for light, or evil for good any more. Their madness will now be gone. Hell will be the unbeliever's bedlam-house, and there God will tame them as to all those bedlam tricks and pranks which they played in this world, but not at all to their profit nor advantage. The gulf that God has placed

and fixed betwixt heaven and hell, will spoil all as to that. (Luke xvi. 23—26.)

But what a joy will it be to the truly godly to think now that they are come to God by Christ ! It was their mercy to begin to come ; it was their happiness that they continued coming ; but it is their glory that they are come, that they are come to God by Christ.

To God ! why ? he is all ; all that is good, essentially good, and eternally good. To God ! the infinite ocean of good. To God in friendly wise, by the means of reconciliation ; for the other now will be come to him to receive his anger, because they come not to him by Jesus Christ. Oh that I could imagine ! oh that I could think, that I might write more effectually to thee of the happy estate of them that come to God by Christ !

But thus have I passed through the three former things, namely,

1. That of the intercession of Christ.
2. That of the benefit of his intercession.
3. That of the persons that are interested in this intercession.

IV. *Every sincere heart certain of salvation.*

Wherefore now I come to the last head, and that is to show you the certainty of their reaping the benefit of his intercession. " Wherefore he is able also to save them to the uttermost that come unto God by him, seeing he ever liveth to make intercession for them."

The certainty of their reaping the benefit of being saved that come unto God by Christ, is thus expressed : " Seeing he ever liveth to make intercession for them." The intercession of Christ, and the lastingness of it, is a sure token of the salvation of them that come unto God by him.

Of his intercession, what it is, and for whom, we have spoken already ; of the success and the prevalency of it, we have also spoken before ; but the reason of its successfulness, of that we are to speak of now. And that reason, as the apostle suggesteth, lies in the continuance of it, " seeing he ever liveth to make intercession." The apostle also makes very much of the continuation of the priesthood of Christ, in other places of this epistle. He abides a priest continually, " Thou art a priest for ever." He " hath an unchangeable priesthood." (Heb. vii. 3, 17, 21, 24.) And here he " ever liveth to make intercession."

Now, by the text is showed the reason why he so continually harpeth upon the durableness of it, namely, for that by the unchangeableness of this priesthood we are saved ; nay, saved demonstratively, apparently : it is evident we are. " He is also able to save them to the uttermost that come unto God by him, seeing he ever liveth to make intercession for them." For,

First. The durableness of his intercession proves that the covenant in which those that come to God by him are concerned and wrapt up is not shaken, broken, or made invalid by all their weaknesses and infirmities.

Christ is a priest according to covenant, and in all his acts of mediation he has regard to that covenant: so long as that covenant abides in its strength, so long Christ's intercession is of worth. Hence when God cast the old high priest out of doors, he renders this reason for his so doing; because they continued not in my covenant, that is, neither priests nor people. Therefore were they cast out of the priesthood, and the people pulled down, as to a church state. (Heb. vii. 6—9.)

Now the covenant by which Christ acteth as a priest, so far as we are concerned therein, he also himself acteth our part, being indeed the Head and Mediator of the body. Wherefore God doth not count that the covenant is broken, though we sin, if Christ Jesus our Lord is found to do by it what by law is required of us. Therefore he saith, " If his children forsake my law, and keep not my commandments, then will I visit their transgressions with a rod," &c. But their sins shall not shake my covenant with my Beloved, nor cause that I for ever should reject them. " My covenant will I not break, nor alter the thing that is gone out of my lips. His seed, also, will endure for ever, his seed shall endure for ever." (Ps. lxxxix. 29—36.) Hence it is clear, that the covenant stands good to us, as long as Christ stands good to God, or before his face. For he is not only our Mediator by covenant, but he himself is our condition to God-ward; therefore he is said to be the covenant of the people, or that which the holy God by law required of us. (Isa. xlii. 6.) Hence, again, he is said to be our justice or righteousness; to wit, which answereth to what is required of us by the law. He is made unto us of God so, and in our room, and in our stead presenteth himself to God. So then, if any ask me by what Christ's priesthood is continued, I answer, By covenant; for that the covenant by which he is made priest abideth of full force. If any ask whether the church is concerned in that covenant, I answer, Yes; yet so as that all points and parts thereof, that concern life and death everlasting, is laid upon his shoulders, and he alone is the doer of it. He is the Lord our righteousness, and he is the Saviour of the body; so that my sins break not the covenant. But them notwithstanding, God's covenant stands fast with him, with him for evermore. And good reason, if no fault can be found with Christ, who is the person that did strike hands with his Father upon our account, and for us, to wit, to do what was meet should be found upon us when we came to appear before God by him.

And that God himself doth so understand this matter is evident, because he also, by his own act, giveth and imputeth to us that good that we never did, that righteousness which we never wrought out: yea, and for the sake of that, transmitteth our sins unto Christ, as to one that had not only well satisfied for them, but could carry them so far,

both from us and from God, that they should never again come to be charged on the committers, to death and damnation. The Scriptures are so plentiful for this, that he must be a Turk, or a Jew, or an atheist, that denies it. Besides, God's commanding that men should believe in his Son unto righteouness, well enough proveth this thing; and the reason of this command doth prove it with an over and above; to wit, " For he hath made him to be sin for us who knew no sin, that we might be made the righteousness of God in him." (2 Cor. v. 19—21.)

Hence comes out that proclamation from God, at the rising again of Christ from the dead, " Be it known unto you therefore, men and brethren, that through this man is preached unto you the forgiveness of sins; and by him all that believe are justified from all things, from which ye could not be justified by the law of Moses." (Acts xiii. 38, 39.)

If this be so, as indeed it is, then here lieth a great deal of this conclusion, " he ever liveth to make intercession," and of the demonstration of the certain salvation of him that cometh to God by him, " seeing he ever liveth to make intercession for them." For if Christ Jesus is a priest by covenant, and so abides as the covenant abides, and if since the covenant is everlasting, his priesthood is unchangeable, then the man that cometh to God by him must needs be certainly saved. For if the covenant, the covenant of salvation, is not broken, none can show a reason why he that comes to Christ should be damned, or why the priesthood of Jesus Christ should cease. Hence, after the apostle had spoken of the excellency of his person and priesthood, he then shows that the benefit of the covenant of God remaineth with us, namely, that grace should be communicated unto us for his priesthood's sake, and that our sins and iniquities God would remember no more. (Heb. viii. 10—12; x. 16—22.)

Now, as I also have already hinted, if this covenant, of which the Lord Jesus is Mediator and High Priest, has in the bowels of it, not only grace and remission of sins, but a promise that we shall be partakers thereof through the blood of his priesthood, for so it comes to us, then why should not we have boldness, not only to come to God by him, but to enter also into the holiest by the blood of Jesus, by that new and living way, &c.

Second. But further, this priesthood, as to the unchangeableness of it, is confirmed unto him " with an oath, by him that said unto him, The Lord sware, and will not repent; thou art a priest for ever." This oath seems to me to be for the confirmation of the covenant, as it is worded before by Paul to the Galatians, (Gal. iii. 15—17,) when he speaks of it with respect to that establishment that it also had on Christ's part, by the sacrifice which he offered to God for us; yea, he then speaks of the mutual confirmation of it, both by the Father and the Son. Now, I say, since by this covenant he stands and abides a Priest, and since "the Lord sware and will not repent, saying, Thou art a priest for ever," we are still further confirmed in the certain salvation of him that cometh to God by Christ.

The Lord by swearing confirmeth to Christ, and so to us in him, the immutability of his counsel, (Heb. vi. 16—18,) and that he is utterly unchangeable in his resolutions to "save them to the uttermost, that come unto God by Christ." And this also shows that this covenant, and so the promise of remission of sins, is steadfast and unmovable. And it is worth your noting the manner and nature of this oath, "The Lord sware, and will not repent." It is as much as to say, What I have now sworn I bind me for ever to stand to; or, I determine never to revoke; and that is, "that thou art a priest for ever." Now, as was said before, since his priesthood stands by covenant, and this covenant of his priesthood is confirmed by his oath, it cannot be but that he that comes by him to God must be accepted of him; for should such an one be rejected, it must be either for the greatness of his sins, or for want of merit in the sacrifice he presented, and urged, as to the merit of it, before the mercy-seat. But let the reason specified be what it will, the consequence falls harder upon the sacrifice of Christ than it can do anywhere else, and so on upon the covenant, and at last upon God himself, who has sworn, and will not repent, "that he is a priest for ever." I thus discourse, to show you what dangerous conclusions follow from a conceit that some that come to God by Christ shall not be saved, though "he ever liveth to make intercession for them."

And this I have further to say, that the Lord's swearing, since the manner of the oath is such as it is, and that it also tended to establish to Christ his priesthood to be unchangeable, it declareth that as to the excellency of his sacrifice he is eternally satisfied in the goodness and merit of it, and that he will never deny him anything that he shall ask for at his hands for his sufferings' sake. For this oath doth not only show God's firm resolution to keep his part of the covenant, in giving to Christ that which was covenanted for by him, but it declareth that, in the judgment of God, Christ's blood is able to save any sinner, and he will never put stop nor check to his intercession, how great soever the sinners be that at any time he shall intercede for: so that the demonstration is clearer and clearer, "He is able to save them to the uttermost that come unto God by him, seeing he ever liveth to make intercession for them."

Third. This unchangeableness of the priesthood of Christ dependeth also upon his own life: "This man, because he continueth ever, hath an unchangeable priesthood." Now, although perhaps at first much may not appear in this text, yet the words that we are upon take their ground from them. "This man, because he continueth ever, hath an unchangeable priesthood: wherefore

he is able also"—that is, by his unchangeable priesthood—"to save them to the uttermost that come unto God by him, seeing he ever liveth to make intercession for them."

The life of Christ, then, is a ground of the lastingness of his priesthood, and so a ground of the salvation of them that come unto God by him. "We shall be saved by his life." (Rom. v. 10.) Wherefore, in another place, this his life is spoken of with great emphasis, the power of an endless life: "He is made (a priest) not after the law of a carnal commandment, but after the power of an endless life." (Heb. vii. 16.) An endless life is, then, a powerful thing; and, indeed, two things are very considerable in it—

1. That it is above death, and so above him that hath the power of death, the devil.

2. In that it capacitates him to be the last in his own cause, and so to have the casting voice.

1. We will speak to the first, and for the better setting of it forth, we will show what life it is of which the apostle here speaks; and then, how, as to life, it comes to be so advantageous, both with respect to his office of priesthood, and us.

What life is it that is thus the ground of his priesthood? It is a life taken, his own life rescued from the power of the grave, a life that we had forfeited, he being our surety, and a life that he recovered again, he being the Captain of our salvation. I lay down my life, saith he, that I may take it again. "This commandment have I received of my Father." (John x. 18.) It is a life, then, that was once laid down as the price of man's redemption, and a life won, gained, taken, or recovered again, as the token or true effect of the completing, by so dying, that redemption. Wherefore it saith again, "In that he died, he died unto sin once; but in that he liveth, he liveth unto God." (Rom. vi. 10.) He liveth as having pleased God by dying for our sins, as having merited his life by dying for our sins. Now, if this life of his is a life merited and won, by virtue of the death that he died, as Acts ii. 24 doth clearly manifest; and if this life is the ground of the unchangeableness of this part of his priesthood, as we see it is, then it follows that this second part of his priesthood, which is called here *intercession*, is grounded upon the demonstrations of the virtue of his sacrifice, which is his life taken to live again: so, then, he holds this part of his priesthood, not by virtue of a carnal commandment, but by the power of an endless life, but by the power of a life rescued from death, and eternally exalted above all that any ways would yet assault it: for "Christ being raised from the dead, dieth no more: death hath no more dominion over him." (Rom. vi. 9.)

Hence Christ brings in his life, the life that he won to himself by his death, to comfort John withal, when he fainted under the view of that overcoming glory that he saw upon Christ in his vision of him at Patmos: "And he laid his right hand upon me" said he, "saying unto me, Fear not, I am the first and the last: I am he that liveth and was dead, and behold I am alive for evermore. Amen." (Rev. i. 17, 18.) Why should Christ bring in his life to comfort John, if it was not a life advantageous to him? But the advantageousness of it doth lie, not merely in the being of life, but in that it was a life laid down for his sins, and a life taken up again for his justification; a life lost to ransom him, and a life won to save him; as also the text affirmeth, saying, " He is able also to save to the uttermost them that come unto God by him, seeing he ever liveth to make intercession for them."

Again: it is yet more manifest that Christ, receiving of his life again, was the death and destruction of the enemy of his people; and to manifest that it was so, therefore he adds—after he had said, "And, behold, I am alive for evermore. Amen "—" And I have the keys of hell and of death." I have the power over them, I have them under me; I tread them down, by being a victor, a conqueror, and one that have got the dominion of life—for he now is the Prince of life—one that lives for evermore. Amen. Hence it is said again, He " hath abolished death, and brought life and immortality to light through the gospel." (2 Tim. i. 10.) He hath abolished death by his death—by death he destroyed him that had the power of death, that is, the devil; and brought life—a very emphatical expression— and brought it from whence? from God, who raised him from the dead; and brought it to light, to our view and sight, by the word of the truth of the gospel.

So then the life that he now hath, is a life once laid down as the price of our redemption; a life obtained and taken to him again as the effect of the merit that was in the laying down thereof; a life by the virtue of which death and sin, and the curse, is overcome; and so a life that is above them for ever. This is the life that he liveth—to wit, this meriting, purchasing, victorious life—and that he improveth, while he ever so lives, to make intercession for us.

This life then is a continual plea and argument with God for them that come to him by Christ, should he make no other intercession, but only show to God that he liveth; because his thus living saith, that he has satisfied for the sins of them that come unto God by him. It testifies, moreover, that those—to wit, death, the grave, and hell—are overcome by him for them; because, indeed, he liveth, and hath their keys. But now, add to life, to a life meritorious, intercession, or an urging of this meritorious life by way of prayer for his, and against all those that seek to destroy them, since they themselves also have been already overcome by his death, and what an encouraging consideration is here for all them that come to God by him, to hope for life eternal! But,

2. Let us speak a word to the second head— namely, for that his living for ever capacitates him to be the last in his own cause, and to have the casting voice; and that is an advantage next to what is chiefest.

His cause; what is his cause? but that the death that he died when he was in the world, was and is of merit sufficient to secure all those from hell, or, as the text has it, to save them that come unto God by him; to save them to the uttermost. Now, if this cause be faulty, why doth he live? Yea, he liveth by the power of God, by the power of God towards us; or with a respect to our welfare, for " he liveth to make intercession"— intercession against Satan our accuser—for us. (2 Cor. xiii. 4.) Besides, he liveth before God, and to God, and that after he had given his life a ransom for us. What can follow more clearly from this, but that amends was made by him for those souls for whose sins he suffered upon the tree? Wherefore, since his Father has given him his life and favour, and that after he died for our sins, it cannot be thought but that the life he now liveth is a life that he received as the effect of the merit of his passion for us.

God is just, and yet Christ liveth, and yet Christ liveth in heaven. God is just, and yet Christ our passover liveth there, do what our foes can to the contrary.

And this note, by the way, that though the design of Satan against us, in his labouring continually to accuse us to God, and to prevail against our salvation, seems to terminate here, yet indeed it is also laid against the very life of Christ, and that his priesthood might be utterly overthrown; and in conclusion that God also might be found unjust in receiving of such whose sins have not been satisfied for, and so whose souls are yet under the power of the devil. For he that objects against him for whom Christ intercedes, objects against Christ and his merits; and he that objects against Christ's intercession, objects against God who has made him a priest for ever. Behold you therefore how the cause of God, of Christ, and of the souls that come to God by him, are interwoven. They are all wrapt up in one bottom. Mischief one, and you mischief all; overthrow that soul, and you overthrow his intercessor; and overthrow him, and you overthrow even him that made him a priest for ever.

For the text is without restriction: " He is able to save to the uttermost, them that come unto God by him." He saith not now and then one, or sinners of an inferior rank in sin, but them that come to God by him, how great soever their transgressions are; as is clear in that it addeth this clause, " to the uttermost:" " He is able to save them to the uttermost."

But if he were not, why did the King send, yea, come and loose him, and let him go free? yea, admit him into his presence, yea, make him Lord over all his people, and deliver all things into his hand?

But he liveth, he ever liveth, and is admitted to

make intercession, yea, is ordained of God so to do: therefore he is "able to save to the uttermost them that come unto God by him."

This therefore that he liveth, seeing he liveth to God and his judgment, and in justice is made so to do, it is chiefly with reference to his life, as Mediator, for their sakes for whom he makes intercession: "He liveth to make intercession." And in that it is said he liveth ever, what is it but that he must live, and outlive all his enemies: for he must live, yea, reign until all his enemies are put under his feet. (1 Cor. xv. 25.) Yea, his very intercessions must live till they are all dead and gone: for the devil and sin must not live for ever, not for ever to accuse. Time is coming when due course of law will have an end, and all cavillers will be cast over the bar; but then and after that Christ our High Priest shall live, and so shall his intercessions, yea, and also all them for whom he makes intercession, seeing they come unto God by him.

Now if he lives, and outlives all, and if his intercession has the casting voice, since also he pleadeth in his prayers a sufficient merit before a just God, against a lying, malicious, clamorous, and envious adversary, he must needs carry the cause, the cause for himself and his people, to the glory of God and their salvation. So then his life and intercession must prevail, there can be no withstanding of it. Is not this then a demonstration clear as the sun, that they that come to God by him shall be saved, "seeing he ever liveth to make intercession for them?"

Fourth. The duration of Christ's intercession, as it is grounded upon a covenant betwixt God and him, upon an oath also, and upon his life, so it is grounded upon the validity of his merits. This has been promiscuously touched before, but since it is an essential to the lastingness of his intercession, it will be to the purpose to lay it down by itself.

Intercession then—I mean Christ's intercession—is that those for whom he died with full intention to save them, might be brought into that inheritance which he had purchased for them. Now then, his intercession must, as to length and breadth, reach no further than his merits. For he may not pray for those for whom he died not. Indeed, if we take in the utmost extent of his death, then we must beware. For his death is sufficient to save the whole world; but his intercessions are kept within a narrower compass. The altar of burnt offerings was a great deal bigger than the altar of incense, which was a figure of Christ's intercession. (Exod. xxvii. 1; xxx 1. Rev. viii. 3.) But this, I say, his intercession is for those for whom he died, with full intention to save them: wherefore it must be grounded upon the validity of his sufferings. And, indeed, his intercession is nothing else that I know of, but a presenting of what he did in the world for us unto God, and pressing the value of it for our salvation.

The blood of sprinkling is that which speaketh meritoriously, (Heb. xii. 24,) it is by the value of that that God measureth out, and giveth unto us, grace and life eternal, wherefore Christ's intercessions also must be ordered and governed by merit. By his own blood he entered into the holy place, having (before by it) obtained eternal redemption for us, for our souls. (Heb. ix. 12.)

Now, if by blood he entered in thither, by blood he must also make intercession there. His blood made way for his entrance thither, his blood must make way for our entrance thither. Though here again we must beware; for his blood did make way for him as Priest to intercede; his blood makes way for us, as for those redeemed by it, that we might be saved.

This then shows sufficiently the worth of the blood of Christ, even his ever living to make intercession for us; for the merit of his blood lasts all the while that he doth, and for all them for whom he ever liveth to make intercession. Oh precious blood! oh lasting merit!

Blood must be pleaded in Christ's intercession, because of justice, and to stop the mouth of the enemy, and also to encourage us to come to God by him. Justice, since that is of the essence of God, must concur in the salvation of the sinner; but how can that be, since it is said at first, "In the day thou eatest thereof, thou shalt surely die;" unless a plenary satisfaction be made for sin, to the pleasing of the mighty God? The enemy also would else never let go his objecting against our salvation. But now God has declared that our salvation is grounded on justice, because merited by blood. And though God needed not to have given his Son to die for us that he might save us, and stop the mouth of the devil in so doing, yet this way of salvation has done both, and so it is declared, we are "justified freely by his grace, through the redemption that is in Jesus, whom God hath set forth to be a propitiation, through faith in his blood, to declare his righteousness for the remission of sins that are past; to declare, I say, at this time his righteousness, that he might be just, and the justifier of him that believeth in Jesus." (Rom. iii. 24—26.) So then here is also a ground of intercession, even the blood shed for us before.

And that you may see it yet more for your comfort, God did at Christ's resurrection, to show what a price he set upon his blood, bid him ask of him the heathen, and he would give him the uttermost parts of the earth for his possession. (Ps. ii. 8.) His blood then has value enough in it to ground intercession upon; yea, there is more worth in it than Christ will plead or improve for men by way of intercession. I do not at all doubt but there is virtue enough in the blood of Christ, would God Almighty so apply it, to save the souls of the whole world. But it is the blood of Christ, his own blood, and he may do what he will with his own. It is also the blood of God, and he also may restrain its merits, or apply it as he sees good. But the coming soul, he shall find and feel the virtue thereof, even the soul that comes to God by Christ; for he is the man concerned in its worth, and he ever liveth to make intercession for him.

Now, seeing the intercession of Christ is grounded upon a covenant, an oath, a life, and also upon the validity of his merits, it must of necessity be prevalent, and so drive down all opposition before it. This therefore is the last part of the text, and that which demonstrateth that he that comes to God by Christ shall be saved, seeing he ever liveth to make intercession for him.

I have now done what I intend upon this subject, when I have drawn a few inferences from this also.

Inferences from the certainty of benefit from Christ's intercession.

First, then, hence I infer that the souls saved by Christ are in themselves in a most deplorable condition. Oh what ado, as I may say, is here, before one sinner can be eternally saved! Christ must die; but that is not all. The Spirit of grace must be given to us; but that is not all; but Christ must also ever live to make intercession for us; and as he doth this for all, so he doth it for each one. He interceded for me before I was born, that I might in time, at the set time, come into being. After that he also made intercession for me, that I might be kept from hell in the time of my unregenerate state until the time of my call and conversion: yet again he then intercedes, that the work now begun in my soul may be perfected, not only to the day of my dissolution, but unto the day of Christ; that is, until he comes to judgment, so that as he begun to save me before I had being, so he will go on to save me when I am dead and gone, and will never leave off to save me until he has set me before his face for ever. (Phil. i. 6.)

But I say, what a deplorable condition has our sin put us into, that there must be all this ado to save us! Oh how hardly is sin got out of the soul, when once it is in! Blood takes away the guilt; inherent grace weakens the filth; but the grave is the place, at the mouth of which sin, as to the being of sin, and the saved, must have a perfect and final parting. Not that the grave of itself is of a sin-purging quality, but God will follow Satan home to his own door; for the grave is the door or gate of hell, and will there, where the devil thought to have swallowed us up, make us (at our coming thence) shine like the sun, and look like angels. Christ all this while ever liveth to make intercession for us.

Second. Hence also I infer, that as Satan thought he struck home at first, when he polluted our nature, and brought our souls to death, so he is marvellous loth to lose us, and to suffer his lawful captives now to escape his hands. He is full of fire against us, full of the fire of malice, as is manifest—

1. Not only by his first attempt upon our first parents, but behold when the Deliverer came into the world, how he roared. He sought his death while he was an infant; he hated him in his cradle, he persecuted him while he was but a bud and blossom. (Matt. ii.)

When he was come to riper years, and began to manifest his glory, yet, lest the world should be taken with him, how politicly did this old serpent, called the Devil and Satan, work. He possessed people that he had a devil, and was mad, and a deceiver; that he wrought his miracles by magic art, and by the devil; that the prophets spake nothing of him, and that he sought to overthrow government which was God's ordinance. And, not being contented with all this, he pursued him to the death, and could never rest until he had spilt his blood upon the ground like water. Yea, so insatiable was his malice, that he set the soldiers to forge lies about him to the denial of his resurrection, and so managed that matter that what they said has become a stumbling-block to the Jews to this very day. (John x. 20. John vii. 12. Matt. ix. 34. John vii. 52. Luke xxiii. 2. Matt. xxviii. 11—15.)

2. When he was ascended to God, and so was out of his reach, yet how busily went he about to make war with his people! (Rev. xii.) Yea, what horrors and terrors, what troubles and temptations, has God's church met with from that day till now! Nor is he content with persecutions and general troubles; but, oh! how doth he haunt the spirits of the Christians with blasphemies and troubles, with darkness and frightful fears; sometimes to their distraction, and often to the filling the church with outcries.

3. Yet his malice is in the pursuit, and now his boldness will try what it can do with God, either to tempt him to reject his Son's mediation, or to reject them that come to God by him for mercy. And this is one cause among many, why he "ever liveth to make intercession for them that come to God by him."

4. And if he cannot overthrow, if he knows he cannot overthrow them, yet he cannot forbear but vex and perplex them even as he did their Lord, from the day of their conversion to the day of their ascension to glory.

Third. Hence I infer that the love of Christ to his is an unwearied love, and it must needs be so; an undaunted love, and it must needs be so. Who but Jesus Christ would have undertaken such a task as the salvation of the sinner is, if Jesus Christ had passed us by? It is true which is written of him, "He shall not fail, nor be discouraged, till he have set judgment in the earth," &c. (Isa. xlii. 4.) If he had not set his face like a flint, the greatness of this work would surely have daunted his mind. (Isa. l. 6, 7.)

For do but consider what sin is, from which they must be saved; do but consider what the devil and the curse is, from which they must be saved, and it will easily be concluded by you, that it is he that full rightly deserveth to have his name called *Wonderful*, and his love such as verily passeth knowledge.

Consider, again, by what means these souls are saved, even with the loss of his life, and together with it the loss of the light of his Father's face. I pass by here, and forbear to speak of the matchless contradiction of sinners which he endured against himself, which could not but be a great grief, or, as himself doth word it, a breaking of heart unto him; but all this did not, could not hinder.

Join to all this, his everlasting intercession for us, and the effectual management thereof with God for us; and withal the infinite number of times that we by sin provoke him to spew us out of his mouth, instead of interceding for us, and the many times also that his intercession is repeated by the repeating of our faults, and this love still passes knowledge, and is by us to be wondered at.

What did, or what doth, the Lord Jesus see in us to be at all this care, and pains, and cost to save us? What will he get of us by the bargain, but a small pittance of thanks and love? for so it is, and ever will be, when compared with his matchless and unspeakable love and kindness towards us.

Oh, how unworthy are we of this love! How little do we think of it! But, most of all, the angels may be astonished to see how little we are affected with that of it which we pretend to know. But neither can this prevail with him to put us out of the scroll in which all the names of them are written for whom he doth make intercession to God. Let us cry, Grace, grace unto it.

Fourth. Hence again I infer that they shall be saved that come to God by Christ, when the devil and sin have done what they can to hinder it. This is clear, for that the strife is now, who shall be Lord of all; whether Satan, the prince of this world or Christ Jesus the Son of God: or which can lay the best claim to God's elect, he that produceth their sins against them, or he that laid down his heart's blood a price of redemption for them. Who, then, shall condemn when Christ has died, and doth also make intercession? Stand still, angels, and behold how the Father divideth his Son "a portion with the great;" and how he divideth "the spoil with the strong: because he hath poured out his soul unto death, and was numbered with the transgressors, and he bare the sin of many, and made intercession for the transgressors." (Isa. liii. 12.) The grace of God and blood of Christ, will, before the end of the world, make brave work among the sons of men. They shall come to a wonderment to God by Christ, and be saved by a wonderment for

Christ's sake. "Behold these shall come from far; and, lo, these from the north, and from the west, and these from the land of Sinim." (Isa. xlix. 12.) Behold, these, and these, and these shall come, and lo, these, and these, and these from the land of Sinim. This is to denote the abundance that shall come in to God, by Christ, towards the latter end of the world; namely, when Antichrist is gone to bed in the side of the pit's mouth; then shall nations come in and be saved, and shall walk in the light of the Lord. But, I say, what encouragement would there be for sinners thus to do, if that the Lord Jesus, by his intercession, were not able to save, "even to the uttermost," them that come unto God by him?

Fifth. Hence again I infer that here is ground for confidence to them that come to God by Christ. Confidence to the end becomes us who have such an high priest, such an intercessor as Jesus Christ; who would dishonour such a Jesus by doubting that, that all the devils in hell cannot discourage by all their wiles? He is a tried stone, he is a sure foundation; a man may confidently venture his soul in his hand, and not fear but he will bring him safe home. Ability, love to the person, and faithfulness to trust committed to him, will do all; and all these are with infinite fulness in him. He has been a Saviour these four thousand years already, two thousand before the law— two thousand in the time of the law—besides the sixteen hundred years that he has in his flesh continued to make intercession for them that come unto God by him. Yet the day is to come, yea, will never come, that he can be charged with any fault or neglect of the salvation of any of them that at any time have come unto God by him. What ground, then, is here for confidence that Christ will make a good end with me, since I come unto God by him, and since he ever liveth to make intercession for me. Let me, then, honour him, I say, by setting on his head the crown of his undertakings for me, by the believing that he is able to save me, "even to the uttermost, seeing he ever liveth to make intercession for me."

Sixth. Hence also I infer that Christ ought to bear and wear the glory of our salvation for ever. He has done it, he has wrought it out: "Give unto the Lord, O ye kindreds of the people, give unto the Lord glory and strength." Do not sacrifice to your own inventions, do not give glory to the work of your own hands. Your reformations, your works, your good deeds, and all the glory of your doing, cast them at the feet of this High Priest, and confess that glory belongs unto him: "Worthy is the Lamb that was slain to receive power, and riches, and wisdom, and strength, and honour, and glory, and blessing." (Rev. v. 12.) "And they shall hang upon him all the glory of his Father's house, the offspring and the issue, all vessels of small quantity, from the vessels of cups, even to all the vessels of flagons." (Isa. xxii. 24.) Oh! the work of our redemption by Christ is such as wanteth not provocation to us to bless, and praise, and glorify Jesus Christ. Saints, set to the work and glorify him in your body and in your souls who has bought you with a price, and glorify God and the Father by him. (1 Cor. vi. 20.)

THE USE.

I come now to make some use of this discourse. And,

First. Let me exhort you to the study of this, as of other the truths of our Lord Jesus Christ. The priestly office of Christ is the first and great thing that is presented to us in the gospel—namely, how that he died for our sins, and gave himself to the cross, that the blessing of Abraham might come upon us through him. (1 Cor. xv. 1—6. Gal. iii. 13—16.) But now because this priestly office of his is divided into two parts; and because one of them—to wit, this of his intercession—is to be accomplished for us within the vail; therefore (as we say among men, out of sight out of mind) he is too much as to this forgotten by us. We satisfy ourselves with the slaying of the sacrifice; we look not enough after our Aaron as he goes into the holiest, there to sprinkle the mercy-seat with blood upon our account.

God forbid that the least syllable of what I say should be intended by me, or construed by others, as if I sought to diminish the price paid by Christ for our redemption in this world. But since his dying is his laying down his price, and his intercession the urging and managing the worthiness of it in the presence of God against Satan, there is glory to be found therein, and we should look after him into the holy place. The second part of the work of the high priests under the law had great glory and sanctity put upon it. For as much as the holy garments were provided for him to officiate in within the vail, also it was there that the altar stood on which he offered incense. Also there was the mercy-seat and the cherubims of glory, (which were figures of the angels,) that love to be continually looking and prying into the management of this second part of the priesthood of Christ in the presence of God. For although themselves are not the persons so immediately concerned therein as we, yet the management of it, I say, is with so much grace, and glory, and wisdom, and effectualness, that it is a heaven to the angels to see it. Oh! to enjoy the odorous scent, and sweet memorial, the heart-refreshing perfumes, that ascend continually from the mercy-seat to the above, where God is, and also to behold how effectual it is to the end for which it is designed, is glorious; and he that is not somewhat let into this by the grace of God, there is a great thing lacking to his faith, and he misseth of many a sweet bit that he might otherwise enjoy. Wherefore I say, be exhorted to the study of this part of Christ's work in the managing of our salvation for us. And the ceremonies of the law may be a great help to you as to this: for though

they be out of use now as to practice, yet the signification of them is rich, and that which many gospellers have got much. Wherefore I advise that you read the five books of Moses often; yea read, and read again, and do not despair of help to understand something of the will and mind of God therein, though you think they are fast locked up from you. Neither trouble your heads though you have not commentaries and expositions; pray and read, and read and pray: for a little from God is better than a great deal from men. Also, what is from men is uncertain, and is often lost and tumbled over and over by men; but what is from God is fixed as a nail in a sure place. I know there are times of temptation, but I speak now as to the common course of Christianity. There is nothing that so abides with us as what we receive from God; and the reason why Christians at this day are at such a loss, as to some things, is because they are content with what comes from men's mouths, without searching and kneeling before God to know of him the truth of things. Things that we receive at God's hand, come to us as things from the minting-house, though old in themselves, yet new to us. Old truths are always new to us, if they come to us with the smell of heaven upon them. I speak not this because I would have people despise their ministers, but to show that there is now-a-days so much idleness among professors, as hinders them from a diligent search after things, and makes them take up short of that that is sealed by the Spirit of testimony to the conscience. Witness the great decays at this day amongst us, and that strange revolting from truth once professed by us.

Second. As I would press you to an earnest study and search after this great truth, so I would press you to a diligent improvement of it to yourselves and to others. To know truth for knowledge-sake, is short of a gracious disposition of soul; and to communicate truth out of a desire of praise and vain-glory for so doing, is also a swerving from godly simplicity; but to improve what I know, for the good of myself and others, is true Christianity indeed.

Now truths received may be improved with respect to myself and others, and that several ways—

1. To myself when I search after the power that belongs to those notions that I have received of truth. There belongs to every true notion of truth a power; the notion is the shell, the power the kernel, and life. Without this last truth doth me no good, nor those to whom I communicate it. Hence Paul said to the Corinthians, "When I come to you again, I will not know the speech of them that are puffed up, but the power. For the kingdom of God is not in word, but in power." (1 Cor. iv. 19, 20.) Search, then, after the power of what thou knowest; for it is the power that will do thee good. Now this will not be got but by earnest prayer, and much attending upon God;

also there must not be admitted by thee that thy heart be stuffed with cumbering cares of this world, for they are of a choking nature.

Take heed of slighting that little that thou hast. A good improvement of little is the way to make that little thrive, and the way to obtain additions thereto: " He that is faithful in that which is least, is faithful also in much ; and he that is unjust in the least, is unjust also in much." (Luke xvi. 10.)

2. Improve them to others, and that,

(1.) By labouring to instil them upon their hearts by good and wholesome words, presenting all to them with the authority of the Scriptures.

(2.) Labour to enforce those instillings on them, by showing them by thy life the peace, the glorious effects that they have upon thy soul.

Lastly. Let this doctrine give thee boldness to come to God. Shall Jesus Christ be interceding in heaven ? Oh, then, be thou a praying man on earth ; yea, take courage to pray. Think thus with thyself—I go to God, to God, before whose throne the Lord Jesus is ready to hand my petitions to him ; yea, " he ever lives to make intercession for me." This is a great encouragement to come to God by prayers and supplications for ourselves, and by intercessions for our families, our neighbours, and enemies. Farewell.

END OF VOL. III.